Lecture Notes in Artificial Intelligence 10085

Subseries of Lecture Notes in Computer Science

More information about this series at http://www.springer.com/series/1244

Minghui Dong · Jingxia Lin
Xuri Tang (Eds.)

Chinese
Lexical Semantics

17th Workshop, CLSW 2016
Singapore, Singapore, May 20–22, 2016
Revised Selected Papers

 Springer

Editors
Minghui Dong
Institute for Infocomm Research
Singapore
Singapore

Jingxia Lin
Nanyang Technological University
Singapore
Singapore

Xuri Tang
Huazhong University of Science
and Technology
Wuhan
China

ISSN 0302-9743　　　　　ISSN 1611-3349　(electronic)
Lecture Notes in Artificial Intelligence
ISBN 978-3-319-49507-1　　　ISBN 978-3-319-49508-8　(eBook)
DOI 10.1007/978-3-319-49508-8

Library of Congress Control Number: 2016959170

LNCS Sublibrary: SL7 – Artificial Intelligence

Printed on acid-free paper

This Springer imprint is published by Springer Nature
The registered company is Springer International Publishing AG
The registered company address is: Gewerbestrasse 11, 6330 Cham, Switzerland

Preface

The 17th Chinese Lexical Semantics Workshop (CLSW 2016) was held during May 20–22, 2016, in Singapore, organized by the Chinese and Oriental Languages Information Processing Society (COLIPS) and Nanyang Technological University (NTU).

Since the first workshop in 2000, the Chinese Lexical Semantics Workshop (CLSW) has been held in different Asian cities, including Hong Kong, Beijing, Taipei, Singapore, Xiamen, Hsin Chu, Yantai, Suzhou, Wuhan, Zhengzhou, and Macao. Over the years, CLSW has become one of the most important venues for scholars to report and discuss the latest progress in Chinese lexical semantics and related fields, including theoretical linguistics, applied linguistics, computational linguistics, information processing, and computational lexicography. CLSW has significantly promoted academic research and application development in the fields.

CLSW 2016 received a total of 182 submissions. Each submission was reviewed by two to four independent expert reviewers. Finally, 94 papers were accepted with 62 scheduled as oral presentations and 32 scheduled as poster presentations in the workshop. The workshop also hosted five invited speeches. For this volume in Springer's LNAI series, only 70 papers (38% of the total submissions) were selected. Among them, 50 are long papers and 20 are short papers. This book is organized in six topical sections: lexicon and morphology, the syntax-semantics interface, corpus and resource, natural language processing, case study of lexical semantics, and extended study and application.

As the editors of this volume, we would like to thank the conference chair, Advisory Committee members, Program Committee members, Publication Committee members, invited speakers, authors, and attendees for their contribution and participation. We would also like to thank the Organizing Committee members from COLIPS and NTU for their dedication in making the event a great success.

September 2016

Minghui Dong
Jingxia Lin
Xuri Tang

Organization

Conference Chair

Li, Haizhou   Institute for Infocomm Research, Singapore

Advisory Committee

Honorary Members

Yu, Shiwen   Peking University, China
Cheng, Chin-Chuan   University of Illinois, USA
Tsou, Benjamin   Hong Kong Institute of Education, SAR China

Members

Diao, Yanbin   Beijing Normal University, China
Huang, Chu-Ren   Hong Kong Polytechnic University, SAR China
Zhuo, Jing-Schmidt   University of Oregon, USA
Ji, Donghong   Wuhan University, China
Lua, Kim Teng   COLIPS, Singapore
Liu, Mei-chun   Taiwan Chiao Tung University, Taiwan
Lu, Qin   Hong Kong Polytechnic University, SAR China
Su, Xinchun   Xiamen University, China
Sui, Zhifang   Peking University, China
Hsieh, Shu-Kai   Taiwan University, Taiwan
Xu, Jie   University of Macau, SAR China
Zan, Hongying   Zhengzhou University, China

Program Committee

Chairs

Dong, Minghui   Institute for Infocomm Research and COLIPS, Singapore
Lin, Jingxia   Nanyang Technological University, Singapore
Ji, Donghong   Wuhan University, China

Members

Ahrens, Kathleen   The Hong Kong Polytechnic University, SAR China
Bai, Xiaojing   Tsinghua University, China
Chen, I-Hsuan   University of California, Berkeley, USA
Chen, Song-Ling   Xiamen University, China
Cheng, Chin-Chuan   National Taiwan Normal University, Taiwan
Dabhur Bayar   Inner Mongolia University, China

Dong, Minghui	Institute for Infocomm Research, Singapore
Du, Jingjing	Xiamen University, China
Duann, Ren-feng	The Hong Kong Polytechnic University, SAR China
E, Chen-chun	National United University, Taiwan
Feng, Wenhe	Wuhan University, China
Fu, Guohong	Heilongjiang University, China
Gao, Hong, Helena	Nanyang Technological University, Singapore
Gao, Zailan	Peking University/The Hong Kong Polytechnic University, SAR China
Guo, Tingting	Wuhan University, China
He, Lin	Wuhan University, China
Hong, Jia-Fei	National Taiwan Normal University, Taiwan
Hou, Ruifen	Chinese Academy of Social Sciences, China
Hsiao, Huichen	National Taiwan Normal University, Taiwan
Hsieh, Shu-Kai	National Taiwan University, Taiwan
Ji, Donghong	Wuhan University, China
Jin, Peng	Leshan Normal University, China
Kang, Shiyong	Ludong University, China
Kwong, Olivia	The Chinese University of Hong Kong, SAR China
Lai, Hui-ling	National Chengchi University, Taiwan
Lee, Lung-hao	National Taiwan Normal University, Taiwan
Li, Baoli	Henan University of Technology, China
Lin, Jingxia	Nanyang Technological University, Singapore
Liu, Mei-chun	City University of Hong Kong, SAR China
Liu, Zhifu	Wuhan University, China
Lu, Qin	The Hong Kong Polytechnic University, SAR China
Ma, Wei-yun	Academia Sinica, Taiwan
Meng, Yao	Fujitsu
Qiu, Likun	Ludong University, China
Shi, Xiaodong	Xiamen University, China
Song, Jihua	Beijing Normal University, China
Song, Zuoyan	Beijing Normal University, China
Sui, Zhifang	Peking University, China
Sun, Yuanyuan	Xiamen University, China
Tao, Hongyin	University of California, Los Angeles, USA
Wan, Jing	Wuhan University, China
Wang, Yubo	Wuhan University, China
Wu, Yunfang	Peking University, China
Xiong, Jiajuan	The Hong Kong Polytechnic University, SAR China
Xu, Hongzhi	University of Pennsylvania, USA
Xu, Jie	The University of Macau, SAR China
Yang, Yuan-Chen	Rutgers University, USA
Yu, Shiwen	Peking University, China
Zan, Hongying	Zhengzhou University, China
Zhang, Yangsen	Beijing Information Science and Technology University, China

Zheng, Zezhi	Xiamen University, China
Zhou, Guodong	Soochow University, China
Zhou, Qiang	Tsinghua University, China

Organizing Committee

Chairs

Chng, Eng Siong	Nanyang Technological University, Singapore
Wang, Lei	Institute for Infocomm Research, Singapore
Song, Zuoyan	Beijing Normal University, China
Jin, Peng	Leshan Normal University, China

Members

Gao, Helena Hong	Nanyang Technological University, Singapore
Zhang, Zhengchen	Institute for Infocomm Research and COLIPS, Singapore
Lu, Yanfeng	Institute for Infocomm Research and COLIPS, Singapore
Tong, Rong	Institute for Infocomm Research and COLIPS, Singapore
Paul, Chan	Institute for Infocomm Research and COLIPS, Singapore
Jiang, Ridong	Institute for Infocomm Research and COLIPS, Singapore

Publication Committee

Chair

| Liu, Pengyuan | Beijing Language and Culture University, China |

Vice Chairs

| Tang, Xuri | Huazhong University of Science and Technology, China |
| Su, Qi | Peking University, China |

Members

Hong, Jiafei	Taiwan Normal University, Taiwan
Kwong, Olivia	City University of Hong Kong, SAR China
Zheng, Zezhi	Xiamen University, China

Invited Speeches

Invited Speech 1 (Keynote)
The Subjectivity of Some Probability Adverbs

Dingxu Shi

The Hong Kong Polytechnic University

Abstract. In Chinese, words like youshi (seldom), wangwang (usually) and zong (generally) are commonly considered frequency adverbs, on a par with words like ouer (rarely), changchang (often) and yizhi (always). It was discovered after analyzing large corpora data that the former are probability adverbs and only the later are frequency adverbs. Frequency and probability are the results of different calculations which require different items. A frequency adverb like the changchang (often) typically requires one set of things only, since the frequency for a given activity will remain constant no matter which time frame is adopted for the calculation. While in the case of probability adverbs, two sets are required for calculating probability. This is why using wangwang (usually) is not acceptable without a proper context. More importantly, youshi (seldom), wangwang (usually) and zong (generally) are subjective adverbs that express the speaker's evaluation of the proposition. Such an evaluation is always against a baseline. The wangwang (usually) means the speaker thinks that the probability is close to the baseline, which should be the statistical average of 0.5. The youshi (probably) may be based on a statistic baseline but it could simply express the speaker's subjective opinion. The sentence "Ni zenme zong bu jie wode dianhua?" (How dare you not answer my call in general?) is a girl's whining against her boyfriend and her baseline for not answering her phone call is 0, a purely subjective decision.

Biography. Dingxu Shi received his MA in Applied Linguistics from University of Pittsburg and his MA and PhD in Linguistics from University of Southern California. He is now a Chair Professor in Chinese Linguistics at the Department of Chinese and Bilingual Studies of the Hong Kong Polytechnic University. His main research interest is on syntax, the interface of syntax and semantics, language contact and language change and Chinese pedagogical grammar. He has published a number of books in publishers such as Cambridge University Press and Peking University Press, and over one hundred papers in journals like *Language, Natural Language and Linguistic Theory, Journal of Chinese Linguistics, Zhongguo Yuwen, Foreign Language Teaching and Research* and *Contemporary Linguistics*.

Invited Speech 2 (Keynote)

Continuous Space Models and the Mathematics of Semantics

Rafael E. Banchs

Institute for Infocomm Research, Singapore

Abstract. In this talk, we present and discuss the most recent advances on the use of continuous space models in natural language processing applications. More specifically, some of the fundamental concepts of distributional semantics and vector space models are presented, followed by a brief discussion on linear and non-linear dimensionality reduction techniques and their implications to the parallel distributed approach to semantic cognition. Finally, some interesting examples about the use of continuous space models in both monolingual and cross-language natural language processing applications are presented.

Biography. Rafael E. Banchs is a Research Scientist at the Institute for Infocomm Research, in Singapore, where he leads the Dialogue Technology Lab of the Human Language Technology Department. He obtained a PhD degree in Electrical Engineering from The University of Texas at Austin in 1998. Since then he has worked on a variety of problems ranging from signal processing, electromagnetic modelling and parameter estimation to natural language processing, across different industries and applications. In 2004, he was awarded a five-year "Ramon Y Cajal" fellowship from the Spanish Ministry of Science and Technology to work on natural language processing related problem. He published over 30 journal papers. He held positions and taught in a number of universities and gave lectures and talks at many international conferences and workshops. His current area of research is focused on the construction and use of semantic representations to support different natural language processing applications, including machine translation, information retrieval, natural language understanding and chat-oriented dialogue.

Invited Speech 3

Activation of the Weak Grammatical Feature [+L] and Its Activator

Jie Xu

Macau University

Abstract. This paper argues that most object/human-denoting nominals, whether N, NP or pronoun, have a weak grammatical feature [+L] ('locative'), and that the feature needs to be activated properly in order to induce its syntactic effects. The feature is activated through different mechanisms in different languages. Along this line of approach, the widely observed construction of 'nominal + place word' in the modern Chinese language such as *zhuozi pang* 'table side' and *Lao Wang zher* 'Lao Wang here' is re-cast and re-captured as a consequence of the weak feature activation.

Biography. Jie Xu obtained his PhD in Linguistics from University of Maryland at College Park in 1993. He taught Chinese language and Linguistics at the National University of Singapore and Central China Normal University from 1993 to 2008 before joining the faculty of University of Macau. He is a professor of Chinese Linguistics in the Department of Chinese Language and Literature, Faculty of Arts and Humanities, University of Macau. His primary academic interests are in syntax, semantics, language acquisition, and language education. His major publications include *Ten Essays on Chinese Descriptive Grammar*, *Grammatical Principles and Grammatical Phenomena*, *Sentence Head and Sentence Structure*, *Language Planning and Language Education*, and over fifty journal articles in his fields. For this academic year, he visits the Nanyang Technological University for academic collaboration.

Invited Speech 4

Manifestation of Certainty in Semantics: The Case of Yídìng, Kěndìng and Dǔdìng in Mandarin Chinese

Jiun-Shiung Wu

National Chung Cheng University, Taiwan

Abstract. This paper examines three modal adverbials in Mandarin Chinese: yídìng, kěndìng and dǔdìng. These three lexical entries can all express epistemic necessity or intensification. However, denoting intensification, kěndìng and dǔdìng have additional semantic requirements. First, they both require that there be at least one alternative to the proposition they present. Second, the speaker uses kěndìng to ascertain the truth of a proposition it takes, although all the alternatives are potentially true. Third, dǔdìng is used to assert the certainty that only the proposition it takes is true. Concerning certainty, two cases are demonstrated here. For yídìng, certainty is used implicitly, because certainty manifests itself through the speaker's attitude. However, for kěndìng and dǔdìng, certainty is revealed explicitly, since (part of) the semantics of these two lexical items is certainty.

Biography. Jiun-Shiung Wu is a professor of Linguistics in Institute of Linguistics, National Chung Cheng University, Taiwan. He received his Ph.D. degree in Linguistics from University of Texas at Austin, Texas, USA. in May, 2003. His research interests include formal semantics, formal pragmatics, computational semantics, discourse analysis, interface between syntax and semantics, etc. In the recent years, he focuses on aspect, tense, temporal relations, discourse structure, anaphor resolution, modality, etc. He has published more than a dozen papers in prestigious journals, including Journal of East Asian Linguistics, Journal of Chinese Linguistics, Language and Linguistics, Taiwan Journal of Linguistics, Cahiers de Linguistique – Asie Orientale, International Journal on Asian Language Processing, Journal of Chinese Language Teaching, etc. He attends at least one conference and presents a paper every year since 2003. He has several book chapters as well. Furthermore, he published a monograph entitled *Temporal and Atemporal Relations in Mandarin* in 2007, and a textbook entitled *Computational Linguistics for Humanities Students: A First Course* [in Chinese] in 2015. In terms of academic service, he served as the Chair of Department of Foreign Languages, National Chiayi University, from August, 2008 to January, 2010. He also served as a board member at Linguistic Society of Taiwan since 2008 to 2014. He was the President of Linguistic Society of Taiwan from 2010 to 2012.

Invited Speech 5

Integrating Character Representations into Chinese Word Embedding

Peng Jin

Leshan Normal University, China

Abstract. We propose a novel word representation for Chinese based on a state-of-the-art word embedding approach. Our main contribution is to integrate distributional representations of Chinese characters into the word embedding. Recent related work on European languages has demonstrated that information from inflectional morphology can reduce the problem of sparse data and improve word representations. Chinese has very little inflectional morphology, but there is potential for incorporating character-level information. Chinese characters are drawn from a fixed set – with just under four thousand in common usage – but a major problem with using characters is their ambiguity. In order to address this problem, we disambiguate the characters according to groupings in a semantic hierarchy. Coupling our character embedding with word embedding, we observe improved performance on the tasks of finding synonyms and rating word similarity compared to a model using word embedding alone, especially for low frequency words.

Biography. Peng Jin, is a professor and Dean of School of Computer Science at Leshan Normal University. He is the founding director of Internet natural language intelligent processing lab authorized by the Education of Department of Sichuan Province. He received his B.Sc., M.Sc. and Ph.D. degrees in computer science from Zhengzhou Textile Institute, Nanjing University of Science and Technology, Peking University, China, in 1999, 2002 and 2009, respectively. From November 2007 to April 2008, sponsored by CSC, he studied as a visiting research fellow in department of informatics, Sussex University, UK. From August 2014 to February 2015, he visited Sussex University for the second time. His research focuses on natural language processing, especially the statistical methods for lexical semantic and language resource. In these areas, he has published more than 30 papers in well-known international journals or conferences and invented one Chinese patent. He has lead two NSFC projects and several collaborative projects with industry. He served as the organization chair of CIS2013 and YSSNLP2014, Program Committee members of NLP&CC'13, NLPOE'09-14, etc.

Contents

Lexicon and morphology

The syntax-semantics interface

Corpus and resource

Natural language processing

Extended study and application

Part I Lexicon and Morphology

Emotion Lexicon and Its Application: A Study Based on Written Texts

Jia-Fei Hong

National Taiwan Normal University, Taiwan
jiafeihong@ntnu.edu.tw

Abstract. Compared with other language forms, journalese, which is characterized as formal, serious, brief, and standard, in Chinese written texts, carries rich information using few words. Expressing textual meanings, especially personal emotions, by means of appropriate words is quite important in Chinese writing. In teaching Chinese writing, it is easier to compose appropriate texts if teachers and learners interpret emotion words through sense divisions, semantic features, related words, and collocations. This study aimed to build a Chinese emotion lexicon that distinguishes emotion expressions in contexts through the classification of semantic features, as well as provides information via related words and collocations. Moreover, this study applied the characteristics of Chinese emotion words to teach Chinese writing with the aim of improving learners' writing.

Keywords. Chinese emotion words, semantic features, collocations, teaching Chinese writing

1   Introduction

The purpose of building a lexicon, which is a reference book that provides related information on words and suggestions for how the words should be used in spoken and written contexts, is to collect words in a language, list them in proper order, and explain their meanings. Lexicons also signal the cultural development of a nation [1] and serve an important role in social life, education, and academic research [2]; in sum, lexicons catalogue human history, culture, and thinking, as well as vastly benefit language learning in both speaking and writing. Constructing a dictionary for professional or special usages is a valuable issue both academically and practically and is an important part of Lexical Semantics. In light of this, the word lists for various vocations or specific purposes that are constructed to match the needs of societal development have a similar value to that of an encyclopedia.

Great strides have been made in constructing a modern Chinese corpus. Corpora for written data, spoken data, Internet data, multimedia data, tutorial material, and learners' data are all of concern to scholars. Moreover, dictionaries have been constructed for specialized subjects and areas, yet thus far a Chinese emotion lexicon has not been built—especially for

© Springer International Publishing AG 2016
M. Dong et al. (Eds.): CLSW 2016, LNAI 10085, pp. 3–17, 2016
DOI: 10.1007/978-3-319-49508-8_1

the needs of Lexical Semantics—from which to extract external linguistic characteristics for the expression of internal human thoughts and emotions.

At the cognitive level of human thoughts, emotions, and feelings, internal emotion activities cannot be realized without language representations. Chinese is characterized by the least linguistic forms representing the most semantic content and information. Among others, Chinese written texts are the best illustration of this phenomenon, especially when expressing emotion in writing. Thus, the Chinese emotion lexicon constructed in this study applied Chinese emotion words to writing to improve learners' ability to use these words when composing written texts, which is a worthwhile issue in teaching Chinese writing.

2   Previous Studies

Basic emotions begin in the early stage of life, and they are distinguished by specific types. Different types of emotions accompany distinct physical reactions or representations, which helps humans adapt to their environment [3], [4]. [5] used the Facial Action Coding System (FACS) to divide human emotions into six major types—happiness, sadness, fear, anger, disgust, and surprise—and each emotion has concordant facial expressions that are accompanied by physical reactions. Moreover, the six basic emotion types are cross-culturally consistent [6], which is to say that people from different cultures have the same recognition of and expressions for the six basic emotions. [7] also proposed six basic emotions, where they grouped 135 emotion adjectives into the categories of joy, love, anger, surprise, sadness, and fear. In another study, [8] suggested that there are 10 basic emotions that can be further divided into three types: positive emotions, neutral emotions, and negative emotions. Positive emotions include interest and joy; neutral emotions include surprise; and negative emotions include anger, contempt, fear, sadness, disgust, guilt, and shame.

The construction of an "emotion word" corpus has already been researched in different languages and has aroused the attention of linguists with different language backgrounds [9], [10], [11], [12], [13], [14], [15]. Taking English as an example. [10] chose four emotion types—happiness, sadness, anxiety, and anger—and asked participants to judge the emotionality of 120 emotion-related and 120 non-emotion-related words to construct a free association norm, while [9] developed the Affective Norms for English Words (ANEW) by selecting about 600 emotion words based on previous studies and rating them in terms of pleasure, arousal, and dominance.

Researches in different languages have suggested that emotion words play an important role in expressing emotional concepts in dialogues and texts. Different emotion words are able to distinguish subtle emotional differences in cognition. In addition, emotion words conveying distinct emotional concepts have been classified as positive or negative across different languages and cultures. On the other hand, research on Chinese emotion words has focused on a variety of areas, for instance, a study on library users' satisfaction evaluation [16], automatic music emotion classification and searches [17], rich research results on sentence emotion classification based on documents and blog posts [18], [19], [20], emotion expressions in the context of Chinese culture [21], a Chinese emotion word dictionary based on an emotion corpus and multiple sources [22], [23], [24], emotion word counts using a concept tagging system [25], and a Chinese emotion corpus based on tagged event information [26], [27]. These investigations and analyses on Chinese emotion words relied heavily on the combination of computer science and Natural Language Processing (NLP).

The ultimate goal of the current study was to obtain a more refined analysis of written texts. Nevertheless, current automatic analyzing technology for Chinese emotion words mostly consists of dictionaries and corpora whose data contain only basic polarity and intensity tagging information, for example, SentiWordNet [28], [29], [30] and SO-CAL [31], [32] in English, as well as NTUSD [33], Chinese Thesaurus [34], HowNet [35], and E-HowNet [36] in Chinese, among others. The results so far suggest only the recognition of texts' emotional positive/negative polarity and intensity. Few studies have distinguished the classification of emotion words and their related words and collocations in texts by digging into their meaning and semantic features. Moreover, little research has been conducted on testing the reliability of emotion word classification using practical experiments on related and collocated words of emotion words listed in dictionaries, or on verifying the prominence of the co-occurrence of related and collocated words in practical writing exercises.

3 Research Motivation and Goal

Previous emotion word studies constructed emotion lexicons in different languages, such as German, French, Indonesian, and English [9], [10], [11], [12], [13], [14], [15]. Other studies have focused on human cognition, human characters, and health [37], [38], [39]. Chinese emotion word researches applied their results to a variety of areas, for instance, text-based emotion classification [18], [19], [40], library users' satisfaction [16], and automatic music emotion classification and searches [17]. Previous studies usually adopted NLP, using algorithm mining [41], automatic detection, and automapping, to find possible emotion words and to analyze their polarity tendency (positive or negative) as the theoretical foundation for future works. Nevertheless, these past studies have not been able to probe the semantic elements/features of the detected emotion words to determine their polarity tendencies or to reveal their interpretations and conceptions with different collocated words in different contexts.

Journalese texts are very special and specific to Chinese written texts. The words used in journalese texts are of particular consideration and usage to ensure that every type of newspaper report has distinguishing features. Texts of newspaper reports, a kind of Chinese written text, are meant to deliver the dynamics and developments of social and topical events, which requires objective writing and realistic points of view to present the original appearance of the event. Therefore, journalese texts often contain many emotion words so that readers can generate an emotional consensus and realize the emotional tendency of the reports by picking up on emotion words and their related/collocated words.

Emotion words in Chinese lexicons are often used to characterize or deliver emotions and feelings [42]. Human emotions are important not only in expressing feelings but also because they are closely connected with other cognitive functions, such as complex thinking, decision-making, and memory [43], [44]. Moreover, Chinese emotion words contain both semantic information and emotional content. Different emotion words used in the same context may be interpreted differently; on the contrary, the same emotion words used in different contexts may convey different semantic and pragmatic information.

The words in Chinese journalese written texts that are categorized by emotion words are sometimes the result of their metaphorical meaning. Since Chinese words often contain literal meanings and metaphorical meanings, readers must rely on the information provided in the context to get the intended meaning. In addition, some polysemous Chinese written words can be interpreted as having different literal meanings and even different metaphorical meanings in different contexts.

Written languages, compared with other language styles, are characterized by formal, serious, brief, and standard words that carry much information. Expressing textual meaning, especially personal emotions, by means of appropriate words is quite important in Chinese writing. In teaching Chinese writing, both the teachers and the learners can comprehend the characteristics of emotion words and their accompanying related/collocated words through their semantic features. This results in Chinese writing that is easier to compose using appropriate emotional expressions.

In sum, based on the above description of lexicons, emotional-expressing words, written texts, and applying emotion words to writing, the current study aimed to establish a Chinese emotion lexicon that distinguishes emotional expressions in contexts through the classification of semantic components/features, as well as provides information on related words and collocations. Moreover, this study applied the characteristics of Chinese emotion words to teach Chinese writing with the aim of improving learners' writing using emotion words.

4   Data Collection

The data collection for the Chinese emotion lexicon in this study was compiled from the Chinese written frequency lexicon (i.e., frequency statistics of the journalese corpus) created by the Chinese Knowledge Information Processing Group, Acdemia Sinica [45], which includes a character frequency list [46], a word frequency list [47], and a word frequency and classification of frequent verbs list [48], and all the words selected, including related words and collocations, had emotion features. For example, 高兴 *gāo xìng* 'happy', 畅通 *chàng tōng* 'clear', and 细腻 *xì nì* 'attentive' are positive emotion words, and 害怕 *hài pà* 'fear', 露骨 *lù gǔ* 'undisguised', and 逾期 *yú qí* 'overdue' are negative emotion words.

5   Data Analysis

5.1   Selecting the Target Words

In this study, the data primarily came from a journalese corpus of Chinese written texts. The semantic components of the data were confirmed by the related words and collocations; in addition, an offline questionnaire task was conducted to evaluate and verify the correlation between the related words and collocations. Furthermore, the semantically-confirmed and collocation-verified Chinese emotion words were applied to writing exercises in language teaching. The procedures of the research were divided into several stages, as shown in Figure 1 below:

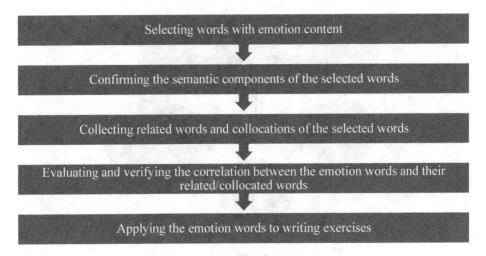

Figure 1: The research design

First, based on the journalese corpora of Chinese written texts outlined in Section 4 above, emotion words were manually collected, and then analyzed and selected objectively. For example, 高兴 *gāo xìng* 'happy', 畅通 *chàng tōng* 'clear', and 细腻 *xì nì* 'attentive' are positive emotion words; 害怕 *hài pà* 'fear', 露骨 *lù gǔ* 'undisguised', and 逾期 *yú qí* 'overdue' are negative emotion words; and 过瘾 *guò yǐn* 'to the full', 长大 *zhǎng dà* 'grownup', and 激烈 *jī liè* 'intense' are context-based neutral emotion words. After retrieving the target words, they were confirmed as Chinese emotion words, and then their related words and collocations were collected. Finally, the Chinese emotion lexicon was built following the classification of the emotion words. The entire process is illustrated in Figure 2 below:

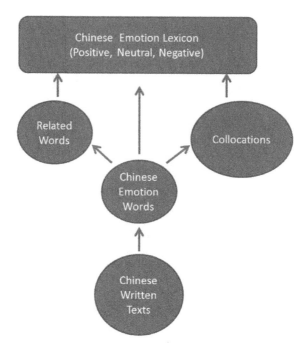

Figure 2: Constructing the Chinese emotion lexicon

5.2   Confirming the Semantic Elements of the Target Words

In building the emotion lexicon, this study adopted the framework proposed by [49], who suggested building an emotion lexicon based on the translation of texts in other languages or existing lexicons, using either an automatic or manual approach. The automatic approach mostly involved a bi-gram incorporating NLP and an intercept information field, with a comparison reference algorithm, to interpret the emotion words in a context by means of analyzing the semantic relationships between two words and their collocational tendency. On the other hand, the manual approach used existing lexicons to probe the semantic components of the emotion words.

The current study referenced online dictionaries—the Ministry of Education Chinese Word Dictionary Revised, Chinese Wordnet of Taiwan, and the Han Dictionary of China—for the semantic analyses of Chinese emotion words, as well as offline dictionaries—the *New Mandarin Daily News Dictionary*, the *Chinese Utilization Dictionary* of Taiwan, and the *Contemporary Chinese Dictionary* and the *Contemporary Chinese Standard Dictionary* of China—to verify and analyze the semantic content and semantic features of the selected Chinese emotion words. The online dictionaries were open source and available to anyone for searches, although Chinese Wordnet was smaller so not all the emotion words were listed with their corresponding information. In Taiwan's Ministry of Education Chinese Word Dictionary Revised (see Figure 3) and China's Han Dictionary (see Figure 4), users can search for not only the word's meaning but also the word's related information.

For example, the synonyms for 高兴 *gāo xìng* 'happy' are listed in the Ministry of Education Chinese Word Dictionary Revised as 得意 *dé yì*, 痛快 *tòng kuài*, 开心 *kāi xīn*, 快乐 *kuài lè*, 快活 *kuài huó*, 欢乐 *huān lè*, 欢喜 *huān xǐ*, 欢跃 *huān yuè*, 喜悦 *xǐ yuè*, 兴奋 *xīng fèn*, 怡悦 *yí yuè*, 愉快 *yú kuài*, 乐意 *lè yì*, and 愿意 *yuàn yì*, and the antonyms as 败兴 *bài xīng*, 悲伤 *bēi shāng*, 悲哀 *bēi āi*, 烦闷 *fán mèn*, 难过 *nán guò*, 苦恼 *kǔ nǎo*, 沮丧 *jǔ sàng*, 伤心 *shāng xīn*, 扫兴 *sǎo xìng*, 忧愁 *yōu chóu*, 厌恶 *yàn wù*, 郁闷 *yù mēn*, 不快 *bú kuài*, and 生气 *shēng qì*. The Han Dictionary lists the synonyms for 高兴 *gāo xìng* 'happy' as 开心 *kāi xīn*, 快乐 *kuài lè*, 欢乐 *huān lè*, 欢快 *huān kuài*, 喜悦 *xǐ yuè*, 愉快 *yú kuài*, 快活 *kuài huó*, 欣喜 *xīn xǐ*, 痛快 *tòng kuài*, 欢喜 *huān xǐ*, 欢畅 *huān chàng*, and 舒畅 *shū chàng*, and the antonyms as 伤心 *shāng xīn*, 悲伤 *bēi shāng*, 悲哀 *bēi āi*, 痛苦 *tòng kǔ*, 难过 *nán guò*, and 生气 *shēng qì*.

Figure 3: Search results in the Ministry of Education Chinese Word Dictionary Revised

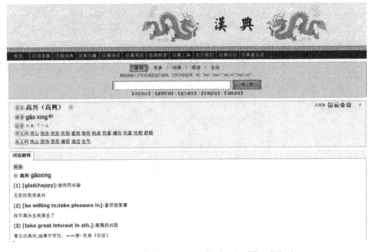

Figure 4: Search results in the Han Dictionary

5.3   Collecting Related Words and Collocations of the Target Words

Related word, collected by observing their co-occurrence with the target word in the context, were used to probe the target word's meaning, sense expressions, and divisions. The distribution of the related words, therefore, was similar to the concept of a thesaurus [50]. To enhance and complete the Chinese emotion lexicon in this study, it was necessary to provide the information of related words and collocations. Thus, after confirming the emotional sense content and semantic features of the chosen words, all the possible related words for each emotion word were collected at this stage by searching Chinese Word Sketch in the one-billion-word Chinese Gigaword Corpus. Chinese Word Sketch has four main features: Concordance, Word Sketch, Thesaurus, and Sketch-Diff. The "Word Sketch" tool accessed the collocations of the emotion words (see Figures 5 and 6), while the Thesaurus feature collected related words (see Figures 7 and 8).

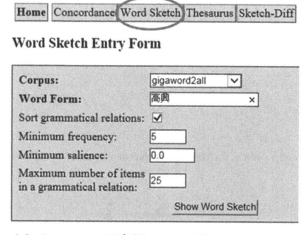

Figure 5: Search for the target word "高興" using the "Word Sketch" tool in Chinese Word Sketch

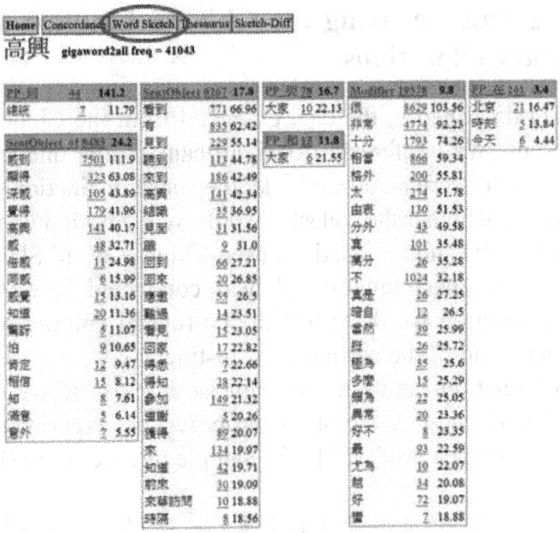

Figure 6: Collocations of the target word "高興" using the "Word Sketch" tool

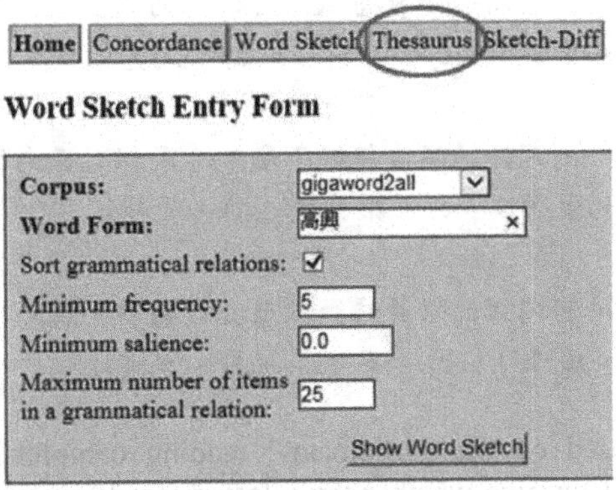

Figure 7: Search for the target word "高興" using the "Thesaurus" tool in Chinese Word Sketch

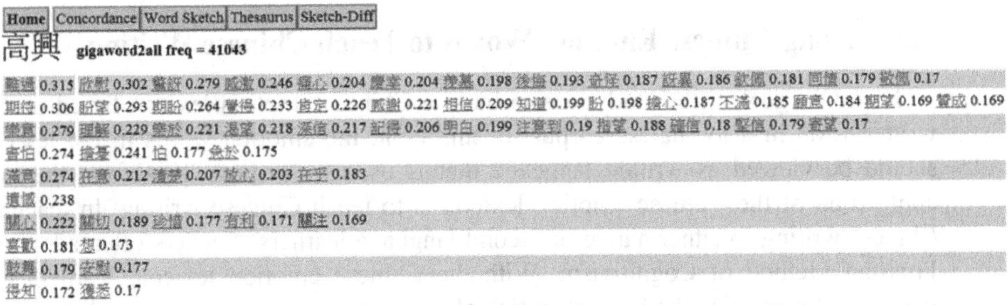

Figure 8: Related words of the target word "高興" using the "Thesaurus" tool

5.4 Evaluating and Verifying the Chinese Emotion Words, Related Words, and Collocations

Adopting the big data theory, the data extracted from the Chinese written texts in the journalese corpus, with reference to significant online and offline dictionaries from Taiwan and China, were analyzed under the sense distinction criteria of Chinese Wordnet [51] to verify whether the collected words were emotion words, and the search for possible related words and collocations used Chinese Word Sketch. Finally, in the fourth stage, an offline questionnaire task was conducted based on the previously confirmed Chinese emotion words to test the co-related emotion words in the same semantic field with the aid of the participants' instinct.

To prove the correlation between the Chinese emotion words and their possible related words and collocations, the study proposed an experimental evaluation by adopting the "multiple-choice task" [52]. The sample questions are shown as below:

(1) 請問下列哪一個詞語的語義特徵不屬於「高興」正向情緒？
a) 期待 ； b) 深感 ； c) 貶值 ； d) 欣慰

(2) 請問下列哪一個詞語的語義特徵不屬於「高興」正向情緒？
a) 下降 ； b) 喜歡 ； c) 分外 ； d) 滿意

(3) 請問下列哪一個詞語的語義特徵不屬於「高興」正向情緒？
a) 珍惜 ； b) 豪邁 ； c) 樂意 ； d) 覺得

(4) 請問下列哪一個詞語的語義特徵不屬於「高興」正向情緒？
a) 感覺 ； b) 慶幸 ； c) 寄望 ； d) 愛護

This method, based on the participants' reading comprehension and semantic cognition, helps to determine whether the selected words are emotion words, further distinguishes their emotion classification, and verifies the correlation between the related words/collocations and the selected target word. The aim of the task was to improve the reliability of the collocation selection.

5.5 Using Chinese Emotion Words to Teach Chinese Writing

The main goal of the study was to build a Chinese emotion lexicon based on the written texts in a journalese corpus. In this light, the emotion words in the lexicon should be viewed as written language that is used in writing. Therefore, the best application of the Chinese emotion lexicon is to teach Chinese writing. In teaching Chinese writing to either native or second-language learners, teachers often adopt the Prussian Method of Cognitivism. With the Chinese emotion lexicon, learners can realize and recognize the characteristics of emotion words through sense distinctions and semantic features, which will facilitate the composition of essay writing using relevant emotion words to appropriately express emotions.

Using this lexicon, learners should also increase their use of emotion words in their writing as they learn more about the semantic features of the words through the task, which in turn will improve their writing ability to manage emotion-content words. In the same vein, the Chinese emotion lexicon will provide teachers with emotion words and their related words and collocations to be used as teaching materials for writing tasks, for example, the positive emotion word 暢通 *chàng tōng* 'clear', its related words 便捷 *biàn jié* 'convenient', 受阻 *shòu zǔ* 'block', 壅塞 *yōng sè* 'congestion', and 疏導 *shū dǎo* 'to dredge', and its collocations 政令 *zhèng lìng* 'government decree', 管道 *guǎn dào* 'way', 交通 *jiāo tong* 'traffic', 目標 *mù biāo* 'target', and 資金 *zī jīn* 'fund'. After the writing task, the written text can be analyzed to measure the learners' ability to use the emotion words appropriately and to count the distribution of the words in a particular context.

6   Conclusion and Future Work

In this study, the main goal was to build a Chinese emotion lexicon based on data collected from a journalese corpus, which can be applied to teaching Chinese writing. The words used in journalese written texts are more formal, precise, and standard, compared with other language styles (e.g., interviews, dialogues, etc.), so appropriate words are needed to express textual meaning, especially personal emotions, in Chinese writing. In teaching Chinese writing, the Chinese emotion lexicon can be used as teaching materials for writing tasks, which can then be analyzed to measure the learners' ability to use the emotion words and their related words/collocations appropriately and to count the distribution of the words in a particular context. Moreover, the study designed context-related pictures for single-topic writing tasks and provided emotion words and related words/collocations in the Chinese emotion lexicon, which can be used to further the study of emotion words in Chinese writing in future research.

Acknowledge

This research is partially supported by the "Aim for the Top University Project" and the "Center of Learning Technology for Chinese" at National Taiwan Normal University (NTNU), sponsored by the Ministry of Education, Taiwan, R.O.C., and the "International Research-Intensive Center of Excellence Program" at NTNU and the Ministry of Science and Technology, Taiwan, R.O.C.

References

1. Zhu, Jia-ning. 1999. Chinese Lexicography. Taipei: Wu-Nan Book Co., Ltd. [In Chinese]
2. Fu, huaiqing. 2008. Modern Chinese Golssary. Taipei: New Sharing. [In Chinese]
3. Eibl-Eibesfeldt, Irenäus. 1973. The Expressive Behavior of the Deaf-and-blind Born. In M. von Cranach & I. Vine (Eds.), Social Communication and Movement, 163–194, London: Academic Press.
4. Plutchik, Robert. 1980. Emotion: Theory, Research, and Experience: 1. Theories of Emotion 1, New York: Academic.
5. Ekman, Paul, & Friesen, W. V. 1976. Pictures of Facial Affect. Palo Alto, CA: Consulting Psychologists Press.
6. Ekman, Paul. 1982. Emotion in the Human Face: Guidelines for Research and An Integration of Findings. 2nd Edition. New York: Cambridge University Press.
7. Shaver, Phillip, Judith Schwartz, Donald Kirson, and Cary O'Connor. 1987. Emotion Knowledge: Further Exploration of A Prototype Approach. Journal of Personality and Social Psychology, 52(6): 1061–1086.
8. Izard, Carroll Ellis. 1977. Human Emotions. New York: Plenum.
9. Bradley, Margaret M., and P. J. Lang. 1999. Affective Norms for English Words (ANEW): Stimuli, Instruction Manual and Affective Ratings. Technical Report C-1. Gainesville, FL: University of Florida.
10. John, Carolyn H. 1988. Emotionality Ratings and Free Association Norms of 240 emotional and non-emotional words. Cognition and Emotion, 2: 49–70.
11. Monnier, C., and A. Syssau. 2014. Affective norms for French Words (FAN). Behavior Research Methods, 46(4): 1128–1137.
12. Schmidtke, D. S., T. Schröder, A. M. Jacobs, and M. Conrad. 2014. ANGST: Affective Norms for German Sentiment Terms, Derived from the Affective Norms for English Words. Behavior Research Methods, 46(4): 1108–1118.
13. Shaver, Phillip, Upekkha Murdaya, and R. Chris Fraley. 2001. Structure of the Indonesian Emotion Lexicon. Asian Journal of Social Psychology, 4: 201–204.
14. Ute Frevert, Christian Bailey, Pascal Eitler, Benno Gammerl, Bettina Hitzer, Margrit Pernau et al. 2014. Emotional Lexicons. Oxford University Press.
15. van Goozen, S., and N. H. Frijda. 1993. Emotion Words used in Six European Countries. European Journal of Social Psychology, 23: 89–95.
16. Kuo, June-Jei, Yu-Jung Zhang. 2013. A Study on Library Users' Satisfaction Evaluation Using Sentimental Analysis. Journal of Library and Information Science Research, 7(2):153–197. [In Chinese]
17. Chen, Juo-Han, Chao-ling Hsu, Jyh-Shing Roger Jang and Feng-chu Lo. 2006. Content Base Music Emotion Analysis and Recognition. 2006 International Workshop on Computer Music and Audio Technology, 68–75. [In Chinese]

18. Yu, Ho-Cheng, Ting-Hao Huang and Hsin-His Chen. 2012. Domain Dependent Word Polarity Analysis for Sentiment Classification. Computational Linguistics and Chinese Language Processing, 17(4): 33–48. [In Chinese]

19. Sun, Yin-Tse, Chien-Liang Chen, Chun-Chieh Liu, Chao-Lin Liu and Von-Wun Soo. 2010. Sentiment Classification of Short Chinese Sentences. Proceedings of the 22nd Conference on Computational Linguistics and Speech Processing (ROCLING 2010), 184–198. September 1-2, Puli, Nantou, Taiwan. [In Chinese]

20. Yang, Changhua, Kevin Hsin-Yih Lin, and Hsin-Hsi Chen. 2007. Building emotion lexicon from weblog corpora. Proceedings of the ACL 2007 Demo and Poster Sessions, 133–136, Prague, the Czech Republic.

21. Bond, Michael Harris. 1993. Emotions and Their Expression in Chinese Culture. Journal of Nonverbal Behavoir. 17(4):245-262.

22. Li, Ji, and Fuji Ren. 2011. Creating a Chinese Emotion Lexicon Based on Corpus REN-CECPS. Proceedings of IEEE CCIS 2011.

23. Xu, Jun, Ruifeng Xu, Yanzhen Zheng, Qin Lu, Kai-Fai Wong, and Xiaolong Wang. 2013. Chinese Emotion Lexicon Developing via Multi-lingual Lexical Resources Integration. In A. Gelbukh (Ed.): CICLing 2013, Part II, LNCS 7817, 174–182. © Springer-Verlag Berlin Heidelberg.

24. Xu, Ge, Xinfan Meng, and Houfeng Wang. 2010. Build Chinese Emotion Lexicons Using A Graph-based Algorithm and Multiple Resources. Proceedings of the 23rd International Conference on Computational Linguistics (Coling 2010), 1209–1217, Beijing, China.

25. Chen, Ying, Sophia Y. M. Lee, and Chu-Ren Huang. 2009. A Cognitive-based Annotation System for Emotion Computing. Proceedings of the Third Linguistic Annotation Workshop, ACL-IJCNLP 2009, 1–9, Suntec, Singapore.

26. Lee, Sophia Yat Mei, Shoushan Li, and Chu-Ren Huang. 2014. Annotating Events in An Emotion Corpus. LREC 2014, 3511–3516.

27. Lee, Sophia Yat Mei, Huarui Zhabg, and Chu-Ren Huang. 2013. An Event-based Emotion Corpus. In P. Liu and Q. Su (Eds.): CLSW 2013, Lecture Notes in Artificial Intelligence (LNAI) 8229, 635–644. © Springer-Verlag Berlin Heidelberg.

28. Baccianella, Stefano, Andrea Esuli, and Fabrizio Sebastiani. 2010. SentiWordNet 3.0: An Enhanced Lexical Resource for Sentiment Analysis and Opinion Mining. Proceedings of the Seventh Conference on International Language Resources and Evaluation (LREC'10), 2200–2204. Valletta, Malta.

29. Bandhakavi, Anil, Nirmalie Wiratunga, Deepak Padmanabhan, and Stewart Massie. 2014. Generating a Word-emotion Lexicon from Emotional Tweets. Proceedings of the Third Joint Conference on Lexical and Computational Semantics (SEM 2014), 12–21. Dublin, Ireland.

30. Esuli, Andrea and Fabrizio Sebastiani. 2006. SentiWordNet: A Publicly Available Lexical Resource for Opinion Mining. Proceedings of the Fifth International Conference on

Language Resources and Evaluation (LREC), 417–422, Genoa, Italy.

31. Taboada, Maite, Caroline Anthony, and Kimberly Voll. 2006. Creating Semantic Orientation Dictionaries. Proceedings of the Fifth International Conference on Language Resources and Evaluation (LREC), 427–432, Genoa, Italy.

32. Taboada, Maite, and Jack Grieve. 2004. Analyzing Appraisal Automatically. Proceedings of the AAAI Spring Symposium on Exploring Attitude and Affect in Text (AAAI Technical Report SS-04-07), 158–161, Stanford, CA.

33. Ku, Lun-Wei, and Hsin-Hsi Chen. 2007. Mining Opinions from the Web: Beyond Relevance Retrieval. Journal of the American Society for Information Science and Technology, 58(12): 1838–1850.

34. Mei, Jia-Ju, Yi-Ming Zhu, Yun-Qi Gao, and Hong-Xiang Yin. 1996. Tongyici Cilin (2nd edition). Shan ghai: Shang wu Press and Shang hai Dictionaries. [In Chinese]

35. Dong, Zhen-Dong and Qiang Dong. 2006. HowNet and the Computation of Meaning. World Scientific Publishing.

36. Chen, Keh-Jiann, Shu-Ling Huang, Yueh-Yin Shih, and Yi-Jun Chen. 2005. Extended-HowNet—A Representational Framework for Concepts. Proceedings of OntoLex. Jeju Island, South Korea.

37. Kiefer, Markus, Stefanie Schuch, Stefanie Schenck, and Klaus Fiedler. 2007. Emotion and Memory: Event-related Potential Indices Predictive for Subsequent Successful Memory Depend on the Emotional Mood State. Advances in Cognitive Psychology, 3(3): 363–373.

38. St-Hilaire, Annie, Alex S. Cohen, and Nancy M. Docherty. 2008. Emotion Word use in the Conversational Speech of Schizophrenia Patients. Cognitive Neuropsychiatry, 13(4): 343–56.

39. van Hooff, Johanna C., Kristina C. Dietz, Dinkar Sharma, and Howard Bowman. 2008. Neural Correlates of Intrusion of Emotion Words in A Modified Stroop Task. International Journal of Psychophysiology, 67: 23–34.

40. Su, Yi-Jen, Shuo-Wen Yu, Huang-Wei Huang and Yue-Qun Chen. 2014. 基于字典树改善中文情绪分类效能之研究. Taiwan Academic Network Conference (TANET2014). 10.22–24, Kaohsiung, Taiwan. [In Chinese]

41. Madden, Sam. 2012. From Databases to Big Data. IEEE Internet Computing, 16(3): 4–6.

42. Cho, Shu-Ling, Hsueh-Chih Chen and Chao-Ming Cheng. 2013. Taiwan Corpora of Chinese Emotions and Relevant Psychophysiological Data -- A Study on the Norm of Chinese Emotional Words. Chinese Journal of Psychology, 55(4): 493–523. [In Chinese]

43. Bechara, Antoine. 2004. The Role of Emotion in the Decisionmaking: Evidence from Neurological Patients with Orbitofrontal Damage. Brain and Cognition, 55: 30–40. Bond.

44. Dolcos, Florin, Kevin S. LaBar, and Roberto Cabeza. 2004. Dissociable Effects of Arousal and Valence on Prefrontal Activity Indexing Emotional Evaluation and Subsequent Memory: An Event-related fMRI Study. NeuroImage, 23: 64–74.

45. Chinese Knowledge Information Processing Group. 1994. 中文书面语频率词典(新闻语

料词频统计). Technical Report No. 94-01. Nankang: Academia Sinica. [In Chinese]

46. Chinese Knowledge Information Processing Group. 1993a. 新闻语料库字频统计表. Technical Report No. 93-01. Nankang: Academia Sinica. [In Chinese]

47. Chinese Knowledge Information Processing Group. 1993b. 新闻语料库词频统计表. Technical Report No. 93-02. Nankang: Academia Sinica. [In Chinese]

48. Chinese Knowledge Information Processing Group. 1993c. 新闻常用动词词频与分类. Technical Report No. 93-03. Nankang: Academia Sinica. [In Chinese]

49. Klebanov, Beata Beigman, Jill Burstein, Nitin Madnani, Adam Faulkner, and Joel Tetreault. 2012. Building Subjectivity Lexicon(s) from Scratch for Essay Data. In Computational Linguistic and Intelligent Text Processing, 591–602. Springer-Verlag Berlin Heidelberg.

50. Jarmasz, Mario. 2003. Roget's Thesaurus as A Lexical Resource for Natural Language Processing. Master's thesis, University of Ottawa, 2003.

51. Huang, Chu-Ren, Dylan Bo Sheng Tsai, Mei-Xin Chu, Wan-Ju Ho, Li-Wan Huang, I-Ni Tsai. 2003. Sense and Meaning Facet: Criteria and Operational Guidelines for Chinese Sense Distinction. Presented at the Fourth Chinese Lexical Semantics Workshops. June 23–25, Hong Kong, Hong Kong City University. [In Chinese]

52. Burton, Steven J., Richard R. Sudweeks, Paul F. Merrill, and Bud Wood. 1991. How to Prepare Better Multiple-choice Test Items: Guidelines for University Faculty. Department of Instructional Science. Brigham Young University Testing Services.

A Study on Semantic Word-Formation Rules of Chinese Nouns from the Perspective of Generative Lexicon Theory*
——A Case Study of Undirected Disyllable Compounds

Xiao Wang   Shiyong Kang   Baorong He   Dian Zhang

School of Chinese Language and Literature, Ludong University
Key Laboratory of Language Resource Development and Application of Shandong Province
Yantai 264025, China
Wangxiaold666@163.com, Kangsy64@163.com

Abstract. This paper mainly applies the qualia structure theory to the study of compound nouns whose lexical meanings cannot be inferred from their morpheme meanings by taking some undirected disyllabic compound nouns as example from the *Chinese Semantic Word-formation Database*. The paper concludes some specific ways by which morpheme meanings can be integrated with lexical meanings. It is hoped that the research result can be conducive to the further study of Chinese semantic word-formation, compilation of dictionaries on motivation, the lexicographical definition and the vocabulary teaching in the teaching of Chinese as a foreign language.

Keywords: disyllabic noun; semantic word-formation; qualia structure; metaphor; metonymy

1   Introduction

There have been many researches about the relationship between morpheme meaning and word meaning. Huaiqing Fu (1981) concluded that there are 5 types of relationship between morpheme meaning and word meaning. In the paper entitled "The Structure Relationship between Compound Morpheme Meanings", Jian Zhou (1991) made a detailed statistical classification study on the semantic structure relationships between the meanings of two morphemes which form compound nouns on a microscopic level by analyzing the structure in which each compound noun is formed by two morphemes. Zhenlan Yang (1993) argued that there are three kinds of relationships between morpheme meanings, namely 'integration, synthesis and combination' so far as the formation of lexical meaning is concerned. Wei Cao(1994) discussed the overt motivation and covert motivation of Chinese lexical meanings from the perspec-

This research is supported by National Social Science Foundation of China (No. 12BYY123) and National Natural Science Foundation of China(No. 61272215).

© Springer International Publishing AG 2016
M. Dong et al. (Eds.): CLSW 2016, LNAI 10085, pp. 18–30, 2016
DOI: 10.1007/978-3-319-49508-8_2

tive of Genetics. Jinxia Li and Yuming Li(2008) proposed the concept "Semantic Transparency" which indicates the scale difference of how easily the whole lexical meaning can be deduced from the meanings of its compositions. According to the scale difference, words are divided into absolute transparent, relatively transparent, relatively obscure and absolute obscure ones. In addition, Yinxin Sun (2003), Shuzhai Wang (1993) and Houyao Zheng (2006) have also done some researches in this aspect. Ludong University has been long committed to the study of Chinese semanticword formation and created Chinese Character Semantic Category Information Database1, and Chinese Semantic Word-formation Database2. After examining the relationship between the lexical meaning and the meanings of two morphemes in more than 50,000 disyllabic compounds, we generalized four rules that morpheme (ziwei) meanings constitute word meaning, including the similar rule, the backward rule, the forward rule, the undirected rule. The similar rule means the two ziwei of a word belong to the same semantic category, and the semantic category of the word is basically same as that of ziwei. The backward rule means the two ziwei of a word belong to different semantic categories, and the semantic category of the word is the same as that of the second ziwei. The forward type means the two ziwei of the word belong to different semantic types, and the semantic type of the word is the same as the first preceding ziwei. The undirected type means the two ziwei of a word belong to different semantic categories, and the semantic category of the words different from that of the first ziwei and the second ziwei. (Shiyong Kang, 2004). The following is an example from the Chinese Semantic Word-formation Database.

Based on the above study, we selected some undirected nouns as research materialto explore the types of undirected words and to interpret why they are undirected with relevant theory. In the same database, Lu Liu (2015) have studiedthe similar rules (such as Aa+ Aa=A, Aa +Ab=A, Ba +Ba=B) and the similar rules in the undirected type (such as Aa +Aa=B, Aa+Ab=C, Ba+Bb=A). In this study we analyzed some disyllabic compound words extracted from the compounds that are formed not by morphemes of the same semantic category in undirected type, which involve such semantic category as EC3, ED, EF, EH, FA , FH, HD, IH, totaling 412.

---

[1]To make it convenient for both man and machine, when we built the Chinese Character Semantic Category Information Database we introduced a concept—"ziwei" (the smallest semantic word-formation unit, that is, a character consisting of form, sound and meaning, with each ziwei having a form, a sound and a meaning). In accordance with the principles of "one-character-one-entry, one-entry-one-meaning, the combination of meaning and grammatical function, non-morpheme characters as separate entries", the Database derived 17430ziwei from 6763 Chinese characters defined by Chinese Standard GB2312 and classified each ziwei according to the three–level semantic classification system with *Tongyici Cilin*or Chinese Dictionary of Synonyms(the major class, the medium class and minor class).

[2]The Database for the Semantic Word-Formation Rules of Chinese Disyllabic CompoundWords is based on *Tongyici Cilin* with more than 50000 disyllabic compound words selected from the Modern Chinese Dictionary and Chinese Neologism Dictionary. The words in the Database followtheprinciple of "one meaning for one word ", namely, each meaning having an entry, so a polysemous word has multiple entries.

[3]EC type means the semantic category of morpheme 1 is E, and the semantic category of mor-

Fig. 1. The Example of Chinese Semantic Word-formation Database

词语	素义义类1	素义义类2	词的义类
▶ 猎户	Hd28, 捕捉禽兽, 打猎的	DI05, 人家, 门第, 户头	Ae08
领队	Hf04, 带, 引	DI10, 具有某种性质的集体, 特指少年先锋队	Af10
录事	Hg11, 记载	Da01, 事情, 事故	Ae01
录象	Hh03, 录制	Dc01, 形状, 样子	Ae17
屠伯	Hd28, 宰杀	Dn04, 在弟兄排行的次序里是老大	Ae08
屠户	Hd28, 宰杀	DI05, 人家, 门第, 户头	Ae08
推事	HI33, 推委, 推脱	DI22, 关系或责任	Ae12
秘书	HI20, 保守秘密	Dk17, 文件, 资料	Ae01
亡命	Hj38, 逃跑	Da17, 生命, 寿命	Ag08

2   A Brief Introduction of GLT

Generative Lexicon Theory (GLT) was proposed in 1995. Since then it has been developed and improved continually, and evolved into a language generation theory
with strong explanatory power which can be applied to various combinations ranging
from the combination of words to the combination of morphemes. This paper mainly
uses the qualia structure theory which is included in Generative Lexicon Theory .

The Qualia structure describes what constitutes the object, what the object refers to,
how it is formed and what purposes and functions it has, respectively corresponding
to constitutive role, formal role, telic role and agentive role (Pustejovsky 1995, Zuoyan Song 2011). Constitutive rolerefers to the relationship between the object and its
components, which includes materials, weight, parts and compositions; Formal role
refers to the properties that distinguish the object from other objects, such as orientation, size, shape and dimensions and so on; Telic role refers to the purpose and function of the object; Agentive role describes how the object is formed or produced
(Pustejovsky1995, Zuoyan Song2011). Conventionalized attributeshave also been
incorporated into the general qualia structure. Conventionalized attributes refer to the
typical characteristicsof things, including regular activities and properties related to
the things. After the qualia structure was introduced to the Chinese study, YulinYuan ,
according to Chinese nouns' basic combination, collocationrulesand semantic interpretation in texts, presented a Chinese noun qualia structure description system, and
defined ten roles (formal, constitutive, unit, evaluation, agentive, material,telic, behavior, disposal and location). The roles defined by YulinYuan are basically consistent
with the above six roles. The material role can be included in constitutive role. Evalu-

---

pheme 2 is C, the semantic category of the word is noun that belongs neither to E nor to C (here
the letter E and C stands for the mark of the major category in Tongyici Cilin). Such as: E+C=A,
E+C=B, E+C=D, the rest can be deduced in the same manner.

ationrole, behavior role, disposal role and location role can be classified under conventionalized attributes, for they all belong to people's common understanding of conventionalized usage of nouns. Take "plaster" for example. Its constitutiverole is "medicine", formal role is "solid", telic role is "cure", agentive role is "production", conventionalized attribute is "paste", unit role is "film".

3   Types of Undirected Words

After data analysis, we conclude several reasons why lexical meaning cannot be inferred from morpheme meaning. They are as follows:

3.1   Lexical meaning deriving from the metaphorical or metonymic use of morpheme.

Lexical meaning derives from the metaphorical or metonymical use of morpheme. For example, the morpheme meanings of "zhaoya" are claws(zhao) and teeth(ya), yet "zhaoya" refers to the members of the evildoers. The reason why it can refer to human beings is that teeth and claws are the powerful weapons of animal. It is based on the similarity of the telic role that people gradually came to refer to the gang of a clique as "zhaoya". "Chengchi" consists of the morpheme meaning of walls and moat, yet its lexical meaning is city. This is because the city includes city walls and moat. It is based on the correlation of the constitutive role that "cheng chi" metonymically becomes a synonym for city.

3.2   The lexical meaning bearing no metaphorical and metonymic meaning of morpheme

Under the premise that there is no metonymy or metaphor or metaphtonymy, there are three reasons why the lexical meaning can't be deduced from the morpheme meanings: Firstly it is because of historical reasons that some words retain the old meaning. Due to the disruption of the etymology, some unprofessional persons are unable to infer the lexical meaning. Secondly it is due to some cultural factors. For example, "zuxia", "tongchui", "wending" are historical allusions. Thirdly there are some proper nouns like "haihong", "yibei", "hongyou", "haisong"; Fourthly there are abbreviated words, dialectal words or colloquial words.
Based on the above review, we analyzed some disyllabic nouns whose meanings have undergone metaphoric and metonymic changes from the perspectives of the qualia structure theory and the metaphtonymy theory, hoping to find new rules for the "exception" that does not follow the semantic word formation rules.

4   Disyllabic Nouns with Metonymy and Metaphor

4.1   Disyllabic Nouns with Metonymy (including the Preceding, Latter or Overall Metonymy)

Morpheme Reflecting the Telic Role of Words.

That a morpheme reflects the telic role of a word means that the morpheme is the telic role of its compound word. The relationship between the morpheme meaning and the meaning of the word composed by the morphemes is shown by the fact that themorpheme reflects the function of the word meaning. It is based on the correlation of this kind of telic role that metonymy occurs. For example, "bubai"refers to "short notes", and its function is to fill in the blank. The morpheme meaning is the telic role of the word, thus, based upon the correlation of telic role, the metonymic meaning of "bubai" here refers to "short notes" which are used to fill in the blanks. "Jiangyi" refers to the textbooks or notes which explain some reasons or meanings. The morpheme is the telic role of the word. As a result, based upon the correlation of telic role, metonymically "jiangyi"refers to the supplementary teaching materials or notes.

Explicit Telic Role.
Explicit telic role means that a morpheme can directly tell the role or function of something or someone signified by a word. Take "jingli" (manager, director of a company) for example. The primary function of "jingli"is to be responsible for the whole operation and management of the company. The specific situations in our corpus are as follow:
E+F=B Latter Metonymy: "Xiaochi" refers to the local delicacy (eating—food)4. Food is to be eaten, and the latter "chi" (eat) is the function of food, namely the morpheme reflects the telic role of words. Based upon the correlation of telic role, the function of food"chi" metonymically refers to food.
E+H=A Latter Metonymy: "Zhubian" refers to the main editorial staff, and "zongbian"refers to the most important editor (editing—editor). The morpheme "bian" (edit) is the telic role of the word meaning (human). Based upon the correlation of telic role, the function of the editorial staff"bianji"metonymically refers to "editorial staff".
Overall Metonymy: "Tongyi" refers to the person who interprets for people with language barriers (interpreting—interpreter). The main function of interpreters is to provide comprehensive linguistic translationfor those who know nothing about the foreign language, that is, to practice"tongyi". The morpheme reflects the telic role of words. Based upon the correlation of this kind of telic role, the function is used metonymically to refer to "the people with this function". "Antan" means spy (spying—

---

[4]The linguistic expression preceding the dash refers to the morphemes and metonymic or metaphorical meaning s of morphemes. The linguistic expression succeeding the dash refers to the meanings of words.

spy). The main function of a spy is to spy on others. Similarwords include "luxiang" (video),"lingdui" (leader),"shexiang" (camera),"jiechai" (escort),"tongshi" (interpreter), "ganshi" (director), "yanhu" (cover) and "baishe" (decoration), etc.

Implicit Telic Role.

Implicit telic role means that the function signified by the morpheme is related to the things or person possessing this kind of function, including both the direct telic role and the indirect telic role. In the direct telic role, what a morpheme signifies is the thing signified by the word or the direct object acted upon by people signified by the word. For example, "fuzhuang" (costume) can be used to refer to those who manage the costume. In the indirect telic role, the content after the transfer of word meaning-maintains the same function as that of the content before the transfer of word meaning. For example, "xinfu" (henchman) represents the trustworthy person. The function of the trustworthy is similar to that of our heart and stomach. In our selected corpus, the direct telic role is the majority; the details are as follow:

E+D=AOverall Metonymy: "Yilu" means companion (whole journey—those who go through the whole journey). Companion's function is to accompany others; "shuwu" refers to officers (general affairs—officer). Officer's main function is to deal with various affairs; "tewu" refers to someone engaged in special tasks (special task—those who handle special task). The main function of a spy is to finish the special task and work. It is based upon the correlation of direct telic role that the whole morpheme takes on the metonymic meaning in which the function of the word is used to refer to the meaning of the word.

So far, according to our analysis of the corpus, there are 126 words with the morpheme reflecting their telic role and having metonymic meanings (including the preceding, latter and overall metonymy) based upon the telic role.

Morpheme Reflecting the Constitutive Role of Words.

In the disyllabic compounds, a morpheme is an integral part of a word;both the morpheme and the word are closely connected, forming a part-and-whole relationship, as well as a relationship between the typical individual and the overall category. Morphemes stimulate and reflect the constitutive role of words, thus bearing metonymic meaning based upon the correlation of constitutive role. For instance, "xumei" refers to male (beard and eyebrows—face—man), "xu" (beard) and "mei" (eyebrows) are parts of man's face, and they are used to refer to male. In our corpus the circumstances are as follow:

Part-whole Relations.

E+C=D Latter Metonymy: "Yiyu" refers to other countries (lands within certain boundaries or territory—country). Countries are usually made up of several localities or territories. Morpheme reflects the constitutive role of words. It is based on the correlation of constitutive role that the metonymy occurs where the parts of a country are used to refer to the country

E+D=A Latter Metonymy--Overall Metonymy: "Guorong" means the most beautiful woman in the country (appearance—face—woman). "Rong" refers to appearance, which is generally manifested in the face and attached to the face. The face is an integral part of human being. Similarly, both "hongyan" and "zhuyan" refer to beauties; and "ciyan" refers to parents.

Relations between Typical Individual and Overall Category.

I+H=D Overall Metonymy: "Yange" refers to the process of development (continuity or revolution—the process of development). Things basically have two forms of development and changes. One is the continuity of the original, and the other is the revolution, both are intended to make it develop. Based upon the correlation of this kind of constitutive role, "yange"metonymically here refers to the process of development and changes of things.

Close Relations.

E+B=A Latter Metonymy: "Nvguan" refers to female Taoist priest (guan: hat—human being). Because female Taoist priests in Tang Dynasty all wore yellow guans, while worldly women wore nothing, hence "nvguan" (female hat) is used to refer to female Taoist priest.

E+D=A Overall Metonymy: "Wansheng"refers to an emperor (tens of thousands of chariots—emperor). Theemperor always takes control of the country's military power which was shown through the number of chariots in the ancient times. "Tongyan" refers to classmates (sharing one ink-stone—classmates). One ink–stone was shared by students to grind ink for brush writing. Rubbing an ink stick on the ink-stone for the ink is usually done by scholars or learners. Based upon this close correlation, "tongyan" is metonymically used to refer to classmates.

According to our present analysis of the corpus, there are 43 words whose morphemes reflecting the constitutive role of words and having metonymic meanings (including the preceding, latter and overall metonymy) based upon the constitutive role.

Morpheme Reflecting the Agentive Role of Words.

Morphemes reflect the agentive role of words, and the morpheme meaning and the meaning of words often form a cause-and-effect relation. Based upon this correlation of agentive role, the metonymic meaning of morphemes usually refers to the result. From the perspective of grammatical category, the meaning of a noun is generally derived from the meaning of a verb, that is, the result comes from action. In our selected corpus the circumstances are as follow:

E+F=D Overall Metonymy: "Jingzhuang"refers to style and decoration (elaborate assembling—style, decoration). Delicate style depends on elaborate assembling. "Cixiu" refers to a kind of handicraft ("ci" means penetrating something with a sharp object; "xiu" meanssewing something with silk threads on clothes—a kind of handicraft).

F+H=D Overall Metonymy: "Nisu" is another kind of handicraft (shaping—a kind of handicraft shaped by clay).

H+A=B Overall Metonymy: "Pushou" refers to the circlet on the doorknob (animal heads made up of materials like gold, silver, bronze and so on—circlets shaped as animal heads on the doorknobs).

I+H=D Overall Metonymy: "Huibian" refers to a series of articles and documents compiled together (collecting and editing—forming articles and documents). Articles and documents are always compiled. "Bianjian" refers to books. During the ancient times, most Chinese scripts were written on bamboo or wooden slips, which must be bound together for collection.Usually two strands of hemp ropes or silk threads are used to link both the upper and lower ends of the bamboo or wooden slips where there is no word; it is much similar to knitting bamboo curtain.

H+D=B Preceding Metonymy: "Zhalei" refers to a kind of food cooked by frying (frying—food). This kind of food is always fried; similar food includes roasted food, quick-fried food, and stir-fried food and so on.

"Suibi" (essay) and "xubian" (continuation) also belong to this category. They are all referred by the agentive role of words, which are reflected by morpheme. At present, according to our corpus, there are 58 such words.

Morpheme Reflecting the Formal Role of Words.

Formal role refers to the forms of manifestation of the words constituted by morphemes, mainly including color, shape, size, etc. For example, the morpheme of "dahuang" ("da" means big, "huang"means yellow) shows the formal role (color) of the word, and thus the formal role of medicinal materials "dahuang" (yellowish-white) is used to refer to the Chinese herbal medicine. "Cangmang"refers to the sky. "Cang" is the gray color, and "mang" means "boundless", which is a formative description of the color and size of the sky. In our selected corpus the circumstances are as follow:

E+D=B Overall Metonymy : "Huaquan" refers to the sacrificial offering (decorated with flowers or decorative pattern, circle shape—sacrificial offering). "Huaquan" ("quan" means circle) is a circle decorated with flowers and decorative patterns; "hengfu" refers to a sign or banner (something hanging above parallel to the ground and as wide as cloth fabric—sign and flag). The hanging banner is generally parallel to the ground and as wide as something like cloth fabric, etc.

H+D=B Latter Metonymy: "Fatiao" refers to a long strip of steel sheet which generates driving force with the help of elasticity when released after tight winding (strip: the elongated shape—the elongated shape of the steel sheet).

Attribute Based on the Conventionalization.

Conventionalized attributes are the typical features of things, mainly including regular activity, direct characteristic, direct space and object-dependent attribute, etc. The regular activity attribute means that the meaning of a word is the related activity it is engaged in; the direct characteristic attribute means that the meaning of a word is the main feature of things; the direct space attribute means that the meaning of a word derives from the activity space which is used to refer to things or human being, such as "jiefang"(neighborhood), in which the spatial meaning of residential places is used to refer to the residents living there; the object-dependent attribute means that the meaning of a word usually depends on the meaning of morphemes, and that the morpheme meaning is generally concrete, yet the meaning of a word is usually abstract. For example, "moshui"is usually used to indicate whether a person has true skill and genuine knowledge or not, and a person's knowledge is measured by how much ink the person uses while reading and writing. In our selected corpus the circumstances are as follows:

Attribute of Regular Activity.

E+H=A Overall Metonymy: "Linju" refers to people living close to one's own dwellings (living in adjacent place— people who live in adjacent place).

F+H=B Overall Metonymy: "Tiaotuo" refers to the bracelet (jumping and breaking away—bracelet).Bracelet worn on the hand is not so tight, so it is easy to fall off the wrist if one jumps up and down;"feizou" refers to birds and animals (birds flap wings and leave—birds and animals). The basic activities of birds and animals are flying and walking (leaving).

H+D=BOverall Metonymy: "Shougong" refers to gecko (keeping the palace—gecko). It is also known as Flat-tailed House Gecko. For the gecko always climbs on the wall to predatemoth, hence "shougong" is used to refer to gecko.

Feature Attribute.

E+C=AOverall Metonymy: "Qingtian"refers to honest and upright officials (the bluesky—incorrupt and upright officials maintaining the same characteristics as the blue sky).

I+H=D Overall Metonymy: "Jiqing"refers to things characterized by good luck and worthy of celebration (auspiciousness and celebration—auspicious things and something worth celebration). "Gaoming" refers to people with smart features (wise— people who maintain smart features). "Duyao" refers to a kind of grass with the characteristic of shaking in the absence of wind. The name of the grass is originated from DouBaicao in Dunhuang QuziCi, namely, "The flower blossoms with tears, the grass shakes alone without winds." It is further proved by a quote by Shizhen Li to interpret the names of plant terms in the Ming Dynasty from Mingyibielu (Supplementary Records of Famous Physicians)in his book Bencaogangmu(Compendium of Materia Medica,Caoer, Duhuo). It goes like this, *"The grass remains still in the wind, but shakes without the wind, hence the name 'duyao' ."*

Spatial and Temporal Attribute.

E+D=A Overall Metonymy: "Tangshang" refers to parents (the principal room which parents live in—parents); "dahu" refers to rich men (big portal--the millionaire who possesses large portal); "fangzhang" refers to the host of the Buddhist temple (the dwelling place of a Buddhist abbot—abbot)

E+C=A Latter Metonymy:"Shaonian" refers to the younger person.

Object-dependent Attribute.

E+C=D Overall Metonymy: "Shangwei"refers to glorious position (top position—

those who are in a top position).

E+H=D Latter Metonymy: "Zhuobi" is a humble term for one's own work (pen: a writing and drawing tool—works).

I+H=DOverall Metonymy: "Xingjian" refers to good conduct (good behavior—good conduct); "fanlian" refers to the sudden change of one's attitudes towards other people, usually changing from good to bad (complexion—attitude). People's attitude, good or not, can easily be seen from the tone and complexion.

According to the statistics of the corpus, there are 140 words with morphemes reflecting the conventionalized attributes and having metonymic meaning (including the preceding, latter and overall metonymy)based on the conventionalized attributes.

1. Morpheme Reflecting the Role of the Unit of Words.

According to the basic combination modes, collocation rules and semantic interpretation of Chinese nouns in the text, YulinYuan proposed a descriptive system of Chinese noun qualia structure and defined 10 qualia roles, including the role of unit which means nouns have a unit of measurement. Take "Linli" for example. In ancient Chinese, five families can be called "Lin" and five neighbors can be called "Li". But now "linli" is used to refer to neighborhood.

E+D=A Latter Metonymy: "Zhuwei" / "gewei" / "nawei" refers to people (wei: the unit of person—human being);

E+D=B Latter Metonymy: "Quanzhang" refers to the paper that has not been cut ("zhang", literally meaning piece: the unit of paper—paper); "dajian"refers to the large objects ("jian", literally meaning piece: the unit of objects—objects).

H+D=B Latter Metonymy: "Suanchi"refers to slide rules (ruler: a unit of length—a tool that is used to measure length—something like a ruler). According to the statistics of the corpus, there are 7 words which have metonymic meaning (includingthe latter and overall metonymy) based on the role of the unit of words.

4.2   Preceding and Latter Metaphor (including Overall Metaphor)

Similarity of Agentive Role.

I+H=D Overall Metaphor: "Zahui" refers to a motley assortment of things (mixing different food and cooking—the food that is mixed and cooked—something mixed).Morphemes reflect indirect agentive role of the word, and there are some similarities inagentive role between the cooked food that is mixed and something mixed.

Similarity of Formal Role.

H+D=B Preceding Metaphor: "Jianguo" refers to olive ("jian": giving some expostulationto correct mistakes—"good advice is harsh to the ear" should be bitter in taste— criticism always makes one feel bitter). Something harsh to one's ear has similarity with the bitterness of olive, this association leads to metaphor, and therefore, "jianguo" is often used to refer to olive. It is worth attention that the part of speech of "jian" here has transformed from a verb into a word with the characteristic of an adjective. In addition, "jiansun" also refers to bitter bamboo shoot.

E+D=A Overall Metaphor: "Changtiao" refers to a tall person (somethingshaped like a long strip—a tall person). This kind of person has similar characteristic as a long strip, and they are both thin and long.

E+H=B Overall Metaphor: "Yudan" refers to the morning star (white and beautiful ball—the morning star). The shape of the morning star is like a beautiful and white ball.

E+D=B Overall Metaphor: "Baiye" refers to the bean products ("ye", meaning page: piece—things with lots of pages—bean products); "baiye" is also called omasum which refers to cattle's stomach (a thing which has a lot of layers and pieces like leaves—stomach).

Overall Metaphor: "Yuchen" is compared to snow (jade-like dust –snow). The snow is as white and flawless as jade and is as tiny as dust; "yulong" is compared to water-fall and spring (jade-like dragon–waterfall, spring).Waterfall and spring look like a long dragon and their color is like jade.

Similarity of Conventionalized Attribute.

Similarity of Feature Attribute.

"Rugou" means "falling into a trap", namely, "gou" refers to "a trap". According to "Anecdotes in Tang Dynasty: On Chin-shihs", when the emperor Taizong of the Tang Dynasty saw crowds of Chin-shihs swarming out through the side door of the Forbidden City, he said excitedly, "All the great minds have been under my control and they will pledge loyalty to me." "Gouzhong" originally referred to the shooting range. "Rugou" is a metaphor based upon the similarity of conventionalized attribute. "Rugou" later took on such metaphorical meaning as "to be put into prison" or "to be under one's control".

E+C=B Overall Metaphor: "Mangcang" refers to the sky (the vast wilderness—the sky). The sky shares the same characteristic of boundlessness with the wilderness.

E+C=D Overall Metaphor: "Jiuquan" refers to the deepest place under the ground (the underground water in the deepest place—the deepest place). "Jiuwei" refers to the world (infinite space—the world). The feature of the world is the infinite space. "Zhenggui"refers to the right way of development (right track—right way for development).

E+D=B : "Guibi" refers to fungi ("gui" literally means "bad", "bi" means "pen"—fungi). This kind of fungi is toxic and is shaped like a pen;the metaphor here involves the overlapping of the two roles, namely, the formative role (shape) and the feature attribute. "Wangpai"refers to a person with outstanding talent (the best card in card games—the strongest ability—talent). Whether "wangpai" refers to a card or a person, they share a common feature, that is, the strongest ability.

In our selected corpus, there are 17 wordswhose meanings derived from metaphors.

5   Summary

After the statistics, we concluded that there are 412 words whose meaning derive from metaphor or metonymicword formation. The main qualia structure roles involved and their numbers are shown in the figure below:

Fig. 2. The Quantity of the Qualia Roles

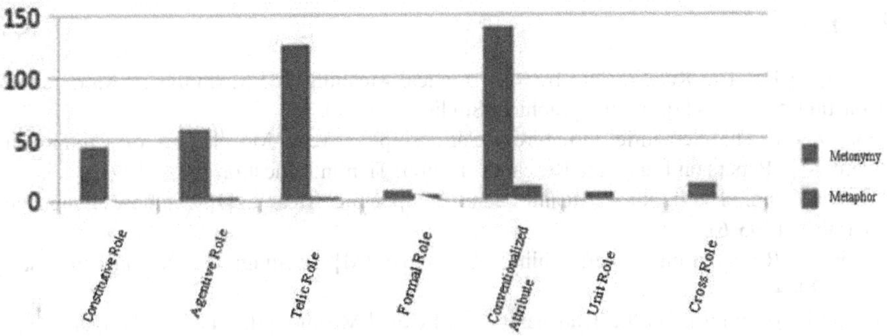

Through the analysis, we can conclude that metaphor and metonymy compound nouns derive their new meanings from the mapping of a single domain or two domains realized by the partial or whole activation of the qualia roles by morphemes. It is obvious that there are more occurrences of metonymy than that of metaphor, namely: metonymy(395)> metaphor(17).So far as the qualia structure is concerned, we can see such an order: conventionalized attributes(140)> telic role (126)> agentive role (58) > constitutive role (43)>cross role (13) > formal role (8) > unit role (7). This result has something to do with our choice of corpus, for in our corpus, most of the morphemes belong to such semantic categories as E (features), C (time and space), H (activity), F (action) and I (phenomenonand state), and a few belong to other minor semantic category as A (person) and D (abstract things). Their characteristics, activities and actions are more related to conventionalized attributes, telic role or agentive role.

In the process of corpus analysis, there are many morphemes with metaphorical or metonymic meanings, such as "daocaoren" (scarecrow), "niren" (clay figure) and "xueren" (snowman), and they are not real man, but things just like man. Other examples are "jiaoshui" (glue) and "huazhuangshui" (lotion). They are not water, but they are of liquid form, and they all contain some water.In other words, they represent things like water. In Modern Chinese Dictionary, many words are defined with the expression "something like.....". For example, one of the definitions of the "er"(ear) is "something like ears". We think that "something like water or man" should also be included in the definition of "water" and "man".

This paper did not interpret all the disyllabic nounswith qualia structure theory. On the one hand, some words (such as allusion words or proper nouns, etc.)indeed cannot be explained with qualia structure theory. On the other hand, the classification in Tongyici Cilin by Jiaju Mei is based on the introspective approach adopted by previous scholars. What's more, the semantic categories classified are controversial, and the scope of the corpus is not large. All in all, because of our limited knowledge and understanding of the qualia structure theory, this paper only selected some of the undirected words for study. In the future, the researcher will continue to expand the corpus so as to make the conclusion more conclusive and representative. The analytic process is not without personal subjective element, we are looking forward to your valuable suggestions.

References:

1. Huaiqing Fu. The Relationship between Lexical Meaning and Meanings of Morphemes Constituting Words [J]. Lexicographical Studies, 1981(1).
2. Jian Zhou. The Semantic Structure Relationship between Morphemes of Compound Words[C]. Papers on Language Research. Tianjin: Tianjin Education Press, 1991.
3. ZhenlanYang, The Lexical Meaning and Morphemic Meaning[J]. Chinese Language Learning, 1993(6).
4. WeiCao. Research on Modern Chinese Vocabulary[M]. Beijing: The Peking University Press, 2004.
5. JinxiaLi, YumingLi. On the Transparency of Lexical Meaning[J].Studies in Language and Linguistics, 2008 (3).
6. Shuzhai Wang. The Relationships between Morpheme Meaning and Lexical Meaning of Chinese Compounds[J]. Chinese Language Learning, 1993, 74 (2).
7. Houyao Zheng.A Study on the Relations between Morpheme Meanings and Lexical Meanings of Disyllabic Compounds of Modern Chinese Language[D]. Ph.D Dissertation. Central China Normal University.
8. Shiyong Kang, Maosong Sun. A Database-based Study on Chinese Semantic Word-Formation[C]. Conference Proceedings of the 3rd Chinese Lexical Semantics Workshop, 2004.
9. Shiyong Kang. A Study of Modern Chinese Grammar for Information Processing[M]. Shanghai: Shanghai Lexicographical Publishing House. 2004.
10. Jiaxuan Shen . Blending and Truncating [J]. Chinese Teaching in the World, 2006 (4).
11. Pustejovsky. The Generative Lexicon[M]. Cambridge, MA: The M IT Press, 1995.
12. Lakoff, George. The Contemporary Theory of Metaphor[A]. In Andrew Ortony (ed.). Metaphor and Thought[M]. Cambridge, MA: Cambridge University Press, pp, 202—251. 1993.
13. Xiusong Zhang, Ailing Zhang .The Brief of the Generative Lexical Theory[J]. Contemporary Linguistics, 2009(3).
14. YulinYuan. On the Descriptive System of Qualia Structure of Chinese Nouns and Its Application in Parsing Complex Chinese Grammatical Phenomena[J]. Contemporary Linguistics. 2014(1):31-48.
15. Zuoyan Song. The Latest Developments of Generative Lexicon Theory[J]. Essays on Linguistics, 2011(44): 202-221.
16. Zuoyan Song. Generative Lexicon Theory and Study of Event Coercion of Mandarin Chinese[M]. Beijing: the Peking University Press，2015.
17. Qingqing Zhao: Study on Chinese Metaphorical Disyllabic Noun-Noun Compounds Based on Generative Lexicon Theory [A]. Conference Proceedings of the 3rd Chinese Lexical Semantics Workshop[C]. 2014.
18. Lu Liu: A Study on Semantic Word-formation Rules of Chinese Nouns——A Case Study of Undirected Disyllable Compounds [D]. MA Thesis, Ludong University.

Polysemous Words Definition in the Dictionary and Word Sense Annotation

Jing Wang[1], Zhiying Liu[2], Honfei Jiang[3]

[1]The institute of Chinese Information Processing, Beijing Normal University, Beijing, 100875

Email: wangjing1204@foxmail.com

[2]The institute of Chinese Information Processing, Beijing Normal University, Beijing, 100875

Email: liuzhy@bnu.edu.cn

[3]The institute of Chinese Information Processing, Beijing Normal University, Beijing, 100875

Email: jianghongfei@bnu.edu.cn

Abstract. By employing Modern Chinese Dictionary as the semantic system for word sense tagging, this paper analyzes the relationships between polysemous words meanings in dictionary and their senses in real corpus. The paper finds that there are three types of relations. First, word meanings in the dictionary can cover all the word senses in the corpus, with some overlapping and repetitive content of each other. Second, word meanings fail to explain word senses in corpus with a lack of meanings or narrow meanings. Third, word meanings exceed the word senses in corpus. The phenomena of overlapping, narrow scope, absence and redundancy of word meanings in dictionary bring difficulties to the work of word sense tagging on real corpus. With an overall consideration of the dictionary and real corpus, reasons behind the phenomena are found out and attempts and methods have been proposed in hope of compiling better dictionaries and completing a better work of word sense annotation on corpus.

Keywords: Polysemous words, Corpus, Definition in dictionary, Word sense annotation

1   Introduction

Word sense annotation refers to tagging the appropriate meanings for a polysemous word on a real corpus based on a certain dictionary (Wu, 2006).A large-scale word sense annotation corpus, which is very important in the field of Natural Language Processing, can also be used to verify the rationality and integrity of

© Springer International Publishing AG 2016
M. Dong et al. (Eds.): CLSW 2016, LNAI 10085, pp. 31–39, 2016
DOI: 10.1007/978-3-319-49508-8_3

word meanings in dictionary [1].

The selection of annotation system and dictionary in word sense annotation mainly contains traditional language dictionary (like *Cihai* and *Modern Chinese Dictionary*), semantic dictionary (like *Chinese Thesaurus*), knowledge base of word sense for natural language processing (like WordNet and HowNet) [2]. Word meaning rationality and integrity is a precondition for word sense annotation and word sense disambiguation when employing traditional dictionary as the semantic system.

By analyzing Modern Chinese Dictionary, Xiao[3] pointed out word meanings of polysemous words in dictionary always overlapping, disjointed and inclusive mutually, which brings adverse effects on the precision of word sense tagging. He believes that word meanings of polysemous words in traditional dictionary always lack of rationality and integrity, which makes it difficult to select a appropriate word meaning or find a corresponding sense for words in corpus. However, apart from the unsuitability of word meanings, the relationships between word meanings and morpheme meanings, the part-of-speech marking would bring difficulties to word sense tagging.

This paper is based on the Word Sense Annotation Corpus for Teaching Chinese as Second Language, which contains 58 sets, 189 volumes of textbooks and about 34 million characters. *Modern Chinese Dictionary* 6th[4]was employed as the semantic system, and 1173 polysemous words have been tagged on the corpus. Based on the word sense annotation corpus, this paper tries to analyze the relationships between word meanings in dictionary and word senses in real sentences, and reveal the reasons behind the contradictions.

2   Paraphrasing relations between word meanings in dictionary and word senses in real corpus

Word meanings and morpheme meanings must be distinguished clearly before tagging. Fu[5] points out that before analyzing different meanings of a word, word meanings must be distinguished from morpheme meanings, a word meaning can be used independently, such as the word meanings (1), (3), (6), (7), (10) and (10) of word "BAI" (white) in picture 1, and a morpheme meaning of a word can only exists in the words and fixed structures which are constructed by it, such as meanings (2),(4),(5),(8) and (9) in picture 1. Distinguishing word meaning and morpheme meaning in dictionary makes it convenient for word sense annotation and word sense disambiguation. For Chinese, word segmentation is done before word sense disambiguation, so word meanings instead of morpheme meanings are the real targets of disambiguation[6,7].

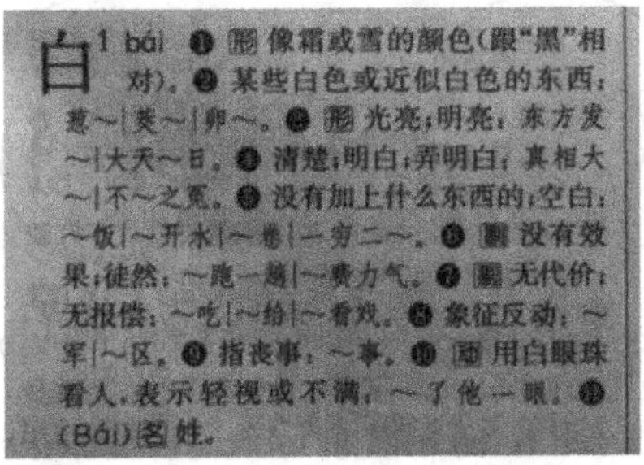

白¹ bái ❶ 形 像霜或雪的颜色（跟"黑"相对）。❷ 某些白色或近似白色的东西：葱～|茭～|卵～。❸ 形 光亮；明亮：东方发～|大天～日。❹ 清楚；明白；弄明白：真相大～|不～之冤。❺ 没有加上什么东西的；空白：～饭|～开水|～卷|一穷二～。❻ 副 没有效果；徒然：～跑一趟|～费力气。❼ 副 无代价；无报偿：～吃|～给|～看戏。❽ 象征反动：～军|～区。❾ 指丧事：～事。❿ 动 用白眼珠看人，表示轻视或不满：～了他一眼。⓫ (Bái) 名 姓。

Fig.1. Meanings of polysemous word "白(*white*)" in Modern Chinese Dictionary 6th

There are 3 types of paraphrasing relations between word meanings in dictionary and word senses in real corpus, that is: 1) word meanings in dictionary can cover all word senses in corpus; 2) word meanings cannot cover all word senses in corpus, sometimes they will lack of meanings or have narrow meanings; 3) word meanings would exceed the word senses.

2.1 Word meanings in dictionary can cover all word senses

Word meanings distinguish with each other clearly

It's the most ideal situation for word sense annotation, word meanings can be selected suitably for word sense of a polysemous word. Supposing that S is the total word senses of a polysemous word in real corpus, and word meaning of the word in dictionary is S1,S2,S3...Sn , so it can be expressed by formula (1):

$$S = S_1+S_2+S_3+...+S_n=S_1 \cup S_2 \cup S_3 \cup ... \cup S_n \quad (1)$$

That is for a polysemous word, all word senses exited in real corpus equals to the sum and union of word meanings listed in dictionary, because all word meanings can be distinguished clearly. Though boundaries of some word meanings may overlap with each, the core meaning is clear enough to tag. It is the most common situation in word sense annotation which proves the feasibility of tagging word senses by dictionary.

Word meanings may overlap with each other.

Though word meanings can cover all word senses in corpus, they may overlap with each other, which make it difficult to select suitable meanings for a word. It can be expressed like this:

$$S = S_1+S_2+S_3+...+S_n<S_1 \cup S_2 \cup S_3 \cup ... \cup S_n \quad (2)$$

That is for a polysemous, all word senses exited in real corpus equals to the sum of word meanings listed in dictionary, but less than the union of the meanings, forsome word meanings would overlap with each other. Two forms of overlapping are partial overlapping and inclusion shown in picture 2.

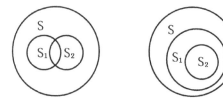

Fig.2. Partial overlapping (left) and inclusion (right) relations of word meanings

If some meanings of a word have partial word senses, they would overlap with each other, when the overlapping part is big enough, a meaning would contain another meaning. Note that overlapping relations would occur among 3 or more word meanings. Word meanings overlapping make it difficult for annotators to select suitable meanings for a word, which also lead to inconsistency of annotation. Table 1 shows some polysemous words with overlapping word meanings.

Table 1. polysemous words with overlapping meanings in dictionary

word	Word meanings	Corpus
地道 Authentic	① 真正是有名产地出产的：～药材. *(real or genuine)* ② 真正的；纯粹：她的普通话说得真～。*(authentic)*	S1 **地道**的炎黄子孙(*real* Chinese descendant) S3 **地道**的广式点心(**authentic** Guangdong Dim Sum)
冻 Freeze /Cold	③【动】受冷或感到冷 *([v]feel very cold:)* ④【动】机体的组织由于温度过低而受损伤(*[v] body issues get hurt because of low temperature)*	S4......，她的脸蛋**冻**得发红。(*Her face red with **cold**.*) S5......，我这才感觉到**冻**得麻木的双脚开始发痛。(*I feel my feet was **cold** to numb and painful*) S6......，车辙上已经有几条**冻**裂的长缝子。(*The tracks have some **frozen** long gap*) S7......，也许她就不会**冻**死。(*She would not **cold** to death*)
世界 World	①自然界和人类社会的一切事物的总和。*(everything that exits anywhere)* ② 佛教用语，指宇宙. *(Buddhism words, refers to universe)* ③地球上所有地方. *(all place on earth)* ④指社会的形势、风气. *(social situations and ethos)* ⑤ 领域；人的某种活动范围。*(people in general; especially a distance group of people with some shared interest)*	S8......，**世界**成了一张涂写得乱七八糟的大字报。(***World** is painted like a messy Dazibao*) S8 现在网络的一个喷嚏，也可能导致全**世界**的感冒。(*A sneezing of Internet **would** make the world catching cold*) S10 网络**世界**不仅改变了我们的整个**世界**，也改变了我们整个**世界**的生活方式。(*Internet **world** changes not only our whole **world**, but also life styles of our whole **world***)

From 2 meanings of word "地道"(authentic), meaning ① and ②both have a core meaning "real", so annotators cannot decide which meaning to tag for S1, S2 and S3.

Meaning ③and meaning ④ of word "冻"(freeze) both express "cold" but are different on cold level. Meaning ④is colder than meaning ③, its core meaning is "very cold and lead to hurt". But in real corpus, such as sentence S4, S5, S6 and S7, we cannot judge whether the cold body is hurt or not.

Meaning ① of "世界"(world) contains the other meanings, which would lead to annotation inconsistency. Meaning 1 is more abstract than the other meanings, especially meanings 2, 3 and 4 which reflect real world.

The three words in table 1 represent 3 kinds of overlapping, one is the some meanings of a word have the same core meaning, such as "地道" (Authentic); the second is some adjective words' meanings would overlap on range, like "冻"(freeze/cold), "强烈"(strong); the third is abstract meaning of a word would cover its concrete meaning, such as "世界"(world), "文化"(culture) and "生活"(live / life).

2.2 Word meanings in dictionary can cover all word senses

Word meanings in dictionary maybe cannot explain a word sense in real corpus, it can be described like this:

$$S > S1+S2+S3+...+Sn \tag{3}$$

This situation have 2 forms that is a word meaning scope is too narrow to cover word sense or lack suitable word meanings to select. Table 2 has shown some words which have a narrow scope.

Table 2. polysemous words with overlapping meanings in dictionary

Word	Word meaning	Question description	语料
地位 posi- tion	①【名】人、团体或国家在社会关系或国际关系中所处的位置。 (position of people, organization or country in society or international relations)	描述对象不能只限于人、团体或国家。 (Description object cannot limit in human, organization or country.)	S11 气候在环境中占据十分重要的**地位**。 (Climate occupy important **position** in environment)
饱 full	①【形】满足了食量（[adj] satisfy appetite）	说明对象不能只限定于食量 (Description object cannot limit in appetite)	S12 如果你还希望睡得饱饱的，…… (If you want to sleep **fully**,…)

Word meaning 1 of "地位"*(position)* limits its description object in human, organization and country which is too narrow to cover word sense in real corpus; word meaning 1 of "饱" *(full)* ask its modifier is appetite, but in some real sentences, "饱"*(full)* is always used to describe "sleeping" and "drink".

In corpus, some words can't find suitable word meanings in dictionary to tag. Table 3 has list some words with their lacked meanings.

Table 3. polysemous words with lacked meanings in dictionary

word	Lacked meaning	corpus
下 download	add[1]-12.【动】下载。 *([v] download)*	S13我正在下一个软件。 *(I am **downloading** a soft ware.)*
冲 (blunt)	add[5]-④【形】说话语气不好。 *([adj] speaks in bad tone)*	S14 他讲话是非常冲的。 *(He speaks **bluntly**)*
放 (fly)	add⑲【动】放飞②：把鸟、风筝放出去，使高飞：~风筝。 *([v] let fly)*	S15我在北京看过放风筝。 *(I have seen people **fly** kites in Beijing)*

The three words in table 3 are all single syllable words which are used very frequently in Chinese, and they all have many meanings in dictionary, but some meanings are lacked.

2.3   Word meanings in dictionary exceed word senses

The corpus are not large enough to cover all words and words senses, so it is normal that word meanings in dictionary may exceed word senses in corpus. But some word meanings exceed word senses because of dictionary definition has its fixed models and some problems. It can be defined like formula 4:

$$S < S_1+S_2+S_3+...+S_n \qquad (4)$$

That is all senses of a word in corpus is less than total meanings of the word in dictionary. Some meanings would not exist in corpus because they are localism meanings or classical Chinese meanings or written language, and most of them are labeled in dictionary, like the 7th meaning of "盖"(wonderful), but some are not, we call it meaning redundancy. Some words and their meanings are showed in table 4.

Table 4. polysemous words with lacked meanings in dictionary

Word	Word meanings that do not appear in corpus
盖	[1]-⑦<方>【形】盖帽儿②：他一连踢进三个球，～了！

(wonderful)	(<localism>[adj] wonderful.)
行 (will)	[1]-⑪<书>【副】将要：~将|~及半岁。 (<written word>[adv] will)
个子 (gezi)	②【名】指某些捆在一起的条状物。 ([n] Some streaks that are bound together.)
对待 (opposite)	②【动】处于相对的情况。 ([v] in opposite status)

The second meaning of "个子"(gezi) would not appear in corpus mostly, and it is a localism meaning, but not marked in dictionary. The second meaning of "对待"(opposite) is a classical Chinese meaning which are often used in classical Chinese poem and sentences, but it is not marked in dictionary also.

3　Reasons of the contradiction between word meanings in dictionary and word senses in corpus

From the analysis above, we may conclude that there are 3 shortages of word meanings in dictionary for explaining words in corpus: the first one is overlapping of meanings make it different to distinguish; the second is the scope of a word meaning is too narrow to cover word sense; the third is word meaning absence for word annotation. Combining real corpus and dictionary paraphrasing, 2 reasons of the phenomenon are summarized in this paper.

3.1　Reasons outside dictionary

(1) With society developing and new things and phenomenon generating, new words and new word meanings are producing. Especially since Internet appeared, computer terminology and internet language emerge one after one, some are eliminated with time goes on, and the others are reserved by society, such as word meanings listed in table 3, these meanings have already become high frequency words in common life, but are not in dictionary.

(2) Word shift phenomenon may make dictionary cannot explain words appeared in real corpus. In written language, especially in literature, rhetorical device is often used which make it difficult to select suitable meanings.

(3) Language has ambiguous boundaries, but word meanings in dictionary must be divided into clear boundaries, this contradiction leads to the difficult of word sense annotation. Such as the word "冻"(freeze) listed in table 2.

3.2　Reasons from dictionary

(4) Distinguish between word meanings and morpheme meanings are marked in the 6th Modern Chinese Dictionary, which make it convenient to tag word senses,

but also have its disadvantage. Some meanings if dictionary are labeled as morpheme meanings, however this meanings would used as word meanings.

Table 5.morpheme meanings of polysemous words in dictionary

word	Morpheme meaning	corpus
木 (wood)	②木头。*(wood)*	S16木球很好玩。 *(Wooden ball is interesting.)* S17两只很大的木船。 *(Two big wooden ship).*
饱 (full/satisfy)	③足足地；充分。*(fully)* ④满足。*(satisfy)*	S18……，就饱蘸墨汁。 *(Dipping in ink fully.)* S19 ……，让我大饱了口福 ((the food) satisfy my appetite.)

According to table 5, two reasons for morpheme would make sense annotation difficult:

One is word meanings in dictionary are marked as morpheme meanings wrongly, such as the second meaning of "木"(wood) and the fourth meaning of "饱" (satisfy).

Second is language shift, sentence S19 is transformed from idiom "大饱口福"(satisfy my appetite), this change make "饱"(satisfy) become a word from a morpheme.

(5) Dictionary are made manually, even the compilers are famous linguistics, there must have some mistakes in it because of great complexity and difficulty of compiling a dictionary.   These mistakes would give rise to difficulties of word sense annotation.

From the 5 reasons above, we may conclude that society development, language usage and paraphrasing forms of dictionary may affect the result of word sense annotation. In order to resolve these questions, on the one hand, dictionary itself must make up the deficiencies in time with the society development and changes of language usages, on the other hand, annotators must make flexible annotation methods to offset the contradiction between dictionary paraphrasing and word sense annotation. For example, set up flexible word meanings for absent meanings, tag more than one meanings for a word when 2 or more meanings are overlapping.

4   Conclusion

Based on the word sense annotation corpus, this paper analyzes the relationship between this paper studies the polysemous words paraphrasing using word meanings in the dictionary. Three types of paraphrasing relationships between word meanings in dictionary and word senses in real corpus have been found. By analyzing the three relations, this paper found that 1) some word meanings may overlap with each other; 2) the scope of a word meaning is too narrow to cover word senses in real corpus; 3) some polysemous words lack suitable meanings from the dictionary to tag; 4) polysemous words have redundant meanings. The former three may result in a difficulty when completing the word sense annotation. Meanwhile, word meaning redundancy can also reflects the deficiencies of the words meaning paraphrasing in the dictionary. Two reasons may give rise to these phenomena: the development of society along with flexible usages of language, the clear distinction of word meaning and morpheme meaning in the dictionary.

For lexicography, this paper may offer large-scale language evidences for lexicographers to overcome deficiencies in order to improve rationality and integrity of polysemous word meaning division. For the construction of word sense annotation corpus, this paper has established some tagging standards which may serve later works of word sense annotation. Along with the development of society and the changing of language use, the contradictions between dictionary paraphrasing and word sense annotation may always exit. In order to resolve the contradictions, a more flexible work of word sense annotation needs to be done.

5   Acknowledgment

This work was supported by the Hi-Tech Research and Development Program of China(2012AA011104), and by China State Language Affairs Commission "Twelfth Five" Scientific Research Project(YB125-124), and by China Postdoctoral Science Foundation (2013M530026).

References

1. Kilgarriff A, Koeling R. An evaluation of a lexicographer's workbench incorporating word sense disambiguation[J]//Computational Linguistics and Intelligent Text Processing. Springer Berlin Heidelberg, 2003: 225-240.
2. Xiao H., Yang L.J. Dictionary Informed Corpus Word Sense Annotation [J]. Applied Linguistics, 2010, (2). [In Chinese].
3. Xiao H., Dictionary Based Corpus Sense Tagging [J],2009. [In Chinese].
4. Dictionary editorial room of Language Institute of Chinese Academy of Social Sciences, Modern Chinese Dictionary(the 6th edition)[M]. The Commercial Press, 2012 [In Chinese].
5. Fu H.Q. Modern Chinese Words[M]. The Peking University Press, 2004.[In Chinese].
6. Wu Y, Jin P, Zhang Y, et al. A Chinese corpus with word sense annotation[J]//Computer Processing of Oriental Languages. Beyond the Orient: The Research Challenges Ahead. Springer Berlin Heidelberg, 2006: 414-421.
7. Wu Y.F, Yu S.W. The Principles and Methods of Sense Discrimination for Chinese Language Processing [J]. Applied Linguistic, 2006: 129:132.[In Chinese]

The Motivated Topicalization and Referentiality
of the Compound Noun in Chinese

Jinghan Zeng[1] and Yulin Yuan[2]

Department of Chinese Language and Literature, Peking University, Beijing 100871

E-mail: woshijinghan@126.com

Abstract: This paper mainly studies the compound noun in Chinese in terms of forming process and motivation. Instead of OV inversion of the Chinese compound noun in previous studies, we claimed that the core of its forming process is topicalization. This involves the object-fronting movement and the relativization based on the downgraded predication structure. The first component stem of the compound is an object-topic, but not an inverted object. This topicalization may be attributed to the topic-prominent feature of Chinese. Moreover, the motivation of the object-fronting movement is to obtain the referentiality resulting in a process of decategorization.

Keywords: Chinese compound noun, OV inversion, topicalization, referentiality

1　1　Introduction：Chinese compound noun and OV inversion

A series of compounds in Mandarin have attracted linguists' attention for several years, because of their specific contradictions on semantic and forms.

(1) a. *zhizhang fensui　ji*　　　b. *meitan kaicai chang*　　　c. *qiche xiuli　gong*

　　paper　shred machine　　　coal　mine　site　　　car　repair worker

　　paper shredder　　　　　coal mining field　　　auto repairing

　　纸张粉碎机　　　　　　　煤炭开采场　　　　　　汽车修理工

(2)*a. *fensui zhizhang ji*　　　*b. *kaicai meitan chang*　　　*c. *xiuli　qiche gong*

　　shard paper　　machine　　　mine　coal　site　　　repair car　　worker

　　粉碎纸张机　　　　　　　开采煤炭场　　　　　　修理汽车工

The kind of compound nouns in (1a-c) often consist of three parts: N_1+V+N_2. There is a verbal government between N_1 and V. The semantic role of N_1 is patient

© Springer International Publishing AG 2016
M. Dong et al. (Eds.): CLSW 2016, LNAI 10085, pp. 40–50, 2016
DOI: 10.1007/978-3-319-49508-8_4

and it is the object of the verb. According to the semantic relations, the order of these three parts should be VN_1N_2 as in (2a-c), but the actual word order is N_1VN_2 in Chinese natural language. As a result, the object (which means N_1) and the verb (which means V) turn out to be inverted, and this is the so called *OV inversion* of Chinese compound nouns.

Many linguists have suggested numbers of detailed explanations why O and V have been inverted such as Duanmu, San [1,2], Gu Yang & Shen Yang [6], Wang Hongjun [17], He Yuanjian [8] and Feng Shengli [7]. However, they might ignore one simple question when explaining the phenomenon that must it be the OV inversion when the patient is in front of a verb or does the so called *OV inversion* truly exist? In this paper, we attempt to explain that the OV inversion does not occur in the process of constructing compound nouns from the perspective of syntax and semantics. Then an explanation about this phenomenon in terms of the topic-prominent feature and specific denotational function is claimed.

2   Viewing the OV inversion on syntactic structure

The primary reason why people suggested OV inversion is that V and N_1 are in the verb-object relation on the syntax tree. Therefore, the syntactic structure should be observed first to check whether the N_1 and V are inverted.

There are mainly two kinds of points about the structure of compound nouns in linguistics circle. One is $[N_1+[V+N_2]]$ represented by Wang Hongjun [17]. Taking *zhizhangfensuiji* (which means paper shredder)as an example, Wang, H. [17] pointed out that *fensui* (shatter) and ji (machine) first combine into *fensuiji* (shredder), which is then modified by the attribute *zhizhang* (paper). In this way, the syntactic structure of *zhizhangfensuiji* should be [zhizhang[fensui-ji]]. Never the less, $[N_1+[V+N_2]]$ means N_2 and V stand in the same level, which is under N_1 on the syntax tree. N_1 and V are neither immediate constituents nor verb-object relation since they do not stand in the same level. Thus, the *OV inversion* does not exist.

Gu Yang & Shen Yang [6], Shi Dingxu [16], He Yuanjian[8], Feng Shengli[7] and Zhou Ren[25] hold another point that the structure of compound nouns should be $[[N_1+V]+N_2]$. For instance, He Yuanjian [8] concluded that N_1 combines with V first and then modifies with N_2 together after studying the compound *bingduchuanbozhe* (people who transmit virus). However, whether N_1 and V are object-verb inverted is still a question. N_1 and V show qualifying relations intuitively, in which N_1 shows class condition. For example, in the compound *zhizhangfensuiji* N_1 is a qualifier that qualifies the target of the verb *fensui* to be *zhizhang* but not others, such as *mutou* (wood) or gangue (nut). Besides, there is a structural particle de that can be put between N_1 and V such as *zhizhang de fensui* (the shredding of papers), *junma de siyang* (the feeding of war-horses), *xiangmu de kaifa* (the development of a peoject). Many examples can be found in authentic materials as in (3):

(3) *dongshihui   dui   xiangmu de   zhixing   jinxing   shidi kaocha,*

Board of Directors   to   project   Aux   execute   dummy verb   on-site   investigate

bing   jiu   xiangmu de kaifa   jiaohuan   yijian.

Conj   Prep   project Aux develop exchange   thought

Board of Directors did on-the-spot investigation towards the execution of the project, and exchanged opinions about the development of the project.

As a consequence, in the compound *zhizhangfensuiji*, N_1 *zhizhang* is actually a qualifier but not the object of V *fensui*, even though the semantic role of N_1 *zhizhang* is patient. N_1 and V are not OV inverted, too.

3   Constructing of compound nouns

In addition to explore the syntactic structure, the mechanism of constructing compound nouns can be figured out by studying the semantic relationship of the three components —— N_1, V, N_2.

3.1   the structure type of N_1V

As what is mentioned above, N_1 and V in a compound noun are not OV inversion, but in qualifying relation. But it does not mean that N_1V is an M-D (modifier-head) construction. This is because regarding N_1V as an M-D construction is obviously on the contrary of the theory of centripetal structure, which claims that the general function of a centripetal structure must correspond to its core component. Let's take the N_1V *zhizhangfensui* (paper shredding) as an example. *Fensui* (shred) is modified by *zhizhang* (paper) so an auxiliary word de can be inserted into the noun as *zhizhang* de *fensui*(the shredding of paper). It is a nominal constituent, which can refer to an event. However, the head *fensui* is a verbal constituent, having a declarative function, which does not correspond to the referential function of *zhizhang fensui*. Thus, N1V *zhizhang fensui* can never be regarded as a centripetal M-D construction.

Actually, the contradiction of *zhizhangfensui* and *zhizhang de fensui* is not rare. Expressions against the centripetal structure like *zhebenshu de chuban* (the publication of the book) and *chuntian de daolai* (the coming of spring) have existed for a long time. Shen Jiaxuan [15] claimed noun includes verb pattern which says that verbs are contained in nouns to solve such problems. Taking *zhebenshu* de *chuban* (the publication of the book) as an example, although the head *chuban* (publication) is a verb, it is contained in noun category, so *chuban* has a referential function which is consistent with *zhebenshu de chuban*. Yuan Yulin [24] doubted Shen's opinion by pointing that a negative marker or adverb can be inserted between *de* and *chuban* as *zhebenshu de bu chuban* (the not-publishing of the book), *zhebenshu de jishi chuban* (the timely publication of the book), in which *chuban* is still a verb that goes against to the theory of centripetal structure. As a matter of fact, *zhebenshu de chuban* is not a centripetal structure. It is formed by a subject-predicate structure *zhebenshu chuban* with a inserted nominalizer *de*. This analysis solves the problem above and not only obeys the theory of centripetal structure but also follows the linguistic facts.

We claimed that N_1V like *zhizhangfensui* is a subject-predicate structure like *zhebenshu chuban*. *Zhizhang de fensui* is similar with *zhebenshu de chuban*, which is formed by a subject-predicate structure *zhizhangfensui* inserted with a nominalizer *de*. Precisely, *zhizhangfensui* is a topic construction. The statement *fensui* illustrates what happens to the topic *zhizhang* as in (4):

(4) *zhizhang fensui, mutou   bu   fensui.*

     Paper   shred wood   Neg   shred

     The paper is shredded while the wood is not shredded.

When zhizhangfensui is inserted with a nominalizer de as zhizhang de fensui, it would get the referential function like any nominal construction as what is shown in (5):

(5) *zhizhang   de   fensui bu feijin,   mutou   de   fensui hen   feijin.*

     paper   Aux   shred Neg   difficult   wood   Aux   shred   very   difficult

     The shredding of paper is not difficult while the shredding of wood is very difficult.

3.2   The combination of N_1, V, N_2

After knowing the relation of N_1, V and N_2, what we want to study next is how they combine to form the compound nouns.

Gu Yang & Shen Yang [6] pointed out that compound nouns have basic argument structures with the movement of nominal constituents. For instance, the compound *qichexiuligong* (auto repairing) has a basic argument structure as *gong-xiuli-qiche* (worker-repair-car). In the first step, the verb *xiuli* (repair) makes an upward movement into the external argument gong (worker).Next, the internal argument *qiche* (car) moves into the verb *xiuli* (repair). However, the analysis in Gu, Y & Shen, Y [6] was made by taking a morphology process as a syntax process which fits sentences well but not compound words. Besides, once V *xiuli* (repair) is combined with N_2 gong (worker), their levels become confused on the syntax tree.

We hold the opinion that the deep structure of compound nouns is a downgraded predication structure formed by the morphemes like N_1, V and N_2. The downgraded predication structure then makes a series of projections and transformations to form the final surface structure of compound nouns. The concept of downgraded predication structure is put forward in Leech, G. [11] to explain similar predication structures which have another predication structure in it as in (6):

(6)   A man who was wearing a wig entered the room.

In (6) the whole sentence is taken as a big predication structure. The attributive clause *who was wearing a wig* is a small predication structure as *man [who.WEAR.wig]*. Since the attributive clause is a modifier, its semantic level is lower than the sentence, making it become a downgraded predication structure of the big predication structure. Yuan Yulin [18] used this concept to explain nouns with complex semantic meanings. For example, the word *yijian* (opinion) has two senses in Chinese as follows:

① something what you think or believe about

②some negative judgment about something or someone

The two senses of *yijian* can be summarized as one: thoughts that someone holds about something. The semantic structure of *yijian* can be described as *yijian: kanfa <mouren dui moushi>* (opinion: thought <someone to something>). In this description *<mouren dui moushi>* (<someone to something>) is a downgraded predication structure of the noun word *yijian* (opinion).

We also find a downgraded predication structure in the deep structure of the compound noun. It makes several transformations to form the final surface structure. The process can be divided into four steps and we would take *zhizhangfensuiji* (paper shredder) as an example to show it. In the first step, the head ji(machine) of the compound contains a downgraded predication: machine:<it shreds paper>. In the predication, <shred paper> is used to describe the application and function of this machine, acting the telic role[1] of the downgraded predication as in (7a). In the second step, the referent ji(machine) is picked out in relativization, with the telic role of the downgraded predication becoming a relative clause as in (7b). *Fensui*(shred) becomes the predicate of the relative clause and *zhizhang*(paper) is the patient role. In the third step, topicalization makes the patient role *zhizhang*(paper) shift forward to the initial position of the compound as in (7c). In the forth step, the unstressed auxiliary word de is deleted because of prosodic restriction with the meaning unchanged, forming the final surface structure *zhizhangfensuiji*(paper shredder) as in (7d). The four steps can be expressed as follows:

(7)   a.   the downgraded predication: $N_2 + V + N_1$

         ji: <*ta   fensui   zhizhang*>

         machine: <it   shred   paper>

    b.   the relativization of the head: $V + N_1 +$ 的 $+ N_2$

         fensui   zhizhang   de   ji

         shred   paper   Aux   machine

         a machine which can shred papers

    c.   the topicalization of the patient role: $N_1 + V +$ 的 $+ N_2$

         zhizhang   fensui   de   ji

         paper   shred   Aux   machine

         a machine which can do paper shredding things

    d.   de deleted: $N_1 + V + N_2$

         zhizhang   fensui   ji

         paper   shred   machine

         paper shredder/paper shredding machine

The processing above is in accordance with the way of information processing in Chinese.   Firstly, Relativization of the headword can reflect the process of extracting core information of human brain. When dealing with the compound nouns N_1VN_2

---

[1] Telic role is one of the qualia roles in Generative Lexicon Theory, being used to describe different semantic features of the target. For more details see J. Pustejovsky [12, 13].

such as *zhizhangfensuiji*, the downgraded predication structure can only show the internal logical relation of the three components other than the semantic structure of the referred object (a machine used for shredding papers). Thus, when integrating *zhizhang, fenzui* and *ji,* human brains will instinctively extract the central component *jiqi*(machine).

Secondly, the topicalization of the patient role shows the linguistic character of Chinese, which emphasizes the topic. We suggested that the initial nominal constituent N_1 in the front of compound nouns N_1VN_2 is a patient topic other than an inverted object, such as *zhizhang fensui wanle* (the papers have been shredded. Li and Tompson [3] claimed that the major difference between Chinese and English is that Chinese emphasizes the topic while English pays more attention to the subject. The existing of numerous S-P predicate sentences and topic sentences proves the emphasis of Chinese on the topic. In the constructing process of compound nouns N_1VN_2, downgraded predication structure N_1 acts as the patient role of the verb. Since the speaker wants to draw the attention of the listener to the patient role, it will be topicalized and moved to the initial of the compound noun.

Moreover, we would provide some other examples of compound nouns N_1VN_2 to prove that the initial nominal constituent N_1 in the front is a patient topic，other than a inverted object as in(8a-d).

(8)   a. *bijibensanreqi*   b. *shuiguoxiaopidao*
          notebook cooler   fruit mitsumane parer

          笔记本散热器   水果削皮刀

      c. *shoujichongdianqi*   d. *chaoshigonghuoshang*
          mobile phone chargers   super-market supplier

          手机充电器   超市供货商

In the compound nouns N_1VN_2 in (8), the initial nominal constituent N_1 is obviously not the object of V. In (8a) the object of the verb *san*（spread）is *re*（heat）; in (8b) the object of the verb *xiao* (pare)is *pi*(peel); in (8c) the object of the verb *chong* (charge)is *dian*(electricity); in (8d) the object of the verb *gong* (supply)is *huo*(goods). Though the initial nominal constituents in (8a-d) are in object-verb relation with the verbal constituents, they are topics with patient roles, other than the objects. [26]

---

[2] To clarify, the structure of compound nouns in (8a-d) is $N_1VN_0N_2$, which not exactly the

4   The referentiality and word order of compound nouns

As what is mentioned above the compound noun is projected and modified from the downgraded predication N_2-V-N_1, along with the key step, in which the topicalization of the patient role N_1 is topicalized and moves to the initial place of the compound. This is mainly because Mandarin is topic-prominent and the topic used to be use to express key information. However, topicalization is not the only way to do express such focus information in Mandarin. Some examples can be shown as(8a-b):

(8) a.   *shi wo   qu,   bu   shi   ni   qu.*

      is   me   go   Neg   is   you   go

      The person who will go there is me but not you.

  b.   *wo   'chi   pingguo. (chi* has a stress accent)

      me   eat   apple

      I will eat the apple.

In (8a) the speaker use a focus marker shi to mark a contrastive focus wo. In (8b) the speaker puts a stress accent on chi to mark the focus.

Then why must the patient role be topicalized and moved to the initial of compound noun instead of using other ways to emphasize *zhizhang* is an important information in *zhizhangfensui ji*? What caused the topicalization of the patient role N_1 and making it move to the initial of the compound(we call it N_1-movement for short)? We suggest the motivation of the movement is that the denotational function of compound nouns need to be transformed, that is, from declarative function to referential function.

To explain in detail, the downgraded predication N_2-V-N_1, such as *ji-fensui-zhizhang* (machine-shred-paper), is a declarative form, which is a dynamic description of an event process. For example, we can say *a machine has shredded the papers*. Even since the patient role N_1 *ji*(machine) is relativized, the whole structure express a declarative process, too. For example, we can say a machine can be used for shredding paper. When the topicalized patient role moves to the initial of compound noun, the declarative process is transformed to referential function. This is because that the patient topic *zhizhang* has a limitation to the predicate, and the whole structure can be seen as a nominal composition. In such structure meaning that anominalization marker *de* can be inserted into the compound noun, such as

---

same as those studied in the paper, but the Semantic relation is similar.

zhizhang-de-fensui-de-ji. Thus, *zhizhangfensui* acquires referentiality, being able to refer to an event, while before the topicalization *zhizhang fensui* only represents a process. *Zhizhang fensui* depicts all the characteristics of the headword *ji*, making the compound noun gain nominal referential function.

Thus, the downgraded predication in deep structure N_2VN_1 of the compound noun N_1VN_2 is originally referential. For example, ji(machine):< it shreds papers>. Meanwhile, its modifier *fensui zhizhang*, which is initially declarative, becomes *zhizhang fensui* with referentiality after the topicalization. Zhou Ren [25] studied the English compound nouns. The author took *language aqcquisition device* as an example to explain that VP undergoes deverbalization, with its initial characteristics changing from [+V] *acquire* to [-V] *acquisition*, in the process of transforming from the deep structure ($_N[_{-V}[_{VP}$[acquire language]–tion] device]) to the surface structure ($_N[_{-V}[_{VP}$[t language] acquisition] device]). Actually, not only VP but also the entire compound noun transforming from declarativity to referentiality have the process of deverblization. Yuan Yulin [24] discussed the kind of structure *zhebenshu de chuban*(the publication of the book), and the conception of de-categorization is used for describing the phenomenon that a verb is posited in the center of nominal phrase. With the inspiration of the study, we claimed that in both the deep structure and the surface structure of a compound noun, V is always a verb, such as *fensui* (shred) in *zhizhang fensui*. The part of speech of V does not change. Thus the transformation from declarativity to referentiality in the construction process of a compound noun can be well explained by de-categorization other than deverbalization. In the transforming process of denotational function, as the initial procedural scope of dynamic process is being weakened with the gradually disappearing of the declarative function, that static state and attributive scope are being strengthened with the appearance of the function of referentiality.

Thus, we concluded that the constructing process of a compound noun, with the topicalized patient moved to the initial position, is a process of de-categorization, and its motivation is to acquire referentiality.

5   Conclusions

By discussing the constructing process of the compound noun in Mandarin, we suggested that the OV inversion does not appear in the compound noun N_1VN_2, as what other researchers believe. Instead, the nominal constituent in the initial of the compound noun is a patient topic. The compound noun is transformed and projected from the downgraded predication in its deep structure. The motivation that the patient role moved from behind the verb to the initial to be topicalized is to make every component of the compound noun more harmonious in terms of denotational function or referentiality.

We have to admit that other compound nouns were not discussed in this study, for example, the patient of the compound noun composed of single syllable does not go through topicalizaion, such as *suizhiji*（paper shredder）and *xiulichang*（Repair shop）, and so on,. Many researchers have analyzed the constructing process of *suizhiji* in the perspective of prosodic morphology and typology. However, the relation between the absence of topicalized patient role with the semantic meaning and denotational function is still unknown, which is expected to be studied in future.

6   Referrences

1.   Duanmu, San: Phonologically motivated word order movement: Evidence from Chinese compounds. Studies in the Linguistic Sciences. Vol. 27, 49-77 (1997).

2.   Duanmu, San: The Phonology of Standard Chinese. Oxford University Press, New York (2006).

3.   Li Charles and Sandra A. Tompson: Subject and Topic: A New Typology of Language. Charles N. Li (ed.). Academic Press. 457-489 (1976).

4.   Duanmu, San: The commonness and characteristics of languages from the stress accent in Chinese. Essays on Linguistics. Vol. 1, 78-84 (1997). [in Chinese]

5.   Duanmu, San: Rhythm in Chinese. Contemporary Linguistics. Vol. 4, 203~209 (2000). [in Chinese]

6.   Gu Yang & Shen Yang: The derivation of synthetic compounds in Chinese. Studies of The Chinese Language. Vol. 2, 122-133 (2001). [in Chinese]

7.   Feng Shengli: Verb-object inversion and prosodic morphology. Linguistic Sciences. Vol. 3, 12-20 (2004). [in Chinese]

8.   He Yuanjian: The loop theory in Chinese morphology. Contemporary Linguistics. Vol. 3, 223-235 (2004). [in Chinese]

9.   He Yuanjian: On the logical form of Chinese synthetic compounds. Linguistic Sciences. Vol. 5, 503-516 (2009). [in Chinese]

10.   Li Qiang and Yuan Yulin: The Structural Description and Conceptual Interpretation of Nouns' Meaning from the Perspective of Generative Lexicon Theory. manuscript in preparation. 2015. [in Chinese]

11.   Leech, Geoffrey: Semantics. Penguin, Harmondsworth(1981).

12. Pustejovsky, James: The Generative Lexicon. Computational linguistics. Vol. 17, 409-441(1991).

13. Pustejovsky, James: The Generative Lexicon. MIT Press, Cambridge (1995).

14. Qi Feng and Duanmu, San: A quantitative study of word-length patterns in Chinese [A N] compounds. Language Teaching and Linguistic Studies. Vol. 5, 83-91 (2015). [in Chinese]

15. Shen Jiaxuan: On nouns and verbs in Chinese. Journal of Sino-Tibetan Linguistics. Vol. 2, 27-47 (2007). [in Chinese]

16. Shi Dingxu: Chinese attributive V-N compounds. Chinese Language. Vol. 6, 483-495 (2003). [in Chinese]

17. Wang Hongjun: The relations between the number of syllable, the tonal range of pitch and the grammatical structure in Chinese. Contemporary Linguistics. Vol. 4, 241-252 (2001). [in Chinese]

18. Yuan Yulin: Valence of Chinese nouns. Social Sciences in China. Vol. 3, 205-223 (1992). [in Chinese]

19. Yuan Yulin: The predicate implying and its syntax results. Chinese Language. Vol. 4, 241-255 (1995). [in Chinese]

20. Yuan Yulin: Topicalization and the relevant syntactic process. Chinese Language. Vol. 4, 241-254 (1996). [in Chinese]

21. Yuan Yulin: On the syntactic and semantic function of *de* in the sentence final position: from a viewpoint of the modern focus theory. Chinese Language. Vol. 1, 3-16 (2003). [in Chinese]

22. Yuan Yulin: Queries about "Part of speech is the class based on denotational function". Chinese Linguistics. Vol. 4, 15-25 (2006). [in Chinese]

23. Yuan Yulin: The equivalent function and the standard of dividing the part of speech. Linguistic Researches. Vol. 3, 24-30 (2006). [in Chinese]

24. Yuan Yulin: The relation between verbs and nouns from de-categorization. Essays on Linguistics. The Commercial Press, Beijing (2010). [in Chinese]

25. Zhou Ren: A study of Chinese VON/OVN compounds under typical evidence: University vs. individuality. Chinese Language. Vol. 4, 15-26 (2006). [in Chinese]

26. Zhu Dexi: Self-reference and transferred reference. Vol. 1, 16-31 (1983). [in Chinese]

27. Zhu Dexi: Syntax analysis notes. The Commercial Press, Beijing (2010). [in Chinese]

An Analysis of Definitions of Poly-meaning Sports' Entries Based on Generative Lexicon Theory

Haixia Feng [1], Wanjing Meng [1]

[1] Ludong University, Yantai, China

Abstract. Applying generative lexicon theory, the paper analyzes several aspects of currently popular Chinese language dictionaries, such as the sense and semantic features of word order and explanation of the multiple-meaning of sports' entries; in addition, the paper analyzes the advantages and disadvantages of the dictionaries, which are explained by related optimized suggestions.

Keywords: language dictionary, sports' entries, definition, generative lexicon theory

1 Introduction

The utility of a specific dictionary is the major criterion according to which its quality is evaluated. A good dictionary requires scientific, systematic, and also contemporary explanations. How a compiler achieves these objectives is dependent on his/her experience and theoretical background. Every advance in the compilation of dictionaries is consequently informed and guided by the authors' linguistic theories. Generative lexicon theory centers on the two concepts of noun structure and semantic type, which provide the theoretical basis for establishing a sememe (especially, a noun) and for both choosing and describing the semantic features for compiling dictionary entries. The *Modern Chinese Dictionary (Sixth Edition)* and the *Longman Contemporary English Dictionary (Fifth Edition)* here serve as examples of typical language dictionaries. It is within this theoretical framework and practical application that we examine the universal terms, characteristics, and properties of sports' entries.

2 Generative Lexicon Theory and its Expansible Sketch

Generative lexicon theory was created by Prof. Pustejovsky at Brandeis University, USA. His theory involves two parts: the semantic generation mechanism of lexical features and the syntax level. At the level of syntax, he constructs four concepts of lexical feature in a word: argument structure, event structure, qualia structure, and lexical typing structure. At the core of his theory is the explanation of the noun concept, which draws on the structure of its environment and lexical derivation.

© Springer International Publishing AG 2016
M. Dong et al. (Eds.): CLSW 2016, LNAI 10085, pp. 51–57, 2016
DOI: 10.1007/978-3-319-49508-8_5

2.1   Qualia Structure

Qualia structure stems from Aristotle's "doctrine of four causes". From this perspective, there are four properties of everything in the world, that is to say, formal cause, material cause, efficient cause, and purpose cause. These four properties underpin our common and conventional senses, informing the way we view and understand the world, as well as reflecting our simplest and deepest perceptions. With the illumination of the above "doctrine of four causes", Pustejovsky suggests qualia structure in vocabulary knowledge, which he specifically breaks down into four levels of semantic knowledge and roles: the constitutive, formal, telic, and agent role (Yuan Yulin 2014). Yuan Yulin proposes ten types of qualia roles, which establish "a bridge between the semantic knowledge and encyclopedia", thereby coding "our common life experience into the system of language knowledge" (Yuan Yulin 2014). That is to say, qualia roles provide generative lexicon theory from detailed and described noun meaning as well as the theoretical basis of the dictionary's definition.

2.2   Lexical Typing Structure

From the semantic view, Pustejovsky (Song Zuoyan 2015:14–17) asserts that nouns can be categorized into three types according to the content of their represented meanings, namely, natural, artefactual, and complex types.

A natural type refers to the natural property of every matter, which does not involve a human being in its creation, such as "stone, rabbit, water, tree, sky", etc. An artefactual type reflects a human's mindset: it features functions and indicates how these have been created, such as "chair, table, stool, beer, knife", etc. A complex type can be represented as "dot object", that is to say, two different categories of matters are mixed into one matter. Specific examples are:

   a. phys_obj•info: book, record (a complexity of matter and knowledge content)

   b. event•info: lecture, play, seminar, exam, quiz, test (a complexity of event and knowledge content)

   c. event•phys_obj: lunch, breakfast, dinner, tea (a complexity of event and matter)

   d. event•(info•sound): concert, sonata, song, symphony (a complexity of knowledge content or sound)

All in all, if a noun can be classified into a natural, artefactual, or complex type, we can easily illustrate and explain how some word phrases can be properly assembled, offering a new way to establish complex noun meanings.

3   The Distinction Sense of Sports' Entries in a Dictionary Based on Generative Lexicon Theory

How many sports' entries there are depends on their sense, which can be categorized into three parts: first, a single sense of sports' entries; second, more than one sense of sports' entries, of which one of the senses is not related to sports' activities; and third, sports' equipment and activities. We focus on the third part.

In the *Modern Chinese Dictionary* there are 35 poly-meaning sports' entries, among which 17 belong to court games, such as "baseball, bowling, squash, ice hockey, rugby, golf, basketball, gate ball, softball, volleyball, hockey, beach volleyball, water polo, tennis, badminton, and football"; 9 belong to gymnastic exercises, such as "vaulting horse, trampoline, rings, uneven bars, balance beam, double balance beam, horse-vaulting, vaulting box, spin-ladder"; and a further 9 belong to other sports activities, such as "putting the shot, curling, weight throwing, javelin, turning board, rowing, kayaking, race horsing, and rowing".

All of the above entries in the *Modern Chinese Dictionary* are separated into two senses: one is events such as sports' activities, and the other is sports' equipment. The explanation of the dictionary accurately describes the entry's meaning. These entries need the separation of the two senses, which are based on linguistics and our perception of reality. Some sports' entries represent complicated nouns of "events or matter"; that is say, they are complicated nouns combining "events or matter", which we are easily able to understand from our life experience, such as the following entries:

（1）中国足球后备人才培养-目前国内青少年足球后备人才的培养。*(The development of reserve talents for Chinese soccer—at present, Chinese is developing junior soccer players as reserve talents.)*

（2）足球俱乐部纷纷"改制"。*(Football clubs are in a stripped-down period.)*

（3）草坪开放时禁止踢足球和烧烤，各种车辆不得入内。*(When the lawn is open, playing football or having barbecues is banned and all kinds of vehicles are prohibited from entering.)*

（4）足球放在后备箱了。*(The football is in the car trunk.)*

But we discover that in the case of "matter" words, some entries are not separated into sememes, such as: "Chinese chess, international chess, army chess, gobang, checkers", etc. Examples of explanations from the *Modern Chinese Dictionary* follow:

【国际象棋】棋类运动的一种，黑白棋子各十六个，分成六种，一王、一后、两象、两车、两马、八兵。棋盘为正方形，由六十四个黑白小方格相间排列而成。两人对下，按规则移动棋子，将（jiāng）死对方的王为胜。

(【Chess】 is a game that is played. Each player has 16 pieces, black and white, including a king, a queen, two elephants, two rooks, two horses, and eight pawns. A chessboard is a square with 64 squares arranged in a black and white grid. The aim is to move your pieces so that your opponent's king cannot escape being taken.)

【围棋】棋类运动的一种。棋盘上纵横各十九道线，交错成三百六十一个位，双方用黑白棋子对着（zhāo），互相围攻，吃去对方的棋子。以占据位数多的为胜。*(【Weiqi】 is a game. The board is crossed with 19 lines, forming 361 intersections. Both players place pieces in turn on the intersections. The aim is to occupy one's opponent's pieces. The winner is the player who occupies the greatest number of positions.)*

【象棋】指中国象棋，棋类运动的一种，双方各有棋子十六个，一将（帅）、两士（仕）、两象（相）、两车、两马、两炮、五卒（兵）。两人对下，各按规则移动棋子。将（jiāng）死对方的将（帅）的一方为胜。*(【Chinese* chess⟧ *is a game. The pieces are red and black. Each player has a knight, two mandarins, two elephants, two horses, two cannons, and five soldiers. You must trap your opponent's king in order to win.)*

【跳棋】棋类游艺的一种。棋盘是六角的星形，上面画着许多三角形的格子。游艺各方的棋子各占满一个犄角，根据规则，或移动，或跳越，先把自己的棋子全部走到对面的那个犄角的为胜。(⟦*Chinese checkers*⟧ *is game played on a six-pointed star by two to six players at opposing corners of the board. The player either moves or jumps in sequence. The winner is the first player to race all of his or her pieces into the opposing camps.)*

【军棋】棋类游艺的一种。有陆军棋和陆海空军棋，棋子按照军职和军械定名。两人对下，双方按照规则走棋，最后以夺得对方军旗者为胜。(⟦*Kriegspiel*⟧ *is a game. The pieces are named after military appointment and weapon. There are two types: land battles and ship battles. The winner is the player who first occupies the other opponent's base.)*

【五子棋】一种棋类游戏，一般常用围棋子在围棋盘上对下，先把五个棋子连成一条直线的为胜。(⟦*Gobang*⟧ *is a game similar to Weiqi. The player take turns on the board. The winner is the first player to get an unbroken row of five stones.)*

The above six chess examples refer to the chess sport or game; however, they can also refer to the chess tool. The following examples are taken from a corpus of contemporary Chinese of Beijing Language University:

（5）另一小房间，放着一张康乐球桌(他是此中高手)，也放着一盘象棋。(《张五常文集》) *(In another small room, there is a named Kangle ball table and a board of Chinese chess. Zhang Wuchang Literature Works)*

（6）身上一无所有，唯一的就是一盒围棋。（《曾国藩》） *(There is only a case of Weiqi with him. Zeng Guofan)*

（7）漳州市新桥文具厂生产的弹子跳棋24000盒，经外贸部门销往日本。(《厦门日报》) *(Xin Qiao stationary factory in Zhangzhou City has produced 24,000 cases of Chinese checkers and will sell them to Japan through the Foreign Trade Department. Xia Men Daily)*

（8）一人一副军棋，一人是一国，只要有"两国"就可以玩"战国七雄"了。(《厦门晚报》) *(Each player has a set of Kriegspiel, each player has belongs to one part. Both "players" can play "Kriegspiel". Xia Men Evening)*

（9）可是我们刚一摆五子棋,几个女人已经过了桥,急急忙忙上楼来了。(《川端康成短篇集》) *(But we had just set up a set of Gobang, when several women passed the bridge and went upstairs in a hurry. Kawabata Yasunari's Short Stories)*

So, from examples (5) to (9), one can observe that all uses refer to the chess tools; in other words, the terms for chess applications are the same as the terms for the "court game"; they can refer to both the event and the matter. Might these terms' entries for the above terms of court game be given as separate senses?

So why is it that the above two sports' entries are easily able to expand their meaning, or to aggregate "event and matter"? From a comprehensive survey of all sports' terms, we discover that their names can be classified into two types. One is named according to the equipment used while doing sports such as baseball, bowling, rugby, vaulting horse, trampoline, rings, uneven bars, balance beam, Chinese chess, weiqi, gobang, shot, curling, weight throw, javelin, turning board, row boat, kayak, racehorse, and rowing, whose meaning is complicated by referring to the sport as well as its equipment; The other is named according to the key act of the generalization of the matter to be constructed, such as pole vault, high jump, long jump, surfing, figure skating, synchronized skiing, weightlifting, boxing, fencing, synchronized swimming, medley swimming, hurdle, etc., which refer to the action rather than the equipment.

The situation is that sports' entries are separated into senses, whereas actually these do not exist. The same finding applies to other dictionaries:

【国际象棋】棋类运动的一种。棋子分黑白两种，每种16个，各有一王、一后、双象、双车、双马、八兵，对弈双方按规则轮流行棋，以"将（jiāng）死"对方为胜。相传起源于古印度，后经阿拉伯传入欧洲。（《现代汉语规范》（3）） (【Chess】 is a game. Each player has 16 pieces, black and white, including a king, a queen, two elephants, two rooks, two horses, and eight pawns. The aim is to move your pieces so that your opponent's king cannot escape being taken. Chess is believed to have originated in India, then came down into Europe via Arab. Modern Chinese Criterion （3）)

【象棋】棋类运动的一种。棋子分红、黑两种，各有一将（帅）、双士（仕）、双象（相）、双车、双马、双炮、五卒（兵），共十六个棋子。对弈双方按规则轮流行棋，以"将（jiāng）死"对方的将（帅）者为胜。(【Chinese chess】 is a game. The pieces are red and black. Each player has a knight, two mandarins, two elephants, two horses, two cannons, and five soldiers. You must trap your opponent's king in order to win.)

【围棋】棋类运动的一种。棋盘上纵横各19条线，相交成361个点(空)。对弈双方分别用黑色和白色的棋子围攻，抢占点的位置，最后以占据点数多者为胜。(【Weiqi】 is a game. The board is crossed with 19 lines, forming 361 intersections. Both of the players place pieces in turn on the intersections. The aim is to occupy one's opponent's pieces. The winner is the player who occupies the greatest number of positions.)

【军棋】棋类游戏。棋子按照军职和武器定名，有陆军棋和海军棋两种。两人对局，以先夺得对方军旗者为胜。(【Kriegspiel】 is a game. The pieces are named after military appointment and weapon. There are two types: land battles and ship battles. The winner is the player who first occupies the other opponent's base.)

【五子棋】棋类游戏。棋具与围棋类似。对弈双方轮流行棋，以先将五子连成一线者为胜。(【Gobang】 is a game similar to Weiqi. The player takes turns on the board. The winner is the first player to get an unbroken row of five stones.)

By "criterion", the five types of board game set up the sports' sememes, but the explanation of "Chinese checkers" defies our expectations.

【跳棋】①棋具，棋盘为六角形，可供2至6人对局。②棋类游戏，下棋各方的棋子各占一个犄角。根据规则，或移动，或跳越，以自己的全部棋子先到对面的犄角为胜。（《现代汉语规范》（3）） (〖*Chinese checkers*〗 *is a game played on a six-pointed star by two to six players at opposing corners of the board. The player either moves or jumps in sequence. The winner is the first player to race all of his or her pieces into the opposing camps. Modern Chinese Criterion（3）)*

The term "Chinese checkers" sets up two senses: one sets up the chess set; the other refers to an event. At the same time, the sense of chess set precedes the event sense.

If we make a comparison between the *Modern Chinese Dictionary* and the *Longman English Dictionary*, we can discover that there are some similarities in both dictionaries: that is to say, there are two senses. An example is:

Basketball ① a game played indoors between two teams of five players, in which each team tries to win points by throwing a ball through a net ② the ball used in this game.

If we make a further comparison between these two dictionaries, we can discover that the separation senses of sports' entries are not the same. There are two separation senses in the *Modern Chinese Dictionary*. On the other hand the two senses in the *Longman English Dictionary* are not clearly differentiated. Some terms only have one sense to illustrate sports and equipment. In the *Modern Chinese Dictionary*, 35 terms have two separation senses, while in the *Longman English Dictionary*, there are 7 terms: "baseball, trampoline, javelin, basketball, softball, kayak, football". There is only one sense corresponding to the 28 entries in the *Modern Chinese Dictionary*.

There are two aspects of the different senses. One is the different word meaning (descriptions) between Chinese and English: for example, a "golf" in Chinese could mean the sport but it also refers to the "ball" in participating (playing) the sport, while in English "golf" only refers to the sport and there is a special term for the ball, namely, "golf ball". There is a similar term for the sport called "rugby", while the "oval ball" refers to the ball. We have also discovered that when some entries have both of the two characters, with one word referring to the sport and to the ball, there is no separation of semenes in the *Longman English Dictionary*, such as "volleyball".

4   Complimentary Close

The development and advance of "a dictionary of idea deduction" and linguistic theories offer a better theoretic basis for dictionaries' definitions of revision and review. Under the direction of generative lexicon theory, we have analyzed the definition of poly-meaning sports' entries in the *Modern Chinese Dictionary* and the *Longman English Dictionary*. We have also pointed out some problems in application of the theory and provided an optimized method to improve dictionaries through revision, thereby making them more scientific.

ACKNOWLEDGMENTS

This work was supported by the National Social Science Foundation of China (No. 13FYY012) and Stage Language Commission Research Project (No.ZDI135-22).

REFERENCES

1. Juri, Apresjan. 2000. Systematic Lexicography. Oxford: Oxford University Press.
2. Chu-Ren HUANG, Jia-Fei HONG, Sheng-Yi CHEN and Ya-Ming CHOU. Exploring event structures in Hanzi radicals: An ontology-based approach. Contemporary Linguistics,2013(15),294-311 [In Chinese]
3. Song Zuoyan. A study on Generative Lexicon Theory and Chinese Event Coercion. Beijing University Press.(宋作艳. 2015. 生成词库理论与汉语事件强迫现象研究. 北大出版社.）[In Chinese]
4. Yuan Yulin, On a descriptive system of qualia structure of Chinese nouns and its application in parsing complex Chinese grammatical phenomena, Contemporary Linguistics,2014(16),31--48 [In Chinese]
5. Zhang Zhiyi. 2012. Lexical Semantics. Beijing: The Commercial Press. （张志毅. 2012. 词汇语义学. 北京：商务印书馆）[In Chinese]

A Finer-Grained Classification of the Morpheme *ke* in the "*ke*+X" Adjectives

Fei Qi

Nanyang Technological University
QIFE0001@e.ntu.edu.sg

Abstract.
This paper reanalyzes the morpheme *ke* in the "*ke*+X" adjectives and categorizes these adjectives into four classes according to their different degrees of lexicalization. This paper also argues from the perspective of grammaticalization that bound morphemes can also develop into affixes or quasi-affixes.

Keywords: lexicalization, grammaticalization, affix, quasi-affix

1 The classification of the "*ke*+X" adjectives

1.1 "*Ke*+X" adjectives from *Contemporary Chinese Dictionary (2012)*

Contemporary Chinese Dictionary (2012) lists 26 entries of "*ke*+monosyllabic X" that are labeled as adjectives[1], which are presented in (1).

(1) 可爱 *ke'ai* 'lovable', 可悲 *kebei* 'deplorable', 可鄙 *kebi* 'contemptible', 可耻 *kechi* 'shameful', 可恨 *kehen* 'hateful', 可怕 *kepa* 'frightening', 可气 *keqi* 'annoying', 可亲 *keqin* 'affable', 可叹 *ketan* 'deplorable', 可恶 *kewu* 'abominable', 可惜 *kexi* 'regrettable', 可喜 *kexi* 'cheerful', 可笑 *kexiao* 'ridiculous', 可憎 *kezeng* 'hateful', 可怜 *kelian* 'pitiful', 可贵 *kegui* 'precious', 可疑 *keyi* 'doubtful', 可观 *keguan* 'considerable', 可靠 *kekao* 'reliable', 可取 *kequ* 'desirable', 可口 *kekou* 'tasty', 可身 *keshen* 'suitable', 可体 *keti* 'fitting', 可心 *kexin* 'nice', 可意 *keyi* 'satisfactory', 可人 *keren* 'pleasant'.

While all being adjectives, the 26 words in (1) are of different degrees of lexicalization. This can be demonstrated by two tests.

Firstly, the degree of fusion between *ke* and X can be tested by examining whether morphemes can be inserted in. The test divides the 26 "*ke*+X" words into two groups. Further examination would find that all adjectives in which morphemes cannot be inserted consist of *ke* and verbal morphemes (e.g., 可爱 *ke'ai* 'lovable' and 可悲 *kebei* 'deplorable'), whereas others which can be expanded consist of *ke* and nom-

---

[1] 可能 *keneng* 'possible' and 可以 *keyi* 'can' are also labeled as adjectives in *Contemporary Chinese Dictionary (2012)*, but they mainly function as auxiliary verbs in the CCL corpus and thus are excluded from the discussion of this study.

© Springer International Publishing AG 2016
M. Dong et al. (Eds.): CLSW 2016, LNAI 10085, pp. 58–64, 2016
DOI: 10.1007/978-3-319-49508-8_6

inal morphemes (e.g., 可意 *keyi*, 'satisfactory'→可人意 *ke+ren yi*, 'suit one's heart'). It can be drawn that the morphemes in "*ke*+V" adjectives has a higher degree of fusion than those in the "*ke*+N" adjectives.

Secondly, the adjectives in (1) can also be tested with regard to meaning transparency, i.e. whether there is any mismatch between the compositional meanings and the meanings of the whole. This test shows that the morphemes in most of the "*ke*+V" adjectives have integrated as a whole, except for 3 words (可观 *keguan* 'considerable', 可靠 *kekao* 'reliable', 可取 *kequ* 'desirable'). However, those in the "*ke*+N" adjectives are not united. In the three "*ke*+V" and "*ke*+N" adjectives, the meanings of the adjectives are just the same as the meaning combination of the two morphemes that compose the words.

In summary, the adjectives such as 可爱 *ke'ai* 'lovable' and 可怜 *kelian* 'pitiful' do not allow insertion of other constituents and their meanings do not directly come from their components, which indicates that they have a higher degree of lexicalization. Adjectives of 可观 *kequ* 'desirable', 可取 *kequ* 'considerable' and 可靠 *kekao* 'reliable' although cannot be separated, their meanings come directly from the components. So the degree of lexicalization is not as high as the first set. Whereas for the "*ke*+N" adjectives, *ke* not only has a concrete meaning, but also can be separated from N, which means this set of words has the lowest degree of lexicalization. In other words, the 26 "*ke*+X" words can be classified into three categories according to their degree of lexicalization, as in (2):

(2) a. *ke*^{1}+V

可爱 *ke'ai* 'lovable', 可悲 *kebei* 'deplorable', 可鄙 *kebi* 'contemptible', 可耻 *kechi* 'shameful', 可恨 *kehen* 'hateful', 可怕 *kepa* 'frightening', 可气 *keqi* 'annoying', 可亲 *keqin* 'affable', 可叹 *ketan* 'deplorable', 可恶 *kewu* 'abominable', 可惜 *kexi* 'regrettable', 可喜 *kexi* 'cheerful', 可笑 *kexiao* 'ridiculous', 可憎 *kezeng* 'hateful', 可怜 *kelian* 'pitiful', 可贵 *kegui* 'precious', 可疑 *keyi* 'doubtful'

b. ke2+V

可观 *keguan* 'considerable', 可靠 *kekao* 'reliable', 可取 *kequ* 'desirable'

c. ke3+N

可口 *kekou* 'tasty', 可身 *keshen* 'suitable', 可体 *keti* 'fitting', 可心 *kexin* 'nice', 可意 *keyi* 'satisfactory', 可人 *keren* 'pleasant'

1.1   Newly-emerged "*ke*+X" adjectives

In addition to "*ke*+monosyllabic X" adjectives introduced in Section 1.1, recent studies have witnessed new nouns consisting of "*ke*+disyllabic verb" as attributives. Some examples are given in (3).

(3)可折叠键盘 *kezhedie jianpan* 'foldable keyboards', 可升降平台 *keshengjiang pingtai* 'lifting platforms', 可移动屏幕 *keyidong pingmu* 'movable screens', 可再生资源 *kezaisheng ziyuan* 'renewable resource', 可持续发展 *kechixu fazhan* 'sustainable development'

These words can be analyzed as [[*ke*+V]+N]. The N takes the head position and even if some verbal morphemes go into this position, they are coerced into nominals.

For instance, in 可持续发展 *kechixu fazhan* 'sustainable development', the head 发展 *fazhan* 'develop' should be analyzed as a nominal referring to 'development', whereas the modifier 可持续 *kechixu* 'sustainable' refers to the attribute of 发展 *fazhan* 'development'.

Syntactically, the "*ke*+disyllabic V" construction behaves similarly to adjectives.

Although it can function as the predicate, the "*ke*+disyllabic V" construction can be transformed to be an attributive and modify nouns without the relative clause marker 的 *de*. It means that it shares more properties with adjectives than with verbal phrases, as is shown in (4).

(4) a. 这种自行车轻便，可折叠。(CCL corpus[2])
zhezhong   zixingche   qingbian   kezhedie
these   cycles   portable   foldable
'These cycles are portable and foldable.'

b. 二等奖奖品为可折叠自行车一辆。(People Daily Online[3])
erdengjiang   jiangpin wei kezhedie zixingche yi liang
the.second.prize award   is foldable cycle   one CLASSIFIER
'The award for the second prize is a foldable cycle.'

The "*ke*+disyllabic verb" constructions can be seen as newly-emerged adjectives. But the meanings of the morphemes within them are not integrated as a whole. For example, the meaning of 可移动 *keyidong* 'movable' equals with that of 可 *ke* 'can' plus 移动 *yidong* 'move'. The lexicalization degree of this set of words is lower than that of the "*ke*[1]+V" adjectives. For convenience, I put them as "*ke*[4]+V".

2   The morphological status of *ke* in the "*ke*+X" adjectives

Ke is analyzed as an affix or a quasi-affix in a number of previous studies, e.g. as an affix in Lü (1980), Shao (2001), Zhu (2001), or as a quasi-affix in Ma (2010), Zeng (2008). However, the adjectives of "*ke*+X" have different degrees of lexicalization as shown in Section 1, accordingly *ke* should be defined differently. According to previous studies such as Lü (1979), Zhu (1982), Zhao (1968/1979), Shen (1986), and Dong (2005), affixes have several characteristics listed in (5).

(5) a. affixes cannot be used independently.
b. affixes can indicate the lexical categories of the whole word.
c. affixes are relatively productive.
d. some affixes may add subjective meanings to their root.

Quasi-affixes differ from affixes in several aspects according to studies such as Lü (1978), Chen (1994), Ma (1995), Wang & Fu (2005), Zeng (2008), as illustrated in (6).

(6) a. quasi-affixes maintain some lexical meanings.
b. quasi-affixes tend to combine with polysyllabic morphemes while affixes always combine with monosyllabic morphemes.

---

[2]   http://ccl.pku.edu.cn:8080/ccl corpus/indux.jsp?dir=xiandai
[3]   http://search.people.com.cn/rmw/GB/bkzzsearch/index.jsp

c. quasi-affixes are more productive than affixes because they can create numerous new words in need of communication.

The morpheme *ke* introduced in Section 1 can be analyzed according to (5) and (6). Table 1 presents the properties of *ke* in different "*ke*+X" adjectives.

Table 1. ,Comparison of *ke*

properties	*ke* in different "*ke*+X" adjectives			
	ke^1	ke^2	ke^3	ke^4
Being used independently	no	yes	yes	no
Indicating the lexical category of the word	yes	no	no	yes
productivity	Relatively high	low	low	Extremely high
Having lexical meanings	no	yes	yes	yes
The number of morphemes it combined with	one	one	one	two

It can be seen from the table that ke^1 in is an affix and ke^4 is a quasi-affix, while ke^2 and ke^3 are free morphemes.

3   The source of *ke* in "*ke*+X" adjectives

Contemporary Chinese Dictionary (2012) lists three meanings of *ke* as an auxiliary verb. One (put as ke^{aux1}) is "should", another (put as ke^{aux2}) is "be worthy of", and the other (put as ke^{aux3}) means possibility and capability. All of them can be traced from ancient Chinese.

3.1 $ke^{aux1} \rightarrow$ adverb *ke* → conjunction *ke*

According to Wang (2010), modal adverb *ke* which functions to strengthen the speakers' attitudes in the interrogative sentences develops from ke^{aux1}. And this is supported by the study of Rao (2012), Wang (2008) and so on. Because ke^{aux1} has little to do with the lexicalization of the adjectives of "*ke*+X", we will not go into a detailed study of this section.

3.2 $ke^{aux2} \rightarrow$ bound morpheme→ affix

Ke^{aux2} indicated how things or people were evaluated, which expressed subjectivity in ancient Chinese, as is in (7) and (8).

(7) 君子在位可畏. <*Zuozhuan*>

Junzi   zai wei   ke   wei
Gentle.man   be high.place   be.worthy.   fearing
'When a gentle man takes a high place, he should be with an air of authority.'

(8) 物大然后可观. <*Zhouyi*>

> *Wu   da   ran   hou   ke   guan*
> Objects big this.way after be.worthy.of seeing
> 'When objects are big enough, it is worthy of seeing.'

The verbs to which ke^{aux2} could attach had two sub-categories: psychological verbs and ordinary verbs. In pre-*Qin* Chinese, psychological verbs and ke^{aux2} were always used as predicate to express the assessment of the speaker. Because they all had subjectivity, they were easily to be lexicalized as one word. When they finished lexicalization, ke^{aux2} became a bound morpheme in the "ke^{aux2}+psychological verb" adjectives. In *Qin* and *Han* dynasties, when the patient became the topic in a sentence, ke^{aux2} was added a meaning of passive. Because of the high frequency of usage, the passive meaning settled but the evaluation meaning was lost. Later, by analogy, ke^{aux2} could be used before all the psychological verbs and thus became an affix before *Tang* dynasty.

However, such a process do not occur to all the constructions of "ke^{aux2}+ordinary verbs", although the three adjectives in (2b) have been lexicalized as words. It is because of the numerous numbers of ordinary verbs and low frequency of usage of each "ke^{aux2}+ordinary verb" construction in both ancient and modern Chinese. Such as 可看 *kekan* 'be worthy of seeing' and 可游览 *keyoulan* 'be worthy of visiting' are verb phrases.

3.3 Ke^{aux3}→ bound morpheme→ quasi-suffix *ke*

Ke^{aux3} occurred before verbs, acting as a part of the predicate of a sentence in ancient Chinese, as is in (9).

(9) 金石可镂. <*Xunzi*>

> *Jin   shi   ke   lv*
> Metal stone can carve.
> '(Even) metal and stone can be carved.'

The difference between ke^{aux2} and ke^{aux3} is that the former has subjectivity and is more easily to be grammaticalized. In the 1970s, ke^{aux3} was always used with some disyllabic verbs to be attributives. In this phase, these "ke^{aux3}+disyllabic verb" constructions gained the properties of adjectives due to the highly frequent usage. Ke^{aux3} was a bound morpheme in these words and could not be used independently. When ke^{aux3} is combined with more and more disyllabic verbs by analogy, its main function turns to changing verbs into adjectives. E.g., 折叠 *zhedie* 'fold' is a verb, but 可折叠 *kezhedie* 'foldable' is an adjective. But because it still has lexical meanings, it should be seen as a quasi-affix which is in the process of grammaticalization.

From the analysis, it can be seen that ke^1 in "ke^{1}+V" being seen as an affix and ke^4 in "ke^4+disyllabic verb" being identified as a quasi-affix is the outcome of the grammaticalization of *ke* and the lexicalization of "*ke*+X" adjectives.

4   Conclusion

From the study of the "*ke*+X" adjectives, we are not with the statement of Wu (2005) that "because there is no morphological changes in Chinese, the path of grammaticalization is 'content word → functional word → internal word component'." The analysis of *ke* in this study shows that when the internal word component has high productivity, it can also be developed into affix or quasi-affix. So the path of grammaticalization in Chinese can be expanded to "content word → functional word → internal word component → affix/quasi-affix".

Acknowledgements

This paper is partially built upon my master's thesis. I would like to thank my thesis advisor Prof. Guosheng Wang who gave me patient guidance and constructive suggestions. I would also like to express my great appreciation to Prof. Jingxia Lin for her valuable comments while revising this paper. I am responsible for all the mistakes in this paper.

References

1. Academy of Social Sciences. (2012). *Contemporary Chinese dictionary*. 现代汉语词典. 6th edition. Beijing: The Commercial Press.
2. Lü, Shuxiang. (1980). *Eight hundred words in contemporary Chinese*. 现代汉语八百词. Beijing, China: The Commercial Press
3. Ma, Biao. (2010). Pragmatic affix system of Chinese state affixes. 汉语状态词缀构成的语用词缀系统. *Chinese Teaching in the World, 2*, 170-218.
4. Ma, Qingzhu. (1995).The property, scope and classification of the affix in Contemporary Chinese. 现代汉语词缀的性质、范围和分类. *Journal of Chinese Linguistics, 6*, 101-137.
5. Rao, Jia. (2012). A study of lexicalization of "Ke+X" words in Chinese. 汉语"可X"的词汇化考察. *Jiannan Literature, 2*, 156.
6. Shao, Bingjun. (2001).The affix of adjectives and additive word formation in Contemporary Chinese. 现代汉语形容词的词缀与附加式构词法. *Journal of Xinjiang University (Philosophy, Humanities & Social Science), 2*, 119-123.
7. Shen, Mengying. (1986). A new tendency of Chinese affixes. 汉语新的词缀化倾向. *Journal of Nanjing Normal University (Social Science Enition), 4*, 93-99.
8. Wang, Hongjun & Fu, Li. (2005). On the quasi-affixes in Contemporary Chinese. 试论现代汉语的类词缀. *Linguistic Sciences, 5*, 3-17.
9. Wang, Meihua. (2008). *Examples of lexicalization from trans-layered structures*. 跨层结构词汇化及其例证. Master thesis. Shanghai Normal University, Shanghai, China.
10. Wang, Mingyu. (2010). *A study on the lexicalization of disyllabic words of "ke+X" and related questions in modern Chinese*. 现代汉语"可X"式双音词的词汇化和相关问题研究. Master thesis. Shanghai Normal University, Shanghai, China.

11. Wu, Fuxiang. (2005).Several typological features of Chinese grammaticalization. 汉语语法化演变的几个类型学特征. *Zhongguo Yuwen* [Studies of the Chinese Language], 6, 483-494.

12. Zeng, Liying. (2008).The quantitative and qualitative research on the affixes in Contemporary Chinese. 现代汉语类词缀的定量与定性研究. *Teaching Chinese in the World, 4,* 75-87.

13. Zhao, Yuanren (1979). *A Grammar of Spoken Chinese*. (Translated by Lü, Shuxiang). . 汉语口语语法. Beijing, China: The Commercial Press.

14. Zhu, Dexi. (1982). *Lectures on Grammar*. 语法讲义. Beijing, China: The Commercial Press.

15. Zhu, Yajun. (2001). Research on the property and classification of affixes in Contemporary Chinese. 现代汉语词缀的性质及其分类研究. *Chinese Language Learning, 2,* 24-28.

Classifiers in Singapore Mandarin Chinese:
A Corpus-based Study

Xuelian Yuan[1] and Jingxia Lin[2]

[1,2] Nanyang Technological University
yuan0051@e.ntu.edu.sg
jingxialin@ntu.edu.sg

Abstract. While the study of classifiers in Modern Standard Mandarin Chinese has been discussed extensively in the literature, there are also key differences in the classifiers between Singapore Mandarin Chinese and other varieties of Modern Standard Mandarin Chinese, such as Mainland China Mandarin Chinese. Yet, classifiers in Singapore Mandarin Chinese have been minimally explored. With a corpus-based approach, involving both the written and spoken data sampled from Singapore Mandarin Chinese, this study aims to carry out a comprehensive and systematic investigation of the classifiers in Singapore Mandarin Chinese, and thereafter compare the classifiers between the (a) written and spoken data of Singapore Mandarin Chinese, and between (b) Singapore Mandarin Chinese and Mainland China Mandarin Chinese. In addition, this study will also look into the "adjective+classifier" adjectival phrase structure in Singapore Mandarin Chinese. The findings of this study will not only serve as an important reference for future studies of Singapore Mandarin Chinese classifiers, but also contribute to the theoretical discussion on classifiers in general and language variation and change.

Keywords: Singapore Mandarin Chinese, classifier, corpus-based approach, "adjective+classifier" adjectival phrase structure

1 Introduction

Singapore Mandarin Chinese (SMC) is a variety of Modern Standard Mandarin Chinese (henceforth Mandarin Chinese). Thus, SMC is generally similar to other varieties of Mandarin Chinese in terms of phonology, vocabulary and grammar ([1], [2]). However, due to a variety of factors, such as the influence of societal background and language environment ([1], [2]), there are key differences between SMC and other varieties of Mandarin Chinese such as Mainland China Mandarin Chinese (MMC). These differences encompass aspects including the usage of classifiers.

To date, few research studies have been carried out to investigate the differences in terms of grammatical use between SMC and other varieties of Mandarin Chinese – particularly on the usage of classifiers. Furthermore, these studies were either limited

© Springer International Publishing AG 2016
M. Dong et al. (Eds.): CLSW 2016, LNAI 10085, pp. 65–75, 2016
DOI: 10.1007/978-3-319-49508-8_7

to written data (such as newspapers, literary works, etc.), or based on the judgments of a few researchers. Studies conducted have yet to systematically explore and analyse the classifier system and hence, the classifiers in SMC. The present study is the first systematic study of the classifier system and classifiers in SMC, based on both the written and spoken data obtained from two fairly large corpora of SMC.

2   Methodology

2.1   Data

The data analysed in this study is based on two fairly large corpora, each representing the written and spoken data sampled from SMC.

The written data is obtained from the Chinese Gigaword Corpus Second Edition ([3]). This corpus consists of an archive of newswire text data from Lianhe Zaobao (Singapore), totaling approximately 30 million Chinese characters, collected from year 2000 to 2003. The spoken data of this study is represented by a selection of Singapore variety shows broadcasted in year 2012 to 2015, including "Behind Every Job S3" (2012, Ep. 1-6), "Home Decor Survivor S5" (2013, Ep. 1-5), "Finding 8 Launch 1" (2014, Ep. 1-8) and "Mars vs. Venus" (2015, Ep. 1-6). These variety shows were selected for the following reasons. First, the spoken data is relatively large with approximately 390 thousand Chinese characters. Second, the spoken data contains a total of 19 hours of unscripted and spontaneous conversations, involving demographically diverse speakers of SMC from Singapore. This is important as the relatively naturally-occurring conversations are able to reflect an accurate representation of the structure of the language. The two corpora of SMC mentioned above have been tagged with part-of-speech (POS) to facilitate linguistic analysis.

2.2   Design

The classifier system adopted in this study mainly follows Huang and Shi's [4] taxonomy of Mandarin Chinese classifiers, with references made to previous comprehensive studies by Tai and Wang [5], Tai [6], Huang and Ahrens [7] and Zhang [8]. The categories of classifiers and their corresponding subcategories in the classifier system are illustrated below in Figure 1.

Specifically, a distinction is made between classifiers (otherwise known as "sortal classifiers" by Huang and Shi [4] to differentiate from the broader grammatical category of "classifiers"; henceforth "sortal classifiers") and measure words "in order to better understand the cognitive basis of a classifier system" ([5], [6]). As Tai and Wang [5] and Tai [6] pointed out, the semantic distinction between classifiers and measure words are as follows: "A classifier categorizes a class of nouns by picking out some salient perceptual properties, either physically or functionally based, which are permanently associated with the entities named by the class of nouns; a measure word does not categorize but denotes the quantity of the entity named by a noun." ([5], [6])

This semantic distinction between sortal classifiers and measure words can be further justified on the basis of two syntactic tests, as pointed out by Tai ([5], [6]). First, "a classifier in Mandarin Chinese can be substituted with the general classifier *ge* without changing the meaning of the expression, whereas a measure word cannot." ([6]) Second, "the modifier marker *de* can be added between a measure word and its head noun but not between a classifier and its head noun." ([4], [6], [7])

Based on the semantic and syntactic distinction, sortal classifiers can be classified into three types: individual classifier, event classifier and kind classifier; whereas measure words can be classified into four types: container measure word, standard measure word, proximation measure word and activity measure word. ([4], [7])

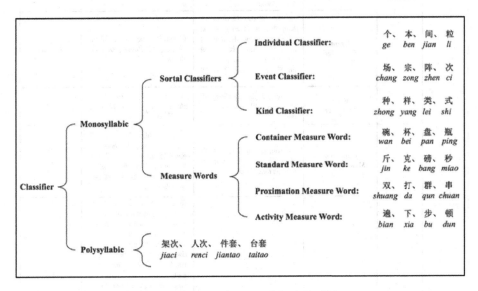

Fig. 1. Classifiers in Singapore Mandarin Chinese

3   Key Findings

3.1   Comparison of classifiers between the written and spoken data of Singapore Mandarin Chinese

Based on data obtained from the two corpora mentioned above, a total of 334 classifiers are divided into their respective categories. Of which, 125 classifiers are shared in common by both the written and spoken data, 199 classifiers only in the written data, and 9 classifiers only in the spoken data. A comparison of the classifiers across the written and spoken data of SMC showed considerable differences in categories of standard measure words and individual classifiers (See Table 1). The classifiers in each of the categories are listed in Table 1.

			Classifiers shared in common by both the written and spoken data	Classifiers in the written data	Classifiers in the spoken data
Mono-syllabic	Sortal Classifiers	Individual Classifier	支 zhi, 本 ben, 名 ming, 幅 fu, 把 ba, 部 bu, 集 ji, 朵 duo, 头 tou, 段 duan, 块 kuai, 张 zhang, 粒 li, 辆 liang, 栋 dong, 根 gen, 艘 sou, 副 fu, 滴 di, 扇 shan, 件 jian, 所 suo, 片 pian, 颗 ke, 尊 zun, 期 qi, 堵 du, 盏 zhan, 座 zuo, 位 wei, 个个 gege, 个 ge, 条 tiao, 间 jian, 面 mian, 只 zhi, 枚 mei, 坨 tuo, 棵 ke, 首 shou, 页 ye, 门 men, 道 dao, 口 kou, 家 jia, 句 ju, 台 tai, 轮 lun, 份 fen, 层 ceng	炷 zhu, 尾 wei, 峰 feng, 柱 zhu, 出 chu, 枝 zhi, 进 jin, 瓣 ban, 卷 juan, 档 dang, 弯 wan, 帧 zheng, 具 ju, 丸 wan, 开 kai, 叶 ye, 付 fu, 株 zhu, 曲 qu, 匹 pi, 册 ce, 管 guan, 蓬 peng, 柄 bing, 项 xiang, 重 chong, 顶 ding, 截 jie, 款 kuan, 封 feng, 纸 zhi, 通 tong, 首首 shoushou, 阕 que, 则 ze, 架 jia, 辑 ji, 栏 lan, 袭 xi, 客 ke, 眼 yan, 篇 pian, 员 yuan, 幢 zhuang, 角 jiao, 方 fang, 户 hu, 处 chu, 节 jie	片片 pianpian, 边 bian, 楼 lou, 等份 dengfen
		Event Classifier	趟 tang, 餐 can, 段 duan, 班 ban, 件 jian, 宗 zong, 期 qi, 阵 zhen, 回 hui, 顿 dun, 门 men, 场 chang, 起 qi, 圈 quan, 盘 pan, 局 ju, 台 tai, 步 bu, 轮 lun, 道 dao, 次 ci, 波 bo	码 ma, 档 dang, 折 zhe, 届 jie, 通 tong, 桩 zhuang, 堂 tang, 幕 mu	环 huan
		Kind Classifier	样 yang, 番 fan, 种 zhong, 式 shi, 类 lei, 门 men, 级 ji, 号 hao	味 wei, 档 dang, 种种 zhongzhong, 款 kuan, 路 lu, 介 jie, 派 pai	NA
	Measure Words	Container Measure Word	碗 wan, 瓶 ping, 杯 bei, 桌 zhuo, 箱 xiang, 盆 pen, 包 bao, 桶 tong, 盘 pan	茶匙 tangchi, 壶 hu, 坛 tan, 盒 he, 床 chuang, 盅 zhong, 缸 gang, 篮 lan, 勺 shao, 袋 dai, 匙 chi, 箩 luo, 罐 guan, 瓢 piao, 筒 tong, 池 chi, 锅 guo, 箩筐 luokuang	NA
		Standard Measure Word	公斤 gongjin, 小时 xiaoshi, 日 ri, 分钟 fenzhong, 毫米 haomi, 平方米 pingfangmi, 块 kuai, 点 dian, 票 piao, 分 fen, 秒 miao, 年 nian, 寸 cun, 公分 gongfen, 秒钟 miaozhong, 股 gu, 毫分 haofen, 尺 chi, 级 ji, 毫升 haosheng, 周 zhou, 磅 bang, 位 wei, 岁 sui, 毛 mao, 代 dai, 元 yuan, 米 mi, 天 tian, 公尺 gongchi, 号 hao, 度 du	微克 weike, 公顷 gongqin, 立方英尺 lifanggongchi, 斤 jin, 吨 dun, 微米 weimi, ℃, 瓦 wa, 码 ma, 品脱 pintuo, 盎司 angsi, 公升 gongsheng, 斗 dou, 克 ke, 升 sheng, 英里 yingli, 卡路里 kaluli, 海里 haili, 平方公里 pingfanggongli, 仞 ren, 宿 su, 晚 wan, %, 圆 wan, 更 geng, 英尺 yingchi, 里 li, 厘 li, 英吋 yingcun, 英亩 yingmu, 马克 make, 分贝 fenbei, 伏特 fute, 哩 li, 坪 ping, 刻钟 kezhong, 里拉 lila, 厘米 limi, 钧 jun, 港元 gangyuan, 兆赫 zhaohe, 月 yue, 立方公尺 lifanggongchi, 公厘 gongli, 公里 gongli, 日元 riyuan, 美分 meifen, 美元 meiyuan, 日圆 riyuan, 英镑 bang, 镑 bang, 法郎 falang, 旬 xun, 载 zai, 周年 zhounian, 时 shi, 钱 qian, 卡 ka, 千瓦 qianwa, 平方公尺 pingfanggongchi, 公克 gongke, 铢 zhu, 瓦特 wate, 文 wen, 钟 zhong, 加仑 jialun, 公吨 gongdun, 两 liang, 便士 bianshi, 畦 qi, 顷 qin, 亩 mu, 贯 guan, 毫克 haoke, 安培 anpei, 星期 xingqi, 卢比 lubi, 角 jiao, 折 zhe, 方 fang, 路 lu, 席 xi, 棒 bang	新币 xinbi

		Approximation Measure Word	幅 *fu*, 把 *ba*, 串 *chuan*, 段 *duan*, 点 *dian*, 票 *piao*, 套 *tao*, 行 *hang*, 班 *ban*, 副 *fu*, 片 *pian*, 组 *zu*, 束 *shu*, 股 *gu*, 些 *xie*, 堆 *dui*, 群 *qun*, 对 *dui*, 笔 *bi*, 声 *sheng*, 摊 *tan*, 排 *pai*, 双 *shuang*, 刻 *ke*	抹 *mo*, 腔 *qiang*, 剂 *ji*, 绺 *liu*, 撮 *cuo*, 捆 *kun*, 丛 *cong*, 点儿 *dianer*, 手 *shou*, 批 *pi*, 帮 *bang*, 缕 *lv*, 丝 *si*, 滩 *tan*, 胎 *tai*, 泓 *hong*, 拨 *bo*, 列 *lie*, 伙 *huo*, 帖 *tie*, 线 *xian*, 窝 *wo*, 簇 *cu*, 泡 *pao*, 打 *da*, 袭 *xi*, 叠 *die*, 队 *dui*, 团 *tuan*, 口 *kou*, 付 *fu*, 派 *pai*, 席 *xi*, 幕 *mu*	阵阵 *zhenzhen*, 系 列 *xilie*
		Activity Measure Word	遍 *bian*, 趟 *tang*, 把 *ba*, 番 *fan*, 下 *xia*, 阵 *zhen*, 周 *zhou*, 笔 *bi*, 声 *sheng*, 顿 *dun* , 招 *zhao*, 圈 *quan*, 任 *ren*, 步 *bu*, 回 *hui*, 度 *du*, 次 *ci*	刀 *dao*, 拳 *quan*, 着 *zhao*, 脚 *jiao*, 掌 *zhang*, 遭 *zao*, 记 *ji*, 鞭 *bian*, 通 *tong*, 针 *zhen*, 架 *jia*, 响 *xiang*, 枪 *qiang*, 眼 *yan*, 箭 *jian* , 关 *guan*	步步 *bubu*
Poly-syllabic			NA		

Table 1. Classifiers in the written and spoken data of Singapore Mandarin Chinese

First, loanwords classified under the category of standard measure words, such as 盎司 *angsi* 'ounce', 便士 *bianshi* 'penny', 伏特 *fute* 'volt', etc. are only adopted in the written data than in the spoken data. Second, units of currency classified under the category of standard measure words, such as 法郎 *falang* 'franc', 英镑 *yingbang* 'pound', 日元 *riyuan* 'yen', etc. are commonly found in the written data as compared to the spoken data, in which only 新币 *xinbi* 'Singapore dollar' has been adopted in the spoken data. In addition, it is also noteworthy to mention that words in different forms with the same meaning are used in the written and spoken data. For instance, 'cents' is expressed as 角 *jiao* in the written data, whereas it is expressed as 毛 *mao* in the spoken data. Third, classifiers denoting a vast variety of shapes classified under the category of individual classifiers, such as 丸 *wan* 'sphere-like', 方 *fang* 'square-like' and 弯 *wan* 'stream-like' shapes, etc. are found in the written data, whereas the spoken data only adopts prototypical classifier, such as 颗 *ke* and 粒 *li*, which denote shapes that are small and round.

3.2　Comparison of classifiers between Singapore Mandarin Chinese and Mainland China Mandarin Chinese

A further comparison of the classifiers across SMC and MMC [9] revealed differences in the category of measure words, particularly in standard measure words (See Table 2). A total of 35 classifiers are found only in SMC, whereas a total of 289 classifiers are found only in MMC. The classifiers in each of the categories are listed in Table 2.

			Classifiers in Singapore Mandarin Chinese	Classifiers in Mainland China Mandarin Chinese
Mono-syllabic	Sortal Classifiers	Individual Classifier	进 jin, 丸 wan, 首首 shoushou, 客 ke	张张 zhangzhang, 颗颗 keke, 粒粒 lili, 滴滴 didi, 瓣瓣 banban, 盏盏 zhanzhan, 条条 tiaotiao, 棵棵 keke, 根根 gengen, 只只 zhizhi, 顶顶 dingding, 朵朵 duoduo, 栋栋 dongdong, 篇篇 pianpian, 块块 kuaikuai, 间间 jianjian, 句句 juju, 门门 menmen, 道道 daodao, 方方 fangfang, 件件 jianjian, 事事 shishi, 户户 huhu, 层层 cengceng, 丝丝 sisi, 家家 jiajia, 节节 jiejie, 处处 chuchu, 枝枝 zhizhi, 重重 chongchong, 锭 ding, 橙 tang, 廛 chan, 截儿 jieer, 兜儿 douer, 兜 dou, 蔸 dou, 驱 qu, 肩 jian, 厢 xiang, 铺 pu, 轴 zhou, 撇 pie, 抬 tai, 例 li, 发 fa, 章 zhang, 帐 zhang, 垛 duo, 炬 ju, 领 ling, 吊 diao, 挺 ting, 驾 jia, 丘 qiu, 羽 yu, 篷 peng, 版 ban, 湾 wan, 编 bian, 孔 kong, 杆 gan, 钩 gou, 围 wei, 份儿 fener, 圈儿 quaner, 片儿 pianer
		Event Classifier	波 bo	回回 huihui, 道道 daodao, 件件 jianjian, 顿顿 dundun, 场场 changchang, 餐餐 cancan
		Kind Classifier	式 shi, 介 jie	样样 yangyang, 门门 menmen, 款款 kuankuan, 品 pin, 流 liu, 辈 bei
	Measure Words	Container Measure Word	茶匙 tangchi, 匙 chi, 箩筐 luokuang	斛 hu, 杯杯 beibei, 簸箕 boji, 盂 yu, 卡车 kache, 塑料袋 suliaodai, 盆盆 penpen, 盘盘 panpan, 麻袋 madai, 箪 dan, 筐 kuang, 篓 lou, 脸盆 lianpen, 锨 xian, 口袋 koudai, 锹 qiao, 听 ting, 碟 die, 挑 tiao, 车 che, 船 chuan, 桶子 tongzi, 网 wang, 篮子 lanzi, 车子 chezi, 书架 shujia, 犁 li, 钵 bo, 框 kuang, 江 jiang, 炉 lu, 板 ban
		Standard Measure Word	公分 gongfen, 毫分 haofen, 公尺 gongchi, 微克 weike, 立方英尺 lifangyingchi, 品脱 pintuo, 晚 wan, %, 日圆 riyuan, 英时 yingcun, 伏特 fute, 坪 ping, 月 yue, 立方公尺 lifanggongchi, 公厘 gongli, 平方公尺 pingfanggongchi, 公克 gongke, 瓦特 wate, 时 shi, 两 liang, 新币 xinbi, 楼 lou	毫 hao, 平米 pingmi, 英寸 yingcun, 摄氏度 sheshidu, 立方米 lifangmi, 千伏 qianfu, 马力 mali, 千克 qianke, 千米 qianmi, 平方 pingfang, 大卡 daka, 千卡 qianka, 立方 lifang, 赫兹 hezi, 市两 shiliang, 平方英尺 pingfangyingchi, 华里 huali, 克拉 kela, 平方厘米 pingfanglimi, 平方英里 pingfangyingli, 铺 pu, 旦 dan, 市斤 shijin, 比特 bite, 毫秒 haomiao, 立方厘米 lifanglimi, 纳秒 namiao, 安 an, 吨 dun, 秤 cheng, 公里 gongli, 伏安 fuan, 帕斯卡 pasika, 毫安 haoan, 毫米汞柱 haomigongzhu, 牛顿 niudun, 毫微米 haoweimi, 毫微妙 haoweimiao, 土方 tufang, 毫升 haoli, 总吨 zongdun, 晌 shang, 雷姆 leimu, 兆位 zhaowei, 费丹 feidan, 垧 shang, 蒲式耳 pushier, 赫 he, 工日 gongri, 丈 zhang, 伏 fu, 焦耳 jiaoer, 纳米 nami, 千瓦时 qianwashi, 澳元 aoyuan, 欧元 ouyuan, 卢布 lubu, 韩元 hanyuan, 比索 bisuo, 加拿大元 jianadayuan, 瑞士法郎 ruishifalang, 先令 xianling, 第纳尔 dinaer, 戈比 gebi, 芬尼 fenni, 克朗 kelang, 塔卡 taka, 林吉特 linjite, 兹罗提 ziluoti, 科朗 kelang, 列伊 lieyi, 兰特 lante, 瑞尔 ruier, 谢克尔 xiekeer, 玻利瓦尔 boliwate, 雷亚尔 leiyaer, 吊 diao, 世 shi, 代代 daidai, 辈 bei, 辈子 beizi, 季 ji, 周岁 zhousui, 周周 zhouzhou, 岁岁 suisui, 年年 niannian, 日日 riri, 天天 tiantian, 夜夜 yeye, 分分 fenfen, 朝朝 zhaozhao, 寻 xun, 国 guo, 乡 xiang, 站 zhan, °, GB, L, cm, nm, T, M, mm, K, V, W, DB, MB, MW, Kg, KV, KW, A, mmHg, ppm, kv, CC, HZ, KB, MHz, Mpa
		Approximation Measure Word	NA	股股 gugu, 堆堆 duidui, 套套 taotao, 对对 duidui, 团团 tuantuan, 排排 paipai, 丝丝 sisi, 双双 shuangshuang, 声声 shengsheng, 点点 diandian, 股子 guzi, 丁点儿 dingdianer, 廛 chan, 丛 cha, 摞 lei, 沓 ta, 嘟噜 dulu, 墩儿 dun, 拨儿 boer, 帙 zhi, 刻刻 keke, 畈 fan, 挂 gua, 园 yuan, 溜 liu, 垄 long, 联 lian, 札 zha, 服 fu, 子 zi, 身 shen, 肚子 duzi, 脸 lian, 掬 ju, 捧 peng, 拱 gong, 坝 ba, 圈儿 quaner, 臂 bi, 帘 lian, 绺 min
		Activity Measure Word	箭 jian, 关 guan, 掌 zhang	跤 jiao, 茬 cha, 仗 zhang, 转 zhuan, 巴掌 bazhang, 拍 pai, 梭 suo, 和 huo, 镐 gao, 巡 xun, 匝 za, 炮 pao, 圈儿 juaner, 下子 xiazi, 画 hua, 次次 cici, 招招 zhaozhao
Polysyllabic			NA	航次 hangci, 人次 renci, 架次 jiaci, 场次 changci, 艘次 souci, 船次, 卷次 juanci, 人份 renfen, 人公里 rengongli, 人年 rennian

Table 2. Classifiers in Singapore Mandarin Chinese and Mainland China Mandarin Chinese

First, units of specific measurement that are classified under the category of standard measure words in SMC, such as 公分 *gongfen* 'centimeter', 公尺 *gongchi* 'meter', 毫分 *haofen* 'millimeter', etc. are expressed in different forms such as 厘米 *limi*, 米 *mi* and 毫米 *haomi* in MMC respectively. Second, standard measure words such as GB 'gigabyte', K 'kelvin', Hz 'hertz', V 'volt', etc. are also expressed as symbols in SMC, whereas these are only expressed as Chinese characters in MMC such as 赫兹 *hezi* 'hertz' and 伏特 *fute* 'volt'. Third, loanwords that are classified under the category of standard measure words such as 帕斯卡 *pakasi* 'pascal', 焦耳 *jiaoer* 'joules', 牛顿 *niudun* 'newton', etc. are commonly found in MMC as compared to SMC. Fourth, temporary measure words (nouns borrowed temporarily as measure words) such as 麻袋 *madai* 'sack', 肚子 *duzi* 'stomach' and 巴掌 *bazhang* 'palm' classified under the categories of container measure words, approximation measure words and activity measure words in MMC respectively, are less common in SMC. Fifth, reduplicative classifiers in MMC, such as 张张 *zhangzhang* 'sheet', 场场 *changchang* 'classifier for events', 款款 *kuankuan* 'models', 堆堆 *duidui* 'pile', etc. are commonly expressed in monosyllabic forms in SMC such as 张 *zhang*, 场 *chang*, 款 *kuan*, 堆 *dui* respectively. Sixth, polysyllabic classifiers such as 航次 *hangci* 'number or sequence of voyages or flights', 架次 *jiaci* 'number of sorties', 场次 *changci* 'number of showings of a play, movie, etc.' are only adopted in MMC than in the SMC.

4 The "adjective+classifier" adjectival phrase structure in SMC

According to Lu et al [2], there is an "adjective+classifier" (henceforth "adj+CL") adjectival phrase structure in SMC, such as **那么大间**的旧屋 *name da jian de jiu wu* 'a huge old house', 这张纸**很大张** *zhe zhang zhi hen da zhang* 'a large sheet of paper', etc. As Lu et al [2] point out, the "adj+CL" phrase structure exhibits syntactic properties similar to that of adjectives such as: (1) occurring in the predicative position and (2) able to be modified by adverbs, particularly degree words such as 很 *hen* 'very', 更 *geng* 'much more', 越 *yue* 'the more…the more', etc. It is also pointed out that the adjective 大 *da* 'big' is frequently used in this phrase structure. In addition, this structure only occurs in SMC and not in MMC.

Despite the above investigation conducted by Lu et al, there are areas on the adjectival "adj+CL" phrase structure that has yet to be explored in detail, such as, the types of classifiers and adjectives which can be used in this phrase structure. The present study therefore aims to conduct an investigation on the "adj+CL" adjectival phrase structure.

4.1 Data and Procedure

The present study conducts the investigation on the "adj+CL" adjectival phrase structure in two stages, namely internet searches and a survey among SMC and MMC native speakers. The following first describes the scope and results of the internet searches, followed by the survey.

4.1.1   Scope of Study (Internet Search)

Internet searches were conducted using the Google site:sg function. The scope of the present study includes the following: (1) To test the types of adjectives which can be used in the phrase structure, a total of 4 adjectives including 大 *da* 'big', 小 *xiao* 'small', 长 *chang* 'long' and 短 *duan* 'short' were selected; of which, 大 *da* 'big' was mentioned by Lu et al [2]; (2) To test the types of classifiers which can be used in the phrase structure, a total of 134 classifiers are taken from the spoken data of SMC. This is due to the reason that the "adj+CL" phrase structure occurs most frequently in spoken SMC; (3) To test if the phrase structure allows reduplication of adjectives. The present study takes into account the first 50 relevant results for each classifier and adjective tested.

4.1.2   Results of Study (Internet Search)

Results of the first stage of study are as follows: First, besides appearing in the predicative position, the syntactic properties of the "adj+CL" adjectival phrase structure also include, occurring in the (a) attributive position, such as **很大只**的蜜蜂 *hen da zhi de mifeng* 'a huge bee', **那么大片**的蛋糕 *name dapian de dangao* 'a big slice of cake', etc.; in the (b) complement position, such as 长得**很大盆** *zhang de hen da pen* 'grown into a huge pot', 变得**很小只** *bian de hen xiao zhi* 'became smaller in size', etc.

Second, the "adj+CL" adjectival phrase structure can occur in (a) comparative sentences, such as 选购**比较大棵**的圣诞树 *xuan gou bijiao da ke de shengdanshu* 'to purchase a bigger Christmas tree', 花生米也都选的**比较大粒** *huashengmi ye dou xuan de bijiao dali* 'select the larger pieces of peanuts', etc.; can be (b) modified by adverbs, particularly degree words, such as 阿婆的船**很小艘** *apo de chuan hen xiao sou* 'the boat that belongs to the old lady is very small' and 有钱人换的车越来**越大辆** *you qian ren huan de che yue lai yue da liang* 'the rich are increasingly getting bigger cars'; (c) adjectives in the "adj+CL" adjectival phrase structure can be reduplicated, such as 一块**大大块**的鸡肉 *yikuai dada kuai de jirou* 'a large piece of chicken', 让他们每一个都眼睛**大大粒** *rang tamen mei yige dou yanjing da dali*, 'leaving everyone astonished, with their eyes wide open', etc. In addition, it is also observed that the "reduplicated adj+CL" phrase structure and "adj+CL" phrase structure exhibit similar syntactic properties mentioned above, thus indicating that it is also an adjectival phrase structure.

Third, the types of (a) adjectives that can be used in the "adj+CL" adjectival phrase structure is limited to 大 *da* 'big' and 小 *xiao* 'small', whereas 长 *chang* 'long' and 短 *duan* 'short' cannot; (b) classifiers that can be used in the "adj+CL" adjectival phrase structure include individual classifiers (支 *zhi* 'classifier for guns, songs, etc.', 幅 *fu* 'piece', 颗 *ke* 'classifier for small and round objects', 尊 *zun* 'classifier for statues, cannons', 棵 *ke* 'classifier for trees, plants', 个 *ge* 'classifier for objects, people, etc.', 条 *tiao* 'strip', 艘 *sou* 'classifier for ships, vessels', 朵 *duo* 'classifier for flowers, clouds', 间 *jian* 'classifier for small buildings, rooms, etc.', 只 *zhi* 'classifier for animals, one of a pair, etc.', 辆 *liang* 'classifier for vehicles', 张

zhang 'sheet', 粒 *li* 'classifier for small and round objects', 块 *kuai* 'lump', 件 *jian* 'classifier for clothing, things', 份 *fen* 'portion', 枝 *zhi* 'classifier for pencils, sticks, etc.', 片 *pian* 'classifier for objects which are flat and thin', 副 *fu* 'classifier for pairs, set of things, etc.'), event classifier (件 *jian* 'classifier for events'), container measure words (碗 *wan* 'bowl', 瓶 *ping* 'bottle', 杯 *bei* 'cup', 包 *bao* 'bag', 桶 *tong* 'pail') and approximation measure words (束 *shu* 'bundle', 群 *qun* 'group'), whereas kind classifiers, standard measure words and activity measure words cannot. The above also applies to the "reduplicated adj+CL" phrase structure. It is noteworthy to mention that the kind classifier 样 *yang* 'kind' only occurs in the "adj+CL" adjectival phrase structure, but does not occur in the "reduplicated adj+CL" phrase structure.

Compared to Lu et al [2], results from the internet searches have not only shown the types of adjectives and classifiers that can be used in the "adj+CL" adjectival phrase structure, but also revealed further syntactic properties of the phrase structure. However, results from the internet searches did not reflect that prototypical classifiers such as 本 *ben* 'classifier for books, periodicals, etc.', 双 *shuang* 'pair', etc. can be used in the "adj+CL" adjectival phrase structure. Furthermore, Shi [10] has also pointed out that the "adj+CL" adjectival phrase structure appears in MMC. In order to ascertain the abovementioned, this study has also conducted an investigation through a survey.

4.1.3   Scope of Study (Survey)

A total of 22 classifiers were selected as tests for this survey. These 22 classifiers form a total of 50 sentences with the "adj+CL" phrase structure occurring in two positions, namely (1) attributive position and (2) predicative position. In other words, 22 classifiers each form a total of two sentences. Two adjectives, 大 *da* 'big' and 小 *xiao* 'small' were then randomly placed in two of the sentences formed by each classifier. Out of the 22 classifiers, 7 classifiers (只 *zhi* 'classifier for animals, one of a pair, etc.', 杯 *bei* 'cup', 棵 *ke* 'classifier for trees, plants, etc.', 碗 *wan* 'bowl', 幅 *fu* 'piece', 包 *bao* 'bag', 束 *shu* 'bundle') which were tested in the first stage of study were also included to control for reliability, while 4 classifiers forming five "adj+CL" phrase structures (很长柄 *hen chang bing* 'long handle', 太整只 *tai zheng zhi* 'whole piece', 很整段 *hen zheng duan* 'whole section', 很长段 *hen chang duan* 'long section', 非常长条 *fei chang chang tiao* 'long strip') mentioned in Shi [10] were included to test for acceptability in SMC and MMC. With the exception of the five "adj+CL" phrase structures mentioned above, the remaining sentences were formed using the adverb 很 *hen* 'very'. 20 participants, inclusive of 15 speakers of SMC from Singapore and 5 speakers of MMC from Mainland China were assigned the survey administered on the Google Form platform. Participants are required to rate the acceptability of the sentences on a 5-point scale, with 1 being the least acceptable and 5 being the most acceptable. Results from the survey would reveal the level of acceptability towards sentences with the "adj+CL" adjectival phrase structure.

4.1.4   Results of Study (Survey)

The responses collected from the survey were computed using the mean value. A mean value greater than 3 indicates high acceptability and vice versa. The tabulated results from the survey are shown in Table 3.

Data		Classifier	Attributive Mean		Predicative Mean	
			SMC	MMC	SMC	MMC
Spoken Data (Test for acceptability)	1.	大 / 小本 *ben*	3.8	2.2	3.6	2.3
	2.	大 / 小盏 *zhan*	3.6	1.2	3.6	2.2
	3.	大 / 小坨 *tuo*	4.1	2.0	3.5	1.1
	4.	大 / 小盘 *pan*	4.1	1.8	3.3	1.8
	5.	大 / 小箱 *xiang*	3.1	2.2	3.9	2.4
	6.	大 / 小盆 *pen*	3.7	2.7	3.4	2.0
	7.	大 / 小串 *chuan*	4.1	2.6	3.5	1.8
	8.	大 / 小 双 *shuang*	3.5	2.0	3.9	2.0
	9.	大 / 小座 *zuo*	3.7	2.4	2.5	1.6
	10.	大 / 小滴 *di*	3.5	1.4	2.5	1.8
	11.	大 / 小段 *duan*	3.1	2.4	1.9	1.4
	12.	大 / 小样 *yang*	3.4	1.6	2.3	1.6
	13.	大 / 小宗 *zong*	2.8	1.8	2.7	1.2
Spoken Data (Control for reliability)	14.	大 / 小棵 *ke*	3.9	2.0	3.7	2.2
	15.	大 / 小只 *zhi*	3.9	2.0	3.7	1.6
	16.	大 / 小幅 *fu*	3.0	2.4	3.0	1.8
	17.	大 / 小碗 *wan*	4.1	2.6	3.7	1.8
	18.	大 / 小杯 *bei*	3.3	1.8	4.0	2.4
	19.	大 / 小包 *bao*	4.3	2.8	3.7	2.6
	20.	大 / 小束 *shu*	3.3	2.2	3.3	2.0
Shi (2013) (Test for acceptability)	21.	很整段 *hen zheng duan* 'whole section'	1.4	1.2	1.5	1.4
	22.	很长段 *hen chang duan* 'long section'	2.0	1.8	1.7	1.2
	23.	很长柄 *hen chang bing* 'long handle'	1.7	2.0	1.6	1.8
	24.	太整只 *tai zheng zhi* 'whole piece'	1.5	1.2	1.5	1.2
	25.	非常长条 *fei chang chang tiao* 'long strip'	1.5	1.8	1.5	1.4

Table 3. Acceptability towards "adj+CL" phrase structure

First, the types of classifiers that can be used in the "adj+CL" adjectival phrase structure has been extended to include kind classifiers such as 样 *yang* 'kind'. Second, with the exception of the five "adj+CL" phrase structure mentioned in Shi [10] and 宗 *zong* 'classifier for cases (legal, medical, etc.)', the remaining sentences with the "adj+CL" phrase structure have been rated as high acceptability by SMC speakers. In addition, "adj+CL" adjectival phrase structure in the attributive position are of higher acceptability than in the predicative position. Second, the five "adj+CL" phrase structure mentioned in Shi [10] have been rated as low acceptability by both the SMC and MMC speakers. This indicates that the phrase structures mentioned in Shi [10] are different to that of the "adj+CL" adjectival phrase structure in SMC. In other words, the "adj+CL" adjectival phrase structure is unique to SMC.

5   Conclusion and Future Studies

This study is the first systematic study of the classifier system and classifiers in SMC, based on both the written and spoken data obtained from two fairly large corpora of SMC. A comparison between the written and spoken data of SMC and between SMC and MMC is made. In addition, this study has also conducted an investigation of the "adjective+classifier" adjectival phrase structure in Singapore Mandarin Chinese. The findings of this study will not only serve as an important reference for future studies of Singapore Mandarin Chinese classifiers, but also contribute to the theoretical discussion on classifiers in general and language variation and change.

The next stage of this study would involve recruiting more participants for the survey, including participants from Mainland China, Taiwan and Hong Kong, to investigate if the "adj+CL" adjectival phrase structure occurs in other varieties of Modern Standard Mandarin Chinese. In addition, classifiers from both the written and spoken data need to be included to obtain more comprehensive results.

Acknowledgements

We wish to acknowledge the funding for this project from Nanyang Technological University under the Undergraduate Research Experience on CAmpus (URECA) programme, and the financial support from MOE Academic Research Fund Tier 1 project (M4011571).

References

1. Li, Linding, Chew, Cheng Hai: Xinjiapo huayu cihui yu zhongguo putonghua cihui bijiao, In: Chew, Cheng Hai: Xinjiapo Huayu Cihui yu Yufa, Lingzi Media, Singapore (2002).
2. Lu, Jianming: Xinjiapo huayu yufa tedian. In: Chew, Cheng Hai: Xinjiapo Huayu Cihui yu Yufa, Lingzi Media, Singapore (2002).
3. Huang, Chu-Ren. 2009. Tagged Chinese Gigaword Version 2.0. Philadelphia: Lexical Data Consortium, University of Pennsylvania. ISBN 1-58563-516-2.
4. Huang, Chu-Ren, Dingxu Shi: A Reference Grammar of Chinese. (eds.) The Cambridge University Press, Cambridge (2016).
5. Tai, James H-Y., and Lianqing Wang: A Semantic Study of the Classifier tiao. Journal of the Chinese Language Teachers Association, 25(1), pp. 35-56 (1990).
6. Tai, James H.-Y.: Chinese Classifier System and Human Categorization. In Honor of Professor William S-Y. Wang: Interdisciplinary Studies on Language and Language Change, Matthew Chen and Ovid Tseng (eds.) Pyramid Publishing Company, pp. 479-494 (1990).
7. Huang, C.-R, Ahrens, K.: Individuals, Kinds and Events: Classifier Coercion of Noun. Language Sciences, 25(4), pp. 353-373 (2003).
8. Zhang, Bin: Xiandai Hanyu miaoxie yufa, Shang wu yin shu guan, Beijing (2010)
9. BCC Corpus: http://bcc.blcu.edu.cn/
10. Shi, Yuan Yuan: "Xingrongci+Liangci" Jiegou Yanjiu. Masters' thesis, Shanghai Normal University (2013).

The "v + n" compound nouns in Chinese: from the perspective of Generative Lexicon Theory

Yaxi Jin

Beijing Language and Culture University
gimahi1980@163.com

Abstract. In Chinese, a verbal morpheme and a nominal morpheme can form a variety of compound words, such as compound verbs, compound nouns, compound adjectives etc. Among them, the 'v + n' compound nouns are not only abundant in quantity, but also rich in meaning. The verbal morphemes show the strong capacity of word-formation. In this paper, we selected nearly 2800 disyllabic "v + n" compound nouns from the "Modern Chinese Dictionary (Sixth Edition)"as the research object and studied their main semantic mode and semantic combination mechanism. We found that the functions of the verbal morphemes were downgraded from predication into identification, and their qualia structure exhibited complex and heterogeneous diversity. The referential transparency of this type of compound nouns is very high, but the semantics is not always simple additive relation and the semantic transparency of part of this type of compound nouns is not high.

Keywords: "v + n" compound nouns; semantic mode; qualia structure; qualia relationship; semantic transparency

ⓒ Springer International Publishing AG 2016
M. Dong et al. (Eds.): CLSW 2016, LNAI 10085, pp. 76–90, 2016
DOI: 10.1007/978-3-319-49508-8_8

1   Introduction

The previous studies on the Chinese compounds mostly focus on the "noun + noun" type compound nouns and the research on the "v + n" compound nouns are not thorough enough. There is a lack of large-scale statistical analyses and a comprehensive system of semantic types has not been set up yet. Besides, the explanations for the combination mechanism of morphemes are not profound enough. The "Modern Chinese Dictionary (the 6th edition)" records about 2800 disyllable "v + n" compound nouns with a huge amount and various semantic relations which can better represent the unique ways of word-formation in Chinese compared to the "n + n" compound nouns. This paper focuses on the "v + n" compound nouns along with their semantic relations and combination mechanism.

2   The types of "v + n" compound nouns in Chinese

2.1   Derived from Syntax

There is one type of the "v + n" compound nouns which are produced from the syntactic ways and are used as verb phrases at the beginning. Owing to the high frequency of use, the gradual lexicalization and the transformation from verbal components to nominal components at the same time, Wang (2010: 57) call it "Lexicalization and Nominalization" and the compound nouns in modern Chinese are abundant like these actually. These compound nouns share something in common that except some verbal morphemes which are directional, others are almost transitive. However, as for the interior, there are great differences since several sub-categories can be divided according to different standards of classification. At first, in terms of the structure, the "v + n" compound nouns from syntax fall into modifier-head and predicate-object construction1 while the former takes up the majority . And the objects the nominal morphemes perform are generalized objects including Target Object, Resultative Object, Instrument Object and so on, such as: "kaoya, jianbing, baoji, shache, peikuan, paocai". However, a few compounds belong to the latter type such as: "laixin, laihan, laidian, laiyuan, huiwei, huixiang, jinkou, chukou, duice" and so on.

---

[1]A few words like "*guanjun, chushen*" and so on can't be included in the two constructions.

And then, there are three types according to the increasing level of lexicalization. The first one is noun-verb ambiguous " verb + noun" type compound nouns, such as "gengdi, laixin, huixin, peikuan, baoche, shache, guanshi, chaofan, jianzhi, guanchang, saiche, peican, defen" and so on. The "v + n" compound nouns from Syntax are originally used as verb-noun verbal phrases. The verbal verb-noun structures still exist and they can be used as verbal compounds in modern Chinese, however, the connections among the morphemes are relatively loose. In the "Modern Chinese Dictionary", " // " is marked among compound morphemes when words of this type are used as compound verbs to reveal that components like auxiliary words, numerals and pronouns can be inserted to extend the phrase to be verb-object. Thus, in modern Chinese, verb-noun constructions in this type form a situation in which the predicate-object compounds verbs and the predicate-object or modifier-head compound nouns exist together and classification and selection on usage can just be made according to the context, thus the level of lexicalization is relatively low. The second one is the "v + n" compound nouns caused by the grammaticalization of nominal morphemes. The nominal morphemes'grammaticalization includes week stress and neutral tone and both or either like "guojiao, bangtui, gaihuo, guotui, doudu, ganshi, jianbing" and so on. Here, the so-called grammaticalization of nominal morphemes is one method which can divide the verb-noun constructions into verb-object type compound verbs and modifier-head compound nouns, namely, when it is not in weak stress and neutral tone, the verb-noun constructions would be interpreted as predicate-object verb phrase or compound verbs; when in weak stress or neutral tone, the construction would be interpreted as compound nous which is more common. Therefore, we suggest that the level of lexicalization in these verb-noun constructions is higher than the former type. The third type are the pure nominal "v + n" compound nouns and some "v + n" compound nouns derived from syntax once performed as verbs or verb phrases only in ancient Chinese, but they are no longer used as verbs or verb phrases in modern Chinese such as "guanjun, tigang, liuyan, duice" and so on (Wang, 2010: 60); besides, there are a large number of "v + n" constructions in modern Chinese just remain their usage as predicate-object constructions theoretically due to the nominal morphemes' fairly low independence. These "v + n" combinations can only be used as compound nouns after Lexicalization and Nominalization with their morphemes tightly linked and have the highest level of lexicalization such as "guanqu, guanpian, rukou, guanqu, bianzhong" and so on.

Wang (2010:57) put forward the notion of "Lexicalization and Nominalization" which refers to the process that the verbal phrases cohere to one single word by lexicalization and the verbal components change to nominal components at the same time. It is a transferred-designation nominalization. We suggest that the "v + n" compound nouns derived from Syntax gain the nominal usage exactly by Lexicalization and Nominalization and the arguments in verbal morphemes are denoted by the whole verb-noun combinations. Besides, five categories can be divided according to arguments in the verbal morphemes from the "v + n" combinations' transferred-designation: (1) objects of transferred-designation, such as "baoche, baoji, gengdi, gugong, jianzhi, jianchai, kaoya, kaoyan, cunkuan, huikuan" and so on; (2) results of transferred-designation, such as "bianhao, huanxiang, duan'an, zuowen, jianbing, qiepian, chenmian, jianying, jianzhi, liefeng" and so on; (3) agents of transferred-designation, such as "lingdui, guanjia, genban, peifang, hufa, dujun, duxue, baobiao, lishi, zhangduo, jiangong, siji, tigong" and so on; (4) experiencers of transferred-designation, such as "guanjun, lichun, lixia, liqiu, lidong, duimen, liushui" and so on; (5) instruments of transferred-designation, here the instruments are generalized including the appliances, facilities, materials and methods called for fulfilling one certain purpose such as "shache, duice, bangtui, guotui, guojiao, baotou, chengchen, tayao, dishui, tiaozhan, fengdi,fengmian, fuchen, hutui, huwan, huxi, huyao, hu'er, kaobei, fushou"and so on.

2.2   Derived from word-formation

Another part of the "v + n" compounds come from word-formation, it is called "Direct Word-formation". (Wang, 2010: 57) which means the verbal morpheme and the nominal morpheme constitute the modifier-head construction compound nouns directly and the connections among the morphemes are tight, any other component cannot be inserted. Zhao Yuanren (1979), Dong Xiufang (2002) once remarked " From the diachronic perspective, the earliest compounds were derived from Syntax and with more and more compounds derived, the compound word-formation emerged." Therefore, the appearance of the "v + n" compound nouns derived from word-formation is later than the appearance of the "verb-noun" type compound nouns derived from Syntax, however, in modern Chinese, compounds of this type are abundant and it is a rather active word-formation mode such as " pei'ou, ankou, cayin, saiyin, liewu, duwu, kuqiang, qiezei, zhenglong, kaoxiang, guocheng, guocuo, baoyi, yanji, shangyuan, shiwu, sixing, huolu, huoti" and so on. The fundamental difference between the above compounds and the "verb-noun" type compound nouns derived from Syntax is that from the perspective of semantic combination, the verbal morphemes and the nominal morpheme can neither form a dominance relationship nor be interpreted as verbs or verbal phrases and thus there is no process of lexicalization and the process of transferred-designationfrom actions to persons or items.

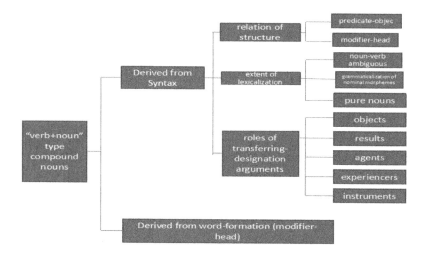

3   Semantic Relations

3.1   Main semantic mode

The main semantic mode of the "v + n" compound nouns in Chinese can be concluded as "prompt feature + category"(Dong, 2005: 132-133), in accordance with the constructional meaning "XY is one kind of Y". The nominal morphemes denote a broad category of items while the verbal morphemes suggest the items' features in certain aspects to specify the category and thus we see the function of the verbal morpheme is downgraded from predication into identification. From the view of types, Chinese verb-noun compound nouns derived from word-formation belong to this semantic mode, however, among those derived from syntax, instruments, agents, experiencers, and some results of transferred-designation of the "v + n" compound nouns disobey the constructional meaning "XY is one kind of Y" and cannot be included in "prompt feature + objects" such as "shache, jiangong, lichun, duan'an" and so on, but the quantity of this kind of compound nous is not much.

However, it should be pointed out that this semantic mode is definitely not the same as the modifier-head construction since the former one is the definition from the functional and cognitive aspect while the latter comes from the aspect of the relation of syntactical construction. In terms of the "verb-noun" type compound nouns in Chinese, both the semantic modes of modifier-head and predicate-object compound nouns can be "prompt feature + category". For example, "paoxie" and "kaoya" are two compound nouns coming separately from modifier-head and predicate-object construction and one refers to the function of something while the other refers to the way something is made. They all perform as hints from different aspects to specify "ban" and "ya".

3.2   Qualia relationship

The Generative Lexicon Theory suggests a set of encyclopedic semantic construction system to manage to analyze the vocabulary and semantic mode based on the semantic compositionality including: argument structure, qualia structure, event structure, and lexical inheritance among which the qualia structure contains the closest relation with we have have discussed in this passage since it focuses on the property and structure and it reveal them from five facets.

Formal role: it depicts properties which are different from other objects in a larger cognitive domain including: orientation, size, shape and dimensionality and so on.

Constitutive role: it describes the relations between objects and their components including: materials, weight, parts and components and so on.

Telic role: it depicts things' use and skills which can further be divided into artificial function and natural function.

Agentive role: it describes the formation and emergence of objects including the artificial and the natural.

Conventionalized attributes: it depicts the typical features including things' regular activities and properties. The so-called "qualia relationship" refers to the semantic relationship between formatives and nouns and accordingly there are five types: constitutive, formal, telic, agentive and conventionalized properties. （Pustejovsky1995; Pustejovsky & Jezek2008; Jezek2012; Song, 2011, 2015）

As for the "v + n" compound nouns in this paper, nominal morphemes'qualia structure determines the nouns' possible collocation. The verbal morphemes must activate some certain qualia role of the nominal morphemes to form valid semantic combination with the nominal morphemes, otherwise, it would result in illegal combination or the reanalysis of morphemes. When legal and valid semantic combination is formed by the verbal morphemes and the nominal morphemes, the items denoted by the verbal morphemes and compound nouns would form certain semantic relation, namely, the qualia relation between verbal morphemes and compound nouns, as shown below:

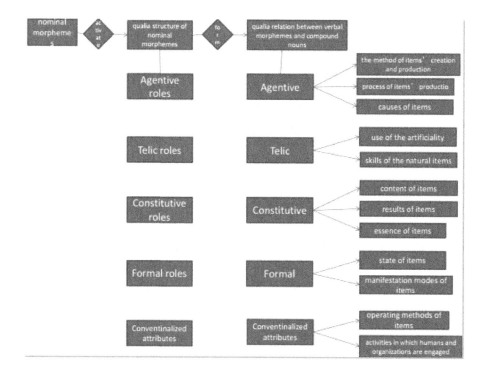

As shown in the above figure, the qualia relationsbetween verbal morphemes in the "v + n" compound nouns and the compound nouscover all the five categories and each category can be further divided into several sub-categories which reveal the verbal morphemes' strong expressive ability in word-formation. For the productivity, Agentive, Telic and Conventionalized attributes these three categories occupy the greatest part. Among them Agentive takes a larger amount. Constitutive and Formal are very few and Formal occupies the least. Seen from the sub-categories, the items representing the "use of artificiality" in Functional are the most and the items representing "meaning of things" are the least.

Qualia relation		Percentage	
Agentive	the method of items' creation and production	22%	31.9%
	process of items' production	6.2%	
	causes of items	3.7%	
Telic	use of the artificiality	23.5%	26.1%
	skills of the natural items	2.6%	
Constitutive	content of items	3.9%	9.4%
	results of items	3.5%	
	meaning of items	2%	
Formal	state of items	3.8%	7.1%
	manifestation modes of items	3.3%	
Convention-alized Attrib-utes	operating methods of items	9.5%	25.5%
	activities in which humans and organizations are engaged	16%	

3.2.1   Agentive

（1）verbal morphemes reveal how the items are made or created, for example:

"chaomian"——fried noodles with oil and condiments after boiled, "yizuo"——works created by translation

（2）verbal morphemes reveal the process of items' production, for example：

"changqiang"——the melody which is sung out, "cayin"——the consonant squeezed by the friction of the airflow in oral cavity

（3）verbal morphemes reveal the causes of items, for example：

"donghai"——the damage to animals and plants caused by low temperature, "yunfei"——fee caused by transportation

3.2.2   Telic

(1)Artificial telic, namely, verbal morphemes reveal the use of the artificiality

Compounds in this category are all artificial nouns and the verbal morphemes represent artificial function, for example:

"kaoxiang"——the box for baking something, "paoxie"——the shoes for running

(2)Natural telic, verbal morphemes reveal the skills of the natural items

Compounds in this category are all natural nouns and the verbal morphemes represent the natural objects' natural function which are unrelated to intention and purpose, for example:

"dongwu"——moving living things, "jiangchen"——solid particles which can precipitate naturally

3.2.3   Constitutive

(1) verbal morphemes reveal the content of items, for example:

"sixun"——to inform others of someone's death, "fugao"——announcement for someone's death

(2) verbal morphemes reveal the results of items, for example:

sizui——crimes which can be sentenced to death, huolu——methods which can keep people alive

（3）verbal morphemes reveal the meaning of items, for example:

"baoyi"——praising meanings, "bianyi"——derogating meanings

3.2.4   Formal

（1）verbal morphemes reveal the state of items, for example:

"sihui"——extinct fire and ash, "diaoqiao"——bridges being hung

（2）verbal morphemes reveal the manifestation modes of items, for example:

"zuofeng"——style showed by acting, "huagong"——skill presented by paint-ing

3.2.5   Conventionalized attributes

（1）verbal morphemes reveal the operating methods of items and the items are passive, for example:

"chouti"——the drawer which is opened or closed by drawing, "lasuo"——the lock which is operated by pulling

（2）verbal morphemes reveal the activities in which independent humans and organizations are engaged, for example:

"chaojia"——people specializing in fraudulent buying and selling, "xiehui"—
—organizations for promoting joint enterprise's development

Nouns in this category can be permanent career or organization, such as "zuojia
, huajia, yihui"and so on, and temporary identification, such as "duzhe,
tingzhong" and so on.

3.3   Referential transparency

Pustejovsky（1995，180-182）put forward the notion of "referential transparency" to
reflect the discrepancy among the amount of information contained in nouns, namely,
the discrepancy of nouns' ability in denoting qualia roles. The higher transparency,
the more accurate qualia information the nouns would provide. Song & Qiu（2013）
suggested that we can get most items' qualia roles in "v + n" compound nouns from
their literal meaning and thus they are very transparent. They also put forward the
rank of the nouns' referential transparency:

common nouns with verbalmorphemes>common nous without verbal mor-

phemes>……>common proper nouns>pronouns

We agree with Song & Qiu's above opinions, but due to the classification
standard, they hold the view that verbal morphemes can just reveal the Telic and
Agentive roles of compound nouns while we believe that the verbal morphemes can
denote all the five qualia roles.

4   Semantic transparency

Semantic transparency refers to the level of difficulty of deducing the meaning of words from the meaning of componental morphemes, as a whole, the semantic transparency of the "v + n" compound nouns is high while the semantic transparency of some types of the "v + n" compound nouns derived from Syntax is not high enough.

(1) "v + n" compound nouns of modifier-head structure like"laixin, laihan, laidian, duice" and so on. The verbal morphemes in these words are either intransitive or cannot form "v + n" combination directly according to syntactical rules, for example, "laixin" should be expressed as "jilaixin" according to syntactical rules; and even they are transitive, the dominance relation cannot be formed in logic, like"duice——＊ duifucelüe". Therefore, the meaning of words belonging to this type cannot be easily deduced from the meaning of componental morphemes.

(2) noun-verb ambiguous words like "gengdi, laixin, huixin, peikuan, baoche, shache, guanshi, chaofan, jianzhi, guanchang, saiche, peican, defen" and words with nominal morphemes grammaticalized like "guojiao, guotui, doudu, ganshi, jianbing, gaihuo" and so on. The above words have the same forms as the predicate-object compound verbs in spelling and thus their meaning cannot be deduced from the the meaning of componental morphemes alone. The syntactical environment should be taken into consideration.

(3) words of instruments of transferred-designation like "shache, bangtui, guotui, guojiao, baotou, chengchen, dayao, dishui, fengdi, fengmian, fuchen, hutui, huwan, huxi, huyao, hu'er, kaobei, kaoshou, fushou, peike, runbi, daixu, tianxiang, chenliao,

chenbu, xiaoye, yantiao, sanshui, pomo, baosha" and so on. Their verbal meaning can

be easily deduced from the the meaning of componental morphemes, but the nominal

meaning are hard to deduce when they are used to express instruments since the in-

strumental arguments cannot be the targets of transferred-designation easily like

agents and patients.

Besides, there are some "v + n" compound nouns whose meaning of verbal

morphemes is not chosen from the meaning of corresponding chinese characters but

the senses of words related to the characters and when they combine with the nominal

morphemes, they are similar to abbreviations with low semantic transparency. For

example, "chengyuan" refers to "zuchengrenyuan", the verbal morpheme "cheng" is

chosen from the meaning of "zucheng"; "hugong" refers to the people who work in

the hospital to look after the patients and "hu" is chosen from the meaning of "huli".

Similarly, we have words like "fanban" (fanyin de banben), "baodan" (baoshuidanju),

"chatiao" (qiancha de tiao) and so on. These compound nouns are formed may due to

Chinese compounds' preference for disyllable in word-formation, and the abbrevia-

tions are formed because of the restrictions on the number of the syllables.

5   Conclusion

The "v + n" compound nouns are one kind of compound nouns in Chinese with

high productivity and distinctive features. The relationships between verbal mor-

phemes and nominal morphemes are well depicted and explained under the guid-

ance of "Generative Lexicon Theory". Verbal morphemes must activate one certain

qualia role of nominal morphemes; otherwise, it will lead to illegal "v + n" combinations or semantic reanalysis of morphemes. Seen from the quantity, the "v + n" type compound nouns of Agentive relation are the most while the "v + n" type compound nouns of Formal relations are the least. Agentive takes a larger amount.

6   Acknowledgement

This research was financially supported by the 2016 Research Project of Wutong Item in Beijing Language and Culture University (16PT01)

Reference

[1]   Jezek, Elisabetta. Acquiring typed predicate-argument structures from corpora. In proceedings of the Eighth Joint ISO-ACL SIGSEM Workshop on Interoperable Semantic Annotation, 28-33.2012

[2]   Pustejovsky, James. The generative lexicon[M]. Cambridge: MIT Press, 1995.

[3]   Pustejovsky, James &ElisabettaJezek. Semantic coercion in language: Beyond distributional analysis. Italian Journal of Linguistics 20: 181-214. 2008.

[4]   Song, Zuoyan, Qiu, Likun. Qualia Relations in Chinese Nominal Compounds Containing Verbal Elements [J]. International Journal of Knowledge and Language Processing, 2013, 4(1):1-15.

[5]   Dong, Xiufang. Lexicalization: The Origin and Evolution of Chinese Disyllabic Words[M].Sichuan: Sichuan Minorities Press, 2002.

[6]   Dong, Xiufang. Chinese lexicon and morphology[M].Beijing: Peking University Press, 2005.

[7] Song, Zuoyan. The Latest Development of Generative Lexicon Theo-
     ry[J].Linguistics（44th Volume）[C].Beijing：The Commercial Press,
     2011.

[8] Song, Zuoyan. A Lexicon of Chinese Compound Nouns with Semantic
     Annotation: General Lexicon Theory Approach[J].Journal of Chinese In-
     formation Processing，2015，（3）.

[9] Wang, Dongmei. Nominalization and Verbalization in Contemporary
     Chinese: A Cognitive Linguistic Inquiry[M].Beijing: China Social Sci-
     ences Publishing House, 2010.

[10] Zhao, Yuanren. A Grammar of Spoken Chinese（Translated by LvShuxiang
     ）[M].Beijing：The Commercial Press, 1979.

A Study on the Referents of Chinese Imposters

Fengcun AN

Yanbian University / Yanji, Jilin, China
Zhejiang University / Hangzhou, Zhejiang, China
afczero@hotmail.com

Lei ZHAO

Yanbian University / Yanji, Jilin, China
zlanssss@qq.com

Gong CHENG

Zhejiang University / Hangzhou, Zhejiang, China
chenggong344@aliyun.com

Abstract. This paper is concerned with the language phenomena in Chinese that some nominal phrases as DPs with the default third person can refer to the speaker with the first person or the addressee with the second person. In English, such nominal phrases are called imposters (Collins & Postal 2012), which refer to the speaker or the addressee and keep the agreement with verbs in third person form when existing in the position of subject. However, unlike English, Chinese is lack of morphological forms to show the subject-verb agreement, and there is no grammatical person form, so the phenomenon of imposter is more popular in Chinese, especially in classic Chinese expressions. The paper, with many instances of such use, intends to interpret the reason why the Chinese nominal phrase in some context have the non-third person interpretation from both syntactic and semantic perspectives.

Keywords: Chinese imposter; referent; syntax

1 Introduction

In Chinese, we often use common nominal phrases (as DPs in the following of the paper) to refer to the speaker or the addressee beyond the first person pronoun as wo (I) or the second person pronoun as ni (you). For example,

(1) a. Mama xihuan kan Tommy tiaowu.
    Mum xihuan see Tommy dance
    'Mum likes to see Tommy dance.'

  b. Mama xihuan kan Tommy tiaowu.
    Mum(I) xihuan see Tommy(you) dance
    'I like to see you dance.'

© Springer International Publishing AG 2016
M. Dong et al. (Eds.): CLSW 2016, LNAI 10085, pp. 91–100, 2016
DOI: 10.1007/978-3-319-49508-8_9

In sentence (1a), generally, we regard the nominal phrases Mama and Tommy as third person DPs, which can be interpreted with the English glossary. However, in a particular discourse context, Mama can refer to the speaker, and Tommy the addressee. So we can have the interpretation as the sentence in (1b).

Such phenomenon in Chinese is very popular, especially in formal conversation and classic Chinese expressions. For example,

(2) a. Xuesheng bucai,   rang laoshi   shiwangle.
      Student   no talent make teacher disappointed
      'I(the student) am not talented, which makes you (the teacher) disappointed. '
    b. Chen   ben   buyi.
      Minister originally commoner
      'Originally, I(minister) was a commoner.'

In above examples, the DPs as Mama, Tommy, xuesheng, chen, etc, all are used as the third person DPs from grammatical sense and have the third person referent from the semantic sense generally, while in the cases like (1b) and (2), the referents of these DPs can be interpreted as the speaker with the first person sense or the addressee with the second person sense. They are quite productive in Chinese.

Collins and Postal (C&P) (2012) discuss and analyze a particular kind of DPs which they call imposters which they define as "An imposter is a notionally n person DP which is grammatically m person, n≠m"(C&P 2012:14). Some typical examples from C&P are given in (3) and (4).

3rd person DPs refers to the speaker:

(3) Yours truly/Daddy/Nixon/This reporter is/*am going to resign.

3rd person DPs refer to the addressee:

(4) Is/*Are Madam not feeling well?

As indicated by the verbal agreement, the subjects in both cases are grammatical 3rd person singular. However, the subject DPs in the above cases actually refer to 1st person or 2nd person in (3) and (4) respectively. That is, the DPs in (3) and (4) with grammatical 3rd person represent either the speaker with the 1st person or the addressee with 2nd person.

So, we can find out that English and Chinese both are quite similar with the phenomenon. And we can say Chinese also has imposters.

In this paper, I will offer extensive evidence based on the comparison of imposters from English and Chinese to show the fundamental differences between them. And I also try to give the interpretation why the grammatical third person DPs can denote the first person sense or the second person sense from the syntactic perspective.

2   Chinese Imposters

Chomsky (1981) divides all the DPs into three categories: anaphors (elements like herslef), pronominals (like she), and R-expressions (i.e. referential expressions, like John, the teacher, no person,et). Pronominals lack a specification for lexical features, and they typically carry only grammatical features, such as person, gender, and number (phi-features) (Reuland 2011).

For most languages, pronominals have inherent phi-features, so does Chinese. The pronouns in Chinese such as wo (I/me), ni (you), ta (he/she/it) have clear inherent phi-features. So we can say pronouns have different person marks or person forms. However, R-expressions are generally regarded as the nominal expressions with the third person form which can be reflected in the sentence through the subject and verb agreement, also called verbal agreement when they function as the subject.

As we know, there is no verbal agreement in Chinese, so it is unnecessary to judge the use of imposters from the morphological form. It seems that in Chinese there is no grammatical person category and no person agreement, however, there are different pronouns with different persons, such as the first person pro-noun wo (I/me), women (we/us); the second person pronoun ni (you), nimen (you plural), and nin (you) as respectful variant; the third person pronouns ta (he, she, it) and tamen (they). So it is obvious that there exist three-person divisions in Chinese.

3.1 The Expressions of Chinese Imposters

We know that the pronouns have very clear person referents in Chinese just the same as English pronouns. Besides, in Chinese, we can refer to the speaker and addressee with DPs with the default 3rd person in discourse context. So we say there are imposters in Chinese, and they are productive, especially in some formal expressions and in daily conversations. The Chinese imposters are very similar with the English imposters. That is the DPs with default 3rd person sometimes have 1st person referents or 2nd person referents as followings:

(5) 1st person imposters:

a. some occupation appellations such as laoshi (teacher), jizhe (reporter), bizhe (writer), etc.

b. names, such as Zhang San, Tom, etc.

c. kinship terms, such as baba (Dad), mama (mum), etc. Also these terms with names such as Li shu (Uncle Li), Tom shushu (Uncle Tom), etc.

d. ben + rank appellations, such as benguan (this official), benxioazhang (this headmaster), also benren (this person), etc.

e. some special phrases like zhe-balaogutou (this handful of old bones), zheshenzigu (this body) etc.

f. the coordination with the above names or kinships terms, such as shushu aiyi (Uncle and Aunt), Zhangsan he Lisi (Zhangsan and Lisi), etc.

h. ni (de) N, like niba (your father), nilaopo (your wife), etc.

(6) 2nd person imposters:

a. some occupation appellations such as laoshi (teacher), jizhe (reporter), bizhe (writer), etc.

b. names, such as Zhang San, Tom, etc.

c. kinship terms, such as baba (Dad), mama (mum), etc. Also these terms with names such as Li shu (Uncle Li), Tom shushu (Uncle Tom), etc.

d. rank appellations, such as furen (Ma-dam), jiangjun (General), xiaozhang (Headmaster), etc.

e. some special phrases like zhe-balaogutou (this handful of old bones), zheshen-zigu (this body) etc.

f. the coordination with the above names or kinships terms, such as shushu aiyi (Uncle and Aunt), Zhangsan he Lisi (Zhangsan and Lisi), etc.

g. zhe +, like zheweijianjun (this general), zheweifuren (this madam), zhegehaizi (this child), etc.

h. wo (de) +N, like womam (my mother), wo(de)er (my child), etc.

The DPs in (5) can refer to 1st person referent wherever they appear in the subject position or object position, even in the attributive position in sentences. For example:

(7) a. Baba bu rang ni   chuqu.
　　　Dad not let you go out
　　　'I(Dad) don't let you go out.'

　　b. Tom re   baba shengqile.
　　　Tom make dad angry-ASP
　　　'Tom makes dad(me) angry.'

　　c. Tom, ba babadexie   naguolai.
　　　Tom,   dad's shoes bring
　　　'Tom, bring dad's(my) shoes here.'

The DPs in (6) can refer to 2nd person referent with the same syntactic distributions as the (7). The example is omitted here.

If we think about the classic Chinese, there are more such expressions to refer to the speaker or the addressee. But now, most of the ancient expressions are not used in modern Chinese, only in the historic films, such as zhen, gujia, guaren, etc, as the first person referents specific for the emperor, and aiqing, jun, dajia, etc. as the second person referent.

3.2　The Cultural Background for Chinese Imposters

In China, there is a respectful system for the lexical expressions. So from the lexical expressions, we can judge who is the speaker or the addressee. For example:

(8) a. Yiding   qu fushang baifang.
　　　certainly go home   call at
　　　'Certainly, I will call at your home. '

　　b. Yiding   guanglin hanshe.
　　　certainly visit   cold home
　　　'Certainly visit my humble home. '

In (8) both contain the expressions of home, but in (8a), from the word fu (home), we know the speaker shows the respect to the addressee, and for the word fu (home) is seldom used for the own house, and it is the word hanshe (cold house) in (8b) to refer to the own house.

From the above instances, we know it originates from the Chinese modesty culture, which influences the language expressions a lot. In Chinese conversations, we tend to show the addressee's social position, and it is impolite to use pronouns, especially to the addressee. So it is natural for Chinese to avoid the pronoun but use some certain expressions to refer to the speaker himself and the addressee.

In classic Chinese, because of the modesty culture, the expressions to denote the speaker and the addressee are plentiful, such as xiao (small), wei(light), bei(low), wei(act as), etc. to form the humble expressions to denote the speaker.

3.3   Chinese Imposters and Binding

We know, in Chinese, there is no grammatical person category, so we can't interpret the referent of different persons from the aspect of the verbal agreement. While, we can rely on the person agreement from the anaphoric relation between imposters DPs and their bound pronouns or reflexives, for example:

(9) a. This reporter lost his/her/*my cool.

    b. Yours truly decided that he/she/*I would not go abroad.

    c. Yours truly will only vote for him-self/*myself.

Collins & Potal 2012:33-39

(10) a. laoshi   yao shiqu *ta/wo de naixinle.

      Teacher will lose s/he/ I POSS pa-tience

      'I (teacher) will lose my patience.'

    b. beren   jueding *ta/wo bu qule.

      This person decide   s/he/ I not go

      'I decided not to go.'

So we can find that the case is quite different between English and Chinese.

This is because there is verbal agreement in English which must be kept in grammatical person agreement. However, Chinese lacks of the verbal agreement and the grammatical person category, so it's easy to form the anaphoric relation.

3   Persons in Language and Participants in Discourse

In the above part, we mention the concept person agreement. Then what is person? "The notion of person in linguistics is primarily conceived of as a grammatical category, on a par with gender, number, case, tense, etc."(Siewierska 2004:1). Then what is the relation between person and referent of the nominal phrase in the discourse sentences?

4.1   Participants in Discourse

It is often stated that the grammatical category covers the expression of the distinction between the speaker of an utterance, the addressee of that utterance and the party talked about that is neither the speaker nor the addressee. So the speaker is said to be the first person, the addressee is the second person and the party talked about is the third person. So there are 3 and only 3 persons in discourse. However, this is not quite correct. In some certain discourse, we can find the person used is not agreeable with the referent in discourse. What is missing from the above characterization is the notion of participant or discourse role.

"A language without the expression of person cannot be imagined."(Benveniste 1971:225) However, in fact, the person in language is quite different from the referent of the corresponding nominal phrase in the context, such as imposters.

The persons in discourse refer to different participants or discourse roles. But they can map onto language to form grammatical person category. So in some languages, the grammatical person category formed, which can be shown on verbal agreement.

4.2   Linguistic Person

"There is a fundamental, and ineradicable, difference between the first and second person, on the one hand, and the third person on the other."(Lyons 1977:638). So we can reference the two person values, + 1st and + 2nd as, so we can have a paradigm of person distributions as following.

	$\pm$ 1st person	$\pm$ 2nd person
First	+ 1	- 2
Second	- 1	+2
Third	- 1	- 2
-----	+ 1	+ 2

Table 1. the tetrachoric table of person

Person is a sort of grammatical category in language with person marker or form. According to Siewierska (2004:16), the person marker is in regard to morphophonological form. The person marker can be reflected on words or the person agreement in sentences. For example:

(11) a. Yau a-mwela
        I   1SG-climb
        'I climbed up. '
    b. Komu ku-mwela
        You   2SG-climb
        'You climbed up. '
    c. Kalitoni i-paisewa.
        Kalitoni 3 SG-work
        'Kalitoni worked. '

                                        Gumawana (Olson 1992:326)

The sentence (11) shows the grammatical persons in language which must keep a grammatical agreement.

4.3   The Relation Between Grammatical Persons and Discourse Roles

We can find the persons in discourse refer to the discourse roles in discourse, but the grammatical person is a sort of grammatical category which must keep unified morphological forms and can cause the covariance, such as between the subject and verb.

Then what is the relation between the grammatical person and the discourse role? We strongly believe that the grammatical person is based on the discourse person.

As we can see, in Chinese, there is no person category, of course no person markers. But in Chinese discourses, we still have person differences.

Discourse role is the basis for the formation of grammatical person. The speaker and the addressee are very clear participants in discourse. So we say person is a grammatical category, but it can't determine the referent of DPs used in language. The referent is something of the semantic category. And the referents of DPs are determined by the discourse participants, which is completely a semantic anaphora.

4   Person Agreement

What is usually meant by agreement is in the word of Steele (1978:610) "some systematic covariance between a semantic or formal property of one element and a formal property of another." So, in the case of person agreement, the property in question is the grammatical category of person.

The person agreement shows the grammatical relation between different syntactic elements in sentences. But we know syntax is relatively dependent. Then can it control the semantic interpretation, such as anaphoric agreement?

Building on Brenan and Mchombo's (1987) grammatical vs anaphoric agreement typology, Siewierska (2004:126) distinguished three types of person agreement markers: syntactic, ambiguous and pronominal, as the followings:

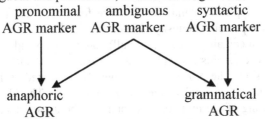

Fig. 1. Relationship between types of agreement markers and type of agreement

So we can find the imposter is a kind of ana-phoric agreement, but it must be on the basis of grammatical agreement, or we can say it is a kind of ambiguous AGR which covers both grammatical AGR and anaphoric AGR.

However, in discourse context, the agreement is represented on the semantic interpretation which is very similar with the anaphora. But it must keep the grammatical agreement and anaphoric agreement. For example:

(12) a. The present authors consider them-selves/ourselves to have been slandered.

　　b. Mommy and Daddy are enjoying themselves/ourselves on the beach.

C&P 2012:158

In (12) there are three types of agreement: the grammatical subject-verb agreement between the authors and consider; the anaphoric agreement with phi-feature agreement such as person and number between themselves and the present author or Mommy and Daddy. But what is the relation between the present author or Mommy and Daddy and ourselves? That is the third type, the ambiguous agreement, for it has both grammatical and anaphoric agreements, besides, it has discourse anaphora.

We can find the person agreement must arouse the covariance of syntactic and semantic aspects.

5   Analysis

5.1   C & P's Analysis

Collins & Postal (2012) argue that the sentence like (13a), where *the present authors* is understood to be the speaker, and *the present authors* contains a null pronoun WE as in (13b).

(13) a. The present authors$_i$ attempt to defend ourselves $_i$.

b. [$_{XP}$ [$_{DP2}$ WE] [$_{DP3}$ the present authors]]

The structure is as (14).

(14) Schematic Structure for English Imposters

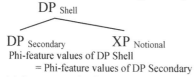

The phi-feature typically stands for the core features of the pronominal system, number, gender and person.(Chomsky 1981)

The XP Notional contains a silent (i.e. null) core pronoun and in this case it is represented as WE since for this particular example *the present authors* refers to 1st person (i.e. the speaker). The process can be roughly illustrated as follows, where the silent core pronoun WE is amalgamated into another DP. The idea of the process is that a XP, consisting of the null core pronoun and the imposter *the present authors*, raises into another higher DP. The imposter *the present authors* then undergoes predicate inversion to the Spec DP.

As a result, the Shell DP is grammatically 3rd person and 1st person simultaneously. According to them, this is exactly why English imposters, while taking a 3rd person agreement, can actually refer to the speaker (1st person), and in other cases of the addressee (2nd person). This is their syntactic analysis for imposters, as opposed to what they call Notional Hypothesis that is based on some semantic or interpretative mechanism.

6.2   Chinese Imposters and Pronoun

In Chinese, we can have an overt pronoun both before the nominal phrases and after. For example:

(15) a. wo Zhangsan buxihuan beiqipian.

b. ni Zhangsan xihuan beiqipian?

c. ta Zhangsan xihuan bei qipian?

(16) a. Zhangsan wo buxihuan beiqipian.

b. Zhangsan ni xihuan beiqipian?

c. Zhangsan ta xihuan bei qipian?

The pronoun before or after the DP is quite different. In (15), there is a pronunciation gap between pronoun and Zhangsan, because it is an appositive. However in (16), we can't pause between Zhangsan and pronouns, if do, Zhangsan tends to have the vocative interpretation. And the pronoun is unnecessary to be the appositive.

So we can say, for imposters, there exists a pronoun after the nominal phrase which is not the appositive but the denotation of the discourse role.

6.3   The Syntactic and Semantic Analysis on Chinese Imposters

On the basis of C & P's (2012) analysis of English imposters, we put forward to the new proposal to interpret the referents of the Chinese imposters.

We strongly believe that in the DPs of imposters, there is a small clause, and that is the XP in (14). But how do we explain the difference between (15) and (16)? We think both of them are generated from the small clause, only if the orders of Zhangsan and the pronoun are different as followings:

(17) Schematic Structure for Chinese Imposters

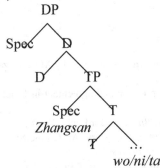

(18) Schematic Structure for Appositive

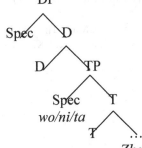

In (17) and (18), Zhangsan and wo/ni/ta both have no case marks in small clause TP. In (17), Zhangsan moves to the D position in DP with the default 3rd person which must agree with the other elements in sentence, but the referent of Zhangsan is determined by the following pronoun wo/ni/ta. When the third person Zhangsan denotes the 1st person or the 2nd person, that is an imposter. While, in (18), the pronoun wo/ni/ta moves to the D position, and the following Zhangsan can only give further interpretative information, so Zhangsan is the appositive.

So we manage to interpret the referent of imposters and the difference between imposters and appositives.

6   Conclusion

The imposters in Chinese are plentiful, which is mainly because of the modesty culture in China. In conversations, especially for the speaker and the addressee, they tend to clearly mark their social status between them to show the respect for the addressee.

In this paper, I have presented a comparative study of the English and Chinese imposters, which shows a sharp contrast in pronominal agreement in these two languages. I hypothesized a small clause as a complement in DP, which can explain the referents of imposters in Chinese and the difference between imposters and appositives.

References

1. Benveniste, Emile. 1971. *Problems in General Linguistics*. Translated by Mary Elizabeth Meek. Cora Gables, FA: University of Miami Papers.
2. Brenan, Joan and Sam A. Mchombo. 1987. Topic, pronoun and agreement in Chichewa. Language 63:741-82.
3. Chomsky, Noam. 1981. *Lectures on Government and Binding*. Dordrecht: Foris.
4. Collins, Chris. Stephanie Guitard and Jim Wood. 2009. Imposters: An Online Survey of Grammatical Judgements. *NYU Working Papers in Linguistics 2*.
5. Collins, Chris and Paul Postal. 2012. *Imposters*. Cambridge, MA:MIT Press.
6. Lyons, John. 1977. Semantics. Cambridge: Cambridge University Press.
7. Olson, Cliff. 1992. Gumawana: grammar sketch and texts. Papers in *Austronesian Linguistics* 2: 251-430.
8. Reuland, Eric. 2011. *Ahaphora and Language Design*. Cambridge, Mass. The MIT Press.
9. Siewierska, Anna. 2004. *Person*. Cambridge University Press, Cambridge, UK.

Quantitative Relation of the Length and the Count of Senses for Chinese Polysyllabic Words

Wei HUANGFU[1,3] and Bing QIU[2,3]

[1]School of Computer and Communication Engineering, University of Science and Technology Beijing (USTB), Beijing, China
[2]College of Humanities and Social Sciences, Beijing Language and Culture University, Beijing, China
[3] Department of Chinese Language Studies, Faculty of Humanities, The Education University of Hong Kong, Hong Kong, China
whuangfu@hotmail.com, bingqiu@tom.com

Abstract. Polysyllabic (i.e. having two or more syllables) words account for a major part in the modern Chinese vocabulary. In Chinese, polysyllabic words are more than a collection of syllables; they are a combination of meaningful morphemes and thus a profound manifestation of the phonetic, semantic and syntactic laws in Chinese language. This study focuses on the polysyllabic words in the Comprehensive Dictionary of Chinese Words and examines the quantitative relation between their number of senses and word length. The data indicate that when the word length increases, the number of senses decreases, and monosemous words are in majority. The negative correlation between number of senses and word length of Chinese polysyllabic words is due to the restriction of word meaning caused by involved morphemic meanings. This reveals a significant difference between Chinese and typical Western languages from a quantitative perspective.

Keywords: Polysyllabic word, Monosemous word, Quantitative linguistics

1   Introduction

Quantitative linguistics is an important sub-discipline of general linguistics. With the adoption of statistic methods, it examines the structure of natural languages as well as the relation between different linguistic properties from a quantitative perspective, explores the mathematical laws behind the natural linguistic phenomena. Since the middle of the 20th century, quantitative linguistics has drawn an extensive attention in the academia and the existing research which covers a wide range of language types and has achieved abundant results.(Kohler 2005)

Quantitative studies on lexis are an important subject in quantitative linguistics. Zipf's law, one of the most classical statistical law in quantitative linguistics (Zipf 1949), is a quantitative statement of the relation between word frequency and its rank. Paul Menzerath introduced the relation known as the Menzerath-Altmann law. (Menzerath 1980) Quantitative studies on lexis especially on word length have been a re-

© Springer International Publishing AG 2016
M. Dong et al. (Eds.): CLSW 2016, LNAI 10085, pp. 101–109, 2016
DOI: 10.1007/978-3-319-49508-8_10

search hot spot in quantitative linguistics(Grzybek 2005). However, quantitative studies on Chinese language are very limited and large quantities of topics are yet to be explored.

In this paper, we will examine the quantitative relation between word length and count of senses of polysyllabic words in Chinese vocabulary. We conclude that monosemous words account for a majority of the whole vocabulary. Furthermore, with the increase of word length or the number of constituent syllables, the average number of senses of the words decreases. Within a group of words with a certain number of syllables, words with a greater number of senses account for a lower proportion. In addition, the above quantitative data comply with the Power Law.

The rest of this paper is organized as follows: Section II introduces the related works and our motivation. Section III discusses the scheme of our quantitative survey and Section IV presents the results. Finally, Section V concludes this paper.

2   Related Works and Motivation

Maria A. Breiter (1994) studied the length of Chinese words in relation to their word frequency, which is among the early achievements in this field. Wang (2009) took the polysemous words in 現代漢語詞典(*Xiandai Hanyu Cidian*, literally *the Contemporary Chinese Dictionary*) as research objects, and after a clear distinction between word meaning and morphemic meaning, examined the frequency, the senses and the length of Chinese words. It was concluded that the longer a word is, the fewer senses it has. Deng and Feng (2013) did a quantitative study on the relation between word length and word frequency in discourses and pointed out that there exists an apparent dependency correlation between them. Their research has enriched observations of word length in relation to word frequency in Chinese language.

Polysyllabic words account for a major part in modern Chinese vocabulary and therefore related research is of great significance in Chinese language studies. Polysyllabic words are words with two or more syllables. According to general linguistics, as speech sounds are the physical form of words, "monosyllabic" and "polysyllabic" merely describe the differences in the phonetic form of words. However, in Chinese, with very few exceptions, each Chinese character is pronounced as an independent syllable and thus "monosyllabic" and "polysyllabic" also indicate the number of characters contained in the word or expression. Since Chinese characters are meaning-phonetic scripts, which mainly convey meanings and at the same time indicate pronunciation, the vast majority of them can function as morphemes. Therefore, Chinese polysyllabic words are more than a collection of syllables, but a combination of meaningful morphemes; they not only represent the external phonetic form of the Chinese language, but also reflect its internal laws concerning phonetics, semantics and syntactics.

Note that in typical Western languages, most of polysyllabic words cannot be resolved into meaning-phonetic morphemes. For instance, phonetically, "potato" can be divided into "po-", "-ta-", "-to", but these three syllables are not meaningful morphemes. In contrast, in Chinese, except for single-morpheme words and other rare circumstances, most polysyllabic words can be resolved into independent morphemes, one character as one morpheme. For instance, "土豆"(*tu dou*, potato) can be divided into "土"(*tu*, earth, ground or land) and "豆"(*dou*, bean). It is true that the word meaning is not a simple sum-up of the morphemic meanings, yet the former is more or less a reflection of the latter. Although each constituent morpheme alone has multiple meanings, once combined into words, the combination usually has no more than a few senses. Therefore, the senses of polysyllabic words which consist of multiple morphemes constitute a special linguistic phenomenon in Chinese language.

Polysyllabic words have particular research values in Chinese lexicology. Note that in Chinese, the word length (in characters) is usually the count of syllables in the word, and also equals the number of morphemes.

The relation between the word length and the count of word senses is among the fundamental issues which reveal the motivation of word formation in Chinese language. In the existing quantitative linguistic studies on Chinese words, the meaning of word has not received much attention. The limited studies on the meaning of word mainly focus on polysemous words and overlook monosemous polysyllabic words, which actually take up a great proportion of the whole vocabulary; meanwhile, few studies are concerned with the peculiarity of Chinese language. Xu said that the peculiarity and inheritance of Chinese language must be taken into consideration in Chinese lexicological studies. He pointed out that ancient Chinese is a monosyllabic isolating language in respect of linguistic typology, in which a syllable alone can express meanings in an independent way. As modern Chinese is an inheritance and development of ancient Chinese, it retains this very characteristic, which has been a major cause of polysyllablization of Chinese vocabulary. The morphemic meanings altogether have a restricting effect on the meaning of the whole word or expression, which consequently turns out to be more precise.

Focusing on the polysyllabic words in 漢語大詞典(*Hanyu Da Cidian*, literally *The Comprehensive Dictionary of Chinese Words*, abbreviated as CDCW in the following text), this study will examine the quantitative relation between word length and number of senses and discuss how the number of constituent morphemes exerts restrictions and influence upon the senses of the word or expression. It will provide fundamental quantitative data for future studies in the polysyllablization of Chinese words and is also expected to reflect the differences between Chinese and typical Western languages from the perspective of quantitative linguistics.

3   Scheme of Quantitative Survey

Starting in 1975, the compilation of CDCW has been the concerted efforts of over one thousand experts and scholars in China. It contains hundreds of thousands of both ancient and modern Chinese words, which cover a range of several thousand years from pre-Qin period to years after the founding of P.R.China. As a comprehensive reflection of the historical change of Chinese vocabulary, this dictionary is called the "Archives of Ancient and Modern Chinese Words" by Lv (1982) and Xu (1994) and has been widely used as one of the most authoritative dictionaries in this academic field. Therefore, in studies of the relation between word length and number of senses of polysyllabic words, using CDCW will better fit the characteristic of inheritance of the Chinese language.

This research adopts the CDROM 2.0 version of CDCW which contains more than 340,000 entries of words. The quantities of polysyllabic words with different numbers of syllables (i.e. in different word length) are shown in Figure 1.

It is observed from the data that words with more constituent syllables usually measure less in their total number contained in CDCW. Among all the polysyllabic words contained in CDCW, disyllabic words add up to 279,719 in number and 81.5% in proportion, which constitute a majority not only in the collection of polysyllabic words, but also in the whole vocabulary, monosyllabic words included. Disyllabliza-tion is a significant feature of the lexis of Chinese language. Trisyllabic and quadri-syllabic words add up to 29,801 and 31,534 in number and 8.7% and 9.2% in propor-tion, respectively. With the increase of the number of constituent syllables, the num-ber of corresponding words included in CDCW significantly decreases: Words with over 5 syllables decrease to about one thousand and those with over 9 syllables are as few as around one hundred. It is worth pointing out that due to the rhyme and the antithetical parallelism of Chinese language, among words with similar numbers of syllables, those with even numbers of syllables exceed those with odd numbers. In general, the average length of polysyllabic words and expression contained in CDCW is 2.3 syllables.

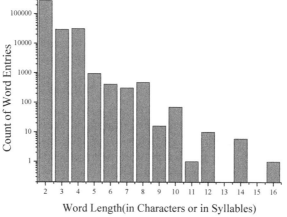

Fig. 1. Count of word entries in CDCW for different word length in characters or syllables.

In CDCW, under each entry of polysyllabic word or expression, its senses are listed out. The polysyllabic word or expression with the most senses in this dictionary is "陰陽"(yin yang, the two opposing principles in nature, the former feminine and negative and the latter masculine and positive), which has as many as 25 senses. However, the majority of polysyllabic words in this dictionary have one single sense.

Since the total entries in CDCW are in large quantities, sampling statistics will be adopted in the below survey. Quantitative observations will be made among the samples and then proportionate assessments will be acquired about the corresponding groups.

4   Numerical Results and Discussions

According to statistics, the average number of senses of all the polysyllabic words contained in CDCW is 1.326. Polysyllabic words with different numbers of senses vary in their quantities in CDCW. Among them, monosemous words are the vast majority, which add up to about 272,000 in number and 79.2% in proportion. As for the rest, those with more senses measure less in quantities. Figure 2 shows the respective proportions of polysyllabic words with different numbers of senses as compared to all the polysyllabic words contained in CDCW.

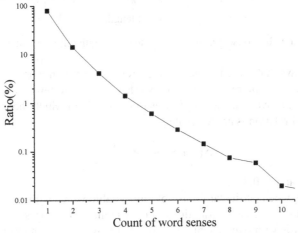

Fig. 2. Ratios of polysyllabic words entries in CDCW for different count of senses.

It is clearly shown in Figure 2 that monosemous polysyllabic words account for the absolute majority of all polysyllabic words. Since polysyllabic words far exceed monosyllabic words, so it can be reasoned that monosemous words outnumber polysemous words in the whole Chinese vocabulary. According to Wang, among all the 65,645 entries in 現代漢語詞典, only 10,632 of them are polysemous. This is in accordance with our conclusion, i.e. monosemous words are in majority in Chinese lexical system. It should be noted that some scholars believe most Chinese words are polysemous, but the statistics do not support their views.

When the number of syllables is taken into consideration, we find that disyllabic words have the biggest average number of senses, which is 1.383. With the increase of the number of syllables, the number of senses decreases: Words with five or more syllables have no more than 1.036 senses in average, which can be treated as monosemous. The average numbers of senses of words in different word lengths in CDCW are depicted in Figure 3.

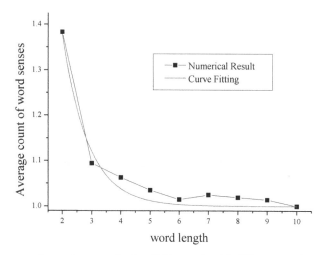

Fig. 3. Average numbers of senses of polysyllabic words with different numbers of syllables.

Figure 3 shows that there is a negative correlation between word length and number of senses, i.e. the more syllables the words contain, the fewer senses they have. Let $S(L)$ denote the average count of senses of the words of which the length equals to L, the numerical relation is approximately

$$S(L) \approx 1 + ae^{-L/b} \tag{1}$$

where a=3.753 and b=0.872.

Furthermore, when particular groups of polysyllabic words with certain numbers of syllables are examined, the distributions of their numbers of senses are shown in Figure 4. Take words with two syllables (i.e. disyllabic words) as an example: 76.0% of them have but one sense, 16.1% two senses and 4.8% three senses; as for those with more senses, their proportions significantly decrease, and it is observed that disyllabic words with five or more senses account for less than 1% of the total of this group. Among words with three syllables (i.e. trisyllabic words), 92.2% of them have but one sense, 6.6% two senses, 1.0% three senses, and 0.1% four and above senses. As for words with more syllables, they are in similar circumstances. Those with more senses account for smaller proportions and monosemous words are always in majority. The curves indicate that the distributions of the numbers of senses comply with the Power Law.

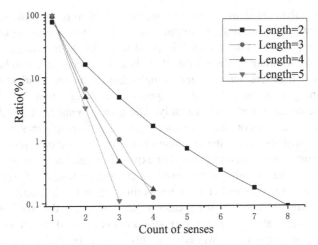

Fig. 4. Respective distributions of the count of senses for different length of polysyllabic words

Figure 5 is an illustration of the proportional distribution of polysyllabic words in regards to word length and numbers of senses. The horizontal axis indicates number of senses, and the vertical axis indicates word length. The darker the bar is, the greater proportion the corresponding polysyllabic words account for. As is shown in the diagram, the lower left corner is a major concentration of words, which tells that words with shorter word length and fewer number of senses are a majority. As for the rest, some words feature in few number of senses and greater word length, and some are characterized by great number of senses and shorter word length. There is hardly any word or expression with great number of senses as well as great word length.

According to the above data, there is a correlation between word length and number of senses. The fewer number of syllables the words have, the greater their average number of senses is, and the greater the proportion of polysemous words is. On the contrary, the greater the number of syllables the words have, the lower their average number of senses is, and the greater the proportion of monosemous words is.

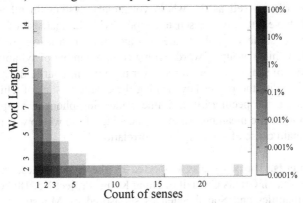

Fig. 5. Proportional distribution of polysyllabic words in regards to word length and number of senses

In Chinese, polysyllabic words are not only a collection of multiple syllables, but also a combination of meaningful morphemes. Although the meaning of a polysyllabic word or expression is not completely consistent with the meanings of its constituent morphemes, it cannot be denied that there is a strong connection in between. The morphemic meanings interact with and complement each other, and as a result, restrict the meaning of the whole word or expression, making it more precise semantically and more concentrated grammatically. The greater number of syllables a polysyllabic word or expression has, the more constituent morphemes there are, the stronger their restrictions upon the meaning of the whole word or expression are, and thus the fewer number of senses the word or expression has. On the contrary, the fewer number of syllables a polysyllabic word or expression has, the fewer constituent morphemes there are, the weaker their restrictions upon the meaning of the whole word or expression are, and thus the greater number of senses the word or expression has. It is concluded that the negative correlation between word length and number of senses of Chinese polysyllabic words is mainly caused by the restrictions of morphemic meanings upon the meanings of the whole word or expression, a peculiar characteristic of Chinese language whose writing system is meaning-phonetic scripts.

5   Conclusion

Quantitative studies on lexis are an important subject in quantitative linguistics, yet such studies on Chinese language are very limited. Since Chinese characters are meaning-phonetic scripts, polysyllabic words in Chinese are not only a collection of syllables, but also a combination of meaningful morphemes, which deeply reflect the internal laws in Chinese phonetics, semantics and syntactics. As polysyllabic words account for a major part of modern Chinese vocabulary system, quantitative linguistic studies on polysyllabic words are of great significance for Chinese language studies.

This study is based on CDCW and examines the quantitative relation between word length and number of senses of polysyllabic words. Conclusions drawn from quantitative data are as follows: First, monosemous words account for a majority of polysyllabic words as well as the whole vocabulary system. In other words, most Chinese words have but only one sense. Second, with the increase of word length or the number of constituent syllables, the average number of senses of the words decreases. Third, within a group of words with a certain number of syllables, words with a greater number of senses account for a lower proportion. Fourth, the above quantitative data comply with the power law. Taking the characteristics of Chinese language into consideration, the peculiarity of Chinese meaning-phonetic scripts and the restrictions of morphemic meanings upon the meaning of the whole word or expression should be the main cause of such negative correlation.

Acknowledgments. The work was supported by the General Research Fund sponsored by the Research Grants Council of Hong Kong (Project No. 18600915), the Key Project of Humanities and Social Sciences sponsored by Ministry of Education of China (Grant No. 15JJD740001), Wutong Innovation Platform of Beijing Language and Culture University supported by the Fundamental Research Funds for the Central Universities(Approval No. 16PT07) and the Foundation of Beijing Engineering and Technology Center for Convergence Networks and Ubiquitous Services.

References

1. R. Kohler, G. Altmann and R.G. Piotrowski(eds.), *Quantitative Linguistics: An international Handbook*, Berlin and New York: de Gruyter (2005)
2. Feng Zhiwei. Study languages by means of quantitative methods. Foreign language teaching and research. 44(2):256-270 (2012) (冯志伟. 用计量方法研究语言. 外语教学与研究, 44(2), 256-270 (2012)). (in Chinese)
3. Liu Haitao, Huang Wei. Current situation, theories and methods of Quantitative linguistics. Journal of Zhejiang University, 43(2):178-192 (2012) (刘海涛,黄伟. 计量语言学的现状、理论与方法，浙江大学学报(人文社会科学版), 43(2):178-192 (2012)) . (in Chinese)
4. George K. Zipf. *Human Behavior and the Principle of Least Effort*. Addison-Wesley Press (1949)
5. Gabriel Altmann. *Prolegomena to Menzerath's law*. Glottometrika. 2:1–10 (1982)
6. Grzybek P. (ed.) *Contributions to the Science of Text and Language: Word Length Studies and Related Issues*. Dordrecht:Springer (2005)
7. Maria A. Breiter. *Length of Chinese Words in relation to their other systemic Features*. Journal of Quantitative Linguistics. 1(3):224-231 (1994)
8. Wang hui. Polysemous words in the Contemporary Chinese Dictionary (5th Edition): meaning, length and frequency. Studies of the Chinese Language. 2:120-130 (2009) (王惠. 词义·词长·词频——《现代汉语词典》(第5版)多义词计量分析.中国语文, 2:120-130 (2009)) . (in Chinese)
9. Deng Yaochen, Feng Zhiwei. A Quantitative Linguistic Study on the Relationship between Word Length and Word Frequency. Journal of Foreign Languages 36(3):29-39 (2013) (邓耀臣,冯志伟. 词汇长度与词汇频数关系的计量语言学研究. 外国语, 36(3):29-39 (2013)) . (in Chinese)
10. Cao Wei. Modern Chinese semantics (Revised Edition). Jinan University Press (2009) (曹炜(Cao Wei). 《现代汉语语义学》（修订本）. 暨南大学出版社 (2009)) . (in Chinese)
11. Xu Weihan. Introduction to Chinese Vocabulary (Revised Edition). Peking University Press (2008). (许威汉.《汉语词汇学导论》(修订版). 北京大学出版社 (2008)) . (in Chinese)
12. Lv Shuxiang. The nature and importanceof *the Comprehensive Dictionary of Chinese Words*. Lexicographical Studies. 3:1-3. (1982) (吕叔湘.《汉语大词典》的性质和重要性. 辞书研究. 3:1-3. (1982)). (in Chinese)
13. Xu Wenkan. On the characteristics and academic value of *the Comprehensive Dictionary of Chinese Words*. Lexicographical Studies. 3:36-45. (1994) (徐文堪. 略论《汉语大词典》的特点和学术价值. 辞书研究. 3:36-45. (1994)) . (in Chinese)
14. Shao Jingmin. An introduction to modern Chinese, Shanghai Education Press (2001) (邵敬敏. 现代汉语通论, 上海教育出版社, 上海 (2001)) . (in Chinese)

Polarity of Chinese Emotion Words: The Construction of a Polarity Database Based on Singapore Chinese Speakers

Chin Loong Ng1; Jingxia Lin1; Yao Yao2

1Nanyang Technological University; 2The Hong Kong Polytechnic University

CNG013@e.ntu.edu.sg; jingxialin@ntu.edu.sg;
ctyaoyao@polyu.edu.hk

Abstract. In this paper, we report a study of the polarity of Chinese emotion words. We conducted a large-scale polarity rating experiment with laymen speakers, and compiled a database of polarity ratings for Chinese emotion words based on these experimental results. The polarity ratings were also compared with previously reported polarity ratings, as well as related emotion word ratings such as emotion category and emotional intensity. The participants in the current study were all Singapore Chinese speakers, but the methodology and the current results will serve as an important reference for future research on sentiment analysis and emotion language in Chinese in a broader context.

Keywords: emotion word, emotion polarity, Singapore Chinese.

1   Background

Sentiment analysis (sometimes also called "opinion mining") refers to automatic analysis and measurement of the semantic orientations of the text (Ding et al. 2008; Esuli & Sebastiani, 2005, etc.). As part of sentiment analysis, polarity analysis aims to determine the sentiment polarity and sentiment polarity intensity of the opinions expressed in text (Esuli & Sebastiani, 2005; Wilson, Wiebe, & Hwa, 2004, etc.). Sentiment polarity is commonly categorized as positive, negative or neutral; sentiment polarity intensity (polarity strength), on the other hand, is usually represented by numerical numbers or levels of degree. Words consisting of semantic orientation are called polarity words or opinion words.

© Springer International Publishing AG 2016
M. Dong et al. (Eds.): CLSW 2016, LNAI 10085, pp. 110–119, 2016
DOI: 10.1007/978-3-319-49508-8_11

Current extraction and analysis of polarity words are generally based on two sources: corpora or dictionaries. The former include studies such as Hatzivassiloglou & McKeown (1997) and Wiebe (2000). Hatzivassiloglou & McKeown (1997) pointed out that conjunctions between adjectives in a sentence provide indirect information about the semantic orientation of the adjectives, thus the semantic orientation of the latter adjective could be deduced by evaluating the linguistic properties of the conjunction and the semantic orientation of the former adjective. They first extracted sentences from a large corpus, then analyzed the semantic orientation of the adjectives with a log-linear regression model combining with supplementary morphology rules, and finally, classified and labeled the adjectives according to polarity by using clustering algorithm. Wiebe (2000) first assigned the subjectivity of seed adjectives manually, then they used a 10-fold cross validation to further refine the polarity of the adjectives which can be automatically learned from corpora. Turney & Littman (2003) adopted two statistical measures of word association (Point Mutual Information and Latent Semantic Analysis) to determine the semantic orientation of a word. The method was tested with adjectives, adverbs, nouns, and verbs. Ding et al.(2008) proposed a holistic lexicon-based approach to solve the problem by exploiting external evidences and linguistic conventions of natural language expressions. This approach allows the system to measure opinion words that are context dependent with higher accuracy. Ding et al. also dealt with many special words, phrases and language construct which have impact on opinions based on their linguistic pattern. Based on the proposed technique, a system named Opinion Observer has been implemented.

Besides the corpus-based approach, there have also been experiments which adopt dictionary-based approach, such as Kamps et al. (2004) and Esuli & Sebastian (2005). Kamps et al. (2004) investigated a graph-theoretic model of WordNet's most important relation, which is synonymy, and proposed measures that determine the semantic orientation of adjectives for three factors of subjective meaning. Their objective was to develop WordNet-based measures for the semantic orientation of adjectives. Esuli & Sebastian (2005) adopted quantitative analysis to determine the semantic orientation of the subjective terms. The experiment made use of the definitions found in online dictionaries to expand its seed words set, and on the use of the resulting term representations for semi-supervised term classification. Andreevskaia & Bergler (2006) proposed a method for extracting sentiment-bearing adjectives from WordNet using the Sentiment Tag Extraction Program (STEP), where the WordNet glosses were adopted to determine semantic orientation of words. Kim & Hovy (2005) expanded a set of manually collected opinion-bearing words with the use of dictionaries. In order to avoid collecting uncommon words, they started with a basic English word list compiled for foreign students preparing for the TOEFL test. Thereafter, 462 adjectives and 502 verbs were randomly selected and then manually annotated by three annotators. As for polarity information of Chinese words, one major Chinese sentiment database is the Affective Lexicon Ontology by Xu et al. (2008). The database was again not constructed based on large-scale manual annotation.

In conclusion, judging from past experiments, the sentiment tagging is either done by machine or by a few annotators (mainly are judgments made by experienced experts). Obviously, even though the annotation process might be deemed as highly effective, it does not necessarily reflect the semantic orientation perceived by average language users. As such, we invited a large number of average language user as participants to take part in the annotation process, and built the first database of normative ratings of polarity information for a list of Chinese emotion words.

2   Experiments

Design of the current study mainly follows Lin & Yao (2015). Lin & Yao (2015) reported a research on emotion classification and emotion intensity of Chinese emotion words rated by Mainland Chinese, Hong Kong, and Singapore Mandarin Chinese speakers. Lin & Yao (2015) used the list of Chinese emotion words from Xu & Tao (2003), and adopted the methodology from Strauss & Allen (2008). In this study, we used the identical list of Chinese emotion words and referred to the methodology from Lin & Yao (2015). With comparison to past experiments (Xu et al. 2008; Khoo et al., 2015; etc.), this current study has fewer words and the words are mainly emotion words. However, our study is a pioneer experiment whereby many average Chinese language users participated in the annotation process, experiment methodology and results will serve as an important reference for future research on sentiment analysis and emotion language in Chinese language in a broader context.

The list we used in this study consisted of 372 emotion words ranging from 1 to 4 syllables in length. These words are further divided into four word lists (Lists 1-4), with 93 words per list, and each participant only to complete one word list. Similar to Lin & Yao (2015), a set of quality control measures for rating consistency was implemented in this study. Firstly, each word list had two test words that each appeared twice so that we could compare a participant's ratings of the repeated items as a measure of consistency within the participant, resulting in 8 intra-list repeated words. Secondly, each word list shared one test word with every other list, resulting in a set of 6 cross-list repeated words, in order to assess rating consistency across participant groups working on different word lists. Lastly, we inserted a non-word item, 几几 *jiji*, to all four word lists, in order to check whether the participants were responding to the judgment task attentively. As a result, each word list contained 97-98 test token in total. Table 1 lists all the items that are repeated within or across word lists.

Table 1 Repeated items

Intra-list repeated words	Cross-list repeated words
List 1: 厌倦yanjuan,　悲痛beitong	List 1, 2: 开心 kaixin
List 2: 担忧danyou,　丧气sangqi	List 1, 3: 焦躁 jiaozao
List 3: 愉悦yuyue, 痛恨tonghen	List 2, 4: 愤怒 fennu
List 4: 愤慨fenkai,　愁闷choumen	List 2, 3: 沉痛 chentong
	List 3, 4: 震惊 zhenjing
	List 1, 4: 畏惧 weiju
	Non-word item (all lists) : 几几 jiji

The participants in this study were mainly native Chinese users. A total of 94 participants (35 males, 59 females) were in the age range of 16-30 years. They live in Singapore and have received compulsory Chinese education in Singapore (lowest education level: Junior College or Polytechnic).

The annotation task was administered in the form of an online survey on the Google Form Platform. Each participant was randomly assigned to work on one word list. The participants' task was to judge and rate the polarity of each test item on the list. Seven polarity scales were available: 3, 2, 1, 0, -1, -2, -3. Option "3" represents very positive, option "0" represents neutral, option "-3" represents very negative. In any case whereby participants did not understand the test word, they could choose the option "不理解词义 bu lijie ciyi/do not understand".

3　Results

A total of 89 participants involved in the annotation process, an average of 22-23 participants for each word list. As mentioned in previous section, 8 intra-list repeated words as well as 6 cross-list repeated words were adopted to assess the consistency and reliability of annotation. We used t tests to verify the two ratings across all repeated words, results showed that the ratings were consistent ($p >$ 0.1). With regards to the annotation of non-word item 几几 jiji, 92.1% of the participants rated it as "neutral" or "do not understand". Even though 7.5% of the participants rated 几几 jiji with a polarity scale, we believe that this would not affect the credibility of the survey. Firstly, the word 几 ji has multiple meanings in Mandarin (几个 jige, 几何 jihe, etc). Secondly, 几几 jiji has homophonic words (唧唧 jiji, 岌岌 jiji, 叽叽喳喳 jijizhazha, etc). This would possibly affect participants' judgment. Furthermore, it is phenomenal that new words are often produced due to the communication across digital media and internet pop culture, some participants might have understood 几几 jiji as a newly created word. In conclusion, the above test results indicate that the annotation obtained from this survey is highly credible.

For the convenience of analysis and discussion, we calculated the mean polarity of 372 emotion words and divided them into three categories: negative emotion words (-3 ≤ Mean Polarity ≤ -1), neutral emotion words (-1 < Mean Polarity < 1) and positive emotion words (1 ≤ Mean Polarity ≤ 3). This is merely one of the ways to categorize the emotion words, researcher may categorize the words accordingly to their needs (for instance, mean polarity > 0 as positive emotion word and mean polarity < 0 as negative emotion words.). Overall, there are 143 negative emotion words (38.4%), 125 neutral words (33.6%) and 104 positive emotion words (28.0%). 挂牵 *guaqian* is the only word within the 125 neutral emotion words which has a mean polarity of 0. The results show that the number of negative emotion words is 10.4% larger than that of positive emotion words. This is a common trend in sentiment analysis. For instance, Khoo et al., (2015) reported that there are more negative emotion words than positive emotion words found in corpus. The 372 words divided into three categories are listed in (1), where the very 10 positive emotion words (2 ≤ Mean Polarity ≤ 3) and 12 very negative emotion words (-3 ≤ Mean Polarity ≤ -2) are underlined. These underlined words are undoubtedly emotion words with the highest degree of sentiment.

Besides mean polarity, we also calculated the range value between the highest and lowest rating of every words, e.g., 骇异 *haiyi* (lowest rating = -2, highest rating = 0, range value = 2) and 快活 *kuaihuo* (lowest rating = -3, highest rating = 3, range value = 6). In all 362 words, the smallest range value is 2, and the biggest range value is 6. To our surprise, the range values for most of the words are bigger than 3, which indicates that the ratings are distributed at different sides of value 0. Specifically, we found that 21.5% (n= 80) of the words has range value of 4, 36.3% (n= 135) of the words has range value of 5, 12.9% (n = 48) of the words has range value of 6. In other words, 70.7% of the words have at least two annotators whom actually held opposite opinion with the word. We suggest that the cause in the big range value could be due to the individual annotators having a difference in semantic orientation of the word. Similar situations can be found in other languages and studies. For instance, Khoo et al., (2015) pointed out that an exact identical word "torrid" could possibly have both semantic orientations, positive in a context, but negative in the other context. Thus, different individuals would rate according to their context resulting in a huge range value. This also indirectly proved the necessity of having multiple annotators in the rating process.

(1) a. Emotion words that are rated as "positive" (1 ≤ Mean Polarity ≤ 3)
    乐于 *leyu,* 拥护 *yonghu,* 放松 *fangsong,* 炽热 *chire,* 神往 *shenwang,* 在乎

zaihu, 快活 kuaihuo, 安宁 anning, 感动 gandong, 赞同 zantong, 可意 keyi, 怡和 yihe, 关切 guanqie, 晓畅 xiaochang, 来劲 laijin, 欢娱 huanyu, 称意 chenyi, 信服 xinfu, 放心 fangxin, 欢 huan, 狂热 kuangre, 称心 chenxin, 带劲 daijin, 康乐 kangle, 安心 anxin, 爱好 aihao, 舒坦 shutan, 关心 guanxin, 高亢 gaokang, 如意 ruyi, 愿意 yuanyi, 相信 xiangxin, 得志 dezhi, 舒畅 shuchang, 松快 songkuai, 乐意 leyi, 动心 dongxin, 欢欣 huanxin, 关怀 guanhuai, 赏识 shangshi, 顺心 shunxin, 珍视 zhenshi, 振奋 zhenfen, 充实 chongshi, 喜欢 xihuan, 宽心 kuanxin, 惊喜 jingxi, 体贴 titie, 欢悦 huanyue, 高昂 gaoang, 景仰 jingyang, 崇尚 chognshang, 崇拜 chongbai, 感激 ganji, 满意 manyi, 爽心 shuangxin, 感谢 ganxie, 喜爱 xiai, 窝心 woxin, 欢喜 huanxi, 激昂 jiang, 乐 le, 欣慰 xinwei, 痛快 tongkuai, 推崇 tuichong, 欢快 huankuai, 自信 zixin, 欢乐 huanle, 钟爱 zhongai, 信赖 xinlai, 快乐 kuaile, 佩服 peifu, 畅快 changkuai, 开心 kaixin, 赞赏 zanshang, 欢愉 huanyu, 崇奉 chongfeng, 自在 zizai, 信任 xinren, 钦佩 qinpei, 欣喜 xinxi, 高兴 gaoxin, 尊敬 zunjing, 珍爱 zhenai, 喜悦 xiyue, 尊重 zunzhong, 珍惜 zhenxi, 舒服 shufu, 器重 qizhong, 兴奋 xinfen, 愉悦 yuyue, 舒心 shuxin, 敬佩 jingpei, 敬慕 jingmu, <u>孝敬 xiaojing</u>, <u>自豪 zihao</u>, <u>尊崇 zunchong</u>, <u>景慕 jingmu</u>, <u>敬仰 jingyang</u>, <u>欢畅 huanchang</u>, <u>崇敬 chongjing</u>, <u>幸福 xingfu</u>, <u>敬重 jingzhong</u>, <u>热爱 reai</u>

b. Emotion words that are rated as "neutral" (-1 <Mean Polarity< 1)

为难 weinan, 烦心 fanxin, 生气 shengqi, 遗憾 yihan, 低沉 dichen, 苦恼 kunao, 愕然 eran, 熬心 aoxin, 窘 jiong, 不满 buman, 困惑 kunhuo, 头疼 touteng, 感伤 ganshang, 操心 caoxin, 烦恼 fannao, 苦闷 kumen, 心虚 xinxu, 发慌 fahuang, 惊慌 jinghuang, 抱愧 baokui, 窝火 wohuo, 惊疑 jingyi, 不好过 buhaoguo, 苦 ku, 心慌 xinhuang, 怀疑 huaiyi, 惊愕 jinge, 担心 danxin, 焦急 jiaoji, 羞怯 xiuque, 心急 xinji, 不平 buping, 失望 shiwang, 惊诧 jingcha, 无奈 wunai, 疑心 yixin, 骇怪 haiguai, 害怕 haipa, 寂寞 jimo, 眼红 yanhong, 伤心 shangxin, 疯狂 fengkuang, 吝惜 linxi, 吓人 xiaren, 挂虑 gualü, 紧张 jinzhang, 多情 duoqing, 骄矜 jiaojin, 诧异 chayi, 悲壮 beizhuang, 担忧 danyou, 对不住 duibuzhu, 解恨 jiehen, 怕 pa, 慌张 huangzhang, 火 huo, 看不惯 kanbuguan, 娇宠 jiaochong, 炫耀 xuanyao, 心浮 xinfu, 可惜 kexi, 害臊 haisao, 痴迷 chimi, 不过意 buguoyi, 憋气 bieqi, 吃惊 chijing, 震惊 zhenjing, 过敏 guomin, 对不起 duibuqi, 狂 kuang, 无聊 wuliao, 消魂 xiaohun, 迟疑 chiyi, 急 ji, 怜惜 lianxi, 疑惑 yihuo, 着急 zhaoji, 不好意思 buhaoyisi, 挂心 guaxin, 痒痒 yangyang, 缠绵 chanmian, 惊讶 jingya, 抱歉 baoqian, 沉静 chenjing, 羞涩 xiuse, 奇怪 qiguai, 挂牵 guaqian, 动摇 dongyao, 感慨 gankai, 牵挂 qiangua, 偏爱 pianai, 害羞 haixiu, 眷恋 juanlian, 怜悯 lianmin, 挂念 guanian, 自满 ziman, 骄傲 jiaoao, 无辜 wugu, 激动 jidong, 同情 tongqing, 留神 liushen, 了解 liaojie, 想 xiang, 心切 xinqie, 关注 guanzhu, 惊奇 jingqi, 亢奋 kangfen, 惦念 diannian, 怀念 huainian,

得意 *deyi*, 情愿 *qingyuan*, 自爱 *ziai*, 可心 *kexin*, 闲适 *xianshi*, 投入 *touru*, 闲雅 *xianya*, 倚重 *yizhong*, 理解 *lijie*, 逍遥 *xiaoyao*, 高涨 *gaozhang*, 快慰 *kuaiwei*, 炽 烈 *chilie*, 瞧得起 *qiaodeqi*, 羡慕 *xianmu*, 体谅 *tiliang*

c. Emotion words that are rated as "negative" (-3 ≤ Mean Polarity ≤ -1)

嫉恨 *jihen*, 憎恶 *zengwu*, 痛恨 *tonghen*, 愤恨 *fenhen*, 忌恨 *jihen*, 鄙夷 *biyi*, 暴怒 *baonu*, 窝囊 *wonang*, 绝望 *juewang*, 忿恨 *fenhen*, 悲恸 *beitong*, 轻蔑 *qingmie*, 怨恨 *yuanhen*, 悲凄 *beiqi*, 颓丧 *tuisang*, 沮丧 *jusang*, 悲愤 *beifen*, 歧视 *qishi*, 郁悒 *yuyi*, 鄙视 *bishi*, 厌恶 *yanwu*, 悔恨 *huihen*, 抑郁 *yiyu*, 沉痛 *chentong*, 惨痛 *cantong*, 哀痛 *aitong*, 忌妒 *jidu*, 惊恐 *jingkong*, 苍凉 *cangliang*, 哀怨 *aiyuan*, 瞧不起 *qiaobuqi*, 懊丧 *aosang*, 愤慨 *fenkai*, 悲凉 *beiliang*, 阴郁 *yinyu*, 揪心 *jiuxin*, 腻烦 *nifan*, 惊惧 *jingju*, 骄慢 *jiaoman*, 沉郁 *chenyu*, 忿怒 *fennu*, 懊 悔 *aohui*, 妒忌 *duji*, 心寒 *xinhan*, 悲切 *beiqie*, 自卑 *zibei*, 悲哀 *beiai*, 悲痛 *beitong*, 蔑视 *mieshi*, 愤怒 *fennu*, 悲怆 *beichuang*, 浮躁 *fuzao*, 愤懑 *fenmen*, 冤 *yuan*, 忧郁 *youyu*, 恐慌 *konghuang*, 愁闷 *choumen*, 敌视 *dishi*, 丧气 *sangqi*, 冤 枉 *yuanwang*, 怅惘 *changwang*, 反感 *fangan*, 惶恐 *huangkong*, 痛心 *tongxin*, 发 憷 *fachu*, 背悔 *beihui*, 忧愁 *youchou*, 烦躁 *fanzao*, 恼恨 *fenhen*, 消沉 *xiaochen*, 惊骇 *jinghai*, 惶惑 *huanghuo*, 愁苦 *chouku*, 焦躁 *jiaozao*, 厌烦 *yanfan*, 憋闷 *biemen*, 悲愁 *beichou*, 犯愁 *fanqiu*, 哀戚 *aiqi*, 困窘 *kunjiong*, 抱委屈 *baoweiqu*, 烦杂 *fanza*, 鄙薄 *bibo*, 恐惧 *kongju*, 负疚 *fujiu*, 焦炙 *jiaozhi*, 颓唐 *tuitang*, 嫉妒 *jidu*, 忧虑 *youlv*, 伤感 *shanggan*, 自负 *zifu*, 发愁 *fachou*, 焦虑 *jiaolü*, 自大 *zida*, 畏怯 *weiqie*, 烦燥 *fanzao*, 狂乱 *kuangluan*, 惭愧 *cankui*, 慌乱 *huangluan*, 羞惭 *xiucan*, 骄横 *jiaoheng*, 心酸 *xinsuan*, 灰心 *huixin*, 酸辛 *xinsuan*, 厌倦 *yanjuan*, 后悔 *houhui*, 溺爱 *niai*, 不快 *bukuai*, 哀愁 *aichou*, 妒嫉 *duji*, 懊恼 *aonao*, 讨厌 *taoyan*, 辛酸 *xinsuan*, 惆怅 *chouchang*, 糟心 *zaoxin*, 委屈 *weiqu*, 冲动 *chongdong*, 捣乱 *daoluan*, 烦 *fan*, 烦乱 *fanluan*, 烦闷 *fanmen*, 畏惧 *weiju*, 自傲 *ziao*, 乏味 *fawei*, 怠慢 *daiman*, 焦渴 *jiaoke*, 低落 *diluo*, 反对 *fandui*, 沉重 *chenzhong*, 沉闷 *chenmen*, 激愤 *jifen*, 烦人 *fanren*, 不安 *buan*, 不悦 *buyue*, 哀伤 *aishang*, 心焦 *xinjiao*, 悲伤 *beishang*, 惊惶 *jinghuang*, 愁 *chou*, 窘促 *jiongcu*, 羞 愧 *xiukui*, 郁闷 *yumen*, 骇异 *haiyi*

4   Discussion

We compared current results with Xu et al. (2008). Xu et al. (2008) divided polarity into four categories: neutral, positive, negative and positive/negative. It is noted that Xu et al. (2008) adopted both human annotation as well as automatic annotation, the study utilized an enormous amount of Chinese words, and among those words 327 were identical to current study. In Xu et al. (2008), these 327 words are categorized into positive (n = 76), neutral (n = 186), negative (n = 64) and positive/negative (n = 1). But a huge difference in annotation was found between Xu et al. (2008) and current study. Among the 76 positive words annotated by Xu et al. (2008), only 10 (13.2%) words are annotated as positive in current study, whereas the other 66 (86.8%) words are annotated as neutral words. Of particular note are 悲壮 *beizhuang* and 沉静 *chenjing*. Their mean polarity is rated as "negative" in this study (-0.62and -0.09 respectively). Similarly, 58 (91%) out of 64 negative words in Xu et al. (2008) were categorized as neutral words, 2 (3%) words are categorized as positive words and only 4 (6%) words are categorized as negative words in current study. As for the 186 neutral words in Xu et al. (2008), only 72 (39%) are categorized as neutral words, and 87 (47%) words categorized as negative words and 27 (15%) words categorized as positive words in current study. Lastly, Xu et al. (2008) categorized the word 挂虑 *gualü* as positive/negative word, it is categorized as a neutral word (mean polarity = -0.71) in current study. Should the word 挂虑 *gualü* categorized as neutral or positive/negative word under different context is arguable, further research has yet to be conducted.

We believe there were at least two reasons responsible for causing the discrepancies between the results of Xu et al. (2008) and current study. Firstly, Xu et al. (2008) targeted at Mandarin used in Mainland China whereas current study targeted at Chinese Mandarin used in Singapore. Therefore the difference may be attributed to the possible variation between the two varieties of Chinese. Secondly, it could be due to the difference in annotation process. Xu et al. (2008) adopted both human annotation (a few experts) and automatic annotation to obtain polarity, whereas we relied on a large number of average language speakers. The large number of laymen participants versus the few expert annotators might cause a difference in semantic understanding of the words. The above mentioned differences still require further study in order to compare the effectiveness and accuracy in different methodologies.

Last but not least, we compared the current results with the emotion categories and emotion intensity reported in Lin & Yao (2015).We noticed there is a correlation between polarity and emotion categories. As shown in table 2, all DISGUST emotion words are annotated as negative polarity words. Most words in the categories of ANGER, ANXIETY, FEAR, and SADNESS are annotated as negative polarity words. HAPPINESS emotion words are all annotated as positive polarity words. SURPRISE emotion words are annotated as neutral polarity words, with only one annotated as negative polarity words. Emotion intensity and polarity are correlated too. We compared and calculated the mean polarity obtained in current study with emotion intensity obtained in Lin & Yao (2015). Results showed that the correlation coefficient values among the negative polarity and positive polarity words were higher (0.57, 0.35 respectively), whereas the correlation was relatively lower in neutral polarity words (0.16). In other words, for polarity words with high positive or high negative mean polarity, the judgment for the word's emotion intensity by average language users was more related.

Table 2 Emotion category and polarity distribution

Emotion category in Lin & Yao (2015)	Current results			Polarity distribution (majority)
	Negative	Neutral	Positive	
ANGER	12(66.7%)	6(33.3%)	0(0%)	66.7% negative
ANXIETY	19(52.8%)	17(47.2%)	0(0%)	52.8% negative
DISGUST	21(100%)	0(0%)	0(0%)	All negative
FEAR	8(66.7%)	4(33.3%)	0(0%)	66.7% negative
HAPPINESS	0(0%)	4(7.1%)	52(92.9%)	92.9% positive
SADNESS	52(78.8%)	14(21.2%)	0(0%)	78.8% negative
SURPRISE	1(9.1%)	10(90.9%)	0(0%)	90.9% neutral

5   Conclusion

In this study, we conducted a large-scale survey of average Chinese language users' annotation of polarity in Singapore. This study generated a polarity database based on Singapore Chinese users. The results of this study also indicated some differences and similarities in comparison with past studies. We hope that the current study will serve as an important reference for future research on sentiment analysis in Chinese in a broader context.

Acknowledgements

This research was partly supported by The Hong Kong Polytechnic University, Department of Chinese and Bilingual Studies under the Departmental General Research Funds [4-ZZEL]. The authors would like to thank the participants of the survey for their time and support.

References

1. Andreevskaia, A., & Bergler, S. (2006). Mining WordNet for a Fuzzy Sentiment: Sentiment Tag Extraction from WordNet Glosses. In *EACL* (Vol. 6, pp. 209–216).
2. Ding, X., Liu, B., & Yu, P. S. (2008). A holistic lexicon-based approach to opinion mining. In *Proceedings of the 2008 International Conference on Web Search and Data Mining* (pp. 231–240). ACM.
3. Esuli, A., & Sebastiani, F. (2005). Determining the semantic orientation of terms through gloss classification. In *Proceedings of the 14th ACM International Conference on Information and Knowledge Management* (pp. 617–624). ACM.
4. Hatzivassiloglou, V., & McKeown, K. R. (1997). Predicting the semantic orientation of adjectives. In *Proceedings of the 35th Annual Meeting of the Association for Computational Linguistics and 8th Conference of the European Chapter of the Association for Computational Linguistics* (pp. 174–181). Association for Computational Linguistics.
5. Kamps, J., Marx, M., Mokken, R. J., & De Rijke, M. (2004). Using WordNet to Measure Semantic Orientations of Adjectives. In *LREC* (Vol. 4, pp. 1115–1118).

6. Khoo, C., Cheon, N., & Basha, J. (2015). Comparison of lexical resources for sentiment analysis. Presentation at the *Singapore Symposium on Sentiment Analysis*. Singapore.
7. Kim, S. M., & Hovy, E. (2005). Automatic detection of opinion bearing words and sentences. In *Companion Volume to the Proceedings of the International Joint Conference on Natural Language Processing (IJCNLP)* (pp. 61–66).
8. Lin, J., & Yao Y. (2015). Encoding emotion in Chinese: Emotion type and intensity of Chinese emotion words. In *Proceedings of the 16ʰ Chinese Lexical Semantics Workshop*.
9. Strauss, G. P., & Allen, D. N. (2008). Emotional intensity and categorisation ratings for emotional and nonemotional words. *Cognition and Emotion, 22*(1), 114–133.
10. Turney, P. D., & Littman, M. L. (2003). Measuring praise and criticism: Inference of semantic orientation from association. *ACM Transactions on Information Systems (TOIS), 21*(4), 315–346.
11. Wiebe, J. (2000). Learning subjective adjectives from corpora. In *AAAI/IAAI* (pp. 735–740).
12. Wilson, T., Wiebe, J., & Hwa, R. (2004). Just how mad are you? Finding strong and weak opinion clauses. In *AAAI* (Vol. 4, pp. 761–769).
13. Xu, L., Lin, H., Pan, Y., Ren, H., & Chen, J. (2008). Constructing the affective lexicon ontology. *Journal of the China Society for Scientific and Technical Information. 27*.2, 180–185.
14. Xu, X., & Tao, J. (2003). Hanyu qinggan xitongzhong qinggan huafen de yanjiu [The study of affective word categorization in Chinese]. In *Proceedings of the 1st ChineseConference on Affective Computing and Intelligent Interaction*, 199–205.

A Structural and Prosodic Analysis of Trisyllabic New Words

Jianfei Luo

Beijing Language and Culture University

nch1980s@163.com

Abstract. The majority of Chinese new words are trisyllabic, which violates the disyllabic norm of Chinese vocabulary. This paper explores reasons underlying this phenomenon by studying the structure and prosody of the trisyllabic new words.

Keywords: new words, trisyllabic words, structure, prosody

1   Introduction

Previous studies on Chinese new words focus mainly on such aspects as their definition, structure, pragmatic analysis and so on. As for the definition, Chen (1984) argues that the four criteria for a new lexical entry include: 1) it is irreplaceable; 2) its formation fits into the language specification and social conventions; 3) it can express certain concept or thought accurately; 4) it is catchy and easily accepted. Liu (2005) proposes further that new words refer to those newly appeared and repeatedly used words, thus gradually becoming stable units in the language system. Therefore, new words are to go through the test of time. Moreover, Yang (2010) takes the public acceptance as the key point in the transition of new words into general vocabulary. Apart from this, in his view, the identification of new words also concerns language rules. Although different opinions can be observed regarding to the definition of new words, the consensus is that the key factors of defining a new word are the test of time and its stability.

With respect to the features of new words, Shen (1995) thinks that the previous arbitrary combinations of the form and meaning are constrained because the creation of new words is motivated. As a result, the meaning of a new word is unicity. Moreover, since the social life and communicative media have changed, new words, are colloquial pragmatically speaking. In terms of their structure, it is found that new words are mostly in the modifier-head structure through a statistical analysis of new words in *Xinhua Dictionary of New Word* by Zhou.

As long as a new word is stabilized and in the common use among social members, it will enter the system of general vocabulary and obey the universal rules of lexical system. As the prosodic structure of modern Chinese vocabulary is a disyllabic one (Feng 1996, 1998), the new words, as members of Chinese lexical system, are

© Springer International Publishing AG 2016
M. Dong et al. (Eds.): CLSW 2016, LNAI 10085, pp. 120–127, 2016
DOI: 10.1007/978-3-319-49508-8_12

expected to follow suit. However, the fact is that the majority of Chinese new words are trisyllabic rather than disyllabic. Therefore, this paper analyzes the structural and prosodic features of trisyllabic new words with the purposes of explaining why trisyllabic new words take a large amount.

2   The features of Chinese new words' syllabic distribution

With new words collected in *Language Situation in China* issued by the print media center for monitoring and studying national language resource from 2011 to 2013 as the sample, this paper makes a classification of these words in term of their syllabic numbers , as shown in Table 1.

Table 1: The distribution of Chinese new word of different syllabic structure

Year	Two syllables	Three syllables	Four syllables	Five syllables	Six syllables	All
2011	85	306	115	60	4	570
2012	76	261	186	43	7	573
2013	86	161	75	17	11	350
All	247	728	376	120	22	1493

It can be seen from Table 1 that the amount of the trisyllabic new words surpasses that of new words in other syllabic structures and that the disyllabic ones are not in the majority. According to the basic conclusion of prosodic study on modern Chinese, the disyllabic words are predicted to be the dominant ones in modern Chinese (Lü 1963; Feng 1996, 1998). The fact, however, is that the trisyllabic new words, flouting the disyllabic rule, take up the advantage among new words. So, what are the underlying reasons for this phenomenon? As no satisfied explanations have been found in previous studies, this paper will make a classification, description and explanation of trisyllabic new words from 2011 to 2013 with the aim of figuring out the fundamental causes of their dominant status.

3   The structural analysis of trisyllabic new words

3.1   Five structural types of trisyllabic new words and a quantitative analysis

(1) Modifier-head structure: an example of new words in this structure is 微信圈 [eixinquan]*(the broadcast massages and friend's latest development in Wechat)*.
(2) Coordinate structure: a new word of this type is 白富美 [baifumei] (*a fire-skinned and pretty good looking rich lady*).
(3) Predicative-object structure: an instance of this kind of new words is 拼同学 [pintongxue] *(friends-privilege-competition, young men from low-income families are sent to noble schools by their parents with the belief that classmates or friends from the elite class will help their children in the future*).
(4) Predicate-Complement structure: a new word of such kind is 伤不起 [shangbuqi] (*to be too delicate to bear a blow*).

(5) Subject-predicate structure: an instance is 习连会 [*xilianhui*] (*President Xi's meeting with the Taiwan's Kuomintang Chairman Lian Zhan*).

Those five structural types of trisyllabic new words exhibit the utmost disproportion in quantitative distribution, as shown in Table 2.

Table 2: The quantitative distribution of Chinese new words of five different structural types

Year	Modifie r-head	Coord inate	Predicat e-object	Predicate-comp liment	Subject-pre dicate	All
2011	235	1	3	2	13	254
2012	191	9	3	0	3	206
2013	125	3	4	0	12	144
All	551	13	10	2	28	604

Table 2 illustrates clearly that the trisyllabic new words of the modifier-head structure take an important part among all the words at hand. There are 551 ones of such kind, accounting for almost 91%, out of a total of 604 trisyllabic new words collected. Given all this, the next section will focus on a further classification, description and interpretation of trisyllabic new words of this structure.

3.2   The structure and amount of trisyllabic new modifier-head words

3.2.1 Three kinds of trisyllabic modifier-head words

(1) Noun as the head: an example is 棱镜门 [*lengjingmen*] (*PRISM, the clandestine surveillance program under which the NSA collects internet communications from at least nine major US internet companies*).

(2) Verb as the head: a word of such kind is 空气游 [*kongqiyou*] (*trips to places of good air quality*).

(3) Adjective as the head: an instance is 火锅红 [*huoguohong*] (*a kind of food additive used to color the hotpot soup red even without pimientos*).

Table 3: The quantitative distribution of trisyllabic modifier-head words with different heads

Year	Noun as the head	Verb as the head	Adjective as the head	All
2011	205	27	3	235
2012	176	11	4	192
2013	108	16	1	125
All	489	54	8	551

3.2.2 The trisyllabic new modifier-head words with nouns as the heads

(1) [2+1] prosodic pattern

There are 374 words in the [2+1] prosodic pattern among all the trisyllabic modifier-head words with nouns as the head and they can be further divided into the following types：

A.   [XX]n+[X]n: this kind of new words are those with the former two syllables as disyllabic nouns, an example of which is 蛋白族[*danbaizu*] (*a term for self-mockery, which refers to the urban white-collar workers who live a dull life instead of the seemingly decent life with a high salary).*

B. [XX]v-o+[X]n: words of this type are those with the former two syllables forming predicate-object structures, and an example is 限奶令 [*xiannailing*] (*the restrictions on mainland purchases of milk powder in Hong kong*).

C. [XX]n-v+[X]n: the former two syllables of this kind of words form verb-noun structures, an example of which is 夜淘族 [*yetaozu*] (*the group of people who do online shopping during the period from 23 p.m. to 5 a.m. in the following day*).

D. [XX]a+[X]n: words of this kind are those with the former two syllables as disyllabic adjectives and an instance is 暴力哥 [*baolige*] (*the guy who is known for paying the extensive fund to lift the stock index*)

E. [XX]a-n+[X]n: words with the former two syllables forming adjective-noun structures, an instance of which is 名表门 [*mingbiaomen*] (*the scandal about Yang Dacai, the Secretary for Work Safety Supervision of Shanxi province, who is known for his expensive timepieces worn in different occasions*).

F. [XX]ad+[X]n: the former two syllables of these words are adverbs, an example of which is 马上体 [*mashangti*] (*a blessing word in the pattern of "you will have ... soon" used in the year of horse to bless others to get what they want*).

G. [XX]ad-v+[X]n: this kind of words are those with the former two syllables forming adverbial-verb structures, and an instance is 裸跑弟 [*luopaodi*] (*a four year old boy who ran, stark naked, in the snowstorm to celebrate the new year of 2012 in New York city*).

H. [XX]conj+[X]n: the former two syllables of this type of words are conjunctions, an example of which is 如果体 [*ruguoti*] (*a semi-open construction in the pattern of "if I do not major in ..., I would like to do...", which reflects the long distance between dream and reality*).

Table 4: The quantitative distribution of different types of modifier-head nouns in the [2+1] prosodic pattern

Year	A	B	C	D	E	F	G	H	All
2011	58	62	2	6	3	2	4	2	139
2012	72	48	4	10	8	0	7	1	150
2013	32	34	8	6	4	1	0	0	85
All	162	144	14	22	15	3	11	3	374

(2) [1+2] prosodic pattern

There are 115 modifier-head nouns in the [1+2] prosodic pattern in total. They are generally combinations of monosyllabic elements that specify properties modifying the disyllabic noun-heads. For instance, 微课程 [*weikecheng*] (*microlecture, referring to the actual instructional content that is formatted for online and mobile learning using a constructivist approach*) .

A further classification can be made in terms of the parts of speech of the monosyllabic modifying element, which are as follows.

A.   [X]n+[XX]n: this kind of words are those with the monosyllabic nouns modifying the disyllabic noun-heads. For example, 碳海绵 [*tanhaimian*] (*a kind of aerogels, which is the lightest object in the world*).

B.   [X]a+[XX]n: words under this category are those with the monosyllabic adjectives (including distinguishing words) modifying disyllabic nouns, such as 微电影 [*weidianying*] (*the short film, an original motion picture that has a running time of 40 minutes or less, including all credits*) and so on.

Table 5: The quantitative distribution of different types of modifier-head nouns in the [1+2] prosodic pattern

Year	A	B	Number in total
2011	22	44	66
2012	5	21	26
2013	9	14	23
Number in total	36	79	115

As is manifested in Table 5, the trisyllabic new words of pattern B significantly outnumber that of pattern A. It suggests that the trisyllabic new words with noun-head in the [1+2] prosodic pattern are more likely to take the form of the adjective-modifier modifying the noun-head.

3.2.3 The trisyllabic new modifier-head words with verbs as the heads

A total of 54 trisyllabic new words of the modifier-head structure with verbs as the heads are collected. In line with the foregoing analysis, they can also be classified into words in the [2+1] prosodic pattern and words in the [1+2] one.

(1) [2+1] prosodic pattern

Altogether 11 new words are collected with 4 in 2011, 1 in 2012 and 6 in 2013.

A.   [XX]n+[X]v: they are words with the former two syllables as nominal structures modifying the monosyllabic verbs. There are altogether 10 words of this kind, with 4 in 2011 and 6 in 2013.

B.   [XX]v-o+[X]v: this type of words are those with the former two syllables as the predicate-object structures modifying the monosyllabic verbs, such as 伤肺跑 [*shangfeipao*] (*a round-the-city race held in the city of Lanzhou regardless of the extremely poor air quality*).

Altogether only one word of such kind is found in 2012 during these three years.

(2) [1+2] prosodic pattern

One example is 微调查 [*weidiaocha*] (*network stages for the online investigations, which offer the one package service from designing, issuing and recycling questionnaire to data analysis and statistics*).

Altogether 43 new words of this kind, including 23 in 2011, 10 in 2012 and 10 in 2013, are found.

3.2.4 The trisyllabic new modifier-head words with adjectives as the heads

There are in total 8 trisyllabic new words of the modifier-head structure with adjectives as the heads, dividing into those in the [2+1] prosodic pattern and those in the [1+2] one as well.

(1) The [2+1] prosodic pattern

　Altogether 6 cases are found, in which 2 are seen in 2011, 3 in 2012 and 1 in 2013.

　　A. [XX]n+[X]a: words of this type are those with the disyllabic nominal structure modifying the monosyllabic adjectives. The relationship between these two components is a noun-adjective one rather than a subject-predicate one. A total of 5 cases at issue are found with 2, 2 and 1 in the year of 2011, 2012 and 2013 respectively.

　　B. [XX]v-o+[X]a: words of this type are composed of the disyllabic predicate-object structure modifying the monosyllabic adjectives, such as 过劳肥 [*guolaofei*] (*the obesity caused by the overwork, high pressure, sleep insufficiency, etc*).

　Only one instance is observed in the data.

(2) The [1+2] prosodic pattern

　An example of words in this pattern is 冷浪漫 [*lenglangman*] (*to illustrate the scientific truth by the romantic language*).

　There are only 2 cases in total, with one in 2011 and the other in 2012.

3.3　The structure and amount of trisyllabic new words of coordinate structure (13 cases altogether)

Trisyllabic new words of such kind of are mostly adjectives or verbs.

　　(1) Adjectives: trisyllabic new words, like *baifumei*, are adjectives and 12 instances of this kind are found in the data.

　　(2) Verbs: only one instance of the verbal nature is seen in the data and it is 调惠上 [*tiaohuishang*] (*the activities carried out under the guidance of the spirits of the twelfth plenum of the ninth Central Committee of the Communist Part of China to adjust the industrial structure, improve people's livelihood and promote economic development*).

3.4　The structure and amount of trisyllabic new predicate-object words

Only a few trisyllabic new words of such kind are observed, 10 in total. For instance, 包小姐 [*baoxiaojie*] (*small advertisements of beauties posted in the street corners to defraud money*).

3.5　The structure and amount of trisyllabic new predicate-complement words

Altogether only two such new words are found. They are *shangbuqi* and *shangdeqi*.

4   Analysis and discussion

4.1   The features of Chinese new words

（1）The trisyllabic ones are dominate in number among Chinese new words of different syllabic structures.

（2）What take up the vast majority among these trisyllabic new words are those of the modifier-head structure. To be more specific, most of them are words with nouns as the heads.

（3）The trisyllabic new words in the [2+1] prosodic pattern outnumber significantly those in the [1+2] prosodic pattern.

（4）As to the structure of words in the [2+1] prosodic pattern, forms of the former two syllables are multiple although they are for the most part nouns.

（5）As to the structure of words in the [1+2] prosodic pattern, the initial syllables generally specify properties while the latter two syllables designate discrete objects or events.

4.2   The analysis of trisyllabic new words in Chinese language

The foregoing features are generalized on the basis of the observation of the data in section 3, from which some further inferences can be made and are listed as follows.

(1) The formation of trisyllabic words is unstable, which turns out to be one significant feature of the new word formation.

In the prosodic system of Chinese language, the disyllables are the most stable ones. Four syllables are composed of two disyllables, thus manifesting the feature of balance. However, the combination of trisyllabic foots, in addition to the parallel [1+1+1] prosodic pattern, have to adopt either the [1+2] prosodic pattern or the [2+1] prosodic pattern. No matter which pattern is chosen, the imbalance is always shown. This kind of imbalance makes words unstable if it is involved in the word formation because these words are in the transition either to disyllables or to phrases. In short, the trisyllabic new words are always in such kind of instability.

(2) The rhythmical differences in various types of trisyllabic word reflect the colloquial feature of new word.

Another feature of the trisyllabic formation of words is colloquial. New words are originally created to represent new things and they are made up from the existing materials in language. Therefore, their acceptability and interestingness are taken as of high value by language users. Although some new words are used with quotes when appearing in newspapers, they are still colloquial in nature.

(3) The trisyllabic new words exhibit the features of nouns.

In light of the statistical analysis above, it is found that the majority of trisyllabic new words are with nouns as the heads while only a few are verb-headed. As a matter of fact, a deeper investigation reveals that these verb-headed trisyllabic words also have the nominal features. For example, *diaocha* in *weidiaocha* still manifest features of nouns. This can be proved by their nominal usages in phrases such as 做了一项调查 [*zuole yixiang diaocha*] (*to make a survey*). Therefore, it is claimed that the verb-headed trisyllabic words in the [1+2] prosodic pattern, like *weidiaocha*, still have features of nouns.

(4) The trisyllabic new words in the [2+1] prosodic pattern have nominal features while those in the [1+2] prosodic pattern are compounds of adjective-noun structures.

The general rule of Chinese trisyllables is that those in the [2+1] prosodic pattern end up as words while those in the [1+2] one as phrases or sentences. Among the new words, those adhering to the [2+1] prosodic pattern are the majority and those in other patterns, as the minority, all have the semantic characteristic of "attributes+ object/event". In other words, the former monosyllables, such as 伪 *wei* in伪基站 *weijizhan* tends to be qualitative adjectives or distinguishing words. Apart from this, some monosyllabic nouns can denote properties as well. This special kind of usage is more likely to be a feature of qualitative words rather than that of common nouns. In consequence, it is assumed that the trisyllabic new words in the [1+2] prosodic pattern are compounds of the adjectives-noun structure.

5   Conclusion

As vocabulary with a high degree of colloquialism, Chinese new words are characterized by their rhythmical differences, which are frequently observed in the trisyllabic word formation. As a result, the vast majority of Chinese new words are trisyllabic. Both new words in the [2+1] prosodic pattern, as in the case of the combination a monosyllable noun and a disyllable one, and those in the [1+2] prosodic pattern, as in the case of the monosyllabic adjective modifying the disyllabic noun, can be realized as trisyllabic nouns.

Acknowledgments. The study is supported by the Beijing Language and Culture University scientific research project (Grant No. 16YJ080207), and the Youth Elite Project of Beijing Language and Culture University.

References

1. Chen, Y.: On the Emergence of New Lexical Entries and Their Social Significance (in Chinese). Studies in Language and Linguistics, no. 2, 151-158 (1984).
2. Feng, S.: On Prosodic Words in Chinese Language (in Chinese). Social Sciences in China, no. 1, 161-176 (1996).
3. Feng, S.: On the "natural foot" in Chinese Language (in Chinese). Studies of the Chinese Language, no. 1, 40-47 (1998).
4. Liu, S.: Chinese Descriptive Lexicology (in Chinese). The Commercial Press, Beijing (2006).
5. Shen, M.: An Investigation on Meaning Composition of New Words (in Chinese). Applied Linguistics, no.4, 66-72 (1995).
6. Yang, B.: The Multi-research on Modern Chinese New Words (in Chinese). Master Degree Thesis of Liaoning Normal University (2006).

On the Notion of "Syntactic Word": its Origin and Evolution

Huibin Zhuang[1], Baopeng Ma[2], Shaoshuai Shen[1], Peicui Zhang[1]

1 Henan University, Kaifeng, China
2 Beijing Language and Culture University, Beijing, China

{zhuanghuibin,mabaopeng1234,wps2005,zpc1981224}@163.com

Abstract. This paper aims to review the previous studies on "syntactic word", with the purpose of analyzing their strengths and weaknesses, and clarifying the advantages and significance of the diversified revisions, especially the one amended by Feng [5-10].

Keywords: Syntactic Word; origin; evolution; significance

1 Introduction

The notion of "syntactic word" is no novelty in the field of Chinese studies. Scholars have discussed the issue [1-15] from different perspectives. Among those scholars, several like Chao [1], Feng [5-10], Furukawa [12], and Zhou [13], have offered definitions of "syntactic word", which are worth to be reviewed for the purpose of a thorough evaluation.

2 Chao's Definition of "Syntactic Word"

Chao [1] first proposes the notion of "syntactic word" in the study of Chinese grammar, particularly that of spoken Chinese, and regards it as a class of bound words.

Concise as it is, Chao's definition is not clear and strict enough, hence difficult to be applied to actual practice. In the case of *bai bu* 'white cloth', *bai-cai* 'Chinese cabbage' and *bai de bu* 'white cloth', *bai bu* and *bai-cai* show only subtle difference and a clear distinction cannot be seen straightforwardly. Only by a certain test can we find the difference [1], [16]. Perhaps this is why Chao has to make a distinction between bound morphemes and free morphemes and why the definition has been revised several times later.

© Springer International Publishing AG 2016
M. Dong et al. (Eds.): CLSW 2016, LNAI 10085, pp. 128–135, 2016
DOI: 10.1007/978-3-319-49508-8_13

3   Furukawa's definition of Syntactic Words

Furukawa [12] has suggested that such disyllabic units as *ke-pa* 'horrible', *ke-qi* 'annoying', *pa-ren* 'timid', *qi-ren* 'irritating', *hao-chi* 'delicious', *nan-chi* 'distasteful' belong to the interface between morphology and syntax, which is said to fall into the category of complex word from a morphological perspective but go beyond the word-hood from a word-formation perspective because they can be categorized as phrases, namely syntactic structures.

It is maintained by Furukawa that these disyllabic units can be regarded as words because the verbal morphemes have lost their original functions and acquired new ones. Such a transformation has been manifested by the argument structure change of those words on the one hand and the sound change of those words in sentences on the other hand. Given those facts, he defines "syntactic word" as a syntactic complex (with syntactic words as an abbreviated name) which belongs to the scopes of both word formation and syntax.

This definition, however, is obtained by generalizing the surface of the linguistic facts and therefore fails to set a clear boundary for syntactic words and other categories, thus being somewhat self-contradictory.

4   Zhou's Definition of Syntactic Words

Zhou's discussion of "syntactic words" mainly involves those compound disyllabic words. His essential proposal can be shown as follows [13]:

> The connection between syllables of compound disyllabic words, particularly of those which can be understood and explained in terms of syntactic patterns, has something in common with that of words in sentences, regardless of their differences in other aspects. On the one hand, some disyllabic words have originated from a particular sentence; on the other hand, the original syntactic relationships between words still exert some influences on that of morphemes of one word which is the lexicalization of the above words. Even if for those which are created independently rather than originate from sentences, they are made by following a similar psychological pattern just like the way the sentences are produced.

Given this fact, Zhou [13] has defined "syntactic words" as words "that can be understood and explained in terms of syntactic patterns, of which some are originated from phrases and others not but can still be attributed to the phrase-forming patterns."

Zhou's argument, interesting as it is, is vulnerable to various problems. For reasons of space, we just list three of them as follows.

Firstly, according to Zhou's definition, "syntactic words" can be classified into two categories, namely, words that "originate from a lexicalization of phrases" and words that "are not but can still be attributed to the phrase-forming patterns". However, the second category above are perhaps not compounded on the syntactic level. If they are defined as "syntactic words", their essence may not be revealed. Zhou argues that those words are "created by following a similar psychological pattern just like the way the sentences are produced". The fact is, however, quite different. As Feng [17-19] proposes, people create disyllabic words to chiefly satisfy the prosodic requirement. Therefore, the syntactic structures do not constitute the fundamental basis for word formation and the words derived then are not created "by following the similar psychological pattern just like the way the sentences are produced". What's more, some words are indeed a lexicalization of syntactic structures, but the syntactic relationships of their two morphemes can only be understood by judging the context. A typical example here is *fouze* 'otherwise' [15] which involves a lexicalization of non-constituent adjacent words. How can we take it as a simplex syntactic structure?

Secondly, Zhou's proposal of the syntactic pattern is too broad, as a result of which the coordinated disyllabic words and the reduplicated disyllabic words are all counted as "syntactic words". However, those words are created because of prosodic requirement [10], [17], [19] rather than syntactic operation.

Thirdly, Zhou's definition, broad as it is, has actually excluded some "syntactic words" in the real sense. In light of the definition, "syntactic words" can be classified into two categories, namely, words that are "originating from a lexicalization of phrases" and words that "are not but can still be attributed to the phrase-forming patterns". However, some words like *bai bu* 'white cloth' belong to neither of the two categories. Obviously, they have not been lexicalized (compared with *bai-cai* 'Chinese cabbage' and therefore should not be "syntactic words" defined by Zhou. It follows that the syntactic words in the real sense are filtered out in Zhou's framework.

5   Feng's Definition of Syntactic Words

5.1   Feng's Definition

Feng has defined "syntactic words" as words derived from syntactic operation:

> It is often held that syntactic operation can generate phrases. As a matter of fact, the same operations can also generate words. For example, some syntactic operations like adjoining (a Y^0 is adjoined to an X^0) and incorporation (a head word is incorporated into another) can also create words" [7].

Thus, some linguistic units like *xiao yusan* 'small umbrella', *da fangjian* 'big room', *dadao* 'knock down', *qiku* 'to anger into tears', *jiang xue* 'to lecture', *fuze* 'to be responsible' are all counted as "syntactic words" [5-10]. Their core structures can be represented as follows [5-6]:

(1)

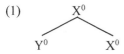

The X^0 and Y^0 here are heads. The point is that, even if such words can be represented with a X-bar structure, a question arises: why do "syntactic words" possess such a structure?

To answer this question, the first thing is to discuss an important syntactic operation, namely, adjoining. As is proposed by Shi:

Adjoining can only be conducted with syntactic elements of the same nature and will produce a syntactic element of the same nature. That is to say, a phrase can only be adjoined to a phrase and the new structure after adjoining is also a phrase; on the other hand, only a head can be adjoined to another head and the new element after adjoining is also a head.

This idea can be represented as follows [5-6], [21-22]:

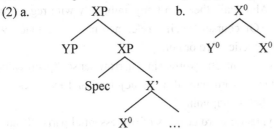

It can be concluded now that the formation of syntactic words must satisfy both of the following two requirements.

(3) Y is adjoined to X to form a syntactic word iff
    1) X is a $\mathbf{X^0}$, and
    2) Y is a $\mathbf{Y^0}$

(4)

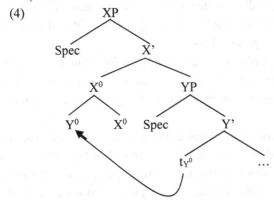

As discussed above, the insertion of an element into another can form a syntactic word and so does another syntactic operation, e.g., derivation. If the Y^0 is moved from another position and then is adjoined to X^0, then we can hardly deny that the newly formed X^0 is a syntactic word. A typical example of this case is those syntactic words formed by incorporation, such as *guan-yan* 'to shut tightly' and *da-po* 'to break' [8], [18], [23].

5.2   Advantages of Feng's Definition

Since Chao [1] has proposed the notion of "syntactic words", why does Feng redefine this notion? Compared to the definitions of other scholars [12-13], what are the special features of Feng's definition then?

We will answer these questions from the following two aspects.

Firstly, Feng has redefined the notion of "syntactic words" and elaborated their formation in a formalized manner, thus clearing all the ambiguities and making it concise and easy to understand. Although some scholars [1], [12-13] define "syntactic words" before Feng, their definitions suffer various kinds of problems which have been discussed in Section 2, 3 and 4. By contrast, Feng has defined "syntactic words" in a formalized way. Consequently, the notion of "syntactic words" is clarified, thus making it easy to understand. Above all, there isn't any ambiguity with regard to the defining of "syntactic words". Of course, specific reference has to be made when deciding whether a word is a syntactic word or not.

Secondly, Feng has defined "syntactic words" in a narrow sense. Specifically, he considers the X^0 to be a syntactic word only if Y^0 is adjoined and excludes all the syntactic atom, namely, the X^0 before adjoining.

Feng [6] stresses that a syntactic word consists of two essential parts, X^0 and Y^0. Actually this idea emphasizes two characteristics: formalization and adjoining.

It should be mentioned that Feng is not the first one to define "syntactic word" in a formalized way. Other scholars [24-28] have employed the formal way to define "syntactic word" too. However, Feng's definition is fundamentally different from those scholars because they have all used the notion of syntactic atom X^0 while Feng only takes the X^0 to be a syntactic word only if Y^0 is adjoined. Slight as it seems, this modification has revealed Feng's profound insight.

We all know that it is a heated issue to distinguish *bai bu* 'white cloth' and *bai-cai* 'Chinese cabbage' and to consider *bai bu* 'white cloth' to be a word or phrase. This issue has posed a challenge to the frameworks of "syntactic words" proposed before Feng's model.

The frameworks [24-36] consider X^0 to be a syntactic word and tend to logically take X^0 after being adjoined with Y^0 as a syntactic word too. Thus *bai bu* 'white cloth' and *bai-cai* 'Chinese cabbage' show no difference. However, if X^0 after adjoined with Y^0 is excluded form syntactic words, then *bai bu* is a phrase and not different from *baicai*, thus falling into the old ruts of traditional analysis [1], [16].

Unlike the above analyses, Feng only takes those X^0 with Y^0 adjoined as "syntactic words" and excludes all the syntactic atoms, i.e., X^0 should be words from lexicon. Moreover, he clarifies the distinctions between syntactic words and phrases, thus setting a clear-cut boundary between *bai bu* and *bai-cai* and also between *bai bu* and *bai de bu*. In this way, *bai bu* and *bai-cai* belong to different categories since the former is a syntactic word while the latter is a compound word.

5.3   Significance of Feng's Redefinition

Feng's redefinition of "syntactic words" has immense significance to the study of Chinese, which can be reflected in the following two aspects.

Firstly, Feng's redefinition has well adapted to the needs of studying Chinese syntactic words, which has long been neglected due to a lack of precise definition.

For instance, though scholars had long realized the phenomenon of "syntactic words", they were compelled (even reluctantly) to categorize them into compound words or phrases. Such an approach was once criticized by Lü [2] who considered it to be improper to take *ji-dan* 'chicken egg' as a phrase while *ya-dan* 'duck's egg' a compound word. What's more, those scholars took different perspectives and were likely to draw different conclusions.

Under such circumstances, some scholars proposed the notion of "syntactic words" or similar concepts to refer to this phenomenon. Among them, Lü [2] was the first one to realize the presence of "syntactic words", but he didn't categorize them into compound words or phrases. Instead, he listed them separately and defined them as "units between words and phrases". He further pointed that "if we take them as phrases, then they should be 'basic phrase' which are different from those 'extended phrases with the insertion of *de*; if we take them as compounds, then they should be 'phrasal words'" [2](p.21).

As we enter the new century, there has arisen even more heated discussion. Feng [5-6] maintains that some prosodic words consisting of an adjective and a noun should also be "syntactic words", such as *da shu* 'big trees', *da panzi* 'big plate', *xiao jisuanji* 'small computers'. Wang [11] takes these words as "word-like phrase". Some other prosodic words like "*bei* + V" and "*ke* + V" are also considered to be "syntactic words" [8]. Besides, some prosodic words as *jiang xue* 'to give lectures' and *shou tu* 'to take somebody as a disciple' taken from *jiang xue Zhongnanhai* 'to give lectures in Zhongnanhai' and *shou tu shaolinsi* 'to accept sb. as a disciple in Shaolin Temple' fall into the category of "syntactic words", too.

Scholars are catching up fast since then. In addition to the studies mentioned above, many other scholars have studied "syntactic words". For example, Dong [14] considers some V-R construction as syntactic words. Cui [29] takes those separable words like *shou tu* 'to take somebody as a disciple' as syntactic words. Huang Mei and Feng [20] maintain that some disyllabic constructions consisting of an adverb and a verb are syntactic words, such as *hu zeng* 'to exchange'.

It can be seen that the notion of "syntactic words" is the natural result of linguistic study in our times. Feng's redefinition has just emerged to adapt to the needs of the times, thus providing a key concept for the interface study between morphology and syntax.

Secondly, Feng's redefinition of "syntactic words" has helped to resolve the old perplexities of distinguishing words and phrases in Chinese.

We all know that the boundary between words and phrases are blurred and some language units can either be defined as words or phrases. As a matter of fact, such a fuzzy distinction is largely due to the existence of syntactic words in Chinese. For instance, some language units like *da shu* 'big trees', *huang meigui* 'yellow roses' are typical ones that cannot be clearly distinguished. To define them, the previous studies have put forward different views. According to the traditional expanding method, they fall into the category of phrases [1], [16]. Nevertheless, Duanmu [4] (pp.135-196) has provided adequate evidence to prove that they are compound words.

Thus, "syntactic words" can be well differentiated from compound words in the traditional sense since the former are derived from syntactic operation while the latter are the results of word-formation. From this, we conclude that *bai-cai* 'Chinese cabbage', *lü-dou* 'enzyme', *bai dagua* 'a white smock', *hong xiaodou* 'red bean' are all lexical words while *bai bu* 'white cloth', *da shu* 'big trees' and *huang meigui* 'yellow rose' are syntactic words.

6   Conclusion

During the 1960s, Chao's proposal of "syntactic words" launched a new era of research on Chinese grammar. However, circumstances change with the passing of time. As people's knowledge of language deepens, Chao's definition is no longer adequate for the needs of current studies. With the introduction of formal linguistics, several revisions of "syntactic words" have been put forward. Among those revisions, Feng's version is distinguished and unique. This is of course due to Feng's profound linguistic knowledge (formalized way to study language). Apart from this, we have concluded through the study that the success is also largely due to Feng's pioneering adaption to the needs of redefinition of "syntactic words" in Chinese in our times.

References:

1. Chao, Y. R.: A Grammar of Spoken Chinese. University of California Press, Berkeley (1968)
2. Lü, S.: Issues in Chinese Grammatical Analysis (in Chinese). The commercial Press, Beijing (1979)
3. Zhu, D.: Lectures on Grammar (in Chinese). The Commercial Press, Beijing (1982)

4. Duanmu, S.: Wordhood in Chinese. New Approaches to Chinese Word Formation, ed. by J. L. Packard, pp.135-196. Mouton de Gruyter, Berlin (1998)

5. Feng, S.: The Prosodic Syntax of Chinese (in Chinese). Shanghai Education Press, Shanghai (2000)

6. Feng, S.: The Multidimensional properties of word in Chinese (in Chinese). Comtemporary Linguistics, no. 3, pp.161-174 (2001)

7. Feng, S.: Prosodically Determined Distinctions between Word and Phrase in Chinese (in Chinese). Studies of The Chinese Language, no.1, pp. 27-37 (2001)

8. Feng, S.: On the Interface between Prosodic Morphology and Prosodic Syntax (in Chinese). Studies of the Chinese Language, no. 6, pp. 515-524 (2002)

9. Feng, S.: On the properties and pedagogy of written Chinese (in Chinese). Chinese Teaching in the World, no.4, 98-106 (2006)

10. Feng, S.: Prosodic Syntax in Chinese (enlarged). The Commercial Press, Beijing (2013)

11. Wang, H.: The prosodic word and prosodic phrase of Chinese (in Chinese). Studies of the Chinese Language, no. 6, 525-536 (2000)

12. Furukawa, Y. Interaction and interface between morphology and syntax (in Chinese). Interface in Chinese: Morphology, Syntax and Phonetics, ed. by J. Xu & Q. Zhong, pp.177-193. Beijing Language and Culture University Press, Beijing (2007)

13. Zhou, J.: A study of word formation, construction and significance in Chinese lexical and syntactic system (in Chinese). Studies of the Chinese language, no. 2, 148-155 (2003)

14. Dong, X.: On the Property of Resultative Construction: From the Perspective of Lexicalization (in Chinese). Linguistic Sciences, no. 1, 40-47 (2007)

15. Dong, X.: Lexicalization (in Chinese). The Commercial Press, Beijing (2011)

16. Wang, L.: A Sketch of Chinese Grammar (in Chinese). New Knowledge Press, Shanghai (1957)

17. Feng, S.: On prosodic words in Chinese (in Chinese). Social Science in China, no. 1, 161-176 (1996)

18. Feng, S.: A formal analysis of the origin of VR-constructions in Chinese (in Chinese). Linguistic Forum, vol. 26, 178-208 (2002)

19. Feng, S.: Interactions between Morphology, Syntax and Prosody in Chinese (enlarged) (in Chinese). Peking University Press, Beijing (2009)

20. Huang, M. & Feng, S.: The syntactic distribution of the monosyllabic words used in disyllabic templates. Studies of the Chinese language, no. 1, 32-44 (2009)

21. Shi, D.: On the syntactic status of compounds and phrases (in Chinese). Research and Exploration of Chinese Grammar, vol. 11, 35-51. The Commercial Press, Beijing (2002)

22. Levin, B. & Rappaport Hovav, M.: Unaccusativity at the Syntax-Lexical Semantics Interface. The MIT Press, Cambridge, MA (1995)

23. Zhuang, H.: The Prosodic History of Chinese Resultatives, Language and Linguistics, vol. 15, pp. 575-595 (2014)

24. Selkirk, E.: The Syntax of Words. MIT Press, Cambridge, MA (1982)

25. Fabb, N.: Syntactic Affixation. Doctoral Dissertation, MIT (1984)

26. Di Sciullo, A. & Williams, E.: On the Definition of Word. MIT Press, Cambridge, MA (1987)

27. Sadock, J. M.: The autolexical classification of lexemes. Theoretical Morphology, ed. by M. Hammond, & M. Noonan, pp. 271-290. Academic, New York (1991)

28. Packard, J.: The Morphology of Chinese. Cambridge University Press, Cambridge (2004)

29. Cui, S.: Ionization and Nucleus Stress (in Chinese). Chinese Language Learning, no. 5, 62-68 (2008)

Part II The Syntax-Semantics Interface

The formation of the "NP1$_{exp}$+V+NP2" construction in Chinese

Mengbin Liu*

School of Foreign Languages, Sun Yat-sen University,
No. 135, Xingang Xi Road, Guangzhou, 510275, P. R. China
greatruth@hotmail.com

Abstract. In this paper, I discuss the formation of the "NP1$_{exp}$+V+NP2" construction from the perspective of historical development and formal syntax. I argue that the "NP1$_{exp}$+V+NP2" construction comes from a morphological or lexical causative construction and has a competitive relationship with the causative constructions in the process of the historical development of Chinese. The "V+NP$_{theme}$" constructions are actually two-place unaccusative sentences with omitted causer or experiencer. Only the "NP$_{theme}$+V" construction is the real one-place unaccusative construction in which the NP$_{theme}$ generates in the object position in deep structure and moves to the subject position in surface structure because of case requirement.

Keywords: The "NP1$_{exp}$+V+NP2" construction; Chinese; Syntax; Historical development

1 Introduction

In this paper, I discuss the formation of the "NP1$_{exp}$+V+NP2$_{theme}$" construction from the perspective of historical development and formal syntax. As shown in (1) and (2).

(1) 王冕死了父親
    wangmian si   le fuqin
    Wangmian die Prt father
    "Wangmian's father died."

(2) 李奶奶瞎了一隻眼
    linainai   xia le yi zhi yan
    Linainai blind Prt one CL eye
    "One of Linainai's eyes is blind."

In (1), the first argument NP1 *Wangmian* 王冕 is an experiencer and the second argument NP2 *fuqin* 父親 "father" is a theme. The verb *si* 死 "die" express non-volitional meaning and it is an unaccusative verb. In (2), NP1 *Linainai* 李奶奶 is an experiencer and NP2 *yan* 眼 "eye" is a theme. The verb *xia* 瞎 "blind" is an unaccusative verb.

© Springer International Publishing AG 2016
M. Dong et al. (Eds.): CLSW 2016, LNAI 10085, pp. 139–148, 2016
DOI: 10.1007/978-3-319-49508-8_14

Xu [1] was one of the first linguists to put forward this construction. Since 1990s, it has been a very hot issue in the Chinese studies. I first briefly summarize previous studies, comment on them and then provide my analysis.

2   Previous studies

Most studies on this construction have been done from a generative perspective. Only a few of them are from cognitive and historical perspectives.

For those studies from generative grammar, linguists focus on the derivation of the structure. Almost all of their analyses are based on the Unaccusative Hypothesis, and there are three different ways in terms of derivation. Details are shown below.

First, based on the systematic description of Guo [2] and Xu [3], Han [4] and Wen and Chen [5] argue that the structure of "NP1$_{exp}$+V+NP2$_{theme}$" is derived from the movement of the possessor in the object position to the subject position. What is debated most is the motivation of movement. As criticized in previous studies, these analyses are problematic because of the existence of sentences with definite NP as object and sentences with indefinite NP as subject [6,7].

I argue that these analyses lack independent syntactic evidence. The biggest problem is that a sentence like *diaole Zhangsan de liangke menya* 掉了張三的兩顆門牙 "missed Zhangsan's two incisors" itself is ungrammatical. There is a lack of independent syntactic evidence for it to be the deep structure of *Zhangsan diaole liangke menya* 張三掉了兩顆門牙 "two incisors of Zhangsan missed".

Second, Pan and Han [6], [8, 9] and Zhuang [10] propose that NP1$_{exp}$ should be analyzed as the topic rather than the subject. According to Pan and Han [8], the object NP2 is generated by extraposition and it undergoes movement twice. For example, in *zhangsan sile fuqin* 張三死了父親 "Zhangsan's father died", *Zhangsan* 張三 stands in the topic position. The object *fuqin* 父親 "father" moves to the subject position for case requirement and then is extraposed to the end of the sentence because of new information requirement.

As pointed out in Han and Pan [9], the extraposition analysis is problematic. We have to explain why in the unergative sentences, like *zhangsan, fuqin tiaowu* 張三,父親跳舞 "Zhangsan, his father dances", the subject cannot be extraposed to the end of the sentence. What is more, I consider that problems may also exist for the NP$_{exp}$ to be analyzed as the topic. One important reason is that a quantified phrase normally cannot stand in the topic position. For example, the sentence *san dao wu ge ren wo jiao guo* 三到五个人我教过 "I taught three to five people" is bad. However, the sentence *san dao wu ge ren si le fuqin* 三到五个人死了父亲 "Three to five people lost their fathers" is good. It is assumed to be as bad as the former sentence if *San dao wu ge ren* 三到五个人 "Three to five people" also behaves as the topic.

Third, Zhu [11], Huang [12] and Zhang [13] argue that NP1$_{exp}$ is a base-generated subject. In Zhang's [13] analysis, a light verb EXP is involved in the causative constructions. Their analyses noticed the relationship between the causative construction and the experience construction, which enlightens my study. However, the case problem is still not solved, because the inherent case proposed in Huang [12] requires the object to be indefinite, but in Chinese there can be definite objects, such as *wo diu le na ben shu* 我丢了那本書 "I lost that book". Zhang [13] argues that the object gets case from the light verb EXP, but no independent evidence is given.

As for the studies from cognitive and historical perspectives, although most of the analyses lack independent syntactic evidence, their description and analyses are enlightening and also abundant data are provided [7], [14,15,16,17,18,19].

It is necessary to mention that both Shi [17] and Liu [18] have noticed the close relationship between the causative constructions and "NP1exp+V+NP2theme" construction. As I discuss in the next section, a close relationship between causatives and experience construction does exist.

3   My analysis

In this section, I will focus on the relationship between the causative construction and the "NP1$_{exp}$+V+NP2" construction. Enlightened by Zhu [11], Huang [12] and Zhang [13]'s analyses, I investigate the relationship between the causative construction and "NP$_{exp}$+V+NP2" from historical perspective. I argue that the "NP1$_{exp}$+V+NP2" construction comes from a morphological or lexical causative construction and has a competitive relationship with the causative constructions in the process of historical development of Chinese.

Pieces of evidence are given below to support my argument.

(i) The existence of middle argument experiencer. Huang[1] [12] argues that in three-place unaccusative constructions, a middle argument experiencer exists. I find that in Archaic Chinese when verbs are used in three-place causative constructions, the middle argument experiencer definitely exists, as illustrated below.

(3)   (敬仲)飲桓公酒。（《左傳·莊公22年》）
  jingzhong yin huangong jiu   [Zuo Zhuan. Zhuanggong 22 Nian]
  Jingzhong drink Huangong wine
  "Jingzhong made Huangong drink wine."

(4)   及食大夫黿（《左傳·宣公4年》）
  ji   si   dafu   bie [Zuo Zhuan. Xuangong 4 Nian]
  wait eat official turtle
  "When treating the official with cooked turtle, he called Zigong to come but didn't give him any."

---

[1] Huang claims that all verbs in Mandarin Chinese can be divided into unergative type and unaccusative type. Transitive verbs (such as *da* 打 "beat", *ma* 罵 "scold" and *xie* 寫 "write") are two-place unergative verbs and three-place rob-type verbs (such as *bo* 剝 "peel", *ti* 踢 "kick" and *qiang* 搶 "rob") are three-place unergative verbs. Causative verbs (such as *kai* 開 "open", *guan* 關 "close", *chen* 沉 "sink" and *xia* 嚇 "frighten") are two-place unaccusative verbs and three-place give-type verbs (such as *song* 送 "send" and *gei* 給 "give") are three-place causative and unaccusative verbs.

In (3)-(4), the two nouns after the verb are obviously not possessive NPs. They are causative constructions. Verbs *yin* 飲 "drink" and *si* 食 "feed" are all pronounced in the fourth tone. It is claimed that the fourth tone in Archaic Chinese comes from the *s-* prefix which morphologically marks the causative verb [20,21]. I argue that in this kind of causative construction, a light verb EXP also exists. The reason is that when the transitive verb is used here, the transitivity is decreased. The external argument of the verb is no longer the volitional agent but the experiencer whose behaviour is forced or caused by something else. Therefore, *Huangong* 桓公 and *dafu* 大夫 "the official" in (3) and (4) are middle arguments. The deep structure of (3) should be as follows:

(5)

As seen from (5), the existence of three-place causative construction and middle argument provides the foundation for forming the "NP1$_{exp}$+V+NP2" construction.

(ii) Since a causative construction involves three arguments: the cause, the experiencer and the theme, it is possible to form a two-place construction with experiencer and patient if the causer does not appear. As for the transitive verb, because of its strong transitivity and agentivity, it involves two arguments, the agent and the patient. As for an intransitive unaccusative verb like *lai* 來 "come", it normally involves only one argument: the theme. In some cases, an experiencer or causer or both arguments can be introduced. I argue that a competitive relationship exists between the experiencer and the causer. The reason is that the causer and experiencer are not inherent arguments of the one-place unaccusative verb argument structure. They are introduced by adding argument at the syntactic level, and the argument is not randomly introduced. Jackendoff [22] proposes the Thematic Hierarchy in which the agent is the most prominent to stand in the subject position and the experiencer is next, as shown in (6) below.

(6) Thematic Hierarchy:
    (Agent (Experiencer (Goal/Source/Location (Theme))))

However, as claimed in Grimshaw [23], Aspectual Hierarchy can override Thematic Hierarchy. The Aspectual Hierarchy is given in (7).

(7)   Aspectual Hierarchy: (Cause (other (…)))

Therefore, as for an intransitive unaccusative verb, if a causer is introduced and stands in the subject position, the experiencer argument is then suppressed. For example, in *taifeng chen le wo yitiaochuan* 颱風沉了我一條船 "The typhoon caused one of my boat to sink", because the causer *taifeng* 颱風 "typhoon" stands in the subject position, the experiencer *wo* 我 "I" is suppressed and appears after the verb. The sentence is then structurally ambiguous. *Wo* 我 "I" may be analyzed as the Experiencer or the possessor. To avoid ambiguity, a light verb *shi* 使 "cause" may be used, as illustrated in (8) below.

(8)   颱風使我沉了一條船。
      taifeng shi wo chen le yi tiao chuan
      typhoon cause me sink Prt a CL boat
      "The typhoon caused me to lose a boat."

As predicted, in the "NP1$_{exp}$+V+NP2" construction, if the experiencer stands in the subject position; the causer or the causing event can be in a higher topic position or in another clause, as illustrated below.

(9)   魯亡叔孫必亡邾,邾君亡國,將焉歸?(《左傳·昭公22年》)
      lu wang shusun bi wang zhu, [Zuo Zhuan. Zhaogong 22 Nian]
      Lu lose Shusun must perish Zhu
      zhu jun wang guo,   jiang yan gui?
      Zhu king perish country will where back
      "Lu will perish Zhu if they don't have Shusun. Where would the king of Zhu go if he lost his country?"

In (9), *Zhujun* 邾君 stands in the subject position, and the causing event is in the preceding clause.

Therefore, I conclude that the competitive relationship between the causer and the experiencer determines which construction is the prominent one in a language. Since the Aspect Hierarchy can override the Thematic Hierarchy, it is natural that the causative construction should be the prominent one if a language has abundant causative morphology.

(iii) The ambiguities of "V+NP$_{theme}$" construction.

As discussed above, the "V+NP$_{theme}$" construction may be ambiguous between the causative meaning and experience meaning[2], as shown below.

(10)剛柔相推而生變化。（《易經·繫辭上傳》）
      gang rou xiang tui er sheng bianhua [Yi Jing. Xi Ci 16 Nian]
      strong soft each push and arise change
      "The strong and the soft push each other and the changes arise."
(11)隕石于宋五,隕星也。（《左傳·僖公 16 年》）

---

[2] The environment is referred to as personified experiencer in this paper.

yun shi yu song wu, yun xing ye [Zuo Zhuan. Xigong 16 Nian]
fall stone in Song five fall star Prt
"In the spring of 16, five stones fell in Song. Those are falling stars."

Since the subject position is empty, (10) and (11) can be understood as either omitting a causer or omitting an environment role. In (10), *gang rou xiang tui* 剛柔相推 "The strong and the soft push each other" should be the causer and the environment role may be *tiandi* 天地 "the world". In (11), there may exist some force which caused the falling of star and the environment role may be *tian* 天 "the sky".

Such ambiguities show the competitive relationship between the causer and the experiencer. If the causer doesn't take the subject position, the experiencer should be free to stand there.

Such ambiguity also exits in Mandarin Chinese. As shown in (12), the omitted subject may be the causer *dafeng* 大風 "wind" or the experiencer *wo* 我 "I".

(12) 沉了一條船。
chen le yi tiao chuan
sink Prt one CL ship
"A ship sank."

In some cases of Mandarin Chinese, no ambiguity exists, as illustrated below.

(13) a. 委屈你了。
weiqu ni le
wrong you Prt
"Let you feel wronged."
b. 這件事情委屈你了。
zhe jian shiqing weiqu ni le
this CL thing wronged you Prt
"This made you feel wronged"
(14) a. 來了一個客人。
lai le yi ge keren
come Asp one CL guest
"A guest came."
b. 我來了一個客人。
wo lai Asp yi ge keren
I come Prt one CL guest
"One of my guests came."

In (13a), obviously the omitted argument is the causer, as shown in (13b). In (14a), the omitted argument is the experiencer, as shown in (14b).

As seen above, although the surface structure is the same, the deep structure may be different. It can be verified that in Archaic Chinese, all the "V+NP$_{theme}$" constructions can be understood as omitting an experiencer or a causer. This is also true in Mandarin Chinese.

Therefore, the problem of why in Mandarin Chinese "V+NP$_{theme}$" construction (like *laile yige ren* 來了一個人 "There comes a man") the NP$_{theme}$ does not need to move to the subject position can now be solved. The reason lies in the fact that an implicit experiencer or causer is always involved. That is to say, in Chinese, no matter whether Archaic Chinese or Mandarin, only the "NP$_{theme}$+V" construction (like *yige ren laile* 一個人來了 "A man Came") is the true one-place unaccusative construction, in which the NP is the only argument and moves from the deep object position to the subject position for case requirement. The essential similarity between the "V+NP$_{theme}$" construction and the "NP$_{theme}$+V" construction lies in that the NP$_{theme}$ occupies the object position in the deep structure. Their difference lies in that the former one involves an omitted experiencer or causer but the later one does not. What is more, the NP$_{theme}$ should satisfy different requirements for it to stand in the subject position or object position in surface structure.

(iv) The historical development of causative constructions and experience constructions in Chinese. In Archaic Chinese, the synthetic causative construction is prominent. As a result, the experience construction was ignored in almost all the studies before. As discussed in Yang and Wu [16], some sentences are much better analyzed as experience constructions, as shown below.

> (15)宋師敗績，公傷股。（《左傳·僖公 22 年》）
> song shi baiji, gong shang gu [Zuo Zhuan. Xigong 22 Nian]
> Song troop fail   Gong hurt leg
> "Song is defeated and Gong got his leg hurt."
> (16)仲尼聞之，出涕曰（《左傳·昭公 20 年》）
> zhongni wen zhi, chu ti yue [Zuo Zhuan. Zhaogong 20 Nian]
> Zhongni hear it   out tear say
> "Zhongni heard it. Tears came down and he said..."

In the traditional literature [24], sentences like (15) and (16) are defined as special kind of causative constructions. Such sentences also exist in Mandarin Chinese. Yang [25] points out that sentences like *ta hongle lian* 他紅了臉 "He blushed" look like causative constructions but actually are experience constructions.

It turns out that experience constructions are rare in Archaic Chinese. I argue that one of the most important reasons for this is that the causative construction in Archaic Chinese is very prominent. In Archaic Chinese, the causative morphology is abundant. Nouns, intransitive verbs and transitive verbs can all be causativized. A causer rather than an experiencer is frequently introduced to the subject position. Therefore, the experiencer is frequently suppressed and the experience constructions are rare.

However, as Chinese developed, the amount of synthetic causative sentences gradually decreased while on the other hand, experience sentences increased. In Mandarin Chinese, there are many more experience sentences than synthetic causative sentences. I argue that there are at least two reasons for this. The most important is the decline of causative morphology. The second is the historical development of the "Num+CL+Noun" phrase in Chinese. As we know, if the object is definite, then the sentence tends to express causative meaning, and if the object is indefinite, then the sentence tends to express experience meaning. In Mandarin Chinese, the indefinite "Num+CL+Noun" phrases are abundant and they are frequently used in the object position, which may greatly increase the possibility of forming experience constructions.

(v) Cross-linguistic evidence. The situation in English is consistent with my argument. Zhang [13] argues that in English the corresponding expressions of the experience sentences in Chinese cannot be found. Zhang argues that this is because in English the light verb EXP does not exist. However, I find the light verb EXP does exist in English, as illustrated below.

> (17)a. I lost my car.
>   b.我丢了我的車。
>   wo diu le wo de che
>   I lose Prt my Prt car
>   "I lost my car."

In (17), both *lost* in English and *diu* 丢 "lost" in Chinese express weak volitional sense and the subjects should be experiencers. This shows that in English the light verb EXP also exists. The question then is that if the light verb EXP does exist in English, why the sentence *Wangmian died his father* is bad. I consider that the lack of experience construction in English is due to the existence of a great deal of synthetic causative constructions. Causative morphemes such as *-en* and *-ize* are abundant. That is to say, for an intransitive unaccusative verb in English, a causer rather than an experiencer is frequently introduced in subject position. Therefore, the experience construction is seldom used.

4   Conclusion

Therefore, I conclude from the above discussion that the "NP1$_{exp}$+V+NP2" construction comes from the synthetic causative construction and has a competitive relationship with the causative constructions in the process of the historical development of Chinese. The "V+NP$_{theme}$" construction is a two-place unaccusative construction with omitted causer or experiencer. Only "NP$_{theme}$+V" construction is a true one-place unaccusative construction in which the NP$_{theme}$ generates in the object position in deep structure and moves to the subject position in surface structure because of case requirement. The essential similarity between the "V+NP$_{theme}$" construction and the "NP$_{theme}$+V" construction lies in that the NP$_{theme}$ occupies the object position in the deep structure in both constructions. Their difference lies in that the former one involves an omitted experiencer or causer but the later one does not. What is more, the NP$_{theme}$ should satisfy different requirements for it to stand in the subject position or object position in surface structure. This analysis is consistent with the Unaccusative Hypothesis proposed by Perlmutter [26].

As for the case problem of the in-situ object of unaccusative verbs, I consider that since this problem also exists in English and it is not much relevant to the main topic of this paper, so I leave it open for further discussions in the future.

Acknowledgments. I would like to express my gratitude to Hsin I Hsieh, Chu-Ren Huang, Jie Xu and Jingxia Lin for their valuable comments and suggestions at the 2016 meeting of Chinese Lexical Semantic Workshop. I benefited a lot from discussing the idea and details of my analysis with Paul.S.Law, Haihua Pan and Liejiong Xu in City University of Hong Kong.

References

1. Xu, Z. Ren.: "Wangmian's father died" [*Wangmian si le fuqin*]. Chinese Knowledge [*Yuwen zhishi*](9), 34-38 (1956) [In Chinese]
2. Guo, J. M.: Possesor-subject and possessum-object constructions [*Lingshu zhubin ju*]. Studies of Chinese Language [*Zhongguo Yuwen*](1), 24-29 (1990) [In Chinese]
3. Xu, J.: Two kinds of retained object constructions and theoretical issues [*Liangzhong baoliu binyu jushi ji xiangguan jufa lilun wenti*]. Modern Linguistics[*Dangdai yuyanxue*]1(1), 16-29 (1999) [In Chinese]
4. Han, J. Q.: A Study of Possessor Raising Movement in relation to Case Theory [*Lingyou mingci tisheng yiwei yu ge lilun*]. Modern Foreign Languages [*Xiandai waiyu*]23(3), 261-272 (2000) [In Chinese]
5. Wen, B. L., Chen, Z. L: A MP Approach to Possessor Raising in Chinese [*Lingyou mingci yiwei: jiyu MP de fenxi*]. Modern Foreign Languages [*Xiandai waiyu*]24(4), 412-416 (2001) [In Chinese]
6. Pan, H. H., Han, J. Q: The Syntax of Surface Unaccusative Constructions [*Xianxing fei binge dongci jiegou de jufa yanjiu*]. Studies in Language and Linguistics [*Yuyan yanjiu*]25(3), 1-13 (2005) [In Chinese]
7. Shen, J. X: The Generative Mechanism of Sentences like "Wangmian si le fuqin" [*"wangmian si le fuqin" de shengcheng fangshi*]. Studies of Chinese Language [*Zhongguo yuwen*](4), 291-300 (2006) [In Chinese]
8. Pan, H. H., Han, J. Q.: The Syntactic Mechanism of Retained Object Constructions in Chinese [*Hanyu baoliu binyu jiegou de jufa shengcheng jizhi*]. Studies of Chinese Language [*Zhongguo yuwen*](4), 511-522 (2008) [In Chinese]
9. Han, J. Q., Pan, H. H.: A Minimalist Account of the Syntactic Derivation of Chinese Retained Object Constructions [*Hanyu baoliu binyu jiegou jufa shengcheng de zui jian fenxi*]. Language Teaching and Linguistic Studies [*Yuwen jiaoxue yu yanjiu*](3), 41-53 (2016) [In Chinese]
10. Zhuang, H. B.: On the Construction "Wangmian si le fuqin": An Account Based on the Split CP Hypothesis [*"Wangmian si le fuqin" jushi de CP fenlie jiashuo jieshi*]. Foreign Language and Literature Studies [*Waiguo yuyan wenxue*](3), 242-250 (2013) [In Chinese]

11. Zhu, X. F.: Light Verb Syntax of Intransitives containing Objects [*Qing dongci he hanyu bu jiwu dongci dai binyu xianxiang*]. Modern Foreign Languages [*Xiandai waiyu*]28(3), 221-231 (2005) [In Chinese]

12. Huang, C. T.: Thematic Structures of Verbs in Chinese and their Syntactic Projections [*Hanyu dongci de tiyuan jiegou yu qi jufa biaoxian*]. Lingui(4), 511-522 (2008) [In Chinese]stic Sciences [*Yuyan kexue*]6(4), 3-21 (2007) [In Chinese]

13. Zhang, H.: Difference among the Object In-situ Constructions in Mandarin Chinese. In: Xiao, Y., Smithfield (eds.) Proceedings of the 21st North American Conference on Chinese Linguistics, Island: Bryant University, Vol.2, pp. 417-435 (2009)

14. Shen, J. X.: The Logical Order and the Historical Sequence [*Luoji xianhou he lishi xianhou*]. Journal of Foreign Languages [*Waiguoyu*]31(5), 91-92 (2008) [In Chinese]

15. Yu, L. M., Lü, J. J.: A Historical Study about "Wangmian's father died" [*"Wangmian si le fuqin" ju de lishi kaocha*]. Studies of Chinese Language [*Zhongguo yuwen*](1), 32-42 (2011) [In Chinese]

16. Yang, Z. L., Wu, F. X.: Possesor-subject and possessum-object constructions in Ancient Chinese [*Xianqin hanyu zhong de ling zhu shu bin ju*]. Studies of Historical Linguistics [*Lishi yuyanxue yanjiu*](8), 70-79 (2014) [In Chinese]

17. Shi,Y. Z.: On Evidence of Linguistic Hypothesis [*Yuyanxue jiashe zhong de zhengju wenti*]. Linguistic Sciences [*Yuyan kexue*]6(4), 39-51 (2007) [In Chinese]

18. Liu, X. L.: Remarks about the Generation of "Wangmian's father died" [*Ye tan "wangmian si le fuqin" de shengcheng fangshi*]. Studies of Chinese Language [*Zhongguo yuwen*](5), 440-443 (2007) [In Chinese]

19. Shuai, Z. G.: The Evolution Process and Mechanisms of "Wangmian's father died" [*"Wangmian si le fuqin" de yansheng guocheng he jizhi*]. Linguistic Sciences [*Yuyan kexue*]7(3), 259-269 (2008) [In Chinese]

20. Mei, T. L.: Chronological Strata in Derivation by Tone Change [*Sisheng bieyi de shijian cengci*]. Studies of Chinese Language [*Zhongguo yuwen*](6), 427-443 (1980)

21. Mei, T. L: The Origin of Voicing Alternation in Old Chinese Verbs [*Shanggu hanyu dongci zhuo qing bieyi de laiyuan*]. Minority Languages of China [*Minzu yuwen*](3), 3-20 (2008) [In Chinese]

22. Jackendoff, R.: Semantic Interpretation in Generative Grammar. Cambridge, MA: MIT Press (1972)

23. Grimshaw, J.: Argument Structure. Cambridge, Mass: MIT Press (1990)

24. Li, Z. F.: Intransitive Verbs and Their Causative Use in Archaic Chinese [*Xianqin hanyu de zidongci jiqi shidong yongfa*]. Linguistics Series [*Yuyanxue luncong*](10), 117-144 (1983) [In Chinese]

25. Yang, S. Y.: The Unaccusative Phenomenon: a study on the relationship between syntax and semantics [*Cong fei binge dongci xianxiang kan yuyi ju jufa jiegou zhi jian de guanxi*]. Modern Linguistics [*Dangdai yuyanxue*]1(1), 30-43 (1999) [In Chinese]

26. Perlmutter, D.: Impersonal Passives and the Unaccusative Hypothesis. In: Proceedings of the 4th Annual Meeting of the Berkeley Linguistics Society, pp.157-190 (1978)

Chinese Word Order Analysis
Based on Binary Dependency Relationships[1]

Yan He, Yang Liu,

Key Laboratory of Computational Linguistics (Peking Uninversity), Ministry of Education,
No.5 Yiheyuan Road, Haidian District, Beijing 100871, China
from.heyan@163.com, liuyang@pku.edu.cn

Abstract. Based on binary dependency relationships of notional words, this paper presents a calculating method of word order and a representation scheme as well. Calculations of sentence examples show that the binary dependency relationship product of SOV, OSV etc. may be turned into the semantic structure of SVO. Therefore, SVO is not only the simplest but also the complete structure of Chinese sentences. Also, modifier-core structure prevents the formation of a sentence, which intends to express more content. From this perspective, SVO order and the disharmony between VO and PPV, are the same law in two opposite ways.

Keywords: Binary dependency relationship, Semantic diagram of waveform, Order calculation, Function of subordinate structures.

1 Introduction

Word order research is one of the most important areas of modern linguistics, especially in linguistic typology. Most languages in the world are divided into six types by Greenberg [1] SOV, SVO, VSO, VOS, OVS, OSV. There is no final conclusion of Chinese word order type yet [2] [3]: Some researchers, such as Shou-hsin Teng, Chauncey C. Chu, Kuang Mei, Meng-Zhen Li, thought that Chinese word order is SVO; Some researchers, such as James H-Y. Tai, C.N Li, Shuan-fa Huang, thought that Chinese word order is SOV; Jin Li-xin thought that Chinese is a mixture of SVO and SOV languages; Some others regarded SSV as the basic sentence pattern in Chinese. In fact, in Chinese, we can observe sentences in a variety of word orders.

(1) SVO:我吃完饭了。
(2) SOV: 我把饭吃完了。
(3) OVS: 一床被盖三个人。
(4) OSV: 一床被三个人盖。
(5) SSV: 他心地善良。

---

[1] This paper is supported by the National Basic Research Program of China (No. 2014CB340504) and the major project of National Social Science fund of China (No. 12&ZD119).

© Springer International Publishing AG 2016
M. Dong et al. (Eds.): CLSW 2016, LNAI 10085, pp. 149–158, 2016
DOI: 10.1007/978-3-319-49508-8_15

(6) VOS: 吃苹果吧, 你!

(7) VSO: 吃你苹果, 少废话！

There are some parameters to help the judgement of word order, such as prepositions, postpositions, the sequence order of the head noun and the genitive phrase or the head noun and the modifiers etc. Lappola pointed out that the word order in Chinese is not harmonious, because there is not only head-initial (such as verb + object), but also head-final (such as genitive/modifiers + verb) in Chinese. The non-harmony derived from Chinese historical change -- with a view to PP placed after the verb in the past and before the verb nowadays [4]. So, what is the reason of the non-harmony?

Based on the practice of semantic role labeling project of Peking University, this paper proposes a new semantic representation of Chinese sentences. We start from the binary dependency relationships in sentences, then investigate the simplest and complete semantic form of the Chinese sentences, which is corresponding to the word order of SVO. Other word orders, such as SOV and OSV, can be transformed into this form. So we can explain the non-harmony of the Chinese word order now: head-initial and head-final are two opposite directions, head-initial order makes the complete Chinese sentences, ending naturally, while head-final order makes the phrases, part of Chinese sentences, by blocking the complete semantic form. So head-initial and head-final follow the same semantic rule: head-initial keeps the complete semantic form, leading to a complete sentence, head-final destroys the complete semantic form, leading to enlarge the sentence by making itself to be a phrase. These two follow the law of excluded middle, just like two sides of a coin.

2   Semantic Representation of a Sentence

This paper comes from the research of the 973 project undertaken by the Institute of Computational Linguistics, Peking University. One of the tasks is to identify the predicates of a sentence and annotate the semantic roles of their related arguments.

2.1   Background

Zhan Weidong [5] drafted *The Specification of Semantic Roles Annotation*. He pointed out, "when starting to do semantic analysis and annotation of large scale real text in modern Chinese, we take the strategy of layering, rendering layer by layer. At the first stage, the project aims at annotating the basic propositional meaning of sentence. Firstly, label the Predicate-Argument Structure, analyze the semantic relationship between predicative components and substantive components of sentences systematically." According to the specification, we labelled 10623 sentences from the machine translation corpus [6]. For more details, please refer to *The Recognition and Practice of Semantic Roles Annotation* by Yu Shiwen [7].

In the annotation, verbs are central. One example of the labelling results is as the following:

(8) 老师来迟了是不平常的。

[%施事 老师 %] [# 来 #] 迟 了 是 不 平常 的 。

[%VP 当事 老师 来 %] [# 迟 #] 了 是 不 平常 的 。

[%VP 当事 老师 来 迟 了 %] [# 是 #] [%AP 系事 不 平常 的 %] 。

[%VP 当事 老师 来 迟 了 %] 是 不 [# 平常 #] 的 。

Based on the results, 1,000 sentences are further tagged as semantic diagram of waveform, a kind of simplified scheme of binary dependency relationships. This tagging process will be described below.

2.2   Definition of Binary Dependency Relationships

We believe that Binary Dependency Relationship is the relationship between a verb and a noun, or between two nouns, which is equivalent to "phrase" in Zhu Dexi's works [8]. In this paper, in order to simplify this issue, we limit Binary Dependency Relationships to the relationships between the verb and the subject, or the verb and the object, namely the relationship between verb and its eight roles (agent, experiencer, relative, patient, dative, result, content and target).

2.3   The Simplified Scheme of Binary Dependency Relationships

In Chinese, the way phrase formed by words is the same as the way sentence formed by phrase. Shen Jiaxuan regarded [9], "The composition is not only an important way for Chinese word formation, but also an important way for Chinese sentence formation. Chinese word formation and Chinese sentence formation follow the same law. Both are the integration of concepts or words." The "composition" is defined as "connection" in Chinese dictionary, and can be defined as "multiplication" in mathematics. The combination relation between two binary dependency relationships is corresponding to combination relation between two phrases in traditional grammatical syntax. In this paper, for the purpose of studying word order, we define the semantic connection between two or more binary dependency relationships as "Vector Multiplication".

For agentive sentence, we define the binary dependency relationship ended by verb or adjective as "up-going relationship", the binary dependency relationship ended by entity role or event role as "down-going relationship". For non-volitional sentence, we define the binary dependency relationship between non-volitional verb and experiencer or relative as "parallel relation". Furthermore, the parallel relation is regarded as a kind of special case of up-going relation or down-going relation, which will be detailed in another paper.

The following table illustrates these simplified relations.

Table 1. The Simplified Scheme of Binary Dependency Relationships

Up-going	Down-going	Parallel
Agent + verb	Verb + patient	Experiencer + verb
Experiencer + adj.	Verb + dative	Verb + relative
	Verb + target	
	Verb + result	
	Verb + content	

2.4   Turn sentence to semantic diagram of waveform

Usually, there are several verbs in a Chinese sentence. By simplified scheme, we turn a sentence to a semantic diagram of waveform. Next, we will show the transformation process by an example.

(9) 已经 出门 的 你 怎么 会 知道 查 煤气 的 人 来 过 了 ?

Step1, Extract word pairs of binary dependency relationships, as following:
(出门,你),(你,知道),(知道,查煤气的人来过了),(查,煤气),(查,人),(查煤气的人,来)

Step2, Determine the word pair's semantic diagram is Up-going or Down-going (Up and Down for short), and judge if the word pair's syntactic word order and the word pair's semantic order are agreed in simplified scheme. There are two directions of a binary dependency relationship, one is the syntactic word order in the sentence, another is the logic order of the semantic relation in Chinese. For example, (查,人) is the syntactic order, while according to the logic order of the semantic relation, (查,人) should be (人,查) , because "agent + verb" is the rightful semantic order. If the syntactic word order of a binary dependency relationship is agreed with its semantic order, we think that its direction is positive going. Positive going includes up positive going and down positive going. If a binary dependency relationship's direction is positive, we do not label extra marks on the semantic diagram of waveform. If the syntactic word order of a binary dependency relationship is not agreed with its semantic order, we think that its direction is negative. Negative going includes up negative going and down negative going. If a binary dependency relationship's direction is negative, we add " ↓ " to the simplified form of the binary dependency relationship. So we have the simplified semantic form of word pairs like this:

```
Up↓, Up, Down, Down, Up↓, Up
```

Step3, Turn the whole sentence to the semantic diagram of waveform, as the following:

```
# Up%(Up↓) *down%(Up%(#down *Up↓#))#
```

"#...#" means two binary dependency relationship share one predicate; "%(...)" means the subordinate binary dependency relationship nested inside the bracket; "↓" means negative going; "*" means "multiply".

Now we have semantic diagram of waveforms of 1,000 sentences. Some more examples are given below.

Table 2. Semantic diagram of waveform and Example Sentences

Semantic diagram of waveform	Example sentences	Word pairs
Up	你 能不能 等 五 分钟 ？	(你,等)
Down ↓	比赛 肯定 已经 被 取消 了 。	(比赛,取消)
# Up *Down #	老人们 从没 见 过 火车 。	(老人,见),(见,火车)
#Up *Down%(#Up *Down #) #	你 知道 他 在 等 谁 吗 ？	(你,知道),(知道,他 在 等 谁 吗),(他,等),(等,谁)
# Down ↓ *Up #	那个 文件 首先 由 秘书 处理 。	(文件,处理),(由秘书,处理)
#Up *Down&O # *Up&S ↓	他 打 碎 了 玻璃 。	(他,打),(打,玻璃),(玻璃,碎)
# Up *Down&O# *U p&s *Up&S	工厂 派 他们 出国 学习 。	(工厂,派),(派,他们),(他们,出国),(他们,学习)
#Up&S *Down # *Up&S	阿珍 他们 吃 完 饭 散步 去 了 。	(阿珍 他们,吃),(吃,饭),(阿珍 他们,散步)

"&" means the subject or object of a binary dependency relationship is the subject or object of another binary dependency relationship. The letter behind the "&" indicates that it is a subject or an object in the word pair.

2.5 The function of semantic diagram of waveform

As mentioned before, there are two kinds of order information included in the semantic diagram of waveform. One is the syntactic word order, and another is the logic semantic order. The syntactic order is obviously known, while the usual logical semantic order is also known. For a sentence, sometime the two kinds of orders match well, sometimes the two kinds of orders cross to each other. The information of the sentence order can be used to calculate the semantic, and the information of logical semantic order will be helpful to judge the word order type.

In section 3, We will use the semantic diagram of waveform to judge Chinese word order type, from phenomena to concrete sentence examples. Examples will illustrate that the word order of SOV, OSV, VOS can be converted to the order of SVO through the semantic diagram of waveform. Although the examples are individual instances, their semantic diagram of waveforms are general forms of SOV, OSV and VOS, so the instances of common significance. The order of SVO, with inborn completeness in syntax and semantics, is corresponding to the simplest complete semantic form of a sentence.

Semantic diagram of waveform not only help us to draw the conclusion that Chinese word order is SVO, but also let us know the inevitable existence of modifier-core structure in Chinese. SVO order contains modifier-core order. We will discuss this point in section 4.

3   Simplest Complete Form of Sentence: The Order of SVO

Chinese word order is SVO. The conclusion is observed from phenomena in part 3.1, and illustrated by examples in part 3.2.

3.1   Phenomena

If we regard "parallel" as a special case of "Up-going" or "Down-going", there are only two kinds of binary dependency relationships, which are "Up-going" and "Down-going". There are four possible outcomes of binary combination of two relationships, which could be described as: {up-going * up-going}, {up-going * down-going}, {down-going * up-going}, {down-going * down-going}, while "*" refers to "multiply". These four types have appeared in Chinese. In these cases, {up-going * down-going} is the most common. If we regard a Chinese sentence as the combination of binary dependency relationship, it is very easy to find that {up-going * down-going} is the typical form of simple sentences in Chinese, and {up-going * down-going} in semantics is corresponding to SVO order in syntax.

3.2   Calculation and Conversion of word order

We put forward that the simplest complete semantic combination form of Chinese sentence is {up-going * down-going}, which is corresponding to structure of Subject Verb Object (SVO). The following example show how to change the sentences from their original semantic diagram of waveforms to "# up-going * down-going #" by calculation. Through the calculation, most Chinese sentences, such as SOV, OSV, VOS, could be changed into SVO order. Of course, some exceptional case appears, for instance, "吃你苹果吧！少废话！", whose semantic diagram of waveform is "# up-going ↓ * down-going #", which aims at expressing certain emotions.

Now, we have the calculation rules that "Up-going" and "Down-going" are two opposing semantic directions. For a binary dependency relationship, if its syntactic word order is consistent with its semantic order of semantic diagram of waveform, its direction value is "1", otherwise, its direction value is "-1". There are some words, such as prepositions, often changing the normal word order. For example, "我 把 苹 果 都 吃 了", the proposition "把" make the object "苹果" in front of the verb "吃". In this paper, a constant "c" is given to represent these words that change the normal word order.

Set:
S represents sentence
A represents Subject-Verb order
B represents Verb-Object order
Up abbreviation of up-going
Down abbreviation of down-going

Then,

if the Subject-Verb order is down-going, then $A\downarrow = -1 * A$

if the Verb-Object is up-going, then $B\downarrow = -1 * B$

$\# A * B \# = \# -1 * (B * A) \#$

$c * A = -1 * A$

$c * B = -1 * B$

The multiplication rule is for the composition of directions. The product rule is in table 3.

Table 3. The product rule

	1	-1
1	1	-1
-1	-1	1

We illustrate how the word order of SOV, OSV, VOS can be converted to the word order of SVO through the semantic diagram of waveform transformation on the semantic level.

(10) 历史 的 车轮 谁 也 不 能 阻挡 。

[%patient 历史 的 车轮 %] [%agent 谁 %] 也 不 能 [# 阻挡 #] 。

Waveform: $\# \text{Down}\downarrow * \text{Up} \#$

Calculation：

$B = ($历史 的 车轮, 阻挡$) = \text{Down}\downarrow = -1 * \text{Down}$

$A = ($谁，阻挡$) = \text{Up}$

$S = B * A = \# \text{down}\downarrow * \text{Up} \# = -1 * (\# \text{Up} * (-1 * \text{Down}) \#) = \# \text{Up} * \text{Down} \#$

(11) 读者 要 对 原文 中 的 内容 批判 地 使用 。

[%agent 读者 %] 要 [%content 对 原文 中 的 内容 %] 批判 地 [# 使用 #] 。

Waveform: $\# \text{Up}\downarrow * (c * \text{Down}\downarrow) \#$

Calculation：

$A = ($读者, 使用$) = \text{Up}$

$B = ($原文中的内容, 使用$) = \text{Down}\downarrow$

$c =$ proposition, "对"

$S = A * (c * B) = \# \text{Up} * (c * \text{Down}\downarrow) \#$

$= \# \text{Up} * (-1 * (-1) * \text{Down}) \#$

(12) 报告 这 一 事故 的 警察 认为 那 是 汤姆 的 错 。

[# 报告 #] [%content 这 一 事故 %] 的 [%agent 警察 %] 认为 内容 那 是 汤姆 的 错 。

Waveform: # Down * Up↓ #

Calculation:

Here the calculation is limited to "报告 这 一 事故 的 警察", if not included the proposition "的".

B= (报告, 这一事故) = Down

A= (报告, 警察) = Up↓

S=B*A= # Down* Up↓ # = # Down * (-1) * Up) #

= # (-1 * (-1) * Up * Down) #

= # Up * Down #

In the above examples, the word order of example (10) is OSV, the word order of example (11) is SOV, the word order of example (12) is VOS, and their semantic diagram of waveforms come to "# Up-going * Down-going #", which is corresponding to the word order of SVO. Example (10) and (11) are grammatical sentences, showing the syntactic and semantic completeness of waveform "# Up-going * Down-going #". Although the waveform of example (12) could be converted to the form of "# Up-going * Down-going #", it is not a sentence, but a phrase. The waveforms of example (10), (11) and (12) are all same, but they are different in grammar. Example (10) and (12) indicate that the functional words play an important role in the products of the waveforms. In the cases like example (10), if the object of a grammatical sentence is between the subject and the verb, propositions etc. must be used to generate the correct word order --- two negatives make a positive. In example (12), there is a proposition "的" between the agent and the verb. Because of the proposition "的" and the negative sequence of the Up-going order, the independent sentence of SVO order "警察 报告 这 一 事故" is turned to modifier-core structure. So, functional words will be take into account in the future research.

We conclude that the word order of Chinese simple sentence is SVO, which is determined by the binary Chinese semantic structure. The other word order can be converted to the order of SVO by semantic diagram of waveforms. In corpus, sentences are far from simple form. There are a variety of incompleteness, shift, cross connection and nesting of binary dependency relationships. How to understand and calculate these complex sentences is the succeeding work.

We lead to the following fourth part by example (12). It is changed from a subject-predicate structure to a modifier-core structure. In Chinese, the modifier (attributive and adverbial) precedes the head words, which means head is behind, and the verb precedes the object, which means head is front. They are inharmonious. Now we can say, the disharmony is inevitable result brought by the SVO word order. In other words, the modifier-core order is contained in the SVO order.

4   Supplement of SVO order: Taking Modifier-Core Order for Instance

According to the definition of Prof. Zhu Dexi, the phrase structure is binary, phrase nesting is not being included, modifier-core structure is composed of two parts -- the modifier and the head word, the head word appears after the modifier. The head word can be substantive or predicative. Relationship between nouns is not involved in this paper, all of our discussion is limited to the phrase with predicative modifier. But in terms of their function, since Prof. Zhu Dexi put the two kinds together, what he stressed is the change of word order, not the combination of various part of speeches. We think that the aim of the word order change is to push the limit, extend the semantic contents, either substantive or predicative phrase.

There are two kinds of modifier-core phrases: with the proposition "的" or without the proposition "的". The two kinds of modifier-core phrases are using different methods to achieve the same purpose.

Modifier-core phrase without the proposition "的" is the only phrase type which is in the opposite order of semantic order. For example, here are two phrases, "美丽 人生", "跳舞 鸟叔", "人生", "鸟叔" are subjects, "美丽", "跳舞" are predicates, the normal semantic forms are "人生 美丽", "鸟叔 跳舞", but as modifier-core phrases, "美丽", "跳舞" are the modifiers, "人生", "鸟叔" are the head words, head words are after modifiers. The phrases must be "Up-going ↓ " in waveform. Such a reverse order results in the independence of the subject-predicate structure, weakening the complete sense of a sentence naturally contained in the waveform "# Up-going * Down-going #", at last not stopping the sentence. So we can continue to develop the sentence, to increase the content size, to express more rich and complex contents.

Therefore, the modifier-core order is like a hindrance, to prevent sentences becoming grammatical sentences. To achieve this purpose, proposition "的" has the same function. The following examples are from Prof. Zhu Dexi:

(13) 手牵手的出去了 / 手牵手出去了

(14) 一声接一声的叹息 / 一声接一声叹息

The subject-predicate phrases are used as adverbial, if the propositions in the phrase are left out, the modifier-core phrases become the conjunction predicate phrases. The proposition "的" cancels the independent property of the sentence, the same as the reverse word order.

Why could we say that the modifier-core order must be contained in SVO order? Because everything has two sides. As described, "# Up-going * Down-going #" is the most minimal semantic form in binary combination of binary dependency relationship, corresponding to the completeness of a Chinese simple sentence. The word order of SVO corresponds to "# Up-going * Down-going #" semantic diagram of waveform, which is the Chinese basic word order. SVO is the front of a coin ---- how to make up a grammatical sentence. Modifier-core order (PPV is included) is the back of a coin---

how to stop making up a grammatical sentence. Reverse word order or propositions are helpful to avoid forming a sentence. So, the SVO order and the modifier-core order follow the same law: should we have a sentence form? They are the same law in opposite way.

5   Conclusion

In this paper, we propose a simplified Chinese semantic representation scheme --- semantic diagram of waveform. We find that SVO order is corresponding to waveform "# Up-going * Down-going #", the other word orders, such as SOV, OSV, OSV, can be converted to SVO order through waveform. People have complete sense to SVO order that form a sentence naturally. Modifier-core order is a kind of negative to SVO order, a kind of negative to completeness of the sentence, for semantic extension, so that more detailed, rich and rigorous information could be included in one sentence. So, we could say that VO/PPV is not opposite, they embody two aspect of the same law, they are examples of the law of the excluded middle.

References

1. Greenberg, J.H.: Some universals of grammar with particular reference to the order of meaningful elements. Lu bingfu, Lu Zhiji: Chinese version. J. Linguistics Abroad, No.2:45--60(1984).
2. Lu bingfu,: word order dominance and its cognitive explanation. Contemporary Linguistics. No.1:1~15(2005).
3. An yuxia,: Research review of Chinese word order. J. Chinese Language Learning, No.6:44~51(2006).
4. Liu dangqing,: Word order Typology and Prepositional theory. The Commercial Press, Beijing. (2003)
5. Zhan weidong: The Specification of Semantic Roles Annotation. to be published.
6. An overview of semantic resources and related theories, http://ccl.pku.edu.cn/973_sem_spec/
7. Yu shiwen: The Recognition and Practice of Semantic Roles Annotation. to be published.
8. Zhu dexi: The Lecture notes of Grammar. The Commercial Press, Beijing (1982)
9. Shen jiaxuan: Six Lecture notes of Grammar. The Commercial Press, Beijing (2011)

From Form to Meaning and to Concept

Hsin-I Hsieh

University of Hawaii

hhsieh@hawaii.edu

We propose a way of connecting the *form* of a sentence to its *meaning* and then to its *concept*. Meaning is the pure, authentic, and unadorned semantic interpretation of form, and concept is meaning adorned by social needs and cultural values in a particular speech community. To frame this view, we borrow the Interface Theory proposed by Chomsky. In that theory, a grammar has three major components: (1) The Computational System, (2) The Conceptual System, and (3) The Sensory-motor System. For a sentence x, the computational system creates a syntactic form f(x), gives it a semantic content, sem(x), then sends it to the conceptual system, to adorn it as a concept, con(x), which the sensory-motor system then processes as a phonetic form, p(x). With this procedure of interface, we can derive a language-specific sentence from its universal origin.

Keywords: Key Words: Merge, Interface, computation, concept, sensory-motor process.

1 Introduction.

Proposed by Noam Chomsky, Generative Grammar has persistently sought to derive language-particular forms from their language-universal origins [1]. Periodically refined, it peaked once at the Theory of Principles and Parameters (P&P), whose one familiar illustration has been the contrast of VO order (in English) with the OV order (in Japanese). The two orders share the same principle at different parameter values. Possibly reacting to criticisms and objections from cognitive grammarians, disagreeing with its exclusive focus on syntax, this P&P approach has been gradually replaced by a more comprehensive Minimalism program, framed in the Interface Theory (Chomsky 2013). Interface Theory on one hand minimizes by employing one single operation, Merge, replacing a set of universal principles, to generate syntactic expressions, and on the other hand enables syntax to interface with meanings, concepts, and sounds, making grammar a comprehensive coherent system for the representation of thoughts

© Springer International Publishing AG 2016
M. Dong et al. (Eds.): CLSW 2016, LNAI 10085, pp. 159–172, 2016
DOI: 10.1007/978-3-319-49508-8_16

expressed as sounds. It's most recent refinement has been stated in Berwick and Chomsky (2016). As previously, the goal of this new version is to link or interface three systems of the grammar: (i) the Computational System, which produces syntax and semantics, (ii) the Conceptual System, which makes use of concepts to facilitate inferences and implications leading to effective actions, and (iii) the Sensory-motor System, which yields sounds. So far cross-linguistic variations are largely left unexplained. As a remedy we propose to add to (ii) the Conceptual System a mechanism that works to explain syntactic and semantic variation among particular languages. And we illustrate this proposed method with pairs of translation-equivalent sentences in English and Chinese.

To set up a sequence of terms, we label the form of a sentence x as $f(x)$, its semantic content as $sem(x)$, and its local or regional concept as $con(x)$. In other words, the computational system creates an $f(x)$, interprets this $f(x)$ as $sem(x)$, and sends them both to the conceptual system of a language to adorn them as $f_a(x)$ and $con(x)$, and finally transports them to the sensory-motor system, for them to be processed on morphology, phonology, and phonetics, and to appear as the phonetic form, $p(x)$.

2   The Interface Theory.

The Interface Theory by Berwick and Chomsky (2011, 2016) is wide in scope and fluid in arrangement, but we try to understand and sketch it in Table 1. The table shows that the components of this interface organization are (1) the Computational System, (2) the Conceptual System, and (3) the Sensory-motor System. We assume that (1) interfaces (2), and then with (3), though a more flexible interface among these components should be possible.

As we see in Table 1, Merge is the single operator in the Computational System. In a binary way, it recursively composes simple, basic units, which are lexical items, into composite units, which are hierarchical structure expressions. These expressions are analyzed forms, denoted as $f(x)$s, that have their semantic content $sem(x)$s. Different languages select different subsets from the infinite universal set $U=\{f(x)_1, f(x)_2, f(x)_3, f(x)_k,...\}$, created by Merge. Chomsky doesn't postulate a regional $sem(x)$ for the original $sem(x)$, but we need this regional $sem(x)$ for cross-linguistic investigation. To produce a regional $sem(x)$, called $con(x)$, we assume that $f(x)$ and $sem(x)$ are sent to the conceptual system of a particular language, where they are adorned as $f_a(x)$ and $con(x)$. In other words, there is the transformation T: $<f(x), sem(x)>$ (in the Computational system) $\rightarrow$ $<f_a(x), con(x)>$ (in the Conceptual system). Merge works in two ways. For example, with the two basic units, x and y, External Merge (EM) forms a set of two elements, $\{x, y\}$. Internal Merge (IM) merges the set so formed, $\{x, y\}$, with one of its element, x, to form another set $\{x, \{x, y\}\}$. Chomsky provides a clear and now familiar example for Merge. Merge creates (1) *{guess, {what₁, {John, {is, {eating, what₂}}}}*.

 The expression *{what$_1$, {John, {is, {eating, what$_2$}}}* means something like "for which thing x, John is eating the thing x'. When the entire sentence reaches the sensory-motor system, the *what$_2$* signifying the object is deleted and the *what$_1$* serving as a quantifier is kept, and the phonetic form p (1) represented in (1) emerges. Chomsky seems ambivalent about whether or not to elaborate a hierarchical expression, such as $\{a, \{b, c\}\}$, into an associated x-bar scheme form <a(head), <b (head), c(complement)> (complement)>. For expository convenience, we might as well label it as an x-bar tree. (But we will soon see the price we pay for this x-bar tree.) We are now ready to explore the notion of a regional or local concept. Let us look at a pair of translation-equivalent sentences in English and Chinese, as (2a, b):

2.

    a. John bought books.

    b. Yuehan mai le shu, John-buy-perf-book.

    'John has bought books.' 约翰买了书。

The two sentences have the same sem(x), sem(2a/2b) in the Computational System, but when they appear in the Conceptual System, they have different con(x)s-- con(2a') and con(2b'):

(2a') λX *Tense-marked*$(X)\lambda x\lambda y$(buy(x, y))(john)(books).

(2b') λX *Aspect-marked*$(X)\lambda x\lambda y$(buy(x, y))(john)(books).

Clearly, (2a') and (2b') share the same sem(x) in the second part of the formula, $\lambda x\lambda y$(buy(x, y))(john)(books), but they differ in being tense marked in (2a')--with λX*Tense-marked*(X),and aspect-marked in (2b') --with λX *Aspect-marked*(X). The derivation of these two different con(x)s is shown in Table 2.

To match an expression f(x) in language L_a with an equivalent expression f(y) in language L_b, the speaker needs to match the con(x) in L_a with the con(y) in L_b. This matching can occur across languages as well as across personal and regional varieties of the same language. For example, given (3)Wo pao(v-1) de kuai(v-2), I-run-get-fast, 'I run fast' 我跑得快 under the assumption of one homogeneous language, it is not clear whether V-1 or V-2 is the main verb (assuming that 'main verb' is defined). But under the assumption that Chinese has several or many varieties, we can choose both, by assuming that they are two configurations, supporting two regional concepts, for two groups of speakers in the Chinese speech community.

3   The issue of whether V-1 or V-2 is the 'main verb' in Mandarin.

To see this, we look at the graphs in (3a) and (3b). They provide two alternative ways of analyzing the same sentence (3). (3a) emphasizes V-1, with -de attached to it, showing that it receives the emphasis, while (3b) stresses V-2, with -de affixed to it, indicating that it obtains the stress. F(3a) and f(3b) are associated with sem(3a) and sem(3b). Due to different intensities, they project into $f_a(3a)$ and $f_a(3b)$, with associated con(3a) and con(3b). So we can resolve the issue on the main-verb status in a sentence like (3) (that contains the phrase V-1 de V-2). It is well-known that Huang (1998) favors V-1 for the main verb, but Huang and Magione (1985) prefers V-2. Since f(3a) relates to sem(3a) and f(3b) relates to sem(3b), it follows that with emphasis marked, sem(3a) has a later con(3a) confirming Huang (1988) and likewise sem(3b) has a later con(3b), supporting Huang and Magione (1985). In meaning, we obtain sem(3a) $\lambda Xkuai(X)\lambda xpao(x)(wo)$, which is adorned as con(3a) $\lambda Xkuai(X)\lambda xpao(x)(wo) \wedge \lambda ZEmp(Z)\lambda xpao(x)(wo)$. We also achieve sem(3b), which equals sem(3a). But sem(3b) is decorated as con(3b) $\lambda Xkuai(X)\lambda xpao(x)(wo) \wedge \lambda Z$ $Emp(Z)\lambda xkuai(x)(wo)$. Con(3a) signifies 'I run fast and my running is emphasized' and con(3b) indicates 'I run fast and my being fast is emphasized'. $F_a(3a)$ and $f_a(3b)$ arise with the -de attachment, and, with their associated con(3a) and con(3b), they are sent to the Sensory-motor System to be processed into p (3). Understood in this way, the V-1 versus V-2 issue is not a pure syntactic issue. It is rather a syntactic, semantic, and conceptual issue that awaits the Interface Theory to provide a solution.

4   Deriving a construction from a structure.

Goldberg (1995, 2006, forthcoming) has persistently and persuasively argued that, some structures are not ordinary structures as the generative grammarians have thought, but are Constructions. Individual constructions are non-compositionally built, and have unpredictable main and ancillary semantic, pragmatic, and discourse meanings. One familiar example is (4a, b):

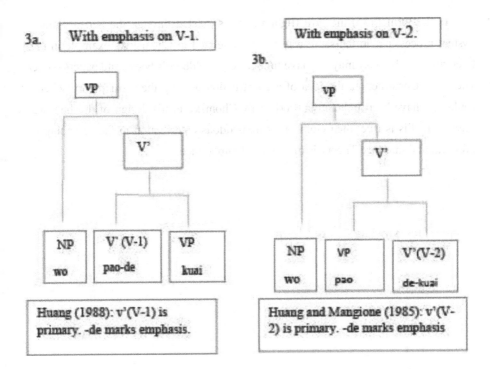

3a. With emphasis on V-1.

3b. With emphasis on V-2.

Huang (1988): v'(V-1) is primary. -de marks emphasis.

Huang and Mangione (1985): v'(V-2) is primary. -de marks emphasis

4.

    a. John baked a cake for Mary. (a structure)

    b. John baked Mary a cake. (a construction)

(4a) is a structure whose meaning can be predicted from whose composite form (because we can draw an x-bar tree for it), but (4b) is a construction, whose meaning contains an element 'give' absent from the composite form and x-bar tree (see the tree F(4b) for the unfilled *give*). (4b) has the meaning 'John baked a cake and gave it to Mary to eat.' So f(4b) has sem(4b) created by Merge, and con(4b) caused by the added *give*. So f(4b) is <John, <<bake, Mary>, a cake>>, and f_a(4b) is <John, <bake, <<give, Mary>, a cake>>>. F_a(4b) moves to the Conceptual System to acquire con(4b) $\lambda x \lambda y \lambda z$Bake(x, y) $\wedge$Give(x, y) $\wedge$ Give(x, z)(John)(a cake)(Mary). 'John baked a cake, John gave a cake, and John gave Mary'. We are constrained by the x-bar theory and the binary composition of the predicate calculus to give a more revealing and less cumbersome formulation than con(4b). Unfortunately, overriding these two restrictions is beyond the scope of this paper.

In the form f_a(4b) the *give* (light verb?) is deleted through the Sensory-motor System processing, in the same way *what₂* is deleted in Chomsky's example in (1). Even though Chomsky may not have time to read Goldberg's books and papers on her Theory of Construction, the idea of a construction defying the x-bar theory scheme could still have been indirectly absorbed by Chomsky in his design of the Interface Theory. If this is true, then Goldberg's tremendous contribution to the reshaping of P&P into the Interface Theory is of historical importance.

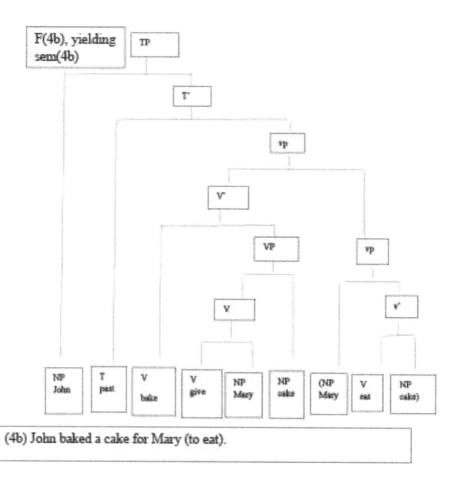

(4b) John baked a cake for Mary (to eat).

5   Tai's (1985, 2002) Principle of Temporal Sequence (PTS)

Equivalent to (4a) and (4b) in English are (5a) and (5b) in Mandarin Chinese:

5.

a. Yuehan wei Mali kao le yige diangao, John-for-Mary-bake-perf-a-cake, 'John baked a cake for Mary'. (cf. (4a))

b.   Yuehan   kao   le   yige   diangao   gei   Mali   chi, John-bake-perf-a-cake-give-Mary-eat, 'John has (e1) baked a cake and (e2) given it to Mary to (e3) eat'. (cf. (4b))

Table 3 provides an x-bar tree for f(5b), where the three events-- e1, e2, and e3-- are temporally sequenced, as Tai would have claimed. Notice that (4) and (5) do not share an f(x). They each have their own f(x)s, renamed as $f_a(x)$s, yielding associated con(x)s in the Conceptual System.

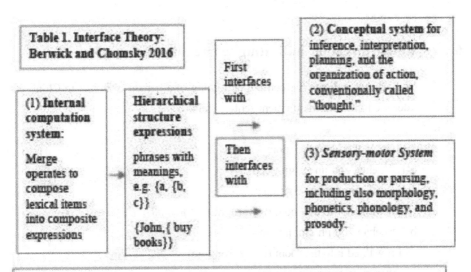

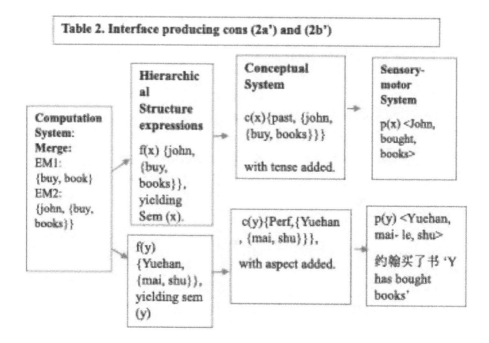

Table 2. Interface producing cons (2a') and (2b')

6   Chinese direction-indicating 'come' and 'go'.

Two particles indicate the coming and going of a person or object in Chinese.
Consider the translation-equivalent sentences in (6):

6.

    a. John walked into the room.

    b.1. Yuehan zou jin fangjian lai.

    John-walk-into-room-coming.

    'John walked into the room (toward me).' 约翰走进房间来

    b.2.Yuehan zou jin fangjian qu.

    'John walked into the room (away from me).' 约翰走进房间去

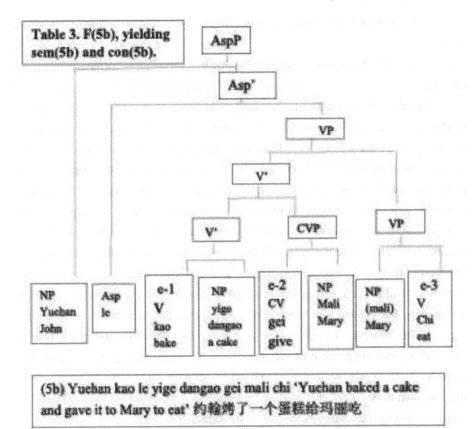

Table 3. F(5b), yielding sem(5b) and con(5b).

(5b) Yuehan kao le yige dangao gei mali chi 'Yuehan baked a cake and gave it to Mary to eat' 约翰烤了一个蛋糕给玛丽吃

The form is f(5b), which yields sem(5b) in the Computational System, and further yields con(5b) in the Conceptual System, where Tai's (1985) PTS applies. In the Sensory-motor System, the events are temporally sequenced, and *give* is reduced to a co-verb.

For (6), Merge creates f(6), and interprets it as sem(6). It is then sent to the Conceptual System in English without adornment, and exists as con(6a), and to the Conceptual System in Chinese, and is adorned as con(6b.1, 6b.2). In steps, this process is:

1. sentence (6)
2. f(6) <John <walked-into, the room>> (by Merge)
3. sem(6)λxλyWalk-into(x, y)(john)(room) (shared by English and Chinese)
4. con(6a) λxλyWalk-into(x, y)(john)(room) (in English)

5a.con(6b.1)λXToward-speaker(X)λxλyWalk-into(x, y)(john) (room) (in Chinese)

5b.con(6b.2)λXAwayfrom-speaker(X)λxλyWalk-into(x, y)(john)(room) (also in Chinese)

Chomsky's Interface Theory has only three major components. We locate the mechanism for generating a con(x) from a sem(x) in the Conceptual System, which, according to Chomsky processes inference, planning, and organization of actions. The examples in (6) serve to support our including con(x) in the Conceptual system. In the pattern of con(6b.1) a person or object is moving toward the speaker, but in the pattern of con(6b.2) a person or object is moving away from the speaker. If the person is a stranger, the speaker could infer that he/she may be an unwelcome intruder, and action would be taken to defend the speaker himself. But if the person is a friend, the speaker would infer that he/she may be a visitor and action would be taken to greet and welcome this visitor. So the 'coming' and 'going' implications are not just wasteful adornments, but convey a message that allows inference, planning, and responsive actions. The 'coming' and 'going' patterns are in this sense invested with cultural values that serve the purpose of community safety and hospitality. If we create for English con(6a.1) John walked into the room to our alert, and con(6a.2) John walked into the room to our relief, they may be grammatical, but they do not have the cultural value enjoyed by the Chinese 'come' and 'go' expressions.

7   Mistake assigned to the agent or to the patient.

A mistake is often assigned to the agent role in Chinese but to the patient role in English, as in (7a, b):

7.

a. John bought the wrong book.

f(a) < john, < buy, <the, <wrong, book>>>>

   sem(a)λxλyBuy(x,y)(john)(book) ∧ λyWrong(y)(book) (Stressing 'the book is wrong')

b. Yuehan mai cuo le shu, john-buy-wrong-perf-book, 约翰买错了书

f(b) <yuehan, <<<mai, cuo>, perf>, shu>>

   sem(b) λxλyBuy(x,y)(john)(book) ∧ λXMistake(X) λ x λ yBuy(x, y)(John)(book) (Stressing 'john is mistaken')

One could infer that, in this example, English is assigning the mistake to the patient role 'the book' but Chinese is assigning the mistake to the agent role 'john'. The Chinese speaker feels responsible for the mistake, but English speaker merely assert that the book bought is different from the book the agent intends to buy. In Chinese, if the agent coincides with the speaker, the speaker-agent is generous and self-blaming, and this generosity is entrenched as a cultural value. In English, the speaker is objective and purely descriptive, and the mistake is reported as a mismatch of book1, actually bought, with book2, intended to be bought. This objectivity is also entrenched as a cultural value.

8 Co-verbs signaling 'control' or 'non-control'

For the distinction of control versus non-control sentences, we consider (8a, b, c):

8.

    a. Yuehan tui kai men, john-push-open-door, 'John pushed open the door', 约翰推开门

    b. Yuehan ba men tui kai, john-hold-door-push-open, 'John pushed open the door', 约翰把门推开

    c. Men bei yuehan tui kai, door-by-john-push-open, 'The door was pushed open by John', 门被约翰推开

We distinguish three types of transitive sentences. 8a is 'simple' transitive, 8b is 'control' transitive, and 8c is 'non-control' transitive. Merge creates

f(8a) <john, << push, open>, the door> >, which is interpreted in the hierarchical structure expressions as sem(8a)λxλypush-open(x,y)(john)(the door), which is then sent to the Conceptual System to become con(8b) and con(8c):

con(8b)λxλypush-open(x,y)(john)(the door) ∧ λxControl(x)(john)

con(8c)λxλypush-open(x, y)(john)(the door) ∧ λxNon-control(x)(the door)

The pattern expressing control is often used to link a result event with a preceding cause event, as in 9 (a, b):

9.

a. Yuehan ba bide *tui/tui dao/tui dao zai dishang/tui dao zai dishang qi bu lai, john-hold-peter-push/push-fall/push-fall-on-ground/push-fall-on-ground-rise-not-com e, 约翰把彼得*推/推到/推到在地上/推到在地上起不来

b. Bide bei Yuehan *tui/ tui dao/tui dao zai dishang/tui dao zai dishang qi bu lai, john-hold-peter-push*/push-fall/push-fall-on-ground/push-fall-on-ground-rise-not-co me, 彼得被约翰*推/推到/推到在地上/推到在地上起不来

If we simply want to say that John pushed Peter, we have to add a frequency phrase, a manner phrase, or a degree phrase, etc., to remove the control implication.

10.Yuehan ba bide tui le yixia/tui kai/tui de yuanyuan de, john-hold-peter-push-once/off/far away.

Obviously, the *ba* for 'control' or *bei* for 'non-control' is not a universal sem(x) shared by all languages, but is a particular con(x) unique to Chinese. The simple transitive sentence is f(x). It has a sem(x). This sem(x) is turned into $con_e(x)$ without any adornment in English, and into $con_c(x)$ to indicate control and non-control in Chinese.

9   Conclusion.

Chomsky's Theory of Interface starts with the single operator Merge. For the sentence x, Merge creates a form, denoted by f(x). F(x) has a semantic interpretation or semantic content, denoted by sem(x). Sem(x) is sent to the Conceptual System to be processed as a concept, con(x), which is processed by the Sensory-motor System as phonetic form, p(x). The Conceptual System performs two functions. As Chomsky intends, it is used to make inference, planning, and decision for actions, before it is uttered as sounds. As we propose, it may also be used to derive regional variation from a common source sentence. We have in effect set up a procedure for deriving from the universal sem(x) a particular con(x). This special procedure, in model, though not in details, is foreseen by Wang (1999) at an early time. At that time most Chinese grammarians were conveniently applying Chomsky's theory of Generative Grammar to describe Chinese sentences, ignoring many interesting Chinese sentence patterns that mirror social and cultural values informing survival strategies unique to the Chinese speech community. Wang (1999) defied this West-obsession and questioned its unwarranted imitation. He had the foresight that Chinese linguists should redirect their attention and start to consider building an Indigenous Chinese Grammar. In that grammar, the sentence patterns that are unique to the Chinese culture should be described in their own terms rather than in terms of a theory that is focused narrowly on English sentence patterns. Many years have elapsed since Wang's sincere urging, and today with Chomsky's Interface Theory, we can describe these peculiarly Chinese sentence patterns as expressing Chinese concepts. Though a Chinese grammar has its forms generated by the universal Computational System, the forms have their semantic contents, which transform into their Chinese-minded concepts. In promoting this genuine Chinese grammar, the dedication and profundity of Wang's scholarship is most brilliantly manifested.

Footnote 1. This is an extensively revised and retitled version of a paper of mine, which appears under the original title 'Transparency and Economy as Two Contending Forces of a Grammar: On deriving a synthesis from an analysis' in the Proceedings of the 17th Chinese Lexical Semantic Workshop. In theory, data, and perspective, it is substantially different from the original version.

References

Chomsky, N. 2013. Problem of projection. Lingua 130: 33-49.

Berwick R. C., Chomsky, N. (2011). The biolinguistic program: the current state of its development, in Di Sciullo A., Boeckx, C. (ed.) 2011, 19-41 (kindle 687-1143).

Berwick, R. C., Chomsky, N. (2016). Why only us: Language and evolution. MIT Press.

Di Sciullo, A., Boeckx, C. (ed.) 2011. Biolinguistic Enterprise: New perspectives on the evolution and nature of the human language faculty. New York: Oxford.

Goldberg, A. 1995. Constructions. Chicago: University of Chicago Press.

Goldberg, A. 2006. Constructions at Work. Oxford University Press.

Goldberg, A. Forthcoming. Explain Me This.

Huang, C-T. 1988. Wo Pao de kuai and Chinese phrase structure. Language 64:274-311.

Huang, C-R. and L. Mangione. 1985. A reanalysis of de: adjuncts and subordinate clauses. Proceedings of West Cost Coast Conference on Formal Linguistics IV (WCCFL IV). pp. 80-81. Stanford: Stanford Linguistics Association.

Larson, R. 1988. On the double object construction. Linguistic Inquiry 19:335-92.

Tai, James H.-Y. 1985. Temporal sequence and Chinese word order. Iconicity in syntax, ed. by John Haiman, 49-72. Amsterdam: John Benjamins.

Tai, James H.-Y. 2002. Temporal sequence in Chinese: A rejoinder. Form and Function: Linguistic Studies in Honor of Shuanfan Huang, ed. By Lily I-wen Su, Chinfa Lien, and Kawai Chui, 331-351. Crane: Taipei.

Wang, W. S.-Y. 1999. Language and people of China. Chinese Languages and Linguistics V: Interactions in Language, ed. by Yuen-mei Yin, I-li Yang, and Hui-chen Chan, 1-26. Taipei: Academia Sinica.

A Corpus-Based Analysis of Syntactic-Semantic Relations between Adjectival Objects and Nouns in Mandarin Chinese

Lin Li, Pengyuan Liu[1]

Language Monitoring and Social Computing Laboratory, National Language Resource Monitoring and Research Center, Faculty of Information Science, Beijing Language and Culture University,

Beijing, China

blculyn@163.com, liupengyuan@pku.edu.cn

Abstract: In this study, we discuss the syntactic and semantic relations between adjectival objects of VA verb-object constructions and specific nouns in Mandarin Chinese. Firstly, it shows that VA verb-object constructions can function as predicates and modifiers in sentences. It also demonstrates that as adjectives represent attributes of nouns, the adjectival objects of VA verb-object constructions have attribute-entity semantic relations with specific nouns. According to the syntactic functions and attribute-entity semantic relations, we point out that there are two main kinds of syntactic relations which are subject-predicate and modifier-head relations between adjectival objects and specific nouns. Moreover, we take adjectival objects as metonymic expressions. At last, we argue that adjectives which function as objects have nominal meanings in semantics, while they are not nominalized in syntax.

Keywords: verb-object constructions, adjectival objects, specific nouns, attribute-entity

---

[1] Corresponding Author

© Springer International Publishing AG 2016
M. Dong et al. (Eds.): CLSW 2016, LNAI 10085, pp. 173–186, 2016
DOI: 10.1007/978-3-319-49508-8_17

1   Introduction

In Mandarin Chinese, linguists have long held that the typical verb-object construc-tions are composed of verbs and nouns which we refer to them as VN constructions. While there are other components can function as objects, for instance, adjectives and verbs, which also have been widely approved by linguists (see Ding Shengshu1961, Chao Yuanren1968, Zhu Dexi1982 etc. for extensive discussions). Examples are: 怕 黑[*pa-hei*](*be afraid of the dark*),喜欢游泳[*xihuan-youyong*](*like swimming*). In this study, we refer to VO constructions which consist of adjectival objects and verbal objects as VA constructions and VV constructions respectively.

These interesting linguistic phenomena arise the following valuable questions in Mandarin Chinese: What are the characteristics of adjectival objects or verbal objects? Are they nominalization phenomena that adjectives or verbs act as objects? What are the similarities and differences among these different combination patterns of VO constructions? What are the properties of VO constructions?

As the typical patterns of VO constructions, there are many research papers and books on VN constructions, especially on the semantic relations between verbs and nouns (see Li Linding1983，Ma Qingzhu1985 etc. for more details). Whereas VA constructions or VV constructions attract relatively much less attention, as a result, all of these above questions are far away from systematical and consistent explanations in recent linguistic literature. VO constructions are important in Mandarin Chinese, however, with only partial thorough research makes it difficult to give detailed de-scriptions and explanations of VO constructions. Therefore, it is necessary to explore and explain VA constructions and VV constructions. In this study, we pay special attention to VA constructions.

Comparing with VN constructions, the noticeable difference between VA construc-tions and VN constructions is the former one have adjectival objects while the latter have nominal objects. Therefore, we will start with adjectival objects to explore VA constructions thoroughly.

It is hard to ignore the nominalization of adjectives when we discuss adjectival ob-jects of VA constructions in Mandarin Chinese. Some researchers argued that adjectives are nominalized in different degrees when they act as objects (see Zhang Guoxian 2006). Others prefer to think VA constructions like 打黑[*da-hei*](*crack down on crime*),招新[*zhao-xin*](*recruit freshmen*) as VN constructions for the reason that the adjectives have nominal meanings in these constructions. In other words, these adjectives represent things rather than attributes. It is no doubt that adjectives have relations with nouns, while the nominalization of adjectival objects need more discussions.

In this study, we will discuss the syntactic and semantic relations between adjectival objects and nouns in attempt to gain a better understanding of the properties of VA constructions. On the one hand, it will provide a new perspective to explain why adjectives can function as objects in Mandarin Chinese. On the other hand, it will help to describe the similarities and differences between VA and VN constructions. Furthermore, it may lead to a comprehensive analysis of VO constructions in Mandarin Chinese.

2   Statistical Analysis of Examples

2.1   Data Collection and Extraction

In this study, we focus on VA constructions which are composed of single verbs and single adjectives.

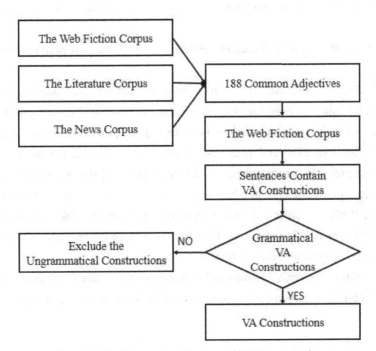

Graph 1 The Extracting Process of VA Constructions

Graph 1 shows the extracting process of VA constructions. Firstly, we extract the common adjectives from three corpora which consist of 1.5 billion words, including a web fiction corpus of 160 million words, a literature corpus of 540 million words and a news corpus of 800 million words. Then we use *The Grammatical Knowledge-base of Contemporary Chinese-A Completed Specification* to exclude the ungrammatical adjectives and we get 188 single adjectives at last. In order to reduce the analytical workload, we only extract VA constructions which consist of these 188 adjectives from the web fiction corpus.

2.2   Statistical Results

We analyze all sentences which contain VA constructions manually and conclude that there are two main syntactic functions of VA construction in the corpus, i.e. they can function as predicates and modifiers, as example (1) and example (2) shows respectively:

(1)豆油价格整体**趋稳**。

Douyou jiage zhengti **qu-wen**.

*Soybean oil price overall **tend to steady**.*

(2)坚决打击任何**售假**行为。

Jianjue daji renhe **shou-jia** xingwei.

*Hitting any **fake-selling** activities firmly.*

It indicates that adjectival objects have relations with nominal subjects or some other specific nouns by analyzing VA constructions in contexts. According to this, we conclude two main syntactic relations between adjectives and their specific nouns: subject-predicate relations and modifier-head relations. In example (1), there is a subject-predicate relation between the main subject 价格[*jia-ge*](*the price*) and the adjectival object 稳[*wen*] (*steady*). In other words, it means 价格稳[*jia-ge wen*] (*the price is steady*). While the adjectival object 假[*jia*](*fake*) represents 'fake commodity' in example (2), that is 假[*jia*](*fake*) modifies the noun 'fake commodity'. The relation between them is modifier-head relation.

Table 1 shows the statistical data and examples of the syntactic relations between adjectival objects and nouns, which the detailed explanations of examples will show in Section 3.

Relations	Numbers	Examples
Sub-ject-Predicate	338	趋稳[*qu-wen*](*tend to steady*) 怕黑[*pa-hei*](*be afraid of the dark*) 回暖[*hui-nuan*](*turn warm*)
Modifi-er-Head	45	售假[*shou-jia*](*to sell fakes*) 打黑[*da-hei*](*crack down on crime*) 揭丑[*jie-chou*](*recrimination*)

Table 1 The Statistical Data and Examples of the Syntactic Relations

We exclude all sentences contain VA verb-complement constructions which are the typical syntactic types of VA constructions. As it shows in Table 1, we totally extract 383 VA constructions from the corpus, 88% of the relations between adjectives and their specific nouns are subject-predicate relations, while only 12% are modifier-head relations. In Section 3, we will provide an explanation for this kind of classification.

3   Analysis of Syntactic-Semantic Relations between Adjectives and Specific Nouns

In this section, firstly, we formulate the semantic relations between adjectives and specific nouns. Secondly, we explicitly discuss the syntactic relations between adjectival objects and nouns based on all instances from the corpus. At last, we argue that some adjectives have nominal meanings in semantics, while keep their adjectival properties in syntax.

3.1   Semantic Relations between Adjectives and Specific Nouns

In VN constructions, linguists concentrate on the complex semantic relations between verbs and nouns. While comparing with nominal objects, we prefer to hold the idea that adjectives have closer relations with nouns than with verbs for the reason that adjectives represent attributes of nouns (see Yao Zhenwu1996 for detailed discussions). In other words, it means when an adjective occurs in a sentence, it needs to connect with a specific noun. For example, the adjective 黑[*hei*] (*black*) should depend on a thing noun which has the attribute of black, and to our knowledge, the thing noun may be the dark night or something else. Therefore, we refer to these semantic relations between adjectives and nouns as attribute-entity relations.

The attribute-entity relations can also be proved by instances from the corpus (see subsection 3.2 for more details). Moreover, the attribute-entity relations between adjectives and their specific nouns have some impacts on their syntactic relations. Therefore, according to the semantic relations we will clearly discuss the syntactic relations between adjectives and their specific nouns.

3.2 Syntactic Relations between Adjectives and Specific Nouns

We analyze the instances from the corpus in accordance with the semantic relations and come to a conclusion that there are two main syntactic relations between adjectival objects and their specific nouns: subject-predicate relations and modifier-head relations. According to our analysis, there are also two different kinds of subject-predicate relations. So in this part, we will focus on three kinds of syntactic relations.

(1)①天气回暖。   ②他的嘴唇发白。

   Tianqi **hui-nuan**.   Zuichun **fa-bai**.

   *The weather **turns warm**.*   *His lips **are white**.*

(2)①夜里我怕黑。   ②这种农作物耐旱。

   Ye li wo **pa-hei**.   Zhe zhong nongzuowu **nai-hai**.

   *I **am afraid of the dark** at night.* *This kind of crop can **tolerant drought**.*

(3)①重庆打黑运动进行正酣。

   Chong Qing **da-hei** yundong jinxing zheng han.

   *The activities of **crime crackdown** are in all swing in Chong Qing.*

   ②日本以揭丑方式连番对美国施压。

   Ri Ben yi **jie-chou** fangshi lianfan dui Mei Guo shiya.

   *Japan continues to put pressure on USA by **recriminating** it.*

Syntactically, there are subject-predicate relations between the main subjects 天气 [*tianqi*](*the weather*), 嘴唇 [*zuichun*](*the lips*) and the adjectival objects 暖 [*nuan*](*warm*),白[*bai*](*white*) respectively in example (1). In other words, they mean 天气暖[*tianqi-nuan*](*the weather is warm*) and 嘴唇白[*zuichun-bai*](*the lips are white*). We can describe weather by feeling temperature, so it is reasonable to say that weather has attributes of 'warm' and 'cold'; lips have an attribute of colour, 'white' is a subordinate of colour, so we can also refer to 'white' as an attribute of lips.

There are no subject-predicate relations between the main subjects 我[*wo*](*I*),农作物[*nongzuowu*](*crop*) and the adjectival objects 黑[*hei*](*black*),旱[*han*](*draught*) in example (2). While these adjectives do depend on some potential nouns which could generate subject-predicate relations with them. In example (2), 黑[*hei*](*black*) does not mean 'I am black', but it means some black things like the darkness, the night. Therefore, 黑[*hei*](*black*) is connected with the dark night, it means 夜黑[*ye-hei*](*the night is dark*). Similarly, 旱[*han*](*arid*) means 天气/环境旱[*tianqi/huanjing han*](*the weather/environment is arid*).

As we can see, the similary between example (1) and (2) is the relations between adjectival objects and their specific nouns are subject-predicate relations, on the other hand, the difference is whether the specific nouns co-occour with the adjectives in the sentences.

Examples in (3) differ from examples in (1) and (2) because of they have different syntactic relations between adjectives and specific nouns. The adjectival objects 黑[*hei*](*black*), 丑[*chou*](*urgly*) represent 黑势力[*hei-shili*](*black powers*), 丑/坏的事情[*chou/huai-de-shiqing*](*urgly/bad things*) respectively. Therefore, we prefer to describe the relations between the adjectives and nouns as modifier-head relations.

It should be noticed that all adjectives in (1)(2)(3) have both subject-predicate relations and modifier-head relations with their specific nouns. 天气暖[*tianqi-nuan*](*the weather is warm*) can also be described as 暖的天气[*nuan-de-tianqi*](*the warm weather*), 夜黑[*ye-hei*](*the night is dark*) can be expressed as 黑夜[*hei-ye*](*the dark night*). We can also transform 丑/坏的事情[*chou/huai-de-shiqing*] (*urgly/bad things*) to 事情丑/坏[*shiqing-chou/huai*](*things are urgly/bad*). The standard of the classification is in consonance with the syntactic functions of VA constructions in the contexts, i.e. VA constructions in example (1)(2) are predicates, while VA constructions in example (3) modify nouns. As a result, the relations between adjectives and their specific nouns in example(1)(2) and (3), we prefer to take them as subject-predicate relations and modifer-head relations respectively.

3.3   Metonymic Analysis of Adjectival Objects

In fact, adjectives act as objects is a kind of metonymic phenomenon. Metonymy as a conceptual phenomenon was proposed by Lakoff and Jonhson (1980). They pointed out that metonymy as an important cognitive pattern exists in our daily life. It has impact on our ideas and actions. In this study, we use the interpretation of F. Ungerer and H-J. Schmid (2009), which taking metonymy as a relationship between a source concept and a target concept in a same cognitive pattern. The relationship within a socially accepted mapping scope that prototypically corresponds to a cognitive model. The source concept is the explaining element, the target concept is the explained element.

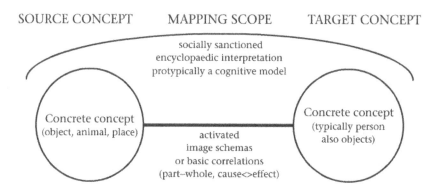

Map 1   The Mapping of Metonymy

As we know, semantic relations between adjectives and nouns are attribute-entity relations, it means people can understand the relationships between the adjectival objects and nouns under some cognitive models according to their cognitive experience. For example, 黑 [*hei*](*black*), 丑 [*chou*](*urgly*) will be referred to as source concepts, 'black powers','urgly/bad things' will be referred to as target concepts. It is obviously that 黑[*hei*](*black*), 丑[*chou*](*urgly*) are the highlighted attributes of the thing nouns. In order to make metonymy plays its role, there must be a relation between the attribute and the thing. The most important point is the thing must be a socially accepted concept. This concept acts as the mapping scope of metonymy. So the mapping scope of 打黑 [*da-hei*](*anti-crime*), 揭丑 [*jie-chou*](*recrimination*) must be a socially accepted cognitive model. The cognitive model is an association pattern between concepts which based on people's cognitive experience. The cognitive model builds a constant connection among the elements. Once one of them is activated, the others are activated too. As a result, the presence of the source concept 'attribute' will activate the target concept 'thing'. Therefore, the explanation for 打黑[*da-hei*](*anti-crime*) is that there is a cognitive model of 打黑 [*da-hei*](*anti-crime*): people know that there are some black powers and bad things in society, and they have very bad influences, so the government takes actions to deal with them. According to this cognitive model, people can use their cognitive experience to understand 黑 [*hei*](*black*), and the connotation of 打黑 [*da-hei*](*anti-crime*).

Besides, the entities of 'attribute-entity' relations in adjectives and nouns have further concretization. For example, 黑[*hei*](*black*) can be concretized as: black <---> [darkness, night, crime...]. This kind of concretization makes the relations clearer.

To sum up, we propose that: the attributions which the adjectival objects represent are salient attributes of the thing nouns. The 'attribute-entity' effective mapping is an 'abstract-entity' mapping. It achieves and expands the usage of 'part-whole' image schema through the intervention of cognitive experience. It further realizes the legitimacy of VA verb-object constructions at syntactic level. This is the connatation of VA verb-object constructions. According to this, the mapping of VA verb-object constructions is in the following:

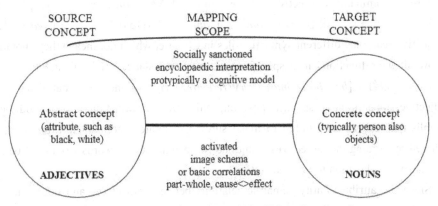

Map 2   The Mapping of VA Verb-Object Constructions

3.4   The Nominalization of Adjectival Objects

At the beginning of this study, we pointed out that some researchers argued that there are variable degrees on the nominalization of adjectival objects and some suggested to take 打黑[*da-hei*](*crack down on crime*),招新[*zhao-xin*](*recruit new people*) as VN constructions. In this paper, neither we deny the possibility of the nominalization of adjectives, nor agree with the idea of 打黑[*da-hei*](*crack down on crime*),招新

[*zhao-xin*](*recruit new people*) are VN constructions. Actually, the following questions about the nominalization of adjectival objects need to figure out:

(1)What does 'nominalization' mean?

(2)Are there some criteria to define 'nominalization'?

(3)Why it is a nominalization phenomenon when adjectives function as objects?

(4)How does this nominalization idea influence the analysis of VA constructions?

First of all, when adjectival or verbal words have nominal functions we can say that they are nominalized. The point is how we define 'nominal functions'. Traditionally, there are two criteria of syntactic nominalization in Chinese: only function as subjects or objects and have some formal signs(mostly followed by '*de*'). Obviously, according to these two criteria, adjectives which function as nouns are not nominalized. For instance, 新[*xin*](*new*) in 招新[*zhao-xin*](*recruit new people*) can function as modifier:新衣服[*xin-yifu*](*new clothes*) and without followed by '*de*'.

Researchers who support nominalization argued that adjectives cannot co-occur with degree words when they appear in object positions and took this as the mainly feature of nominalized adjectives. For example, 你放轻松[*ni fang qingsong*]([*You*] *Take it easy*)→ 你放很轻松[*ni fang hen qingsong*] ([*You*]*Take it very easy*) *. Adjectives can play different syntactic roles in Chinese, which not means they should show all their functions in a specific position. For instance, 红花[*hong hua*] (*red flowers*)→很红花[*hen hong hua*] (*very red flowers*) *. It indicates that when an adjective appears in a specific position, only one or two functions should be highlighted, others are limited to make sure to generate grammatical expressions. Therefore, arguing that adjectives cannot co-occur with degree words would not be a persuasive explanation to nominalization.

Since the attribute-entity semantic relations between adjectives and nouns, it is noticable that some adjectives in VA constructions have nominal meanings, and the referential functions of the adjectival objects become stronger in pragmatic.What needs to mention is that it is not because of the adjectival objects tend to be nominalized, but the objects demand the elements which appear in these positions must highlight the referential functions. The possible reason that many sholars hold the assumption of the adjectival objects tend to nominalization, is that they take the standards of nonimal objects as the standards of objects. In other words, when we discuss what kind of elments can act as objects and the reason, the standards come from the nominal objects, not the objects.

In sum, according to our syntactic analysis of adjectival objects and their specific nouns, we prefer to hold the idea that these nominal meanings only occur in semantics, it does not mean that the adjectives have already been nominalized in syntax. On the one hand, this non-nominalization comes from the analysis of instances from the corpus which can provide wider explanation to VA constructions. On the other hand, it shows that adjectives function as objects have some properties which differ from nominal objects. It will provide a new perspective to discuss VA and VN constructions.

According to the above analysis, we summarize the syntactic and semantic relations of VA constructions as the following:

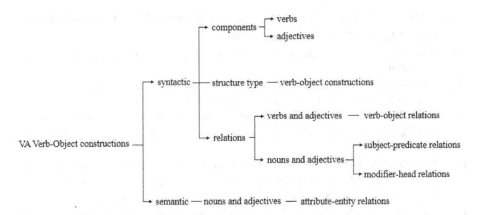

Graph 2   Syntactic and Semantic Relations of VA Verb-Object Constructions

4   Conclusions

In this study, we discuss the relations between adjectival objects of VA constructions and specific nouns both in semantic and syntax and arrive at the conclusions that adjectives have attribute-entity relations with specific nouns, and they have two main different syntactic relations: subject-predicate relations and modifier-head relations. What should be emphasized again is that some adjectives have nominal meanings in semantics, while keep their adjectival properties in syntax.

Although we have already explored some aspects about adjectival objects, we still cannot give persuasive and thorough descriptions and explanations about VA constructions. The further work what we will focus on is to explore the factors or limitations that adjectives function as objects. We do hope the following work will provide new research perspectives to VA constructions and VO constructions in Mandarin Chinese.

Acknowledgements

This research was supported by the Major Project of the National Language Committee of the 12th Five-Year Research Plan in 2015 (ZDI 125-55) and by the Open Foundation of Shandong Key Lab of Language Resource Development and Application.

References

[1]   Adele E.Goldberg. Constructions: a new theoretical approach to language [J].TRENDS in Cognitive Sciences, 2003.

[2]   Chao Yuanren. A Grammar of Spoken Chinese [M]. The Commercial Press, 1968:439.

[3]   Charles N.Li and Sandra A. Thompson. Mandarin Chinese: A Functional Reference Grammar [M]. University of California Press, 1981.

[4]   Ding Shengshu. The Modern Chinese Language Phrasing Talk [M]. Beijing: The Commercial Press, 1968 丁声树.现代汉语语法讲话[M].商务印书馆,1961 [In Chinese]

[5]   Feng Shenli. Interactions Between Morphology, Syntax and Prosody in Chinese(Revised Edition) [M].Perking University Press,2009 冯胜利.汉语的韵律、词法与句法（修订本）[M].北京大学出版社, 2009 [In Chinese]

[6]   Lv Shuxiang. First Exploration of single and double words in Mandarin [J]. Studies of The Chinese Language, 1963(1)吕叔湘.现代汉语单双音节问题初探[J].中国语文,1963(1)[In Chinese]

[7]   Lv Shuxiang. An Exploration of the Usage of Adjectives [J]. Studies of The Chinese Language, 1965(6)吕叔湘.形容词使用情况的一个考察[J].中国语文,1965(6)[In Chinese]

[8]   Lv Shuxiang. Formulate Grammar Questions in Mandarin   [M].The Commercial Press, 23-26,40-53,77-80(1979)吕叔湘.汉语语法分析问题[M].商务印书馆,23-26,40-53,77-80(1979)[In Chinese]

[9]   Lv Shuxiang. Research on Monosyllabic Adjectives in Mandarin [J]. Studies of The Chinese Language, 1982(1) 吕叔湘.单音形容词用法研究[J].中国语文,1982(1)[In Chinese]

[10] Li Linding. The Chinese Verbs [M]. Chinese Social Science Press,151-170(1990) 李临定.现代汉语动词[M].中国社会科学出版社,151-170(1990)[In Chinese]

[11] Lakoff.G and M.Jonhson.Metopher We Live By[M].Chicago:The University of Chicago Press,1980.

[12] Li, Yongzhong. Metonymy and Construction Coercion[J]. *Journal of PLA University of Foreign Languages*, 2004, 27(2):10-14 李勇忠. 构式义、转喻与句式压制[J].解放军外国语学院学报 2004, 27(2):10-14[In Chinese]

[13] Li, Yongzhong. The Conceptual Essence and the Pragmatic Significance of Metonymy[J]. *Foreign Language and Their Teaching*, 2005, 197(8):1-4. 李勇忠. 转喻的概念本质及其语用学意义[J].外语与外语教学, 2005, 197(8):1-4[In Chinese]

[14] Lu, Jianming. On Metaphor and Metonymy[J]. *Journal of Foreign Language*, 2009, 32(1):44-50 陆俭明.转喻、隐喻散议[J].外国语, 2009, 32(1):44-50 [In Chinese]

[15] Ronald W.Langacker. Foundations of Congnitive Grammar:Theoretical Prerequisites[M].Stanford University Press,1987.

[16] Ma Qingzhu. The Chinese Verb and Verbal Constructions [M]. Peking University Press,12-85(2004) 马庆株,汉语动词和动词性结构[M].北京大学出版社,12-85(2004) [In Chinese]

[17] Meng Cong. Dictionary of Chinese Verbs Usage [M]. The Commercial Press,2012 孟琮等.汉语动词用法词典[M].商务印书馆,2012[In Chinese]

[18] Shen, Jiaxuan. A Metonymic Model of Transferred Designation of De-constructions in Mandarin Chinese[J]. *Contemporary linguistics*, 1999, 1(1):3-15 沈家煊.转指和转喻[J].当代语言学, 1999, 1(1):3-15[In Chinese]

[19] Xu, Shenghuan. Metonymy and the Logic of Taxonomy[J]. *Foreign Language Teaching and Research*, 2008, 40(2):93-99 徐盛桓.转喻与分类逻辑[J].外语教学与研究, 2008, 40(2):93-99[In Chinese]

[20] Yuan, Yulin. On a descriptive system of qualia structure of Chinese nouns and its application in parsing complex Chinese grammatical phenomena[J]. *Contemporary linguistics*, 2004, 16(1):31-48.s 袁毓林[J].汉语名词物性结构的描写体系和运用案例当代语言学, 2004, 16(1):31-48.s[In Chinese]

[21] Yao Zhenwu. Reasons and Rules of the Nominalization of Verb Phrases [J]. Studies of The Chinese Language, 1996(1) 姚振武.汉语谓词性成分名词化的原因及规律[J].中国语文,1996(1) [In Chinese]

[22] Yu Shiwen. The Grammartical Knowledge-base of Contemporary Chinese-A Complete Specification [M]. Tsinghua University Press,2003 俞士汶等.现代汉语语法信息词典详解（第二版）[M].清华大学出版社,2003[In Chinese]

[23] Zhu Dexi. Research on Adjectives in Mandarin [J]. Linguistic Research,1956(1) 朱德熙.现代汉语形容词研究[J],语文研究,1956(1)[In Chinese]

[24] Zhu Dexi. Grammar Notes [M]. The Commercial Press,110-124(1982)朱德熙.语法讲义[M].商务印书馆,110-124(1982)[In Chinese]

[25] Zhang Guoxian. The Selective Differences of Monosyllabic and Disyllabic Adjectives [M]. Chinese Language Learning.1996(3)张国宪.单双音节形容词的选择性差异[M].汉语学习.1996(3)[In Chinese]

[26] Zhang Guoxian. A Study on the Function and Cognition of Adjectives in Modern Chinese [M]. The Commercial Press,42,359-361(1979)张国宪.现代汉语形容词功能与认知研究[M].北京商务印书馆,42,359-361(1979) [In Chinese]

[27] Zheng Huaide: Dictionary of Chinese Adjectives Usage [M]. The Commercial Press,2010 郑怀德等,汉语形容词用法词典[M].商务印书馆,2010[In Chinese]

A Corpus-based Study on the Structure of V in "进行 [jin4xing2]+V" in Modern Chinese

Yujie Liu, Pengyuan Liu[1]

Language Monitoring and Social Computing Laboratory, National Language Resource Monitoring and Research Center, School of Information Science, Beijing Language and Culture University,
Beijing, China

lovely6968@126.com，liupengyuan@pku.edu.cn

Abstract This paper argues for the necessity of study on the structure of "V" in "进行[jin4xing2][2]+V" based on the analysis of the previous research , and gives a full description and analysis of it based on the large-scale corpus. In the choice of verb of predicate-object structure, only verbs that have external object in semantic are allowed to enter "进行[jin4xing2]+V" structure. In the syllable, only double-syllable or tri-syllable verbs can be the verb object of "进行 [jin4xing2]", and those tri-syllable verbs are mainly composed in additional morphology, with affixes like"化[hua4]、热[re4]、再[zai4]"and so on.

Keywords: dummy verb   structure   syllable   word formation

1   Introduction

Dummy verb is a special part of speech, Lv_Shuxiang (1980) first proposed the name "dummy verb" in Chinese, which is also known as "colorless verb" (Song Yuke, 1982), "virtual of verb", "quasi predicate object verb" (Zhu Dexi, 1985) and "leading verb" (Fan Xiao, Hu Yushu 1987), "delexical verb" (Diao Yanbin, 2004), but most of the scholars are used to using the name "dummy verb" in their studies, such as Zhou Gang (1987), Li Linding (1990), Hu Yushu, Fan Xiao (1995), Shao Jingmin (2003), Shen Jiaxuan, Zhang Jiangzhi(2013) and so on. In Zhao Yuanren's book *A Grammar of Spoken Chinese*, it is called dummy word, from which the names of all the Chinese translations are derived. In English, dummy word often refers to a kind of form which is introduced into the structure or analysis to ensure that a legal sentence is produced while in Chinese dummy word tends to have different performance in different situations. when collocated with a verb, it is only functioning in structure, but with nominal object, it's unable to deny the lexical meaning of it. Many scholars don't distinguish the

---

[1] Corresponding author

[2] Since "进行[jin4xing2]" in this paper doesn't have lexical meaning, only help construct a grammatical sentence, so we don't list its lexical meaning in this paper.

ⓒ Springer International Publishing AG 2016
M. Dong et al. (Eds.): CLSW 2016, LNAI 10085, pp. 187–198, 2016
DOI: 10.1007/978-3-319-49508-8_18

different situations when they discuss the dummy verb. Moreover, thought the syntactic functions and pragmatic functions of this kind of verbs are analyzed, the analysis on its structure is still not clear enough. Scholars have realized that there are still different syntactic and semantic features within these verbs, so they divide them into two categories: "加以[jia1yi3]" and "进行[jin4xing2]" ,and make a comparative study, such as Zhou Gang、Hu Yushu etc. Other scholars have studied their grammatical function and syntactic performance from different perspectives. Yuan Jie、Xia Yunyi(1984)、Zhu Dexi(1985)、Shen Jiaxuan、Zhang Jiangzhi(2013)、DiaoYanbin (2004)、Chen Yongli(2006)、Li Guimei(2012)、Du Qun'er(2013)、Yu Lili(2008) all have made a lot of researches on the use and functions of dummy verb.

"进行[Jin4Xing2]" is a typical member of the dummy verb and many scholars take it out for separate analysis and discussion. For example, Song Yuke (1982) has studied the grammatical functions of "进行[Jin4Xing2]". DiaoYanbin (2004) has analyzed the use and function of "进行[Jin4Xing2]" in his doctoral dissertation. Jiang Zixia, Ding Chongming (2011) and Qiu Wei (2013) has discussed the forming mechanism of the function of the "进行[Jin4Xing2]" sentences. Pang Jiaguang (2012) has conducted a study on "进行[Jin4Xing2]" from the perspective of cognitive grammar.

In previous studies, few of the "进行[Jin4Xing2]+V" structures has been directly discussed, scholars tended to discuss the case of noun object and verb object together. This paper argues that the most significant feature of the dummy verb is that it's lexical meaning is weaken or even disappear when it is collocated with the verb object, and the action of the whole sentence is assumed by the verb object. Therefore, it is very necessary to focus on the "V" in the structure of "dummy verb +V". This paper will take the typical dummy verb "进行[Jin4Xing2]"as an example, and conduct analysis and researches on the "V" in the structure of "进行[Jin4Xing2]+V"[3]. At the same time, in view of the previous studies which lack supports from a large number of corpus data, the study of this paper will give an objective description and analysis of the actual use of such structure and a further research on the basis of retrieval, statistical and econometric analysis based on a large corpus of BCC (hereinafter called BCC)[4].

---

[3]This study doesn't include other forms that other constituents appear between "进行[Jin4Xing2]" and "V".

[4] In this paper, we use the BCC Chinese corpus of Beijing Language and Culture University. This corpus is the largest Chinese corpus in China at present, total number of characters are about 15 billion, including comprehensive(1 billion)、literature(3 billion)、microblg(3 billion)、newspapers(2 billion)、science (3 billion) and ancient Chinese. This paper uses the data from literature、newspapers、microblog and science and technology(about 11 billion characters in total) to conduct our studies.

2   Structural characteristics of "V" in "进行[Jin4Xing2]+V"

Through the BCC query statistics and primarily screening, we get 1605 common verb objects of "进行[Jin4Xing2]".These 1600 words are legitimate collocations which all appear in the literature, newspapers, and science and technology works and micro-blog. We temporarily call them common words, and the data coverage of the more than 1600 common words has reached 95%. As a result, we will analyze the data in the context of common words. The data below is the coverage of common words.

Table 1. Coverage of common words

The first N common words	the quantity of language data	Word coverage rate	Corpus coverage
20	172627	1.25%	34.73%
50	231178	3.12%	46.51%
100	282729	6.23%	56.89%
200	345063	12.46%	69.43%
300	381141	18.69%	76.69%
400	406862	24.92%	81.86%
500	427161	31.15%	85.95%
1605	497010	100.00%	100.00%

We can see from Table 1 that in the "进行[Jin4Xing2]+V" structure, the top 400 high frequency verb collocations account for 24.92% species of common words, whose corpus coverage rate reaches 81.86%. The distribution of the verbs which can be used as the object of "进行[Jin4Xing2]" is more concentrated and also has a larger coverage area. Therefore, this section of the analysis of the structure of V in the structure of "进行[Jin4Xing2]+V" will focus on these 400 verbs.

2.1   Investigation of word formation

Yuan Chunfa and Huang Changning (1998) have conducted a statistical research on the compound word formation of Chinese parts of speech. The distribution of the five main types of verb in the conclusion of the thesis is shown in Table 2.

Table 2.the word formation of Chinese verb from the statistic of Yuan & Huang[5]

combined structure	adverbial-centered structure	predicate-object Structure	predicate-complement structure	subject-predicate structure
4257	3647	7134	927	243

---

[5] We only choose five word formations in Yuan & Huang's article which are the same as that of high frequency verb, so it's sum of proportion is not equal to 1.

| 27.17% | 23.3% | 39.7% | 5.92% | 1.55% |

From Table2 we find the word formation of Chinese verb are mainly predicate-object structure、combined structure and adverbial-centered structure and they account for 90% of the total amount of the double syllable verb. Generally speaking, the word formation of Chinese compound word is mainly predicate-object structure. The number of verbs in predicate-object structure is almost two times that of the adverbial-centered structure, followed by combined structure and adverbial-centered structure. And verbs in the predicate-complement structure and subject-predicate structure are much more less.

We analyze the structure of the first 400 high frequency verb object. The results are as follows.

Table 3. Analysis of the structure of the top 400 high-frequency words

combined structure	adverbial-centered structure	predicate-object structure	predicate-complement structure	subject-predicate structure
151	137	51	52	8
37.75%	34.25%	12.75%	13.00%	2.00%

From Table3 we find that the distribution of the word structure of Chinese verb collocated with "进行[Jin4Xing2]" is not the same as the distribution of word structure of general verbs. In the first 400 high-frequency verbs, combined structure and adverbial-centered structure are the main structure of verbs, such as "分析[fen1xi1](*analyze*)/计算[ji4suan4](*calculate*)/控制[kong4zhi4](*control*)/学习[xue2xi2](*study*)/处理[chu4li3](*deal with*)" in combined structure and "统计[tong3ji4](*count*)/总结[zong2jie2](*summarize*)/反击[fan3ji1](*counterattack*)/座谈[zuo4tan2](*symposium*)" in adverbial-centered structure. Predicate-object structure and predicate-complement structure also occupy a certain proportion while subject-predicate structure is at least which only contains eight words in the first 400 high frequency words. Except for the predicate-object structure, Table 3 is consistent with the basic word formation rules of verbs in Table 2.

As for the predicate-object structure which accounts for nearly 40% in the original word formation of Chinese verbs, the number of verbs in it only accounts for about one eighth. We roughly analyze the statistics of one thousand and six hundred common words and find out some of the verbs in predicate-object that can be used as the verb object of "进行 [Jin4Xing2]", such as "评价 [ping2jia4](*evaluate*)、规范[gui1fan4](*regularize*)、动员[dong4yuan2](*mobilize*)、采样 [cai3yang4](*sampling*)、抽样 [chou1yang4](*sampling*)、分流 [fen1liu2](*divert*)、立案[li4an4](*place a case on file*)、合资[he2zi1](*joint venture*)、充电 [chong1dian4](*charge*)、投票 [tou2piao4](*vote*)、排队 [pai2dui4](*wait in a line*)、定位 [ding4wei4](*locate*)、减压 [jian3ya1](*decompression*)、消毒[xiao1du2](*disinfect*)、罚款[fa2kuan3](*fine*)、

投标[tou2biao1](*bid*)、融资[rong2zi1](*finance*)、反腐[fan2fu3](*anti-corruption*)、立法[li4fa3](*legislation*)、备案[bei4an4](*filing*)、筹资[chou2zi1](*finance*)、排名[pai2ming2](*rank*)、征税[zheng1shui4](*taxation*)、联网[lian2wang3](*connect with the internet*)、立项[li4xiang4](*project establishment*)、备课[bei4ke4](*prepare lesson*)、排序[pai2xu4](*sort*)、敛财[lian3cai2](*accumulate wealth*)、分类[fen1lei4](*classify*)"etc. The number of words in this kind of structure is no more than one hundred which only accounts for 6% in the whole of more than one thousand words. Let's take a look at some example sentences:

(1) 不应根据在其他人眼中的属性，而应基于某个人能干什么来对其**进行评价**。

We should judge one person based on what he is capable to rather than his personal attribution in other's eyes.

(2) 活动受到来自全国数千万玩家朋友的关注，百万玩家通过网络投票方式**进行投票**。

The activity has attracted attention from tens of millions game players around the country, and millions of game players can vote by internet voting.

(3) 因此，检察机关根据报案、控告和举报途径获取立案材料**进行立案**，无法获取犯罪嫌疑人的口供。

Therefore, the office of the public prosecutor filing a case according to the report of the prosecution, the prosecution and the way to obtain filing materials.

(4) 在机械表表面涂有黑色吸光条，当表盘转动光电管对其**进行采样**。

The mechanical watch is coated with a black light absorbing strip, and when the dial is rotated, the photoelectric tube is sampled.

From the examples above, we can see that in addition to its inner patient "value", the word"评价[ping2jia4](*evaluate*)" also has its object in semantic, namely "people". In addition to its inner patient " ballot", the word"投票[tou2piao4](*vote*)" also has its object in semantic, namely "internet game". In addition to its inner patient " case", the word"立案[li4an4](*put a case on file*)" has its object in semantic, namely "event". In addition to its inner patient " sample", the word"采样[cai3yang4](*sampling*)" has its object in semantic, namely "population". But structures like "进行吃饭[jin4xing2 chi1fan4]/进行喝水[jin4xing2 he1shui3]/进行唱歌[jin4xing2 chang4ge1]……" are all grammatically wrong for the fact that "吃饭[chi1fan4](*have a meal*)、喝水[he1shui3](*drink*)、唱歌[chang4ge1](*sing*)" only have their inner patient without any external object。"吃饭[chi1fan4](*have a meal*)" only has one inner patient "rice". "喝水[he1shui3](*drink*)" only has one inner patient "water"."唱歌[chang4ge1](*sing*)" only has one inner patient "songs". That's why those words are not allowed to enter "进行[jin4xing2]+V".

Diao Yanbin (2004) has put forward an opinion that the "进行[jin4xing2]" sentence is a kind of stress. It emphasizes the content of the relevant actions through the focus shift. According to the analysis above we find that the idea that the V which is allowed to enter "进行[jin4xing2]+V" must has external object is in accordance with Diao's study. Because only when the verb has external object, "进行[jin4xing2]" sentence has object to shift when shifting the focus of this sentence, although sometimes the external object does not necessarily appear in the original sentence, but we can find out it based on the context. Accordingly, we believe that the main reason why verbs in predicate-object structure have access to "进行[jin4xing2]+V" is because the structure emphasizes the external object and usually the external object can be brought to the front of "进行[jin4xing2]+V" using preposition like "对[dui4]、将[jiang1]、向[xiang4]、把[ba3]".Taking a few sentences as examples:

(5)   目前一些企业在***进行赞助***时，存在误区。

At present, some enterprises have misunderstanding in the sponsorship.

(5')   目前一些企业在***对平台进行赞助***时，存在误区。

At present, some enterprises have misunderstanding in the sponsorship.

(6)   高尔夫模拟器采用电脑软件***进行控制***，可自动调节各种打法和击球距离，并能真实模拟高尔夫球的运动轨迹.

The golf simulator is controlled by computer software, can automatically adjust a variety of play and hitting distance and can truly simulate the trajectory of golf.

(6')   高尔夫模拟器采用电脑软件***对高尔夫球进行控制***，可自动调节各种打法和击球距离，并能真实模拟高尔夫球的运动轨迹.

The golf simulator is controlled by computer software, can automatically adjust a variety of play and hitting distance and can truly simulate the trajectory of golf.

(7)   一些村民害怕侵犯中国领土，不愿意去，公安人员就***进行训斥***和威胁。

Some villagers fear the invasion of Chinese territory and do not want to go, the public security personnel rebuked and threatened them.

(7')   一些村民害怕侵犯中国领土，不愿意去，公安人员就***对村民进行训斥***和威胁。

Some villagers fear the invasion of Chinese territory and do not want to go, the public security personnel rebuked and threatened them.

(8)   对这些商品的价格，国家物价局和各级地方政府要按管理权限，分别***进行整顿***，严格管理。

The State Price Bureau and local governments at all levels shall shake up and tightly regulate the price of those commodities in accordance with the administrative authority.

(8')   对这些商品的价格，国家物价局和各级地方政府要按管理权限，分别***对商品价格进行整顿***，严格管理。

The State Price Bureau and local governments at all levels shall shake up and tightly regulate the price of those commodities in accordance with the administrative authority.

The examples above show that we can usually highlight the external object by advancing it using prepositions. While most of verbs in predicate-object structure only have their inner patient which cannot be separated , only a few verbs in predicate-object structure have external object and only those words will be allowed to enter "进行 [jin4xing2]+V" structure. So the verb in "进行 [jin4xing2]+V" is selective in structure. When directly collocated with "进行 [jin4xing2]",the verb object prefers verbs in combined structure and adverbial-centered structure. while in the selection of verbs in predicate-object structure, only words which have external object can be the verb object of "进行 [jin4xing2]". It is this kind of restriction that greatly reduces the proportion of verbs in predicate-object structure in the"进行[jin4xing2]+V" structure.

2.2   syllable

Through the statistics of the feature of syllables of V, we have found that there are certain rules in the syllable, as shown in the table below:

Table 4.statistics of syllable of common words

Single syllable	Double-syllable	Tri-syllable
0	1588	17

According to the corpus retrieval and statistical results, we find that there is no single syllable verb in "进行[jin4xing2]+V" structure and double-syllable words accounts for most proportion and there are also a few tri-syllable verbs. For why there is no single syllable verb in this structure, many scholars have given their views. A typical view is what early Zhu Dexi (1985) has put forward, "the object of the request of the virtual verb is the nominal composition of the action. In line with the requirements of the syntax, there are only two categories: pure noun that represents an action and denominatives with the dual nature of the noun and verb. These two kinds of words are almost all produced in a short history of the written word double syllable words. In the spoken language, there is no denominatives in the single syllable or no pure noun that represents an action. This is the real reason why the object of virtual verb can only be double syllable word."[6] DiaoYanbin (2004) also has proposed that from the point of view of syllable, all of the single verb objects are double syllables, and most of the people have interpreted it as the requirement of "2+2" structure in syllable. It's true that according to the viewpoint of prosody, the combination of two standard foot are

---

[6]Zhu Dexi, a virtual verb and noun-verb in modern written Chinese, for the first International Conference on Chinese language teaching and learning, Journal of Peking University (Humanitie and Social Sciences), 1985 (5).

the most basic and most natural on the combination of Chinese phrases. And in predicate-object structure,"2+2" structures and "1+2" structures are acceptable while "2+1" structure is not acceptable. So it is reasonable that there is no single syllable verb object in our statistics. But many scholars have ignored the three syllable verbs in the "+V" structure, the total number of their data is about 1300 and most of it are those with suffix " 化 [hua4]", such as " 系统化 [xi4tong3hua4](systematization)、格式化 [ge2shi4hua4](formatting)、专业化 [zhuan1ye4hua4](specialize) 、 数字化 [shu4zi4hua4](digitalize) 、 精细化 [jing1xi4hua4](refine) 、 立体化 [li4ti3hua4](three-dimensional) 、 形象化 [xing2xiang4hua4](visualize) 、 个人化 [ge4ren2hua4](personalize) 、 全球化 [quan2qiu2hua4](globalize) 、 公式化 [gong1shi4hua4](formulate) 、 理论化 [li3lun4hua4](theorize) 、 理想化 [li3xiang3hua4](idealize) 、 形式化 [xing2shi4hua4](formalize) 、 规模化 [gui1mo2hua4](large-scale) 、 程序化 [li3xiang3hua4](programming)、产业化[chan3ye4hua4] (industrialize)、本土化 [ben3tu3hua4](localize) 、 国际化 [guo2ji4hua4](internationalize) 、 抽象化 [chou1xiang4hua4](abstract)、 多元化 [duo1yuan2hua4](diversify) 、 指数化 [zhi3shu4hua4](indexing) 、 私有化 [si1you3hua4](privatize) 、 拟人化 [ni3ren2hua4](personify)" etc.

According to Zhu Dexi's view that the verb object of "进行[jin4xing2]" are those denominatives with the dual nature of both noun and verb, we are going to discuss if the nominal features are obvious in those three syllable words mentioned above like " 系统化 [xi4tong3hua4](*systematization*) 、 格式化 [ge2shi4hua4](*formatting*) 、 全球化 [quan2qiu2hua4](*globalize*) 、 抽象化 [chou1xiang4hua4](*abstract*)" whose predicative nature is indisputable evident.

The nominal features of the double-syllable denominatives in " 进行 [jin4xing2]+V" displayed in the previous studies are as follows:

a. Can be directly affected by the noun modifier to form a modification-center structure

(数据)分析	(社会)调查	(科学)研究
Shu4ju4 fen1xi1	she4hui4 diao4cha2	ke1xue2 yan2jiu1
data analysis	*social survey*	*science research*
(课堂)讨论	(人口)统计	(结构)优化
Ke4tang2 tao3lun4	ren2kou3 tong3ji4	jie2gou4 you1hua4
class discussion	*demographic*	*structural optimum*

b. Some words can be modified by some quantitative words

一些 [yi4xie1](*some*)：进行 [jin4xing2]~ 调查 [diao4cha2](*research*)/ 分析 [fen1xi1](*analysis*)/ 研究 [yan2jiu1](*study*)/ 统计 [tong3ji4](*count*)/ 评价 [ping2jia4](*evaluate*)

不少 [bu4shao3](*not a few*)：进行 [jin4xing2]~ 修改 [xiu1gai3](*revise*)/ 解释 [jie3shi4](*explain*)/改进[gai3jin4](*improve*)

From the analysis of double-syllable verb object, we have confirmed their nominal features. Then let's have a look at those tri-syllable verbs whether they also have those nominal features[7]:

系统化：	（规则）系统化	（知识）系统化
Xi4tong3hua4	gui1ze2 xi4tong3hua4	zhi1shi2 xi4tong3hua4
Systematization	*Rule systematization*	*Knowledge systematization*
	*一些系统化	*不少系统化
	Yi4xie1 xi4tong3hua4	bu4shao3 xi4tong3hua4
	Some systematization	*not a few systematization*

全球化：	（资本）全球化	（经济）全球化
Quan2qiu2hua4	zi1ben3 quan2qiu2hua4	jing1ji4 quan2qiu2hua4
Globalization	*Capital globalization*	*economic globalization*
	*一些全球化	*不少全球化
	Yi4xie1 quan2qiu2hua4	bu4shao3quan2qiu2hua4
	Some globalization	*not a few globalization*

抽象化：	（概念）抽象化	（问题）抽象化
Chou1xiang4hua4	gai4nian4chou1xiang4hua4	wen4ti2 chou1xiang4hua4
Abstract	*concepts abstraction*	*problem abstraction*
	*一些抽象化	*不少抽象化
	Yi4xie1 chou1xiang4hua4	bu4shao3 chou1xiang4hua4
	Some abstraction	*not a few abstraction*

格式化：	（数据）格式化	（电脑）格式化
Ge2shi4hus4	shu4ju4 ge2shi4hua4	dian4nao3 ge2shi4hua4
Formatting	*data formatting*	*computer formatting*
	*一些格式化	*不少格式化
	Yi4xie1 ge2shi4hua4	bu4shao3 ge2shi4hua4
	Some formatting	*not a few formatting*

From the analysis above, we can easily notice that tri-syllable verbs with "化 [hua4]" as their suffix tend to be constituted in combined structure rather than in modification-center structure when collocated with a noun. Also they doesn't show strong nominal feature, instead its predicative nature is more obvious. In other words, the view of Zhu Dexi seems to be not too strict. In the discussion on this issue, Shen Jiaxuan (2012) has pointed out that once we accept the idea that denominatives are verbs when modified by adverbs or take an object and are nouns when modified by attributes or quantitative words, we would find that

---

[7] Here "*" means it is ungrammatical.

almost every verb in Chinese can be analyzed like this, including single syllable verbs. Let's take some single syllable verbs as examples[8]:

(9)   去 是 有　道理　的。
        It makes sense to go.

(10)   不 去 是 有　道理　的。
        It makes sense not to go.

(11)   跳　　很　重要。
        It is important to jump.

Therefore, Shen Jiaxuan has put forward the theory that nouns contain verbs and proposed the regularity of the change between nouns and verbs. He holds the view that Chinese verbs are part of nouns and the only difference between them is the degree of their nominal feature, and the predicative nature and nominal feature of the dummy verb and its verb object change synchronously. Since dummy verb is strongest in predicative nature, although its lexical meaning is empty, the verb object of it always presents strong nominal feature. Shen Jiaxuan's theory has solved the deficiency of Zhu Dexi's theory. But we still have problems when we use it to explain the tri-syllable verbs. As we analyzed above, the tri-syllable verbs present strong predicative nature , which means "N+XX 化" tends to be a subject-predicate structure and this kind of structure can't be modified by quantitative words. As a result, we think it's not very strict to explain the collocation with tri-syllable verbs using Shen Jiaxuan's theory.

In fact, through the observation of the double-syllable word we find there are some verbs with suffix "[化 hua4]" such as "虚化[xu1hua4](*virtual*)、简化 [jian3hua4](*simplify*)、深化[shen1hua4](*deepen*)、同化[tong2hua4](*assimilate*)" etc. Those tri-syllable verbs with suffix "[化 hua4]" have the same properties as these double-syllable verbs with suffix "[化 hua4]". They all represent a change in behavior and have strong predicative nature. Tri-syllable verbs like "热处理 [re4chu3li3](*heat treating*)、再加工[zai4jia1gong1](*reprocessing*)" also have access to "进行[jin4xing2]+V". The main characteristics are that they all consist of a double-syllable compound verb and an affix. So they are much similar to the double-syllable compound verb in many respects. However, the biggest difference between those tri-syllable verbs and traditional tri-syllable verbs is that those tri-syllable verbs are constituted in additional way. We hold the view that with the development of Chinese language and the contact with other languages, the length of Chinese word is getting longer and the collocation between Chinese phrase are not limited to "2+2" on syllable any more. "2+3" structure has appeared and developed and more tri-syllable verbs will be allowed to enter "进行 [jin4xing2]+V" structure.

---

[8]The examples here are derived from the article "talk about the function of dummy verbs" written by Shen Jiaxuan and Zhang Jiangzhi. Other examples in this paper are derived from BCC Chinese Corpus.

3   Conclusion

Through the investigation and statistics of large scale corpus BCC, this paper has described and analyzed the structure of V in the structure of "进行 [jin4xing2]+V". And we have proposed that it is selective on the structure of the verbs which can be used as the object of "进行[jin4xing2]". From the perspective of the formation of V, the main choice of the verb object of "进行[jin4xing2]" are verbs in combined structure and adverbial-centered structure and verbs in other structure only occupy a small part. Especially for verbs in predicate-object structure which account for a large proportion in the formation of whole Chinese verbs, the proportion of them in "进行[jin4xing2]+V" is unbelievable low. That is because most of verbs in predicate-object structure are intransitive verbs, so they don't have external object in semantic, which is in contrary to the function of emphasis of "进行[jin4xing2]+V" structure because they emphasize by shifting the focus(generally refers to the external object of V). As a result, only those verbs who have external object in semantic are allowed to enter "进行 [jin4xing2]+V" structure. From the perspective of the syllable of V, V in "进行 [jin4xing2]+V" structure are mostly double-syllable verbs and a few tri-syllable verbs. The reason why single-syllable verbs can't be the object of "进行 [jin4xing2]" is the limitation of morphology. "进行[jin4xing2]+V" structure itself is a predicate-object structure, so the limitation of morphology makes it un-grammatical to form a "2+1" structure. While tri-syllable verbs are not limited by morphology. That is because those tri-syllable verbs have much in common with double-syllable verbs except for the difference in syllable, which makes it possi-ble for those tri-syllable to become the object of "进行[jin4xing2]".

Acknowledgements

This research is supported by National Natural Science Foundation of China (No.61272215) and the project of Beijing Language and Culture University ("the Fundamental Research Funds for the Central Universities", No.16YJ030003).

Reference

1. DiaoYanbin.2004. Function of Modern Chinese Dummy verb. Journal of Ningxia University (Social Science Edition). Vol3. [in Chinese]
2. DiaoYanbin.2004. On Delexical verb. Doctoral Dissertation of Nankai University. [in Chinese]
3. Du Quner.2010. A Tentative Study on Dummy Verbs of Contemporary Chinese Language. master's degree thesis of Shanghai Normal University. [in Chinese]
4. Fan Xiao, Hu Yushu.1987. An Overview of Chinese Verbs. Shanghai: Shanghai Education Press. [in Chinese]
5. Hu Yushu, Fan Xiao.1995. Study of Verbs. Kaifeng: Henan University press. [in Chinese]
6. Kim Na'ai.2013. Study on Sentences with Dummy Verb "Jinxing" in Modern Chinese. mas-ter's degree thesis of Fudan University. [in Chinese]
7. Li Guimei.2012. the effect of the expression of dummy verb sentence pattern. Language

Teaching and Linguistic Studies. Vol4. [in Chinese]

8. Li Guimei.2015. a review of the research on Modern Chinese formal verbs. Journal of Zhejiang University of Science and Technology, Vol4. [in Chinese]

9. Li Linding.1990. modern Chinese verb, Beijing: Chinese Social Science Press. [in Chinese]

10. LvShuxiang.1980. the "modern Chinese" eight hundred words. Beijing: the Commercial Press. [in Chinese]

11. Pang Jiaguan.2012. a cognitive grammar study on the "verb" of the virtual verb. Chinese language learning. Vol4. [in Chinese]

12. Shao Jingmin.2007. the "modern Chinese theory". Shanghai: Shanghai Education Press. [in Chinese]

13. Shen Jiaxuan.2012. "the verb" Reflection: Problems and solutions. Chinese teaching in the world. Vol1. [in Chinese]

14. Shen Jiaxuan, Zhang Jiangzhi.2013. talk about the function of dummy verbs. TCSOL Studies. Vol2. [in Chinese]

15. Song Yuke.1982. the grammatical function of "carry out". Language Teaching and Linguistic Studies. Vol1. [in Chinese]

16. Xun Endong, Rao Gaoqi, Xiao Xiaoyue, Zang Jiaojiao.2016. Development of BCC corpus in the context of large data. Corpus Linguistics. Vol1. [in Chinese]

17. Yang Lixue.2015. The Research on Dummy Word Syntax in Modern Chinese. master's thesis of Jilin University. [in Chinese]

18. Yu Lil.2008. Research on Dummy Verb in Modern Chinese. master's degree thesis of Soochow University. [in Chinese]

19. Yuan Chunfa and Huang Changning.1998. Chinese morpheme and word building research based on morpheme database. Chinese teaching in the world. Vol2. [in Chinese]

20. Xia Yunyi, Yuan Jie.1984. random talks on virtual verbs. language studies. Vol2. [in Chinese]

21. Zhu Dexi.1985. a virtual verb and noun-verb in modern written Chinese. for the first International Conference on Chinese language teaching and learning, Journal of Peking University (Humanitie and Social Sciences), Vol5. [in Chinese]

A Study on Causative meaning of Verb-Resultative Construction in Mandarin Chinese Based on the Generative Lexicon Theory

Yiqiao Xia[1], Daqin Li [2]

[1]School of Communication&Animation, Qingdao University of Science&Technology,
Laoshan District, Qingdao, 266061, China
xiayiqiao58@126.com
[2]Faculty of Literature&Law, Communication University of China,
Chaoyang District, Beijing, 100024, China
liidaaqiin@163.com

Abstract. Based on the Generative Lexicon Theory, this paper analyses the co-compositon and the qualia projections of the predicate verb denoting an action and the complement verb describing the result in the Verb-Resultative Construction. The paper reveals that the co-compostion of the qualia structures results in a derived causative sense of the VP, where the AGENTIVE role of the action verb matches that of the complement verb, and the FORMAL role of the action verb matches that of the complement verb. In consequence, under the qualia unification $(QS\ \alpha\ (\beta) = QS\ \alpha \cap QS\ \beta)$, the FORMAL role of the complement verb is shared with that of the VP, and the AGENTIVE role of the action verb is shared with that of the VP, resulting in a derived causative and aspectually telic interpretation.

Keywords: Verb-Resultative construction· Causative· Generative lexicon theory

1   Introduction

Verb-Resultative Construction in Mandarin Chinese is a representative expression, which expresses the meaning of the causation, and its syntactic representation and semantic structure are very complicated. The study on it not only involves the study on lexical-semantic features, but also involves the study on the interface between semantics and syntax. Based on the GLT, the paper attempts to explore why the VRC can generate causative meaning. Through the analysis of the co-composition, the qualia unification, and the qualia projections of a predicate verb denoting an action and a complement verb describing the result, we explore the argument structures, the event structures, and the qualia structures of two verbs in the VRC, and we also explore the interaction among these structures. In addition, we explore the syntactic encoding of the causative event schema, and thus providing a novel theoretical

ⓒ Springer International Publishing AG 2016
M. Dong et al. (Eds.): CLSW 2016, LNAI 10085, pp. 199–213, 2016
DOI: 10.1007/978-3-319-49508-8_19

perspective and study methods on the studies of the interface between semantics and syntax of Mandarin Chinese.

2   The VRC represents a left-headed binary event

The Verb-Resultative Construction expressing the causative meaning is the product of the syntactic encoding of the causative event schema. By the co-composition of a predicate verb denoting an action and a complement verb describing result, the VRC projects the information of the verbs to the syntactic level. According to the Extended Event Structure, the VRC represents a TRANSITION EVENT, focusing the action bringing about a state. As a kind of causative expression, the VRC is a binary event structure constituted of 2 subevents, a causing event e_1 and a caused event e_2, and the initial event $e1$ is headed. There are 2 kinds of sequential relations between subevents, that is "$e_1 <^\propto e_2$" and "$e_1 <o^\propto e_2$". The causing event can completely precede or precede and overlap the resulting event.

$$e_1 <^\propto e_2 \tag{1}$$

A complex event constituted of two subevents, the causing event e_1 and the caused event e_2, where e_1 and e_2 are temporally ordered such that the first completely precedes the second, can be lexicalized with a relation we will call "exhaustive ordered part of ", $<^\propto$. For example:

1. 我打碎了杯子。(*I broke the cup.*)

$$e_1 <o^\propto e_2 \tag{2}$$

A complex event constituted of two basically simultaneous subevents, the causing event e_1 and the caused event e_2, where the causing event starts before the caused event, can be lexicalized with a relation we will call "exhaustive ordered overlap", $<o^\propto$. It involves a precede and overlap relation between the process and the resulting state. For example:

2. 水泡湿了鞭炮。(*The water wet the firecracker.*)

The event schema of the VRC expressing Causative meaning is described as follows:

$$
\begin{aligned}
EVENT=E1 &=e_1: \text{ process} \\
E2 &=e_2: \text{ state} \\
RESTR&=e_1 <\propto e_2 \text{ or } e_1 <o^\propto e_2 \\
HEAD&=e_1 \\
QUALIA=FORMAL &= a\_\_Result\ (e_2,\ y) \\
AGENTIVE&= a\_\_act\ (e_1,\ x,\ y)
\end{aligned}
\tag{3}
$$

3   The co-composition and the qualia projections of the predicate verb and the complement verb in the VRC

The co-composition operation is the function application $(QS\alpha(\beta) = QS\alpha \cap QS\beta)$ caused by the qualia unification. The causative meaning of the VRC is closely related to the qualia structures of the 2 verbs in the VP. The operation of the qualia unification generates the causative meaning of the VRC. When the operation of co-compostion in the VRC occurs, the function application binds the FORMAL role of the complement verb into the qualia structure of the action verb as its FORMAL role, and binds the AGENTIVE role of the action verb into the qualia structure of the complement verb as its AGENTIVE role. A type of feature unification occurs, licensed by the identity of qualia values for AGENTIVE and FORMAL respectively in two verbs. The complement verb co-specifies the action verb. The operation of co-compositon results in a qualia structure for the VP that reflects aspects of both constituents. The co-compostion of the qualia structures results in a derived causative sense of the VP, where the AGENTIVE role of the action verb matches that of the complement verb, and the FORMAL role of the action verb matches that of the complement verb. In consequence, the AGENTIVE role of the action verb acts as the AGENTIVE role of the entire VP, and the FORMAL role of the complement verb acts as the FORMAL role of the entire VP.

According to the traditional linguistics, verbs are divided into 2 subcategories, that is the transitive verbs and the intransitive verbs. It is somehow a vague taxonomy. In this paper, we adopt the classifying criteria of the Modern Linguistics, and divide Chinese verb into 3 subcategories, that is the accusative verbs, the unaccusative verbs and the unergative verbs. We analyse the co-compostion and syntactic projection of these verbs. The dual combination of three kinds of verbs should generate 9 kinds of combination form, but we only find 7 in the VRC.

3.1 The collocation of an accusative verb and an unergative verb

The first verb is an accusative verb, and the second verb is an unergative verb in the VRC.

3.张三赶跑了李四。(*Zhang San chased Li Si away.*)

According to the argument coherence, the events must cohere in some way, such that the lexical item is predicated of the same individual over at least two consecutive events. The relation expressed by the causing event and that expressed by the resulting event must make reference to at least one parameter in common. This reference can be direct or indirect. The causing event e_1 and the resulting event e_2 have a common argument "李四" (*Li Si*).

$$\left[\begin{array}{l} \text{赶}\ (chase) \\ \text{EVENTSTR} = \left[\begin{array}{l} E_1 = e_1{:}process \\ E_2 = e_2{:}state \\ RESTR = e_1 <_{\propto} e_2 \\ HEAD = e_1 \end{array}\right] \\ \text{ARGSTR} = \left[\begin{array}{l} ARG1 = \boxed{1}\left[\begin{array}{l} animate_ind \\ FORMAL = physobj \end{array}\right] \\ ARG2 = \boxed{2}\left[\begin{array}{l} animate_ind \\ FORMAL = physobj \end{array}\right] \end{array}\right] \\ \text{QUALIA} = \left[\begin{array}{l} FORMAL = leave\ or\ move(e_1, \boxed{2}) \\ AGENT = utterence\ or\ action_act(e_1, \boxed{1}, \boxed{2}) \end{array}\right] \end{array}\right]$$

Fig. 1. The lexical representation for the verb "赶" *(chase)*

The accusative verb "赶"(*chase*) represents a binary event, and its subevents are the action of "赶"(*chase*), and the result of "赶"(*chase*). It has 2 TRURE ARGUMENTS, that is an agent argument and a patient argument, both of which are the animate individual. "The utterence" or "push" acts as its AGENT role and the "leave" or "move" acts as its FORMAL role and TELIC role.

$$
\begin{bmatrix}
跑 \qquad (r u n) \\[4pt]
E V E N T S T R = [E_1 = e_1 : p r o c e s s] \\[4pt]
A R G S T R = \begin{bmatrix} A R G 1 = \boxed{1} \begin{bmatrix} i n d \\ F O R M A L = p h y s o b j \end{bmatrix} \end{bmatrix} \\[4pt]
Q U A L I A = \begin{bmatrix} F O R M A L = m o v e (e_1, \boxed{1}) \\ A G E N T = r u n\_a c t (e_1, \boxed{1}) \end{bmatrix}
\end{bmatrix}
$$

Fig. 2. The lexical representation for the verb "跑" *(run)*

The unergative verb "跑"(*run*) represents a simple event, and it has a TRUE ARGUMENT. The argument is an agent argument, and it might be an animate individual, or it might be a motor vehicle such as "train" or "car". "Making sth/sb move or leave" acts as the TELIC role of the verb "赶"(*chase*), and "move" acts as the FORMAL role of the verb "跑"(*run*). A type of feature unification occurs, and thus the TELIC role of "赶"(*chase*) and the FORMAL role of "跑"(*run*) matches. "李四"(*Li Si*) is an animate individual, so it satisfies the requirement of the object of the verb "赶"(*chase*) and 跑 (*run*).

$$
\begin{bmatrix}
李 四 (\quad L \quad i \quad S \quad i) \\[4pt]
A R G S T R = [A R G 1 = x : h u m a n] \\[4pt]
Q U A L I A = [F O R M A L = a n i m a t e\_i n d]
\end{bmatrix}
$$

Fig. 3. The lexical representation for the noun "李四"(*Li Si)*

Given these three expressions, the qualia structure resulting from co-compostion within the VP[vp 赶跑李四]*(chase Li Si away)* can be expressed as follows:

$$
\begin{bmatrix}
赶 \, 跑 \, 李 \, 四 \qquad (c h a s e\ L i\ S i\ a w a y) \\[4pt]
E V E N T S T R = \begin{bmatrix} E_1 = e_1 : p r o c e s s \\ E_2 = e_2 : s t a t e \\ R E S T R = \angle_\alpha \\ H E A D = e_1 \end{bmatrix} \\[6pt]
A R G S T R = \begin{bmatrix} A R G 1 = \boxed{1} \\ A R G 2 = \boxed{2} \begin{bmatrix} 李 四 (L i S i) \\ Q U A L I A = \begin{bmatrix} p h y s o b j - l c p \\ F O R M A L = \boxed{3} \end{bmatrix} \end{bmatrix} \end{bmatrix} \\[6pt]
Q U A L I A = \begin{bmatrix} c a u s e - l c p \\ F O R M A L = P (e_2, \square [\boxed{3}]) \\ A G E N T = 赶 \ (C h a s e)\_a c t (e_1, \boxed{1}, \boxed{2}) \end{bmatrix}
\end{bmatrix}
$$

Fig. 4. The lexical representation for the VP [vp 赶跑李四]*(chase Li Si away)*

" 赶 跑 "(*chase away*) make " 李 四 "(*Li Si*) leave the original position, and □ represents the change of the location or state of "李四" (*Li Si*).

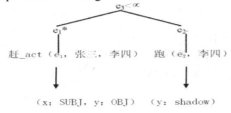

Fig. 5. The qualia projection of "张三赶跑了李四" (*Zhang San chased Li Si away*)

This can also be represented by the mapping given below:

a. Qi: R (e₁*, "张三" (*Zhan San*), "李四"(*Li Si*)) $\rightarrow$ x: SUBJ, y: OBJ   (4)

b. Qj: P (e₂, "李四" *(Li Si)*) $\rightarrow$ shadowed

According to the HEADEDNESS theory, only arguments associated with the headed event are obligatorily expressed at surface structure. The headless events, along with their arguments are shadowed, resulting in an interpretation with quantification closure over these arguments. "张三赶跑了李四" (*Zhang San chased Li Si away*) is a left-headed event structure, so it foregrounds the AGENTIVE predicate, and projects all arguments "张三" (*Zhang San*) and "李四" (*Li Si*) therein. And the resulting event is the headless event, consequently shadowing the arguments "李四" (*Li Si*).

3.2   The collocation of an unergative verb and an accusative verb

The first verb is an unergative verb, and the second verb is an accusative verb in the VRC.

4.我跑忘了一件事。(*I forgot to do something because of running.*)

The lexical representation for the unergative verb "跑"(*run*) is illustrated above, and the lexical representation for the accusative verb "忘" (*forget*) is illustrated as follows:

$$
\begin{bmatrix}
忘 \quad (forget) & & \\
ARGSTR = \begin{bmatrix} ARG1 = \boxed{1}\begin{bmatrix} animate\_ind \\ FORMAL = physobj \end{bmatrix} \\ ARG2 = \boxed{2}\begin{bmatrix} ind \\ FORMAL = physobj \end{bmatrix} \end{bmatrix} \\
QUALIA = \begin{bmatrix} AGENT = forget\_act(e_1, \boxed{1}, \boxed{2}) \end{bmatrix}
\end{bmatrix}
$$

Fig. 6. The lexical representation for the accusative verb "忘" *(forget)*

The accusative verb "忘" (*forget*) has two TRUE ARGUMENTS. The ARG1 is an agent argument, and the ARG2 is a patient argument. The ARG1 must be an animate individual.

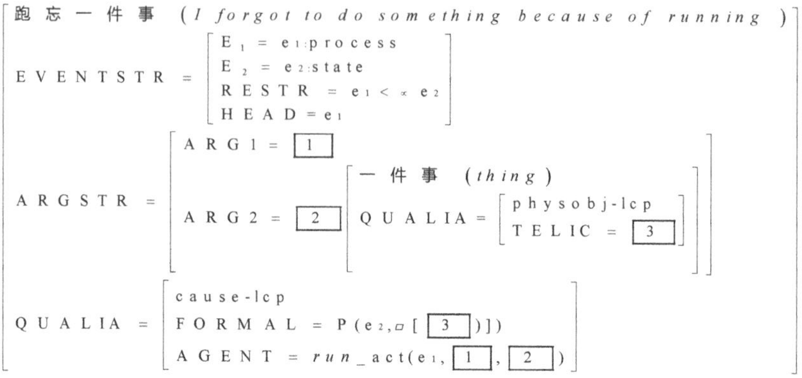

$$
\begin{bmatrix}
跑 忘 一 件 事 \quad (I\ forgot\ to\ do\ something\ because\ of\ running\ ) \\
EVENTSTR = \begin{bmatrix} E_1 = e_1\text{:process} \\ E_2 = e_2\text{:state} \\ RESTR = e_1 <_\propto e_2 \\ HEAD = e_1 \end{bmatrix} \\
ARGSTR = \begin{bmatrix} ARG1 = \boxed{1} \\ ARG2 = \boxed{2} \begin{bmatrix} 一 件 事 \quad (thing) \\ QUALIA = \begin{bmatrix} physobj\text{-}lcp \\ TELIC = \boxed{3} \end{bmatrix} \end{bmatrix} \end{bmatrix} \\
QUALIA = \begin{bmatrix} cause\text{-}lcp \\ FORMAL = P(e_2, \square\ [\ \boxed{3}\ )]) \\ AGENT = run\_act(e_1, \boxed{1}, \boxed{2}) \end{bmatrix}
\end{bmatrix}
$$

Fig. 7. The lexical representation for the VP "跑忘一件事" *(I forgot to do something because of running)*

In the VP "我跑忘了一件事"(*I forgot to do something because of running*), the AGENTIVE role of the action verb "跑"(*run*) matches that of the complement verb "忘"(*forget*), and the FORMAL role of the complement verb "忘"(*forget*) matches that of the action verb "跑" (*run*). In consequence, the AGENTIVE role for "跑"(*run*) acts as the AGENTIVE role of the entire VP, and the FORMAL role of "忘"(*forget*) acts as the FORMAL role of the entire VP.

The qualia projection of "我跑忘了一件事"(*I forgot to do something because of running*) is illustrated as follows:

$$\text{a. Qi: R}(e_1\text{*, "我"}(I)) \rightarrow \text{x: SUBJ} \tag{5}$$
$$\text{b. Qj: P}(e_2, \text{"我" }(I), \text{一件事}(thing)) \rightarrow \text{x: shadowed, y: OBJ}$$

3.3 The collocation of an unergative verb and an unaccusative verb

The first verb is an unergative verb, and the second verb is an unaccusative verb in the VRC.

5.我哭肿了眼睛。 (*My eyes are swollen for crying.*)

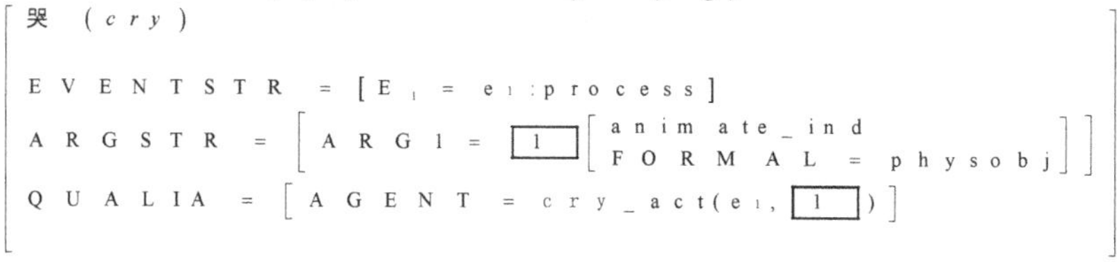

$$
\begin{bmatrix}
哭 \quad (cry) \\
EVENTSTR = [E_1 = e_1\text{:process}] \\
ARGSTR = \begin{bmatrix} ARG1 = \boxed{1} \begin{bmatrix} animate\_ind \\ FORMAL = physobj \end{bmatrix} \end{bmatrix} \\
QUALIA = [AGENT = cry\_act(e_1, \boxed{1})]
\end{bmatrix}
$$

Fig. 8.   The lexical representation for the verb "哭"*(cry)*

The unergative verb "哭"(*cry*) represents a TRANSITION event, and has a TRUE ARGUMENT. The ARG1 is an animate individual.

$$\begin{bmatrix} \text{肿} \ (swollen) \\ \text{ARGSTR} = \begin{bmatrix} \text{ARG 1} = \boxed{1}\begin{bmatrix} animate\_ind \\ FORMAL = physobj \end{bmatrix} \\ \text{D-ARG 1} = x : T_1 = \boxed{2} \end{bmatrix} \\ \text{EVENTSTR} = \begin{bmatrix} E_1 = e_1{:}state \\ D\text{-}E_1 = e_2{:}\sigma \\ RESTR = e_2 < \propto e_1 \\ HEAD = e_1 \end{bmatrix} \\ \text{QUALIA} = \begin{bmatrix} FORMAL = swollen(e_1, \boxed{1}) \\ AGENT = exp\_act(e_2, \boxed{1}, \boxed{2}) \end{bmatrix} \end{bmatrix}$$

Fig. 9. The lexical representation for the verb "肿"*(swollen)*

The unaccusative verb "肿"*(swollen)* represents a right-headed binary event, and it has a TRUE ARGUMENT, a DEFAULT ARGUMENT and a Default PROCESS. The Default PROCESS e_2 acts as the AGENT role that brings about the state.

$$\begin{bmatrix} \text{哭 肿 眼 睛} \ (eyes\ are\ swollen\ for\ crying) \\ \text{EVENTSTR} = \begin{bmatrix} E_1 = e_1{:}process \\ E_2 = e_2{:}state \\ RESTR = e_1 < o \propto e_2 \\ HEAD = e_1 \end{bmatrix} \\ \text{ARGSTR} = \begin{bmatrix} \text{ARG 1} = \boxed{1} \\ \text{ARG 2} = \boxed{2}\begin{bmatrix} eye \\ QUALIA = \begin{bmatrix} physobj.info\text{-}lcp \\ FORMAL = \boxed{3} \end{bmatrix} \end{bmatrix} \end{bmatrix} \\ \text{QUALIA} = \begin{bmatrix} dc\text{-}lcp \\ FORMAL = P(e_2, \sigma[\boxed{3}])]) \\ AGENT = cry\_act(e_1, \boxed{1}, \boxed{2}) \end{bmatrix} \end{bmatrix}$$

Fig. 10. The lexical representation for the VP "哭肿眼睛"*(eyes are swollen for crying)*.

The AGENTIVE role of the qualia structure of the complement verb "肿"*(swollen)* implies a stage-level predicate. This stage-level predicate represents a Default Causative Paradigm. In the VRC, the co-composition activates the stage-level predicate. And therefore the stage-level predicate facilitates or licenses reference to that which brings about that state, but only in specific constructions under co-compostional operation.

In the VP "我哭肿了眼睛"*(My eyes are swollen for crying)*, the AGENTIVE role of the action verb "哭"*(cry)* matches that of the complement verb "肿"*(swollen)*, and the FORMAL role of the complement verb "肿"*(swollen)* matches that of the action verb "哭"*(cry)*. In consequence, the AGENTIVE role of the verb "哭"*(cry)* acts as the AGENTIVE role of the entire VP, and the FORMAL role of the verb "肿"*(swollen)* acts as the FORMAL role of the entire VP. "我的眼睛"*(my eyes)* undergoes the change of the state, and the state of"不肿" *(being not swollen)* converts to the state of "肿" *(being swollen)*.

The qualia projection of "我哭肿了眼睛" (*My eyes are swollen for crying*) is illustrated as follows:

a. Qi: R (e₁*, "我"*(I)*) → x:SUBJ   (6)

b. Qj: P (e₂, "眼睛"*(eyes)*) → y:OBJ

"我哭肿了眼睛" (*My eyes are swollen for crying*) represents a left-headed binary event. The event e₁ "我哭" (*I cry*) results in the event e₂ "我的眼睛肿" (*My eyes are swollen*). The word "眼睛" (*eyes*) and "我" (*I*) is the whole and part.

3.4   The collocation of an unergative verb and an unergative verb

The first verb is an unergative verb, and the second verb is also an unergative verb in the VRC.

6.他气哭了我。(*I was angered to tears by him.*)

The experiencer predicates predicate a certain state of the person performing a certain act, and it exhibits the experienced causation. The underlying semantics of experiencer predicates is a causative structure where the surface subject is the logical object of an experiencing event. A complex event constituted of two basically simultaneous subevents, the causing event e₁ and the caused event e₂, where the causing event starts before the caused event, can be lexicalized with a relation we will call "exhaustive ordered overlap", <o ∝ . The temporal restriction involves a precede and overlap relation between the experiencing process and resulting experienced state. The sequential relation between the subevents of the experiencer predicate is illustrated as "e₁<o ∝ e₂". That is, if doing something angers me, then I need not complete the activity before I become angry. Taking the sentence "一句话气哭了那个老头" (*The old man was angered to tears by hearing the sentence*) as an example, the sentence means that the old man cry because of being angry, and when he is crying he does not stop being angry. However, "赶跑"(*chase away*) is different from "气哭" (*angered to tears*). In the sentence "张三赶跑了李四" (*Zhang San chased Li Si away*), the causing event e₁ completely precedes the caused event e₂, and the temporal restriction is illustrated as "e₁<∝ e₂".

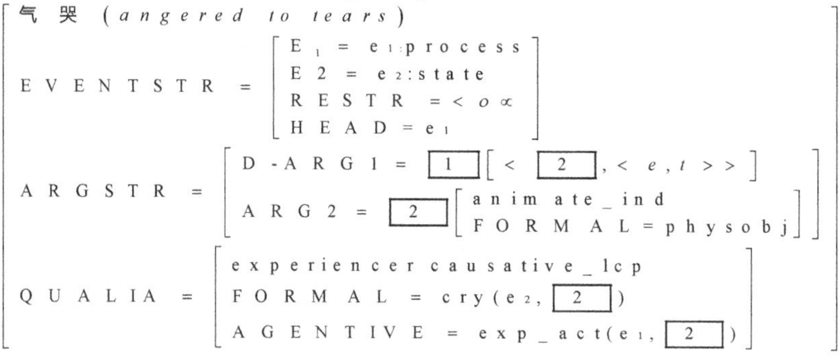

$$
\begin{bmatrix}
\text{气 哭 } (angered\ to\ tears) \\
\text{EVENTSTR} = \begin{bmatrix} E_1 = e_1:process \\ E_2 = e_2:state \\ RESTR = <o\ \alpha \\ HEAD = e_1 \end{bmatrix} \\
\text{ARGSTR} = \begin{bmatrix} D\text{-}ARG1 = \boxed{1}\ [\ <\boxed{2},\ <e,t>>\ ] \\ ARG2 = \boxed{2}\ \begin{bmatrix} animate\_ind \\ FORMAL = physobj \end{bmatrix} \end{bmatrix} \\
\text{QUALIA} = \begin{bmatrix} experiencer\ causative\_lcp \\ FORMAL = cry(e_2,\ \boxed{2}) \\ AGENTIVE = exp\_act(e_1,\ \boxed{2}) \end{bmatrix}
\end{bmatrix}
$$

Fig. 11. The lexical representation for the VP "气哭" (*angered to tears*) .

Experiencer predicates select for an event function in subject position. According to the type theory of the formal semantics, e represents a individual, <e, t> is a one-element predicate function, <e, <e, t>> means e is substituted into <e, t>, then we can get t after rearranging. The ARG2 is e, and e is substituted into <e, t>, then we can get t. So the causer of the VRC "气哭" (*angered to tears*) is an event which represents a proposition, and it is the event that the ARG2 experienced. "他气我" (*He make me angry*) results in the change of the state.

$$
\begin{bmatrix}
\text{气 哭 我} \quad (angered \ to \ tears) \\[4pt]
\text{EVENTSTR} = \begin{bmatrix} E_1 = e_1\text{:process} \\ E2 = e_2\text{:state} \\ \text{RESTR} = \angle o_\propto \\ \text{HEAD} = e_1 \end{bmatrix} \\[4pt]
\text{ARGSTR} = \begin{bmatrix} \text{ARG1} = \boxed{1} \ [\ <\ \boxed{2}\ ,\ <\ e\ ,\ t\ >\ >\ ] \\[4pt]
\text{ARG2} = \boxed{2} \begin{bmatrix} \text{我} \ (I) \\ \text{QUALIA} = \begin{bmatrix} \text{animate\_ind} \\ \text{TELIC} = \boxed{3} \end{bmatrix} \end{bmatrix} \end{bmatrix} \\[4pt]
\text{QUALIA} = \begin{bmatrix} \text{experiencer causative\_lcp} \\ \text{FORMAL} = P(e_2, \sigma\ [\ \boxed{3}\ ])\ ]) \\ \text{AGENTIVE} = \text{exp\_act}(e_1, \boxed{1}, \boxed{2}) \end{bmatrix}
\end{bmatrix}
$$

Fig. 12. The lexical representation for the VP "气哭我" (*I was angered to tears*)

The ARG2 is a TRUE ARGUMENT, while the ARG1 is a DEFAULT ARGUMENT (D-ARG1), such as "我气哭了" (*I was angered to tears*) must implies that there is an event that makes me cry.

The qualia projection of "他气哭了我" (*I was angered to tears by him*) is illustrated below:

a. Qi: R (e$_1$*, "他"(*he*), "我"(*I*)) $\rightarrow$ x: SUBJ, y: OBJ   (7)

b.Qj: P (e$_2$, "我"(*I*)) $\rightarrow$ y: shadow

3.5   The collocation of an unaccusative verb and an unaccusative verb

The first verb is an unaccusative verb, and the second verb is also an unaccusative verb in the VRC.

7. 我累倒了他。   (*Helping me made him so tired that he finally fell ill.*)

$$
累 \quad (tired) \\
\begin{bmatrix}
\text{ARGSTR} = \begin{bmatrix} \text{ARG1} = \boxed{1} \begin{bmatrix} \text{animate\_ind} \\ \text{FORMAL} = \text{physobj} \end{bmatrix} \\ \text{D-ARG1} = x : T_1 = \boxed{2} \end{bmatrix} \\
\text{EVENTSTR} = \begin{bmatrix} E_1 = e_1 : \text{state} \\ \text{D-}E_1 = e_2 : \sigma \\ \text{RESTR} = e_2 < \propto e_1 \\ \text{HEAD} = e_1 \end{bmatrix} \\
\text{QUALIA} = \begin{bmatrix} \text{FORMAL} = tired\,(e_1, \boxed{1}\,) \\ \text{AGENT} = \exp\_\text{act}(e_2, \boxed{1}, \boxed{2}\,) \end{bmatrix}
\end{bmatrix}
$$

Fig. 13.   The lexical representation for the verb "累"(tired)

$$
倒 \quad (fell\ ill) \\
\begin{bmatrix}
\text{ARGSTR} = \begin{bmatrix} \text{ARG1} = \boxed{1} \begin{bmatrix} \text{animate\_ind} \\ \text{FORMAL} = \text{physobj} \end{bmatrix} \\ \text{D-ARG1} = x : T_1 = \boxed{2} \end{bmatrix} \\
\text{EVENTSTR} = \begin{bmatrix} E_1 = e_1 : \text{state} \\ \text{D-}E_1 = e_2 : \sigma \\ \text{RESTR} = e_2 < \propto e_1 \\ \text{HEAD} = e_1 \end{bmatrix} \\
\text{QUALIA} = \begin{bmatrix} \text{FORMAL} = 倒\,(fell\ ill)(e_1, \boxed{1}\,) \\ \text{AGENT} = R(推\,(push),打\,(hit),绊\,(stumble),摔\,(fall),病\,(sick),累\,(tired)\text{ect.})\_\text{act}(e_2, \boxed{1}\,\boxed{2}\,) \end{bmatrix}
\end{bmatrix}
$$

Fig. 14.   The lexical representation for the verb "倒" *(fell ill)*

In the VRC, the complement verb "倒" (*fell ill*) denotes the resulting state, and the AGENTIVE role of the qualia structure of the complement verb implies a stage-level predicate which represents a DEFAULT CAUSATIVE PARADIGM, and it is a derived interpretation and is not lexicalized into one lexical item. The unaccusative verbs can denote only a state and not a transition, as with the adjective. Stage-level predicates, therefore, facilitate or license reference to that which brings about that state, but only in specific constructions such as the VRC under co-compositional operations.

Here we are assuming that R is a predicate that is sortally structured to subsume "推"(*push*), "打"(*hit*), "绊"(*stumble*), "摔"(*fall*), "病"(*sick*), "累"(*tired*) and related predicates. The stage-level predicate acts as a function over the VP "累倒" (he was so tired that he fell ill), and under the qualia unification, the FORMAL role of "倒" (*fell ill*) unifies with that of the VP "累倒" (*he was so tired that he fell ill*), resulting in a derived causative and an aspectually telic interpretation.

The qualia projection of VP "我累倒了他" (*Helping me make him so tired that he finally fell ill*) is illustrated as follows:

a. Qi: R (e_1*, "我" *(I)*, "他"*(He)*) $\longrightarrow$ x: SUBJ, y: OBJ   (8)

b. Qj: P (e_2, "他" *(He)*) $\longrightarrow$ shadowed

3.6 The collocation of an unaccusative verb and an unergative verb

The first verb is an unaccusative verb, and the second verb is an unergative verb in the VRC.

8.宝宝累跑了保姆。(*Taking care of the baby was so tired that the babysitter left.*)

The lexical representation for the unaccusative verb "累" (*tired*) and the lexical representation for the unergative verb "跑" (*run*) are illustrated above. In the VP "宝宝累跑了保姆" (*Taking care of the baby was so tired that the babysitter left*), the AGENTIVE role of the action verb "累" (*tired*) matches that of the complement verb "跑"(*run*), and the FORMAL role of the complement verb "跑"(*run*) matches that of the action verb "累"(*tired*). In consequence, the AGENTIVE role for "累" (*tired*) acts as the AGENTIVE role of the entire VP, and the FORMAL role of "跑" (*run*) acts as the FORMAL role of the entire VP. "保姆"(*babysitter*) undergoes the change of the location and the state.

The qualia projection of "宝宝累跑了保姆" (*Taking care of the baby was so tired that the babysitter left*)is illustrated as follows:

a. Qi: R (e_1*, 宝宝*(baby)*, 保姆*(babysitter)*) $\rightarrow$ x: SUBJ, y: OBJ   (9)

b. Qj: P (e_2, 保姆*(babysitter)*) $\rightarrow$ shadowed

3.7 The collocation of an accusative verb and an unaccusative verb

"打碎" (*broke*), "杀死" (*kill*), and "擦干净" (*wipe clean*)

9. 玛丽擦干净了桌子。(*Mary wipes the table clean.*)

$$
\begin{bmatrix}
\text{干 净 (clean)} \\[4pt]
\text{EVENTSTR} = \begin{bmatrix} E_1 = e_1:\text{state} \\ D\text{-}E_1 = e_2:\text{process} \\ \text{RESTR} = e_2 <_{\propto} e_1 \\ \text{HEAD} = e_1 \end{bmatrix} \\[20pt]
\text{ARGSTR} = \begin{bmatrix} \text{ARG1} = \boxed{1}\begin{bmatrix} \text{physobj} \\ \text{FORMAL} = \text{entity} \end{bmatrix} \\ \text{D-ARG1} = \boxed{2} \end{bmatrix} \\[16pt]
\text{QUALIA} = \begin{bmatrix} \text{FORMAL} = \text{clean}(e_1, \boxed{1}) \\ \text{AGENTIVE} = \text{R}(e_2, \boxed{1}, \boxed{2}) \end{bmatrix}
\end{bmatrix}
$$

Fig. 15. The lexical representation for the unaccusative verb "干净"*(clean)*

In the VRC, the complement verb "干净"(*clean*) denotes the resulting state, and the AGENTIVE role of the qualia structure of the complement verb implies a stage-level predicate which represents a DEFAULT CAUSATIVE PARADIGM, and it is a derived interpretation and is not lexicalized into one lexical item.

Here we are assuming that R is a predicate that is sortally structured to subsume "擦" (*wipe*), "洗" (*wash*) and related predicates. The stage-level predicate acts as a function over the VP "擦桌子" (*wipe the table*), and under the qualia unification, the FORMAL role of "干净" (*clean*) unifies with that of the VP "擦桌子" (*wipe the table*), resulting in a derived causative and an aspectually telic interpretation. The accusative verb can denote only a state and not a transition, as with the adjectives. Stage-level predicates, therefore, facilitate or license reference to that which brings about that state, but only in specific constructions such as VRC under co-compositional operations.

10.我摔碎了杯子。 (*I break the cup.*)

$$
\begin{bmatrix}
杯子（\qquad cup\qquad) & & & & & & \\
QUALIA & = & \begin{bmatrix}
CONST & = 有形物质人造物器皿 & & physobj\_l & cp \\
FORMAL & = 圆柱状下部略细 & & cylinder & (y,x) \\
TELIC & = 盛放液体 & hold & liquid(e, & w, \ x\,.y) \\
AGENTIVE & = 制作、加工、烧制 & & make & (e',v,x\,.y)
\end{bmatrix}
\end{bmatrix}
$$

Fig. 16.   The qualia structure of the noun "杯子"*(cup)*

$$
\begin{bmatrix}
摔\ 碎\ 杯子\ (break\ the\ cup) & & \\
EVENTSTR & = & \begin{bmatrix} E_1 = e_1:process \\ E_2 = e_2:state \\ RESTR = < \propto \\ HEAD = e_1 \end{bmatrix} \\
ARGSTR & = & \begin{bmatrix} ARG1 = \boxed{1} & \\ ARG2 = \boxed{2} & QUALIA = \begin{bmatrix} 杯子\ (cup) \\ \begin{bmatrix} physobj.info\text{-}lcp \\ TELIC = \boxed{3} = \varnothing \end{bmatrix} \end{bmatrix} \end{bmatrix} \\
QUALIA & = & \begin{bmatrix} dc\text{-}lcp \\ FORMAL = P(e_2, \neg\ \Box\ [\boxed{3}\ )]) \\ AGENT = 摔\ (break)\_act(e_1, \boxed{1}, \boxed{2}) \end{bmatrix}
\end{bmatrix}
$$

Fig. 17.   The qualia structure of the VP[ᵥₚ 摔碎杯子] (*break the cup*)

$\neg\Box$ represents the conversion of the opposite state. "摔碎杯子" (*break the cup*) represents a TRANSITION event. The resulting state of a transitional event of "摔碎杯子" (*break the cup*) refers to the inability to use the object i.e., "杯子" (*cup*) for that which it is intended; i.e., its TELIC role "盛放液体" (*hold or contain liquid*). Because the cup is broken, the change of the state causes the cup can no longer play the original function. The co-composition of the verb "摔" (*break*) and "碎" (*smash*) has contextual influence on the object "杯子" (*cup*), resulting in a derived causative and an aspectually telic interpretation.

喝醉 (*get drunk*)

11.我喝醉了酒。 (*I drink wine and get drunk.*)

$$
\begin{bmatrix}
喝 \quad (drink) \\
EVENTSTR = \begin{bmatrix} E_1 = e_1:process \\ E_2 = e_2:state \end{bmatrix} \\
ARGSTR = \begin{bmatrix} ARG_1 = animate\_individual \\ ARG_2 = 流食 、 液体 \ (liquid) \end{bmatrix} \\
QUALIA = \begin{bmatrix} FORMAL = 醉 \ (drunk) \ or \ 饱 \ (full) \\ AGENT = 喝 \ (drink)\_act(e_1,x) \end{bmatrix}
\end{bmatrix}
$$

Fig. 18. The lexical representation for the accusative verb "喝" *(drink)*

$$
\begin{bmatrix}
醉 \quad (drunk) \\
ARGSTR = \begin{bmatrix} ARG1 = \boxed{1} \begin{bmatrix} animate\_ind \\ FORMAL = physobj \end{bmatrix} \\ D\text{-}ARG1 = x:T_1 = \boxed{2} \end{bmatrix} \\
EVENTSTR = \begin{bmatrix} E_1 = e_1:state \\ D\text{-}E_1 = e_2:\sigma \\ RESTR = e_2 <\!\propto e_1 \\ HEAD = e_1 \end{bmatrix} \\
QUALIA = \begin{bmatrix} FORMAL = 醉 \ (drunk)(e_1,\boxed{1}) \\ AGENT = R\,喝 \ (drink)\_act(e_2,\boxed{1},\boxed{2}) \end{bmatrix}
\end{bmatrix}
$$

Fig. 19. The lexical representation for the unaccusative verb "醉" *(drunk)*

$$
\begin{bmatrix}
我 喝 醉 了 酒 \quad (I \ drink \ wine \ and \ get \ drunk) \\
EVENTSTR = \begin{bmatrix} E_1 = e_1:process \\ E_2 = e_2:state \\ RESTR = e_1 <\!\propto e_2 \\ HEAD = e_1 \end{bmatrix} \\
ARGSTR = \begin{bmatrix} ARG_1 = \boxed{1} \begin{bmatrix} 我 \ (I) \\ QUALIA = \begin{bmatrix} animate\text{-}lcp \\ FORMAL = \boxed{3} \end{bmatrix} \end{bmatrix} \\ ARG2 = \boxed{2} \begin{bmatrix} 酒 \ (wine) \\ QUALIA = \begin{bmatrix} physobj.info\text{-}lcp \\ TELIC = 醉 \ (get \ drunk) \end{bmatrix} \end{bmatrix} \end{bmatrix} \\
QUALIA = \begin{bmatrix} Cause\text{-}lcp \\ FORMAL = P(e_2,\sigma[\boxed{3}])]) \\ AGENT = 喝 \ (drink)\_act(e_1,\boxed{1},\boxed{2}) \end{bmatrix}
\end{bmatrix}
$$

Fig. 20. The lexical representation for the VP "我喝醉了酒" *(I drink wine and get drunk)*

e_1"我喝酒"(*I drink wine*) causes e_2"我醉"(*I get drunk*), the AGENTIVE role of the qualia structure of the verb "醉" *(get drunk)* is a stage-level predicate R, and the embodiment of R is "喝" *(drink)*. One of the FORMAL role of the qualia structure of "喝"*(drink)* is "醉"*(get drunk)*, and thus the qualia unification occurs, licensed by the identity of qualia values for AGENTIVE and FORMATIVE respectively in two verbs. The co-compostion of the qualia structures results in a derived causative sense of the VP, where the AGENTIVE roles of the action verb"喝"*(drink)* matches that of the complement verb"醉"*(get drunk)*, and the FORMAL role of the complement verb"醉"(*get drunk*) matches that of the action verb "喝"(*drink*). In consequence, the AGENTIVE role of the action verb"喝"(*drink*) acts as the AGENTIVE role for the entire VP, and the FORMAL role of the complement verb"醉"(*get drunk*) acts as the FORMAL role of the entire VP. Eventually the co-composition causes the change of my state, that is the state of "not being drunk" converts to the state of "being drunk".

The qualia projection of "我喝醉了酒"(*I drink wine and get drunk*) is illustrated as follows:

a. Qi: R (e_1*, "我" (*I*), "酒" (*wine*)) $\rightarrow$ x:SUBJ, y:OBJ   (10)

b. Qj: P (e_2, "我" (*I*)) $\rightarrow$ shadowed

4   Conclusion

This paper analyses the co-compostion of the action verb and the complement verb in the VRC. The dual combination of three kinds of verbs should generate nine kinds of collocations, but we only find seven kinds of collocations in the VRC as follows:

A. The collocation of an accusative verb and an unergative verb, e.g., "张三赶跑了李四" (*Zhang San chased Li Si away*);

B. The collocation of an unergative verb and an accusative verb, e.g., "我跑忘了一件事" (*I forgot to do something because of running*);

C. The collocation of an unergative verb and an unaccusative verb, e.g., "我哭肿了眼睛" (*My eyes are swollen for crying*), and "我哭湿了手帕" (*I cry and make my handkerchief wet*);

D. The collocation of an unergative verb and an unergative verb, e.g., "他气哭了我" (*I was angered to tears by him*);

E. The collocation of an unaccusative verb and an unaccusative verb, e.g., "我累倒了他" (*Helping me make him so tired that he finally fell ill*);

F. The collocation of an unaccusative verb and an unergative verb, e.g., "宝宝累跑了保姆" (*Taking care of the baby is so tired that the babysitter leave*);

G. The collocation of an accusative verb and an unaccusative verb, e.g., "我摔碎了杯子"(*I break the cup*), and "我喝醉了酒"(*I drink and get drunk*).

However, we did not find the following two kinds of collocations:

I. The collocation of an unaccusative verb and an accusative verb;

II. The collocation of an accusative verb and an accusative verb.

As discussed above, some interesting phenomena are found:

First of all, we find that the unaccusative verb as the component of the resultative complement of the VRC has an absolute dominance, and its combine with other kinds of verbs more freely, and its combinations with other verbs are the richest. Why? The reason is that the complement of the VRC emphasizes the state of the participant, and thus the unaccusative verb which mainly represents the state is more suitable for the composition of the resultative complement than others.

What's more, we calculate the collocations of the verbs in *the collocations of the verb and resultative complement dictionary in Mandarin Chinese*, and we find that there are 266 collocations of an unergative verb and an unaccusative verb, which account for 22% of the collocations of the verbs in the whole dictionary. And there are 157 collocations of an unaccusative verb and an unaccusative verb, which account for 13% of the collocations of the verbs in the whole dictionary. And there are 787 collocations of an accusative verb and an unaccusative verb, which account for 65% of the collocations of the verbs in the whole dictionary.

Among all of the collocations of an unaccusative verb and the other verbs, the collocations of an accusative verb and an unaccusative verb have an absolute dominance, when the unaccusative verb acts as the complement in the VRC. While the proportion of the collocations of an unaccusative verb and an unaccusative verb is the lowest. Why? The reason is that an accusative verb denotes an action, while an unaccusative verb denotes a state. In the VRC the first verb describes an action, therefore the accusative verb as the first verb of the VRC has an absolute dominance. The second verb of the VRC describes the result, and thus the collocations of an accusative verb and an unaccusative verb have an absolute dominance, and the subtypes of this kind of collocations are the richest.

Last but not the least, the collocation of an accusative verb and an accusative verb can not be found in the VRC. Why? The reason is that this kind of collocation can not satisfy the requirement of the VRC. The accusative verb denotes the action, so the collocation of an accusative verb and an accusative verb can not denote the state of the verb, while the complement of the VRC requires a component that denotes the state of the verb.

Acknowledgment. This research was supported by the Social Science Funding project of Qingdao University of Science and Technology "A Study on Causative meaning of Verb-Resultative Construction in Mandarin Chinese Based on the Generative Lexicon Theory" (2015). We hereby express our sincere thanks.

References

1. Pustejovsky, James. and Elisabetta Jezek.: An Introduction to Generative Lexicon Theory. Oxford, UK: Oxford University Press(2012)
2. Pustejovsky, James.: Lexical Semantics. Handbook of Semantics. Ed. Paul Dekker and Maria Aloni. Cambridge, UK: Cambridge University Press(2015)
3. Pustejovsky. James.: A type composition logic for generative lexicon. Advances in Generative Lexicon Theory. Ed. Pustejovsky, J., P. Bouillon, H. Isahara, K. Kanzaki, and C. Lee. Springer(2012)
4. Pustejovsky, James.: Type Theory and Lexical Decomposition.Advances in Generative Lexicon Theory. Ed. Pustejovsky, J., P. Bouillon, H. Isahara, K. Kanzaki, and C. Lee. Springer(2012)
5. Pustejovsky, James. : The Generative Lexicon. MIT Press(1995)
6. Pustejovsky, James., Patrick Hogan.: Qualia Roles. The Cambridge Encyclopedia of the Language Science(2010)

Lexical Semantic Constraints on the Syntactic Realization of Semantic Role Possessor[1]

Shiyong Kang   Minghai Zhou   Qianqian Zhang

School of Chinese Language and Literature, Ludong University
Key Laboratory of Language Resource Development and Application of Shandong Province
Yantai 264025, China
kangsy64@163.com

Abstract. When mapped to syntactic elements, semantic roles are constrained by lexical semantic categories of words that assume the semantic roles. Based on a large-scale annotated corpus, this paper takes the semantic role "Possessor" as an example and analyzes its syntactic-semantic pattern, the influence of lexical semantic category upon its mapping to syntactic elements, the collocations of the semantic categories of noun-core structures and verb-core structures. The research initially reveals the constraints of lexical semantic categories upon the mapping of the semantic role "Possessor" to syntactic elements.

Keywords:semantic role; syntactic element; lexical semantic category

1   Introduction

When mapped to the corresponding syntactic elements, semantic role of a word is constrained by its lexical semantics. Supported by National Social Science Foundation of China, entitled "Research on the Lexical Semantic Constraints on the Syntactic Realization of Semantic Roles Based on a Large-scale Annotated Corpus", we built a large-scale Chinese corpus and generalized the rules that govern the syntactic realization of semantic roles.

Based on the related researches in the field, we defined the syntactic elements, semantic roles and the labels as shown in Table 1 and Table 2, respectively.

Table 1. Syntactic Elements and Labels

Labels	Meaning	Labels	Meaning
S	Subject chunk	D	Adverbial Chunk
P	Predicate Chunk	C	Complement Chunk
O	Object chunk	J	Concurrent Chunk
A	Attributive chunk	T	Independent Chunk

---

1 This research is supported by National Social Science Foundation of China (No.12BYY123) and National Natural Science Foundation of China(No.61272215).

M. Dong et al. (Eds.): CLSW 2016, LNAI 10085, pp. 214–222, 2016
DOI: 10.1007/978-3-319-49508-8_20

Table 2.Semantic Roles and Labels

Labels	Meaning	Labels	Meaning	Labels	Meaning	Labels	Meaning
S	Agent	Z	Causer	V	Verb	P	Location
D	Theme	R	Result	I	Instrument	A	Direction
L	Genitive	T	Dative	M	Material	E	Range
Y	Comitative	X	Relative	Q	Manner	C	Reason
O	Patient	F	Partitive	W	Basis	G	Aim
K	Objective	B	Source	H	Time	N	Quantity
J	Standard	U	Miscellany				

As to the lexical semantic category, we adopted the classification system and labels proposed inTongyiciCilin.

Based on the tagged corpus, this paper generalized the lexical semantic constraints that semantic role "Possessor" confronts when mapped to the syntactic elements. In this research, "Possessor" is defined as the subject with possessive relationship, where the predicate usually means possession or occupation. For example, [我] (wo. Literally it means "I") L 有一本书 (you yi ben shu, literally it means "have a book"). With the above labels, we annotated the Chinese texts of primary and secondary school Chinese textbooks published by People's Education Press.

2   Possessor's Syntactic Semantic Patterns

According to the statistics of the annotated corpus, Possessor has 6 types of syntactic semantic patterns, they are: SLPV>JLPV>PVSL>PVOL>OLPV>PVJL. Please see Table 3 for more details.

Table 3. Distribution of syntactic-semantic patterns

Label Number	Syntactic-Semantic Pattern	Number	Percent
1	SLPV	1040	93.95%
2	JLPV	24	2.17%
3	PVSL	19	1.72%
4	PVOL	15	1.36%
5	OLPV	6	0.54%
6	PVJL	3	0.27%
	Total	1107	100.00%

In the table above,"SLPV"means PossessorL plays the role of "subject S", "P"refers to the predicate, and "V" stands for the verbs that correspond with the semantic roles. Other syntactic semantic patterns can be interpreted in the same way. The statistics reveal that Possessor can also be mapped to concurrent and objectin addition to subject.

First of all, Possessor is mapped to subject. There are 1059 such uses, accounting for 95.66% of the total. Some sentences are inverted. The following is a detailed classification.

(1) SLPV

Most of the Possessor follows this pattern when mapped to subject. There are 1040 such uses, accounting for 93.95% of the total. For example:

1) 可是/c[S 他/r]L1D2[P 有/v]V1[O 足够/a 的/u 勇气/n]K1[D 把/p 今天/t 的/u 功课/n]KB2[P 坚持到底/I]V2

Literal translation:But/c[S he/r]L1D2[P have/v]V1[Oenough/ade/ucourage /n]K1[Dba/ptoday/tde/uhomework/n]KB2[P stick it out/I]V2

(2) PVSL

In this pattern the predicate is fronted, therefore forming a predicate-subject pattern. There are 24 such uses, accounting for 2.17% of the total number of subject. For example:

2) [P 没有/v]V1[O 爱/vn]K1[S 你/r]L1L2[D 就/d[P 没有/v]V2[O 欢乐/an]K2，[S 你/r]S3[D 就/d[D 不/d[D 愿/v[P 游玩/v]V3。

Literal translation: [P do not have/v]V1[O love/vn]K1[S you/r]L1L2[D will/d[P do not have/v]V2[O happiness/an]K2，[S you/r]S3[D will/d[D do not/d[D want to/v[Pplay/v]V3.

Second, Possessor is mapped to concurrent. There are 27 such uses, accounting for 2.44% of the total. It is further divided into two sub-patterns.

(1) JLPV

There are 24 Possessor used as concurrent, accounting for 2.17% of the total. For example:

3) [P 让/v]V1[J 他们/r]O1+L2S3L4S5[D 既/d[P 没有/v]V2[O 淡水/n]K2O3[P 喝/v]V3，[D 也/d[P 没有/v]V4[O 淡水/n]K4[P 种/v]V5[O 庄稼/n]O5。

Literal translation: [P let/v]V1[J them/r]O1+L2S3L4S5[D not only/d[P do not have/v]V2[Ofreshwater/n]K2O3[Pdrink/v]V3，[D but also/d[Pdo not have/v]V4[O freshwater /n]K4[Pplant/v]V5[Ocrops/n]O5.

(2) PVJL

This pattern is formed when a concurrent is followed by a predicate-complement structure with thecomplementary meaning orientated to the concurrent. There are 3 such uses, accounting for 0.27%. For example:

4) [S 这/r 虾/n]K1[D 照例/d[D 是/d[P 归/v]V1[J 我/r]L1+S2[P 吃/v]V2 的/u。

Literal translation:[S this/rshrimp/n]K1[D as usual,/d[D is/d[Pbelong to/v]V1[J me/r]L1+S2[P eat/v]V2de/u.

Third, Possessor is also mapped to object. There are 21 such uses, accounting for 1.90% of the total. Possessor as object include the following two sub-patterns.

(1) PVOL

There are 15 Possessor used as object, accounting for 1.36% of the total. For example:

5) [D 莫非/d，[S 艺术/n]K[D 是/d[P 属于/v]V[O{弱者/n}@、{失败者/n}@]L 的 /u?

Literal translation:[D could it be/d，[Sart/n]K[D is/d[P belong to /v]V[O{weak/n}@、{loser/n}@]Lattributive marker /u?

(2) OLPV

In this pattern, Possessor is semantically related to verb-core structure cross sentences. Object here means that noun-core structure plays the role of object in the preceding clause. For example:

6) [S 他/r]S1[P 做/v]V1[O 各种/r 事/n]O1L2，[P 有/v]V2[O 各种/r 意义 /n]K2，......

Literal translation:[S he/r]S1[P do/v]V1[O all kinds/rthing/n]O1L2 ， [P have/v]V2[Oall kinds /rsignificance/n]K2，......

3   The Influence of Lexical Semantic Categories on the Mapping of Possessor to the Syntactic Elements

3.1   Major Semantic Categories

Possessor can be mapped to a variety of syntactic elements, but the mapping capacity is constrained by lexical semantic categories. See Table 4 for details.

Table 4. Distribution of major lexical semantic categories

Syntactic Elements / Semantic Category	Subject	Concurrent	Object
A human being	477	14	7
B object	207	4	8
C Time and space	37		2
D Abstract things	271	7	4
E feature	42	0	0
F movement	1	0	0
G psychological activity	2	0	0
H activity	11	1	0
I Phenomena & state	6	1	0
J relevance	5	0	0
TOTAL	1059	27	21

From the table above, we can see the mapping capacity of each semantic category which isshown by inequation as follows:

Semantic categories for possessor as subject:A>D>B>E>C>>H>I> J> G>F>K=F

Semantic categories for possessor as concurrent:A> D>B >H=I

Semantic categories for possessor as object:B> A> D >C

Though semantic categories that play the role of Possessor are scattered, they, relatively speaking, are focused on A (human being), D (abstract things), B (object), E (features) and C (time and space), accounting for 97.56% of the total.

3.2   Middle semantic categories

The distribution of middle lexical semantic categories is shown in Table 5.

Table 5. Distribution of middle lexical semantic categoies

Semantic category	Number	percent	Semantic category	Number	percent
Aa wide title	407	36.77%	AbMen and women	19	1.72%
Acposture	/	/	AdMembership genus	5	0.45%
AeOccupation	9	0.81%	AfIdentity	6	0.54%
Agsituation	2	0.18%	AhFamily dependents	20	1.81%
AiSeniority	2	0.18%	Ajrelationship	7	0.63%
AkMoral character	9	0.81%	Alability and insight	9	0.81%
Amfaith	1	0.09%	AnBad sort	2	0.18%
BaCollectively called	60	5.42%	BbQuasi-like	17	1.54%
BcPortion of an object	/	/	BdAstronomical	/	/
BeGeomorphology	10	0.90%	Bfmeteorological	6	0.54%
BgNatural world	30	2.71%	Bhplant	34	3.07%
Bianimal	19	1.72%	Bjmicroorganism	/	/
Bkwhole body	11	0.99%	BlFecal secretions	/	/
Bmmaterial	5	0.45%	Bnbuilding	15	1.36%
BoMachines and tools	4	0.36%	BpArticles	6	0.54%
BqClothing	2	0.18%	BrFood and Drug Drugs	/	/
Catime	15	1.36%	Cbspace	24	2.17%
DaWhat circumstances	42	3.79%	DbAffair	19	1.72%
Dcappearance	3	0.27%	Ddperformance	13	1.17%
DeCharacter talent	6	0.54%	Dfawareness	10	0.90%
Dgmetaphor	2	0.18%	DhImaginary object	1	0.09%
DiSociety and government	52	4.70%	Djeconomic	2	0.18%
DkCulture and education	123	11.11%	Dldisease	/	/
Dmmechanism	2	0.18%	DnNumber of Units	7	0.63%
Eashape	/	/	EbIdea	3	0.27%
EcColor taste	/	/	Ednature	37	3.34%
EeMoral talent	2	0.18%	Efsituation	/	/
FcHead movements	/	/	FdSystemic action	1	0.09%
GaMentation	/	/	GbMental activity	2	0.18%
GcModal	/	/	HaPolitical activity	1	0.09%

HbMilitary activities	3	0.27%	HcAdministration	/	/
Hdproduce	1	0.09%	HeEconomic activity	/	/
HfTransportation	/	/	HgEducation and health research	1	0.09%
HhSports activities	/	/	HiSocially	3	0.27%
Hjlife	3	0.27%	HkReligious activities	/	/
IbPhysiological phenomenon	2	0.18%	Icexpression	/	/
IdObjects status	1	0.09%	Iesituation	2	0.18%
IfCircumstance	1	0.09%	IgStart and end	/	/
IhVariety	1	0.09%	Jacontact	/	/
Jdexist	2	0.18%	Jeinfluences	3	0.27%

The top 20 semantic categories follow the sequence:

Aa>Dk>Ba >Di >Da >Ed >Bh>Bg>Cb>Ah >Ab>Bi >Db>Bd>Bn>Ca>Dd>Bk>Be >Df

Horizontally, there are three types.

(1) Full projection. Semantic categories in this type can be projected to any syntactic element served by Possessor. It consists of 5 semantic categories: Aa, Af, Ba, Da, Dk.

(2) Zero projection. Semantic categories that belong to this type can not be projected to any syntactic element served by Possessor. This type includes 36categories, they are: Ac, Bb, Bc, Bj, Bl.

(3) Restricted projection. Semantic categories that belong to this type can be selectively projected to the syntactic elements served by Possessor. There are 54 semantic categories such as Ab, Ad, etc.

58 semantic categories can be mapped as subject, 11categories be mapped as concurrent, 5 as object. Of all the semantic categories, Aa precedes the others.

4   Collocation of Possessor's Noun-core Structure (NS) Semantic Category and Verb-core Structure (VS) Semantic Category

4.1   The semantic characteristics of verb-core

The syntactic realization of semantic roles is a process in which noun-core structure semantic category and verb-core structure semantic category constrain each other reciprocally. When we study the characteristics of the syntactic realization of semantic roles, we have to take into consideration the semantic categories of the verbs that collocate with Possessor. The following table shows the verb-core structure collocating with Possessor.

Table 6. Distribution of semantic categories of verbs

Major Semantic Categories	Number	Percent	Cumulative Percentage
J	842	76.06%	76.06%

K	202	18.25%	94.31%
H	48	4.34%	98.64%
I	10	0.90%	99.55%
E	4	0.36%	99.91%
G	1	0.09%	100.00%
Total	1107	100.00%	

According to the number of verb-core structure semantic categories that collocate with Possessor, we can see such a sequence: J(relevance)>K(expletive)>H (activity)>I (phenomenon and state)> E (feature)> G (psychological state).

The collocation of Possessor's syntactic elements and verb-core structure semantic categories is shown in the table below.

Table 7. Collocation of syntactic elements and verb-core semantic categories

Middle Semantic category	Subject	Concurrent	Object
E	4	/	/
G	1	/	/
H	47	1	/
I	9	/	1
J	799	23	20
K	199	3	/
TOTAL	1059	27	21

From the vertical perspective, not a kind word can freely onto the possessor syntactic component matched the predicate, but the subject is projected onto the possessor matched the predicate more, followed by the possessor as pivot

Vertically, predicates that collocate with Possessor as Subject can be any semantic category listed in Cilin. More semantic categories collocate with concurrent. Fewer semantic categories go with Possessor as object. Horizontally, semantic categories like J(relevance) and K(expletive) can collocate with any syntactic element of Possessor.

4.2   The rule of verb core match noun core

Lexical semantic constrains on the syntactic realization of semantic roles are not only reflected in their respective semantic features of noun-core structure and verb-core structure but also in their mutual collocation constrains. They are shown in the two-dimensional collocation rule table. The following two-dimensional table shows the collocation rules of semantic categories of Possessor.

Table 8. Collocation of NS and VS semantic categories

noun core verb core	A	B	C	D	E	F	G	H	I	J	K	L	Total
E	1	/	/	3	/	/	/	/	/	/	/	/	4
G	1	/	/	/	/	/	/	/	/	/	/	/	1
H	23	17	/	5	2	/	/	1	/	/	/	/	48

I	3	5	1	1	/	/	/		/	/	/	/	10
J	336	172	30	246	37	1	2	8	6	4	/	/	842
K	134	25	8	27	3	/	/	3	1	1	/	/	202
L	/	/	/	/	/	/	/	/	/	/	/	/	/
Total	498	219	39	282	42	1	2	12	7	5			1107

From the table it can be seen laterally and J class can either type in the name of nuclear-defined classes except L, K outside combination; from the verticalperspective, there is no name for a class of nuclear and free to move with nuclear, but A, D, B, C class more than other categories, accounting for 93.85 percent of the total, This also shows that A, B, D, C class act as possessor more. The above the top ten rules are : A+J（336）> D+J（246）>B+J（172）> A+ K（134）> E+J（37）>C+J（30）>D+K（27）>B+K（25）> A+ H（23）>B+H（17）,accounting for 97.76% of the total. Consul with the rules and dynamic nucleus concentrated, formulated for the exclusionary rule is very favorable.

The meanings of verbs and nouns are intertwined in a sentence. The precondition for the combination of two lexical semantic units is that they have common semanteme, that is to say, the well-formedness of a sentence is the result of the synergy of the lexicalmeanings of both verbs and nouns. Here we would like to show the constrain characteristics of the syntactic realization of Possessor through collocation rules of semantic categories. CategoriesK and L are very special for they seldom combine with other categories, so we exclude them in our discussion. From the table above, horizontally we can see Category J can collocate with any semantic category of noun-core structure. Vertically, no semantic category of noun-core structure can freely collocate with those of verb-core structure. Only Category A, B and D have more collocations than others, accounting for 90.24% of the total. This means Possessor is mainly realized by Category A, B and D. The top ten collocation rules are: A+J(336)> D+J(246)>B+J(172) >A+K (134) > E+J (37) >C+J(30) >D+K(27) >B+K(25) > A+ H(23) >B+H (17),accounting for 97.76% of the total. Meanwhile, in the closed domain the above table can also be seen as a two-dimensional truth table. It can provide useful knowledge for automatic tagging of semantic roles together with probability statistics.

5   Conclusions

In this paper, we analyzed the lexical-semantic constraints on the syntactic realization of the semantic role Possessor. We conclude that Possessor can be realized as subject, object and concurrent syntactically, and subject is the most popular one. In addition, the words that belong to the A, B and C category are the main types of words that act as Possessor.

References

1. WordNet: http://wordnet.princeton.edu/.
2. Changlai Chen. Research on the Semantic Issues of Modern Chinese [M]. Shanghai: Xuelin

Press, 2003.
3. Fillmore, C.J. Case for Case [M]. Mingyang Hu (Trans.). Beijing: Commercial Press, 2002.
4. Xiao Fan, Yufeng Zhang. A Compendium of Grammar Theory [M]. Shanghai: Shanghai Translation Publishing House, 2003.
5. Kang Shiyong, XiaoxingXu, Yongteng Ma. Semantic Constrains on the Syntactic Realization of Agent and Patient [J]. Linguistics Research. 2011(4):36-40.
6. Xingguang Lin, Chuan Lu. Subjective and Objective Information of Chinese Sentences on the Semantic Dimension [J]. Chinese Language Learning, 1997(5):8-11.
7. Chuan Lu. Parataxis Network of Chinese Grammar [M]. Beijing: Commercial Press, 2001.
8. Jianming Lu. On Interface between Syntax and Semantics [J]. Journal of Foreign Languages, 2006(3):30-35.
9. Jiaju Mei et al. TongyiciCilin [M]. Shanghai : Shanghai Lexicographical Publishing House,1983.
10. Yanqiu Shao, Zhifang Sui, Yunfang Wu. On the Tagging of Chinese Semantic Roles based on the Lexic-semantic Characteristics [J]. Journal of Chinese Information Processing, 2009(6):3-10.
11. Jingmin Shao. On Bi-directional Semantic Selection Principle of Chinese Grammar [J]. Journal of Chinese Language, 1997(8).
12. Daogong Sun, Baojia Li. A Study on the "Lexical-semantic and Syntactic-semantic" Cohesion in Verb-core Structures [J]. Applied Linguistics, 2009(1):134-141.
13. Baohua Wang. On the Relationship Between the Lexical Meaning of Verbs and Their Argument Realization [J]. Chinese Linguistics, 2006(1):76-82.
14. Yulin Yuan. The Fineness Hierarchy of Semantic Roles and its Application in NLP [J]. Journal of Chinese Information Processing, 2007(4):10-20.

Research on Collocation Extraction Based on Syntactic and Semantic Dependency Analysis

Shijun Liu[1], Yanqiu Shao[1*], Lijuan Zheng[1], Yu Ding[2]

[1]Information Science School, Beijing Language and Culture University, Beijing, China
liusjliusj@126.com, yqshao163@163.com
[2]Computer Science and Technology School, Harbin Institute of Technology, Harbin, China
dingyu008@gmail.com

Abstract. In this paper we present a kind of collocation extraction method based on automatic semantic analysis. On the basis of semantic dependency analysis, we use co-occurrence frequency and mutual information to extract collocation. Compared with the accuracy of collocation extraction based on syntactic dependency parsing, the one based on semantic dependency analysis can achieve 77.7% accuracy.

Keywords: semantic dependency parsing, collocation extraction, syntactic dependency parsing.

1 Introduction

Domestic and foreign scholars have had many in-depth research on collocation. Earlier foreign researchers Choueka, Klein and Neuwtiz defined collocation as adjacent words of which co-occurrence frequency reaches a certain threshold value [1]. Church and Hanks improved the automatic collocation extraction technology by defining mutual information as the standard of collocation [2]. Smadja's Xtract system could achieve 80% accuracy by proposing strength calculation formula of collocation, and combining it with location information, calculation formula of dispersion degree and automatic part of POS technology of corpus linguistics [3]. Lin extracted collocation based on shallow syntactic parsing [4]. Shouxun Yang integrated decision tree with many other indexes such as frequency, likelihood ratio, pointwise mutual information and variance to achieve higher accuracy of collocation extraction

*Correspondent Author
Foundations: National Natural Science Foundation of China (NSFC) via Grant 61170144,Major Program of China's National Linguistics work Committee during the twelfth five-year plan (ZDI125-41), young and middle aged academic cadre support plan of Beijing Language and Culture University (501321303),BLCU supported project for young researchers program (supported by the Fundamental Research Funds for the Central Universities)(16YCX159).

© Springer International Publishing AG 2016
M. Dong et al. (Eds.): CLSW 2016, LNAI 10085, pp. 223–232, 2016
DOI: 10.1007/978-3-319-49508-8_21

[5].

In recent years, domestic research on collocation has significant development. Sun Maosong played an initial role in the field of collocation extraction based on large-scale corpus and proposes three indexes: strength, dispersion and spike to extract collocation [6]. Sun Honglin used rule-based approach to identify verb-object structure [7]. Qv Weiguang presented a method of collocation extraction based on framework [8]. Che Wanxiang counted the number, distance and variance of word-pairs based on 1.8 GB corpus and used the improved t-test to gain the value of "collocation intensity coefficient" that is used to evaluate collocation relations [9]. Xu Runhua compared two methods of automatic collocation extraction based on syntactic parsing and builds a large-scale collocation repository [10].

Currently, collocation extraction technology is gradually combining with linguistics. Compared with the former method only based on statistics, the automatic collocation extraction now has integrated with more linguistic knowledge such as POS Tagging and syntax. We extract collocation from the data which have been separately analyzed with syntactic dependency parsing and semantic dependency analysis. By comparing results of the two methods, we propose a method of collocation extraction based on semantic dependency parsing hoping to provide new ideas for collocation extraction.

2   Related instructions of collocation extraction

2.1   Definition of collocation

Different scholars have different definitions of collocation. Firth in Modes of Meaning defined collocation from lexical level thinking that collocation is a relationship in which a word's meaning is determined by another word that often occurs with it [11]. Benson thought that collocation are non-accidental cases with certain degree of circulation, which means that if a word-pair is defined as collocation it should be accepted by people within a certain range. And he thought that collocation is not arbitrary and unpredictable, which means that collocation is constraint combination instead of free combination. For example, "warmest greetings" is collocation because it is a habit of saying so there is no rule to follow. Lin Xingguang further proposed a principle called "fewer but better" when compiling collocation dictionary. The principle advocates that common combinations such as "good dictionary" and "bad dictionary" should not be included in collocation dictionary because they are all free combinations, but some such as "encyclopedic dictionary" and "English-Chinese Dictionary" should be included because these sayings are more fixed [12]. Shen Xiuying pointed out that the nature of collocation is between free combinations and idioms in Research on the Collocation of Modern Chinese [13].

In this paper we define collocation as constraint combinations with certain degree of co-occurrence frequency. The collocation we study here are constraint combinations with limited extensibility such as "受到批评" (be criticized) and "受到谴责" (be condemned) instead of free combinations such as "好词典" (good dictionary) and "好学生" (good student). The "co-occurrence" means a relationship in which words involved are related syntactically or semantically and this relation will not be influenced by the distance between them. For example:

(1) 她 脸色 很 难看，好像 病 了。
    ta_lianse_nankan_haoxiang_bingle
    she_face_very_pale_seem_ill
    She looks pale as if she were ill

"她脸色很难看，好像病了" (She looks pale as if she were ill) "她" (she) and "病了" (ill) are co-occurrence though they are far from each other, because "她" (she) is the subject and "Experiencer" of "病了" (ill). So we define words having syntactic or semantic relations as co-occurrence regardless of the distance between them.

2.2 Corpus for the Research

The corpus for the present study is from Beijing Language and Culture University National Language Resource Monitoring Center. The corpus includes the data of People's Daily, Guangming Daily and other 18 mainstream print media, from which we select the data of 2006 as our research materials. The corpus size is 2.3 GB with 1,087,660 word types, and the word frequency is 205471302. The corpus for the research is segmented, POS-tagged and analyzed with automatic semantic dependency analysis. For example:

(2) 他 参加 运动会
    ta_canjia_yundonghui
    he_attend_sports_meet
    He attends sports meet.

As is shown in Table 1, "参加" (take part in) is the root of the whole sentence, and "他" (he) and "运动会" (sports meet) are the Agent and Content of it.

Table 1. Example sentence of SDP

Number	Word	POS	Father node	Semantic role
1	他 (he)	NN	2	Agt
2	参加 (attend)	VV	0	Root
3	运动会 (sports meet)	NN	2	Cont

2.3 Extracted Objects

We define collocation as constraint combinations with certain degree of co-occurrence frequency. The co-occurrence here refers to the relationship in which words are related semantically. In this paper we mainly focus on the collocation of verb-object structure because this structure is the core of most sentences in SVO language and it can outline the syntax structure and meaning of the whole sentence. We choose two representative semantic roles as the object of our study: Patient which means the direct object changed by the verb, for example, the "旷工者" (absenteeism people) of "公司处分了旷工者" (the company punished absenteeism people) and Content which means object influenced but not changed by the verb such as the "炮声" (guns) of "难民听到炮声" (Refugees heard guns).

2.4   Semantic Dependency Parsing and Syntactic Dependency Parsing

The general way to extract collocation is opening windows within a certain range. This method works well when words taken as collocation are next to each other but it fails to extract collocation correctly when words involved are far from each other. Besides, words that co-occur frequently do not necessarily have grammatical or semantic relations so this will lead to the error of extraction. To solve this problem, we use semantic dependency analysis to extract collocation. And we also conduct the experiment based on syntactic dependency in order to compare the results respectively based on the two methods.

We change the corpus into syntactic trees based on dependency parsing in order to describe the structure and the relations between words better and since the relations will not be influenced by distance, it can reduce the interference caused by unrelated components. We analyze the corpus with the open source tool on the platform of LTP [14] provided by Social Computing and Information Retrieval Research Center of Harbin Institute of Technology. And then we extract collocation on the basis of the corpus analyzed with syntactic parsing. This is illustrated in Fig 1.

(3) 我们 邀请 他 参加 学校 举行 的 运动会
women_yaoqing_ta_canjia_xuexiao_juxing_de_yundonghui
We_invite_him_attend_school_hold_sports_meet
We invited him to attend the sports meet held by school

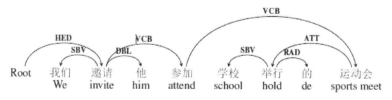

Fig. 1. Result of syntactic dependency parsing

The direction of arc is from parent node to child node, and there are labels representing syntactic relations on the arc. The arc that connects "举行" (hold) and "运动会" (sports meet) is marked with "VOB" which means that "运动会" (sports meet) is the object of "举行" (hold). The syntactic analysis system has 14 types of syntactic relations such as HED (core relationship), SBV (subject-predicate relationship), VOB (verb-object relation), ATT (modifier-head relationship).

The semantic dependency analysis system for the present study is based on SVM semantic dependency graph. Semantic dependency graph is a kind of directed acyclic graph (DAG), the nodes of which are made of words and there are semantic labels on it. Compared with tree structure, the semantic relation system of dependency graph is more normative and efficient [15]. Dependency Graph allows a node with multiple father nodes and non-projection. The only node without father node is the root. As is illustrated in Fig 2: "他" (he) has two father nodes: "邀请" (invite) and "参加" (attend). It is true that dependency graph is more suitable for parataxis language such as Chinese.

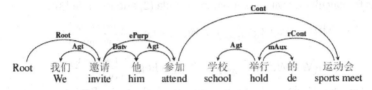

Fig. 2. Example of semantic dependency graph

3   Algorithm for Collocation Extraction

The collocation extraction algorithm based on syntactic dependency parsing and semantic dependency analysis is as follows:

Step 1: Analyze the corpus based on automatic syntactic dependency and automatic semantic dependency respectively.

Step 2: Generate semantic and syntactic triples. According to the results of semantic dependency analysis, we can get semantic triples like {(w1, w2, Rela-Sem)}, in which w1and w2 respectively mean parent node and child node. Rela_Sem means the semantic relationship between w1 and w2. For example, （参加(attend)，运动会 (sports meet)，Cont）"参加" (attend) and "运动会" (sports meet) are parent node and child node. "Cont" means that "运动会" (sports meet) is the Content of "参加" (attend). And then we can get syntactic triples like {（w1，w2，Rela_Syn）} through dependency parsing. Like the semantic triples, w1 and w2 respectively mean parent node and child node. But the difference is that Rela_Syn means the syntactic relationship between w1 and w2. For example, （参加(attend)，运动会(sports meet)，VOB）"参加" (attend) and "运动会" (sports meet) are parent node and child node. "VOB" means that "运动会" (sports meet) is the object of "参加" (attend). The total number of semantic triples we have got is 200,769,237 and the one of syntactic triples is 27,856,336.

Step 3: Add frequency information to the semantic triple and syntactic triple in order to generate two quadruples { (w1, w2, Rela_Sem, Freq_Sem) } and { (w1, w2, Rela_Syn, Freq_Syn) }, in which Freq_Sem and Freq_Syn mean the frequency of the triples (w1,w2,Rela_Sem) and (w1,w2,Rela_Syn).

Step 4: Construct candidate set of semantic roles and syntactic relations. In this paper we build a candidate set of Patient and Content called S1, and a candidate set of VOB relation called S2.

Step 5: Add weighted mutual information to S1 and S2 respectively to generate a semantic and a syntactic quintet. In order to highlight the importance of dependency, we use the formula (1) to calculate the weight of semantic mutual information W_Sem. The Sum means the total number of triples extracted:

$$W_{sem} = Freq\_Sem_{(w1, w2, Rela\_Sem)} / sum \qquad (1)$$

Formulas for calculating MI are shown in formula (2) and formula (3):

$$MI(W1, W2, Rela_{sem}) = W_{Sem} * Log\frac{p(w1,w2,Rela_{sem})}{p(w1)p(w2)} \qquad (2)$$

$$MI(W1, W2, Rela_{Syn}) = W_{Syn} * Log\frac{p(w1,w2,Rela_{Syn})}{p(w1)p(w2)} \qquad (3)$$

In this way, we attain a semantic quintet {(w1, w2, Rela_Sem, Freq_Sem, MI_Sem)} after adding the weighted mutual information MI_Sem to S1. Similarly, we can get a syntactic quintet by adding weighted mutual information MI_Syn to S2.

Step 6: Extract all the semantic and syntactic collocations with the frequency of co-occurrence (Freq) more than 10 and the threshold of mutual information beyond 0.0001.

4   Results and analysis of experiment

Through the experiment, we draw out 3386 collocation based on semantic dependency analysis and 268102 collocation based on dependency parsing. The results are illustrated in Table 2 and Table 3.

Table 2. Top 10 of semantic collocation labeled as Pat and Cont

W1	W2	Rela_Sem	Freq_Sem	MI_Sem
解决(solve)	问题(problem)	Pat	21647	0.7927
降低(reduce)	成本(cost)	Pat	2737	0.1240
推进(push on)	建设(construction)	Pat	4011	0.1179
骑(ride)	自行车(bike)	Pat	1936	0.1139
买(buy)	车(car)	Pat	3582	0.1066
采取(take)	措施(measure)	Cont	14268	0.7010
承担(take)	责任(responsibility)	Cont	6689	0.3182
做出(make)	贡献(contribution)	Cont	5801	0.3164
满足(satisfy)	需求(demand)	Cont	5363	0.2642
提供(provide)	服务(service)	Cont	8286	0.2525

Table 3. Top 10 of syntactic collocation

W1	W2	Rela_Syn	Freq_Syn	MI_Syn
说(say)	是(is)	VOB	97509	1.7935
解决(solve)	问题(problem)	VOB	43088	1.6853
发挥(play)	作用(role)	VOB	25128	1.2546
采取(take)	措施(measure)	VOB	21328	1.0459
接受(accept)	采访(interview)	VOB	22385	1.0453
认为(think)	是(is)	VOB	47229	1.0416
加大(increase)	力度(intensity)	VOB	14610	0.8000
告诉(tell)	记者(reporter)	VOB	24090	0.7695
加强(enhance)	建设(construction)	VOB	20025	0.6841
开展(develop)	活动(activity)	VOB	18547	0.6718

In order to compare the results, we select 5 verbs with high frequency through sampling and respectively calculate their precision and recall rate of collocation extraction. To maintain the accuracy, we narrow the range of collocation to the dictionary, which means that only the collocation included in *Collocation Dictionary of Modern Chinese* [16] are defined as qualified ones. The result is illustrated in Table 4.

Table 4. Results of evaluation

Method	Word	Dic_N	Corr_N	All_N	P(%)	R(%)	F(%)
Semantics	做(Do)	232	103	432	23.8	44.4	31.0
	参加(Attend)	64	40	416	9.6	62.5	16.6
	受到(Suffer)	122	79	260	30.4	64.8	41.4
	感到(Feel)	48	24	241	10.0	50.0	16.7
	加强(Reinforce)	68	38	226	16.8	55.9	25.8
Average		106.8	56.8	315	18.1	55.5	26.3
Syntax	做(Do)	272	153	1147	13.3	56.3	21.5
	参加(Attend)	67	49	737	6.6	73.1	12.1
	受到(Suffer)	129	86	316	27.2	66.7	38.4
	感到(Feel)	58	29	352	8.2	50.0	14.1
	加强(Reinforce)	42	32	493	6.5	76.2	12.0
Average		113.6	69.8	609	12.4	64.5	19.6

In Table.4. Dic_N refers to the number of extracted collocation included in dictionary. Corr_N refers to the number of collocations we extracted correctly. All_N refers to the total number of collocation we extract. Formulas of accuracy rate, recall rate and F-value are shown as follows:

$$P = Corr\_N / All\_N \qquad (3)$$

$$R = Corr\_N / Dic\_N \qquad (4)$$

$$F = 2*P*R*/(P+R) \qquad (5)$$

From the result above, we can see that the P-value and F-value of collocation extraction based on semantic analysis are higher than the ones based on dependency parsing though the recall rate is lower. This is because the annotation system of semantic dependency analysis is more fine-grained than syntactic analysis's. Semantic dependency analysis includes 98 semantic labels while syntactic analysis has only 11 syntactic tags. The coarse-grained tags will make the number of each role higher, therefore we draw out 3610129 arcs labeled "Pat" and "Cont", and 27856336 arcs labeled "VOB". It can be seen from Table 3 that combinations such as "认为是" (think is), and "说是" (say is) are labeled "VOB" so the coarse-grained tags will increase the interference factors and lower the extraction accuracy.

What is more, we find that accuracy rate is lower than recall rate no matter which theory we based on. This is because we evaluate the results based on the collocation dictionary. In another word we are only concerned with the collocation included in dictionary. However, actually many collocation we extract are qualified though they are not listed in dictionary. To compensate this shortcoming we then evaluate the results by introspection. For example, through our evaluation the 123 words listed in Table 5 can also form collocation with "受到" (suffer) though they are not included in collocation dictionary. By combining the reference of dictionary and artificial judgment we think the precision rate of collocation extraction based on semantic dependency analysis can reach 77.7%, and the one based on dependency parsing is 74.7%.

Table 5.Collocations of "受到 'suffer'"

关注(focus)	伤害(hurt)	处罚(punish)	青睐(favor)	追捧(sought)
重视(value)	教育(educate)	侵害(hurt)	保护(protect)	批评(criticize)
处理(deal)	质疑(doubt)	谴责(condemn)	指控(accuse)	挑战(challenge)
惩处(punish)	肯定(sure)	严惩(punish)	损伤(damage)	约束(constraint)
指责(criticize)	损坏(damage)	认可(approve)	赞誉(praise)	追究(investigate)
挤压(press)	震撼(shock)	抑制(press)	考验(test)	接见(receive)
对待(treat)	罚款(punish)	推崇(praise)	监督(watch)	照顾(take care)
审判(trial)	重创(hit)	起诉(sue)	抨击(attack)	危害(damage)
牵连(involve)	触动(move)	认同(approve)	礼遇(treat)	削弱(weaken)
波及(spread)	监控(watch)	创伤(damage)	恐吓(intimidate)	响应(response)
非议(criticize)	欺骗(cheat)	抵制(resist)	款待(hospitality)	重用(useful)
遏制(contain)	侵袭(attack)	赞许(praise)	局限(limit)	阻力(resistance)
资助(fund)	争议(criticize)	赞赏(praise)	洗礼(baptism)	接待(reception)

5   Conclusion

In this paper, we define collocation as constraint combinations with certain degree of co-occurrence frequency and we define co-occurrence as a relationship in which words involved have semantic relations. We calculate the weighted mutual information and extract collocations respectively based on semantic dependency analysis and dependency parsing. Through comparing the results, we find that the F-value and accuracy of collocation extraction based on semantic dependency are higher than the ones based on dependency parsing, the reason of which is that semantic tags are more fine-grained. Besides, we propose a method of collocation extraction based on dependency analysis that can improve extraction accuracy. The collocation corpus with semantic tags can provide support for machine learning, information retrieval and other fields of natural language processing. At present, our study is only a preliminary discussion due to the accuracy of automatic semantic parser is not very ideal with only 71.7% accuracy. And the size of dictionary adopted by our study is small, which will also have a negative effect on the evaluation. To improve the efficiency of semantic dependency analysis and collocation dictionary will be the focus of our following work.

Acknowledgement

We appreciatively acknowledge the support of the National Natural Science Foundation of China (NSFC) via Grant 61170144, Major Program of China's National Linguistics work Committee during the twelfth five-year plan (ZDI125-41), young and middle aged academic cadre support plan of Beijing Language and Culture University (501321303) and BLCU supported project for young researchers program (supported by the Fundamental Research Funds for the Central Universities) (16YCX159).

Reference

[1] Choueka, YandKlein, TandNeuwitz, E. Automatic Retrieval of Frequent Idiomatic and Collocational Expressions in a Large Corpus. Journal of Literary and Linguistic Computing, 1983, 4.

[2] K.church, P.Hanks. Word Association Norms.Mutual information and Lexicography. Computational Linguistics, 1990, 16 (1): 22-29.

[3] Smadja,F. Retrieving Collocation from Text : Xtract. Computational Linguistic, 1993, 19(1): 143-177.

[4] Lin D. Extracting Collocations from Text Corpora[C]. In First Workshop on Computational Terminology, Montreal, Canada, 1998: 8-12.

[5] Yang S. Machine Learning for Collocation Identification. In 2003 IEEE International Conference on Natural Language Processing and Knowledge Engineering (NLP-KE 03).Beijing, 2003: 315-320.

[6] Maosong Sun. Preliminary study on quantitative analysis of Chinese Collocation. Studies of theChinese Language, 1997(1).

[7] Honglin Sun. Generalizing Grammar Rules from Annotated Corpus: analysis of "V + N". The Forth China National Conference on Computational Linguistics, 1997. Beijing: TsinghuaUniversity Press.

[8] Weiguang Qu, Chen Xiaohe, Ji Genlin. A Frame-based Approach to Chinese Collocation Automatic Extracting. Computer Engineering, 2004.12.

[9] Wanxiang Che, Ting Liu, Bing Qin. A Method to Fetch Collocations Orienting

Dependency Grammar. The sixth China National Conference on Computational Linguistics, 2001. Beijing: TsinghuaUniversity Press.

[10] Runhua Xu. A Grammar Parser Based on Collocation Knowledge Base and Grammar Function Match. Nanjing Normal University.2013.

[11] Firth，J.R. Modes of Meaning. In Essays and Studies.The English Association，1951.Reprinted in J.R. Firth Pagers in Linguistics 1934-1951.London：Oxford University Press，1964:190-215.

[12] Xingguang Lin. Research on Collocation. Chinese Teaching & Studies, 1994(4).

[13] Xiuying Shen. A study on Chinese Collocatino.Fudan University. 2007.

[14] Wanxiang Che, Zhenghua Li, Ting Liu. LTP: A Chinese Language Technology Platform. In Proceedings of the Coling 2010: Demonstrations. 2010.08, pp13-16, Beijing, China.

[15] Yu Ding, Yanqiu Shao, Wanxiang Che, Ting Liu. Dependency Graph based Chinese Semantic Parsing. Harbin: Harbin Institute of Technology, 2014.

[16] Shoukang Zhang, Xingguang Lin. The dictionary of modern Chinese words collocation. The commercial press.

Comitative Relational Nouns and Relativization of Comitative Case in Mandarin

Xin Kou

Department of Chinese Language and Literature, Peking University, Beijing, China

e-mail: snjdkx@163.com

Abstract. This paper discusses unmarked comitative relative clauses activated by comitative relational nouns. Different from canonical relative clauses, these clauses are restricted syntactically and semantically. This paper points out that comitative relative clauses are directly generated by the conceptual structure of comitative relational nouns rather than by transformation, since the semantic structures of these nouns contain comitative prepositions and their arguments. Therefore, comitative relative clauses are presentations of the downgraded predications of comitative relational nouns at the syntactic level. Besides, a questionnaire survey is conducted in this research to investigate the grammaticality of comitative relative clauses, through which, we find that these constructions, which are triggered by comitative relational nouns, are less grammatical than canonical relative clauses, which are generated by syntactic transformation.

Keywords: Relational nouns, Comitative Relative clauses, Semantic structure

1 Introduction

Relativization means to make a syntactic operation of a noun argument in a clause, by which, the whole clause will change to be a modifier of the noun argument. In Mandarin, we are used to prepositioning relative clauses by using the complementizer *de* (的) to connect adnominal clauses and head nouns. Keenan & Comrie proposed the famous theory of "Noun Phrase Accessibility Hierarchy" through a large number of investigations on languages, which reveals the possibility of relativization of nouns on various syntactic positions. [1] The accessibility hierarchy shows as follow:

Subject > Direct object > Indirect object > Oblique> Possessive > Comparative

Among them, the subjects of clauses have the highest accessibility, while comparatives are most impossible to be relativized. According to implicational universals, if the noun argument ranking behind is allowed to be relativized, those ranking in the front should also get approved. In Mandarin, subjects and direct objects can be relativized directly while arguments behind indirect objects can only achieve marked relativization

© Springer International Publishing AG 2016
M. Dong et al. (Eds.): CLSW 2016, LNAI 10085, pp. 233–240, 2016
DOI: 10.1007/978-3-319-49508-8_22

by means of pronominal anaphora in clauses [1]. However, Ning found that oblique is permissible to get unmarked relativization. For example: location, time, way and tool. While other oblique such as comitative can achieve relativization only by means of pronominal anaphora. [2] Such as:

（1）a. 我　和　那　个　女孩儿　跳舞。
　　　　1sg and that CL　girl　　dance
　　　　I danced with that girl.

　　b. *我　跳舞　的　那　个　女孩
　　　　1sg dance de that CL girl
　　　　*the girl that I danced

Yet Huang pointed out that comitative relational nouns can be relativized directly sometimes [3]. For example:

（2）我　　跳舞 的　舞伴
　　　1sg　dance de　dancing partner
　　　the dancing partner with whom I danced

Based on this idea, we find that, in addition to the word 舞伴 (dancing partner), there still exist other relational nouns allowing unmarked relativization with comitative categories. Such nouns usually refer to people, which are usually constituted by morphemes such as -友 (friend), -伴 (companion) or 同- (together) and 对- (oppose). These words include:

酒肉朋友 (a mercenary friend) 盟友 (ally) 难友 (fellow sufferer) 战友 (comrade-in-arms) 队友 (teammate)

伙伴 (partner) 旅伴 (travelling companion) 同伴 (companion) 舞伴 (dancing partner)

同窗 (classmate) 同党 (partisan) 同僚 (colleague) 同谋 (accomplice)

对头 (enemy) 对手 (opponent) 对象 (object)

In this paper, these nouns are considered as exceptions in accessibility of relativization in Mandarin. Meanwhile, this special kind of relative clauses can reveal the competitive relationship between syntactic rules and lexical semantics. Therefore, this paper aims to discuss unmarked comitative relative clauses caused by comitative relational nouns and has an in-depth exploration of their semantic, syntactic features and generative mechanisms.

2 Semantic and Pragmatic Constraints of Comitative Relative Clauses

Although comitative relational nouns can activate unmarked comitative relative clauses, these constructions are restricted semantically and pragmatically. The constraints are also important features that makes these constructions different from other unmarked (canonical) relative clauses.

2.1 Content of Comitative Relative Clauses

Although comitative relational nouns such as 舞伴 (dancing partner), 同伴 (companion) and 队友 (teammate) can get relativized as comitative, what the relative clauses describe must be consistent with what the comitative nouns connate in order to make the constructions reasonable. For example, 舞伴 (dancing partner) is interpreted as "the person with whom you dance". Thus, the example (2) can be accepted, yet 他吃饭的 舞伴 (the dancing partner with whom he had dinner) cannot. The contrast in the following example also demonstrates this restriction. For example:

（3）a. 他　打　　排球　　　的　队友

    3sg　play　volleyball　de　teammate

    the teammate　with whom he plays volleyball

b. 他　争夺　　　　奥运冠军　　　　的 对手

    3sg　compete (for)　Olympic champion　de　opponent

    the opponent with whom he compete for Olympic champion

It is seen from the above that the semantic contents of the comitative relative clauses are strictly restricted by meaning of their noun heads. Only events in comitative relational nouns' semantic frames can become the contents of comitative relative clauses.

2.2 Focus Restriction in Comitative Relative Clauses

When comitative relational nouns get relativized, the comitative relative clauses can only be limited as event relevant to words' meaning. Therefore, from the perspective of pragmatic function, the key information expressed in these relative clauses can only be the subjects or the elaboration parts. Take 他跳舞的舞伴 (the dancing partner with whom I danced) as an example. When the accent falls on 他 (he), the whole construction is more grammatical, yet it gets less reasonable when the accent falls on 跳舞 (dance), since 舞伴 (dancing partner) has already embodied the meaning of "dance". While in the example 他打排球的队友 (the teammate with whom he plays volleyball), the accent is allowed to fall on 他 (he) or 排球 (volleyball), since both of them can be the comparative focus.

We mentioned in Section 2.1 that the events described in relative clauses must be a part of the lexical contents. Therefore, if a relative clause only repeats the meaning the head noun conveys, the entire noun phrase will be redundant semantically. If the speaker is to convey some new information to the hearer by a comitative relative clause, the information may be the identity of the subject of the clause, or a more meticulous part of the event described by the head noun.

3 Syntactic Constraints on Comitative Relative Clauses

Comitative relative clauses have many syntactic restraints, which are mainly reflected in syntactic category of each part in the clauses.

3.1 Non-process Feature of Comitative Relative Clauses

The syntactic feature of the comitative relative clauses is that there cannot exist any tense or aspect information in the clauses, which is called the "non-process" feature. For example:

（4）a. 他 跳舞 的 舞伴

    3sg dance de dancing partner

    the dancing partner with whom he danced

  b. *他 跳 了 舞 的 舞伴

    3sg dance ASP dance de dancing partner

    the dancing partner with whom he has danced

  c. *他 跳 了 一 支 舞 的 舞伴

    3sg dance ASP one CL dance de dancing partner

    the dancing partner with whom he has danced once

Comitative relative clauses are definitely devoid of the time feature. Examples such as（4b）that reflects completion and（4c）that shows bounded are both unaccepted.

3.2 Comitative Relative Clauses Exclude Adverbs and Complements

Adverbs or complements are not allowed in the comitative relative clauses, so the elaborate description of events cannot using these categories. Such as:

（5）a. 他 去 北京 旅行 的 同伴

    3sg go (to) Beijing travel de companion

    the companion with whom he traveled to Beijing

  b. *他 一起 偷偷地 去 北京 旅行 的 同伴

    3sg together furtively go(to) Beijing travel de companion

    *the companion with whom he traveled to Beijing furtively

In addition, comitative relative clauses also exclude degree complements or result complements.

（6）a. 他 一起 学习 的 同窗

    3sg together study de classmate

    the classmate with whom he studied

b. *他　学　得　　非常 认真　的 同窗
3sg study de-comp very　earnest de　classmate
*the classmate with whom he studied very earnestly

3.3 Subjects of Comitative Relative Clauses

The subjects of the comitative relative clauses must be definite. For example:

（7）*一 个 士兵　一起　　战斗　的 战友
　　　 one CL soldier together combat de comrade-in-arms
　　　 *the comrade-in-arms (with) who a soldier combat together

On the one hand, a definite subject always reduces the definiteness of the event referred by the relative clause; on the other hand, it is also the requirement of the relational noun head, since a relational noun is used to having a definite noun argument.

4 The Generative Mechanism and Grammaticality of Comitative Relative Clauses

Through the above analysis, we can find that although there exist some nouns that can trigger unmarked comitative relative clauses, these constructions have so many restraints in types of head nouns and content of clauses, even the meaning of the relative clauses is redundant sometimes since it is corresponding to the lexical meaning. We believe that comitative relative clauses are lexicon internally motivated, and only the nouns that satisfy the special lexical structure of the comitative can be the heads of these constructions.

4.1 The Generative Mechanism of Comitative Relative Clauses

The main reason for the significant differences that exist between comitative relative clauses and canonical relative clauses at semantic and syntactic levels lies in their different generative mechanisms. Canonical relative clauses come from syntactic transformation by moving arguments out from the argument positions in clauses to be head nouns with the gaps left. But generally speaking, there is no space left among comitative relative clauses. Besides, the head nouns of comitative relative clauses can't be restored to the clauses through topicalization. Therefore, from this point of view, comitative relative clauses don't belong to relative clauses in a strict sense. [4] Through the previous discussion, it can be seen that comitative relative clauses are based upon comitative relational nouns. Only when the comitative relational nouns serve as the head nouns of the relative clauses, can these constructions have the possibility to be achieved. So the concept structure of the comitative relational nouns is the syntactic and semantic pivot for the whole noun phrases. A common point of these comitative relational nouns is that this kind of nouns is explained as "*one* do something with *somebody*" in the dictionary. For example:

舞伴(dancing partner)：someone you dance with.

队友(teammate): someone you make a team with him and compete with others together.

同伴(companion): someone with whom you do things together.

So these relational nouns not only contain arguments referring to persons but also include event-arguments. Hence we believe that comitative relative clauses are internally motivated by the special lexical structure of the head nouns.

Compared with monovalent nouns, a comitative relational noun can adopt downgraded predication structure for demonstrating its semantic structure. The concept structure of a comitative relational noun contains a predicate and a preposition frame showing comitative meaning [5]:

Comitative relational nouns: <who. WITH sb.> <who. DO. sth.>

That is to say, a comitative relational noun contains two variables. *Sb.* has a pure noun meaning. For example, the nominal argument 他 (he) of 舞伴 (dancing partner). At the same time, a relational noun also contains a predicate component *DO sth.* The preposition frame with a comitative sense and the predicate structure of "doing something" are both compressed into lexical meaning of the comitative relational noun, and can be released as an adnominal clause at the syntactic surface. According to Leech (1987), the downgraded predication structure can often be achieved at the surface syntactic level with adjective function. Obviously, the downgraded predications can be expressed by comitative relative clauses. But this kind of release is very limited that must satisfy and match the lexical meaning of the comitative relational nouns, and should be non-processing and non-descriptive. Therefore, we can think that the comitative relative clauses are more like noun complements than modifiers.

4.2   Grammaticality of Comitative Relative Clauses

Comitative relative clauses triggered by lexical meaning are against the "Noun Phrase Accessibility Hierarchy" in Mandarin, which makes the grammaticality of these constructions questioned. We believe that the grammaticality of this kind of clauses should be less than those triggered by syntactic rules. We investigate the validity of this kind of clauses through a questionnaire. A total of 60 questionnaires were distributed and 54 were valid. Three types of sentences are designed in the questionnaire. The first category is unmarked comitative relative clauses triggered by relational nouns; the second is subject relative clauses; the third type is unmarked comitative relative clauses with entity nouns as the heads. As the following table shows, the grammaticality is divided into four grades. **A** is perfectly legal; **B** is understandable, which speakers can understand, but rarely use it. It will not be judged as faulty; **C** is that this expression is somewhat unnatural, but can be understood; **D** is completely ungrammatical. The statistical results of the investigation are as follows:

Table 1. the statistical results of grammaticality of comitative relative clauses

clause types	Examples	A	B	C	D

unmarked comitative relative clauses with relational noun heads	张三打球的队友	38.19%	53.94%	7.87%	0%
subject relative clauses	跟张三打球的队友	84.72%	12.96%	1.39%	0.93%
unmarked comitative relative clauses with entity noun heads	张三打球的男孩	2.47%	16.05%	42.59%	38.89%

It can be seen that the comitative relative clauses with relational noun heads are grammatical, but these constructions such as 张三打球的队友(the teammate with whom Zhang San plays basketball) is less used than the subject relativization structures such as 跟张三打球的队友 (the teammate who plays basketball with Zhang San). However the comitative relative clauses with relational noun heads are more grammatical than comitative relative clauses with entity noun heads such as 张三打球的男孩 (the boy with whom Zhang San plays basketball). So we can believe that unmarked comitative relative clauses are less acceptable than subject relative clauses. We think that this is because the constructions activated by semantics are weaker than that done by the syntactic rules.

5   Conclusion

In this paper, we discuss the semantic and syntactic features of the comitative relative clauses, which are triggered by comitative relational nouns. Different from canonical relative clauses, comitative relative clauses are restricted syntactically and semantically. This paper argues that the generative mechanism of these relative clauses is the conceptual structure of comitative relational nouns rather than transformation. The semantic structure of a comitative relational noun contains a comitative preposition and its argument, by virtue of which, an unmarked comitative relative clause forms. The comitative relative clauses are reflections of the downgraded predications of their noun heads. In addition, this article has carried on the questionnaire survey for the grammaticality of these relative clauses. The survey shows that the comitative relative clauses triggered by comitative relational nouns are far more grammatical than those with heads of entity nouns, but less than subject relative clauses. This result demonstrates the fact that constructions generated by the semantic structure are weaker than those formed by syntactic rules, whether in terms of syntactic and semantic conditions or grammaticality.

References

1. Keenan, E., Comrie, B.: Noun Phrase accessibility and universal grammar. *Linguistic Inquiry*, pp63-99, (1977)
2. Ning, C.: *The Overt Syntax of Relativization and Topicalization in Chinese*, University of California, Irvine: PhD Dissertation, (1993)

3. Huang, Z. D.: The noun phrases of head postposition: construction or composition, In the 5th conference of oversea Chinese scholars, Xuzhou: Jiangsu Normal University, (2015) [In Chinese]
4. Dixon, R. M. W.: *Basic Linguistic Theory Vol.II: Grammatical Topics*, Oxford University Press, Oxford, (2009)
5. Leech, G.: Semantics: The Study of Meaning 2ed edition. Penguin Books, Harmondsworth, (1981)
6. Yuan, Y.: hidden predicates and the syntactic results: the reference rule of "de" construction, In: Studies of the Chinese Language, No.4, pp241-255, (1995) [In Chinese]
7. Yuan, Y.: The Study of Valency Grammar in Mandarin, Shangwu Press, Beijing, (2010) [In Chinese]
8. Zhu, D.: Self-reference and transformation reference: the function of nominalization markers *de zhe suo zhi* in Chinese, *Dialect*, No.1, pp16-31, (1983) [In Chinese]
9. Cha, J. Y.: *Constraints on Clausal Complex Noun Phrases in Korean with Focus on the Gapless Relative Clause Construction*. Phd Dissertation in University of Illinois, Urbana, (2005)
10. Huang, C-J., Li, A., Li Y.: Relativization: Order and Structure, In: Presented at the 9th International Conference of Chinese Linguisitcs (Annual Conference of International Association of Chinese Linguistics, IACL-9), National University of Singapore, June 26-28, (2000)

A Corpus-Based Study on Pseudo-ditransitive Verbs in Mandarin Chinese

Pei-Jung Kuo

Department of Foreign Languages, National Chiayi University, Chiayi, Taiwan
domo@mail.ncyu.edu.tw

Abstract. Based on the search in the Sinica Corpus, in this paper I present a novel syntactic observation for pseudo-ditransitive verbs in Mandarin Chinese. That is, the internal argument order of certain pseudo-ditransitive verbs in the previous proposal is not complete. The internal arguments of certain pseudo-ditransitive verbs in fact can have two different orders, which is reminiscent of locative alternation observed in English. Consequently, in addition to the proposed lexical categorization in the literature, it is suggested that Mandarin pseudo-ditransitive verbs should also be categorized based on their genuine syntactic behaviors in order to get a full picture of these verbs in Mandarin verbal categorization.

Keywords: Pseudo-transitive verb · Internal arguments · the Sinica Corpus · Locative alternation

1 Introduction

Lin et al. [9] propose a new verbal category of pseudo-ditransitive verbs in Mandarin Chinese. A typical ditransitive construction is shown in (1). In this example, the ditransitive verb *song* ('give') takes three arguments: one external argument and two internal arguments postverbally. Interestingly, as proposed by Lin et al. [9], there also exists a group of verbs which has to take three arguments in Mandarin Chinese. However, for this special group of verbs, their two internal arguments cannot both stay postverbally, as shown in (2). One of the internal arguments has to be placed in the preverbal position, which can be achieved via the BA construction in (3), the BEI construction in (4), or the external topic construction in (5).

(1) Zhangsan song-le   Lisi   yi-ben shu.
     Zhangsan give-ASP   Lisi   one-CL book
     'Zhangsan gave Lisi a book.'

(2) *Zhangsan   tu-shang   mianbao   naiyou.
     Zhangsan   spread-onto   bread   butter
     'Zhangsan spread better onto the bread.'

(3) Zhangsan ba   mianbao   tu-shang   naiyou.
     Zhangsan BA   bread   spread-onto   butter
     'Zhangsan spread better onto the bread.'

© Springer International Publishing AG 2016
M. Dong et al. (Eds.): CLSW 2016, LNAI 10085, pp. 241–248, 2016
DOI: 10.1007/978-3-319-49508-8_23

(4) Mianbao   bei   Zhangsan   tu-shang   naiyou.
    bread   BEI   Zhangsan   spread-onto   butter
    'The bread was spread with butter by Zhangsan.'

(5) Mianbao, Zhangsan   tu-shang   naiyou.
    bread   Zhangsan   spread-onto   butter
    'On the bread, Zhangsan has spread butter.'

The preverbal internal argument phenomenon is quite similar to the one found in pseudo-transitive verbs, which also exhibit preverbal internal arguments. (see also Li and Thompson [7]; Chang et al. [1]; Paul [12]; Tang [14]; C.-R. Huang [3]; Mo [10]; Her [2]; Zhuang et al. [15] and so on). The relevant examples are given in (6).

(6) a. *Zhangsan   jie-hun   Li   xiaojie.
        Zhangsan   get-married   Li   miss
       'Zhangsan got married with Miss Li.'
    b. Zhangsan   gen   Li   xiaojie jie-hun.
       Zhangsan   with   Li   miss   get-married

Lin et al. [9] therefore names this group of verbs as pseudo-ditransitive verbs.

2   The Three Subtypes

In this section, I present the three subtypes of pseudo-ditransitive verbs categorized by Lin et al. [9]. Lin et al. [9] analyze the pseudo-ditransitive verbs from the perspective of lexical semantics. The pseudo-ditransitive verbs examined are basically compounds composed of a verb and a complement. According to Lin et al. [9], a common semantic property shared by these three subtypes is "movement" since these verbs all involve the movement of an object to a goal or resulting in a change of state (a kind of movement metaphorically). The first subtype is shown in (7), whose verbs are composed of the so-called *spray/load* verbs or *fill* verbs (i.e. Levin [5]) plus a resultative complement. The first part of the compound verb involves the movement of an object to a goal, and the second part of the compound verb indicates that a state has been achieved after the action. An example of this kind is shown in (8) and the pseudo-ditransitive verb here is *tu-shang* 'spread onto'. The first part of the compound *tu* 'spread' involves movement of the theme "butter" to the goal "bread". Notice that the second part of the compound *shang* 'onto' indicates the state that the butter is fully over the bread.

(7) *Put*-verb + *shang* 'onto' / *man* 'full'
    ex: *tu-shang* ('spread onto'), *tian-shang* ('fill in'), *bang-shang* ('tie onto'), *tie-shang* ('stick onto'), *zhuang-man* ('load with'), *dao-man* ('fill with'), etc.

(8) Zhangsan   BA   mianbao   tu-shang   naiyou.
    Zhangsan   BA   bread   spread-onto   butter
    'Zhangsan spread better onto the bread.'

The second subtype is composed of a transitive verb plus a direction verb, as shown in (9). For this subtype, the first part of the compound verb also involves movement of an object from one place to another, and the second part of the compound specifies the exact direction of the involved movement. An example is shown in (10). The first part of the compound *gan* 'drive' shows that *Lisi* was moved unwillingly and the second part *chu* 'out' indicates that *Lisi* was moved from inside the classroom to the outside of the classroom.

(9) verb + direction-verb (*chu* 'exit/out', *ru* 'enter/into', *jin* 'enter/into'...)
     ex: *shou-jin* ('put into'), *guan-jin* ('lock into'), *pai-chu* ('eject'), *xie-ru* ('write into'), *fang-ru* ('place into'), etc.

(10) Zhangsan   ba   Lisi   gan-chu   jiaoshi.
     Zhangsan   BA   Lisi   drive-out   classroom
     'Zhangsan drove Lisi out of the classroom.'

The last subtype in (11) is composed of a transitive verb plus a *become* verb. This last subtype is slightly different from the above two subtypes. The first part of the compound verb shows how the change of state is applied to an object, while the second part of the compound verb indicates the change of state has been achieved or the goal has been reached. An example is shown in (12). The first part of the compound verb *yi* ('translate') shows that the change of state is to "translate", and the second part of the compound verb *cheng* ('become') indicates that this article of a certain language has become an English one.

(11) verb + *become*-verb (*cheng* 'become', *wei* 'be', *zuo* ,'be')
     ex: *juan-cheng* ('roll into'), *shi-wei* ('see as'), *kan-zuo* ('view as') *yi-cheng* ('translate as'), etc.

(12) Zhangsan ba   zhe-pian wenzhang   yi-cheng   yingwen.
     Zhangsan BA   this-CL   article   translate-into English
     'Zhangsan translated this article into English.'

Note that for the third subtype, there is no actual physical movement involved as in the first or the second subtype. However, Lin et al. [9] propose that for this subtype, the movement is a metaphorical one. In (12), the article has changed from a certain language to English, indicating a change of its original property. Also note that a metaphorical movement may also involve the process of assigning a property to someone, or mapping someone to a set of people with a certain quality. In example (13), *Lisi* is considered as a good friend by *Zhangsan*, which can be viewed as a "goal" bearing the same property of *hao-yao* 'good friend' under *Zhangsan*'s categorization for his friends.

(13) Zhangsan   ba   Lisi   shi-wei   hao-yao.
     Zhangsan   BA   Lisi   see-as   good-friend
     'Zhangsan see Lisi as a good friend.'

Lin et al. [9] therefore conclude that no matter it is physical or metaphorical, pseudo-ditransitive verbs all involve the common semantic property: movement.[1]

---

[1] There are different opinions regarding the categorization, though. As one of the reviewers points out, the use of "movement" is not quite suitable for the third type which is simply a

3   Mandarin Pseudo-Ditransitive Verbs in the Corpus Study

In this section I present a new observation regarding Mandarin pseudo-ditransitive verbs from the Sinica Corpus study. And I discuss the consequences following the new observation.

3.1   The New Data

One interesting phenomenon can be found if one compares the syntactic behaviors of these three subtypes of pseudo-ditransitive verbs by Lin et al. [9]. The syntactic behaviors of example (8), (10) and (12) are summarized in (14).

(14) a. Type 1: Goal – V – Theme
      b. Type 2: Theme – V – Goal
      c. Type 3: Theme – V – Goal

As one can see, for the first subtype, the Goal argument is in the preverbal position, while the Theme argument is in the postverbal position. On the other hand, the second and the third subtypes show the opposite pattern. Their Theme arguments simply precede the Goal arguments.

However, the syntactic patterns of pseudo-ditransitive verbs seem not to be fixed in (14) if one tries to search the listed pseudo-ditransitive verb examples in the Sinica Corpus [17]. Take the pseudo-ditransitive verb *dao-man* 'fill with' as an example. We in fact can find the syntactic pattern "Theme – V – Goal" for *dao-man* as shown in (15).

(15) ... zuihou   yi   fengmi   dao-man   guanzi ...
          finally   use   honey   fill-with   pot
      '... finally fill the pot with honey ...'

The other verb *zhuang-man* ('load with') in the first subtype may also show the "Theme – V – Goal" pattern. In other words, for *zhuang-man* and *dao-man*, their internal arguments can exhibit two different word orders.

This free-order phenomenon is not unique for the two verbs *zhuang-man* and *dao-man* in the first subtype. Most of the verbs in the second subtype also exhibit two opposite syntactic patterns for their internal arguments as well. That is, in addition to the listed pattern "Theme – V – Goal", verbs such as *fang-ru* ('place into') also allows the syntactic pattern "Goal – V – Theme", as shown in (16).

(16) ... chaoguo   zhong   fang-ru   liang-da-chi   you ...
          fry-pan   inside place-into   two-big-spoon   oil
      '... place two big-spoon of oil into the frying pan...'

---

change on internal property of the Theme. In addition, there are differences observable in the third subtype itself. For example, *shi-wei* in example (13) is a stative verb and should be different from *yi-cheng* in example (12). Obviously, while the former can be modified by the frequency adverbial *yizhi* ('always), the latter cannot.

The verbs in the second subtype which show two different internal argument patterns are *xie-ru* ('write into'), *fang-ru* ('place into'), *shou-jin* ('put into') and *pai-chu* ('eject').

As for the third subtype, the syntactic behavior of the listed verbs is quite consistent. That is, only one syntactic pattern "Theme – V – Goal" for the internal arguments can be found in the Sinica Corpus.

3.2   Discussions

The findings for the pseudo-ditransitive verbs in the Sinica Corpus are summarized in (17), (18) and (19):

(17) Type 1:
　　a. *tu-shang* ('spread onto'), *tian-shang* ('fill in'), *bang-shang* ('tie onto'), *tie-shang* 'stick onto': **Goal – V – Theme**
　　b. *zhuang-man* ('load with') and *dao-man* ('fill with'): **Goal – V – Theme** and **Theme – V – Goal**

(18) Type 2:
　　a. *guan-jin* ('lock into'): **Theme – V – Goal**
　　b. *xie-ru* ('write into'), *fang-ru* ('place into'), *shou-jin* ('put into') and *pai-chu* ('eject'): **Theme – V – Goal** and **Goal – V – Theme**

(19) Type 3:
　　juan-cheng ('roll into'), *shi-wei* ('see as'), *kan-zuo* ('view as'), *yi-cheng* ('translate as'): **Theme – V – Goal**

The above new observation regarding pseudo-ditransitive verbs in Mandarin Chinese lead to the following two issues: Firstly, the free alternation of internal arguments in (17b) and (18b) is reminiscent of locative alternation in English (i.e. Pinker [13]; Levin [5]). The relevant examples are shown in (20).

(20) a. John loaded [$_{NP}$ books] [$_{PP}$ in the car].
　　b. John loaded [$_{NP}$ the car] [$_{PP}$ with books].

In English, it is well-known that verbs such as *load* or *spray* exhibit two different syntactic patterns as shown in (20). In (20a), the internal argument order is "V – Theme – Goal", while the one in (20b) is "V – Goal – Theme". Not surprisingly, in the literature it has been proposed that the patterns in (20) can be found in Mandarin Chinese as well (see Wang [15]; Pao [11]). For example, the main verb in (21) is *zhuang* ('put'), and it shows two orders of its internal arguments: "Theme – V – Goal" in (21a) and "Goal – V – Theme" in (21b).

(21) a. Zhangsan ba [$_{NP}$ shui]   zhuang [$_{PP}$ zai   pingzi li].
　　　　Zhangsan BA   water   put   at   bottle inside
　　b. Zhangsan ba [$_{NP}$ pingzi] zhuang-le [$_{NP}$ shui].
　　　　Zhangsan BA   bottle   put-ASP   water
　　　　'Zhangsan filled the bottle with water.'

Compared to the examples in (20) and (21), it seems that some of the pseudo-ditransitive verbs also have this kind of internal argument alternation. That is, in addition to verbs like *zhuang* ('put'), it should be fair to say that locative alternation can be found in pseudo-ditransitive verbs in Mandarin Chinese as well. However, a salient characteristic of the locative alternation in the pseudo-ditransitive verbs lies in the syntactic categories employed in the structures. Note that in the English example (20), the syntactic categories for the internal arguments of *load* are NPs and PPs, no matter in which order. Its Chinese counterpart in (21a) also needs a NP and a PP for the "Theme – V – Goal" order. On the other hand, it is not necessary for Mandarin pseudo-ditransitive verbs to use PPs to host its internal argument in the "Theme – V – Goal" order. For example, in (15), both Theme and Goal arguments are realized in the format of NPs. Moreover, the constructed examples in (22) show that no PPs are required to host the internal arguments of *zhuang-man* ('load with') in either order.[2] Note that *ba* in the BA construction is not a preposition. It has been argued to be a light verb (C.-T. Huang [4]; Lin [8]) or a head in a *ba* projection (Li, [6]).

(22) a. Zhangsan   ba   shui   zhuang-man-le   beizi.
        Zhangsan   BA   water   load-with-ASP   cup
     b. Zhangsan   ba   beizi   zhuang-man-le   shui.
        Zhangsan   BA   cup   load-with-ASP   water
     'Zhangsan filled the cup with water.'

Secondly, with the new data from the Sinica Corpus, it is suggested that the syntactic categorization of pseudo-ditransitive verbs should be re-arranged. So far there are three syntactic patterns observable for pseudo-ditransitive verbs in Mandarin Chinese. Some verbs allow locative alternation as in (23a). Others exhibit only one syntactic pattern for their internal arguments: in either the order of (23b) or the order of (23c).

(23) Syntactic representations of Mandarin pseudo-ditransitive verbs:
     a.   Pattern 1: Locative alternation
     b.   Pattern 2: Goal – V – Theme
     c.   Pattern 3: Theme – V – Goal

Compared to the new data found in the Sinica Corpus, it is clear that the original categorization based on lexical components by Lin et al. [9] does not guarantee a particular syntactic pattern (see (17) to (19)). Therefore in addition to the semantic categorization, the genuine syntactic behaviors of the pseudo-ditransitive verbs like the ones in (23) should be presented as well. The new semantic and syntactic interactions of the pseudo-ditransitive verbs are shown in Table 1. Under the new categorization, the only intact subtype is the third one, which exhibit only the "Them – V – Goal" syntactic pattern. For both the first and the second subtypes, each of them has two syntactic patterns individually, and the locative alternation pattern is the shared syntactic representation of these two subtypes.

---

[2]   It is also allowed for Mandarin pseudo-ditransitive verbs to use PPs to host their Goal arguments in the order of (22b), but this is optional.

Table 1. The new categorization of Mandarin pseudo-ditransitive verbs

		Semantic categorization		
		Subtype 1	Subtype 2	Subtype 3
Syntactic pattern	Locative alternation	*zhuang-man* ('load with') *dao-man* ('fill with')	*xie-ru* ('write into') *fang-ru* ('place into') *shou-jin* ('put into') *pai-chu* ('eject')	
	Goal – V – Theme	*tu-shang* ('spread onto') *tian-shang* ('fill in') *bang-shang* ('tie onto') *tie-shang* ('stick onto')		
	Theme – V – Goal		*guan-jin* ('lock into')	*juan-cheng* ('roll into') *shi-wei* ('see as') *kan-zuo* ('view as') *yi-cheng* ('translate as')

4   Conclusion

In this paper I have re-examined the syntactic patterns of pseudo-ditransitive verb in the Sinica Corpus. The syntactic behaviors of certain pseudo-ditransitive verbs in Mandarin Chinese are similar to locative alternation observed in verbs such as *load* or *spray* in English, but are also unique in the syntactic categories chosen for the internal arguments. Because of this new finding, it is therefore recommended that the syntactic categorization of the pseudo-ditransitive verbs in Mandarin Chinese should be re-arranged and incorporated with the original semantic categorization. In this way, we then can have a better understanding of the pseudo-ditransitive verbs both semantically and syntactically.

Acknowledgement. This paper is part of my research sponsored by the Ministry of Science and Technology, Taiwan (Grant No. MOST 104-2410-H-415-020). I hereby acknowledge the financial support of the MOST. The author would also like to thank the two anonymous reviewers for their valuable comments and suggestions on the previous version of this paper. All errors remain mine.

References

1. Chang, L.-P., Huang, C.-R., Chen, K.-J.: The phenomenon of Mandarin Pseudo-Transitive Verbs. In: The 2nd Conference of Mandarin Teaching, pp. 213-22. (1988)
2. Her, O.-S.: Interaction and Variation in the Chinese VO Construction. Crane Publishing, Taipei (1997)
3. Huang, C.-R.: Subcategorized topics in Mandarin Chinese. In: the 1989 CLTA Annual Meeting, Boston, November 17-19 (1989)
4. Huang, C.-T. J.: On lexical structure and syntactic projection. Chinese languages and Linguistics 3, 45-89 (1997)
5. Levin, B: *English Verb Classes and Alternations.* University of Chicago Press, Chicago (1993)
6. Li, Y.-H. A. : Chinese *ba.* In: Everaert, M., Van Riemsdijk, H., Goedemans, R., Hollebrandse, B. (eds.) The Blackwell Companion to Syntax, vol. 1, pp. 374-468. Blackwell, Oxford, UK (2006)
7. Li, C. N., Thompson, S. A.: Mandarin Chinese: A Functional Reference Grammar. Berkeley and Los Angeles: University of California Press (1981)
8. Lin, T.-H. J.: Light Verb Syntax and the Theory of Phrase Structure. Doctoral dissertation, University of California, Irvine. (2001)
9. Lin, C. C.-J., Wei W.-C., Huang, C.-R.: Mandarin Pseudo-Ditransitive Verbs. In: Proceedings of the 9th North American Chinese Conference on Linguistics, pp. 191-201. (1997)
10. Mo, R.-P.: Mandarin Chinese Subcategorized Topics: A Lexical Functional Grammar account. Master thesis, Fujen Catholic University, Taipei (1990)
11. Pao, Y.-Y.: Delimitedness and the locative alternation in Chinese. In: Ingemann F. (ed.) 1994 Mid-America Linguistics conference Papers, vol. 1, pp. 202-214. University of Kansas, Lawrence (1996)
12. Paul, W.: The Syntax of Verb-Object Phrases in Chinese: Constraints and Reanalysis. Editions Languages Croisés, Paris (1988)
13. Pinker, S.: 1989. Learnability and Cognition: The Acquisition of Argument Structure. MIT Press, Cambridge, MA (1989)
14. Tang, T.-C. C.: On the notion "possible verbs of Chinese". Tsing Hua Journal of Chinese Studies 18.1, 43-69 (1988)
15. Wang, L.: Eventuality and argument alternations in predicate structures. Doctoral dissertation. Chinese University of Hong Kong, Hong Kong (1998)
16. Zhuang, H., Liu Z., Zhang, Y.: VO Verbal Compounds and the Realization of Their Objects. In Ji, D., Xiao G. (eds.) Chinese Lexical Semantics: 13th Workshop, CLSW 2012, Wuhan, China, July 6-8, 2012, Revised Selected Papers, pp. 26-279. Springer, Heidelberg (2013)
17. The Sinica Corpus, http://app.sinica.edu.tw/kiwi/mkiwi/

Part III Corpus and Resource

Construction of the Dynamic Word Structural Mode Knowledge Base for the International Chinese Teaching

Dongdong Guo[1], Shuqin Zhu[2,1], Weiming Peng[1(✉)], Jihua Song[1] and Yinbing Zhang[1,3]

[1]College of Information Science and Technology, Beijing Normal University,
Beijing 100875, China
dongdongguo@mail.bnu.edu.cn, {pengweiming,songjh}@bnu.edu.cn
[2]Teachers' College of Beijing Union University, Beijing 100011, China
185904496@qq.com
[3]School of Mathematical Science, Huaibei Normal University, Huaibei 235000, China
zyb79225@126.com

Abstract. The different definition about "word" in international Chinese teaching and Chinese information processing leads to many achievements in the field of Chinese information processing cannot directly serve international Chinese teaching. In this paper, by studying the dynamic words which are frequently appeared in the international Chinese teaching materials we design a set of symbols which describe the structural relationship between the internal components of dynamic words, put forward a method to describe the dynamic word structural mode. Finally, the dynamic word structural mode knowledge base is created simultaneously when building the international Chinese teaching materials Treebank. The knowledge base provides a resource for research and information processing in the field of international Chinese teaching.

Keywords: Dynamic word · Dynamic word structural mode · International Chinese teaching · Knowledge base

1   Introduction

The international Chinese teaching materials Treebank is a basic resource to serve the international Chinese teaching which is based on Sentence-based Grammar founded by Li Jinxi [1]. The Treebank uses influential international Chinese teaching materials designated by Hanban or welcomed by the market as its raw corpus, adopts Diagrammatic Analyzing Method based on Sentence Pattern Structure to analyze Chinese sentences [2,3,4,5], and selects the Modern Chinese Dictionary (Sixth Edition) as the basic lexicon to annotate parts of speech (POS) and senses. Diagrammatic Analyzing Method, namely the use of visual diagrammatic tagging tool, achieves the conversion between syntactic structure annotating and XML storage.

In the actual process of annotating corpus, a large number of dynamic words appear which are not included in the Modern Chinese Dictionary, such as proper nouns (中国人[zhongguo ren](Chinese people), 铁路工人[tielu gongren](locoman)), verb-resultative verbs or verb-trending verbs (看清[kan qing](see clearly), 举起[ju qi](hold

M. Dong et al. (Eds.): CLSW 2016, LNAI 10085, pp. 251–260, 2016
DOI: 10.1007/978-3-319-49508-8_24

up)), quantifiers (一只[yi zhi](a), 十多个[shi duo ge](more than ten)), reduplicated forms (看看[kan kan](have a look), 听一听[ting yi ting](listen)), etc. These temporary dynamic words usually have to be segmented according to segmentation specification in the field of Chinese information processing and finally be analyzed into syntactic structure. However, it may be easier for students to accept these words as a whole in the international Chinese teaching. Based on the practical experience of the Treebank construction and the reality of international Chinese teaching, we advocate that this kind of combination structure with high cohesion is separated from syntactic analysis and treated with lexical analysis [6].

Early in the Treebank construction, we deal with dynamic words as follows: using spaces to separate the internal components, annotating the POS (an English letter) and sense (three digits) for each internal component. Diagrammatic analysis of the dynamic word "铁路工人[tielu gongren](locoman)" is shown in Fig. 1.

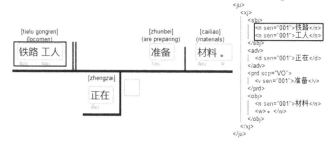

Fig. 1. Diagrammatic Analysis of "铁路工人"

In the corpus annotating process, we found: although the types of dynamic words are defined in the annotating specification and some examples are given, annotators are still vague about the dynamic words and can't distinguish dynamic words from phrase structures well. This not only lowers the tagging efficiency but also makes the Treebank lack of standardization and consistency.

Dynamic words in the international Chinese teaching have very important value for dynamic words reflect the basic principles of Chinese collocation which contributes to the production of standardized Chinese expression and the formation of Chinese language sense. In order to make the dynamic word processing more accord with the teaching practice, at the same time to ensure the standardization of the international Chinese teaching materials Treebank, this paper presents a method to describe the structural mode of dynamic words, and sets up a dynamic word structural mode knowledge base for the international Chinese teaching.

2   Dynamic Word Structural Mode

Dynamic words are sentence units which are generally not included in the lexicon and are not appropriate to be done further analysis as phrase structure in the syntactic analysis. Limited by structural stability, degree of significance cohesion and syllable prosodic features, dynamic words have obvious patternization. Some research and practice on dynamic words have been done [7,8,9,10]. On the basis of existing research results and Treebank building practice, four types of information including the whole POS of a dynamic word, the POS of each internal component, the syllable number of each internal component and structural relationship between the internal components are used to describe the dynamic word structural mode. Specific work done is: in the first place, adding POS information for non-word morphemes in the Modern Chinese Dictionary, and then designing a set of symbols to describe the structural relationship between the internal components, finally determining the specific method to describe the dynamic word structural mode.

Table 1. Symbols of Structural Relationship

Structural Relationship	Symbol	Samples	Notes
Coordination	...	花...草[hua cao] (flowers and plants); 中[zhong](middle)...小学[xiaoxue] (primary school)	Including reduced coordination
Attribute-head	↗	鸡[ji](chicken)↗蛋[dan](egg); 文字[wenzi](character)↗改革[gaige](reform); 北京[Beijing]↗师范[shifan](normal)↗大学[daxue](university); 刘[Liu](Liu)↗队[dui](captain); 周[Zhou](Zhou)↗副[fu](vice)↗主席[zhuxi](chairman)	Including "name-title" structure
Adverbial-head	→	极[ji](extremely)→具[ju](possess); 深[shen](deeply)→感[gan](feel); 代[dai](replace)→写[xie](write); 改[gai](instead)→用[yong](use)	Including auxiliary verb, serial verb construction
Verb-compliment	←	赶[gan](drive)←跑[pao](run); 看[kan](see)←清[qing](clear); 拿[na](grasp)←下[xia](dow); 举[ju](lift)←起[qi](up)	verb-resultative structure; verb-trending structure
Verb-obj	|	调[tiao](mix) | 酒[jiu](wine)↗师[shi](worker)	Usually use with other operators
Sbj-prd	‖	你[ni](you)‖争[zheng](fight)...我[wo](I)‖夺[duo](capture)	
Reduplication	.	看·看[kan kan](have a look); 研究·研究[yanjiu yanjiu](try a research); 看·一·看[kan yi kan](have a look); 看·了·看[kan le kan](have a look); 看·不·看[kan bu kan](to look or not); 看·没·看[kan mei kan](see or not)	except AABB and ABB forms of adj.
Other	-	桌[zhuo](desk)-上[shang](upside); 一[yi](one)-只[zhi]; 一[yi](one)-大[da](big)-碗[wan]; 看[kan](look/see)-了[le]; 看[kan](look)-着[zhe]; 看[kan](look)-过[guo]; 同学[tongxue](classmate)-们[men](-s); 学习[xuexi](learn)-者[zhe](-er); 拿[na](pick)-得[de]-起[qi](up); 华山[Huashan](Hua Mountain)-之[zhi](of)-巅[dian](summit); 付[fu](put)-诸[zhu](into)-实践[shijian](practice); 翩然[pianran](lightly)-而[er]-至[zhi](come)	locative structure; quantitative structure; affix/auxiliary word structure; other fixed format

2.1 The POS Information for Non-word Morphemes

The internal components of dynamic words often contain non-word morphemes, while in the Modern Chinese Dictionary only the morphemes which are words are annotated POS information [11]. According to the functions of non-word morphemes when they are combined into words, the non-word morphemes are divided into noun morphemes, verb morphemes, adjective morphemes, adverbial morphemes and other categories, which could help to explain the functional relationship between a morpheme and the word formed by the morpheme and the relationship between internal components of a word [12]. According to morpheme senses in the Modern Chinese Dictionary and word formation functions of morphemes we added POS information for non-word morphemes which follows lexical category names. It should be noted that affixational morphemes, such as "-儿、-子、老-、阿- (-er, -zi, lao-, a-)", are unified into auxiliary morpheme. In order to facilitate the text below, the following are no longer strictly distinguish between POS and POS of morpheme.

2.2   Symbols of Structural Relationship

Using the approach similar to syntactic combination to produce words is the most common way. The internal structural relationship of dynamic words is also from the syntactic relationship, in addition, including locative structures, quantitative structures, auxiliary structures and reduplicated structures, etc.

The symbols of dynamic word structural relationship are shown in Table 1. Locative structure, quantitative structure and auxiliary structure are all represented by the "-" symbol, because they could be distinguished each other by the POS information of their internal components.

2.3   Structural Mode Expression

The formalization of dynamic word structural mode is as follows:

- <dynamic word structural mode> ::= <the whole POS of dynamic words>: <internal component information>[<structural relationship symbol><internal component information>]+
- <internal component information> ::= <the POS of the internal component><the syllable number of the internal component> | <the internal component>
- <the whole POS of dynamic words> ::= n | t | f | m | q | r | v | a | d | p | c | u | e | o
  (The meaning of the letters can refer to the literature [5].)
- <the POS of the internal component> ::= n | t | f | m | q | r | v | a | d | p | c | u | e | o
- <the syllable number of the internal component> ::= <NULL> | 2 | 3 | 4 | 5
  (The syllable number is the default value 1 when it is NULL.)

Examples of dynamic word structural mode are shown in Table 2.

The structural mode of "爱国心[aiguo xin](patriotism)" is "n: v2↗n". Its internal component information takes the form of "<the POS of the internal component><the syllable number of the internal component>". In "n: v2↗n", the "n" before the colon indicates the whole POS is noun; the "v2" indicates the POS of "爱国[aiguo]" is a verb and its syllable number is 2; the final "n" represents "心[xin]" is a noun and its syllable number is 1; the "↗" represents attribute-head relationship.

The structural modes of "城市化[chengshi hua](urbanize)", "听了听[ting le ting](listen)" and "翩然而至[pianran er zhi](come lightly)" contain the internal component information which is fixed internal components "化[hua]", "了[le]" and "而[er]". The internal components can be uniquely identified or one of the several types identified. The structural modes with the fixed component are discovered in the process of building the dynamic word structural mode knowledge base. Detailed content will be discussed in step 3 of Part 3.

Table 2. Dynamic Word Structural Mode

Dynamic Word	Structural Mode	Dynamic Word	Structural Mode
木桥[mu qiao] (wooden bridge)	n: n↗n	看清[kan qing] (see clearly)	v: v←a
爱国心[aiguo xin] (patriotism)	n: v2↗n	城市化[chengshi hua] (urbanize)	v: n2-化
小白兔[xiao bai tu] (little white rabbit)	n: a↗a↗n	听了听[ting le ting] (listen)	v: v·了·v
铁路工人[tielu gongren] (locoman)	n: n2↗n2	翩然而至[pianran er zhi] (come lightly)	v: a2-而-v

Diagrammatic style and XML structure of dynamic words with structural mode are shown in Fig. 2. "n: v001↗n002" is located under the diagrammatic style of "爱国心 [aiguo xin](patriotism)", in which "001" and "002" are sense codes of "爱国[aiguo]" and "心[xin]" respectively. Syllable numbers of the internal components are not displayed in the diagrammatic style, which could be get by the diagrammatic tagging tool automatically. The "n" in the outermost layer of XML structure represents the whole POS of the dynamic word. The "mod" attribute takes the form of "<the POS of the internal component><the syllable number of the internal component>[<structural relationship symbol><the POS of the internal component><the syllable number of the internal component>]+". The "sen" is sense code attribute of the internal component. For a structural mode with a fixed component, the "mod" attribute of the XML structure is also a sequence including POS of the internal components, syllable numbers of the internal components and structural relationship symbols.

Fig. 2. Diagrammatic Style and XML Structure of Dynamic Words

Some of the problems that need to be explained are:

1. Word Segmentation: When a dynamic word is analyzed in the diagrammatic tagging tool, we separate its internal components with spaces until the corresponding POS and sense of every component can be found in the Modern Chinese Dictionary. The diagrammatic tagging tool will automatically give candidate senses and corresponding POS for each internal component.

2. Syllable Problem: Because the syllable number of very few words (about 200 or so) in the Modern Chinese Dictionary is greater than 5, and these words are generally not as a component of dynamic words, so the syllable number of the internal component is limited to 5.

3. Hierarchy Problem: In theory, dynamic words with more than two internal components have the problem of combination sequence, namely hierarchy problem. But the hierarchy ambiguity is little when the POS, syllable number and structural relationship of dynamic words are certain. Therefore we don't take hierarchy relationship into account.

3   The Process of Building Knowledge Base

The dynamic word structural mode knowledge base is created simultaneously when building the international Chinese teaching materials Treebank. In order to ensure the quality of corpus annotation, postgraduate students of linguistics participate in manual annotating and the annotating results would been given professional staffs proofreading strictly. The work of annotating and the dynamic word structural mode knowledge base are constantly improved and perfected in the process of mutual assistance. The specific process of building the knowledge base is as follows:

Step 1: Initialize the dynamic word structural mode knowledge base. First of all, the basic framework of the knowledge base is designed, and the meaning of each field is shown in Table 3. The contents of the knowledge base are added gradually in the process of building the international Chinese teaching materials Treebank.

The initial knowledge base contains a variety of typical dynamic word structural modes which were obtained from the actual situation of using words in the international Chinese teaching, the practical experience of the Treebank's early construction and the research results of the dynamic words in the field of linguistics. In the initial knowledge base, seven fields of each structural mode are decided which are "id", "mode", "example", "POS", "syllable", "xml_mod" and "sequence".

Table 3. The Structure of the Knowledge Base

Fields	Illustration
id	the id of the dynamic word structural mode
mode	the structural mode of dynamic words
example	examples of the dynamic word structural mode
POS	the whole POS of the dynamic word
syllable	the syllable number of the dynamic word
xml_mod	the "mod" attribute in XML structure of dynamic words
sequence	character sequence about the POS and syllable numbers of internal components
rule	regular expression rules rule for dynamic words
freq	the frequency of corresponding mode in the Treebank

Step 2: The initial knowledge base assists manual annotating. Apart from tagging POS and senses for the internal components, annotators need to tag the whole POS and the internal structural relationship of dynamic words. In order to enable annotators better to identify dynamic words, improve the efficiency of annotating and ensure the standardization and consistency of the Treebank data, the lexical analysis of dynamic words is done by the aid of computer automatic prompts.

The initial knowledge base was integrated into the diagrammatic tagging tool. When annotators complete word segmentation and POS tagging of the internal components for a dynamic word, the tool will automatically get POS and syllable numbers of all internal components of this dynamic word. The information would be compared with all records in the initial knowledge base, if there are records which can be matched, then the corresponding dynamic word structural modes are suggested. As shown in Fig. 3, the tool will automatically complete the annotating of the whole POS and internal structure relationship just when annotators choose a right mode.

Fig. 3. Prompts of Dynamic Word Structural Modes

Step 3: Update the dynamic word structural mode knowledge base. More dynamic word structural modes are extracted through statistically analyzing periodic annotating data (XML file). After a discussion and examination for the new discovered structural mode with relatively high frequency, if it is defined as a new dynamic word structural mode, its internal components need for further analysis. If one of the internal components is unique or one of the several types identified, the internal component information will be described as follows: <internal component information> ::= <internal component>. If there isn't the internal component which is fixed, the internal component information will be described as follows: <internal component information> ::= <the POS of the internal component><the syllable number of the internal component>. In the end, we update these new dynamic word structural modes to the knowledge base.

For instance, for the reduplicated structure "V了V" contains a fixed internal component "了", its structural mode is "v: v·了·v". For the modes of double syllable nouns plus affix, the affix usually is: "-们", "-儿" or "-性", thus the structural modes are defined as "n: n2-们", "n: n2-儿" and "n: n2-性".

Step 4: Add regular expression restriction rules for some dynamic word structural modes. With the increase of the number of dynamic word structural modes, there will be too many prompts just according to the POS and syllable numbers of internal components. For example, "爱国者[aiguo zhe](patriot)", its structural mode is "n: v2-者" and its character sequence about the POS and syllable numbers of internal components is "v2u". Since character sequence of the structural modes "n: v2-性" and "n: v2-率" is also "v2u", it will produce three prompt modes. It is obvious that the latter two don't meet the condition.

To alleviate this problem, the regex restriction rules are added to the records of the dynamic word structural modes with distinct features or fixed components, which are used to limit the number of prompt modes. For instance, the last component of the mode "n: v2-者" is "者", thus we add regular expression "..者" for it. The diagrammatic tagging tool not only compares character sequence about the POS and syllable numbers of internal components, but also matches the regular rule. If the match fails, all corresponding dynamic word structural modes would be returned, otherwise, only the correct mode corresponding to the regular rule would be returned.

Step 2 to step 4 will be repeated and constantly optimized.

Step 5: Create the final dynamic word structural mode knowledge base. From the international Chinese teaching materials Treebank, the frequency of each structural mode could be obtained, which will be integrated into the "freq" field of the final knowledge base.

Following the steps above, 8 sets of international Chinese textbooks have been annotated with the scale of 29465 sentences (498965 words). The knowledge base with 836 kinds of dynamic word structural modes for international Chinese teaching is finally established.

4   Overview of the Knowledge Base

The 836 kinds of dynamic word structural modes cover all POS. The dynamic word structural modes the whole POS of which are noun and verb have the largest number, accounting for 38.88% and 25.36% of the total number of modes respectively. According to the number of syllable, dynamic word structural modes could be divided into double-syllable, three-syllable, four-syllable and more than four syllables, their numbers are 166 (19.86%), 246 (29.43%), 288 (34.45%) and 136 (16.27%). In addition, dynamic word structural modes with regular expression rules reach 143, accounting for 17.11% of the total number.

Limited to space, 6 kinds of structural modes which have the highest frequency in the three-syllable nouns of the knowledge base are displayed, as shown in Table 4. Through the "freq" field, the frequent structural modes in the international Chinese teaching materials could be known.

Table 4. The Dynamic Word Structural Mode Knowledge Base

id	mode	example	POS	syllable	xml_mod	sequence	rule	freq
1	n: n2↗n	棒球场[bangqiu chang](baseball field)	n	3	n2↗n	n2n		1786
2	n: a↗n2	矮个子[ai gezi](shorty) 白瓜子[bai guazi](white melon seeds)	n	3	a↗n2	an2		813
3	n: v2↗n	爱国心[aiguo xin](patriotism)	n	3	v2↗n	v2n		506
4	n: n↗n2	癌细胞[ai xibao](cancer cells) 丁先生[ding xiansheng](Mr.Ding)	n	3	n↗n2	nn2		488
5	n: n2-们	同学们[tongxue men](students)	n	3	n2-u	n2u	..们	254
6	n: a2↗n	好奇心[haoqi xin](curiosity) 烦心事[fanxin shi](troubles)	n	3	a2↗n	a2n		184

On the basis of the existing international Chinese teaching materials Treebank and dynamic word structural mode knowledge base, this paper extracted specific dynamic words corresponding to each structural mode. Due to various types and large amount of modes, only part of them are listed below:

1. affix word structure

- "n: v2-者":
  消费者[xiaofei zhe](customer);
  来访者[laifang zhe](visitor);
  旅游者[lvyou zhe](traveler).
- "n: a2-性":
  合理性[heli xing](rationality);
  可能性[keneng xing](possibility);
  重要性[zhongyao xing](significance).
- "v: a2-化":
  多样化[duoyang hua](diversify);
  合法化[hefa hua](legitimize);
  绝对化[juedui hua](absolutize).

2. verb-resultative or verb-trending structure

- "v: v←a":
  长大[zhang da](grow up);
  做好[zuo hao](complete);
  吃饱[chi bao](glut).
- "v: v←v":
  带来[dai lai](bring);
  走进[zou jin](walk into);
  关上[guan shang](turn off).

3. quantifiers

- "m: 一-q • q":
  一天天[yi tian tian](day by day);
  一个个[yi ge ge](one by one);
  一点点[yi dian dian](a little bit).
- "m: m-a-q":
  一小块[yi xiao kuai](a patch of);
  一大堆[yi da dui](a heap of);
  一小撮[yi xiao cuo](a handful).

These dynamic words are in line with actual needs of the international Chinese teaching. Because of the large number of Chinese words, it is very difficult for the second language learners to master. Only by using some Chinese word-formation rules can they produce standardized and customary Chinese expression, which makes learning easier. In addition, the dynamic word, which is larger than a word unit, is helpful for learners to quickly search and extract linguistic units, thus the difficulty of language learning would be reduced.

5   Conclusion

The different definition about "word" in international Chinese teaching and Chinese information processing leads to many achievements in the field of Chinese information processing cannot directly serve international Chinese teaching. Through the study of frequent dynamic words in international Chinese teaching, this paper constructs the dynamic word structural mode knowledge base for international Chinese teaching. At the lexical level, it provides a way of thinking and method for the communication of international Chinese teaching and Chinese information processing. This paper makes preparation for automatic lexical and syntactic analysis in the field of international Chinese teaching.

Acknowledgement. Supported by: Beijing Normal University Young Teachers Fund Project (No: 2014NT39); Natural Science Foundation of the AnHui Higher Education Institutions of China (No: KJ2016B002).

References

1. Jinxi, L.: The New Chinese Grammar. Commercial Press, Beijing (2001)
2. He, J., Peng, W., Song, J., Liu, H.: Annotation schema for contemporary chinese based on JinXi Li's grammar system. In: Liu, P., Su, Q. (eds.) CLSW 2013. LNAI, vol. 8229, pp. 668–681. Springer, Heidelberg (2013)
3. Min, Z., Weiming, P., Jihua, S.: Development and Optimization of Syntax Tagging Tool on Diagrammatic Treebank. Journal of Chinese Information Processing 06, 26–33 (2014)
4. Tianxin, Y., Weiming, P., Jihua, S.: High Efficiency Syntax Tagging System Based on the Sentence Pattern Structure. Journal of Chinese Information Processing 04, 43–49 (2014)
5. Peng, W., Song, J., Sui, Z., Guo, D.: Formal Schema of Diagrammatic Chinese Syntactic Analysis. In: Lu, Q., Gao, H.H. (eds.) CLSW 2015. LNAI, vol. 9332, pp. 701-710. Springer, Heidelberg (2015)
6. Weiming, P., Jihua, S., Shiwen, Y.: Lexical Issues in Chinese Information Processing: in the Background of Sentence-based Diagram Treebank Construction. Journal of Chinese Information Processing 28(02), 1–7 (2014)
7. Zhendong, D., Qiang, D.: Introduction to HowNet - Chinese Message Structure Base, http://www.keenage.com/zhiwang/aboutMessage.html
8. Xiufang, D.: Chinese Lexicon and Morphology. Peking University Press, Beijing (2004)
9. Xingquan, T.: The Study of Dynamic Words in Chinese Understanding Processing. Science Press, Beijing (2012)
10. Jinxia, L.: The Theory and Practice of Distinguish between Words and Phrases. China Social Sciences Press, Beijing (2013)
11. The Dictionary Editing Room in the Linguistics Institute of Chinese Academy of Social Sciences. Modern Chinese Dictionary. Commercial Press, Beijing (2012)
12. Bin, Z.: The modern Chinese grammar. Commercial Press, Beijing (2010)

EVALution-MAN 2.0: Expand the Evaluation Dataset for Vector Space Models

Hongchao Liu, Chu-Ren Huang

The Hong Kong Polytechnic University, Hung Hum, Hong Kong
E-mail: jiye12yuran@126.com; karlneergaard@gmail.com;
churen.huang@polyu.edu.hk

Abstract. We introduce EVALution 2.0, a simplified Mandarin dataset for the evaluation of Vector Space Models. We take a psycholinguistics-based methodology through the use of a verbal association task, which differs from previous datasets that use corpus and ontology to construct word relation pairs. Semantic neighbors were created for 100 target words and surprisingly, to which participants produced 1129 word relation pairs. In a separate agreement-rating task, only 62 pairs showed were rejected. The methodology has proven to be a way to expand the existing resources quickly while maintaining a high level of quality.

1   Introduction

Vector Space Model (VSM) has been used for the measurement of document similarity since Salton (1971). A VSM measure the similarity between items ranging from word to document by constructing a vector matrix. Usually we use w_i to refer to the *i-th* words, d_j to refer to the *j-th* documents, and f_{ij} to refer to frequency of the word i in document j.

Table 1. Word-document matrix

	d_1	d_2	...	d_j	...	d_m
w_1	f_{11}	f_{12}	...	f_{1j}	...	f_{1m}
w_2	f_{21}	f_{22}	...	f_{2j}	...	f_{2m}
...	...	...	...	...	...	...
w_i	f_{31}	f_{i2}	...	f_{ij}	...	f_{im}
...	...	...	...		...	
w_n	F_{n1}	f_{n2}	...	F_{nj}	...	f_{nm}

© Springer International Publishing AG 2016
M. Dong et al. (Eds.): CLSW 2016, LNAI 10085, pp. 261–268, 2016
DOI: 10.1007/978-3-319-49508-8_25

Based on several hypotheses, the matrix can be used to measure the similarity between words, documents, patterns and pairs respectively. Hypothesizes include distributional hypothesis and latent relation hypothesis (Turney & Pantel, 2010). Deerwester, Dumais, Furnas, Landauer, and Harshman (1990) and Landauer and Dumais (1997) are applications of the distributional hypothesis while Lin and Pantel (2001) and Turney (2006) are applications of the latent relation hypothesis. Both the hypotheses and applications will be introduced.

(1) The distributional hypothesis: if two words tend to appear within similar context, they tend to express similar meaning (Harris, 1954). Thus, if we replace the columns with contexts instead of documents, vectors in rows actually represent words' distribution in different context. Thus, the rows of vectors can be used to measure the similarity between words based on this hypothesis.

Deerwester et al. (1990) uses the word-context (the window size is 151 words) to measure the similarity between words based on *cosine* which is widely accepted for the measurement of vectors similarity (Turney & Pantel, 2010):

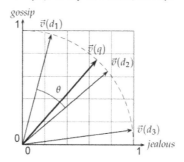

Cosine similarity illustrated. $\text{sim}(d_1, d_2) = \cos\theta$.

Fig. 1. Cosine between vectors

It is much reasonable to measure the similarity between vectors by using *cosine* instead of others such as length or direction along. *Cosine* tend to ignore the difference of vector length. Length of the vectors represent how many different context the word appear. However, the similarity depends on whether two words appear in the same contexts.

Although Deerwester et al. (1990) applied the measurement of word similarity, they didn't give evaluation. Thus Landauer and Dumais (1997) introduces TOEFL test to evaluate Deerwester et al. (1990)'s model.

The TOEFL test contains 80 multiple-choice synonym question. Such as for the synonym of *levied*, there are four candidates: *imposed, believed, requested* and *correlated* while *imposed* is the correct answer. The model is required to "answer" these questions by giving the most similar word to the target word. Since then, different evaluation dataset such as *BLESS* (Baroni & Lenci, 2011) and *EVALution 1.0* (Santus, Yung, Lenci, & Huang, 2015) etc. have been constructed to evaluate the performance of VSMs on measuring the similarity between words. For Chinese, *Cilin* (Mei, Zhu, Gao, & Yin, 1983) is also regarded as an evaluation dataset for VSMs.

(2) Latent relation hypothesis: word pairs that occurs in similar patterns tend to express similar semantic relation. In other words, in a pair-pattern matrix, if a row of vectors is similar to another, words in word pairs tend to hold similar semantic relation.

While (1) and word-context matrix is used for the measurement of word similarity, (2) and pair-pattern matrix is used for the measurement of relational similarity. The pair-pattern matrix is firstly introduced by Lin and Pantel (2001).

If we replace the words in rows of table 1 with word pair like "*cat: animal*" and "*penguin: bird*" and replace the column of table 1 with pattern like "X is a kind of Y" or "X belongs to Y" etc. Then a pair-pattern matrix will be constructed.

The measurement of relational similarity is very similar to the measurement of words. Both are based on *cosine*.

Turney (2006) evaluate the VSM that measure the similarity between word pairs introduced by Turney and Littman (2003) . The evaluation dataset contains 374 analogy questions. Taking *mason: stone*, which serves as the stem of the question, as an example. Several choices are offered:

(3) a. *teacher: chalk*

b. *carpenter: wood*

c. *soldier: gun*

d. *photograph: camera*

e. *book: word*

As shown above, both "*mason:tone*" and "*capenter:wood*" hold worker-working material relation between the words in pairs. Thus, the answer is (3b).

Thus, models of the measurement of both word similarity and relation similarity need evaluation dataset.

However, most of the evaluation datasets are single-purpose. They are usually designed one certain relation similarity measurement[1]. It is a reasonable way to use different datasets to evaluate one model or models applied within one study (Baroni, Dinu, & Kruszewski, 2014) but different datasets usually means different criteria and quality which can be blocks for evaluating VSMs effectively and completely. New evaluation datasets are necessary for VSM. The dataset should contains more relations between target words (hence relata) and be with high quality.

2   Related Work and Motivation

In this section, related work on datasets with different relations between word pairs are introduced. Some classical datasets for the measurement of word similarity such as *TOEFL* (Landauer & Dumais, 1997) and the measurement of relational similarity such as Turney (2006) have been reviewed in the first section.

---

[1] Actually, word similarity also belongs to relational similarity since similar words hold synonymy with each other. From this point of view, VSMs are used for the measurement of relational similarity.

We will only focus on datasets which are similar to ours and studies related to our work including *BLESS* (Baroni & Lenci, 2011), *EVALution 1.0* (Santus et al., 2015) and *EVALution-MAN* (Hongchao Liu, Karl, Enrico, & Huang, 2016).

BLESS is specially designed for the evaluation of VSMs[2]. It contains 26554 relata distributed in the relation of coordinate (such as *cat* and *dog* are coordinate knots of the hypernym *animal*), hypernym, meronym, attributes, events etc. The raw relata are selected from ontology like WordNet (Fellbaum, 1998) and text resources like Wikipedia.

EVALution 1.0 is a dataset with more than 7000 word pairs holding relations of synonym, antonym, meronym and hypernym relation with each other. They also add frequency, PoS and semantic information for the word pairs. The information is useful when weighting the vectors in the matrices. The pairs are selected from *Concept 5.0* (Hugo Liu & Singh, 2004) and *WordNet*.

EVALution-MAN is a specially designed Chinese evaluation dataset (in traditional Chinese) for VSM. It is featured with 376 relata distributed in the relation of synonym, antonym, hypernym, meronym and variant (homomorphy relation) based on *EVALution 1.0*. The raw word relation pairs are selected from Chinese WordNet (Huang et al., 2010) and word relation pairs are all judged as acceptable by human in a reliability test. While BLESS and EVALution 1.0 are English evaluation dataset, EVALution-MAN, though in Chinese, has other problems:

(1) It is in traditional Chinese. The raw word relation pairs are selected from Chinese WordNet which is constructed for the language used in Taiwan. There are language variation between Taiwan and Mainland, China. Thus, simplified Chinese word relation pairs should be added.

(2) The dataset is small in size. It is expected to expand the dataset in an effective way. There is no similar language resources like WordNet or Chinese WordNet in simplified Chinese except HowNet (Dong & Dong, 1999) for us to collect raw word relation pairs. However, the semantic relation is holding between features instead of words which make it impossible for us to extract the word relation pairs directly from HowNet. Thus we turn to human elicitation task to collect raw word relation pairs.

3   Construction of the Dataset

There are three steps for constructing the dataset including relata collection, reliability test and semantic information tagging.

3.1   Relata Collection

Relata refers to the words that hold different relations with the target word. We randomly select 100 target words. For the target words, we mainly focus on the relata that

---

[2]   Baroni and Lenci (2011) call it distributional semantic model (DSM) to stress the distributional hypothesis which is the basic hypothesis behind the vector space model. However, according to Turney and Pantel (2010), there are different hypothesis used for the constructing of vector space model (VSM) while distributional hypothesis is only one of them which have been discussed in the first section. We intend to use the general name i.e. VSM.

hold the relation of synonym, antonym, hypernym and meronym. For example, for the target word of 锚 (*mao*, anchor), we design the questionnaire in the following format:

Table 2. Relata Collection Questionnaire (sample)

Target	Relation Statement	Relatum
锚 (*mao*, anchor)	is similar with	
锚 (*mao*, anchor)	has the opposite meaning of	
锚 (*mao*, anchor)	__ is a kind o f 锚 (*mao*, anchor)	
锚 (*mao*, anchor)	is a kind of__	
锚 (*mao*, anchor)	is a part of__	
锚 (*mao*, anchor)	__ is a part of 锚 (*mao*, anchor)	

Each row forms a word relation pair. For table 2, the rows actually represent the relation of synonym, antonym, hyponym, hypernym, meronym and holonym.

Three linguistics Ph.D. students filled in the relatum column. Then all of the word relation pairs will be extracted and finally, 1129 pairs were collected. Repeated pairs are counted according to their appearing times.

Table 3. Word Relation Pairs (sample)

X	Relation	Y	Relation Statement	Count
直径 (*zhijing*, diameter)	holo	圆 (*yuan*, circle)	*Zhijing* is a part of *yuan*	1
云 (*yun*, cloud)	syno	云朵 (*yunduo*, cloud)	*Yun* is similar with *yunduo*	1
白云 (*baiyun*, white cloud)	hyper	云 (*yun*, cloud)	*Baiyun* is a kind of *yun*	2
乌云 (*wuyun*, dark cloud)	hyper	云 (*yun*, cloud)	*Wuyun* is kind of *yun*	3

Note: X and Y are relata in a word relation pairs; Count refers to the repeated times.

3.2   Reliability Test

A questionnaire was designed for the reliability check. In the questionnaire, word relation pairs are placed in a sentence like "*cat* is kind of *animal*" following by choices of *totally agree, agree, don't know, don't agree, totally don't agree, don't know X* and *don't know Y* from left to right respectively.

Another five subjects (different from the participants in relata collection task) are involved into the reliability check of the collected word relation pairs.

The subjects are asked to vote among *totally agree, agree, don't know, don't agree,* and *totally don't agree* according to the relation statement for the word relation pairs. In case of unfarmilar with the words, we suplly extra choice of *don't know X* and *don't know Y*.

All of the word relation pairs and the participants' votes will be extracted into one rough dataset.

Finally, word relation pairs are classified into different dataset according to the votes result.

We set the classification standard as the following: If three or more subjects chose *totally agree* or *agree*, the word relation pair will be collected into positive dataset. The other word relation pairs which don't reach this requirement will be collected into negative dataset.

Table 4. Result of Reliability Test

X	Y	Relation Statement	Result								
毒箭	箭	*Dujian* is a kind of *jian*	3	1	0	1	0	0	0	0	0
(*dujian,* position arrow)	(*jian,* arrow)										
弓箭	箭	*Gongjian* is a kind of *jian*	3	1	0	0	1	0	0	0	0
(*gongjian,* bow and arrow)	(*jian,* arrow)										
摔箭	箭	*Shuaijian* is kind of *jian*	2	1	1	0	0	1	0	0	0
(*shuaijian,* hand- throw arrow)	(*jian,* arrow)										
铁箭	箭	*Tiejian* is a kind of *jian*	4	1	0	0	0	0	0	0	0
(*tiejian,* iron arrow)	(*jian,* arrow)										

Note: Column Result include *totally agree, agree, don't know, don't agree, totally don't agree, don't know X* and *don't know Y* from left to right respectively.

After applying the classification standard to the rough dataset, 1067 word relation pairs are judged as positive and only 62 word relation pairs are judged as negative which make the reliability rate 94.5%. The reliability rate of the raw word relation pairs extracted from Chinese WordNet is only 73.2% in *EVLution-MAN*.

Table 5. Distrubution of Word Relation Pairs

Relation	Postive_Dataset	Negative_Dataset	Total
Synonymy	98	23	121
Antonymy	19	19	38
Hyponymy	620	8	628
Meronymy	330	12	342
合计	1067	62	1129

3.3   Semantic Information Tagging

One of the tasks of VSMs is the clustering task which aims to classify words into their semantic type (Baroni & Lenci, 2011). If semantic type information is annotated for the relata, the dataset can also be used for evaluating the performance of VSMs in clustering task.

The semantic tags of *EVALution 1.0* are accepted in our dataset. We add Action and Attribute tags as too many words cannot be classified according to *EVALution 1.0*.

(1) Basic/Subordinate/Superordinate: for example, *vehicle* can be tagged as *Superordinate*, *automobile* can be tagged as *Basic* and *Volkswagen* can be tagged as *Subordinate*;

(2) General/Specific: for example, *position* can be tagged as *General* and *President Obama* can be tagged as *Specific*;

(3) Abstract/Concrete: for example, *creation* can be tagged as *Abstract* and *oil painting* can be tagged as *Concrete*;

(4) Event/Action/Time/Space/Object/Animal/Plant/Food/Color/People/Attribute: for example, *gate* can be tagged as *Space* and *bear* can be tagged as *Animal*.

In addition, we added frequency information for all of the relata. The frequency information is calculated in a combined corpus of sinica (Chen, Huang, Chang, & Hsu, 1996) and Chinese Gigaword (Hong & Huang, 2006).

4   Conclusion

In this paper we presented the construction of EVALution-MAN 2.0 which serve as an evaluation dataset for vector space models.

The construction includes three steps: relata collection, reliability test and semantic information tagging.

A human elicitation task was designed for the relata collection which is different from method taken in previous studies. *BLESS*, *EVLution 1.0* and *EVLution-MAN* use language resources such as *WordNet* and Wikipedia to collect word relation pairs.

1129 word relation pairs were collected and 1029 word relaiton pairs were judged as positive.

Our results showed that the human elicited semantic neighbors were 94.5% reliable when tested in a human judgment task. This was much higher than that of the words extracted from Chinese WordNet (73.2% reliability). The rate shows that it is an effective way to collect word relation pairs which can be used for the construction of evaluation dataset for vector space models.

References:

1. Baroni, M., Dinu, G., & Kruszewski, G. (2014). Don't count, predict! A systematic comparison of context-counting vs. context-predicting semantic vectors. Paper presented at the ACL (1).

2. Baroni, M., & Lenci, A. (2011). How we BLESSed distributional semantic evaluation. Paper presented at the Proceedings of the GEMS 2011 Workshop on GEometrical Models of Natural Language Semantics.

3. Chen, K.-J., Huang, C.-R., Chang, L.-P., & Hsu, H.-L. (1996). Sinica corpus: Design methodology for balanced corpora. Language, 167, 176.

4. Deerwester, S., Dumais, S. T., Furnas, G. W., Landauer, T. K., & Harshman, R. (1990). Indexing by latent semantic analysis. Journal of the American society for information science, 41(6), 391.

5. Dong, Z., & Dong, Q. (1999). HowNet. http://www.keenage.com

6. Fellbaum, C. (1998). WordNet: Wiley Online Library.

7. Harris, Z. S. (1954). Distributional structure. Word, 10(2-3), 146--162.

8. Hong, J.-F., & Huang, C.-R. (2006). Using chinese gigaword corpus and chinese word sketch in linguistic research. Paper presented at the The 20th Pacific Asia Conference on Language, Information and Computation (PACLIC-20). November.

9. Huang, J., Hsieh, S.-K., Hong, J.-F., Chen, Y.-Z., Su, I.-L., Chen, Y.-X., & Huang, S.-W. (2010). Chinese Wordnet: Design, implementation, and application of an infrastructure for cross-lingual knowledge processing. Journal of Chinese Information Processing, 24(2), 14--23.

10. Landauer, T. K., & Dumais, S. T. (1997). A solution to Plato's problem: The latent semantic analysis theory of acquisition, induction, and representation of knowledge. Psychological review, 104(2), 211.

11. Lin, D., & Pantel, P. (2001). DIRT@ SBT@ discovery of inference rules from text. Paper presented at the Proceedings of the seventh ACM SIGKDD international conference on Knowledge discovery and data mining.

12. Liu, H., Karl, N., Enrico, S., & Huang, C.-R. (2016). EVALution-MAN: A Chinese Dataset for the Training and Evaluation of DSMs. Paper presented at the Proceedings of the Tenth International Conference on Language Resources and Evaluation (LREC 2016), Paris, France.

13. Liu, H., & Singh, P. (2004). ConceptNet—a practical commonsense reasoning tool-kit. BT technology journal, 22(4), 211-226.

14. Mei, J., Zhu, Y., Gao, Y., & Yin, H. (1983). Cilin-Chinese thesaurus: Shanghai Lexicographical Publishing House.

15. Salton, G. (1971). The SMART retrieval system—experiments in automatic document processing.

16. Santus, E., Yung, F., Lenci, A., & Huang, C.-R. (2015). EVALution 1.0: an Evolving Semantic Dataset for Training and Evaluation of Distributional Semantic Models. ACL-IJCNLP 2015, 64.

17. Turney, P. D. (2006). Similarity of semantic relations. Computational Linguistics, 32(3), 379-416.

18. Turney, P. D., & Littman, M. L. (2003). Measuring praise and criticism: Inference of semantic orientation from association. ACM Transactions on Information Systems (TOIS), 21(4), 315-346.

19. Turney, P. D., & Pantel, P. (2010). From frequency to meaning: Vector space models of semantics. Journal of artificial intelligence research, 37(1), 141-188.

Constructing the Verb Sub-library in the Electronic Dictionary of *NIGEN DABHVR ASAR*

Dabhurbayar, Xiaojuan

School of Mongolian Studies, Inner Mongolia University
Daxue West Street, No.235, Hohhot, P.R.China
dabhvrbayar@163.com; 297772760@qq.com

Abstract

The Mongolian Classic literature *NIGEN DABHVR ASAR* is one of the main representative works by famous Mongolian writer *Yinzhannashi*. The Electronic Dictionary of *NIGEN DABHVR ASAR* is greatly useful to Mongolian researchers and learners. In this paper, 33634 verbs in the text of *NIGEN DABHVR ASAR* were analyzed and processed from the perspective of the Mongolian information processing and the compilation methods and the content of the Electronic Dictionary of *NIGEN DABHVR ASAR* are mainly introduced. It described the verb entries selection, phonetic notation, part of speech information, syllable structure, interpretation, frequency rank, Morphological changes and examples. Then, it covered the significance of constructing the verb section in the Electronic Dictionary of *NIGEN DABHVR ASAR* and a brief talk about the subsequent tasks related to the dictionary construction.

1 Introduction

The compilation of the electronic dictionary is one of the most fundamental functions of corpus. The compilation work of Mongolian electronic dictionary for information processing started to pick up some speed since 1990s. Representative research results include *Mongolian Grammatical Information Dictionary* and *Modern Mongolian Fixed Phrase Grammar Information Dictionary* aimed at automatic analysis and automatic generation of Mongolian. *Mongolian Grammatical Information Dictionary* is provided with the relational database form and composed of different layers. The first layer is the general library for various kinds of attribute fields of all entries such as phonology, orthography, syntax, semantics and pragmatics. Second layer is the sub-libraries for various word classes like noun, verb and adjective etc. The structure of Modern Mongolian *Fixed Phrase Grammar Information Dictionary* and *Mongolian Grammatical Information Dictionary* are similar in

© Springer International Publishing AG 2016
M. Dong et al. (Eds.): CLSW 2016, LNAI 10085, pp. 269–279, 2016
DOI: 10.1007/978-3-319-49508-8_26

structure and provide various information about Mongolian fixed phrases in the form of relational database.

NIGEN DABHVR ASAR by *Yinzhannashi* is a masterpiece in contemporary Mongolian literature. As a Mongolian famous writer, poet, thinker and eminent writer, *Yinzhannashi* was proficient in both Chinese and Mongolian and with a sound knowledge of Mongolian contemporary society, history and culture, whose main works such as *HOHESODOR, NIGEN DABHVR ASAR, VLAGAN_A VHILAHV TINGHIM, VLAGAN UNGETEN-U NILBVSV* laid a solid foundation for the formation of contemporary Mongolian normative written language. At present, the development of each individual database for the Electronic Dictionary of *HOHESODOR* has been completed. Compilation of the Electronic Dictionary of *NIGEN DAVHVR ASAR* by corpus-based approach is a worthwhile effort. Eventually the success is practically valuable for Mongolian researchers and students. In Mongolian information processing, combination of corpus and lexicography is a significant research project. Some remarkable achievements have been obtained in this respect. Corpus-based electronic dictionary not only could accurately reflect the usage of words in a specific language environment, but also could provide direct evidences and instances to entries, which allows users to obtain more comprehensive but authentic information on grammar, semantics, and pragmatics etc.

2 Preparation work for the compilation of verb sub-library in the Electronic Dictionary of *NIGEN DABHVR ASAR*

2.1 Introduction to the original corpus of NIGEN DABHVR ASAR

Inner Mongolia University has started the construction of Contemporary Mongolian Corpus since 1984. In 2005, being funded by the Project of Education Ministry and State Language Commission Project, previous 5 million words level Contemporary Mongolian Corpus was continuously expanded and updated to 10 million words level. This expanded part of the library included works by *Yinzhannashi* and *NA.SAINCHOGT*. *NIGEN DABHVR ASAR* (1978 edition) by Inner Mongolia People's Publishing House was used for the corpus construction. In addition, according to the needs of compilation, the translated version of *NIGEN DABHVR ASAR*(1963 Edition) by *Jia Yimu* was also used and quoted.

Figure 1 original text of the corpus of *NIGEN DABHVR ASAR*

```
NOA用词片.txt - 记事本
文件(F) 编辑(E) 格式(O) 查看(V) 帮助(H)
page1
    . HEBLE/N NEYITELEGCI-YIN UGE

    << NIGEN DABHVR ASAR ( I=ceNG=LeU ) >>-I []
INJENNESI JOHIYA/BA . []INJENNESI-YIN BAG_A-YIN
NER_E []HASCILAGV ,
HITAD NER_E []B0V=heNG=$AN , C0LA []rUN=TING . 1837
0N-V TABVDVGAR SAR_A-YIN ARBAN TABVN ( TORO
GERELTU-YIN
ARBAN D0L0DVGAR 0N-V VLAGCIN TAHIY_A JIL-UN
DORBEDUGER SAR_A-YIN ARBAN JIRGVGAN )-DV
JVSVTV-YIN CIGVLGAN-V
```

2.2 Corpus tagging

Compilation of the Electronic Dictionary of *NIGEN DABHVR ASAR* has been carried out progressively mainly based on the method of establishing sub-libraries for different word classes like verb, noun and adjective etc. POS tagging is the premise of constructing all sub-libraries. Therefore, corpus POS tagging is the significant step for constructing the Electronic Dictionary of *NIGEN DABHVR ASAR*. Tagging proceeds according to the following steps:

The fixed phrases tagging was conducted first. Mongolian Lexical Analyzer was applied to conduct fixed phrases tagging. During the procedure, artificial supplement and annotation were carried out for those fixed phrases left behind under the reference of Modern Mongolian Fixed Phrase Grammar Information Dictionary. In the continuous text, tagging format of fixed phrase adopts symbol "="to link two or more words and record lexical category tag code behind slash "/". The tagging format goes: fixed phrase/ fixed phrase tag codes. For example: BOTOGEN = BAYIGVLHV / Yv（which means "to build" in Mongolian）, Yv means verbal compound words。

Then, lexical tagging is followed. In 2010, Mglex, a lexical tagging system based on statistics, was developed under the collaboration of Inner Mongolia University and Chinese Academy of Sciences. We conducted lexical tagging to the text corpus of *NIGEN DABHVR ASAR* by applying Mglex which could segment words and add corresponding lexical tagging. Tagging formats are as follows :(1) Stem forms: stem / POS tag code. For example: YABV/Ve2 (it means "togo"in Mongolian). (2) The link writing of stems and configuration additional component: "stem / POS tag code +Constitutive additional component / configuration tag code." For example: BICI/Ve1+JU/Fn1 (it means "to write" in Mongolian.)(3) The separate writing of stems and configuration additional component: "stem / POS tag code - Constitutive additional component / configuration tag code." For example: CAG/Ne1-VN/Fc11 (it means "hand's" in Mongolian.)

According to the relevant papers, the accuracy rate of Mglex system is up to 97.7%, while there are still some errors in tagging. For correcting these mistakes, we referred to Mongolian-Chinese Dictionary (revised edition,1999) and Contemporary Mongolian Language (Mongolian Institute of Inner Mongolia University,1964) to conduct manual correction and modification.

Figure 2 sample of tagged corpus

```
e10 {{{{AJV=AHVI/Yn-YIN/Fc11 AJILLAG_A/Ne2+N/Zx-
DAHI/Fh3}NP2d {JARIM/Ri {T0B0I/Ve2+GSAN/Ft11
{{JORICEL/Ne2 BA/Cj}NP2s ASAGVDAL/Ne1}NP3h}
NP4d}NP5d}NP7d {NELIYED/Dx NAMDA/Ve2+BA/Fs14}
VP2b}VP9u ./Wp1}S10
e10 {{{{ANGHADVGAR/Mu VDAG_A/Qn-YIN/Fc11}QP2d
{{0RCIL/Ne2 AJV=AHVI/Yn-YIN/Fc11}NP2d
{{TVRSILTA/Ne1-YIN/Fc11 CEG/Ne2-UN/Fc11}NP2d
AJIL/Ne2-I/Fc31}NP3d}NP5d}NP7d
{J0HIYAN=BAYIGVLVN/Yv
HEREGJI/Ve2+GUL/Fe11+BE/Fs14}VP2h}VP9t ./Wp1}S10
e10 {{{{ARAD-VN/Fc11=AMIDVRAL/NT-I/Fc31
```

2.3 Extraction of verbs

All verbs were extracted from the lexical tagging corpus of *NIGEN DABHVR ASAR* by making use of Excel spreadsheet and text editor. The extraction methods are as follows :(1) Lexical tagging corpus of NIGEN DABHVR ASAR was imported into three different fields of Excel spreadsheet. Previous part of slash "/", namely stem and configuration additional components, was stored in the first field. In the second field, lexical category information after slash"/" of corresponding stem, namely lexical category tag code, was stored. In the third field, lexical category information after slash"/" of corresponding configuration additional components, namely lexical category tag code, was stored.(2) By using Excel sorting capabilities, to sort the second field which has been stored POS tagging code according to the order of Latin alphabet. At the same time, verbs with related information are extracted and saved in the Excel.

3   Framework of verb sub-library

There is a close relation between the compilation of the Electronic Dictionary of *NIGEN DABHVR ASAR* and the selection, pronunciation, sylla-ble structure, interpretation, number of occurrences, frequency rank, variation forms and application message of verb entries. There are 13 fields in the verb sub-library as following: traditional Mongolian form of entries, （field as MU ）, Latin transliteration form of entries （GU ）, pronunciation （DDG）, part of speech （UA）, syllable structure （UB）, the tradi-tional Mongolian form of Interpretation （MVT）, Latin transliteration form

of the interpretation （GVT）, Chinese translation of interpretation
（HVT）, occurrence frequency （IT）, frequency rank （DD）,
inflectional forms （HH）, traditional Mongolian form of examples
（MJU）, Latin transliteration of examples（GJU）。

Figure 3 sample of verb sub-library

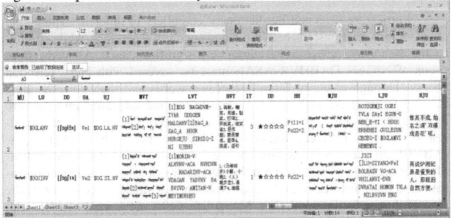

3.1 selections of entries

In Mongolian, Verbs can be divided into four categories such as general verbs, pronoun verbs, link verbs and auxiliary verbs. The general verbs
are subdivided into transitive and intransitive categories. Auxiliary verbs are
subdivided into first kind auxiliary verb and second kind auxiliary verbs.

Verb is one of the most important word classes in Mongolian. There
are altogether 132918 words in the text corpus of *NIGEN DABHVR ASAR*.
Among them, the number of the verb is 33634, occupying 25.30% of all
words. From this data, we could see the importance of verb.

Table1 Statistical Classification of verbs in the text corpus of *NIGEN
DABHVR ASAR*

Classifications of verbs		Number of words	Percentage in all verbs
General verb(Ve)	transitive	16502	49.06%
	intransitive	12190	36.24%
Pronoun verb(Vt)		173	0.51%
Link verb(Vx)		2757	8.21%
Auxiliary verb(Vz)	First level auxiliary	84	0.25%

	Second level auxiliary	1928	5.73%
In total		33634	100%

As we could see from table 1, general verbs account for the highest proportion among all verbs, over 85%. However, pronoun verbs occupy less than 1%.

Entries are designed by dictionary compilers in order to explain and reflect various relationships between language units. Therefore, while compiling the dictionary, selection of entries is a significant task. All verbs from corpus of NIGEN DABHVR ASAR must be covered with entry selection process. Through category filtering repeated words and their corresponding variation forms, 1262 verb entries were selected and subsumed into the verb library. For example: "YABVBA (left)"and "YABVN_A (to go)" are considered to be two different forms of YABV. In the verb sub-library, as YABVHV an entry, previous two change forms are recorded into the in lexical variation field. Grammatical information, also known as syntactic information, is the most basic level of information. Grammatical condition is the basis of dictionary interpretation. Mongolian verbs are a kind of POS with many complicated morphological changes. There is suffix variation besides morphological change of stems. In the verb library, grammatical information is an important part for the interpretation. Related grammatical information of Mongolian verb includes voice of the verbs (active, dynamic, passive, mutual, codynamic, homogeneous), categories of aspect and time, declarative and imperative etc. In the national standard of Information Technology and Processing for Mongolian Lexical Markers, various forms of these categories have corresponding codes. In Figure 3, K field value indicates the category of additional components by marks begin with F. the value behind the symbol "=" indicates the number of times the word appeared in the text corpus of NIGEN DABHVR ASAR. For example:

$ANGNAHV Fs14=1 Fn72=3 Ft11=1 Ft11+Fc22=2 Ft11+Fc51=1 Fe11+Fn1=1 Ft12=5 Ft13+Fc22=1 Fn1=6 Fn3=2 Fb12=1

Fs14=1: the mark code "BA/BE", namely "$ANGNABA" appeared once;

Ft11+Fc51=1: the mark code "GSAN/GSEN-BAR/IYAR/BER/IYER", namely "$ANGNAGSAN-IYAR" appeared once.

Table2Statistical Classification of verb entries in the sub-library

Classification of verbs	Number of verb entries	In total
Ve1	628	1262
Ve2	625	
Vt	4	

Vx	3	
Vz	2	

It can be seen from table 2 that, main categories of verbs could be classified into transitive verbs and intransitive verbs which could separately accounts for 49.76% and 49.52% of the total number of verbs.

3.2 phonetic notation

Phonetic notation refers to the tagging of pronunciation to entries. Currently, there are many different phonetic systems around the world among which International Phonetic Alphabet is the most popular. Pronunciation of entries is tagged under the reference of Mongolian- Chinese Dictionary edited by Mongolian Institute of Inner Mongolia University. For example, GAJAR [gadʒɪr](ground), VNGSIHV[ʊŋʃɪx](to read)

3.3 POS information

Part of speech means the different classification of vocabularies in a language according to the various grammatical functions. POS information is closely related to the construction of POS sub-libraries of the Electronic Dictionary of *NIGEN DABHVR ASAR*. Mongolian POS can be divided into content words and function words: content words include verbs, nouns, adjectives, numerals, measure words and pronouns; the function words are divided into adverbs, prepositions, conjunctions, auxiliary word, onomatopoeia and interjection. Word classification is helpful to understand the grammatical function of words. POS tagging for entries is essential to Mongolian researchers, Mongolian instructors and learners.

3.4 syllable structure

Generally, Mongolian word length is measured by the number of syllables. Recording syllable boundaries of entries has great significance to the studies on the Mongolian studies and language teaching. Syllable is the unit of speech sequence construction and the most natural and minimal phonetic structure. In the written language, it could be seen as structural components of word formation. In Mongolian, a word consists of one or more syllables. Usually each syllable must have a vowel; the vowel can be a single syllable, which is an important element of word formation, yet the consonant cannot be used as a single syllable. In the verb sub-library we built, "." is the separator between syllables. In Figure 3, the value of D field indicates the syllable structure of entries. For example: Vel $ANGNAHV[$ANG.NA.HV] is consisting of three syllables such as "$ANG", "NA", "HV". (It means "to reward" in Mongolian.)

Common active syllables in Mongolian include: (V indicates vowel, G indicates consonant)

V:[E.JI] (mom)
VC:[0R] (to enter)
CV:[SI.RE.GE] (table)
CVC:[GAR] (to go out, hand)
Table3distribution of syllable type of entries in the verb-library

Syllable class	Number of word
monosyllabic word	1
Two-syllable word	27
Three-syllable word	511
Four-syllable words	516
Five-syllable words	189
Six-syllable words	16
Seven-syllable words	2
total	1262

From table 3, we can see that, three-syllable words and four-syllable words are in the majority and separately accounts for 40.56% and 40.95%. Monosyllabic words occupy the smallest proportion.

3.5 interpretation

Semantic information refers to the information provided by any meaningful language, text, symbols, data, formulas and theories. Semantic is an important component and a level of language. Semantics is the study of meaning, yet the meaning itself is an extremely complicated subject. Polysemy is very common in Mongolian. For example, besides its own meaning, one word has other grammatical meaning and rhetoric meaning, and they could convey different meanings by combining with different words. Semantics affects all aspects of human society and it is an indispensable part for information processing, and they are closely related to each other.

We are currently working on the Mongolian interpretation (traditional Mongolian and Inner Mongolia University Latin) of verbs from verb sub-library of Electronic Dictionary of NIGEN DABHVR ASAR with the help of Mongolian Dictionary compiled by Mongolian Dictionary Compilation Group and adding the Chinese definition with the reference of Mongolian Chinese Dictionary. Examples of the F, G and H field values are shown below. Interpretation in traditional Mongolian:

[1] ᠬᠠᠷᠢᠶ᠎ᠠ ᠮᠤᠩᠭᠤᠯ ᠤ ᠠᠭᠤᠯᠭ᠎ᠠ ᠶᠢᠨ ᠪᠣᠳᠣᠯᠭ᠎ᠠ ᠲᠡᠢ ᠪᠠᠢᠢᠭ᠎ᠠ

[2] ᠲᠣᠬᠢᠶᠠ ᠠᠭᠤᠯᠭ᠎ᠠ ᠪᠠᠷ ᠵᠠᠰᠠᠯ ᠠᠴᠠ ᠲᠤᠰᠤᠨ ᠲᠤᠰ ᠠᠭᠤᠯᠭ᠎ᠠ ᠲᠠᠢ

[3] ᠬᠠᠷᠢᠶᠠᠲᠤ ᠰᠢᠨᠵᠢᠯᠡᠬᠦ ᠤ ᠬᠠᠷᠢᠶᠠᠲᠤ ᠭᠡ ᠬᠠ ᠲᠠᠢᠢᠯᠪᠤᠷᠢ᠎ᠠ

[4] ᠲᠣᠬᠢᠶᠠ ᠮᠤᠩᠭᠤᠯ ᠤᠨ ᠬᠡᠯᠡᠨ ᠤ ᠠᠷᠠᠯᠵᠢᠶᠠᠨ ᠲᠠᠷᠬᠠᠭ᠎ᠠ ᠠᠭᠤᠯᠭ᠎ᠠ ᠪᠠᠷ ᠬᠡ ᠠᠭᠤᠯᠭᠠ᠎ᠠ ᠬᠠᠷᠢᠶᠠ • ᠰᠠᠢᠢᠨ • ᠵᠠᠰᠠᠯᠭᠠᠲᠤ

[5] *(Mongolian script text)*

[6] *(Mongolian script text)*

[7] *(Mongolian script text)*

[8] *(Mongolian script text)*

Interpretation in Inner Mongolia University Latin:

[1]SINGGEN YAGVMAN-V D0TVR_A H0LILDVGSAN ODGEN B0DAS-I
ILGAN GARGAHV

[2]VSVN D0TVR_A-ACA JIGASV-YI T00R-IYAR T0RG0N BARIHV

[3]SAGSVN BOMBUGE-YI SAGSVN-DV NI 0RVGVLHV

[4]OLAN YAGVM_A-YI JAH_A DARAGALAN AJIGLAJV D0TVR_A-ACA
NI YAGVM_A ERIHU , TEGUHU , BORIDGEHU

[5]N0M BICIG-I TVGVLVN VNGSIJV JOB BVRVGV-YI HINAHV BVYV
YAMAR NIGEN BARIMTA MAteRIYAL ERIHU , TEGUHU,
BORIDGEHU[6]JIGAGSANN0M-IYAN VNGSIGVLJV CEGEJILEGSEN
ESEHU-YI SILGAHV

[7]ELDEB HEREG JARGV-YI BAYICAGAN ASAGVJV OCIGLEGULHU

[8]TEMECEGEN MOROICEGEN BA T0GLAGAM-DV H0NJIHV BA
DAYILHU

Interpretation in Chinese:

[1]捞

[2]过滤

[3]（棋、牌、赌博中）赢

3.6 occurrence number and frequency rank

In the text of NIGEN DABHVR ASAR, some words occur repeatedly and some occurs relatively few. It is beneficial for describing the characteristics of word usage from NIGEN DABHVR ASAR to examine the occurrence time of entries and then to put this information into the verb-library.

Occurrence number refers to the occurred time of different forms of a word in the text corpus of NIGEN DABHVR ASAR. In figure 3, I field value indicates the occurrence number of words. For example: $ANGNAHV[$ANG.NA.HV] vel (24) (it means "to reward" in Mongolian). "24" in parentheses indicates that "$ANGNA/" appeared with different forms in the text corpus of NIGEN DABHVR ASAR for 24 times. Frequency rank refers to the level of occurrence time of a certain word in the corpus and which is indicated with an asterisk.

Table 4 the relation between frequency and stars

Frequency	Star ranks	occurrence in the corpus	Percentage of occurrence in the corpus
1-10	★☆☆☆☆	913	72.35%
11-50	★★☆☆☆	254	20.13%

51-100	★★★☆☆	43	3.41%
101-500	★★★★☆	43	3.41%
>500	★★★★★	9	0.70%

It can be seen from table 4 that, verbs in the one star rank occupies the largest proportion. Statistics shows that verbs occurred less than 100 times in the text corpus of *NIGEN DABHVR ASAR* occupies 95.89%.However, verbs occurred more than 500 times only occupies 0.70%.

We have done statistical investigation to the verb classes, occurrence time and the relation between frequency and stars in the verb-library.

Table 5   statistical investigation of verb classes, occurrence time and frequency stars

	★☆☆☆☆	★★☆☆☆	★★★☆☆	★★★★☆	★★★★★
Ve1	419	154	23	29	3
Ve2	492	99	19	12	4
Vt	2	1			
Vx			1	1	1
Vz				1	1
total	913	254	43	43	9

From table 4 and table 5, we could see that the occurrence of verbs gradually reduce while the frequency star increases, whether observing from the verb as a whole, or from the perspective of the internal category of verbs,

3.7 Application

It is quite difficult and time-consuming to find an appropriate example in the process of dictionary compilation. At present, for the compilation of modern electronic dictionary based on Corpus, it is very simple, convenient and time-saving. Of course, such convenience depends on the size of the corpus, the selection of materials and many other factors.

Each entry in this study comes with an example which is from the text corpus of *NIGEN DABHVR ASAR*. Traditional Mongolian and latin forms are listed with corresponding Chinese definitions referred from the translated edition of *NIGEN DAVHUR ASAR* (JiaYimu 1963). Three field values of L, M, and N are shown in the table 3.

4   Conclusion

Dictionary compliationis an important content of Applied Linguistics. In a narrow sense, applied linguistics involves dictionary compilation besides language teaching. Modern applied linguistics and its methods are characterized by computer, which demonstrates the status of computer in linguistics and related sciences. The application of computer in the compilation of dictionary becomes one of the main content of modern applied linguistics.

In Mongolian information processing field, it is a meaningful task to compile the Electronic Dictionary of *NIGEN DABHVR ASAR* based on its text corpus. For dictionary compilation, we have to make sure that it is practical, accurate and scientific. Some problems and tagging errors need to be corrected manually. These works take a lot of time. At present, we have just finished the verb sub-library of the compilation of the Electronic Dictionary of *NIGEN DABHVR ASAR*. The remaining part still needs to be improved for implementation. Moreover, more time, manpower and material resources are needed to finish the construction work of other sub-libraries in order to meet the Mongolian researchers, learners and enthusiasts' need to have a more convenient, accurate and practical one.

References

Mongolian Institute of the Inner Mongolia University. 1964. *Contemporary Mongolian Language*. Inner Mongolia People's Publishing House, Hohhot.

D.Chingelt. 2005. *Mongolian Fixed Phrase Grammar Information Dictionary*. Inner Mongolia Education Press, Hohhot.

Zhao, Yurong. 2009.*Adjective sub-library for the Electronic Dictionary of HUHSODOR*. Inner Mongolia University,Hohhot.

Bao, Xiaorong. 2009.*Verb sub-library for the Electronic Dictionary of HUHSODOR*. Inner Mongolia University, Hohhot.

Zhang Yihua. 2002.*Semantics and Dictionary Interpretation*. Shanghai Dictionary Press, Shanghai.

Dabhurbayar. 2014.The *Relevant Research on Mongolian Phrase Structure Knowledge Base*. Liaoning People's publishing House, Shenyang.

Zhang, Jianmei et al. 2006.On developing the Yinzhannashi Dictionary.In *the third symposium on the student computational linguistics*, Taiyuan.

Mongolian Institute of the Inner Mongolia University. 1999. *Mongolian–Chinese Dictionary* (revised edition). Inner Mongolia University Press, Hohhot.

Compilation group of Mongolian Dictionary. 1997.*Mongolian Dictionary*. Inner Mongolia People's Publishing House, Hohhot.

Li, Kai. 1990.*Modren Lexicography*. Nanjing University Press, Nanjing.

Zheng, Shupu. 1987. Sematics and Lexicography. in*Dictionary Research*. Shanghai Dictionary Press, Shanghai.

Ye, Peisheng and Xu, tongqiang. 2010.*Introduction to Lingguistics* (revised edition). Beijing University Press, Beijing.

The Construction Scheme of a Graded Spoken Interaction Corpus for Mandarin Chinese

Yuelong Wang

College of Humanities, Huaqiao University, Quanzhou 362021, China
wangyuelong@hqu.edu.cn

Abstract: This paper introduces the construction scheme of a graded spoken interaction corpus for Mandarin Chinese. Material selection and collection principals, corpus annotation and assistant software development are explained. This paper also points out the important and difficult issues in the construction process. The corpus proposed in this paper consists of 1 million words (transcribed from 1.5 TB data), and it is graded and tagged with interaction annotation. This corpus can provide naturally occurring interactions with transcriptions and annotations for researchers, by which the quantitative analysis of SI can be realized. In addition, exemplars grading according to Conversation Analysis (CA) is also provided in the corpus for the reference of other researchers.

Keywords: spoken interaction, graded SI corpus, conversation analysis

1 Introduction

With the development of linguistic research and the global promotion of Chinese language, the proficiency evaluation of Mandarin Chinese is getting more and more scientific. However, although there are already some researches about spoken interaction (SI), the research on grading of SI with Mandarin Chinese has not been given due attention to in the research cycles, and there are no national grading standards for the classification of SI as of now. Therefore, it is an obstacle to the research of Chinese language proficiency evaluation. Establishing the national grading standards would be helpful for the promotion of scientific evaluation to language ability and for the grading test for Mandarin Chinese. It is thus the most urgent task to build a SI corpus, which is reasonably sampled with large scale and SI annotation, as the foundation of the grading research of SI.

Research on SI has recently become a new hotspot (Clayman and Gill 2004). SI is richly varied from spoken language in many aspects. The most distinctive feature of spoken interaction is that response is always expected (Stenstrom and Anna-Brita 1994:2). SI is a consolidated work of language knowledge including speech, vocabulary and syntax, and is a communication process using spoken language. It is primarily through interaction that children are socialized, and culture is transmitted (Clayman and Gill 2004).

© Springer International Publishing AG 2016
M. Dong et al. (Eds.): CLSW 2016, LNAI 10085, pp. 280–290, 2016
DOI: 10.1007/978-3-319-49508-8_27

From the perspective of language education, apprehending the grading differences of SI would be helpful and useful for training the SI ability of students and enhancing the effect of SI. However, there are no distinctive criteria of distinguishing SI from spoken in the language proficiency test of Mandarin Chinese, and it therefore is a weak pocket. SI research can already be found in English, such as the levels of SI proficiency of the Common European Framework of Reference for Languages (CEFR), which provides a set of six common reference levels. Nevertheless, there are still obvious problems in the existing SI grading system.

Firstly, the grading levels of SI proficiency are usually based on the complexity of a topic, which is a simple but not absolute standard. This was due in part to the oral test tradition. The complexity of a topic could be an important reference index, but not the most important or unique index. Moreover, the judgment for the complexity of a topic has a highly subjective content. The same topic may be difficult for someone meanwhile may be easy for others. Therefore, there is no enough uniformity in the operation.

Secondly, the complexity of the task belongs to the outside observation of a language and the inside analysis of a turn is neglected. Therefore, it is not a perfect grading criterion. Conversation Analysis (CA) offers a rigorous methodology for data analysis, and can be used as an inside index of SI grading. The combination of inner and outside standard is thus a reasonable option for establishing the grading standard for SI classification.

Thirdly, SI research is traditionally based only on a few transcribed data but not on big data. Therefore, there are still shortages in the research on the grading levels of proficiency of SI, and more advanced researches are needed.

Corpus is already the indispensable resource of linguistic research, and more and more research is based on large corpus for the investigation. Research on SI also needs large scale corpus. There are already a few small SI corpora for Mandarin Chinese, such as Mandarin Conversational Dialogue Corpus of Sinica (Tseng and Low 2002). However, corpus with large-scale, themed on graded SI data, served on researching on SI classification, is not seen yet.

2   The necessity of building a graded SI corpus

Although there are already many corpora of spoken language, they are yet not suitable for the research on grading SI proficiency and are difficult for lateral and vertical comparison.

Firstly, although the content of SI in the existing spoken corpus accounts for large percentage, we find that the scenes of SI are yet richly varied and complicated. The distribution of topics is thus scattered and easy to lead to sparse data. Therefore, it is not suitable for statistical analysis and for the lateral and vertical comparison. As we know, spoken language corpus of Indo-European language has an early start and large scale, such as London-Lund corpus, the earliest spoken corpus of English. In London-Lund spoken corpus, the scenes of SI include dialogue, telephone conversation, discussion, interview, argument, and so on. They are varied and not suitable for the lateral and vertical comparison. Therefore, it is not an ideal corpus for SI research. The same problem also exists broadly in other spoken corpus.

Secondly, the coverage of age scale of participants in the examples is incomplete. Along with the intricacies of scenes, the ages of participants are also random and disorderly. It may be due to the thoughtless of the corpus constructor. Although some of the exemplars in corpus can be compared, we cannot see the complete development of the ability of SI.

Thirdly, studies of spoken corpus are usually based on transcripts of audio recording, which is a long-historical tradition. Transcript is not a substitute for the recording, but an analytical tool. With the rapid development of network and information technology over the years, online transition of video becomes possible, which makes it possible to record nonvocal behaviors with the stream of speech. Information encoded in audio and video is much more than word transcription, which can only infinitely close but cannot take the place of audio and video. Inquiry system, which can synchronously index character, audio and video, can make up the disadvantage to make the investigation more credible.

In summary, it is necessary to build a multi-dimensional corpus with complete age scale of participant, which can support the lateral and vertical comparison and reflect the development of SI ability. This is the actual demands of SI research and information construction. Meanwhile, it can also increase the types of language resource. Proposed corpus in this paper can basically satisfy the need with the characters of large scale, rich annotations and synchronous inquiry system.

3   The value and significance of building a graded SI corpus

The graded SI corpus proposed in this paper is designed to help researchers with SI research, the development of national standards of SI proficiency, SI teaching, compiling of SI text books, and thus has higher theoretical and practical value. The theoretical value is characterized by the following three aspects.

Firstly, it is useful and helpful to know the complete state of SI ability development of students. Exemplars in the proposed corpus are all actual SI materials recorded in testing scene. They are well selected and annotated with SI features. This corpus has large scale, and can represent and reflect the actual state of SI development. This can change the existing situation of relying heavily on the perceptual knowledge which lacks of objective evaluation.

Secondly, it will prove helpful to the research of SI grading and SI teaching. The application of the graded SI corpus can bring the SI research closer to SI teaching. From this corpus, we can know the actual states of SI ability development of students, and then formulate reasonable teaching goals for students of all ages. SI teaching and training are becoming a prominent lightspot in language teaching. For example, there are already SI textbooks compiled in Singapore for SI teaching in primary and secondary schools. This will possibly be the new trend of education in primary and middle schools in China.

Thirdly, it can improve the normalization and standardization of SI research. As we all know, human interaction lies at the very heart of children's life. However, the development of SI ability is still inconspicuous, and is lack of explicit guidelines. By exemplars in the corpus and statistical data, we can know the real state of current SI and analysis of distinctions in different ages. In addition, it can be used as the foundation of developing the national standards of grading SI proficiency. The construction of large scale SI corpus can provide a data platform for the research of national regulations of SI grading.

The practical value of the construction of a graded SI corpus includes the following aspects:

Firstly, it can provide actually occurred language materials with transcription and SI annotation for different researchers. Nowadays, most researches on SI are executed by individual researchers, and rely heavily on the transcript of video and audio and related information annotation. This is usually an extremely labor-intensive and time-consuming work. Due to the limitation of individual research, the field range of inquiry is usually small. The reliability of the research result is therefore often questionable. Building a large scale SI corpus for the usage can spare the time of transcription and annotation for individual researcher and may save a great deal of manpower and financial resource.

Secondly, the construction of a graded SI corpus can also realize the consistency of annotation. The transcribing of data can be affected by many factors, such as the ability of researcher, the understanding about the data, the transcription system and the reader of transcription. Building a corpus with unified transcriptions can provide a unified platform as the dialogue and research foundation for different researchers to make the conclusion more reliable. More importantly, it allows researchers to independently access the analytic claims by others. Therefore, conclusions based on this corpus are all observable and verifiable.

Thirdly and the most importantly, the construction of a graded SI corpus can support the quantitative analysis of different SI indicators. Most previous studies are case-based and general qualitative analysis. The large scale SI corpus can assist the quantitative analysis for indicators in larger range, and the results are more precise. It is helpful for the combination of quantitative and qualitative research.

4   The main research content of the graded SI corpus

This study will explore the theory and method of the construction of a graded SI corpus, according to the features of SI and utilizing the theoretical and methodological experience of corpus construction for spoken language. There are many similarities between the construction of SI corpus and the building of spoken language corpus, but there are still some unique features. We propose the material selection and collection principals, corpus annotation guidelines and the development schemes of assistant software. As a result, this will be a multi-layer annotated, easily used and large scale SI corpus for the SI research of Mandarin Chinese.

The overall framework of the construction of a SI corpus can be shown in Figure 1.

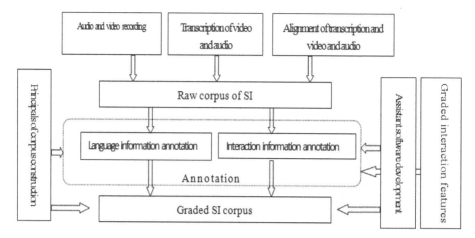

Fig. 1. General framework of the construction of graded SI corpus

The focal points of building the graded SI corpus include establishing scientific and appropriate principals for material selection and annotation, executing careful data collection, linguistically and interactional information annotation and SI grading. The specific research content can be explained as follows.

4.1   Corpus construction principles

As to SI grading, the first thing we need to consider is the comparability among the language materials. Nothing but materials with similar form and content can be laterally and vertically compared. Therefore, it is necessary to restrict the form and topic of interaction when collecting the language materials. Moreover, it is also necessary to consider other external influencing factors, such as voice, light, time, location, and so on.

Theoretically, there are two options for restricting the external influence factors. One possible option is to eliminate all the influence factors; the other is to obtain the consistence of external factors. Since the external factors cannot be completely eliminated, it is better to choose the second option as a feasible strategy. Furthermore, material collection should strictly comply with the completely principle, which means that the age of participants in exemplars should cover all ages.

Considering the operability, we choose students from grade 1 in primary school to grade 3 in high school as the representative participates of SI. This age bracket can basically represent and reflect the complete course of development of students' SI ability.

We determine the background of SI as testing scene. Naturally occurring interactions are preferred for interaction research. Just like Sack (1992) pointed, there will be astonishing discoveries in working with actual interactions. SI in the testing background is also a naturally occurring scene, but a restricted form. Moreover, testing scene can also keep the consistence of external influencing factors to realize the relative justice.

The recording time of exemplars should also be nearly identical. In this situation, the exemplars can be laterally and vertically compared to discover the similarities and differences.

4.2   Data collection scheme

The specific scheme of data collecting include: specifying the testing topic, maintaining the comparability of exemplars, determining the form of SI, and choosing the data sampling cities to reflect the development course of Chinese students. Data collected from students should be large in number and widely distributed.

The testing topics should not affect the performance of SI ability, while can keep the possibility of lateral and vertical comparison among them. Therefore, the topics used for testing should not only be concentrative, but also be appropriate for all the students to talk. After discussion and sampling, we asserted two topics as the testing topics for SI. As shown in Table 1.

Table 1. Testing topics for SI

Topic	Content
Topic 1	What do you do in spare time?
Topic 2	What is your opinion for tutorial class?

There are at least two forms for SI, two players and multi-players. Interaction happened among multi-players is different from interaction occurred between two players in many aspects, such as turn-taking, transfer, watching, and so on. Therefore, different testing forms are needed for the interaction differences. Furthermore, the identity acted in the interaction could also be optional. It could be interaction between teacher and student; it could also be interaction between students. Interaction between teacher and student is mostly used in the existing grading standards, such as the Common European Framework of Reference for Language, which is clearly affected by the spoken test tradition.

There are however obvious disadvantages in the form of interaction between teacher and student. In this situation, the SI ability of investigator is much higher than the respondent. They can easily define the framework of SI and the development of topic, that is the 'manipulation' named by Heritage and Atkinson (1984:2-3). As a result, the students cannot show their best performance in SI. Meanwhile, the form of interaction between students can avoid this disadvantage, because the students have similar age and common interest in the same topic. Therefore, it is perhaps not surprising that the form of interaction between students is the preferred testing form, and can better exert students' ability.

According to the data collection principals, stratified sampling will be used to collect the exemplars by age group. Moreover, gender differences at the interactions need also to be strictly considered. From grade 1 in primary school to grade 3 in high school, we gather 300 exemplars in each grade, where the female-to-male ratio of students is 1:1, which are 150 students each. Students come from five main cities organized geographically in China. The sampling cities can be seen in Table 2.

Table 2. Sampling cities of SI

Location	East	West	North	South	Center
City	Shanghai	Xi'an	Beijing	Guangzhou	Wuhan

The availability of audio and video recording technology made it possible to capture and preserve the stream of speech and the nonvocal behaviors unfolded in the interactions.

4.3   Corpus annotation principals

Corpus annotation is notoriously a labor-intensive and time-consuming work. It is necessary to use strict guidelines to keep the consistency of transcription and annotation. Transparent annotation guidelines can increase the reusability of the corpus. According to the reality of SI research and teaching, multi-layer information annotations are needed in the corpus proposed.

Our annotation consists of three parts. First part is the meta-message which is the non-language information annotated for language materials, including the source of material, recording time, speaker ID, gender, age of students, grade of students, topic, level, and so on. Meta-message can provide basic query condition and evidence for corpus indexing and analysis. Second part of annotation is about language information, including word segmentation, part of speech, sentence, and so on. Third part is interaction information annotation, including specific interaction features such as turns, action, backchannels, maintenance, stress, and so on. That is the investigation foundation for SI grading.

4.4   Annotation schedule for data

Corpus annotation is the actual demands of formalization of SI, and is the key point of corpus construction. The quality of annotation will directly affect the diversity and precision of data mining.

We use the transcription system commonly used in CA to transcribe the recording of audio and video. Transcriptions make features of the interaction more transparent and accessible. The content includes speech, voice, unclear speech, silences, overlapping speech, speed, duration, stress, volume, and nonvocal behaviors such as gaze direction, gestural displays, body positioning, and so on.

Transcription system used in this corpus is mostly the transcription symbols used in American CA sects (Atkinson and Heritage. 1984) and is simplified to fit the reality as a symbol assembles. As shown in Table 3.

Table 3. Outline of the transcription symbols for SI

Symbol	Meaning	Symbol	Meaning
201 202	speaker	[	overlapping start
// //	overlapping speech	]	overlapping end
=	close engagement	\<hhh\>	inhale
(1)(2)(3)	number means pausing time	hhh	asperaion
?	rising tone	(hhh)	laugh
!	falling tone	( )	comment
yes.	'.' represent falling tone	...	unclear
:	prolong speech	[a]	voice transcript
yes-	'-'means pause	(( ))	description
yes	underline means stress	> <	fast word speed
yes	'* *'means reducing volume	<>	slow word speed
+yes+	'+ +'means enlarging volume	→	attention
*	needs discussion	yes	bold letters represent repeated usage
1.2.3.	number means turn order	#	tone unit boundary
ə( )	brief voiced pause	ə:( )	long voiced pause

4.5   Assistant software for corpus construction and application

The construction of a graded SI corpus needs a software platform to use existing technology and develop related assistant software. Assistant software can speed the construction of corpus, improve the science and efficiency and keep the consistency of construction.

Specifically, software needed in SI corpus construction can be classified into four categories. The first one is the assistant software for data collection, which serves for data collection, transcription, alignment and data storage. The second one is the annotation software, which serves for the annotation of meta-message, language information and interaction. The third one is management software, which serves for the quality inspection. The fourth one is statistical and index software, serving for statistical analysis for the usage of SI features and index service for word, annotation, sentence, text, and so on. As shown in Figure 2.

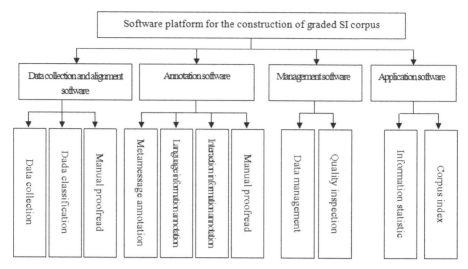

Fig. 2. Software classifications for the graded SI corpus

5   Focuses and difficulties of building a graded SI corpus

The construction of a graded SI corpus is a new attempt, and has no precedents for such a procedure. Therefore, it is necessary to explore and improve during the construction. More attentions need to be paid on some focuses and difficulties.

The followings are some key problems of the construction of a graded SI corpus.

- Defining the differences between spoken and SI.

It is important to define the differences between spoken and SI for establishing the standard of SI. There is different emphasis between spoken and SI. How to properly define SI is a guiding point. The differences of them are unclear till now, and it is the first thing need to be clarified.

- Developing the specific assistant software.

Previous language material is usually written form of transcription. The availability of online transfer technology made the video corpus possible to capture the conversational interaction. The corpus we proposed is a multi-dimensional corpus which can simultaneously index character, audio and video. That places higher request to assistant software development.

- Establishing the grading standards of SI.

As the existing grading levels of SI proficiency are based on the complexity of topics, which is the observation outside of language and is unstable, we propose to grade SI according to CA features. Using CA features to grade SI levels is a new attempt, and has no previous experience. It is necessary to cluster the features from bottom to top according to the data-based investigation. Therefore, it is a difficult problem to solve.

- Building the quality control system

The construction of a graded SI corpus is a complicated project, and multiple person cooperation is needed. Therefore, it is very important to keep the consistence of transcript and annotation. To accomplish this purpose, strict manpower proofread is needed. We need both the inside self check system and other person's check, to keep the consistence of data processing.

The difficulties of the construction are mainly about data collecting, annotation and SI grading.

- Data collection problems in testing scene

It is the first time to include testing scene in SI data collection. How to keep the consistence of external influencing factors in SI is a problem. In addition, how to motivate the best performance of the students in testing scenes is also a difficult problem.

- Annotation problems

Although traditional annotation has been good at describing how speech, vocabulary and grammar work in spoken language, the distinctions between SI annotation and spoken annotation are not very clear till now. Therefore, how to definitely distinguish them is a difficult point.

- Grading problem of SI

There would be two grading levels in the corpus proposed. One is the natural grading according to the grade of students. As to the similarity of age in the same grade, it can be regarded as the grading according to the ages. It is the simply clustering of the ages. The other is the SI grading according to the interaction features. This grading is based on data investigation and statistical analysis. How to statistically analyze the SI features and cluster the distinctive features is also a difficult point.

6   Conclusion

In this paper, we propose the construction scheme of a graded SI corpus, including principals establishing, topic choosing, data collection, data processing, integration, and so on. The construction of a graded SI corpus is the actual demands of the development of SI research, and should be a constituent part of national strategy. It is a basic and useful resource for SI research. Meanwhile, the project involves many domains, such as linguistics, sociology, computer science, and so on. It has the prominent features of originality, pioneering and integration.

This research will rectify the status of weakness in SI research and the shortage of basic corpus resource for statistical research. It can provide quantitative evidence of

SI features for researchers, and would be beneficial for SI teaching and text compiling of SI. In addition, this research will cover the shortage of similar research, and will offer a reference for the construction of similar corpora.

Acknowledgements. This work was supported by the Scientific Research Foundation for the Returned Overseas Chinese Scholars, State Education Ministry (Z1534014), and the Initial Research Foundation for High-level Talents of Huaqiao University (13SKBS219).

References

1. Council of Europe. The Common European Framework of Reference for Languages. London: Cambridge University Press, 2007.
2. Ministry of Education and the State Language Commission. Spoken Chinese Proficiency Grading Standards and Testing Guideline. Beijing: Language and Literature Press, 2011.
3. Tseng S.C. and Low Y.F.: Annotation system description of Mandarin conversational dialogue corpus. Technical Report, No. 02-01, 2002.
4. Clayman, S. and V. T. Gill.: Conversation Analysis// Hardy M, Bryman A. Handbook of Data Analysis. London: SAGE Publications. 2004.
5. Heritage J, and J. Atkinson.: Introduction // Atkinson J, Heritage J. Structures of social action: studies in conversation analysis. Cambridge: Cambridge University Press. 1984.
6. Sacks, H.: Lectures on Conversation. Oxford:Blackwell. 1992.
7. Stenström and Anna-Brita.: An introduction to spoken interaction. Longman, London and New York, 1994.
8. Svartvik, J. and R. Quirk (eds).: A corpus of English conversation. Lund: Lund University Press, 1980.

Study on Modality Annotation Framework of Modern Chinese

Kunli Zhang[1], Lingling Mu[1], Hongying Zan[1], Yingjie Han[1], Zhifang Sui[2]

[1] School of Information Engineering, Zhengzhou University, Zhengzhou, Henan 450001, China
{ieklzhang,iellmu,iehyzan,ieyjhan}@zzu.edu.cn
[2] Key Laboratory of Computational Linguistics, Ministry of Education, Peking University, Beijing 100871, China
szf@pku.edu.cn

Abstract. Modality is the speaker's subject idea processed and expressed for sentence objective express system. Modal meaning is important for deep understanding of sentence semantics. In this paper, a Chinese modality annotation framework aimed for deep semantic understanding is preliminarily practiced, which constructed a modal meaning classification system on the basis of existing research results, built the modal operator dictionary, established rules for annotation, and annotated modal operators of a sentence which have been tagged basic proposition arguments.

Keywords: Modality, Modality Classification System, Modal Operator Dictionary, Modality Annotation Framework

1   Introduction

Since natural language understanding is based on the semantic understanding, digging deep semantic understanding with obvious form will be the breakthrough in natural language understanding in the future. It is often believed that a sentence is the relatively complete meaning expression unit of natural language. So if someone wants to understand natural language, he/she needs to understand the semantics of the sentence. In the abstract semantics structure of a sentence "{[<|(proposition component) tense and aspect component| modal component>mood component] tone component}" [1],

© Springer International Publishing AG 2016
M. Dong et al. (Eds.): CLSW 2016, LNAI 10085, pp. 291–305, 2016
DOI: 10.1007/978-3-319-49508-8_28

the modal meaning conveyed by the modal components is an important level for level for the deep semantic understanding of a sentence.

Taking sentence (1) and (2) as examples, sentence (1) describes an objective fact "这座山是华山*(The mountain is Huashan Mountain)*", while sentence (2) adds the speaker's subjective attitude "可能[*keneng*] (*might*) " which expresses an inaccurate judgment on the proposition's truth. The meaning expressed by "可能[*keneng*] (*might*) " is called modal meaning or modality, and the word "可能[keneng] (might be)" is called modal operator or modal mark. Modality is often represented by different names in different literatures, such as "模态[*motai*](*modality*)", "情态[*qingtai*](*modality*)", "语气[*yuqi*] (*mood*)", etc., and in this paper we use the name "模态[*motai*] (*modality*)".

(1)这座山是华山。 (*The mountain is Huanshan Mountain.*)

(2)这座山可能是华山。 (*The mountain might be Huanshan Mountain.*)

Modality refers to the subjective concept expressed by the speaker in the course of processing language meaning of the sentence's objective expression system. In the linguistic field, the Chinese language modality has been extensively researched and discussed [2-6]. Some Scholars have focused on one or several types of modality research [7-17], while some have focused on case study [18-20]. Such research analyzed the classification of modality, modal operators and typical cases, however, divergences in different studies are quite obvious [6].In the computational linguistics field, the analysis and annotation of modality in sentences have attracted attention of many researchers. For example, Baker et al. studied the English modality expression framework and analyzed the corpus annotation [21]. To the best of our knowledge Chinese modality annotation framework has not been explored yet. In this paper, from the perspective of semantic understanding, we try to establish a modality annotation framework and annotate the modality of Chinese sentences which have been annotated the basic proposition arguments.

The rest part of this paper is organized as follows. In Section 2, we review the related works of modality. In Section 3, we introduce the annotation framework of Chinese modality and the modal operator dictionary. In Section 4, we describe the process of modality annotation and analyze the result. At last, we conclude the paper and list further works.

2   Related Work

In the logic study, modality starts from ancient Greek philosophy. Aristotle, in his theory of modality logic, proposed four modal operators including "certainty", "possibility", "contingency" and "impossibility", and discussed the modal propositions formed by the four modal operators. In the study of Chinese grammar, modality has been also explored for a long time. In particular, researchers presented general modality study or case study. However, they have different opinions about questions such as "What is modality?" and "How many kinds of modalities are there?" .

He Y. [2] and Qi H. Y. [3] referred to modality as "语气[*yuqi*](*mood*)" and considered that "Mood is the subjective consciousness of a speaker that expresses the proposition through the grammatical form". He Y. summarized that modality has two basic features: semantically, a sentence is divided into proposition and modality, and formally, modality is the grammatical meanings expressed through the grammatical form. The modality of a sentence is mainly expressed through formal marks such as punctuation marks which reflect intonation, special sentence patterns, co-occurrence restriction, auxiliaries, modal particles, interjections, etc. He Y. divided modern Chinese system into three categories including functional modality, judging modality and emotional modality, while Qi H. Y. divided it into functional mood (the communicative purpose that a speaker wants to achieve) and volitional mood (the attitude or emotion that a speaker wants to express) with 8 categories and 15 sub-categories. Wen S. L. [4] considered modality as "口气[*kouqi*] (*tone*)" and defined it as "feelings and attitudes of a speaker expressed for the proposition". He proposed that evidentiality, which concerns the reliability and truth of objective information, and modality, which has a certain degree of subjectivity, constitute a complete set of "tone modality" system. Lu C. [5] pointed out that the modality is "judgments" and "comments" of a speaker expressed for objective matters based on his/her subjective standpoint and viewpoint. And he divided modality into two categories, namely, judgments and comments. Peng L. Z. [6] provided a detailed analysis for the concept of modality and proposed the semantic system expressed by modal verbs.

Some researchers explored sub-classes or cases of modality including the detailed analysis and research on certainty[9], probability[10], intention[11], conjecture[12], rhetorical[13,14], comprehension[15], and persuading[17], and the research on cases of "竟然[*jingran*](*unexpectedly*)"[16], "能[*neng*](*can*)"[18], "可以[*keyi*] (*may*)"[19], and "大概[*dagai*](*probably*), 也许[*yexu*](*perhaps*), and 恐怕[*kongpa* (*supposed-*

ly)"[20]. These studies mentioned above analyze and illustrate the modality from different angles on markers, syntax and semantics, but none of them focus on systematical modality annotation of sentences. Based on annotation of semantic role of predicate in corpus of 973 subtopic *Acquisition and Organization of the Chinese Language Knowledge and World Knowledge that Integrates Three-dimension Space*, we carry out systematic research and annotation for modal meaning of the sentence.

3   Modality Annotation Framework

The annotation of modality will be taken on the foundation of the annotated basic proposition arguments, and the modality annotation framework includes a modality classification system based on the existing modality research, the modal operator dictionary, and guidelines for annotation.

3.1   Modality Classification System

Because modality annotation in this paper aims to provide a foundation for the semantic understanding of the natural language, only the "modal components" in abstract semantic structure is considered, which mainly includes the marked volitional modality that affects the meaning of a proposition and the speaker's subjective attitude. The modality annotation framework mainly relies on the modality classification systems proposed in literature [2] and [3] and studies of other researchers. Modality mainly consists of probability (including possibility and certainty), ability and intention, acquittal (including permission and requirement), comment (including anticipate, comprehend, felicitating, unexpected, and emotion) [2, 3], advice and judgment [1, 6] that express volitional modality. Except of these, rhetorical modality is also included in volitional modality because of its relatively strong subjectivity. Torsion[7] is also included as an individual category; and other modalities are classified into the emphasis that are difficult to fall into other categories but show the emphasis of a speaker on basic propositions[1]. Noting that literature [2] and [3] considered function moods (including indicative mood, interrogative mood, imperative mood and exclamation mood) as modality , we categorize them into "mood components" in abstract semantic structure because they mainly express the speech function of sentences in the communication processing and they will not be discussed in this paper. As shown in Table 1, the modality classification system can be divided into 9 categories and 16 subclasses.

The modal operators of various types are often auxiliary verbs, adverbs or phrases etc. , and some of typical operators are listed in Table 1. The "Tag" representation is shown in Section 4.

Table 1. The classification system of modality

Category		Typical operator	Operator No.	Tag
probability	certainty	一定[*yiding*](*must*)/d	26	mod_possibility
	possibility	可能[*keneng*] (*may*)/vu	93	mod_possibility
modal	intention	愿意[*yuanyi*] (*will*)/vu	27	mod_intention
	ability	能[*neng*] (*can*)/vu	5	mod_ability
acquittal	permission	可以[*keyi*](*may*)/vu	7	mod_permission
	requirement	必须[*bixu*](*must*)/d	37	mod_requirement
	comprehend	怪不得[*guaibude*](*no wonder*)/d	5	mod_comment_1
	anticipate	果然[*guoran*](*as expected*)/d	2	mod_comment_2
comment	felicitating	幸亏[*xingkui*](*fortunately*)/d	7	mod_comment_3
	unexpected	居然[*juran*](*unexpectedly*)/d	6	mod_comment_4
	emotion	老是[*laoshi*](*always*)/d	7	mod_comment_5
advice		最好[*zuihao*](*had better*)/d	4	mod_advice
judgment		值得[*zhide*](*deserve*)/v	3	mod_judgement
interrogative		何不[*hebu*](*why not*)/d	30	mod_rhetorical
torsion		反倒[*fandao*](*instead*)/d	8	mod_torsion
emphasis		的确[*dique*](*really*)/d	31	mod_emphasis
Total			298	

1) Probability

Probability modality represents the speaker's inference and judgment for the truth of the proposition in the sentence, which can be divided into certainty and possibility.

a. Certainty

Certainty modality indicates that the speaker speculates the proposition in the sentence might be true and might not be false, which is a kind of awareness to the inevitability of the matter [2]. The adverbs "一定[*yiding*](*definitely*)", "必然[*biran*](*necessarily*)", "必定[*biding*](*certainly*)", "势必[*shibi*](*undoubtedly*)", etc. act as modal operators of certainty. The following sentence (3) is an example of certainty modality[1].

(3)反动派{<必定[*bingding*](*certainly*)>mod_certainty 失败}。(*The reactionaries will certainly fail.*)

b. Probability

Probability modality indicates that the speaker cannot determine the proposition's veridicality in the sentence, and infers that it might be true [2]. The auxiliary verbs

---

[1]   See modal tag's specification in Section 4.

"会[hui](will)", "可能[keneng](may)" and the adverbs "也许[yexu](maybe)",
"或许[huoxu](perhaps)", "大概[dagai](probably)", "大约[dayue](approximately)",
"多半[duoban](mostly)", etc. can act as modal operators of possibility modality. The
following sentence (4) is an example of possibility modality.

(4)他{<可能[keneng](may)>mod_possibility回家去了}。(He might go home.)

Except for the operators that conjecture (such as "也许[yexu](perhaps)") the proposition's veridicality, the probability modal operator of this classification system also includes the operators that indicate the inference to the minimum or maximum of quantity or extent (such as "至少[zhishao](at least)") , or the certain extent of incidents or situations (such as "差不多[chabuduo](almost)")[8,10,12,20].

2) Ability and Intention

a. Ability

Ability modality indicates that the speaker estimates whether a person or something has the ability to achieve the proposition or has the function to realize the proposition in the sentence.   The   auxiliary   verbs   "能[neng](can)",   "能够[nenggou](can)",
"可以[keyi](may)",   "会[hui](be   able   to)"   and   the   negative   form   of
"不能[buneng](cannot)",   "不会[buhui](be   not   able   to)"   and   the   verb
"得以[deyi](can) " can act as modal markers of ability modality. The following sentence (5) and (6) are examples of ability modality.

(5)计算机{<能[neng](can)>mod_ability模仿人的思维}。(Computers can simulate human thinking.)

(6)发扬民主，使每个人的意见{<得以[deyi](can)>mod_ability充分发表出来}。(Promote democracy so that everyone can fully express their opinions.)

b. Intention

Intention modality indicates that the speaker estimates whether someone has the willingness to achieve the propositions in a sentence [2,7]. Auxiliary verbs such as
"肯[ken](will) ", "愿意[yuanyi](be inclined to) ", "情愿[qingyuan](be willing to) ",
"乐意[leyi](be willing to) ", "想[xiang](want to) ", "要[yao](would like to) " and other possible negative forms can all act as modal operators of intention modality. The following sentence (7) is an example of intention modality.

(7)小王{<想[xiang](want to)>mod_intention去北京}。(Xiaowang wants to go to Beijiing.)

In addition, there is another kind of intention modality that expresses the speaker's prominent subjectivity. In this modality, the speaker makes choices based on his/her subjective intention with the admission of objective conditions, and gives up other choices. According to the different semantic features, this kind of modality can be divided   into   four   types   including   "偏偏[pianpian](deliberately)",

"宁可[*ningke*](*would rather*)", "只好[*zhihao*](*have no choice but to*)" and "索性[*suoxing*](*might as well*) " [11].

3) Acquittal

Acquittal modality indicates the attitude that the speaker adopts to achieve the proposition in a sentence with the restriction of moral principle or objective environment [2]. Acquittal modality can be divided into permission and requirement.

a. Permission

Permission modality indicates that the speaker considers that the moral principle or objective environment allows for the realization of propositions in the sentence, and non-realization of this proposition can also be accepted [2]. Auxiliary verbs "能[*neng*](*can*)", "能够[*nenggou*](*can*)", "可以[*keyi*](*may*)" can act as modal operators of permission. The following sentence (8) is an example of permission modality.

(8)持有特别通行证的人才{<能[*neng*](*can*)>mod_permission进入}。(*People with special pass can enter.*)

b. Requirement

Requirement modality indicates that according to the moral principle or objective requirements, the speaker believes that it is necessary to realize the proposition in a sentence [2]. According to the different extents of emphasis on achieving propositions, requirement modality can be divided into "必须[*bixu*](*must*)" type that subjective order is given to the motion and "应当[*yingdang*](*should*)" type that reasonably or morally expresses responsibility or obligation. The following sentence (9) and (10) are examples of requirement modality.

(9)我们{<必须[*bixu*](*must*)>mod_requirement按时到达指定地点}。(*We must arrive at the given place on time.*)

(10)大家的事情{<应当[*yingdang*](*should*)>mod_requirement大家办}。(*Matters of all should be done by all.*)

4) Comment

Comment modality indicates the speaker's comprehension, anticipation, unexpected feeling, felicitating or other unclear emotions to the basic propositions of a sentence.

a. Comprehension

Comprehension modality is also known as disillusion modality, which indicates that the speaker understands the reason of the stated matters in the propositions and doesn't feel strange for the results or discovers something he/she doesn't know. The typical modal operators include "原来[*yuanlai*](*so*)", "难怪[*nanguai*](*no wonder*)",and

"怪不得[*guaibude*](*no wonder*)", etc.[2,7,15]. The following sentence (11) is an example of comprehension modality.

(11)下雪了，{<难怪[*nanguai*](*no wonder*)> mod_comment_1这么冷}。(*It's snowing; no wonder it's so cold.*)

b. Anticipation

Anticipation modality indicates that the stated matter in the proposition has been expected by the speaker, and the matter is consistent with the expectation of the speaker or is of certainty. The typical modal operators of this kind include "果然[*guoran*](*as expected*)" and "果真[*guozhen*](*as expected*)". The following sentence (12) is an example of anticipation modality.

(12)他{<果然[*guoran*](*as expected*)> mod_comment_2没有辜负大家对他的期望}。(*He doesn't fail the expectation of all as expected.*)

c. Felicitating

Felicitating modality indicates that possible bad results are avoided to happen in some favorable conditions and the speaker feels felicitating. The typical modal operators include adverbs "幸亏[*xingkui*](*thanks to*) ", "幸好[*xinghao*](*fortunately*) " etc.[2,7] The following sentence (13) is an example of felicitating modality.

(13){<幸好[*xinghao*](*fortunately*)>mod_comment_3地上有很厚的积雪}，他掉下来才没有摔伤。 (*Fortunately, there was thick snow on the ground so he didn't get hurt after falling.*)

d. Unexpected

Unexpected modality indicates the stated propositions is out of the speaker's expectation or it is not consistent with the expected results [2,16]. The typical modal operators include adverbs "竟敢[*jinggan*](*how dare*) ", "竟然[*jingran*](*unexpectedly*) ", and "居然[*juran*](*to one's surprise*)", etc. The following sentence (14) is an example of unexpected modality.

(14)你{<竟敢> mod_comment_4酒后驾车}！ (How dare you drive after drinking!)

e. Emotion

Emotion modality indicates that the speaker takes a certain emotion when expressing the basic proposition of a sentence. The emotion can usually be felt but it is hard to express clearly, or the emotion cannot be categorized into other subclasses of comment modality. The typical modal operators include adverbs "本来[*benlai*]()", and "原来[*yuanlai*]()", etc. The following sentence (14) is an example of emotion modality.

(15)他的病没好，{<本来[*benlai*]( )> mod_comment_5就不能去}。(*He hasn't recovered yet, and he shouldn't have gone.*}

5) Advice

Advice modality indicates that the speaker persuades and expects the listener to take relevant measures according to the speaker's own willingness [17]. The typical modal operators include adverbs such as "最好[zuihao](had better)" and "不妨[bufang](might as well)" etc. The following sentence (16) is an example of advice modality.

(16)这些刺人的话，{<最好[zuihao](had better)>mod_advice别说}。(It's better not to say these hurtful words.)

6) Judgment

Judgment modality indicates the speaker's judgment to the value of the matter, including the typical modal operators of "值得[zhide](deserve)", "配[pei](be worthy of)"[17], etc. The following sentence (17) is an example of judgment modality.

(17)只有这样的人，才{<配[pei](be worthy of)> mod_judgement称为先进工作者}。(Only this kind of people is worthy of the title of advanced worker.)

7) Rhetorical

Rhetorical modality is a kind of emphasis. It confirms or denies one obvious truth or fact to strengthen the mood or to blame someone [7,13,14]. The typical modal operators include adverbs such as "何必[hebi](why) ", "何不[hebu](why not) ", "何妨[hefang](not that) ", etc. The following sentence (18) is an example of rhetorical modality.

(18) 既然你还能再找人，{<何必[hebi](why)>mod_rhetorical再找我}? (Since you could find someone else, why do you find me?)

8）Torsion

Torsion indicates the semantic meaning [17] that is opposite to the context above or common sense, including the adverbs "反而[faner](instead) ", "反倒[fandao](on the contrary) ", etc. The following sentence (19) is an example of torsion modality.

(19) 帮他做了事情，他不领情，{<反倒[fandao](on the contrary)>mod_ torsion骂你是个靠不住的坏蛋}。 (He didn't feel grateful for the help. On the contrary, he said you were a badass.)

9）Emphasis

Emphasis indicates the intensifying mood. Adverbs such as "的确[dique](indeed)", "恰恰[qiaqia](exactly)", "才[cai]( )", "到底[daodi](after all) ", etc. can act as modal marks of emphasis modality.

(20) 他下意识地回敬：你{<才[cai]( )>mod_emphasis瞎眼了}，差点没有打起来。(He replied subconsciously: you are the one who is blind. And they almost fight with each other.)

3.2   Modal Operator Dictionary

The words in the modal operator dictionary are mainly extracted from the literatures on monographic study and on case study, and have been analyzed and selected when they were included in the dictionary. Considering the needs of annotating modality, we describe modality words from different properties such as ID, words, POS, sources, definition, sentences, full-pinyin, modality class and annotation tag, etc. It is interesting to note that most modal operators are adverb and adverb is one kind of dictionaries from the existing *Chinese Function word Knowledge Base*, abbreviated as CFKB[22,23], which includes dictionaries of adverbs, conjunctions, prepositions, modal particles, location words and auxiliary etc. So on the basis of CFKB, we extract the properties of modal operators from the adverbs dictionary, and then take the *Modern Chinese Dictionary* (h), the *Dictionary of Modern Chinese Grammar* (y) and other (z) contents as the supplement. In order to use the CFKB's results of usage automatic recognition for the further automatic modality annotation, the words from CFKB in the modal operator dictionary remain the granularity partitioning of usage, and those from other sources are described according to semantic granularity. Samples from the modal operator dictionary are shown in Fig. 1.

ID	词语	词性	来源	释义	例句	用法	情态标记	标记	全拼音
d_bi4ding4_1	必定	d	CFKB	表示判断的确凿或推论的必然	他这样说，"有他的道理。"〈x〉修饰形容词或动词短语。〈x〉		必然	mod_certainty	bi4ding4
d_xu3_1	许	d	CFKB	也许！或许。表示对情况的推测	那本书"是老张留下的吧〈x〉	大多数修饰动词"是"。〈x〉	或然	mod_possibility	xu3
d_xu3_2	许	d	CFKB	表示爱憎的肯定，带有商讨	东方红铁路当"是全国最大的	大多数修饰动词"是"。〈x〉	或然	mod_possibility	xu3
d_xu3_3	许	d	CFKB	表示对数量的估测，相当于	这杂鱼太大了，"三二十多斤	常修饰动词"有"、"要"。修饰	或然	mod_possibility	xu3
gs_bu4hao3bu5	不好不	gs	z	表示主体由于客观条件的限制	计算机已经邀请我好多次了，我"去。〈z〉		意愿	mod_intention	bu4hao3bu
vu_neng2_1	能	vu	h	表示具有某种能力或达到某种	计算机"模仿人的思维。〈z〉		能力	mod_ability	neng2
vu_neng2_2	能	vu	h	表示有条件或情理上许可。	明天的晚会家属也"参加。〈z〉		许可	mod_permission	neng2
d_bu4ke3bu4	不可不	d	CFKB	表示"必须"，加强肯定的	行于所当行，止于所"止。〈x〉修饰动词或动词短语。〈x〉		要求	mod_requirement	bu4ke3bu4
d_guai4bu5de5	怪不得	d	CFKB	表示醒悟（明白了原因，不再	"这么冷〈b〉"吐下"修饰形容词或动词最小句。〈x〉		评注-料惜	mod_comment_1	guai4bu5d
d_xing4er2_1	幸而	d	CFKB	指由于某种有利条件而侥幸	没遇到明天这样出发，"我们早一般用在主谓前。"…"。		评注-庆幸	mod_comment_3	xing4er2
jing4gan3	竟敢	v		出乎意料的大胆。〈z〉	在光天化日之下胆你为]你"酒后驾车，真不象话。[胆敢-意外			mod_comment_4	jing4gan
d_zui4hao3	最好	d	CFKB	表示"最为合适"，多用于	这些整人的话，"别说〈x〉"还是把时期事情调查清楚，在		建议	mod_advice	zui4hao3
v_pei4	配	v	h	够得上资格、符合。	只有这样的人，才"称为先进工作者。		评判	mod_judgement	pei4
d_nan2dao4_1	难道	d	CFKB	加强反问语气。〈b〉	"让我们看一下都介么？〈b〉句末常有"吗"。〈z〉用于动		反诘	mod_rhetorical	nan2dao4
d_fan3dao4	反倒	d	CFKB	表示转折语气。〈x〉表示跟原	我好意劝他，他"倒我多事〈z〉常用于后一小句，引出与前		转折	mod_torsion	fan3dao4

Fig. 1. Examples of the modal operator dictionary

ID in the modal operator dictionary is constructed based on the coding rules[22,23] of CFKB, and these words extracted from CFKB still remain the ID codes in CFKB. For example, in Figure 1，"许[yu](*maybe*)" has three semantic meanings ("d_xu3_1", "d_xu3_2" and "d_xu3_3")which all belong to the probability modality, while "能 [*neng*](*can*)" has two semantic meanings ("vu_neng2_1" and "vu_neng2_2") which belongs to ability modality and permission modality respectively. Except for the adverbs (d) and auxiliary (vu) included in the dictionary, a few verbs (v) and phrases(gs) such as the verbs "竟敢[*jinggan*](*how dare*)" and "配[*pei*](*be worthy of*)" representing a subjective emotion and judgment of the speaker respectively in the context, double negative phrase "不得不[*budebu*](*have to*) " which shows the subject voluntarily makes the only choice due to the limitation of the objective conditions, are also included in the modality dictionary as modality annotation unit. The parentheses mentioned in literature [1] as the modality markers, such as "我想呀[*woxiangya*](*I think*)", "我估计呀[*wogujiya*](*I guess*)", etc., are not included in modality dictionary. So far, the modality dictionary contains 298 operators and 186 of them come from CFKB, accounting for 62.4% of the total. The number of each modality operator is shown in Table 1.

4   Annotation and Analysis of Modality

Modality annotation mainly aims to annotate semantic function and scope of modal operators in the argument structure. The tags of "mod_category" (as shown in Table 1) are added as the symbol behind modal operators and "{}" is used to show their scope. In this way, the annotated sentence not only tells the scope dominated by verbal composition, but also shows that the language expression of modality in " {}" is a non-reality assertion.

We have preliminarily annotated the modal operators and their scopes in 10634 segmented sentences which have been marked basic proposition arguments. In the annotated corpus, modal operators have been annotated 2024 times, and a total number of 146 modal operators appeared. Frequencies of top 10 annotated words' tag is listed in Table 2. They amounted to 1082 times, accounted for over 50% of the total annotation frequency.

Table 2. Top-10 words' tag in corpus

Word&tag	No.	Word&tag	No.
<必须[*bixu*](*must*)>mod_requirement	214	<能[*neng*] (*can*)>mod_ability	94
<别[*bie*] (*don't*)>mod_requirement	173	<能[*neng*] (*might*)>mod_possiblity	87
<不要[*buyao*] (*don't*)>mod_requirement	117	<想[*xiang*](*want to*)>mod_intention	77
<可以[*keyi*](*may*)>mod_permission	95	<要[*yao*](*want to*)>mod_intention	70
<会[*hui*](*might*)>mod_possiblity	95	<要[*yao*](*should*)>mod_requirement	60

In the process of annotation, special cases listed below are marked with different ways.

1) Co-occurrence of modal operators and negation operators

There are positive form and negative form in possibility modality and acquittal modality. As far as possibility modality, the positive form can be divided into probability and certainty, so be the negative form. Relationship between these two forms is that proposing negation to the positive form of a probability modal component will produce a negation form of certainty. For example, "可能[kneng](may)" is of probability modality, and "不可能[bukeneng](impossible)" is of certainty modality. On the contrary, proposing negation to the positive form of a certainty modal component will produce a negation form of probability. For instance, "一定[yiding](must)" is of certainty modality, and "不一定[buyiding](uncertain) " is of probability modality.

The modality annotation is only a part of the semantic annotation, and negative meaning of the sentence should also be considered. As a result, if negative operators (like "不[bu](not)") and modal operators co-occur, modality and negativity should be annotated separately. Then, corresponding modality can be determined by logic calculation. In sentence (21), "不[bu](not)" is negative, and "可能[keneng](may) " is probability modality, while "不可能[bukeneng](impossible) " means certainty modality. In this case, " 不 [bu](not)" (temporarily set mark as "neg") and " 可能 [keneng](may) " will be marked respectively. Annotated result is shown in sentence (21).

(21) 他 {<不[bu](not)>neg   {<可能[keneng](may)>mod_possibility 在六点钟回到家}}。 (It is impossible for him to get home at six o'clock.}}

2) Same word belongs to different modal meanings

In the modal operator dictionary, some words belong to multiple modality categories. In Figure 1, "能[neng](can)" belongs to both ability category and permission category. For sentence (5) and (8), it's easy to distinguish which type of modality it belongs depending on the context. But in sentence (22), due to the lack of context, "能 [neng](can) " can be interpreted as "ability" or "permission". It's hard to distinguish which category it belongs to. Two annotations should be marked temporally in this situation. See sentence (22) and (23).

(22) 比 尔 不 {< 能 [neng](can)>mod_permission 骑 那 匹 马 } , 但 黛 安 娜 {< 能 [neng](can)>mod_permission}。 (Bill cannot ride that horse, but Diana can.}

(23) 比 尔 不 {< 能 [neng](can)>mod_ability 骑 那 匹 马 } , 但 黛 安 娜 {< 能 [neng](can)>mod_ability} 。 (Bill has not the ability to ride that horse, but Diana has.)

5 Conclusions

Aiming for deep semantic understanding, we firstly integrated the existing research results and constructed the modality annotation classification framework. And then we built the modal operator dictionary on the basis of the CFKB. Finally, we established rules of modality annotation, and annotated modal operators appeared in 10634 sentences.

So far we have only carried out a preliminary discussion of modality annotation framework. The annotation of coexisting of multiple modalities and that of modality and negative will be covered in the next phase of work. We will try to annotate more typical sentences, and develop machine learning methods to automatically annotate modal operators on the base of annotated corpus. Meanwhile, according to abstract semantic structure, further analysis and annotation of tense and aspect components, mood components and tone components will be taken for the deep semantic understanding combining with the modality annotation results. In addition, as an important mark of modality analytic form of modal operator for distinguishing reality assertion and non-reality assertion, modality annotation achievements could be tried to apply in subjective sentence recognition, or consumption intention exploration and other fields.

Acknowledgments. We thank the anonymous reviewers for their constructive comments, and gratefully acknowledge the support of National Basic Research Program of China(2014CB340504), National Natural Science Foundation of China (No.61402419, No.60970083), National Social Science Foundation (No.14BYY096), Basic research project of Science and Technology Department of Henan Province(No. 142300410231,No.142300410308) and Key Technology Project of the Education Department of Henan Province (No.12B520055, No. 13B520381, No. 15A520098).

References

1. Zhang, X.H.: An Initial Study on Modality Category of Modern Chinese. Master Thesis. Sichuan Normal University, Chengdu(2008).(In Chinese)

2. He,Y.: On the Modality System of Modern Written Chinese. Journal of Renmin University of China, Vol.6No.5:59-66(1992)(In Chinese)

3. Qi, H.Y.: Modality Words and Modality System. Anhui Education Press, Hefei (2002)(In Chinese)

4. Wen, S. L.: Study on Pragmatics Plane of Modern Chinese. Beijing Library Press, Beijing(2001)(In Chinese)

5. Lu, C.: Grammar Subjective Information and Modality Tag of Chinese. China Commercial Press, Shanghai(2003)(In Chinese)

6. Peng, L.Z.: On Modality of Modern Chinese. Doctor Dissertation. Fudan University, Shanghai(2005)(In Chinese)

7. Xiao,X.Q.:Analysis of Syntax and Semantic of Model Adverb. Journal of Language Studies, Vol.2003No.4:10-17(2003)(In Chinese)

8. Deng, Y.Q.: Modern Chinese Probabilistic Modality Logics Study. Master Thesis.Guangxi Normal University, Nanning(2006)(In Chinese)

9. Zhou, Z.L.:Study on Chinese Modal Adverbs Denoting "Certain". Master Thesis.Shanghai Normal University, Shanghai(2007)(In Chinese)

10. Yao, J.: Study on Chinese Modal Adverbs Denoting "Probable". Master Thesis.Shanghai Normal University, Shanghai(2005)(In Chinese)

11. Chen, B.Y.: Studies on Chinese Modality Adverbs Denoting "subjective Wishes". Master Thesis.Fujian Normal University, Fuzhou(2007)(In Chinese)

12. Zhu, L.: Conjectural Modality and Conjectural Modality Adverbs. Master Thesis.Fujian Normal University, Fuzhou(2005)(In Chinese)

13. Qu, H.Y.: The Function of the Interrogative Adverbs. Master Thesis. Yanbian University, Yanji(2004)(In Chinese)

14. Qi, H.Y., Ding C.C.: A Study on Negative Function of Interrogative Modal Adverbs.Journal of Chinese Learning,Vol.2006No.5:4-13(2006)(In Chinese)

15. Deng, X.L.: Studies on Chinese Modality Adverbs Denoting "Comprehend". Master Thesis.Shanghai Normal University, Shanghai(2005).(In Chinese)

16. Luo, S.L.: A Pragmatic Function Analysis on Modality Adverbs of "Jingran" Category. Master Thesis.Guangxi Normal University, Nanning(2007)(In Chinese)

17. Ma, S.J.: Study on Chinese "Persuading" Modality Adverbs. Master Thesis. Henan University, Kaifeng(2008)(In Chinese)

18. Wang, W.: Semantic Representation of Mandarin Modal *neng*(can) in Communications. Journal of Zhongguo Yuwen,Vol.2000No.3:238-246(2000)(In Chinese)

19. Zhang, Q.: The Research of the Volitive Auxiliary "Keyi" in Teaching Chinese as a Foreign Language. Master Thesis. Huazhong Normal University,Shanghai(2014)(In Chinese)

20. Sheng, L.C.:A Functional Analysis of the Probable Modal Adverbs "Dagai", "Yexu" and "Kongpa". Master Thesis. Yanbian University, Yanji(2003)(In Chinese)

21. Baker, K., Bloodgood, M., Dorr, B. J., Filardo, N. W., Levin, L., Piatko, C.: A modality Lexicon and its Use in Automatic Tagging. In Proceedings of LREC'10, Valletta, Malta. ELRA, 1402-1407.

22. Zan, H.Y., Zhang, K.L., Zhu, X. F., Yu, S.W.: Research on the Chinese Function Word Usage Knowledge Base. International Journal on Asian Language Processing.Vol.21 No.4: 185-198(2011)

23. Zhang, K.L.,Zan, H.Y.,et al.: A Survey on the Chinese Function Word Usage Knowledge Base. Journal of Chinese Information Processing.Vol.9 No.3:1-8(2015)(In Chinese)

The Construction of Sentence-Based Diagrammatic Treebank

Tianbao Song, Weiming Peng, Jihua Song(✉), Dongdong Guo, and Jing He

College of Information Science and Technology, Beijing Normal University, Beijing 100875, China

{songtianbao,dongdongguo,hejing8}@mail.bnu.edu.cn,
{pengweiming,songjh}@bnu.edu.cn

Abstract. The Sentence-based Diagrammatic Treebank is built under the annotation scheme of diagrammatic Chinese syntactic analysis. This scheme implements Sentence Component Analysis (SCA) as its main idea and highlights the importance of sentence pattern structure. This paper first reviews the researches on diagrammatic Chinese syntactic analysis, then illustrates the typical characteristics of this Treebank around sentence pattern structure, and then introduces the engineering implementation of this Treebank from the perspective of practice.

Keywords: Sentence-based Diagrammatic Treebank · Sentence Component Analysis · Sentence Pattern Structure

1 Introduction

Building large-scale annotated corpus is the foundation of natural language processing and also a cutting-edge subject in corpus linguistics research [1]. Treebank is a kind of text corpus that has annotated syntactic or semantic sentence structure under certain annotation schema based on some kind of grammar theory [2]. In the field of Chinese information processing, phrase structure Treebank and dependency Treebank are the two main categories, both of which have adopted Analytical Hierarchy Process (AHP) advocated by the structuralism grammar school. The typical Treebanks of these two categories in China are the TCT Treebank built by Tsinghua University and the CDT Treebank built by Harbin Institute of Technology [3].

Phrase structure Treebank considers syntactic analysis of the sentence as hierarchical structure analysis of phrases. In this kind of Treebank, a sentence is broken down into its Immediate Constituent (IC) and analysis is based on these ICs. Dependency Treebank considers syntactic analysis of the sentence as relation analysis of words. In this kind of Treebank, a sentence is determined by its words and the relations between them. Both phrase structure and dependency can be regarded as IC analysis, and IC analysis is the core of AHP.

In Chinese grammar teaching and research, besides AHP, Sentence Component

© Springer International Publishing AG 2016
M. Dong et al. (Eds.): CLSW 2016, LNAI 10085, pp. 306–314, 2016
DOI: 10.1007/978-3-319-49508-8_29

Analysis (SCA) is another kind of grammar theory that is advocated by the traditional grammar school. It takes "sentence component", such as Subject, Predicate and Object, as the basic element of analysis and emphasizes the integral pattern of the sentence. In terms of Chinese grammar teaching and research, especially in the field of teaching Chinese as a foreign language, educational thoughts have been transformed from "structure-based teaching" into "function communication-based teaching". To fulfill the combination of grammar and communication function, sentence pattern structure plays an irreplaceable role. But both phrase structure and dependency focus on the hierarchical division and relation description in the aspect of phrases and do not take sentence pattern structure into account directly, thus causing the gap between Chinese information processing and grammar teaching and research.

This paper will use the method of SCA to build a Sentence-based Diagrammatic Treebank on Chinese teaching materials. The formal scheme of this Treebank has been introduced in previous research papers, but many detailed and important problems have not been mentioned. So we first review the previous researches, and then discuss some problems that are inevitable during the construction of Treebank including the typical characteristics around sentence pattern structure and the engineering implementation.

2   Reviews of Previous Researches

The Sentence-based Diagrammatic Treebank is built under the annotation scheme of diagrammatic Chinese syntactic analysis that is based on the grammar theory created by linguist Li Jinxi. This grammar theory claims to do grammatical analysis from the perspective of sentence and emphasizes the syntactic structure of "sentence component". Li designed the diagrammatic parsing method to demonstrate the sentence pattern structure in a diagram vividly [4].

An annotation schema for contemporary Chinese based on Li's grammar system was proposed by He Jing et al. for the first time [5]. Then a preliminary scheme of diagrammatic Chinese syntactic analysis was proposed by Peng Weiming et al., which improved Li's diagrammatic parsing method [6].

The latest research puts forward a new formal scheme of diagrammatic Chinese syntactic analysis, which combs the sentence pattern system to make it more normative and logical and adds lexical analysis into it [7]. This scheme still uses diagram to present the syntactic structure of sentence and XML to store data. But it classifies the sentence pattern structures into "basic sentence pattern", "extend sentence pattern", "complex sentence pattern" and "special sentence pattern and complex sentence" and adds lexical analysis process to analyze dynamic words and their structure modes. The diagram of each kind of sentence pattern structure is shown in Fig. 1.

The latest research has given the specification of syntactic and lexical analysis at the macroscopic level, but in the process of annotation, annotators still have a lot of confusions. The next two sections will explain the typical characteristics of this Treebank around sentence pattern structure and its engineering implementation respectively from the perspective of practice.

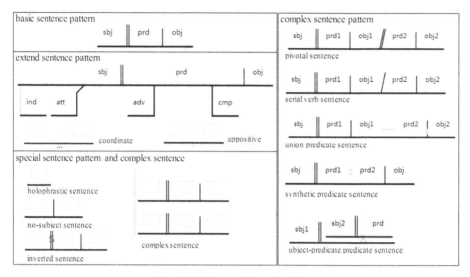

Fig. 1. Sentence pattern structures

3   Typical Characteristics

We attempt to bring sentence pattern structure into Chinese information processing and provide a new way of thinking for Chinese automatic syntactic analysis by the extraction and induction of fundamental sentence pattern structure and the analysis of argument structure around the predicate. So the key point in this Treebank is to keep the information and facilitate the extraction of sentence pattern structure. All the design principles are subjected to this point. This section will introduce the typical characteristics that have confused the annotators so as to explain the design principles.

3.1   Absence of Components

Subject, Predicate and Object in a sentence pattern structure can be omitted, but there must remain a corresponding position both in the diagram and in the XML storage. The examples of omitting these three components are shown in Fig. 2.

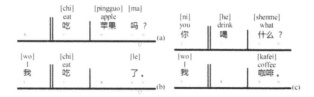

Fig. 2. Absence of components

From the perspective of Chinese information processing, not only does this contribute to maintaining the unity of sentence pattern structure，but also this can make it convenient to extract sentence pattern structure and analyze argument structure around the predicate.

From the perspective of Chinese grammar teaching and research, the omitted components indeed play a semantic role under certain context, so this analytical method conforms more to Chinese grammar teaching and research. For example, the sentences shown in Fig. 2(a)(b)(c) omit the Subject "你 (you)", the Object "饭 (meal)", and the Predicate "喝 (drink)" respectively.

3.2 Division of Clauses

The theory of "Clause driven Grammar" advocated by Xing Fuyi states that clause is the smallest grammatical unit which can make a statement independently and completely and that clause is in the central position among various kinds of Chinese grammar entities [8]. The Sentence-based Diagrammatic Treebank takes clause as the basic object to do syntactic analysis.

The division of clauses is based on the following principles. First, the clause must be followed by a pause usually marked by punctuations. Second, the clause must express a relatively complete meaning, i.e., it will make a statement. The text fragments that conform to the above principles are analyzed separately as clauses.

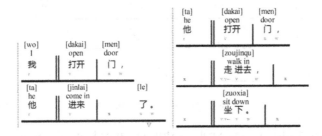

Fig. 3. Division of clauses

See the sentences shown in Fig. 3. The left one is divided into two clauses, and each one has the complete structure of SVO. The right one is a singular-topic paratactic sentence which is very common in Chinese. It contains three clauses, and each one makes a statement about the common Subject.

As for this kind of situation, many other Treebanks treat it as coordinate structure or consecutive predicate structure. Our analytical method can avoid too long sentence pattern structure and make sure that the components around the long horizontal trunk line in a diagram can represent a finite and definite sentence pattern structure.

3.3 Hierarchy of Sentence

All the sentences must be analyzed under constraints of the basic framework of sentence pattern structure. The components that cannot directly adhere to the trunk line according to the diagrammatic formula should use a hierarchical analytical method.

If the content on the position of nominal component is a VP or a clause, it should be scaffolded to produce a new pattern structure layer. The nominal component includes Subject, Object, the component after preposition, the component before localizers and the component in appositive structure. An example is shown in Fig. 4(a).

Fig. 4. Hierarchy on the position of nominal component and Predicate

If the content on the position of Predicate is a clause that has Subject or a Subject-Predicate phrase, it should be scaffolded to produce a new pattern structure layer. An example is shown in Fig. 4(b).

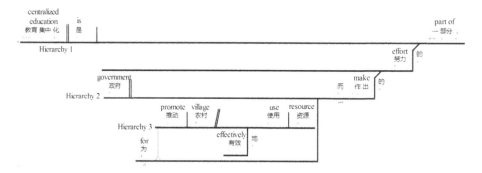

Fig. 5. Hierarchy of a sentence

Besides, a particular sentence pattern structure already implies some internal hierarchies like [subject-[adverbial-[[predicate-complement]-object]]], but when the component sequences in a sentence are beyond a certain range, the sentence needs the hierarchical analytical method. See the sentence shown in Fig. 5, it can be divided into three pattern structure layers around the predicate which have the corresponding node hierarchy in XML: (1) 教育集中化 ‖ 是 | (努力 的)一部分 (Centralized education is part of the effort); (2) 政府 ‖ [为{3}]作出 | 努力 (effort), (Government did sth. for sth.); (3) 政府 (government) ‖ 推动 | 农村 // [有效 地]使用 | 资源 (Sb. promotes the village to use resources effectively).

This hierarchical analytical method can avoid the ambiguity of the sentence pattern structure and make its extraction and induction more convenient.

3.4   Particularity of Complex Sentence Pattern

The complex sentence pattern in the Sentence-based Diagrammatic Treebank includes pivotal sentence, subject-predicate predicate sentence, synthetic predicate sentence, union predicate sentence and serial verb sentence. The first two types are in accordance with the mainstream Treebanks, while the last three types have some special characteristics. The examples are shown in Fig. 6.

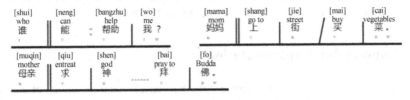

Fig. 6. Complex sentence pattern

The synthetic predicate sentence refers to the sentences that have the structure of "S || V_1 : V_2 | O" in which V_1 is an generalized auxiliary verb including modal verb and directional verb such as "来 (lai)". "是 (be) + NP" and "V + directional verb" are not treated as synthetic predicate. So the synthetic predicate here is slightly different from that in the "Temporary System of Chinese Teaching Grammar" [9].

This kind of structure is usually processed as verb-object structure or adverbial-head structure in other Treebanks, but considering that V_2 semantically plays a more important role than V_1 and V_1 conforms to the characteristics of predicate, we import the synthetic predicate sentence.

The serial verb sentence refers to the sentences that have the structure of "S || V_1 | O_1 / V_2 | O_2" in which V_1 and V_2 have a strict sequential relationship. The sentences in which V_1 and V_2 have other relationships similar to complex sentence such as co-ordinate relation, selection relation and so on are treated as union predicate sentence.

3.5   Lexical Analysis

The definition of word in Chinese is a difficult problem because Chinese has no white space to mark word boundaries and Chinese words are lacking in morphological signs and morphological changes. In the field of Chinese information processing, this problem is solved by the specification of word segmentation and lexicon. Although the lexicon has recorded a part of phrases, there are still a lot of words in linguistics not included. So some tasks of lexical analysis are done through syntactic analysis causing the higher complexity of syntactic analysis.

In the Sentence-based Diagrammatic Treebank, it also brings about some other problems. First, some words such as "大灰狼 (timber wolf)" and "小白兔 (little white rabbit)" are regarded as a whole in Chinese teaching and learning, so it is not reasonable to segment them especially in our Treebank that seeks to find a balance between Chinese information processing and Chinese grammar teaching and research. The two examples are analyzed as "小白兔 (n:a↗a↗n)" and "大灰狼 (n:a↗a↗n)" respectively. Second, lexical analysis can avoid the sentence pattern structure being too many and diverse, for example, "调酒师 (bartender)" and "办事员 (clerk)" that have the same internal structure of "n:v↗n↗n" will result in different sentence pattern structures without lexical analysis, because not both of them are in dictionary. Third, the segmentation of some words may cause the backbone components not to form a correct sentence. Forth, the ambiguity in the definition of word brings up the inconsistency problems during the construction of Treebank.

Based on the analysis above, we add lexical analysis process to get dynamic words and their structure modes during the construction of Treebank.

4   Engineering Implementation

For the construction of Treebank, having only theoretical specification is not enough. This section will introduce the engineering implementation of the Sentence-based Diagrammatic Treebank from the perspective of practice.

4.1   Supporting Tool

A convenient and efficient annotation tool plays a vital role in the construction of Treebank. An annotation tool of Client-Server mode for the construction of Sentence-based Diagrammatic Treebank was developed by Peng Weiming [10]. Yang Tianxin et al. implemented an annotation tool of Browser-Server mode [11]. Zhao Min et al. optimized the tool aiming at its shortcomings [12].

We improve the human-computer interaction graphical interface of the tool to make it accord more with people's cognitive psychology, and simplify the operation steps and methods in order to improve the annotation efficiency. What is much more important is that we integrate the theoretical specification into the annotation tool so as to guarantee the uniformity between specification and annotation process and the consistency among different annotators.

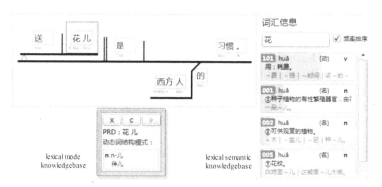

Fig. 7. Supporting tool

Take the sentence shown in Fig. 7 as an example. The tool does not allow the annotators to split the Subject of sentence directly into the predicate-object structure, and the only way to solve it is using the scaffold to avoid the incorrect analysis. The tool integrates the "Modern Chinese Dictionary" as its lexical semantic knowledgebase. When a diagrammatic unit matches with some item in the knowledge-base, the tool will list the semantic information of this item including Chinese phoneticize, parts of speech, meaning, use cases and so on. The tool gets and displays the statistical distribution of semantic information for each item, and the dominant semantic information can be annotated automatically. Besides, the tool integrates a lexical mode knowledge-base so as to display the lexical modes in accordance with a diagrammatic unit dynamically. If a diagrammatic unit matches with a specific mode in the lexical mode knowledge-base, it can be annotated automatically.

4.2   Audit and Management Mechanism

In the construction of Sentence-based Diagrammatic Treebank, we adopt a strict audit and management mechanism.

All sentences must undergo preliminary annotation stage and the audit stage. In preliminary annotation stage, each sentence can be annotated by multiple annotators, and the annotation results will not be directly stored into the main table in Treebank. The auditors examine the annotation results and choose the correct one to go into the main table or return the incorrect ones to the annotators for modification. The tool provides the bidirectional communication channels through which the annotators can submit questions and the auditors can express audit opinions. High frequency questions will be sorted out and published on the annotation platform.

4.3   Effective Searching

During the construction of Treebank, there will be inevitably some incorrect or inconsistent annotations. In such circumstances, the annotators may need to refer to or modify the previous annotations. The annotation tool provides effective searching methods including searching based on keywords, searching based on regular expressions and searching based on XPath. The annotators can choose from these methods flexibly to search the sentences annotated or not annotated.

In addition, because the Treebank focus on the sentence pattern structure, each sentence is analyzed into a diagram that has strict linear and hierarchical structure, and the components in a sentence pattern structure have a relatively stable relationship, so it is convenient to use XPath to extract information directly, such as the Chinese grammar points [13], sentence pattern structures and so on.

5   Conclusion

The construction of Treebank is a laborious as well as significant project. This paper introduces the key problems during the construction of Sentence-based Diagrammatic Treebank from both the aspects of theory and engineering practice. The sentence-based Treebank adopts the grammar theory of SCA, which is different from the mainstream Treebanks. It tries to search for a balance between Chinese information processing and Chinese grammar teaching and research from the perspective of sentence pattern structure. We build this Treebank based on Chinese teaching materials, and up to now we have more than 30,000 sentences that have been annotated syntactic and lexical information. The Treebank will be released soon, and we hope that it can make some contributions to both Chinese information processing and Chinese grammar teaching and research. Meanwhile we hope that related scholars can use it and give valuable suggestions.

Acknowledgement. Supported by: Beijing Normal University Young Teachers Fund Project (No: 2014NT39).

References

1. Jurafsky, D., Martin, JH.: Speech and Language Processing. Pearson Education India (2000)
2. Manning, CD., Schütze, H.: Foundations of Statistical Natural Language Processing. The MIT Press, Cambridge (1999)
3. Jihua, S., Erhong, Y., Qiangjun, W.: Chinese Information Processing, p. 94. China Higher Education Press, Beijing (2011)
4. Jinxi, L.: A New Chinese Grammar. The Commercial Press, Beijing (2001)
5. He, J., Peng, W., Song, J., Liu, H.: Annotation schema for contemporary chinese based on JinXi Li's grammar system. In: Liu, P., Su, Q. (eds.) CLSW 2013. LNCS, vol. 8229, pp. 668–681. Springer, Heidelberg (2013)
6. Weiming, P., Jihua, S., Ning, W.: Design of Diagrammatic Parsing Method of Chinese Based on Sentence Pattern Structure. Computer Engineering and Applications 50(06), 11–18 (2014)
7. Peng, W., Song, J., Sui, Z., Guo, D.: Formal Schema of Diagrammatic Chinese Syntactic Analysis. In: Lu, Q, Gao, H.H. (eds.) CLSW 2015. LNCS. vol. 9332, pp. 701-710. Springer, Heidelberg (2015)
8. Fuyi, X. The theory of clause as nucleus. Chinese Language. 06, 420-428(1995)
9. Zhigong, Z.: Grammar and Grammar Teaching: Introduction to the Temporary Grammatical System. People's Education Press, Beijing (1956)
10. Weiming, P.: Digital Platform Construction of Sentence-based Grammar and Its Application Study. Beijing Normal University, Beijing (2012)
11. Tianxin, Y., Weiming, P., Jihua, S.: High Efficiency Syntax Tagging System Based on the Sentence Pattern Structure. Journal of Chinese Information Processing 04, 43–49 (2014)
12. Min, Z., Weiming, P., Jihua, S.: Development and Optimization of Syntax Tagging Tool on Diagrammatic Treebank. Journal of Chinese Information Processing 06, 26–33 (2014)
13. Zhang, Y., Song, J., Zhu, X., Peng, W.: The Identification of Grammar Points in International Chinese Language Teaching Materials Based on Sentence-Based Annotation. In: International Conference of Educational Innovation through Technology (EITT), pp.29-36 IEEE Press, New York (2014).

Dictionary as Corpus:
A Study Case to Reveal the Statistical Trend of Polysyllablization of Chinese Vocabulary

Bing QIU[1,2]

[1] Faculty of Humanities and Social Sciences, Beijing Language and Culture University, Beijing, China
[2] Department of Chinese Language Studies, Faculty of Humanities, The Education University of Hong Kong, Hong Kong, China

bingqiu@tom.com

Abstract. From a macro-level viewpoint, a dictionary is indeed a lexical corpus. 漢語大詞典(*Han Yu Da Ci Dian*, or literally *the Comprehensive Dictionary of Chinese Words*), as a summary of ancient and modern vocabulary, provides abundant information with respect to its construction of entry. Based on the classification of entry's emerging year in it, the information of new-created words in different periods is obtained to analyze the development of Chinese vocabulary system. Thus the quantitative trend of polysyllablization in different periods is revealed, which demonstrate a novel perspective of Chinese historical lexicology as a study case. The lexical evidence for the periodization of the historical Chinese language is also discussed.

Keywords: Corpus · Polysyllablization · Chinese historical lexicology

1 Introduction

Corpus linguistics is one of the fastest-growing methodologies in contemporary linguistics.(Stefan 2009) It was noticed, in the recent years, a shift in the way some linguists find and utilize data. Lots of paper use corpora as their primary data.

A corpus is a large, principled collection of naturally occurring examples of language. As one of the most important dictionaries in Chinese lexicology study, 漢語大詞典 (*Han Yu Da Ci Dian*, literally *the Comprehensive Dictionary of Chinese Words*, abbreviated as CDCW in the following text) itself is a corpus for historical lexical research.

CDCW has been widely referred to during these twenty years since the publication of the first volume in 1986. According to the incomplete statistics by the writer, there are nearly ten academic works and more than 2,000 journal and conference papers and dissertations which are in relation to CDCW.

In general, these researches can be divided into two categories: taking it as a searching tool of certain words, e.g. Qi (2000), Liu (2007) etc., and detecting the

© Springer International Publishing AG 2016
M. Dong et al. (Eds.): CLSW 2016, LNAI 10085, pp. 315–324, 2016
DOI: 10.1007/978-3-319-49508-8_30

weaknesses of it based on achieved researches of lexicology, such as the omission of entries and examples, the wrong judgment of word's emerging year, the lack of textual criticism of examples, and so on, which offers the basic support for the revision of *The Comprehensive Dictionary of Chinese Words*, e.g. Wang (1990), Wu (1997), Shi (1998) etc. Supplementary to each other, these two researches promote the development of the study of Chinese lexicology, as well as dictionary itself.

However, most of present researches focus on the micro-level, namely the search, verification, correction and supplement of certain words, and few of them explore its value from the macroscopic corpus linguistics perspective.

When referring to the macroscopic importance of CDCW, Lv (1982) defines it as an archive of ancient and modern vocabulary. And Xu (1994) further even argues that "before the publication of CDCW, there is no such a dictionary, which includes ancient and 'not ancient and not modern' words". "With it, researchers not only can, from a diachronic perspective, observe the change of one word in different periods, but also can, from a synchronic perspective, analyze the semantic structure of a group of words in one period. Apart from that, such a magnificent historic dictionary itself is a database of great value, for it collects hundreds of thousands of ancient and modern words from abundant materials, and arranges and explains them in a certain sequence." Both Lv and Xu regard CDCW as a lexical database from the point of view of corpus linguistics.

There are about fifty million characters in CDCW, and the number of polysyllabic word entries is around three hundred and seventy-five thousand. As a grand dictionary, CDCW, from the corpus viewpoint, provides us with abundant information through the construction of entries, the arrangement of sense and the explanation of meaning etc. If we compare CDCW to a mountain, the present works mainly focus on the handling of stones, while ignore the present of panorama of it.

Therefore, if we can cross the boundary of concrete words and analyze CDCW from an aspect of corpus linguistics with corresponding methods, it will make a great contribution to the deep study of it and to the improvement of Chinese lexicology study.

In the following sections, CDCW will be explored as a valuable corpus. By this means, we will endeavor to reveal the quantitative tendency of the polysyllablization of Chinese vocabulary as a study case in order to demonstrate the macro academic value of the dictionary as a corpus.

2   Perspective and Methodology

From an aspect of corpus linguistics, hundreds of thousands of entries in CDCW offer a wealth of information and therefore, reveal relative rules of vocabulary. Because of the variety of entry's features, such as part of speech, meaning, form of pronunciation and construction, this paper particularly takes the emerging year of entry as it research focus. And due to its indication of word's formation time, the emerging year is of great value to historical lexicology. In CDCW, the definitions of entries usually contain several senses, and most of them can be testified by examples in books. According to the emerging year of the example, we can deduce the formation time of the word.

Taking the disyllablic word文化(Wen Hua, culture) as an example, it has four senses in CDCW, and the first one is 文治教化(Wen Zhi Jiao Hua, political doctrine), which is first seen in 劉向《說苑•指武》(Liu Xiang's Shuo Yuan·Zhi Wu of the Western Han Dynasty). All the other examples are seen in books appeared after the Western Han Dynasty, thus indicating that the word 文化 is first used in Western Han Dynasty.

Figure 1 is an example of the analysis of emerging time. Supposing we can draw the conclusion from its emerging time of word entry 1 that it emerges in Han Dynasty, we can, theoretically, deduce the appearing time of all words in CDCW.

Given that the previous step is practical, we can achieve all the new words in one period through gathering words produced at the same time in *The Comprehensive Dictionary of Chinese Words*. Taking Figure 1 as an instance, by assuming that word entry 1 and 3 and so on are created in the Western Han Dynasty, we can draw the conclusion, if we take the year as the index to gather all the words generated in Western Han Dynasty, then will get word entry 1 and 3 and so on.

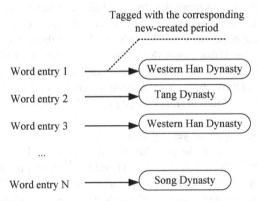

Fig. 1. The emerging years of examples and deduction of their new-created times

By the analysis of the production of new words in different periods, we can see the overall development of Chinese vocabulary system from a macro perspective. However, although it is theoretically feasible to sum up the emerging year of all entries in CDCW, the workload to analyze more than three hundred thousand words is too huge. As a result, this paper applies the method of random sampling, analyzing the randomly chosen entries and accordingly deducing the general feature of all entries.

The specific steps of the method are as follows:

1. Choosing quite a number of examples randomly from more than three hundred entries in *The Comprehensive Dictionary of Chinese Words*, and determining the emerging year of each entry by checking the sense and its quotation book;
2. Counting the number of polysyllabic words of examples in different periods which is on the basis of the emerging year of new words

3. Calculating the amount of polysyllabic words and presenting the quantitative tendency of polysyllablization in the form of figures

It is of no doubt that there are some omissions and mistakes in CDCW and the new words of certain period it includes are not completely equal to all the new words indeed created in that period. Nevertheless, the definition and explanation in CDCW are the products of more than 1,000 experts; thus, compared with the number of entries, the proportion of deficiencies and errors in this dictionary is comparatively low. As "the archive of ancient and modern vocabulary", CDCW has been one of the most authoritative dictionaries in the lexicology area so far. Therefore, it is practical and, to some extent, objective to do the diachronic research of lexicology from the perspective of entry's emerging year in CDCW.

3   Numerical Trend of Polysyllablization

This paper is based on the CD-ROM version of *The Comprehensive Dictionary of Chinese Words* which is published in 1998, and it includes 279,720 disyllabic words and 63,587 words of three or more than three syllables. Among them, 2,000 disyllabic words and 1,000 three-or-more syllabic ones are randomly chosen to be analyzed. Excluding the homophones in CDCW, only 1,904 disyllabic words (95.2% of the samples) and 876 polysyllabic words (87.6% of the samples) are valid.

According to the randomness of sampling theory, there is quite a large proportion of homophones in CDCW; thus, it is estimated that there about 266,293 disyllabic words (279,720×95.2%≈ 266,293) and 55,702 (63587×87.6%≈55,702) three-or-more-syllable words in it.

In the light of the emerging year of entries, there are 246 disyllabic words in the samples which are created in the pre-Qin period, occupying 12.9 percentages of the overall valid samples (246÷1,904≈12.9%). Therefore, the total number of words produced in the pre-Qin period in CDCW is around 34,406 (266,293×12.9%≈34,406). By analogy, we can estimate the amounts of words produced in different periods, which are shown in Table 1.

Table 1. Number of New-created words in different periods

Period	Syllables	Samples	Percent (%)	Count
Pre-Qin	=2	246	12.9	34406
	≥3	55	6.3	3497
	Subtotal			*37903*
Western Han	=2	135	7.1	18881
	≥3	33	3.8	2098
	Subtotal			*20979*
Eastern Han	=2	128	6.7	17902
	≥3	22	2.5	1399
	Subtotal			*19301*
	=2	115	6.0	16084

Jin	≥3	23	2.6	1462
	Subtotal			*17546*
Northern	=2	238	12.5	33287
and	≥3	48	5.5	3052
Southern				
Dynasties	*Subtotal*			*36339*
	=2	275	14.5	38461
Tang	≥3	97	11.1	6168
	Subtotal			*44629*
	=2	243	12.8	33986
Song	≥3	110	12.6	6995
	Subtotal			*40981*
Yuan,	=2	391	20.5	54685
Ming and	≥3	306	34.9	19458
Qing	*Subtotal*			*74143*
	=2	133	7.0	18601
Modern	≥3	182	20.8	11573
	Subtotal			*30174*
			Total	**321995**

Although Table 1 demonstrates the number of new-created polysyllabic words in different periods, it is unable to indicate the speed of word-creation. Taking the words of the Northern and Southern Dynasties and Tang Dynasty as an example, despite the fact that there are more new polysyllabic words in Tang Dynasty (36,339 in the Northern and Southern Dynasties and 44,629 in Tang Dynasty), it cannot be neglected that Tang Dynasty lasts for 327 years, while the Northern and Southern Dynasties only exist for 160 years. Consequently, if we calculate the average number of new-generated words, it is evident that the amount of polysyllabic words produced per year of Tang Dynasty is only as half as that of the Northern and Southern Dynasties (136 for Tang Dynasty and 227 for the Northern and Southern Dynasties). Therefore, it is of necessity to take the duration of each period into consideration when we calculate the rate of newly born words, and the result is presented in Table 2.

Figure 2 is the data graph of words produced each year, with the horizontal axis showing the year and the vertical presenting the annual number of new-created words.

Table 2. Number of New-created words per year in different periods

Period	Span (Years)	New-created word count	New-created words per year
Pre-Qin	about 1000	37903	37.9
Western Han	245	20979	85.6
Eastern Han	195	19301	99.0
Jin	200	17546	87.7
Northern and Southern	160	36339	227.1

Dynasties			
Tang	327	44629	136.5
Song	372	40981	110.2
Yuan, Ming and Qing	670	74143	110.7
Contemporary Period	44	30174	685.8

From Figure 2, we can find that the number enjoys an incline since the Western Han Dynasty, reaching to the peak in the Northern and Southern Dynasties with 227 new words created. After that, the speed shows a gradual slowdown, with 11 0 words produced each year from Song Dynasty to Qing Dynasty. When it comes to the contemporary Chinese, there was a fast growth of polysyllabic words. Although it was until 1949 that the words of contemporary Chinese were gathered, there were many words of the Opium War and the May 4th Movement; thus, in spite of some deviation of statistics, it generally reflects the rapid growth of contemporary Chinese.

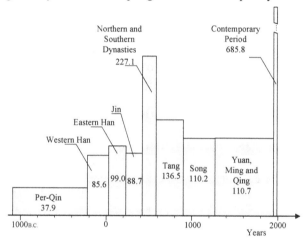

Fig. 2. The trend of polysyllablization of Chinese words

The Chinese vocabulary system of ancient times, which is represented by pre-Qin and the Western Han Dynasty, are predominated by monosyllabic words; while, for that of modern and contemporary Chinese which is after Tang and Song Dynasty, polysyllabic words are the main streams. Hence, polysyllablization is one of the crucial features of Chinese development, which is consistent with the statistics of entry's emerging year in CDCW. Zhu (1992) argues for the rapid growth of polysyllabic words (mainly disyllabic ones) in the Northern and Southern Dynasties, "although in the view of the inherent laws of Chinese development, disyllablization will be finally realized, it is quite a slow process before Wei and Jin Dynasty. And it is after the middle age that the process of disyllablization accelerates, fundamentally changing Chinese lexicology system (mainly in literature) which is predominated by monosyllabic words in a short period of two and three hundred years". All of these are in accordance with the quantitative tendency of polysyllablization. As a discreet work of more than one thousand researchers, it is not a coincidence that the macro information contained in CDCW is consistent with the result of historical lexicology, which, as a result, indicates the macro academic value of it in the area of lexicology. According to Guo (2011), there are more than six thousand published papers and more than eight hundred dissertations about vocabulary in middle age and modern Chinese, and quite a large proportion of them are concerned with polysyllablization. Nevertheless, because of the subjectivity in defining polysyllabic words and limitation of corpus (monograph), no overall quantitative features of lexicology system are achieved in academia. And researchers are still haunted by many problems: how the polysyllablization is achieved in Chinese vocabulary step by step, what is the degree of polysyllablization in different periods, whether the process of polysyllablization is at a constant rate or not, which period enjoys a dramatic growth and which witnesses a gentle increase. Therefore, it is of no doubt those drawing samples of entry's emerging year providing a new access to the quantitative analysis of polysyllablization, which directly provides the trend of polysyllablization and thus breaks through the predicament of polysyllablization researches.

4   Lexical Evidence for the Periodization of Chinese Language

Historical Chinese is usually divided into the following basic periods: Old Chinese, Middle Chinese and Modern varieties. The periodization of Chinese Language is determined by the evidences of phonology, syntactic or lexicology. However, there are kinds of periodization of historical Chinese. Bernhard Karlgren (1940) defines Middle Chinese as the historical variety of Chinese that is phonologically recorded in the Qieyun, a rime dictionary first published in 601. Wang (1957) figured that Middle Chinese covers from the 4th century to the 12th century. Liu (1959) considered that the span of Middle Chinese is mainly referred to as Wei Dynasty, Jin Dynasty and Northern and Southern Dynasties. Pan (1989) indicated that Middle Chinese began in the 3rd and ended in the 10th century. Zhu (1992) pointed out that Middle Chinese spans from Eastern Han Dynasty to Northern and Southern Dynasties.

Hence the polysyllablization is one of the crucial features of Chinese development. Our results provide novel quantitative evidences for the periodization of Chinese Language, as shown in Figure 3.

From Figure 3, we can find that the polysyllablization reaches to the peak near 600, which means Chinese language changed acutely in Northern and Southern Dynasties. Thus it implies that Northern and Southern Dynasties are the center of the span of Middle Chinese from the viewpoint of Chinese lexis. The conclusion agrees with other researchers, among which the intersection is obvious Northern and Southern Dynasties.

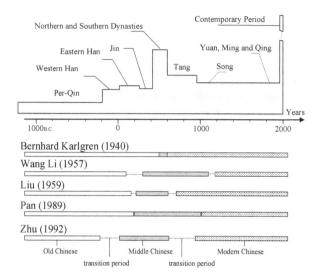

Fig. 3. Lexical evidence for the periodization of historical Chinese language

5   Conclusion

The academic value of CDCW can be recognized in many fields such as the field of linguistics, history and culture; but it is of the most direct and significant value for the study of Chinese lexicology. The relevant researches conducted in the academia in recent years not only promote the study in lexicology, but provide resourceful materials for the revision of CDCW. However, the existing researches mainly focus on the description and explanation of specific word or word of certain range, the macro academic value of the hundreds of thousands of vocabulary entries in CDCW from an aspect of corpus linguistics has not been fully explored for a long time.

CDCW is the archives for ancient and modern Chinese vocabulary. The vocabulary entries, selected by thousands of experts from thousands of ancient Chinese books and records, are of great authority. This paper, from the perspective of the emerging year of the vocabulary entry, judges and quantizes the classification of the formation time of the vocabulary in CDCW. Besides, this research aims to present the development status of ancient Chinese in different periods and provide the quantized basic data for the in-depth study of polysyllablization of Chinese vocabulary. As a result, it may exploit the abundant information of the dictionary in the macro level and offer a novel corpus perspective for the study of Chinese historical lexicology.

Acknowledgments. The work was supported by the key project of Humanities and Social Sciences sponsored by Ministry of Education of China (Grant No. 15JJD740001), the General Research Fund sponsored by the Research Grants Council of Hong Kong (Project No. 18600915), and the Faculty Project (No. 16YJ010003) and the Wutong Innovation Platform (No. 16PT07) of Beijing Language and Culture

University supported by the Fundamental Research Funds for the Central Universities of China.

References

1. Stefan Th. Gries. What is Corpus Linguistics? Language and Linguistics Compass, v3:1–17, doi:10.1111/j.1749-818x.2009.00149.x (2009)
2. Cheng Xiangqing. Study of the disyllabic words in Selected Chinese books. The Commercial Press, Beijing (2003) (程湘清. 汉语史专书复音词研究. 商务印书馆,北京 (2003)). (in Chinese)
3. Bernhard Karlgren. Chinese phonology. the Commercial Press, Beijing (1940) (高本汉. 1940. 中国音韵学研究. 商务印书馆,北京 (1940)) . (in Chinese)
4. Guo Zuofei. A brief summary of the study on the lexis of the middle and modern Chinese in the recent century(Part I). Frontier. 4:145-150 (2011) (郭作飞.中古近代汉语专书词汇研究的历史回望——百年中古近代汉语专书词汇研究述略（上）.前沿, 4:145-150 (2011)) . (in Chinese)
5. Guo Zuofei. A brief summary of the study on the lexis of the middle and modern Chinese in the recent century (Part II). Frontier. 6:141-143 (2011) (郭作飞.中古近代汉语专书词汇研究的历史回望——百年中古近代汉语专书词汇研究述略（上）.前沿, 6:141-143 (2011)) . (in Chinese)
6. Han Huiyan. On the formation of the polysyllabic words in *Shi Shuo Xin Yu*. Journal of Guyuan Teachers College. 1:19-24(1990). (韩惠言.《世说新语》复音构词方式初探. 固原师专学报,1:19-24 (1990)) . (in Chinese)
7. Liu Shiru. On the classifier in the Wei, Jin, southern and Northern Dynasties. Studies of the Chinese Language, 11 (1959) (刘世儒. 论魏晋南北朝的量词. 中国语文, 11 (1959)) . (in Chinese)
8. Liu Yanping. The monosemic metonymy words in *the Comprehensive Dictionary of Chinese Words*. Doctoral dissertation of Shandong University (2007) (刘艳平.《汉语大词典》单义项借代词语研究. 山东大学博士学位论文. (2007)). (in Chinese)
9. Lv Shuxiang. The nature and importanceof *the Comprehensive Dictionary of Chinese Words*. Lexicographical Studies. 3:1-3. (1982) (吕叔湘.《汉语大词典》的性质和重要性. 辞书研究. 3:1-3. (1982)). (in Chinese)
10. Pan YunZhong. A summary of the history of Chinese vocabulary. Shanghai ancient books Press (1989) (潘允中. 汉语词汇史概要. 上海古籍出版社,上海 (1989)) . (in Chinese)
11. Qi Xiaopeng. On the words of *Lun Heng* included by *the Comprehensive Dictionary of Chinese Words*. Master degree thesis of Hebei University (2000) (齐霄鹏.《汉语大词典》收录《论衡》词语研究. 河北大学硕士学位论文 (2000)) . (in Chinese)
12. Qiu Bing. Study on ancient Chinese polysyllabic words. Nanjing University press, Jiangsu Province (2012) (邱冰.中古汉语词汇复音化的多视角研究. 南京大学出版社,江苏南京. (2012)) . (in Chinese)
13. Qu Wenjun. The errors and amendments of *the Comprehensive Dictionary of Chinese Words*. Shandong People's Press. Jinan, Shandong Province (2012) (曲文军.《汉语大词典》疏误与修订研究. 山东人民出版社,山东济南. (2012)) . (in Chinese)
14. Shi Guanghui. Compilation problems of *the Comprehensive Dictionary of Chinese Words* from the words in *Qi Min Yao Shu*. Southeast academic. 5: 115-118. (1998) (史光辉. 从《齐民要术》看《汉语大词典》编纂方面存在的问题. 东南学术. 5:115-118. (1998)) . (in Chinese)

15. Wang Li. The history of Chinese Language. Zhonghua Press. Beijing (1957) (王力. 汉语 史稿. 中华书局, 北京. (1957)) . (in Chinese)

16. Wang Weihui. The errors and amendments of *the Comprehensive Dictionary of Chinese Words.* Journal of NingBo University. 2:86-90 (1990) (汪维辉. 《汉语大词典》摘瑕. 宁 波大学学报, 2:86-90 (1990)) . (in Chinese)

17. Wang Weihui. On the evolutionof common words from East Han Dynasty to Sui Dynasty. Nanjing University press, Jiangsu Province (2000) (汪维辉. 东汉－隋常用词演变研究. 南京大学出版社,江苏南京. (2000)) . (in Chinese)

18. Wang Ying. The amendments and supplements of *the Comprehensive Dictionary of Chinese Words.* Mount Huangshan Press, Hefei, Anhui Province, China (2006) (王瑛.《汉语 大词典》商补. 安徽合肥, 黄山书社(2006)) . (in Chinese)

19. Wu Jinhua. The amendments and supplements of *the Comprehensive Dictionary of Chinese Words.* Journal of Nanjing Normal University. 1:129-135 (1997) (吴金华.《汉语大 词典》商补.南京师范大学学报(社会科学版), 1:129-135. (1997)) . (in Chinese)

20. Xiang Yujian. Documentary tracing of *the Comprehensive Dictionary of Chinese Words.* Mount Huangshan Press, Hefei, Anhui Province, China (2012) (相宇剑 《汉语大词典》 书证溯源. 黄山书社,安徽合肥. (2012)) . (in Chinese)

21. Xu Wenkan. On the characteristics and academic value of *the Comprehensive Dictionary of Chinese Words.* Lexicographical Studies. v(3):36-45. (1994) (徐文堪. 略论《汉语大词 典》的特点和学术价值. 辞书研究. v(3):36-45. (1994)) . (in Chinese)

22. Zhu Qingzhi. On the influence of Buddhist scripture translation on the development of Chinese vocabulary in the middle ancient times. Studies of the Chinese Language, v(4): 297-305. (1992) (朱庆之. 试论佛典翻译对中古 汉语词汇发展的若干影响. 中国语文, v(4): 297-305. (1992)). (in Chinese)

Yet Another Resource to Sketch Word Behavior in Chinese Variation

Meng-Hsien Shih and Shu-Kai Hsieh

Graduate Institute of Linguistics, National Taiwan University,
Taipei, Taiwan (R.O.C.)
{d00142002,shukaihsieh}@ntu.edu.tw

Abstract. Most corpus-based lexical studies require considerable efforts in manually annotating grammatical relations in order to find the collocations of the target word in corpus data. In this paper, we claim that the current technique of natural language processing can facilitate lexical research by automating the annotation of these relations. We exploit the above technique and report an online open-resource for the comparison of lexical behaviors in cross-strait Chinese variations. The proposed resource is evaluated by juxtaposing the results with previous lexical research based on the same corpus data. The results show that our resource may provide more comprehensive and fine-grained grammatical collocation candidates in the case study.

Keywords: Lexical resource · Corpus construction · Chinese variation

1 Introduction to Grammatical Collocation Extraction

Collocation is *a tendency for words to occur together* [1]. In order to find word collocation, most researchers devote considerable efforts to manual annotation of the corpus data in corpus-based lexical studies. With the advancement of corpus development, however, there have been many lexical resources such as Word Sketch Engine[1] (WSE) [2] designed to display automatically extracted grammatical collocations.

For example, in Fig. 1 this online English resource shows that the collocations of the noun *team* include the words management, spirit, lead and so on, and each with the grammatical relations of modifier, verb-object, etc.

Among Chinese language resources, the Chinese WSE [3] has also applied these automatic techniques to large-scale corpus data in simplified Chinese and traditional Chinese corpora, which provides lexical comparison of language variation. In this paper, we will focus on similar construction of lexical resources for Chinese variation. The next section will briefly review the current issues of WSE and other resource; in Section 3 we describe the design of the proposed approach and the corpus data used in our lexical resource; Section 4 discusses the evaluation issue and presents a case study based on our results; in Section

---

[1] http://www.sketchengine.co.uk

© Springer International Publishing AG 2016
M. Dong et al. (Eds.): CLSW 2016, LNAI 10085, pp. 325–332, 2016
DOI: 10.1007/978-3-319-49508-8_31

team *(noun)* Alternative PoS: verb (478)
British National Corpus (BNC) freq = 22,482 (200.21 per million)

modifiers of "team" 13,919 0.62		nouns and verbs modified by "team" 3,166 0.14		verbs with "team" as object 4,616 0.21		verbs with "team" as subject 6,300 0.28		"team" and/or ... 2,244 0.10	
management +	433 9.31	spirit +	112 9.15	lead +	205 8.48	win	98 7.97	football	12 7.15
management team		*team spirit*		*head*	63 8.26	*team won*		cast	8 6.75
football +	207 8.63	mate	53 8.75	*team headed by*		play +	105 7.86	search	9 6.71
football team		*his team mates*		join +	113 8.04	work +	109 7.53	group	31 6.55
project +	166 8.35	leader +	133 8.26	pick	47 7.79	*team working*		squad	7 6.55
the project team		*team leader*		field	26 7.43	lose	40 6.78	individual	12 6.41
england +	143 8.05	coach	40 8.09	assemble	25 7.17	*team lost*		husband	12 6.37
the england team		*the team coach*		beat	34 7.01	consist	31 6.78	*husband and wife team*	
research +	164 7.83	manager +	133 8.05	negotiate	26 7.00	*team consists of*		player	10 6.35
the research team		*team manager ,*		*negotiating team*		perform	27 6.74	supporter	7 6.19
rescue	98 7.76	member +	197 8.01	captain	18 6.92	compete	22 6.70	afternoon	7 6.17
mountain rescue team		*team members*		send	55 6.86	*teams competing in*		fan	6 6.11
display	91 7.60	effort	72 7.94	strengthen	22 6.79	find	57 6.55	panel	6 6.11
the national display team		*a team effort*		investigate	27 6.77	*team found*		specialist	6 6.08
cup	96 7.45	championship	49 7.77	*the investigating team*		comprise	21 6.46	sale	10 6.07
cup team		*team championship*		select	27 6.74	*team comprising*		member	16 6.01
design	87 7.38	selection	38 7.73	visit	36 6.53	prepare	22 6.45	department	10 5.93
the design team		*team selection .*		*visiting teams*		take +	105 6.36	management	12 5.91
care	90 7.32	captain	28 7.65			*team took*		manager	13 5.88

Fig. 1. Word sketch of the English noun *team* (Source: www.sketchengine.co.uk)

5 we demonstrate our online system; this paper ends with a conclusion of the proposed lexical resource for Chinese variation research.

2 Toward Grammatical Collocations as Dependency Relations

Among the resources of automatically extracting grammatical collocations from sentences, the WSE used regular expressions over part-of-speech (POS) tags to achieve this. For instance, to capture the verb-object relation, they would manually devise the following expression:

```
1:V (DET | NUM | ADJ | ADV | N)* 2:N
```

That is, for any sequence that matches the following condition, the first word would be treated as the 1st argument (verb) in the verb-object relation, with the ending word as the 2nd argument (object): the condition in which the first word is tagged as V followed by either a determiner, number, adjective or noun, and the ending word tagged as N.

Although the Chinese version of WSE[2] has gained its popularity among corpus linguists and language teachers [4] [5] [6] [7], it is proprietary, limited to 27 grammatical relations, and requires a POS-annotated corpus in advance. In the following study, we will investigate the approach of exploiting a dependency parser to automatically tag 45 relations, which can also be applied upon a raw corpus even without any segmentation if necessary.

---

[2] http://wordsketch.ling.sinica.edu.tw

Unlike the more known constituent grammar which decompose a sentence into constituents in a hierarchical manner, dependency grammar [8] analyzes the grammatical relations between words in a sentence in a flat manner. For example, in Fig. 2 there is a *direct object* relation *dobj*(搞,賭場) between 搞[gao3] (do) and 賭場[du3chang3] (gambling house) in the Chinese sentence 兩人合搞 賭場(Two people together do gambling house). This kind of relations may be useful in lexical research if properly defined.

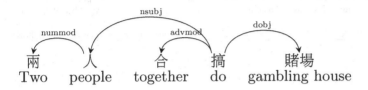

Fig. 2. The structures of the Chinese sentence 兩人合搞賭場[liang3ren2 he2 gao3 du3chang3] (Two people together do gambling house) in dependency grammar.

Though among those resources of dependency parses the manually annotated Chinese Dependency Treebank [9] has been available with a license fee, this parsed corpus contains only simplified Chinese newswire stories from People's Daily. In this paper, however, we aim to further compare grammatical relations of words in not only simplified Chinese but also traditional Chinese variation. On the other side, the LIVAC corpus [10] also collected simplified and traditional Chinese texts, but it mainly focused on KWIC (Key Word In Context) search without annotation of grammatical relations. In order to compare fine-grained grammatical relations of words in the two language varieties, in this study we attempt to use a dependency parser [11] to automatically parse a simplified Chinese corpus and a traditional Chinese corpus.

3 Methodology

In the proposed approach, we apply Stanford Dependency Parser 3.6[3] upon one simplified Chinese corpus and one traditional Chinese corpus respectively. The parser could tag words in a sentence with up to 45 relations as mentioned before (see Table 1 for some examples of the relations).

Our datasets include 744,536 sentences of traditional Chinese Sinica Corpus 3.0[4] and 764,943 sentences of simplified Chinese Xinhua News. After parsing, the output contains the grammatical relations between words in every sentence, which will be later counted as grammatical collocations when properly defined. Fig. 3 shows the schematic structure of our lexical resource designed for comparative research in Chinese variation.

---

[3] http://nlp.stanford.edu/software/lex-parser.shtml
[4] http://app.sinica.edu.tw/cgi-bin/kiwi/mkiwi/kiwi.sh

Table 1. Chinese grammatical relations and examples [11]

Abbreviation	Example	Relation
1. nn	服務中心(service center)	nn(中心,服務)
2. punct	海關統計表明(statistics from the customshouse indicate)	punct(表明,，)
3. nsubj	梅花盛開(plum blossoms are blooming)	nsubj(盛開,梅花)
...	...	...
45. nsubjpass	鎳被稱作現代工業的維生素(nickel is called vitamin of modern industry)	nsubjpass(稱作,鎳)

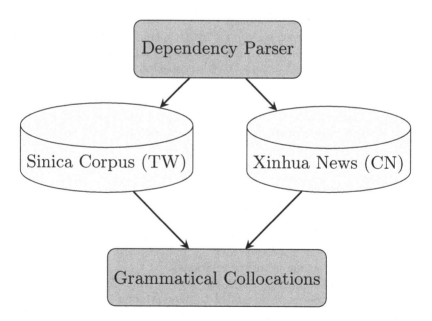

Fig. 3. Design of the proposed resource for language variation

An online user interface has been also available for querying the word of interest in the parsed data.[5]

4   Evaluation Issues

To evaluate the whole parsed corpus, it will require manual annotation of this large-scale corpus data, which is not available yet. Even if we could manually annotate the whole corpus and calculate the accuracy rate, the overall performance will still rely on the assessment of each stage in Chinese language pre-processing. For example, when we intend to compare our overall performance with that of other resources such Chinese WSE, we have to take into consideration the assessment of word segmentation and POS-tagging in each resource respectively, which has complicated the evaluation or even makes the results not comparable on the same base.

For the above two reasons, here we choose to present one case study comparable with previous literature, and evaluate the annotation in this case study: Cai[12] has studied the pro-verb 搞[gao3] (do) both in the simplified and traditional Chinese variation. 418 sentences of 搞[gao3] (do) in Sinica Corpus 3.0 (the same corpus used in our parsing approach) were manually annotated, and 213 instances of 搞[gao3] (do) + noun phrase were found as shown in Table 2 and 3.

Table 2. Collocation comparison of the verb 搞[gao3] (do) in simplified and traditional Chinese [12]

Colligation	Simplified Chinese	Traditional Chinese
搞[gao3] (do) + complement	269 26.9%	144 26.5%
搞[gao3] (do) + noun phrase	579 57.9%	213 39.1%

To be comparable with other research, we queried on the proposed resource for the same word 搞[gao3] (do), and found in the parsed traditional Chinese corpus 211 cases of gao + noun phrase. By juxtaposing our results with those from WSE and Cai's study, we can observe in Table 4 that our resource has provided more comprehensive collocations for the case of 搞[gao3] (do) + noun phrase, based on the same Sinica corpus 3.0.

By further examining the entry of 搞[gao3] (do) + 運動[yun4dong4] (movement) which is absent in other research, we also found that most of the six cases are long-distance dependency relations, which may need much more efforts for human annotation:

1. 所以他們經常搞一些民主運動
   (so they frequently do some democratic movements)
2. 搞訴苦運動
   (do complaint movement)

---

[5] http://140.112.147.131:8000/variation

Table 3. Prototypical collocations of the verb 搞[gao3] (do) in traditional Chinese [12]

Colligation	Type frequency	Instances
搞[gao3] (do) + complement	9	不清楚(unclear)17, 清楚(clear)8, 迷糊(dazed)3, 大(big)3, 不懂(not understand)3, 得泥濘不堪(to be muddy)2, 得破損(to be broken)2, 得熱熱鬧鬧(to be bustling)2, 得人心惶惶(to be panic)2
搞[gao3] (do) + noun phrase	12	社會主義(socialism)5, 政治(politics)5, 共產主義(communism)4, 迷信(superstition)3, 躍進(leap)3, 這個領域(this field)2, 花樣(trick)2, 新項目(new item)2, 小圈圈(small group)2, 多媒體(multimedia)2, 臺獨(Taiwan independence)2, 文革(Cultural Revolution)2
搞[gao3] (do) + verb	5	統一(unite)3, 研究(research)2, 改革(reform)4, 抗日(anti-Japanese)2, 干擾(interfere)2

Table 4. Comparison of the noun phrase counts for the verb 搞[gao3] (do) in Cai [12], WSE and our proposed resource, all based on the same data from Sinica Corpus 3.0

Noun phrase	Cai	WSE	Proposed
社會主義(socialism)	5	8	7
政治(politics)	5	12	9
共產主義(communism)	4	-	2
迷信(superstition)	3	-	2
躍進(leap)	3	-	2
花樣(trick)	2	-	2
項目(item)	2	-	2
圈圈(small group)	2	-	2
臺獨(Taiwan independence)	2	-	2
文革(Cultural Revolution)	2	-	2
這個領域(this field)	2	-	-
多媒體(multimedia)	2	-	-
運動(movement)	-	11	6
個(piece)	-	11	6
鬼(ghost)	-	-	5
什麼(what)	-	-	4
工程(engineering)	-	-	3

3. 喜歡搞運動
   (like to do movement)
4. 大學裡很多有名的老師也搞社會運動去了
   (in the university many famous teachers also went doing social movement)
5. 各地的黨組織按照搞運動的慣例
   (party organizations around follow the convention of doing movement)
6. 還有一些同志不注意在工業方面搞大規模的群眾運動
   (there are still some comrades unaware of the large-scale mass movement in industries)

5   System Demonstration

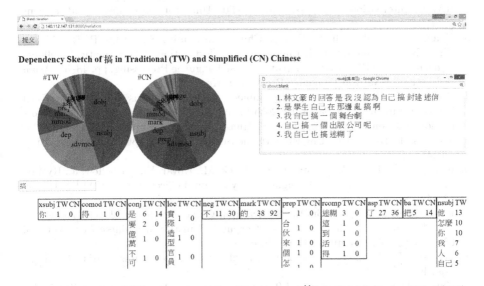

Fig. 4. Comparison of the grammatical collocations of 搞[gao3] (do) in simplified (CN) and traditional (TW) Chinese in our proposed resource

As mentioned before, the proposed lexical resource has been online for users to query the word of interest. Fig. 4 illustrates the structure of the output with a sample query of 搞[gao3] (do). The system has provided for the query word grammatical collocations in simplified and traditional Chinese variation respectively. Since the Stanford Parser is trained mostly on simplified Chinese data, we may find more errors in the traditional Chinese output. However, in this demonstration we can also observe the collocations of the fine-grained *advmod* (adverbial modifier) and *mmod* (modal verb modifier) relations such as *advmod*(搞[gao3],也[ye3]) and *mmod*(搞[gao3],要[yao4]), while in WSE it will be treated just as the more coarse-grained *modifier* relation.

6   Conclusion

In summary, though the accuracy rate of the current parsed corpus could not be as good as human annotators, the parser is able to capture long-distance relations and thus find more grammatical collocations as shown in the case of *dobj*(搞[gao3],運動[yun4dong4]), which is absent in previous research. In the future, we will continue further examining other grammatical relations in our online resource such as predicate and complement.

References

1. Sinclair, J.: Corpus, Concordance, Collocation. Oxford University Press, Oxford (1991)
2. Kilgarriff, A., Rychly, P., Smrz, P., Tugwell, D.: The Sketch Engine. In: 11th EU-RALEX International Congress, pp. 105–116. Université de Bretagne-Sud, Lorient (2004)
3. Huang, C.-R., Kilgarriff, A., Wu, Y., Chiu, C.-M., Smith, S., Rychly, P., Bai, M.-H., Chen, K.-J.: Chinese Sketch Engine and the Extraction of Grammatical Collocations. In: 4th SIGHAN Workshop on Chinese Language Processing, pp. 48–55. Asian Federation of Natural Language Processing, Korea (2005)
4. Hong, J.-F., Huang, C.-R.: Using Chinese Gigaword Corpus and Chinese Word Sketch in Linguistic Research. In: 20th Pacific Asia Conference on Language, Information and Computation, pp. 183-190. Huazhong Normal University, Wuhan (2006)
5. Thomas, J.: Discovering English with the Sketch Engine. Laptop Languages, Brno (2014)
6. Kilgarriff, A., Baisa, V., Busta, J., Jakubicek, M., Kovar, V., Michelfeit, J., Rychly, P., Suchomel, V.: The Sketch Engine: Ten years on. Lexicography ASIALEX 1, 7–36 (2014)
7. Kilgarriff, A., Keng, N., Smith, S.: Learning Chinese with the Sketch Engine. In: Zou, B., Smith, S., Hoey, M. (eds.) Corpus Linguistics in Chinese Contexts, pp. 63–73. Palgrave Macmillan, Hampshire (2015)
8. Tesniere, L.: Elements of Structural Syntax. John Benjamins, Paris (1959) [In French]
9. Chinese Dependency Treebank 1.0, http://catalog.ldc.upenn.edu/LDC2012T05
10. Tsou, B.K., Kwong, O.Y.: Toward a Pan-Chinese Thesaurus. In: 5th International Conference on Language Resources and Evaluation, pp. 2391–2394. European Language Resources Association, Genoa (2006)
11. Chang, P.-C., Tseng, H., Jurafsky, D., Manning, C.: Discriminative Reordering with Chinese Grammatical Relations Features. In: 3rd Workshop on Syntax and Structure in Statistical Translation, pp. 51–59. Association for Computational Linguistics, Boulder (2009)
12. Cai, C.: The Semantic Prosody of Pro-verb Gao "do" in Cross-strait Varieties between Modern Chinese. Journal of Chinese Language Teaching, 11(3), 91-110 (2014)

Part IV Natural Language Processing

Integrating Character Representations into Chinese Word Embedding

Xingyuan Chen[1], Peng Jin*[1], Diana McCarthy[2], John Carroll[3]

[1] Key Lab of Internet Natural Language Processing of Sichuan Provincial Education Department, Leshan Normal University, China
{1045258214@qq.com; jandp@pku.edu.cn}
[2] Department of Theoretical and Applied Linguistics, University of Cambridge, UK
diana@dianamaccarthy.co.uk
[3] Department of Informatics, University of Sussex, UK
j.a.carroll@sussex.ac.uk

Abstract. In this paper we propose a novel word representation for Chinese based on a state-of-the-art word embedding approach. Our main contribution is to integrate distributional representations of Chinese characters into the word embedding. Recent related work on European languages has demonstrated that information from inflectional morphology can reduce the problem of sparse data and improve word representations. Chinese has very little inflectional morphology, but there is potential for incorporating character-level information. Chinese characters are drawn from a fixed set – with just under four thousand in common usage – but a major problem with using characters is their ambiguity. In order to address this problem, we disambiguate the characters according to groupings in a semantic hierarchy. Coupling our character embeddings with word embeddings, we observe improved performance on the tasks of finding synonyms and rating word similarity compared to a model using word embeddings alone, especially for low frequency words.

Keywords: word embedding, Chinese character, *Cilin*.

1   Introduction

Word embeddings represent a word as a low dimensional dense vector (Bengio et al., 2003; Mikolov et al., 2013a); the technique has been successfully applied in many natural language tasks (Turian et al., 2010; Collobert et al., 2011). Introducing global contexts (Pennington et al., 2014) or dependency relationships between words (Levy and Goldberg, 2014a) can improve word embedding. However, rare words are often represented poorly due to data sparsity. To obtain better vectors for both high and low frequency words, recent work has taken morphology into account. Luong et al.(2013) combine recursive neural networks, where each morpheme is a basic unit, with neural language models to produce morphologically-aware word vectors, thus improving language models. Botha and

© Springer International Publishing AG 2016
M. Dong et al. (Eds.): CLSW 2016, LNAI 10085, pp. 335–349, 2016
DOI: 10.1007/978-3-319-49508-8_32

Blunsom (2014) exploit inflectional morphology to improve the performance of word embedding representations on word similarity rating and machine translation.

Unlike Western European languages, such as German and to a lesser degree English, Chinese has very little morphology, and individual Chinese characters play a central role in word formation. In Western languages, inflections carry some meaning, such as the English prefix *dis*-conveying "not" or "opposite of" (e.g. *dis-connect*).Chinese words draw on a fixed set of Chinese characters. Although Leng and Wei (1994) list 85,568 characters in their dictionary, there are only 3,500 characters in common usage (covering 99.48% tokens). Out of these, 2,500 characters cover 97.97% tokens and are called "often-used" characters; the remaining 1,500 cover 1.51% tokens and are called "second often-used" characters. There is thus almost no data sparseness in character usage.

However, the character has more influence on a word's meaning than western suffixes and prefixes in two respects. Firstly, Chinese words are only composed of characters (many characters are also words by themselves). Secondly, Chinese characters convey a much wider range of meanings compared to Western affixes and are strongly related semantically to their containing words (most commonly through a hypernym relationship). For instance, the bi-character word"火车" (*train*) consists of"火" (*fire*) and "车" (*vehicle*), so "火车" is a kind of"车" which is driven by burning something. Tseng (2003) attempts to predict the semantic category of a word from its characters. He uses characters whose functions are similar to suffixes or prefixes, such as "家" (*expert*) which can generate"音乐家" (*musician*) and "艺术家" (*artist*).Unlike suffixes and prefixes, which provide quite a specific meaning to only a restricted set of words, Chinese characters provide semantic information for nearly all Chinese words[1]. Our intuition is that for Chinese words, in particular for low frequency words such as "车轱辘" (*wheel rim*), if we can use the vector for "车" then we will obtain a better word embedding than a word-based model which uses only a vector for the whole word.

In this paper, we propose two compositional models to improve Chinese word embedding. In the first model, based on the Mikolov et al. (2013a) skip-gram model, a word vector is obtained by combining the vectors for the characters comprising the word. The second model additionally combines character vectors with the original word vector. We compare these to a baseline word embedding model and to a character embedding which does not use word segmentation.

One major issue with character-level processing of Chinese is that most Chinese characters are ambiguous. For instance, in the examples above, the usual usage of "车" is a chessman in Chinese chess; and "家" is more commonly used with the meaning of 'home' or 'family' rather than 'expert'. Therefore, directly integrating the character vector into a word embedding model could return only limited benefits.

In order to alleviate character ambiguity, we use the Chinese thesaurus

---

[1]Transliterations are exceptions to this generalization.

TongYiCiCiLin (Extended Version) (Mei et al., 1984). This thesaurus is hierarchically organized similarly to WordNet. Each word is decomposed into characters. For any character, if the lexicographer places it at different levels (semantic categories), we assume it has different meanings and our system produces different vector representations of the character during training reflecting these different categories. Finally, these character vectors are combined using addition to get word vectors.

2   Related Work

2.1   Distributional Word Representation

Compared with traditional vector representations, a distributional word representation uses low dimension dense vectors v_w to represent a word w in a vocabulary W. A neural network is used to obtain word vectors (Bengio et al., 2003). Mnih and Hilton (2007) propose a log-bilinear language model (LBL) which predicts the current word w_m via its preceding words $w_1, w_2, \cdots, w_{m-1}$; the predicting vector is $v = \sum_{j=1}^{m-1} v_{w_j} C_j$, where v_{w_j} is the vector of w_j, and C_j is the weight matrix between w_j and w_m.

In contrast to previous work on continuous space language models (Schwenk, 2007), Mikolov et al. (2013a) propose two efficient models which do not involve dense matrix multiplications: the continuous bags-of-words model (CBOW) and the continuous skip-gram model. In this paper, we extend the latter, which usually performs better than CBOW (Levy and Goldberg 2014a).

In the skip-gram model, the current word w_t is used as an input to predict the context word w_j. The objective function is:

$$\frac{1}{T} \sum_{t=1}^{T} \sum_{t-c \leq j \leq t+c} \log p\left(w_j \mid w_t\right)$$

where c is the size of the context window, and T is the number of tokens in the training corpus.

One way to solve the objective function is negative sampling as described by Goldberg and Levy (2014b):

$$\sum_{(w_O, w_I) \in D} \log \sigma\left(v_{w_O}'^T v_{w_I}\right) + \sum_{(w_O, w_I) \in D'} \log \sigma\left(-v_{w_O}'^T v_{w_I}\right) \qquad (1)$$

where $\sigma(x) = \frac{1}{1+e^{-x}}$, D is the positive pairs set, and D' is the negative pairs set.

There has been a great deal of recent work improving these word embedding models. For example, Yu and Dredze (2014) improved word embedding by integrating prior knowledge about synonyms from two semantic resources: WordNet and a paraphrase database. Zou et al. (2013) improve performance on various tasks by producing bilingual (Chinese-English) word embeddings using machine translation alignments. We focus our attention on improving word embeddings for a non-inflectional language, using compositional morphology.

2.2   Improved Embedding for Inflectional Languages

Botha and Blunsom (2014) take advantage of compositional morphology to improve word embedding for languages that have some inflectional morphology, such as English, Spanish, German and Russian. Their approach links the vectors for words sharing the same affix. They use an additive LBL model via matrix decomposition, training the vectors for stems and affixes in two separate steps. Unfortunately, their work is limited in its applicability. Specifically, in English a large number of words do not contain any prefix or suffix. Moreover, agglutinative languages such as Japanese and isolating languages such as Chinese have an almost complete lack of inflection. Fortunately, Chinese characters provide semantic morphemes, which can be used to help infer Chinese word meaning by composition.

There are at least three advantages to taking account of Chinese characters in Chinese natural language processing: (1) it can avoid the need for word segmentation, which is an open problem; (2) characters are enumerable, thus overcoming data sparseness; and (3) characters carry information about word meaning to some extent. Although the word is still the fundamental unit for most Chinese natural language processing tasks, the character has been drawing researchers' attention, particularly for lexical semantics.

In particular, many researchers have used Chinese characters to improve lexical semantic processing. Tseng (2003) predicts the semantic category of an unknown Chinese word by using the semantic categories of similar words that share at least one component character. Lu (2007) further combines two knowledge-based models with a corpus-based model and tries to utilize context information. However, he finds that context information does not help. Jin et al. (2012) simply assign a higher similarity score to a word if it shares a component character with the target word regardless of whether this character is ambiguous or not. Besides lexical semantics, characters are also used for improving dependency parsing (Li et al., 2001), and for Chinese machine translation evaluation (Li et al., 2011; Liu and Ng, 2012).

In this paper, we propose a novel approach to Chinese word embedding based on the skip-gram model by using the compositional morphology. In contrast to Botha and Blunsom (2014), we obtain both the word vector and character vector together in one step.

However, a disadvantage of the character is its higher ambiguity compared to affixes in inflectional languages. Many Chinese characters are ambiguous: of the 200 most productive morphemes (characters), about 51.5% of them are polysemous (Huang et al., 1997) and there are on average 3.5 senses for each character. In order to deal with this problem, we describe an extension to our approach, in which we integrate a thesaurus to resolve character ambiguity.

3   Models

Let W be the vocabulary of the Chinese corpus M. For any subset $A \subset W$, we use $C(A)$ to denote the set of all Chinese characters that form the words in A. Let $C(w)$ be the set of characters in word w. We define two mappings to describe the compositional relationship between words and characters:

$$v_c : C(W) \to R^n, v_c = v_c(c) \quad s : W \to R^n, \ s_w = s(w)$$

where R^n is a n-dimensional real space. The mapping v_c assumes one vector per character independent of which words it appears in. Since a word is not represented well enough only by combining its component characters,(because words vary as to how compositional they are) (Reddy et al, 2011), a surface vector s_w for the form of a word(as in Botha and Blunsom, 2014) is combined to represent the word w.With the above two mappings, addition is used to express compositional morphology:

$$v_w = as_w + b\sum_{c \in C(w)} v_c, \tag{2}$$

where v_w is the vector of word w, parameters $a, b \in \{0,1\}$ which determine whether s_w and v_c are selected or not.

This additive function is used to revise the skip-gram model. In equation (1) in section 2.1, there are two word vectors: the input word vector and the output word vector. Although both of them could be used by addition, we only apply composition to the output, leaving exploration of composition on input vectors for future work. We therefore re-write equation (1) as follows:

$$S = \sum_{(w_O, w_I) \in D} \log \sigma\left(v'_{w_O}{}^T v_{w_I}\right) + \sum_{(w_O, w_I) \in D'} \log \sigma\left(-v'_{w_O}{}^T v_{w_I}\right) \tag{3}$$

where

$$v'_{w_O} = as_{w_O} + b\sum_{c \in C(w_O)} v_c, \ a, b \in \{0,1\} \tag{4}$$

For equation (3), we can obtain a number of models by varying the values of a and b in equation (4). In this paper, we investigate two models:(i) the *character model*, where $a=0$ and $b=1$, and (ii) the *character-word model*, where $a=b=1$. We compare these models against two baselines (*W-unit* and *C-unit*) where $a=1$ and $b=0$; these are similar to Mikolov et al. (2013a),with W-unit using the word as the basic unit, and C-unit using the character as the basic unit (therefore not needing word segmentation on training corpus).

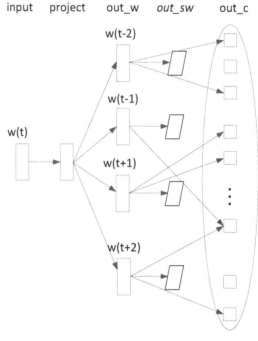

input   project   out_w   *out_sw*   out_c

Fig. 1. The architecture of our models. The character model (represented by the parts without italics) is used to produce a word vector representation which is the sum of the component character vectors. For the character-word model, the surface word form vectors (illustrated as parallelograms) are combined with the component character vectors.

Character model and Character-word model are formulated, respectively:

$$v'_{w_O} = \sum_{c \in C(w_O)} v_c \quad (5) \qquad v'_{w_O} = s_{w_O} + \sum_{c \in C(w_O)} v_c \quad (6)$$

Figure 1 illustrates the architecture of this model. In fact *out_sw*(s_{w_O}) is located at the same layer as the character vectors *out_c*(v_c), though in the diagram it appears between *out_w*(v'_{w_O}) and *out_c*. For example, the tri-character word "排水沟"*(drain)*is represented in our two models as follows.

Character model:
$$\overrightarrow{\underset{\text{drain}}{排水沟}} = \overrightarrow{\underset{\text{discharge}}{排}} + \overrightarrow{\underset{\text{water}}{水}} + \overrightarrow{\underset{\text{trench}}{沟}}$$

Character-word model:

$$\overrightarrow{排水沟}_{drain} = \overrightarrow{排水沟}_{drain} + \overrightarrow{排}_{discharge} + \overrightarrow{水}_{water} + \overrightarrow{沟}_{trench}$$

Both models described by equation (3)can be trained using stochastic gradient descent in equation (7)

$$\frac{\partial S}{\partial v_c^{(i)}} = a \frac{\partial S}{\partial v_{w_O}'^{(i)}}, \frac{\partial S}{\partial s_{w_O}^{(i)}} = b \frac{\partial S}{\partial v_{w_O}'^{(i)}} \quad (7)$$

where $v_{w_O}^{(i)}$ is the *i-th* element of the vector v_{w_O}.

The above two models integrate both word sequence information and the compositional relationship between a word and its component characters. Equation (4) allows for words sharing a character to benefit from occurrences of the character in other words during training. This is aimed at improving word embedding especially for low frequency words. One outstanding issue is the assumption that one vector per character is sufficient to capture the meaning within all words. We introduce a thesaurus to help combat character ambiguity.

4   Unambiguous Chinese Characters Integration

The two models described in the above section assume there is one vector per character. However, it is very common for a Chinese character to be ambiguous (Huang et al., 1997). To solve this problem, we use the Chinese thesaurus TongYiCiCiLin (Extended Version) (Mei et al., 1984)[2].

4.1   The Cilin Thesaurus

TongYiCiCiLin (Extended Version) – which we refer to as 'Cilin' from now on – organizes 77,343 words in a semantic tree with five levels. In contrast to WordNet, there are no words in the non-leaf nodes. Instead all words are listed in the fifth level as leaf nodes. Figure 2 shows an example. Circles indicate non-leaf nodes, and the labels above them are their semantic codes. At the fifth level (the leaf nodes), ovals indicate synonym sets.

In Cilin, there are a total of 12 large semantic classes (on the first level), 97 medium semantic classes (on the second level), 1,400 small semantic classes (on the third level), and 17,817 word clusters (on the fourth level). Each of the 77,343 words is a member of one or more of the 17,817 synonym sets.

We assume that there is only one meaning for any given character shared by words that are grouped together at a given level of the hierarchy. In our experiments, for example, if we use the second level of the hierarchy, all words are classified into the 97 classes at this level. Therefore, each character will have as many meanings, and therefore vector representations, as there are word classes

---

[2]TongYiCiCiLin (Extended Version) can be downloaded from http://ir.hit.edu.cn

containing this character at this level. For any test word, we assume the character vectors selected are those that share the same semantic grouping from Cilin as other characters within the word.

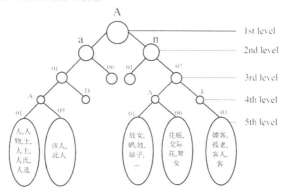

Fig. 2. The structure of the Cilin thesaurus.

For a polysemous word, if it only appears in one semantic class – given the level being used by our model – then it will be decomposed into characters; however if it appears in more than one class at this level it will not be decomposed and not used for training the character vectors. Table 1 shows the numbers of polysemous and unambiguous words if we consider the semantic groupings at levels 1, 2 and 3 in Cilin.

	Level 1	Level 2	Level 3
# Polysemous	663	1,630	3,496
# Unambiguous	8,146	7,179	5,313

Table 1. The ambiguity of words in levels 1 to 3 in Cilin.

4.2   Revising Models by Integrating Cilin

As stated above, we use the semantic categories at a given level to determine whether a word is polysemous or unambiguous. Each word will be used for training provided all its senses (occurrences in Cilin) occur within the same grouping for the level being used by our model. The word will be used once regardless of how many times it occurs in Cilin within this level. If it occurs in more than one semantic category at the given level then it is not used for training. The words in category k are denoted as T_k and let $T = \bigcup_{k=1}^{K} T_k$.

In order to leverage T , we introduce a new mapping:

$$v_k : C(T_k) \to R^n, v_{k,c} = v_k(c)$$

This mapping allows a character to be represented with multiple vectors. It maps the character c into as many vectors as the number of T_k that the character occurs in, thereby reducing the ambiguity.

Replacing v_k with $v_{w,c}$ in equation (4), we get equation (8).

$$v'_{w_O} = as_{w_O} + b \sum_{c \in C(w_O)} v_{k,c} \qquad (8)$$

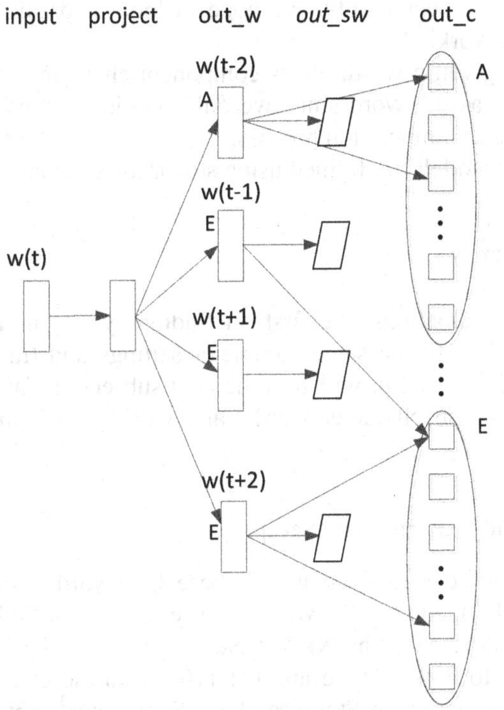
input
project
out_w
out_sw
out_c
w(t-2)
A
w(t-1)
E
w(t)
w(t+1)
E
w(t+2)
E
A
E

Fig. 3. Revised models when the first level of Cilin is integrated into them. A Chinese character will have as many meanings, and therefore vector representations, as there are word classes containing this character at this level.

Similarly to section 3, our character model and character-word model are expressed by equations(9) and (10) respectively.

$$v'_{w_O} = \begin{cases} \sum_{c \in C(w_O)} v_{k,c}, & w_o \in T \\ s_{w_o}, & w_o \notin T \end{cases} \qquad (9) \qquad v'_{w_O} = \begin{cases} s_{w_o} + \sum_{c \in C(w_O)} v_{k,c}, & w_o \in T \\ s_{w_o}, & w_o \notin T \end{cases} \qquad (10)$$

For a word w_o,if $w_o \notin T$, then v'_{w_O} will not be decomposed into characters and will be represented only by its surface vector.

In contrast to Figure 1, each set of words from the same semantic category, at a given level, containing a given character provides a grouping-- so that during training a vector will be produced using these words as context for this specific semantic grouping of that character. The number of these groups amounts to the number of semantic categories at a specific level in Cilin. In Figure 3, the capital letter at the right top of the oval denotes the semantic label. "A..." denotes the semantic category code for w(t-2); so does "E...". During training, words that don't appear in Cilin, exemplified by *w(t+1)* in our diagram, will be represented by the word surface vector only. We hope to look at predicting their semantic category in future work.

What is more, given a word, all its component characters will be in the same semantic category as the word since we only consider unambiguous words at a given level for the decomposition process.

These two new models are trained using stochastic gradient descent.

5   Experiments

We conduct two evaluations: the first on finding synonyms and the second on word similarity. We use the same parameter settings and training data for both evaluations; the details are provided in the next subsection. We experiment on all words including single character words, and words consisting of two or more characters.

5.1   Dataset and Experimental Setup

The training corpus comes from the Chinese Gigaword Second Edition (LDC catalog number LDC2005T14). We only use the simplified Chinese files. It covers all the news released by Xinhua News Agent (the largest news agency in China)from 1991 to 2004. There are 471,110K Chinese characters in total. We segment the corpus with the Stanford Word Segmenter[3], obtaining almost 0.25 billion word tokens.

For the word model, we use word2vec[4] with all the parameters in the default settings. Our models have the same parameters as Mikolov et al. (2013) for ease of comparison.

5.2   Evaluation on Synonym Acquisition

For this evaluation we use the fifth level of Cilin as our gold standard. As described in section 4.1, this level provides all the synonym sets. We use an evaluation metric proposed by Curran and Moens (2002). Given a word *w*, we compute the cosine similarity between its vector and any other word's vector, and then rank them according to the cosine similarity value. The measure *P@n* is the percentage of matches in the top *n* similar words appearing in the corresponding

---

[3] http://nlp.stanford.edu/software/segmenter.shtml
[4] https://code.google.com/p/word2vec

w's synonyms gold standard lists.

Tables 2 and 3 show the results in detail. The left-most column lists the ranges of word frequency from low to high. The baseline model is the word model. *C-unit* uses this model, treating each character rather than a word as a unit in the training corpus. *W-unit* denotes the word model treating the word as a training unit. In these tables, *NT* indicates no thesaurus is integrated, thus showing the performance of the model described in Section 3. *1st*, *2nd* and *3rd* denote the models that use the first, second and third levels of Cilin respectively to reduce the ambiguity of characters.

Word freq.	#Word types	Baseline model		Character model				Character-word Model			
		C-unit	W-unit	NT	1st	2nd	3rd	NT	1st	2nd	3rd
5-50	17084	14.8	6.80	14.5	24.4	33.5	45.1	15.2	28.7	35.9	44.0
50-10^2	7197	15.0	13.6	14.8	26.8	35.7	45.0	16.9	29.6	33.7	38.9
10^2-500	15961	15.5	18.2	14.9	27.4	34.8	41.7	19.7	28.0	31.5	34.7
500-10^3	5135	15.2	18.2	14.7	25.9	32.2	35.9	19.1	24.3	26.1	28.5
10^3-5000	7305	14.5	19.0	12.6	27.4	33.7	35.6	20.0	23.9	25.5	26.8
5000-10^4	1799	11.5	15.6	11.7	26.5	32.3	31.3	17.8	21.8	22.5	24.3
>10^4	2707	10.6	14.0	10.4	26.0	30.4	31.2	16.1	18.7	20.3	20.5
all	57188	14.7	14.0	14.2	26.2	33.9	41.0	17.8	26.9	31.0	35.4

Table 2. P@1 (%) on Cilin.

Word freq.	#Word types	Baseline model		Character model				Character-word Model			
		C-unit	W-unit	NT	1st	2nd	3rd	NT	1st	2nd	3rd
5-50	17084	9.21	4.00	9.34	15.9	22.2	29.4	10.0	18.6	22.8	27.1
50-10^2	7197	10.5	9.09	10.8	18.5	24.1	28.9	11.9	19.6	22.0	24.5
10^2-500	15961	10.5	11.3	10.6	17.9	21.8	24.9	13.0	17.8	19.2	20.6
500-10^3	5135	10.6	11.1	10.3	17.3	20.3	21.1	12.5	15.3	16.1	17.0
10^3-5000	7305	10.3	11.5	9.72	18.6	21.0	21.5	13.0	15.3	15.7	16.5
5000-10^4	1799	9.24	10.1	8.72	17.9	20.3	19.2	11.2	13.5	13.7	14.2
>10^4	2707	8.72	9.63	7.47	18.3	20.3	18.7	11.6	13.5	13.8	13.9
all	57188	9.98	8.74	9.90	17.5	21.9	25.5	11.8	17.4	19.5	21.7

Table 3. P@5 (%) on Cilin.

All character-based approaches perform better than the W-unit baseline, particularly on lower frequency words. The C-unit baseline, which does not even rely on word segmentation does better than W-unit, and comparably to our models without character disambiguation – apart from the character-word model which does best of all. For example, in Table 2, the P@1 of the character-word model without Cilin is 17.8% on all words. This is a significant improvement on the 14.0% achieved by the word model.

Our hypothesis is that character disambiguation, using Cilin, improves the ability of the character vectors to convey the appropriate semantics in the composition of word meaning. Our models' results improve for lower layers of Cilin, since the models are effectively exploiting more specific semantic information from the groupings in the thesaurus. When Cilin is used for disambiguation we notice particularly that while there is improvement across the board, low frequency words benefit the most, and actually perform better than the words of higher frequency. This is particularly noticeable at the 3rd level of Cilin where the gains for low frequency words are stronger for the character-word model. When disambiguation at the 3rdlevel is used, the character model outperforms the character-word model.

While the actual percentages we achieve are modest, it should be noted that our task is difficult. Although Curran and Moens (2002) achieved 64.5%, they created a gold standard thesaurus containing the union of the synonym lists from three thesauri, giving a total of 23,207 synonyms for the 70 terms, i.e. each term had on average 330 synonyms in their gold standard. In contrast we evaluate on nearly all words in Cilin; 57,188 terms are evaluated and each term has only 4.33 synonyms. Moreover, for evaluating a polysemous word in Cilin, rather than merging all synonyms from all its senses as a gold standard set, we separately use each sense's synonym set as a gold standard.

5.3   Evaluation on Word Similarity

The second experiment evaluates word pair similarity based on human judgments. Jin and Wu (2012) translated English WordSim 353 (Finkelstein et al., 2002) to Chinese and re-assigned the similarity scores provided by twenty native speakers. These word pairs are ranked according to each pair's similarity score. This rank is used as the gold standard. The metric for this evaluation is Spearman rank correlation.

In order to observe the behavior of our model on low frequency words, we randomly removed instances of the terms in the test data subject to a frequency threshold n, set to 5, 10, 20, 40, 60, and 100[5]. Then we trained all models on this new corpus. Each word pair's similarity is the cosine of their vector. Figure 4 shows the results.

C_NT and *CW_NT* denote the character model and character-word model respectively without integrating the thesaurus. *C_1st* and *CW_1st* denote these two models integrating the first level of Cilin. We also experimented with the second and the third levels, but the results were so similar to the first level that for clarity we omit them.

In Figure 4 we can see that when all words in those pairs are less frequent, the Spearman *rho* values of our models (whether they integrate Cilin or not)are higher than the baseline word model. The word model does not catch up with our models until test terms to appear 100 times.

For our two models, when they do not integrate Cilin, the character-word model is always better than the character model and even better than the latter when leveraging Cilin for character disambiguation. However, our two models are both improved with character disambiguation.

---

[5]If some word's frequency is already less than n, we just retain all occurrences.

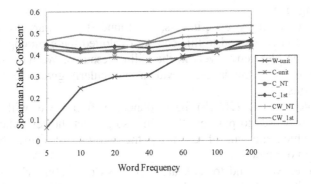

Fig. 4. Performance of all models on different word frequencies.

Regardless of word frequency, the word model which treats a word as a gram has to learn about 0.5 million parameters for all words. However, a model which treats a character as a gram only has to learn several thousand parameters. So, when the word frequency is low (from 5 to 40), its performance is better than a model using each word as a gram. When more and more contexts are observed the word model surpasses its character-based counterpart since there are sufficient contexts for training.

Table 4 shows the Spearman correlations when all of the tokens are used. For a similar task, Zou et al. (2013) achieved 0.593 (monolingual word embedding) and 0.608 (bilingual word embedding). The likely reason for the difference is that they used the Chinese Gigaword Fifth Edition, so the size of training corpus is almost four times as large as in our experiments.

Model	rho	Model	rho
C-unit	0.456	C-1st	0.519
W-unit	0.564	CW_NT	0.538
C_NT	0.413	CW-1st	**0.569**

Table 4. Spearman rank correlation without a word frequency threshold.

6   Conclusions

We have proposed a method of representing Chinese words using the skip gram model operating on word embeddings coupled with character embeddings. This model has two attractive features: (1) the additive property; and (2) allowance for embedding a thesaurus. We have demonstrated that results are superior using these character embeddings, particularly for low frequency words. Adapting such embedding models to cope with low frequency data is crucial because while a large portion of language usage involves high frequency words, it is the large body of low and mid frequency words that provide much of the content of everyday language.

From our preliminary experiments, we found it necessary to deal with the ambiguity of characters and to this end we exploited the groupings of characters provided by the hierarchy levels in the Cilin thesaurus. We have not dealt with word ambiguity since this is less prevalent, particularly given the focus on lower frequency terms.

As Mikolov et al. (2013b) have done, in future we will extend from embeddings of words to phrases. We will also predict the semantic category for the words which are out of Cilin for the purpose of using their character information in our models.

Furthermore, we intend to look at other ways of dealing with character and word ambiguity, possibly using clustering of contexts. We also plan to look at whether these word representation models improve performance when used within deep learning tasks.

Within a word, the characters composing it should have different weights when adding them together. Inspired by Levy and Goldberg (2014a), we plan to weight the character vectors according to the characters' structure inside a word (Li 2011).

Acknowledgments

This work is partially supported by Leshan Normal University Cultivating Project (No. Z1411), Nature Science Fund of China (No. 61373056), and Opening Project of State Key Laboratory of Digital Publishing Technology. Peng Jin is the corresponding author.

References

Yoshua Bengio, Réjean Ducharme, Pascal Vincent and Christian Jauvin. 2003. A neural probabilistic language model. Journal of Machine Learning Research, 3:1137–1155.

Jan Botha and Phil Blunsom. 2014. Compositional Morphology for Word Representations and Language Modeling. Proceedings of ICML.

Ronan Collobert, Jason Weston, Leon Bottou, Michael Karlen, Koray Kavukcuoglu, and Pavel Kuksa. 2011. Natural language processing(almost) from scratch. Journal of Machine Learning Research, 12:2493–2537.

James Curran and Marc Moens. 2002. Scaling Context Space. Proceedings of ACL, pp.231 - 238.

Lev Finkelstein, Evgenity Gabrilovich, Yossi Matias, Ehud Rivlin, Zach Solan, Gadi Wolfman, and Eytan Ruppin. 2002. Placing Search in Context: The Concept Revisited. ACM Transactions on Information Systems, 20(1):116-131.

Chu-Ren Huang, Keh-Jiann Chen, and Chinghsiung Lai. 1997. Mandarin Daily Classification Dictionary, Taipei: Mandarin Daily Press.

Peng Jin and Yunfang Wu. 2012. SemEval-2012 Task 4: Evaluating Chinese Word Similarity. Proceedings of First Joint Conference of Lexical and Computational Semantics, pp. 374–377.

Omer Levy and YoavGoldberg. 2014a. Dependency-basedWordEmbedding. Proceedings of ACL, pp. 23-25.

Omer Levy and Yoav Goldberg. 2014b. Word2vec Explained: Deriving Mikolov et al.'s Negative-Sampling Word-Embedding Method.arxiv1402.3722v1.

Maoxi Li, Chengqing Zong and Hwee Tou Ng. 2011. Automatic Evaluation of Chinese Translation Output: Word-Level or Character-Level? Proceedings of ACL, pp. 159-164.

Zhongguo Li. 2011. Parsing the Internal Structure of Words: A New Paradigm for Chinese Word Segmentation. Proceedings of ACL, pp.1405-1414.

Chang Liu and Hwee Tou Ng. 2012.Character-Level Machine Translation Evaluation for Languages with Ambiguous Word Boundaries. Proceedings of ACL, pp.921-929.

Minh-Thang Luong, Richard Socher and Christopher D. Manning. 2013. Better Word Representations with Recursive Neural Networks for Morphology. Proceedings of CoNLL, pp.104 - 113.

Jiaju Mei, Yiming Zheng, Yunqi Gao and Hungxiang Yin. 1984. TongYiCiCiLin. Shanghai: the Commercial Press.

Tomas Mikolov, Kai Chen, Greg Corrado and Jeffrey Dean. 2013a. Efficient Estimation of Word Representations in Vector Space. Proceedings of Workshop at ICLR.

Tomas Mikolov, Ilya Sutskever, Kai Chen, Greg Corrado, and Jeffrey Dean. 2013b. Distributed Representations of Words and Phrases and their Compositionality. Proceedings of NIPS.

Andriy Mnihand Geoffrey Hinton. 2007. Three New Graphical Models for Statistical Language Modelling. Proceedings of ICML.

Frederic Morinand Yoshua Bengio. 2005. Hierarchical Probabilistic Neural Network Language Model. AISTATS.

Jeffrey Pennington, Richard Socher and Christopher D. Manning. 2014. GloVe: Global Vectors for Word Representation. Proceedings of ACL, pp. 1532-1543.

Siva Reddy, Diana McCarthy and Suresh Manandhar. 2011. An Empirical Study on Compositionality in Compound Nouns. Proceedings of IJCNLP, pp. 210-218.

Holger Schwenk. 2007. Continuous space language models. Computer Speech and Language, 21:492-518.

Huihsin Tseng. 2003. Semantic classification of Chinese unknown words. Proceedings of ACL.

Joseph Turian, Lev Ratinov and Yoshua Bengio. 2010. Word representations: A simple and general method for semi-supervised learning. Proceedings of ACL, pp. 384-394.

Mo Yu and Mark Dredze. 2014. Improving Lexical Embedding with Semantic Knowledge. Proceedings of ACL, pp. 545-550.

Will Y. Zou, Richard Socher, Daniel Cer and Christopher D. Manning. 2013. Bilingual Word Embeddings for Phrase-Based Machine Translation. Proceedings of EMNLP, pp.1393 - 1398.

Parallel Corpus-based Bilingual Co-training for Relation Classification

Haotian Hui, Yanqun Li, Longhua Qian *, Guodong Zhou
(1.Natural Language Processing Lab of Soochow University, Suzhou, Jiangsu 215006,
China;
2.School of Computer Science & Technology, Soochow University, Suzhou, Jiangsu
215006, China)

E-mail: hht0414@163.com; 20154227023@stu.suda.edu.cn;
qianlonghua@suda.edu.cn; gdzhou@suda.edu.cn

Abstract. This paper proposes a bilingual co-training paradigm for relation classification based on an instance-level parallel corpus aligned between Chinese and English on entity and relation level. Given a small-scale seed set and a large-scale unlabeled corpus, reliable instances induced from the Chinese classifier are iteratively augmented to the English classifier, and vice versa, in order to enhance both classifiers. Experimental results on the Chinese and English parallel corpus show that bilingual co-training can improve relation classification in both languages, especially in English. Moreover, as the size of the seed set and of the iteration batch increases, bilingual co-training can always make consistent improvements, demonstrating its better robustness.

Keywords: Relation Classification, Bilingual Co-training, Bootstrapping, Parallel Corpus

1   Introduction

Relation extraction, a sub task of three main tasks of ACE [1], aims to determine the semantic relation between two entities and keep it in a structured format for further usage. Relation extraction also plays a significant role in many applications of natural language processing, such as Question Answering, Information Infusion, Social Network Construction and Knowledge Mining etc.

The emergence of multilingually annotated corpora has enabled the development of cross-language information extraction, but few research was carried out in this field. Besides comparing the difference between the information extraction tasks on different languages, Chen et al. [2] conducted joint recognition and alignment of named entities on a Chinese-English parallel corpus, aiming to improve the named entity recognition performance on both languages. Based on the idea of mapping the

---

* Corresponding author. This research is supported by the National Natural Science Foundation of China [Grant No. K111817913, 61373096 and 90920004].

© Springer International Publishing AG 2016
M. Dong et al. (Eds.): CLSW 2016, LNAI 10085, pp. 350–361, 2016
DOI: 10.1007/978-3-319-49508-8_33

entities and relations of the source language into the target language, Kim et al. [3] perfromed cross-lingual relation extraction from English to Korean using a parallel corpus.

The above studies indicate that parallel corpora are of great significance to improve the performance of cross-lingual information extraction. Nevertheless, they only focus on one-way cross-lingual information extraction, ignoring the redundance and complementarity between two languages. In order to take advantage of the complementarity between two languages, Li et al. [4] proposed a semi-supervised co-training approach for Named Entitiy Recognition (NER) between Chinese and English using a parallel corpus. The experimental results showed the improved performance of NER on both Chinese and English. Qian et al. [5] adopted the machine translation method to translate both Chinese and English ACE2005 corpora to construct a high-quality pseudo parallel corpus for bilingual relation classification, and thus improved the relation classification performance on both languages.

So far, however, the mainstream methods for relation extraction are supervised learning [6,7,8,9] ,semi-supervised learning [10,11,12,13] and unsupervised learning [14,15]. Supervised learning needs annotated corpora of high quality and large volume, while semi-supervised learning is used when less training instances are available. Based on a parallel corpus with entities aligned between Chinese and English [16] , this paper presents a bilingual co-training method for relation classification. We first generate parallel entity relation instances in Chinese and English from the parallel corpus, then add Chinese relation instances automatically recognized with high confidence to the English training dataset during each iteration, and vice versa, to improve the performance of relation classification on both languages.

2 Parallel Corpus and Baseline

This section introduces the basic notion of the instance-level parallel corpus and the features used in the relation classification experiments, as well as the semi-supervised baseline system based on the bootstrapping algorithm.

2.1 Parallel Corpus

This paper uses a high quality Chinese and English parallel corpus for information extraction adapted from the OntoNotes Corpus. Specifically, the instance-level corpus not only contains the entities and their mutual relations, but is also aligned between Chinese and English on entity and relation level. Entities are annotated with entity type, mention scope, mention level and entity class etc. while relations are annotated with relationship type, syntactic class and tense etc. For example, in the following sentence pair (c1, e1):

(c1) [乍得]*1-1* 新 [总统]*2-2* [依迪斯 代比]*2-3* 十二日 到达 [巴黎]*3-4* 访问 。 [密特朗]*4-5* [总统]*4-6* 同 [他]*2-7* 进行 了 半 小时 秘密 会谈 。

(e1) [Chad]*1-1* 's New [President]*2-2* [Idriss Deby]*2-3* arrived in [Paris]*3-4* on the 12th for a visit . [President]*4-5* [Mitterrand]*4-6* had a half - hour 's secret meeting with [him]*2-7* .

What is enclosed within square brackets denotes an entity mention, with the sub-scription its mention id, and the underlined part means the leftest entity and the right-est entity have a semantic relationship. We can see that the sentence pair has 7 entity mentions, 4 entities (2-2, 2-3 and 2-7 are mentions of Entity 2; 4-5 and 4-6 are men-tions of Entity 4), 2 relationships (Entity 1 and Entity 2 has a relationship of ORG-AFF.Employment; Entity 2 and Entity 3 has a relationship of PHYS.Located).

2.2   Features

We adopt the feature-based method for relation classification, rather than tree ker-nel-based method, since semi-supervised learning including co-training needs a large number of iterations and the kernel-based one usually performs much slower than the former. Following is a list of features, much similar to Zhou et al. [17]:

- Lexical features of entities and their contexts

  WM1: bag-of-words in the 1st entity mention (M1)
  HM1: headword of M1
  WM2: bag-of-words in the 2nd entity mention (M2)
  HM2: headword of M2
  HM12: combination of HM1 and HM2
  WBNULL: when no word in between
  WBFL: the only one word in between
  WBF: the first word in between when at least two words in between
  WBL: the last word in between when at least two words in between
  WBO: other words in between except the first and last words when at least three
      words in between

- Entity type

  ET12: combination of entity types
  EST12: combination of entity subtypes
  EC12: combination of entity classes

- Mention level

  ML12: combination of entity mention levels
  MT12: combination of LDC mention types

- Overlap

#WB: number of other mentions in between
#MB: number of words in between

2.3   Baseline

Following Zhang [10], we have implemented a self-bootstrapping procedure as the baseline system, which keeps augmenting the training data by applying the classification model trained from previously available training data, to the unlabeled data as shown in Figure 1.

Since the SVMLIB[1] package used in classification can output probabilities that it assign to the class labels on an instance, we adopt an entropy-based metric to measure the confidence with regard to the classifier's prediction. With a sequence of K probabilities at some iterations, denoted as $\{p_1,p_2,...p_K\}$ with p_i the probability for the i-th class, we compute the entropy as follows:

$$H = -\sum_{i=1}^{K} p_i \log p_i \qquad (1)$$

Where K denotes the total number of relation classes. Intuitively, the smaller the H is, the more reliable the prediction is.

Algorithm self-bootstrapping

Input:
   - L, labeled data set
   - U, unlabeled data set
   - n, batch size

Output:
   - SVM, classifier

Repeat:
   1. Train a single classifier SVM on L
   2. Run the classifier on U
   3. Find at most n instances in U that the classifier has the highest prediction confidence
   4. Add them into L

Until: no data points available or the stoppage condition is reached

---

Fig. 1. Self-bootstrapping algorithm

---

[1] https://www.csie.ntu.edu.tw/~cjlin/libsvm/

3   Bilingual co-training for relation classification

3.1   Task definition

The main task of this paper is to apply the co-training paradigm to classify the relation instances in the parallel corpus into multiple semantic relationships. With Chinese and English (designated as c and e) as two languages used in our study, this paper intends to show that our method can improve the task of bilingual relation classification, i.e., assigning relationship labels to candidate instances in two languages that have semantic relationships.

Suppose we have a small-scale labeled instance sets in both languages, denoted as L_c and L_e respectively, and a large-scale unlabeled instance sets in both languages, denoted as U_c and U_e. The test instance sets in both languages are represented as T_c and T_e. Note that all the above instance sets are parallel. We adopt bilingual co-training method to acquire two SVM classifiers SVM_c and SVM_e in two languages respectively.

Algorithm bilingual co-training

Input:
 - L_c and U_c, labeled and unlabeled instances in Chinese
 - L_e and U_e, labeled and unlabeled instances in English
 - n, batch size
Output:
 - SVM_c and SVM_e, two classifiers for Chinese and English respectively
Repeat:
 1. Learn the Chinese classifier SVM_c from L_c
 2. Use SVM_c to classify instances in U_c
 3. Choose the n most confidently classified instances E_c from U_c and find their parallel counterparts E_{ep} in U_e
 4. Learn the English classifier SVM_e from L_e
 5. Use SVM_e to classify instances in U_e
 6. Choose the n most confidently classified instances E_e from U_e and find their parallel counterparts E_{cp} in U_c
 7. Remove E_c from U_c and E_e from U_e
 8. Add instances $E_c \cup E_{cp}$ to L_c with their automatically annotated labels
 9. Add instances $E_e \cup E_{ep}$ to L_e with their automatically annotated labels
Until no instances available

Fig. 2. Bilingual co-training algorithm

3.2   Bilingual co-training algorithm

The intuition of bilingual co-training for relation classification is that reliably classified relation instances in one language may not be easily classified in another language and therefore their addition to another language will help its classifier. This idea is embodied in the bilingual co-training algorithm in Figure 2, where n is the batch size, i.e., the number of instances added at each iteration. Specifically after Step 3, we add the n most reliably classified instances E_c to the Chinese training data, then their parallel counterparts E_{ep} in English are further added to the English training data, and vice versa.

4   Experiments

4.1   Experimental corpus and setting

We use a Chinese and English parallel corpus with alignment on instances, which defines 7 entity types, 6 major relation types and 18 relation subtypes, the same with the standard ACE guideline [ACE, 2004]. We select those aligned instances that have semantic relationship as positive instances. The number of Chinese and English mentions is 14,738, and the number of relation instances is 4,732. The number and its percentage of each entity type as well as of each relation type are shown in Table 1.

Table 1. Number and percentage of entities and relations

Entity Mention			Relation Instance		
Type	No	%	Type	No	%
PER	3,290	22.3	PHYS	562	11.9
ORG	3,458	23.5	PART-WHOLE	1,339	28.3
GPE	**6,146**	**41.7**	PER-SOC	51	1.1
LOC	1,381	9.4	ORG-AFF	1,079	22.8
FAC	398	2.7	ART	49	1.0
VEH	65	0.4	GEN-AFF	**1,652**	**34.9**
WEA	0	0.0	-	-	-
Total	14,738	100.0	Total	4,732	100.0

In our experimentation, SVMLIB is selected as our classifier since it supports multi-class classification and there is also probability distribution available on class prediction. The training parameters C (SVM) is set to 2.4, which had been empirically verified to exhibit the best performance in previous relation extraction research. Relation classification performance is evaluated using the standard Precision (P), Recall (R) and their harmonic average (F1).

In order to reduce the performance fluctuation caused by different divisions of training and test datasets, overall performance scores are averaged over 10 runs. For each run, 1/30 and 1/5 randomly selected instances are used as the training and test set respectively while the remaining instances are used as the unlabeled set.

4.2   Experimental methods

The following experimental methods are compared:

SL-MONO (Supervised Learning with monolingual labeled instances): only the monolingual labeled instances are fed to the SVM classifiers for both Chinese and English relation classification respectively. No any unlabeled instances are involved. That is, the training data only contain L_c and L_e for Chinese and English respectively.

SSL-MONO (Semi-Supervised Learning with monolingual labeled and unlabeled instances): the labeled and unlabeled data for bootstrapping only contain monolingual instances. That is, the data contain L_c and U_c for Chinese, or L_e and U_e for English respectively (Fig. 2).

CO-BI (Co-training with bilingual labeled and unlabeled instances): the involved data sets are the same as those of **SSL-MONO**, their usage, however, is different (Fig. 2).

4.3   Experimental results and analysis

4.3.1   Method comparison

Table 2 compares the performance P/R/F1 scores of relation classification on the Chinese-English parallel corpus for various methods. In the three learning methods, namely, SL-MONO, SSL-MONO and CO-BI, the batch size n set to 100 and the performance scores are the highest ones ever obtained during iterations until all the unlabeled instances have run out.

Table 2. Performance comparison of different methods

Methods	Chinese			English		
	P(%)	R(%)	F1	P(%)	R(%)	F1
SL-MONO	80.47	80.40	80.43	77.35	77.28	77.31
SSL-MONO	82.69	82.57	82.62	80.46	80.08	80.26
CO-BI	**82.89**	**82.58**	**82.73**	**82.03**	**81.23**	**81.62**

The table shows that among the three learning paradigms, CO-BI and SL-MONO achieve the best and the worst performance scores respectively, and both CO-BI and

SSL-MONO outperforms SL-MONO by 2-3 units in F-score for Chinese and English. Comparing with SSL-MONO, CO-BI can boost the English performance by1.4 units in F1score, but for Chinese the performance is almost the same.

This is probably due to the better performance for Chinese relation classification than the English counterpart, thus the instances selected by the Chinese classifier have relatively high reliability, therefore, when their parallel instances are added to English, the English Classifier will have a better performance improvement. On the contray, the instances selected by the English classifier have relatively low reliability, thus they will have little help to the Chinese classifier.

4.3.2 Influence of the number of iteration

In order to examine the impact of number of iteration on two semi-supervised learning methods, Figure 3 depicts the curve of the F1 scores relative to the initial performance, with respect to the number of the iteration. Where the x-axis is the number of iteration, the y-axis represents the F1 scores substracted by the initial one, and "C" and "E" denote Chinese and English respectively.

- For English, with the addition of English parallel instances corresponding to high reliability Chinese instances, CO-BI acquires constant improvements. Moreover, It is consistently higher than SSL-MONO. This demonstrates that the Chinese classifier has a consistent role in enhancing the English classifier.
- For Chinese, in the previous stage of the iterations, CO-BI is slightly higher than SSL-MONO, that is, English has a slight contribution to Chinese. However, with the addition of higher reliability instances, this contribution is gradually disappearing.

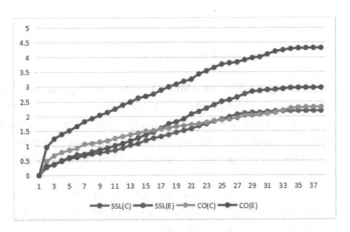

Fig. 3. Influence of the number of iteration

In summary, for English, the CO-BI is always superior to SSL-MONO; for Chinese, CO-BI is better than SSL-MONO during the initial iterations.

4.3.3 Influence of batch size *n*

Figure 4 depicts the F1-score gains, i.e, the difference between the highest score during the iteration and the initial score for SSL-MONO and CO-BI with different batch sizes *n*. Due to the prohibitive computational cost, we do not try all the possible batch sizes with a fixed interval, rather, we only select the typical ones. Nevertheless, it clearly shows the tendency difference between SSL-MONO and CO-BI.

- For SSL-MONO, the performance gains in both Chinese and English are basically in a downward trend when the batch size increases, although English reaches the highest value when *n* is about 400.
- For CO-BI, the performance gains for Chinese and English develop relatively stable in a wide range of batch size, therefore, CO-BI has a better robustness than SSL-MONO.

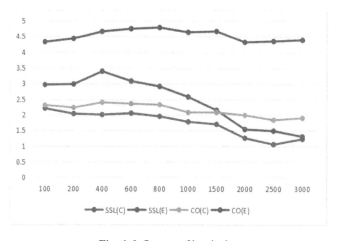

- **Fig. 4.** Influence of batch size

The above results suggest that SSL-MONO performance gains for Chinese and English diminish progressively with the increasing batch size while CO-BI performance gains maintain relatively stable. This implies that adding training instances from another language can always make up the deficiency of its own training instances due to the complementary nature of two languages like Chinese and English.

4.3.4 Influence of seed size

Figure 5 depicts the performance gains for SSL-MONO and CO-BI in both languages. The x-axis represents the available seed sizes (160, 320, 480, 640, 800, 960 respectively) while the y-axis represents the F1-score gains compared with SL-MONO.

Although both SSL-MONO and CO-BI decrease their performance gains when the number of training instances increases, the CO-BI performance gains for both languages outperform SSL-MONO consistently.

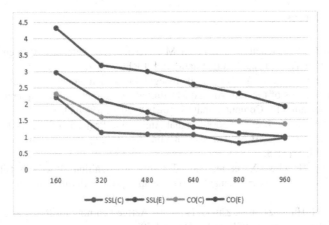

Fig. 5. Influence of seed size

In addition, the difference between CO-BI and SSL-MONO in Chinese first increases and then keeps stable with the increase of seed size while for English this difference always maintains stable. This indicates that, when we have a larger seed size, the classification performance of English has been significantly improved, therefore it has a positive effect on enhancing the Chinese classifier.

It can be concluded from Figure 4 and Figure 5 that CO-BI consistently outperforms SSL-MONO regardless of the scale of seed size as well as of the batch size.

5   Conclusion

Based on a parallel corpus, this paper presents a bilingual co-training method for Chinese/English relation classification. Its idea is that, given two small-scale seed sets of relation instances in two languages and a large-scale unlabeled corpus (seed sets and unlabeled corpus are both parallel), we add the parallel instances of the relation instances with high confidence from one language into another language in a bilingual co-training fashion. The experimental results show that the bilingual co-training can boost the performance of relation classification, and the Chinese classifier with high classification performance has greater contribution to the English counterpart with relatively low performance. However, English also can help Chinese in the beginning of iterations. Different from the monolingual bootstrapping method, our method has a steady positive effect with the the increase of the batch size and of the seed set size.

In our work, both the annotated and unlabeled corpora are parallel, which are usually unavailable in practical scenario. We are trying to apply this parallel corpus to other Chinese-English corpora (such as ACE2005 corpus) to further explore its effect on a wide spectrum of corpora.

References

1. Doddington G R, Mitchell A, Przybocki M A, et al. The Automatic Content Extraction (ACE) Program-Tasks, Data, and Evaluation[C]//LREC. 2004.
2. Chen Y, Zong C, Su K Y. On jointly recognizing and aligning bilingual named entities[C]//Proceedings of the 48th Annual Meeting of the Association for Computational Linguistics. Association for Computational Linguistics, 2010: 631-639.
3. Kim S, Jeong M, Lee J, et al. Cross-Lingual Annotation Projection for Weakly-Supervised Relation Extraction[J]. ACM Transactions on Asian Language Information Processing (TALIP), 2014, 13(1): 3.
4. Li Y, Huang H, Zhao X, et al. Named Entity Recognition Based on Bilingual Co-training[M]//Chinese Lexical Semantics Workshop. Springer Berlin Heidelberg, 2013: 480-489.
5. Qian L, Hui H, Hu Y, Zhou G, Zhu Q. Bilingual Active Learning for Relation Classification via Pseudo Parallel Corpora[C]//ACL 2014:582-592.
6. Liu D, Zhao Z, Hu Y, et al. Incorporating lexical semantic similarity to tree kernel-based Chinese relation extraction[M]//Chinese Lexical Semantics Workshop. Springer Berlin Heidelberg, 2013: 11-21.
7. Culotta A, Sorensen J. Dependency tree kernels for relation extraction[C]//Proceedings of the 42nd Annual Meeting on Association for Computational Linguistics. Association for Computational Linguistics, 2004: 423.
8. Qian L, Zhou G, Kong F, et al. Exploiting constituent dependencies for tree kernel-based semantic relation extraction[C]//Proceedings of the 22nd International Conference on Computational Linguistics-Volume 1. Association for Computational Linguistics, 2008: 697-704.
9. Chan Y S, Roth D. Exploiting syntactico-semantic structures for relation extraction[C]//Proceedings of the 49th Annual Meeting of the Association for Computational Linguistics: Human Language Technologies-Volume 1. Association for Computational Linguistics, 2011: 551-560.
10. Zhang Z. Weakly-supervised relation classification for information extraction[C]//Proceedings of the thirteenth ACM international conference on Information and knowledge management. ACM, 2004: 581-588.
11. Chen J, Ji D, Tan C L, et al. Relation extraction using label propagation based semi-supervised learning[C]//Proceedings of the 21st International Conference on Computational Linguistics and the 44th annual meeting of the Association for Computational Linguistics. Association for Computational Linguistics, 2006: 129-136.
12. Zhou G D, Li J H, Qian L H, et al. Semi-Supervised Learning for Relation Extraction[C]//IJCNLP. 2008: 32-39.
13. Qian L, Zhou G. Clustering-based stratified seed sampling for semi-supervised relation classification[C]//Proceedings of the 2010 Conference on Empirical Methods in Natural Language Processing. Association for Computational Linguistics, 2010: 346-355.
14. Hasegawa T, Sekine S, Grishman R. Discovering relations among named entities from large corpora[C]//Proceedings of the 42nd Annual Meeting on Association for Computational Linguistics. Association for Computational Linguistics, 2004: 415.
15. Zhang M, Su J, Wang D, et al. Discovering relations between named entities from a large raw corpus using tree similarity-based clustering[M]//Natural Language Processing–IJCNLP 2005. Springer Berlin Heidelberg, 2005: 378-389.

16. Hui H T, Li Y J, Qian L H, et al. A Chinese-English Parallel Corpus for Information Extraction[J]. Computer Engineering and Science, 2015, 37(12): 2331-2338.
17. GuoDong Z, Jian S, Jie Z, et al. Exploring various knowledge in relation extraction[C]//Proceedings of the 43rd annual meeting on association for computational linguistics. Association for Computational Linguistics, 2005: 427-434.

Named Entity Recognition for Chinese Novels in the

Ming-Qing Dynasties

Yunfei Long, Dan Xiong, Qin Lu, Minglei Li, Chu-Ren Huang

Department of Computing, The Hong Kong Polytechnic University
{csylong,csdxiong,csluqin,csmli}@comp.polyu.edu.hk

Abstract. This paper presents a Named Entity Recognition (NER) system for Chinese classic novels in the Ming and Qing dynasties using the Conditional Random Fields (CRFs) method. An annotated corpus of four influential vernacular novels produced during this period is used as both training and testing data. In the experiment, three novels are used as training data and one novel is used as the testing data. Three sets of features are proposed for the CRFs model: (1) baseline feature set, that is, word/POS and bigram for different window sizes, (2) dependency head and dependency relationship, and (3) Wikipedia categories. The F-measures for these four books range from 67% to 80%. Experiments show that using the dependency head and relationship as well as Wikipedia categories can improve the performance of the NER system. Compared with the second feature set, the third one can produce greater improvement.

Keywords: Named entity recognition, dependency parsing, Wikipedia, Chinese vernacular novels

1   Introduction

Chinese classic novels are much more complicated for both readers and researches because named entities in earlier literature make use of different words and forms reflecting the social and historical customs of those eras. The lack of properly annotated data and other relevant resources makes automatic

© Springer International Publishing AG 2016
M. Dong et al. (Eds.): CLSW 2016, LNAI 10085, pp. 362–375, 2016
DOI: 10.1007/978-3-319-49508-8_34

system for NER particularly challenging. This work aims to develop an NER system specialized for Chinese vernacular novels produced during the Ming and Qing dynasties. The training corpus used for this work contains four influential works of vernacular fiction, namely, A Dream of Red Mansions (《紅樓夢》), Romance of the Three Kingdoms (《三國演義》), Water Margin (《水滸傳》), and The Golden Lotus (《金瓶梅》), referred to as the four novels in the following sections. The corpus, which has been segmented, includes manually annotated named entities (Xiong et al., 2013) and automatically added Part-of-Speech (POS) (Chiu et al., 2015). Our attempt is to investigate that with limited resources, how an NER system can perform, and what additional resources may help us to improve performance. The algorithm- we choose is the CRFs method. Experiments show that additional features such as head words using dependency parsing and external knowledge in Wikipedia can help improve the system's F-score in the range of 6% to 11%.

2   Related Work

Compared with researches of NER in modern Chinese, much less efforts have been made for Chinese vernacular novels due to the lack of resources. There was an annotated corpus, called Tagged Corpus of Early Mandarin Chinese (Wei et al., 1997; Academia Sinica, 2001), including some Chinese classic novels produced in the Ming and Qing dynasties. In this corpus, personal names are treated as proper nouns (tagged with "Nb") but not further classified. For example, in *Water Margin*, the surname "宋(Nb)", the given name "江(Nb)", and the courtesy name "公明(Nb)" are all tagged with "Nb". In addition, terms of address and official positions in this corpus are just treated as common nouns (tagged with "Na"), for instance, "父親(Na)宋(Nb)太公(Na)" (*fùqin(Na) Sòng(Nb) tàigōng(Na), his father Mr. Song*) and "蔡(Nb)太師(Na) " (*Cài(Nb) tàishī(Na), Imperial Tutor Cai*). In the four novels used for this work, these named entities are further classified and annotated in a more systematic way, which will be introduced in details in Section 3.

Researchers have explored the effectiveness of different features used for NER. One of them is the dependency head and relationship, which has long been used as indicators for named entities. Kazama and Torisawa (2008) introduced dependency relations between verbs and multi-word nouns to construct a gazetteer for NER in Japanese. Affected by the difference in lexical meanings, putting raw Chinese classic text sequence into a parser will return an unreliable result. So, few researches put effort into using dependency parsing in classical Chinese NER.

Other work made use of Wikipedia as a knowledge base for NLP tasks. Bunescu and Pasca (2006) presented a method for disambiguating ambiguous entities exploiting internal links in Wikipedia as training examples. Kazama and Torisawa (2007) conducted an experiment to exploit Wikipedia as external knowledge for NER. The two structures built into Wikipedia, redirections and disambiguation pages were used in the NER system for Wikipedia corpus. Study to use Wikipedia in NER was expended from single language to multi-language (Nothman et al 2013) and produced promising results because a fully constructed high quality and high coverage gazetteer from Wikipedia has been extracted. Based on our investigation, the Wikipedia categories provide a more direct indication for Chinese classics, for example: 宰相/nu1 (*zǎixiàng/nu1, the Prime Minister in Ancient China*) has categories like [政府首脑] (the head of the government) to indicate it is an official position. But this entry has 17 disambiguation pages and 12 re-direction sub-pages. Implement this two features would bring huge amount of noises.

3   Named Entities in the Corpus

In accordance with the specification, a corpus of four classical novels in the Ming and Qing dynasties, namely, A Dream of Red Mansions (《紅樓夢》), Romance of the Three Kingdoms (《三國演義》), Water Margin (《水滸傳》), and The Golden Lotus (《金瓶梅》), has been annotated through a computer-aided method followed by manual review in Xiong et al.(2013). In the annotated corpus of the four Chinese classic novels, named entities are mainly classified into six categories: personal name (tagged with /nr), titles including name of official position and title of nobility or honor (/nu), term of address (/na), place name (/ns), organization name (/nt), and building name (/nv). Table 1 lists the categories of the named entities, their subcategories, their tags, and examples for each category. Figure 1 shows the classification system tree of named entities and their tags in the corpus.

As shown in Table 1, there are some com-pound named entities which contain several terms and even other types of named entities. In this case, the annotation method of Peking University for corpus processing (Yu et al., 2003) is adopted: square brackets ([]) are used to enclose compound named entities and the slash sign (/) is used to separate different units. The terms in the square brackets are annotated according to the specification for Chinese classic novels in the Ming and Qing dynasties (Xiong et al., 2013). For example, the compound official position, [幽州/ns2# 太守]/nu1 ([Yōuzhōu/ns2# tàishǒu]/nu1, Prefect of Youzhou), is bracketed, in which the place name is also tagged. We provide the detailed named entity by distribution in the table 2.

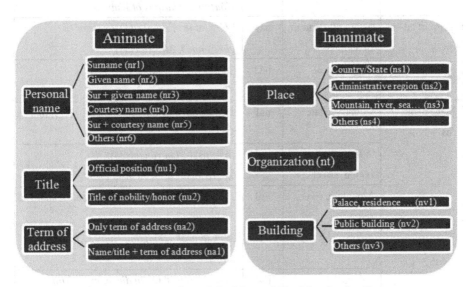

Figure 1. Categories of the Named Entities in the Corpus.

Category		Tag	Example
Personal name /nr	Surname	nr1	劉/nr1# (*Liú/nr1#*)[1];
	Given name	nr2	備/nr2# (*Bèi/nr2#*);
	Sur + given name	nr3	劉備/nr3# (*Liú Bèi/nr3#*);

---

[1] In the corpus, real named entities are labeled with "#" to distinguish them from fictional ones to facilitate future researches. But in this paper, the real and fictional ones are treated in the same way.

Category		Tag	Example
	Courtesy name	nr4	玄德/nr4# (*Xuándé/nr4#*);
	Sur + courtesy name	nr5	劉玄德/nr5# (*Liú Xuándé/nr5#*);
	Others	nr6	阿瞞/nr6# (*Ā'mán/nr6#, infant name of Cao Cao*)
Title /nu	Official position	nu1	[幽州/ns2# 太守]/nu1 (*[Yōuzhōu/ns2# tàishǒu]/nu1, Prefect of Youzhou*)
	Title of nobility/honor	nu2	[武平/ns2# 侯]/nu2 (*[Wǔpíng/ns2# Hóu]/nu2, Marquis of Wuping*)
Term of address /na	Name/title + term of address	na1	[玄德/nr4# 公]/na1# (*[Xuándé/nr4# gōng]/na1#, Mr. Xuande*)
	Only term of address	na2	父/na2 (*fù/na2, father*)
Place name /ns	Country, State	ns1	鮮卑國/ns1# (*Xiānbēi Guó/ns1#, the Xianbei State*)
	Administrative region, street...	ns2	洛陽/ns2# (*Luòyáng/ns2#*); 紫石街/ns2 (*Zǐshí Jiē/ns2, Zishi Street*)
	Mountain, river, sea...	ns3	北邙山/ns3# (*Běimáng Shān/ns3#, Beimang Mountain*); 洞庭湖/ns3# (*Dòngtíng Hú/ns3#, Dongting Lake*)
	Others	ns4	西津渡口/ns4# (*Xījīn dùkǒu/ns4#, Xijin Ferry*)
Organization name /nt		nt	樞密院/nt (*Shū Mì Yuàn/nt, the Privy Council*)
Building name /nv	Palace, residence ...	nv1	長樂宮/nv1# (*Chánglè Gōng/nv1#, Changle Palace*)
	Public building	nv2	鎮國寺/nv2 (*Zhènguó Sì/nv2, Zhenguo Temple*)
	Others	nv3	楓橋/nv3 (*Fēng Qiáo/nv3, Feng Bridge*)

Table 1. Named Entities in the Corpus.

	Romance of the Three Kingdoms t	Water Margin	The Golden Lotus	A Dream of Red Mansions
nv1	84	137	739	427
nv2	17	162	134	207
nv3	66	23	16	123
nu1	2213	634	162	1389
nu2	709	14	289	88
na1	1398	6154	9270	3539
na2	5303	11254	8271	7794
nt	3	131	85	145
ns1	14	0	12	0
ns2	4390	944	320	3665
ns3	778	88	48	763
ns4	235	23	35	775
nr1	988	154	246	460
nr2	10654	3100	7885	514
nr3	17707	9927	5629	27653
nr4	4579	19	96	12
nr5	450	43	61	355
nr6	1194	9236	6569	3759

Table 2. Named Entities distribution in corpus by types.

4   CRFs and Features Used

4.1   Algorithm

We treat NER as a sequential labeling issue and apply the CRFs model (Lafferty et al., 2001). To detect and classify a named entity through the sequence labeling technique, it is necessary to determine the beginning and the end of a named entity. In this case, the CRFs model is used. Let $x = x_1, x_2 \ldots x_t, \ldots, x_T$ $1 \leq t \leq T$ be a sequence of Chinese words with length T and $y = y_1, y_2 \ldots y_t, \ldots, y_T$ $1 \leq t \leq T$ be a corresponding sequence of output labels. Each observation x_t is then associated with a label, for example: $y_t \in$ {B-nr1, I-nr1, B-ns1, I-ns1, O...}, which indicates whether the character x_t is a part of a named entity. B-ns1 indicates the beginning of a Chinese country/state name, and I-ns1 is the continuation of the name. O (outside) refers to the fact that the character is not a part of a named entity.

The effectiveness of any learning method is also dependent on the features used. We evaluate different feature sets for NER. For the baseline feature set, we explore three types of commonly used features in a context window including word context, their corresponding POS, and bigrams in the window. These features are widely used in NER for modern Chinese texts. The annotated corpus for Chinese classics is very limited, we explore two additional feature sets related to lexical meaning representation: the dependency parsing based feature and Wikipedia feature.

4.2   Dependency Parsing Feature

Using words from sentences, a parser generates labeled dependency links between a head and its dependent. With respect to the dependency tree of a sentence, the relationship between the dependency head and its dependents has some properties which may provide useful hints to NER. Although many Chinese dependency parsers are available, most of them are trained on modern Chinese text and are not suitable for Ming-Qing Chinese novels. The performance of dependency parsing in Chinese is highly dependent on correct word segmentation and POS tagging. This is particularly challenging to perform segmentation on Ming-Qing Chinese novels. However, in this corpus, the segmentation and POS are manually annotated already. So we can directly feed the segmented text with POS into a dependency parser. We choose the HIT dependency parser (Che, 2010) and extract two features: dependency head and its relationship. **Figure 2** gives us an example about dependency head and relationship features.

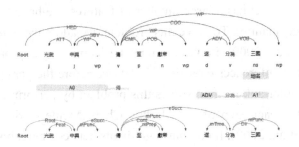

Figure 2: The dependency parsing feature

4.3   Wikipedia Feature

Wikipedia articles have many useful structures for knowledge extraction such as headings, lists, internal links, categories, and tables. These are marked up by using the Wikipedia syntax in source files, annotated naturally by authors.

In Wikipedia, categories are particularly useful as it can be applied to cluster pages of similar subjects. Categories help readers to find, and navigate around a subject area to see pages sorted by title, and to thus find articles in similar areas. If available, it provides the semantic information for entity identification for NER task[2]. The categories of an entry can be extracted by Python wiki API[3].

Table 2 shows the features used for an example sentence "光武/n 中興/n，/w 傳/v 至/p 獻帝/n ，/w 遂/m 分/v 為/p 三/m 國/n 。/w" (*Guāngwǔ/n zhōngxīng/n ，/w chuán/v zhì/p XiànDì/n ，/w suì/m fēn/v wéi/p sān/m gu ó/n 。/w, Emperor Guangwu restored the Han dynasty, but after the reign of Emperor Xian, the realm was split into three kingdoms.*). The word "獻帝" (*Xiàn Dì, Emperor Xian*) is set as the current word. Note that since there is an entry for Emperor Xian, that category is used as a feature.

---

[2] https://en.wikipedia.org/wiki/Help:Category

[3] https://pypi.python.org/pypi/wikipedia

Since the CRFs model has a large number of features, we have to estimate parameters in large quantity. To solve this problem, we adopt the SampleRank algorithm (Wick et al., 2009). Previous parameter learni ng approach (Wallach, 2002) requires inferences over the full dataset before the parameters are updated. The SampleRank method solves this problem by performing parameter updates within each step of the Markov Chain Monte Carlo (MCMC) inference (Wick et al., 2009). It computes gradients between neighboring configurations in an MCMC chain. When disagreement occurs between model ranking and objective ranking, a higher model score is assigned to the sample that has a lower loss. By so doing, the SampleRank algorithm reduces the number of iterations in parameter estimation.

Feature Set	Representation	Explanation	Examples
1 Baseline feature set	C_n (n=-3, -2, -1,0,1,2,3)	The current word and its neighboring words in window size 3	C_{-3}= '中興'(ZhongXing) C_{-2}='傳'(Chuan) C_{-1}=' 至 '(Zhi) C_0='獻帝'(XianDi) C_1= '遂 '(Sui) C_2= ' 分 '(Fen) C_3=' 為 '(Wei)
	T_n (n=-3, -2, -1,0,1,2,3)	POS of the current word and its neighboring words in window size 3	T_{-3}=n T_{-2}=o T_{-1}=p T_0=n T_1=m T_2=v T_3=p
	C_nC_{n+1}(n=-2, -1,0,1)	Word bigram in window size 2	$C_{-2}C_{-1}$='中興/傳' $C_{-1}C_0$='傳/至' C_0C_1=' 至 / 獻 帝 ' C_1C_2='遂/分'
2 Dependency feature	P	Dependency head of the current word based on parser	P('獻帝') = '至'
	R	Semantic relationship be-	R('獻帝') = 'POB'

		tween the current word and its dependency parent	
3 Wikipedia feature	WikiDictCategory	Category of the current word in Wiki page	WikiDictCategory('獻帝') ='東漢皇帝','181年出生','234年逝世','三國人','中國末代皇帝','末代帝王','諡孝獻','諡孝愍'.

Table 2. Description of Feature Sets.

5 Performance Evaluation

5.1 Statistics of the Named Entities

Because the huge overlap of Named entities in this four novels, cross validation within novels would lead to overfitting. In our experiments, three novels are used as training data and one novel is used for testing so that there is no closed test. Table 3 lists the number of the named entities in each novel. The same named entity is counted only once no matter how many times it appears in the corpus. The data indicates the variety of the named entities in a novel. To assess the effectiveness of the system to handle out of training data, the overlapping ratio of the named entities in the training and testing data is calculated. When A Dream of Red Mansions is used as testing data and the other three novels are used for training, the lowest overlapping ratio is only 4.09% and the highest is 6.71% (Water Margin), still quite small.

Testing Dataset	Number	Overlapping Ratio
Romance of the Three Kingdoms	4,372	5.54%
Water Margin	4,142	6.71%
The Golden Lotus	3,544	6.40%
A Dream of Red Mansions	2,567	4.09%

Table 3. Statistics of the Named Entities.

5.2   Experimental Results

Each novel is tested in turn while the other three novels are used as training data. To evaluate which feature set is more effective, four experiments are conducted by using different feature sets from **Table 2**:

(1) Baseline: using the baseline feature set only, that is, word/POS (tuned for optimal window size of [-3,3]) and bigram (tuned for optimal window size of [-2, 2]),

(2) B + D: using (1) and the two dependency features, head and relation-ship,

(3) B + W: using (1) and Wikipedia category,

(4) All: Using all the three feature sets

Weighted precision (P), recall (R), and F-score (F) of all named entity cat-egories are used as the performance measures. For a compound named entity, such as [幽州/ns2# 太守]/nu1 (*[Yōuzhōu/ns2# tàishǒu]/nu1, Prefect of Youzhou*), correct recognition means that the whole compound is recognized without any mistake or loss. **Table 4** lists the results of the four experiments using different feature sets.

Feature Set	Romance of the Three Kingdoms			Water Margin			The Golden Lotus			A Dream of Red Mansions		
	P	R	F	P	R	F	P	R	F	P	R	F
(1) Baseline	88.72	57.61	69.86	91.34	61.81	73.73	79.30	51.01	62.08	81.36	48.73	60.95
(2) B + D	90.72	58.91	71.43	91.73	65.86	76.67	79.80	57.58	66.89	81.52	52.74	64.05
(3) B + W	92.31	62.47	74.51	92.36	69.86	79.55	81.82	58.76	68.40	82.51	55.47	66.34
(4) All	92.29	62.77	**74.72**	91.74	71.42	**80.31**	81.95	60.03	**69.3**	82.52	56.31	**66.94**
Net increase	3.57	5.16	4.86	0.4	9.61	6.58	2.65	9.02	7.22	1.16	7.58	5.99
Improvement from (1) to (4)	4.02	8.96	**6.96**	0.44	15.55	**8.92**	3.34	17.68	**11.63**	1.43	15.56	**9.83**

Table 4. Experimental Results.

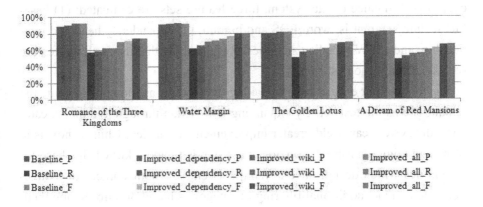

Figure 2. Results of Experiment 1.

Table 4 and **Figure 2**. shows that the best results are achieved when all the three feature sets are used. This indicates that all the selected feature sets are helpful for NER. Compared to using only the baseline feature set, the F-scores of the four novels in the experiments using all the three feature sets improve by at least 6.96% with the greatest improvement to over 11.63%, as listed in **Table 4**. The overlapping ratio shown in **Table 3** affects the results of each novel. In the four experiments, *Water Margin* with the highest overlapping ratio achieves the best results, and *A Dream of Red Mansions* with the lowest overlapping ratio has the lowest F-scores. However, there is an exception: *The Golden Lotus*, with a higher overlapping ratio than *Romance of the Three Kingdoms*, gets lower F-scores. This is because the former one, focusing on urban life at the time, depicts details of people's daily lives and uses various informal ways for addressing. This proves to be difficult for the system.

By considering dependency and Wikipedia categories as two independent features, Wikipedia categories give larger improvement.

6   Conclusion

This paper presents a CRFs-based system for NER in Chinese classic novels. An annotated corpus of four influential novels of the Ming and Qing dynasties is used for training and testing. To find the best method to improve the overall performance of the system, three feature sets are evaluated: (1) baseline feature set, that is, word/POS and bigram, (2) dependency head and relationship, and (3) Wikipedia categories. Results show that using all the feature sets can achieve the best results.

We conduct our experiments by taking three books as training set while the remain one as the test set. By expanding knowledge through Wikipedia category, the system can yield greater improvement for ancient Chinese novels in Ming and Qing dynasty. An obvious next step is to adopt knowledge base for the entities which do not have a Wikipedia entry. Another interesting direction is to conduct additional filtering of categories based on information theory to reduce noise in the feature set.

Acknowledgement

The work was partially supported by Hong Kong Polytechnic University (PolyU RTVU and CERG PolyU 15211/14E).

References

1. Razvan Bunescu and Marius Pasca. 2006. Using Encyclopedic Knowledge for Named entity Disambiguation. Proceedings of EACL-06: 9-16.

2. Wanxiang Che, Zhenghua Li, and Ting Liu. 2010. LTP: A Chinese Language Technology Platform. Proceedings of the Coling 2010, Demo Volume: 13-16.

3. Tin-shing Chiu, Qin Lu, and Jian Xu, et al. 2015. PoS Tagging for Classical Chinese Text. Chinese Lexical Semantics (CLSW2015 Revised Selected Papers), LNAI, vol. 9332: 448–456. Springer, Heidelberg

4. Jun'ichi Kazama and Kentaro Torisawa. 2007. Exploiting Wikipedia as external knowledge for named entity recognition. Proceedings of the 2007 Joint Conference on Empirical Methods in Natural Language Processing and Computational Natural Language Learning (EMNLP-CoNLL): 698-707.

5. Jun'ichi Kazama and Kentaro Torisawa. 2008. Inducing gazetteers for named entity recognition by large-scale clustering of dependency relations. Proceedings of ACL-08: HLT: 407-415.

6. John Lafferty, Andrew McCallum, and Fernando Pereira. 2001. Conditional Random Fields: Probabilistic Models for Segmenting and Labeling Sequence Data. Proceedings of the Eighteenth International Conference on Machine Learning, 282-289.

7. Joel Nothman, Nicky Ringland, and Will Radford, et al. 2013. Learning multilingual named entity recognition from Wikipedia. Artificial Intelligence 194: 151-175.

8. Academia Sinica. 2001. Academia Sinica Tagged Corpus of Early Mandarin Chinese: http://app.sinica.edu.tw/cgi-bin/kiwi/pkiwi/kiwi.sh

9. Hanna Wallach. 2002. Efficient Training of Conditional Random Fields. Proc. 6th Annual CLUK Research Colloquium.

10. Pei-chuan Wei, P.M. Thompson, and Cheng-hui Liu, et al. 1997. Historical Corpora for Synchronic and Diachronic Linguistics Studies. International Journal of Computational Linguistics & Chinese Language Processing, 2(1): 131–145.

11. Michael Wick, Khashayar Rohanimanesh, Aron Culotta, and Andrew McCallum. 2009. SampleRank: Learning Preferences from Atomic Gradients. Neural Information Processing Systems (NIPS), Workshop on Advances in Ranking.

12. Dan Xiong, Qin Lu, and Fengju Lo, et al. 2013. Specification for Segmentation and Named Entity Annotation of Chinese Classics in the Ming and Qing Dynasties. Chinese Lexical Semantics (CLSW2012 Revised Selected Papers), LNCS, vol. 7717: 280-293. Springer, Heidelberg

13. Shiwen Yu, Huiming Duan, and Xuefeng ZhuYu, et al. 2003. Specification for Corpus Processing at Peking University: Word Segmentation, POS Tagging and Phonetic Notation. Journal of Chinese Language and Computing 13(2): 121–158.

14. Help: Category. (n.d.). In Wikipedia. Retrieved August 10, 2004, https://en.wikipedia.org/wiki/Help:Category

Chinese Text Proofreading Model of Integration of Error Detection and Error Correction

Yizhuo Sun, Yangsen Zhang, and Yanhua Zhang

Institute of Intelligence Information Processing, Beijing Information Science & Technology University, Beijing 100192

zys@bistu.edu.cn

Abstract. In text proofreading area, the error detection and error correction are reversible process to each other. In this paper, considering them in the same angle, we put forward an idea of "scattered string concentration", and combine the bidirectional Pinyin knowledge bases to improve the accurate of positioning error. We fill the gaps between error detection and error correction fundamentally, so as to achieve the effective integration of error detection and error correction. In this paper, the error detection model of today's text is optimized and the sorting algorithm of the error correction is discussed. The experimental results show that the recall rate of this method is 95.37%, the accuracy rate is 83%, and the method has good application prospect.

Keywords: Scattered string, Error detection and error correction, Bidirectional pinyin knowledge base.

1 Overview

In recent years, the studies of text error detection and text error correction have made great progress, while most of the previous studies divided these two methods separately, which would affect accuracy and practicability of text correction. In this paper, considering the correlation of error detection and error correction, we expanded the contents of existing error detection knowledge base, and optimized error detection model according to the characters of main stream input method's frequent errors, so that we could dispatch the knowledge base reasonably, at the same time error correction suggestions candidate set was given by converse solution thought.

2 The Research Status at Home and Abroad

Foreign text proofreading technology has reached a certain degree of maturity, and has launched a series of practical business systems, such as "Word" which is commonly used software and so on. English text automatic proofreading mainly focuses on non-word errors and context dependent errors[2].

There are many excellent proofreading commercial softwares such as "Black-Horse", "JINSHAN", "Wen Jie" and so on in domestic. There are three levels errors in Chinese text: word level errors, grammar level errors and semantic level errors [4].

© Springer International Publishing AG 2016
M. Dong et al. (Eds.): CLSW 2016, LNAI 10085, pp. 376–386, 2016
DOI: 10.1007/978-3-319-49508-8_35

Word level research has got preferable results, for example the literature [5] proposed error algorithm of the word level based on continuous word. The literature [6] showed the algorithm based on combination of rules and statistics. Based on pattern matching and combination of sentence pattern composition analysis method to Grammar level error detection is presented in literature [7]. Literature [8] proposed semantic level error detection algorithm based on sememe matching of HowNet, and achieved better effect. As a result, the text proofreading is widely applied, in many areas, the basis of natural language processing research is dependent on it, a lot of application systems need to rely on its reform and development. Therefore text proofreading has an indispensable position in the field of natural language processing and is valuable of academic research.

3   Error Detection Model

3.1   The Basic Thought of Error Detection

The word error mainly contains typo, translocation, multi word etc. It mainly contains the true multi-word error and non-multi-word error. The true multi-word error is the existence of a dictionary, but does not conform to the context, however, the non-multi-word error is not included in the dictionary.

Literature [6] clearly pointed out that after the segmentation of the text, the words contained in the text are generally more than two words, in general the single word basically is auxiliary, preposition, adverb, conjunction and so on, such as "的" (de), "了" (le).

After the text segmentation, the general appearance of the length of the "scattered single string" does not exceed two, it can be assumed that, in the text after the word segmentation, the word string may contain errors if there are more than two single words in the text.

N-gram model is one of the most commonly used models in Natural Language Processing. It is assumed that the appearance of element W_i is only related to the sequence $W_{i-n+1} \cdots W_{i-1}$ which is composed of the former N-1 elements.

$$P(W_i|W_1...W_{i-1}) = P(W_i|W_{i-n+1}...W_{i-1}) \tag{1}$$

As it can be seen from the formula (1), the N-gram model is a local analysis method based on historical information. When the N value is greater, the structure of the sentence is more accurate. But with the increasing of N value, it will increase the requirements of storage resources, generally in the practical application, we choose the value of N for 2 or 3. Using the N-gram model, when N=2, we can judge the connection relationship between word and word in the string $S=X_1X_2X_3... X_{i-1}X_i...$, namely the transition probability of the P $(X_i|X_{i-1})$. Further, if X_1 and X_2 are adjacent words, we have the following formula:

$$P(X_1) = \frac{R(X_1)}{N}, P(X_2) = \frac{R(X_2)}{N} \qquad (2)$$

$$P(X_1, X_2) = \frac{R(X_1, X_2)}{N} \qquad (3)$$

The R (x_1), R (x_2), R (x_1, x_2) denote the string frequency and co-occurrence frequency of words in the training corpus, N is the number of strings in the training corpus. In the process of the text proofreading, calculating the co-occurrence frequency between two adjacent words, if the co-occurrence frequency is greater than a certain threshold, we believe that these two words are connected in a continuous relationship. Otherwise, the connection is not clear, the word may be wrong, we give the word a certain weight value.

Mutual information is another criterion in NLP area. It is a good reflection to measure the co-occurrence probability between two words in the corpus. The bigger Mutual information is, the greater the co-occurrence possibility will be.

The formula is as follows:

$$MI(A_i, A_j) = \log \frac{P(A_i, A_j)}{P(A_i) \times P(A_j)} \qquad (4)$$

Among them, P (A_i, A_j) expresses the common occurrence frequency of the A_i and A_j in the training corpus.

Errors in Chinese texts are mostly expressed in terms of characters and words, so it is very important to find out the errors of words. Word error detection is mainly aimed at the error detection between adjacent character and character, adjacent single character and word, adjacent word and word, and can check out the errors caused by the destruction of the surface structure of words, from the characters, words and other languages. N-gram model can effectively reflect the consecutive relationship of every single character, single character and word, word and word. And Mutual information model can clearly show the co-occurrence probability between every single character, single character and word, word and word.

3.2   Construction of knowledge Base of Error Detection

According to the characteristics of N-gram model and Mutual information model, in this paper we design and build a large amount of knowledge base, which is the basis of the whole error detection model, including: for word level error detection "single-character into word knowledge base", "2-character-word knowledge base", "2-character-word comprehensive knowledge base". The construction of Knowledge bases is as follows in table 1:

Table 1. Knowledge Base of Error Detection

Type	Name	Quantity	Example
The knowledge bases of error detection	single-character into word knowledge base	4558	朝:1410
	2-character-word knowledge base	1461960	做做:30
	2-character-word comprehensive knowledge base	2359544	主动 克服:1 2.22408236438723

According to the above discussion and description, the word error detection model is shown in algorithm 1.

Algorithm 1. Word Error Detection Model

Step1: Input the original text and preprocessing it with word segmentation tool. Then turn to step 2;

Step2: Scanning text to find the scattered single-word string in the original text. If the length of the string is 1, then estimate that whether this word can form a phrase itself basing on the single-word-phrase knowledge base. If the result is negative, then put this word and its position into the error array. Otherwise, turn to step 3;

Step3: If the length of the scattered single-word string is not 1, record this string as $W_1W_2......W_i$ and process it's sub strings. Then turn to step 4;

Step4: Starting from W1, estimate that whether this word can form a phrase itself. If the result is positive, set the error factor K as 1.6. Otherwise, turn to step 5;

Step5: Merge current word respectively with the last word of its preceding phrase and the first word of its following phrase into a two-word phrase. Set the value of K according to this two-words phrase's frequency in the two-words-phrase knowledge base, referred as Freq. If Freq>=1 and Freq<3, K +=0.8. If Freq>=3, K-=1.0. If Freq=0, K+=0.8. Then turn to step 6.

Step6: Merge current word respectively with its preceding word and following word into a two-word phrase. Find its corresponding two-word phrase in the mutual information knowledge base using the first letter of the first word of this phrase and get its frequency, referred as Freq, and the value of its mutual information, referred as MI. Then turn to step 7;

Step7: determine the value of Freq and MI, so as to give the error factor K weighting. If Freq>=1 and Freq<2, K-=0.5, if Freq>=2, K-=1.0, if Freq=0, that does not exist, K+=1.0 to Step8;

Step8: determine the value of MI. If K+=0.1, if MI<=2 and MI>1, K-=0.5, if MI>2, K-=1.0, if not exist, MI<=1, K+=1.0, Step9;

Step9: determine the K value, if K>1.6, think the word is wrong, will the current word added to the error string array. Step10;

Step10: end.

4   Error Positioning Model

4.1   The Basic Thought of Error Positioning

Scattered string centralized strategy: After text error detection, a certain strategy is proposed to determine whether the combination (character with wrong sign and other characters) could be composed into an integrated word which may need to be corrected. This method is described as "scattered string centralized".

Because error detection is based on the scattered string, there is a common phenomenon, that there are errors in the adjacent or nonadjacent characters in the word, after the text of the error detection ,only one word can be marked in red, and not the whole can be marked in red, such as "售/v 书亭/n 琳琅满目/i ，/w 一/m 本本/n 刊物/n 争/v 奇/ag 斗/v 燕/ng", only "燕" will be marked in red. When using the knowledge base for error detection, although the wrong character could be detected and marked in red，it will bring great difficulties to the follow-up work that is error correction [16] I believe that error detection and error correction are interrelated and are very close in terms of ideology. The error correction is error detection reverse solving process, both of them focus on differences. The former is to detect the error, the latter is likely to generate the correct candidate set and gives the error correction suggestion. So both of them need to be considered from the angle of unified perspective, we should use the corresponding reverse error correction model. Previous studies have always separate the two parts, it has a great impact on the validity and usefulness of the system. In view of the error detection model based on the single character scattered string, after the error detection is completed, using the knowledge base of bidirectional Pinyin, the characters will be combined into a word according to the number of characters，then they will be marked in red and be programed to the next step that is error correction as the error word, so error detection and error correction can be combined together effectively and we fill the gap between the error detection and the error correction fundamentally.

Text description method: In the text, if the current word's formal description is $Word_i$, thus the former is $Word_{i-1}$ and the latter is $Word_{i+1}$, we could describe the whole text by any word description. The specific formal description methods shown in Table2.

Table2. Formal Description Text mode

...	$Word_{i-1}$	$Word_i$	$Word_{i+1}$	...

In the error detection system of this paper, three kinds of cases, including two words, three words and four words, are mainly focused on scattered string concentration, and determination of whether these characters can be combined into words, the specific strategies of combination as shown in table 3.

As it can be seen from table 3, after the completion of the error detection, the current wrong word can combine with the front characters or back characters of this current word, the number of characters is not more than three. The order of scattered string centralized is that any word which contains more characters would be higher priority, thus the continuous scattered string would be firstly determined whether it could be combined into a 4-character-word, and then a 3-character-word, final a 2-

character-word, and then the combined word would be regarded as a candidate word marked in red, and at the same time error correction suggestions set about this word would be given according to those knowledge bases constructed in the error detection step.

Table 3. Scattered String Concentration Policy Table

					Current word			
Double words	1				W_i	W_{i+1}		
	2			W_{i-1}	W_i			
Three words	3				W_i	W_{i+1}	W_{i+2}	
	4			W_{i-1}	W_i	W_{i+1}		
	5		W_{i-2}	W_{i-1}	W_i			
Four Words	6				W_i	W_{i+1}	W_{i+2}	W_{i+3}
	7			W_{i-1}	W_i	W_{i+1}	W_{i+2}	
	8		W_{i-2}	W_{i-1}	W_i	W_{i+1}		
	9	W_{i-3}	W_{i-2}	W_{i-1}	W_i			

4.2 Construction of knowledge Bases of Error Positioning

In this paper we design and build a large amount of bidirectional pinyin knowledge bases, which is the basis of the error positioning model, the bidirectional pinyin knowledge base is made up of three parts, including: " single-character-bidirectional-pinyin knowledge base", "2-character-bidirectional-pinyin knowledge base", "multi-character-bidirectional-pinyin knowledge base". The function of the knowledge base of bidirectional-pinyin is to read the "2-character-word comprehensive knowledge base", concentrate scattered string and position the error. The Structural form of knowledge bases of error positioning is as follows in table 4.

According to the discussion and description above, the construction of the word error positioning model is shown in algorithm 2.

Table 4. Bidirectional-pinyin Knowledge Base

Type	Name	Quantity	Example
Bidirectional-pinyin Knowledge base	Single-character bidirectional-pinyin Knowledge base	20902	宫 Gong Gong 宫
	2-character- bidirectional-pinyin Knowledge base	29145	Zuzong 祖宗 祖宗 Zuzong
	Multi-character- bidirectional-pinyin Knowledge base	24546	Aihaozhe 爱好者 爱好者 Aihaozhe

Algorithm 2. Error Positioning Model

Step1: Scan text after the error detection algorithm, find words whose flag is true, turn to step 2;

Step2: Record this word. Process this word with the four-character-word strategy shows in table 4.2(6-9) basing on its position index. If this word can form a word, then turn to step 6, otherwise turn to step 3;

Step3: Process this word with the three-character-word strategy shows in table 4.2(3-5). If this word can form a word, turn to step 6, otherwise turn to step 4;

Step4: according to table two in the 4.2 word strategy (1-2) to match, if the current word can be a word, then turn Step6, or Step5

Step5: the current word with the upper and lower words, so only the current word into the wrong array, turn Step6;

Step6: with combination of words constitute the current word added to array errors, and the word in the knowledge base corresponding to the word as the error correction suggestions added to propose candidate set 1,Step7;

Step7: all the wrong words in the standard red string array, display output, Step8;

Step8: end.

5   Error Correction Model

5.1   The Basic Thought of Error Correction

As we have already mentioned previously, the error correction and the error detection are connected, but their strategies are reciprocal, according to this characteristic we constructed the following error candidate set and sorted the candidate set.

The candidate-set-1: The candidate-set-1 is composed of correct words in the knowledge base which are corresponding to the error strings we got through error positioning.

The candidate-set-2: The candidate-set-2 is composed of all the words which have the same Pinyin with the error words in bidirectional-Pinyin.

The candidate-set-3: The candidate-set-3 is composed of all the correct words which are corresponding to the current error string in the knowledge base of confusable words.

According to the discussion and description above, the construction of the word error correction model is shown in algorithm 3.

The merging principle of candidate set 2 and 3: Using 2-character-word and 2-character-mutual information to carry out the merger, the greater the co-occurrence frequency and mutual information value they have, the higher the ranking will be. And the set after the merger is called the candidate-set-4.

The principle of the finally error correction suggestion set: Merge the candidate-set-1 and the candidate-set-4 following the principle of that element of candidate-set-1 is the first element of the error correction suggestions set.

Combining with the above description of the error correction proposed generation model and combining strategy, we generated a complete flow chart as shown in Fig 1 (the sub module in the flow chart is mentioned in the fourth chapter).

Algorithm 3. Error Correction Model

Step1: Scan the text with the wrong identifier string, placed them in the wrong array, to Step2;

Step2: cycling error words, to Step3;

Step3: find Confusable words Knowledge base, if the current error word in the knowledge base, to Step4, if not to Step5;

Step4: By getting the correct word corresponding to the current error word from the Confusable words Knowledge base as candidate set 3, to Step6;

Step5: Get all the words with the same spelling as his candidate set 2, through the Bidirectional-pinyin Knowledge base, to step6;

Step6: cycling error array until the end of the array, to Step7.

Step7: merged with the candidate set 1, to Step8

Step8: end

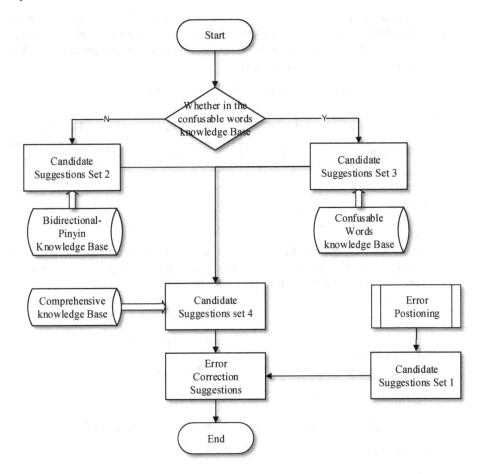

Fig 1. Error Correction Proposal Generating and Sorting Flow Chart

5.2   Construction of knowledge Base of Error Correction

According to the idea proposed in [16], based on the establishment of confusable words knowledge base, the corresponding correction suggestions could be got by consulting this knowledge base during error correction process. The knowledge Base format is shown as table 5:

Table 5. The knowledge Base of Confusable Words

Type	Name	Quantity	Example
Error correction knowledge base	Confusable words Knowledge base	74502	精粹 精萃

6   Test and Analysis of Experimental Results

Through the above proposed Chinese text proofreading model of integration of error detection and error correction, the experiment is carried out, and experimental sample set is composed of **247** real texts, which contains **231** error texts, **16** correct texts. The results are shown in the following table 6.

Table 6. Experimental Results of Error Detection

	Correct rate%	Recall rate%	F-Score%
Other documents	65.89	89.6	75.85
The results in this paper	83.00	95.37	88.76
Black-Horse results	91.53	93.68	92.59

Comparison of experimental results of positioning: Comparing with the results of "Black-Horse", our error positioning is more accurate obviously, part of experimental results are shown in the figure below. As shown in Fig 2, 3.

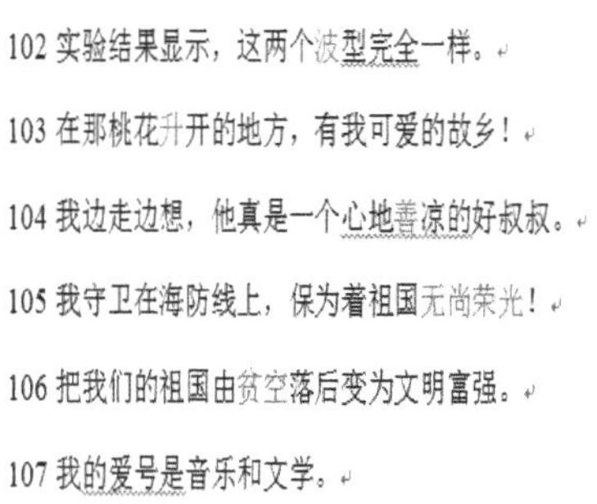

102 实验结果显示，这两个波型完全一样。

103 在那桃花升开的地方，有我可爱的故乡！

104 我边走边想，他真是一个心地善凉的好叔叔。

105 我守卫在海防线上，保为着祖国无尚荣光！

106 把我们的祖国由贫空落后变为文明富强。

107 我的爱号是音乐和文学。

Fig 2. Part Results of Black-Horse

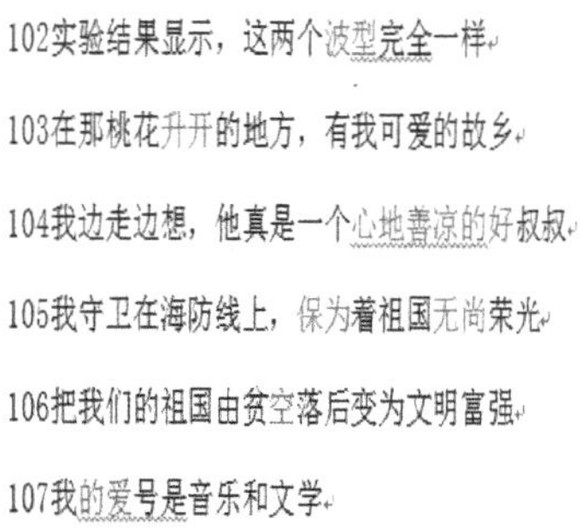

102实验结果显示，这两个波型完全一样。

103在那桃花升开的地方，有我可爱的故乡。

104我边走边想，他真是一个心地善凉的好叔叔。

105我守卫在海防线上，保为着祖国无尚荣光。

106把我们的祖国由贫空落后变为文明富强。

107我的爱号是音乐和文学。

Fig 3. Part Results in This Paper

Table 6 shows that the accuracy of error detection is significantly improved, and the positioning accuracy is also improved, the improvement of these laid the good foundation for error correction. Through the algorithm of the model, we have the results of error correction statistics, the principle of evaluation is whether the first five error correction suggestions contain the correct correction word or not. The correct rate of error correction is 80.03%, and the earlier research's correct rate is 71.24%, the correct rate of this model is increased by 8.79 percentage points. The experimental results show that the correct rate of the proposed error correction is significantly improved.

Acknowledgment. Research of this paper is funded by the National Natural Science Foundation of China (61370139),The Project of Construction of Innovative Teams and Teacher Career Development for Universities and Colleges Under Beijing Municipality（IDHT20130519）.

Reference

1. Zhang, Y.S., Yu, S.W.: Summary of Text Automatic Proofreading Technology [J]. Application Research of Computers, 6 (5), 8-12 (2006) (in Chinese).
2. K.Kukich: Techniques for automatically correcting words in text [J]. ACM Computing Surveys, 24(4), 377-439 (1992)
3. Zhang, Y.S., Ding, B.Q.: Present Condition and Prospect of Chinese Text Automatic Proofread Technology [J]. Journal of Chinese Information Processing, 12(3), 51-57 (1998) (in Chinese)
4. Zhang, L., Zhou, M., Huang, C.N.: Automatic Chinese Text Error Correction Approach Based on Fast Approximate Chinese Word-matching Algorithm[C]. Microsoft Research China Paper Collection, 231-235 (2000) (in Chinese)
5. Zhang, Y.S., Ding, B.Q.: Automatic Errors Detecting of Chinese Texts Based on the Bi-neighbor ship [J]. Journal of Chinese Information Processing, 15(3), 36-43 (2001) (in Chinese)
6. Zhang, Y.S., Cao, Y.D., Yu, S.W.: A Hybrid Model of Combining Rule-based and Statistics-based Approaches for Automatic Detecting Errors in Chinese Text [J].Journal of Chinese Information Processing, 20(4), 1-7 (2005) (in Chinese)
7. Gong, X.J., Luo, Z.S., Luo, W.H.: Automatically Detecting Syntactic Errors in Chinese Texts [J]. Journal of Computer Engineering and Applications, 39(8), 98-100 (2003) (in Chinese)
8. Guo, C., Zhang, Y.S.: Study of semantic automatic error-detecting for Chinese text based on sememe matching of Hownet [J]. Computer Engineering and Design, 31(17), 3924-3928 (2010) (in Chinese)
9. Wu, L., Zhang, Y.S.: Reasoning Model of Multi-level Chinese Text Error-detecting Based on Knowledge Bases [J]. Computer Engineering, 38(20), 21-25 (2012) (in Chinese)

10. Zhang, Y.S.: The Structuring Method of Correcting Knowledge Sets and the Producing Algorithm of Correcting Suggestion in the Chinese Text Proofreading System [J]. Journal of Chinese Information Processing, 15(5), 33-36 (2001) (in Chinese)

11. Yu, M., Yao, T.S.: A Hybrid Method for Chinese Text Collation [J]. Journal of Chinese Information Processing, 02, 32-37 (1998) (in Chinese)

12. Li, R.: A Chinese Spelling Check System for the OCR Output [J]. Journal of Chinese Information Processing, 05, 92-97 (2009) (in Chinese)

13. Joseph J Pollock. Automatic Spelling Correction in Scientific and Scholarly Text [J]. Communication of the ACM, (4), 358-368 (1984)

14. Zhang, Y.S., Tang, A.J., Zhang, Z.W.: Chinese Text Proofreading for Political News Fieid [J]. Journal of Chinese Information Processing, 28(6), 79-84+128 (2014) (in Chinese)

15. Liu, L.L., Wang, S., Wang, D.S., Wang, P.Z., Cao, C.G.: Automatic Text Error Detection in Domain Question Answering [J]. Journal of Chinese Information Processing. 27(3), 77-83 (2013) (in Chinese)

16. Zhang, Y.S., Cao, Y.D., Xu, B.: Correcting Candidate Suggestion Algorithm and Its Realization Based on Statistics [J]. Computer Engineering, 30(11), 106-109 (2004) (in Chinese)

A Sentence Segmentation Method for Ancient Chinese Texts Based on NNLM

Boli Wang[1], Xiaodong Shi[1,2,3] (✉), Zhixing Tan[1], Yidong Chen[1], Weili Wang[1]

[1] Department of Cognitive Science, Xiamen University, Xiamen 361005, China
[2] Collaborative Innovation Center for Peaceful Development of Cross-Strait Relations, Xiamen University, Xiamen 361005, China
[3] Fujian Province Key Laboratory for Brain-inspired Computing, Xiamen University, Xiamen 361005, China
mandel@xmu.edu.cn

Abstract. Most of ancient Chinese texts have no punctuations or segmentation of sentences. Recent researches on automatic ancient Chinese sentence segmentation usually resorted to sequence labelling models and utilized small data sets. In this paper, we propose a sentence segmentation method for ancient Chinese texts based on neural network language models. Experiments on large-scale corpora indicate that our method is effective and achieves a comparable result to the traditional CRF model. Implementing sentence length penalty, using larger Simplified Chinese corpora, or dividing corpora by ages can further improve performance of our model.

Keywords: Ancient Chinese · Sentence segmentation · Neural network language model

1   Introduction

In ancient Chinese texts, characters are written or printed one by one without any punctuations or extra spaces to denote boundaries of words or sentences. To make texts more readable, readers must use their language expertise and understanding of context to mark the end of clauses and sentences by themselves, which is called Judou (句读, whose literal meaning is division of sentences and clauses). Because Judou is time-consuming, only a small amount of digitalized ancient Chinese texts have been manually segmented so far. Those unsegmented texts are hard to be understood by modern laymen and also difficult to process by computer programs.

Therefore, some researches apply NLP methods to automatic sentence segmentation of ancient Chinese texts. Popular methods [1,2,3] regard sentence segmentation as a sequence labeling task and exploit classical statistical models like conditional random fields (CRF) [4]. These models use handcrafted and fixed features, including characters in local context and their properties.

Intuitively, understanding of meanings in local and global context is indispensable for accurate sentence segmentation. Therefore, we regard sentence segmentation as a

© Springer International Publishing AG 2016
M. Dong et al. (Eds.): CLSW 2016, LNAI 10085, pp. 387–396, 2016
DOI: 10.1007/978-3-319-49508-8_36

sequence generation task and employ the new neural network language model (NNLM), which introduces semantic information into the model. Giving a paragraph of unsegmented ancient Chinese text, we use a segmented ancient Chinse language model to generate punctuated text. In this paper, we only generate one type of punctuation mark (i.e. "。", which denotes the end of clauses). But our model can be extended to more complex punctuation sets.

Experimental results show that our model is comparable to the state-of-the-art CRF-based model. We also implement our model as a web service, which is available in http://jf2.cloudtranslation.cc/dj.html.

2   Related Work

2.1   Sentence Segmentation Method for Ancient Chinese Texts

[5] first proposed an n-gram model with a smoothing algorithm for ancient Chinese sentence segmentation. [6] handled sentence segmentation with a pattern-based string replacement approach. The precision of these early researches is rather low.

Later works treated sentence segmentation as a sequence labeling problem and tried CRF model with handcrafted feature templates. [1] used characters in local context. [2] implemented mutual information and T-test difference. [3] employed phonetic information, including modern Mandarin phonetic symbols Hanyu Pinyin (汉语拼音), and ancient Chinese phonetic symbols Fanqie (反切) and Guangyun (广韵). Experimental results show that CRF-based models are effective in ancient Chinese sentence segmentation. However, these methods rely mainly on handcrafted and limited features and are unable to utilize semantic information.

These existing researches trained and tested their models only on small-scale ancient Chinese corpora. Besides, there is no sentence segmentation toolkit or online service for ancient Chinese texts available yet.

2.2   Neural Network Language Model

Different from traditional statistical language model, neural network language models use distributed representation to represent semantic information of context [7]. [8] first introduced word embedding to language modeling. Words in context window are first projected to vectors and then feed into a neural network to estimate the conditional probability of next word. [9] proposed recurrent neural network based language model (RNNLM) which is capable to utilize information from full context. RNNLM is now a typical application of deep learning in natural language processing.

Note that the sentence segmentation model proposed in this paper is compatible with any kind of NNLM, despite the fact that we use RNNLM in our current implementation.

3   Our Approach

3.1   Sentence Segmentation Model

We regard ancient Chinese sentence segmentation as a sequence generation problem, which can be illustrated by the following formula:

$$\hat{Y} = \underset{Y, Y \in U(X)}{\mathrm{argmax}}\, P(Y) \tag{1}$$

where X is the input character sequence, i.e. unsegmented text; Y is the corresponding segmented text with extra punctuation marks added; $U(X)$ is a set of all possible segmentation results of X. For instance, giving $X =$ "三人行", then $U(X) =$ {"三人行","三。人行","三人。行","三。人。行"}.

Given a segmented sequence Y, we use language model to score the segmentation,

$$P(Y) = P_{lm}(Y) \tag{2}$$

where $P_{lm}(Y)$ is the joint probability of sequence Y estimated by a neural network language model.

However, language models prefer short sequences. Initial experimental results also show that this simple model tends to add a small number of punctuation marks. To address this issue, we introduced length penalty into our model:

$$P(Y) = P_{lm}(Y) + \lambda Len(Y) \tag{3}$$

where $Len(Y)$ is the length of sequence Y; λ is the weight of length penalty. Meanwhile, to make length penalty and probability of language model comparable, we transform $P_{lm}(Y)$ by taking its logarithm.

Given an unsegmented ancient Chinese paragraph, we use the beam search algorithm to find the optimal segmentation. In decoding, we keep N-best candidates temporarily for each step. We set N=15 in our experiments.

Furthermore, we use a heuristic method to deal with headlines, where no punctuation marks should be added. We propose following rules to judge whether an extra punctuation mark should be added to the end of the given sequence or not:

— If any punctuation marks have been added in decoding result, a punctuation mark should be added to the end of the sequence (because it seems to be a common paragraph).
— If no punctuation mark has been added in decoding result, no punctuation mark should be added to the end of the sequence either (because it seems to be a headline).

3.2   Neural Network Language Model

In this paper, we use character level recurrent neural network language models. We train two types of language models on segmented ancient Chinese texts. The first one is character-level language model with six punctuation types (CLM6), which means the training corpus only contains six types of punctuation marks, i.e. "。", "？", "！", "，", "；", and "：", and other punctuation marks are all removed. For the second one, we replace all six types with a unified segmentation mark, i.e. "。" and call this CLM1.

Given a sequence $S = w_1, w_2, ..., w_n$, RNNLM use a vector x_t to represent the semantic information of each character w_t. The conditional probability is estimated by a recurrent neural network as follow:

$$P(w_{t+1} = i | w_t \cdots w_1) = \frac{exp(W_i h_t)}{\sum_{j=1}^{K} exp(W_j h_t)} \tag{4}$$

where K is the size of the vocabulary; W_j is the j-th row of the weight matrix; and h_t is the encoded hidden state of RNN, which is regarded as compressed representation of current context.

At each step, RNN updates the hidden state,

$$h_t = f(x_t, h_{t-1}) \tag{5}$$

where x_t is the current input, i.e. the vector representation of current character w_t; h_{t-1} is the hidden state of the previous step; and f is a non-linear function. In this paper, we employ the new Gated Recurrent Unit (GRU) as the non-linear function f [10,11].

GRU updates h_t as follows:

$$r_t = sigmoid(W_r x_t + U_r h_{t-1}) \tag{6}$$

$$z_t = sigmoid(W_z x_t + U_z h_{t-1}) \tag{7}$$

$$\tilde{h}_t = tanh(W_h x_t + U_h(r_t \circ h_{t-1})) \tag{8}$$

$$h_t = z_t \circ h_{t-1} + (1 - z_t) \circ \tilde{h}_t \tag{9}$$

where r_t is called reset gate; z_t is called update gate; $W_r, W_z, W_h, U_r, U_z,$ and U_h are weights; $\circ$ denotes the element-wise product of the vectors.

4   Experiments

4.1   Setup

Different from existing works, our experiments are based on large scale corpora. We extract manually punctuated or segmented ancient Chinese texts from the Superfection Traditional Chinese Corpus (STCC) [1] and construct a training set of 237 million Chinese characters. Besides, we also construct a development set and two test sets, using segmented ancient Chinese texts in Traditional Chinese extracted from Hanchi

---

[1]   http://cloudtranslation.cc/corpus_tc.html

Database of Sinica Taiwan (HDST)[2] and 4HN website[3]. Table 1 shows the details of these datasets.

Table 1. Details of datasets.

Dataset	# of chars	Charset size	Source	Content
Training Set	237M	23905	STCC	
Dev. Set	0.01M	1890	HDST	Chap. 1 of *Yue Wei Cao Tang Bi Ji (阅微草堂笔记)*
Test Set 1	0.32M	6188	4HN	*Bin Tui Lu (宾退录)* *Chao Ye Qian Zai (朝野金载)* *Nan Bu Xin Shu (南部新书)* *Chu Ci Bu Zhu (楚辞补注)* *Zhong Wu Ji Wen (中吴纪闻)*
Test Set 2	0.36M	5755	HDST&4HN	Chap. 2 to Chap. 24 of *Yue Wei Cao Tang Bi Ji (阅微草堂笔记)* *Jing Zhai Gu Jin Tou (敬斋古今黈)*

We calculate precision P, recall R, and $F1$ score for sentence segmentation evaluation.

$$P = \frac{TP}{TP+FP} \tag{10}$$

$$R = \frac{TP}{TP+FN} \tag{11}$$

$$F_1 = \frac{2 \cdot P \cdot R}{P+R} \tag{12}$$

where TP, i.e. true positive, is the number of correct segmentation tags the model outputs; FP, i.e. false positive, is the number of wrong segmentation tags the model outputs; FN, i.e. false negative, is the number of wrong non-segmentation tags the model outputs.

---

[2] http://hanchi.ihp.sinica.edu.tw/ihp/hanji.htm

[3] http://www.4hn.org/

We reproduce the CRF-based sentence segmentation method as a baseline using the open-source toolkit CRF++[4]. We use the same feature template and training algorithm as [1]. We set the minimal frequency of features to 3 and use the default setting of the toolkit for other hyper-parameters.

4.2   Parameter Selection

The weight of length penalty λ is a significant hyper-parameter of our model. We evaluate the segmentation performance of CLM6 with different λ on development set. The results are shown in Fig. 1. With λ growing up, the recall increases and the precision drops accordingly. We find that when setting $\lambda = 0.65$, CLM6 achieves the highest $F1$ score.

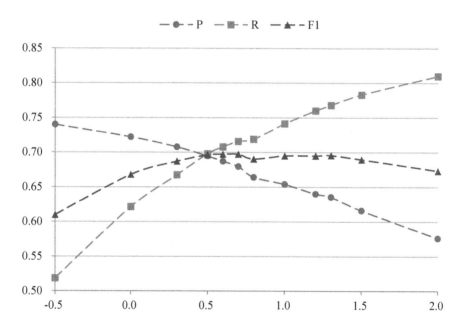

Fig. 1. Performances of CLM6 on different weights of length penalty λ.

4.3   Results

We compare our models, CLM6 and CLM1, with the baseline CRF-based model on two test sets. The experimental results are shown in Table 2. On precision, CLM6 outperforms CLM1 but cannot beat CRF-based model. CLM1 achieves higher recall

---

4   http://taku910.github.io/crfpp/

than CLM6 and CRF baseline. On $F1$ score, both CLM1 and CLM6 cannot outperform CRF baseline, but are comparable.

Table 2. Experimental results on sentence segmentation.

	Test Set 1			Test Set 2		
	P	R	F1	P	R	F1
CLM6 (λ =0)	0.7822	0.5767	0.6639	0.7283	0.6364	0.6793
CLM6 (λ =0.65)	0.7492	0.6727	0.7089	0.6861	0.7205	0.7029
CLM1 (λ =0.65)	0.7212	**0.7325**	0.7268	0.6393	**0.7691**	0.6982
CRF	**0.8163**	0.6617	**0.7309**	**0.7856**	0.7100	**0.7459**

4.4 Experiments on Large-Scale Simplified Chinese Corpus

Actually, there are much more segmented ancient Chinese texts available in Simplified Chinese (SC) than those in Traditional Chinese (TC). And the total amount of SC characters is smaller than TC characters, which may help alleviate the problem of data sparsity. Therefore, we suspect that models trained on larger SC corpus should perform better on sentence segmentation.

We extract 629 million characters of ancient Chinese texts in SC from Superfection Corpus[5]. Furthermore, we use a public toolkit[6] to convert the previous 237M TC training set into SC and combine these two corpus into a larger SC training set. We use the same method and setups as CLM1 to train a new language model on this SC set. We name this larger SC language model CLM1-S.

When segmenting sentences, we first convert the given TC sequence into SC and then generate the segmented sequence using the same method mentioned in Section 3.1. Since characters in TC sequence and SC sequence are corresponding one to one, it's easy to transfer the segmentation marks to the original TC sequence.

The experimental results are shown in Table 3. CLM1-S outperforms CLM1 in both two test set and achieves much higher $F1$ scores. This proves that employing SC-to-TC conversion does help to alleviate the data sparsity problem and improves performance of ancient Chinese sentence segmentation. Furthermore, this time the performance is better than the CRF model.

---

[5] Although the scale of this SC corpus is more than 2 times larger than the TC corpus mentioned previously, the charset size of SC one is only 21697, that is smaller than the TC one, which confirms our intuition.

[6] http://jf.cloudtranslation.cc/

Table 3. Experimental results on large-scale Simplified Chinese corpus

	Test Set 1			Test Set 2		
	P	R	F1	P	R	F1
CLM1 (λ=0.65)	0.7212	0.7325	0.7268	0.6393	0.7691	0.6982
CLM1-S (λ=0.65)	**0.8243**	**0.7988**	**0.8113**	**0.7180**	**0.8339**	**0.7716**

4.5   Experiments on Fine-Grained Model.

Our training set contains ancient Chinese texts from different times. However, lexicon and grammar of ancient Chinese varied a lot during long ages. Intuitively, subdividing training corpus by ages may lead to more accurate language models and achieve better segmentation.

Referring to the standard of Academia Sinica Ancient Chinese Corpus[7], we divide our 237M TC training set into three subsets, namely Remote Ancient Chinese (上古汉语) (up to West Han Dynasty), Middle Ancient Chinese (中古汉语) (from East Han Dynasty to the Southern and Northern Dynasties), and Modern Ancient Chinese (近古汉语) (from Tang Dynasty). Since both Test Set 1 and Test Set 2 only contain Modern Ancient Chinese texts, we train a smaller language model on Modern Ancient Chinese subset (114M), using the same method and setup as CLM1. We call this fine-grained model CLM1-J.

Experimental results are shown in Table 4. CLM1-J outperform CLM1 on Test Set 2 but achieves a lower *F*1 score on Test Set 1. Considering that *Chu Ci Bu Zhu (楚辞补注)* in Test Set 1 contains lots of texts of *Chu Ci (楚辞)*, which actually belongs to Remote Ancient Chinese, we construct Test Set 3 with all texts in Test Set 1 except *Chu Ci Bu Zhu (楚辞补注)*. As shown in Table 4, CLM1-J achieves higher *F*1 score than CLM1 on Test Set 3.

To summarize, a fine-grained model trained on less than half of the corpus can even perform better in sentence segmentation.

Table 4. Experimental results on Fine-Grained Model

	Test Set 1			Test Set 2			Test Set 3		
	P	R	F1	P	R	F1	P	R	F1
CLM1 (λ=0.65)	**0.7212**	0.7325	**0.7268**	0.6393	0.7691	0.6982	**0.6496**	0.7478	0.6952
CLM1-J (λ=0.65)	0.6659	**0.7544**	0.7074	0.6442	**0.8267**	**0.7241**	0.6387	**0.8076**	**0.7133**

---

[7]   http://app.sinica.edu.tw/cgi-bin/kiwi/akiwi/kiwi.sh

5   Conclusion

In this paper, we propose an ancient Chinese sentence segmentation method based on NNLM. Experimental results show that sequence generation model based on NNLM can achieve comparable segmentation results with traditional CRF-based models. Moreover, introducing length penalty to our model is effective to improve recall and F1 score of sentence segmentation.

Further experiments indicate that training datasets are important to improve performance of ancient Chinese sentence segmentation. Subdividing training corpus by ages or using larger SC corpus can lead to more effective NNLM and achieve better segmentation.

In further studies, we will try to implement CRF model to our sequence generation model to compensate the language models and boost segmentation performance. Moreover, inspired by experimental results in Section 4.4, we will try to normalize variant characters in ancient Chinese texts to further reduce data sparsity. Replacing variant characters in both training set and test set with the normalized ones should result in better segmentation.

Acknowledgments. The work described in this paper is supported by the Special Fund Project of Ministry of Education of China (Intelligent Conversion System from Simplified to Traditional Chinese Characters), National High-Tech R&D Program of China (No. 2012BAH14F03), the National Natural Science Foundation of China (No. 61573294 and No. 61303082) and the Research Fund for the Doctoral Program of Higher Education of China (No. 20130121110040).

References

1. Zhang, H., Wang, X., Yang J., Zhou, W.: Method of sentence segmentation and punctuating for ancient Chinese literatures based on cascaded CRF. Application Research of Computers, 26(9):3326–3329 (2009) (in Chinese)
2. Zhang, K., Xia, Y., Hang, Y. U.: CRF-based approach to sentence segmentation and punctuation for ancient Chinese prose. Journal of Tsinghua University, 49(10):1733–1736 (2009) (in Chinese)
3. Huang, H. H., Sun, C. T., Chen, H. H.: Classical Chinese sentence segmentation. In: Proceedings of CIPS-SIGHAN Joint Conference on Chinese Language Processing (2010)
4. Lafferty, J. D., McCallum, A., Pereira, F. C. N.: Conditional random fields: Probabilistic models for segmenting and labeling sequence data. In: Proceedings of ICML (2001)
5. Chen, T., Chen, R., Pan, L., Li, H., Yu, Z.: Archaic Chinese punctuating sentences based on context N-gram model. Computer Engineering, 33(3), 192–193 (2007). (in Chinese)
6. Huang, J., Hou, H.: On sentence segmentation and punctuation model for ancient books on agriculture. Journal of Chinese Information Processing, 22(4):31–38 (2008) (in Chinese)
7. Hinton, G. E.: Learning distributed representations of concepts. In: Proceedings of CogSci (1986)
8. Bengio, Y., Ducharme, R., Vincent, P.: A Neural Probabilistic Language Model. In: Proceedings of NIPS (2001)
9. Mikolov, T., Karafiat, M., Burget, L., Cernockk, J. H., Khudanpur, S.: Recurrent neural network based language model. In: Proceedings of Interspeech (2010)

10. Cho, K., Merrienboer, B. V., Gulcehre, C., Bahdanau, D., Bougares, F., Schwenk, H., Bengio, Y.: Learning phrase representations using RNN encoder-decoder for statistical machine translation. arXiv preprint arXiv:1406.1078 (2014)
11. Chung, J., Gulcehre, C., Cho, K., Bengio, Y.: Empirical evaluation of gated recurrent neural networks on sequence modeling. arXiv preprint arXiv:1412.3555 (2014)

A Stack LSTM Transition-Based Dependency Parser with Context Enhancement and K-best Decoding

Fuxiang Wu[1], Minghui Dong[2], Zhengchen Zhang[2] and Fugen Zhou[1]

[1]Image Processing Center, School of Astronautics, Beihang University, Beijing, China
{fxwuedu, zhfugen}@buaa.edu.cn
[2]Institute for Infocomm Research (I2R), A*STAR, Singapore
{mhdong, zhangzc}@i2r.a-star.edu.sg

Abstract. Transition-based parsing is useful for many NLP tasks. For improving the parsing accuracy, this paper proposes the following two enhancements based on a transition-based dependency parser with stack long short-term memory: using the context of a word in a sentence, and applying K-best decoding to expand the searching space. The experimental results show that the unlabeled and labeled attachment accuracies of our parser improve 0.70% and 0.87% over those of the baseline parser for English respectively, and are 0.82% and 0.86% higher than those of the baseline parser for Chinese respectively.

Keywords: Context enhancement • LSTM • K-best decoding • Transition-based dependency parsing • NLP

1   Introduction

Recently, the following two parsing algorithms have been widely used: graph-based parsing [1,2,3,4] and transition-based parsing [5, 6]. The graph-based parsing searches for the best dependency structure from all possible structures of a sentence. It is time-consuming because of its huge searching space, especially for a long sentence. Transition-based parsing contains two data structures: a buffer of words and a stack. It takes actions, such as shift, reduce, etc., to incrementally build the dependency structure. Typically, an action in a transition step is determined using a greedy strategy. Because of its efficiency and high accuracy, many researches focus on the transition-based parsing [5].

Traditional feature-based parsers predict the next action using the features extracted from the buffer and the stack. There are many feature-based parsers which have achieved high parsing accuracy such as ZPar [6]. However, such kind of parser may suffer from the sparse feature problem, and highly relied on feature engineering. Thus, many research works, such as integrating neural network structures into the parsing algorithm, were conducted to alleviate the problems. Le and Zuidema [7];

© Springer International Publishing AG 2016
M. Dong et al. (Eds.): CLSW 2016, LNAI 10085, pp. 397–404, 2016
DOI: 10.1007/978-3-319-49508-8_37

Table 1. An example of transition-based parsing

Step	Action	Stack S	Buffer B
1	SHIFT	[]	[Yes, ,, he, did, ., ROOT]
2	SHIFT	[Yes]	[,, he, did, ., ROOT]
3	SHIFT	[,, Yes]	[he, did, ., ROOT]
4	SHIFT	[he, ,, Yes]	[did, ., ROOT]
5	L-ARC	[did, he, ,, Yes]	[., ROOT]
6	L-ARC	[did, ,, Yes]	[., ROOT]
7	L-ARC	[did, Yes]	[., ROOT]
8	L-ARC	[did]	[., ROOT]
9	R-ARC	[., did]	[ROOT]
10	SHIFT	[did]	[ROOT]
11	L-ARC	[ROOT, did]	[]
12		[ROOT]	[]

Zhu et al. [8] employed recursive neural networks or recursive convolutional neural networks to rank dependency trees in a list of K-best candidates, and improved the parsing accuracy. Ballesteros et al. [9]; Dyer et al. [10] employed stack long short-term memory (LSTM) recurrent neural networks in a transition-based parser and yielded state-of-the-art parsing accuracy.

In this paper, we propose a transition-based parser with stack LSTM, which is enhanced via exploiting the context of each word in a sentence and utilizing K-best decoding. Additional buffers and stacks, which track the context word of a word, are beneficial to the parsing accuracy. Besides, during dependency structure decoding, only an action of the best local score is considered in the current step. However, an action of the ith best local score on a step may not be the ith best score globally in the K-best decoding. Thus, we employ a K-best searching strategy with global scoring to expand the searching space.

2   Transition-based Dependency Parser

Given a sentence x, a transition-based parser builds a dependency tree y by searching a series of transition actions. Our parsing model is based on the arc-standard transitions parsing algorithm [11]. In that system, a configuration C describes the current state of the parser, which consists of a buffer B, a stack S, and a series of completed actions A_{sr}. We denote the ith word in B as b_i and the ith top word in S as s_i. In each parsing step, an action is predicted from the corresponding configuration C. There are three actions in the arc-standard system: SHIFT, L-ARC, R-ARC. SHIFT moves a word b_1 from the buffer B to the stack S. L-ARC adds an arc $s_1 \rightarrow s_2$ and

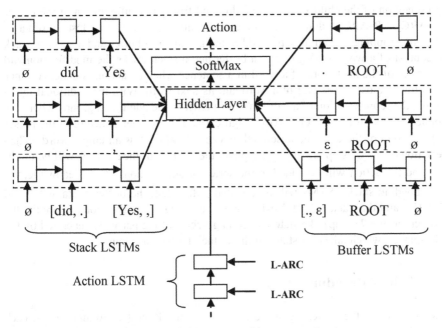

Fig. 1. The structure of the parser with context enhancement.

removes s_2 from S. R-ARC adds an arc $s_2 \rightarrow s_1$ and removes s_1 from S. An example for the sentence "Yes, he did." is shown in Table (1). (We ignore the label of an arc of a dependency structure for simplifying).

3   Context Enhancement Parser

Our work is based on the transition-based parser with stack LSTM described in Dyer et al. [10]. The parser contains three stack LSTMs: B_{LSTM} for the buffer B, S_{LSTM} for the stack S and A_{LSTM} for the series of actions. When the parser takes an action, according to the type of the action, the buffer and the stack are modified by pushing (popping) the corresponding words into (off) it. Meanwhile, according to the operations applying to B, the corresponding operations would operate on B_{LSTM}: The pushing operation corresponds to the operation of pushing the word representation to B_{LSTM}; The popping operation corresponds to the operation of rewinding to the last state of B_{LSTM}. In the same way, S_{LSTM} is handled except that it tracks S. For A_{LSTM}, since actions are taken incrementally, the corresponding operations sequentially push the representation of the action to A_{LSTM}.

The stack LSTMs extract the representation of the current configuration by tracking the change of the stacks of the configuration when an action is done. However, the stack LSTMs may not fully track and represent the changes of the configuration due to the complicated interaction between the buffer B and the stack S. Moreover, the representation of the child word will be dropped from the configuration of the parser if L-ARC or R-ARC is done. Thus some useful information may be lost. In order to delay the dropping, we employ two additional groups of a buffer and a stack to track the context of a word. One group of a buffer and a stack tracks the modification and movement of the next word of a word in a sentence when an action is done. Another group tracks those of the pair of a word and its next word. With the additional information, the representation of a word may still exist in the additional groups when it is dropped by taking L-ARC or R-ARC. Figure 1 shows an inner structure of the parser at the 7th step of the example described in Table 1, where ε is an empty word. When the action of the 6th step "L-ARC" is applied, the content of the stack S will be modified, and the action will be added to the series of done actions A_{sr},. Meanwhile, the corresponding stack LSTMs will be updated. After that, the buffer contains "." and "ROOT", and the stack is [did, Yes] as depicted in Fig. 1. Furthermore, to predict the next action (the 7th step), the state embedding vector of the parser is generated by the hidden layer, which takes the states of three stack LSTMs as inputs.

4   K-best Decoding

Since expanding the searching space by tracking the K-best configurations at each step is beneficial to the parser, we adopt K-best decoding algorithm in the parsing procedure. Besides, global score accumulated from the previous steps is employed to generate the correct K-best candidates, and the parser tracks K best contents to suppose K-best decoding. The following equation depicts the content Ψ^j,

$$\Psi^j = \{B^j, B^j{}_{LSTM}, S^j, S^j{}_{LSTM}, A^j{}_{sr}, A^j{}_{LSTM}\},\tag{1}$$

where the superscript j indicates that the object belongs to the jth best parsing state. As describing in section 3.1 in Dyer et al. [10], the following function $p^j(\alpha)$ defines the probability of a possible action α for a content Ψ^j,

$$p^j(\alpha) = p(\alpha, \Psi^j).\tag{2}$$

Denoting $\{\tau^j\}_{j=1}^K$ as the scores of the previous K-best parsing state, the pseudo-code of the K-best decoding procedure is defined as follows,

1.   Given K contents $\{\Psi^j\}_{j=1}^K$, we generate the possible set $\tilde{A}^j$ of actions for each Ψ^j.
2.   For each $\alpha \in \tilde{A}^j$, the following equation calculates the global score $g^j(\alpha)$,

$$g^j(\alpha) = p^j(\alpha) + \tau^j,\tag{3}$$

and then all $\{\alpha, j, g^j(\alpha)\}$ are stored into a set Q.
3.   The K-best actions Q_K are selected by sorting Q according to its item score.

Table 2. The data splits of PTB and CTB

	training	development	test
PTB	2-21	22	23
CTB	001-815, 1001-1136	886-931, 1148-1151	816-885, 1137-1147

Table 3. The configurations of the parsers

Parser	$P_{baseline}$	P_k	P_c	P_{kc}
K-best decoding	✗	✓	✗	✓
context enhancement	✗	✗	✓	✓

4. For the ith best item $\{\alpha, j, g^J(\alpha)\} \in Q_K$, the content Ψ^i is copied from Ψ^J, and j in the item is set to i.

5. For each item $\{\alpha, j, g^J(\alpha)\} \in Q_K$, the action α is applied on Ψ^J.

6. If there is a Ψ^J that is not finished, the procedure will go to step a).

The stack LSTM contains the previous memory cells and outputs, and a content Ψ^J is modified after taking an action. Thus, we copy the content Ψ^i instead of linking it in step d) in the decoding procedure.

5 Experiments

5.1 Experimental Setup

We conduct experiments on the English Penn Treebank (PTB) and Chinese Treebank 5.1 (CTB) and follow standard splits of PTB and CTB as shown in Table 2. Since the treebanks consist of phrase structures, the Stanford Parser is employed to transform the structures of PTB to dependency structures, and their format is Stanford Dependency (SD) [12]. For Chinese transformation, Penn2Malt is employed with head rules compiled by Zhang and Clark [5]. Besides, parsing accuracy is measured by unlabeled attachment score (UAS) and labeled attachment score (LAS). UAS is the percentage of words with the correct head. LAS is the percentage of words with the correct head and label.

The baseline parser is the one built by Dyer et al. [10]. Similar to their work, the number of iterations in training is determined by the testing result on the development set. To explore the effects of context enhancement and K-best decoding, we build four parsers as described in Table 3. Since the training algorithm cannot guarantee that the final weights are global optimum, we train six times for a parser and select the model with the best accuracy on the development set as the final model for this parser.

Table 4. The results on the development set of PTB

Parser	$P_{baseline}$	P_k	P_c	P_{kc}
LAS	92.67%	93.04%	93.05%	93.21%
UAS	94.12%	94.46%	94.43%	94.59%
K	-	3	-	5

Table 5. The results on the testing set of PTB

Parser	$P_{baseline}$	P_k	P_c	P_{kc}
LAS	92.3%	92.6%	93.02%	93.17%
UAS	93.67%	93.9%	94.25%	94.37%
K	-	3	-	5

5.2   Results and Discussion

The results on the development set of PTB are shown in Table 4. For the parser exploiting K-best decoding, we select the best K by finding the best accuracy on the development set, which is shown in the last row of the table. The results demonstrate that both the context enhancement and the K-best decoding improve the accuracy. Table 5 depicts the results of the testing set of PTB. With the context enhancement, the UAS of P_c and P_{kc} are 0.58% and 0.47% higher than those of $P_{baseline}$ and P_k respectively. With the K-best decoding, the UAS of P_k and P_{kc} improve 0.23% and 0.12% over those of $P_{baseline}$ and P_c respectively.

For CTB, the results on the development set are shown in Table 6. It is shown that the context enhancement improves the accuracy, but the effect of the K-best decoding is small. Finally, Table 7 describes the results on the testing set of CTB. With the context enhancement, the UAS of P_c and P_{kc} improve 0.80% and 0.76% over those of $P_{baseline}$ and P_k respectively. However, the improvement of those with the K-best decoding is little, which may cause by training with the simple stochastic gradient descent algorithm. Thus, more sophisticated training algorithms may bring further improvement.

6   Conclusion

We propose two improvements on the transition-based dependency parser with stack LSTM. With two additional groups of stack LSTMs to track the context, at least 0.58% UAS for English and 0.80% UAS for Chinese improvements were observed. And then the further improvement is achieved with the K-best decoding. Finally, the accuracy of our parser has 0.70% UAS and 0.87% LAS improvement for English over

Table 6. The results on the development set of CTB

Parser	$P_{baseline}$	P_k	P_c	P_{kc}
LAS	85.61%	85.57%	86.17%	86.18%
UAS	87.07%	87.18%	87.52%	87.53%
K	-	5	-	5

Table 7. The results on the testing set of CTB

Parser	$P_{baseline}$	P_k	P_c	P_{kc}
LAS	85.13%	85.17%	85.97%	85.99%
UAS	86.53%	86.59%	87.33%	87.35%
K	-	5	-	5

those of the baseline. For Chinese, UAS and LAS of our parser are 0.82% and 0.86% higher than those of the baseline respectively.

References

1. McDonald, R., Pereira, F., Ribarov, K., Hajič, J.: Non-projective dependency parsing using spanning tree algorithms. In: Proceedings of the conference on Human Language Technology and Empirical Methods in Natural Language Processing, pp. 523-530. Association for Computational Linguistics, (2005)
2. McDonald, R., Pereira, F.: Online learning of approximate dependency parsing algorithms. In: 11th Conference of the European Chapter of the Association for Computational Linguistics, EACL 2006, April 3, 2006 - April 7, 2006, pp. 81-88. Association for Computational Linguistics (ACL), (2006)
3. Ma, X., Zhao, H.: Fourth-Order Dependency Parsing. In: COLING, pp. 785-796. Association for Computational Linguistics (ACL), (2012)
4. Wu, F., Zhou, F.: Hybrid dependency parser with segmented treebanks and reparsing. In: Chinese Intelligent Automation Conference, 2015, 2015, pp. 53-60. Springer Verlag, (2015)
5. Zhang, Y., Clark, S.: A tale of two parsers: investigating and combining graph-based and transition-based dependency parsing using beam-search. In: Proceedings of the Conference on Empirical Methods in Natural Language Processing, pp. 562-571. Association for Computational Linguistics, (2008)
6. Zhang, Y., Clark, S.: Syntactic Processing Using the Generalized Perceptron and Beam Search. Computational Linguistics 37, 105-151 (2011)
7. Le, P., Zuidema, W.: The inside-outside recursive neural network model for dependency parsing. In: 2014 Conference on Empirical Methods in Natural Language Processing, EMNLP 2014, October 25, 2014 - October 29, 2014, pp. 729-739. Association for Computational Linguistics (ACL), (2014)
8. Zhu, C., Qiu, X., Chen, X., Huang, X.: A re-ranking model for dependency parser with recursive Convolutional neural network. In: 53rd Annual Meeting of the Association for Computational Linguistics and the 7th International Joint Conference on Natural Language Processing of the Asian Federation of Natural Language Processing, ACL-IJCNLP 2015,

July 26, 2015 - July 31, 2015, pp. 1159-1168. Association for Computational Linguistics (ACL), (2015)

9. Ballesteros, M., Dyer, C., Smith, N.A.: Improved Transition-based Parsing by Modeling Characters instead of Words with LSTMs. In: Proceedings of the 2015 Conference on Empirical Methods in Natural Language Processing, pp. 349-359. (2015)

10. Dyer, C., Ballesteros, M., Ling, W., Matthews, A., Smith, N.A.: Transition-based dependency parsing with stack long short-term memory. In: 53rd Annual Meeting of the Association for Computational Linguistics and the 7th International Joint Conference on Natural Language Processing of the Asian Federation of Natural Language Processing, ACL-IJCNLP 2015, July 26, 2015 - July 31, 2015, pp. 334-343. Association for Computational Linguistics (ACL), (2015)

11. Ballesteros, M., Nivre, J.: MaltOptimizer: Fast and effective parser optimization. Natural Language Engineering 1-27 (2014)

12. De Marneffe, M.-C., MacCartney, B., Manning, C.D.: Generating typed dependency parses from phrase structure parses. In: Proceedings of LREC, pp. 449-454. (2006)

An Analysis of the Relation between Similarity Positions and Attributes of Concepts by Distance Geometry *

Hui Liu[1] and Jianyong Duan[2]

[1] Shanghai University of International Business and Economics,
1900 Wenxiang Rd., Shanghai 201620, China,
liuh@suibe.edu.cn,
[2] North China University of Technology,
No. 5, Jinyuanzhuang Rd., Beijing 100144, China,
duanjy@ncut.edu.cn

Abstract. In this paper, we discussed the relation between the attributes of a concept and its similarity position with other concepts. We constructed a function to map a similarity position of a concept to its coordinates in a geometry space. The coordinates can be further mapped to the attributes through another function. We constructed the functions by distance geography methods and proved that such functions do exist under some conditions. This work will benefit attribute retrieval tasks.

Keywords: attribute computing, semantic similarity, distance geometry

1   Introduction

Similarity and attributes are two popular topics in semantic computing. In this paper, we want to establish a theoretical link between these two topics. The initial idea is quite simple. From observation, we know that if two concepts are similar, they will have similar parts. The problem is: *which* parts are similar? And *why*?

We explore the answer to the above questions quantitatively in this paper. If the similarity measure could be viewed as a kind of distance measure, we could try to embed the similarity matrix of a set of concepts into a high-dimensional space in which each point represents one concept and the distances between points are transformed similarity values between concepts. If we could further map the coordinates of the points in the space to the attributes of the concepts, we can establish a theoretical relation between similarity and attributes. In this way, we convert our problem into a geometry problem. Ideally, if we know the *similarity position* of a concept, i.e. the similarity with other concepts, we can calculate its attributes mathematically. In this way, our result will benefit future studies on attribute retrieval.

The paper is structured as the following. First, we discuss some related works in the next section. Then, we introduce the basic concepts of concept space and similarity

* This work is supported by the Ministry of Education of China (Project of Humanities and Social Sciences, Grant. 13YJC740055) and the National Science Foundation of China (Grant No. 61103112).

© Springer International Publishing AG 2016
M. Dong et al. (Eds.): CLSW 2016, LNAI 10085, pp. 405–415, 2016
DOI: 10.1007/978-3-319-49508-8_38

position in section 3. In section 4 we discuss how to create a mapping from similarity positions to points in the concept space using distance geometry methods under given conditions. Section 5 is devoted to some further discussions. The last section is the conclusion.

2 Related Works

Many researchers who have discussed the relation between similarity and attributes focused on the definition of similarity. The first group of researchers used the feature model such as the contrast model [19] to represent similarity. For example, [5] introduced a definition of similarity by generalizing measure functions to high dimension attribute spaces. Lin's work on the information-theoretic definition of similarity [9] can also be included in this category. The second group of researchers defined similarity on the hierarchy of an ontology, such as WordNet . [15] proposed a semantic similarity measure between concepts based on semantic neighbourhoods. Such methods are also popular in similarity computing, such as [14] [10]. The third group of researchers such as [4] considered similarity as a distance metric. Gärdenfors [3] introduced the *conceptual space* theory which is also a geometric description of concepts. In his work the similarity is described as a function of distances in the space.

Another related area is attribute retrieval, which focus is on real applications rather than theories. Some researchers such as [7] [17] analysed structured or semi-structured text, like HTML tables and encyclopedias. Others, such as [18] [12], used lexico-syntactic templates to extract attributes from plain text especially Web text. Only a few researchers started to use similarity as a tool for attribute retrieval, such as [1] [11].

This paper is different from previous works. In previous works the theoretical discussions focus on the similarity side, especially how attributes (or other concept structures) will affect definition and characteristics of similarity. However, in this paper, our analysis is in the opposite direction. We focused on how the values of attributes in a concept are related to the similarity values of the concept with other concepts. On the other hand, unlike previous works in attribute retrieval, we provide a similarity based theoretical framework to solve the problem based on instances and similarities.

3 Concept space and similarity positions

3.1 Concept space

Let C be a set of all concepts in a domain. The intension of a concept $c \in C$ is commonly represented by an "attribute-value structure" (AVS), which contains attributes and their values that can be atom values or other sub-AVS.

First, in order to simplify further discussions, we "flatten" the AVS to be a set of attribute-value pairs, $\{\langle a_1, v_1 \rangle, \langle a_2, v_2 \rangle, ..., \langle a_N, v_N \rangle\}$. A possible flattening method is to join the attribute names from the root of the AVS to the deepest value. For example, in a LAPTOP concept, we can have an attribute *cpu*, while the value of the cpu is another concept INTEL CORE which has an attribute *speed* with the value of 2.4G. Then, the *speed* attribute which is denoted as LAPTOP.*cpu*.*speed* in a recursive AVS could be rewritten as LAPTOP.*cpu_speed* which is a single attribute under the concept LAPTOP. Second, we just assume that all attributes have only one value, not multiple values.

If we have an order on the set of all the possible attributes in C, we can construct the representation of the concept c as a vector of values while the subscripts of the vector components correspond to attribute names.

Definition 1. *The* concept vector *of a concept c is a vector $v = (v_1, v_2, ..., v_N)$, in which N is the number of attributes and v_i is the value of the i_{th} attribute.*

A *concept space* $\mathfrak{C}$ is a set of concept vectors. In other words, the concept space is a set of "known" concepts.

3.2   Similarity models and similarity positions

Similarity is first a cognitive measurement. Two concepts are similar because they have something in common. In order to quantify the amount of commonness, we need similarity models. A similarity model is a method that will output a similarity value for two concepts in the domain.

Definition 2. *A similarity model is a function* $s_i : C \cup \mathfrak{C} \times C \cup \mathfrak{C} \to [0, 1]$. S *is the set of all similarity models.*

The inputs for a similarity model could be concepts or concept vectors. Though similarity values could be given by humans, in NLP applications similarity models are algorithms that based on different resources, such as WordNet, corpus or the Web [14][10]. A similarity model in practice could capture some aspects of similarity between two concepts. Since similarity models could be computed by different methods, we do not always need the full concept representation of concepts to know their similarities.

Given a concept space and a similarity model, we have the following definition of the *similarity position* of a concept c_u.

Definition 3. *For* s_i, *the similarity position* sp *of c_u in concept space* $\mathfrak{C} = \{v_1, v_2, ..., v_M\}$ *is defined as:*

$$sp = (s_i(c_u, v_1), s_i(c_u, v_2), ..., s_i(c_u, v_M))$$

The set of all similarity positions is denoted as $\mathfrak{P}$.

4   The link between similarity positions and concept vectors

Let us repeat our prime problem: if two concepts are similar, they should have similar parts. But which parts are similar? In this section, we will provide a theoretical solution to this problem. We try to find the mathematical link between similarity positions and concept vectors. We consider all the values as numerical ones in this section. We will discuss other situations in Section 5.

We re-state our prime problem as the following:

Problem 1. Given:

1. A concept space $\mathfrak{C}$ which size is M;
2. A *similarity matrix* of $\mathfrak{C}$ is defined as $\boldsymbol{S_i} = (s_{mn})_{M \times M}$ where $s_{mn} = s_i(\boldsymbol{v_m}, \boldsymbol{v_n})$.
3. A similarity position $\boldsymbol{sp}$ which correspondent concept vector is $\boldsymbol{vp}$.

We want to find a function f: $2^{\mathfrak{C}} \times \mathfrak{P} \to \mathfrak{C}$, s.t. f($\mathfrak{C}, \boldsymbol{sp}$) = $\boldsymbol{vp}$.

4.1 Preliminary assumptions

First, we are going to make two assumptions which will simplify our problem.

Assumption 1. *The similarity of two concepts c_1 and c_2 only depends on their intensions.*

Assumption 1 is taken by a lot of researchers in NLP such as [14], as they calculated the similarity between concepts through ontologies or lexical resources, which are representations of concept intensions.

Assumption 2. *Similarity is a function of distance. [3][6]*

Apart from linguists, we can also find support for Assumption 2 in psychological literature, in which similarity is viewed as an exponentially decaying function of distance [13]:

$$s(x, y) = e^{-c \cdot d(x,y)} \tag{1}$$

In Equ.1, c is the decay factor.

4.2 Similarity and distance

From Assumption 1 and 2, we can arrive at the conclusion that similarity value, which is a function of distance, can be induced by the concept vectors. So the calculation of the aforementioned distance also involves two concept vectors. Because different attributes contribute differently to similarity, we can assume that the distance is calculated between weighted concept vectors. Therefore, we have the following definitions and assumption.

Definition 4. *A simple weight matrix $\boldsymbol{W_i^*} = (w_{ij}^*)_{N \times N}$ is a diagonal matrix depending on the similarity model s_i, where $\forall j, k, \ j \neq k \to w_{jk}^* = 0$ and w_{kk}^* is the weight for the k_{th} attribute.*
A weight matrix $\boldsymbol{W_i} = (w_{ij})_{N \times N}$ is also a diagonal matrix where $w_{ij} = c \cdot w_{ij}^*$, in which c is the decay factor.
A distance vector $\boldsymbol{d}$ is a weighted concept vector i.e. $\boldsymbol{d} = \boldsymbol{W_i} \cdot \boldsymbol{v}^{\mathrm{T}}$. The set of all distance vectors is denoted as $\mathfrak{D}$.

Assumption 3.

$$s_{12} = e^{-c\|\boldsymbol{W_i^*} \cdot v_1, \boldsymbol{W_i^*} \cdot v_2\|} = e^{-\|\boldsymbol{d_1}, \boldsymbol{d_2}\|} \tag{2}$$

where $\| \cdot \|$ is the Euclid distance.

In Assumption 3, $(W_i^* \cdot)$ can be viewed as a linear weighting function.

Let $v_1 = (v_{11}, ..., v_{1N})$, $v_2 = (v_{21}, ..., v_{2N})$. From Assumption 3, we can have the following:

$$- \ln s_{12} = \|d_1, d_2\| = \left(\sum_{k \in [1,N]} w_{kk}^2 (v_{1k} - v_{2k})^2 \right)^{\frac{1}{2}} \tag{3}$$

The first problem is, given a similarity model s_i, how to estimate W_i? The initial idea is to estimate it through the concept space. Suppose we have M concepts and N attributes in the concept space. Let us introduce the following definitions.

Definition 5. *The subscript vector* $r = ((1,1), (1,2), ..., (1,M), (2,3), ..., (2,M), ..., (M-1, M))$.

r is a vector of all possible combination of subscripts in a concept space $\mathfrak{C}$.

Definition 6. *The coefficient matrix* $A = (a_{ij})_{M(M-1)/2 \times N}$, *where* $a_{ij} = (v_{r_{i1}j} - v_{r_{i2}j})^2$.

Here, r_{i1} *means the first number of the* i_{th} *component of* r. v_{xy} *means the* y_{th} *component of* v_x. *Similarly, the support vector* b *is a* $M(M-1)/2 \times 1$ *matrix.*

$$b = (\ln s_{12}^2, \ln s_{13}^2, ..., \ln s_{1m}^2, \ln s_{23}^2, ..., \ln s_{m-1\,m}^2)^{\mathrm{T}}$$

The augmented matrix $B = [A, b]$ *is a row block matrix consisting of* A *and* b.

Lemma 1. *Given a concept space* $\mathfrak{C}$, *there exists a weight matrix* W_i *satisfying:*

$$\forall u, v \quad - \ln s_{uv} = \|W_i \cdot v_u^{\mathrm{T}}, W_i \cdot v_v^{\mathrm{T}}\|$$

if $\mathrm{rank}(A) = \mathrm{rank}(B) = N$.

Proof. Let w be a matrix of $N \times 1$. $A \cdot w = b$ is a linear equation system.

Since $\mathrm{rank}(A) = \mathrm{rank}(B) = N$, there exists the only solution $w_0 = \{w_1, w_2, ..., w_k, ..., w_N\}$. So, for any two concept vectors v_u and v_v, there is one correspondent linear equation:

$$\sum_{k \in [1,N]} w_k^2 (v_{uk} - v_{vk})^2 = (\ln s_{uv})^2$$

Let's construct W_i from w s.t. $w_{kk} = w_k$. Rewriting the left-hand side of the equation, we will have:

$$\|W_i \cdot v_u^T, W_i \cdot v_v^T\|^2 = (\ln s_{uv})^2$$

Since $s_{uv} \in [0, 1]$, $\ln s_{uv}$ is negative. We reach our target. $\square$

Because we need to estimate N parameters, we need at least N equations. Assume we have m concept vectors, m should satisfy:

$$m \geq \frac{1}{2}(1 + \sqrt{1 + 8n}) \tag{4}$$

As our condition in Lemma 1 is quite strong, in practice we may get the slack solution of the equation by LSE or other estimation methods.

Corollary 1. $v = \mathbf{W_i}^{-1} \cdot \mathbf{d}$, *if* $\forall k$, $W_{kk} \neq 0$.

If $\mathbf{W}_i^{-1}$ does not exist, i.e. $\exists k, w_{kk} = 0$, we can exclude v_k from the concept vectors because $w_{kk} = 0$ means that v_k does not contribute to this similarity model implying that v_k will not be helpful for further calculations.

4.3   The Distance Geometry Problem

From the above section, we have constructed the weight matrix $\mathbf{W_i}$ which can convert any concept vector v into a distance vector d and vice versa. We also know that $\|d_i, d_j\| = -\ln s_{ij}$. In other words, the Euclid distance of two distance vectors equals to the similarity distance of the correspondent concept (vectors).

Reviewing Problem 1, now we are going to find a function that can map a similarity position sp into a distance vector d given a set $\mathfrak{D}$ of distance vectors. Since sp is actually the distance from other points in the $\mathfrak{D}$, we have a sub-problem to finding a point's coordinates given its distance with other points in a Euclid space.

Such problem has been discussed in Distance Geometry which concerns some geometric concepts in terms of distances. The fundamental problem in distance geometry is the *distance geometry problem* (DGP) [8].

Given an integer $K > 0$ and a simple undirected graph $G = (V, E)$ whose edges are weighted by a nonnegative function d $: E \rightarrow \mathbb{R}_+$, determine whether there is a function x $: V \rightarrow \mathbb{R}^K$ such that: $\forall \{u, v\} \in E$ $\|x(u) - x(v)\| = d(\{u, v\})$.

Though started as a purely mathematical problem, DGP is gaining more and more popularity in bio-informatics, in which researchers use related algorithms to construct molecular structures. Our problem is also a sub-problem of DGP, which can be stated as the following:

Problem 2. How to find a function f* s.t. $f^*(\mathfrak{D}, p) = d_j$, given

1. The coordinates of all vectors in $\mathfrak{D}$;
2. The distance of a distance vector dp with all points in $\mathfrak{D}$. The distances are noted as a vector p, which is called a distance position. It is easy to find out that $p_i = -\ln s_i(vp, v_i)$, where vp is the correspondent concept vector of dp.

The general DGP in N-dimension is NP-Hard. However, since we have all the interpoint distance values, we can have an algorithm in $O(|\mathbf{D}| \cdot N^3)$ [2]. This algorithm was designed for three dimension spaces. We extended it to N-dimension in which N is the size of our distance vector as well as the number of attributes.

The coordinates of any distance vectors $d_j (j \in [1, M])$ in $\mathfrak{D}$ are already known, in which M is the size of the concept space. To simplify our discussion, we will denote the unknown vector dp as d_0. We can have the following representation of any distance vector d_k in $\mathfrak{D} \cup \{d_0\}$.

$$d_k = (u_{k1}, u_{k2}, ..., u_{kN})^\mathrm{T} \quad k \in [0, M] \tag{5}$$

The distance between any known d_j and the unknown d_0 can be calculated as the following. Remember that p_j is a component in p, which identifies the distance between d_0 and d_j. So by definition we have:

$$\|d_0 - d_j\|^2 = p_j^2 \tag{6}$$

Expanding the left-hand side of the equation we will have Equ. 7.

$$\|d_0 - d_j\|^2 = \|d_0\|^2 - 2d_0^T d_j + \|d_j\|^2 = p_j^2 \tag{7}$$

Expand d_0 and d_j in Equation 7 in their full vector forms as in Equ. 5, we have the general distance constraint Equ. 8.

$$\|d_0\|^2 - 2u_{01}u_{j1} - \dots - 2u_{0N}u_{jN} + \|d_j\|^2 = p_j^2 \tag{8}$$

Let us make a copy of Equ. 8 by setting j as 1.

$$\|d_0\|^2 - 2u_{01}u_{11} - \dots - 2u_{0N}u_{1N} + \|d_1\|^2 = p_1^2 \tag{9}$$

Subtract Equ. 9 from 8, we will have:

$$2u_{01}(u_{11} - u_{j1}) + \dots + 2u_{0N}(u_{1N} - u_{jN})$$
$$= (\|d_1\|^2 - \|d_j\|^2) - (p_1^2 - p_j^2) \tag{10}$$

Through a closer look of Equ. 10, we can see that the right-hand side has nothing to do with d_0, so the value is known to us. On the left-hand side, u_{01} to u_{0N} are the components of the unknown d_0, while the "coefficients" of them can be calculated by d_1 and d_j. So, let us create M copies of Equ. 10 with the values of j ranging from 1 to M. The equations form a linear equation system which can be rewritten as:

$$A^* d_0 = b^* \tag{11}$$

$A^* = (a_{mn})_{M \times N}$ and $b^* = (b_1, b_2, ..., b_M)^T$ where

$$a_{mn} = 2(u_{1n} - u_{mn}) \tag{12}$$

$$b_m = (\|d_1\|^2 - \|d_m\|^2) - (p_1^2 - p_m^2) \tag{13}$$

Lemma 2. $\mathfrak{D}$ *is a set of distance vectors, dp is a distance vector and p is the distance position of dp. There exists a function* $f^* : 2^{\mathfrak{D}} \times \mathfrak{P} \to \mathfrak{D}$ *s.t.* $f^*(\mathfrak{D}, p) = dp$ *if* $rank(A^*) = rank(B^*) = N$, *in which* $B^* = [A^*, b^*]$.

Proof. Let f' be a function that will solve a linear equation system. For any p, we can construct correspondent A^* and b^* using p and $\mathfrak{D}$. So the domain and range of f' are the same as f*.

Since $rank(A^*) = rank(B^*) = N$, $A^* d = b^*$ has only one solution d_0. So $f'(\mathfrak{D}, p) = d_0$.

Also from Equ. 11, we can see that d_0 satisfies Equ. 7 for all vectors in $\mathfrak{D}$. So $d_0 = dp$, and consequently $f' = f^*$.   □

Having the above Lemmas, we can have the following theorem.

Theorem 1. $\mathfrak{C}_1$ *is a concept space.* sp *is a similarity position and* v *is the correspondent distance vector.* N *is the number of attributes. There exists a function* $f: 2^{\mathfrak{C}} \cup \mathfrak{P}$ *s.t.* $f(\mathfrak{C}_1, sp) = v$ *if we meet the following conditions:*

1. $rank(A) = rank(B) = N$ *and* W_i^{-1} *exists;*
2. $rank(A^*) = rank(B^*) = N$

The matrices in the above conditions are defined in the previous sections.

Proof. From Lemma 1, since $rank(A) = rank(B) = N$, there exists the weight matrix W_i. Let T $: 2^{\mathfrak{C}} \to 2^{\mathfrak{D}}$ be a function that maps a concept space to the a set of distance vectors, i.e.

$$T(\mathfrak{C}_1) = \{W_i \cdot v_i^{\mathrm{T}}\}_{i \in [1,M]} = \mathfrak{D}_1$$

Let $p = -\ln sp$. From Lemma 2 we know f^* exists because $rank(A^*) = rank(B^*) = N$.

$$f^*(\mathfrak{D}_1, p) = dp$$

So,

$$f^*(T(\mathfrak{C}_1), -\ln sp) = dp$$

Also from Corollary 1, we can rewrite the above equation to get our target function:

$$(W_i^{-1} \cdot f^*(T(\mathfrak{C}_1), -\ln sp))^{\mathrm{T}} = (W_i^{-1} \cdot dp)^{\mathrm{T}} = v$$

$\square$

5   Further discussions: non-numerical attribute values

For a concept, some values are not numerical. In this case, we have to extend our framework. Here we just discuss two common situations.

5.1   Case 1

Definition 7. *Let* V_i *be the set of all possible values of an attribute* a_i. $t_i : V_i \times V_i \to [0,1]$ *is a similarity function on* V_i.
A dual mapping function is $m_i : V_i \to \mathbb{R}$ *s.t.* $\forall v_1, v_2 \in V_i$, $sim(v_1, v_2) = | m_i(v_1) - m_i(v_2) |$

To construct m_i is still a DGP problem. Let S^* be the similarity matrix of value pairs in V_i. According to [16], S^* can be embedded in $\mathbb{R}^K$ but not $\mathbb{R}^{K-1}$ if and only if:

- There is a principal $(K+1) \times (K+1)$ submatrix $D \in S^*$, the Cayley-Menger determinant of D is non-zero;
- For $\mu \in 2, 3$, every principal $(K+\mu) \times (K+\mu)$ submatrix E that includes D has zero Cayley-Menger determinant.

If S^* could be embedded in $\mathbb{R}$, i.e. there exists a dual mapping function m_i on V_i, we can construct m_i as the following. Given two values v_1 and v_2, we set $m_i(v_1) = u_1$, $m_i(v_2) = u_2$. Here, $t_{ij} = t_i(v_i, v_j)$. We know that:

$$t_{12} = \|m_i(v_1), m_i(v_2)\|$$
$$= |m_i(v_1) - m_i(v_2)|$$
$$= |u_1 - u_2| \tag{14}$$

So, given two already mapped value u_1 and u_2, we will have

$$t_{k1}^2 = (m_i(v_k) - u_1)^2 \tag{15}$$

$$t_{k2}^2 = (m_i(v_k) - u_2)^2 \tag{16}$$

Let us expand the above two equations and we will have the following for any v_k:

$$m_i(v_k) = \frac{1}{2}\left(\frac{t_{k1}^2 - t_{k2}^2}{u_2 - u_1} + u_1 + u_2\right) \tag{17}$$

Having m_i for each V_i, we can define the *dual vector*.

Definition 8. *For any concept vector v that contains non-numerical attributes, a dual vector u of v is a real number vector $(u_1, u_2, ..., u_N)$, in which $u_i = m_i(v_i)$.*

It is easy to prove that:

$$\forall i, j \quad s_i(v_i, v_j) = \|u_i, u_j\|$$

It is also easy to prove that if $rank(A) = N$, the dual vector d is the only reconstruction of v.

5.2 Case 2

A more complicated situation is that S^* could only be embedded into $\mathbb{R}^k$ in which $k > 1$. Therefore, we introduce the pseudo dual function $m_i' : V_i \to \mathbb{R}^k$, which also satisfies the following:

$$\forall v_1, v_2 \in V_i, \ t_i(v_1, v_2) = \|m_i'(v_1), m_i'(v_2)\|$$

For any V_i, constructing m_i' is a DGP problem similar to our main problem, so we will not give details here.

Definition 9. *A pseudo-dual vector u' of a concept vector v is a vector $(m_i'(v_1), m_i'(v_2), ..., m_i'(v_N))$, in which $m_i'(v_j) = u_{j1}, ..., u_{jK_j}$. K_j is the size of $m_i(v_j)$. The size of d is equal to or greater than v.*

It is also easy to prove that:

$$\forall i, j, \quad s_i(v_i, v_j) = \|u_i', u_j'\|$$

6 Conclusions

In this paper, we discussed the relation between similarity and attributes. We showed how to construct a function to map a concept's similarity position to its attribute vector by embed the similarity matrix of a concept space into a geometry space. Then we proved that under some given conditions the function exists. We also discussed how to handle non-numerical attributes. Our results will benefit future works in attribute retrieval.

This work is in its early stage. We are still facing some difficulties. One problem is that the proposed conditions on matrix ranks are quite strong. In future studies, we would like to find if there are alternate weaker conditions. Moreover, it is not actually that easy to find the weight matrix to the attribute vector. Though we suggested using LSE for estimation, we may resort to other machine learning methods. In a worse scenario, the weight matrix may even not exist. In this case, we will try to find another mapping function from concept vectors to distance vectors other than the linear weight function. Our preliminary calculation showed that our results still hold as long as the mapping function has an inverse function.

References

1. Alfonseca, E., Pasca, M., Robledo-Arnuncio, E.: Acquisition of instance attributes via labeled and related instances. In: Proceeding of the 33rd international ACM SIGIR conference on Research and development in information retrieval. pp. 58–65. ACM (2010)
2. Dong, Q., Wu, Z.: A linear-time algorithm for solving the molecular distance geometry problem with exact inter-atomic distances. Journal of Global Optimization 22(1-4), 365–375 (2002)
3. Gärdenfors, P.: Conceptual spaces: The geometry of thought. MIT press (2004)
4. Gärdenfors, P.: The geometry of meaning: Semantics based on conceptual spaces. MIT Press (2014)
5. Gust, H., Umbach, C.: Making use of similarity in referential semantics. In: Proceedings of the 9th Conference on Modeling and Using Context (2015)
6. Jin, P., Qiu, L., Zhu, X., Liu, P.: A hypothesis on word similarity and its application. In: Chinese Lexical Semantics, pp. 317–325. Springer (2014)
7. Kopliku, A., Boughanem, M., Pinel-Sauvagnat, K.: Towards a framework for attribute retrieval. In: Proceedings of the 20th ACM international conference on Information and knowledge management. pp. 515–524. ACM (2011)
8. Liberti, L., Lavor, C., Maculan, N., Mucherino, A.: Euclidean distance geometry and applications. SIAM Review 56(1), 3–69 (2014)
9. Lin, D.: An information-theoretic definition of similarity. In: ICML. vol. 98, pp. 296–304 (1998)
10. Liu, H., Bao, H., Xu, D.: Concept vector for semantic similarity and relatedness based on wordnet structure. Journal of Systems and software 85(2), 370–381 (2012)
11. Liu, H., Duan, J.: Attribute construction for online products by similarity computing. ICIC Express Letters 9(1), 99–105 (2015)
12. Pasca, M., Van Durme, B.: What you seek is what you get: Extraction of class attributes from query logs. In: Proceedings of the 20th International Joint Conference on Artificial Intelligence (IJCAI-07). pp. 2832–2837 (2007)
13. Reisberg, D.: The Oxford handbook of cognitive psychology. Oxford University Press (2013)

14. Resnik, P.: Using information content to evaluate semantic similarity in a taxonomy. In: Proceedings of the 14th International Joint Conferences on Artificial Intelligence. pp. 448–453 (1995)
15. Rodríguez, M.A., Egenhofer, M.J.: Determining semantic similarity among entity classes from different ontologies. Knowledge and Data Engineering, IEEE Transactions on 15(2), 442–456 (2003)
16. Sippl, M.J., Scheraga, H.A.: Cayley-menger coordinates. Proceedings of the National Academy of Sciences 83(8), 2283–2287 (1986)
17. Suchanek, F., Kasneci, G., Weikum, G.: Yago: A large ontology from wikipedia and wordnet. Web Semantics: Science, Services and Agents on the World Wide Web 6(3), 203–217 (2008)
18. Tokunaga, K., Kazama, J., Torisawa, K.: Automatic discovery of attribute words from Web documents. Natural Language Processing–IJCNLP 2005 pp. 106–118 (2005)
19. Tversky, A., Gati, I.: Studies of similarity. Cognition and categorization 1(1978), 79–98 (1978)

Computation of Word Similarity Based on the Information Content of Sememes and PageRank Algorithm

Hao Li, Lingling Mu*, Hongying Zan

School of Information Engineering, Zhengzhou University, Zhengzhou, 450001, China

lihao_zzunlp@foxmail.com iellmu@zzu.edu.cn
iehyzan@zzu.edu.cn

Abstract: Based on sememe structure of *HowNet* and PageRank algorithm, this article proposes a method to compute word similarity. Using depth information of *HowNet* as information content of sememes and considering sememe hyponymy, this method builds a transfer matrix and computes sememe vector with PageRank algorithm to obtain sememe similarity. Thus, the word similarity can be calculated by the sememe similarity. This method is tested on several groups of typical Chinese words and word sense classification of nouns in Contemporary Chinese Semantic Dictionary (CSD). The results show that the word similarity computed in this way quite conforms with the facts. It also shows a more accurate result in word sense classification of nouns in the CSD, reaching 71.9% consistency with the judgment of human.

Keywords: word similarity, HowNet, sememe, PageRank, word sense classification

1   Introduction

Word similarity computing is widely used in the field of natural language processing, such as information retrieval, information extraction, text classification, word sense disambiguation and machine translation.

HowNet[1] is a knowledge base created by Dong Zhendong, an expert in natural language processing. Taking the concepts referred by Chinese and English words as the targets it describes, *Hownet* makes itself a large base of general knowledge so as to reveal the relationships among different concepts and their different properties. Concept is a description of lexical semantic meaning. Each word has several concepts and each concept is described by a number of sememes, which have hyponymy relations.

Based on Sememe Information Content(SIC) and PageRank[2], this article

---

*Corresponding author: Lingling Mu, E-mail: iellmu@zzu.edu.cn

© Springer International Publishing AG 2016
M. Dong et al. (Eds.): CLSW 2016, LNAI 10085, pp. 416–425, 2016
DOI: 10.1007/978-3-319-49508-8_39

proposes an algorithm of word similarity computing, including the following steps: 1) To build the sememes tree hierarchical structure according to the hyponymy of sememes in *HowNet*; 2) To compute SIC on the basis of depth information of the sememe and its descendants; 3) To build a transfer matrix by sememe hyponymy and SIC then calculate sememe vector with PageRank algorithm; 4) To calculate sememe similarity through sememe vector; 5) To calculate word similarity based on the sememe similarity.

2   Related Work

Structures of many knowledge bases which are created to describe the world knowledge such as WordNet[3] and HowNet have hyponymy between concepts. These hyponymy and concepts construct the knowledge map.

At present, several approaches to apply knowledge base in word similarity computing have been proposed, among which Liu and Li[4] used edge-based approach to consider the similarity as a function of distance in the knowledge map; Wu[5] proposed a method based on HNC to calculate word similarity; Tian [6] calculated it based on Tongyici Cilin.

The concept similarity can be also measured by the Node Information Content(NIC). According to the hyponymy and level of the nodes, the information contained in nodes can be measured. David Sanchez[7] proposed a NIC calculation model based on the subsumers of leaf nodes. Zhou[8] proposed a method to compute NIC through the number of descendant nodes and the depth information of nodes. Singh J[9] combined the least common subsumer and the NIC of concept to calculate concept similarity.

Referring to the above methods, this article proposes a method to calculate sememe similarity based on SIC. This method utilizes the PageRank algorithm and the depth information of sememe and its descendants to calculate the similarity of sememes so as to calculate the word similarity.

3   Word Similarity Computing Based on SIC and PageRank Algorithm

3.1   Word Similarity

Each word in *HowNet* can be interpreted by one or more concepts. Suppose the concepts of word w_1 are $m_{11}, m_{12} ..., m_{1m}$, the concepts of word w_2 are $m_{21}, m_{22} ..., m_{2n}$. Then the similarity between the two words equals the maximum similarity of all their concepts [4]:

$$sim_w(w_1, w_2) = \max\left(sim_m(m_{1i}, m_{2j})\right) \tag{1}$$

Where, $i = 1 \ldots m, j = 1 \ldots n$, $\text{sim}_m(m_{1i}, m_{2j})$ is the similarity of two concepts.

The concepts of word in *HowNet* are defined by some sememe sets, which included four types of sememes: the first basic sememes, other basic sememes, the relation sememes and the sign sememes. Each of them represents a different part of concept.

Therefore, the similarity of (m_1, m_2) is composed of four parts[4]: The first basic sememe similarity $\text{sim}_1(s_1, s_2)$, other basic sememe similarity $\text{sim}_2(s_1, s_2)$, the relation sememe similarity $\text{sim}_3(s_1, s_2)$, the sign sememe similarity $\text{sim}_4(s_1, s_2)$. Then the similarity of the two concepts can be calculated as follows:

$$\text{sim}_m(m_1, m_2) = \sum_{i=1}^{4} \beta_i \prod_{j=1}^{i} \text{sim}_j(s_1, s_2) \tag{2}$$

Where, β_i is the adjustable parameter, and $\beta_1 + \beta_2 + \beta_3 + \beta_4 = 1$, $\beta_1 \geq \beta_2 \geq \beta_3 \geq \beta_4$

3.2   The Similarity of Sememe Set

As we have discussed that the word similarity can be determined by the concept similarity, and the concept similarity is determined by the similarity of the four sememe sets. As each sememe set in *HowNet* consists of one or more sememes, to calculate the sememe similarity is to calculate the similarity of two sets:

1. As for the similarity between the non-empty and empty sets, it is defined as a small value γ;
2. Define the similarity of two empty sets as 1;
3. For two non-empty sets, their similarity is calculated in the following method:

Assuming two sememe sets are X and Y, l_X is the number of elements in set X and l_Y is the number of elements in set Y.

The similarity between the two sememe sets can be calculated by equation (3):

$$\text{sim}_{\text{set}}(X, Y) = \frac{\text{Avg}(X,Y) + \text{Avg}(Y,X)}{2} \tag{3}$$

Where, Avg(X, Y) is the average maximum similarity of each sememe in set X to all sememes in set Y, that is:

$$\text{Avg}(X, Y) = \frac{\sum_{i=1}^{l_X} \text{sim}_s(X_i, Y)}{l_X} \tag{4}$$

Where, $\text{sim}_s(X_i, Y)$ represents the maximum similarity of X_i to all sememes in set Y, that is:

$$\text{sim}_s(X_i, Y) = \max(\text{sim}_s(X_i, Y_j)) \ j=1...l_Y \tag{5}$$

Where, $\text{sim}_s(X_i, Y_j)$ is the similarity between X_i and Y_j, it will be described in section 3.3.

Since one word instead of one sememe may be used to describe the concepts in *HowNet*:

1) If the similarity is between a sememe and a word, the value is 0;

2) If the similarity is between two same words, the value is 1, otherwise the value is 0.

3.3   Sememe Similarity

In *HowNet*, the sememes have hyponymy, according to it we can build a tree hierarchy called G. In G, the topmost layer is root node, and each node corresponds to a sememe, the sememe hyponymy forms the links between these nodes. SIC can be calculated through the depth of the sememe. Then a transfer probability matrix M can be constructed by SIC and those links. Therefore, sememe vector can be obtained with PageRank algorithm.

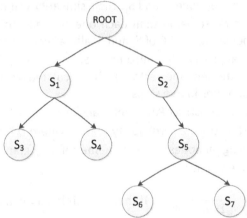

Fig. 1. The hyponymy of knowledge base

3.3.1   Sememe Information Content (SIC)

SIC refers to the information contained in sememes. It is an important feature to distinguish sememes. The closer the content of the sememes is, the higher the similarity is, and vice versa.

In *HowNet*, the depth of sememe is an important feature to calculate SIC. Sememes at different depths have different SIC. Sememes at the same depth with their descendants at different depths also have different SIC. According to figure 1, the nodes represent sememes, S_5 and S_1 are at different depths, so the SIC they contain is not the same; S_1 and S_2 are at the same depth, but the descendants nodes of S_1 are S_3 and S_4, the descendant nodes of S_2 are S_5, S_6, S_7. S_1 and S_2 have different depths of descendant nodes, therefore S_1 and S_2 contain the different SIC. By reference[10], the SIC can be calculated in the following way:

$$IC_s = \frac{\log(\text{deep}(s)+1)}{\log(\text{deep}_{max}+1)} \times (1 - \frac{\log(\Sigma_{\alpha \in \text{hypo}(s)}\frac{1}{\text{deep}(\alpha)}+1)}{\log(\text{node}_{max})}) \tag{6}$$

Where, deep (s) is depth of sememe s, root is the first layer and its depth is 1, deep_{max} is the maximum depth of all sememes, hypo(s) is the descendants sememe of s, node_{max} is the total number of all sememes.

3.3.2   SIC_PageRank and Sememe Vector

PageRank algorithm was proposed by Larry Page and Sergey Brin to rank web pages. It is an algorithm to reflect the relevance and importance of web pages. It uses traditional thought of citation analysis. When there is a link from web page A to page B, B is considered to obtain the contribution value of A, and the value depends on the importance of A.

In calculating the sememe similarity, weighed graph is constructed by sememe hyponymy. For sememe S_i and S_j, their similarity will be higher if S_i and S_j connects to the same sememe than each one connects to different sememes. The differences between the SIC of S_i and S_j also affect their similarity. Therefore, we define the approach to introduce SIC into PageRank algorithm as SIC_PageRank and the sememe vector can be calculated by SIC_PageRank.

The calculation runs in two steps:

1)   Using SIC to construct PageRank transfer probability matrix M

Let M be a N×N transfer probability matrix, where N is the total number of sememes. Traversing all nodes in the sememe relation graph, then calculate the value of each element in M:

$$M_{ji} = \begin{cases} \frac{SIC_j}{\Sigma_{k \in Out(i)} SIC_k}, & \text{If there is a link between i and j} \\ 0, & \text{otherwise} \end{cases} \tag{7}$$

Where, Out(i) is a set of sememes which have links to sememe i.

2)   Calculating the sememe vector $\vec{s}$

The calculation of the sememe vector is equivalent to resolving equation (8):

$$\vec{s} = cM\vec{s} + (1 - c)\vec{v} \tag{8}$$

In the equation, c is a damping factor, a value between 0 and 1; M is the transfer probability matrix; $\vec{s}$ is an N-dimension sememe vector and its initial value-- $\{\frac{1}{N}, \frac{1}{N} ..., \frac{1}{N}\}$, is modified during iterative process; $\vec{v}$ is also an N-dimension vector which is called smoothing factor in PageRank. As pointed out by reference[11], if there is a link between sememe i and j, $\vec{v}_i(j) = \frac{IC_j}{\sum_{k \in Out(i)} IC_k}$, other-

wise, $\vec{v}_i(j) = 0$.

3.3.3   Calculating the Similarity of Sememe

After using SIC_PageRank to calculate the sememe vector, each sememe has a corresponding vector. We can use the cosine to compute distance of sememe S_i and S_j:

$$dis(i,j) = \cos\left(\theta(\vec{s_i}, \vec{s_j})\right) = \frac{\vec{s_i} \cdot \vec{s_j}}{\|\vec{s_i}\| \|\vec{s_j}\|} \tag{9}$$

Then the similarity of two sememes can be obtained, that is:

$$sim_s(i,j) = \frac{dis(i,j)}{\alpha + dis(i,j)} \tag{10}$$

Where, α is an adjustable parameter.

4   Experiments and Results

We calculate the similarity between several groups of typical Chinese words and verify the validity of the method. We also apply this method in automatical identification of the semantic class of nouns in Contemporary Chinese Semantic Dictionary. Our experiments use the same version of *HowNet* with reference[4], and the parameters are set as follows: $c = 0.85$，$\alpha = 0.5$，$\beta_1 = 0.4, \beta_2 = 0.3, \beta_3 = 0.17, \beta_4 = 0.13$，$\gamma = 0.3$，the PageRank iterative number is 30.

4.1   Experiment of Word Similarity

The table 1 is the word similarity of several groups of words by using two methods respectively.

From table 1, we can see in group 1~5, the calculated results of the two methods are quiet consistent, but in group 6~12, the results are different. In group 6~8, "粉红(pink)" and "深红(crimson)" are both colors and similar in semantic. Their similarity calculated by our method is 0.606001, which is consistent with the actual situation. The same examples can also be found in "吃(eat)" and "喝(drink)", "跑(run)" and "跳(jump)", which represent similar actions. They should have a high degree of similarity. For the words in group 9~12, "采掘(mining)" and "采集(collection)" are not the same action, "祸(disaster)" and "电(electricity)" are not the same thing. Therefore, the similarity of these two groups should not be 1. Generally speaking, the similarity of SIC_PageRank method in this paper is reasonable, and it quite conforms with the actual situation.

Table 1. Word Similarity

Group	Word 1	Word 2	Reference [4]	SIC_PageRank
1	男人(man)	女人(woman)	0.861111	0.900000
2	男人(man)	财产(property)	0.208696	0.220341
3	香蕉(banana)	苹果(apple)	1.000000	1.000000
4	财富(fortune)	财产(property)	0.600000	0.552701
5	中国(China)	美国(America)	1.000000	0.935000
6	粉红(pink)	深红(crimson)	0.074074	0.606001
7	吃(eat)	喝(drink)	0.444444	0.666667
8	跑(run)	跳(jump)	0.444444	0.666667
9	壮举(feat)	善举(kindness)	0.621429	0.403829
10	采掘(mining)	采集(collection)	1.000000	0.580001
11	祸(disaster)	电(electricity)	1.000000	0.580001
12	驾驶室(cab)	眼泪(tear)	0.582987	0.412078

4.2 Experiment of Word Sense Class Recognition

The method of reference[4] and SIC_PageRank are applied in the sense class identification of words, and the results are compared with the judgment of human.

The proofreading and revision of the sense class of Contemporary Chinese Semantic Dictionary was carried out in Natural Language Processing Laboratory of Zhengzhou University in 2014[12]. The semantic category of the words in the dictionary is corrected by the way of subjective adjustment, and the sample terms of the document are used as the semantic classification standard.

We determine the sense class of nouns by the similarity between nouns in CSD, the progress runs in four steps:

1) Select the sample nouns in proofreading document as the standard word set S (a total of 269), and then take out the nouns in CSD which have the same sense class with the standard word in set S as the test word set T;

2) Calculate the similarity of each word in S and T;

3) For each word in T, select the words with the highest similarity in S (may be one or more), and make them a set C; if the maximum similarity is less than 0.5, then delete those words from T;

4) Calculate the proportion of standard words corresponding to sense class in C, regard the sense class of highest proportion as the word's semantic class. If there is the same proportion of the sense class, then choose one randomly;

Through the experiment, a total of 9535 conditions are extracted. Compare the calculated sense class with the judgment of human in the CSD, the consistency of the results is shown in Table 2

Table 2. The results of sense class identification

Method	Reference [4]	SIC_PageRank
The number of consistent words	6610	6859
consistency	69.3%	71.9%

As we can see from table 2, the results calculated by the SIC_PageRank method have a high consistency with the judgment of human. Table 3 lists some Chinese word similarity which is derived from the experiment. Word 1 is the test words, and word 2 is the standard words.

From table 3, we can seen that the similarity values of "角尺(angle square)" and "花(flower)", "空调(air conditioner)", "尺子(ruler)" calculated by the method in reference [4] are the same. From the semantic perspective, the similarity of "角尺(angle square)" and "尺子(ruler)" is higher than that of "花(flower)" and "空调(air conditioner)". In the same way, "恋情(romance)" and "爱情(love)" expressed emotions, "兴趣(interest)" expressed consciousness, the similarity of "恋情(romance)" and "爱情(love)" is higher than that of "兴趣(interest)" and "爱情(love)". Compared with "煤炭(coal)", "铺盖(blanket)" is more closer with "被子(quilt)" in semantic meaning. "虹膜(iris)" and "鼻子(nose)" are body organs of human beings or animals, the similarity of the two should be higher than that of "虹膜(iris)" and "环节(link)". Generally speaking, the word similarity through our method is reasonable, and it has a better effect on the recognition of the sense class.

Table 3. Word similarity in sense class identification

Word 1	Word 2	Reference [4]	SIC_PageRank
角尺 (angle square)	花(flower)	0.896000	0.870039
角尺 (angle square)	空调(air conditioner)	0.896000	0.870020
角尺 (angle square)	尺子(ruler)	0.896000	0.967500
家常便饭(potluck)	早餐(breakfast)	0.602632	0.400635
家常便饭(potluck)	米饭(rice)	0.600000	0.580001
恋情(romance)	兴趣(interest)	0.807692	0.794768
恋情(romance)	爱情(love)	0.800000	0.850020
铺盖(blanket)	煤炭(coal)	0.578989	0.505303
铺盖 blanket	被子(quilt)	0.575040	0.541007
虹膜 iris	鼻子(nose)	0.875200	0.935007

| 虹膜(iris) | 环节(link) | 0.896000 | 0.873319 |

Conclusions

In this paper, we propose a method based on *HowNet* to calculate the word similarity. The method makes full use of the *HowNet* sememe structure and the hyponymy information, and it calculates sememe similarity in the way of the depth of sememe and PageRank, then it obtains the word similarity according to the weight of each part of the sememe. Through experimental verification, the calculation results show that the word similarity is more reasonable, and it can get better effect in the recognition of sense class.

With more word knowledge bases being constructed, we will propose a much better calculation method of word similarity by considering more other information of word and combine multiple knowledge bases and various features of word in the future work.

Acknowledgments. This paper is supported by the National Social Science Foundation Project (No. 14BYY096), the National Natural Science Foundation of China (No. 61402419), the National key basic research and development program (No. 2014CB340504), Basic research project of Henan provincial science and Technology Department(No. 142300410231, 142300410308) and the Key scientific research projects of Henan Province Universities(No. 15A520098).

References

1. Dong Zhendong, Dong Qiang: Hownet Literature [OL] , http://www.keenage.com.(1999) (In Chinese)
2. Page L, Brin S, Motwani R, et al. The PageRank Citation Ranking: Bringing Order to the Web[J]. Technical Report, Stanford Digital Libraries. (1998)
3. Fellbaum C. WordNet: An Electronic Lexical Database. Language, Speech, and Communication[M].The MIT Press.(1998)
4. Liu Qun，Li Sujian. Word Similarity Computing Based on How-net(基于《知网》的词汇语义相似度计算)[C]. Proceedings of Chinese Lexical Semantics:3th Workshop. 2002：59-76. (2002) (In Chinese)
5. Wu Zuoxian, Wang Yu. A New Measure of Semantic Similarity Based on Hierarchical Network of Concept(基于 HNC 理论的词语相似度计算)[J]. 中文信息学报, 2014,02:37-43+50. (2014) (In Chinese)
6. Tian Jiule, Zhao Wei. Words Similarity Algorithm Based on TongyiciCilin in Semantic Web Adaptive Learning System(基于同义词词林的词语相似度计算方法)[J]. Journal of Jilin University (Information Science Edition),2010,06:602-608. (2010) (In Chinese)
7. David Snchez, Montserrat Batet, and David Isern. Ontology Based Information Content Computation[J]. Journal on Knowledge-Based Systems, 2011, Volume 24 Issue 2:297-303. (2011)
8. Zhou Z, Wang Y, Gu J. A new model of information content for semantic similarity in Word-

Net[C]. Proceedings of Future Generation Communication and Networking Symposia, 2008. FGCNS"08. Second International Conference on. IEEE, 2008, 3: 85-89. (2008)

9. Singh J, Saini M, Siddiqi S. Graph Based Computational Model for Computing Semantic Similarity[J]. Emerging Research in Computing, Information, Communication and Applications, ERCICA, 2013: 501-507. (2013)

10. Adhikari A, Singh S, Dutta A, et al. A novel information theoretic approach for finding semantic similarity in WordNet[C]. Proceedings of TENCON 2015-2015 IEEE Region 10 Conference. IEEE, 2015: 1-6. (2015)

11. Haveliwala T H. ToSIC-sensitive PageRank[C]. Proceedings of the 11th international conference on World Wide Web. ACM, 2002: 517-526. (2002)

12. Mu lingling, Li hao, Zan hongying et al. Proofreading and Revision of the Semantic Classes in the Contemporary Chinese Semantic Dictionary[C]. Proceedings of Chinese Lexical Semantics:16th Workshop, CLSW2015. Springer International Publishing, 2015: 222-233. (2015)

Joint Event Co-reference Resolution and Temporal Relation Identification

Jiayue Teng[1], Peifeng Li[1], Qiaoming Zhu[1], Weiyi Ge[2]

1: School of Computer Science & Technology, Soochow University, Suzhou, Jiangsu, 215006;
2: Science and Technology on Information Systems Engineering Laboratory, Nanjing, China
tjyemail@sina.com, {pfli,qmzhu}@suda.edu.cn, geweiyi@163.com

Abstract. Event co-reference and event temporal relations are two important types of event relations, which are widely used in many NLP applications, such as information extraction, text summarization, question answering system, etc. Event temporal relations provide much useful semantic and discourse information for more accurate co-reference resolution. However, traditional event co-reference resolution neglects those event temporal relations, leading to inconsistent resolutions in temporal logic. This paper proposes a joint model for event co-reference resolution and event temporal relation identification in Chinese event corpus. The experimental results on the ACE corpus show that our model can improve the performance of the above two tasks.

Keywords: Event Co-reference, Temporal Relation, Joint Model.

1 Introduction

Event co-reference resolution and event temporal identification are widely used in many NLP applications such as information extraction, topic detection, text summarization and question answering system. As two important types of event relations, co-reference and temporal relation are not independent and have close relation each other. Commonly, those co-reference events always have the same occurrence time, which is helpful for event temporal identification. Meanwhile, those events which have the same occurrence time always are co-reference events. In contrast, those events with different occurrence times usually are not co-reference events. Take the following two instances for examples:

a) 重庆市公安局日前**抓获**（*EV1*）持枪杀人抢劫案张君及其同伙。被**逮捕**（*EV2*）的6人，有张君及其情妇杨明燕，以及杨明燕的哥哥杨明军。*(Chongqing public security bureau recently **arrested (EV1)** armed robbery Zhang Jun and his associates. Six **arrested (EV2)** people include Zhang Jun, Yang Mingyan who is his mistress, and Yang Mingjun who is Yang Mingyan's brother.)*

b) 据警方称监狱里面有2名囚犯引火**自焚**（*EV3*）。当警方和安全部队突击监狱时，射死第3名朝着军警冲去**自焚**（*EV4*）的囚犯。*(The police announced that there are two prisoners who **burned themselves (EV3)** in prison. When the police*

M. Dong et al. (Eds.): CLSW 2016, LNAI 10085, pp. 426–433, 2016
DOI: 10.1007/978-3-319-49508-8_40

*and security forces raided the prison, the third **self-burning (EV4)** prisoner who rushed towards the police was shot to die.*)

In example a), event EV1 and EV2 are co-reference events. However, they have different triggers, i.e. 抓获*(arrest)* and 逮捕*(arrest)*. General co-reference resolution is difficult to identify because the above two events have only one same argument (张君*(Zhang Jun)*). In example b), Event EV3 and EV4 are not co-reference events. However, they have the same trigger (自焚*(self-burning)*) and several similar arguments, which leading to the error result of co-reference resolution in general. In fact, it is easily to infer that EV4 occurred after EV3 according to token 第三名 *(third)*.

According to the definition of event co-reference, co-reference events occur in the same time. In most cases, those events with different temporal relation do not have co-reference relation.

Event co-reference is different from entity anaphora which regularly occurs in adjacent sentences. Those co-reference events often cross sentences and paragraphs, and even discourses. Besides, Chinese event co-reference resolution is a challenge task, due to its language characteristics. As is well-known, English grammar is more rigorous and less polysemy. Unfortunately, Chinese often omits the subject and has no obvious tenses and plural forms, bringing about a complex and free Chinese grammar.

To solve those mentioned issues above, this paper combines event co-reference and event temporal information with some semantic and distance constraints, to establish a joint inference model. The experimental results on the ACE corpus show that our model can improve the performance of the above two tasks.

2   Related works

2.1   Event Co-reference Resolution

Event co-reference resolution is an important task in information extraction and most previous work focused on pairwise model. The pairwise model first lets any two events make up into one event pair with effective features such as words, sentences, distances, etc. Then, a machine learning method is used to train a classification model for predicting [1]. For examples, Bejan [2] proposed some structure features; Chen [3] provided a feature impact method based on maximum entropy model; Teng [4] used trigger semantics and combined features to resolve Chinese event co-reference. However, most of the pairwise models assume that the events in a document are independent and ignore those relations between all event pairs, which easy to create inconsistent event co-reference chains.

Optimizing co-reference event chains is helpful for reducing defects of pairwise model and improving resolution performance. For examples, graph model optimization uses vertexes as events, edges as co-reference relations. It maximizes the sum of the measures of every edge to achieve a best decision. Nicolae [5] employed entity relation graph based on cluster algorithm to optimize co-reference event chains.

Chen [6] used spectral partitioning which allows the incorporation of pronoun co-reference information. Sangeetha [7] proposed Mincut algorithm to optimize event relation graph. Song [8] used Markov logic network for global inference. Teng [9] applied integer linear programming to optimizing event co-reference chains.

2.2 Event Temporal Identification

Researches on event temporal identification are similar to event co-reference resolution, which mainly used pairwise model. On event temporal identification, Chambers [10] introduced many lexical, contextual and syntactic features to a pairwise model. Cheng [11] used dependency syntax tree to construct the sequence tag model. Bethard [12] appended syntactic relation and semantic features. D'Souza [13] introduced discourse features. Considering the defects of pairwise model, global optimization and inference method can be applied to the temporal relation identification, which furthers its performance based on temporal relation constraints. Chambers [14] and Xuan [15] used integer linear programming to improve performance of event temporal relation identification. Zheng [16] employed global optimization model on Chinese event temporal relation corpus which contains four categories temporal relations: before, after, overlap and unknown.

2.3 Joint Model

Combining several relational tasks which can acquire abundant event semantics and discourse information is helpful for each task. Lee [17] joint event and entity co-reference on across documents. Araki [18] employed structured perceptron to partial event co-reference resolution and event trigger extraction. From the angle of granularity, event is much larger than entity or trigger because event contains trigger and several entities which played the role of event arguments. Whereas many relations between events, this paper propose a method of joint event temporal relation and co-reference relation from linguistics logic.

Unlike the current joint model, both event temporal relation and co-reference relation are not two tasks in a pipeline model. Nevertheless, the two event relations have close correlation and supply much semantic information each other from a linguistic logic point of view, as shown in example a) and b). In this paper, we construct a joint model for event co-reference resolution and temporal relation identification with semantic and distance features.

3   Joint Model of Event Co-reference Resolution and Temporal Relation Identification

This section introduces the joint model of event co-reference resolution and temporal relation identification based on integer linear programming for global optimization. We also proposed various kinds constraints to further improve this joint model and improve the performance of both two tasks.

3.1   Joint Inference Model

Two Maximum Entropy (ME) model and a Condition Random Field (CRF) are used in our joint model as the basic classifiers. Although the ME model has been widely used in various NLP tasks and achieved certain success in capturing the global information, our experimentation shows that it suffers from low precision. To overcome this problem, a CRF model is introduced to capture the local sequential information. Our preliminary experimentation shows that the CRF model is much complementary to the ME model in our task.

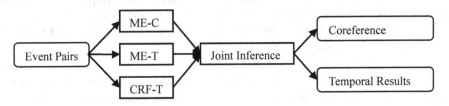

Fig. 1. Joint Inference Model

The joint inference model contains two event temporal classification and one event co-reference resolution. As figure 1 shown, ME-C is a ME model of event co-reference resolution, while ME-T and CRF-T are the ME and CRF models of event temporal relation classification, respectively.

3.2   Optimization Objective

The objective of our joint inference model is to maximize the probabilities of event co-reference and temporal relation identification. Let $p_{ME}(e_i, e_j|rc)$ be the probability of event e_i and e_j which have co-reference relation by ME-C. Event temporal relation contains four categories: before, after, overlap and unknown. This paper only focuses on the overlap relation because only the overlap relation has close linguistics logic with co-reference relation. Let $p_{ME}(e_i, e_j|rt)$ be the probability of overlap relation between events e_i and e_j by ME-T. Several formulas of probability profit are defined as follows:

$$pc_{ij}^c = logp_{ME}(e_i, e_j|rc) \tag{1}$$
$$pc_{ij}^u = log(1 - p_{ME}(e_i, e_j|rc)) \tag{2}$$
$$pt_{ij}^o = logp_{ME}(e_i, e_j|rt) \tag{3}$$
$$pt_{ij}^u = log(1 - p_{ME}(e_i, e_j|rt)) \tag{4}$$

pc_{ij}^c indicates the probability profit of the co-reference event e_i and e_j, pc_{ij}^u indicates the probability profit of the unco-reference event e_i and e_j; pt_{ij}^o and pt_{ij}^u indicate the probability profits of the overlap and other relations respectively between event e_i and e_j. Besides, we introduce two variables x, y to ensure that each event pair has only one co-reference resolution and one temporal identification. The objective function of our joint inference model is as follows:

$$max \sum_{ei,ej\in E}(x_{ij} \cdot pc_{ij}^c + (1 - x_{ij}) \cdot pc_{ij}^u + y_{ij} \cdot pt_{ij}^o + (1 - y_{ij}) \cdot pt_{ij}^u) \qquad (5)$$

Subject to

$$x_{ij} \in \{0,1\}, \quad y_{ij} \in \{0,1\}, \quad i \neq j.$$

3.3   Constraints

Two global optimization models, i.e. event co-reference resolution and event temporal relation classification, are used as our baselines, mentioned in [9] and [16]. In our joint inference model, we apply two kinds of constraints: temporal-co-reference (C1-C3) and co-reference-temporal (C4-C5) constraints, respectively.

(C1) Trigger consistency: if the two events have consistent triggers and temporal relations, they are co-reference events.

$$x_{ij} \geq \hat{y}_{ij} \quad \forall trigger_i \approx trigger_j \wedge \hat{y}_{ij} = 1 \qquad (6)$$

$trigger_i$, $trigger_j$ are triggers of event e_i, e_j, which are measured by semantic similarity and word matching. $\hat{y}_{ij}$ is a fusion variable which balance the ME and CRF classifier. This variable is only involved in the constraints and not in the optimization objective, the same below.

(C2) Neighbor events in long distance sentences: if the two neighbor events in nonadjacent sentences have the same argument and temporal relation, they are co-reference events.

$$x_{ij} \geq \hat{y}_{ij} \quad \forall bias_{ij} = 1 \wedge segment_{ij} \geq 2 \wedge arg_{ij} \geq 1 \qquad (7)$$

Where $bias_{ij} = 1$ indicates event e_i, e_j are neighbor events, $segment_{ij} \geq 2$ means there is more than one sentence between event e_i and e_j, $arg_{ij} \geq 1$ express event e_i and e_j have the same argument.

We employ two kinds of event distances: one is measured by event; the other is measured by sentence. As the ACE corpus shows, the close events in the same sentence or neighbor sentence usually have no co-reference relation. However, the neighbor events often have high probability of being co-reference relation when they have the same argument and temporal relation (overlap).

(C3) Different temporal relation: when the different temporal events are in the same sentence or neighbor sentence and there is temporal conjunction, they are not co-reference events.

$$x_{ij} = 0 \quad \forall \hat{y}_{ij} = 0 \wedge segment_{ij} \leq 1 \wedge conj_{ij} \geq 1 \qquad (8)$$

According to the analysis of experimental data, more than 98% of co-reference events have been identified as overlap relation and the events with non-overlap relation are not co-reference events. To get more scientific and rigorous constraint, two events are not co-reference events when they have the obvious conjunction [16], such as later, cause, therefore, etc. Nevertheless, we only constrain the events in the same sentence or neighbor sentence.

(C4) Co-reference events have overlap relation: when the two events have co-reference relation, they are overlap events especially they have the same argument.

$$y_{ij} \geq x_{ij} \quad \forall arg_{ij} \geq 1 \qquad (9)$$

(C5) Non-coreference events have non-overlap relation: if the two non-coreference events are in non-adjacent sentence and do not have same argument, they do not have overlap relation. This constraint only identifies overlap temporal relation or not as follows.

$$y_{ij} \leq arg_{ij} \quad \forall x_{ij} = 0 \wedge segment_{ij} \geq \theta \qquad (10)$$

where $\theta = 6$, adjusted by the development set.

4   Experiments

This section introduces the corpus and experimental setting firstly, and then gives the experimental results and analysis.

4.1   Corpus and Experiment Setting

To facilitate the joint model for event co-reference resolution and temporal relation identification, we choose the intersection of the two corpora, namely, the ACE 2005 Chinese corpus and the temporal relation corpus based on the ACE 2005 Chinese corpus by Zheng [20]. Our final corpus contains 4834 overlap event pairs (22.87%) and 4364 co-reference event pairs (20.39%). We randomly select 30 documents as the development set, and maintain the ratio of training and test set is about 4:1 to perform 5 fold cross validation. We employ Gurobi Optimizer 6.0[1] to process the integer linear programming, and Conll2012 scorer 8.0[2] to evaluate performance of event co-reference resolution under the MUC-6. Afterward, we calculate micro average precision (P), recall (R) and F1 for two tasks.

4.2   Experiment Results of Joint Model

Table 1 shows the experimental results within the joint inference model and two baselines. After significant test, event co-reference resolution part: p=0.0002, and event temporal relation identification part: p=0.0005, indicates that our joint model has significant differences compared with the baselines.

Table 1. Experiment Results

Experiments	Event Co-reference Resolution			Event Temporal Identification (Overlap)		
	P/%	R/%	F1/%	P/%	R/%	F1/%
Baseline	68.54	72.52	70.47	67.48	71.23	69.30
Joint Model	71.45	73.37	72.40(+1.93)	68.48	71.51	69.96(+0.66)

From Table 1, our joint method has great improvement for event co-reference resolution by 1.93% and it illustrates that event temporal relation is effective for identify co-reference event pairs. If an event pair does not have overlap temporal relation, our joint model can infer that they do not have co-reference relation. Table 1

---

[1] http://www.gurobi.com/

[2] http://conll.cemantix.org/2012/software.html/

shows that the improvement of event temporal relation identification is not high (0.66%), because most co-reference events are also identified as overlap relation. Even if we use the gold co-reference events, our model improve the F1-score of overlap temporal identification by 1.2%.

4.3   Contributions of Constraints for Co-reference Resolution

Table 2 shows the contributions of constraints C1~C3 for co-reference resolution.

Table 2 Contributions of Constraints for Co-reference Resolution

Experiment	P/%	R/%	F1/%
Baseline	68.54	72.52	70.47
+C1	68.85	73.97(+1.45)	71.32(+0.85)
+C2	68.41	73.88(+1.36)	71.04(+0.57)
+C3	71.31(+2.77)	71.64	71.47(+1.00)

Table 2 shows that the constraints C1 and C2 achieve relative high improvement on recall (1.45% and 1.36). However, their improvement of precision is limited. The reasons are that about 2/3 of event pairs are not co-reference events in those overlap event pairs and those exceptions. The Constraint C3 achieves the highest accuracy improvement (2.77%). The reason is that about 99% of co-reference events are classified as the overlap temporal events

5   Summary

In this paper, we propose a joint method of combining the event co-reference resolution and temporal relation identification. We also introduce many constraints such as trigger consistencies, temporal relations, conjunctions, arguments, distances, etc. to enhance the performances of the joint model. In future work, we will combine the event argument extraction and co-reference resolution to further improve the performances of each tasks.

Acknowledgments

The authors would like to thank the anonymous reviewers for their comments on this paper. This research was supported by the National Natural Science Foundation of China under Grant Nos. 61472265, 61331011 and 61273320.

References

1. David Ahn. The Stages of Event Extraction. In Proceedings of the ACL 2006. Sydney, 2006:1-8.
2. Cosmin Adrian Bejan, Sanda Harabagiu. A Linguistic Resource for Discovering Event

Structures and Resolving Event Coreference. In Proceedings of the ACL 2008. Marrakech, 2008:2881-2887.

3. Zheng Chen, Heng Ji, Robert Haralick. A Pairwise Event Coreference Model, Feature Impact and Evaluation for Event Coreference Resolution. In Proceedings of eETTs 2009. Borovets, 2009:17-22.

4. Jiayue Teng, Peifeng Li, Qiaoming Zhu. Chinese Event Co-Reference Resolution Based on Trigger Semantics and Combined Features. Chinese Lexical Semantics, Springer International Publishing, 2015:494-503.

5. Cristina Nicolae, Gabriel Nicolae. BESTCUT: A Graph Algorithm for Coreference Resolution. In Proceedings of EMNLP 2006. Sydney, 2006:275-283.

6. Bin Chen, Jian Su, Sinno Jialin Pan, Chew Lim Tan. A Unified Event Coreference Resolution by Integrating Multiple Resolvers. In Proceedings of IJCNLP 2011. Chiang Mai, 2011:102-110.

7. Satyan Sangeetha, Michael Arock. Event Coreference Resolution Using Mincut Based Graph Clustering. In Proceedings of the Fourth International Workshop on Computer Networks & Communications 2012. Coimbatore, 2012:253-260.

8. Yang Song, Jing Jiang, Wayne Xin Zhao. Joint Learning for Coreference Resolution with Markov Logic. Research Collection School of Information Systems, 2012:1245-1254.

9. Jiayue Teng, Peifeng Li, Qiaoming Zhu. Global Inference for Co-reference Resolution between Chinese Events. Acta Scientiarum Naturalium Universitatis Peinensis, 2016, 52(1):97-103 [In Chinese].

10. Nathanael Chambers, Shan Wang, Dan Jurafsky. Classifying Temporal Relations between Events. In Proceedings of the ACL 2007. Prague, 2007:173-176.

11. Yuchang Cheng, Masayuki Asahara, Yuji Matsumoto. NAIST.Japan: Temporal Relation Identification Using Dependency Parsed Tree. In Proceedings of the 4th International Workshop on Semantic Evaluations 2007. Prague, 2007:245-248.

12. Steven Bethard, James Martin. Temporal Relation Classification Using Syntactic and Semantic Features. In Proceedings of the ACL 2007. Prague, 2007:129-132.

13. Jennifer D'Souza, Vincent Ng. Classifying Temporal Relations with Rich Linguistic Knowledge. In Proceedings of NAACL-HLT 2013. Georgia, 2013:918-927.

14. Nathanael Chambers, Dan Jurafsky. Jointly Combining Implicit Constraints Improves Temporal Ordering. In Proceedings of EMNLP 2008. Honolulu, 2008:698-706.

15. Quang Xuan Do, Wei Lu, Dan Roth. Joint Inference for Event Timeline Construction. In Proceedings of EMNLP-CoNLL 2012. Jeju Island, 2012:677-687.

16. Xin Zheng, Peifeng Li, Qiaoming Zhu. Global Inference for Temporal Relations between Chinese Events. Journal of Chinese Information Processing, 2015 [In Chinese].

17. Heeyoung Lee, Marta Recasens, Angel Chang. Joint Entity and Event Coreference Resolution across Documents. In Proceedings of EMNLP-CoNLL 2012. Jeju Island, 2012:489-500.

18. Jun Araki, Teruko Mitamura. Joint Event Trigger Identification and Event Coreference Resolution with Structured Perceptron. In Proceedings of EMNLP 2015. Lisbon, 2015:2074-2080.

19. Peifeng Li, Qiaoming Zhu, Hongjun Diao. Joint Modeling of Trigger Identification and Event Type Determination in Chinese Event Extraction. In Proceedings of COLING 2012. Mumbai, 2012:1635-1652.

20. Xin Zheng, Peifeng Li, Qiaoming Zhu. An Approach to Recognize Temporal Relation between Chinese Events. Chinese Lexical Semantics, Springer International Publishing, 2015:507-512.

Automatic Classification of Classical Chinese Lyrics and Songs

Yuchen Zhu; Tianqi Qi; Xinning Dong

School of Chinese Language and Literature, Beijing Normal University, Beijing 100875, China
zhuyuchen81@qq.com

Abstract. We proposed a text classification model for classical Chinese lyrics and songs in this paper. 596 Song lyrics and Yuan songs are represented in vectors with Vector Space Model. The classifiers are based on Naive Bayes and Support Vector Machine algorithms, which both performed well in the experiment (with SVM, the F-measure up to 92.6%). In addition, we examined the performance of the classifiers in sorting atypical texts, with lyrics and songs in Ming dynasty as the test set. Although the F-measure drops to 79.2%, it still demonstrates stylistic changes in lyrics in Ming dynasty.

Keywords: lyric· song· text classification· Naive Bayes· support vector machine

1   Introduction

Tang poetry (唐诗), Song lyric (宋词) and Yuan song (元曲), are considered as the three gems on the crown of ancient Chinese verse literature. Among them, lyrics and songs are closely related: they both took shape from folk songs and ditties, and are featured with sentences uneven in length. However, they developed into quite different styles in literary. Therefore, researchers have spent tremendous effort on the distinction between lyrics and songs.

Traditionally, we discussed the similarities and differences between lyrics and songs centering on the aesthetic intuition and experience, which is to some extent capable of telling the unique spirits and tastes of lyrics and songs. But pragmatically, the classification standard is still vague. A typical example is that, the *Sunny Sand ·Autumn Thoughts* (天净沙·秋思) by Ma Zhiyuan (马致远) is often selected by both lyric anthologies and song anthologies.

In recent years, researchers started to apply natural language processing (NLP) to text classification problems in literary study. Hu et al [1] incorporated computer technology into the study of lexical semantics of Tang poetry and developed a computer-aided system to assist the study of ancient Chinese poetry and lyric. Kuang et al [2] and Hu et al [3] tried to figure out how to automatically classify different themes of Tang poetry. Mu [4] designed a text classifier for different genres of Song lyrics. These studies transformed poem texts into vectors, and then applied classification algorithms, such as Rocchio, Naive Bayes (NB), Support Vector Machine (SVM), and K-

© Springer International Publishing AG 2016
M. Dong et al. (Eds.): CLSW 2016, LNAI 10085, pp. 434–440, 2016
DOI: 10.1007/978-3-319-49508-8_41

Nearest Neighbor (KNN), to theme classify the poems. The features of the documents, such as text, title, and genre were extracted from characters, words, and N-gram.

With the previous research, we transformed the texts of lyrics and songs in vectors with Vector Space Model, and designed contrast experiments to identify the most effective way to extract features. Two classifiers were successfully built with NB and SVM algorithms to classify lyrics and songs. Furthermore, we conducted a case study with lyrics and songs in Ming dynasty, to explore the application of our classifiers in the literature research.

2   Data Source and Framework

The complete flow of establishing our classifier is as followed: 1. Took 596 classical texts from *Three hundred Lyrics of the Song Dynasty* (宋词三百首) [5] and *Three hundred Songs of the Yuan Dynasty* (元曲三百首) [6] as our corpus. 2. Preprocessed the corpus with single-word segmentation policy and word segmentation policy respectively, and transformed the characters and words into feature vectors with Vector Space Model. 10-fold cross validation was employed to examine the result. 3. By comparing the Precision, Recall and F-measure, the most suitable classifying algorithm for our corpus was selected. 4. To explore the further application of our classifier, we performed atypical texts categorizing experiment, with classical texts of Song lyrics and Yuan songs as the training set and lyrics & songs in Ming dynasty as test set. We used the data mining software--Weka3.7 for the experiment.

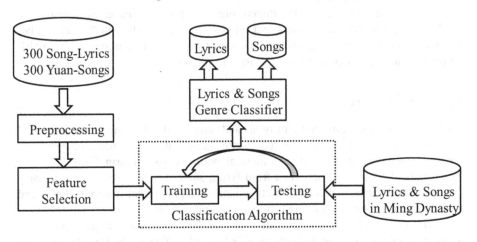

Fig. 1. Flow chart of the classification model of lyrics and songs

3   Classifier Designing

3.1   Vector Representation

The classifier is developed from Vector Space Model proposed by Salton *et al.* In VSM, a text is represented as a feature set composed of a series of word vectors. Each feature has its own weight, together they formed a multi-dimensional feature vector, $d= \{t_1, w_1; t_2, w_2; \ldots\ldots; t_i, w_i\}$, in which d represents the text, t_i represents a feature (a word), and w_i is the weight of t_i, calculated by TF-IDF weighting.

3.2   Preprocessing

Opinions are divided on the unit of segmentation for ancient Chinese verse texts like lyrics and songs. Some scholars[4] prefer single-word segmentation because there is a large amount of monosyllabic in ancient Chinese and an ancient Chinese character may contain rich connotations since poets paid so much attention selecting characters and words. Some researchers[2], however, claimed that the words appeared frequently or have metaphorical meaning should be retained, including proper nouns and phrases with parallel or subordinate structure, such as fallen petal (落花), green hill (青山) and spring water (春水). To compare these two methods, we apply both single-word segmentation policy and word segmentation policy in text processing. The word segmentation dataset is obtained with the help of NLPIR/ICTCLAS 2015 and some artificial proof. In the experiment, the advantages and disadvantages of the two sets of data were compared first.

Besides, in order to reduce the dimensions of the vector space, we counted the word frequency of the two datasets, and set characters or words with frequencies below 4 as threshold. We also eliminated the words with no contribution to the classification, such as not(不), one(一), no(无), is(是), either(也) and *etc.*.

3.3   Other Features

Moreover, we used tune name of lyrics and songs as the dividing factor and tested the result of the classification with tune name. Tune is the music name of lyrics and songs, which represents the particular musical mode and textual form. Since 1/3 of the tune names of songs were inherited from lyrics, some different musical modes may share the same names. Therefore, the tune name is an important feature of lyrics and songs, rather than the determining factors on text classification.

Previous studies have taken the title of the work as a feature, but many lyrics and songs are untitled. We assumed that the title has little effect on the text classification and didn't take the titles as a feature.

3.4   Algorithm

The previous studies showed that NB, SVM and KNN, rather than Rocchio delivered better results. However, the K-measure of the KNN algorithm is not employed since it requires a much finer adjustment when handling text classification for small datasets. We finally chose NB and SVM as the algorithm of our classifier.

Naive Bayes algorithm is a common algorithm[7], which can classify texts by calculating the conditional probability (P) of each text of lyrics or songs, and select the maximum one as the output result:

$$P(c_i|d) = \frac{P(d|c_i)P(c_i)}{P(d)} \tag{1}$$

In the formula, $P(c_i|d)$ stands for the probability of text d pertaining to c_i (lyrics or songs) and $P(d|c_i)$ is the probability of d in c_i. Due to the limited space, further deduction is not demonstrated here.

The basic principle of SVM is to find a support vector in hyperplane which can partition the points (text d) in the space into different spaces, namely, finding a vector w and a constant b to build a hyperplane with the formula $w^T x + b = 0$. We used Sequential minimal optimization (SMO) to solve the equation -- defining Lagrangian at first and the calculation of w and b can be transformed into that of the Lagrange multipliers α_i[8]. After some trials, we selected Polynomial Kernel, that is $K(d, d_i) = \langle d, d_i \rangle + 1$, and set the regulation parameter C as 1.

4   Results

We tested the performances of different feature selection plans by comparing their Precision (P), Recall (R) and F-measure (F) with 10-fold cross validation. The results of different feature selections (single-word segmentation/ word segmentation; with tune name/without tune name) in NB and SVM are shown in table 1:

Table 1. Experiment performance of lyrics and songs classification

Features	Naive Bayes			SVM		
	P(%)	R(%)	F(%)	P(%)	R(%)	F(%)
Single-word segmentation	91.2	90.9	90.9	90.5	90.4	90.4
Single-word segmentation + Tune name	91.9	91.8	91.8	92.6	92.6	92.6
Word segmentation	87.3	85.1	84.8	91.2	91.1	91.1
Word segmentation + Tune name	89.0	87.4	87.3	92.6	92.6	92.6

As shown in table 1, only the plan with word segmentation and NB algorithm was less satisfying. However, there is no difference between single-word segmentation and word segmentation when adding tune name of lyrics / songs in SVM. Adding tune name of lyrics / songs as a feature will improve the overall efficiency of the classifier. As for the algorithm, SVM is better than NB in helping building the classifier. We believe that the single-word segmentation would be a smarter choice.

When integrating tune names as our feature, all classifiers performed better, which validated our assumption that musical factor profoundly affect lyrics & songs writing, that is, musicality is a defining characteristic to classification.

5   Application Case

The classifier was developed to assist the research of Chinese ancient verse literature, especially of lyrics & songs' genre. After achieved good results in studying Song and Yuan dynasty, we tried to expand its application to classifying atypical texts.

For this purpose, we designed another experiment to test the accuracy performance of our classifier for lyric & song texts written after Yuan dynasty and tried to find some rules of the literary evolution. We chose the dataset in the previous experiment as our training set and extracted 100 lyrics in Ming dynasty from *Lyric anthologies of the Jin, Yuan and Ming Dynasty* [9] and 100 songs in Ming dynasty from *Song anthologies of the Jin, Yuan and Ming Dynasty* [10] as our test set. We used single-word segmentation and took the tune names of lyrics / songs as a feature in this study. The results are outlined in Table 2.

Table 2. Experiment result of Ming dynasty's lyrics and songs classification

	P(%)	R(%)	F(%)
Naive Bayes	75.5	75.0	74.9
SVM	81.5	79.5	79.2

As shown above, SVM delivered a better result than NB. However, comparing to the classical Song lyrics and Yuan songs in the previous experiment, the F-measure of lyrics & songs in Ming dynasty was down by 13.4%. The changes of lyrics in Ming dynasty in words, imagery and style might lead to this confusion. Therefore, we explored further on what decreased the F-measure.

With the output result of the experiment, we found that the misclassified texts were mostly from lyrics, especially from those short songs(小令), such as *As in a Dream*(如梦令), *Remembering the Prince*(忆王孙) and *Goddess in Xiaoxiang*(潇湘神). All *Dreaming of the South*(忆江南) in lyrics texts were mistaken for songs, so does Qu Dajun's(屈大均) lyrics. In addition, we found that the misclassified lyrics, such as Liu Ji's(刘基) *As in a Dream* (如梦令), were mainly talking about ambitions, rather than romantic love and sentimental aspects which were much more common in Song lyrics. And a sense of desolate broadness in such misclassified texts could always be felt when reading Yuan songs, which is quite different from the delicacy of Song lyrics. Besides, the reduplicated words and rhetoric repetition, an obvious characteristic of typical song texts, also resulted in the changes in word frequency and other characteristic values in those misclassified texts.

In another word, we extracted those poetic variants of Ming lyrics through the classifier. The results provide some interesting perspectives for our further research, such as the changes of Ming lyrics in language, rhetoric and emotions. An interesting example is that the writing style of Qu Dajun(屈大均), a lyrics writer in Ming dynasty, is more similar to a typical text of Yuan songs, rather than to that of Song lyrics. Thus, the application of NLP can efficiently assist researchers in the study of Chinese ancient verse literature.

6   Conclusion

The application of text classification is proved to be valuable in the realm of Chinese ancient verse literature study. It helps researchers distinguishing the genre of lyrics and songs effectively, and sparks new ideas in literature study.

In this paper, we adopted vector space model to process the text of lyrics & songs and set classical texts of Song lyrics and Yuan songs as our corpus. Then we built two classifiers with Naive Bayes and SVM algorithm respectively, the latter of which achieved a satisfying result in the classification (F-measure is 92.6%). The experiment also proved that the single-word segmentation policy was more cost-and-time-effective.

Since our corpus is not large enough, it is still a preliminary study on the text classification. More data should be included in the future work, and the advantages of different classifiers when dealing with larger corpus are to be tested.

For the atypical texts, such as lyrics & songs in Ming dynasty, the performance of our classifier is still to be improved. In the further study, our corpus will be enlarged, and some other factors, such as epoch, metrics and context or semantic information extracted from the texts, will be taken as features to improve the classification accuracy. Our study is far from over.

References

1. Junfeng, H., Shiwen, Y.: Word Meaning Similarity Analysis in Chinese Ancient Poetry and Its Applications. Journal of Chinese Information Processing 4(2002).(in Chinese)
2. Haibo, K., Xiaohe C.: Research on Algorithms of Tang-Poetry-Text Automatic Classification. Proceedings of YWCL-2010.(in Chinese)
3. Renfen, H., Yuchen, Z.: Automatic Classification of Tang Poetry Themes. Acta Scientiarum Naturalium Universitatis Pekinensis 2(2015).(in Chinese)
4. Yong, M.: Using Keyword Features to Automatically Classify Genre of Song Lyrics Poem. Chinese Lexical Semantics, Springer International Publishing Switzerland 2015, 478-485.
5. Xiaozang, Z. Three Hundred Lyrics of the Song Dynasty. Zhonghua Book Company, Beijing(2006).(in Chinese)
6. Zhongmin, R.: Three Hundred Songs of the Yuan Dynasty. Zhejiang Ancient Books Publishing House, Hangzhou(2010).(in Chinese)
7. Yong, Y., Yan, Z., Zhongshi, H., Liangyan, L.: Studies of Traditional Chinese Poet Identification Based on Machine Learning. Mind and Computation 3(2007).(in Chinese)

8. Zhao, Z., Guoxing, H., Yu, B.: An improved SMO Algorithm. Computer Science 8(2003).(in Chinese)
9. Chengtao, X., Zhang, Z.: Lyric anthologies of the Jin, Yuan and Ming Dynasty. People's Literature Publishing House, Beijing(1983).(in Chinese)
10. Qi, W., Baizhao, H., Boyang, X.: Song anthologies of the Jin, Yuan and Ming Dynasty. People's Literature Publishing House, Beijing(1988).(in Chinese)

Clustering of News Topics Integrating the Relationship among News Elements

Jiaying Hou[1,2], Zhengtao Yu[1,2,*], Xudong Hong[1,2], Feng Li[3]

[1] School of Information Engineering and Automation, Kunming University of Science and Technology, 650500 Yunnan, China
[2] Key Laboratory of Intelligent Information Processing, Kunming University of Science and Technology, 650500 Yunnan, China
[3] Logistics Science Research Institute of PLA, Beijing 100166, China
ztyu@hotmail.com

Abstract. To make full use of news document structure and the relation among different news documents, a news topic clustering method is proposed of using the relation among document elements. First, the word characteristic weight was calculated by the TF-IDF method based on word frequency statistics to generate document space vector and news document similarity was calculated using text similarity measurement algorithm to obtain the initial news document similarity matrix. Then, the initial similarity matrix was modified with the relation among different news elements as semi-supervised constraint information, the clustering of news documents was realized using Affinity Propagation algorithm, and news topics were extracted from news clusters. As a result, the construction of news topic model was finished. At last, the contrast experiments were performed on manually-annotated news corpus. The results show that the Affinity Propagation clustering methods integrating the relation among document elements can achieve a better effect than those without constraint information.

Keywords: relationship among news elements; news topic; affinity propagation algorithm; semi-supervised constraints.

1   Introduction

With the development of the Internet, a large amount of data renders internet users difficult to extract news topics, and have access to the cues of and relation among events of one topic. Against this backdrop, many mainstream portal websites launch popular events and news topics within a certain period through manual editors or computer tools. For example, Baidu news updates daily hot news rankings, and Sina micro-blog updates hot topic list according to the popularity of the news. This has brought great convenience to internet users. Therefore, it is important and urgent to realize the clustering of news topics through the machine learning.

The research on finding topics both at home and abroad mainly focuses on the establishment of specific topic models, which can be roughly divided into the following categories. One is vector space models. For example, Makkonen constructed space

© Springer International Publishing AG 2016
M. Dong et al. (Eds.): CLSW 2016, LNAI 10085, pp. 441–448, 2016
DOI: 10.1007/978-3-319-49508-8_42

vector of such models according to persons, time and places [1]. Lee converted the problem of finding topics into the clustering problem of the news text. To be specific, he realized the clustering and found topics by extracting news important words as the characteristic to calculate text similarity [2]. The second category is probabilistic topic models. Through the integration of evolutionary clustering algorithm and topic models, Ahmed et al. realized topic detection and tracking. This integrated model can achieve a better result in news topic detection and tracking [3]. D.Newman extracted figure entity in the news, and then integrated figure entity characteristics and topic models. This integrated model can also achieve a better result in topic detection [4]. The third category is Graphic Models. In 2000, Ogilvie constructed a Graphic Models with the feature words as the centroid gathered from text sets [5]. In 2004, Cathy used WordNet [6] to convert similar or related words of text sets into the lexical chain. Such a model was also constructed by Liu Ming et al in 2010 by using How net language dictionary [7].

For some of the above methods, different news elements are also used to realize news topic clustering, but the relation among them is not taken into consideration. In fact, there can be many kinds of relation among different news elements, which play a great supporting role in finding news topic.

2   Affinity Propagation algorithm

In 2007, Frey et al proposed an AP algorithm [8]. In this algorithm, the similarity among data points was used as the basis, all data points were considered as potential representative point and trust propagation theory was applied to the exchange of information among data points to find the representative point for each data point, which can make the sum of the similarity among all the data points and their nearest representative point of similarity largest. Thus clustering was completed. In figure 1 as below:

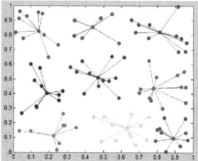

Fig. 1. Clustering results based on the algorithm of AP

AP algorithm was selected as the clustering algorithm based on similarity matrix after the adjustment. According to the literature [8-10], AP algorithm can achieve a higher accuracy and a better effect in processing large quantities of data, the accuracy and effectiveness of the algorithm is much higher than K-means [11].

3 Building the model of news topic clustering integrating relation among news elements

AP clustering algorithm can be seen as one kind of graph-based clustering. Each data point can be seen as a node in the graph, and AP is performed along the edges to find the optimal representative set of points. The most important two parameters in the algorithm are the similarity matrix S and the bias parameter P. The definition of the similarity matrix directly affects the performance of the clustering algorithm based on similarity matrix. The construction process of the news topic clustering model integrating relation among news elements is described in detail as follows.

3.1 Constructing the initial similarity matrix of the news-documents

"Topic detection and tracking is defined as the technique which can be used to automatically find topics in data flow from the newswire and broadcast news and link the piece of news with other pieces about the same topic"[12]. It can be seen that the research on topics is converted into the clustering problem of news text. Firstly, taking the new-pages collections as graph $G = (V, E, S)$, where V is the node set of the new pages, S indicates the similarity matrix between the new-page notes. E is the edge set. Assign a weight to the edge between two nodes according to the similarity between them. After some pretreatment for the retrieved new-pages, such as stripping tags, Chinese words segmentation and the stop word removal, we entirely consider the occurrence frequency of different words in all the texts and the resolution capabilities of the word to the different texts and then use the TF-IDF based on word frequency statistics to calculate the word feature weights of the two new-pages nodes. The cosine of the vector space angle of the documents is employed for defining the similarity between the two new-page nodes, based on which we can get the initial similarity matrix S.

Suppose there are two arbitrary new-page nodes $\forall x_i, x_k \in V$, TF-IDF as follows:

$$W_{t,x} = TF_{t,x} \times IDF_{t,x} \quad (1) \qquad TF_{t,x} = N/M \quad (2) \qquad IDF_{t,x} = \log(x/x_N) \quad (3)$$

Where $W_{t,x}$ is the weight of the feature item t in the document x; $TF_{t,x}$ represents the occurrence frequency of t in the document x. $IDF_{t,x}$ is known as the document frequency of features to reflect the distribution of feature item t in the whole document set and the distinction ability of this feature item to a certain extent, The following we use the angle cosine of the two document vectors to define the initial similarity S between two new-page nodes.

$$S_{ik} = Sim(x_i, x_k) = \cos \theta = \frac{\sum_{t=1}^{n} W_{t,x_1} \times W_{t,x_2}}{\sqrt{\left(\sum_{t=1}^{n} W_{t,x_1}^2 \right) \left(\sum_{t=1}^{n} W_{t,x_2}^2 \right)}} \quad (4)$$

Where $W_{t,x1}, W_{t,x_2}$ is respectively devotes the weight of the feature item t in the new-page documents x_1, x_2 and further obtain the initial similarity matrix S.

3.2 Correcting the initial similarity matrix based on the relation among news elements

Selecting the structural characteristics of new documents .
The html code of news documents was analyzed to find news document structural features. News report not only gives the text describing the event, but also the report title, entity name, keywords, links, classes and other factors. The relation among these factors plays a pivotal role in the initial adjustment of the initial similarity of news pages. After the analysis, 5 kinds of news documents structural features were selected:

Table 1. Structural features of new documents

Serial number	Structural characteristics
1	title
2	entity
3	keywords
4	links
5	category

Annotation was conducted using CRF-TF tool developed in the laboratory, and the recognition model was trained using the above tool. The structured features of the test corpus were identified and extracted through the recognition model.

Analysis of relation among document elements and their characteristic value.

Table 2. Relationship among document elements and their characteristic value

Serial number	Elements-associated relationship	Feature type	Eigenvalue f_m	Feature weight α_m
1	Title association	Boolean	0,1	α_1
2	Entity co-occurrence	Boolean	0,1	α_2
3	Keywords co-occurrence or high correlation	Boolean	0,1	α_3
4	Links pointed to each other	Boolean	0,1	α_4
5	Whether belongs to the same category	Boolean	0,1	α_5

In order to avoid the frequent appearance of 0, TF-IDF to calculate feature weight was not used. Instead, the method of calculating the semantic extension of words was introduced which was based on Tongyici Cilin in semantic [14] put forward by Liu Duanyang and Wang Liangfang [13].

3.3   Page-associated feature constraints and similarity correction

Add the weights to the different relations through training the relation characteristic among the elements of the page as shown in table 1, assume two arbitrary new-page nodes , define a adjustment matrix as follows:

$$S'_{ik} = \sum_{m=1}^{4} \alpha_m f_m + \alpha_5 f_5 \qquad (5)$$

Where, α_m is the elements-associated feature weight obtained by training, as the two page is belong to the same category is a important factor to determine whether two pages should be gathered to a class. Therefore set $\alpha_5 = 0.5$, $\sum_{m=1}^{4} \alpha_m = 0.5$ and f_m de-

votes the elements-associated eigenvalue mentioned in table 2.

Wagstaff etc [15] had introduced two kinds of pairwise constraints the first time, say must-link and cannot-link constraints to facilitate clustering search.

According to the rules of heuristic judgment and integrating the relation among documents elements with the adjustment matrix S'_{ik} .Define the elements-associated feature constraints (including the "must-link" and "cannot-link") shown in formula (6) as the supervision constraint information, and then do the correction of the initial similarity matrix S based on the "must-link" and "cannot-link" constraints to obtain the final similarity matrix S''_{ik} .

$$\begin{cases} S''_{ik} = S''_{ki} = 1, \left(S'_{ik} \geq 0.5 \right) \Leftrightarrow \left(x_i, x_k \right) \in must-link \\ S''_{ik} = S''_{ki} = 0, \left(S'_{ik} = 0 \right) \Leftrightarrow \left(x_i, x_k \right) \in cannot-link \\ \qquad S''_{ik} = S_{ik} \left(0 < S'_{ik} < 0.5 \right) \end{cases} \qquad (6)$$

For formula (6), it is represented that it has the same category at least or that the previous four eigenvalues are all 1 in the two new-pages together are a "must-link" constraint. The same reason is that all elements-associated eigenvalues are all 0 when $S'_{ik} = 0$.

4   Experiments and Analysis

4.1   Experiment Data Preparation

In this paper, different templates were formulated using HtmlUnit to gather the exper-imental data from different sites. The gathered data were stored in MongoDB data-base. The use of HtmlUnit to gather news data can obtain more accurate structured data of the news webpage, such as titles, URL links, keywords, category, etc.

In the experiment, the test set was selected 4 times. Each time, 10 news texts in each of 10 fields (politic, economy, culture, etc.) were extracted from the database and these 100 texts were used as the test set. 1000 high-frequency words were chosen based on word frequency statistics method and their feature weight were calculated using TF-IDF method. Then 1000 dimensional feature space was constructed. In the experiment, the number of the feature constraints of the relation among the elements of the page ranged from 0 to 400. The feature constraint of the relation among the page elements was randomly generated from the training data set. The randomly gen-erated constraints were used to guide the analysis of all the data with the clustering algorithm. At last, the clustering result of the test data sets was evaluated according to the clustering evaluation index.

4.2   Experimental Evaluation

Here the F-value will be employed. The F-value is defined as below:

$$\mathrm{Pr}\,e = \frac{T_p}{T_p + F_p}, \mathrm{Re}\,c = \frac{T_p}{T_p + F_n}, F = \frac{2\,\mathrm{Pr}\,e \times \mathrm{Re}\,c}{\mathrm{Pr}\,e + \mathrm{Re}\,c} \tag{7}$$

Where T_p is the number of new-page documents that the two documents together in one cluster are classified correctly, F_p represents the number of new-page documents that the two should not be placed in one cluster are divided into one falsely, F_n is the number of new-page documents that the two should not be separated are parted wrongly.

4.3   Experimental Design and Analysis

Experiment 1 was performed to evaluate the influence of different number of relation characteristic constraints on clustering. For any given number of constraints, the ex-periment was done 30 times. The average output results represented the performance of the Affinity Propagation model integrating relation among page elements and with a fixed number of constraints to cluster some test set. Each test set had 200 texts, of which 50 were used as the test set, and the rest were used as the training set. So figure

1 reveals the changes of the F-value indexes on the four test sets with the different numbers of associated constraints.

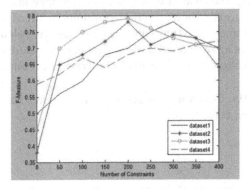

Fig. 2. The impact of different numbers of associated constraints on the F-values indexes of the four test sets

It can be seen from figure 1 that the F-value index obtained by our approach show upward trend as a whole with the increase in the number of constraints, when the number of constraints is between 150 and 300, the corresponding F-value reached the maximum and the number of clusters obtained at this time is optimal.

Experiment 2 is the clustering performance comparison of the AP clustering method integrating the relation among page elements of news (T_1) and without constraint information (T_2). There are results of experiment 2 given in table 3.

Table 3. Results of clustering of news topics with different algorithms

datasets	T_1			T_2		
	P (%)	R (%)	F (%)	P (%)	R (%)	F (%)
TestSet1	67.67	50.75	58.00	83.00	92.00	87.26
Test Set 2	76.00	84.00	79.8	85.64	82.35	83.97
Test Set 3	71.64	75.00	73.28	83.65	80.01	81.78
Test Set 4	55.56	73.45	63.26	86.17	83.57	84.86

Seen from Table 3, the P, R and F-value obtained by using the AP, which integrating the relation among page elements are significantly improved than those without constraint information. Therefore, it can be known that adding constraint information can largely enhanced the clustering performance of the entire data set.

5   Conclusions

In this paper, an Affinity Propagation clustering method integrating the relation among page elements of news is proposed. By this method, the characteristic weight obtained using the relation among page elements of news was made full use of to modify the initial page similarity matrix, through which large change took place of data similarity matrix. The contrast experiments demonstrate that the use of the relation among page elements of news as priori constraint is effective and it can play a guiding role in generating the Affinity Propagation clustering algorithm. The further work is to take the initiative to provide affinity propagation clustering algorithm rich constraint information, so that the news topic clustering effect can be improved.

Acknowledgments. This work was supported by National Natural Science Foundation of China, Contract No.61472168.

References

1. Makkonen, J., Ahonen-Myka, H.: Simple Semantics in Topic Detection and Tracking. Information Retrieval 7(3-4), 347-368(2004)
2. Wei, C., Lee, Y., Chiang, Y.: Discovering Event Episodes from News Corpora: A Temporal-based Approach. In: Proceedings of ACM ICEC2009, Taipei, Taiwan, pp.72-80(2009)
3. Ahmed, A., Ho, Q., Eisenstein, J.: Unified analysis of streaming news. In: Proceedings of the 20th international conference on World Wide Web. ACM, pp.267-276(2011)
4. Newman, D., Chemudugunta, C., Smyth, P.: Statistical entity-topic models. In Kdd, New York, NY,USA, pp.680-686(2006)
5. Ogilvie, P.: Extracting and Using Relationships Found in Text for Topic Tracking(2000)
6. Carthy, J.: Lexical Chains versus Keywords for Topic Tracking. In: Proceedings of the 5th International Conference on Intelligent Text Processing and Computational Linguistics (2004)
7. Liu, M., Wang, X., Liu, Y.: Research of Key-Phrase Extraction Based on Lexical Chain. Chinese Journal of Computers(33),1246 – 1255(2010)
8. Frey, B., Dueck, D.: Clustering by passing messages between data points. Science315(5814),972-976(2007)
9. Frey, B., Dueck, D.: Response to Comment on "Clustering by passing messages between datapoints". Science319(1151268),726(2008)
10. Xiao, Y., Yu, J.: Semi-Supervised Clustering Based on Affinity Propagation Algorithm. Journal of Software19(11),2803-2813(2008)
11. Guan, R., Shi, X.: Text Clustering with Seeds Affinity Propagation. IEEE Trans, on Knowledge and Data Engineering23(4),627-637(2011)
12. Luo, W., Liu, Q., Cheng, X.: Development and Analysis of Technology of Topic Detection and Tracking . Association for Compu-tational Linguistics(2004)
13. Liu, D., Wang, L.: Extraction Algorithm Based on Semantic Expansion Integrated with Lexical chain. Computer Science40(12),264-269(2013)
14. Tian, J., Zhao, W.: Words Similarity Algorithm Based on Tongyici Cilin in Semantic Web Adaptive Learning System. Journal of Jilin University28(6), (2010)
15. Wagstaff, K., Cardie, C.: Clustering with instance-level constraints. In: Langley P, Ed. Proc. of the 17th Int'l Conf. on Machine Learning. Morgan Kaufmann Publishers, pp.1103−1110(2000)

Part V Case Study of Lexical Semantics

Manifestation of Certainty in Semantics:
The Case of *Yídìng*, *Kěndìng* and *Dǔdìng* in Mandarin Chinese

Wu, Jiun-Shiung

Institute of Linguistics, National Chung Cheng University, 168, University Road, Minhsiung, Chiayi County, Taiwan, 621
Lngwujs@ccu.edu.tw

Abstract. This paper examines three modal adverbials in Mandarin Chinese: *yídìng*, *kěndìng* and *dǔdìng*. These three lexical entries can all express strong epistemic necessity or intensification. However, denoting intensification, *kěndìng* and *dǔdìng* have an additional semantic requirement: they both require that there be at least one alternative to the proposition they present. They are different in that the speaker uses *kěndìng* to ascertain the truth of a proposition it takes, although all the alternatives are potentially true, while *dǔdìng* is used to assert the speaker's certainty that only the proposition *dǔdìng* takes is true. Concerning certainty, two cases are demonstrated here. For *yídìng*, certainty is expressed implicitly, because certainty manifests itself through the speaker's attitude. However, for *kěndìng* and *dǔdìng*, certainty is revealed explicitly, since (part of) the semantics of these two lexical items is certainty.

keywords: kending, duding, yiding, epistemic modality, intensification, certainty

1   Introduction

In Mandarin Chinese (henceforth, Chinese), there are lexical items that present an inference, conjecture or stipulation, or indicate an emphasis, such as *yídìng*, *kěndìng* and *dǔdìng*. Let's look at a few examples below.

(1)a. Jīntiān   fēngyǔ   zhème   dà,   wǒ   tuīcè
today   wind.rain   so   big   1st.SG[1]   conjecture
yídìng/kěndìng/dǔdìng   bù   bì   shàngbān.
YÍDÌNG/KĚNDÌNG/DǓDÌNG[2] not   need   go.to.work
'It is very stormy today. I conjecture that it must be the case that we definitely

---

[1]   The abbreviations used in this paper include: 1st for a first-person pronoun, 3rd for a third-person pronoun, ASSO for an associative marker, CL for a classifier, DEON for a deontic modal expression, DYN for a dynamic modal expression, EPI for epistemic modal expression, PL for a plural marker, Prc for a sentential particle, RCP for a reciprocal prefix, SG for singular.

[2]   Due to their multiple semantics, these lexical items are glossed with their smallcapped Pinyins. Their accurate meaning is reflected in the English translations of sentences.

© Springer International Publishing AG 2016
M. Dong et al. (Eds.): CLSW 2016, LNAI 10085, pp. 451–463, 2016
DOI: 10.1007/978-3-319-49508-8_43

don't need to go to work.'

b. Lǎobǎn qiángdiào   míngnián   yídìng/kěndìng/dǔdìng
   boss   emphasize   next.year   YÍDÌNG/KĚNDÌNG/DŮDÌNG
   jiā   xīn.
   raise   salary
   'The boss emphasized that there definitely would be a raise next year.'

In (1a), *yídìng*, *kěndìng* and *dǔdìng* present a conjecture or stipulation because the matrix verb *tuīcè* 'conjecture' selects a stipulation or a conjecture as its clausal complement. When the three lexical entries present a stipulation or conjecture, they are suggested to express a strong epistemic necessity reading.

The conjecture/stipulation reading is referred to as "strong" epistemic necessity because the speaker uses them to express a high degree of certainty toward the conjecture or stipulation. Let's look at the following examples. Assume the following scenario. A wants to talk to Laozhang but is not certain whether Laozhang is at home. Knowing Laozhang's schedule very well, B looks at his watch and utters:

(2)a. Lǎozhāng   xiànzài huì   zài   jiā.   Qù   zhǎo   tā
      Laozhang   now   EPI   at   home   go   find   3rd.SG
      ba.[3]
      Prc
      ''Laozhang must be at home now. Go find him.'

   b. Lǎozhāng   xiànzài yídìng zài   jiā.   Qù   zhǎo   tā
      Laozhang   now   YÍDÌNG at   home   go   find   3rd.SG
      ba.
      Prc
      'It must be the case that Laozhang is definitely at home now. Go find him.'

(2a) contains epistemic *huì* and (2b) includes *yídìng*. Both clauses are Speaker B's conjecture based on his understanding of Laozhang's schedule. If we compare (2a) with (2b) carefully, we can find that (2b) is a conjecture of a higher degree of certainty. Because *kěndìng* and *dǔdìng* behave similarly in this respect, the conjecture reading is referred to as a 'strong' epistemic necessity reading.

On the other hand, in (1b), the matrix predicate *qiángdiào* 'emphasize' does not select a clausal complement describing a stipulation or conjecture. Instead, it selects an emphasized proposition. Therefore, *yídìng*, *kěndìng* and *dǔdìng* in this example express emphasis. [1,2] argue that emphasis is actually an intensification on the degree of the speaker's certainty toward the truth of a proposition. Therefore, the emphasis reading is referred to as an intensification reading.

Moreover, *yídìng* can function as a modal adverb, as in [3,4,5]. [5] is a dictionary of modal adverbs but it does not include *kěndìng* or *dǔdìng*. This is probably because *kěndìng* and *dǔdìng* can function as a verb taking a clausal complement. One might

---

[3] I thank Hsu-Te Cheng for this example.

wonder whether *kědìng* and *dǔdìng* can function as modal adverbs. Let's compare the examples below.

(3) a. Zhāngsān   hěn   kěndìng/dǔdìng   míngtiān   huì
    Zhangsan   very   KĚNDÌNG/DǓDÌNG   tomorrow   EPI
    xià   yǔ.
    fall   rain
    'Zhangsan is very certain/positive that it will rain tomorrow.'
  b. Zhāngsān   kěndìng/dǔdìng   yíngdé   zhè-cì
    Zhangsan   KĚNDÌNG/DǓDÌNG   win   this-CL
    bǐsài-de   guànjūn.
    competition-ASSO   championship
    'It must be the case that Zhangsan definitely will win the championship at this competition.'

(3a) is a typical example where *kěndìng* and *dǔdìng* function as matrix predicates, taking a clausal complement. How about (3b)? Is it possible that (3b) includes an open complement, whose subject is coindexed with the matrix one?

The answer to this question is negative, and the evidence comes from the source of certainty. The source of certainty for (3a) is the matrix subject, Zhangsan. That is, the speaker expresses Zhangsan's certainty toward a certain situation. But, as epistemic modal adverbs, the source of certainty for (3b) is the speaker. Since the source of certainty is different and modal expressions describe the speaker's attitude, I take *kěndìng* and *dǔdìng* in (3b) as modal adverbs and hence *kěndìng* and *dǔdìng* are the target of discussion of this paper.

While (1) show that *yídìng*, *kěndìng* and *dǔdìng* are interchangeable, they are not always so. Let's look at some examples.

(4) a. Wǒ   yídìng/*kěndìng/*dǔdìng   quánlì   xiāngzhù.
    1st.SG   YÍDÌNG/*KĚNDÌNG/*DǓDÌNG   all.force   RCP-help
    'I definitely will try my best to help you.'
  b. Guóhuì   xuǎnjǔ jiēxiǎo,   kē'ěr   dǔdìng/*kěndìng
    parliament   election announce   Cole   DǓDÌNG/*KĚNDÌNG
    dāngxuǎn   zǒnglǐ.
    win.election   Prime.Minister
    'The result of parliament election is announced. Cole definitely will be elected Prime Minister.'
  c. Qǐng   yídìng/*kěndìng/*dǔdìng   zhǔnshí   chūxí.
    please   YÍDÌNG/*KĚNDÌNG/*DǓDÌNG   on.time   present
    'Please be present on time.'

As shown in (4), *yídìng*, *kěndìng* and *dǔdìng* are not always interchangeable. In this paper, I attempt to address two questions. First, how are *yídìng*, *kěndìng* and *dǔdìng* semantically different? Second, how is expression of certainty related to the semantic differences among *yídìng*, *kěndìng* and *dǔdìng*?

The data used in this study is retrieved from the on-line version of Academia Sinica Balanced Corpus (for short, Sinica Corpus). I substitute one of *yídìng, kěndìng* and *dǔdìng* in a sentence with the other two to test whether any grammatical change or semantic change occurs, to examine their semantic similarities and differences.

This paper is organized as follows. Section 2 is literature review, where I briefly review literature on *yídìng* (and *kěndìng*). Section 3 provides relevant data and generalizations. Section 4 concludes this paper.

2   Literature Review

In this section, I review descriptive studies on *yídìng* (and *kěndìng*) in chronological order, i.e. [4,6,7,5,8]. I also briefly review the dynamic semantics for *yídìng* (and *shìbì*) proposed in [1,2].

[4] distinguishes *yídìng₁* from *yídìng₂*, and states that the former expresses strong volition or determination whereas the latter presents an inference or conjecture. He further claims that the former often goes with *yào* 'DEON', while the latter usually with *huì* 'EPI', or *shì* 'be'.

[6,7] also tells *yídìng₁* from *yídìng₂*, similar to [4]. She also suggests that *yídìng₁* expresses strong volition or determination, and *yídìng₂* an inference or conjecture. In addition, she also compares *yídìng* with *kědìng*. She suggests that, when expressing epistemic necessity, *yídìng* presents a subjective inference, while *kěndìng* an objective one, and that *yídìng*, expressing strong volition or determination, cannot be substituted for by *kěndìng*.

[5] is a dictionary of mood and modal expressions in Chinese. He suggests that *yídìng* can express strong volition or affirmative judgment. He does not discuss *kěndìng* or *dǔdìng*, probably because *kěndìng* and *dǔdìng* can function as a verb, as illustrated above, or a predicative adjective.

The main topic of [8] is the grammaticalization of *yídìng*, and states that *yídìng* can denote strong determination/volition or inference/conjecture, a conclusion very similar to [4,6,7,5].

One of the problems concerning *yídìng* shared by all of the above studies is that none of them takes the intensification reading, as in (1b), into consideration. Moreover, it is not clear how the subjective vs. objective distinction proposed in [6,7] can explain the examples in (4). Moreover, why can't *yídìng* expressing strong volition or determination be replaced by *kěndìng* or *dǔdìng*?

[1] proposes a dynamic semantics for *yídìng* and [2] compares *yídìng* with *shìbì*. Observing that *yídìng* expresses either strong epistemic necessity or intensification, and that context plays a significant role in the semantics of *yídìng*, [1] utilizes [10,11] and proposes an affirmative[4] ordering and others as follows:

---

[4] Please note that in [1,2] the term *affirmative(ness)* is used because certainty is usually used to describe epistemic necessity, as in [9]. In this paper, I adhere to *certainty* and the distinction between epistemic necessity and intensification is specified by means of an additional prepositional phrase, that is, certainty <u>toward a conjecture or stipulation</u> vs. certainty <u>toward</u>

(5) a. An information state σ is a pair $\langle\mathcal{A}, s\rangle$, where s is a proposition and $\mathcal{A}$ an affirmative ordering.

b. For possible worlds v, w, $w \leq_{\mathcal{A}} v$ iff the degree of speaker's affirmativeness toward a proposition in w is at least as high as in v.

c. Absolutely affirmative worlds (cf. $n_{\langle\epsilon, s\rangle}$ on p14 of [10]):
Aff$_{\mathcal{A}}$ = $\{w\in W: \forall v\in W, w \leq_{\mathcal{A}} v\}$, where W is the set of all possible worlds.

d. Updating an affirmative ordering:
$\mathcal{A} \bullet \phi = \{\langle w, v\rangle: w \leq_{\mathcal{A}} v$ and if $v\in\phi$, then $w\in\phi\}$

(6) a. Strong epistemic necessity
$\sigma [\text{yíding}(\phi)]^{M}$
= $\langle\mathcal{A}\bullet\phi, s\subseteq\phi\rangle$ if Aff$_{\mathcal{A}} \cap \{w: [\phi]^{w, M} = 1\} \neq \varnothing$ and s represents the speaker's knowledge in w; or = absurd state, otherwise.

b. Intensification
$\sigma [\text{yíding}(\phi)]^{M}$
= σ if Aff$_{\mathcal{A}} \cap \{w: [\phi]^{w, M} = 1\}$ = Aff$_{\mathcal{A}}$ and $s \neq$ speaker's knowledge in w; or = absurd state, otherwise.

Following [10], [1] proposes that an information state is a pair, but the pair is composed of $\mathcal{A}$, an affirmative ordering, and s, a proposition, as defined in (5a). (5b) defines an affirmative ordering $\leq_{\mathcal{A}}$. (5c) defines absolutely affirmative worlds as the set of worlds where each world is ranked higher than all the other worlds in W, according to the affirmative ordering.

Yíding updates the information state if it denotes strong epistemic necessity, as defined in (6a): $\mathcal{A}$ is updated with the proposition ϕ presented by *yíding*, that is, the possible worlds are ordered based on the affirmativeness of ϕ, which stands for an intensification reading because the degree of affirmativeness is intensified; furthermore, s is specified to be a subset of ϕ, i.e. ϕ is true in all of the possible worlds where s is true, which represents an epistemic necessity reading, according to [11].

On the other hand, *yíding* simply checks whether the set of possible worlds where ϕ is true is a (proper) subset of the absolutely affirmative worlds, rather than updating the information state, as in (6b). Because s does not equal to the speaker's knowledge, no epistemic reading can be derived. Therefore, only an intensification reading is reached.

The semantics for *yíding* in [2] is similar to that in [1] except for the definition of affirmative ordering. Following the definition of ordering source in [12,13], the affirmative ordering is revised as:

(7) Affirmative ordering
v, w are possible worlds. p is a proposition.
$w \leq_{\mathcal{A}} v$ iff $\{p: p$ is affirmed in $v\} \subseteq \{p: p$ is affirmed in $w\}$

---

the truth of a proposition. But, when [1,2] are reviewed, the term used in these two studies are adopted.

As for the semantic difference between *yídìng* and *shìbì*, [2] suggests that *s* in the information state for *shìbì* is underspecified while it is identified to the speaker's knowledge in the information state of *yídìng*, as shown in (6a). And, this underspecification must be resolved by information provided in the discourse. That is, the dynamic semantics for *shìbì* is the same as that of *yídìng* given in (6), plus the following:

(8) a. $<\mathcal{A}, s=?>$ ⟦shìbì(ϕ)⟧^{M}

b. Suppose that α, ϕ forms a (mini-) discourse. α, ϕ are propositions. If $<\mathcal{A}, s=?>$, ⟦shìbì(ϕ)⟧^{M} and $R(\alpha, \phi)$, then $s = R$.

In (8a), $s = ?$ stands for an underspecified *s*. (8b) states how the underspecification is resolved by the information provided by sentences in the discourse. $R(\alpha, \phi)$ stands for the possible relationship between α and ϕ. The underspecified *s* is resolved to *R*.

While [1,2] are interesting in that these studies are the first attempt to provide a dynamic semantics for *yídìng* (and *shìbì*) and to discuss the semantic difference between *yídìng* and *shìbì*, underspecification is not how *yídìng*, *kěndìng* and *dǔdìng* differ. I focus on this part in this paper.

3   Certainty: Implicit vs. Explicit

As shown in (1), *yídìng*, *kěndìng* and *dǔdìng* can express strong epistemic necessity or intensification and they are interchangeable at either case. Furthermore, these lexical entries can present a sentence which already contains a modal expression, and remain ambiguous as usual. Let's look at two examples.

(9) a. Tā   yídìng/kěndìng/dǔdìng   huì   qí   jiǎotàchē.
he   YÍDÌNG/KĚNDÌNG/DǓDÌNG DYN   ride   bicycle
'It must be the case that he definitely can ride a bicycle.'
Or, 'He definitely can ride a bicycle.'

b. Yīzhào   zhè-zhǒng   qūshì,   jīnnián
based.on   this-cl   trend   this.year
jūnwēn   bǎozuò   yídìng/kěndìng/dǔdìng
average.temperature   winner's.chair   YÍDÌNG/KĚNDÌNG/DǓDÌNG
yào   huàn   rén   le.
DEON   change   person   Prc
'Based on this trend, it must be the case that the city which has the highest average temperature definitely will change this year.'
Or, 'Based on this trend, the city which has the highest average temperature definitely will change this year.'

(9a) contains a dynamic modal expression *huì* and (9b) a deontic one *yào*. Both (9a) and (9b) show that *yídìng/kěndìng/dǔdìng* can present a sentence with a modal expression, and remain ambiguous between strong epistemic necessity and intensification.

However, *yídìng/kěndìng/dǔdìng* are not always interchangeable. There are examples where *yídìng* is good, but *kěndìng/dǔdìng* are not, and examples where *yídìng* is not good, but *kěndìng/dǔdìng* are. Let's look at some examples.

(10) a. Qǐng   yídìng/*kěndìng/*dǔdìng   zhǔnshí chūxí.
     please YÍDÌNG/*KĚNDÌNG/*DǓDÌNG   on.time present
     'Please <u>do</u> be present on time.'

   b. Wǒ   yídìng/*kěndìng/*dǔdìng   quánlì   xiāngzhù.
     1st.SG YÍDÌNG/*KĚNDÌNG/*DǓDÌNG   all.force   RCP.help
     'I definitely will try my best to help you.'

   c. Guóhuì   xuǎnjǔ jiēxiǎo,   kē-ěr   dǔdìng/*kěndìng
     Parliament   election announcement   Cole   DǓDÌNG/*KĚNDÌNG
     dàngxuǎn   zǒnglǐ.
     win.election   Prime.minister
     'The result of parliament election is announced. Cole definitely will be elected Prime Minister.'

   d. Zài huālián shì tíngchē, sān fēngzhōng nèi,   guǎnlǐyuán
     at Hualian city park   three minute in   parking.staff
     yídìng/*dǔdìng   qiánlái kāidān   shōufèi, jué   wú
     YÍDÌNG/*DǓDÌNG   come issue.ticket charge absolutely   no
     miǎnfèi   tíngchē-zhī   shì.
     free   parking-ASSO matter
     'If you park in Hualian City, a parking staff definitely will come, in three minutes, to give you a notice for parking fee. There is absolutely no such thing as free parking.'

   e. Parkway Parade   kěndìng/*dǔdìng   shì   xiāpīngzú-de
     Parkway Parade   KĚNDÌNG/*DǓDÌNG   be   shopper-ASSO
     zuì'ài.
     favorite
     'Parkway Parade is definitely shoppers' favorite.'

(10a, b) are examples where *yídìng* is good, but *kěndìng* and *dǔdìng* are not. (10a) is an imperative and (10b) a promise. (10c) is an example where *yídìng* is not good, but *dǔdìng* is. (10d) is the other way around: *yídìng* is good, but *dǔdìng* is not. (10e) is an example where *kěndìng* is good, but *dǔdìng* is not.

The first observation about the examples in (10) is that in these examples *yídìng*, *kěndìng* and *dǔdìng* all express intensification. But, why are they not interchangeable in these examples?

The other usages of *kěndìng* and *dǔdìng*[5] shed light on this question. *Kěndìng* and *dǔdìng* can function as a main verb. Let's look at *kěndìng* first.

(11) Lǎoshī   hěn   kěndìng   wǒ-men zhè-cì bǐsài-de   nǔlì.

---

[5]   In fact, *yídìng* can function as an attributive adjective, in addition to a modal adverb. But this function is irrelevant to our discussion here and hence is not addressed.

teacher   very   ascertain.value   1st-PL   this-CL   game-ASSO   effort
Lit. 'The teacher ascertains the value of our efforts spent in this game.'
'The teacher thinks highly of our efforts spent in this game.'

As shown in (11), *kěndìng* functioning as a main verb means 'think highly of', and this meaning comes from the literal meaning *ascertain the value of*. *Kěndìng* is used to express the speaker's positive attitude toward a proposition when there can be either positive or negative attitude toward the same proposition.

On the other hand, *dǔdìng* means 'be certain' when it functions as a verb. See below.

(12) Zhāngsān   hěn   dǔdìng   zìjǐ   huì   yíngdé
     Zhangsan   very   be.certain   self   EPI   win
     guànjūn.
     championship
     'Zhangsan is very certain that he will win the championship.'

As shown in (12), *dǔdìng* is used when the speaker is certain that no proposition other than the one presented by *dǔdìng* is true.

To ascertain something, there must be different ways to evaluate the thing. To be certain that something is true, the thing should have a chance, however slim, to be false. Hence, I propose a semantic requirement for *kěndìng* and *dǔdìng*:

(13) a. Requirement of Alternatives:
     Kěndìng and *dǔdìng* require that there be at least one alternative to the
     proposition they present, e.g. p vs. ¬p; p vs. q vs. r, etc.
   b. ALT(p) =$_d$ {p} $\cup$ {q: $q \neq p$}, where p, q are propositions and $p \approx q$.
   c. $p \approx q$ iff $p \rightarrow \neg q$.

(13a) is Requirement of Alternatives for *kěndìng* and *dǔdìng*. This requirement is formalized as in (13b). ALT(p) stands for the alternatives of p. ALT(p) is the union of {p} and the set of propositions which are not p. But, obviously, this definition includes all propositions in the world and many of them are not relevant. Hence, (13b) contains an additional constraint: $p \approx q$, which means p must be related to q in certain ways. This 'relatedness' is defined by means of truth conditions as in (13c): p is related to q iff the following condition holds: if p is true, then q is not true. Relatedness is defined in this way because the set of alternatives of a proposition are related in terms of truth conditions, on which the semantic difference between *kěndìng* and *dǔdìng* depend, as discussed below.

To ascertain something, all the alternatives should have an equal chance to be true, and then the speaker can identify one alternative, based on whatever information he/she has, and ascertains the truth of the alternative.

On the other hand, since *dǔdìng* indicates that only the proposition it presents is true, the other alternative(s) are considered false by the speaker. Hence, I propose that the semantic difference between *kěndìng* and *dǔdìng* lies in whether the propositions in ALT(p) other than p are considered potentially true:

(14) a. For *kěndìng*, while both (or all) of the alternatives are possibly true, the speaker uses *kěndìng* to ascertain the truth of the proposition presented by *kěndìng*.

    b. For *dǔdìng*, the speaker uses it to assert his certainty that only the proposition presented by *dǔdìng* is true.

    c. *kěndìng*(p) = 1 iff (($p \in$ ALT(p) $\wedge p = 1$) → ($\forall s \in$ ALT(p) ($s \neq p \rightarrow s = 0$)))

    d. *dǔdìng*(p) = 1 iff $\forall q \in$ ALT(p) ($q = 1 \rightarrow q = p$)

(14a, b) are the semantic constraints for *kěndìng* and *dǔdìng* respectively, and (14c, d) are the formalizations of the two constraints. (14c) says that, for *kěndìng*(p) to be true, the following condition must be satisfied: if p is in the alternatives of p and p is true, then all the other propositions in the alternatives of p are not true. (14d) says that, for *dǔdìng*(p) to be true, any proposition in the alternatives of p which is true must be p.

Now, we can understand why $p \approx q$ is defined in terms of truth conditions. ALT(p) needs to be a set of propositions where, if one of the propositions is true, the others are not true, so that (14c, d) can be defined and the semantic characteristics of *kěndìng* and *dǔdìng* can be captured. As a result, any proposition whose truth cannot be determined when p is decided to be true is not relevant to the semantics of *kěndìng* and *dǔdìng*.

One last comment on *dǔdìng* is about potential intuition difference.[6] It has been brought to my attention that some native speakers of Chinese do not accept (9a) if *dǔdìng* is used in this sentence. A possibility is that for those who share this intuition *dǔdìng* needs it to be explicitly present in the discourse, the information based on which *dǔdìng* is used. Let's compare (9a) to (9b). In (9b), *zhè-zhǒng qūshì* is the information based on which an inference or an intensification is made. Hence, *dǔdìng* is good here. (9a) does not have such information, and hence *dǔdìng* is not good (at least for some people).

Let's look at how (13) and (14) can explain the examples in (10). (10a) is an imperative, which the speaker uses to ask (or order) the addressee to do something. Hence, this proposition does not allow for another alternative, except for the order to be carried out. As a result, *kěndìng/dǔdìng* are not good here. (10b) is a promise. Just like an imperative, a promise allows for no other alternative, except for the promise to be kept. This is why *kěndìng/dǔdìng* are not good.

(10c) is an intriguing example. Only 34 instances of *dǔdìng* are found on the online version of Sinica Corpus, and 14 of them are examples where *dǔdìng* is located at the adverbial position, as defined on p231 of [3]. Furthermore, the majority of the 14

---

[6] Thanks also go to the CLSW 17 audience for bringing to my attention plausible regional differences regarding the usages of *dǔdìng* and *kěndìng*. As reported in Section One, this paper relies on the data retrieved from the on-line version of Sinica Corpus and the possible regional differences are left for future study.

examples are of the type as (10c): the speaker asserts his/her certainty that the only proposition which is true is the one presented by *dŭdìng*. For (10c), the speaker asserts his/her certainty that *Cole be elected Prime Minister* is the only proposition which is true, based on the parliament election result. The reason why the speaker can assert that the proposition is the only true one is because of the political system of Germany. In Germany, the leader of the majority political party at the parliament serves as Prime Minister. In this context, the political party led by Cole won more than half of the seats in the parliament. Therefore, according to German political system, it is the only possibility that Cole will become Prime Minister. This is why *dŭdìng* is good here, but *kěndìng* is not. One might ask whether *yídìng* can be used here. The answer is positive. But, if *yídìng* is used, only intensification is expressed and the sense of alternatives disappears.

An anonymous reviewer points out that *kěndìng dāngxuǎn* 'KĚNDÌNG win.election' is also possible due to google search. I agree with this comment. However, *kěndìng* is not good in this context. *Kěndìng* will be good under other contexts. For example, someone predicts that Cole won't be elected Prime Minister. However, after the result of parliament election is announced, Cole will be. Under this scenario, *kěndìng* is good, but *dŭdìng* is not.

For (10d), there are two alternatives concerning whether parking is free in Hualian City. And the proposition under discussion is an argument against free parking. Since there are two alternatives and both are possibly true, *dŭdìng* is not good, but *yídìng* is, since *yídìng* does not have to obey (14b). Of course, *kěndìng* can be used in this example. If *kěndìng* is used, the sense of alternatives is brought out.

For (10e), there are many good shopping places and the speaker ascertains the truth of *Parkway Parade be shoppers' favorite*. Since there are more than one alternative and the alternatives are all potentially true, *kěndìng* is used, rather than *dŭdìng*.

To sum up, while *yídìng*, *kěndìng* and *dŭdìng* all express strong epistemic necessity and intensification, *kěndìng* and *dŭdìng* have a semantic requirement when they denote intensification. That is, they both require that there be at least one alternative to the proposition they present. They are different in that *kěndìng* is used to ascertain the truth of the proposition it presents, though all (both) of the alternatives are potentially true, whereas *dŭdìng* is used to express the speaker's certainty that only the proposition it takes is true.

With respect to certainty, *yídìng* represents the speaker's attitude of certainty, whereas both *kěndìng* and *dŭdìng* directly denote certainty, rather than attitude or opinion about certainty. *Yídìng* stands for the speaker's attitude because a modal expression is used to describe the speaker's attitude in a proposition, e.g. [16]. To put it another way, for *yídìng*, certainty is expressed implicitly, because certainty manifests itself through the speaker's attitude. However, for *kěndìng* and *dŭdìng*, certainty is revealed explicitly, since (part of) the semantics of these two lexical items is certainty.

4   Conclusion and Implications

This paper examines the modal adverbial usages of *yídìng*, *kěndìng* and *dǔdìng*. These three lexical items can all describe an inference/conjecture or intensify the degree of the speaker's certainty concerning the truth of a proposition being a fact. However, they have subtle semantic differences.

Kěndìng and *dǔdìng* have an additional semantic requirement. They both require that there be at least one alternative to the proposition they present. The speaker uses *kěndìng* to identify an alternative and ascertains its truth, although all/both of the alternatives are potentially true. On the other hand, *dǔdìng* is used to assert the speaker's certainty that only the proposition *dǔdìng* takes is true.

Regarding certainty, *yídìng* stands for the speaker's attitude of certainty, while *kěndìng* and *dǔdìng* denote certainty directly, rather than attitude or opinion of certainty. Hence, for *yídìng*, certainty is implicit, while, for *kěndìng* and *dǔdìng*, certainty is explicit.

The distinction between explicit expression of certainty and implicit one has at least two theoretical significances. First, [12,13] directly adopts the idea of modal force in modal logic. But, where does modal force come from? This study suggests that there are at least two sources for modal force. First, a modal expression carries an inherent modal force, such as *must* in English or *yídìng* in Chinese. If a lexical entry of such type does not carry an inherent modal force, then we cannot know what it means. On the other hand, the modal force of *kěndìng* and *dǔdìng* are not inherent. Instead, their modal force is inferred from (part of) their semantics: certainty.

To put it another way, when the speaker implicitly expresses certainty through his/her attitude by using a modal expression, the modal force is inherent in the modal expression and is not inferable from other sources. But, when the speaker explicitly expresses certainty, the modal force is inferred from certainty and is not inherent in a lexical entry.

In terms of explicitness of expression of certainty, there is a hierarchy: *quèdìng* > *kěndìng/dǔdìng* > *yídìng*. *Quèdìng* is the highest on the hierarchy because it means 'certainty'. *Quèdìng* does not have an epistemic necessity reading, but only an intensification reading. *Kěndìng/dǔdìng* rank second on this hierarchy. They can express epistemic necessity and, when certain conditions are satisfied, intensification. *Yídìng* ranks lowest on this hierarchy and it can freely express epistemic necessity and intensification. It is worthwhile to further consider the interaction between the hierarchy and an epistemic necessity/intensification reading.

Second, the explicit vs. implicit expression of certainty is related to whether a modal adverb can be negated. *Bù yídìng* 'not YÍDÌNG' is good, but *bù kěndìng/dǔdìng* 'not KĚNDÌNG/DǓDÌNG' are not good (when *kěndìng* and *dǔdìng* serve as modal adverbs).

A plausible explanation for the above difference is as follows. The modal force of *yídìng* is inherent, but not inferred from other sources, and can be negated directly. Oppositely, the modal force of *kěndìng* and *dǔdìng* is inferred from their semantics 'certainty'. Unless we can negate the semantic source, it is contradictory to directly negate the modal force of *kědìng* and *dǔdìng*. That is to say, if the modal force for a modal adverb is inferred from the lexical semantics of the adverb, negating the modal adverb is not possible since there is no way to cancel the lexical semantics of these modal adverbs. This generalization is supported by another modal adverb *shìbì*. As noted in [14,15], *shìbì* is historically derived from *shì*, which means "trend", and *bì*, which is a modal adverb expressing strong epistemic necessity. The modal force of *shìbì* comes from the etymology of *shìbì*. And therefore it cannot be negated. This is why *bù shìbì* 'not SHÌBÌ' is not good.

Acknowledgements

I thank anonymous reviewers for valuable comments and the CLSW 17 audience for enlightening discussion. I am grateful to Ministry of Science and Technology, Taiwan, for financial support, under the grant number MOST 103-2410-H194-037. I also thank my part-time research assistant, Xuan-Xiang Wang, for collecting data and for a preliminary classification of data.

Reference

1. Wu, J. : Context-dependency of Adverbial *Yídìng*: A Dynamic Semantic Account. Paper presented at the 4th Syntax and Semantics in China. Xi'an, China (Nov. 28th-29th, 2015)
2. Wu, J.: Dynamic Semantics for Intensification and Epistemic Necessity: The Case of *Yídìng* and *Shìbì* in Mandarin Chinese. In: Proceedings of the 29th Pacific Asia Conference on Language, Information and Computation, 241-248. Shanghai Jiaotong University, Shanghai (2015)
3. Guo, R.: Xiàndài hànyǔ cílèi yánjiù [Research on Parts of Speech in Modern Chinese]. Shāngwù yìnshūguǎn, Beijing (2002)
4. Li, C.: Fùcí *yídìng* shuōluè [On Adverb *yídìng*]. Lǐlùn yuèkān [Theory Monthly], Year 2005, Issue 5, 126-127 (2005)
5. Qi, H. (Eds.): Xiàndài Hànyǔ Yǔqì Chéngfèn Yòngfǎ Cídiǎn [Dictionary of Mood and Modal Expressions in Modern Chinese]. Shāngwù yìnshūguǎn, Beijing (2011)
6. Ding. P.: Yě shuō fùcí yídìng [Adverb *Yídìng* Revisited]. Journal of Northwest University for Nationalities (Philosophy and Social Sciences), Year 2008, Issue 8, 108-112 (2008)
7. Ding, P.: Yídìng yǔ kěndìng zuò zhuàngyǔ shí de bǐjiào [Comparison of Adverb *Yídìng* and Adverb *Kěndìng*]. Journal of Southwest University for Nationalities (Humanities and Social Sciences), Year 2008, Issue 8, 236-240 (2008)
8. Chen, Y.: Yídìng de xūhuà jí liáng zhǒng yǔyì de fānhuà [Grammaticalization of *Yídìng* and Two Types of Modality Diversification]. Journal of Wuhan University of Science & Technology (Social Science Edition), 13, 5, 605-609 (2011)
9. Matthewson, L., Rullmann, H. & Davis, H.: Evidentials are epistemic modals in St'át'imcets. UBCWPL, 18, 221-263 (2006)
10. Veltman, F.: Defaults in Update Semantics. Journal of Philosophical Logic, 25, 221-261 (1996)
11. Yalcin, S.: Epistemic Modals. Mind, 116, 983-1026 (2007)
12. Kratzer, A.: Modality. In: Semantics: An International Handbook of Contemporary Research, 636-650, de Gruyter, Germany (1991)

13. Kratzer, A.: The Notional Category of Modality. In: Modals and Conditionals, 21-69, Oxford University Press, Oxford (2012[1981])
14. Li, S.: Yŭqì fùcí shìbì de xíngchéng [On the Formation of Modal Adverb *Shìbì*]. Yŭwén xuékān [Journal of Language and Literature], Year 2009, Issue 10, 42-44 (2009)
15. Wang, M.: Shìbì de cíhuìhuà [Lexicalization of *Shìbì*]. Journal of Hunan First Normal College, 7, 1, 101-103 (2007)
16. Palmer, F. R.: *Mood and Modality*. 2nd Ed. Cambridge University Press, Cambridge (2001)

On the Intersubjectivity of Sentence Final Particle-*Ne*
--A Case Study between Degree Modifiers and SFP-*Ne*

Yifan He

The Hong Kong Polytechnic University

yifanhe324@yahoo.com.hk

Abstract. This research aims at identifying the intersubjectivity information encoded in SFP-*ne* in Mandarin. Built upon the theoretical framework of sub-jectivity and intersubjectivity, we find degree adverbs *ke, zhen* and *tai* are in complementary distribution when co-occurring with SFPs based on large-scale corpus data. We summarize the semantic properties and syntactic characteriza-tion between *ke* and SFP-*ne* via analyzing its stylistic function, it semantic rele-vance to the lead and answer sentences. We ultimately propose the interactional functions revealed by SFP-*ne* including reminding, informing, correcting and refuting.

Keywords: intersubjectivity, SFP-*ne, ke*

1   Introduction

Sentence final particles (henceforth Sfps) have been the object of intensive linguistic scrutiny for the past several decades. A large voluminous body of literature (e.g. Chao 1968, Li and Thompson 1981, Wu 2005, Constant 2011 among others) has been de-voted to the study of structural properties, historical development as well as the se-mantic and pragmatic features of Sfps.

Zhu (1982:208) accurately observes the hierarchical structures of Sfps and clearly proposes a three-layer classification on them, which is excerpted below:

Table 1. Three-layer classification on Chinese SFPs

C_1 ([1]Tense and Aspect)	C_2 (Force)	C_3 (Attitude)
Le Currently relevant	*Ma* Interrogative	*A* Astonishment
Laizhe Recent past	*Ba* Imperative	*Ou* Impatience
Ne$_1$ Continued State	*Ne$_2$* Interrogative	*Ne$_3$* Exaggeration

Three senses of SFP-*ne* are exemplified in (1). In order to give elaborate and precise

---

[1]   C here abbreviates for the highest layer of the Complementizer. It is generally acknowledged in the generative paradigm that SFPs in Chinese occupy the head position of the CP layer.

© Springer International Publishing AG 2016
M. Dong et al. (Eds.): CLSW 2016, LNAI 10085, pp. 464–471, 2016
DOI: 10.1007/978-3-319-49508-8_44

accounts of SFP-*ne,* this research has, by necessity, restricted itself to examining only the SFP-*ne₃* in assertion.

(1)   a.Ta zai jia   kan   dianshi   ne.
       He PROG   home   look   television   *ne.2*
       He is watching television at home.
       b. Ni   mama   ne?
       You   mum   *ne?*
       Where is your mum?
       c. Ta   chi le   shi   wan   mifan   ne.
       He   eat PERF   10   CL   rice   *ne.*
       He has eaten ten bowls of rice.

2   Literature Review

2.1   Review on SFP-*Ne.*

The literature on SFP-*ne* can be summarized as following two opposite directions, as Wu (2005: 48) points out, one is the "meaning maximalist", enumerating all the possible meanings of SFP-*ne* in the descriptive tradition. The other is the "meaning minimalist", endeavoring to extract a unified core meaning of SFP-*ne*. This paper takes the basic stand of the latter, i.e., "meaning minimalist".

In the literature, as for the core meaning of SFP-*ne,* Li and Thompson (1981: 300) propose that SFP-*ne* is used as a "response to the hearer's claim, expectation or belief". Shao (1996: 21) suggests the core meaning for SFP-*ne* is "reminding". The recent work by Fang (2014: 16) puts forward the "interactive function" as the core characterization of SFP-*ne.*

All of these studies identify the interactional function signaled by SFP-*ne,* be it the "response" or "remind". However, their proposals are deduced from the few examples they listed on the paper, seldom do the corpora data are involved. Moreover, previous research focuses only on SFP-*ne,* seldom do they take other constituents within the sentence into consideration.

Then we may ask what exactly is the interactional function signaled by SFP-*ne*? In what ways can their marking of interactional function be proved?

These points were left unattended and our study here aims at investigating the interactional function of SFP-*ne* and unveiling the mechanism of interaction between certain modifiers and SFP-*ne.*

2.2   Review on Intersubjectivity

In the literature, subjectivity has been investigated from functional and cognitive linguistics (see Portner 2009: 126-132 for a recent overview). Represent works from

---

2   It is hard for us to translate the meaning of SFPs, therefore we retain its original form in all the glosses. The abbreviations used in this paper are glossed as follows: PROG: progressive aspect marker; CL: classifier; NEG: negative morpheme; PERF: perfective aspect marker; DE: prenominal modifier marker, post-verbal resultative marker. DOU: universal quantifier.

functional approach include Lyon (1977), Traugott (1998, 2010). They in general treat subjectivity as the speaker's attitudes and perspective in describing an event or state of affairs. (It is termed as speaker's imprint in Finegan 1995:1). Langacker (1985,1990) theory is developed within cognitive semantics and treats subjectivity as speaker's conceptualization of a situation.

Intersubjectivity 3 evolves from subjectivity and is considered to be the speaker/writer's commitment in terms of hearer/audience interaction, speaker no longer just focuses on his/her alone, but taking into hearer's attitude or belief into consideration as well. (Traugott and Dasher 2001)

With respect to the investigation of intersubjectivity in Chinese, one group of researchers (Zhang and Yao 2009, Wang and Yang 2010) investigates the intersubjectivity encoded in Chinese honorifics, kinship terms and pronouns. The other group of scholars (Zhang and Li 2009, Zhang 2012) researches on the intersubjectivity reflected in certain grammatical constructions, for instance, *lian/dou, geng-bu-yong -shuo* (Even X, needless to say).

To summarize, the review on SFP-*ne* indicates that previous investigations recognize the interactional function trigger by SFP-*ne*. However, no concrete empirical evidence or testing mechanism has been put forward. Moreover, to what extent is the notion of intersubjectivity applies to SFP-*ne* is still a research area needs our further investigation.

3   Characterizations of *"Ke X Ne"* construction

3.1   Co-occurrence Distribution

According to our large-scale corpus data investigation of the CCL corpus. We find there exists a complimentary distribution between degree modifiers and SFPs in Mandarin Chinese. The degree modifiers here include *ke* (so/such), *zhen* (really/truly) and *tai* (excessively/very). SFPs include SFP-*ne,* SFP-*a* and SFP-*le.* The figure below presents a frequency counts of co-occurrence between degree modifiers and SFPs.

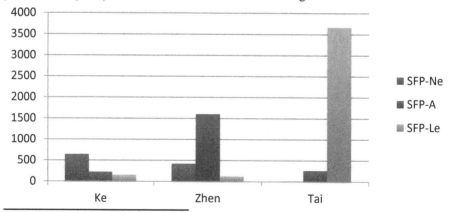

---

[3] The origin of intersubjectivity is still controversial and debatable. Some scholars (e.g. Benveniste 1971, Kärkkäinen 2006, among others) did not treat subjectivity as prior to intersubjectivity, but rather the other way around.

Fig. 1. Frequencies of the co-occurrence between Degree Modifiers and SFPs in CCL

The above-mentioned data indicate that *ke* is in high frequency of co-occurring with SFP-*ne*, *zhen* is in high frequency of co-occurring with SFP-*a* and *tai* is in high frequency of co-occurring with SFP-*le*.

Co-occurrence between *ke* and SFP-*ne* far outnumbers the rest two pairs, which refer to *zhen* and SFP-*a*, *tai* and SFP-*le*. Sentences in (2)-(4) illustrate this contrast.

(2)   xianggang   xiatian   ke   re   ne

          Hong Kong   summer so   hot   *ne.*

          It is so hot in Hong Kong in summer.

(3)   xianggang   xiatian   zhen   re   a

          Hong Kong   summer really   hot   *a.*

          It is really hot in Hong Kong in summer.

(4)   xianggang   xiatian   tai   re   le

          Hong Kong   summer excessively   hot   *le.*

          It is excessively hot in Hong Kong in summer.

The three sentences above provide us with the same description of the hotness in summer in Hong Kong. Nevertheless, when this "hotness" is modified differently, they tend to choose different SFPs.

In (2), *ke* here not only marks degree, it also implicitly entails the existence of a contrastive proposition, indicating that the summer in Hong Kong is not that hot. Sentences in (3) and (4) are descriptions of the speaker's subjective judgment of the hotness in summer in Hong Kong. Since SFP-*ne* is obligatory in the *ke* sentences, we will discuss the characterization of their co-occurrence in the following discussion.

3.2   Structural Description

The general characterization of "*Ke* X *Ne*" construction can be established through both corpus search and introspect. First, *ke* needs to be stressed. Second, the predicate part of X can be gradable adjectives, psychological verbs and measurable verb phrase. Sentences 4in (5)-(7) illustrate these points.

(5)   "jiaqian ke   gui   ne"   Ma   Wei   shuo

          "Price   so   expensive   *ne*"   Ma   Wei   say.

          "It costs a lot" said Ma Wei.

(6)   Women lingdao dui   xiashu   de   We   leader

               for   subordinate   DE   jiating   wenti

               ke   guanxin ne.

          Family   problem so   care   *ne.*

          Our leader cares so much about his subordinates' family affairs.

(7)   Nongchang   jin   wan   zhe   ge   dianyi   keyi

          Farm   today   night   this   CL   movie   can

          kan   yi   kan,   ke   kai   yanjie   ne.

---

[4] All the examples below, if not specified, come from the CCL corpus. The latest access: www.ccl.pku.edu.cn

| look | one | look | so | open | eye-horizon | *ne.* |

You may watch this movie tonight in the farm, it quite eye-   opening.
The adjective *"gui* (expensive)" in (5) belongs to the type of gradable predicates (Kennedy and McNally 2005). The psychological verb *"guanxin* (care for)" and verb phrase *"kai yanjie* (widen one's horizon)" in (6) and (7) are both gradable and measurable, and hence *ke* is used to mark the degree.

Moreover, the construction of *"Ke X Ne"* is always found to appear in the declarative and exclamative sentences. It is almost forbidden to appear in the imperative and interrogative sentences.

In the context of conversational exchange, we find that the construction of *"Ke X Ne"* appear both in the lead sentence and answer sentence (Yin 2008, Zhao and Shi 2015)

(8)	Qing	gaosu	xiaoqingtongzhi,	jiaxiang	zhe	ji
	Please	tell	Xiaoping	comrade, hometown	this	few
	nian	bianhua	ke	da	ne.
	year	change		so	big	*ne.*

Please tell Comrade Xiaoping, great changes have taken place   in his hometown these days.

(9) A:	lili, ni		ma	jin	wan	zuo	de	cai
	Lili, you mum		today	night	do	DE	dish	dou
	mei	zenme		chi.
	DOU	NEG	how		eat.
B:	Ba,	wo	ma	zuo	de	hongshao
	Daddy, I		mum	do	DE	braised with soy	niurou
	ke	haochi		ne
	Beef	so	yummy	*ne.*

A: Lili, the dishes cooked by your mum tonight has not been touched so much.

B: Daddy, the beef braised with soy sauce actually tastes very   good.
The speaker in (8) is asserting that great changes have taken place in his hometown. The *"Ke X Ne"* construction is used in the lead sentence to inform or remind the hearer of this unexpected change. In (9), the lead question by the speaker/daddy implicitly implied that the dishes
cooked by the Mum is not that tasty. The construction of *"Ke X Ne" is* used in the answer sentence to indicate that the tastiness of the dishes is unexpected to the hearer, and it also serve as a refutation to the precedent sentence.

3.3   Intersubjectivity encoded in SFP-*ne.*

Based on previous observation and investigation, we summarize that *ke* is not limited to mark degree, this degree information is highly associated with conversational participants' expectations and assumptions. This interactional context and intersubjectivity information need to be marked by SFP-*ne.*

| (10) | Zhe | liang | tiao | wugong | ke | bu | xiao | ne |
| | This | two | CL | centipede | so | NEG | small | *ne.* |

These two centipedes are not small at all.

| (11) | Na | shi, | wo | ke | lihai | ne. | ying |
| | That | time, | I | so | aggressive | *ne.* | Britain |

zhengfu	gongzuo	renyuan	yilun		wo		
government	work		Personnel		discuss	I.	zhe
ge	nv		lingshi	zhen	rang		
This	CL	female	Consul		really	let	
tamen	tou	teng.					
They	head	hurt.					

I was very aggressive at that time. British government officials always say that this Consul is a headache for them.

The speaker in (10) is informing and reminding the hearer that the size and length of these two centipedes are out of the hearer's previous expectation or assumption. This intersubjectivity information needs to be marked by SFP-*ne*. In a similar vein, the speaker in (11) is informing or reminding the hearer that the degree of her toughness is beyond the hearer's previous expectation or assumption as well.

This intersubjectivity information, or to be more specific, the discourse function of informing or reminding needs to be marked by SFP-*ne*.

Zhang and Li (2009) propose that degree modifier *ke* in conversation is used to activate the speaker and hearer's expectation. This research is in line with our investigation on the construction of *"Ke X Ne"* so far.

Besides the discourse function of informing and reminding, we also find the construction of *"Ke X Ne"* suggests the discourse function of correcting and refuting as well.

(12) A: Lao Li, wo   duibuqi nimen, ben   xiang   jie   dian
     A: Old Li, I sorry you,   originally   want borrow little
         bai   mian, ke   wei   le   bao   mi   jiu
         white   flour, but   for   ASP   keep secret then
         mei   jie.
         NEG   borrow.
     B: Gui-ying,   na   you,   ke   haochi   ne.
     B: Gui-ying,   where have, so   yummy   ne.

     A: Old Li, I feel sorry for you, I originally planned to borrow some flour,
        however for the sake of keeping secret, I gave it up.
     B: Gui Ying, you are wellcome, the meal you provided is very delicious.

(13)   A: Nan-nan, qu Dalian pai   xi   zenme yang?
         A: Nan-nan, go Dalian clap   drama how   way?
         Jiang   Jiang   ni   de   mingxing   shenghuo.
         Tell   tell   you   DE   star   life.
         B: ba,   pai   xi   ke   zao   zui   ne.
         B:Daddy, clap drama so   suffer guilty ne.

     A: Nan-nan, how does it feel like to participate the movie shooting in
Dalian? Tell me about your life of being a star?
     B: Daddy, I had such a hard time there!

The lead sentence in the conversation (12) implies that the meal is not tasty, the *"Ke X Ne"* construction is used in the answer sentence to correct this assertion and confirm that the meal actually is delicious. Similarly, the speaker in (13) is correcting or refuting the hearer/ daddy's assertion that being a movie star equals to an easy life.

Sometimes, the expectation or assumption cannot be deduced from conversational background information, but need to be implied from world knowledge or social norms.

(14) A:ni   lai   wan   le,   zao   dian   keyi   kanjian
      A:you   come   late PERF, early little can   see
            Hushi gei   zhe   xie   bing   er
            Nurse give   this CL   sick   child
xizao,   Zhe   ke   you   da   xuewen   ne.
            Shower, This   so   have   big   knowledge   *ne.*

A: you are late, if you come earlier, you would see these nurses give
shower to these sick children. It is such a knowledge-demanding   work.

Unlike the sentences in (12) and (13), where the contrastive proposition or to be more
specific, the proposition that is corrected or refuted, is deduced from the conversational context. Here the construction of *"Ke X Ne"* is used to correct or refute the
background world knowledge, i.e. the general social perception that showering for
small kids is not a big deal.

Therefore, we may conclude from these empirical evidences that the construction of
"Ke X Ne" serves the following discourse function of informing, reminding, correcting and refuting. *Ke* is used not only to mark degree, but also indicate conversational
participants' expectations and assumptions. The existence of the expectations that are
negotiated intersubjectively needs to be marked by SFP-*ne*.

4 Conclusion

To conclude, this paper proposes the intersubjectivity information encoded in SFP-*ne,*
and more importantly, the identification of co-occurrence between degree modifier *ke*
and SFP-*ne*, i.e. the construction of *"Ke X Ne"* as the traceable clue to prove the interactional function of SFP-*ne*.

The observation and investigation of co-occurrence between certain constituents or
more specifically, the adverbial part and SFPs may apply to other final particles both
in Chinese and cross-linguistically.

References

1. Benveniste, E. (1971). Problems in General Linguistics. Coral Gables, FL: University of Miami Press.
2. Kennedy, C. & L, McNally. (2005).Scale structure, degree modification, and the semantics of gradable predicates. Language 81(2): 345-381.
3. Fang, M. (2014). Re-Analysis of *"Ne"*—Investigation on the syntactic differences of final particles from the perspective of interactive function. Paper presented at the 18th Conference on Modern Chinese Grammar. October, Macau.
4. Finegan, E. (1995). Subjectivity and subjectivisation: An introduction. In Subjectivity and Subjectivisation. Linguistic Perspectives, D. Stein and S. Wright (eds.), 1–15. Cabridge: Cambridge University Press.
5. Kärkkäinen, E. (2006). Stance taking in conversation: From subjectivity to intesubjectivity. Text & Talk-An Interdisciplinary Journal of Language, Discourse Communication   Studies, 26(6), 699-731.
6. Li, Charles N. & Sandra A, Thompson. (1981). Mandarin Chinese: A Functional Reference Grammar. Berkeley: University of California Press.
7. Lyons, J. (1977). Semantics. Cambridge: Cambridge University Press.
8. Portner, P. (2009). Modality. Cambridge: Cambridge University Press.
9. Shao, J.-M. (1996). Xiandai Hanyu Yiwenju Yanjiu [Research on Modern Chinese Interrogatives] Shanghai: East China Normal University Press.
10. Traugott, E.C. & R.B, Dasher (2001). Regularity in Semantic Change. Cambridge: Cambridge University Press.
11. Traugott, E. C. (2003). From subjectification to intersubjectification. In Hickey(eds) Motives for language change. Cambridge: Cambridge University Press. 124-139.
12. Traugott, E. C. (2010). (Inter) subjectivity and (inter) subjectification: a reassessment. In Davidse, Vandelanotte and Cuyckens (eds) Subjectification, intersubjectification and grammaticalization, New York: De Gruyter Mouton.29-71.
13. Wu, G. (2005). The discourse function of the Chinese particle ne in statements. Journal of the Chinese Language Teachers Association. 40(1): 47-82.
14. Yin, S.-C. (2008). The Response Sentence Patterns of Chinese. Chinese Language Learning 2: 15-22.
15. Zhang Y. (2010). A semantics-syntax interface study of SoA qualification—Based on cognitive intersubjectivity. Foreign Language Teaching and Research 203-210
16. Zhang, W.-X. & H-M, Li. (2009). Interlocution and Inter-subjectivity of the adverb "Ke" Language Teaching and Linguistic Studies. 2:1-8.
17. Zhao, C-L. & D-X, Shi. (2015). Attitudinal Orientations and Semantic Source of Sentence Final Particle *Bei*. Language Teaching and Linguistic Studies. 4: 68-78.
18. Zhu, D-X. (1982). Yufa Jiangyi [Lecture Notes on Grammar]. Beijing: Commercial Press.

When Degree Meets Evaluativity: A Multidimensional Semantics for the Ad-adjectival Modifier *hǎo* 'well' in Mandarin Chinese*

Qiongpeng Luo[1] and Yuan Wang[2](✉)

[1]School of Liberal Arts, Nanjing University, China
qpluo@nju.edu.cn
[2]School of Chinese Language and Literature, Nanjing Normal University, China
wy_cathy@163.com

Abstract. This study provides a semantic account of the Mandarin ad-adjectival modifier *hǎo* '(lit.) well', which is a member of a family of adverbs that yield intensification, display subjectivity and parallel with speaker-oriented intensifiers in resisting nonveridical contexts. We argue that *hǎo* is a mixed expressive item. On the one hand, it is like canonical degree adverbs, meaning some individual x holding to a high degree with respect to some gradable property. On the other, it is a conventional implicature (CI) trigger that contributes an expressive content, expressing the speaker's strong emotion (surprise, approval, etc.) towards x holding to high degree. We propose a formal analysis of *hǎo* by incorporating the degree semantics into the multidimensional logic.

Keywords: Expressive modification · Multidimensional Semantics · Intensifier · Mandarin Chinese

1   Introduction

This study provides a semantic account for the ad-adjectival 好 *hǎo* 'well' in Mandarin Chinese. When used as an adverb, *hǎo* can modify an adjective (AP).[1] In traditional descriptive linguistics, *hǎo* is always termed as a "degree word/adverb", alongside with other canonical degree words such as *hěn* 'very'. For instance, in [9], both the adverbial *hǎo* and *hěn* are defined as "expressing high degree", and can be used interchangeably:

(1) a. The definition of the adverbial 好 *hǎo*:
表示程度深 *biǎoshi chéngdù shēn* 'expressing high degree' (p. 258)
b. The definition of the adverbial 很 *hěn:*
表示程度高 *biǎoshi chéngdù gāo* 'expressiving high degree' (p. 266)

---

* Corresponding author: Yuan Wang, School of Chinese Language and Literature, Nanjing Normal University, 122 Ninghai Road, Nanjing, 210097, China.
[1] *hǎo* also has an adjectival use. This study focuses on the adverbial, ad-adjectival one.

ⓒ Springer International Publishing AG 2016
M. Dong et al. (Eds.): CLSW 2016, LNAI 10085, pp. 472–482, 2016
DOI: 10.1007/978-3-319-49508-8_45

(2) 街上{很/好}热闹。
    Jiē   shàng {hěn/ hǎo} rènào.
    street LOC very/WELL boisterous[2]
    'It is very/well boisterous in the street.'

Many descriptive works follow suit to treat *hǎo* as a degree adverb (cf. [16] and references therein). This line of thought runs into some empirical problems. First and foremost, it misses some important semantic differences between *hǎo* and other canonical degree adverbs. Even [9] admits that the use of *hǎo* signals some additional exclamatory mood, which is lacking for *hěn*. Some other works have pointed out that the adverbial *hǎo* also has some subjectivity flavor, i.e., it describes the speaker's subjective evaluation towards the propositional content that is being said (cf. [7]). However, without a precise and formal account as for how the exclamatory mood, or the subjectivity, associated with *hǎo* is achieved, such analysis is at best descriptive, and at worst speculative.

The goals of this paper are twofold. First, we report fresh observation to demonstrate that *hǎo*, differing from canonical degree adverbs such as *hěn*, systematically resists the non-veridical contexts such as negation, questions, modals, and the antecedents of conditionals. To our knowledge, this distributional pattern of *hǎo* has received very little attention in the theoretical literature. Second, we develop a precise and formal analysis of *hǎo* to explicate both of its degree and subjectivity senses. Drawing insights from recent studies on expressive items ([14, 15], [4]), we propose that *hǎo* is a mixed expressive in the sense that it conveys simultaneously descriptive and expressive meanings. On the one hand, it sides with canonical degree adverbs, taking an adjective (AP) as its argument and meaning some individual x holding to a high degree of ADJ-ness. On the other, it is a conventional implicature (CI) trigger that expresses some evaluative attitude or emotion of the speaker (or agent) towards x holding to a high degree. We provide a formal analysis of *hǎo* by incorporating degree semantics into an extension of the multidimensional logic L_{CI} of [14, 15].

2   Some empirical generalizations

2.1   The subjectivity of *hǎo*

The "*hǎo*+AP" constructions always have some additional subjectivity flavor, i.e., they express the speaker is strongly emotional (i.e., surprise, approval, positive evaluation, and so forth) about the propositional content. This speaker-orientation sets *hǎo* apart from canonical degree adverbs that merely manipulate the standard of comparison. For example, the following (3a) has some "double assertion" sense, as shown in (3b) ("d" for degrees):

(3) a. 晓丽好漂亮。
      Xiǎolì hǎo piàoliang.

---

[2] Abbreviations used in this paper are as follows: LOC: locatives; NEG: negation; WELL: *hǎo*; Q: question marker.

Xiaoli WELL pretty
Lit.: 'Xiaoli is very pretty.'
b. (i) ∃d [Xiaoli is d-pretty & d≥d_c], where d_c is some contextually provided standard;
(ii) The speaker is strongly emotional about Xiaoli being pretty at such a high degree.[3]

For *hǎo* to be felicitously used, two conditions (as demonstrated by (3bi) and (3bii)) must be satisfied: (i) the degree that the relevant entity holds must be greater than some contextually salient standard; (ii) the speaker has some heightened emotional state towards the entity holding to such a high degree. Unlike *hǎo*, *hěn* 'very' only has the degree-related reading. The use of *hěn* is more often to make an objective report, not a subjective judgment:

(4) a. 晓丽很漂亮。
    Xǐaolì hěn pìaolìang.
    Xiaoli very pretty
    'Xiaoli is very pretty.'
    b. (i) Xiaoli is d-pretty, d≥some norm-related standard.[4]
       (ii) ∃d[pretty(d)(XL)∧ d≥norm$_C$([[pretty]])]

This emotional meaning of *hǎo* serves as the speaker's ancillary commitment to other discourse participant(s), and cannot be denied or even "played down" (in contrast to *hěn*). Observe the contrast between (5a) and (5b) below:

(5) a. 晓丽好聪明，#但这也没什么。
    Xǐaolì hǎo cōngmíng, #dàn zhè yě
    Xiaoli WELL smart   but this also/even méishenme.nothing-significant
    (Intended:) 'Xiaoli is well smart, but this is nothing significant.'
    b. 晓丽很聪明，但这也没什么。
    Xǐaolì hěn cōngmíng, dàn zhè yě méishenme.
    'Xiaoli is very smart, but this is nothing significant.'

2.2   *Hǎo* and (non)veridical contexts

Previous studies on *hǎo* fail to observe another significant syntactic distributional pattern. A more comprehensive examination of the data indicates that *hǎo* cannot occur in the immediate semantic scope of negation, conditionals, questions and modals. To illustrate, consider the examples in (6):

---

[3] (3a) can be used as an exclamation. When it is used as an exclamation, it means Xiaoli is d-pretty, and d≥the degree such that it takes the speaker by surprise (we take "surprise" as the illocutionary force of exclamations).

[4] We take the standard of comparison that *hěn* manipulates to be a norm-related one, see [11] for details.

(6) a. 晓丽没有{*好/很}聪明。
   Xǐaolì méiyǒu {*hǎo/ hěn } cōngmíng.
   Xiaoli NEG   WELL very   intelligent
   Lit.: 'Xiaoli is not well/very intelligent.'
 b. 如果晓丽{*好/很}聪明，她就会挣很多钱。
   Ruguo Xǐaolì {*hǎo/ hěn } cōngmíng, tā jìu huì zhèng hěnduo   qían.
   if   Xiaoli WELL very   intelligent she then will earl very:much money
   Lit.: 'If Xiaoli is well/very intelligent, she will earn much money.'
 c. 晓丽{*好/很}聪明吗？
   Xǐaolì {*hǎo/ hěn } cōngmíng ma?
   Xiaoli WELL very   intelligent Q
   Lit.: 'Is Xiaoli well/very intelligent?'
 d. 晓丽可能{*好/很}聪明。
   Xǐaolì kěnéng {*hǎo/ hěn } cōngmíng.
   Xiaoli may-be WELL very intelligent
   Lit.: 'Xiaoli may be well/very intelligent.'

Those contexts (negation, conditionals, questions and modals) are all entailment-cancelling ones. To be precise, these contexts are all non-veridical ones. A non-veridical context is the context where the truth of the proposition cannot be asserted. The definition of (non-)veridicality is provided as below (1: true; 0: false):

(7) (Non)veridicality ([17])
   (i) Let O be a monadic sentential operator. O is veridical iff Op $=1 \Rightarrow$ p$=1$, other-
       wise O is nonveridical;
   (ii) A nonveridical operator O is averidical iff Op$=1 \Rightarrow$ p$=0$.

Given the definition in (7), negation is of course nonveridical (and also averidical by (7ii)). Questions and the antecedents of conditionals are also nonveridical: questioning p does not entail p, nor do conditionals. Why *hǎo* resists the nonveridical contexts remains unexplained in the literature. Another relevant question that needs to be addressed is how this distributional pattern is related to its subjectivity flavor.

As a further note, *hǎo*'s systematic resistance to being embedded in nonveridical contexts has placed it in parallel with speaker-oriented, evaluative adverbs ([3]) and expressive items ([14-15]). Most of the speaker-oriented, evaluative adverbs cannot occur in the semantic scope of nonveridical operators. The following examples (8) and (9) are from [3] and [15] respectively:

(8) a. Unfortunately, John disappeared.
   b. *John didn't unfortunately disappeared.
   c. *Has he unfortunately disappeared?
   d. *If he has unfortunately disappeared,…
(9) a. *He isn't fucking calm.
   b.* Is he fucking calm?

To capture the semantics of expressive items such as *damn, fucking*, [14-15] propose a multidimensional semantics of conventional implicatures (CIs). Conventional implicatures are non-truth-conditional inferences that are not derived from the pragmatic principles (maxims of quality, quantity, manner and relevance), but are simply attached by convention to particular lexical items. Potts makes a further step by arguing that CIs are expressive content, and as such they can also be semantically computed. Expressive items, as CI-triggers, express the speaker's heightened emotional state. The meaning of a sentence that contains an expressive item is thus bi-dimensional in the sense that it expresses both an at-issue content in the descriptive (truth-conditional) dimension and a CI content in the expressive dimension. *Fucking*, for example, expresses the speaker's negative attitude towards the state of affairs under discussion. In a bi-dimensional semantics framework, the semantics of (9a), for instance, is represented as (10) below:

(10) *He isn't fucking calm.
    a. At-issue content: $\neg$ (**calm** (**he**$_i$))
    b. CI content: The speaker expresses a negative attitude at him being calm.
    c. CI's presupposition: **calm** (**he**$_i$).

As shown by (10b) and (10c), *fucking* contains a CI content that expresses the speaker's negative attitude. This CI carries a presupposition that he$_i$ is calm. But this presupposition contradicts with the at-issue content, which asserts that he$_i$ is not calm. This semantic contradiction renders (9a) ill-formed.

    Inspired by this analysis, we can also treat *hǎo* as contributing some expressive content in the expressive dimension. As a consequence, the meaning conveyed is speaker-oriented and cannot be contradicted in the same manner as asserted meaning. This may provide a straightforward account of the distributional pattern of *hǎo*, i.e., its systematic resistance to being embedded in nonveridical contexts. However, there is strong empirical evidence indicating that to treat *hǎo* as merely contributing some expressive content is missing the whole picture.

2.3   *Hǎo* as a degree word

Despite the apparent subjectivity sense, *hǎo* manifests certain similarities with canonical degree adverbs like *hěn*: (i) the adjectives they modify must be gradable (11a); (ii) they must immediately precede the modified AP at the surface syntax, and are not floatable (11b); (iii) they resist modification by other degree adverbs (11c); (iv) they are in complementary distribution with comparative morphemes like *geng* '(even) more' (11d):

(11) a. *晓丽{好/很}未婚。
       *Xiǎolì　{hǎo/hěn}　wèihūn.
       Xiaoli　WELL very　unmarried
    b. (*好/*很)晓丽{好/很}聪明。
       (*hǎo/*hěn)　Xiǎolì　(hǎo/hěn)　cōngmíng.
       well　very　Xiaoli　WELL/very smart

c. 晓丽（*非常）{好/很}聪明。
Xĭaolì (*féichang)   hăo/hěn   cōngmíng.
Xiaoli extraordinarily WELL/very smart
d. 晓丽（*更）{好/很}聪明。
Xĭaolì (*gèng) hăo/hěn cōngmíng.
Xiaoli   more WELL/very smart

The examples in (11) demonstrate that *hăo* is a degree word, that is, it has some degree component in its (lexical) semantics.

2.4 Interim summary

To recap, *hăo* has some mixed properties. On the one hand, it parallels with canonical degree adverbs in being subject to the same constraint in syntactic configuration and meaning some individual x holding to a high degree with respect to some gradable property. On the other, it patterns with (strong) evaluative adverbs in resisting to being embedded in nonveridical contexts and contributing an expressive content that expresses the speaker's strong emotion (surprise, approval, etc.) towards x holding to high degree. In the next section, we will develop a formal account for such mixed properties in a multidimensional semantics.

3   A multidimensional account

This section is devoted to providing a multidimensional semantic account of *hăo*. In his influential works on the logic of conventional implicature, [14-15] develops a multidimensional logic L_{CI} to deal with expressive meaning (as a conventional implicature). The most fundamental assumption is that meanings operate on different dimensions. Thus, an utterance may express both an at-issue (truth-conditional) content in the descriptive dimension and a conventional implicature in the expressive dimension. Informally, the expressive meaning is like "double assertion", or some side comment by the speaker. [14-15] introduce a new semantic type for CI (expressive content) in the semantic system. The semantic types organize the semantic lexicon, and they index the denotation domains. The semantic types in L_{CI} are defined as in (12) below:

(12) a. e^a and t^a are basic at-issue types.
b. e^c and t^c are basic CI types.
c. If τ and σ are at-issue types, then $\langle \tau, \sigma \rangle$ is an at-issue type.
d. If τ is an at issue type and σ is a CI type, then $\langle \tau, \sigma \rangle$ is a CI type.
e. The full set of types is the union of the at-issue and CI types.

The at-issue content is marked by the superscript "a", and the expressive content by the superscript "c". Potts proposes the following CI application rule for semantic composition when an expressive item (such as *damn*) combines with an item that only has descriptive meaning (such as *Republicans*):

(13) CI application rule in L_{CI}

$$\beta: \sigma^a \bullet \alpha(\beta): \tau^c$$

$$\alpha: <\sigma^a, \tau^c> \qquad \beta: \sigma^a$$

At its core, (13) is just the standard rule of functional application. It states that if α is a term of type $<\sigma, \tau>$, and β is a term of type σ then $\alpha(\beta)$ is a term of type τ. The bullet "$\bullet$" is a metalogical symbol to separate the at-issue content from the CI content. (13) applies the CI functor to the descriptive, at-issue meaning to produce a CI meaning, but in addition, pass along the at-issue content unmodified.

According to Potts, the at-issue meaning in the descriptive dimension and the expressive meaning (i.e., the speaker's emotional attitude) in the expressive dimension are independent of each other. He proposes the following claims to highlight this independence thesis:

(14) Claim 1: expressive types are only output types, i. e.:
   a. At-issue content never applies to expressive content. ([14], §3.5.1)
   b. Expressive content never applies to expressive content. ([14], §3.5.2)
(15) Claim 2: No lexical item contributes both an at-issue and a CI meaning. ([14]: 7)

This fact is reflected in the composition system as shown in (12) and (13). However, the afore-mentioned *hǎo* facts pose an empirical problem for this system. As shown before, *hǎo* has some mixed properties: it "fuses" both degree and expressivity simultaneously. To captures such mixed properties, we adopt the composition system as developed in [13] and [4], which is an extension of Potts' L_{CI}. To make a difference, we call this system L_{CI+}. The type definition for L_{CI+} is provided as below:

(16) a. e^a and t^a are (at-issue) descriptive type.
   b. e^c and t^c are basic expressive type.
   c. If σ and τ are descriptive type, then $<\sigma, \tau>$ is a descriptive type.
   d. If σ is an at issue type and τ is an expressive type, then $< \sigma, \tau>$ is an expressive type.
   e. If σ and τ are expressive types, then $<\sigma, \tau>$ is an expressive type.
   f. If σ and τ are descriptive type and ν is an expressive type, then $< \sigma, \tau> \diamond <\sigma, \nu>$ is a mixed type.

As shown in (16f), a mixed expressive has two types, one for each dimension of meaning. It takes a descriptive argument as its input and generates an output which conveys meanings in both dimensions. These two components are separated by the diamond symbol $\diamond$, and they simultaneously combine with the same descriptive input, and yield two different outputs, one in the descriptive dimension and the other in the expressive one. This composition is shown by the Mixed Application Rule (17) ([4]: 15):

(17) The Mixed Application Rule

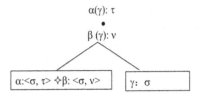

With the afore-mentioned types and composition rules at hand, we are now in a position to provide a formal semantic account of *hǎo*. To capture the expressive content, we adopt the **speaker.involvement (SI)** function of [1]. **SI** is a function from propositions to degrees of the speaker's emotional involvement in that proposition. We also introduce a context-sensitive function **good**, which states that the speaker is strongly emotional (surprise, evaluation, approval of, and so forth) about the propositional content. The general lexical entry for *hǎo* is provided as (18):

(18) $[\![h\check{a}o]\!]= \lambda G_{<d,\ et>}\lambda x.\exists d[G(d)(x)\wedge d>!s]$ $\diamond\lambda G_{<d,et>}\lambda x\lambda w.\exists d[d>!s\wedge G(d)(x)]=1$
$\rightarrow$**good**(**SI**$(G(d)(x)))(w)$

(18) states that *hǎo* takes a gradable predicate (G) as its argument, yielding a meaning that some individual holding to a high degree of G-ness; while in the meantime, the speaker is strongly emotional about x holding to such a high degree. Following [5], we assume that gradable adjectives are functions from degrees to individuals (for a degree-based analysis of adjectives in Chinese, see [10-11]). The adjectives such as *cōngmíng* 'intelligent' receive a representation as shown in (19).

(19) $[\![c\bar{o}ngm\acute{i}ng]\!]=\lambda d\lambda x.$ **intelligent**$(d)(x)$ $(<d, et>)$

(20) below illustrates the semantic derivation of *hǎo*+AP constructions. For comparison, (21) is the semantic derivation for the *hěn*+AP constructions. As it is manifested by (20) vs. (21), *hǎo* and *hěn* have a common semantic component related to degrees, yet they differ from each other in the presence vs. absence of an expressive content.

(20) 晓丽好聪明。
　　 Xiǎolì hǎo cōngmíng.

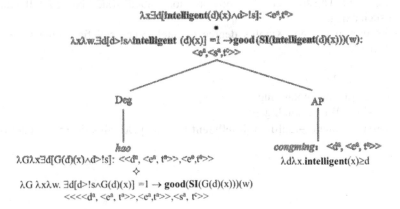

(21) 晓丽很聪明。

Xĭaolì hĕn cōngmíng.

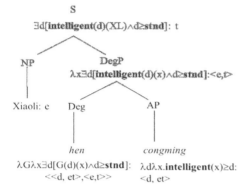

4   Discussion

The present analysis reaps three immediate advantages. First, as shown in (20), it captures the intuitive degree flavor of *hǎo*. It is this degree flavor that has led many (descriptive) linguists to treat it as a pure degree adverb. Second, it intuitively captures the subjectivity flavor of *hǎo*. The expressive meaning is performative, and as a consequence, it cannot be denied (cf. (5a-b)). Third, *hǎo*'s resistance to negative contexts follows naturally. The expressive component of *hǎo* carries a presupposition that the speaker is committed to the descriptive content. A non-veridical context, by contrast, is one in which the truth of a propositional content cannot be asserted, and this contradicts with such a presupposition. This is illustrated by the contrast between (22) and (23):

(22) 晓丽好聪明。

Xĭaolì hǎo cōngmíng.

i.   At-issue content: $\exists d[d \geq !s \land$ **intelligent** ($\textbf{XL}$)(d)] (Xiaoli's degree of intelligence satisfies some salient standard)

ii. CI content: The speaker is strongly emotional about Xiaoli being intelligent at such a degree.

iii. CI's presupposition: Xiaoli's degree of intelligence satisfies some salient standard.

(23) *晓丽没有好聪明。

*Xĭaolì méiyŏu hǎo   cōngmíng.

Xiaoli NEG   WELL intelligent

i.   At-issue content: $\neg \exists d[d \geq !s \land$ **intelligent** ($\textbf{XL}$)(d)] (Xiaoli's degree of intelligence fails to satisfy some salient standard.)

  ii. CI content: The speaker is strongly emotional about Xiaoli being intelligent at a certain degree.

  iii. CI's presupposition: Xiaoli's degree of intelligence satisfies some salient standard.

(23iii) contradicts with (23i), and this semantic contradiction results into the ill-formedness of (23). Questions, modals and the antecedents of conditionals are also nonveridical. As a consequence, when a *hǎo*+AP construction is embedded in them, some contradiction between the descriptive content and the presupposition of the expressive content would arise, resulting into in-formedness. This semantics correctly derives the nonembedablility of *hǎo*.

5 Conclusion

Although our analysis focuses on *hǎo* out of practical reasons, we would like to stress that *hǎo* is just one of a family of adverbs in Mandarin Chinese that bear similar mixed properties. Other candidates include the adverbial use of *guài* '(lit.) odd', *tǐng* '(lit.) outstanding', and *lǎo* '(lit.) old' (cf. [12]). [5] reports similar mixed modifiers (*sau/total/voll*) in German (see also [2]). Such adverbs form a small yet interesting class and are worth further exploration. For now, this preliminary study of the ad-adjectival modifier *hǎo* not only provides new, cross-linguistic evidence for an enhanced multidimensional approach to expressive meaning, but also suggests a plausible means of incorporating degree semantics into a multidimensional logic for expressive/descriptive mixed meaning.

Acknowledgements. We are grateful to three anonymous reviewers for helpful suggestions and comments on an earlier draft of this paper. This work was financially supported by the National Social Science Foundation of China under grant No. 16BYY006 to Qiongpeng Luo and the Humanities and Social Science Fund, the Ministry of Education, China under grant No. 14YJC740089 and the Jiangsu Provincial Social Science Foundation under grant No. 14YYC002 to Yuan Wang. All errors remain our own.

References

1. Beltrama, A., Bochnak, R.: Intensification without degrees cross-linguistically. Natural Language and Linguistic Theory 33, 843-879 (2015).

2. Castroviejo, E: Adverbs in restricted configurations. In: Bonami, O., Hofher, P.C. (eds.), Empirical Issues in Syntax and Semantics 7, 53-76. CNRS, France (2008).

3. Ernst, T.: Speaker-oriented adverbs. Natural Language and Linguistic Theory 27, 497-544 (2009).

4. Gutzmann, D.:Expressive modifiers & mixed expressives. In: Bonami, O., Hofher, P.C. (eds.), Empirical Issues in Syntax and Semantics 8, 123-141. CNRS, France (2011).

5. Gutzmann, D., Turgay, K: Expressive intensifiers in German: Syntax-semantics interfaces. In: Piñon, C. (ed.), Empirical Issues in Syntax and Semantics 9, 149-166. CNRS, France (2012).
6. Kennedy, C., McNally, L.: Scale structure, degree modification, and the semantics of gradable predicates. Language 81, 345-381 (2005).
7. Li, J.: The grammaticalization and subjectivity of *hǎo*. Chinese Teaching in the World 1: 44-49 (2005). (*hǎo* de yufahua he zhuguanxing. Shijie Hanyu Jiaoxue)[In Chinese]
8. Liu, M.: Multidimensional Semantics for Evaluative Adverbs. Brill, Leiden, the Netherlands (2012).
9. Lü, S.: The Eight Hundred Words in Modern Chinese. The Commercial Press, Beijing, China (1999). (Xiandai Hanyu Babai Ci) [In Chinese]
10. Luo, Q.: Degree, scale and the semantics of *zhen* and *jia*. Studies in Language and Linguistics 2, 94-100 (2016). (Chengdu, liangji yu xingrongci "zhen" he "jia"de yuyi. Yuyan Yanjiu) [In Chinese]
11. Luo, Q., Wang, Y.A contrastive analysis of *hen* and *ting* in Chinese. In: Lu, Q. and Gao, H. (eds.), *CLSW 2015, LNAI 9332*, 33-41, (2015).
12. Ma, Z.: On the degree adverbs *hen*, *ting*, *guai* and *lao* in Mandarin Chinese. Chinese Language Learning 2, 8-13 (1991). (Putonghua li de chengdu fuci hen, ting, guai, lao. Hanyu Xuexi) [In Chinese]
13. McCready, E.: Varieties of conventional implicature. Semantics and Pragmatics 3, 1-57 (2010).
14. Potts, C.: The Logic of Conventional Implicatutre. Oxford University Press, Oxford, UK (2005).
15. Potts, C.: The expressive dimension. Theoretical Linguistics 33, 165-198 (2007).
16. Zhang, B.: A Descriptive Grammar of Modern Chinese. The Commercial Press, Beijing, China (2010). (Xiandai Hanyu Miaoxie Yufa)[In Chinese]
17. Zwarts, F.: Nonveridical contexts. Linguistic Analysis 25, 286-312 (1995).

Verbal Plurality of Frequency Adverbs in Mandarin Chinese: The case of *cháng* and *chángcháng*

Hua-Hung YUAN [1(✉)] and Daniel Kwang Guan CHAN [2(✉)]

[1] Taipei city, Taiwan
`yuan.huahung@gmail.com`
[2] Centre for Language Studies, National University of Singapore, Singapore
`daniel.chan@nus.edu.sg`

Abstract. This paper looks at the similarities and differences between two frequency adverbs, *cháng* and *chángcháng*, which have been often confused with each other in the Sinologist literature. Since both denote a multiplicity of 'occasions', they can be treated as markers of verbal plurality operating at the occasion-level in the sense of Cusic (1981). They present differences in two aspects: (i) the sentence types that they can occur in (respectively, characterizing vs. particular sentences) and (ii) their semantic functions (respectively, the expression of habituality vs. iterativity).

Keywords. Verbal plurality · Frequency adverbs · Mandarin Chinese · Habituality · Iterativity · Reduplication

1 Introduction: "Often" in Chinese

This paper seeks to gain a basic understanding of the similarities and the differences between two frequency adverbs in Mandarin Chinese, *cháng* and *chángcháng*, which are almost always glossed identically as 'often' or 'frequently' in Sinologist literature in Chinese.

1.1 Differences cited in the literature

To our knowledge, the main differences that have been mentioned in the literature relate mainly to their phonological, pragmatic and semantic properties. For example, some authors think that constraints on monosyllabic or dissyllabic verbs determine the choice of *cháng* and *chángcháng* (Diao (2011: 32); Yang & Jia (2005: 198–199)). On the semantic level, some linguists think that the two adverbs express different frequencies (Diao (*op. cit.*) and Zou (2006: 44)). Others have claimed that *cháng* is used in formal texts while *chángcháng* is more of a spoken form (Li, 2005: 25; Li, 2007).

© Springer International Publishing AG 2016
M. Dong et al. (Eds.): CLSW 2016, LNAI 10085, pp. 483–496, 2016
DOI: 10.1007/978-3-319-49508-8_46

1.2   Counterexamples

However, it is not difficult to find counterexamples to the above-cited differences between *cháng* and *chángcháng*. In this sub-section, we present counter-examples for each of the type of differences cited in the previous literature.

As example (1a) shows, both the dissyllabic verb, *késòu* 'cough', and the monosyllabic one, *kū* 'cry', can indifferently be placed after *cháng* and *chángcháng*. Moreover, the short clause expressing the frequency 'ten times per day' can be added to complement the sentence in (1a), showing that both *cháng* and *chángcháng* can refer to exactly the same frequency. The syllable structure of verbs and the reference to different frequencies are therefore of insignificant consequence for the choice of use between *cháng* and *chángcháng*.

(1)   a.以前，小明{**常/常常**}咳嗽/哭…
       *Yǐqián,   Xiǎomíng **cháng/chángcháng** késòu / kū*
       In the past Xiaoming cháng/chángcháng cough / cry
       'In the past, Xiaoming coughed/cried often.'

      b. …一天就咳/哭了十次.
       …yì-tiān   jiù   ké   / kū-le   shí-cì.
       one-day then cough cry-Acc[1]. ten-times
       'In one day, he coughed/cried 10 times.'

Last but not least, the example (2) below, taken from an online book review, shows that *chángcháng* has no problems occurring in a so-called formal text, thereby refuting the claim that text type has anything to do with the choice between *cháng* and *chángcháng*.

(2)   在巴比伦的金融史中，词语的意思**常常**随时间的变化而变化.
       Zài Bābǐlún de jīnróng shǐ   zhōng,
       Loc. Babylon de financial history within
       *cíyǔ   de yìsi   **chángcháng** suí   shíjiān de biànhuà er   biànhuà*
       words de meaning *chángcháng* follow time   de change Conj. change
       'In Babylon's financial history, the meaning of words often changed
       with the time.' (Taken from http://www.beduu.com/read-1273.html)

---

[1] List of abbreviations: Acc.= Accomplished aspect; Cl.= Classifier; Conj.=conjunction; de= Mandarin *de* (的) genitive; Dur.= Durative aspect; Loc.= Locative; neg = Negation marker.

1.3   Research question

We have shown in this section that the differences between the two adverbs *cháng* and *chángcháng* are not what other researches have made them out to be.

In view of the above, our research questions are as follows:

(i)   What are the actual similarities and differences between *cháng* and *chángcháng*?

(ii)   How do we analyze these adverbs to account for their similarities and differences?

In the following sections, we will show the similarities and the differences of *cháng* and *chángcháng* in section 2 and in section 3 respectively.

2   Similarities between *cháng* and *chángcháng*

We propose to analyze *cháng* and *chángcháng* as markers of 'verbal plurality' (Cusic, 1981: 64). In other words, we claim that the common function of *cháng* and *chángcháng* is to mark plurality in the verbal domain. This will be shown in section 2.1. In section 2.2, we look at the different levels of verbal plurality and we argue that *cháng* and *chángcháng* belong to a class of verbal plurality markers that operate at the occasion-level in the sense of Cusic (1981).

2.1   The common function of *cháng* and *chángcháng*

According to Cusic (1981), verbal plurality (PLv) markers transform a predicate denoting a single occurrence of an action into a predicate denoting multiple occurrences of that action. This transformation can be represented as follows.

Fig. 1. The function of verbal plurality (PLv) markers

The denotation of the multiple occurrences described by the predicate is illustrated in (3). If *cháng* or *chángcháng* is absent from the sentence, then the interpretation of the multiple occurrences described by the predicate is no longer possible – see (4).

(3)   他{**常/常常**}抓着我的手(每次都抓得我好痛).
       *Tā **cháng/chángcháng** zhuā-zhe wǒ-de shǒu.*
       he *cháng chángcháng* grab-Dur. my   hand
       (*měi-cì   dōu zhuā dé   hǎo tong*).
       every-time all grab until very pain

'He grabbed my hand often. (Every time, I was in pain from the grabbing.).

(4)   他抓着我的手. (#每次都抓得我好痛).
     Tā zhuā-zhe wǒ-de shǒu, (#*měi-cì   dōu zhuā dé   hǎo tong*).
     he grab-Dur. my   hand   every-time all   grab until very pain
     'He was grapping my hand. (#Every time, I was in pain from the grabbing.)

To sum up, we will treat *cháng* and *chángcháng* as PLv markers, in the sense illustrated above. In other words, one similarity between the two frequency adverbs is that they both contribute to the denotation of a plurality of occurrences of a certain action.

In the next sub-section, we will argue that the verbal plurality of both adverbs is at the "occasion-level", in the sense of Cusic (1981).

2.2   Different levels of verbal plurality

In Cusic (1981)'s framework, PLv can occur at three different levels: **phases**, **events** and **occasions**. The three different levels are illustrated in his examples reproduced below:

(5)   The mouse nibbled the cheese.
     ➔ **plurality of phases**

(6)   The mouse nibbled the cheese again and again on Thursday.
     ➔ **plurality of events**

(7)   Again and again, the mouse nibbled the cheese on Thursday.
     ➔ **plurality of occasions**

Phases refer to the plurality of event-internal parts; this is evident with certain lexical verbs (e.g. *to nibble*) that inherently express sub-events within an event. As pointed out by Tovena and Kihm (2008, p. 14), event-internal plurality is often expressed at the lexical level (French: *chanter* vs. *chantonner*; Italian: *mordere* vs. *mordicchiare*). In Mandarin, this is also the case: *chī miànbāo* 'eat bread' vs. *kěn miànbāo* 'nibble bread', etc.. In addition, Chinese contains verbal classifiers like *xià*, which overtly express phases, as in *kěn-sān-xià miànbāo* 'nibble bread three bites' (Paris, 2013).

Events can be pluralized with help of certain adverbs within a single time frame, making up one occasion occupying that said time frame. In (6) above, the pluralizing adverbial phrase is the post-verbal *again and again*: there is a single occasion (i.e. a particular Thursday) during which many events of mouse-nibbling took place. As we will show below, in Mandarin Chinese, *pínpín* 'repeatedly' is one such event-pluralizing adverb.

Occasions, in Cusic's three-tiered framework, are larger than events, and each occasion must occur within different time frames. Due to the topicalization of *again and again* in (7) above, there is a pluralizing effect on the occasion (the time frame provided by the temporal noun "Thursday").

The difference with "**events**" and "**occasions**" can be made clear in Mandarin Chinese, as illustrated in the ambiguous example below – see (8).

(8)　约翰生了三年的病.
　　Yuēhàn shēng-le sān-nián   de bìng.
　　John   fell-Acc three-years de ill
　　'John fell ill for three years'.
　　(a) First reading: The illness of John lasted three years.
　　(b) Second reading: John fell ill several times over a period of three years.

In the first reading, the single event of John being sick lasted for three years. In the second reading, there are multiple events of John being sick, and these events make up a group of events (or in our framework, they make up an occasion), which lasted three years.

2.2.1　The level of verbal plurality for *cháng* or *chángcháng*

Coming back to the adverbs *cháng* or *chángcháng*, we now argue that they are markers of PLv at the occasion-level only. In other words, they have a pluralizing effect only on occasions. *Cháng* and *chángcháng* can commute with *dōu*. *Dōu* is a marker of plurality for occasions (Cf. Yuan (2011:267). This can be seen in (9), where it co-occurs with a temporal subordinate introduced by *shí* 'while', an overt marker of occasions. In (9), the only interpretation possible is that there are different speeches (i.e. different occasions) that are being referred to.

(9)　他听演讲时，{**常**/**常常**/**都**}点头.
　　Tā tīng   yǎnjiǎng shí,   cháng/chángcháng/dōu   diǎn tóu.
　　he listen speech   while   cháng/chángcháng all   nod head
　　a. for *chǎng/chángcháng* : 'He <u>often</u> nodded while listening to a [different] speech.'
　　b. for *dōu* : '<u>Every time</u> when he listened to a speech, he nodded.'

This is in contrast with the adverb *pínpín* 'repeatedly', which induces plurality of actions at the "events" level instead, within a single occasion (i.e. during the same speech).

(10)　他听演讲时，{**频频**}点头.

*Tā tīng   yǎnjiǎng shí,   **pínpín**   diǎn tóu.*

he listen speech while   repeatedly nod head

'He repeatedly nodded while listening to the [same] speech.'

2.2.2　Further evidence that *cháng*/*chángcháng* marks occasion-level PLv

We will now provide four further tests to support our claim that *cháng* and *chángcháng* are occasion-level PLv markers, unlike *pínpín*, which is an event-level PLv marker. The four tests that we put forward relate to their (1) compatibility with durational complements, (2) compatibility with specific reference to a single occasion, (3) scope relative to a temporal subordinate clause and (4) requirement for longer unbounded reference time frames:

Firstly, durational complement can only specify the duration of a single event or a single occasion. However, the adverb *cháng* or *chángcháng* forces the interpretation of a plurality of occasions. As a result, occasion-level PLv markers (like *cháng* or *chángcháng*) are incompatible with durational complements because the multiple occasions cannot be distributed over the duration expressed by the post-verbal durational complement, as Yuan (2011: 255) observed. Hence *cháng* and *chángcháng* can never co-occur with durational complements – see (11).

(11)　*他不说话，只是**常/常常**点头，点了十五分钟.

Tā bú shuōhuà, zhǐshì **cháng/**chángcháng** diǎn tóu, diǎn-le shíwǔ fēnzhōng.*

he neg speak   only *cháng*/*chángcháng* nod head nod-Acc fifteen minutes

On the other hand, the adverb *pínpín*, which merely pluralizes events within a single occasion, can co-occur with durational complements. For example, in (12), it is the duration of the single occasion (consisting of multiple nodding events) that is being expressed.

(12)　他不说话，只是**频频**点头，点了十五分钟.

*Tā bú shuōhuà, zhǐshì **pínpín**　diǎn tóu, diǎn-le   shíwǔ fēnzhōng.*

he neg speak   only repeatedly nod head nod-Acc fifteen minutes

'He did not speak; all he did was to nod repeatedly for 15 minutes.'

Secondly, because PLv markers signal a plurality of occasions, they are incompatible with the explicit reference to a single occasion. In example (13), the specific reference of a particular occasion is made explicit through the use of the demonstrative-classifier phrase *nà-cì*; this blocks the use of *cháng* and *chángcháng* because these adverbs must operate at the occasion-level. However, the adverb *pínpín* is perfectly acceptable with since it merely marks the plurality of events, which can all occur within a single occasion – see (14).

(13) *他<u>那次</u>听演讲时，**常/常常**点头.
     *Tā <u>nà-cì</u> tīng yǎnjiǎng shí,   **cháng/chángcháng** diǎn tóu.
     he that-Cl. listen. speech   while cháng/chángcháng nod head
     (Intended: 'He often nodded while listening to that speech.')

(14) 他<u>那次</u>听演讲时，**频频**点头.
     Tā <u>nà-cì</u> tīng yǎnjiǎng shí,   **pínpín**   diǎn tóu.
     he that-Cl. listen speech while   repeatedly nod head
     'He repeatedly nodded while listening to that speech.'

Thirdly, occasion-level PLv markers can have temporal subordinate clauses within their scope, like in (15): the pluralizing effect is on the action described in the temporal subordinate clause, and the example in (15) is interpreted as saying that there are many speech occasions, such that someone nods during the speech. This is impossible with an event-level PLv marker such as *pínpín*, as (16) shows.

(15) 他**常/常常**听演讲时点头.
     Tā **cháng/chángcháng** tīng yǎnjiǎng shí   diǎn tóu.
     he cháng/chángcháng listen speech   while   nod head
     'He often nodded while listening to a [different] speech.'

(16) *他**频频**听演讲时点头.
     *tā **pínpín**   tīng yǎnjiǎng shí   diǎn tóu.
     he repeatedly listen speech   while   nod head
     (Intended: 'He repeatedly nodded while listening to a speech.')

Fourthly, the reference time for occasion-level PLv markers should preferably be longer and unbounded, as it must be possible to perceive of that reference time as one in which multiple occasions can occur. Example (17) shows that when the adverb *cháng* or *chángcháng* is used, then a longer unbounded reference time like *xiǎoshíhòu* 'in one's youth' is perfectly acceptable while a shorter bounded reference time like *zuótiān* 'yesterday' is less acceptable. Example (18) shows that the converse is true: when the adverb *pínpín* is used, then it is the reference time *zuótiān* 'yesterday' that is acceptable, while the reference time *xiǎoshíhòu* 'in one's youth' is less acceptable.

(17) {小时候/^{??}昨天}他**常/常常**搭错车.
     Xiǎoshíhòu /^{??}Zuótiān   tā **cháng/chángcháng** dā cuò   chē.
     When-young   yesterday   he cháng/chángcháng take wrong bus
     <u>When he was young</u>/(??Yesterday), he often took the wrong bus.'

(18) {$^{??}$小时候/昨天}他**频频**搭错车.
$^{??}$*Xiǎoshíhòu/ Zuótiān,   tā pínpín   dā cuò   chē.*
When-young yesterday   he *repeatedly* take wrong bus
'Yesterday/($^{??}$When he was young), he repeatedly took the wrong bus.'

The above tests all point to the conclusion that *cháng* and *chángcháng* are occasion-level PLv markers – unlike *pínpín*, which is an event-level PLv marker.

2.3   Summary: Properties of *cháng*(*cháng*)

To sum up, we have established that *cháng* and *chángcháng* both express verbal plurality, and that they apply on the occasion-level only, i.e. these adverbs quantify only over occasions. The specific differences between *cháng* / *chángcháng* (markers of occasion-level PLv) and *pínpín* (marker of event-level PLv) are given below.

Table 1. Properties of *cháng* / *chángcháng* vs. *pínpín*

	Properties of *cháng/chángcháng*	Properties of *pínpín*
Level of verbal plurality	Occasion-level PLv	Event-level PLv
Durational complements	No	Yes
Specific singular occasion	No	Yes
Scope over temporal clause	Yes	No
Time frames	Longer and unbounded	Shorter and bounded

3   Differences between *cháng* and *chángcháng*

We now present some basic differences between *cháng* and *chángcháng*. We shall focus on the two following differences: (i) the different sentence types that they can occur in, and (ii) their different semantic functions.

3.1   Sentence types: characterizing vs. particular sentences

Although the two frequency adverbs are both PLv markers, they appear in different types of sentences: *cháng* occur in sentences that express timeless characterizing properties while *chángcháng* occur in sentences that describe episodes that take place in time. The difference between characterizing (generic) sentences and particular (episodic) sentences is due to Krifka *et al* (1995: 19–23).

We provide two tests below to show the differentiation of the two frequency adverbs: (1) compatibility with the two negation markers and (2) the compatibility with the *shi...de* construction.

3.1.1 Property negation vs. episodic negation

One way of differentiating the different sentence types that *cháng* and *chángcháng* appear in is by looking at their compatibility with the types of negation in Mandarin Chinese. Chan (2011: 52) demonstrated that in Chinese, the two negation markers function differently: *bù* negates a property (individual-level predication) while *méi* negates the existence of an episodic actions (stage-level predication), as (19) illustrates. In other words, with *bù*, the sentence is a characterizing (generic) sentence regarding a property of Zhangsan, while with *méi*, the sentence is a particular (episodic) sentence.

(19) 张三**不/没**等迟到的人。
    *Zhāngsān **bù** /**méi** děng chídào-de rén.*
    Zhangsan neg/neg wait late   person
    With *bù*: 'ZS does not wait for latecomers' (characterizing property)
    With *méi*: 'ZS did not wait for latecomers' (particular episode)

Example (20) further shows that the sentence with *cháng* can be negated with *bù*, but not with *méi*, while example (21) shows that the sentence with *chángcháng* can be negated with *méi*, not with *bù*.

(20) 张三不/*没**常**游泳。
    *Zhāngsān bù /*méi **cháng** yóuyǒn.*
    Zhangsan neg/neg   *cháng* swim
    'ZS <u>does</u> not swim often'   (characterizing property)

(21) 张三*不/没**常常**游泳。
    *Zhāngsān *bù /méi **chángcháng** yóuyǒng.*
    Zhangsan neg/neg *chángcháng* swim
    'ZS <u>did</u> not swim often'   (particular episode)

3.1.2 Individual-level predication and stage-level predication

Another way of differentiating between the characterizing sentence and particular sentences is through the use of the *shi* VP *de* construction, which "changes the value of the VP" (Paris, 1998: 149): in example (22), where the *shi* VP *de* construction is absent, the predication is a stage-level predication, but in example (23), where the *shi* VP *de* construction is present, the predication is an individual-level predication. The distinction between individual-level and stage-level predication is due to Kratzer (1995).

(22) 玛丽弹钢琴。
Mǎlì tán gāngqín.
Mary play piano
'Mary plays the piano.'

(23) 玛丽是弹钢琴的。
*Mǎlì **shì** tán gāngqín de.*
Mary be play piano   *de*
'Mary is a pianist.'

Since *cháng* helps to denote a generic property, it is expected that this adverb can occur as part of the VP in the *shi* VP *de* construction. This expectation is borne out, as shown in (24); however, when *chángcháng* is used instead, there is a perceived mismatch between the reference to particular episodes taking place in time and the timeless individual-level predication introduced by the *shi* VP *de* construction.

(24) 玛丽是**常**/***常常**弹钢琴的
*Mǎlì shì **cháng** / *****chángcháng** tán gāngqín de*
Mary be *cháng   chángcháng*   play piano   *de*
With *cháng:* 'It is often that Mary plays piano.' / Mary OFTEN plays piano.' (characterizing property)
With *chángcháng:* impossible.

In sum, we have shown that *cháng* and *chángcháng* appear in different sentence types, i.e. characterizing and particular sentences respectively.

3.2   Semantics: Habituality vs. Iterativity

The second difference between *cháng* and *chángcháng* that is worthy of mention resides in their semantic functions: *cháng* marks **habituality** and *chángcháng* marks **iterativity**. According to Bertinetto and Lenci (2012), "habituality consists of attributing a property to a given referent" (*ibid.*: 857) while iterativity merely involves repetition (*ibid.*: 852). Therefore, (25) can be interpreted differently depending on whether *cháng* or *chángcháng* is used: (25a) shows the semantic function of *cháng* is to assert a property while (25b) shows that the semantic function of *chángcháng* is to express a repetition of an action, taking place in time.

(25) 玛莉{**常**/ **常常**}看书.
*Mǎlì {**cháng** / **chángcháng** }kàn shū*
Mary *cháng   chángcháng*   read book
(a) With *cháng* (habitual):   'Mary often reads [PRESENT] books.'
(b) With *chángcháng* (iterative): 'Mary often read [PAST] books.'

The four following tests provide further evidence to our claim regarding the different semantic functions: (i) numerical specifiability, (ii) strictness of time frame, (iii) interpretation of framing time adverbials, and (iv) co-occurrence with an adverb expressing habit.

Firstly, Bertinetto and Lenci (2012: 855) explain that a habitual sentence, like (26) cannot be numerically specifiable, while an iterative sentence, as in (21), is numerically specifiable.

(26)   When he lived in Paris, Franck would often take the 8 o'clock train.
*/??**Specifically 30 times.**

(27)   In the past few years, Franck has often taken the 8 o'clock train.
Specifically 30 times.

Similarly, in (28), it is not possible to specify the number of occurrences of going to France when the adverb used is *cháng*, but when the adverb is *chángcháng*, then the numerical specification is acceptable.

(28)   保罗{常 / 常常}去法国。#他总共去了二十次。
Bǎoluó ***cháng* /*chángcháng*** qù Fǎguó. #*Tā zǒnggòng qù-le **èrshí** cì.
Paul   *cháng   chángcháng*   go France   He in-total go-Acc. **twenty** times
(a) With *cháng* (**Habitual**): # *impossible to specify numerically*
(b) With *chángcháng* (**Iterative**): 'Paul often went to France.
'He has gone there a **total of 20 times**''

Secondly, a habitual sentence like (29) cannot easily be framed by a strict time adverbial such as *between 1ˢᵗ May 2009 and 31ˢᵗ March 2010*, but with an iterative sentence like (30), this is completely acceptable (*ibid.*: 858).

(29)   ??**Between 1ˢᵗ May 2009 and 31ˢᵗ March 2010**, James used to cook at home. (= **Habitual**)

(30)   **Between 1ˢᵗ May 2009 and 31ˢᵗ March 2010**, James cooked at home. (= **Iterative**)

In the same way, the predication with *cháng* cannot easily be framed by such an adverbial of strict time frame, while this is not a problem with the predication with *chángcháng*.

(31)   从五月一号到六月二十号，保罗{??常/常常}在家下厨。
Cóng wǔyuè yī-hào dào liùyuè èrshí-hào,
From May First to June Twentieth,
*Bǎoluó {??**cháng/chángcháng**} zài jiā   xiàchú.*
Paul   *cháng/chángcháng*   at home cook

(a) With *cháng* (**Habitual**): **??**
(b) With *chángcháng* (**Iterative**): '**From 1/5 to 20/6,** Paul often cooked at home.'

Thirdly, a time adverbial such as *last year* can be interpreted differently: either as a reference time when it co-occurs with a habitual sentence, like in (32), or as a strict time adverbial when it co-occurs with an iterative sentence as (33) (*ibid.*: 857).

(32)   **Last year**, the members used to wear black ties in their meetings.
(➔ "**Last year**" is the reference time for the habitual sentence).

(33)   **Last year**, the members wore black ties in their meetings.
(➔ "**Last year**" is a strict time adverbial for the actual occurrences).

In (34), the time adverbial *nà-duàn shíjiān* 'that period of time' or *xiǎo-shíhòu* 'when-young' can also be considered as a reference time for the sentence with *cháng*; but the same time adverbial is interpreted as a strict time adverbial the iterativity induced by *chángcháng*.

(34)   <u>那段期间 / 小时候</u>，保罗的母亲{**常/常常**}在家下厨。
Nà-duàn shíjiān /*Xiǎo-shíhòu*, *Bǎoluó de mǔqīn* ***cháng*** /***chángcháng***
zài jiā   xiàchú.
That-Cl. period /When-young, Paul de mother *cháng* /*chángcháng*
at home cook
(a) With *cháng* (**Habitual**): 'During that period of time/When he was young, Paul's mother used to often cook at home.
(b) With *chángcháng* (**Iterative**): 'During that period of time/When he was young, Paul's mother often cooked at home.

Fourthly, since *cháng* denotes habituality, it is expected to be compatible with the adverb expressing habit *àn tā-de xíguàn* 'according to his habit'. The expectation is borne out: (35) also shows that the adverb expressing habit cannot co-occur with *chángcháng*.

(35)   按他的习惯，保罗**常**/*/??**常常**到户外跑步。
àn tā-de xíguàn,   Bǎoluó **cháng**/*/??**chángcháng*** *dào hùwài pǎobù.*
according to one's habits Paul   *cháng* / *chángcháng* go-to outdoor jog
'**According to his habits**, Paul often goes outdoors for a jog.'

In this section, we have accounted for the distinction in semantic function between *cháng* and *chángcháng* with the four tests. *Cháng* is a marker of habituality while *chángcháng* is a marker of iterativity.

3.3   Summary of semantic differences

The four tests distinguishing *cháng* and *chángcháng* with respect to habituality and iterativity are summarized in the table below.

Table 2.   Tests of the semantic difference between *cháng* and *chángcháng*

	chángcháng (Iterativity)	*cháng* (Habituality)
Numerical specifiability	Yes	No
Strictly delimiting time frame	Yes	No
Determinability of framing time adverbial	Potentially determinable	Non-determinable
Co-occurrence with adverb expressing habit	No	Yes

4   Conclusion

In this paper, we have presented the similarities and the differences between the two frequency adverbs, *cháng* and *chángcháng*. Both are PLv markers at the occasion-level since they denote a multiplicity of occasions during which events described by the predicate take place. They appear in different sentence types: *cháng* is used in a **characterizing sentence**, *while chángcháng* is used to denote **particular events**. Their semantic functions are different: *cháng* marks **habituality**, *while chángcháng* marks **iterativity**.

References

1. Bertinetto, P. M., Lenci, A: Habituality, pluractionality, and imperfectivity. In: Binnick, Robert I. (ed.) The Oxford Handbook of Tense and Aspect. Oxford University Press, New York (2012)
2. Chan, K.G.D.: La Négation et la Polarité en Chinois Contemporain. Unpublished doctoral dissertation, Université Paris-Diderot, France (2011)
3. Cusic, David: Verbal Plurality and Aspect, Unpublished PhD dissertation, Stanford University, Stanford (1981)
4. Diao, Y. J.: A Comparative Study of the Historical Evolution of the Adverbs cháng and chángcháng. Master's thesis, Qingdao University, China (2011). (刁玉娟:副词常和常常历史演变比较研究) (in Chinese)
5. Kratzer, A. Stage-level/individual-level predicates. In: Carlson, G. and Pelletier, F. J. (eds.) The Generic Book, pp. 125–175. University of Chicago Press, Chicago (1995).
6. Krifka, M., Pelletier, F.J., Carlson, G.N., ter Meulen, A., Link, G., Chierchia, G.: Genericity: an introduction. In: Carlson, G. and Pelletier, F. J. (eds.) The Generic Book, pp. 2–124. University of Chicago Press, Chicago (1995).
7. Li, D.: Learner's Chinese-English Dictionary. Tuttle Publishing, Vermont (2005)
8. Li, S.: Analysis of the acquisition of synonyms chángcháng and cháng. Adult education 242(3): 83–84 (2007). (李姝:试析同义词常常和常的习得, 成人教育) (in Chinese)
9. Paris, M.-C.: Focus operators and types of predication in Mandarin. Cahiers de Linguistique Asie-Orientale, 27(2): 138–159 (1998).
10. Paris, M.-C.: Verbal reduplication and verbal classifiers in Chinese. In: Cao, G., Chappell, H., Djamouri, R. and Wiebusch, T. (eds.) Breaking Down the Barriers, pp. 257–278. Academia Sinica, Taipei (2013).

11. Tovena, L.M., Kihm, Alain.: Event internal pluractional verbs in some Romance languages. Recherches linguistiques de Vincennes, **37**: 9–30 (2008).
12. Yang, J. Z., Jia, Y. F.: 1700 Groups of Frequently Used Chinese Synonyms. (Chinese Reference Series for Foreigners) Beijing Language and Culture University Press, Beijing. (2005)
13. Yuan, Hua-Hung: Quelques aspects de la quantification en chinois mandarin: pluralité et distributivité, PhD dissertation, Université Paris-Diderot (2011).
14. Zou, H. Q.: The scope and types of frequency adverbs. Chinese Teaching in the World 77, 36–45 (2006). (邹海清:频率副词的范围和类别, 世界汉语教学) (in Chinese)

On the distributive nature of adverbial *quan* in Mandarin Chinese

Lucia M. Tovena[1] and Yan Li[2]

[1] Université Paris VII
tovena@linguist.univ-paris-diderot.fr
[2] Université Paris VII
liyanlf@hotmail.com

Abstract. The Chinese adverbial *quan* is analysed as an event predicate modifier that can force a distributive reading on a sentence by targetting a nominal that expresses a plural participant in the event, and encapsulating the distributive function in the θ-role associated with such a participant. This solution enables us to model the speakers' intuition of an 'overall evaluation' associated with *quan*.

Keywords: Formal semantics, distributivity, non-differentiation, adverbial *quan* in Chinese

1 Introduction

This paper is about the distributive nature of adverbial *quan* in Mandarin Chinese. *Quan* is a single morpheme[1] that means something like 'all', 'entirely' or 'entire', and can be an adjective (1a,b) or an adverbial (1c,d) (Lü, 1980).[2]

(1)   a. Quan ban yiqi qu tubu.
          Whole class together go hiking
          The whole class goes hiking together.

      b. Zhe xilie congshu quan-bu-quan?
          DEM collection book complete-negation-complete
          Is this book collection complete?

      c. Zhe shi quan xin de shu.
          DEM be completely new DE book
          This is a brandly new book.

      d. Zhexie nansheng quan shi wo de boshisheng.
          DEM-pl boy all be pro.1sing DE PhD student
          These boys are all my PhD students.

---

[1] In terms of morphology, *quan* can combine with another morpheme and form a new word. Ex. *quan-bu* also means 'all' in Chinese. It can occur either in the determiner position, or the head position of a nominal phrase, or an adverbial position.

[2] Abbreviations used throughout in the glosses: ASP = perfective aspect; ASPExp = experiential aspect; BEI = bei-construction; Cl = classifier; DEM = demonstrative; pl = plural; pro = pronoun; sg = singular.

© Springer International Publishing AG 2016
M. Dong et al. (Eds.): CLSW 2016, LNAI 10085, pp. 497–511, 2016
DOI: 10.1007/978-3-319-49508-8_47

We focus on *quan* with a single semantic type and functioning like an adverb as shown in (1d). In (1d), *quan* is interchangeable with *dou*. More generally, in its adverbial use, *quan* exhibits many syntactic and semantic similarities with *dou*, e.g. it must occur immediately before the verb and it forces a distributive reading of the subject (2) or preverbal object (3), which act as sorting keys (Choe, 1987). They differ insofar as *quan* has a more restricted distribution.

(2)   Xuesheng quan/dou pao-le.
       Student   all   run-ASP
       The students all ran away.

(3)   Zhexie   pingguo Mali quan/dou chi-wan-le.
       DEM-Pl apple   Mali all   eat-finish-ASP
       These apples, Mali has eaten them all.

Quan has been discussed mainly by comparing it with *dou*, at least in the recent literature on formal linguistics written in English. The role of distributor and/or universal quantifier of the Mandarin Chinese functional morpheme *dou* has been studied extensively, (Lee, 1986; Cheng, 1995; Lin, 1998, i.a.). We acknowledge the relevance of the comparison for their adverbial uses, where there are similarities. However, we consider that one must leave aside the scalar use of *dou*, in the *lian* ... *dou* construction, because *quan* does not admit a scalar interpretation. We also leave aside cases where adverbial *quan* cooccurs with *dou*, e.g. (4).

(4)   Tamen   quan-dou huidao-le   faguo.
       Pro.3.pl all   go-back-ASP France
       They all went back to France.

In our view, adverbial *quan* is an event predicate modifier that can force a distributive reading on a sentence by targetting a nominal that expresses a plural participant in the event, and encapsulating the distributive function in the θ-role associated with such a participant. This treatment avoids decomposing the distributive quantification into sets of assignments, hence sub-participants and subevents are not accessible. This solution enables us to model a property that could be termed 'wholeness', for want of a better term, that shows in *quan*'s resistance to event differentiation.

The paper is organised as follows. The main properties of *quan* and some of its peculiarities are recalled while discussing previous literature in §2. Next, we look specifically at the distributivity of *quan* in §3 and present cases where the sorting key is a single individual or a bare noun in generic phrases. We also discuss the incompatibility of *quan* with adverbs that differentiate subevents among them. This empirical evidence motivates our analysis in terms of event-predicate modifier developed in §4. The main contributions of the paper are summarised in §5.

2 The adverbial use of *quan*

Tomioka and Tsai (2005) have claimed that *quan* is not a distributive quantifier by itself. *Quan* is acceptable in a sentence with intrinsically distributive predicates such as *leave*, e.g.(5a), but it is not acceptable in a sentence with an ambiguous predicate that gets only collective reading in the absence of a distributive marker (5b), and acquires distributive only reading when *dou* is present (5c). These data are taken to show that *quan* is compatible with sentences with distributive reading and incompatible with collective reading, and that it is unable to induce distributivity. As a consequence, Tomioka and Tsai (2005) claim that *quan* is a domain regulator that ensures a good fitting cover (Brisson, 1998). The good fitting cover is the value assigned to the domain variable (Cov) of a distributive operator. *Dou* can function as a distributive operator, and *quan* can constrain its domain of quantification. The acceptability of example (5d) is taken to confirm that the acceptability of *quan* depends on the presence of a distributive operator.

(5) a. Tamen quan likai-le.
         pro.3.pl all   leave-ASP
         They all left.
     b. *Tamen quan mai-le   yi bu chezi.
         pro.3.pl all   buy-ASP one Cl car
         They all bought a car.
     c. Tamen dou mai-le   yi bu chezi.
         pro.3.pl all buy-ASP one Cl car
         They all bought a car.
     d. Tamen quan-dou mai-le   yi bu chezi.
         pro.3.pl all   buy-ASP one Cl car
         They all bought a car.

In their analysis, Tomioka and Tsai also point out that *quan* is unacceptable with a *wh*- in (6) and a *mei* 'every' NP in (7). We come back to these examples when discussing the property of 'wholeness' of *quan*.

(6) shei dou/*quan lai-le
     who all   come-ASP
     Everyone has come.

(7) Mei ge laoshi dou/*quan lai-le.
     Every Cl teacher all   come-ASP
     Every teacher has come.

Tomioka and Tsai's argument for the unacceptability of *quan* in (5b), is rejected by Lee et al. (2013), who ascribe its unacceptability to the 'once-only' interpretation of *buy one x*. In their view, this interpretation is a consequence of the specificity of the object, as NPs with the numeral 'one' tend to have a specific interpretation in Chinese. Lee et al. point out that it is not the case that the buy-type predicates cannot co-occur with *quan*, as shown by example (8), where the numeral is *wu* 'five'.

(8)   Tamen quan mai-le   wu ben shu
      pro.3.pl all   buy-ASP five Cl   book
      They all bought five books.

Lee et al. claim that a treatment of *quan* cast exclusively in terms of domain regulation is inadequate, contra Tomioka and Tsai. They propose that *quan* has two functions, it is a domain regulator when there is a distributivity operator, or else a universal quantifier. Cases like (8), where the predicate, in principle, admits collective and distributive readings, and where there in no overt distributive operator, are instances of *quan* as a universal A-quantifier (Bach et al., 1995). In cases where a distributive operator such as *dou* is overtly present (5d), *quan* is analysed as a domain regulator.

However, Lee et al. do not note the possibility of a kind reading for the nouns phrase in object position in (5b). This reading is not accounted for under their claim is that ungrammaticality follows from the specific only interpretation of postverbal NPs with the numeral *yi* 'one', a claim that cannot apply to (5c) either. Under the kind reading, the sentence is interpreted distributively and more than one buying event of the same type of car can take place. We concede that this reading is subject to speaker variation. Next, Lee et al. also impose a plurality condition that rules out potentially ambiguous predicates with singular objects such as *mai le yi bu chezi* 'buy one car' in (5b). This would account for the difference between (5b) and (8). However, the data are not complete, as plurality is not always required. Singular NPs can play the role of distributive key for *quan*, see (17) below, and (9) from Tomioka and Tsai (2005). Moreover, *yi* can occur in direct object position in a distributive sentence and get non-specific interpretation. The truth conditions of (10) require each child to recite one poem, without specifying whether the same or different poems are recited.

(9)   Zhe   ben shu   wo   quan kan-wan-le
      DEM Cl   book pro.1.sing all   read-finish-ASP
      I finished reading all parts of this book.
(10)   Zhexie   haizi quan langsong-le yi shou shige
      DEM-pl boy   all   recite-ASP a Cl   poem
      All the boys recited a poem.

Sentence (10) needs a more sophisticate approach to predicate classification, one that takes into consideration the properties of thematic roles. The nature of the thematic role discharged by the phrase with *yi* matters, given that *yi* can occur in the distributed share (Choe, 1987) provided the referent of the nominal is not affected. Non-affectedness makes it possible to iterate through all the members of the sorting key in (10). On the contrary, a set of individuals cannot be exclusively separate buyers of the same car, without being sellers in the next buying subevent (5b). From this it does not follow that buying-a-car is a once-only event, since a car can be bought many times. But *buy* being a transfer of possession verb, a car cannot be bought repeatedly in a context where only the buyer is checked to vary systematically.

Now that is clear that cases like (5a), (8) and (10) do not require a double analysis of *quan*, the empirical ground in support of such a distinction reduces to the three specific cases Lee et al. insist on when illustrating where *quan* functions as a universal quantifier, namely when it combines with a collective predicate such as *shi pengyou* 'be friends', see (11); when it quantifies on a domain of degrees such as *quan ping ganjue* 'completely on feeling', see (12); and when it associates with focus in a focus structure, see (13).

(11) Women quan shi tongxue/pengyou.
      pro.1.pl all   be classmates/friends
      We are all classmates/friends.
(12) Ta   quan ping   ganjue daqiu
      pro.3.sg all   depend feeling play-ball
      He plays ballgames depending totally on his intuition.
(13) Ta   quan xie   de [xiaoshuo]$_f$
      pro.3.sg all   write DE novel
      All he wrote are novels.

At least three different collective predicates are discussed by Tomioka and Tsai and Lee et al. They are provided in (11), (14) and (15).

(14) *Women quan shi yi   ge da tuanti.
      pro.1.pl all   be one Cl big group
      We are all a big group.
(15) Women quan zai dating jihe.
      pro.1.pl all   in hall   gather
      We all gathered in the hall.

Lee et al. tackle the variation between (14) and (15) by endorsing the analysis that Tomioka and Tsai take from Brisson (1998), cast in terms of predicates endowed/not endowed with a DO$_{plural}$ component and invoking a plurality condition. The predicate *jihe* 'gather' has such a subcomponent and example (15) is fine. On the contrary, the predicate *shi yi ge da tuanti* 'be a big group' doesn't and (14) is out. As for the predicate *shi tongxue/pengyou* 'be classmate/friends', it is said not to have such a component according to such a classification, but (11) is fine. Lee et al. rule this case in by assuming a different analysis of *quan*, namely as a universal quantifier. In short, the grammaticality judgements on the three cases in (11), (14) and (15) require assuming two types of collective predicates and two functions of *quan*, according to Lee et al.

However, the property of symmetry naturally splits collective predicates into the same two groups that yield (un)acceptable sentences when *quan* is added. The predicates *jihe* 'gather' and *shi tongxue/pengyou* 'be classmate/friends' are both symmetric, and sentences (15) and (11) are fine. The predicate *shi yi ge da tuanti* 'be a big group' is not symmetric, and (14) is out. Symmetry is a relevant property because symmetric predicates enforce a strong form of equity among individuals, hence condition (27) discussed below, is bypassed. In short, the acceptability of (11) is not strong evidence for assuming that *quan* plays a distinct function from what it does in (15).

Second, we observe that the case in (12) is much closer to (13) than suggested by Lee et al.'s discussion. Indeed (12) can be understood as 'he plays ballgames only on his intuition', in which case the set of alternatives that is evoked and the whole information structure is close to that of (13). Alternatives are ordered in such a 'only' interpretation, but *quan* is known not to have scalar uses. Example (12) is peculiar also because it may have a syntactic structure that differs from all the other cases, insofar as *quan* takes scope on the right.

Beside the partial similarity with *dou*, a second characteristics of *quan* that has been discussed in the literature concerns a property of wholeness. Zhou (2011) notices that speakers have the intuition of a global predication on the key, and calls it the property *zhengti xing* 'integrity' in Chinese. Zhou's proposal is cast in informal terms and cannot be easily integrated in a formal analysis of *quan*. Furthermore, what he calls 'global predication' must satisfy distributivity anyway, since (16) is true in a situation where twenty five flowers are bought.

(16)   Zhe   wu ge xuesheng quan mai-le   wu duo hua.
       DEM five Cl student   all   buy-ASP five Cl flower
       These five students have all bought five flowers.

Lee et al. invoke a set-prominent property when they discuss Tomioka and Tsai's treatment of *wh-* and *mei* cases. Recall that Tomioka et Tsai argue that *quan* is neither distributive nor quantificational, and they do not take a clear stand on the compatibility of *dou* with *wh-*. For them *dou* is either a distributive operator, or an adverb of quantification. As for *mei*, Tomioka and Tsai follow Lin (1996, 1998), according to whom *mei* itself imposes a good-fitting cover and has a maximality function. As a consequence, *mei* would completely trivialise the function of *quan*, and this accounts for their unacceptable cooccurrence. Following a different approach, Lee et al. argue that the incompatibility of *quan* with *mei* should not be explained in terms of redundancy. They argue that *mei* 'inherently demonstrates an individual-prominent property', and emphasizes that there is no exception among individuals. On the contrary, *quan*, like *suoyou* 'all', is compatible only with quantified NPs with a set-prominent property. As a consequence, they say, 'one cannot attribute the incompatibility between *quan* and *mei* merely to the fact that both can serve as a good-fitting cover to its associated NP and compete for the same NP'. The compatibility of *quan* with the sum operator *suoyou* is taken to show that their semantics share an inherent set-prominent property. As for *wh*-universals, these are said to operate at the level of individuals as well. Hence, they are compatible with the individual-prominent property of *dou*, and incompatible with *quan*.

However, it is not clear how the set-prominent property Lee et al. argue for meshes with the rest of their analysis. They do not explain why the fact that *quan* is a domain regulator should matter for the fact that *mei* has the individual-prominent property. Other unanswered questions are whether *quan* still has such a set-prominent property when it is a universal quantifier, and if it does, what is the difference with a collective reading; and how come *quan* can cooccur with individual-prominent *dou* in sentences like (4).

3   The distributivity of *quan*

3.1   Extending the empirical coverage

The treatment of *quan* must be extended to cover cases where the sorting key is one individual, and a distributive thematic role relates its parts to subevents. This type of data with singular nominals working as key show that *quan* is not just licensed by a distributive predicate or operator, but plays a more active role in bringing about a distributive reading. Let's start by example (17), where there is no obvious source of distributivity alternative to *quan*, and *quan* is acceptable. The book is the sorting key and there is a form of contextually relevant equipartition applied on it, where each cell is a suitable patient in a doodling event. The book is doodled if scribbled pages occur here and there, but a bit everywhere.

(17)   Zhe   ben shu   quan bei   luan tu luan hua-le
       DEM Cl   book all   BEI doodle-ASP
       This book is all doodled.

Next, consider (18). No obvious difference in meaning is observed between (18) and (19). Furthermore, *dou* is not acceptable in the same context, see (20).

(18) Zhe ge pingguo, Mali quan chi-wan-le.
      DEM Cl apple   Mali all   eat-finish-ASP
      This apple, Mali has eaten it all.
(19) Zhe ge pingguo, Mali chi-wan-le.
      DEM Cl apple   Mali eat-finish-ASP
      This apple, Mali has eaten it.
(20) *Zhe ge pingguo, Mali dou chi-wan-le.
      DEM Cl apple   Mali all   eat-finish-ASP
      This apple, Mali has eaten it all.

Again, *quan* appears to impose a partition on a participant so that the predicate applies to the cells of the partition, and all the cells are related to subevents by the same thematic role. Further evidence that this is the correct analysis comes from the fact that, if the predication cannot meaningfully apply to the cells, the sentence is out, whether *quan* or *dou* is used, see (21). In (18) each portion of the apple is a patient in the eating event. On the contrary, it is not the case that each portion of the boy in (21) is an 'initiator-theme' in the event of arriving. The contrast between (18) and (20) suggests that it is not the case that the distribution of adverbial *quan* is a proper subset of the distribution of *dou*.

(21) *Zhe ge haizi quan/ dou lai-le.
      DEM Cl boy all/   all arrive-ASP
      This boy has all arrived.

Moreover, *quan* is acceptable even in a sentence where it is stated explicitly that the domain of the sorting key is an individual and there is an event with a single temporal or spatial trace, which at first sight is a problem for distributivity at large, see (22). By emphasising that every bit of the fish is a patient of my eating, the fact that the whole fish has been eaten gets emphasised too, and vice-versa. This is compatible with my eating the fish in a single go.

(22) Zhe tiao yu, wo   yi kou   quan chi-le
      DEM Cl fish pro.1.sg one mouth all   eat-ASP
      This fish, I have eaten it all in one mouthful.

Finally, consider generic sentences with bare nouns. *Quan* differs from *dou* insofar as it cannot occur in generic sentences featuring individual-level predicates, e.g. *shi buru dongwu* 'be a mammal' in (23).

(23) a. *Shizi quan shi buru dongwu.
          Lion all   be mammal
          Lions are all mammals.
      b. Shizi dou shi buru dongwu.
          Lion all   be mammal
          Lions are all mammals.

Although the unacceptability of (23a) cannot be imputed directly to distributivity, otherwise the acceptability of (23b) would be surprising, we hypothesise that distributivity has got something to do with it. Note that *quan* is acceptable in generic sentences that differ from (23a) in a subtle way, illustrated by (24).

(24) (Na ge xingqiu shang de) Shizi quan shi buru dongwu.
      That Cl planet on DE lion all be mammal
      Lions (on that planet) are all mammals.

The bare noun *shizi* 'lion' in (23a) intensionally denotes the kind lion, including individuals that exist and that do not exist in specific worlds. The sentence states a definitional characteristics of lions. On the contrary, the denotation of the bare noun in (24) is restricted to lions that exist in that particular planet, because of the modifier that sets the context. In other words, sentence (24) expresses a contingent generalisation, and *quan* is acceptable. The bare noun can act as the sorting key of *quan*, which must be extensional. Another interesting case of contingent generalisation arises with descriptive generics with predicates such as *xihuan* 'like', see (25).

(25) a. Nüren   quan xihuan chengshu de   nanren.
        Woman all   like   mature DE man
        All women like mature men.
     b. Meiguoren quan xihuan chi hanbao.
        American all like   eat hamburger
        All Americans love eating hamburgers.

Example (25) illustrates a case of descriptive generic, whereas example (23a) is an *in virtue of* generic, in the words of Greenberg (2006). Greenberg is interested in the type of law-likeness of different forms of generics and in a mechanism to model their exception tolerance. She notes that the *in virtue of* generalisation illustrated by (23a) is true in virtue of a certain property, that the speaker has in mind, and the listener is supposed to accommodate. With descriptive generalisations, speakers do not characterise in what exact sense the possible worlds in which the generalisation is asserted to hold are similar to the actual world. Her distinction is relevant for us insofar as in descriptive generalisations, there is no commitment to an in virtue of factor that would make the proposition hold across worlds. In our view, the assertion is grounded in the contingency of the actual world. This allows us to build a bridge between cases with contextual restrictions such as (24) and descriptive generics such as (25), because it is plausible to assume that in both cases there is an extensional domain that can be the sorting key of *quan*. On the contrary, truly in virtue of generics such as (23a) are intensional and cannot host *quan*.

3.2 Drawing analogies

Adverbial *quan* can impose a distributive reading on a sentence, see (10), but clearly seems to be against event differentiation, as it appears from its incompatibility with adverbs such as *gezi* that differentiate subevents (Yang, 2013), see (26).

(26) *Tamen gezi   quan huidao-le   Faguo.
       pro.3.pl separately all   go-back-ASP France
       They all went back to France separate ways.

Event differentiation is one of the criteria that current research on scopal properties of distributive lexical items is exploring. The differentiation condition in (27) was proposed by Tunstall (1998) for modelling restrictions on lexically distributive determiners. The distributivity requirement for English *each* is stated to concern the event, which must be completely distributed, and the subevents that make up such a distributed event, which must be differentiated in some way. These two requirements are put together in condition (27).

(27) The Differentiation Condition (Tunstall, 1998)
       A sentence containing a quantified phrase headed by *each* can only be true of event structures which are totally distributive. Each individual object in the restrictor set of the quantified phrase must be associated with its own subevent, in which the predicate applies to that object, and which can be differentiated in some way from the other subevents.

For instance, *each* takes inverse scope in the preferred reading of (28a), so that subevents involve different agents and (27) is satisfied. *Every* is not subject to (27), and no preference for wide scope is reported with respect to (28b).

(28) a. A helper dyed each shirt
      b. A helper dyed every shirt

The incompatibility of *quan* with *mei*, the equivalent of 'each', can be interpreted as expressing a strong form of non-differentiation. Such a sensitivity is confirmed by the ungrammaticality of *quan* in sentences with other marks of inherent distributivity such as reduplicated classifiers (29).

(29) gege xuesheng dou/*quan mai-le   hua.
       ClCl student   all   buy-ASP flower
       Each student bought one flower/flowers

Going back to example (26), the event it describes is completely distributed, the subevents are in direct correspondence with the sub-bearers of the thematic role discharged by the sorting key constituent, and the sentence is unacceptable. Sentence (26) becomes acceptable if *gezi* is taken out, as if subevents were not to be differentiated and predication on the members of the key had to be homogeneous. Which subevent matches which sub-participant is information that should not be accessible if *quan* obeys a strong form of non-differentiation. Sentence (26) might be improved by altering the linear order (Shi Dingxu p.c.), which in Chinese tends to match semantic scope. But although it is slightly better, (30) is not accepted by most speakers.

(30)   ?*Tamen quan gezi   huidao-le   Faguo.
       pro.3.pl all   separately go-back-ASP France
       They all went back to France separate ways

More data confirming the incompatibility of *quan* with a differentiated distributive share, feature the adverbs *fenbie* 'disjointly' (31a), and *fenfen* 'successively' (31b). These examples confirm that no internal difference among subevents can be overtly expressed in the same clause.

(31)   a.   *Zhexie xuesheng fenbie   quan qu-le   Bali.
            DEM-pl student   disjointly all   go-ASP Paris
            These students all went to Paris seprately.
       b.   *Zhexie baogaozhe zai huiyi shang fenfen   quan fa-le   yan.
            DEM-pl participant at conference successively all make-ASP speech

            These participants all made a speech/speeches at conference successively.

The criterion of event differentiation helps us to make a fresh start on adverbial *quan*. First, non-differentiation gives us a way to characterise the form of homogeneous predication that cannot bring in differences within the key, and that is required by *quan* and incompatible with differentiating quantifiers such as *mei*. This homogeneity is behind the wholeness effect. Second, differentiation always concerns subevents, because *quan*—like floated *all* and unlike binominal *each* and distributive numerals—roughly speaking, need not distributively relate two (sets of) participants, but can do so, compare (5a) and (16). More precisely, the relevant θ-role relates individuals to events, and the individuals may well be the unique expressed participants in those events. This is usually not the case with share markers and binominal quantifiers.

4   A formalisation as event predicate modifier

The incompatibility of *quan* with a differentiated distributed share is reminiscent of the impossibility of having a sentence internal reading of *different* in clauses containing the distributor *one by one*, see (32) that has only a sentence external reading. The unavailable reading, where recited poems must differ among themselves, is the one that would obey the differentiation condition (27).

(32)   The boys recited a different poem one by one.

Brasoveanu and Henderson (2009) build on the reading restriction on (32) to argue for two routes to distributivity, one based on the decomposition of the distributive quantification into sets of assignments, exemplified by *each*, the other based on encapsulation into a function, exemplified by *one by one*. We assume that the ungrammaticality of sentences with *mei* and other forms of inherent distributivity such as reduplicated classifiers, follows from the fact that *quan* encapsulates part of a θ-role function. By modelling *quan* as event predicate modifier that targets a nominal discharging a θ-role, as in (33), we get a unified treatment of the distributivity and of the wholeness of adverbial *quan*.

(33) $\lambda^* P_{\varepsilon t} \ \lambda e_\varepsilon \ [^*P(e) \wedge \forall x \in Part(^*\theta(e)) \ \exists e' \leq e \ [\theta(e')=x \ ] \ ]$
      where Part is a non-trivial function

In prose, (33) says that *quan* contributes the dependency encapsulated in the θ-role function associated with the targeted participant. It requires the event to be plural, with subevents that are more than one because they are θ-associated with the cells of a non-trivial partition imposed on the referent of the nominal. The domain of the distribution relation is made of the cells of the partition returned by the function Part applied to $^*\theta(e)$, and the subevents are the range. The temporal dimension being irrelevant, subevents e' are equivalent distributed shares. Their characterisation is done in various ways. It can be provided mainly by a simple predicate, i.e. intransitive verbs (5a) and passives with suppressed agent (17), or a transitive verb with singular proper noun as subject when the key is the preverbal object (3). From the point of view of distributivity, these cases can be likened to quantifier float examples. Alternatively, it can be done by a transitive verb with its object, like in cases of binominal *each* and distributive numerals, e.g. (8) and (10). In this last case, numerical information from the object is crucial. We come back to this issue when discussing example (35) below.

Differently from Brasoveanu and Henderson, we keep fixed the semantic function of sorting key for the participant, because *quan* does not distribute over events. It is the information on its partition that is encapsulated, and consequently the identification of the subevents θ-related to the cells. $^*\theta(e)$ in (33) is independently valued and e is the dependent variable in the distributive relation. Encapsulation turns out to have an effect *à double détente*, on the share AND on the key. First, subevents cannot be differentiated other than by the participant whose value comes from a cell of the partition on the key, as illustrated by (26), and (31). Second, non-differentiation has an impact on the sorting key. When a quantificational structure is introduced by *mei* or other distributive items subject to condition (27), and the distributive share is the nuclear scope, incompatibility with the non-differentiated predication required by *quan* ensues, see (7). Conversely, when no distributive quantifier in the key NP imposes the satisfaction of condition (27), the condition is not triggered. The impossibility for the share/nuclear scope to introduce a differentiation among the elements of the key/restriction, licences the inference of a predication verified for the whole from a predication that is verified distributively and undiscriminatively on the parts. This implements a form of homogeneous inner distribution that we have called wholeness. The value of the whole key, which is the only value directly assigned by the assignment function, does not look partitioned by the predicate. This cumulative inference meshes with the status of dependent variable of e, which is required to be a plurality because the partition on the key is non-trivial.

The use of the partition on the key in (33) makes it possible to distribute over a key which is a singular individual, since the partition can 'split up' an entity. There is a restriction, though. The cells are related to subevents via the θ-role, thus each cell must be suitable for discharging such a role, recall the contrast between (18) and (21). Nothing requires that the cells of the key be anonymous, as supported by the acceptability of (34). The constraint of non visibility applies only to the share.

(34)   Mali, Lisi he   Wang quan lai-le
        Mali, Lisi and Wang all   come-ASP
        Mali, Lisi and Wang came.

In a distributive interpretation, constant shares are paired with constant key units (Tovena, 2016), whereas no constant size is required in cumulative interpretations. When the key is a sum of atoms, distribution may but need not be done over atoms. Atomicity and size identity of the key units seems a default that cannot be easily overturned when there is a numeral in the share, see (16). However, it appears that the cells of the key no longer have to be atomic or of equal size when the share is a subevent with a participant contributed by a bare noun. Indeed, example (35) has both distributive and cumulative readings. The lack of cardinality on the patient seems to have the effect of making it impossible to define subevents of constant size, and this seems to hamper the equipartition of the key. Thus, Part in (33) can be characterised as an equipartition only by default, not by definition. The mechanism by which non-constant shares block such a default is not clear at the moment. Nevertheless, it is clear that those who might consider *quan* to be a share marker, crucially have to concede that it is different from numeral modifiers like in Tlingit.

(35) Zhe wu ge xuesheng quan mai-le   hua.
      DEM five Cl student   all   buy-ASP flower
      These five students have all bought a flower/flowers

Definition (33) captures the distributivity effect via a universal quantifier on the key. The non-trivial partition on the key requires e to be a plural event. Pluralisation is directly exploited by Cable (2014), who takes a pair $<e,x>$ of individual and event pluralities to be basic, and claims to distribute within them via cumulation. Distribution is properly handled by the cumulation/sub-division mechanism, when the event plurality is the key. But when the key is an individual plurality, the mechanism does not specify how subevents are distributed over the key, because the plurality of individuals x in the pair $<e,x>$ is necessarily part of the share and corresponds to the participant with constant cardinality that identifies subevents, cf. the constraint '$\langle e,x \rangle = \sigma_{<e',y>}.y<x\wedge|y|=n\wedge e'<e\wedge$Participant$(e',y)$' in his formalisation. This cannot be correct for Chinese though, because (8), (16) and (10) are not ambiguous and are not felicitous in a scenario where e.g. the referent of the subject acts collectively or cumulatively in buying-five-books events. Moreover, we doubt that constant shares in general can be paired with non constant units of the key—be the latter a plurality of individuals or events—and still yield a true distributive dependency (Tovena, 2016).

The universal quantifier in (33) may seem too strong for the treatment of examples with collective predicates such as *he-xie* 'co-write' (Luo Qiong-peng p.c.). However, its function is to use up the sorting key, and no strong reciprocity ensues with symmetric predicates, in the sense of Dalrymple et al. (1998). The domain is exhaustified only for the key under the $\forall\exists$ mechanism, no need to exhaust the domain of co-authors for each author. What is waived by symmetry is the need to check that coauthors vary, hence condition (27) is not met.

5   Summing up

The distributive adverbial *quan* of Chinese is treated as an event predicate modifier that forces a distributive reading on a sentence by targeting a nominal that expresses a plural participant and modifying the θ-role that relates it to the event.

Distribution is only over participants, and it is subject to restrictions coming from the relevant θ-role. Examples where the sorting key is a singular individual, and descriptive generalisations based on extensional domains provide evidence for the distributivity of *quan*.

The incompatibility with adverbs that differentiate subevents, such as *gezi*, points toward a non-differentiation condition that also helps to explain native speakers' intuitions, who consistently describe *quan* as distributing over the members of the key while focussing on the whole key.

Bibliography

Bach, E., E. Jelinek, A. Kratzer, and B. Partee H. (1995). *Quantification in Natural Languages*. Dordrecht: Kluwer.

Brasoveanu, A. and R. Henderson (2009). Varieties of distributivity: *One by One* vs *each*. In *Proceedings of SALT XIX*, pp. 55–72.

Brisson, C. (1998). *Distributivity, maximality and floating quantifiers*. Ph. D. thesis, University of Rutgers.

Cable, S. (2014). Distributive numerals and distance distributivity in Tlingit (and beyond). *Language 90*, 562–606.

Cheng, L. (1995). On dou-quantification. *Journal of East Asian Linguistics 4*, 197–234.

Choe, J.-W. (1987). *Anti-Quantifiers and a Theory of Distributivity*. Ph. D. thesis, University of Massachusetts Amherst.

Dalrymple, M., M. Kanazawa, Y. Kim, S. Mchombo, and S. Peters (1998). Reciprocal expressions and the concept of reciprocity. *Linguistics and Philosophy 21*, 159–210.

Greenberg, Y. (2006). Tolerating exceptions with 'descriptive' and 'in virtue of' generics. In K. von Heusinger and K. Turner (Eds.), *Where Semantics Meets Pragmatics*, pp. 197–222. Amsterdam: Elsevier.

Lee, P.-L. P., H.-H. Pan, and L. Zhang (2013). Chinese adverbial *quan* as a dual-function operator: a domain restrictor and a universal quantifier. *Linguistics and the Human Sciences 8*, 169–204.

Lee, T. H.-t. (1986). *Studies on Quantification in Chinese*. Ph. D. thesis, University UCLA.

Lin, J.-w. (1996). *Polarity Licensing and Wh-phrases Quantification in Chinese*. Ph. D. thesis, University of Massachusetts, Amherst.

Lin, J.-w. (1998). Distributivity in Chinese and its implications. *Natural language semantics 6*, 201–243.

Lü, S.-X. (1980). *800 Major Words in Contemporary Chinese*. Beijing: Shangwu Yinshuguan. (现代汉语800词, 北京: 商务印书馆)[In Chinese].

Tomioka, S. and Y. Tsai (2005). Domain restrictions for distributive quantification in Mandarin Chinese. *Journal of East Asian Linguistics 14*, 89–120.

Tovena, L. M. (2016). Le type ratio parmi les configurations distributives. *Travaux de linguistique 72*.

Tunstall, S. L. (1998). *The interpretation of quantifiers: semantics and processing*. Ph. D. thesis, University of Massachusetts Amherst.

Yang, T.-H. T. (2013). Distributivity in Mandarin Chinese. *USTWPL 7*, 21–35.

Zhou, R. (2011). The semantic feature 'integrity' of *quan* (全) and its syntactic consequences. *Zhongguo Yuwen* (2). [In Chinese]

The Use of "Ná" and "Hold" Verbs by Bilingual Pre-School Children in Singapore

Ying Tong Yap, Helena Hong Gao

School of Humanities and Social Sciences,
Nanyang Technological University, 14 Nanyang Drive, Singapore 637332
yapy0022@e.ntu.edu.sg; helenagao@ntu.edu.sg

Abstract. Verb forms a major category of lexicon in any language. As our daily actions consist of mostly hand actions, it is important for bilingual speakers to be able to use different specific hand action verbs to describe the corresponding actions. This study focuses on one particular type of hand action, namely, holding actions, to examine Singaporean bilingual preschoolers' competencies in both English and Mandarin through their usage of holding verbs.

Thirty bilingual children between the ages of 3 and 6 were recruited for the study. In the experiment of the study, we used the standard PPVT-IV pictures and self-selected pictures of different holding actions as stimulus and asked the children to describe the actions in English and Chinese. The results show that most of the children used the Mandarin word "*ná*" (□) and the English word "*hold*" for almost all the scenarios of holding in the experiment.

Keywords: Mandarin, English, holding action verb, bilingual children, language acquisition

1   Introduction

Singapore is a multi-racial country where many languages co-exist in a single society. The four official languages of Singapore are namely English, Mandarin, Malay and Tamil, with English being the lingua franca of communication among all the ethnic groups, while the rest of the languages being the mother tongues of the respective ethnic groups. As Singapore implements a bilingual education policy, children are all taught in English and their mother tongues when they begin to go to kindergartens around at the age of three years old. All students are taught English in schools as their first language for most of the subjects and their mother tongues language as a second language during the language lesson.

Even though Singaporean children are bilingual, most of them are English-dominated in terms of language performance. With a final goal to help our children in becoming balanced bilinguals, this study is designed to explore English-Chinese bilingual children's varying competencies in their use of holding verbs in English and Mandarin. Factors that might be responsible for bilingual children in using holding

© Springer International Publishing AG 2016
M. Dong et al. (Eds.): CLSW 2016, LNAI 10085, pp. 512–523, 2016
DOI: 10.1007/978-3-319-49508-8_48

action verbs appropriately in both languages would be discussed. It is hopedthat the results of such a study could help language teachers in understanding more specifically in terms of the degree of proficiency the bilingual children have learned the two languages, accounting for some of the verbs being easier to learn over others, and what teaching methods could be applied in their teaching of domain-specific words to bilingual children.

2   Methodology

Thirty English-Chinese Singaporean bilingual children between the ages of 3 and 6 years old were recruited for this study.

There are in total four parts designed for this study. The first part consists of a parental report designed by Gao (2014) for the investigation of Singaporean bilingual children's lexical development.

The second part is a standard PPVT-IV test where children were being asked to identify pictures of simple objects. We used the results to determine whether the children's vocabulary size was within the normal range, which would serve as the benchmark for the children to continue with the third and fourth tests accordingly.

The third part is a picture test. Children were being asked to describe the different physical actions as shown in the picture.

The fourth part consists of pictures depicting different holding actions. Children were shown several pictures of a hand holding an object, one at a time. This test aims to investigate whether children are able to use different hand action verbs, that is, near-synonyms, in both languages, to identify holding actions in different manners. The objects being held by hands as shown in the pictures were commonly seen objects and thus are familiar to the children. Pictures were shown randomly in the slides. Some of them which were shown are as follow:

- two pictures with a hand holding a same object in two different manners appearing one after another
- two pictures with a hand holding a same object in different manners placed further apart; and
- two pictures with a hand holding different objects but are being held in a same manner.

3   Results and Analysis

3.1   Different Verbs Used in Describing Two Pictures with a Hand Holding a Same Object

In describing two pictures with a hand holding an identical object, the bilingual children were found to be able to apply different verbs particularly when the two pictures were placed in between other pictures. For example, Pictures 1 and 2 below illustrate that the manners of how the keys were being held are somewhat similar. The only directional difference is that the key in Picture 1 was facing upwards while the keys in Picture 2 were facing downwards.

Picture 1. Holding Action 1

Picture 2. Holding Action 2

The children were asked in both languages pertaining to what the hand was doing in the two pictures. The verbs that the children used in English included "hold", "take", "grab", and "carry". Among these, "hold" was used the most frequently, accounting 46.67% and 40.00% respectively for both figures. (See Table 1 and 2)

Most of the children who did not manage to say out the verbs responded instead by identifying the objects being held in the hand. Some also imitated the hand actions as shown in the figures or simply remained silent.

English	Verbs/Non-verbs	Children (no.)	%
	Hold	14	46.67%
	Take	1	3.33%
	Key	7	23.33%
	Don't know	5	16.67%
no hand	*Imitates action	1	3.33%
action	*Silence	2	6.67%
verbs used	Total Responses	30	100%

Table 1. Children's responses when being asked to describe Picture 1 in English

English	Verbs/Non-verbs	Children (no.)	%
	Hold/Holding	12	40.00%
	Carrying	1	3.33%
	Grabbing	1	3.33%
	Take	3	10.00%
	Key	9	30.00%
	Don't Know	2	6.67%
no hand action verbs used	*Imitates action	2	6.67%
	Total Responses	30	100%

Table 2. Children's responses when being asked to describe Picture 2 in English

When being asked to describe Pictures 1 and 2 in Mandarin, the children's responses varied significantly. In Picture 1, the Mandarin verbs used included "ná" (" 口 ": "to hold"_, "tōu" ("口 ": "to steal"), "zhuā" ("口 ": "to catch"), and "dǎ kāi" ("打开": "to open") (see Table 3). However, in describing Picture 2, the children used merely one verb, which was "ná" ("口 ": "to hold").

Mandarin	Verbs/Non-verbs	Children (no.)	%
	拿	13	43.33%
	偷	1	3.33%
	抓	1	3.33%
	Hold/Holding	3	10.00%
	打开	1	3.33%
	key	3	10.00%
	锁匙	1	3.33%
	Don't know	4	13.33%
no hand action verbs used	*Imitates action	2	6.67%
	*Silence	1	3.33%
	Total Responses	30	100%

Table 3. Children's responses when being asked to describe Picture 1 in Mandarin

Mandarin	Verbs/Non-verbs	Children (no.)	%
	拿	14	46.67%
	Hold/Holding	5	16.67%
	key	3	10.00%
	锁匙	2	6.67%
	Don't Know	2	6.67%
no hand	*Imitates action	2	6.67%
action	*Silence	2	6.67%
verbs used	Total Responses	30	100%

Table 4. Children's responses when being asked to describe Picture 2 in Mandarin

Tables 3 and 4 list the different verbs used to describe Pictures 1 and 2. This indicates that even though the same object was being held, the participants were able to differentiate the varying manners used in holding the same object. This is particularly true of the children's responses in English.

3.2   Varieties of Verbs used in English but not in Mandarin for Similar Pictures Shown Consecutively

Pictures 3 and 4 illustrate a hand holding some 10 dollar Singapore bills. The children used a variety of English holding verbs to describe them when these two pictures were placed next to each other.

Picture 3. Holding Action 3

Picture 4. Holding Action 4

The above two pictures differ from each other in terms of the manner of holding. Picture 3 shows simply a hand holding the dollar bills in a "relaxed" manner whereas in Picture 4, the hand is being clenched in a "tensed" manner.

Table 5 lists the different verbs used by the children to describe Picture 3 as "hold", "take" and "count". The verbs used to describe Picture 4 also include those verbs used in describing Picture 3 but with an additional 3 verbs which are namely "catch", "grab" and "squeeze" as listed in Table 6. This implies that the participants knew that the manners were different and they could use a variety of English verbs to differentiate the varying manners of a hand holding an identical object.

In reality, when one catches, grabs or squeezes an object, the hand tends to close up and clench. The children seemed to understand these physical differences and therefore used them accordingly to describe Picture 4. Their demonstration of these use of verbs also suggests that they knew that these verbs are different in that each verb indicates certain features that could be used to describe different holding actions. In this case, the semantic features of the English holding verbs "catch", "grab", and "squeeze" that can be differentiated from that of *hold* would be in terms of +more strength and +clenched fistetc.

English	Verbs/Non-verbs	Children (no.)	%
	Hold/Holding	9	30.00%
	Take	5	16.67%
	Counting	1	3.33%
	*Imitates action	4	13.33%
	Don't know	3	10.00%
no hand action verbs used	Money	8	26.67%
	Total Responses	30	100%

Table 5. Children's responses when being asked to describe Picture 3 in English

English	Verbs/Non-verbs	Children (no.)	%
	Hold/Holding	11	36.67%
	Take	4	13.33%
	Squeeze	1	3.33%
	Catching	2	6.67%
	Grabbing	3	10.00%
	*Imitates Action	4	13.33%
	Don't know	1	3.33%
no hand action	Money	4	13.33%
verbs used	Total Responses	30	100%

Table 6. Children's responses when being asked to describe Picture 4 in English

However, when the children were being asked to describe the same pictures in Mandarin, they used merely one verb "*ná*"("口 ") in describing the two actions. (See Table 7 and 8) This may imply that the participants had not yet acquired the different hand action verbs in Mandarin and hence were unable to use a different verb even though they were cognitively aware of the differences between the two scenarios. This explanation could be corroborated by their usage of a variety of English holding verbs.

Mandarin	Verbs/Non-verbs	Children (no.)	%
	拿	16	53.33%
	hold	1	3.33%
	count	1	3.33%
	take	1	3.33%
	Money	4	13.33%
	钱	2	6.67%
no hand	*Imitates action	4	13.33%
action	*Silence	1	3.33%
verbs used	Total Responses	30	100%

Table 7. Children' responses when being asked to describe Picture 3 in Mandarin

Mandarin	Verbs/Non-verbs	Children (no.)	%
	拿	11	36.67%
	Hold/Holding	2	6.67%
	Take	1	3.33%
	Squeeze	2	6.67%
	Catching	1	3.33%
	Money	2	6.67%
	钱	2	6.67%
	Don't know	3	10.00%
no hand	*Imitates Action	3	10.00%
action	*Silence	3	10.00%
verbs used	Total Responses	30	100%

Table 8. Children's responses when being asked to describe Picture 4 in Mandarin

3.3 Similar Verbs Used for Pictures of Hand Holding in a Similar Manner

It was also observed that the verbs used by the children were relatively similar in describing the pictures of hands holding different objects in a similar manner.

For example, as illustrated in Pictures 5 and 6, the holding manners of the objects are very similar.

Picture 5. Holding Action 5

Picture 6. Holding Action 6

Tables 9 and 10 list the same variety of English holding verbs used in the description of the above pictures. They are "hold", "take" and "carrying" (in its present participle form). The percentage of these verbs used is also relatively equal. For "hold" and "holding", the percentages of their usage are 40.00% and 36.67% respectively. The usage of the verb "take" are also relatively equal for both pictures, with the respective percentages being 16.67% and 20.00%. The usage of "carrying" is 3.33% for both pictures. This implies that this holding action to the children corresponded to the three English holding verbs as mentioned above since no other variety of verbs were used by the children for the description of these two pictures.

English	Verbs/Non-verbs	Children (no.)	%
	Hold/Holding	12	40.00%
	Take	5	16.67%
	Carrying	1	3.33%
	Bag	6	20.00%
	Small	1	3.33%
no hand	Don't know	3	10.00%
action	*Imitates action	2	6.67%
verbs used	Total Responses	30	100%

Table 9. Children's responses when being asked to describe Picture 5 in English

English	Verbs/Non-verbs	Children (no.)	%
	Hold/Holding	11	36.67%
	Take	6	20.00%
	Carrying	1	3.33%
	Don't Know	4	13.33%
	Cage	1	3.33%
no hand	Bird	5	16.67%
action	*Imitates action	2	6.67%
verbs used	Total Responses	30	100%

Table 10. Children's responses when being asked to describe Picture 6 in English

Likewise, there is one identical Mandarin verb "ná"("囗 ") being used to describe both Pictures 5 and 6, as listed in Tables 11 and 12. The English verb "hold" was used by the children, which indicates that although they did not know the verb of the action depicted by the pictures in Mandarin, they regarded "hold" as the equivalent of "ná"("囗 ") that could be used to describe the action.

In cases where no verbs were used, some participants merely named the object which the hand was holding, while the others imitated the action of the hand, and there were also some who did not know at all .

Mandarin	Verbs/Non-verbs	Children (no.)	%
	拿	12	40.00%
	Hold/Holding	1	3.33%
	纸袋/包	2	6.67%
	Bag	5	16.67%
	Don't know	5	16.67%
	*Silence	2	6.67%
no hand	*Imitates action	3	10.00%
action			
verbs used	Total Responses	30	100%

Table 11. Children's responses when being asked to describe Picture 5 in Mandarin

Mandarin	Verbs/Non-verbs	Children (no.)	%
	拿	11	36.67%
	Hold/Holding	1	3.33%
	Catch	1	3.33%
	Cage	1	3.33%
	鸟	3	10.00%
	Bird	1	3.33%
	Don't know	7	23.33%
no hand	*Silence	2	6.67%
action	*Imitates action	3	10.00%
verbs used	Total Responses	30	100%

Table 12. Children's responses when being asked to describe **Picture 6** in Mandarin

3.4   Discussion

In this study, an experiment was conducted in which 3-to-6-years-old bilingual pre-schoolers were being asked to identify hand holding actions in English and Mandarin. There were altogether 43 pictures of hands holding different objects shown to the children and they described them in both English and Chinese.

The most common English and Mandarin verbs used by the children in describing the 43 pictures are "hold" in English (76.63%) and "ná"("□ ") in Mandarin (79.01%) respectively. It then appears that the perception of similar actions of a typical young child is simplified. This could be possible due to the fact that a child's focus while conversing with an adult would be to convey what he or she saw in the most direct and simplistic manner possible. The Mandarin and English holding verbs "ná"("□ ") and "hold" are considered to be the more basic verbs in describing prototypical holding actions.

The results listed in the tables demonstrate that the participants were able to differentiate certain hand actions in the pictures by using a variety of English holding verbs. However, when describing the actions in Mandarin, the children used fewer varieties of verbs significantly. There was a total of 7.38% more varieties of other English holding verbs used as compared to other Mandarin holding verbs used.

According to Gao (2015), "the types and the ordering of children's learning of physical action verbs may advance in parallel with their experience and understanding of the physical world around them." This suggests that in the cases of holding actions, children would find it easier to choose a word to express themselves if they had experienced the holding actions in the corresponding different manners. The children's performance in Mandarin reveals that they might not have been using the language as often as compared to that in English. When being asked in Mandarin what the hands were doing in the pictures, most of the younger children whom are aged 3 and 4 years old did not answer the questions; instead, they merely named the objects being held in the hands. As mentioned previously, it might be due to the fact that the objects in the pictures caught the children's attention more easily as compared to the hand action itself. Another reason could be that even though they knew (they were all able to imitate the actions) and had seen those scenarios before, they had not yet acquired or used the linguistics terms before in their daily expressions.

4   Conclusion

The verb "hold" in English and "ná" ("□ ") in Mandarin are the most commonly used hand action verbs in both languages. It is one of the earliest lexical items acquired by young children.

The results of this study demonstrate that most of the children used the Mandarin word "ná" ("□ ") and the English word "hold" correctly even though the children were mostly English dominated speakers. They tended to give responses in English despite being asked to describe the scenarios in Mandarin. In addition, they also used more English holding verbs than the Mandarin counterparts. It is possible that the children had not yet learnt the different 'hold' action verbs in Mandarin. Moreover, the limitation of the design of the study could have also restricted the children from giving more detailed responses. Consequently, further studies could be conducted to refine these questions.

Acknowledgements. We thank the children and their parents for their active participation in this study. We express our gratitude to the principals and teachers in Wiggle Learners Childcare and Early Learning's Fun Childcare in Singapore for assisting us to get in touch with the parents and allowing us to conduct the experiments in their respective centres. We are also thankful to the supporting staff, Ms Li Meiyan and Mr

Neo Keng Hwee, in the Bilingual Development Lab at NTU who provided great help in the collection and proofreading of the data.

We acknowledge the funding support for this project from Nanyang Technological University under the Undergraduate Research Experience on CAmpus (URECA) programme.

References:

1. Chin, S.-C., & Gao, H. (2014). Malaysian Chinese Independent High School Students' Cognitive Understanding of Take "Na" Action Verbs in Chinese: Examples from "V + N" structures. In The Taiwan Journal of Chinese as a Second Language, Vol. 8, Pp.19-41. (in Chinese)

2. Tan, J.M. (2015). Descriptions of physical actions by Singapore Bilingual Chinese Children aged 3-5: Positive Actions. Nanyang Technological University, School of Humanities and Social Sciences. Pp. 1-10. (in Chinese)

3. Wang, H. (2014). The acquisition of hand action verbs by English-Chinese bilinguals in Singapore. Nanyang Technological University, School of Humanities and Social Sciences. Pp. 70-98. (in Chinese)

4. Wang, M. (2015). A comparative study of the application of the Chinese "La" hand action verbs by monolingual and bilingual children. Nanyang Technological University, School of Humanities and Social Sciences. Pp. 14-31. (in Chinese)

5. Gao, H. (2001). Dǎ 打 Polysemy. In The Physical Foundation of the Patterning of Physical Action Verbs: A Study of Chinese Verbs. Pp. 321-324

6. Gao, H. (2014).Parent Report Form for the Studies of Lexical Development in Bilingual Children in Singapore, English and Chinese Bilingual Versions. Singapore: Nanyang Technological University.

7. Gao, H. (2015). Children's Early Production of Physical Action Verbs in Chinese. In Wang, W.S-Y, Sun, C. (eds) The Oxford Handbook of Chinese Linguistics. , Oxford, UK : Oxford University Press. Chapter 48.Pp. 654-665.

8. Tardif, T. (2015). Early Vocabulary Learning in Chinese-Speaking Children. In Wang, W.S-Y, Sun, C. (eds) The Oxford Handbook of Chinese Linguistics. Oxford, UK : Oxford University Press. Chapter 49.Pp. 641-653.

The Polysemy of the Chinese Action Verb "Dǎ" and Its Implications in Child Language Acquisition

Hui Er Sak and Helena Hong Gao

School of Humanities and Social Sciences,
Nanyang Technological University, 14 Nanyang Drive, Singapore 637332

sakh0001@e.ntu.edu.sg, helenagao@ntu.edu.sg

Abstract. The Chinese verb *"dǎ"* is a polysemous and frequently used verb. Studies have shown that it is one of the earliest verbs acquired by monolingual children by the age of five year old, they can use most of the commonly used senses in their daily life. But whether it is an easy task for bilingual children to acquire and use the verb in different contexts is unknown. Our study investigated the usage pattern of *"dǎ"* by 30 Chinese-English bilingual preschool children in Singapore. Visual stimuli depicting *"dǎ"* actions were used to elicit descriptions from the participants. The results reveal that the meaning representations of *"dǎ"* in the semantic domains such as "social interaction" and "physical punishment" are most commonly used by the children while the meaning representations of *"dǎ"* in the semantic domains such as "fastening" and "possession" are the least used by the children. This paper will discuss the factors that affect the children's use of the polysemous verb.

Keywords: *Dǎ* polysemy, Chinese language acquisition, bilingual language acquisition, pre-school children

1 Introduction

1.1 The *Dǎ* Polysemy

The verb "打" [dǎ] (hit) in Chinese is commonly used as a typical physical action verb. Its prototypical meaning refers to a single or repeated "physical contact between a human agent's hand(s) and a patient object" (Gao, 2001:157). The prototypical meaning is exemplified in *the* set phrases of *"dǎ"*such as "打屁股" [dǎ pìgǔ] (spank on the buttock), "打门" [dǎ mén] (knock on the door), etc.

However, *"dǎ"* is highly polysemous in actual language usage. Xiàndài Hànyǔ Cídiǎn (The Contemporary Chinese Dictionary) itself lists 24 meanings of the verb. Gao (2001) analysed the *"dǎ"* polysemy based on the Taiwan Sinica Corpus and the Peking University Contemporary Corpus (CCL Corpus) and calculated here are 152 distinct meaning representations of *"dǎ"*. These meaning representations were then grouped into 27 semantic domains. Based on Gao's (2001) framework pertaining to

© Springer International Publishing AG 2016
M. Dong et al. (Eds.): CLSW 2016, LNAI 10085, pp. 524–533, 2016
DOI: 10.1007/978-3-319-49508-8_49

the categorisation of the meaning representations of *"dǎ"*, this paper will explore the application of different meanings of *"dǎ"* by 30 Chinese-English bilingual preschool children in Singapore.

1.2 Child Language Acquisition

Much research has been done to understand the multiple aspects of language development in children, particularly in their lexical development. For example, investigations of the types of words children first acquired in their lives have been the interest of many researchers (e.g. Gentner, 1982; Gentner & Boroditsky, 2001; Imai et al., 2008; Tardif, 1996). There are also studies which explore the factors influencing children's lexical development. Non-linguistic factors such as language exposure, family SES status, and parents' education background have been examined and found to be correlated to children's vocabulary use (e.g. Dixon et al., 2012; Duursma, 2014; Huttenlocher et al., 1991). Linguistic characteristics such as the polysemous nature of a word, the relationship with its near-synonyms may also affect children's acquisition of a particular lexical item (e.g. Gao, 2015; Germann et al., 2010).

Bilingualism is the emerging trend in today's globalised world. However, established studies on bilingual acquisition are often constrained to bilingualism in English and other Indo-European languages (Yip & Matthews, 2013). In addition, most studies focus more on the development of English in bilingual speakers than that of their ethnic languages (Dixon et al., 2012).

Previous studies show that *"dǎ"* is one of the earliest verbs acquired by monolingual children and by the age of 5 years old, they can use most of the commonly used senses in their daily life (Gao, 2001; 2015). However, little is known about the acquisition and application of the variety of the meanings of *"dǎ"* by bilingual children.

Therefore, we hope that our study can fill the above-mentioned gaps by focusing on the Chinese lexical acquisition by Chinese-English bilingual children, particularly in the acquisition of polysemous verbs.

2   Literature Review

Studies targeting specifically on the acquisition of Chinese polysemous words have highlighted various characteristics of child language acquisition of such words. For example, Zhang et al. (2010) examined the acquisition of 8 polysemous words in Mandarin Chinese by 3 monolingual children and found that their acquisition of the polysemous meanings typically followed the chronological order of the derivation of the meaning extensions, unless driven by functional motivations. That is, the more frequently used meanings in the children's daily lives were generally acquired before other meanings. However, the existing studies merely address mainly on the acquisition order in monolingual children.

Regarding early child language acquisition, Gao (2015) examined the Chinese monolingual children's acquisition of physical action verbs based on the data extracted from Child Language Data Exchange System (CHILDES). The results revealed that factors such as children's physical development, growth environment, and cognitive understanding of the actions have direct correlations with the children's acquisition of corresponding physical action verbs. Besides, it was found that children's personal experience with the actions had a positive correlation with the number of near-synonyms they acquired.

There are also studies which research upon bilingual child language acquisition in Singapore. For instance, Dixon et al. (2012) conducted an empirical study on 6-years-old preschool children, testing the lexical development of their mother tongue (Chinese, Malay, and Tamil) based on translated versions of the American-based Peabody Picture Vocabulary Test-III (PPVT-III). The study indicated that parents speaking their mother tongues to their children create a positive effect on the children's mother tongue vocabularies, while parents speaking English to their children yield a negative effect on the children's mother tongue vocabularies.

Gao & Wang (2013) conducted a domain-specific lexical development study on preschool children in Singapore with the use of two vocabulary checklists. The results showed that parents who spoke English to their children at home restricted their children's lexical development in Chinese. On the other hand, , parents who spoke Chinese to their children at home did not result in any observable impediment on their children's lexical development in English.

In recent years, more domain-specific studies on verbs have been conducted in Singapore. For example, Tan (2015) and Wang (2015) investigated the preschool children's lexical development in positive actions and pulling actions respectively. These studies underscored the trend that bilingual children were more inclined to use a hypernym or a more general verb to describe the relevant actions. Both studies highlighted that the Chinese-English bilingual children have a smaller size of vocabulary in Chinese than in English.

3   Methodology

3.1   Participants

Thirty child participants aged between 3;4 and 5;9 (mean: 4;5) were recruited in this study. They were all Chinese-English bilingual children enrolled in bilingual preschools in Singapore. In terms of dominant language, 14 children were Chinese-dominant, 7 were English-dominant, and 9 were balanced bilinguals. Based on the demographic information collected, these children came from middle-income families and thus represented the typical average Singapore families.

3.2   Materials

Questionnaire. A parent report form designed by Gao (2014) was used for the parents of eligible child participants to provide relevant information such as the child's age, gender, languages spoken at home and his or her parents' education background etc.

Visual Stimuli. A list of *"dǎ"* constructions of "Verb + Object" were first searched and selected from different resources, such as oral productions of Singaporean speakers, preschool storybooks, frequently occurring set phrases of *"dǎ"* in the Taiwan Corpus of Child Mandarin (TCCM), and Peking University CCL corpus. Relevant pictures or videos of the set phrases of *"dǎ"* were self-filmed or selected from the internet and used as visual stimuli for the test. Forty-one actions were prepared and tested accordingly. Thirty-one of them were analysed in details and discussed in this paper.

3.3   Procedure

The experiment was conducted in the children's pre-schools and the children were tested individually. They were first reassured that there were no right or wrong answers before being asked to describe the actions shown to them. The experiment was video-recorded for the ease of transcription. Transcribed responses were then coded and analysed afterwards.

4   Results

Table 1 below presents the usage rate[1] of individual meaning representations for the actions. The 10 actions (out of 31 actions analysed) which did not elicit any use of *the* meaning representations of *"dǎ"* from the children are excluded from Table 1.

Table 1. Usage rate of *dǎ* for each action

Rank	*Dǎ* Set Phrase	Semantic Domain	Usage Rate of *Dǎ* (%)
1	打电话 [dǎ diànhuà] (make a phone call)	Social Interaction	80.0
2	打耳光 [dá ěrguāng] (slap in the face)	Physical Punishment	63.3
3	打蚊子 [dǎ wénzǐ] (hit the mosquito)	Battle	56.7
4	打针 [dǎ zhēn] (inject)	Insertion	53.3
5	打屁股 [dǎ pìgǔ] (spank on the	Physical Punishment	50.0

---

[1]   Usage rate refers to the percentage of children who used *dǎ* in their descriptions.

	buttock)		
6	打手心 [dá shǒuxīn] (beat on the palm)	Physical Punishment	43.3
7	打鼓 [dá gǔ] (drum a drum)	Sound Source	36.7
8	打棒球 [dǎ bàngqiú] (play baseball)	Game	30.0
8	打架 [dǎ jià] (fight)	Battle	30.0
10	打油 [dǎ yóu] (refuel)	Insertion	26.7
11	打高尔夫球 [dǎ gāoěrfūqiú] (play golf)	Game	20
12	打喷嚏 [dǎ pēntì] (sneeze)	Physiological Reaction	16.7
13	打篮球 [dǎ lánqiú] (play basketball)	Game	6.7
13	打哈欠 [dǎ hāqiàn] (yawn)	Physiological Reaction	6.7
13	打招呼 [dǎ zhāohu] (greet someone)	Verbalisation	6.7
13	打麻将 [dǎ májiàng] (play mahjong)	Game	6.7
17	打灯笼 [dǎ dēnglóng] (hold up a lantern)	Upholding	3.3
17	打呼噜 [dǎ hūlu] (snore)	Physiological Reaction	3.3
17	打扑克 [dǎ pūkè] (play poker)	Game	3.3

| 17 | 打嗝
[dǎ gé]
(burp) | Physiological
Reaction | 3.3 |
| 17 | 打门
[dǎ mén]
(knock on the door) | Sound Source | 3.3 |

The 10 actions in which the meaning representations of *"dá"* were not used by the children are:

1. 打口哨 [dá kǒushào] (whistle) / sound source,
2. 打游戏机 [dǎ yóuxìjī] (play video game) / game,
3. 打结 [dǎ jié] (knot) / fastening,
4. 打毛衣 [dǎ máoyī] (knit a sweater) / fastening,
5. 打鱼 [dǎ yú] (catch fish) / possession,
6. 打秋千 [dǎ qiūqiān] (swing on a swing) / game,
7. 打瞌睡 [dǎ kēshuì] (doze off) / physiological reaction,
8. 打伞 [dá sǎn] (hold up an umbrella) / upholding,
9. 打领带 [dá lǐngdài] (tie a tie) / fastening, and
10. 打水 [dá shuǐ] (fetch water) / possession.

The most frequently used meaning representation was 打电话 [dǎ diànhuà] (call on the phone), with a usage rate of 80%. Meaning representations belonging to "social interaction", "physical punishment", "battle" and "insertion" were most commonly used by the children - the actions tested in these semantic domains ranked top 10 or higher. On the other hand, none of the meaning representations of *"dǎ"* belonging to the semantic domains of "fastening" and "possession" were used by the children.

5   Discussion

5.1   Experience

The results indicate that the children were more familiar with the meanings of *"dǎ"* in the semantic domains of "social interaction", "physical punishment", "battle" and "insertion". This might be due to the fact that children were more familiar with the corresponding actions or events.

For instance, 80% of the children used *dǎ* for 打电话 [dǎ diànhuà] (call on the phone) even though the meaning of the action of *"dǎ"* is somewhat abstract and far from being prototypical. Since most children would have personal experience of making a phone call, frequent exposure to this particular verb phrase could have motivated its early acquisition. In addition, the meaning representation of *"dǎ"* in 打针 [dǎ zhēn] (inject) was also used very frequently in the study (53.3%), despite it not being prototypical. The reason could be that most children had prior frightening experiences with injections and they might also have learned the expression at an early age.

Due to the restrictions of their physical capability, young children mostly participate in events that are typical of simple actions as being easily manipulated. Meaning representations in "physical punishment" and "battle" had high usage rate owing to the simplicity in the corresponding actions. These actions include the use of a hand, and a goal-directed action with strong force and motion. Features as such make it easier for children to imitate the action, thus supporting their cognitive understanding of the actions and resulting in early acquisition of the lexical item. In fact, Gao (2015) mentioned that physical abilities, cognitive abilities, and personal experiences would aid in the learning of linguistic expressions of these physical actions.

However, we note that experience with the actions was not an accurate predictor of the acquisition of the meaning representations of "dǎ". For example, despite the fact that the action of knocking on the door is common in the children's daily lives, the usage rate is one of the lowest out of all actions tested. Moreover, some actions in the same semantic domains have vastly different usage rate. This thus shows that there are other factors alongside experience which are involved in the process of acquisition. We will discuss these factors in Sections 5.2 to 5.4.

5.2   Competition between *Dǎ* Meaning Representation and its Near-synonyms

A closer examination into the verbs (apart from "dǎ") used by the children revealed that *the* meaning representations of "dǎ" which have more near-synonyms were less likely to be used.

"打门" [dǎ mén] (knock on the door), for example, has only a usage rate of 3.3%. 63.3% of the children used 敲 [qiāo] (knock) instead. Both "dǎ" and "qiāo" have similar semantic properties - both actions involve a force, contact and motion. The observed usage pattern above concurs with the occurrence rate in CCL corpus: "qiāo mén" occurs 2110 times while "dǎ mén" occurs only 377 times. With a much higher occurrence rate in daily lives, "qiāo" entered the children's vocabulary before the respective meaning of "dǎ" did. Another example would be "打秋千" [dǎ qiūqiān] (swing on a swing), the respective meaning representation of "dǎ" was not used by any children. In fact, the near-synonyms "荡" [dàng] and "玩" [wán] were used in preference instead, with a usage rate of 20% and 26.7% respectively. A search in CCL corpus shows that *dàng qiūqiān* (115 times) is more common than *dǎ qiūqiān* (33 times). "*Wán qiūqiān*" is the least common, occurring only 5 times.

All in all, the results reveal that near-synonyms could affect the acquisition of the meaning of "dǎ", particularly if the near-synonyms are more commonly used in daily lives.

5.3   Children's Understanding of Actions

The analysis of the verbs used other than "dǎ" also revealed that certain meanings of "dǎ" were not acquired because of a lapse in the understanding of the action itself. For example, while only 6.7% of the children used "dǎ" to describe the action of "打篮球" [dǎ lánqiú] (play basketball), most of the children (36.7%) used "丢" [diū] (throw) to describe it. The meaning of *"dǎ"* in *dǎ lánqiú* encompasses a much more abstract meaning, involving a series of actions that can be defined as defeat, physical contact, interaction between players, etc (Gao, 2001). As such, young children without a complete understanding of the process of a basketball game may find it difficult to map such a complex process onto *"dǎ"*.

5.4   Bilingual Cross-Language Effects

Growing up in Singapore entails a challenge in language acquisition. Most children are exposed to two languages since birth. As such, it brings about an exclusive challenge when it comes to language acquisition. Language transfer, or more specifically lexical transfer, arises as a result of language contact between English and Chinese.

For example, the meaning of *"dǎ"* in the phrases, such as "打游戏机" [dǎ yóuxìjī] (play video game) and "打扑克" [dǎ pūkè] (play poker) were hardly used by the children. They used "玩" [wán] (play) in replacement instead. This is quite possibly due to the fact that the English descriptions of these actions involve the verb "play", such as "play video game" and "play poker". The language transfer resulted in the children usage of the Chinese translational equivalent, which is *"wán"*. Although *"wán"* has similar semantic properties as *"dǎ"* in these contexts, it is not a colloquial expression in Mandarin. We assume that this type of word usage by the children in Chinese was due to the English interference.

6   Conclusion

In summary, this study has shown that the different meaning representations of *"dǎ"* are acquired through a complicated process involving an interplay of several factors. First of all, our results show that exposure to action events was advantageous for children to acquire the corresponding meanings of *"dǎ"*, particularly if the actions are simple. Secondly, we found that *"dǎ"* and the complex relationships with its near synonyms might have impeded the children's acquisition of the relevant *"dǎ"* meanings. Thirdly, non-linguistic factors such as children's understanding of the actions would also affect the children's acquisition of certain meanings of the verb. Lastly, bilingual children's use of the *"dǎ"* verb was found to have been negatively affected by their use of English.

As the study was based solely on a sample size of 30 children, the results might not be representative of the child population in Singapore. Besides, this study was restricted to a small number of the *"dǎ"* meanings. Future studies could investigate the acquisition of the other meanings of *"dǎ"*. Comparative studies between the acquisition of *"dǎ"* polysemy and its English translational equivalents could also be explored.

Acknowledgements. We thank all the participants, their parents and teachers for their support to our study. We would also like to thank Dr Connie Lum, Dr Haoshu Wang,

Ms Meiyan Li for their help in the recruitment of participants and Mr Neo Keng Hwee for his proofreading of the data.

We acknowledge the funding for this project from Nanyang Technological University under the Undergraduate Research Experience on CAmpus (URECA) programme and the Academic Research Fund (AcRF) of Ministry of Education, Singapore.

References

1. Centre for Chinese Linguistics Peking University. *CCL Corpus.* See Website: http://ccl.pku.edu.cn:8080/ccl_corpus/ Date of Visit: 3 Aug 2016. [In Chinese]
2. Cheung, H., Chang, C.-J., Ko, H-W., & Tsay, J. (2011). *Taiwan Corpus of Child Mandarin (TCCM).* (NSC96-2420-H-002-030) [In Chinese]
3. Chinese Academy of Social Sciences Research Institutes of Language Department of Dictionary. (2012). *Xiandai Hanyu Cidian (The Contemporary Chinese Dictionary) (6th ed.).* Beijing: The Commercial Press. [In Chinese]
4. Dixon, L. Q., Zhao, J., Quiroz, B. G., & Shin, J.-Y. (2012). Home and Community Factors Influencing Bilingual Children's Ethnic Language Vocabulary Development. *International Journal of Bilingualism*, 16(4), 541-565.
5. Duursma, E. (2014). The Effects of Fathers' and Mothers' Reading to Their Children on Language Outcomes of Children Participating in Early Head Start in the United States. *Fathering: A Journal of Theory and Research about Men as Parents*, 12(3), 283-302.
6. Gao, H. (2001). *The Physical Foundation of the Patterning of Physical Action Verbs.* Sweden: Lund University Press.
7. Gao, H. H., & Wang, H. (2013). *Bilingual Children's Domain Specific Lexical Development.* Project Report Funded by Early Childhood Research Fund. Singapore: Ministry of Family and Social Development.
8. Gao, H. (2014). *Parent Report Form for the Studies of Lexical Development in Bilingual Children in Singapore. English and Chinese Bilingual Versions.* Singapore: Nanyang Technological University.
9. Gao, H. H. (2015). Children's Early Production of Physical Action Verbs in Chinese. In C. F. Sun, W. S-Y Wang & Y. Tsai (Eds.), *The Oxford Handbook of Chinese Linguistics.* Oxford, UK: Oxford University Press. Chapter 49. 654-665.
10. Gentner, D. (1982). Why Nouns Are Learned Before Verbs: Linguistic Relativity Versus Natural Partitioning. In S. A. Kuczaj (Ed.), *Language Development: Vol. 2. Language, Thought and Culture.* Hillsdale, N.J.: Lawrence Erlbaum. 301-334.
11. Gentner, D., & Boroditsky, L. (2001). Individuation, Relativity and Early Word Learning. In M. Bowerman & S. Levinson (Eds.), *Language Acquisition and Conceptual Development.* Cambridge, UK: Cambridge University Press. 215-256.
12. Germann, D.C., Villavicencio, A. & Siqueira, M. (2010). An investigation on polysemy and lexical organization of verbs. *Proceedings of the NAACL HLT 2010 First Workshop on Computational Neurolinguistics*, 52-60.
13. Huttenlocher, J., Haight, W., Bryk, A., Seltzer, M., & Lyons, T. (1991). Early Vocabulary Growth: Relation to Language Input and Gender. *Developmental Psychology*, 27(2), 236-248.
14. Imai, M., Li, L., Haryu, E., Okada, H., Hirsh-Pasek, K., Golinkoff, R. M., & Shigematsu, J. (2008). Novel Noun and Verb Learning in Chinese-, English- and Japanese-Speaking Children. *Child Development*, 79(4), 979 – 1000.

15. Tan, J. M. (2015). *Descriptions of Physical Actions by Singapore Bilingual Chinese Children Aged 3-5: Positive Actions.* B.A. Thesis. Singapore: Nanyang Technological University. [In Chinese]
16. Tardif, T. (1996). Nouns are Not Always Learned before Verbs: Evidence from Mandarin speakers' Early Vocabularies. *Developmental Psychology*, 32(3), 492-504.
17. Wang, M. (2015). *A Comparative Study of the Application of the Chinese "La" Hand Action Verbs by Monolingual and Bilingual Children.* B.A. Thesis. Singapore: Nanyang Technological University. [In Chinese]
18. Yip, V., & Matthews, S. (2013). *The Bilingual Child: Early Development and Language Contact.* (Translated by Tsai, Y.) Beijing: Beijing World Publishing Corporation. [In Chinese]
19. Zhang, Y., Zhou, J., & Fu, J. (2010). Learning Strategies for Polysemous Words by Chinese Children. *Zhongguo Yuwen*, 1, 34-43. [In Chinese]

A Metaphorical and cognitive study on Idioms with of "Ru"

Zhimin Wang[1], Lei Wang[2*], Shiwen Yu[2]

[1]Beijing Language and Culture University, 100083, China
wangzm000@qq.com
[2]Peking University, 100871, China
{wangleics,yusw}@pku.edu.cn

Abstract. This paper explores the structural characteristics of idioms with "如
（Ru）", focuses on the similarities and differences between the format
"1+Ru+2" and "2+Ru+1", and summarizes the selection restriction and metaphorical mapping between tenor and vehicle, through the analysis of word "Ru"
in different position. This study shows that although the word "Ru" is in the idiom of the four kinds of positions, among which the number of the third positions is the largest. The "Ru" idioms have different mapping regularities, that is,
the tenor is not the abstract and unfamiliar things, but the choice of human
body, the body parts. The concept of the five elements such as "gold, wood, water, fire, earth" usually is selected as sources in the format "2+Ru+1",as well as
the living things familiar with the ancient ancestors as a metaphor.

Keywords: Metaphorical mapping; Event structure; Metaphorical
comparison; Ground

1   Introduction

Lakoff and Johnson (1980) argue that when one conceptual domain is understood
in terms of another conceptual domain. Based on the perceived experience, they
understand the abstract and unfamiliar things with the concrete and familiar ones.
For the concept of mapping, both the simile and the metaphor in Chinese are the
figure of speech. In modern Chinese, "像(xiang)", "好 像(hao xiang)" and
"像……一样(xiang…yi yang)" are usually labeled as the simile while "如(ru)",
"若(ruo)", and "譬如(bi ru)" were generally used as the simile in ancient Chinese,
which are commonly used in Chinese idioms. The Chinese four-character idioms
are shown as followed:

如临大敌	奉如神明	举步如飞	泣血涟如
ru lin da di	feng ru shen ming	ju bu ru fei	qi xue lian ru
如沐春风	爱如己出	一见如旧	开合自如
ru mu chun feng	sheng ru yin ling	yi jian ru gu	kai he zi ru
如鱼似水	动如脱兔	惜财如命	挥洒自如

© Springer International Publishing AG 2016
M. Dong et al. (Eds.): CLSW 2016, LNAI 10085, pp. 534–545, 2016
DOI: 10.1007/978-3-319-49508-8_50

ru yu si shui	dong ru tuo tu	xi cai ru ming	hui sa zi ru
如前所述	爱如珍宝	趁心如意	猪狗不如
ru qian suo su	ai ru zhen bao	chen xin ru yi	zhu gou bu ru

In four-character idioms mentioned above, the word "ru" can be used in four positions including the first, the second, the third and the last one. Further research should be carried out including the combined forms of position for the word "ru" and expression mode for the vehicle(source domain)and the tenor(target domain).

For the four-character idioms for the word of"ru",it is found by Yin Wang(2010)through the detailed study that the occurrence frequency for 14 words of simile in four-character idioms is great difference, among which such 4 words reach the frequency of over 40 as "如(ru)"," 若(ruo)","比(bi)"and "拟(ni)" ranged from high frequency to low frequency. The word of "ru" has the highest frequency with 66 percent of 642 examples. The research on four-character idioms with the word of simile has also been studied including position and type of word of "ru"in the four-character idioms. Jie Cheng(2012)applied the conceptual integration theory to the cognitive mechanism of vehicle integration for four-character idioms with double words of simile. For the cross-cultural study on the four-character idioms with word of metaphor, Wang Yin (2010) collected 969 simile idioms in Chinese, and analyzed their internal collocation rules according to the coexistence and position of the four elements, i.e. tenor, vehicle and ground. Thease idioms can be classified into six types and 11 varieties. The study mentioned above can be used for a reference to specialize in the research on four-character idioms with word of "ru".

This paper collects all four-character idioms with word of "ru" in accordance with the knowledge base for idioms by Institute of Computational Linguistics of Beijing University and labels and classifies idioms with word of "ru" in order to offer help for the student to learn the metaphor with the summary of real distribution of word of "ru" in four-character idioms based on the statistics results and with exploration of rules of metaphor mapping.

2   Features of Distribution for four-character idioms with word of "ru"

The knowledge base for idioms collected 38093 four-word idioms by Institute of Computational Linguistics of Beijing University is one of the largest knowledge base recently. This paper collects 679 idioms with the word of "ru" accounting for 1.78 percent of the total idioms. There are obvious differences in the position and amount of the word of "ru" in the idioms. It is shown as table.

Table 1.   Table I Quantitative Distribution for the different position of "ru" in four-character idioms

Position of word of "ru"	Amount	Proportion
Position 1	141	20.77%
Position 2	158	23.27%
Position 3	343	50.52%
Position 4	44	6.48%
Other Position	11	1.62%

Based on the statistical results, it is found that there are 343 four-character idioms in which the word of "ru" is in position 3 with 50.52 percent of total idioms, in position 2 with 23.27 percent and in position 1 with 20.77 percent of total idioms respectively. There are only 44 four-character idioms in which the word of "ru"is in position 4 with 6.48 percent of total idioms. There are other useful expressions in which the word of "ru" is in other position with the form of "bu ru",for example, "尽信书不如无书（jin xin shu bu ru wu shu）Believing in books without any doubt is no better than no books." and "君子之交淡如水（jun zi zhi jiao dan ru shui）The friendship between gentlemen is as plain as water", which shall not be discussed here.

For four structures mentioned above, position 1 and position 4 are reverse the same as the position 2 and position 3 with the form of position echo, which are shown as follows:

Position 1 "ru" __ __ __

Position 2 __ "ru" __ __

Position 3 __ __ "ru" __

Position 4 __ __ __ "ru"

It is found in the four-character idioms with the word of "ru "that the tenor and the vehicle also exist co-occurrence difference. For the structure with the position 1 or position 4, the co-occurrence of the tenor and the vehicle cannot be existed. But for the structure of position 2 or position 3, the mapping relation of the tenor and the vehicle is shown fully to form the essential patter of the metaphor, e.g. "风雨如磐(feng yu ru pan) wind and rain are as hard as the huge stones", 目光如炬(yue guang ru ju) One's eyes are as bright as torches."," 心如止水(xin ru zhi shui) One's heart remains as calm as still water.". This paper firstly studies the structure of metaphor and the mapping relation of tenor and vehicle in the idioms with word of "ru" in the position 2 and position 3. The analysis on the idioms with the word of "ru"in the position 1 and position 4 shall be made in another paper.

3   The structure analysis of the word of "ru"in the position 2

If the word of "ru"is in the position 2 of the idioms, then the structure of idioms will be "N1+"ru"+N2", which is shown as follows:

肤如凝脂(fu ru ningzhi), the color of the skin is the same as the color of the milk

情如兄弟(qing ru xiongdi), the emotion between two man is the same as the emotion of the brothers

文如其人(wen ru qiren) ,The writing mirrors the writer

Generally, N1 stands for the word with one syllable and N2 for the words with two syllables, which are connected with the word of "ru"to form the structure of "N1+"ru"+N2"in which the co-occurrence of the tenor(N1) and the vehicle(N2)makes a metaphor mode of "the tenor+"ru"+the vehicle". The structure of "N1+"ru"+N2"can be changed into the structure of "X 像(xiang) Y 一样（yiyang）A"(X is the same as Y). For example, we can say that "皮肤像凝脂一样(pifu xiang ningzhi yiyang)，the color of the skin is the same as the color of the milk "and "情像兄弟一样(qing xiang xiongdi yiyang), the emotion between two man is the same as the emotion of the brothers". However, the ground(A) is not shown in the structure of "X is the same as Y".

If the word of "ru"is in the position 2 of the idioms, then the structure of idioms will be "A1+"ru"+N2". For example,

安如磐石 (an ru pan shi), as steady as a rock

稳如泰山 (wen ru tai shan) , as steady as Taishang mountain

美如冠玉 (mei ru guan yu) , as beautiful as a gem

轻如鸿毛 (qing ru hong mao) ,as light as a feather

易如反掌 (yi ru fan zhang) , as easy as turning one's hand over

A1 is the adjective with one syllable and N2 are usually the nouns with two syllables that are the relation of modification. For the form of metaphor, N2 is the vehicle and A1 is the ground, which form the metaphor mode of "the ground+"ru"+the vehicle". It can be expressed as "as steady as a rock, as steady as Taishang mountain and as beautiful as a gem ". Beside this, N2 is also the nouns with two syllables，which are the relation of coordination, for example.

浩如烟海(hao ru yanhai),as vast as the smoke and sea

凛如霜雪(lin ru shuangxue), as cold as frost and snow

急如风火(ji ru fenghuo), as fast as wind and fire

疾如雷电(ji ru leidian),as fast as thunder and lighting

昭如日星(zhao ru rixing),as shining as the sun and the star

亲如手足(qin ru shouzu), as close as the hand and foot

亲如骨肉(qin ru gurou), as close as the flesh and blood

明如指掌(ming ru zhizhang), as clear as the hands

皓如日星(hao ru rixing), as bright as the moon and star

The vehicles (N2) mentioned above are familiar natural phenomenon (e.g. the smoke and sea, frost and snow, wind and fire, ice and frost, thunder and lighting, the sun and the star), and human's body(e.g. the hand and foot, the brothers, flesh and blood, the hands).As the vehicle of metaphor, all N2 are familiar things for us.

The structure of "A1+"ru"+N2"can be transformed into the structure of "X is as A as Y" whose variant form is "as A as Y" without the tenor X. Another structure of "V1+"ru"+N2"can also be formed when the word of "ru"of the idioms is in the position 2, which is shown as follows:

视如草芥(shi ru caojie), see someone as the dust

动如脱兔(dong ru tuotu), someone run as fast as the rabbit

视如陌路(shi ru molu), see someone as the stranger

视如寇仇(shi ru kouchou), see someone as the enemy

视如敝屐(shi ru biji), see someone as the discarded shoes

The V1 is the verb with one syllable and N2 is the words with two syllables. The structure of "V1+"ru"+N2"can also be transformed into "X is as A as Y" in which the vehicle Y is the complex form. For example,

The vehicle Y=V1+N2 视如草芥-〉像视草芥一样

shi ru caojie-> see somebody as the humble people

The vehicle Y=N2+V1 动如脱兔-〉像脱兔动一样

dong ru tuotu-> someone run as fast as the rabbit

We can say "see somebody as the humble people". But for "动如脱兔",We can say "someone run as fast as the rabbit". So, it is found that the combination of the tenor X and the vehicle Y will not be a simple structure but an event structure that results in the occurrence of the verb V1. The event structure will be used with the different forms of the vehicle Y, for example, "hate" and "see" are marked as the second-order verb. The form of V1+N2 can be used in the expression of event structure.

There is another structure of "N1+"ru"+NV"closely behind the structure mentioned above, which is shown as follows:

心如刀锯(xin ru daoju) , feel pain as if the heart is cut by a knife

汗如雨下(han ru yuxia) ,feel hot as if rain drops in the face

心如刀锉(xin ru daocuo) ,feel pain as if the heart is cut by a knife

谋如涌泉(mou ru quanyong),feel tactical as if water flows freely

心如刀绞(xin ru daojiao),feel pain as if the heart is cut by a knife

胆如斗大(dan ru douda) ,feel brave as if the gallbladder is the same as the 10 litre container"

The N1 is the noun with one syllable and the NV is two- syllable phrase with the function of a subject and a verb. The structure of "N1+"ru"+NV"can also be transformed into the structure of "X is as A as Y". So, we can say in Chinese "心如刀割(xin ru dao ge)feel pain as if the heart is cut with a knife " and "汗如雨下 (han ru yu xia)feel hot as if the rain drops in the face". The structure in Chinese isn't the same as one in English. The vehicle is still the event structure to form the special mode of the tenor X and the vehicle Y. Beside this, only a few four-character idioms with the word of "ru" is the structure of "N1+"ru"+NV". For example, "洞如观火 dong ru guan huo, see something as clearly as a blazing fire; 势如破竹 shi ru po zhu, deal with something as easily as a splitting bamboo, 味如嚼蜡 wei ru jiao la, taste as insipidly as a sawdust"。

There are 158 four-character idioms with the word of "ru" in position 2. The 124 four-character idioms discussed above are 79 percent of all idioms, which are shown in numerical order as follows:

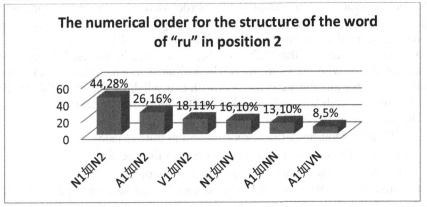

Fig. 1. The numerical order for the structure of the word of "ru" in position 2

The structure of "N1+"ru"+N2" ranks the first with 44 idioms, the "A1+"ru"+N2" is the second with 26, the "V1+"ru"+N2" is the third with 18, the "N1+"ru"+NV" is the fourth with 16, the "A1+"ru"+NN" is the fifth with 13 and the "A1+"ru"+VN" is the last with 8. The idioms with the beginning of the noun are almost the same as the one with beginning of the adjective in number.

4   The structure analysis of the word of "ru" in position 3

The four-character idioms with the word of "ru" in position 3 are in the majority of all idioms. The structure of "N2+"ru"+N1" is contrary to the structure of "N1+"ru"+N2", which is ranks the first with the metaphor mode of "the tenor +"ru"+the vehicle" , such as,

胜友如云(shengyou ru yun) ,many good friends gather as much as the clouds

人生如梦(rensheng ru meng) ,life is just like a dream

巧舌如簧(qiaoshe ru huang),talk as eloquently as a smooth spring

日月如梭 (ruyue ru suo),time flies as quickly as a shuttle

日夜如梭(riye ru suo) ,Day and night go as quickly as a shuttle

风雨如磐 (fengyu ru pan), wind and rain is as heavy as the huge stones

宾客如云(binke ru yun) ,many guests accumulate as much as the clouds

侯门如海(houmen ru hai), noble's home is as deep as an ocean

军令如山(jun ling ru shan), military orders are as unshakeable as the mountains

For the structure of "N2+"ru"+N1", the N2 stands for the two-syllable nouns with the relation of modification, such as, good friends, life, sweet tongue, and the N2 is also two-syllable nouns with the relation of coordination to express the meaning of synonym or antonym, such as, sun and moon, Day and night, wind and rain. The N1 is the noun with one syllable that is familiar to us in our daily life, such as, cloud, ocean, mountain. The structure of "N2+"ru"+N1" can also be changed into the structure of "X is as A as Y", e.g. many guests is as much as the cloud. However, the ground (as much) will be emitted in Chinese.

Another structure of the "V2+"ru"+N1" can usually be used in the four-character idioms with the word of "ru" in position 3 in which the N1 is the noun with one syllable and the V2 is the verb with two syllables. Based on the function of grammar, the verb V2 can be divided into the following structures:

The structure of "VN+"ru"+N1":

守身如玉(shoushen ru yu) , keep oneself as pure as jade

挥金如土 (huijin ru tu), to squander money like the dust

挥汗如雨(huihan ru yu) ,sweat as much as raindrops.

The structure of "VN+"ru"+N1" can be transformed into the structure of "X is as A as Y". The tenor X is the event structure with the verb and the noun. For example, "守身如玉(shoushen ru yu), keep oneself as pure as jade".

The structure of "NV+"ru"+N1":

胆小如豆(danxiao ru dou),the gallbladder is as small as the bean

心细如发(xinxi ru fa),the heart is as thin as the hair

血流如注(xue liu ru zhu), bleed as much as water-jet

The structure of "VV+"ru"+N1"

堆集如山 (duiji ru shan) ,pile up as highly as a mountain

暴跳如雷(baotiao ru lei) ,stamp and jump as fiercely as thunder

应答如流 (ying da ru liu) , answer fluently

The structure of "V2+"ru"+N1"

一清如水(yiqing ru shui) ,as clear as water

烂醉如泥(lanzui ru ni) , as drunk as a lord

不绝如缕(bujue ru lv) , hang as precariously as a thread

For the above structures, the N1 is the common word that is the vehicle of the metaphor, and the tenor is an event structure with a complex form. The structures mentioned above are asymmetric forms with the tenor and the vehicle. There are differences in the co-occurrence of the N1 and the V with restrictions of selection. In the structure of "NV+"ru"+N1", the property or action of V usually derives from the N1. For example, "胆小如豆(danxiao ru dou)the gallbladder is as small as the bean", "心细如发(xinxi ru fa)the heart is as thin as the hair".

The adjective can also be put before the word of "ru" besides the noun and verb to form the structure of "A2+"ru"+N1" which there are only a few examples. For example,

吉祥如意(jixiang ru yi) , wish good luck and fortune

甘之如饴 (gan zhi ru yi) , as sweet as sugar

依然如故 (yiran ru gu) ,remain as before

The structures for the four-character idioms with the word of "ru" in the position 3 are shown as fig.1.

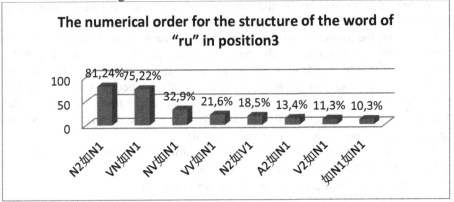

Fig. 2. The numerical order for the structure of the word of "ru" in position3

The structure of the "N2+"ru"+N1" ranks the first with 81 idioms accounting for 24 percent of all idioms, and the "VN+"ru"+N1", the "NV+"ru"+N1", the "VV+"ru"+N1" with 75, 32 and 21 for the 22, 9 and 6 percent respectively. The structures mentioned above have a common in the form of verb phrase before the word of "ru", such as, VN, NV, VV and the form of N1 after the word of "ru", which shows the asymmetric structure.

There are more than four-character idioms, such as

人生如朝露 (rensheng ru zhaolu),human life goes as quickly as the morning dew

病去如抽丝(qu bing ru chou si),illness will not go easily

兵败如山倒(pingbai ru shandao),the army collapsed as fast as a mountain

磕头如捣蒜(ke tou ru dao suan) , kowtow is just like the pounding garlic

5   The comparative analysis on the metaphor of four-character idioms with the word of "ru"

As far as the syllable is concerned, in the structure of "1+"ru"+2" with the word of "ru" in position 2 and the structure of "2+"ru"+1 with the word of "ru" in position 3, 1 stands for the word with one syllable and 2 stands for the word with two syllables. How many changes will be made with the difference of position? How to reflect the tenor, vehicle and the ground of the metaphor in the four-character idioms? This paper finds in a survey that most of the structures of the "1+"ru"+2" and "2+"ru"+1" are the structure of the metaphor. The words with one syllable will be picked up in the form of the metaphor.

There are 83 words with one syllable in the structure of the "1+"ru"+2" and 122 words in the structure of "2+"ru"+1". The choice of word varies with the different position of word with one syllable before or after the word of "ru" . If the one-syllable word is before the word of "ru", the tenor will be the word with one syllable, which is related to the people or people's body(e.g. the heart, the face, the tear, the tooth, the sound, the mouth, the sweat, the gallbladder, the skin, the man and the appearance), the people's living place(e.g. the room and the house) and to the word of animal(e.g. horse).In addition, the structure of "1+"ru"+2" can also choose the verbs related with the people's action and the sense(see, kiss, learn, love, think of, move, argue, hate, surprise, keep) and the adjective with the expression of the property(easy, stable, steady, rapid, bright, splendid, quiet, broad, clear，light and difficult).

The structure of "V1+"ru"+N2" is the transformation form of the metaphor with the ground without the tenor. For example:

视如敝屣 (shi ru bixi) , to regard as worn-out shoes

多如牛毛 (duo ru niumao), as many as the hairs on an ox

危如累卵 (wei ru leiluan),as precarious as a pile of eggs

The structures mentioned above can also be changed into "as A as Y" to form the structure of ""ru"+N2"+一样(yiyang)"+V1/A1". e.g. to regard as worn-out shoes, be as many as the hairs on an ox, as precarious as a pile of eggs. For the structure discussed above, it shows the importance of the ground.

The one-syllable word in the structure of "2+"ru"+1" behind the word of "ru" is usually the vehicle of the metaphor whose function changes with the different position. It is a familiar word for the ancient Chinese in connection with the gold, wood, water, fire and earth(the gold, forest, water, rain, sea, fire, earth, wind, thunder, cloud, rainbow, frost, mountain, rock), with article sindaily life(drawings, mirror, thread, linen, bottle, arrow, stove, letter and torch) ,with the word of animals (mouse, bull, tiger, jackal and dragon) and with the word of time(year, day)

In addition, there are also the words are related to the action of people(wash, smile, see, hurt, eager, practice) and to the property of the adjective (old, closely), which are the vehicle of the metaphor to form the structure of "X +"像(xiang)"

+Y+"一样(yi yang)"",for example.

春山如笑（chun shan ru xiao）,the sun is shining brightly as if the hills smile in spring

碧空如洗（bi kong ru xi）,the sky is blue and clear as if it is cleaned.

一面如旧(yi mian ru jiu) , feel like old friends at the first meeting

讳莫如深 (huimo ru shen), keep sth as carefully as a secret

A conclusion will be drawn that the two structures mentioned above are differences in the choice of word, the position and the form of the metaphor. The one-syllable word in the structure of "1+"ru"+2" can also be used as the tenor and the ground of the metaphor while the one-syllable word in the structure of "2+"ru"+1" can be used as the vehicle of the metaphor without the tenor and the ground. With the restriction of four-character idiom, the form of metaphor in the structure can be shown in part.

People usually describe something unfamiliar with the metaphor or with something familiar. So, the tenor is an abstract concept that is not easy to understand while the vehicle is the concrete concept easy to understand. There are some exceptions for the four-character idiom with the word of "ru" in which the tenor in the structure of "1+"ru"+2" is not the abstract word but the part of the body or the familiar word.

In the paper, the words with one syllable in the structure of "1+"ru"+2" and "2+"ru"+1" are studied with one example in the "2+"ru"+1", which are shown as follows table2.

Table 2.   The common one-syllable word in structure of "1+"ru"+2"and "2+"ru"+1"

One-syllable word	Structure of "1+"ru"+2"	Structure of "2+"ru"+1"
Face	面如土色(mian ru tuse),面如满月(mian ru manyue),面如死灰(mian ru sihui),面如冠玉(mian ru guanyu),面如灰土(mian ru sihui),面如傅粉 (mian ru fufen),面如凝脂(mian ru ningzhi)	人心如面 Renxin ru mian

The two structures mentioned above have a common in the one-syllable word, but its function of the grammar is totally different in the two structures. For example, in the structure of "1+"ru"+2", the face is the tenor of the metaphor with the specificity which refers to the specific person's face while the face in the structure of "2+"ru"+1" only refers to the appearance without specific person that is the vehicle of the metaphor.

It is found in the study of the two-syllable words in the structure of "1+"ru"+2" and "2+"ru"+1" that there isn't an repeatable example, which shows that the one-syllable word or two-syllable words is or are in different position of the four-character idioms with the word of "ru" with few repetitions of one-syllable words and with no repetition of two-syllable words. The one-syllable or two-syllable words are the tenor and the vehicle of the metaphor with the different function in the structure.

6   The conclusion

This paper makes an analysis on the four-character idioms with the word of "ru" in the position 2 and the position 3 and provides the features of the structure with the word of "ru". Furthermore, it is discussed in detail for the differences and similarities of the one-syllable words in the structure of "1+"ru"+2" and "2+"ru"+1", for the selection restrictions in the one-syllable word as the tenor and vehicle of the metaphor and for the mapping rule of four-character idioms with the word of "ru". It is found that the word of "ru" can be in 4 positions of the four-character idioms and the word of "ru" in the position 3 is the largest number of all ones. The four-character idioms with the word of "ru" reserve the simile mark, but they are a metaphor with tenor and the vehicle whose cognitive paths show the special mapping rules in which the tenor is not something abstract and strange but something concrete and familiar including the words of people's body. In the structure of "2+"ru"+1", the most ancient words can be used for the vehicle of the metaphor (e.g. gold, wood, water, fire and earth) and daily articles known to the ancient people can also be used.

Acknowledgments. The work was supported by the National Science Foundation of China (No. 61170163); the support program of young and middle-aged backbone teachers for Beijing Language and Culture University; Funding Project of Education Ministry for Development of Liberal Arts and Social Sciences(16YJA740036); Wu Tong Innovation Platform of Beijing Language and Culture University (supported by "the Fundamental Research Funds for the Central Universities(16PT03,14YJ160502)). The authors also gratefully acknowledge the helpful comments and suggestions of the reviewers, which have improved the presentation.

References

1. Lakoff, George, Mark Johnson. Metaphors We Live By. Chicago and London:The University of Chicago Press,1980.
2. Lakoff,George.Woman,Fire,and DangerousThings: What Categories Reveal about the-Mind.Chicago and London:The University of Chicago Press,1987.
3. Wang Yin Wang Tiancheng. A Cognitive Analysis of Simile Idiom Construction in Chinese.Language Teaching and Linguistic Studies,2010.4.
4. Chen Jie, Xie Shijian. Conceptual Blending of Two Vehicles of Similes in Chinese Four-Character Idioms.Journal of Guangxi Normal University,2012.6.
5. Wang yin Wang tianyi .A Cognitive Analysis of Simile Idiom Construction in Chinese.Language Teaching and Linguistic Studies,2010.4.
6. Su Dingfang. Studies in Metaphor, Shanghai Foreign Language Education Press, 2004.
7. Sun Mengming. Idioms with figurative words and their combinations. Rhetorical study,

1994,4.
8. Li Shengmei. System analysis of figurative categories. Rhetorical study, 1994,1.
9. Hu Zhuanglin. Metaphor and Cognition.Chinese university press, 2004.
10. Wang Zhimin. Chinese Noun Phrase Metaphor Recognition. Applied Linguistics, 2007.2.
11. Zhao Yanfang. An Introduction to Cognitive Linguistics. Shanghai Foreign Language
Education Press, 2002.

Semantic Development: From Hand Act to Speech Act ---Metaphors and Different Image Schemas

Minli Zhou

School of Liberal Arts, Jiangxi Normal University, Nanchang, Jiangxi Province, P.R. China

minlizhou@163.com

Abstract: For the speech act verbs "*fureru*" in Japanese and "*ti2*" in Chinese, the function of speaking is derived from the meaning of hand act under the action of metaphor. However, this semantic development is based on different image schemas. "*Fureru*" is based on "far to near" schema, while "*ti2*" is based on "low to high" schema, container schema, and focus schema. There also exist similar semantic development paths in English. This study is designed to provide an example for the research of semantic development based on the same cognitive mechanism and different image schemas, thus deepening the understanding of semantic development rules about the verbs of hand act.

Keywords: Metaphor • Image schema• Action of hands • Verbs denoting speaking

1   Introduction

It is showed in cross-linguistic studies that the semantic development from hand act verbs to speech act verbs may be universal in human languages. For instance, by taking the Chinese verbs "提"[*ti2*] (*to raise or lift something*) and "扯"[*che3*] (*to pull something*) for example, [1] made a detailed analysis on how their meaning moved from hand act to mouth act and then developed into speech act. [1] further pointed out that some hand act verbs and related phrases or idioms in English could also develop a function of saying or speaking (e.g., *beat about the bush*, "to talk about something for a long time without coming to the main point"; *hold forth*, "to speak for a long time about something in a way that other people might find boring"; *pull somebody up*, "to criticize somebody for something that they have done wrong"), suggesting that this pattern of semantic development has a typological value. [2] revealed that the hand act verb "*ti2*" caused its recipient to change position, which was the premise of its semantic development. It was metaphor that made the hand act verb "*ti2*" project a new meaning of mouth act and finally endowed it with the function of saying or speaking. In addition, [3] discovered that there were nearly one hundred body act verbs in Chinese from which speech act verbs derived, and the same was true in Mongolian. It is worthwhile to note that the body act verbs mentioned in this paper also include hand act verbs such as "摆"[*bai3*](*to place or set something in order*),

© Springer International Publishing AG 2016
M. Dong et al. (Eds.): CLSW 2016, LNAI 10085, pp. 546–556, 2016
DOI: 10.1007/978-3-319-49508-8_51

"释"[*shi4*](*to unfasten something or take things off, to put down something*), "指" [*zhi3*] (*to show with finger*), "敲" [*qiao1*] (*to knock or beat something*), "举"[*ju3*] (*to raise or lift up something*) etc. Besides, many other relevant studies can also be found in [4], [5], and [6] etc.

The researches mentioned above indicate that the semantic development of hand act verbs has drawn considerable attention. As it was pointed out in [2], "it is an issue worthy of an in-depth investigation and discussion that in what other languages the hand act verbs could generate the function of speaking". What's more, "do all hand act verbs generate this function under the action of metaphors?[2]" Another closely related question is that whether there are different image schemas behind the same cognitive mechanism regarding those speech act verbs derived from hand act verbs.

2   Semantic Development of Japanese Verb *"fureru"*

According to *Japanese-Chinese Dictionary*, the verb "触れる" [*fureru*] basically means to touch something or contact with something:

(1) 手で軽く触れる[1]。 [*Te de karuku fureru*] (*Touch lightly with hand.*)

(2) 髪にそっと触れた。 [*Kami ni sotto fureta*] (*Touch the hair lightly.*)

However, the verb *"fureru"* also has some other uses as shown in the two examples below:

(3) そのことには触れないでくれ。 [*Sono koto ni wa furenaide kure*] (*Please don't bring that up again.*)

(4) 時間がないので簡単にしか触れられない。 [*Jikan ga nai node kantan ni shika furerarenai*] (*I cannot but touch upon it briefly since time is running out.*)

The verb *"fureru"* in Examples 3 and 4 can be interpreted as idioms in English such as *"bring something up"*(to mention a subject or start to talk about it) or *"touch upon something"*(to mention or deal with a subject in only a few words, without going into detail). Obviously, it not only denotes hand act, but also denotes speech act.

2.1   The Effect of Metaphor Mechanism

The contemporary cognitive linguistics holds that metaphor is not only a linguistic phenomenon, but also a cognitive phenomenon, known as a humans' basic mode of thinking, cognition and conceptualization [7]. Metaphor refers in essence to understanding and experiencing one kind of things by another kind of things [8]. Here *"another kind of things"* can be comprehended as the source domain, while *"one kind of things"* is the target domain. And *"another kind of things"*---the source domain, which is the basis for metaphorical cognition, is usually something tangible and familiar to people, while *"one kind of things"*---the target domain, is usually something strange and abstract. Metaphor, psychologically based on the association by similarity be-

---

[1]   The explanations, examples, and translations of the Japanese words are cited from an electronic version of *Japanese-Chinese Dictionary*, unless otherwise specified.

tween things of the two domains, is a cognitive projection from one domain (*source domain*) onto another domain (*target domain*).

In order to describe the semantic development of *"fureru"* from denoting hand act to denoting speech act more clearly, we will start with linguistic facts.

(5) 直接手を触れないでください。[*Chokusetsu te o furenaide kudasai*] (*Don't touch with bare hands.*)

(6) 軽く触れるだけでスイッチが入る。[*Karuku fureru dakede suicchi ga hairu*] (*A light touch will turn the switch on.*)

(7) 電線に触れて感電した。[*Densen ni furete kandenshita*] (*(Somebody) touched the wire and got an electric shock.*)

When the verb *"fureru"* means touching something or contacting with something, it indicates a spatial connection between the agent or subject of an act (the doer of the act in a sentence, generally living individuals, such as "a person") and the recipient or object of an act (generally living or lifeless materials, such as "髪"[*kami*](*hair*) in Example 2 or "電線"[*densen*] (*wire*) in Example 7) by means of tools, such as hands. When serving as a tool, hands sometimes will appear in sentences, as shown in Examples 1 and 5. No matter whether it is translated into "摸"[*mo1*](*to touch something*) or "碰"[*peng4*](*to contact with something*) in Chinese, it always stresses the contact between hands and materials. So the verb *"fureru"* denotes an act of hands and it emphasizes that hands act on materials.

When the verb *"fureru"* means involving something or mentioning something, its object and tool starts to become abstract although the subject is still a living person. For example:

(8) 過去には触れないでほしい。[*Kako ni wa furenaide hoshii*] (*Please do not mention the past.*)

(9) この点についてはあとで触れる。[*Kono ten ni tsuite wa atode fureru*] (*This point will be touched upon later.*)

(10) ついでに少し触れておきます。[*Tsuide ni sukoshi furete okimasu*] (*I will mention this point now in passing.*)

As the objects of the verb *"fureru"*, "過去"[*kako*] (*the past*) in Example 8, "この点"[*kono ten*](*this point*) in Example 9, and "そのこと"[*sono koto*](*that thing*) in Example 3 hereinbefore, are, relatively speaking, an abstract being. Moreover, in these uses, the tools used by the verb *"fureru"* are abstract "words". That is to say, if the meaning of the verb *"fureru"* is still understood as a kind of contact, it will be a kind of abstract contact. This can be comprehended from a perspective of metaphor, as shown below: a person, as a cognitive subject, associates himself with a concrete object by hands. Likewise, a person, as a cognitive subject, associates himself with related things or events by words. The similarity of the two cases is that the subjects of the act are associated with the objects of the act, so "saying (something)" can also be compared to abstractly "touching (something)", and in this way, the verb *"fureru"*, which originally represents hand act, is given a function of speaking. In Example 4 hereinbefore, the verb *"fureru"* can be translated into "谈"[*tan2*] (*to talk*) in Chinese.

2.2   "Far to Near" Schema

Image schema is one of the most important concepts in cognitive linguistics. Images, according to [9], are abstract representations formed by people in a process in which they perceive and experience objective things, and are different psychological impressions formed by different methods (being different in highlights, perspectives, and abstraction degrees) in that process. Moreover, [7] and [10] also thought that image schema was a simple and basic cognitive structure formed by people in daily association with objective things, which, as a schematic representation, showed a fixed type.

Basically the verb "*fureru*" means a spatial connection and contact between a person (the agent or subject of the verb) and a concrete object by hand, which is the tool of the verb. Its image schema is shown in Fig.1. When the behavior the verb "*fureru*" denotes and the object "*fureru*" involves are perceived by language users again and again, its core meaning "to contact with (something)" will be highlighted, thus forming a more abstract "far to near" schema, as shown in Fig.2.

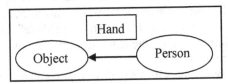

Fig.1. Basic "Far to Near" Schema

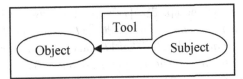

Fig.2. Abstract "Far to Near" Schema

When the tool which the subject of the verb uses is not hands but words, and the object which the subject contacts with is not concrete materials but abstract events, such as "*sono koto*" (*that thing*) or "*kono ten*" (*this point*), it is only that the parameters in the image schema in Fig.2 need to be concretized. The image schema is illustrated in Fig.3.

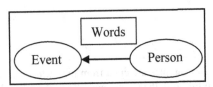

Fig.3. Extended "Far to Near" Schema

In short, the hand act verb "*fureru*" stresses a spatial contact between the subject and the object, namely, the subject contacts with the object from far to near. So its function of speaking is based on a cognitive "far to near" schema.

2.3   Related Phenomena

The English verb *"touch"* is similar to the Japanese verb *"fureru"*. No matter whether it serves as a transitive verb or an intransitive verb, it can express hand act, that is, to put one's hand onto somebody or something. Moreover, when serving as an intransitive verb, it also has a function of speaking. For example, the idiom *"touch on/upon something"* means to mention or deal with a subject in only a few words, without going into detail.

(11) Can you *touch* your toes (=bend and reach them with your hands)?[2]

(12) In his speech he was only able to *touch* on a few aspects of the problem.

3   Semantic Development of Chinese Verb *"ti2"*

"提"[*Ti2*] is a pictophonetic character in which the left part，as a pictographic element, is related to the meaning of the whole character and the right part, as a phonetic element, is related to the pronunciation of the whole character. According to *Shuowen Jiezi*[3], the verb *"ti2"* means *"to raise, lift or carry something"*. In *Contemporary Chinese Dictionary* (Edition VI)[4], both the hand act verb *"ti2"* and the speech act verb *"ti2"* are explained as follows:

Sense 1: to carry (something with a handle or rope) with hands down.

(13) 我去提一壶水来。[*Wo3 qu4 ti2 yi1hu2shui3 lai2*] (*I will go and fetch a bucket of water.*)

Sense 2: to hold something up: 提高[*Ti2gao1*] (*To raise somebody or something or be raised to a higher position or level*)、提升[*Ti2sheng1*] (*Move upwards, to lift or move something to a higher level*)、提价[*Ti2jia4*] (*To raise or increase prices*)、提神[*Ti2shen2*] (*To keep one's spirits up, to refresh oneself*)。

Sense 4: to point out or enumerate: 提意见[*Ti2 yi4jian4*] (*To offer comments or suggestions, to advice on something*)、提问题[*Ti2 wen4ti2*] (*To ask questions*)。

Sense 7: to speak of; to mention:

(14) 旧事重提。[*Jiu4shi4 chong2ti2*] (*Rake up the past.*)

(15) 他跟父亲提到要考大学的事。[*Ta1 gen1 fu4qin1 ti2dao4 yao4 kao3 da4xue2 de shi4*] (*He mentioned to his father that he would take the university entrance examination.*)

---

[2]   All the following English examples are cited from the *Oxford Advanced Learner's English-Chinese Dictionary* (7th Edition), the Commercial Press & Oxford University Press, 2009.

[3]   *Shuowen Jiezi*说文解字 is a dictionary written by Xu Shen(Han Dynasty). It systematically discussed the structures and formation rules of Chinese characters. The edition used here is verified by Xu Xuan(Song Dynasty) and published by Zhonghua Book Company, 2014.

[4]   The explanations and examples of the Chinese words are cited from *Contemporary Chinese Dictionary*现代汉语词典 (Edition VI. The Commercial Press, 2012), unless otherwise specified.

3.1   The Effect of Metaphor Mechanism

For the use of the verb "*ti2*" in Sense 1, a more accurate interpretation should be "to carry something with hands down, to hang it in the air". In order to "*hang something in the air*", one must first "raise it up". This sememe is most apparent in compound words such as "提高"[*ti2gao1*] and "提升"[*ti2sheng1*] whose structures are composed of the verb "*ti2*" and its result complement. As a verbal morpheme, "*ti2*" can also be combined with some nominal morphemes to form compound words such as "提价"[*ti2jia4*], "提级"[*ti2ji2*] (*to promote to a higher level*), "提职"[*ti2zhi2*](*to promote to a higher position*), "提速"[*ti2su4*](*to increase speed*) etc. As more and more nominal morphemes are used to collocate with the verbal morpheme "*ti2*", the original sememe that "an act which needs to be realized by 'hands'" has disappeared, but the core sememe— "*raising something up*", which corresponds to "*hanging something in the air*", still works through metaphor mechanism. Taking "提价"[*ti2jia4*](*to raise or increase prices*) for example, the "prices" is seen as a "real object", and "*to raise or increase prices*" is taken as "to raise an object up". Moreover, there is a change in height before and after an "object" is "raised up", and the same is true for the things represented by those nominal morphemes, since in these things there also exists differentiation in grade or degree, which can be comprehended as a kind of abstract height.

For the use in Sense 4, "advices" or "questions" are regarded as something that can be "raised up" like a real object. The associational basis for this metaphor is that they exist in human consciousness, especially for the native Chinese speakers, they exist in the mind, and it is through words that people advice on something or raise a question about it. So the "advices" or "questions" just seem to be "raised up" and "hung in the air" like a concrete object. In other words, they come out of speakers' mind and become perceptible to both speakers and listeners. This is similar to the process in which "a person, as an agent of an act, hangs something in the air by hand", only that the former has the aid of words, so the verb "*ti2*" can be understood as a verb of speech act in Sense 4.

In Sense 7, the object of the verb "*ti2*" is an abstract "event". Here, the basis for association by similarity is that these events are originally not in the scope of attention in the current state, but the speaker transfers them from the scope of inattention to the scope of attention by words. So there is a similarity between this transfer and the process in which a subject raises something up and then hangs it in the air by hand. Therefore, the verb "*ti2*" in Sense 7 also has a corresponding function of speaking.

In a word, the semantic development of "*fureru*" and "*ti2*" shows that the metaphorical projection relations between hand act verbs and speech act verbs are not built directly, and they, actually, experience a process from "object metaphor" to "event metaphor". For language users metaphorical cognition aims to concretize some abstract concepts, but not to make concrete concepts abstract, so when cognizing a behavior or an act, people do not directly perceive a concrete act as an abstract one, but always first concretize the object of the act in an event, and then dominate it by using this act verb. Meanwhile, the metaphorization of a cognitive object also requires the metaphorization of the verb that dominates it, otherwise semantic disharmony will arise. In this way, under the influence of the abstract object, the concrete act verb will be metaphorized and become an abstract act verb.

3.2   "Low to High" Schema, Container Schema, and Focus Schema

The verb "*ti2*" basically means "to carry something with hands down, to hang it in the air". Its image schema is shown in Fig.4. After further abstract conceptualization, this image schema can evolve into a more basic "low to high" schema, as shown in Fig.5. It well embodies the use in Sense 2, for example, "提价" [*ti2jia4*] (*to raise or increase prices*) and "提神" [*ti2shen2*] (*to keep up one's spirits*). This is because "价" [*jia4*] (*prices*) and "神" [*shen2*] (*spirits*) are increased in quantity or degree by the subject of the act under a certain acting force or in a certain way.

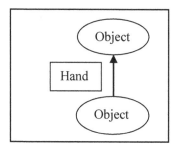

Fig.4. Basic "Low to High" Schema

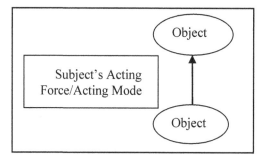

Fig.5. Abstract "Low to High" Schema

It is noteworthy that although a function of speaking is given to the verb "*ti2*", it is still explained in two items (in Senses 4 and 7) in dictionary. From a perspective of cognitive image schema, there is also a difference between them. As mentioned above, in such uses as "提问题"[*ti2 wen4ti2*](*to ask questions*) and "提意见"[*ti2 yi4jian4*](*to offer comments or suggestions, to advice on something*), in native Chinese speakers' eyes, "意见" [*yi4jian4*] (*comments, suggestions, and advices*) and "问题" [*wen4ti2*] (*questions*) exist in human consciousness, that is, they "exist in human mind". At this point, "mind" is metaphorized into a container, and people advice on something or ask questions as if to take "advices" or "questions" out of "mind", so it is often said that

"提出一个问题" [*ti2chu1 yi1ge4 wen4ti2*] (*to ask a question*) or "提不出什么意见" [*ti2bu4chu1 shen2me yi4jian4*] (*somebody cannot offer any comments*). Here the directional verb "出"[*chu1*], as a result complement, means "out of somewhere". For the uses in Sense 4, the image schema is a coincidence of "low to high" schema with container schema, as shown in Fig.6.

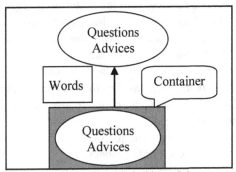

Fig.6. Sense 4 - based Coincidence Schema
"Low to High" Schema
Container Schema

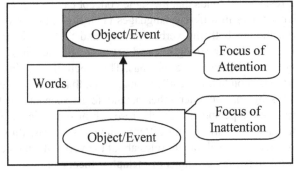

Fig.7. Sense 7 - based Coincidence Schema
"Low to High" Schema
Focus Schema

In the uses listed in Sense 7, an "event" is metaphorized into a "liftable" object, and it is transferred from the scope of inattention to the scope of attention to make it the current focus through the act which the verb "*ti2*" denotes. Taking "旧事重提"[*jiu4shi4 chong2ti2*](*rake up the past*) for example, "旧事"[*jiu4shi4*](*the past*) is originally not in the scope of attention for the speakers or listeners, it is transferred to the present scope of attention through words by the speakers. Therefore, when a text starts by "提起某件事" [*ti2qi3 mou3jian4 shi4*](*to mention something*) or "提到某个人*" [*ti2dao4 mou3ge4 ren2*](*to mention somebody*), usually "某件事"[*mou3jian4 shi4*](*something*) or "某个人"[*mou3ge4 ren2*](*somebody*) will serve as a text topic and thus remind the listeners to pay attention to it. Its image schema is a coincidence of "low to high" schema with focus schema, as shown in Fig.7.

3.3   Related Phenomena

Like the verb "*ti2*" mentioned above, both the verb "举"[*ju3*](*to lift something up*) in Chinese and the verb "*raise*" in English are also used as a hand act verb and a speech act verb. Moreover, their functions of speaking are based on the same metaphorical cognitive mechanism and similar image schemas.

(16) 举重[*Ju3zhong4*](*To lift weights*)、举手[*Ju3shou3*](*To raise one's hands*)、高举着红旗[*Gao1ju3 zhe hong2qi2*](*Holding the red banner high*)。

(17) 举个例子。[*Ju3ge4 li4zi*] (*To illustrate, to give an example*)

(18) She *raised* the gun and fired.

(19) The book *raises* many important questions.

(20) I'm glad you *raised* the subject of money.

4   Conclusion

Cognitive linguistics puts the relationship between language, thought and reality as the core of language research. It holds that the same concept can be expressed with different images and metaphors in different languages [11]. It can be seen from the above analysis that even though both the verbs "*fureru*" and "*ti2*" generate a function of speaking from their original meaning of hand act under the action of metaphor, they are different from each other in image schemas. The function of saying or speaking of "*fureru*" is mainly based on "far to near" schema, while that of "*ti2*" is primarily based on "low to high" schema, container schema, and focus schema. So this paper can provide an example and a perspective for the research of semantic development based on the same cognitive mechanism and different image schemas, thus deepening the understanding of semantic development rules about the verbs of hand act.

One of the most important opinions of metaphor theory in cognitive linguistics is that "there are interconnecting and conventional metaphorical expression systems in every language, and they jointly embody basic conceptual metaphors or fundamental analogies. The reasons why different languages have these commonalities are that they all come from humans' common feelings of the world, and have become part of people's common notions"[12]. To fully verify whether the metaphorical expression from hand act to speech act is a universal law or not in human languages, we still need to conduct lots of corpus analyses. But the research in this paper at least shows that for the semantic developments occurring in different language systems or in the same language system, it is absolutely possible that they may be based on different image schemas even if they have the same start and end points.

As far as the paths for the semantic development from hand act verbs to speech act verbs are concerned, this paper outlined two basic schemas, but it is an issue worthy of further discussing whether other image schemas exist and what they are, e.g., the

Chinese verbs "扯" [*che3*] and "掰" [*bai1*], as well as the English verbs "*put*" and "*bring*" in the examples below.

(21) 没等他说完扯着他就走。 [*Mei2 deng3 ta1 shuo1wan2,che3 zhe ta1 jiu4 zou3.*] (*He was drawn away before finishing his words.*)

(22) 闲扯[*Xian2che3*](*Chattering*)、扯谎[*Che3huang3*](*To lie*)、扯闲篇[*Che3 xian2pian1*](*To make pointless chitchat.*)

(23) "我实话跟你说吧，他收下那套红木家具了！" 田曼芳淡然一笑："瞎掰！" [5][*"Wo3 shi2hua4 gen1 ni3 shuo1 ba, ta1 shou1xia4 na4tao4 hong2mu4 jia1ju4 le!" Tian2 Man4fang1 dan4ran2 yi1xiao4: "xia1bai1!"*] (*"To be frank with you, he accepted the mahogany furniture!" Manfang Tian smiled drily, "You're lying!"*) (*God Is Watching*)

"掰"[*Bai1*] is a meaning-joint character, literally meaning "to break off something with hands". It also has an extended meaning, that is, "to argue questions or things out". There is such a use in the verb "掰扯"[*bai1che3*] in Tianjin dialect [13]. For example,"这件事，我得跟他掰扯掰扯!"[*Zhe4jian4 shi4, wo3 dei3 gen1ta1 bai1che3 bai1che3!*] (*I'm going to argue this matter out with him!*). In the above Example 23, "瞎掰"[*xia1bai1*] means "to talk nonsense or tell a lie".

(24) *Put* the cases down there, please.

(25) She *put* it very tactfully.

(26) The meat was---how shall I *put* it---a little overdone.

The verb "*put*" basically means "to move something into a particular place or position", but it also has a function of speaking, that is, "to express or state something in a particular way", as can be seen in Examples 25 and 26. The verb "*bring*" means "to come to a place with somebody or something", as shown in Example 27. It also denotes speaking when used in some idioms, for instance, the idiom "*bring something up*" in Example 28, means "to mention a subject or start to talk about it".

(27) Don't forget to *bring* your books with you.

(28) *Bring* it up at the meeting.

References

1. Zhengcun Dong. : The Shift from Hand Act to Speech Act in Semantic Development. ZHONGGUOYUWEN, no.2 (2009). (董正存. 词义演变中手部动作到口部动作的转移. 中国语文，2009/02). (in Chinese)
2. Zhengcun Dong. : How does the Verb "*Ti*(提)" Get the Meaning of Speaking? Chinese Linguistics, no.2 (2012). (in Chinese)
3. Yunxia Ma & Yuzhu Bao. : Speaking Meanings of Body Action Verbs in Chinese and Mongolian. Journal of Minzu University of China, no.2 (2013). (in Chinese)
4. Yanqing Zeng & Huaizhi Wu. : Meaning Extension and Shift of Hand Act Verbs. JOURNAL OF BINGTUAN EDUCATION INSTITUTE, no.2 (2000). (曾艳青、吴怀智. "扌"(手) 部动作动词的意义伸展与转用. 兵团教育学院学报，2000/02). (in Chinese)

---

[5] This example is cited from a novel in the corpus of Center for Chinese Linguistics PKU.

5. Hong Wei. : From Body Act to Speech Act---An Analysis on One Kind of Semantic Development in Shandong Dialect during the Ming and Qing Dynasty. JOURNAL OF DAIZONG, no.3 (2006). (魏红. 从肢体行为到言说行为——试析明清山东方言里一类词义的演变. 岱宗学刊，2006/03). (in Chinese)
6. Yunxia Ma. : From Body Act to Speech Act---The Function Expansion of Verbs of Speaking Driven by Rhetoric. DANGDAI XIUCIXUE, no.5 (2015). (马云霞. 从身体行为到言说行为——修辞动因下言说动词的扩展. 当代修辞学，2010/05). (in Chinese)
7. Ungerer F. & Schmid H. : An Introduction to Cognitive Linguistics. Addison Wesley Longman Limited, London (1996).
8. Lakoff G. & Johnson M. : Metaphors We Live By. The University Of Chicago Press, Chicago (1980).
9. Langacker R. W. : Concept, Image and Symbol. Mouton de Gruyter, New York (1990).
10. Croft W. & Cruse D. A. : Cognitive Linguistics. Cambridge University Press, Cambridge (2004).
11. Shikai Zhao. : Cognition-based Contrastive Studies of English and Chinese. In: Studies and Applications of Chinese Linguistics. Shanghai Foreign Language Education Press, Shanghai (2001). (赵世开. 基于认知的英汉对比研究，《中国的语言学研究和应用》. 上海：上海外语教育出版社，2001). (in Chinese)
12. Feng Zhang. : A Comparative Study of Spatial Metaphors in Russian and Chinese. Journal of PLA University of Foreign Languages, no.1 (2001). (in Chinese)
13. Ruwei Tan. About the Lexicon in Tianjin Dialect: 掰 [*bai1*], 掰扯 [*bai1che3*], 瞎掰 [*xia1bai1*]. http://blog.sina.com.cn/s/blog_4b6668a101009gsi.html. (2008). (谭汝为. 天津方言词语趣谈：掰·掰扯·瞎掰. 新浪网博客, 2008). (in Chinese)

Computer semantic identification of the adverb "Dou"

Yong Lu[1], *Pengyuan Liu[2]

[1]Institute for Language Monitoring and Social Computing,
Beijing Language and Culture University
Beijing 100083, China
ly_yonglu@163.com

[2]Institute for Language Monitoring and Social Computing,
Beijing Language and Culture University
Beijing 100083, China
*Corresponding author
liupengyuan@pku.edu.cn

Abstract. Semantic identification of adverbs in Modern Chinese is regarded as an exploration and attempt in improving semantic analysis on sentence level. This paper mainly focuses on two problems. Firstly, how to make computer identify the meanings of adverb "Dou". Secondly, how to make computer identify the semantic orientation of adverb "Dou". Based on the real large-scale corpus, the authors investigate the meanings of adverb "Dou" which are restricted by various factors and formal features, summarize the formal rules in a systematic way, and build a flow chart that computers are capable of identifying. We hope that this research will contribute to computer understanding and generating in the sentence that contains the adverb "Dou".

Keywords: Adverb, "Dou", Semantic Orientation, Semantic Identification

1   Introduction

The adverb "Dou" has always been a focus in the field of Chinese linguistics. Relevant studies on the adverb "Dou" boost an extensive scope, present multiple perspectives and make breakthrough in profundity. Achievements have been made in relevant studies, especially in the studies of analyzing the adverb "Dou" by means of semantic

© Springer International Publishing AG 2016
M. Dong et al. (Eds.): CLSW 2016, LNAI 10085, pp. 557–576, 2016
DOI: 10.1007/978-3-319-49508-8_52

orientation. However, it is worth noting that early studies on semantic orientation give priority to the discussion of linguistics itself and fail to put those research results into practice to some extent. With the development of information processing, it is a basic requirement for the realization human-machine interaction that having computers understand languages, and the key to understand languages is semantics. So studying the computer-oriented identification of semantic orientation is an important practice of improving the semantic analysis of sentence level via computers. Aiming at the need of natural language processing, based on the predecessors research achievements, this paper make full use of a large number of real corpus and try to inquire the constraints of judging meaning and semantic orientation of adverb "Dou", systematically summing up the structural regularity and describing them formally, building a flow chart of semantic identification of adverb "Dou". We hope that our research work above can provide some methods and help for the computer to understand and generate Dou-sentence and semantic identification of other parts of speech as well.

The classification of "Dou[1]" in this paper refers to the Modern Chinese Dictionary(6th edu) [2].

This Paper will discusses and analyses the following two questions:

1. For any Dou-sentence, how to make computer identify the meanings of "Dou".

2. For any Dou-sentence, how to make computer identify the semantic orientation of "Dou".

If computer can successfully resolve the above two questions, it will play an important role in natural language processing technologies, such as disambiguation of

---

[1] Dou₁ denotes the meaning of "sum up", except for question, the components locate in front of "Dou", for example, "全家都搞文艺工作[quán jiā dōu gǎo wén yì gōng zuò]". Dou₂ denotes the meaning of "even", for example, "今天一点儿都不冷[jīn tiān yī diǎn ér dōu bú lěng]". Dou₃ denotes the meaning of "already", for example, "饭都凉了,快吃吧[fàn dōu liáng le, kuài chī ba]". Dou₄ combines with the character "是[Shi]",which denotes the meaning of "reason", for example, "都是你要我也不会迟到[dōu shì nǐ mó cèng , yào bú wǒ yě bú huì chí dào]" . In addition, we put forward the Dou₅ which denotes the meaning of "sun up" and "even" simultaneously. For example, "说起跳水,这里连小孩子都知道,荷荷有名的"跳水皇后"高敏就是他们的老乡[shuō qǐ tiào shuǐ,zhè lǐ lián xiǎo hái zǐ dōu zhī dào,hé hè yǒu míng de "tiào shuǐ huáng hòu "gāo mǐn jiù shì tā men de lǎo xiāng]" .

[2] Linguistics Institute of Chinese Academy of Social Sciences: The Contemporary Chinese Dictionary, 6th edn. The Commercial Press(2012).(in Chinese)

the meaning of Dou-sentence[3], English-Chinese machine translation, and automatic question answering about Dou-sentence[4] et al.

In this paper, the second part discusses how to make computer indentify the meanings of "Dou"; the third part analyses how to make computer identify the semantic orientation of "Dou"; Finally, the fourth part reveals the shortcomings of our research and look to the research in future.

2   How to make computer identify the meanings of "Dou"

Zhan Weidong(2004) investigated the classification of "Dou", and proposed some form features for computer judges, which had enlightenment and practicality for us. Integrating his research, we continue to explore the form features to distinguish the meanings of "Dou", so as to provide a little help for the computer identification. It is important to say that Zhan proposed a flow "$Dou_2 \rightarrow Dou_3 \rightarrow Dou_1$", which can judge the

---

[3] The sentence "饭我们都吃完了[fàn wǒ men dōu chī wán le]" is actually an ambiguous sentence. If the semantic of "都" in the sentence orients "我们", the meaning is all of us have finished the meal. If the semantic of "都" orients "the "饭", the meaning is the meal has been ate up. This proves that if the semantic orientation of "都" is different, the meaning of the sentence will be different too. If we cannot judge the semantic orientation of "都" correctly, we will not comprehend the meaning of the sentence accurately, even misunderstand it. Therefore, for sentence processing, if we make computers understand and recognize the meaning of sentences by themselves, it will be a great advancement of improving the semantic analysis of sentence level.

[4] Supposing that the presupposition is "昨天上午, 陈校长和何副校长都会见了美国的麦阿密教授[zuó tiān shàng wǔ, chén xiào zhǎng hé hé fù xiào zhǎng dōu huì jiàn le měi guó de mài ā mì jiāo shòu]". If be asked that "昨天上午谁 (哪些人) 会见了美国的麦阿密教授[zuó tiān shàng wǔ shuí (nǎ xiē rén) huì jiàn le měi guó de mài ā mì jiāo shòu?]", the computer can arrive at three points of cognition based on the knowledge of the semantic orientation of "都": ①昨天上午, 陈校长会见了美国的麦阿密教授(Yesterday morning, Headmaster Chen met with Professor Miami from America). ②昨天上午, 何副校长会见了美国的麦阿密教授(Yesterday morning, Vice-headmaster He met with Professor Miami from America). ③昨天上午, 陈校长和何副校长一起会见了美国的麦阿密教授(Yesterday morning, Headmaster Chen met with Professor Miami from America together with Vice-headmaster). Obviously, the computer arrives at these answers based on understanding of the semantic orientation of "Dou". And adopting methods based on statistic or other rules can make computer choose the best answer about the semantic orientation object of "Dou" for us.

meanings of "Dou". We found that it is realistic, but there is a sort of meaning which denotes the "reason", Although Zhan mentioned in his work, it didn't pit it into the flow of meanings judgment. In view of this shortcoming, Thus in this paper, through investigating the realistic rate[5] of all kinds of meanings in corpus and the importance of form features, we summarized a new and scientific flow of meanings identification, which is "$Dou_5 \rightarrow Dou_2 \rightarrow Dou_3 \rightarrow Dou_4 \rightarrow Dou_1$[6]". We will particularly discuss the formal features and structural regularities of the meanings of "Dou" in the next section.

2.1 Through investigating exhaustively the 240 Dou_2-sentences, we sum up three following structural regularities[7]. The characters "Dou" and "Lian" occur together;

---

[5] Scholars generally thought that "Dou_1" is superiority meaning, However, in order to ensure that our research is scientific and objective, we based on the real corpus, through artificially judging the meaning and then get a result that is the number of the Dou_1-sentences, Dou_2-sentences, Dou_3-sentences, Dou_4-sentences, and Dou_5-sentences respectively are 9114, 240, 34, 8 and 4. In addition, there remains 600 unqualified sentences in which the "Dou" either refers to location, name or common nouns. According to the result, the data proved to the "Dou_1" is superiority meaning, also known as common meanings, "Dou_2" is more common meaning and others is not commonly used meaning.

[6] Specifically, let computer traverse the before and after Dou-sentence firstly, searching form features of the "Dou_5". if there are these futres, it's "Dou_5". If there are no these, secondly, let computer search form features of the "Dou_2", if there are, it's "Dou_2". The rest can be done in the same manner. Finally, if thre are no features of "Dou_4" in sentence, it's "Dou_1".

[7] We found that examples from (4) to (10) actually omit the character "Lian" before underlines, in other words, we actually can add the "Lian" to sentence or replace "竟[Jing]" to "Lian", which cause to the meaning of each sentence above dose not changed. In addition, due to the appearance of "Lian", the prominence of the meaning of "even" denoted by "Dou" become more clear. We thought that the above three structure regularities can merge into one in essence and ultimately, that is the regularity of the character "Dou" and "Lian" occur together. However, considering that the computer can not judge and analyse like the brain of human after all, therefore, this paper reduce to 3 regularities, aimed at making computer get rid of the constraint and to better identify through getting other regularities.

"Dou" is followed by negative verb phrases[8]; In front of "Dou" is "Yi+number" phrases and then comes the negative verb phrases. There are some examples[9].

（1）她干脆连下一次的机会［都］不给你了。

[tā gàn cuì lián xià yī cì de jī huì [dōu]bú gěi nǐ le。]

（2）连冯先生这样的中国哲学大家［都］说 "不懂"。

[lián féng xiān shēng zhè yàng de zhōng guó zhé xué dà jiā [dōu]shuō "bú dǒng"。]

（3）我连看［都］没有看。[*wǒ lián kàn [dōu]méi yǒu kàn。*]

（4）她想［都］没想过。[*tā xiǎng [dōu]méi xiǎng guò。*]

（5）走了一天了，午饭［都］没回来吃。[*zǒu le yī tiān le，wǔ fàn [dōu]méi huí lái chī。*]

（6）因病不得不摘除一个肾脏，出院后竟一天［都］不休息，揣着导尿管出现在会场。

[yīn bìng bú dé bú zhāi chú yī gè shèn zāng，chū yuàn hòu jìng yī tiān [dōu]bú xiū xī，chuāi zhe dǎo niào guǎn chū xiàn zài huì chǎng。]

（7）一个字［都］听不进。[*yī gè zì [dōu]tīng bú jìn。*]

（8）一点男子气概［都］没有。[*yī diǎn nán zǐ qì gài [dōu]méi yǒu。*]

（9）一个老得眼睛［都］睁不开的干瘪老头瘫坐在沙发上。

[yī gè lǎo dé yǎn jīng [dōu]zhēng bú kāi de gàn biě lǎo tóu tān zuò zài shā fā shàng。]

As you can see, for a Dou-sentence, if the sentence in line with the above three structural regularities, computer can indentify the "Dou" in sentence is "Dou_2".

2.2 We also conclude three structural regularities [10] by analyzing 34 Dou_3-sentences. Firstly, "Dou" is followed by noun phrase that has semantic characteristics of "pass in sequence[11]" and the modal particle "le". Secondly, "Dou" is followed by verb complement structure and the modal particle "le". Thirdly, "Dou" is

---

[8] The negative verb phrases here refer to the pattern of "negation like '不*bu*]', '没[*mei*]' + verbal components" or patterns of "Dou + verbal components which include the negation such as '不*bu*]' and so on". Computer can complete the task of identification through the identification of these negation makers.

[9] Examples in this paper, without special instructions, all come from the Peking University modern Chinese corpus(CCL).

[10] The structure regularity order listed in this paper is same with the flow order of computer identification.

[11] "pass in sequence" is a kind of semantic feature that belongs to the specific normal words in the syntactic pattern of "noun phrase+le". For more detailed information, please see Lu Jianming(2005).

followed by time words, negative verb phrases and the modal particle "le". For example:

（10）［都］大学生了。[[*dōu*]*dà xué shēng le*。]

（11）谁炒谁呀，［都］市场经济了。[*shuí chǎo shuí ya*，[*dōu*]*shì chǎng jīng jì le*。]

（12）你看几点啦？［都］快12点了。

[*nǐ kàn jǐ diǎn lā ?[dōu*]*kuài 12diǎn le*。]

（13）［都］七十多了，还闹什么气哟！[*dōu*]*qī shí duō le*，*hái nào shí me qì yō !*]

（14）"郝处长，上次您老走得匆忙，这件工作服忘带走了，你看我［都］洗干净了。

["*hǎo chù zhǎng*，*shàng cì nín lǎo zǒu dé cōng máng*，*zhè jiàn gōng zuò fú wàng dài zǒu le*，*nǐ kàn wǒ [dōu]xǐ gàn jìng le*。]

（15）宋郁彬点点头："您放心吧，［都］锁好了。

[*sòng yù bīn diǎn diǎn tóu : "nín fàng xīn ba*，*[dōu]suǒ hǎo le*。]

（16）哎，我［都］三天没看见我爸了，他七十多又有老年痴呆症，急死人了。

[*āi*，*wǒ [dōu]sān tiān méi kàn jiàn wǒ bà le*，*tā qī shí duō yòu yǒu lǎo nián chī dāi zhèng*，*jí sǐ rén le*。]

（17）谢延红说，上岸前，我都5个多小时没吃东西了。

[*xiè yán hóng shuō*，*shàng àn qián*，*wǒ [dōu]5gè duō xiǎo shí méi chī dōng xī le*。]

Similarly, for a Dou-sentence, if the sentence in line with these regularities, computer can recognize that the "Dou" in sentence is "Dou$_3$". Besides, we found that Dou$_3$-sentences all end with the modal particle "le", which expresses time changing or new circumstance. The semantic of "Dou" is correspond with the modal particle "le" (Strictly, the "already" meaning of "Dou" might be loaded by the modal particle "le"). If delete "le", the mood of sentence will be incomplete or uncomfortable. Therefore, strictly speaking, the modal particle "le" at the end of the sentence is a necessary condition but not a sufficient for "Dou$_3$". However, one thing to be noted is that given a Dou$_3$-sentence, e.g. "我都成大人了"[12] (*I am grown-ups*)", if replaces "i" with "we", then we should regard "Dou" in sentence as "Dou$_1$". Because when "Dou$_3$" compete with "Dou$_1$", we usually take the principle which slants to the "Dou$_1$". In addition, If the

---

[12] The symbol * indicates that the sentence, although it is made by the author, is a qualified sentence in that it conforms to the natural language rule and used in the daily life communication.

character "Dou" is followed by the signal word, such as 已(yǐ) or 已经(yǐ jīng), which denote completion of action, change or reaching a certain level, we might though that the "Dou" no longer has the meaning of "already" in that it is already deprived by these signal words. In other words, the significance of the relationship between them, in fact, is a kind of reciprocal relationship. For example "这碗都(已经)凉了(The soup is already cold)", The "Dou" in the sentence seems to express the meaning of "sum up" or "already" at the same time, but combine with practice[13], no matter the "Dou" is followed by signal words like 已[yǐ] or 已经[yǐ jīng], we all judge "Dou$_1$".

2.3 Through investigating 8 Dou$_4$-sentences, we found that the character "Dou" which denotes the meaning of "reason" is followed by the character "是(Shi)". So this is an important characteristic for judging "Dou$_4$". Moreover, be same as the semantic function of mentioned above signal words, if there are markers revealing "reason" such as 因(yīn) or 因为(yīn wéi) in sentence, we consider that the "Dou" in sentence no longer reveals the meaning of "reason" in that it was deprived by these signal words. For example, "那位聪明的伯爵小姐今天所以没着被找来，而且近些日被缺勤都是因为这个缘故呢!(That intelligent count lady is not called for today, and often absent recently, because of this reason)", the "Dou" in sentence denotes the meaning of "sum up", containing two things about "not called for today" and "often absent recently". There are more examples.

（18）这[都]是引用道德解释历史，操切过急将牵引的事实过于简化所造成的。

[zhè [dōu]shì yǐn yòng dào dé jiě shì lì shǐ , cāo qiē guò jí jiāng qiān yǐn de shì shí guò yú jiǎn huà suǒ zào chéng de。]

（19）换句话说，[都]是人们自作自受，非干鬼神之事。

[huàn jù huà shuō, [dōu]shì rén men zì zuò zì shòu , fēi gàn guǐ shén zhī shì。]

---

[13] Specifically, if markers like "已[yǐ] or已经[yǐ jīng]" appear in the back of "Dou", then we should judge "Dou$_1$". Oppositely, if there is no markers in the back of "Dou", the current "Dou" denotes the meaning of "sum up" and "even" simultaneously in facts , but in view of this instances is not used commonly meaning, it's rate in corpus is so little, the "Dou$_1$" is advantage meaning, and it's impossible to identify the underling pragmatic meaning currently, So we adopt the strategy that let computer identify "Dou$_1$" in general.

（20）他们每天涌进涌出濠江大小赌场，［都］是当地开放内地旅个人游以后出现的现象。

[tā men měi tiān yǒng jìn yǒng chū háo jiāng dà xiǎo dǔ chǎng , [dōu]shì dāng dì kāi fàng nèi dì lǚ gè rén yóu yǐ hòu chū xiàn de xiàn xiàng。]

（21）这种强烈的心理落差，［都］是与那纵横捭阖颐指气使的"８０年代批评热"参照得来的。

[zhè zhǒng qiáng liè de xīn lǐ luò chà , [dōu]shì yǔ nà zòng héng bǎi hé yí zhǐ qì shǐ de "8 0nián dài pī píng rè "cān zhào dé lái de。]

We found that Dou$_4$-sentences mainly imply the speaker subjective attitude towards facts or evaluation, and negative emotional color. Unfortunately, unlike human being, computer can't understand the speakers' feelings, so we should look for a suitable path for computer indentify precisely. We take a view that if the Dou-sentence in line with the above characteristics, then the "Dou" in sentence is "Dou$_4$". However, the rule is also flawed for the identification of computer. Because the Dou-sentences following by "Shi" not always denote the meaning of "reason". For example sentences.

（22）在社会教育中，人人都是施教者，又都是受教育者。

[zài shè huì jiāo yù zhōng , rén rén dōu shì shī jiāo zhě , yòu dōu shì shòu jiāo yù zhě。]

（23）这些现象在通常情况下都是正常的生理现象，随着青春期的过去，会自然消失。

[zhè xiē xiàn xiàng zài tōng cháng qíng kuàng xià dōu shì zhèng cháng de shēng lǐ xiàn xiàng, suí zhe qīng chūn qī de guò qù, huì zì rán xiāo shī。]

（24）社会教育对任何人来讲都具有终身性，活到老学到老对任何人来讲都是不以你的意志为转移的。

[shè huì jiāo yù duì rèn hé rén lái jiǎng dōu jù yǒu zhōng shēn xìng, huó dào lǎo xué dào lǎo duì rèn hé rén lái jiǎng dōu shì bú yǐ nǐ de yì zhì wéi zhuǎn yí de。]

（25）一系列新兴工业，如高分子合成工业、原子能工业、电子计算机工业、半导体工业、宇航工业、激光工业等，都是建立在新兴科学的基础上的。

[yī xì liè xīn xìng gōng yè, rú gāo fèn zǐ hé chéng gōng yè、yuán zǐ néng gōng yè、diàn zǐ jì suàn jī gōng yè、bàn dǎo tǐ gōng yè、yǔ háng gōng yè、jī guāng gōng yè děng, dōu shì jiàn lì zài xīn xìng kē xué de jī chǔ shàng de。]

The "Dou" in the above sentences all denote the meaning of "sum up", and the utilization rates   of such sentences are very high and very common in practice. So just relying on the marker "Shi" to judge the type of "Dou" is obviously unfair. Thereupon, on the investigation of Dou-sentence that "Dou" is followed by "Shi", we concluded a scientific rule to resolve. Specifically though "Dou" and "Shi" combine together, the condition of judging "Dou_1" is the formal features of "Dou_1" has appeared in front of "Dou". The condition of judging "Dou_4" is the formal features of "Dou_1" has not appeared in front of "Dou" or there are singular noun components in front of "Dou". That is to say, on the precondition of "Dou" is followed by "Shi", if "Dou_4" competes with "Dou_1", then indentify "Dou_1".

2.4 In addition, there are some Dou-sentences denote the meaning of "sum up" and "even" simultaneously. In order to facilitate discussion, it's defined as "Dou_5". There are some instances.

（26）老寿首先表现了自己的耐心，一脸的笑，笑得眼睛[都]弯了起来。

[*lǎo shòu shǒu xiān biǎo xiàn le zì jǐ de nài xīn, yī liǎn de xiào, xiào dé yǎn jīng [dōu]wān le qǐ lái。*]

（27）肩伤对我的发挥有很大影响，最后和他对拉时我的胳膊[都]在抖。

[*jiān shāng duì wǒ de fā huī yǒu hěn dà yǐng xiǎng ,zuì hòu hé tā duì lā shí wǒ de gē bó [dōu]zài dǒu。*]

（28）说起跳水, 这里连小孩子[都]知道, 赫赫有名的"跳水皇后"高敏就是他们的老乡。

[*shuō qǐ tiào shuǐ ,zhè lǐ lián xiǎo hái zǐ [dōu]zhī dào ,hè hè yǒu míng de "tiào shuǐ huáng hòu "gāo mǐn jiù shì tā men de lǎo xiāng。*]

（29）他自己呢，连铺盖，衣服，和罐头筒子，[都]没能拿出来，就一脚被日本兵踢出了英国府！

[*tā zì jǐ ne , lián pù gài , yī fú , hé guàn tóu tǒng zǐ , [dōu]méi néng ná chū lái , jiù yī jiǎo bèi rì běn bīng tī chū le yīng guó fǔ !*]

The word "yǎn jīng", "gē bó", "xiǎo hái zǐ" and "pù gài, yīfú, guàn tóu tǒng zǐ" are respectively plural noun and nounal combinative phrase in above sentences. We argued that in the front of the underlines of sentences like example (26) and example(27) are omit the adverb "连[*Lian*]". If we add the word "Lian" to it, then the meaning of "even" denoted by "Dou" will prominent. so the "Dou" in sentences is "Dou_5". However, given a certain Dou-sentence, if the word of "甚至[*shen zhi*]" and "lian" appear together, we thought that the "Dou" in sentence might not denote the "even" meaning. Because when the word "shen zhi" appears in sentence, the "even" meaning of "Dou" might be deprived, on the contrary, when the word "shen zhi" implies or there is not the word "shen zhi", then the meaning of "even" can be showed prominently. For example,

"他们药知道少，神至连一些最基常识都没有(*They know little about drugs, and even some of the basic *common sense)"*.If we delete the word "shen zhi", we can judge "Dou$_5$", otherwise, we can judge "Dou$_1$". Besides, the word "Dou$_1$", "Dou$_2$" and "Dou$_3$" might be overlapped in specific context, and have ambiguity. Zhan Weidong(2004) has analysed, so it's no need for us to say more here.

2.5 Through analyzing 9114 Dou$_1$-sentences, we summarized some formal features, such as there are conditional connectives like "不论[*bú lùn*]", "无论[*wú lùn*] and "不管[*bú guǎn*]" and feature words like "每[*měi*]", "各[*gè*]", "满[*mǎn*]", "整个[*zhěng gè*]", "所有[*suǒ yǒu*]" and "任何[*rèn hé*]" or some combinative phrases or other specific structures in front of "Dou" in sentences. According to these formal markers, we can consider the "Dou" as "Dou$_1$". These formal markers of "Dou$_1$", however, is not a closed set, in view of the space, we do not list one by one here, and we just list some formal markers at appendix for readers.

（30）见了亚母，一高兴<u>什么</u>[都]说出来了。

[*jiàn le yà mǔ, yī gāo xìng shí me [dōu]shuō chū lái le。*]

（31）<u>各企业</u>[都]有自己实力雄厚的科研队伍。

[*gè qǐ yè [dōu]yǒu zì jǐ shí lì xióng hòu de kē yán duì wǔ。*]

（32）泰国是一个<u>大多数人</u>[都]信奉佛教的国度。

[*tài guó shì yī gè dà duō shù rén [dōu]xìn fèng fó jiāo de guó dù。*]

（33）<u>谁</u>[都]不可心里谋害邻舍，也不可喜爱起假誓。

[*shuí [dōu]bú kě xīn lǐ móu hài lín shě, yě bú kě xǐ ài qǐ jiǎ shì。*]

（34）这样，<u>他们每周</u>[都]要乘公共汽车去购物，安全就很难保证。

[*zhè yàng ,tā men měi zhōu [dōu]yào chéng gōng gòng qì chē qù gòu wù ,ān quán jiù hěn nán bǎo zhèng。*]

（35）雷斯林自从和大伙在索拉斯碰面之后，<u>不管是能力还是力量</u>[都]在提升当中。

[*léi sī lín zì cóng hé dà huǒ zài suǒ lā sī pèng miàn zhī hòu , bú guǎn shì néng lì hái shì lì liàng [dōu]zài tí shēng dāng zhōng。*]

（36）记者昨天是通过日本同行朋友才得知<u>评估团</u>和<u>新闻中心</u>[都]在里佳皇家饭店。

[*jì zhě zuó tiān shì tōng guò rì běn tóng háng péng yǒu cái dé zhī píng gū tuán hé xīn wén zhōng xīn [dōu]zài lǐ jiā huáng jiā fàn diàn。*]

In general, the semantic of "Dou$_1$" orients the front components of it, but it can also orients components that behind it. This circumstances mostly appear in questions. For example, "你都知道谁来了？ *[nǐ dōu zhī dào shuí lái le。*]", the "Dou" in sentence orients interrogative pronoun "Shui". It's need to be mentioned that "Dou_1" can also forward orients pronoun "Shui", however, at this point pronoun "Shui" refers to any one or the whole in full set not question. It denotes the concept of "sum up", for example(33). So, we argued that the semantic orientation of "Dou" is relatively complicated, it can be divided into forward and backward[14].

It is important to say the rates of "Dou_3", "Dou_4" and "Dou_5" in Dou-sentences are 34(0.36%),11 (0.09%) and 4 (0.04%) .They are so little, compared to the superiority meaning "Dou_1" that accounts for 96.96%,. It also reflects the actual usage of all kinds meaning of adverb "Dou" in people's daily conversation. In addition, they also involve some conversational implicature, which need to take some pragmatic elements such as stress, tone, intonation, presupposition and context et al into account to understand. Unfortunately, now information processing can not let the computer combine context to identify the conversational implicature. So, it's strict to indentify them for computer(even say "hard"),and we put forward a strategy that if there is a circumstance that something compete with the superiority meaning "Dou_1", we usually consider it as "Dou_1".

3   How to make computer indentify the semantic orientation of "Dou"

The basic purpose of language information processing is how to make computer to understand natural language, generate sentences complied with natural language rules, and achieve human-machine interaction harmoniously. How to let computer understand precisely the meanings of Dou-sentence, it's important to indentify the semantic orientation of "Dou".

3.1   Current state of the semantic orientation research of adverb[15] "Dou".

The semantic orientation analysis of blanket range adverb "Dou" can date back to 1989 when the Wang Ming discussed the question that the semantic orientation of "Dou" is

---

[14] The forward and backward orientation refers to the objects of semantic orientation of "Dou" span the "Dou" itself, and appear in before and after the "Dou".

[15] Some scholars refer to "Dou_1" as the blanket adverb or range adverb, "Dou_2" as modal adverb and "Dou_3" as time adverb.

ether forward or backward. Later, a lot of scholars such as Shi Jianping(1995), Chen Zijiao(1996) investigated the semantic orientation problems of "Dou$_1$" and "Dou$_2$" from the view of relation meaning. Liu Chuanping(1997), Li Wenfu(2005) and Nan Xiaoming(2010) all investigated the semantic orientation of "Dou" from the perspective of sentence pattern. Fu Manyi(2001) from the angle of the cognition and commutation to analysis the semantic orientation problems of "Dou". More specifically, Liu Chuanping summarized all kinds of regularities of internal orientation and external orientation through researching 4 different attribute objects in the "S都是O" sentence pattern. Li Wenfu found that the usage of blanket range adverb "Dou$_1$" had an important significance to "Ba + NP +Dou+ VP" structure and the development of the modal adverbs "Dou$_2$" by analyzing the regularity of "Dou$_1$" and "Dou$_2$" of "Ba+NP+Dou$_1$/Dou$_2$+VP". Nan Xiaoming thought that the semantic orientation of "Dou$_1$" usually orientes forward and the semantic orientation of "Dou$_3$" usually orientes backward, but the "Dou$_2$" could either orients forward and backward at the same time. Specifically, forward orientation is in typical Lian-sentence, and orientation of forward and backward is in non-typical Lian-sentence.

It is worth mentioning that the problem about semantic orientation of "Dou" also has attracted the attention of computational linguistics. Zhan Weidong comprehensively investigated the distribution of semantic orientation of blanket range adverb "Dou" and presented common principles judging the semantic orientation of "Dou". He also discussed the relationship between the "Dou" as adverbial verbal phrase and the "De" structure and other problems such as the respective location relation between "Dou" and other adverbial components. We thought that the research results of Zhan Weidong were comprehensive analysis about information processing. Not only does it accumulate materials for theory of semantic orientation ,but also provides linguistic theoretical guidance for language information processing. Especially, it plays an important significance in understanding and generating Dou-sentence and Chinese-English transformation technologies and so on. In general , it is an excellent work that combining with theory and practice, linguistics and computer science.

3.2   The semantic orientation of "Dou"

From wide views of semantic orientation researches, specialists and scholars nearly tended to study the problems of blanket range adverb "Dou" such as Wang Ming, Chen Zijiao, Zhan Weidong and so forth. They all made comprehensive and detail research form different points and levels. So the issues mentioned above will not be involved in the essay. Unfortunately, linguistic academia pay less attention to study the semantic orientation of "Dou$_2$" and "Dou$_3$", and some results are only fragmentary and brief analysis. for the "Dou$_4$", the study of semantic orientation is more extremely weak. This paper which provides some guidance and scientific basis for computer semantic identification is aiming to discuss the situation of "Dou$_2$" and "Dou$_3$" and propose a semantic orientation problem of "Dou$_4$",. Therefore, on the basis of former achievements, through analyzing a great number of real linguistic datas, we had a comprehensive investigation of the semantic orientation of the adverb "Dou".

3.2.1 In Lian-sentence[16], the semantic of "Dou$_2$" usually forward orients[17] the nominal components or predicate components leaded by the word "Lian". If there is no "Lian" or it is omitted, the semantic orientation object of "Dou$_2$" is only the predicate components behind the "Lian".

（37）连腿[都]伸不直。[lián tuǐ [dōu]shēn bú zhí。]

（38）连房子[都]拆了。[lián fáng zi [dōu]chāi le。]

（39）连声音[都]没有？[lián shēng yīn [dōu]méi yǒu？]

（40）连手[都]不敢碰一下。[lián shǒu [dōu]bú gǎn pèng yī xià。]

（41）连哭[都]哭不上来了。[lián kū [dōu]kū bú shàng lái le。]

（42）他屁[都]没敢放，就重新给了人家真钞。

[tā pì [dōu]méi gǎn fàng, jiù zhòng xīn gěi le rén jiā zhēn chāo。]

（43）连办理出国手续，私营企业[都]要比国有、集体企业复杂得多。

[lián bàn lǐ chū guó shǒu xù, sī yíng qǐ yè [dōu]yào bǐ guó yǒu、jí tǐ qǐ yè fù zá dé duō。]

3.2.2 The semantic orientation of "Dou$_3$" usually backward orients[18] the normal words featured by "pass in sequence", predicate pronouns and verbal phrases and so on.

（44）三十几？我[都]快五十啦！[sān shí jǐ ？wǒ [dōu]kuài wǔ shí lā！]

（45）这个女人也是，[都]什么时代了，这点事还这么斗硬。

[zhè gè nǔ rén yě shì, [dōu]shí me shí dài le, zhè diǎn shì hái zhè me dòu yìng。]

（46）你[都]这样了，还不高兴，那我们还有什么盼头儿？

[nǐ [dōu]zhè yàng le, hái bú gāo xìng, nà wǒ men hái yǒu shí me pàn tóu ér？]

（47）我听一回[都]会啦："数九寒天冷飕飕，转年春打六九头……"哪向绕嘴？

---

[16] The Lian-sentence in this paper is the sentence in which the adverb "Dou" and "lian".

[17] "Forward orientation" refers to the object of semantic orientation is in front of the "Dou".

[18] "Backward orientation" refers to the object of semantic orientation is in back of the "Dou".

[wǒ tīng yī huí [dōu]huì lā : "shù jiǔ hán tiān lěng sōu sōu, zhuǎn nián chūn dǎ liù jiǔ tóu ……"nǎ jù rào zuǐ ?]

（48）丽娟[都]等不及了，她认为亚平态度很好，曾经的愤怒失手完全可以原谅。

[lì juān [dōu]děng bú jí le, tā rèn wéi yà píng tài dù hěn hǎo, céng jīng de fèn nù shī shǒu wán quán kě yǐ yuán liàng。]

In spoken language, because of the style of speaking or the demands of expression, the "Dou$_3$" might move to the sentence end, which causes circumstance of forward orientation of "Dou". For example, "我这儿有几封读者来信，您帮我回一下儿吧，我拖了好几天了，都。[wǒ zhè ér yǒu jǐ fēng dú zhě lái xìn , nín bāng wǒ huí yī xià ér ba , wǒ tuō le hǎo jǐ tiān le , dōu。]", we argued that it was just a variety of "我都拖了好几天了。[wǒ dōu tuō le hǎo jǐ tiān le。]" sentence and its meaning dose not change[19]. Therefore, based on the basic sentence pattern, we thought that the semantic of "Dou" backward orients the phrase "拖了好几天了[tuō le hǎo jǐ tiān le]".

3.2.3 We consider that the "Dou$_4$" also has the attribute of semantic orientation, and its object of semantic orientation is the component that denotes "reason" in sentence.

（49）碗里从来没有见过鱼肉，也从来没有穿过一件新衣裳，[都]是用旧衣服补补缝缝。

[wǎn lǐ cóng lái méi yǒu jiàn guò yú ròu , yě cóng lái méi yǒu chuān guò yī jiàn xīn yī shang, [dōu]shì yòng jiù yī fú bǔ bǔ féng féng。]

（50）这当然[都]是妈妈教得好了，尽管她只有一只手，不能操做，可她很会指点。

[zhè dāng rán [dōu]shì mā mā jiāo dé hǎo le , jìn guǎn tā zhǐ yǒu yī zhī shǒu , bú néng cāo zuò , kě tā hěn huì zhǐ diǎn。]

（51）换句话说，[都]是人们自作自受，非干鬼神之事。

[huàn jù huà shuō, [dōu]shì rén men zì zuò zì shòu, fēi gàn guǐ shén zhī shì。]

---

[19] This paper considers the meaning of sentence only from the perspective of semantic, with no thought of small differences on the context caused by the transform of syntactic position of the "Dou".

（52）大家一定和和气气的办好了这件事。[都]是<u>多年的老邻居</u>了，谁还能小瞧谁？

[dà jiā yī dìng hé hé qì qì de bàn hǎo le zhè jiàn shì。 [dōu]shì duō nián de lǎo lín jū le, shuí hái néng xiǎo qiáo shuí ?]

3.3 How to make computer indentify the semantic orientation of "Dou"

When we determine semantic orientation of a composition, it seems to be sure through   language sense. However, there are no objective laws to verify and only by a vague language sense which results in semantic orientation analysis tend to arise disagreements. Therefore, some scholars, striving to provide some science evidences for determining semantic orientation, began to explore scientific principles and methods of semantic orientation. There is no doubt that their research played an important significance to the construction and perfection of semantic orientation theory system, but it is a pity that their research on principle of judging semantic orientation is based on the   human. However, it's particularly difficult for computer which has no linguistic competence to determine and identify the semantic orientation of target word. Therefore, this paper that is based on predecessors' study keeps a foothold for information processing, and tries to explore formal features of semantic orientation to apply to computer identification. We sincerely hope that the work will provide a little help for understanding and generating Dou-sentence.

The semantic orientation identification of "Dou" is based on semantic entry identification, and it is the second identification of orientation followed semantic entry identification. So, the flow of semantic orientation identification also follow the process of semantic entry identification, that is "$Dou_5 \rightarrow Dou_2 \rightarrow Dou_3 \rightarrow Dou_4 \rightarrow Dou_1$" . In conclusion, according to the priority, we can draw the flow charts of the semantic entry and orientation identification of adverb "Dou". Please look at the chart.

Flow chart of computer semantic identification of the adverb "Dou"

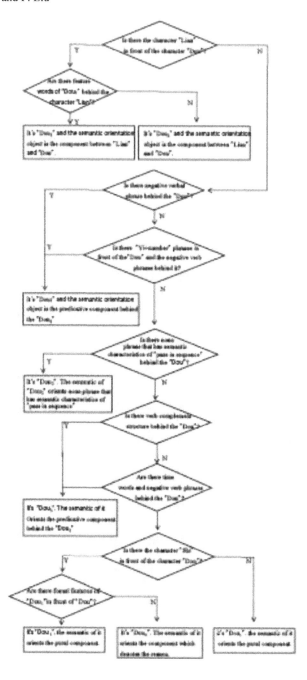

4 Conclusion

This paper mainly discusses two questions about the adverb "Dou": how to make computer identify the meaning and semantic orientation of "Dou" (In this paper, both are considered as computer semantic identification of "Dou"). We think that these knowledge and methods might contribute to computer understanding and generating in the sentence that contains the adverb "Dou". However, this research also has a certain degree of limitation as follows. Firstly, judgments of the meanings of "Dou" are inevitably committed to some subjectivity. Secondly, research pertaining to structure regularities and form features fails to have comprehensive investigations and conclusions. Thirdly, the method of identification is relatively single, only through the formal description of structure regularities. In addition, some problems that are worth studying have no further analysis and exploration, leading to a lack of research scope and depth in this paper. However, we hope that the results of this research will provide some inspiration and assistance to relevant researches in identifying the semantic meaning of other parts of speech.

We think that studies on computer-oriented semantic identification are considered as an important practice and representation of semantic processing in language information. The mentioned above not only exerts important implications on the ontology studies of semantic orientation, but also gives some support to language information processing. Generally speaking, studies on computer-oriented semantic identification provide us a new research point of view to reflect some language phenomenon in linguistics, which makes us rethink and redefine semantic orientation, have a new understanding of theoretical building and improvement related to semantic orientation, as well as the application of this theory to the analysis of language facts. In addition, studies on semantic orientation of adverbs and other parts of speech will be conducive to semantic analysis on syntactical level as well as computer calculation, understanding and disambiguation in syntactical meanings. Overall, the combination of semantic orientation and computers will produce theoretical and practical significance in researches of semantic orientation and information processing.

Acknowledgement This research project is supported by National Natural Science Foundation of China(Grant No.61272215) and the Fundamental Research Funds for the Central Universities, and the Research Funds of Beijing Language and Culture University(Grant No.16YCX156).

Appendix

Dou₁
Singal words

Common nouns	动物[dòng wù]; 孩子[hái zǐ]; 村民[cūn mín]; 大家[dà jiā]; 人（们）[rén (men)]; 儿童[ér tóng]; 国人[guó rén]; 朋友（们）[péng yǒu(men)]; 百姓[bǎi xìng]; 衣服[yī fú]; 人民[rén mín]; 学生[xué shēng]......
Personal pronoun	我们[wǒ men]; 你们[nǐ men]; 他们[tā men]; 它们[tā men]; 她们[tā men]......
Quantifier reduplication	个个[gè gè]; 村村[cūn cūn]; 人人[rén rén]......
Universal reference component	整个[zhěng gè]; 全[quán]; 满[mǎn]; 所有[suǒ yǒu]; 此/这/那些（类）[cǐ /zhè /nà xiē (lèi)]; 到处[dào chù]; 诸（多、如）[zhū(duō、rú)]、从来[cóng lái]; （一）直（到）[(yī)zhí(dào)]; 一般[yī bān]; 随时[suí shí]; 一辈子[yī bèi zǐ]; 基本（上）[jī běn(shàng)]......
Seriatim reference component	每[měi]; 各[gè]; 彼此[bǐ cǐ]; 分别[fēn bié]......
Arbitrary reference component	什么[shí me]; 任何[rèn hé]......
Condition component	凡[fán]; 无论[wú lùn]; 不管[bú guǎn]; 不论[bú lùn]......
Quantitative phrase	/
Quantitative Adjective	许多[xǔ duō]; 大多（数）[dà duō(shù)]; 众多[zhòng duō]......

Syntactic patterns

Combine structure	...和（与）... [...hé(yǔ)...]; ...以及.. [...yǐ jí ...]; ...等[...děng]......
Other patterns	除..之外[chú ...zhī wài]; 有的..有的.. [yǒu de ...yǒu de ...]; ...也好，...也好[...yě hǎo , ...yě hǎo]......

Questions	
Interrogative words	谁 (你猜都谁来了?*) [*shuí (nǐ cāi dōu shuí lái le?)*]......
Derogatory sense component	她都看无聊的电影。*[*tā dōu kàn wú liáo de diàn yǐng。*]......

Reference

[1] Lu, J: On Semantic Orientation Analysis. China linguistics review (First Edition). BeiJing Language and Culture University Press (1997). (陆俭明.关于语义指向分析[J],中国语言学论丛（第一辑）[M],北京:北京语言文化大学出版社,1997.)

[2] Zhan, W: Semantic Orientation Analysis of Range Adverb of "All". Chinese Linguistics 1,74-84(2004). (詹卫东.范围副词'都'的语义指向分析[J].汉语学报,2004,01:74-84.) (in Chinese)

[3] Linguistics Institute of Chinese Academy of Social Sciences: The Contemporary Chinese Dictionary, 6th edn. The Commercial Press(2012). (中国社会科学院语言语言研究所词典编辑室编. 现代汉语词典<第6版>[M].北京：商务印书馆, 2012.) (in Chinese)

[4] Lu, J: A Study of Modern Chinese Grammar. Peking University Press (2005). (陆俭明.现代汉语语法研究教程[M].北京: 北京大学出版社, 2005) (in Chinese)

[5] Wang, M: Discussion on Semantic Orientation of Blanket Range Adverb of "All". Journal of Nanjing Normal University(Social Science Edition) 4,85-87(1989). (王敏.试论范围副词'都'的语义指向[J].南京师大学报(社会科学版),1989,04:85-87.) (in Chinese)

[6] Chen, Z: Semantic Orientation of "All". Chinese Language Learning 6,54-56(1996). (陈子骄."都"的语义指向[J].汉语学习,1996,06:54-56.) (in Chinese)

[7] Shi, J: Pragmatic Feature and Semantic Orientation of Adverb "All". Journal of Changshu Institute of Technology 1,91-93(1995). (施建平.副词"都"的语用特征和语义指向[J].吴中学刊,1995,01:91-93.)(in Chinese)

[8] Liu, C: Semantic and Pragmatic Analysis on Sentence of "S都是O". Chinese Language Learning 4,42-45(1997). (刘川平.句式"S都是O"中'都'的语义、语用分析[J].汉语学习,1997,04:42-45.) (in Chinese)

[9]   Li, W: 'Ba+NP+Dou+VP' Construction and Dou's Semantic Orientation. Journal of Yunnan Normal University 4,39-44(2005). (in Chinese)

[10] Nan, X: On Semantic Analysis of Adverb "all"——Also on the Focus Perspective of Sentence with "all". Journal of Tibet University S1,25-29(2010).(in Chinese)

[11] Hao,L and Wu, D: Computer Identification of the Adverb Semantic Orientation: Path & Case. Wuhan University Journal(Humanity Sciences) 4,459-463(2009). (in Chinese)

"净" (jìng) and "都" (doū), which one has exclusiveness?*

Qiang Li

Department of Chinese Language and Literature, Shanghai University, Shanghai 200444, China
leeqiang2222@163.com

Abstract. This paper argues that "jìng" has exclusiveness, while the basic exclusive meaning does not exist in "doū". The exclusiveness of "doū" is deduced from the collective meaning. Thus, we can say that "doū" triggers the exclusive meaning or "doū" sentence has exclusiveness. In some context, the exclusive meaning of "doū" sentence is defeasible. Moreover, this paper points out that besides the quantifying direction of "jìng" and "doū", contrastive focus and stress also play an important role in the generation of the exclusive meaning.

Keywords: "jìng", "doū", exclusiveness, "doū" sentence, contrastive focus, contrastive stress

1   Introduction

"净" (jìng) and "都" (doū) are two common adverbs in Chinese and overlap in the meaning, namely, they are both with the function of universal quantification and have the meaning of "all". Hence, they can be used interchangeably, for instance, "满天净是乌云~满天都是乌云" (*All over the sky are dark clouds*). Besides, "净" has the meaning of "光，只" (*just*), which has been clearly stated in the books *Eight Hundred Words in Modern Chinese* and *Exemplification on Functional Words in Modern Chinese* (hereinafter *Eight hundred words* and *Exemplification on functional words* for short). *Eight hundred words* points out that "净" which shows the meaning of "光，只" (*just*) usually collocates with verb phrases, such as "~顾着说话，忘了时间了" (*forget the time due to talking*). *Exemplification on functional words* points out that "净" has the same usage with "光，只", such as "别的都已经运走了，~剩下棉花了" (*All have been removed except cotton*). So "净" has the exclusive meaning, which is an undisputable fact. However, whether "都" similar to "净" on the meaning and usage has exclusiveness remains disputable. Pan (2006), Jiang and Pan (2013) suggested that "都" has exclusiveness, while Xu (2014) and Shen (2015) argued that "都" does not have the absolute exclusive meaning. Zhang (2015) held the opinion

---

* This research is sponsored by the National Social Science Fund Major Project "Chinese parataxis characteristic research and large knowledge base and corpus construction under the background of international Chinese language education" (Approval No. : 12&ZD175). We hereby express our sincere thanks.

© Springer International Publishing AG 2016
M. Dong et al. (Eds.): CLSW 2016, LNAI 10085, pp. 577–587, 2016
DOI: 10.1007/978-3-319-49508-8_53

that the exclusive meaning of "都" is derived, but not innate. So does "都" have exclusiveness? Can exclusiveness be applied on "都" or "都" sentence?

2   The analysis on exclusiveness of "净" and "都" in Zhang (2015)

Zhang (2015) has conducted a detailed research on the meaning of "净" and made the following statement: the innate exclusive feature exists in "净", and a candidate set is derived from the constituent right related to "净" as the assertion value, which comprises one member at least. The function of "净" is that only the assertion value relative to other candidates can satisfy the open statement. Therefore, "净" has the meaning of "只" when it is right related to the constituent. She illustrated with the examples below.

1. 他净吃油炸食品（，不吃非油炸食品）。

"He eats fried food, but not non-fried food."

In this sentence, "净" relates to "油炸食品" (fried food). Under the semantic influence of "净", the possibility that x in "他吃x" is not equivalent to "油炸食品" is excluded. In this case, "净" equals to "只".

As to "都", Zhang (2015) argued that the exclusiveness does not exist in "都" when it left relates to the constituent, and "都" has exclusiveness when it right relates to the contrastive focus, which is exhaustive. In other words, the exclusiveness of "都" is derived from the contrastive focus, but not innate.

It is thus clear that Zhang (2015) holds different opinions on the exclusiveness of "净" and "都". Nevertheless, I feel that this difference sounds farfetched, and cannot be the sufficient evidence to illustrate that "都" does not have the innate exclusiveness. I will explain from three perspectives.

Firstly, also take sentence 1 for example. We can substitute "净" for "都" to form the sentence below.

2. 他都吃油炸食品（，不吃非油炸食品）。

"He always eats fried food, but not non-fried food."

Actually we can also hold that "油炸食品" right related to "都" as an assertion value leads to a candidate set. Relative to other candidates, only "油炸食品" can satisfy the truth of this sentence. From this perspective, "都" is the same with "净", and the exclusiveness can be considered innate, but not derived. Moreover, if the contrastive focus related to "都" has exclusiveness and exhaustiveness, so "都" does not have the innate exclusiveness. Then, we can also think that the object related to "净"

is the contrastive focus, because of which the exclusiveness of "净" is also derived, but not innate.

Secondly, Zhang (2015) has pointed out that "净" has the three features of focus particle proposed by König (1991), namely, quantifying ability, quantifying operation on candidate set and exclusion of the relevant characteristics of candidates. On this basis, she considered "净" as an exclusive adverb. Then, according to these three criteria, we can easily find that "都" also has them. So "都" can also regarded as an exclusive adverb.

Moreover, Zhang (2015) has pointed out that as a universal quantifying adverb, "净" can trigger its tripartite structure. When "净" only relates to its right constituent, it can trigger a tripartite structure determined by focus rule: the constituent related to "净" as a focus is projected into the nuclear scope, while other parts in the sentence are mapped into the restrictor. Take the sentence below for example.

3. a. 前排的票已经卖完了，净剩下后排的了。
   "*The tickets for front rows have already been sold out, now only the back rows left.*"
   b. 净x [剩下x了][x=后排的]
   ∀x [剩下x了→x=后排的]
   "对于每个x来说，如果'剩下x了'，那么x等于'后排的'。"

The thought of analyzing "净" by tripartite structure is from Pan (2006). As we know, Pan (2006) made an analysis on the meaning of "都" using tripartite structure earlier. Similarly, if "净" in the above sentence is replaced by "都", the tripartite structure of the corresponding "都" sentence is the same with the semantic expression as b. Then, we would ask: since the logical semantic expressions of "净" and "都" are the same, why does "净" have exclusiveness, but "都" does not?

In short, I argue that the conclusion "都" does not have the innate exclusiveness cannot be arrived at from the relevant discussion in Zhang's paper.

3 "都" does not have exclusiveness

Does "都" have exclusiveness or not? My opinion is that if "都" is considered independently, it does not have exclusiveness, or as Zhang (2015) said, "都" does not have the innate exclusiveness. However, the method in this paper is different from Zhang's.

Before analyzing "都", let's talk about "净". The same with *Eight hundred words* and *Exemplification on functional words*, *Modern Chinese Dictionary* also sets an independent exclusive meaning "只" for "净", which can be supported with some proof in the period of word meaning evolution. The adjective "净" initially means "not have impurity", which can lead to the simple nature of things. Hence, "净" has the strong exclusiveness. Then, with grammaticalization the meaning of "simple nature" can become the meaning of "restriction". According to Deng (2010), the exclusiveness of "净" has already appeared in Qing Dynasty. For instance:

4. a. 展爷是一语不发，净听着徐三爷他一个人不住口的骂。

（清·石玉昆《小五义》）

"Zhan is silent, listening to Xu cursing ceaselessly."

b. 咱们就该着净找乐儿了！怎么倒添了想不开了呢？

（《儿女英雄传》第十九回）

"We should find fun! How would take things to heart?"

c. 一时小丫头点上灯来，袭人道："你不吃饭，喝半碗热粥儿罢，别净饿着。"

（《红楼梦》第八十九回）

"A little girl lighted a lamp. Xi Ren said: "since you do not eat, drink half a bowl of hot congee, and do not be hungry."

d. 这么件大事，咱们一点摸不着，净当苦差。

（《红楼梦》第一一零回）

"We cannot deal with this event, but only do the all-consuming task."

In the sentences above, VP is modified by "净", which is considered as "not involve other entities except the specific object". For instance, what "净" emphasizes is the simplicity of actions "听 (*listen*), 找乐儿 (*find fun*), 饿 (*hungry*), 当苦差 (*do the all-consuming task*)". That only these actions but not others exist is revealed.

If "净" in above sentences shows the sum meaning of "都" more or less, then the exclusive meaning of "净" is apparent in the sentences below.

5. a. 听说又娶了位少太太，净嫁妆就是十万黄金，十万白银。

（《儿女英雄传》第三十一回）

"I heard that he married with a woman again. Only the dowry is ten thousand gold and ten thousand silver."

b. 金头虎在千佛寺真武顶学习这一招的时候，净筋斗栽了足有三千六百个。

（《三侠剑》第一回）

"When Jin Douhu learned this skill in Zhenwuding of Qianfo Temple, he practiced the somersault for three thousand and six hundred."

c. 眼看小英雄指东打西，犹如虎入羊群，净滚楼梯的四五个。

（《三侠剑》第一回）

"The hero fought with others, like a tiger entering a flock of sheep. There were several people rolling stairs."

In the above sentences, "净" modifies NP and limits the number of the same entity, excluding the quantity more than the specific number and emphasizing the big number.

There are many cases of the exclusive "净" in modern Chinese. For instance:

6. a. 可是，净咱一个人儿对得起政府不行啊，这得大家伙齐心哪。

（老舍《龙须沟》）

"*However, that just I follow the government is not OK. We should get together.*"

b. 你说，腰里带着硬的，净弄些个暗门子，算哪道呢？

（老舍《上任》）

"*He carried hard things with the waist, and only did some tricks. What means?*"

c. 十月下工的时候，老万按春天的粮价一算，工钱就完了，净欠那三十块钱的利钱十块零八毛。

（赵树理《福贵》）

"*When he did work in October, Lao Wan counted by the price of spring grain. Wages would be none, and he owes ten and eight cents, the interest of thirty.*"

In conclusion, it is clear to see the grammaticalization process of the adjective "净" meaning "干净" (*clean*) to the adverb "净" meaning "只，光" (*just*). Therefore, it is reasonable to set an independent sense for the exclusive meaning of "净".

As to "都", its meaning can be summarized as "sum up", "universal quantification" in formal semantics. Its semantic effect is that "in a certain range, the same feature exists in some nature, action and event". For instance, "他们都是学生" (*They are all students*), in the set of "他们" (*they*), everyone has the feature of "是学生" (*being student*), so "是学生" is the same in the set of "他们". In the sentence "他都说法语" (*He always speaks France*), there exists a hidden time variable, such as "一直以来，他都说法语" (*All the time, he speaks France*). "都" left quantifies the hidden variable "一直以来", which means that in the time range of "一直以来", the event of "他说法语" always happens, namely, the event is the same. Hence, the basic meaning of "都" is "sum up", while the exclusive meaning is derived from the meaning of "sum up". Since in a certain range, the same feature exists in some nature, action and event, those which do not have the same feature are excluded. For instance, in the sentence "小明一直都买名牌货" (*Xiao Ming always buys good things*), the event that relates to the time variable "一直" (*always*) is "买名牌货" (*buy good things*), so "买二手货" (*buy second-hand goods*) or "买冒牌货" (*buy counterfeit goods*) is naturally excluded. Therefore, we can feel that "都" has exclusiveness. However, the more accurate statement is that "都" triggers the exclusiveness, but not have exclusiveness in nature, and the "都" sentence has exclusiveness.

From the perspective of word meaning grammaticalization, the trace of "净" is from the restrictive adverb to the collective adverb. That is to say, the exclusive usage appears first, then the collective usage, which appeared in modern Beijing spoken language (Wei 2014). The adverb "都" is developed from the verb "都" meaning "collect". As an adverb, the basic usage of "都" is "sum up", then the usage of universal quantification appeared (Zhang 2005). Nevertheless, "都" is not in the transitional direction to restrictive adverb. Hence, it is reasonable to say "净" has exclusiveness, but inaccurate to state that "都" has exclusiveness.

Moreover, when "净" and "都" right relate to the interrogative phrase, it is evident to see which one has exclusiveness. For instance (cited from Zhang 2015):

7. a. 他都买什么？
   b. 他净买什么？
   (*What does he always buy?*)
8. a. 他都说了些什么！
   b. 他净说些什么！
   (*What he said!*)

As pointed out by Zhang (2015), "都" has universality and generality, but "净" has exclusiveness. Sentence (7a) means "what things is he ready to buy", and (8a) means "what he said makes people unpleasant". Sentence (7b) means "what does he always buy in the every event of buying goods", and (8b) means "what he said always makes people unpleasant". In the contrast of (7) and (8), we can find that the exclusiveness of "净" is apparent, but "都" does not have exclusiveness.

Zhang, Li and Pan (2012) argued that "都" has exclusiveness when it right relates to the interrogative phrase. They illustrate with the sentence below.

9. 他都不吃什么水果？（"什么水果" is the focus）
   "*What fruits does not he eat?*"

They pointed out that when answering the question above, the answer must be "水果" (*fruit*), but not entities irrelevant with fruit, for instance, "他都不吃饼干和苹果", so "都" here has the exclusive meaning. Nevertheless, we suggest that the function of "都" is to sum up the entities in the range of fruit, and the exclusive meaning is weak. The meaning of sentence (9) is equivalent to "他不吃的水果都是什么/有哪些？". From the opposite perspective, if "都" here has exclusiveness, then in general the exclusive object should contain some specific but not vague objects, otherwise exclusive operation cannot be done. Interrogative phrase "什么" (*what*) is a variable, and its referent is vague, so the exclusive operation cannot be imposed on "什么" and the exclusive meaning of "都" cannot appear naturally. Meanwhile, as (7a) shows, the main function of "都" is to sum up, and "都" does not have the exclusive meaning.

4   The "都" sentence has exclusiveness

As the last section points out, "都" does not have exclusiveness. The reason why sentence "他都说法语" (*He always speaks France*) has the exclusive meaning lies on the universal quantification of "都", which makes "说法语" (*speak France*) be the event always happening in a certain period. Hence, the possibility of speaking other languages is eliminated. The "都" sentence has exclusiveness.

However, some scholars have challenged the exclusive meaning of "都" sentence. Jiang and Pan (2013) argued that "都" does not have exclusiveness in the case of right quantification. They referred that, in the sentence "小李都买呢子的衣服" (*Xiao Li always buys woolen clothes*), as long as the clothes *Xiao Li* buys is mostly woolen, even if he buys a piece of cotton clothes, the sentence can also be spoken. This case can also be paraphrased into that *Xiao Li* always buys woolen clothes, occasionally cotton. I think language is an elastic system. The semantic loss and inaccuracy may appear in the communication process, but on the whole the semantic system is sufficient. Even though the phenomenon that "都" means the most cases indeed exists, we cannot deny that the sentence above can mean that *Xiao Li* only buys woolen clothes, but not clothes made of other material. Therefore, we can say that "都" sentence has the exclusive meaning.

Shen (2015) referred that the exclusive meaning "只是" (*just*) of "都" is a conversational implicature derived from the quantity maxim principle, which belongs to pragmatics and can be eliminated by context. For instance, the second half of each sentence below can directly exclude the hidden meaning of "只是".

10. a. 他都买的呢子衣服，除了一件纯棉的。
   "Except a piece of cotton clothes, he always buys woolen clothes."
   b. 书架上都是外文书，只有这一本是中文的。
   "Except this Chinese book, on that bookshelf are all foreign language books."

Actually, as to (10), we can also think that speakers firstly exclude the exception from the descriptive object set, then use "都" sentence to illustrate the case about the left object, emphasizing the unique of object. Hence, "都" sentence has exclusiveness. Example (10) is equivalent to:

11. a. 除了一件纯棉的，其余的他都买的呢子衣服。
   "Except a piece of cotton clothes, the clothes he always buys is woolen."
   b. 只有这一本是中文的，书架上其余的都是外文书。
   "Except this Chinese book, on that bookshelf are all foreign language books."

Xu (2014) also questioned the opinion that "都" has the exclusive meaning when right relates. He took the sentences below to illustrate.

12. a. 他去百货商店，都买呢子衣服，还买些别的东西。
   "When he goes to the market, he always buys woolen clothes and other things."
   b. *他去百货商店，只买呢子衣服，还买些别的东西。
13. a. 每次旅游，他都带妻子去，而且都带儿子去。
   "He takes his wife and son when traveling."
   b. *每次旅游，他只带妻子去，而且只带儿子去。
14. a. ? 小王都看英文书，不做别的事。
   "Xiao Wang only reads English books but not do other things."
   b. 小王只看英文书，不做别的事。

He referred that in (12) and (13), contrasted with unacceptable "只" sentences with exclusiveness, "都" sentences are OK. In (14), "只" sentence is acceptable, while "都" sentence is not. These contrasts show that "都" sentence does not have exclusiveness. However, I argue that the exclusiveness generates in a certain range, namely, "都" sentence has exclusiveness in a limited scope. If we contrast "呢子衣服"

(*woolen clothes*) with "别的东西" (*other things*), sentence (12a) does not have exclusiveness. But we cannot consider that "都" sentence do not show the exclusive meaning. In the category of clothes made of different materials, "都买呢子衣服" means "woolen clothes, not clothes made of cotton, silk, nylon and so on, is chosen". Hence, the sentence has the exclusive meaning. Likewise, "都看英文书" (*always read English books*) in sentence (14a) also show exclusiveness. In the category of books, "都看英文书" means "'英文书' is chosen, but not '法文书，中文书，俄文书'". As to "都" sentence in (13a), I think it can also show the exclusive meaning.

15. a. 每次旅游，他都带妻子去，不带儿子去。
   "*He always takes his wife but not his son when traveling.*"
   b. 每次旅游，他只带妻子去，不带儿子去。
   "*He only takes his wife but not his son when traveling.*"

Analogous to "只" in (15b), "都" in (15a) can right relate to "妻子" (*wife*), and the sentence stress can be on "妻子", which contrasts with "儿子" (*son*). In this case, the meanings of sentence (15a) and (15b) are the same, and the exclusive meaning exists. As to "都" in (13a), it is likely to sum up the events of "旅游" (*traveling*), which is equivalent to a sum operator, namely, he takes his wife and son the first traveling, he takes his wife and son the second traveling……. The sentence stress can be on "每次旅游" (*each traveling*), which can lead to the meaning that he takes his wife and son when traveling. Hence, "都" in (13a) is not totally the same with "只".

To sum up, I argue that even if the exclusive meaning of "都" sentence can be eliminated, the fact that it has the exclusive meaning cannot be denied.

5   Contrastive focus, contrastive stress and the realization of exclusiveness

The difference of right quantification and left quantification of "净" and "都" is whether exclusiveness exists, namely, exclusiveness does not exist in the case of left quantification, while exists in right quantification. With regard to this difference, Zhang (2015) and Jiang and Pan (2013) have made a detailed analysis. The distinct of the quantifying direction is indeed an important factor affecting the semantic exclusiveness. However, I argue that the contrastive stress and focus can also have a vital impact on the realization of the exclusive meaning.

As mentioned above, *Eight Hundred Words*, *Exemplification on Functional Words* and *Modern Chinese Dictionary* all set two senses "都，全" (*all*) and "只，光" (*just*) for "净". Then, faced with the sentences below, how do we distinguish the meaning?

16. a. 满天净是乌云。
   "*All over the sky are dark clouds.*"

   b. 这片地方净是工厂。
   "*All over the place are factories.*"

17. a. 他净说法语。

"*He always speaks France.*"

　b. 别的都已经运走了，净剩下棉花了。

"*All the things have been removed except cotton.*"

According to the language sense, "净" in (16) is usually considered to mean "都, 全", while "净" in (17) means "只, 光". Then, there appears a question: why cannot "净" in (16) mean "只, 光" and in (17) mean "都, 全"? That is to say, there is an overlap between the meaning "都, 全" and "只, 光".

Jiang and Pan (2013) has pointed out that there are two semantic explanation rules about "都" sentence. P1 is the left quantification rule ("topic rule"), and P2 is the right quantification rule ("focus rule"). The content of P1 and P2 is as follows.

P1: there are phrases which can be quantified on the left of "都", or focus, context can derive the quantification scope of "都".

P2: a contrastive focus is contained in the comment on the right of "都".

Besides, P1 is prior to P2 in the application order.

I think that the semantic explanation rule of "都" can also be applied on "净", because "净" can left quantify on the basis of right quantification (Zhang 2015). Then the application order that P1 is prior to P2 can be used to illustrate why "净" in (16) means "都, 全". In the sentence (16a), there is a natural plural quantification scope on the left of "净", and "满天" can be seen as a plural set which consists of many smaller areas of the sky. When "净" left quantifies the plural expression, it is equivalent to "都". Hence, relative to the right quantification of "乌云" (*dark cloud*), "净" firstly left quantifies "满天" (*all the sky*). In this case, "净" means "都" and the whole sentence means that all over the sky are dark clouds.

Likewise, in the sentence (16b), "这片地方" (*all over the place*) can be seen as a plural set which consists of many smaller areas, which is firstly left quantified by "净", then the semantic interpretation "都" generates. In the sentences (17), because there is not an overt quantification scope on the left of "净", "净" firstly quantifies its right object "法语, 棉花", which are considered as contrastive focuses. For instance, "法语" (*France*) in (17a) contrasts with "汉语, 英语" (*Chinese, English*), while "棉花" (*cotton*) in (17b) contrasts with "别的" (*others*). Therefore, "净" in these two sentences are easily regarded as having the meaning of "只, 光" (*just*). Actually, as to (17a), we can also hypothesize that there exists a covert time quantification scope "这几个月" (*these several months*) on the left of "净". Then, according to the application rule of P2 prior to P1, "净" here relates to "这几个月", which can be seen as "总" (*always*). However, if the contrastive stress of the sentence is on "法语", the object that "净" relates to would be pulled to its right. The contrastive stress can highlight the contrastive focus status of "法语". In this case, "净" has exclusiveness. Similarly, the same occurs on "都" sentence.

18. a. 他们都是学生。

"They are all students."
b. 他都说法语。
"He always speaks France."

In the sentence (18a), "都" relates to "他们" (*they*) on its left, being equivalent to "全" (all). In (18b), because there is not an overt quantification scope on the left of "都", which directly relates to "法语" (*France*) on its right, "法语" becomes the contrastive focus, making sentence b have the exclusiveness. Of course, if we assume that there exists a covert time quantification scope "一直以来" (*all along*) on the left of "都", then "都" can relate to it and shows the universal meaning. However, if the contrastive stress is on "法语", the object "都" relates to would be pulled to "法语", which makes it become the contrastive focus. In this case, the sentence also has the exclusiveness.

In short, I argue that in "净" and "都" sentences, besides the difference of quantifying direction, the contrastive focus and stress also have an important effect on the realization of the exclusive meaning.

6   Summary

The exclusiveness of "都" has been involved in some literature, on the basis of which this paper rethinks the accuracy and reliability of the statement that "都" has exclusiveness. Zhang (2015) has pointed out that "净" has the innate exclusive meaning, while that of "都" is derived. On the whole, I am in favor of this opinion. But different from the analysis in Zhang's paper, I argue that the exclusive usage of "净" had already appeared in modern Chinese. Moreover, the collective usage of "净" generates on the basis of its exclusive usage. Hence, "净" has the exclusiveness. Nevertheless, the basic meaning of "都" is "sum up", from which the exclusive meaning is deduced. Because in a certain range, some nature, action and event have the same feature, then those which do not have the same feature can be naturally excluded. Therefore, "都" does not have the exclusive usage, but triggers the exclusive meaning. Or we can say "都" sentence has exclusiveness. Actually, the exclusive meaning of "都" sentence can be eliminated in a specific context. Finally, this paper points out that in the research of exclusiveness of "净" and "都" sentences, besides the difference of quantifying direction, the contrastive focus and stress cannot be ignored.

References

1. Deng, H.: A Study on Diachronic Changes of Modified Verbs. MA thesis of Hunan Normal University (2010) [In Chinese]
2. Jiang, J., Pan, H.: How many DOUs do we really need? Studies of the Chinese Language. 1, 38-50 (2013) [In Chinese]

3. König, Ekkehard: The meaning of focus particles—A comparative perspective. Routledge, London (1991)
4. Li, Z.: A Research on the Evolution of Chinese Common Words. Chinese Dictionary Press, Beijing (1999) (汉语常用词演变研究. 北京：汉语大词典出版社, 1999) [In Chinese]
5. Lv, S.: Eight Hundred Words in Modern Chinese. The Commercial Press, Beijing (1980) (现代汉语八百词. 北京：商务印书馆, 1980) [In Chinese]
6. Pan, H.: Focus, tripartite structure and *Dou* quantification. Research of Grammar. 13, 163-184 (2006) [In Chinese]
7. Shen, J.: Leftward or rightward? The quantifying direction of *Dou*. Studies of the Chinese Language. 1, 3-17 (2015) [In Chinese]
8. The 1955/1957 language class in the department of Chinese Language and Literature of Peking University: Exemplification on Function Words in Modern Chinese. The Commercial Press, Beijing (1982) (现代汉语虚词例释. 北京：商务印书馆, 1982) [In Chinese]
9. The Language Institute of Chinese Academy of Social Sciences: Modern Chinese Dictionary (6th edition). The Commercial Press, Beijing (2012) [In Chinese]
10. Wei, Z.: The Scope Adverbs "Jing", "Jin" and "Jing" in Early Beijing Dialect. Journal of Langfang Teachers College. 1, 41-44 (2014) [In Chinese]
11. Xu, L.: Is *Dou* a universal quantifier? Studies of the Chinese Language. 6, 498-507 (2014) [In Chinese]
12. Zhang, L.: A Semantic Study of the Adverb of Universal Quantification "Jing" and Constraints on Its Use. Chinese Teaching in the World. 3, 336-349 (2015) [In Chinese]
13. Zhang, L., Li, B., Pan, H.: The Semantic Requirements of *Dou*: a Study of Its Rightward Association. Studies in Language and Linguistics. 2, 63-71 (2012) [In Chinese]
14. Zhang, Y.: On the Grammaticalization and Subjectivisation of the Adverb *Dou*. Journal of Xuzhou Normal University. 1, 56-62 (2005) [In Chinese]

Constructional Coercion in the Evolution of Contemporary Chinese Morphemes—Taking "fen"(粉) as an Example[1]

Xiaoping Zhang

School of International Education and Exchange, University of Jinan,
Jinan, 250022, China

sh_zhangxp@ujn.edu.cn

Abstract. In contemporary Chinese, morphemes are changing with the development of vocabulary. During the evolution of morphemes, constructional coercion has played an important role. It is a mechanism to adjust semantic conflict and type mismatch, and will sometimes cause the change of meaning in the component of the construction. Chinese morpheme "fen"(Chinese character "粉")has evolved from a meaningless transliterated syllable to a nominal morpheme and then a verb to express events, which is a semantical evolution chain from specific to abstract, and from special indication to general reference. Constructional coercion has played a vital role in the process. This paper takes the new Chinese morpheme "fen（粉）" as an example in order to analysis and explain the reason of its evolution using the theory of constructional coercion on the bases of a clear semantical evolutional trace of "fen（粉）".

Key words: constructional coercion; morpheme; "fen（粉）"; semantical evolution

1 Introduction

Chinese vocabulary has undergone tremendous changes ever since the reform and opening- up. New words and meanings have been emerging in large numbers and have triggered the evolution of Chinese morphemes and the meaning of morphemes. "fen（粉）" (Chinese character "粉") means "powder", "become powder", "pink" and others in modern Chinese, which can be used as a noun, a verb and an adjective. In recent years, a new morpheme "fen（粉）" comes into beings with the growing popularity of the network and the micro blog. It has demonstrated a relatively powerful productivity as the frequent appearance of new words made up by the morpheme "fen

---

[1] This paper is funded by Ministry of Education's humanities & social sciences research program "A Study of the Forming and Evolution of Chinese Morphemes Based on Quantitative Analysis"（11YJC740146）and Social Science Planning Study Program of Shandong Province（10DWXJ05）.

© Springer International Publishing AG 2016
M. Dong et al. (Eds.): CLSW 2016, LNAI 10085, pp. 588–599, 2016
DOI: 10.1007/978-3-319-49508-8_54

（粉)" and the gradual formation of constructions of words and expressions with the morpheme "fen（粉)" ("fen（粉)" construction for short in the following), mainly "X fen" or "fen X". "fen（粉)" originates from the transliteration of the English word "fans" ("粉丝fensi" in Chinese)[2], which has nothing to do with the "fen（粉)" in the word "粉末fenmo" (powder) in modern Chinese. It is just a coincidental homonyms caused by the transliteration of a foreign word. The academic circle has paid attention to the study of the word "fans" (粉丝fensi), for example Zhou Ri'an[1], Chen Liufang, Qu Weiguo[2] and others, whose researches focus on the introduction of "fans" (fensi), its meaning and influence on the breeding social culture and psychology, and other aspects. Few scholars have probed into the meaning and breeding social culture of "fen（粉)", for example, Wang Huanling[3]. However, hardly ever scholars have applied the theory of constructional coercion into the study of the semantic evolution of "fen（粉)".

According to the general constructional grammatical understanding of constructional connotation, constructional can be understood as a special unity of form and meaning (or function). Morphemes, words, phrases, sentences, a piece of writing, and even type of writings and literary forms can be regarded as construction. Constructional coercion is a mechanism to solve semantic conflict and type mismatch between constructions and words. Constructions have their independent meanings. If words cannot meet the requirement of constructional semantic, they can be forced to shift type, including the change of argument structure, meaning, and others. For example:

John sneezed the napkin off the table.

The word "sneeze" should be a one-valence verb, however, in this sentence, it has undergone a trivalent caused-motion construction and gained the semantic features of a trivalent verb, thus the causative meaning is added. [4] On this basis, Shi Chunhong combines the constructional grammatical understanding of constructional coercion and generational lexicon understanding of semantic compulsion to give the definition of constructional coercion: "constructional coercion refers to the phenomenon when the component enters the construction; the structure requires entry conditions for the component. If the function, meaning and form of the component are totally different from those of the construction, then some aspects of the function, meaning structure and form structure of the component should be adjusted to meet the entry conditions. If the two agree with one another, then the constructional coercion is successful; otherwise it fails."[5] This paper uses Shi Chunhong's definition of construction and constructional coercion and takes the theory of constructional coercion as a basis to study the semantic evolution of "fen（粉)" in modern Chinese.

---

[2] In modern Chinese, "fen（粉)" also means "very, very much", an adverb of degree, for example, "fen like" means "like (it) very much". This is a network word influenced by dialectical sound, which is not included in the study of homonyms "fen（粉)" in this paper.

2   The Forming of "Fen（粉）" Construction and the Morphemic of "Fen（粉）"

The Appearance of "fensi（粉丝）" and the Forming of "Fen（粉）" Construction

"Fen（粉）" originates from the abbreviation of "fensi（粉丝）" (fans). The word "fensi（粉丝）" first appeared in Taiwan media and entered mainland China in 2004. It became popular with a large-scale talent show on a satellite TV in 2005[6] and refers to "someone who adores a certain famous person"3. From the perspective of constructional coercion, the forming of the word "fensi（粉丝）" is closely tied up with the internalization of construction in Chinese native speakers. First of all, "fensi" is suppressed by the phonetic form of English word "fans" and the existing Chinese morphology "fensi （粉丝）". "fensi（粉丝）" is transliterated from the English word "fans" imitating the sound and using the existing Chinese form "fensi（粉丝）". Next, "fensi（粉丝）"is suppressed by Chinese diplophonia construction. "Diplophonia construction is the most frequently used and a morphological construction of prototypical effect in modern Chinese. It has the absolute pre-emption【7】in word-building." 1 Either from the aspect of syllable rhythm or the culture psychology of Han Chinese, Diplophonia construction has the absolute pre-emption in word-building. "Fan" corresponds with the monosyllable "fen（粉）" in Chinese, however, "fen（粉）" fails to be a new expression in Chinese but translates the plural form of "fans" to be a disyllable "fensi （粉丝）". This not only connects to an enthusiastic devotee to something or someone as the English word "fan" refers to, but also closely relates to Chinese diplophonia construction. When transliterating a foreign word, if it is a single-syllable word, Chinese diplophonia construction will suppress it and transform it to be a diplophonia structure. For example, foreign word "卡车truck, 啤酒 beer, 酒吧bar" and others are transliterated by adding a morpheme to express its semantic generic. "Fen si" uses the plural form "s" to fill the vacancy in order to meet the requirement of Chinese diplophonia construction.

The popular of"fensi(粉丝)" opens the gate for "fen（粉）" construction. In the beginning of 2005, talent shows like "Super Girl" and "Super Boy" were hot nationwide. The word"fensi(粉丝)" was used more and more frequently and gradually became a fixed construction in Chinese vocabulary system, which started to facilitate the forming of other new constructions. At that time, star fans divided themselves into different star camps and fans club by their fancy idols. This phenomenon was soon conceptualized, categorized and symbolized in linguistics. Then some words appeared, for example, "凉粉liangfen

---

3 This definition is founded in the Editorial Office of Language Research Institute, Chinese Academy of Social Sciences: *Modern Chinese Dictionary* (version 6), Beijing: The Commercial Press, 2012.

(fans of Jane Zhang张靓颖)", "通心粉tongxinfen (fans of Pinky孙艺心)", "职粉"zhifen (professional fans)", "散粉sanfen" (refers to fans who do not join in any fan club or who like many stars), "粉头fentou" (a leading figure in the fan club). Gradually, "X fen" and "fen X" construction were found, in which "X" is usually a single or disyllabic noun morpheme or an adjective morpheme. "X fen" and "fen X" are all nouns. In the two structures, "fen X" creates fewer words. According to our knowledge, there is only "粉头fen tou". On the contrary, "X fen" demonstrated more powerful word-formation ability. Words like "铁粉tiefen, 忠粉zhongfen, 脑残粉naocanfen, 理智粉lizhifen" appeared later. For example:

①职粉分为不同等级，收入可达每月几百元到上万元不等。
（Zhífěn fēnwéi bùtóng děngjí，shōurù kě dá měiyu èjǐbǎiyuán dào shàngwànyuán bùděng。）

（There are different degrees of "zhi fen" (professional fans) whose income range from hundreds to over ten thousands of RMB a month.）

②社区网络采用多种方式吸引居民，让居民真正成为社区网络平台的铁粉。(Shèqū wǎngluò cǎiyòng duōzhǒng fāngshì xīyǐn jūmín，ràng jūmín zhēnzhèng chéngwéi shèqū wǎngluò píngtái de tiěfěn。)

(Community network attracts residents in different ways to make them "tie fen"(loyal fans) of the community network platform.）

(2) The Morphemic of "Fen（粉）"

"X fen（粉）" construction mainly comes from the simplification of word creation, for example, "职粉zhifen (pro fans), 铁粉tie fen (ironfans), 忠粉zhongfen (loyal fans)" are shorted from "职业粉丝professional fans,铁杆粉丝iron-like fans, 忠实粉丝loyal fans". Under the influence of the ideographic and discreteness nature of Chinese characters[8], the seemingly fixed and unanalytical word "fans (粉丝fensi)" is split and "fen（粉）" is extracted as the abbreviation of "粉丝fensi (fans)" to make new words with other morphemes, forming new word constructions. Su Xinchun regards monosyllablization and repetition rate as a necessary condition for the morphemic of complex tone foreign words [9]. Judging from the current usage of "fen（粉）", it is a monosyllable that can create new words repeatedly while has a specific meaning. That is to say, "fen（粉）" has updated to a morpheme from a meaningless syllable. During the process of morphemic "fen（粉）", abbreviation word creation is just the inducement and the blasting fuse, while the critical factor lies in constructional coercion. Analyzed from the syntactic and semantic, "X fen" is an "attributive + head word" form of constructional coercion with "X" modifying and restricting "fen（粉）". Since Medieval Chinese, "attributive + head word" has been the priority of construction, which has been solidified in our mentality and will suppress the semantic features of certain component in a new construction. It is certain that the central component in an "attributive + head word" construction must be a meaningful language sign. "If the head word is not an ideographical syllable, it cannot meet the requirement of the construction and will be forced to be morphemic, that is, changing from a meaningless syllable to a morpheme of alleges meaning" [10]. In "X fen（粉）", "fen（粉）" is such a meaningless head word of this "attributive + head word" construction that is mismatched and will be suppressed by this construction. In this way, the meaningless syllable becomes meaningful and morphemic. In terms of the construction itself, "X fen" is a Simi-open construction abstracted from the repeated expression which has a fixed form and semantic type. In this construction, "fen（粉）" is fixed which independently decides the referring and semantic content of the construction while "X" is a dependent changeable modifier that distinguishes the construction. Because of the unknowable and changeable of "X", the openness and inclusiveness of the construction is stronger and thus has a higher productivity, which in a sense promotes the morphemic of "fen（粉）".

In other word, under the dual influences of simplification of word creation and constructional coercion, "fen（粉）" gains the meaning of "fensi(粉丝)" (fans) to refer to "someone who adores a certain famous person" and completed the process of becoming a morpheme.

3   The Semantic Generalization of "Fen（粉）"

As above mentioned, in the early "fen（粉)" construction, "X fen(粉)" can be divided into two cases. One is "N+fen（粉）", in which "X" mainly refers to morphemes that means somebody except "职粉zhifen", for example "姚粉yaofen (fans of Yao Ming), 翔粉xiangfen (fans of Liu Xiang)". Another is "Adj+fen（粉）", In which "X" refers to the status or degree of the adoration, for example, "理智粉lizhifen, 狂热粉 kuangrefen". These two types can be regarded as preference rules system of "fen （粉)" construction. As the constant increasing of "fen（粉）" construction, its connection between form and meaning are gradually stabilized. The semantic information of this construction not only carries the humorous of a foreign word, but also embodies a positive attitude. It gradually becomes popular in a special social culture environment. The popular elements in "fen（粉)" construction attract people to use it as often as they can regardless the context. In this way, "X fen（粉）" construction camp is enlarging in pragmatics and noun morpheme gradually refers to something besides someone, for example, "果粉guofen (fans of iPhone), 星粉xingfen (fans of Samsung), 书粉shufen (fans of books), 茅台粉maofen (fans of Maotai liquor), 舌尖 粉shejianfen (fans of TV show "A Bite of China")". For example:

③为了买到苹果手机，"果粉"们彻夜排队。（Wèile mǎidào píngguǒshǒujī, "guǒfěn"men chèyè páiduì。）

（*In order to buy iPhone ("pingguo" in Chinese), "guo fen" line up all night.*）

④2012年纪录片《舌尖上的中国》在央视首播后，引起了全国轰动，成功笼络了大批忠实的"舌尖粉"。(2012nián jìlùpiàn《shéjiānshàngdezhōngguó》zài yāngshì shǒubō hòu，yínq ǐle quánguó hōngdòng，chénggōng lǒngluò le dàpī zhōngshí de "shéjiānfěn"。)

（*The first-run of 2012 documentary "A Bite of China" ("舌尖上的中国she jian shang de zhong guo" in Chinese) in CCTV was a hit nationwide and gained many loyal "舌尖粉she jian fen".*）

Michaelis proposes that the semantic and syntax context of a lexical item are in compatible with one another, the meaning of the lexical item will be determined by the syntax structure of its embedding form.[11] This override principle is suitable for the meaning of a morpheme that constitutes a compound word. Theoretically, though the cognize conceptual framework that is activated by "X fen" can make a new expression by conceptual blending with "fen（粉）" structure, in a "attributive + head word" construction, if the head word does not has the nature that the attributive activated, the construction will force the morpheme of the head word to change meaning in order to realize semantic harmony. In the above example, "果guo" is a morpheme referring to an object, which is incompatible with the requirement of a morpheme referring to a person in the prior construction. In this case, the construction will force the semantic change of "fen（粉）" so that it no longer refers to a person only but also an object. With the appearing of other similar words like "书展粉shuzhanfen, 堂粉 tangfen (fans of an auditorium), 锤粉chuifen (fans of hammer phone), 朝代粉 chaodaifen (a joint name for fans of all dynasties in Chinese history)", this semantic feature of "fen（粉）" is further proved to be dominated. In other word, the meaning of "fen（粉）" is generalized. It no longer refers to "someone who adores a certain famous person", but "the supporter or favorer of some people or some object".

In about 2010, with the heat of micro blog in China, "fen（粉）" construction is also applied to micro blog's relating area, which makes its word creation ability increased further. Words like "jiang shifen", "sifen", "huofen", "beidongfen" appear, for example:

⑤经营者告诉代理如何让"陌生人转粉""僵尸粉转活粉"。(Jīngyíngzhě gàosu dàilǐ rúhé ràng "mòshēngrén zhuǎnfěn" "jiāngshīfěn zhuǎn huófěn"。)

（*The operator told to the agent how to make "strangers turn to fans (fen)", and "jiang shi fen turn into huo fen".*）

⑥"这些都是被动粉，也就是俗称的死粉，他们的背后并非真实的活跃用户，只是为了让你能快速踏进认证公众账号的门槛而已。"该店客服告诉商报记者。("zhèxiē dōushì bèidòngfěn，yě jiùshì súchēng de sǐfěn，tāmen de bèihòu bìngfēi zhēnshí de huóyuèyònghù，zhǐshì wèile ràng nǐ néng kuàisù tàjìn rènzhèng gōngzhòng zhànghào de ménkǎn éryǐ。"gāidiàn kèfú gàosu shāngbào jìzhě。)

（*"These are "bei dong fen", also called "Si Fen". They are not real active users, but a method that can bring a normal account into a public account quickly." The services assistant told to reporter of commercial news.*）

In micro blog,"fensi(粉丝)" (fans) refers to a person of group that continues to pay attention to a certain blogger. "僵尸粉jiangshifen" (zombie fan) refers to some false fans that can be bought with money, which are titular micro blog fans that is usually malicious registration users auto-generated by the system. "活粉huofen" is the update version of "僵尸粉jiangshifen" which means paid part time net friends to update blog articles and comments periodically and is seemingly not different from real fans. "死粉sifen" refers to fans that are not active in micro blog, which are not managed or seldom updated. "死粉sifen" and "活粉huofen" are "Adj + fen(粉)" construction referring to the nature and statues of micro blog fans while "僵尸粉jiang shi fen" is "N + fen" construction in which the modifier and central word is semantically mismatched. "僵尸jiang shi" is not the object that the fans adores, but becomes an adjective through the metaphorical meaning of "as inactive and false as a zombie ("僵尸 jiang shi" in Chinese)". In fact, all "死粉si fen" "活粉huo fen" and "僵尸粉jiang shi fen" are semantically mismatched. In reality,"fensi(粉丝)" that refers to a person cannot be divided into "死si (dead), 活huo (alive)" or even "僵尸jiang shi (zombie)". The classification in this "attributive + head word" construction is different from a conventional one so that it's the semantic meaning of the central component will be reanalyzed. The concerning object of "fen（粉）" in micro blog is no longer bound to a person or an object in reality, but also refers to virtual things like micro blog. In addition, the object "fen（粉）" referring to can be both a real man in the actual world and a imagined man in the virtual world. Later, as the appearance of WeChat, these words are also used in WeChat. So far, both the concerning object and referring object of "fen（粉）" are enlarged as a result of the coercion of "X fen" construction and the meaning of "fen（粉）" is also generalized. In micro blog and WeChat context, "fen（粉）" refers to a person or group that constantly pays attention to micro blog or WeChat.

The appearance of these words is closely related to the user of micro blog and WeChat. The registered users of micro blog and WeChat are mainly common people and the majority of which is young people. Generally, they lack the sense of identity in reality and wish badly to gain attention and support in virtual world. As a result, many bloggers value their fans and work hard to add the number of their fans so that "fen（粉）" construction words frequently appear in micro blog and WeChat. As the constant increasing of "fen（粉）" combination ability, the "scaffold" function of "preference rules system" is weakened for "X fen". In pragmatics, "X fen" construction has new combinations besides "N + fen" and "Adj + fen", for example, "增粉 zengfen (the increasing of fans number), 涨粉zhangfen, 掉粉diaofen (the decreasing of fans number), 路转粉luzhuanfen (a passer-by who becomes a fan), 求粉qiufen (seek for fans), 骗粉pianfen, 刷粉shuafen, 互粉hu fen". For example:

⑦动漫营销不仅是增粉利器，更是产业多元化发展之路。(Dòngmàn yíngxiāo bùjǐn shì zēngfěn lìqì，gèng shì chǎnyè duōyuánhuà fāzhǎn zhīlù。)

（*The marketing of cartoon is not only a good way to increase fans (zeng fen), but also a way for industrial diversified development.*）

⑧警务工作涉及面广泛，和老百姓生活息息相关，开博求粉的动力强。(Jǐngwù gōngzuò shèjímiàn guǎngfàn，hél ǎobǎixìng shēnghuó xīxīxiāngguān，kāibó qiúfěn de dònglì qiáng。)

（*Police work covers many aspect that is closely related people's life so that it is strongly recommended to register a micro blog account and seek for its fans (qiu fen).*）

In above combination, "路转粉luzhuanfen" is a subject-predicate structure. Others can be divided into "V + fen（粉）" and "Adv + fen（粉）" two types, which are verb-object construction and adverb-head word structure respectively. In pragmatics, the application range of these types of words is enlarging beyond the context of micro blog and WeChat and enters into daily life. For example:

⑨录制节目再苦再累，她也坚持每天起床跑步，元气满满的形象为她疯狂涨粉。(Lùzhì jiémù zàikǔ zàilèi，tā yě jiānchí měitiān qǐchuáng pǎobù，yuánqìmǎnmǎn de xíngxiàng wéi tā fēngkuáng zhǎngfěn。）

（*No matter how hard and tired she shot the program, she insisted to run every morning. This energetic image makes her attract more and more fans (zhang fen).*）

⑩这一场看下来，火箭队"掉粉"情况严重。（Zhè yì chǎng kàn xiàlái，huǒjiànduì "diàofěn" qíngkuàng yánzhòng。）

（*After this competition, Houston Rockets has lost many fans (diao fen).*）

In this way, as the enlargement of application context and the enhancement of constructional productivity, "fen（粉）" totally generalized to "supporters or followers of someone or something".

What is more interesting is that, influenced by constructional coercion, the two "fen（粉）" construction types such as "求粉qiufen, 骗粉pianfen, 互粉hufen" begins to verbalize their grammatical feature. "求粉Qiufen" and "骗粉pianfen" do not mean to "ask for fans" and "cheat fans", but to "ask others to be his or her fans" and "cheat others to be his or her fans". In this two constructions, the objects "请qing (ask)" and "骗pian (cheat)" are verbs, and verbalize "fen（粉）" which is in the position of an object. The meaning of "互粉hufen" is "to be each other's fans". Modified by adverb "互hu", the verbal feature of "fen（粉）" is clearer. From this aspect, "fen（粉）" is translating from noun to verb, which is the beginning of its verbalization.

4   The Verbalization of "fen（粉）" and Its further Generalization

In social life, in order to express more level of conception category, "fen（粉）" construction is generating more and more new expressions. Its meaning is further generalized on the basis of new expressions and the category function is also intensified. As the enhancement of its combination ability and repetition rate, "fen（粉）" tends to be an independent word gradually. For example:

⑪粉一回十。(Fěn yì huí shí。）

（*fen（粉）" one and replies ten.*）

⑫这样多好，亲切。回答问题再好，板着个脸，高高在上的，又有什么意思？就冲这个我粉她。(Zhèyàngduōhǎo，qīnqiè。Huídá wèntí zài hǎo，bǎn zhe gè liǎn，gāogāo zài shàng de，yòu yǒu shénme yìsi？Jiù chòng zhège wǒ fěn tā。）

（*It's so good, warm and genial. It's meaningless if one can answer questions well but looks to high of himself or herself with an aloof looking. This is why I "fen（粉）" her.*   ）

⑬粉一粉，积分将来还能抵票款。(Fěn yi fěn, jīfēn jiānglái hái néng dǐ piàokuǎn。)

（*"fen（粉）" me, and the credit can be a substitute for money in the near future.*）

⑭他说在国外的时候，和小伙伴一起"粉"了一首歌，叫《不变的信仰》。(Tāshuōzàiguówàideshíhou ， héxiǎohuǒbànyìqǐ"fěn"leyìshǒugē ， jiào 《búbiàndexìnyǎng》。)

（*He said, when he was abroad, he "fen（粉）" a song entitled "Faith Never Change" together with his friends.*）

In above examples, "fen（粉）" has been an independent word and presents the grammatical feature of a verb in the context. For example, in sentence ⑪, we can add quantity complement after "fen（粉）"; in sentence ⑫, we can add an object directly after "fen（粉）"; sentence⑬ uses the repetition form of "fen（粉）"; ⑭ modified by adverb "一起yiqi (together)", we can add auxiliary word "了le" after "fen（粉）". In these instances, all "fen（粉）" are in the position of a verb and present the function of a verb. This is category mismatch in constructions, which means a syntax category appears in the position of other syntax category and the syntax category is mismatched with its semantical function. [12] The category mismatch in above "fen（粉）" constructions suppresses "fen（粉）" and make it to transform its type and be reanalyzed. The reanalysis includes two aspects. One is the verbalization from a noun; another is to be reanalyzed as a word. The verbalization of a noun is a common grammar case in Chinese, especially ancient Chinese. Chinese is an isolating language which lacks the morphologic change. There are no morphologic changes to demonstrate the grammar properties of a part of speech. As a result, a word can both have the grammar properties of a noun and a verb. According to the statistics by Wang Dongmei, monosyllable nouns are more likely to be verbalized than disyllable nouns; in most cases, the verbalization of noun is a disyllable noun getting rid of a syllable to be a monosyllable one other than the other way around. For example, "纳米技术，谁都可以纳一把？"("Nàmǐ jìshù, shuídōu kéyǐ nà yì bǎ？") [13] (Nanotechnology, anyone can own it？)" The verbalization of "fen（粉）" is in accordance with this rule. In a sense, "fen（粉）" is verbalized through the abbreviation of "fensi(粉丝)".

The verbalization of noun is certainly to change its meaning. With the verbalization of "fen（粉）", the meaning extends from "the supporter or follower of someone or something" to the statement meaning of "pay attention to and support". The change of meaning can be explained by constructional coercion. Generally speaking, when a noun appears in the position of a verb, it is suppressed by this construction, and the referring meaning of the noun will be implicit while the statement meaning presented. Shi Chunhong indicates that the premise of a successful constructional coercion lies in that some features of the suppressed lexical item must accord with that of the construction so that when it enters the construction, the features are presented. [14] The constructional coercion can never happen if the lexical item does not share some features that the construction requires. There is semantic basis for the verbalization of a noun. Specifically, the semantical meaning of the verbalized "fen（粉）" is closely related to its nature as a noun. Generative Lexicon Theory comes up with the idea that the meaning of a word including four layers, namely, argument structure, event structure, qualia structure and lexical typing structure. Qualia structure is the core content which decides the meaning of a noun. It is made up with four roles, that is, formal role, constitutive role, agentive role and telic role. [15] Besides the four roles, conventionalized attribute is also included in the qualia structure. Conventionalized attribute is a typical feature of an object, including its regular activities, features and others. For example, the conventionalized attribute of a "dog" is "bark", of "food" is "digest". [16] For "fen（粉）", the essential role in the conceptual framework it activated is the conventionalized attribute of a noun. In the setting of micro blog, you can be the blogger's fan by clicking the "attention" button of his or her homepage. In daily life, the regular activity of "fensi(粉丝)" is to support and pay attention to someone or something they like. As a result, the regular feature of "fen si" is to pay attention to and to support. When category mismatch appears in "fen（粉）" construction, "fen （粉）" will be reanalyzed as a verb, then its conventionalized attribute "to pay attention to and to support" will be presented. Song Zuoyan noted that "nouns that has specific, single function and agentive role are more easily to verbalize". [17]This rule is also suitable for conventionalized attribute. "To pay attention to and to support" is the specific and single feature of "fensi（粉丝）", accordingly, the referring meaning of its verbalized word is clearer and will not be semantically vague. In this sense, it is more easily to be rebuilt in understanding and explaining. In short, by constructional coercion, the constructional meaning will suppress the lexical meaning and change its semantic type. The noun morpheme "fen（粉）" that has r conventionalized attribute will enter the construction and realizes the syntax and semantic transformation.

5   Conclusion

In modern Chinese, the meaning of "fen（粉）" has evolved in many aspects. First, as the abbreviation of "fensi（粉丝）", "fen（粉）" is used to create words and form "X fen（粉）" and "fen（粉）X" constructions. Type mismatch happens in "fen（粉）" construction and its nature is changed from meaningless transliterated syllable to a noun morpheme which means "someone who adores a certain famous person". Later, with the enhancement of word-formation ability of "fen（粉）" construction and its innovative using in micro blog and WeChat context, the [+ object] feature is added to the concerning object of "fen（粉）" and its meaning is generalized to "the supporter and follower of someone or something". In order to express more layers of category conceptions, the scaffold function of "preference rules system" in the pragmatic of "X fen（粉）", such as "N + fen（粉）" "Adj + fen（粉）" and others, is weaken and "V + fen（粉）" and "Adv + fen（粉）" construction appear. In addition, "fen

（粉）” begins the trend of independence. In above construction, the category "fen （粉）" is mismatched and influenced by constructional coercion. Thus, "fen （粉）" is reanalyzed from a noun morpheme to a verb. At the same time, the conventionalized attribute of "fensi（粉丝）" is presented and it gains the event referring meaning "to pay attention to and to support". In conclusion, influenced by constructional coercion, the semantic evolution of "fen（粉）" is transformed from specific to abstract, from special indication to general reference. This paper roughly clarifies the semantic evolution trace of "fen（粉）", and analyzes and explains the reason of the generation of its new meanings using the theory of constructional coercion.

References:

1. Zhou Ri'an: "fensi""tiesi" and "gangsi", Rhetoric Learning, 2006(6).(In Chinese)
2. Chen Liufang, Qu Weiguo, "A Study of the Semantic Complementation of Foreign Words and Native Words: Take the Introduction of 'Fen' as an Example". Contemporary Rhetoric. 2011 (2). (In Chinese)
3. Wang Huanling, "New Meanings of 'Fen'". Modern Chinese 2012(4). (In Chinese)
4. Goldberg，Adele Eva: Constructions：A construction grammar approach to argument structure, Chicago: University of Chicago Press,(1995).
5. Michaelis , Laura A. Type shifting in construction grammar: An integrated approach to aspectual coercion. Cognitive Linguistics 15:(2005), pp.1-67.
6. Shi Chunhong, "Zhao Pin" and "Qiu Zhi:" Bilateral Interaction Joint Force Mechanism. Contemporary Rhetoric, 2014(2). (In Chinese)
7. Guo Lixia: From "Fensi" to "Shanzi",Journal of North China Electric Power University(Social Sciences), 2007(3). (In Chinese)
8. Liu Yumei, "A Study of the Cognitive Mechanism of 'Ba' Construction". Journal of PLA University of Foreign Languages, 2010(1). (In Chinese)
9. Yan Chensong: On the Discreteness of Zi, Foreign Languages Research, 2009(2). (In Chinese)
10. Su Xinchun: On formation and extraction of monosyllabic morphemes of foreign origins in Contemporary Chinese, Chinese Language, 2003(6). (In Chinese)
11. Song zuoyan: Construction Coercion in Modifier-Head Compound Nouns. Chinese Teaching in the World, 2014(4). (In Chinese)
12. Michaelis，L: Entity and event coercion in a symbolic theory of syntax．In J. Ostman & M. Fried (eds.) Construction Grammars: Cognitive Grounding and Theoretical Extensions．John Benjamins Publishing Company．Talmy,L. (2000) Toward a Cognitive Semantics. MIT Press, (2005).
13. Francis，Elaine J. & Laura A. Michaelis (eds.) Mismatch: Form-function incongruity and the architecture of grammar. Stanford, CA:CSLI，(2003).
14. Wang Dongmei, Nominalization and Verbalization in Contemporary Chinese: A Cognitive Linguistic Inquiry. Graduate School of Chinese Academy of Social Sciences, 2001(5):112-113. (In Chinese)
15. Shi Chunhong, The Grammatical and Rhetorical Interaction of Constructional Coercion. Contemporary Rhetoric，2012（1）. (In Chinese)
16. Pustejovsky, James: The generative lexicon. Cambridge: MIT Press, (1995).61, pp85-86.

17. Pustejovsky, James & Elisabetta Jezek: Semantic coercion in language: Beyond distributional analysis, Italian Journal of Linguistics 20, (2008).pp.181-214.
18. Song Zuoyan: Logical Metonymy, Event Coercion and Noun-to-verb Transformation, Linguistic Sciences, 2013(2). (In Chinese)

Applying Chinese Word Sketch Engine to Distinguish Commonly Confused words

Yang Wu and Shan Wang*

Dept. of Chinese Language Studies, Faculty of Humanities,
The Education University of Hong Kong,
Tai Po, New Territories, Hong Kong
s1051341@s.eduhk.hk, swang@eduhk.hk

Abstract. Recently, as the popularizing of Chinese language learning on a worldwide scale and the rapid expansion of Confucius Institutes, teaching Chinese as an international language (TCIL) develops rapidly all over the world. As a result, teaching commonly confused words from the perspective of non-native Chinese learners has become a necessary concern. Traditional commonly confused words discrimination stands much more on authoritative Chinese dictionaries for senses definition or meanings of a word. However, some scholars in and out of China now promote a new technology for collocation extraction in Chinese which is based on corpora. The latest concept of commonly confused words discrimination is using Chinese Word Sketch (CWS), a powerful tool for extracting meaning grammatical relations and presenting non-native Chinese learners an in-depth analysis of synonyms phrase. This method can not only embrace learners' better understanding about the discrimination between synonym words or commonly confused words, but also built up their capability of choosing a suitable word in different Chinese contexts. This study takes a pair of commonly confused words 接收 *jiēshōu* 'receive' and 接受 *jiēshòu* 'accept' which non-native Chinese learners would always confuse as an example, and based on Chinese Gigaword Corpus, as well as using CWS, to explore the discrimination between 接收 *jiēshōu* 'receive' and 接受 *jiēshòu* 'accept', showing how to adopt CWS to distinguish commonly confused words and apply the results in error analysis and vocabulary learning.

© Springer International Publishing AG 2016
M. Dong et al. (Eds.): CLSW 2016, LNAI 10085, pp. 600–619, 2016
DOI: 10.1007/978-3-319-49508-8_55

Keywords: Key words: Chinese Word Sketch, Commonly Confused Words, Teaching Chinese as an International Language.

1   Introduction

In the world at large, under the background of information globalization and big data, we have witnessed the transformation of dictionaries from printed versions to electronic dictionaries, the electronic dictionaries moving from computer screens to mobile phone touch screens. With the tendency of search engines popularization, linguistic corpora have attracted more and more interests in the field of language study. Before corpus linguistic was introduced into China in 1980s, it already had developed for more than 50 years abroad. Moreover, its vast potential for further application prospects has attracted many scholars' interest (He, 2004; Guo, 2013). Currently, corpus-based studies are welcome in language studies, but most corpora just can provide rich data, such as the widely used corpus of *Center for Chinese Linguistics* PKU (short for CCL)[1]. Yet, in the past ten years, corpora designers and linguists have promoted and proven a very effective corpus tool, Word Sketch Engine (Kilgarriff & Tugwell 2002, Kilgarriff et al. 2004). It has not only provided general keyword search and contextual inquiry, but also presented a list of automatically grammatical knowledge that includes word sketch, grammatical relations and synonyms analysis. For the family of languages, Chinese Word Sketch Engine (CWS) was also developed (Huang, Kilgarriff et al. 2005).

This paper took HSK Dynamic Composition Corpus[2] as the main source of corpus, using CWS as a research tool, referred to sense definitions in several authoritative Chinese dictionaries as well as some popular learners' dictionaries, so as to discuss and analysis the differences between commonly confused words 接收 *jiēshōu* 'receive' and 接受 *jiēshòu* 'accept'. Meanwhile, with the data analysis, this paper tried to propose a discrimination method on commonly confused words, which is based on corpus, and the results can be applied in TCIL.

---

[1] http://ccl.pku.edu.cn:8080/ccl_corpus/
[2] http://202.112.195.192:8060/hsk/login.asp

2   Research Motivation and Goals

Under the background of information globalization, social software has already been in-depth in all areas of life. What interested the authors is that when one transfers files, the word-wide used social software, MSN (2007 edition), and the popular social software in Mainland China, Tencent QQ, use different wordings in the Chinese version. For example, MSN (2007 edition) prompt 等待XX的**接受** "Wait for XX to **accept**", while Tencent QQ prompt language is XX 发给您的文件XX，**接收**另存为还是拒绝XX文件 "XX send you the file XX, **receive**, save as or deny".

On this basis, the study searched HSK dynamic composition Corpus, referred to commonly confused words misused sample statistics of 接收 *jiēshōu* 'receive' and 接受 *jiēshòu* 'accept' in Chinese as a second language (CSL) teaching. According to the data, the misuse frequency of接收 *jiēshōu* 'receive' is 6, while the misuse frequency 接受 *jiēshòu* 'accept' is 31. Examples of major errors (the suitable word in parentheses), as follows:

(1)   我可以接收各种各样的工作。（接受）

   wǒ kěyǐ jiēshōu gèzhǒnggèyàng de gōngzuò。　(jiēshòu)

   I can receive a wide variety of work. (accept)

(2)   孩子们也要接收过去的优良传统。（接受）

   háizǐmen yě yào jiēshōu guòqù de yōuliáng chuántǒng。　(jiēshòu)

   Children need to receive the splendid tradition of the past. (accept)

(3)   这个意见绝对不能接收。（接受）

   zhègè yìjiàn juéduì bùnéng jiēshōu。　(jiēshòu)

   This suggestion absolutely cannot be received. (accept)

(4)   可是周围的人抽烟，所以一直不得不接收自己被动吸烟的无奈的情况。（接受）

   kěshì zhōuwéi de rén chōuyān，suǒyǐ yīzhí bùdébù jiēshōu zìjǐ bèidòng xīyān de wúnài de qíngkuàng 。　(jiēshòu)

   However, the people around me keep smoking, so, I have no alternative but to receive the situation that I smoke passively. (accept)

(5)   那么我们怎么接收教育呢？（接受）

   nàme wǒmen zěnme jiēshōu jiāoyù ne？　(jiēshòu)

   Then how can we receive education? (accept)

(6)   这样果然是让人难以接收的结果。（接受）

   zhèyàng guǒrán shì ràngrén nányǐ jiēshōu de jiéguǒ。　(jiēshòu)

It's hard for us to receive such a result. (accept)

(7) 他们大学今年主要<u>接受</u>一万名新生。（接收）

tāmen dàxué jīnnián zhǔyào <u>jiēshòu</u> yīwànmíng xīnshēng。 (jiēshōu)

Their university plans to accept ten thousand freshmen this year. (receive)

(8) 我每天靠国际互联网<u>接受</u>新闻。（接收）

wǒ měitiān kào guójì hùliánwǎng <u>jiēshòu</u> xīnwén。 (jiēshōu)

I rely on the internet every day to accept news. (receive)

Generally speaking, there are two main reasons that the CSL learners would make such mistakes between commonly confused words. One possible reason is simply because the pronunciations of one or both of the morphemes are similar. While the other reason is because they are a pair of commonly confused word. In this paper, the author mainly focusses on discrimination of the meanings of the two words.

Discrimination of commonly confused words and how to choose the suitable word are difficult and important language teaching points in CSL teaching. Scholars carried out a lot of research on how to discriminate commonly confused words in Chinese contexts, mainly aimed to help CSL learners to discern similarities and differences between synonyms and commonly confused words, so that learners can better understand and use words correctly as well as improve the efficiency and accuracy during Chinese learning. In traditional vocabulary teaching, teachers mainly use sense definitions to present the discrimination of commonly confused words. However, for CSL learners, error analysis cannot simply be based on a small number of observed samples. On the contrary, data analysis that established on the basis of large amount of real corpus data is not only comprehensive but also in-depth. This paper attempted to take Chinese Gigaword Corpus as a main language source, using CWS as an analytical tool, focused on how CWS can help distinguish commonly confused words and facilitate lexicography though comparative study on 接收 *jiēshōu* 'receive' and 接受 *jiēshòu* 'accept'.

3   Literature Review

Zhang (2013) believed that in the progress of language acquisition, it is easy and unavoidable for language learners to mistake A as B, or take B for granted as A. Therefore, those A and B words should be classified as commonly confused words which is valued in the field of CSL teaching. Earlier, Zhang (2007) has pointed out that synonym discrimination in teaching Chinese as an international language should change its perspective from Chinese language ontology research into inter-language research.

However, traditionally commonly confused words teaching mainly depends on sense definitions of major authoritative dictionaries, such as *Contemporary Chinese Dictionary (Xiàndài hànyǔ cídiǎn), Standard Modern Chinese Dictionary (xiàndài hànyǔ guīfàn cídiǎn),* and *High Frequency Words of Chinese Dictionary (hànyǔ chángyòngzì dàcídiǎn)* and so on. Though it is easy and quick to supply sense of definition by means of major dictionaries, it is still difficult for CSL learners to discriminate subtle differences and similarities between commonly confused words, and easily leads to a variety of wrong usages in real communication. Meanwhile, the traditional synonyms teaching mainly be "with meaning as the standard, with little regard for the structure, pragmatic and other factors" (Zhao, 2014). From Table 1 and Table 2 below, it is obvious to see that although all the major authoritative dictionaries have labelled the word's part of speech, senses definition, illustration, and even listed the semantic difference between the commonly confused words or synonyms, itis still lack of comprehensive and in-depth analysis. Therefore, it is difficult for CSL learners to master the right usage of these two commonly confused words. For CSL learners, to understand the meaning of a word is not so difficult, but how to apply it correctly and master its specific usages thoroughly are not easy tasks.

Table 1: Sense Definitions of 接收 jiēshōu 'receive'

Dictionary	Sense	Example
Contemporary Chinese Dictionary (xiàndài hànyǔ cídiǎn) (6th Edition)	Verb 1. 收受 'get in, fetch'; 2.根据法令把机构、财产等拿过来 'take property or institution by law'; 3.接纳 'adopt'。	1.～来稿 '～manuscript' 2.～遗产 '～heritage' 3.～新会员 '～member'
Standard ModernChinese Dictionary (xiàndài hànyǔ guīfàn cídiǎn) (2ⁿᵈ Edition)	Verb , 1. 收受 'get'; 2.接纳、吸收 'take in, absorb'; 3.依法接管（机构、财产等）'take by law（property or institution etc.）'。	1.～信号 '～signal' 2.～新生 '～freshmen' 3.～敌伪财产 '～puppet army's

		possessions'
High Frequency Words of Chinese Dictionary (hànyǔ chángyòngzì dàcídiǎn) (1ˢᵗ Edition)	Verb，1接受 'take in'； 2.根据法令把机构、财产等拿过来 'take property or institution by law'； 3.接纳 'adopt'。	1.～无线电信号 '～radio signal' 3.～新会员 '～member'
Ancient and Modern Chinese Dictionary (gǔjīn hànyǔ shíyòng cídiǎn) (1ˢᵗ Edition)	Verb 1.接纳；收受 'adopt；get'； 2.依照法令收归己方所有 'take over something by law'。	1.～新会员 '～member' 2.～敌伪财产 '～ puppet army's possessions'
New Multifunction Chinese Dictionary (xīnbiān hànyǔ duōgōngnéng cídiǎn) (1ˢᵗ Edition)	Verb 1.收受 'get'； 2.根据法令接管机构、财产、人员等 'take over property, institution or staff etc. by law'。	1.～无线电信号 '～radio signal' 2.～敌伪财产 '～ puppet army's possessions'
HSK Word Usage Annotation Dictionary (HSK cíyǔ yòngfǎ xiángjiě) (1ˢᵗ Edition)	verb，～+人/ 事物 '～+person/ things'.	～新会员 '～members' ～毕业生 '～graduates' ～无线电信号 '～radio signal'
800Chinese Words Dictionary (hànyǔ 800cí cídiǎn) (1ˢᵗ Edition)	verb，1. 收受，接到 'get, come to hand'； 2、根据法令把机构、财产等拿过来 'take property or institution by law'； 3、对事物容纳而不拒绝 'hold things, not refuse'.	1、～电视节目 '～ TV programme' 2、～工厂 '～factory' 3、～病人 '～patient'
Business Hall Chinese Learner's Dictionary (shāngwùguǎn xué hànyǔ cídiǎn) (1ˢᵗ Edition)	verb，1、得到（送来或发来的东西） 'obtain（things being sent）'； 2、同意或采纳（别人的意见、建议等） 'agree or accept（others' opinions or suggestions, etc.）'。	1、～信件 '～letter' 2、～留学生 '～ oversea students'

Table2: Sense Definitions of 接受 jiēshòu 'accept'

Dictionary	Sense	Example
Contemporary Chinese Dictionary (Xiàndài hànyǔ cídiǎn) (6th Edition)	verb, 1、收取（给予的东西）'take（things given）'; 2、对事物容纳而不拒绝 'accommodate things, not refuse'	1、～礼物 '～gift' 2、～任务 '～task'
Standard Modern Chinese Dictionary (xiàndài hànyǔ guīfàn cídiǎn) (2ⁿᵈ Edition)	verb, 领受；采纳 'receive；adopt'。	～惩罚 '～punishment'
High Frequency Words of Chinese Dictionary (hànyǔ chángyòngzì dàcídiǎn) (1ˢᵗ Edition)	verb, 对事物容纳而不拒绝 'accommodate things, not refuse'	～犯罪 '～criticism'
Ancient and Modern Chinese Dictionary (gǔjīn hànyǔ shíyòng cídiǎn) (1ˢᵗ Edition)	承受；采纳 'bear；adopt'	～任务 '～task'
New Multifunction Chinese Dictionary (xīnbiān hànyǔ duōgōngnéng cídiǎn) (1ˢᵗ Edition)	领受、容纳而不拒绝 'Get; accommodate things, not refuse'	～教育 '～education'
HSK Word Usage Annotation Dictionary (HSK cíyǔ yòngfǎ xiángjiě) (1ˢᵗ Edition)	verb, ～+ 事物 '～+ things'	～礼物 '～gift' ～批评 '～criticism'
800 Chinese Words Dictionary (hànyǔ 800cí cídiǎn) (1ˢᵗ Edition)	verb, 对事物容纳而不拒绝 'accommodate things, not refuse'	～邀请 '～invitation'
Business Hall Chinese Learner's Dictionary (shāngwùguǎn xué hànyǔ cídiǎn) (1ˢᵗ Edition)	verb, 1、收下（别人送的礼物、钱财等）'take（gift or money etc. given by others）'; 2、同意或采纳（别人的意见、建议等）'agree or adopt（others' opinions or suggestions etc.'.	1、～礼物 '～gift' 2、～邀请 '～invitation'

Table 3: Sense Discrimination to 接收 jiēshōu 'receive' and 接受 jiēshòu 'accept'

Dictionary	接收 jiēshōu 'receive'	接受 jiēshòu 'accept'
Standard Modern Chinese Dictionary (xiàndài hànyǔ guīfàn cídiǎn) (2nd Edition)	1、为了使用、管理等目的而收下，对象多是具体的事物或人； 'take over for the purpose of using or management, mostly focus on detailed things or a certain people.' 2、所指动作行为多带主动意味。 'such behavior has initiative meaning.'	1、应承他人所施予的行为或要求，对象多是抽象事物； 'reply to requirement or behavior given by others, mostly focus on abstract things.' 2、多带被动意味。 'mostly with passivity meaning.'
Modern Chinese Synonymy Dictionary (xiàndài hànyǔ tóngyìcí cídiǎn)	1、主动地收取、吸取； 'initiatively charge or absorb'; 2、对象多为信件、订单、信号等； 'most objects are mail, order, signal, etc.' 3、可以表示接纳新的成员。 'It means take in new members.'	1、表示承认、承受、收下，不拒绝； 'it means admit, bear, take without refusing.' 2、对象是别人给予的东西，如意见、任务、观点、条件、批评、教育、处分、邀请等。 'most objects are things that given by others, such as viewpoints, task, opinion, condition, criticism, education, punishment, invitation, etc.'
New Multifunction Chinese Dictionary (xīnbiān hànyǔ duōgōngnéng cídiǎn) (1st Edition)	1、对象一般是具体的，或者是人员；或者是财务、机关、企业等；或者是信息； 'most objects are specific, people, finance, organization, enterprise, etc.' 2、可带动词宾语。 'It may be linked with verb object.'	1、对象可以是具体的，也可以是抽象的； 'objects may be specific or abstract.' 2、不带动词宾语。 'could not be linked with verb object.'
1700 pairs of Synonyms Dictionary	宾语既可以是抽象名词，也可以是具体名词。 'Object may be specific or abstract.'	主要是心理活动，它的宾语一般是抽象名词。 'mainly means mental activity. The object is mostly abstract noun.'

(1700 duì jìnyì cíyǔ yòngfǎ duìbǐ) (*1ˢᵗ Edition*)		
Business Hall Chinese Learner's Dictionary (shāngwùguǎn xué hànyǔ cídiǎn) (*1ˢᵗ Edition*)	同：都表示受到、得到。 'Similarity: both with meaning of get and obtain.' 异：对象不能是抽象的；对象是具体的，除了物品以外，还可以是"信件、稿件"； 'Difference: object cannot be abstract. Only specific things like mail, manuscript can be the object.' 还可以表示接纳新成员和依照法令把某些机构、财物拿过来。 'It may describe taking in new members or fetching money or institution by law.'	同：都表示受到、得到。 'Similarity: both with meaning of get and obtain.' 异：对象可以是抽象的。 'Difference: object may be abstract.'
Synonyms Discrimination Dictionary (tóngyìcí biànxī cídiǎn)	多义词，词义范围大，而适用范围小，限于同表具体事物的名词搭配。 'Polysemous word, with wide range of meaning but small range of usage, only matching the specific noun.'	单义词，词义范围小，而适用范围较大，可同表具体事物的名词搭配，而多数时候同表抽象事物的名词搭配。 'Univocal word, with small range of meaning but wide range of usage. It may match specific noun while mostly be with abstract noun.'
HSK Word Usage Annotation Dictionary (HSK cíyǔ yòngfǎ xiángjiě) (*1ˢᵗ Edition*)	1、后面不能加"着"； 'cannot be followed by "zhe".' 2、后面可加量动词"下、次、回"； 'can be followed by verbs like "again, more, next"' 3、后面可加趋向词"起、起来"； 'Can be followed by direction words "up, on"' 4、后面可加介词"到"； 'Can be followed by preposition "dào"' 5、不能重叠。 'Cannot be repeat.'	1、后面可加动量词"次、回"； 'can be followed by verbal measure words like "time"' 2、后面可加趋向词"下来、起来"； 'can be followed by direction words "up"' 3、后面不能加介词短语。 'Cannot be followed by prepositional phrase.'

Table 3 is the comparative analysis of some major authoritative dictionaries and learner's dictionaries. Seen from the details, it basically focuses on the definitions of senses, and taking these two commonly confused words as a simple vocabulary issues of Chinese language itself, yet does not refer to distinguish them from perspectives of the grammar and contexts, as well as error analysis for CSL learners. What's more, except for the definitions of senses in major dictionaries, there is no paper or other research on the comparative study of 接收 jiēshōu 'receive' and 接受 jiēshòu 'accept' as a pair of commonly confused words.

According to studies and papers of semantic fields, generally speaking, there are three main approaches on sense discrimination. The first and primary approach is sense interpretation through various authoritative dictionaries or learners' dictionaries. Representative works of this type includes *Chinese Thesaurus Discrimination* (Yang, 2005), *1700 pairs of Synonyms Usages Comparison* (Yangand Jia,2005), *Chinese Synonyms Dictionary* (Wang, 1997) and so on. The second approach is based on corpus data, dynamically and visually presenting similarities and differences between commonly confused words. For instance, Hao and Xing (2010) proposed a corpus-based synonyms discrimination method, mainly summarizing the frequency of synonyms when they occur in different sentence structures and the statistics of specific collocations. However, because the corpora they used is not segmented and tagged, their data collocations cannot make deeper grammatical analysis and it is hard to compare a given word from grammatical perspective. Liu (2010) suggested to distinguish synonyms with word collocation through corpus. At last, the third approach suggests to explore the possibility of deeper and comparable Chinese grammatical information via the powerful Word Sketch Engine. CWS has proven to be a very effective and useful tool for automatic description of lexical information which includes collocation extraction, deeper grammatical analysis, and grammatical relations. Much research has used it in getting suitable data (Huang, Kilgarriff, *et al*, 2005; Wang, 2012; Wang & Huang, 2011, 2013a, 2013b; Hong & Huang, 2013). For example, Huang, Kilgarriff,*et al* (2005)introduced their corpora thoroughly with examples of extraction of collocation information, and in particular showed the robustness of CWS by achieving better and deeper results thought grammatical knowledge. Wang and Huang (2013), in the paper of facilitating lexicography study, presented how to apply Chinese Word Sketch Engine into sense definitions via a comparative study on two emotional words 愉快 yúkuài 'pleasant' and 高兴 gāoxìng 'happy', as well as focusing on how CWS functions on synonymous words discrimination and its significant advantages in collocation robustness and comprehensiveness. However, current research that used CWS has not applied the results to TCIL.

4   Research Methodology

This paper, based on Chinese Gigaword Corpus, via Chinese Word Sketch Engine, carried out a comparative study of a pair of commonly confused words 接收 *jiēshōu* 'receive' and 接受 *jiēshòu* 'accept', to deepen explore their similarities and differences.

According to the grammatical distribution graphs provided by CWS, we can extract various subtle differences between commonly confused words 接收 *jiēshōu* 'receive' and 接受 *jiēshòu* 'accept' in actual language usages, through their common patterns and single word patterns only. Figure 1, 2, 3 is the data extracted from CWS.

接受 21 14 7 0, -7 -14 -21 接收

SentObject_of	24238	1145	6.9	8.0	Object	24232	10228	4.1	4.2	Subject	54973	2460	3.7	4.0	Modifier	78553	2276	3.9	2.8
拒絕	4839	121	86.0	44.3	天線	6	160	2.7	54.4	衛星	16	141	2.0	41.3	無法	5089	55	64.1	24.5
願意	3190	68	75.6	34.8	信號	29	153	5.8	43.7	中共	491	242	17.0	34.1	不能	3701	19	61.4	14.9
願	1957	49	62.0	28.4	電台	1904	6	43.3	3.9	他	2646	13	32.9	2.6	不會	1902	5	48.2	5.2
同意	1472	52	53.4	27.4	電話	3123	27	43.3	10.3	他們	881	18	28.0	8.8	必須	2263	12	48.1	9.7
注意	14	234	3.2	52.7	電視台	1674	18	40.4	10.2	人	2052	9	27.3	0.5	不	6463	45	46.5	12.4
開始	1782	60	52.2	26.6	訊號	7	79	1.9	39.3	民政部門	5	13	7.4	26.4	是否	1608	9	45.6	8.8
準備	865	61	43.7	29.0	裝置	18	116	0.8	35.9	民政部	8	15	8.8	26.0	可以	2691	100	45.6	28.3
負責	92	96	16.0	36.6	畢業生	43	137	3.9	35.8	信號	6	24	3.1	25.9	共	339	138	21.9	42.8
代為	117	9	36.4	19.2	香港	450	694	0.5	34.5	代表	1011	8	23.3	1.9	能	3171	132	41.6	27.8
繼續	820	15	35.6	10.9	捐款	518	13	30.9	11.1	電視	21	49	0.6	23.1	正在	1084	9	40.8	9.5
需要	641	8	34.9	7.6	難民	186	121	12.8	30.7	民眾	574	5	21.0	1.7	所	1965	34	40.6	16.4
不予	101	11	33.4	21.0	電子郵件	13	44	4.0	29.8	畢業生	26	22	7.7	20.9	不肯	157	5	38.4	13.9
專門	36	37	13.0	29.3	電視	1164	23	27.2	8.8	當局	242	11	18.6	8.5	能夠	766	47	38.3	26.5
希望	760	23	28.3	11.5	訊息	48	6	5.3	26.9	它	176	23	18.4	16.2	定期	388	5	38.2	9.6
停止	171	12	26.8	14.8	節目	289	117	13.5	26.9	單位	154	58	6.5	17.8	曾	1434	10	37.1	7.3
有意	128	16	25.3	18.7	病人	476	72	24.4	24.9	用戶	24	17	6.4	17.3	並	2002	20	35.5	9.6
堅持	193	6	23.6	7.5	請願信	30	9	24.1	22.7	政府	956	108	14.1	15.9	不准	201	6	35.1	13.0
顯示	145	8	20.2	9.4	衛星電視	8	19	4.7	23.9	期間	233	5	15.1	3.1	不再	351	18	33.5	19.2
擬	45	5	17.9	10.6	各界	892	18	23.8	7.2	細胞	7	11	1.1	14.0	將	3730	161	32.5	23.1
打算	38	5	17.5	11.2	管轄權	15	21	6.8	23.2	官員	314	5	14.0	1.7	不得	397	11	32.5	13.3
派員	26	10	13.9	17.4	群眾	1119	11	23.0	2.9	權	30	6	12.6	11.3	隨時	280	40	32.1	31.5
															應	1079	9	31.8	6.3

Figure1 ： 接收 jiēshōu 'receive' and 接受 jiēshòu 'accept' common patterns

"接收" only patterns

SentObject_of 1145 8.0		Object 10228 4.2		Subject 2460 4.0		Modifier 2276 2.8	
報請,	17 26.8	主權,	197 34.4	衛星電視	53 45.9	強行,	7 15.2
用來,	15 22.3	設施,	262 32.5	雲圖,	31 44.4	**Modifies 411 0.1**	
		好望角	18 31.9	天線,	34 37.5	畢業生,	15 24.1
		設備,	206 30.6	飛彈營,	8 30.2	光線,	6 23.3
		專用卡	10 29.9	款物,	9 22.7	節目,	12 17.9
		日產,	33 29.8	訊號,	13 22.2	訊號,	5 17.3
		轉播站	18 27.7	接收機,	6 21.1	銀行,	8 8.4
		系統,	211 25.4	實時,	8 20.3		
		澳門,	109 24.5	接收器,	6 19.9		
		衛星,	83 24.4	電視機,	11 19.3		
		架,	64 23.6	日共,	5 18.8		
		資訊,	101 22.8	整體,	23 16.7		

Figure 2： 接收 jiēshōu 'receive' only patters

"接受" only patterns

PP_由 477 9.0		SentObject_of 24128 6.9		PP_以 446 4.5		PP_被 107 4.2	
周人,	5 20.1	自覺,	766 66.8	電台,	38 33.6	事實,	9 21.2
聯合國,	21 19.0	樂於,	280 58.6	武力,	14 22.8	巴勒斯坦人	5 17.1
徐立德,	6 17.2	樂意,	225 54.3	電視台,	16 22.1	命運,	5 17.0
南韓,	11 15.8	勉強,	208 53.8	方式,	25 19.5		
美國,	21 12.4	勇於,	227 46.9	名義,	8 17.4		
法官,	5 11.5	被迫,	269 41.6	原則,	11 14.7		
國際,	13 8.9	自願,	139 37.4	民調,	5 13.7		
成員,	5 8.4	涉嫌,	253 31.8	土地,	10 13.3		
組織,	7 6.8	敢,	148 31.8	臨時,	5 12.5		
國家,	8 5.1	肯,	53 30.1	身份,	5 9.9		
人,	6 3.9	顧不顧意	19 29.7	媒體,	6 8.7		
總統,	5 3.1	無意,	62 28.1	美國,	7 5.2		

PP_對 219 0.7		PP_在 389 0.5		Modifies 5617 0.1	
指控,	5 14.4	伊拉克,	7 10.6	方案,	270 39.1
他,	17 14.1	聯合國,	5 7.8	程度,	152 35.9
大選,	5 11.2	國際,	8 6.5	人道,	150 35.7
台,	5 9.4	記者,	8 3.5	條件,	221 33.6
他們,	5 8.3	地區,	5 3.3	方式,	267 32.1
台灣,	5 5.4	台北,	5 2.8	範圍,	145 31.3
		PP_把 87 0.5		彥線,	26 28.5
		自覺,	5 19.6	平衡點,	16 27.3
		PP_向 53 0.1		協議,	125 26.8
		報告,	6 13.6	事實,	62 26.0
				潮法,	95 25.6

Object 242332 4.1		Modifier 78553 3.9		Subject 5493 3.7		PP_朝 9 2.0	
媒體,	11847 59.4	欣然,	970 77.6	會前,	41 35.3	記者,	5 11.4
手術,	3162 53.4	愉快,	642 62.2	雙方,	652 31.3	**PP_將 299 0.9**	
新聞網	1007 50.4	絕不,	656 53.1	我們,	687 30.5	同時,	8 12.6
記者,	41614 49.5	無條件,	380 52.5	患者,	327 28.9	醫院,	6 9.7
本報,	474 49.0	難以,	1065 51.2	我方,	111 28.8	總統,	6 5.2
探訪,	2017 47.9	拒不,	283 51.0	巴方,	65 26.9	人,	5 4.3
訓練,	4017 45.0	不可能,	489 43.8	病人,	215 26.6		

Figure 3： 接受 jiēshòu 'accept' only patterns

5　Data Analysis

Figure 1 illustrates the common patterns of 接收 *jiēshōu* 'receive' and 接受 *jiēshòu* 'accept'. The words listed in color chain which is from green to red are suitable to the two words. Seen from color values in Figure1, the redder in the color chain, the more possible that it will collocate with 接收 *jiēshōu* 'receive'; on the contrary, the greener in the color chain, the more possible it collocates with 接受 *jiēshòu* 'accept'. By analyzing and categorizing with Figure 1, we can summarize a list of concordance and grammatical relation of common patterns as Table 4 as below.

Table 4: Distribution of Words co-occurrence and grammar functions

语法功能 Grammatical functions	"接收" 常见搭配 Common collocation with "receive"	两词皆可以的常见搭配 Common collocation with both words	"接受" 常见搭配 Common collocation with "accept"
SentObject_of	注意 *zhùyì* 'pay attention to'、负责 *fùzé* 'be responsible to'、专门 *zhuānmén* 'be specialized to'。	有意 *yǒuyì* 'intend to'、打算 *dǎsuàn* 'plan to'、派员 *pàiyuán* 'sent to'、包括 *bāokuò* 'include'、可望 *kěwàng* 'expect to'、要求 *yàoqiú* 'require'。	拒绝 *jùjué* 'refuse to'、愿意 *yuànyì* 'willing to'、同意 *tóngyì* 'agree to'、开始 *kāishǐ* 'start to'、继续 *jìxù* 'continue to'、需要 *xūyào* 'need to'。
Object	天线 *tiānxiàn* 'antenna'、信号 *xìnhào* 'sign'、讯号 *xùnhào* 'signal'、装置 *zhuāngzhì* 'appliance'、毕业生 *bìyèshēng* 'graduates'、难民 *nánmín* 'refugee'、邮件 *yóujiàn* 'mail'、讯息 *xùnxī* 'message'。	病人 *bìngrén* 'patient'、请愿信 *qǐngyuànxìn* 'requirement letter'、指令 *zhǐlìng* 'order'。	电台 *diàntái* 'radio station'、电话 *diànhuà* 'telephone'、电视台 *diànshìtái* 'TV station'。
Subject	卫星 *wèixīng* 'satellite'、信号 *xìnhào* 'signal'、电视 *diànshì* 'TV'。	它 *tā* 'It'、政府 *zhèngfǔ* 'government'、干部 *gànbù* 'cadre'、院校 *yuànxiào* 'Institute'。	他们 *tāmen* 'them'、代表 *dàibiǎo* 'delegate'。
Modifier	共 *gòng* 'together'。	随时 *suíshí* 'anytime'、已 *Yǐ* 'already'、可 *kě* 'can'。	无法 *wúfǎ* 'Can't'、不能 *búnéng* 'unable to'、不会 *búhuì* 'Won't'、必须 *bìxū* 'must'、是否 *shìfǒu* 'whether'、正在 *zhèngzài* 'be doing'、不肯 *búkěn* 'unwilling

			to'、定期 *dìngqī* 'at regular intervals'、不准 *bùzhǔn* 'mustn't'。
Modifies	信息 *xìnxī* 'information'	问题 *wèntí* 'question'	

Based on the data extracted from CWS, while comparing to some major authoritative dictionaries and learners' dictionaries, there is not any sense definitions, yet, it illustrates different levels of contrast from the grammatical and contextual perspective. From Figure 1, 2, 3, it is clear that CWS provides not only various distributions of concordance, but also more information than simply sense definition, such as, POS-tagged, grammatical relations and distributional thesaurus. Therefore, judging from data analysis results from CWS, it is clear that we can classify the differences between this pair of commonly confused words into four aspects: the range of application, whether to collect with abstract nouns or not, sentimental coloring of each word, whether to collect with negative modifiers.

Viewing from Figure1, despite this pair of commonly confused words 接收 *jiēshōu* 'receive' and 接受 *jiēshòu* 'accept' share lots of common usages and collocations, we find that it illustrates more examples on differences. For instance, CWS provides word lists of collocations with verbs, which in particular lists out different occasions when 接收 *jiēshōu* 'receive' and 接受 *jiēshòu* 'accept' match with various verb phrases forming a formation of modifier-noun phrases or serial verb constructions, linked with the other verb phrases (See SentObject_of); when 接收 *jiēshōu* 'receive' and 接受 *jiēshòu* 'accept' become a predicate, how they separately collocate with different noun phrases(see Subject); when the modifier places either in the front of or behind 接收 *jiēshōu* 'receive' and 接受 *jiēshòu* 'accept'(see Object, Modifier and Modifies).Figure 2 接收 *jiēshōu* 'receive' only pattern and Figure 3 接受 *jiēshòu* 'accept' only patterns, show CSL learners a vivid picture of word collocations on high frequency words in real language usage as well as marking its total frequency and robustness. Word collocations in Figure 1, 2, and 3, display different grammatical relations, which not only helps CSL learners jump out of confusion caused by abstract and vague sense definitions in authoritative dictionaries, but also guides them to get more rational analysis of subtle differences between this pair of commonly confused words in the grammatical structures in different contexts.

By contrast, the sense definition in major dictionaries has only a few words, combined with simple illustrations. It is still challenging for Chinese native speakers to discern the similarities and difference between synonyms or pairs of commonly confused words simply from concise summary in dictionary descriptions which sometimes are used in a circulatory way, let alone the CSL learners. When we refer to learners' dictionaries which on the basis of sense definitions can provide more comparisons from semantic and grammatical level, yet, still basically literary statements. Moreover, different learner's tools sometimes have different opinions on the same concept. For example, on the issue of whether the object of 接收 *jiēshōu* 'receive' is abstract or not, *1700 Pairs of Synonyms for Contrast* and *Business Learning Chinese Synonyms Dictionary* held different opinions. And such kinds of learners' dictionaries will confuse CSL learners and build up more blocks for them. However, corpora and computational linguistic tools can offer a better and effective answer to the above issue. Based on vast amount of data, with KWIC concordances, corpus present lots of sentences of a given word so that the learners can analyze these data. As Huang, Kilgarriff,*et al* (2005) pointed out that availability of grammatical information depends on corpus annotation. Currently, one of the most popular Chinese corpora CCL which just allows users to process extracted information of a given word, doesn't have POS tags, and not to mentions the most salient grammatical information, such as subject, object, adjunct etc. But the Chinese Word Sketch Engine offers not only KWIC concordances, but also word sketches, thesaurus and sketch difference which are all annotated and automatic (Huang, *et al* 2005).

In contrast to Figure 2 (the 接收 *jiēshōu* 'receive' only patterns) and Figure3 (the 接受*jiēshòu* 'accept' only patterns), we can see that 接收 *jiēshōu* 'receive' has smaller scope of use, while 接受 *jiēshòu* 'accept' has a wider scope. But when we analyze the common nouns related to 接收 *jiēshōu* 'receive' and 接受*jiēshòu* 'accept', we could not conclude that 接受 *jiēshòu* 'accept' mainly connect to abstract nouns as synonyms dictionary does. Conversely, in real corpus data, whether it is 接收 *jiēshōu* 'receive' or 接受 *jiēshòu* 'accept', both of them can connect to nouns which represent specific things. Besides, both of them can be used in conjunction with abstract nouns, but the situation of which appears rare. Figure 3 shows 接受 *jiēshòu* 'accept' is usually represented with mental noun phrase, with a strong emotional component, but we cannot see much passive meaning of it from Figure 3. From the 接收 *jiēshōu* 'receive' only pattern in Figure 4, it is clear that this word usually has an initiative meaning, but from the robustness and total frequency, we can propose that 接收 *jiēshōu* 'receive' is used more for the objective situation, and has more neutral emotion. In addition, by comparing Figure2 and 3, we obviously can conclude that 接受 *jiēshòu* 'accept' can constitute a prepositional phrase with different prepositions. Meanwhile, from grammatical functions such as subject, object, adjunct and the frequency of which, we can see that 接受 *jiēshòu* 'accept' has a larger use scope than 接收 *jiēshōu* 'receive', which provide concrete evidence for synonym dictionaries. To sum up, the above corpora data analysis and real life language usage contexts which cannot be extracted from printed dictionaries, are what CWS advantage all the printed dictionaries as well as other corpora. All the salient grammatical information and distributional thesaurus that CWS provided is what CSL learners look for. It helps them acquire correct usages of synonyms so as to improve the efficiency and accuracy of Chinese language learning.

6   Apply CWS Analysis to Commonly Confused Words in TCIL

From the above analysis, we can conclude that 接受 *jiēshòu* 'accept' mainly matches with nouns of mental activity, and it is an active action; while 接收 *jiēshōu* 'receive', on the other hand, is often used in conjunction with objective things. By analyzing the wrong collocations in sentences of CSL learners which is selected from the HSK Dynamic Composition Corpus, with CWS as a query tool, we can help learners distinguish this pair of commonly confused words in aspects of range of sematic, emotion, whether being referring to mental activity, and connect with negative modifiers and so on.

In error analysis of the selected sentences of HSK Dynamic Composition Corpus, take Sentence (3) as an example, we can compare 接收 *jiēshōu* 'receive' with 接受 *jiēshòu* 'accept' by means of modifier, and therefore can conclude that 接受 *jiēshòu* 'accept' can connect with negative modifier while 接收 *jiēshōu* 'receive' doesn't. Hence, this sentence should be corrected as 'this suggestion absolutely cannot be accepted'. As for Sentence (7), judging from the color chain of common patterns of 接收 *jiēshōu* 'receive' and 接受 *jiēshòu* 'accept', it is clear that "freshmen" equal to "graduation", only collocating with 接收 *jiēshōu* 'receive' in Chinese. When we refer to Sentence (8), judging from the emotions of the words in Figure 1 as well as grammatical functions in Figure 2, we can suggest that 新闻 *xīnwén* "news", similar to 信息*xìnxī* "information", can collocate with 接收 *jiēshōu* 'receive', yet, from Figure 3 接受 *jiēshòu* 'accept' only patterns, we cannot find out such usages.

In addition, in the error analysis of 接收 *jiēshōu* 'receive' and 接受 *jiēshòu* 'accept', from Chinses second language learner's perspective, we cannot exclude that they made mistakes simply because this pair of commonly confused words have a same morpheme or similar pronunciation, but not they completely cannot master their correct usages.

At last, when we go back to the original research question that who has a correct choice of this pair of commonly confused words, MSN or Tencent QQ? According the data and analysis we get from CWS, the answer is "both of them are correct". For MSN, it chooses 等待XX的**接受** "Wait for XX to **accept**", which in Figure 1 "wait" is similar to the grammatical function of 同意 *tóngyì* "agree", 继续 *jìxù* "continue", 开始 *kāishǐ* "begin" that included active and usually collocate with nouns of mental activity. While Tencent QQ chooses XX发给您的文件XX，**接收**另 存为还是拒绝XX文件 "XX send you the file XX, **receive**, save as or deny", which just matches the data conclusion that 接收 *jiēshōu* 'receive' is consistent with more objective and specific things. Hence, the paper can propose that both MSN and Tencent QQ stands on different perspectives, and thus both have a correct choice between this pair of commonly confused words based on different kinds of information that they want to convey to the recipients.

7   Conclusion

The Error Analysis of commonly confused words in Chinese language teaching and research methods attract more and more attention of many scholars in and out of China. In addition to the traditional sense definitions which based on authoritative canonical dictionaries and learners' dictionaries, more and more attention can be turned to the use of the technological query tool CWS to explore more information of commonly confused words. This paper proves the Chinese Sketch Engine is an efficient and powerful tool for deeper linguistic analysis and the findings can help CSL learners to improve their Chinese proficiency. In the case study of a pair of commonly confused words 接收 *jiēshōu* 'receive' and 接受 *jiēshòu* 'accept', we presented its significant advantages in automatic display of lexical information as well as grammatical functions that other corpora don't have. In particular, we showed the robustness of CWS and how it can be applied to TCIL.

* **Corresponding author.**

Acknowledgement: This research is supported by Internal Research Grant of The Education University of Hong Kong. The reference number is RG 6/2015-2016R and the project code is R3648.

References

Dictionary Editing Room of Institute of Linguistics of China Academy of Social Sciences. (2012). *Contemporary Chinese Dictionary (xiàndài hànyǔ cídiǎn) (6th Edition)*. Beijing: Commercial Press.

Guo, S. L. (2013). *Chinese corpus application course book (hànyǔ yǔliàokù yīngyòng jiāochéng)*. Shanghai: Shanghai Jiaotong University Press.

Hao, Y.X., Xing, X.B. (2010). Based on Large-scale Corpus Synonym Discrimination: A Case Study of 美丽 *měilì* and 漂亮 *piàoliàng (jīyú dàguīmó yǔliàokù de xuéxíng tóngyìcí biànxī móshì chūtàn ——yǐ "měilì"、"piàoliàng " wéi lì)*. In Shi-Yong, Kang. et al. (Eds.), *Development of Lexical Semantics - Tenth Vocabulary Semantics Forum*, Singapore: Oriental Languages Information Association.

He, A.P. (Ed.). (2004). *Applying Corpora in Foreign Language Teaching - Theory and Practice (yǔliàokù zài wàiyǔ jiāoyù zhōng de yīngyòng ——lǐlùn yǔ shíjiàn)*. Guangzhou: Guangdong Higher Education Press.

Huang, C.-R., Kilgarriff, A., Wu, Y., Chiu, C.M., Smith, S., Rychly, P., Bai, M. H., and Chen, K. J. (2005). Chinese Sketch Engine and the Extraction of Collocations, *Proceedings of The Fourth SIGHAN Workshop on Chinese Language Processing*, Jeju, Korea, pp. 48-55.

Huang, N.S., & Sun, D. J. (Ed.). (2000). *HSK Word Usage Annotation Dictionary (HSK cíyǔ yòngfǎ xiángjiě) (1ˢᵗEdition)*. Beijing: Beijing Language and Culture University Press.

Hong, J. F., and Huang, C. R. (2013). Cross-Strait Lexical Differences: A Comparative Study based on Chinese Gigaword Corpus, *Computational Linguistics and Chinese Language Processing*, 18 (2). pp. 19-34.

Kilgarriff, A., Pavel, R., Pavel, S., & David, T. (2004). The Sketch Engine. In Geoffrey, W. & Sandra, V., Lorient. (Eds), *Proceedings of the 11th EURALEX International Congress*, France: pp.105-116.

Kilgarriff, A.& David, T. (2002). Sketching Words Lexicography and Natural Language: A Festschrift in Honour of B.T.S. Atkins (EURALEX 2002). In Marie-Hélène Corréard. (Ed). Copenhagen, Denmark: pp.125-137.

Li, X. J. (Ed.). (2010). *Standard Modern Chinese Dictionary (xiàndài hànyǔ guīfàn cídiǎn) (2nd edition)*. Beijing: Foreign Language Teaching and Research Press.

618   Y. Wu and S. Wan

Liu, F. Q. (2010). Based on Corpus Collocation Study and CSL Vocabulary Teaching (*jīyú yǔliàokù de cíyǔ dāpèi yánjiū yǔ duìwàihànyǔ cíhuì jiāoxué*). *Language Teaching and Research*, (6). pp.115-117.

High Frequency Words of Chinese Dictionary (hànyǔ chángyòngzì dàcídiǎn) (1ˢᵗ Ed). (2009). Beijing: International Commercial Press.

Lu, J. Y., & Lv, W. H. (Ed.). (2006). *Business Hall Chinese Language Learning Dictionary (shāngwùguǎn xué hànyǔ cídiǎn) (1ˢᵗ edition)*. Beijing: Commercial Press.

Lv, S. X. (Ed.). (2000).*800 Chinese Words Dictionary (hànyǔ 800cí cídiǎn) (1ˢᵗEdition)*. Beijing: Beijing Language and Culture University Press.

Wang, S. (2012). *Semantics of Event Nouns*. (Ph.D), The Hong Kong Polytechnic University, Hong Kong.

Wang, S., & Huang, C-R. (2011). A Generative Lexicon Perspective to Possessive Relation in Mandarin Chinese *Proceedings of The 12th Chinese Lexical Semantics Workshop (CLSW-12)* (pp. 201-213). National Taiwan University, Taipei.

Wang, S., & Huang, C.-R. (2013a). Apply Chinese Word Sketch Engine to Facilitate Lexicography. In Kwary, D. A., Wulan, N., & Musyahda, L. (Eds.), *Lexicography and Dictionaries in the Information Age*: Selected paper from the 8ᵗʰ ASIALEX International Conference, Bali, Indonesia, pp.285-292.

Wang, S., & Huang, C.-R. (2013b). The Semantic Type System of Event Nouns. In S. Z. Jing (Ed.), *Increased Empiricism: Recent Advances in Chinese Linguistics* (Vol. 2, pp. 205-221). Amsterdam / Philadelphia: John Benjamins Publishing Company.

Wu, C. H. (2000). *Ancient and Modern Chinese Dictionary (gǔjīn hànyǔ shíyòng cídiǎn) (1ˢᵗEdition)*. Sichuan: Sichuan People's Press.

Xu, A. C., & Zhao, D. P. (Ed.). (1997). *Synonym Discrimination Dictionary (tóngyìcí biànxī cídiǎn)*. Beijing: Chinese Language Press.

Yang, J. Z., & Jia, Y. F. (Ed.). (2005). *1700 pairs of Synonyms Dictionary (1700duì jìnyì cíyǔ yòngfǎ duìbǐ) (1ˢᵗEdition)*. Beijing: Beijing Language and Culture University Press.

Zhao, X., & Li, Y. (Ed.) (2009). *Business Hall Chinese Synonyms Dictionary (shāngwùguǎn xué hànyǔ jìnyìcí cídiǎn)*. Beijing: Commercial Press.

Zhang, B. (2007). Synonyms, Near-synonyms, commonly confused words: Perspective transfer from Chinese ontology to inter-language (*tóngyìcí, jìnyìcí, yì húnxiáocí: cóng hànyǔ dào zhōngjièyǔ de shìjiǎo zhuǎnyí*). *World Chinese Teaching*, (3).

Zhang, W. X. (2013). *Chinese Ontology of Teaching Chinese as an International Language (duìwàihànyǔ běntǐ jiāoxué gàilùn)*. Beijing: Commercial Press.

Zhou, X. J. (Ed.). (2009). *New Multifunction Chinese Dictionary (xīnbiān hànyǔ duōgōngnéng cídiǎn) (1ˢᵗ Edition)*. Hainan: Hainan Press.

Domain Restrictor *Chúfēi* and Relevant Constructions

Lei Zhang

Chinese Language and Literature School, Northeast Normal University
Zhangl120@nenu.edu.cn

Abstract. This paper argues that *chúfēi* is a domain restrictor, which restricts the domain of quantification. More precisely, it has two functions: it can serve as either a marker of the only condition or an exceptive operator. As an only-condition marker, *chúfēi* marks the condition denoted by its associate element to be the only condition which is quantified by a universal/negated existential quantifier. As an exceptive operator, *chúfēi* subtracts the condition denoted by its associate element from the domain of a quantifier. In the case that *chúfēi* occurs in the first clause of a complex sentence, *chúfēi* usually requires some element such as *cái* or *fǒuzé* to co-occur with it because as a unary operator, *chúfēi* can only take its interacting element to be its argument. Since it fails to take both the subordinate clause and the main clause to be its arguments, the two clauses cannot be related semantically by *chúfēi*, and a co-occurring element in the main clause is thus needed.

Keywords: semantics of *chúfēi*· relevant constructions· domain restrictor· only-ly-condition marker· exceptive operator.

1 Introduction

As observed by previous studies such as Lü (1980), in Mandarin Chinese 除非 [*chúfēi*] (*unless, only*) generally co-occurs with adverbs or conjunctions such as 才 [*cái*] (*only (if)*) and 否则 [*fǒuzé*] (*otherwise*), and they form constructions like '*chúfēi···cái···*' and '*chúfēi···fǒuzé···*'. Moreover, in many cases the appearance of such an adverb or conjunction is needed, otherwise the relevant sentences would be unacceptable. Consider (1)-(5).[1]

(1) 除非　　你　答应 我 的　条件，　我＊（才）告诉 你。
　　CHUFEI you consent I DE condition I　CAI　tell you[2]
　　'I won't tell you unless you consent to my conditions.'
(2) 除非　　临时　　有 事，＊（否则）　八点　　　一定　动身。

---

[1] In this paper, the description on *chúfēi* is mainly based on observing the data of some commonly used corpora such as CCL corpus, BCC corpus and the corpus of Chinese Complex Sentences, and previous studies like Lü (1980). Further, most examples used in this paper are cited from the above-mentioned corpora and Lü (1980), which are not pointed out one by one.
[2] Abbreviations used in this paper include-CL: classifiers; ASP: aspect markers; SFP: sentence final particles; and NEG: negative markers.

© Springer International Publishing AG 2016
M. Dong et al. (Eds.): CLSW 2016, LNAI 10085, pp. 620–629, 2016
DOI: 10.1007/978-3-319-49508-8_56

CHUFEI temporarily have-thing otherwise eight o'clock certainly start-out

≈*'We will start out at eight o'clock unless something comes up.'*

(3) 除非　你 去，他 不 会 去。

CHUFEI you go　he NEG will go

'He won't go, unless you go.'

(4) 他　平时　　　除非　不　喝酒，喝起 酒来 谁　也　比 不上他。.

he in-normal-times CHUFEI NEG drink drink up liquor come who also compare NEG up he

'Ordinarily, unless he does not drink, if he drinks, no one can compare with him.'

(5) 要　战胜　困难，除非 把 群众 发动 起来。

want conquer difficulty CHUFEI BA masses arouse up

'In order to conquer the difficulties, you must mobilize the masses.'

It is an issue of debate about the semantics of *chúfēi*. Some linguists give *chúfēi* a unified account, i.e. Lü (1980) claims that *chúfēi* emphasizes that some condition is the only condition; Jiang (1990) suggests that it indicates 'except'.[3] Other studies hold that *chúfēi* takes two meanings, namely it can imply both 'except' and 'only', cf. *Modern Chinese Dictionary* and so forth.

What's the semantics of *chúfēi*? Why does it need some element such as *cái* to license the relevant sentences?

In this paper, I will investigate the semantics of *chúfēi* from a perspective of formal semantics, and attempt to explain why *chúfēi* occurring in the first clause need some element to support it. It is argued that *chúfēi* is a domain restrictor which has two uses: one is to mark the only condition, and the other is to act as an exceptive operator.

The rest of this paper is organized as follows. Section 2 explores the cases that *chúfēi* serves as a marker of the only condition. Section 3 deals with the exceptive operator *chúfēi*. Section 4 discusses the cases of *chúfēi* with two possible semantic analyses and suggests that in these cases it is more appropriate to treat *chúfēi* as an exceptive operator. Section 5 concludes this paper.

2   *Chúfēi* as an only-condition marker

In the case that *chúfēi* functions as a marker of the only condition, its meaning approximately corresponds to the adverb *zhǐyǒu* occurring in the first clause of a complex sentence. In this case, *chúfēi* operates on its interacting element and marks this element as the only condition, which is quantified by a particle with universal/negated existential quantificational force. In which the only condition refers to the condition which is contrary to the alternatives under consideration and only it can satisfy the result denoted.

Generally speaking, in the construction of '*chúfēi* ⋯*cái* ⋯', '*chúfēi* ⋯ (*cái*) ⋯ fǒuzé ⋯ (不 [*bù*] (NEG)) ⋯', or '如果 [*rúguǒ*] (*if*) 要 [*yào*] (want) ⋯, *chúfēi* ⋯', *chúfēi* plays this role.

---

[3] Actually, there is a debate between Wu and Hu in 1920's. In his letter to Hu, Wu considers that the meaning of *chúfēi* is equivalent to 只有 [*zhǐyǒu*] (*only if*), while Hu (1922a, 1922b) argues that *chúfēi* indicates 除了 [*chúle*] (*except*).

2.1   The construction of '*chúfēi* ⋯*cái* ⋯'

The division of labor of *chúfēi* and *cái*. The construction of '*chúfēi*⋯*cái*⋯' not only can occur in complex sentences, as shown in (6), but also can appear in simple sentences, as seen in (7).

(6) 除非   你   给 我   二百   元，我 才   肯   冒 这 个 险。
CHUFEI you   give I two-hundred dollar I   CAI be-willing-to take this CL risk
'*Only if you give me two hundred dollars will I be willing to take this risk.*'
(7) 如今   除非   神仙   才   能   救活 他 的 命。
Nowadays CHUFEI immortal CAI can   save he DE life
'*Now only immortals can save his life.*'

The data from corpora such as CCL shows that in a '*chúfēi*⋯*cái*⋯' construction, the relative position between *chúfēi* and *cái* is fixed. To be more specific, in complex sentences, *chúfēi* occurs in the first clause, and *cái* is present in a preverbal position of the second clause. See also (6); in simple sentences, *chúfēi* appears in a preverbal position, and *cái* occurs in a post-*chúfēi* and preverbal position. Still consider (7).

As pointed out by *Exemplification of functional words in Modern Chinese* (*Xiàndài Hànyǔ Xūcí Lìshì*), in a sentence with the construction of '*chúfēi*⋯*cái*⋯', after deleting *chúfēi*, the basic semantics of the relevant sentence is maintained. Without regard for the role of focus, this description accords with the relevant Chinese language fact. For instance, omitting *chúfēi*, the basic meanings of sentences (6) and (7) are not changed, as shown in (8) and (9).

(8) 你   给 我   二百   元，我 才   肯   冒 这 个 险。
you give I two-hundred dollar I CAI be-willing-to take this CL risk
'*Only if you give me two hundred dollars will I be willing to take this risk.*'
(9) 如今   神仙   才   能 救活 他 的 命。
Nowadays immortal CAI can   save he DE life
'*Now only immortals can save his life.*'

However, deleting *cái*, the complex sentences under consideration become marginal or even unacceptable. Consider (10), which is derived from (6) via deleting *cái*.

(10) * 除非   你   给我   二百   元，我   肯   冒 这 个 险。
CHUFEI you give I two-hundred dollar I be-willing-to take this CL risk
'*Only if you give me two hundred dollars will I be willing to take this risk.*'

The above-mentioned phenomena show that *cái* plays a crucial role in completing the complex sentences considered, whereas *chúfēi* cannot take this job. Therefore, *chúfēi*'s scope should be the clause in which it occurs.

It is proposed that, in a '*chúfēi*⋯*cái*⋯' construction, *cái* is still an exclusive adverb which takes negated existential/universal quantificational force, and its scope is the whole sentence; the semantic contribution of *chúfēi* is to emphasize that the condition associating with it is the only condition in contrast to the alternatives.

The role of focus. In many cases, focus influences the composition of the alternative set, namely the alternatives only differ in the position of focus. More specifically, in simple sentences, when the interacting element or part of it is in focus, the focus will affect the alternative set, as illustrated in (11).

(11) 除非　　　[优秀]_F 学生　才　能　被　录取。⁴

    CHUFEI excellent student CAI can BEI enroll

    'Only [excellent] _F students can be enrolled.'

In (11), the alternatives introduced by the asserted value 优秀学生 [*yōuxiù xuéshēng*] (*excellent students*) can be generalized as 'x students', which differ in the position of the focus *yōuxiù*.

In complex sentences, the focus in the c-command domain of *chúfēi* influences the set of alternatives, as shown in (12).

(12) a. 除非　　　[你]_F 请　我，我　才　去。

    CHUFEI you invite me   I CAI go

    'Only if [you] _F invite me will I go.'

  b. [你]_F 除非　　　请　我，我　才　去。

    you   CHUFEI invite me I CAI go

    ≈*'Only if [you] _F invite me will I go.'*

In (12a), the focus 你[*nǐ*] (*you*) will affect the alternatives introduced by the asserted condition 你请我 [*nǐ qǐng wǒ*] (*you invite me*). The alternative conditions can be generalized as 'x invites me', in which the value of x is determined by the context. Suppose there are four individuals in the domain of discourse: 张三[*Zhāngsān*] (*Zhangsan*), 李四[*Lǐsì*] (*Lisi*), 王五[*Wángwǔ*] (*Wangwu*) and 赵六[*Zhàoliù*] (*Zhaoliu*), and 我[*wǒ*] (*I*) and 你[*nǐ*] (*you*) refer to *Zhāngsān* and *Lǐsì* respectively. Then the alternative set is composed of two members: 'Wangwu invites me' and 'Zhaoliu invites me'. In (12b), the focus is out of the c-command domain of *chúfēi* and thus it does not have an influence on the alternative set.

The tripartite structure triggered. In a '*chúfēi···cái···*' construction, the exclusive adverb *cái* will trigger a tripartite structure. The details are shown below.

In simple sentences, *chúfēi* operates on its interacting element and marks it as the only condition, and thus a binary partition is arrived. Next, *cái* triggers a tripartite structure: the *chúfēi*-construction is mapped to the nuclear scope and the rest of the sentence to the restrictor. For example, the possible tripartite structure of sentence (7) is shown in (13).

(13) 如今除非神仙才能救活他的命。

    才 x [如今 x 能救活他的命] [x=神仙]

    ¬∃_{x'} [如今 x' 能救活他的命 & x'≠神仙]

    'There is no such an x', if now x' can save his life, and then x' is not equal to immortals.'

In complex sentences, the tripartite structure triggered is a little complicated. The adverb *cái* triggers the first layer partitioning, in which the clause containing *chúfēi* is mapped to the unclear scope and the main clause to the restrictor. In the restrictor of *cái*'s tripartite structure, there is the second level partitioning composed of operator [topic] [comment]. If there is a focus in the co-command domain of *chúfēi*, an implicit operator, usually the assertion operator will trigger the third level partitioning in the

---

⁴ '[ ]_F' represents that the element in the brackets is in focus.

nuclear scope of *cái*'s tripartite structure. Given 二百元 [*èrbǎi yuán*] (*two hundred dollars*) is in focus, the possible tripartite structure of sentence (6) is illustrated in (14).

(14) 除非你给我 [二百元] ꜰ, 我才肯冒这个险.

    a. The first level partitioning

        才 ₚ [P, 我肯冒这个险] [P=你给我二百元]

        ¬∃ₚ' [P', 我肯冒这个险 & P'≠ 你给我二百元]

    b. The second level partitioning

        OP [P] [我肯冒这个险 if p]

        OP [P→我肯冒这个险]

    c. The third level partitioning

        ASSERT ꜰ [你给我 f] [f=二百元]

    'There is no such a P', if P' can make 'I will be willing to take this risk' true, then P' is not equal to the condition 'you give me two hundred dollars', in which it is asserted that f in 'you give me f' is 'two hundred dollars'.'

A short summary. In a nutshell, for a '*chúfēi…cái…*' construction, in complex sentences *chúfēi* operates on the clause in which it occurs; in simple sentences *chúfēi* associates with the element that is in its c-command domain. When there is more than one element can serve as the focus in *cái*'s c-command, the position of focus will influence the alternative set. The semantic contribution of *chúfēi* to the sentence considered is to mark its associate element as the only condition. Here *chúfēi* is a unary operator. The exclusive *cái* taking the whole sentence as its scope quantifies over the *chúfēi*-construction and indicates that only the condition marked by *chúfēi* can satisfy the relevant sentence.

2.2   The construction of '*chúfēi…(cái…), fǒuzé…(bù…)*'

In the construction of '*chúfēi…(cái…), fǒuzé…(bù…)*', the *cái*-expression and sometimes the negative *bù* can be absent, as shown in (15).

(15) a. 除非　　你告诉我, （我才会相信, ）（否则）我不　会　相信。

      CHUFEI you tell me　　I CAI will believe　　FOUZE I NEG will believe

      'Only if you tell me, will I believe. Otherwise, I will not believe.'

    b. 除非　　下大雨, （我们才会取消比赛, ）*（否则）比赛会按时进行。

      CHUFEI rain heavy rain we CAI will cancel game FOUZE game will on-time play

      'Only if it rains heavily will we cancel the game. Otherwise, the game will play on schedule.'

In (15a), *fǒuzé* is optional due to the occurrence of *bù* in the main clause; in (15b), *fǒuzé* is obligatory. Deleting *fǒuzé*, this sentence becomes unacceptable.

The conjunction *fǒuzé* implies an adversative relation, which indicates 'if not…, then…', and can be written as 'if ~P, then Q'. In this construction, *fǒuzé* establishes such a relation between the condition and result: if the condition is the negation of the only condition P, in another word, if the condition belongs to the set of alternative conditions in contrast to the only condition P, then the result Q is satisfied. *Chúfēi* is still used to mark its associate element as the only condition.

2.3   The construction of '(*rúguǒ*) *yào*···, *chúfēi* ···'

In a '(*rúguǒ*) *yào*···, *chúfēi*···' construction, the appearance of the conditional marker *rúguǒ* is optional. In the first clause, the deontic modal particle *yào* indicates 'be will-ing to'; in the second clause *chúfēi* is used to mark the only condition. The whole construction expresses that, the willing of getting some result and the only condition which can make this result true. As usual, here the only condition is still relative to the alternatives. Consider (16).

(16) a. 要　　　　想 取得 第一手 资料，除非 你 亲自 去 做 调查。
　　　　be-willing-to want gain first-hand data CHUFEI you in-person go do research
　　　　'*In order to get first-hand data, you must do research in person.*'
　　b. 如果你 要 得到 他 的 同意，　除非　 找 老何 去 跟 他 谈谈。
　　　　if　you want get　he DE consent CHUFEI find Laohe go with he talk
　　　　'*If you want to get his approval, you must let Laohe talk with him.*'
In this construction, the semantic relation between the two clauses is clear, and consequently no other element is needed to link up these two clauses. Here *chúfēi* operates on the clause it occurs and emphasizes that the condition denoted by this clause is the only condition.

3   *Chúfēi* as an exceptive operator

I put forward that, in the case of indicating 'except', *chúfēi* serves as an exceptive operator. In this case, *chúfēi* and its interacting element form an exceptive construc-tion to restrict the domain of quantification. Subtracting the entity denoted by the *chúfēi*-construction from the domain of the quantifier in question, the restricted quan-tificational domain is gotten.

The construction of '···, *chúfēi*···' is a typical case, in which *chúfēi* functions as an exceptive operator. In this construction, the exceptive construction is to restrict the domain of a quantifier, which is generally an implicit universal quantifier over the whole sentence. Moreover, the first clause denotes the result, and the second clause in which *chúfēi* occurs denotes the condition which cannot satisfy the result. Consider (17).

(17) a. 他 不 会 来，除非　 你 去 请。
　　　　he NEG will come CHUFEI you go invite
　　　　'*He won't come except you go to invite him.*'
　　b. 他 不 会 听 的，除非　 你 亲自 去 劝 他。
　　　　he NEG will listen DE CHUFEI you in-person go persuade he
　　　　'*He will not listen, unless you persuade him in person.*'
In (17a), the exceptive operator *chúfēi* and its interacting element 你去请[*nǐ qù qǐng*] (*you go to invite*) form an exceptive construction to restrict the quantificational domain of an implicit universal quantifier. *Chúfēi* subtracts the condition 'you go to invite' from the domain of discourse, and thus the restricted quantificational domain of this quantifier is gotten. In the same fashion, in (17b), the exceptive construction composed of *chufei* and 你亲自去劝他[*nǐ qīnzì qù quàn tā*] (*you persuade him in person*) is utilized to restrict the domain of the implicit quantifier.

In such a case, an implicit quantifier will trigger the tripartite structure. For instance, the possible tripartite structure of (17a) is elaborated as in (18).

(18) ∀ s [s∈S & s≠你请我)][我不去 in s]

'*For every situation s, if s is a member of S and s is not equal to 'you invite me', then I won't go in s.*' (Where 's' represents a situation variable, and 'S' refers to the set of situations.)

4   The cases of *chúfēi* with two possible solutions

Theoretically speaking, in the following three cases *chúfēi* may be endowed with two possible semantic solutions. In this section, I will focus on these cases and provide my own analysis.

4.1   Three cases

Case 1. *Chúfēi* and the negative adverb *bù* form the construction of '*chúfēi···bù···*', which can occur in both complex sentences and simple sentences. Look at (19a) and (19b) respectively.

(19) a. 除非   你   请   我，我 不   会   去。
    CHUFEI you invite I   I NEG will go
    '*I won't go except you invite me.*'
    b. 除非   特殊 情况，一般   不   宜   提倡   加班。
    CHUFEI special case generally NEG appropriate advocate work-overtime
    '*Except special cases, generally it is inappropriate to advocate working over-time.*'

It can be observed that, in complex sentences, *chúfēi* appears in the first clause and *bù* occurs in the preverbal position of the second clause. See also (19a).

Moreover, deleting the negative marker *bù*, the sentences in question will become ungrammatical, as shown in (20a), or their basic meaning will be changed, as shown in (20b).

(20) a. *除非   你   请 我，我 会 去。
    CHUFEI you invite I   I   will go
    '*I will go except you invite me.*'
    b. 除非   特殊   情况，一般   宜   提倡   加班。
    CHUFEI special   case   generally appropriate advocate work-overtime
    '*Except special cases, generally it is appropriate to advocate working overtime.*'

Case 2. The case that *chúfēi* co-occurs with both a verb (phrase) and its negative form can be generalized as a '*chúfēi···V/ ¬ V···,··· ¬ V/V···*' construction. Its salient characteristic is that the main verb in the main clause is the same as that in the subordinate clause, and one takes the affirmative form and the other holds the negative form, as illustrated in (21).

(21) a. 他   除非 不   出去，一   出去 就是   一 天。
    he CHUFEI NEG go-out once go-out   is   one day

'Unless he does not go out, once he goes out he will spend the whole day.'
b. 湖上　　　除非　不　　下雨，一　下，便是　势若倾盆。
lake-on CHUFEI NEG rain once rain is   like-downpour
'Unless it does not rain on the lake, once it rains, it will be a heavy downpour.'
In (21a) and (21b), the verbs 出去[*chūqù*] (*go out*) and 下[*xià*] (*rain*) occur in both
the first and the second clause. Furthermore, in the former they take the negative
forms and in the latter they are with the affirmative forms.

Case 3. The construction of '*chúfēi···měi···*' is composed of a *chúfēi*-construction
and a 每[*měi*] (*every*)-clause. [5] See (22).
(22) a.除非　　不　钓，每　　钓运气都　很　好。
CHUFEI NEG fish every fish luck all very good
≈ *'Except the case of not fishing, every time when I fish, luck is very good with me.'*
b. 摆摊既是为了糊口，苦是不屑说的，除非下雨落雪，每天都得早出摊晚收
摊。
set-up-a-stall since is for make-a-living bitter is scorn say DE CHUFEI rain snow
everyday all have-to early open-the-marker-stall late pack-up-the-stall
*'Since setting up a stall is to make a living, it disdains to say bitter, except it rains
or snows, every day I have to open the stall early and pack up it late.'*

4.2   Two possible solutions

Possible solution 1. One possibility of the semantics of *chúfēi* in the above three cases is that it acts as an exceptive operator which subtracts the condition denoted by its
interacting element from the domain of the quantifier in question. Look at (19a), (21a)
and (22a). Suppose *chúfēi* is an exceptive operator, (19a) means that, under the condition s, I won't go. In which s belongs to the set of conditions which is composed of
the domain of discourse minus the condition 'you invite me'. In a similar fashion,
(21a) expresses that, except the condition that 'he does not go out', under the other
condition 'he goes out', the result 'he spend the whole day' is met. In (22a), due to the
semantics of *chúfēi*, 不钓[*bú diào*] (*not fishing*) is subtracted from the domain of the
quantifier 都[*dōu*] (*all*). This analysis endows the relevant sentences with the correct
interpretations.

Possible solution 2. The other possible semantics of *chúfēi* is that it functions as the
only condition marker. To maintain this proposal, some studies resort to the assumption that there is some implicit operator such as *fǒuzé* to build up a correct semantic
relation between the *chúfēi*-construction and the rest of the sentence. Still consider
(19a), (21a) and (22a). When *chúfēi* is glossed as a marker of the only condition, an
implicit adversative *fǒuzé* is needed to help the sentence under consideration. Hence
(19a) can be interpreted as 除非你请我，否则我不会去. [*Chúfēi nǐ qǐng wǒ, fǒuzé
wǒ bú huì qù.*] (*Only if you invite me (will I go,) Otherwise, I won't go.*) This is the

---

[5] Lü (1980) treats sentences like (22) as special examples of the construction of '*chúfēi···bù···*'.

correct meaning of this sentence. In the same fashion, (21a) can be interpreted as 他除非不出去，否则，一出去就是一天. [*Tā chúfēi bù chūqù, fǒuzé, yī chūqù jiùshì yī tiān.*] (*Only if he does not go out, otherwise, if he goes out, he will spend the whole day*). The basic meaning of this sentence is also maintained. As for (22a), it can be translated into 'Only if not fishing, otherwise, every time when I fish, luck is very good with me.'

4.3   The opinion of this paper

However, either from a diachronic perspective or from a synchronic perspective, there is no enough evidence to support the existence of such an implicit element that builds up a semantic relation between the relevant two parts of the sentence under consideration. As a result, I prefer solution 1, namely the analysis that in these constructions *chúfēi* is an exceptive operator.

5   Concluding remarks

This paper puts forward that, in Mandarin Chinese *chúfēi* is a domain restrictor which is generally to restrict the domain of a quantifier and it takes two functions. As an only-condition marker, *chúfēi* marks its interacting element as the only condition, on which a particle with the universal/negated existential quantificational force such as *cái* usually operates. Being an exceptive operator, *chúfēi* and its associate element form an exceptive construction. After subtracting the entities denoted by the exceptive construction from the domain of the quantifier, the quantificational domain is restricted.

In complex sentences with the constructions of '*chúfēi*⋯*cái*⋯', '*chúfēi*⋯*fǒuzé*⋯', or '*chúfēi*⋯*bù*⋯', the occurrence of *cái*, *fǒuzé* or *bù* is obligatory. This is because *chúfēi* as a unary operator cannot establish a semantic relation between the subordinate clause where it occurs and the main clause, and thus the relevant complex sentence needs some operator to support it. The exclusive adverb *cái* and the conjunctive *fǒuzé* can link up the two clauses, and they both operate on the whole sentence considered. The adverb of negation *bù* makes the relation between the two clauses clear, and an implicit quantifier will quantify over the whole sentence. Consequently, in many cases when *bù* is present, no other element such as *fǒuzé* is need to license the relevant sentences.

Acknowledgements. I would like to thank Dr. Lee Peppina Polun, audiences of LSHK-ARF2015 and CLSW2016, and anonymous reviewers of CLSW2016, for discussion and comments on an earlier version of this paper. My thanks also go to The National Social Science Fund Project (Project No. 15BYY141), HKSAR-GRF (Project No. Cityu 143113), and The Fundamental Research Funds for the Central Universities and The Funds for Young Team Projects of Northeast Normal University (Project No. 14QT009), for the generous support of these relevant parties.

References

1. Cao, X: On the Appearing Time of the Conjunction *Chúfēi*. Research in Ancient Chinese Language. 2, 88-91+96 (2011) (In Chinese)
2. Dictionary Editorial Office, Institute of Linguistics, Chinese Academy of Social Sciences: Modern Chinese Dictionary. The Commercial Press, Beijing (2005) (In Chinese)
3. Grade 1955 and 1957, the Class of Language, Department of Chinese Language, Beijing University: Exemplification of Functional Words in Modern Chinese. The Commercial Press, Beijing (1980) (In Chinese)
4. Hajičová, E., Partee, B.H., Sgall, P.: Topic-focus Articulation, Tripartite Structures and Semantic Content. Kluwer Academic Publishers (1998)
5. Heim, I.: The Semantics of Definite and Indefinite Noun Phrases. PhD Dissertation. University of Massachusetts, Amherst (1982)
6. Jiang, X. Y.: A Study on *Chúfēi*. J. of Shanghai Normal University. 3,138-142 (1990) (In Chinese)
7. König, E.: The Meaning of Focus Particles—a Comparative Perspective. Routledge: London and New York (1991)
8. Lappin, S.: Generalized Quantifiers, Exception Phrases, and Logicality. J. of Semantics. 13, 197-220 (1996)
9. Liu, W., Zhang, H.Q.: A Study on the Diachronic Changes of the Constructions of *Chúfēi*-sentences. The Northern Forum. 4, 51-54. (2011) (In Chinese)
10. Lü, S. X: Eight Hundred Words in Modern Chinese. The Commercial Press, Beijing (1980) (In Chinese)
11. Von Fintel, K.: Restriction on Quantifier Domains. PhD Dissertation. University of Massachusetts (1994)
12. Xing, F. Y: A Study on Complex Sentences in Chinese. The Commercial Press, Beijing (2001) (In Chinese)
13. Zhang, L., Lee, Peppina P.L.: A Semantic Study of Mandarin *Cái* as a Focus Adverb in Simple Sentences. In: Chinese Lexical Semantics--13th Workshop, CLSW2012 Wuhan, China, July 6-8, 2012 Revised Selected Papers, pp.685-695. Springer (LNCS) (2013)
14. Zhao, X., Liu R. Y.: The Semantic and Pragmatic Analysis of *Chúfēi* Conditional Clause. Studies in Language and Linguistics. 1, 17-21 (2006) (In Chinese)

A Corpus-based Study on Near-synonymous Manner Adverbs: *"yiran"* and *"duanran"*

Helena Yan Ping Lau and Sophia Yat Mei Lee

Department of Chinese and Bilingual Studies,
The Hong Kong Polytechnic University, Hong Kong
helena.lau@connect.polyu.hk, ym.lee@polyu.edu.hk

Abstract. Manner adverb is one of the major groups of adverbs describing how an action is carried out. Although a number of near-synonymous manner adverbs are found in Chinese, most dictionaries use rather general or even circular definitions for these items which persistently confuse second language learners. The subtle yet important differences between near-synonymous manner adverbs are invisible by definitions but observable in collocational behaviors. Thus, this work aims to examine the semantic differences between a pair of near-synonymous manner adverbs 毅然 and 斷然 (resolutely). We propose that near-synonymous manner adverbs can be differentiated in terms of the event structures constructed by the collocated verbs, conjunctions, and nouns.

1 Introduction

Manner adverbs in Chinese 'modify the verb phrase by signaling the manner in which the action of the verb phrase is carried out' (Li and Thompson 1981:322). According to Shi (2003), manner adverbs can be further classified into six sub-types, namely 意志 (volition), 時機 (occasion), 同獨 (collectivism-individualism), 依照 (accordance), 狀態 (state) and 方式 (manner). As one of the major types of adverbs, manner adverbs are found to contain a number of near-synonyms. However, most dictionaries, if not all, use rather general or even circular definitions for these near-synonyms and entirely neglect their semantic differences. Given that these nuanced yet important

© Springer International Publishing AG 2016
M. Dong et al. (Eds.): CLSW 2016, LNAI 10085, pp. 630–642, 2016
DOI: 10.1007/978-3-319-49508-8_57

differences between near-synonymous manner adverbs are seemingly undetectable by definition, the phenomenon undoubtedly poses a great challenge to second language (L2) learners of Chinese.

In view of this, the paper aims to uncover the semantic differences between a pair of near-synonymous manner adverbs by means of exploring their collocational behaviors. In doing so, we first examine the selected pair of words 毅然 and 斷然 (resolutely). We then propose various distinctive features of the two adverbs in terms of their collocated verbs, conjunctions, and nouns. We believe this study will contribute to a better understanding of manner adverbs and enrich the existing near-synonym differentiation frameworks.

2   Related Work

2.1   Near-Synonyms

Research on near-synonyms has been a well-studied topic in the field of Chinese lexicology and semantics. There is a series of papers working on near-synonyms. Tsai et al. (1998) proposed using distributional differences between near-synonyms to deduce the relevant semantic features by investigating three pairs of near-synonymous verbs including 累 and 疲倦 (be exhausted), 高興 and 快樂 (be happy), and 勸 and 說服 (convince). Chang et al. (2000) explored seven subgroups of emotion verbs by identifying the distinctive syntactic features in terms of the distribution of grammatical functions, aspect, the transitivity etc. They concluded that the contract is motivated by event structure properties. Huang et al. (2000) proposed the Module-Attribute Theory of Verbal Semantics (MARVS) can even interpret lexical knowledge of near-synonym pairs. They conducted four case studies in order to demonstrate the correlation between lexical semantic specifications and event-structure attributes.

2.2   Chinese Adverbs

A number of studies have attempted to differentiate different types of near-synonymous adverbs. Tian (2015) discriminated a pair of near-synonymous time adverb 一直 and 一向 (always) in terms of their semantic features. E (2015) examined the lexical semantics and syntactic distributions of three degree adverbs 更, 還 and 再 (more) in comparative structures. Ai (2012) illustrated the subtle and nuanced functional and distributional differences across different genres by comparing modal adverbs 的確 and 確實 (really). Despite a growing body of research on near-synonymous adverbs, not much work has been done on manner adverbs. Li and Jin (2008) described the different usages of 成心 and 存心 (intentionally). Shao (2016) proposed an approach for the meanings of adverbs to be accurately denoted by exploring a set of manner adverbs ending with 然 "-ran2", such as 悻然 (irritatingly), 憤然 (irritatingly), 悄然 (silently), 默然 (silently), 斷然 (resolutely), 截然 (entirely), 毅然 (resolutely), 決然 (resolutely) etc.

Although 毅然 and 決然 are reasonably grouped as a pair of near-synonyms in Shao (2016) due to their semantic similarities, we find a large number of instances of 決然 preceded by 毅然 in both the Academia Sinica Balanced Corpus of Modern Chinese (Sinica Corpus)[1] and the Modern Chinese Corpus developed by the Centre for Chinese Linguistics at Peking University (CCL Corpus)[2] (Percentages of the instances where 決然 is preceded by 毅然 in Sinica Corpus and CCL Corpus: 92.9% and 57.4%). It indicates that these two adverbs frequently co-occur and the semantic differences between them may not be as important as the two we selected. As for the pair of 斷然 and 截然 in Shao (2016), we do not consider them near-synonyms as they convey different semantic meanings. Therefore, we group 毅然 and 斷然 as a pair of near-synonyms for further differentiation.

---

[1] http://www.sinica.edu.tw/SinicaCorpus/

[2] http://ccl.pku.edu.cn:8080/ccl_corpus/

3   Corpus Data

The denotational meanings of the selected items 毅然 and 斷然 are highly close to each other. In the Contemporary Chinese Dictionary (6th Edition), 毅然 conveys the meaning of 堅決地/毫不猶豫地 and 斷然 as an adjective refers to 堅決/果斷, and 斷乎 as an adverb. However, 斷然 is found to function more frequent as an adverb denoting 堅決/果斷 in the Sinica Corpus, meaning that the two adverbs are indeed used in a rather similar way.

Instead of using introspective examples, the present study extracts naturally occurring data of 毅然 and 斷然 from the Sinica Corpus. After manual checkup, 37 valid tokens of 斷然 and 74 of 毅然 functioning as an adverb are found in the corpus. They are all under examination. By examining the two manner adverbs with the aid of Chinese Word Sketch Engine[3], generalizations about the semantic differences between 毅然 and 斷然 are made.

4   Corpus Analysis

In the following subsections, we analyze semantic information unveiled by the collocated verbs, conjunctions, and certain nouns which express temporal relations.

4.1   Collocations of 毅然 and 斷然 - Verbs

Frequency of Co-occurrences

毅然 and 斷然 mostly modify actions denoted by the verbs adjacent to the adverbs. In order to gain an insight into the event types taken by these two adverbs, we extract the collocated verb of each sentence that is closest to the selected adverb. For example, in 翁智光**毅然**踏出第一步，接掌當時還附屬於中華民國跳傘協會的滑翔翼委員會主任委員 '*Weng Zhiguang resolutely took his first step to become the chairperson of Hang Gliding Committee that was formerly affiliated with the Chinese Taipei Aero-*

---

[3]   http://wordsketch.ling.sinica.edu.tw/

sports Federation', the extracted verb is 踏出 as it is closer to the adverb than 接掌.
The collocated verbs co-occurring with the two adverbs are shown in Table 1.

Table 1. Frequencies of Collocated Verbs

Node	Category and collocated verbs	Frequency	
毅然	Beginning: 踏出(第一步)、邁開(步伐)、投入、出來找(…工作)、走入(婚姻)、創辦、開設、獻身(行醫濟世)、決定改當、轉往、輟學赴(美)、下嫁、出家、移民、送(到)	15/74	
	End: 分手、辭職、辭去、辭退、罷黜、放棄、放下、揚棄、捨棄、離開、搬離開來、簽字離婚、退出、轉身往(…走去)、決定離開	22/74	
	Return: (啟程)返回、返(國)、回(國/台灣)、回到、決定返台、送(返)	7/74	
	Decision-making: 選擇、做出(撤場告示)、(另)擇、交給、指定、接下(…任務)、整裝前往、決定到、參加、生(下來)、剪下、決定學、推動、帶領、反抗、偷走、衝(了下來)、周遊	18/74	
	Expression: 宣布	1/74	
	Others: 睡、拖(著…的身軀)	2/74	
斷然	End: 取消、停止、結束、了去、出脫、拋棄、脫離、轉身	9/37	
	Expression: 說、道	2/37	
	Negation: 否認、否定、表示否定、斲殺	4/37	
	Elimination: 排除	1/37	
	Decision-making: 投下、決定保留、引進、(不)予(鼓勵)	5/37	
	Others: 劃分、領略、是、無、處理	6/37	
毅然 & 斷然	Decision-making: 決定	7/74	1/37
	Expression: 表示	1/74	1/37
	Rejection: 拒絕	1/74	8/37

As shown in Table 1, there are six types of verbs that are collocated with 毅然. These collocated verbs refer to the events or actions of *beginning, end, return, decision-making, expression*, and *others*, with verbs of *end* being the most frequent ones. As for 斷然, the collocated verbs can also be classified into six categories, including *end, expression, negation, elimination, decision-making*, and *others*. Comparing the categories of the two adverbs, both 毅然 and 斷然 collocate with the *end* verbs, *expression* verbs and *decision-making* verbs. Those *end* verbs collocated with 毅然 are more associated with responsibility or work, while those with 斷然 refer to an end of an event. For the *expression* verbs, 毅然 tends to collocated with formal announcements than 斷然. In addition, the number of *decision-making* verbs collocated with 毅然 are larger than that with 斷然, meaning that things are more often done after serious consideration in the manner of 毅然. Apart from that, three verbs are found to co-occur with both 毅然 and 斷然 respectively, of which each of them belongs to different groups. These groups are *decision-making* (e.g. 決定), *expression* (e.g. 表示), and *rejection* (e.g. 拒絕).

Interchangeability of 毅然 and 斷然

As there are some common categories, we hypothesize that 毅然 and 斷然 are interchangeable in some cases. We therefore conduct a substitution test. The adverb 毅然 is substituted with 斷然 in all the tokens, and 斷然 is replaced by 毅然 in all the tokens. We then verify the grammaticality of these sentences with native speaker intuition. When the grammaticality of a particular pattern is too difficult to judge, we search for the same pattern in the CCL corpus. We consider it interchangeable only if there is a reasonable frequency. The interchangeability of the two adverbs is illustrated in Table 2.

In Table 1 and 2, the categories of verbs are classified in a coarse-grained way for easier comparison. Some verbs belonging to a particular category may not literally refer to the meaning suggested by the category name, but they must imply the shared meaning of the category. For example, 創辦 refers to 'establish' which connotes the meaning of a start.

Table 2. Properties of Potential Collocated Verbs

Node(s)	Category	Potential Collocated Verbs
毅然	Beginning	踏出(第一步)、邁開(步伐)、投入、出來找(…工作)、走入(婚姻)、創辦、開設、獻身(行醫濟世)、轉往、輟學赴(美)、下嫁、出家、移民、送(到)
	Return	(啟程)返回、返(國)、回(國/台灣)、回到、送(返)
	Decision-making	接下(…任務)、整裝前往、參加、生(下來)、推動、帶領、反抗、衝(了下來)、周遊
	Others	睡、拖(著…的身軀)
斷然	Negation	否定、否認、斷殺
	Elimination	排除
	Decision-making	(不)予(鼓勵)
	Others	劃分、領略、是、無、處理
毅然 & 斷然	Beginning	決定改當
	End	分手、辭職、辭去、辭退、罷黜、放棄、放下、揚棄、捨棄、離開、搬離開來、簽字離婚、退出、轉身往(…走去)、決定離開、取消、停止、結束、了去、出脫、拋棄、脫離、轉身
	Return	決定返台
	Negation	表示否定
	Decision/ choice-making	選擇、做出(撤場告示)、(另)擇、交給、指定、決定到、決定學、偷走、引進、剪下
	Expression	表示、說、道、宣布
	Rejection	拒絕

As demonstrated in Table 2, there are differences between the properties of the verbs modified by 毅然 and 斷然. First, *elimination* verb 排除 can only be preceded by 斷然. Second, except for 表示否定, *negation* verbs can only be modified by 斷然.

Although there is one exception, we consider *negation* a distinctive category because the exception is preceded by the *expression* verb 表示 which is found to be modified by both adverbs in our data. Similar to *negation* verbs, *beginning* verbs and *return* verbs can only be modified by 毅然 with the exceptions of 決定改當 and 決定返 台. These exceptions are accepted simply because they are preceded by the *decision-making* verb 決定 which is the shared collocation of the two adverbs. Thus, the categories of *beginning*, *return* and *negation* are still useful in discriminating the two adverbs.

Third, most *decision-making* verbs can be taken by both 毅然 and 斷然, but those events of long-duration nature such as 參加 and 反抗 can only be done in the manner of 毅然.

Lastly, 毅然 and 斷然 are interchangeable when they collocate with *end* verbs, *expression* verbs, *rejection* verbs and some *decision-making* verbs (events of short-duration nature).

4.2　Collocations of 毅然 and 斷然 - Conjunctions

Since the focus sentences (sentences containing the keyword) mostly come after a comma, we hypothesize that there must be some hints in the preceding sentences that help distinguish 毅然 and 斷然. Table 3 demonstrates the conjunctional collocates.

There are various conjunctions found in the concordance lines of 毅然. The collocates are grouped in terms of their functions such as *cause-and-effect*, *transition*, and *conditional*. *Cause-and-effect* refers to conjunctions that introduce the cause such as 因 or the effect such as 所以, 因此. The span window size is +15 (i.e. 15 words of the left context), and those occurred before a period, exclamation mark, question mark or ellipsis are not counted even within the span window. For example, in 但內部黨派紛 擾，政局相當不穩定。為此，斯賓諾莎毅然放下… '*But there was a disruption within the party. The political situation is rather unstable. For that reason, Spinoza resolutely gave up...*', the *transitional* conjunction 但 is not considered a relevant token as the conjunctive relation is ended by the period. As for *cause-and-effect*, those conjunctions introducing effects should only be counted as relevant only if they precede the selected adverbs and are not used to describe another statement. For example, the conjunction 因此 in 張振得希望能夠提供更完善的學習空間，因此毅然開設一間實習教室 'Zhang Zhende wished to be able to provide a more well-equipped space for learning. Therefore, he resolutely set up a classroom for practical studies' is a valid token as the elicited event did in the manner of 毅然 is directly introduced by that conjunction.

Table 3. Frequencies and Percentages of Collocated Conjunctions

Function	Collocation	Frequency & Percentage of 毅然		Frequency & Percentage of 斷然	
Cause-and-effect	於是	5		0	
	因	3		0	
	因此	2		0	
	所以	3	15 (20.3%)	0	1 (2.7%)
	故	1		0	
	而	1		0	
	之所以	0		1	
Transition	然而	1		1	
	可是	1	5 (6.8%)	0	2 (5.4%)
	但	2		1	
	但是	1		0	
Conditional	否則	0	0 (0%)	1	1 (2.7%)

As illustrated, conjunctions functioning as *cause-and-effect* are more likely to co-occur with 毅然 (20.3%), comparing to 斷然 (2.7%). It indicates that someone 毅然 does something is usually because he/she is triggered by a cause event. For example, in ...不能放棄追求與學習的機會，於是毅然決然的辭去教職 '... could not give up his/her chance of learning, he/she therefore resolutely decided to quit teaching', the elicited event is introduced by 於是 indicating that the agent resolutely quit teaching because he considered the learning opportunity a rare one which should not be given up. Hence, it can be seen that actions done in the manner of 毅然 are often with a reason or trigger while actions can be done in the manner of 斷然 for no reasons.

Since the co-occurrence between *transitional* conjunctions and 斷然 (6.8%) are nearly the same as 毅然 (5.4%), *transitional* conjunctions cannot serve as a distinctive feature for this pair. For *conditional*, the frequencies are rather low with only one token found in 斷然 and none in 毅然. No conclusion can therefore be made.

In this section, it is proved that conjunctions functioning as *cause-and-effect* are noted to be of great value in providing deep-level semantic information that helps distinguish the selected pair.

4.3   Collocations of 毅然 and 斷然 - Nouns

Apart from verbs and conjunctions, it is suggested that nouns expressing temporal relations also provide hints to uncover the motivation of the actions done in the manner of 毅然 or 斷然. The co-occurrence of the adverbs and temporal nouns are demonstrated in Table 4.

Table 4. Frequencies and Percentages of Collocated Nouns

Collocations	Frequency & Percentage of 毅然		Frequency & Percentage of 斷然	
後	6		1	
之後	3		0	
最後	2	13 (17.6%)	0	1 (2.7%)
後來	1		0	
災後	1		0	
時	5		3	
(之)際	3	9 (12.2%)	0	4 (10.8%)
當時	1		1	

The span window size is set as +15, and those within the specific window but separated from the focus sentence by a period, exclamation mark, question mark, and ellipsis are considered irrelevant. Adding onto this, temporal items modifying a specified component are also screened out. For example, in 但是當時的行政院長… 'But the President of the Executive Yuan of the time…', the temporal noun 當時 is obviously modifying the term of office of the President but not the temporal point of an action. 當時 is considered invalid in that case.

As shown in Table 4, the collocates are divided into two types in terms of their semantic meanings, namely 後-related and 時-related type. 後-related words are more frequently collocated with 毅然, reaching 17.6% as in 藝術總監李國修前天晚上徹夜未眠，精確算計後，毅然做出撤場公告 'The Artistic Director Li Guoxiu didn't sleep a wink the night before. After careful calculation, he resolutely decided to make the announcement of leaving the venue'. Yet, only 2.7% are found with 斷然. Statistics indicate that someone 毅然 does something after the occurrence of another event, meaning that the agent is triggered by a past event. As for 時-related words, the frequencies are similar, with 毅然 achieving 12.2% and 斷然 10.8%. It is suggested that someone 毅然/斷然 does something when another event is taking place as in …蜜桃以及水梨事件，當時政府為了杜絕果樹的持續蔓延，斷然引進美國蘋果 '… the peach and pear incident. The government resolutely imported apples from the USA to put an end to the continuous spread of apple trees'.

4.4   Summary of the Distinctive Structures of 毅然 and 斷然

In Section 4.1 – 4.3, we discuss the semantic differences between 毅然 and 斷然, be it significant or not. Collocations including verbs, conjunctions, and nouns provide us with deep-level semantic information for the differentiation of the two adverbs. The distinctive structures of 毅然 and 斷然 are summarized as below:

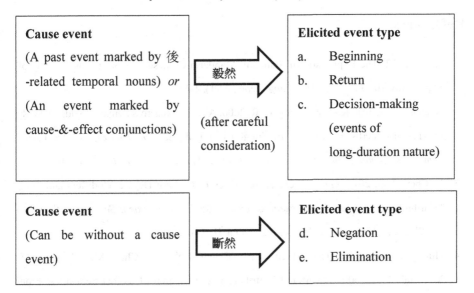

5   Conclusion

In this study, 毅然 and 斷然 are proved to be semantically distinguishable in terms of their event structures. Although they both convey the meaning of 堅決, 毅然 is usually used when someone is triggered by a cause event, marked by *cause-and-effect* conjunctions or temporal nouns. As for elicited events, the distinctive verb groups that can be modified by 毅然 are *beginning, return,* and *decision-making* (events of long-duration nature), while *negation* and *elimination* can only co-occur with 斷然.

Since manner adverbs are syntactically similar, we discriminate them in terms of semantics. We propose that not only content words are of value in semantics, function words such as conjunctions can also be beneficial. Apart from shedding light on the study of manner adverbs, the current study is also useful for many real world applications, such as language pedagogy, language acquisition, and machine translation.

Acknowledgements. The work is supported by an Early Career Scheme (ECS) project sponsored by the Research Grants Council (Project no. PolyU 5593/13H).

References

1. Ai, H. 2012. The Expression of Stance in Mandarin Chinese: A Corpus-based Study of Stance Adverbs. *Int. J. of Asian Lang. Proc.*, 22(1), 1-14.

2. Chang, L. L., Chen, K.-J., & Huang, C. R. 2000. Alternation across Sematic Fields: A Study of Mandarin Verbs of Emotion. In Yung-O Biq. (Ed.) *Special Issue on Chinese Verbal Semantics. Computational Linguistics and Chinese Language Proceeding.* 5.1: 61-80.

3. E, Chen-chun. 2015. On the Lexical Semantics of Chinese Degree Modifiers and Their Distribution in Syntax. In *Proceedings of the 16ᵗʰ Chinese Lexical Semantics Workshop (CLSW2015).* May 9-11, 2015. Beijing, China. [In Chinese]

4. Huang, Chu-Ren, Kathleen Ahrens, Li-Li Chang, Keh-Jiann Chen, Mei-Chun Liu, & Mei-Chih Tsai. 2000. The Module-Attribute Representation of Verbal Semantics: From Semantics to Argument Structure. In Yung-O Biq. (Ed.) *Special Issue on Chinese Verbal Semantics. Computational Linguistics and Chinese Language Processing* 5.1.19-46.

5. Li, C. N. & Thompson, S. A. 1981. *Mandarin Chinese: A Functional Reference Grammar.* Berkeley: University of California Press.

6. Li, Xiao-jun & Jin, Mu-gen. 2008. "Chengxin" and "Cunxin". Language Planning, 10, 51-52. ("成心"與"存心". *語文建設*, 10, 51-52.) [In Chinese]

7. Shao, Jing-min. 2016. The Accuracy of the Interpretation of Adverbs and Its Methodological Exploration – Take the Situation-Depicting Adverbial Group "X-*ran*" for Example. *Jinan Journal (Philosophy & Social Science Edition)*, vol 38 (1): 9-18. [In Chinese]

8. Shi, Jin-sheng. 2003. On the Categories and Co-occurrence Orders of Manner Adverbs. *Studies in Language and Linguistics,* 23(4) 1-9.

9. Tsai, M. C., Huang, C. R., Chen, K. J., & Ahrens, K. 1998. Towards a Representation of Verbal Semantics--An Approach Based on Near Synonyms. *Computational Linguistics and Chinese Language Processing*, 3(1), 61-74.

10. Tian, Jia-long. 2015. The Semantic Features of the Time Adverbs "Yi Zhi" ("一直") and "Yi Xiang" ("一向"). In *Proceedings of the 16ᵗʰ Chinese Lexical Semantics Workshop (CLSW2015).* May 9-11, 2015. Beijing, China. [In Chinese]

The lexicalization of the word "Jinqing" (尽情) in Chinese

Xiujuan Chen , Qing Wang , Gaowu Wang

Beijing Normal University，Beijing, China

Abstract. The lexicalization and grammaticalization of Chinese word "Jinqing" (尽情) has been studied in this paper, with examples from Old Chinese, Middle Chinese, and modern Chinese. The word has undergone three phases: V+N phrase, verb, and adverb. Reasons of the grammaticalization have been proposed and discussed. In addition, the lexicalization of "Jin+X" structure has also been examined.

Keywords: lexicalization, grammaticalization, language change

1 Introduction

"Jinqing" (尽情) is an adverb in modern Chinese with the meaning of "freely, fully, enjoyably". However, the meaning of the word "Jingqing" is different in Old Chinese. For examples:

1). Old Chinese (OC):致命尽情，天地乐而万事销亡。（庄子.外篇.天地）
Interpretation in English (Eng): Enjoying our life and **giving up private feeling**, that makes everything to be happy and dissovled.

2). OC: 虽获归骨于晋，犹子则肉之，敢不尽情？（左传.昭公.十三年）
Eng: Although I could come back and be buried in Jin State, it is you that give me the chance. How couldn't I **spare no effort working** for you?

In these cases above, "Jinqing" (尽情) is a V+N phrase ("尽/v 情/n"). Moreover, another example shows that "Jinqing" (尽情) could be separated.

3). OC:其余外事，有所不从，以尽痛慕之情。（魏收.魏书.文明皇后列传）
Eng: In order to **express my deep sadness and respects**，you can decide whether comply with my orders.

In the following period from Old Chinese to modern Chinese, "Jin-qing" has experienced a process of lexicalization. Lexicalization refers to a linguistic phenomenon that a non-lexical component changed into a lexical component (Dong, 2006). The unit of "Jin-qing" in syntactic level was incorporated gradually into lexical level when promoted by some certain reasons. We investigated The Online Corpus which contains a total of one hundred million ancient words and ten million modern Chinese words. Based on the data collected from the corpus, in the lexicalization of "Jinqing" (尽情), three phases can be identified, ie. V+N phrase, verb, and adverb, from ancient Chinese to modern Chinese.

© Springer International Publishing AG 2016
M. Dong et al. (Eds.): CLSW 2016, LNAI 10085, pp. 643–649, 2016
DOI: 10.1007/978-3-319-49508-8_58

2   Lexicalization timeline of "Jinqing" (尽情)

2.1   Pre-Qin Dynasty: "JING(verb)+QING(noun)"

Two cases have been found in Pre-Qin Chinese, in both of which "Jinqing" were used as predicates.

4)OC: 子曰："圣人立象以尽意，设卦以**尽情伪**，系辞焉以尽其言。（周.易经.系辞）

Eng: …, Saint creates Gua (卦) to **distinguish truth and false**,….

"JIN" (尽) means "distinguish" and "情伪" （QINGWEI） means truth and false. The whole unit is a verb-object construction and "情伪" （QINGWEI） is an Parallel Phrases.

Fig. 1. the internal structure of "JIN(尽)QINGWEI(情伪)"

2.2   Wei and Jin Dynasty:"JING(verb)+QING(noun)"+conjunction +verb

In Wei & Jin Dynasty, "Jinqing" (尽情) began to appear with another verb and a conjunction must be presented. There are about 8% materials in the corpus we introduced above.5)OC: 夫务学不如择师，师所闻素狭，又不**尽情**以教之，因告云，为道不在多也。(东晋.葛洪.抱朴子)

Eng: Choosing a teacher is more important than studying hard. Because the teacher may have a poor knowledge and he might not **teach with a whole heart**. So the most important thing for knowledge is not the amount but to understand it.

2.3   Song and Ming Qing Dynasty :"JING(verb)+QING(noun)"+verb

In Song Dynasty, the construction of " Jinqing " +verb appeared, without any conjunction between. But it is not a common phenomenon, only 28% materials are founded.

6)OC: 钱大尹大怒，教左右索长枷把和尚枷了，当厅讯一百腿花，押下左司理院，教**尽情**根勘这件公事。(宋代话本.简帖和尚)

Eng: Qian Dayin gets angry and commands the subordinate **make an effort** to survey this thing.

In Ming and Qing Dynasty, " Jinqing " （尽情） +verb has become a common phenomenon.

7)OC: 到了郫县，果然两船上东西**尽情**搬上去住了。（明末.凌濛初.二刻拍案惊奇）

Eng: When arrive at Pi county, all the goods are **entirely** transported to the home

8)OC: 我要不把姐姐当亲姐姐待，上回那些家常烦难事，我也不肯**尽情**告诉

你了。（清.曹雪芹.红楼梦）
Eng: If I don't treat you as my sister, I would not **completely** tell you the affairs in my home.

2.4   Modern Chinese: "JINQING" (adverb)+verb & "JINQING" + "地" （DE）+verb

In modern Chinese, "Jinqing"(尽情) became an adverb and only used as adverbial construction. What's more, an adverbial maker "地"（DE）appeared.
    9)modern Chinese: 灯亮了，火苗蹿起来了，在每个人的脸上尽情地跳跃着璀灿的光斑……（肖复兴.精神文明的灯光)   Eng: The splendid lights and flames **completely** jump irradiate at everyone's faces.

3   Causes for Lexicalization of "Jin Qing"

3.1   Phonetically: disyllable

Feng (2005) argued that Chinese language has experienced the transformation from monosyllabic foot to two-syllable foot roughly in Han Dynasty. The original two-syllable phrases meet the requirement of single two-syllable foot, which led to constituting a prosodic word. With other causes (such as high-frequency use, extended meaning), two-syllable phrases is very likely to solidify into a word. "Jingqing", a verb-object phrase in Old Chinese, is a good example under the process of disyllablization and finally solidified into a word.

3.2   Grammatically: intransitive verb causative usage

Disyllablization is only a necessary but not sufficient condition for lexicalization. "Jin Qing"'s solidification into a word is also due to the grammatical relation between internal components of the phrase.
    "Jin" is an intransitive component, "Jin Qing" is an intransitive verb causative usage constituted phrase. In causative usage, syntactic relation between verb and object is not so obvious as transitive verb with object structure, the relation between them is likely to be diluted, so they are easier to solidify into a unit.

3.3   Semantically:

(1) Weak action of verb component.
    The so-called weak action means the verb action shows no obviously visible action, so it does not constitute a physical process. Some verbs identify strong action, so they can form a clear physical process. For instance, as the verb "kick" ("踢" in Chinese), the whole process can clearly emerge in our mind. The "Jin" action is weak, it is

difficult for us to think about the "Jin" process, or we can say that "Jin" is not a typical verb, and its syntactic feature is weak after combination with object.

(2) Non-specificity of object component.

Taylor (1989) has summarized typical characteristics of noun: discrete, tangible, occupy three-dimensional space> entity in non-spatial domain> collective entity> abstract entity.

The so-called non-specificity means that noun represented object does not occupy defined space. In ancient Chinese, common interpretation of "Qing" is: i) emotion. ii) truth. Interpretations are relatively abstract.

"Qing" is a typical abstract noun, and does not represent specific thing. When people understand discourse, they tend to combine packaged components for understanding, which cognitive psychology calls "chunking" mental process. (Lu Bingfu, 1986) when a component itself expressed meaning is non-specific, it relies on other components, and tend to combine with adjacent components into a more clear unit, people also tend to understand and memorize it as a unit, this is in line with psychological process of chunking.

(3) Ambiguity of object component.

The meaning of "Qing" is very complicated in the ancient Chinese, and it is difficult to define "Qing". In Shuo Wen Jie Zi, the meaning of "Qing" (with a seal character " 情 ") roughly refers to "a kind of spirits which desires something".

It is very difficult to define it accurately.

(4) Low affected extent of object.

Affected extent refers to the effect degree of object imposed by the verb. In general, after verbs of strong action collocating with specific nouns, the nouns get a high degree of influence, such as scissor cut(Jian Zhi:剪纸), embroidered flower (Xiu Hua: 绣花), threatened to kill（Si Piao: 撕票）, add snacks (Jia Can: 加餐) and so on. On the contrary, after verbs of weak action collocating with non-specific nouns, the nouns get a low degree of influence, so it will be easier to package it with verb and use as a language unit. "Jin Qing" belongs to object of lesser affected extent situation, "Qing" has no significant changes in appearance, and it is difficult to imagine a physical process of "Jin".

3.4   Syntactically: universality of "Jin Qing" cross-level usage.

Language has linear feature. The so-called linear feature means that language symbols can only appear sequentially in time sequence. On the other hand, the internal language system is layered, and language unit is not a haphazard arrangement, which result in many phenomenon of the same on voice line but differ in internal structure. In corpus, we found some phenomenon "Jin", "Qing" are cross-level but adjacent to each other in line. Such as:

10)OC: 闲作《东武吟》，曲尽/情未终。(唐.李白.东武吟)

Eng: I spend my free time creating one poem. The Singing is over but not the end of my emotion.

11)OC:恩劳未尽/情先尽，暗泣嘶风两意同。(唐.张祜.杂曲歌辞.爱妾换马)

Eng：Kindness yet finished but my love came to the end.

12)OC:琪树长青资玉润。鸳鸯不老眠沙稳。此去期程知远近。君休问。山河有尽/情无尽。（宋.杨无咎.渔家傲.十月二日老妻生辰）

Eng：.......Mountains and rivers could disappear, but I still have lots to talk about to you.

"Jin" and "Qing" in cross-level usage is very common, especially in poetry. An important reason for the non-word components into higher grammar level is high frequency usage. High-frequency use of "Jin Qing" also contributed to the generation of lexicalization.

3.5   Pragmatically: antiquing

Frequency of occurrence of "Jin Qing" collocation is high in ancient literature, especially in ancient poetry, probably because of the need of lyrical substance. Out of antique psychology, posterity often imitates such usage, which also contributed to further lexicalization of "Jin Qing".

4   "Jin + x" structure

Similar to "Jin Qing", there are a group of words starting with "Jin" in modern Chinese. These words were called as "Jin + X" class words, and they would be investigated in this section.

According to Modern Chinese Dictionary (sixth edition), "Jin" in modern Chinese is a free morpheme, indicating "end", "death", "reach extreme", "used up" and other meanings. The word beginning with"Jin"(falling tone) are: Jin Li (Try: 尽力), Jin Liang (As much as possible: 尽量), Jin Xiao(Filial: 尽孝), Jin Xin (Dedicated: 尽心), Jin Xing (Enjoy: 尽兴), Jin Ze (Do their duty: 尽责), Jin Zhi (Do their duty on their position: 尽职), Jin Zhong (Be loyal to: 尽忠), Jin Qing (almost: 尽情), Exhaustively (Jin Shu: 尽数). In tone 3, Jin is only used as a prefix in Jin Liang (尽量).

It can be found that "Jin+ X" series of entries have both verbs and adverbs. Moreover, some words show grammatical features of ambiguous verb and adverb. "Jin Li" can be used alone as predicate, and it can also be used as an adverbial modifier before a verb, indicating the level of effort to do things, such as

"Jinlizuo"(try to do: 尽力做), "Jinli Wancheng（try to complicate: 尽力完成）".
Another example is "Jin Liang"（As much as possible or Reached the limit: 尽量），
which even shows phonetic differentiated meaning. We believe that "jin3 Liang" is a
result of grammaticalization of "jin4 Liang", while "jin4 Liang" is the result of
lexicalization of verb-object phrase from the ancient Chinese, which is similar to "Jin
Qing"'s lexicalization situation. The difference is, "Jin Liang" verb usage survives,
and by phonetic differentiated meaning, it is also reserved in modern Chinese
vocabulary system together with the adverb usage. This may also provide an evidence
for "Jin + X" lexicalization.

Different lexicalization degree of "Jin + X" structure is related to X meaning.
When X is abstract, indicating component of degree, the structure is more easily
grammaticalization, and more inclinable into an adverb with higher degree of
grammaticalization, such as "Jin Liang", and "Jin Shu". While X has a more specific
denotation, it is less prone to further grammaticalization. It is likely to generate
further grammaticalization in the middle, such as "Jin Li".

Based on the above considerations, a sequence of lexicalization tendency of "Jin +
X" structure was found as follows:

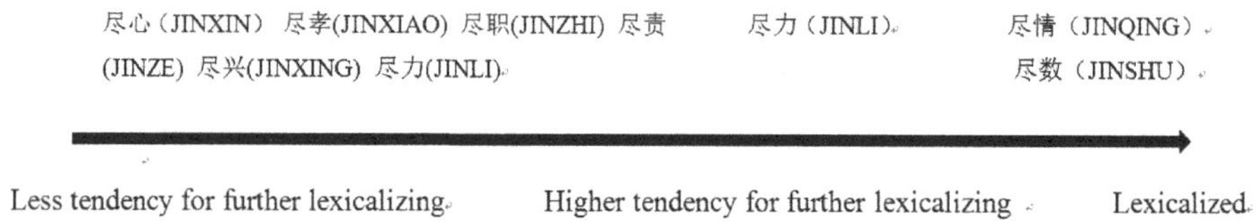

尽心（JINXIN） 尽孝(JINXIAO) 尽职(JINZHI) 尽责   尽力（JINLI）.   尽情（JINQING）.
(JINZE) 尽兴(JINXING) 尽力(JINLI).   尽数（JINSHU）.

Less tendency for further lexicalizing.   Higher tendency for further lexicalizing .   Lexicalized.

Fig. 2. the lexicalization sequence of "Jin + X"

5   Conclusion

By investigating the usage of "Jin Qing" in each period, we come to the conclusion
that the word "Jin Qing" has experienced a lexicalization, grammaticalization process
from a verb-object phrase to a verb, and then to an adverb. There are many causes for
the word lexicalization, including linguistic sign linear adjacent, two-syllable
phonetically, grammatical intransitive causative usage, ambiguity, non-specificity of
object component, low action of verb component, object component which is affected
to a lesser extent, syntactic "Jin Qing" cross-level high-frequency use and the like.
"Jin + X" structure members are in different degree of continuity in the lexicalization
process, and its lexicalization degree is related to whether X meaning is abstract, and
the degree of expression.

Acknowledgements
Sincerely appreciate the discussion and help from Associate Professor Song Zuoyan.
This research is supported by Young Scholar Fund of Beijing Normal University
(SKXJS2014020).

References

1. Dong Xiufang. 2002. Lexicalization: Derivation and Development of Chinese Disyllables. Sichuan Ethnic Publishing House.
2. Dong Xiufang. 2006 (5). Vocabulary Evolution and Lexicalization of Chinese. Chinese Language.
3. Feng Shengli. 2005 (1). The Historical Resource of DiSyllabification. Modern Chinese Research.
4. Ancient Chinese Dictionary (forth edition). Commercial Press.2005, p312-313
5. Lu Bingfu. 1986 (2). Description and theProcess of Sentence Understanding. Chinese.
6. Taylor. 1989. Linguistic Categorization: Prototypes in Linguistic Theory. Clarendon press.
7. The website of corpus http://www.cncorpus.org/ The Online Corpus contains abundant language literal materials, including ancient and modern Chinese. Ancient Chinese corpus materials cover a wide range, from Pre-Qin period to Qing Dynasty, with a total of one hundred million ancient words. Modern Chinese corpus is established by State Language Work Committee. It is an a'large-scale and balance corpus which contains ten million modern Chinese words.

On the Case of Zheyangzi in Mandarin Words of Taiwan and Mainland China

Xiaolong LU

Jinan University, Guangzhou City, China

collinlew007@gmail.com

Abstract. As a mandarin word, Zheyangzi has been widely used in the accent of Taiwan, where the usages and part of meanings in this word are the same as its application in mainland China, but there can be some disparities on the features of Zheyangzi through comparison between two areas. This paper will illustrate these disparities by analyzing corpus and explain the reasons behind the features shared by this word.

Keywords: Zheyangzi; usages; comparison; disparities; reasons

1   Introduction

The study of mandarin words in Taiwan has developed early since 1980s, some researches concern the verb You (Robert Cheng, 1990), the noun Nansheng or Nvsheng (Shao Jingmin, 2011), the function word Eryi (Diao Yanbin, 2012) and Hui (Li Lei, 2014), the preposition Touguo (Chu Zexiang, 2014) and so on. By referring to the previous study, we find that most researches aim at analyzing the mandarin words in Taiwan in macroscopic ways including range of words usage, syntactic and semantic differences in words, as well as reasons for words differences. This paper mainly illuminates the differences in Taiwan mandarin word Zheyangzi(這樣子), and expounds its reasons for these disparities from synchronic and diachronic perspectives, which are rarely conducted in former study. Now we overally analyze the differences in this word through Chinese data, including CCL Corpus (mainland China) and Sinica Corpus (Taiwan), to find out the reasons for the word disparity across the Taiwan straits.

Firstly, we can make clear that the word Zheyangzi, as a demonstrative pronoun in mandarin, is widely used in Taiwan, especially in spoken mandarin. Here are three examples like (1) from Sinica Corpus,

(1) a. Keshi ni zhaobudao yige zheyangzi de   gege.
    but 2SG can't.find CLF this.kind ASSO brother
    "But you can't find this kind (of) brother."

In this sentence, the word Zheyangzi serves as an attributive, which is followed by structural particles like "de", and Zheyangzi means "this way" or "this kind of thing".

© Springer International Publishing AG 2016
M. Dong et al. (Eds.): CLSW 2016, LNAI 10085, pp. 650–659, 2016
DOI: 10.1007/978-3-319-49508-8_59

From the analysis of discourse function, we also know that Zheyangzi can be ana-phoric in the context, because we don't know what kind of brother is by reading this sentence only, there must be a pre-context which tells us the brother's characteris-tics (i.e. Zheyangzi de gege). So the word Zheyangzi is a demonstrative pronoun.

b. Suoyi ni yao zheyangzi jieshi gei wo ting.
   so 2SG should this.way explain to 1SG listen
   "So you should explain (it) to me to listen (in) this way."

In this sentence, we see that the word Zheyangzi serves as an adverbial, which fol-lows an auxiliary verb like "yao" (should) , and Zheyangzi is also followed by a no-tional verb like "jieshi" (explain). From discourse function we see that this word can be also anaphoric, that is, there must be some way in the pre-context "you should use to explain it to me (i.e. Zheyangzi jieshi gei wo ting)".

c. Zheyangzi ba, wo xian bang ta mai yifen biandang.
   this.way PRT 1SG firstly help 3SG buy CLF bento
   "(Let's do it) this way, I help him buy a box of bento firstly."

In this sentence, we find that the word Zheyangzi serves as an adverbial, which is an independent element, followed by a modal particle like "ba", to suggest doing some-thing in this way (i.e. Zheyangzi ba). From discourse function we see that this word can be cataphoric, because the clause following this independent element can tell us that we should do something in this way.

From above, we see that in some cases, the semantics, syntax, and pregmatics in Zheyangzi is the same as Zheyang (這樣), which is often used by people from main-land China, that is, two words can be replaced for each other to express the same idea in three sentences above.

However, based on field survey, we find that in some conditions, the word Zheyangzi shares several unique meanings and usages in Taiwan mandarin, which can hardly be used by people from mainland China now, in the following example (2) we can see these different features,

(2) a. Lvyou jiche yiding yao baochi henhao de wendingxing zheyangzi.
    travell motorcycle must / keep excellent ASSO stability that's.all
    "(The) travelling motorcycle must keep excellent stability, that's all."

b. Ranhou ta jiu xiwang ni neng haohao nianshu, zheyangzi.
   then 3SG only hope 2SG can well study that's.all
   "Then he only hopes that you can study well, that's all."

c. Wo bu keneng bang ni xie, zheyangzi, wo bu hui xie nide huaihua, jiu zheyangzi.
   1SG not can help you write that's.all 1SG not can write your cuss just that's.all
   "I cannot help you write, that's all, I cannot write (down) your cuss, just that's all."

Interestingly, we find that the word Zheyangzi mentioned above can be placed at the end of these three sentences, sometimes more than one words are used in the end, but these words have no content as demonstrative pronouns, that is, if this word Zheyangzi could be removed from one sentence, the whole meaning of the sentence would not be changed. More likely, the function of this word can be the same as modal particle's, in order to show some pregmatic effects. Therefore, we know that the word Zheyangzi has its change in semantics, and so do its syntax and pragmatics, these findings motivate us to figure out what the changes are and how to describe them by combining qualitative and quantitative methods.

2   Differences in Taiwan

2.1   Semantic Change

Further study tells us, the semantic change in this word is a transition from notional word to function word, and this change, which makes Zheyangzi unique in its usage of modern Taiwan mandarin, is different compared with the word Zheyang used in mainland China. How does the meaning of this word Zheyangzi change? Let's see semantics analysis from example (1) to (2).

Firstly, the meaning of Zheyangzi in example (1) is contentive, and the word Zheyangzi serves as an attributive or adverbial, to illustrate some attributes or states in something which is modified by Zheyangzi. This is a vital process in the transition of meaning, see, this word can be removed from one sentence like in example (1), the whole meaning of this sentence is incomplete (lacking modifier in each sentence) but still keeps its main idea.

Secondly, the word Zheyangzi can be removed from sentences like in example (2a) and (2b), the whole meaning of each sentence is never changed, as we said, the word Zheyangzi is not contentive but functional at this time, which is called semantic bleaching, say, its meaning starts to weaken, is just like that's all in English, and this word can serve as a discourse marker 1 gradually, to show personal mood like subjective attitude or emotion.

Lastly, as it happens, the word Zheyangzi in example (2c) is used in succession, see, two words are used as independent element, separated by comma, to show pause between clauses. And sometimes we see more than two words are used in one sentence, people in Taiwan tend to use Zheyangzi for more times in the spoken mandarin without attention, these are just pauses in their words, to slow the flow of speech when speaking.

Looking at the following table which shows a gradual semantic change as well as features of syntax and pregmatics in the word Zheyangzi,

Table 1. Differences in the Word Zheyangzi

Scope			

---

[1] Discourse maker is put forward by Deborah Schiffrin (1987), it's a word or phrase which is attached to some place in one sentence, with a weakened meaning, to only highlight the pragmatic factors like mood, attitude and emotion in the sentence, and speakers often use this maker to lead listeners to a right understanding. In English, we see *well, or, you know, I mean, as I said* etc. as the discourse maker; In mandarin, we see *dajia zhidao*（大家知道）, *wo de yisi shi*（我的意思是）, *ye jiushi shuo*（也就是說）etc. as the discourse maker.

Features \ Options	Taiwan/ Mainland China	Taiwan	Taiwan
Semantics Change (word meaning)	contentive (this way/this kind)	weakened (that's all)	functional (no meaning)
Syntactic Function	attributive / adverbial	discourse marker	independent element
Pregmatics Effects	anaphoric/ cataphoric reference	subjective mood	pause between clauses
Examples	1a、1b、1c	2a、2b	2c

2.2 Frequency of Use

By comparing CCL with Sinica Corpus to count the total number of cases about the word Zheyangzi, we find that 1) for the frequency of use, people in Taiwan are more likely to use this word in their life from Sinica corpus, similarly we often choose to use "Zheyang" or "Zhegeyangzi" in mainland China, but the word Zheyangzi is relatively less used by us according to CCL corpus; 2) for the stylistics, this word is used both in written and spoken mandarin in Taiwan, especially for its generalization in the speaking, while in mainland China the word Zheyangzi is confined to informal styles like network language and dialects. Here is a table which shows the difference in frequency of word use between Taiwan and mainland China.

Table 2. Difference in Frequency of Word Use in Two Areas

Counting \ Area	Sum of Total Cases in Corpus (A)	Sum of Zheyangzi in Corpus (B)	Frequency of use (B/A)
Mainland China (CCL)	581,794,456	1539	0.00026%
Taiwan (Sinica)	112,459,32	808	0.007%

From table 2 we know that although the total cases as well as the word Zheyangzi in CCL is more than Sinica's, but as to the frequency of word use, it is 0.007% in Taiwan, and 0.00026% in mainland China, so the frequency of word use in Taiwan is about 27 times (B/A = 0.007%/ 0.00026% ≈ 27) larger than that in mainland China.

2.3 Effect of Expression

As a colloquial word, Zheyangzi has been widely used in Taiwan, as we said, it has served as discourse marker or independent element, to show some effects of expression in the speaking.

Firstly, the generalization of this word makes its suffix Zi (Zheyangzi) grammaticalize gradually. Here Zi doesn't have a contentive meaning but has the function of modal particle, it can just show a sense of euphemism like Haole or Eryi, as a modal particle, is also used to do the trick in Taiwan, where the elegant speech has prevailed for a long time. So the euphemism in the word Zheyangzi meets the requirements of language use in Taiwan society.

Secondly, the suffix Zi can be followed by some modal particles such as A, MA, Ye etc., to show a sense of feminine tone at the end of one sentence, because Zi plus these modal particles can heighten the effect of euphemism in the expression, which is preferred by women in the speaking. Besides, some typical colloquial words like Na, Ranhou, Suoyi etc., can be followed by Zheyangzi, to stand out the accent of Taiwan. Let's see example (3),

(3) a. Ranhou wo juede wo ye hui zheyangzi ye.
     then 1SG think 1SG also can that's.all PRT
     "Then I think I can also (do it) that's all."

In this sentence we see that the word Ranhou is often used as the beginning word in one sentence by people in Taiwan, and Ye is a typical modal particle in mandarin. These two words are widely used by people in Taiwan, especially for young women.

    b. Shengming bu jiu shi zheyangzi eryi ma?
     life not only is this.way PRT PRT
     "Isn't life only (like) this way?"

In this sentence we also find that the modal particle Eryi and Ma can obviously straighten a sense of euphemism in the disjunctive question, which can be preferred by people in Taiwan.

    c. Suoyi wo ma hen xiaoshun jiu zheyangzi a!
     so 1SG mother very filial just that's all PRT
     "So my mother (is) very filial, just that's all!"

In this sentence the conjunction Suoyi and modal particle A are the typical words in Taiwan mandarin, so people can use them to express their elegant and easy-going language style.

    d. Na zheyangzi haole, ni meige libai yiding yao hui waipo jia.
     so this.way PRT 2SG every weekend must / return.to grandma home
     "So (like) this way, you must return to (your) grandma's home every weekend."

In this sentence we see that the conjunction Na and the modal particle Haole are also the symbols of euphemism in language use, so people get accustomed to using them in their speaking, to convey their subjective comments or attitudes.

3   Causes of Difference

The difference of mandarin word Zheyangzi in Taiwan and mainland China, has its historical basis. And the causes of difference are attributed to two practical factors, say, language environment and contact.

3.1   Disparity in Language Environment

In macroscopic view, mandarin including words in Taiwan and mainland China shares common ground, that is, both of them date back to ancient Chinese, let's see two cases in ancient Chinese books firstly,
(4) a. Yi zheyangzi zuo, zuo de heshi bianshi he   tianli   zhi ziran.
according.to this.way do do PRT suitably is   fit heavenly.law PRT nature
    "Doing (it) according to this way, doing suitably is (to) fit the nature (of) heavenly law."
This case is from the book called Zhuzi's Language Category, which was finished in Earlier Song dynasty (960-1127).
    b. Zheyangzi, ni wo de   shuying,   yisuan ding zhun le.
    that's.all 2SG 1SG PRT losing.or.winning PFV decide exactly PRT
    "(The) losing or winning (to) you (and) me (has been) decided exactly, that's all."
This case is from the book called Enlightenment in The Eight Immortals, which was completed in Qing dynasty (1644-1911).
And because of different political systems and language policies, mandarin can be developed in different ways. Here are three factors related to language environment.

3.1.1 Source and Branch in The Development of Mandarin
Firstly, the Debate on Ancient and Modern Chinese happened during the New Culture Movement (around the time of the May 4th Movement in 1919, China) prompted modern Chinese to be accepted in the society at that time, and then modern Chinese had a different development in two main political regions from late 1920s to late 1940s, see, the written or classical style in mandarin had been kept in Kuomintang-controlled areas, while the spoken or plain style in mandarin was advocated in liberated areas controlled by Communist Party.
Secondly, mandarin in mainland China was always basing on northern China dialects which were the source of spoken Chinese, so the word Zheyangzi in mandarin tended to be colloquial and varying, but it was not widely used in written language according to corpus; while mandarin in Taiwan had developed independently since 1950s (because of Chinese Civil War in history), its written style could be advocated as a branch of modern Chinese but separated from mainland mandarin, from the data we see that the word Zheyangzi could exist both in the written and spoken language, so the scope of its application had been enlarged. Let's see the following cases taken from Taiwan literary works,
(5) a. Tian zhidao zheyangzi de biaoyan Jiang Yanrong juran   caidechulai.
    God know this.kind PRT performance 3SG unexpectedly figure.it.out
"God knows that (the girl) Jiang Yanrong figures out this kind (of) performance unexpectedly."
This case is from one of Qiong Yao's (瓊瑤) romantic fictions.
    b. Jianghu zhong qifei you henduo ren   doushi zheyangzi de?
    world inside isn't.it exist many people are.all this.kind PRT
    "Inside (the) world, isn't it (like that there are) many people (who) are all (of) this

kind?"

This case is from one of Gu Long's (古龍) Kung fu novels.

c.zheyangzi duidai waidiren, nin zhen diu beijingren de lian!
this.way   treat outsiders 2SG really lose Beijingnese PRT face
"Treating outsiders (in) this way, you really lose face (as a) Beijingnese!"

This case is from one of Long Yingtai's (龍應台) modern cultural novels.

3.1.2 Language Policy in Two Areas

Since 1949, government in mainland China had carried out some policies about standardization of Chinese like popularizating and promoting mandarin (1956), simplifying Chinese characters (1956), designing Chinese Spelling and Pronunciation Plan (1958) etc., to make sure that mandarin should base on northern China dialects and its grammar should come from the standard modern Chinese written works, language use had been unified as a result; while Taiwan authorities had kept the written style in mandarin for a long time because they emphasized ancient Chinese and classical culture in school education, but as social situation changed, the local government had implemented some policies like Local Language Education and Free to Choose a Language since 1990s, to diversify language use along with liberal politics in Taiwan. Therefore, the mandarin word Zheyangzi can be used more freely in Taiwan than that in mainland China.

3.1.3 Time of Openness in Two Areas

From the history we know, the government in Taiwan had a close relationship with America and British since 1950, and its society was also affected by Japan, which had controlled Taiwan for 50 years (1895-1945), hence Taiwan was open to the western countries earlier, but at the same time, the mainland China had witnessed a long seclusion to the outside especially during the Great Cultural Revolution (1966-1976) until the Reform and Opening-up Policy had been proposed since 1978, which was to declare that mainland China had started to be open to the world since then. Therefore, mandarin in two areas had definitely been affected by other foreign languages but the extent of the impact in Taiwan could be more intense than that in mainland China.

3.2   Disparity in Language Contact

From the micro perspective, the word Zheyangzi owns its unique features in Taiwan because of the following factors.

3.2.1 The Influence From Southern China Dialect

In Taiwan, mandarin mainly contacts with Southern Min Dialect, as well as little Hakka language, Shanghainese and Cantonese etc., which are all dialects from southern China, thus the whole style of Taiwan mandarin becomes not only decent and elegant, but also diversified in the communication. More importantly, the word Zheyangzi can be found in some southern China dialects, which means these dialects become a source of Taiwan mandarin, especially for the word. By investigating dialectical vocabulary in mainland China, we can demonstrate this influence. For example, the demonstrative pronoun in Nanjing dialect is called Zhegeyangzi (proximal deixis) and Nageyangzi (distal deixis), which is similar to the word Zheyangzi. And in Jiangle (belongs to Fujian Province) dialect, the word Zheyang is called Zheyangzi, Nayang is called Nayangzi, Zenyang is called Nayangzi. Also the places where people use Zheyangzi as a demonstrative pronoun include Hechuan, Leshan, Rongxian, Weiyuan in Sichuan province, Binchuan, Qiaojia in Yunnan province, and Wuhan in Hubei province etc., as a result, we find that the suffix Zi in Zheyangzi appears in many words of southern dialects, but this suffix is just a modal particle in the speaking, the real meaning comes from Zheyang, as a proximal deixis. Therefore, because of war and policy in history, large numbers of mainland Chinese immigrants who could speak southern dialects came to Taiwan and their dialects had penetrated Taiwan mandarin through constant communication. It was a blending process which could reflect a regional variant in mandarin word, just as Zheyangzi in Taiwan.

3.2.2 The Influence From Japenese

In history, Japan has occupied Taiwan for almost 50 years as we said, during the colonial period, the authority imposed Japanese education all the island, as a policy of language assimilation, the popularity rate of Japanese came to nearly 70% among other languages because of this strong policy at a time, so mandarin in Taiwan was influenced by Japanese inevitably. Now we can find some Japanese traces in Taiwan mandarin, for the grammar, there is an auxiliary verb (〜そうだ) which can show a kind of state, condition or sign at the end of one Japanese sentence, its meaning is almost equal to "幾乎/看起來/好像...的樣子" in Taiwan mandarin. Look at example (6) for translations in Taiwan,

(6) a. ああ、寒い。風邪をひきそうだ。
啊，冷。幾乎要患感冒了（的樣子）。
"Oh, (it is) chilly. Nearly catching a cold."

In this sentence, the auxiliary verb "〜そうだ" is to estimate the current condition, say, the speaker feels that he or she is catching a cold because of the chilly day.

b. このリンゴはおいしそうだ。
這個蘋果看起來好吃（的樣子）。
"This apple looks delicious."

In this sentence, the auxiliary verb "〜そうだ" is to predict the coming condition, say, the speaker thinks that this apple will be delicious because it looks tasteful.

c. 昨夜、雨が降ったようだ。
昨夜好像下了雨（的樣子）。
"Last night it seemed to have had a rain."

In this sentence, the auxiliary verb "～ようだ" is to judge the past condition, say, the speaker reflects that it probably had a rain last night.
From example (6) we can learn that the translation between Taiwan mandarin and Japanese made people at that time keep parts of characteristics in Japanese grammar, that is, for the auxiliary verb at the end of one sentence, people tried to use the word "好像", "看起來", "幾乎" to translate, and the word "樣子(Yangzi)" was added to the end of translation, to emphasize a kind of state or condition as a rule. The three mandarin translations in example (6) all have the word "樣子", which can demonstrate this translation behavior can be common among local people. With the popularity of this behavior, people in Taiwan were accustomed to adding "的樣子", "這樣子", "就這樣子" to the end of one sentence whose meaning was complete, just to convey the mood of judgment or prediction on the fact, the word "樣子(Yangzi)" could become a modal particle gradually. Therefore, the word Zheyangzi can be influenced because its latter two morphemes are Yang (樣) and Zi (子), which constitute the word "樣子(Yangzi)". That's the reason why the word Zheyangzi had became a modal particle at the end of one sentence, and this phenomenon had a connection with Japanese grammar. From the point of linguistic typology, we see that the grammar in Taiwan mandarin and Japanese share some similar features because of language contact.

4   Conclusion

From this study we know that the mandarin word Zheyangzi across the Taiwan straits displays some disparities, 1) for semantic change, it is a transition from notional word to function word (contentive→weakened→functional) in Taiwan. Also, features of syntax which are not found in mainland China can be discourse marker and independent element in Taiwan. Besides, the pregmatics effects can be anaphoric and cataphoric reference both in two areas but the subjective mood and pause between clauses are found in Taiwan; 2) for frequency of use in this word, the number of cases in Taiwan is much higher than that in mainland China; 3) for effect of expression, this word has served as discourse marker or independent element, to show a sense of euphemism or elegance, which can meet language style in Taiwan society.
And the reasons for these differences contain 1) different language environment in two areas, like source (mainland China) and branch (Taiwan) in the development of mandarin, and language policy as well as time of openness at that time; 2) disparities in language contact like the influence from southern China dialect and Japenese.
Honestly, we hope this passage could serve as a prototype for the study of mandarin words across the Taiwan straits and provide some effective methods for lexicon research.
However, we may question: compared with spoken mandarin in Taiwan, why is the word Zheyangzi not widely used in written style? And how to predict its usage in the future? Later study will try to settle down these questions we believe.

Appendix

1SG 1st person singular 2SG 2nd person singular 2PL 2nd person plural
3SG 3rd person singular 3PL 3rd person plural ASSO associative marker
CLF classifier   COMP complementizer   EM emphasis marker
NEG negator   NOM nominalizer/nominalization PRT particle PASS passive
PFV perfective   PST past tense

References

1. Diao Yanbin: A Microscopic Comparison of Cross-strait Varieties: The Case of Eryi (而已),
   Journal of Beijing Normal University (Social Sciences) 232 (4), pp. 44-51 (2012)
2. Rober Cheng: Theory of Lexical Diffusion Applied to Syntactic Change and on the Case of
   You-sentence in Taiwan Mandarin, Language Teaching and Linguistic Studies 43 (1), pp.
   66-73 (1990)
3. Li Lei: Auxiliary Verb *Hui* in the Mandarin Dialect in Taiwan, Journal of Hebei Normal University (Philosophy and Social Sciences Edition) 37 (2), pp. 68-71 (2014)
4. Yang Haiming, Shao Jingmin: Comparing the Address Terms Nansheng and nvsheng across
   the Taiwan Straits, Applied Linguistics 4, pp. 54-63 (2011)
5. Chu Zexiang, Zhang Qi: The Diversity and Tendentiousness Investigation of *Touguo* in Both
   Sides of the Taiwan Straits. Applied Linguistics 4, pp. 70-79 (2013)
6. Qiu Zhiqun, Fan Dengbao: The History and Current Situation of Mandarin Implementation
   in Taiwan, Taiwan Studies 4, pp. 77-82 (1994)
7. Nanjing Dialect Compiling Committee: A Survey of Nanjing Dialect. Nanjing Press, pp. 212-
   213 (1993)
8. Li Rulong. A Survey on Twelve Fujian Cities (Counties) Dialects. Fujian Education Press, pp.
   349 (1999)
9. Xu Baohua, Miyada Ichiro: Dictionary of Chinese Dialects. Beijing: Zhonghua Book Company, pp. 2845. (1999)
10. Xiong Nanjing: A Study on Language Policy in Taiwan After the World War II (1945-2006),
    Beijing: Minzu University of China. pp. 1 (2007)
11. Xing Mei: The Variation of Taiwan Chinese Grammar, Shanghai: Fudan University, pp. 62
    (2003)
12. Lakoff, George & Johnson, Mark. 2003. Metaphors We Live By. London: The University of
    Chicago Press, pp. 8-10 (2003)
13. Wang Yin: The Pragmatic Analysis of Iconicity Principles. Modern Foreign Languages 26 (1),
    pp. 2-12 (2003)
14. Beijing Language and Culture University, Taipei Language Institute: Modern Chinese Cross-
    Strait Dictionary. Beijing: Beijing Language and Culture University Press (2003)
15. Deborah Schiffrin: Discourse Analysis. Cambridge University Press (1987)

Dou in Kaifeng Dialect

Shaoshuai Shen[1], Bing Lu[2], Huibin Zhuang[1]

1 Henan University, Kaifeng, China
2 Shanxi University, Taiyuan, China

{wps2005,Zhuanghuibin}@163.com

Abstract. Compared with *dou* in Mandarin, *dou* in Kaifeng dialect shows a higher frequency of use and reflects a richer diversity of usages. The investigation finds that *dou* in Kaifeng dialect has two pronunciations of, i.e. *dou*$_{k1}$ [təu33] and *dou*$_{k2}$ [təu214]. Among all the usages of *dou*$_{k1}$, four of them correspond to that of *dou* in Mandarin, one demonstrates a unique feature, and the rest of the usages of *dou*$_{k1}$, together with that of *dou*$_{k2}$, largely correspond to that of *jiu* in Mandarin. This new collection of data can shed light on the study of *dou* in Chinese.

Keywords: *dou* in Mandarin, *dou* in Kaifeng dialect, *jiu* in Mandarin

1   Introduction

In recent year, the usage of *dou* in modern Chinese attracted the attention of many scholars, such as Gao [1]; Huang [2]; Xu & Yang [3]; Yuan [4]; Zhang, Li, & Pan [5]; Zhou & Wang [6], etc. Their research has put forward new opinions from different perspectives, and deepen the understanding of *dou*. However, their main objects of study are the Mandarin *dou*, and more focused on its meaning of universal quantification, which lead to limitations of their studies. The usage of *dou* in the dialect is far richer than the meaning of universal quantification, which is worth to explore in depth.

Although there are some literatures about the *dou* in the dialect (Li [7]; Li [8]; Wang [9]; Guo [10]), the study of specific usage of *dou* in the dialect is not enough. Compared to the *dou* in Mandarin, *dou* in Kaifeng dialect is a frequently used word, and its usage is very flexible. Therefore, this paper investigates *dou* in Kaifeng Dialect, and systemically explores its usage.

In the second section of this paper, by contrasting the usage of *dou* in Mandarin (hence after *dou*$_m$), we find the *dou* in Kaifeng dialect (hence after dou$_k$) has two pronunciations, referred to as *dou*$_{k1}$ [təu33] and *dou*$_{k2}$ [təu51], which respectively represent different usages. The usage of *jiu* in Mandarin (hence after *jiu*$_m$) will be contrasted with *dou*$_k$. In the third section, the findings of the study are presented in the way of semantic map, with the purpose of further clarifying the relationship between those words.

M. Dong et al. (Eds.): CLSW 2016, LNAI 10085, pp. 660–667, 2016
DOI: 10.1007/978-3-319-49508-8_60

2   The usage of *dou* in Kaifeng dialect

By comparing the usage of *dou*$_m$, we explore the usage of *dou*$_k$. According to The Institute of Linguistics of Chinese Academy of Social Sciences [11], the usage of *dou*$_m$ is listed as follows:

dou$_m$

1) *adv.* whole extent or quantity of; all
他无论干什么都很带劲。
Tā wúlùn gànshénme dōu hěn dàijìn.
'Whatever he did, he did with vigor.'

2) *adv.* used with *shì* to show the cause
都是你磨蹭，要不我也不会迟到。
Dōu shì nǐ móceng, yào bù wǒ yě bù huì chídào.
'It was all because of your dawdling that I got late.'

3) *adv.* even
今天一点都不冷。
Jīn tiān yīdiǎn dōu bù lěng.
'It is not cold at all today.'

4) *adv.* already
饭都凉了，快吃吧。
Fàn dōu liángle, kuài chī ba.
'The food is already cold. Hurry and eat.'

    With respect to the above usage of *dou*$_m$, we can find the corresponding expressions in the usage of *dou*$_{k1}$ [təu33], as shown in the following examples:

dou$_{k1}$

1) *adv.* whole extent or quantity of; all
   a. 他两口都$_{开1}$是搞传销哩。
Tā liǎngkǒu dōu shì gǎo chuánxiāo lī.
'That couple are both engaged in illegal pyramid selling.'
   b. 他俩哥都$_{开1}$个北京上班嘞。
Tā liǎ gē dōu gè běijīng shàngbān lei.
'His two brothers are both worked in Beijing.'

2) *adv.* used with *shì* to show the cause
   a. 都$_{开1}$是你口（[ke33]）这耽误事，要不现在都$_{开1}$快到了。
Dōu shì nǐ □([ke33]) zhè dānwù shì, yào bù xiànzài dōu kuài dàole.
'If you were not delayed, we would have been almost there right now.'
   b. 都$_{开1}$是停电哩事，叫我这一晌啥都$_{开1}$弄不成。
Dōu shì tíngdiàn lī shì, jiào wǒ zhè yī shǎng shà dōu nòng bùchéng.
'It was all because of the power outage that I cannot do anything for this period.'

3) *adv.* even
   a. 你别[pe53]看外面刮着风，今（[tɕi]）个一点都$_{开1}$不冷。
Nǐ bié [pe53] kàn wàimiàn guāzhe fēng, jīn ([tɕi]) gè yīdiǎn dōu bù lěng.
'Even though the wind blowing outside, it's not cold at all today.'
   b. 他抠死了，一个（[yo51]）糖都$_{开1}$不给。
Tā kōu sǐle, <u>yīgè</u> ([yo51]) táng dōu bù gěi.

'He was very stingy, and even didn't want to share a piece of candy.'

4) *adv.* already

a. 饭都_{开1}有点凉了，赶紧吃吧。

Fàn dōu yǒudiǎn liángle, gǎnjǐn chī ba.

'The food is a little bit cold, please hurry and eat!'

b. 我都_{开1}说罢了，他不来了。

Wǒ dōu shuō bàle, tā bù láile.

'I've already said that he was not coming.'

The above usage of *dou*_{k1} is consistent with that of *dou*_m. We then explore the further usage of *dou*_{k1} as follows:

***dou*_{k1}**

5) *adv.* at once; right away

a. 别[pe53]急，饭都_{开1}快做中了。

Bié [pe53] jí, fàn dōu kuài zuò zhōngle.

'No hurry. The meal will be ready soon.'

b. 再少等一会儿，司机都_{开1}快到了。

Zài shǎo děng yīhuǐ'er, sījī dōu kuài dàole.

'Just wait a little while, the driver will be here right away.'

6) *adv.* as early as, already

a. 夜黑雨都_{开1}停了。

Yè hēi yǔ dōu tíngle.

'The rain stopped already last night.'

b. 我都_{开1}说了吧，你还不信。

Wǒ dōu shuōle ba, nǐ hái bùxìn.

'I've already told you, but you don't believe it.'

7) *adv.* as soon as; right after

a. 咿！弄啥类，还冇[məu33] 刚到都_{开1}又叫走类。

Yī! Nòng shà lèi, hái mǎo [məu33] gāng dào dōu yòu jiào zǒu lèi.

Ah! What's the problem! I just arrived here, then you ask me to leave.'

b. 还冇[məu33] 刚会走了，都_{开1}想跑了，那会中！

Hái mǎo[məu33] gāng huì zǒule, dōu xiǎng pǎole, nà huì zhōng!

'You want to run before you have learnt to walk, and that would never do!'

8) *adv.* indicating a natural result under certain conditions or circumstances; in that case; then

a. 你要是不去，那我都_{开1}不去了。

Nǐ yàoshi bù qù, nà wǒ dōu bù qùle.

'If you don't go, I will not go.'

b. 明个要是下雨，那都_{开1}不去恁干娘家了。

Míng gè yàoshi xià yǔ, nà dōu bù qù nèn gàn niángjiāle.

'If it rains tomorrow, you will not go to visit your godmother.'

9) *adv.* as much as; as many as

a. 我心里说俩人都_{开1}中了，他叫来哩一下都_{开1}十人嘞。

Wǒ xīnlǐ shuō liǎ rén dōu zhōngle, tā jiào lái lī yīxià dōu shí rén lei.

'I thought two people were enough, but he called up ten people at last.'

b. 你还说沉哩，叫我松松儿嘞[le55]都_{开1}扛起来了。

Nǐ hái shuō chén lī, jiào wǒ sōng sōng er lei [le55] dōu káng qǐláile.

'You feel it heavy, but I can carry it easily.'

10) *adv.* used between two identical elements to express resignation

a. 大点儿都_{开1}大点儿吧，过两年了[lou]还能穿。

Dà diǎn er dōu dà diǎn er ba,guò liǎng niánle [lou] hái néng chuān.

'Though it's a little too big, you can still wear it two years later.'

b. 中吧，两块都_{开1}两块吧。

Zhōng ba, liǎng kuài dōu liǎng kuài ba.

'Oh, well. Two Yuan is okay.'

11) *adv.* begin with; as expected

a. 这路本来都_{开1}不宽，你都不能_{开1}让让！

Zhè lù běnlái dōu bù kuān, nǐ dōu bùnéng ràng ràng!

'The street is not wide. Can't you make a way for us.'

b. 这油本来都_{开1}少，你都_{开1}不能省着点用！

Zhè yóu běnlái dōu shǎo, nǐ dōu bùnéng shěng zhuó diǎn yòng!

'We don't have much oil. You can't waste it like that.'

12) *adv.* indicating determination; just; simply

a. 我都_{开1}不信弄不住他。

Wǒ dōu bùxìn nòng bù zhù tā.

'I don't believe that I can't pick him up.'

b. 我都_{开1}不信我学不会。

Wǒ dōu bùxìn wǒ xué bù huì.

'I don't believe that I can't manage it.'

13) *adv.* exactly; precisely

a. 我都_{开1}给你说了吧，他这不是有[məu33]来么！

Wǒ dōu gěi nǐ shuōle ba, tā zhè bùshì mǎo [məu33] lái me!

'I have told you. Now it turns out that he didn't come!'

14) *adv.* enough

a. 恁走吧，我一个（[yo51]）人都_{开1}中。

Nèn zǒu ba, wǒ yīgè ([yo51]) rén dōu zhōng.

'You can leave now. I can handle it myself.'

b. 别[pe53]拿多了，俩都_{开1}中了。

Bié [pe53] ná duōle, liǎ dōu zhōngle.

'Don't take too much. Two is enough.'

The above examples are the usage of *dou*_{k1} [təu33]. For *dou*_{k2} [təu214], there are also abundant examples to show its usage.

dou_{k2}

1) *adv.* only; merely; just

a. 天天值班嘞[le55]都_{开2}我一个（[yo51]）人，恁谁都_{开1}不个这儿。

Tiāntiān zhíbān lei [le55] dōu wǒ yīgè ([yo51]) rén, nèn shuí dōu bù gè zhè'er.

'Every day I am the only one on duty, all of you are absent.'

b. 都_{开2}他一个人会，其他都_{开1}不会。

Dōu tā yīgè rén huì, qítā dōu bù huì.

'He is the only one to know this, no one else knows.'

2) *adv.* indicating determination; just; simply

a. 我都开2不吃饭，你想咋吧！

Wǒ dōu bù chīfàn, nǐ xiǎng zǎ ba!

'I simply refused to have the meal. So what?'

b. 我都开2是不给你说，你能咋着？

Wǒ dōu shì bù gěi nǐ shuō, nǐ néng zǎzhe?

'I simply refuse to tell you the thing. So what?'

3) *adv.* exactly; precisely

a. 那都开2是他家。　Nà dōu shì tā jiā. 'That is precisely his home.'

b. 这都开2是他哥。　Zhè dōu shì tā gē. 'This is precisely his brother.'

4) *conj.* indicating a supposition

a. 你都开2是口（[ɕin51]）送给我，我都开1不要。

Nǐ dōu shì □([ɕin51]) sòng gěi wǒ, wǒ dōu bùyào.

'Even if you give it to me free of charge, I won't receive it.'

b. 你都开2是叫谁说情都开1不中，这个分数我不会给你改！

Nǐ dōu shì jiào shuí shuō qíng dōu bù zhòng, zhège fēnshù wǒ bù huì gěi nǐ gǎi!

'No matter whoever you asked for help, I absolutely won't change your score.'

5) used with *shì* to show agreement

a. 都是开2都是开2，你说了很对。

Dōu shì dōu shì, nǐ shuōle hěn duì.

'Yes, yes, you're quite right.'

The above observation shows that the usage of dou_{k1} is richer than that of dou_{k2}. The consistency can be observed in their usage when they are used to express the meaning of "simply" and "exactly".

Further observations reveal that the usage of dou_k that is different from dou_m is systemically consistent with that of *jiu* in mandarin. The following examples of *jiu* is from The Institute of Linguistics of Chinese Academy of Social Sciences [11].

jiu_{m1}

1) *v.* come near; move towards

就着灯看书 jiùzhe dēng kànshū 'read a book by the light of a lamp'

2) *v.*　undertake; engage in

就业　　jiùyè 'obtain employment'

3) *v.* suffer; be subjected to

就擒　jiùqín 'be seized'

4) *v.* accomplish; make

功成业就　　gōng chéng yè jiù　'(of a person's career) crowing success'

5) *v.* take advantage of; accommodate oneself to

就便　　　jiù biàn　'at somebody's convenience'

6) *v.* (dishes, fruit, etc.) be eaten (or drunk) with (staple food or wine); go with

花生仁儿就酒　huāshēng rén er jiù jiǔ　'have peanuts with one's drinks'

7) *prep.* with regard to; concerning; on

他们就这个问题进行了讨论。

Tāmen jiù zhège wèntí jìnxíngle tǎolùn.

'They had a discussion on this question.'

jiu_{m2}

1) *adv.* at once; right away

我就来。　Wǒ jiù lái.　'I'll come right away.'

2) *adv.* as early as, already

他十五岁就参加革命了。

Tā shíwǔ suì jiù cānjiā gémìngle.

'He joined the revolution when he was only 15 years old.'

3) *adv.* as soon as; right after

卸下了行李，我们就到车间去了。

Xiè xiàle xínglǐ, wǒmen jiù dào chējiān qùle.

'As soon as we unloaded our luggage, we went to the workshop.'

4) *adv.* indicating a natural result under certain conditions or circumstances; in that case; then

只要用功，就能学好。

Zhǐyào yònggōng, jiù néng xuéhǎo.

'As long as one works hard, one can learn it well.'

5) *adv.* as much as; as many as

他三天才来一次，你一天就来三次。

Tā sān tiāncái lái yīcì, nǐ yītiān jiù lái sāncì.

'He comes here once every three days.'

6) *adv.* used between two identical elements to express resignation

大点儿就大点儿吧，买下算了。

Dà diǎn er jiù dà diǎn er ba, mǎi xià suànle.

'Even though it's a little too big, just buy it.'

7) *adv.* begin with; as expected

我就知道他会来的，今天他果然来了。

Wǒ jiù zhīdào tā huì lái de, jīntiān tā guǒrán láile.

'I knew he would come, and he came toady as expected.'

8) *adv.* only; merely; just

以前就他一个人知道，现在大家都知道了。

Yǐqián jiù tā yīgè rén zhīdào, xiànzài dàjiā dōu zhīdàole.

'He used to be the only one to know this, now it is known to all.'

9) *adv.* indicating determination; just; simply

我就做下去，看到底成不成。

Wǒ jiù zuò xiàqù, kàn dàodǐ chéng bùchéng.

'I just continue to do it, to see whether it will succeed or not.'

10) *adv.* exactly; precisely

幼儿园就在这个胡同里。

Yòu'éryuán jiù zài zhège hútòng lǐ.

'The kindergarten is exactly in this alley.'

jium3

1) *conj.* indicating a supposition

你就是送来，我也不要。

Nǐ jiùshì sòng lái, wǒ yě bùyào.

'Even if you send it to me, I won't accept it.'

Observation of the above examples reveal that the usage of dou_{k1} is systemically consistent with jiu_{m2} and jiu_{m3}. They can be used as adverb and conjunction, and express similar meaning.

3   The Comparison of dou_k with Corresponding Expressions

According to the usage of dou_k, dou_m, and jiu_m listed above, we can draw the following table and figure to reveal their connection. Table 1 shows the contrast of their part of speech.

Table1 Contrast of Part of Speech

		v.	*adv.*	*prep.*	*conj.*
Mandarin	dou_m	–	+	–	–
	jiu_m	+	+	+	+
Kaifeng dialect	dou_k	–	+	–	+

As indicated by Table 1, dou_m can only be used as adverb; jiu_m can be respectively used as verb, adverb, preposition, conjunction; dou_k can be used as adverb and conjunction. From the perspective of part of speech, we can draw a conclusion that compared to the status of dou_m in Mandarin, dou_k is more prominent in Kaifeng dialect.

According to their specific usage, we can draw Figure 1 to show their semantic contrast.

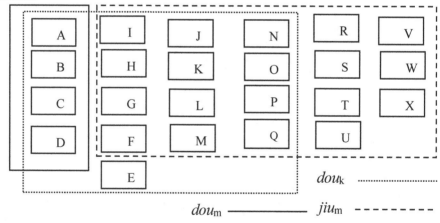

Figure 1 Semantic Map of dou_k, dou_m, and jiu_m

The capital letters enclosed by rectangle indicate the specific usage. A. all; B. used to show the cause; C. even; D. already; E. enough; F. as early as; G. right after; H.in that case; I. at once; J.as much as; K. used to express resignation; L. begin with; M. indicating determination; N. exactly; O. merely; P. indicating a supposition; Q. showing agreement; R. come near; S. engage in; T. be subjected to; U. accomplish; V. take advantage of; W. go with; X. with regard to

As indicated by Figure 1, the usage of dou_m encloses the area from A to D in the semantics map. The usage of jiu_m encloses the area from F to X. The usage of dou_k

encloses the area from A to Q, which overlap with dou_m and jiu_m. Therefore, we can draw a conclusion that the usage of dou_k is a prominent category in Kaifeng dialect, which requires further explanation.

4   Conclusion

From the firsthand data, we observe that in Kaifeng dialect dou_k can be used as adverb and conjunction, and its usage includes all that of dou_m and most part of the usage of jiu_m in Mandarin. Dou_k is a prominent category in Kiafeng dialect, and its meaning is far richer than universal quantification meaning of dou_m, which is worth to explore further.

Acknowledgements. The study is supported by Humanities and Social Sciences by the Ministry of Education (14YJC740115).

References

1. Gao, M. L. A Survey of the Binding Scope and Function of Chinese "$d\bar{o}u$"(都) (in Chinese). Language Teaching and Linguistic Studies, no. 3, pp. 33-34 (2002)
2. Huang, W. F.: A On the Question of $d\bar{o}u$ Functioning to Quantify the Time Adverb (in Chinese). Chinese Teaching in the World, no. 3, pp. 373-382 (2010)
3. Xu, Y. Z., & Yang, Y. M.: The Subjectivity, Objectivity and Pragmatic Ambiguity of Chinese Adverb "Dou(都)" (in Chinese). Linguistics Study, no. 3, pp. 24-29 (2005)
4. Yuan, Y. L.: On the Implicit Negation and NPI Licensing of dou (都) (in Chinese). Studies of the Chinese Language, no. 4, pp. 306-320 (2007)
5. Zhang, L., Li, B. L. & Pan, H. H.: The Semantic Requirements of Dou(都): a Study of Its Rightward Association (in Chinese). Studies in Language and Linguistics, no. 2, pp. 63-71 (2012)
6. Zhou, X. B. & Wang, Y.: An Analysis of the Grammatical Errors Concerning "Dou" as an Adverb of Scope (in Chinese). Chinese Language Learning, no. 1, pp. 71-76 (2007)
7. Li, B.: Study of the Range Adverbs Like "Dou" in Chinese Dialects (in Chinese). Journal of Hunan Institute of Engineering, no. 2, pp. 31-35 (2012)
8. Li, S. R.: "$d\bar{o}u$"[təu] in Shanxian Dialects in Shandong (in Chinese). Modern Chinese, no. 4, pp. 89-90 (2016)
9. Wang, S. G.: On the Prepositive Topic Marker [tou] in Puyang Dialect, Henan Province (in Chinese). Dialect, no. 4, pp. 367-371 (2012)
10. Guo, D. Y.: Plural Marker of "$d\bar{o}u$"(都) in Zhongmu Dialect (in Chinese). Chinese Knowledge, no. 4, pp. 58-59 (2013)
11. The Institute of Linguistics of Chinese Academy of Social Sciences. The Contemporary Chinese Dictionary (Chinese - English Edition). Foreign Language Teaching and Research Press, Beijing. (2002)

About "好说歹说[*haoshuodaishuo*]"*

Bin Liu

Department of Chinese Language & Literature, Peking University, Beijing 100871
liubin198903@126.com

Abstract. This paper mainly discusses the structural, semantic and pragmatic features of "好说歹说[*haoshuodaishuo*]". Firstly it can be viewed as a parallel structure of "好说[*haoshuo*]" and "歹说[*daishuo*]", whose main syntactic function is to be part of the predicate. Then its meaning "repeatedly requesting or persuading by various arguments or means" is formed through the mechanism of metaphor. In addition, "*haoshuodaishuo*" is usually used in a pragmatic situation of asking for a favor or persuading another. Especially, for the universal principle of optimism, "*haoshuodaishuo*" usually implicates an anticipated positive result.

Keywords: "好说歹说[*haoshuodaishuo*]", formation mechanism of meaning, metaphor, pragmatic features, optimism

1   Introduction

"好说歹说[*haoshuodaishuo*]" is one of the most frequently used idioms in daily Chinese, but its structure and meaning albeit abundant in distinctions as well as research significance, has not yet received corresponding specialized study. This paper, however, is to discuss "*haoshuodaishuo*" and reveal its features in structure, meaning and usage through investigating linguistic data from real texts.

In *Modern Chinese Dictionary* (the sixth edition), "*haoshuodaishuo*" is defined as "repeatedly requesting or persuading by various arguments or means". As we can hardly catch this connotation by character-by-character interpreting it, there emerge questions like how its connotation comes into being and what are its pragmatic features in practical use. Focused on these questions, the paper is to emphasize explorations of the semantic features, meaning formation mechanism and pragmatic features of "*haoshuodaishuo*".

---

* This research is sponsored by the National Social Science Fund Major Project "Chinese Parataxis Characteristic Research and Large Knowledge Base and Corpus Construction Under the Background of International Chinese Language Education" (Approval No. : 12&ZD175). I would like to extend my sincere thanks.

M. Dong et al. (Eds.): CLSW 2016, LNAI 10085, pp. 668–675, 2016
DOI: 10.1007/978-3-319-49508-8_61

2   The Structural Features and Syntactic Functions of "*haoshuodaishuo*"

"*haoshuodaishuo*" forms a parallel structure by juxtaposing "好说[*haoshuo*]" and "歹说[*daishuo*]" in which "好[*hao*]" and "歹[*dai*]" a pair of antonyms both followed by the head verb "说[*shuo*]" constitute an attributive structure.

After an exhaustive investigation of linguistic data from Corpus of Center for Chinese Linguistics Peking University (CCL Corpus), we find that the main and most important syntactic function of "*haoshuodaishuo*" is to serve as part of the predicate in a sentence. For example:

(1) 众人<u>好说歹说</u>，这才把他"请"进了办公室。
All people *haoshuodaishuo*, just BA he "invite" into the office
After continuous persuasions, we finally "invited" him into the office.

(2) 韵梅<u>好说歹说</u>，把老人劝了回去。
Yunmei *haoshuodaishuo*, BA the elderly persuade LE back.
After unremitting efforts, Yunmei finally persuaded the elderly to go back.

(3) 刘老板<u>好说歹说</u>，掏几个钱才算了事。
Liu boss *haoshuodaishuo*, hand out some money get it over
Mr. Liu, the boss, kept requesting before he finally managed to spend a small sum of money to have the disputes settled.

All "*haoshuodaishuo*" in the above examples function as main part of the predicate while in other examples albeit comparatively rare "*haoshuodaishuo*" can also constitute an adverbial modifier or an attributive modifier. For instance:

(4) 几个胆子大的冒着危险骗走他的枪，然后又<u>好说歹说</u>地护送他回家了事。
Several the bold take risk cheat his gun, then *haoshuodaishuo* accompany him home
Several bold men cheated him of the gun at great risk and then accompanied him home while keeping on persuading.

(5) 晚上见面的时候，我<u>好说歹说</u>地让他开了口，可他却说"我找工作是我自己的事情，怎么样你管不着？！"
In the evening meet time, I *haoshuodaishuo* let him talk, but he just says "I look for a job is my self's business, it's none of your business ?! "
When we met in the evening, I was asking all the time before he finally blurted "Finding a job is my business, not yours!"

(6) 而且公馆里来对她<u>好说歹说</u>的说客又是如此之多。
But from the Mansion to her *haoshuodaishuo* lobbyists are so many
So large was the number of the lobbyists from the Mansion to keep persuading her.

What is interesting is that in linguistic data from real texts there is usually an ellipsis of subject in a "*haoshuodaishuo*" sentence making the idiom more like an adverbial modifier clause as in:

(7) <u>好说歹说</u>，邓承东就是不同意……
haoshuodaishuo, Deng Chengdong still disagree…

In spite of repeated requests, Deng Chengdong still disagreed...

(8) 好说歹说，他就是不去。

haoshuodaishuo, he still NEG go

In spite of repeated requests, he still refused to go.

(9) 好说歹说，才把大贵的火头煞下去。

haoshuodaishuo, finally Dagui's fury damp down

After continuous persuasions, we finally succeed in damping down Dagui's fury.

Adverbial modifier clauses above indicate some degree of grammaticalization of "*haoshuodaishuo*" which in all likelihood will go further.

Moreover, we also find that "*haoshuodaishuo*" is hardly syntactically self-sufficient, that is, it is rarely or never used by itself but generally followed by a complementary result clause. This applies to Example (1) to (9) and more examples are as follows:

(10) 父母好说歹说，儿子还是不改主意，为每天0.14元零花钱而放弃学业。

The parents *haoshuodaishuo*, the son still NEG change his mind, for everyday 0.14 RMB pocket money to give up on school

Though his parents kept on convincing him, he still dropped out only to earn 0.14 RMB a day for pocket money.

(11) 好说歹说，才给他剃了头。

haoshuodaishuo, finally cut his hair

After being repeatedly demanded, he finally had his hair cut.

(12) 好说歹说，他才答应由他娘陪去看。

haoshuodaishuo, he finally agree by his mother accompany to see

After being asked over and over again, he finally agreed to be accompanied by his mother.

In Example (10), (11) and (12), "*haoshuodaishuo*"s are all followed by their adverbial clauses of result.

3   The Meaning Features and Formation Mechanism of "*haoshuodaishuo*"

As mentioned in the Introduction, "*haoshuodaishuo*" means "repeatedly requesting or persuading by various arguments or means" rather than a combination of the respective meanings of "*haoshuo*" and "*daishuo*" despite its parallel structure. We find that "repeatedly," the core of the meaning of "*haoshuodaishuo*", cannot be literally drawn from the parallel structure, which implies the Principle of Compositionality does not apply in this case. Then comes the question how does the meaning of "*haoshuodaishuo*" come into being?

In fact, "*haoshuodaishuo*" can be considered as a construction formalized into "A_+VA_-V" in which "A_+" and "A_-" represent a pair of antonymous adjectives like those in "紧赶慢赶[*jinganmangan*]", "左想右想[*zuoxiangyouxiang*]", etc. We find that all "A_+VA_-V" constructions can be understood as "repeatedly V.". For example, "*haoshuodaishuo*" means "repeatedly *shuo*", "*zuoxiangyouxiang*" means "repeatedly *xiang*", "*jinganmangan*" means "repeatedly *gan*". In sum, "repeatedly" constitutes the core of the meaning of the "A+VA_V" construction and its meaning formation mechanism is to be discussed below.

Then I will take "*haoshuodaishuo*" as an instance to elaborate on the meaning formation mechanism of the "A+VA_V" construction. But before that, we need to revisit a theory of metaphor.

From a cognitive linguistic perspective, a metaphor contains a projection from one cognitive domain to another. In a famous example in Lakoff and Johnson's study (1980) "Time is money" is considered to contain a metaphorical projection from money to time. In other words, "time" the target domain is conceptualized from "money" the source domain. So the study of metaphor concerns not only linguistics but also way of thinking which indicates that way of thinking itself is metaphorical and the conceptual systems we build our thinking and actions on can mostly be constructed and defined by metaphors (Zhang, 1998). Metaphors are not only conceptual but also systematic and it is its systematicness that allows us to understand a concept in the light of another. For example, to understand "debate" in term of "battle" may highlight the battlefulness of the former (Lakoff & Johnson, 1980). To sum up, through metaphorical projections between different domains, the individual characteristics of the target domain can be highlighted and extra meanings generated.

Likewise the meaning of "*haoshuodaishuo*" is also formed in this metaphor mechanism and its core "repeatedly" is highlighted through metaphorical projection from the space domain to the time domain. In the idiom, the two antonyms "*hao*" and "*dai*" stand at the two ends of the spectrum of various manners and methods. After the two antonyms are combined with "*shuo*" their original meanings are grammaticalized from which new meanings of means and arguments are derived and the meaning of "repeatedly" in term of time course is derived afterwards. In other words, through metaphorical projection from the space domain to the time domain, the original meanings of "*hao*" and "*dai*" are grammaticalized and the new meaning of "repeatedly" is thus highlighted. In this way, the meaning of "repeatedly requesting or persuading by various arguments or means" is formed.

On the whole, we think the reason why instead of a combination of the respective meanings of "*haoshuo*" and "*daishuo*" or either of the two, "repeatedly" or the repetition of the verb is stressed in "*haoshuodaishuo*" is because "repeatedly" is what is highlighted through the metaphorical projection. So we may say metaphor is the main meaning formation mechanism of the "A+VA_V" construction.

4   The Pragmatic Features of "*haoshuodaishuo*"

As mentioned above, "*haoshuodaishuo*" is syntactically self-insufficient and cannot be used by itself but followed by a complementary result clause for further explanation. Besides, after investigating plenty of linguistic data, we find that "*haoshuodaishuo*" is usually used in narrative style and a pragmatic situation of asking for a favor or persuading another to do something with particular emphasis on the great difficulty to do the favor. As the favor is usually not easy to do or requires great efforts from the hearer, or the hearer feels reluctant to do the task in question, after "repeated requests or persuasions" two results may come. If the hearer finally takes the speaker's request, the follow-up clause will contain a positive result the speaker anticipates and adverbs of fulfillment such as "才 [*cai*](*just*)", "总算 [*zongsuan*](*at last*)" and "终于[*zhongyu*] (*finally*)". For instance:

(13) 众人好说歹说，这才把他"请"进了办公室。

    All people *haoshuodaishuo*, just he "invite" into the office

    After continuous persuasions, we finally "invited" him into the office.

(14) 好说歹说，他才答应由他娘陪去看。

    haoshuodaishuo, he finally agree by his mother accompany to see

    After being asked over and over again, he finally agreed to be accompanied by his mother.

(15) 看这个倔强的老人，钟书记好说歹说几经动员，这位老人才愿离开家。

    Look this stubborn aged man, Secretary Zhong *haoshuodaishuo* repeatedly mobilize, this elderly just willing to leave home

    Let's take a look at this stubborn aged man who finally agrees to leave his house after Secretary Zhong repeatedly mobilizes him.

After analyzing the contexts of the three examples above, we find that in Example (13) going "into the office" used to be difficult to realize because of the hearer's unwillingness; in Example (14) "he" used to be reluctant to be accompanied by his mother; in Example (15) the aged man used to be disinclined to leave his house. But after speakers spare no efforts to "*haoshuodaishuo*" the hearers finally agree to do the thing they used to feel reluctant about, which are thus demonstrated with adverbs implying fulfillment in the follow-up clauses of results the speakers anticipate.

In the other case, however, if after unremitting efforts the hearer still does not take the speaker's request, the follow-up clause will contain a result against the speaker's anticipation and thus with transitional adverbs like "就是 [*jiushi*](*still*)", "还是 [*haishi*](*still*)", "硬是[*yingshi*](*still*)", "却[*que*](*yet*)" and "但[*dan*](*yet*)" constitute a transitional relation between the main clause and the subordinate one. For example:

(16) 好说歹说，邓承东就是不同意……

    haoshuodaishuo, Deng Chengdong still disagree…

    Despite others' incessant persuasions, Deng Chengdong still disagreed…

(17) 好说歹说，他就是不去。

    haoshuodaishuo, he still NEG go.

    In spite of repeated requests, he still refused to go.

(18) 父母好说歹说，儿子还是不改主意，为每天0.14元零花钱而放弃学业。

    The parents *haoshuodaishuo*, the son still NEG change his mind, for everyday 0.14 RMB pocket money to give up on school.

    Though his parents kept on convincing him, he still dropped out only to earn 0.14 RMB a day for pocket money.

In the three examples above, the hearers, namely, Deng Chengdong, "he" and "son" in the end still refuse to take the speakers' requests, to establish a transitional relation which may be made more explicit by adding the transitional conjunction "但[*dan*] (*yet*)" as follows:

(16') 好说歹说，但邓承东就是不同意……
haoshuodaishuo, yet Deng Chengdong still disagree…
Despite others' incessant persuasions, Deng Chengdong yet still disagreed…
(17') 好说歹说，但他就是不去。
haoshuodaishuo, yet he still NEG go.
In spite of repeated requests, he yet still refuses to go.
(18') 父母好说歹说，但儿子还是不改主意，为每天0.14元零花钱而放弃学业。
The parents *haoshuodaishuo*, yet the son still NEG change his mind, for everyday 0.14 RMB pocket money to give up on school.
Though his parents kept on convincing him, he yet still dropped out only to earn 0.14 RMB a day for pocket money.

To sum up, "*haoshuodaishuo*" is usually used in narrative style and a pragmatic situation when one is asking for a favor or persuading another. In practice, an adverbial clause of a positive result of fulfillment or a negative result of refusal is required to follow "*haoshuodaishuo*" in the sentence. So "*haoshuodaishuo*" always comes with the speaker or the narrator's subjective attitudes and emotions.

Next we are to discuss whether the numbers of positive clauses and negatives ones are equivalent and if not, why.

After consulting CCL Corpus for "*haoshuodaishuo*", we obtain 115 examples with "*haoshuodaishuo*" in modern Chinese and 8 in ancient Chinese among which 107 and 8 are respectively validated after screening. If we classify the follow-up clauses by whether it contains a result positive to the speaker, we will find 7 out of 8 in ancient Chinese are with positive clauses accounting for 87.5% while only 1 or 12.5% is negative; 82 out of 107 or 76.7% in modern Chinese are positive while the left 25% or 23.3% are negative.

In brief, the follow-up clauses in "*haoshuodaishuo*" sentences show great bias that as many as nearly 80% are positive while only 20% are negative. But why?

We think it is due to the optimism principal universal to human mentality, namely, the Pollyanna Hypothesis proved through psychological experiments by Boucher and Osgood (1969), implying people are generally more willing to see or talk about positive things (good news and virtues) than negative ones. Universal optimism gives rise to a universal propensity: words for positive evaluation always outnumber negative ones in frequency, diversity and free choice (Shen, 1999; Yuan, 2013).

One potent proof is that the adverb "终于[*zhongyu*] (*finally*)" which means something happens after long period of time is more frequently used in sentences with anticipated results (Lü, 2008/1980). For example:
(19) a. 反复试验，终于成功了。
After repeated tests, we finally make it.
  b. *反复试验，终于失败了。
*After repeated tests, we finally fail.
(20) a. 等了很久，他终于来了。
After long wait, he finally shows up.
  b. *等了很久，他终于没来。

*After long wait, he finally does not show up.

We may easily find that (19a) and (20a) with positive results are more idiomatic while (19b) and (20b) with negative results are not idiomatic nor semantically suitable due to the universal principle of optimism of preferring positive things (good news and virtues) to negative ones in particular after long period of efforts have been invested.

As "*haoshuodaishuo*" discussed in this paper concerns a speaker's repeated requests or persuasions by various arguments or means through great efforts, consequently in most cases a follow-up clause contains an anticipated positive result due to the universal principle of optimism.

In summary, we think the pragmatic features of "*haoshuodaishuo*" can be summarized as follows: it is usually used in narrative style and a pragmatic situation of repeated requests or persuasions; it is always followed by a biased result clause of positive results the speaker anticipates due to the optimism principle universal to human mentality.

If the above research results of "*haoshuodaishuo*" are included in the dictionary, its definition will be more complete as well as accurate. Therefore lexicographers are advises to make an adjustment of "repeatedly requesting or persuading with various arguments or means and always with a follow-up clause of positive results".

5   Conclusion

Based on investigation of linguistic data from real texts, this paper mainly discusses the structure, meaning features and meaning formation mechanism as well as pragmatic features of "*haoshuodaishuo*". To begin with, the paper points out that "*haoshuodaishuo*" is a parallel structure of "*haoshuo*" and "*daishuo*" in which "*hao*" and "*dai*" are a pair of antonyms and it generally serving as part of the predicate is rarely used by itself but followed by a result clause for complement. Next, it finds the metaphor theory rather than the Principle of Compositionality applies to the meaning formation mechanism of "*haoshuodaishuo*" whose meaning is "repeatedly requesting or persuading by various arguments or means". Besides, "*haoshuodaishuo*" is usually used in a pragmatic situation of asking for a favor or persuading another and with the speaker's anticipated positive results in the follow-up clause due to the optimism principle universal to human mentality. Finally, we also deliver according advice to improve the dictionary definition of "*haoshuodaishuo*".

References

1. Boucher, J. & C. E. Osgood: The Pollyanna Hypothesis, Journal of Verbal Behavior **8**, 1-8 (1969).
2. Lakoff, George & Mark Johnson: Metaphors we live by. University of Chicago Press, Chicago (1980).
3. Ungerer, F. & Schmid, H.—J.: An Introduction to Cognitive Linguistics. Longman, London & New York (1996).

4. Lü, S.: Eight Hundred Words of Modern Chinese. The Commercial Press, Beijing (2008/1980). (现代汉语八百词, 北京: 商务印书馆, 2008/1980).（In Chinese）
5. Shen, J.: Asymmetry and the Markedness Theory. Jiangxi Education Publishing House, Nanchang (1999). (不对称和标记论, 南昌: 江西教育出版社, 1999)（In Chinese）
6. Yuan, Y.: On the Implicit Negation Hidden in Chadianer(差点儿) and its Grammatical Effects, Studies in Language and Linguistics **02**, 54-64(2013) (In Chinese)
7. Zhang, M.: Cognitive Linguistics and Chinese Noun Phase. China Social Sciences Press, Beijing (1998). (认知语言学与汉语名词短语, 北京: 中国社会科学出版社,1998)（In Chinese）
8. Institute of Linguistics Chinese Academy of Social Sciences: Modern Chinese Dictionary (the sixth edition). The Commercial Press, Beijing (2012). (现代汉语词典（第6版）, 北京: 商务印书馆, 2012)（In Chinese）

On the Semantic Patterns and Features of "Shao" Serving as Adverbial in Imperative Sentences

Pu Li

College of Language Study, Xinjiang University, Urumqi, China
lipu0312@sina.com

Abstract: Ambivalent words are seen as a difficult point both in machine translation and Chinese language teaching. Although some more research has been made on them, none is done in respect to machine translation and Chinese language teaching. This article, based on the previous research, studies the Ambivalent word "shao", including its syntactic and semantic features and the conditions and formal marks when a meaning appears, exploring new ways of studying Ambivalent words for machine translation and Chinese language teaching.

Keywords: Shao; syntactic features; semantic features; conditions; formal marks; machine translation.

1 Introduction

1.1 The translation of "Shao" often confronts problems

Based on Eight Hundred Chinese Modern Words by Lv Shuxiang, the meanings and usages of "Shao" (少) as adjectives can be concluded into two cases. First, "Shao" serves as predicate and complement to indicate an objective quantity. No ambiguity will occur under this situation. Second, "Shao" serves as adverbial. Its usages are complicated. In non-imperative sentences, "Shao" indicates an objective quantity. No ambiguity will occur under the situation. However, in imperative sentences, the usages of " shao" can be categorized into the following two groups . Examples:

Group A:
- *Shao chi yi dian ba! 少吃一点吧!* (don't eat too much)
- *Shao fang yan, tai xian bu haochi 少放盐，太咸不好吃。* (put less salt, or not tasty)

Group B:
- *Shao duozui! 少多嘴!* (don't interrupt)
- *Nimen chao nimen de, shao ba wo che jinqu! 你们吵你们的，少把我扯进去!* (don't drag me into your quarrel !)

Group A can be marked as "Shao X" and group B can be marked as "Shao Y". Their differences and controversies are mirrored in machine translation. Normally, there would not be too much problems in the translation of group A.

© Springer International Publishing AG 2016
M. Dong et al. (Eds.): CLSW 2016, LNAI 10085, pp. 676–683, 2016
DOI: 10.1007/978-3-319-49508-8_62

But the translation of group B is often problematic, since the "Shao" under this situation cannot be understood as "small in quantity". For example:

- *Shao duozui!* 少多嘴！ Less talkative!*1 (http://fanyi.baidu.com/) The right translation: Mind your own business!
- *Nimen chao nimen de, shao ba wo che jinqu!* 你们吵你们的，少把我扯进去！ You fight yours, less drag me into this. *(http://fanyi.baidu.com/) The right translation should be: Don't drag me into your quarrel!

What happens in online translation would also happen in Chinese language teaching.

1.2 Reasons for the problems

In Eight Hundred Chinese Modern Words, "Shao" serves as adjectives to modify two kinds of predicates, one of which is not followed by quantifiers. Under this situation, "Shao" indicates small in number (shorted for shao1). For example:

Group C：

- *bing gang hao, shao huodong.* 病刚好，少活动。 *(*take a rest since you have just recovered)

Another kind of predicate is followed by quantifiers. Now "Shao" indicates smaller in number (shorted for shao2). For example,

Group D：

- *ni shao shuo jiju ba* 你少说几句吧。 (don't make too much comments)

In other words, in Eight Hundred Chinese Modern Words, "Shao X" in Group A is divided into cases of "Shao1 X" and "Shao2 X". "Shao1 X" only represents a comparatively static and isolated quantifier, namely, less VP in X. For instance, "Shao huo dong" means "do less exercises"; "Shao fang yan" means " put less salt". To be specific, the receptor of V should be small in number. "Shao zhong shan dao" forms in the same way as "Shao fang yan". Whereas, "Shao2 X"indicates two related quantifiers, one of which has been possessed by X, while that of the other assumes to decrease the original quantifier (shao X). For example, "Shao shuo ji ju" means "don't say too much as you would like to say", namely "to decrease the quantity'; "Shao chi dian tang" means "you have eaten too much sugar and the quantity should be decreased next time".

In a word, in *Eight Hundred Chinese Modern Words,* the distinctions in Shao X ("A1X" and "A2X") in group A are analyzed as the differences of A ("Shao"), namely, A1 represents "small quantity" and A2 represents "decrease in quantity". "Shao Y" in group B is simply categorized into the only group to represent "small quantity". To some extent, it is the kind of neglect, carelessness and tendency that results in the difficulties in online translation and teaching Chinese to foreign students. To solve the problem, we have to study more on "Shao Y".

Therefore, the paper, with regard to the syntactic features of "Shao" which serves as adverbial in imperative sentences, will investigate "Shao Y" by summarizing its

---

[1] Sentences with* mean a mistranslation.

semantic patterns and the conditions and formal markers[2] when a meaning appears. This shall contribute to machine translation and teaching Chinese as a foreign language.

2 Syntactic patterns modified by "Shao" and syntactic features of "Shao + VP" when "Shao" functions as adverbial in imperative sentences

As have been explained in section 1, since group C can be rendered into "small quantity in X" or "the decrease of X", "Shao X yidian" = "X shao yidian" and group D "Shao Y" = "bie Y", such as "Shao duoshi! 少多事！" = "bie duoshi! 别多事！". Are the two cases of "Shao" in group C and group D all related to quantity? How to distinguish their semantic meanings? Can the conditions and formal markers when a meaning appears be discerned?

First, let's exam the syntactic patterns and syntactic features when "Shao" functions as adverbial in imperative sentences.

The syntactic patterns can be classified according to quantifiers' category. Quantifiers' category can be understood in wide and narrow senses. For convenience, only the narrow sense is considered in the paper, namely, apply quantifiers and words indicating quantity. As to the form, it refers to formations with words indicating quantity(these/those), quantifiers or verbs and adjectives being followed by "yi dian er 一点儿", "yi hui er 一会儿" which indicate transitional small quantity. When "Shao" functions as adverbial in imperative sentences, there are two conditions for the syntactic patterns and the syntactic features of " shao VP".

2.1 Category 1: Without quantifier

1. Modifying verb phrases: The following examples try to include derogatory, neutral and commendatory phrases.
   (a) Without adverbial: For example: *shao huodong.* 少活动 (do less exercises!) (+verb)
   (b) With adverbial. For example: *Nimen chao nimen de, shao ba wo che jinqu.* 你们吵你们的，少把我扯进去！(don't drag me into your quarrel !)
2. Modifying adjectives and adjective phrases such as in *ni shao luosuo!* 你少啰嗦！(don't say too much!)
3. Modifying phrases for comparison such as in *Shao xiang gen mutou shide.* 少像根木头似的！ (don't be like a piece of wood!)
4. Modifying idioms, fixed phrases and slang such as in *Shao zhuangfengmaisha* 少装疯卖傻！(don't play the fool!)
5. Other special patterns. *shao hejiu, duo chicai !* 少喝酒，多吃菜！(drink less, eat more!)

---

[2] formal marker: the meaning of a word or a sentence can be found by the marker.

2.2 Category 2: With quantifiers

1. With indicating phrases such as "this/that, these/those: "ni shao guan zhe shi. 你少管这事.
2. With phrases indicating quantity. "Shao"+ V + quantifier (+ noun) such as in *Shao guang jici jie* 少逛几次街 (don't go shopping frequently)!
3. Words indicating transitional small quantity like "yi dian er 一点儿", "yi hui er 一会儿" serve as complement

The above section only concludes syntactic patterns and syntactic features of "Shao VP" from the perspective of linguistic forms. In the next section, we will discuss the semantic patterns indicated by "Shao".

3 Semantic patterns of "Shao" when serving as adverbial in imperative sentences

3.1 Indicating objective small number or decrease in number

This semantic pattern is corresponding to that of group C. Lv Shuxiang has already clarified that this pattern is included in the two conditions when adjective "Shao" is used as adverbial to modify predicate verbs.

"Shao 1" refers to the condition when predicate verb is not followed by quantifiers. "Shao" here means "small quantity". For example, "*Shao fangyan*" in sentence "*Shao fangyan, tai xian bu haochi* 少放盐，太咸不好吃。*" "Shao" under this situation is based on objective weighing and is compared to standard quantity.

"Shao 2" refers to the condition when predicate verb is followed by quantifiers. "Shao" gets the meaning of comparison. In non-imperative sentences, the meaning is obvious, such as in the sentence "*duo xiu xi le ban xiao shi, shao shou ru le shang wang yuan* 多休息了半小时，少收入了上万元*". According to Xiao Guozheng (2004), the comparative meaning of adjectives has three dimensions: compared with itself, compared with others and compared with the standard. This is the semantic basis for adjectives. Exam the following sentence, "*duo xiuxi le ban xiaoshi, shao shouru le shang wang yuan*" can be understood in three ways:

a. rest half an hour more than before, and lose ten thousand yuan. (compared with itself);
b. rest half an hour more than others, and lose ten thousand yuan.(compared with others);
c. rest half an hour more than being required, and lose ten thousand yuan. (compared with the standard).

In imperative sentences, influenced by the sentence patterns and the specific meaning and collocation of adjectives, some "Shao" possess the three meanings and some "Shao" possess partial meaning.

"Shao 1" and "Shao 2" in group A are all adjectives. Both "Shao 1" which indicates small quantity and "Shao 2" which indicates smaller in quantity, are directly related to quantity. When a quantifier is added to "Shao 1", "Shao 1" can easily be converted into "Shao 2" .The semantic meaning of "Shao" can still indicate "small quantity or the decrease of quantity".

Moreover, the two conditions will not generate ambiguity both in machine translation and Chinese language teaching. Therefore, in this paper we consider the two cases as one.

3.2 Indicating imperative and subjective negation

This semantic pattern is corresponding to group B, namely "Shao Y". As to this pattern, its meaning and grammatical function have been less studied. Even if it has been mentioned, it is always classified into group A, just like what Lv Shuxiang has done in Eight Hundred Chinese Modern Words. However, the phenomenon has attracted attention of some scholars in recent years. Chen Shuang (2005) and Yao Zhanlong (2014) directly named "Shao3" as "imperative and negative adverb". Yao thinks, in the dialects of northern China, "Shao" partially loses its adjective function and is converted into negative form and gradually develops into an imperative and negative adverb. The disappearance of the occurrence when "Shao" is used to indicate quantity and the enforcement of the speaker's negative subjective attitude has essentially resulted in its state being grammaticalized.

Compared with group A, the semantic meaning of group B is obviously different. The precondition of group A is that the listener has done too much. The purpose is to persuade the listener to reduce the quantity of his action. Thus, "Shao" in group A is compared with "duo" and has nothing to do with quantity. It means "less than the normal quantity or a decrease of the original quantity".

The precondition of group B is that the speaker and the listener are in opposing positions. "Shao" has nothing to do with quantity and indicates forbidding. In other words, the semantic function of group A is to "inform and persuade" and the semantic function of group B is to "warn and blame". Therefore, "Shao" in group B can be replaced by imperative and negative adverd "bie". For instance,

- *Ni shao lai zhe yi tao* 你少来这一套。*(don't make tricks)*
  equals to
- *Ni bie lai zhe yi tao* 你别来这一套。(don't make tricks)

Obviously, "Shao" has a stronger flavor of "warn and blame" than "bie". But when "Shao" serves as imperative and subjective negation, it can be replaced by "bie". Under the condition, only the meaning of "warn and blame" becomes weaker. On the contrary, not all "bie" can be replaced by "Shao".

However, semantic meaning of group B has something to do with that of group A. Group A presumes the listener has done too much. The meaning of the sentence is to persuade the speaker to decrease his action quantity and the destination goal is to extinguish the action. Thus, it is the disappearance of the quantity meaning and the enforcement of the negative and subjective attitude of the speaker that make it grammatical and generate the meaning of group B.

4   Conditions and formal markers when a meaning appears

We can conclude from the above analysis that the semantic patterns of "Shao" is closely related to the derogatory or commendatory meaning of the words or phrases it modifies such as in *"Shao qu shangjie!* 少去上街！" ("shang jie" is neutral, can be understood as "inform and persuade").

Moreover, the greater the derogatory meaning of the words or phrases "Shao" modifies is, the greater the possibility is when the whole sentence being understood as "warning and blaming" and the greater the possibility is when "Shao" is used to indicate imperative and subjective negation. But, even for this, we find the conditions and formal markers when the two meanings of "Shao" still exist.

Li Shengxi (1992) proposed 20 ways to strengthen or abate the mood of imperative sentences. In the paper, the author borrows his outline, based on the syntactic features and semantic features when "Shao" functions as adverbial in imperative sentences, checks thousands of imperative sentences with "Shao" as adverbial in CCL data base, Chinese Language Research Center, Beijing University, finally concludes the formal markers.

4.1 When "Shao" indicates objective small quantity or decrease in quantity, the following formal markers appear

1. With Quantifier's category:
   V + "yi hui er", "yi dian er"or quantifier such as in
   Shao xiuxi hui er! 少休息会儿 (don't take too much rest) ("yi hui er", "yi dian er")
2. Overlapping of verbs: such as in
   Shao fa fa laosao, duo zuo zuo shi. 少发发牢骚，多做做事。 (don't complain too much and just do it).
3. With euphemism or mood words:
   "qing, ma fan, lao jia"can increase the politeness of a sentence, such as in
   qing shao yidian zhize, duo yifen guan ai 请少一点指责，多一份关爱。 (less blame and more care)
   Mood word "ba"in *shao ai wo yidian ba*(love me less)
4. Use"hai shi", "zui hao", "gu qie", "bu fang"to ease the mood such as in
   Hai shi shao shuo ji ju ba 还是少说几句吧。 (don't say too much)
   "hai shi", "zui hao"to some extent, abates the mood.
5. Use "wokan" , "woxiang", "woshuo", "wo renwei" to indicate the insert of subjective opinion. For example,
   Wokan haishi shao zhu liangtian ba.(don't live here too long) 我看还是少住两天吧。
6. Use juxtaposing elements and comparison. For example,
   Duo heshui, shao chouyan 多喝水，少抽烟！ (drink less and smoke less) (comparison of"duo", "Shao")

4.2 When "Shao" indicates imperative and subjective negation, there are the following formal markers.

1. Words and fixed phrases (idioms, fixed phrases and slang) with derogatory meaning will be accompanied. For example, *Ni shao fangsi!* 你少放肆！ (don't be too relaxed)
2. Adjectives and adjective phrases are used as predicate. Example: *Ni shao shahuhu de!* 你少傻乎乎的! (don't be silly)

3. with phrases for comparison. Example: *shao xiang gen mutou shide* 少像根木头似的！(don't be like a piece of wood!)

4. use sentences with "ba" Example: S*hao ba zeren wang wo shenshang tui* 少把责任往我身上推！(don't put the responsibility on me!)

5. use sentences with "bei". Example: S*hao bei ren pian!* 少被人骗！(don't be cheated!)

6. use emphasizing markers like "geiwo", "genwo" Example: N*i shao geiwo zhuangfengmaisha* 你少给我装疯卖傻！(don't play fool!)

7. use pronouns such as "zhe, zhe er, zheli, zhezhong, na er, nali"to show emphasis. Example:*Ni shao zai nali chong haoren!* 你少在那里充好人！(don't pretend to be a good man!)

The author of the paper thinks the markers are closely related to the semantic functions of group A and group B. Group A indicates "informing and persuading" while group B indicates 'warning and blaming'. In group A, the speaker and the listener maintain a good communicative relationship, based on which the speaker can persuade the listener to be cautious of something and the listener can accept it and keeps or decreases his action to the degree of "Shao". The speaking mood of the speaker is cordial. Formally, on one hand, words with quantifier's category and words for comparison are usually applied and on the other hand, ways to abate mood are more often used. In group B, there is controversy between the speaker and the listener and the two parties are on opposing positions. Thus the speaker speaks with toughness and discontent when he tries to stop the listener's action. Thus, formally, adjective phrases and comparative phrases with derogatory and subjective meanings are always used. Emphasizing markers "geiwo", "genwo" are used to enforce the mood of order. Sentences with "ba" are more often used to express the strong meaning of deposition.

The above listed conditions and formal markers are only a tendency and cannot be generalized all linguistic facts. In the process from weak imperative (informing and persuading) to strong imperative (blaming and warning), the meaning of a sentence depends on the specific context. Without phrased indicating comparison and specific context, there would be ambiguity.

Therefore, it is the logical relation of "Shao-wu" among shao1, shao2 and shao3 that generates the ambiguity "Shao" which functions as adverbial in imperative sentence.

5   Conclusion

The paper investigated the conditions when "Shao" functions as adverbial in imperative sentences. Then what are the conditions for "Duo", the antonym of "Shao"? In the book Eight Hundred Chinese Modern Words, Lv Shuxiang classifies "Duo" into adjectives and verbs. As a pair of antonyms, the usages of "duo" and "Shao" are not completely the same When serving as adjectives. One typical difference is that "Duo" can modify nouns and follow adjectives to indicate a great distinction in comparison while "Shao" does not have such a function. However, in imperative sentences, "Duo" indicates: 1, large quantity; 2, larger or smaller in quantity; increase or decrease in quantity. That is to say, under any conditions, the meaning of "Duo" is directly related to quantity. However, the usage of "Shao" is more complicated.

If applying the conclusions of the research, especially the conditions and formal markers when a meaning appears in machine translation, more integrated rules would be generated to make machine translation more intelligent. In Chinese language teaching, ambivalent words are usually taught simply by making sentences and explaining of their meanings and usages while overlooking the systematic of the meaning, the relation between the meanings and the syntactic elements and the conditions and formal markers when a meaning appears. If the condition is improved, Chinese language teaching would make great progress.

Acknowledgment

This paper is financially supported by the Youth Fund Project of communication strategy of Chinese learners in different backgrounds of the Ministry of Education of China (12XJJC740003). The author would like to thank all the people involved in the research projects for their help.

References

1. Guozheng Xiao, A Tentative Research on the Connotative Structure Development and Choice of Modern Chinese Grammar Study in the 21st Century [M], Journal of East China Nornal University, 2004(3):32-40. [In Chinese]
   萧国政.21世纪现代汉语法研究的内涵构成与发展选择[J].华东师大学报,2004(3):32-40页.
2. Zhanlong Yao. the Negative Adverb "less" and its Pragmatic Interpretation [J].Linguistic Research, 2014(1):pp43-46. [In Chinese]
   姚占龙.祈使性否定副词"少"的产生及其语用解释[J].语文研究,2014(1):43-46页.
3. Shuang Chen. The Imperatively Negative Adverb "Shao(少)" [J]. .Journal of Liuzhou Vocational & Technical College, 2005(3):pp68-71
   陈爽. 祈使性否定副词"少"[J]. 柳州职业技术学院学报，2005（3）:68-71页.
4. Shuxiang Lv. Eight Hundred Chinese Modern Words, [M]. The Commercial Press.2010: pp 184-186, pp 480-481. [In Chinese]
5. Yulin Yuan, A Study of Imperative Sentences in Modern Chinese, [M] . Beijing: Publishing House of Beijing University, 1993: pp.42-56. [In Chinese]
6. Shengxi Li, A Study of Chinese Imperative Sentence System, Journal of Yiyang Normal College, 1992(3): pp.57-60 . [In Chinese]
   李胜昔.关于汉语祈使句系统的研究[J].益阳师专学报，1992（3）： 57-60页.

Part VI Extended Study and Application

The MFCC Vowel Space of [ɤ] in Grammatical and Lexical Word in Standard Chinese

Yu Chen[1,2,3], Ju Zhang[2], Huixia Wang[2], Jin Zhang[1], Yanting Chen[1], Hua Lin[3],
Jianwu Dang[2]

[1] Tianjin University of Technology, Tianjin, China
{chenyu, zhangjin, chenyanting}@tjut.edu.cn
[2] Tianjin University, Tianjin, China
juzhang@tju.edu.cn, jdang@jaist.ac.jp
[3] University of Victoria, Victoria, Canada
luahin@uvic.ca

Abstract. This study investigated the phonetic quality of [ɤ] in the light sylla-bles of grammatical words and the non-light syllables of content words. By us-ing the Mandarin Speech Test Materials as the main linguistic materials, audio data of 10 native speakers of Standard Chinese was collected for this study. Af-ter the audio data collection, the Mel Frequency Cepstral Coefficents of [ɤ] in both conditions were extracted as the acoustic feature. Then, the dimension of MFCCs was reduced through Laplacian eigenmaps in order to construct the 3D acoustic space. Also, an independent T-test was applied to test the differences of the three-principal-dimension data be-tween the light and non-light [ɤ]. The results of 3D vowel space and independent T-test jointly show that the quality of [ɤ] in light syllables distinguish from that in non-light syllables. Therefore, results of the present study may suggest that the traditional term light-tone is not an accurate term for describing the phenomenon of light syllable in Manda-rin. Furthermore, considering any possible variations of vowel quality under different lexical context may improve the output of natural speech processing of Standard Chinese.

Keywords: MFCCs, Vowel Space, Grammatical word, Lexical word, Mid vowel, [ɤ], Standard Chinese

1   Introduction

As the only mid vowel in Mandarin Chinese, [ɤ] has a high function load in building up various syllables which in turn form a great number of words in the language. In the set of grammatical words, for instance, [ɤ] and its onset consonants form some most frequently used auxiliaries (e.g., "*de*" and "*le*")[1].

---

[1] According to the Frequency list of Standard Chinese Corpus, BCC, "*de*" and "*le*" ranked the 1st and 3rd separately among the 1055378 words in this corpus. Interesting readers may want to check http://bcc.blcu.edu.cn for detail.

© Springer International Publishing AG 2016
M. Dong et al. (Eds.): CLSW 2016, LNAI 10085, pp. 687–699, 2016
DOI: 10.1007/978-3-319-49508-8_63

Meanwhile, [ɤ] is also found in many everyday lexical words. Due to its ultra-high frequency count in the language's lexicon, [ɤ] is also an important entry in the natural language processing in the language.

In spite of its prominence in the language, the fundamental nature of [ɤ] is still an open question both for phonologists and phoneticians. In the area of phonology, a consensus is that [ɤ] is the only mid vowel in the language, and most phonologists acknowledge the complexity in its realization. For instance, some phonologists argue that [ɤ] is a monophthong with a less-constrained status than other vowels in Mandarin vowel, and lacks phonemic counter-parts both in vertical and horizontal direction in the vowel chart [1,2,3]. In phonetics, a few researchers notice the quality change during the production of this mid vowel [4,5]. In particular, [5] argues that [ɤ] is a transitional vowel because it experiences a successive target transition from [ɯ] to [ʌ] during its production.

Making things more complicated is the fact that the syllables[2] of the gram-matical words such as "*de*" and "*le*" are usually light as opposed to the regular or, henceforth, non-light syllables such as "*gē*" (elder brother) and "*hé*" (riv-er). [ɤ] in the former may have different phonetic qualities than in the latter. Since the light syllable has a shorter duration than the non-light one, from early on, practices in speech processing often used a shorter duration, such as 60% of the normal value, for the light syllables [6]. However, such treatment is too simplistic and does not seem to account for the full spectrum of differ-ences between the two types of syllables. The [ɤ] in the light syllable may simply have not enough time to achieve its targets which are fully achieved in non-light syllable. In that case, the shape and quality of the light [ɤ] should be very different from that of the normal [ɤ]. And if the sound qualities of [ɤ] are significantly different in the two types of syllables, two sets of parameters may need to be established for the two variations of [ɤ] to achieve better speech processing results.

Based on the aforementioned considerations, we conducted an experiment in which the phonetic quality of [ɤ] was investigated in both the light and the non-light syllables using Mel Frequency Cepstral Coefficents (MFCCs). The following sections are organized as follows: Section 2 describes data acquisi-tion and processing; Section 3 reports the results of the experiment; Section 4 contains a brief discussion and some remarks of conclusion.

---

[2] Since the light syllable of Standard Chinese always has a shorter tonal duration than non-light syllable, while its intensity is not necessary lower than the latter, Chinese linguists coined a term "*qīngshēng*" (light tone) to refer this phenomenon in Mandarin.

2   Data Acquisition and Processing

2.1   Participants

Ten native speakers of Chinese, five males and five females, were recruited in Tianjin. The age range was 20 to 29. All grew up in Northern China and speak Standard Chinese as their first language. They reported no history of speech and hearing impediment at the time of data recording. (All volunteered their participation in the experiment, and each was paid 50 yuan for the 2 hours he/she contributed to the experiment.)

2.2   Materials and Recording

The main linguistic materials used in the present experiment is the Mandarin Speech Test Materials (MSTMs) developed by Beijing Institute of Otolaryngology [7]. Although this instrument is designed to facilitate the use of speech audiometry in audiology clinics, we found it suitable to the current research with its balanced word- and sentence-lists[3].

MSTMs has 951 items, including 800 words, 150 sentences and a short passage. Every participant was recorded reading all of them. However, only the 150 sentences and the short passage were selected for analysis. We also added the passage *"běifēng hé tàiyáng"* (North wind and the Sun) since we felt the one short passage from MSTMs was not giving us enough passage reading results.

Among the 152 recorded materials, 155 [ɤ]s were in light syllables of which 111 were in grammatical words (57 *"de"* and 54 *"le"*), and 70 [ɤ]s were in non-light syllables of which 62 [ɤ]s were in high-frequency lexical words such as *"chē"* (car) *"hé"* (river) *"rè"* (hot). The 111 light [ɤ]s and the 62 non-light [ɤ]s were extracted for later analysis.

All data were recorded at a quiet classroom of the School of Chinese Language and Culture, Tianjin University of Technology. As shown in Fig. 1, the recording hardware consists of a Hasee UT-47 D1 laptop, a Mivsn T 6-2 usb audio card, a Mivsn MS-2H Microphone and a monitor headphone.

---

[3] Interesting reader may want to check http://trhos.com/mstms/indexe.asp for more information, including all of the materials of MSTMs.

Fig. 1. Audio Data Recording Setups

The recording software is developed on the platform of Matlab 12.0b by the 3rd author. Fig. 2a shows the PC window with three items: Practice, Actual Recording, and Additional Recording. Fig. 2b shows that the item for recording is promoted at the upper-center of the window. The participant can control the recording pace by clicking the menus on the right.

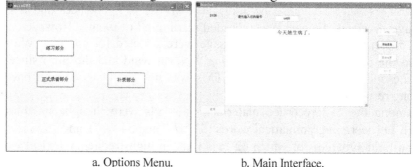

a. Options Menu.   b. Main Interface.

Fig. 2. Audio Data Recording System.

After the data recording, each item was stored as an individual audio file in .wav format (mono soundtrack, 16 KHz, 32-bit resolution).

2.3   Data Annotation

Totally, there were 90 items (88 sentences and 2 paragraphs) that contained the target phonemes were selected for annotating and analysis. The Penn Phonetics Lab Forced Aligner (P2FA) was used to complete the phoneme and word level automatic annotation. P2FA is now a popular automatic phonetic alignment system [8] based on the Hidden Markov Model (HMM) Speech Recognition Toolkit [9]. The acoustic models included in the P2FA are Gaussian Mixture Model-based (GMM) monophone HMMs. Each HMM has 32 Gaussian mixture components on 39 Perceptual linear predictive (PLP) coefficients. To improve alignment accuracy, the acoustic model also included a robust short-pause ("sp") HMM inserted optionally between words. According to [8], the P2FA can achieve 93.92% agreement (of phone boundaries) within 20ms, compared to manual segmentation.

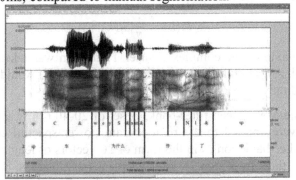

Fig. 3. Example of Automatic Annotation by P2FA.

As shown in Fig. 3, the word layer (at bottom) divided the sentence *"chē wèishénme tíng le?"* (Why did the car stop?) into the words which were annotated in Chinese characters, and the phone layer correctly separated all of the phonemes of the sentence. In this example, the sentence contains two targets, one a noun *"chē"* (car) and the other a tense auxiliary *"le"*.

2.4   MFCCs Feature Extraction

One of the most significant acoustic features currently used is the MFCCs. They take human perception sensitivity with respect to frequencies into consideration, and the frequency bands are equally spaced on the Mel-scale, which approximates the human auditory system's response more closely than the linearly-spaced frequency bands used in the normal cepstrum [10].

[11] have suggested that the auditory image, i.e. acoustic space, can be described by affine transformed logarithm of power spectrum, and some acoustic space studies involved MFCCs [12,13,14]. In our study, the MFCCs were used as the acoustic feature of phoneme to construct the acoustic space.

For a speech signal, MFCCs are commonly derived as follows [15]:
1) Frame the signal into 20-40 ms frames. 25ms is standard. Frame step is usually something like 10ms (160 samples), which allows some overlap to the frames.
2) To take the Discrete Fourier Transform (DFT) of the frame, perform the following:

$$S_i(k) = \sum_{n=1}^{N} S_i(n)h(n)\, e^{-j2\pi kn/N} \quad 1 \le k \le K, \tag{1}$$

where $S(n)$ is the time domain signal. n ranges over samples and i ranges over the number of frames. $h(n)$ is an N sample long analysis window (e.g. hamming window), and K is the length of the DFT. The periodogram-based power spectral estimate for the speech frame $S_i(n)$ is given by:

$$P_i(k) = \frac{1}{N}|S_i(k)|^2 \tag{2}$$

The absolute value of the complex Fourier Transform was taken, and the result is squared. A 512 point Fast Fourier Transform (FFT) would be generally performed and only the first 257 coefficients are kept.

3) Compute the Mel-spaced filter-bank. A set of 20-40 (26 is standard) triangular filters were applied to the periodogram power spectral estimate from step 2). The filter-bank comes in the form of 26 vectors of length 257 (assuming the FFT settings from step 2). Each vector is mostly zeros, but is non-zero for a certain section of the spectrum. To calculate filter-bank energies, each filter-bank with the power spectrum is multiplied, and then the coefficients are added up. Once this is performed, the 26 numbers are left to indicate that how much energy was in each filter-bank.

4) Take the log of each of the 26 energies from step 3), and 26 log filter-bank energies are left.

5) Take the Discrete Cosine Transform (DCT) of the 26 log filter-bank energies to give 26 Cepstral coefficients. And only the lower 12-13 of the 26 coefficients are kept.

The resulting features are called Mel Frequency Cepstral Coefficients (MFCCs).

Using the method advanced by [16], the middle 20ms of the stable periods of [ɤ] were chosen for calculating MFCCs features in the current study. To build up the vowel space that [ɤ] occupies, the cardinal vowels [a], [i] and [u] in monosyllables were also selected from which MFCCs features were extracted. Different from [16], the present work does not consider tonal information. Therefore, the MFCCs feature extracted for each vowel has 13 dimensions.

2.5   Further Data Processing

After extracting the MFCCs features, a Laplacian eigenmaps was applied to reduce the vectors of MFCCs features into three principal dimensions [12].

For the dimension-reduced data, the vowel space including [ɤ] under light and non-light syllables was built up, and an independent T-test was also applied to test the differences of the three-principal-dimension data between the two versions of [ɤ].

3   Results

The current study first tested the differences between light and non-light [ɤ] produced by all the subjects. Then, the tests were carried out separately for gender to see whether there is any possible variance in producing light and non-light [ɤ] between male and female participants.

3.1   Vowel Space

Using the data collected as described in Section 2, the 3D vowels spaces of the three groups are constructed, as shown in Figure 4. To clearly show the differences between light and non-light [ɤ], the spaces of the three cardinal vowels /i, a, u/ are also plotted in the figure.

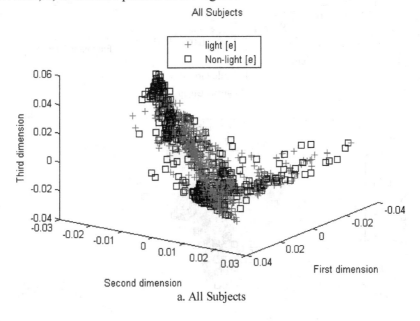

a. All Subjects

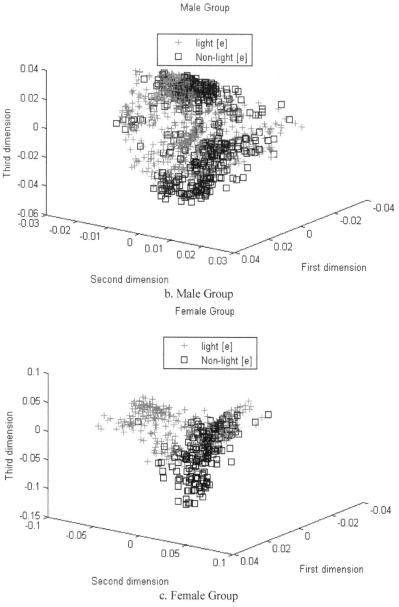

Fig. 4. 3D Vowel Spaces of [ɚ] in Light and Non-light Syllables for the Three Groups[4].

From Fig. 4, one may note that there is some overlapping of [ɚ] between the two conditions, but the light [ɚ]s do distinguish from the non-light ones in

---

[4] Because MATLAB cannot process the IPA fonts correctly, [ɚ] is represented as [e] instead in Figure 4.

all of three groups. Both for the male and female group, as shown in Fig. 4b and Fig. 4c, the non-light [ɤ]s concentrate at the front-right-bottom of the space, while the light ones are locating at back-left-upper positions. Comparing with the case of Fig. 4a, Fig. 4b and Fig. 4c jointly shows a gender effect on acoustic feature in producing vowels: both of the two versions of [ɤ] are converged in the vowel spaces of the male and female group, while the vowels in the vowel space of all subjects are more divergent in Fig. 4a.

Overall, visual observation of the vowel spaces seems to support the idea that [ɤ] is different in light and non-light syllables.

3.2   Independent T-test

Figure 5 demonstrates the distribution of acoustic data of the three groups. Observing the three boxplots, one may notice that, except for the third dimensional data of the group of all subjects, all of the data demonstrate a convergent distribution. Considering [ɤ] is such a flexible vowel in Mandarin, this result may indicates that, the dimension-reduced MFCCs features by the Laplacin eigenmaps still can properly reflect the common features across the different speakers.

To check if the difference of the two versions of [ɤ] shown in the vowel spaces is statistically significant or not, a series of independent T-tests were applied between each dimension of the data of light [ɤ] and not-light [ɤ] of the three groups, excluding the outliers (the values larger or smaller than 2 deviations of average), which are shown as red crosses in Figure 5.

For the group of the all subjects, two-sample T-test results are, for the first dimension, $t(772.496) = 1.853$, $p = 0.64$ (2-tailed); for the second dimension, $t(983.020) = 9.760$, $p < 0.001$ (2-tailed); and for the third dimension, $t(1112.439) = -11.120$, $p < 0.001$ (2-tailed). Except for the first dimension, the acoustic data of two versions of [ɤ] are significantly different both in second and third dimensions. That is to say, assembling the data of male and female subjects together does not eliminate the differences of sound quality between light and non-light [ɤ].

For the male group, two-sample T-test results are: for the first dimension, $t(546.835) = -2.847$, $p = 0.005$ (2-tailed); for the second dimension, $t(362.230) = 6.105$, $p < 0.001$ (2-tailed); and for the third dimension, $t(588.609) = -9.424$, $p < 0.001$ (2-tailed). All the three dimensions show significant differences between light and non-light [ɤ].

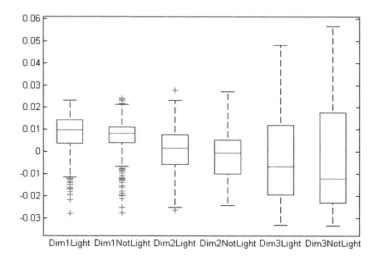

a. All Subjects

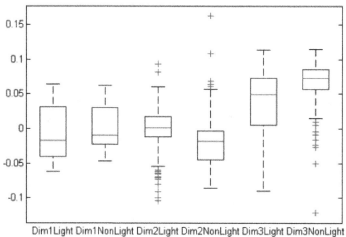

b. Male Group

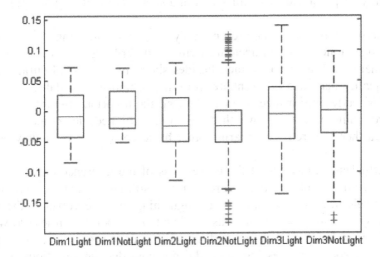

Dim1Light Dim1NotLight Dim2Light Dim2NotLight Dim3Light Dim3NotLight

c. Female Group

Fig. 5. Distribution of the Acoustic Data. (From left to right: First dimension + light [ɤ]; First dimension + non-light [ɤ]; Second dimension + light [ɤ]; Second dimension + non-light [ɤ]; Third dimension + light [ɤ]; Third dimension + non-light [ɤ])

For the female subjects, two-sample T-test results are: for the first dimension, $t(490.241) = -2.354$, $p = 0.019$ (2-tailed); for the second dimension, $t(276.938) = 2.356$, $p = 0.19$ (2-tailed); and for the third dimension, $t(375.890) = -1.138$, $p = 0.256$ (2-tailed). The results show that the two versions of [ɤ] significantly differ from each other in the first and second dimensions, but there exists no significant difference in the third dimension.

4   Discussion and Conclusion

In the current study, the qualities of mid vowel [ɤ] under two lexical contexts, namely in the light syllables of grammatical words and in the non-light syllables of lexical words, are studied by using the method of extracting the MFCCs features and then reducing the dimensions through Laplacian eigenmaps. And the result, as shown by 3D vowel space, indicates that the two versions of [ɤ] are separately located at the central zones of the space, with a small degree of overlapping. Meanwhile, the independent T-test results support the visual observation of the vowel spaces, which indicates that the light [ɤ] and non-light [ɤ] are significantly different in most situations for all the three groups of subjects. Therefore, it could now be safely concluded that the quality of [ɤ] in light syllables distinguishes from that in non-light syllables.

Furthermore, results of the present study support the idea that the traditional term light-tone is not an accurate term for describing the phenomenon of light syllable in Mandarin. In fact, besides shortening the tonal duration, the vowel quality may also differentiate from that of non-light syllables. Considering this study only inspect the case of [ɤ], the notorious flexible vowel in Standard Chinese, to verify whether the aforementioned viewpoint is correct or not, further researches comparing other basic vowels are obviously necessary.

Nevertheless, regardless of the correctness of the inference on light syllable, our fresh insight into the nature of [ɤ] is still significant. As one of the basic vowels in Standard Chinese, distinguishing the sole vowel in the most frequent grammatical words such as "*de*" and "*le*" from that in lexical words would be very helpful for the area of natural language processing. In the past, practices of speech processing often did not consider the variations or allophones of the same phoneme under different lexical contexts. The present work suggests that, at least for the case of [ɤ], that approach is outdate and inaccurate to say the least.

To conclude, the current paper suggests that the further practice of speech processing of Standard Chinese should consider setting up a couple of controlling parameters for the vowel quality of grammatical words. After assigning different vowel values to these grammatical words from that of lexical words, the naturalness of speech synthesis and the precision of speech recognition could get a promising improvement.

5   Acknowledgement

This paper is sponsored by Humanity and Social Science Foundation for Young Scholars of Ministry of Education of China (15YJC740005) and partly supported by Art Fund of Tianjin (No.A14037).

References

1. Wu, Y. 1994. *Mandarin Segmental Phonology*: PhD Dissertation. University of Toronto, Toronto.
2. Duanmu, S. 2007. *The phonology of standard Chinese*. Oxford University Press, Oxford, UK.
3. Lin, Y. 2007. *The Sounds of Chinese (Vol. 1)*. Cambridge University Press, Cambridge, UK.
4. Howie, J. M. 1976. *Acoustical studies of Mandarin vowels and tones*. Cambridge University Press, Cambridge, UK

5. Shi, F. 2002. *The vowel pattern of Beijing Mandarin.* Nankai Linguistics, 1(1):30–36. (In Chinese)
6. Zhang J. 1986. *Acoustic Parameters and Phonological Rules of a Text-ti-speech System for Chinese.* ICASSP 86, Tokyo.
7. Zhang H., Wang S., Chen J., Wang L., Shao G., Li Y., Jiang W. 2008. *The Mandarin Speech Test Materials (MSTMs): Development and application.* Chinese Scientific Journal of Hearing and Speech Rehabilitation, 31(6):16–18. (In Chinese)
8. Yuan, J., Ryant, N., Liberman, M., Stolcke, A., Mitra, V., Wang, W. 2013. *Automatic phonetic segmentation using boundary models.* Proceedings of the Annual Conference of the International Speech Communication Association: 2306–2310.
9. Young, S., Evermann, G., Gales, M., Hain, T., Kershaw, D., Moore, G., Odell, J., Ollason, D., Povey, D., Valtchev, V., et al. 1995. *The Hidden Markov Model Toolkit Book (version 3.4).* Entropic Cambridge Research Laboratory, Cambridge.
10. Feng, X. and Meng, Z. 2010 *Distinctive parameter survey of Mandarin consonants for speech evaluation.* Technical Acoustics, 29(3):297-305. (In Chinese)
11. Wang K., and Shamma S. 1995. *Spectral shape analysis in the central auditory system.* IEEE Transactions on Speech and Audio Processing, 3(5): 382-395.
12. Belkin, M. and Niyogi, P. 2003. *Laplacian eigenmaps for dimensionality reduction and data epresentation.* Neural computation, 15(6):1373-1396.
13. Dang J., Tiede M., Yuan J. 2009. *Comparison of vowel structures of Japanese and English in articulatory and auditory spaces.* INTERSPEECH 2009: 2815-2818.
14. Lu X., Dang J. 2010. *Vowel production manifold: Intrinsic factor analysis of vowel articulation.* IEEE Transactions on Audio, Speech, and Language Processing, 18(5): 1053-1062.
15. Huang, X., Acero, A., Hon, H. 2001. *Spoken language processing: A guide to theory, algorithm, and system development.* Prentice Hall PTR.
16. Wang, H., Dang, J., Feng, H., Wang, H., Yu, Y., Honda, K. 2015. *Investigation of Learning Trajectory of Mandarin for Tibetan Speakers.* APSIPA 2015. Hongkong.

On the Lexical Characteristics of Deception

Qi Su

School of Foreign Languages, Peking University, Beijing, China 100871

Sukia@pku.edu.cn

Abstract. The use of language reflects the way of people thinking. Some research indicate that, people show significant differences in their cognitive state when they are lying. And the differences further reflect in their external language behaviors, which suggests the possibility of distinguishing truth from deception through verbal cues. Expanding the previous studies which mainly focus on the analysis of fabricated events or facts, in this study, we construct a Chinese opinion-oriented deception corpus. Based on the observation and statistics of different word usages in the deceptive and non-deceptive speech, this paper examined the possible word categories which may serve as cues to distinguish between genuine and deceptive reviews, e.g. the second-person pronouns, direct speech and so on.

Keywords: Chinese language, Deception, Corpus, Lexical Characteristics

1   Introduction

As one of the main carriers of everyday interpersonal communication, languages convey both truthful and deceptive information. Lying, which is commonly witnessed in social behavior, takes place both in face-to-face interactions between people, as well as in mediated conversations (e.g., e-mails, weblogs, forums, tweets, and other forms of electronic content) [Hancock et al. 2008]. According to a report in [DePaulo et al. 1996], most people tell one or two lies every day, and one third of daily conversations involve some sort of deception. In fact, people deceive more frequently in their speech than dare to admit. Even more deception exists among the crowd than between individuals [Cohen et al. 2009].

Discerning lies from truths is a challenging task and a significant research topic, which has been widely developed in psychology, sociology, criminology, and linguistics. To model the psychological process of lying, and further understand the factors influencing deception behaviors, researchers have developed several theories, hypotheses and models [Sun 2008], which include Leakage Theory, Information Manipulation Theory, Reality Monitoring Theory, Interpersonal Deception Theory and deception process model to name a few.

An emerging body of research has shown that liars often behave differently than truth-tellers, which include both their language usages and body behaviors. Therefore,

© Springer International Publishing AG 2016
M. Dong et al. (Eds.): CLSW 2016, LNAI 10085, pp. 700–707, 2016
DOI: 10.1007/978-3-319-49508-8_64

cues for identifying deception are numerous, which can be accordingly categorized into verbal cues and non-verbal cues. Non-verbal cues refer to the observable signs during communication, e.g., the speaker's body movements, facial expressions and eye contact with the listeners, while verbal cues focus upon the specific linguistic strategies adopted by the speaker. Currently, most studies in this research field concentrate mainly on the non-verbal cues to deception. Some researchers have employed electronic biofeedback devices to record speakers' physiological responses while lying. Those records can act as quantitative indicators of telling lies [Zhang & Zhang 2008].

According to [Ekman 1984]'s leakage theory, compared with non-verbal behaviors, it is easier for lying people to control their verbal utterances in the communication process. Therefore, non-verbal behavior is more likely to betray a lie. When people verbalize something but their body languages do differ, non-verbal leakage happens. For example, when people are engaged in deception, they are quite likely to have more smiles on faces, change their postures frequently, blink more than usual, make more speech errors and slow down their speaking speed. Although many signs of lying can be observed, the effectiveness of non-verbal cues for deception detection remains limited and unreliable. Some studies even indicate that no scientific evidence exists to support the effectiveness of using those nonverbal behaviors when trying to detect deception. And the overall accuracy rate of catching lies reported in most research is around 55%~60%, only slightly above chance levels [Sun 2008].

Research on verbal cues to deception analyzes lies by inspecting the content of deceptive speeches, and tries to develop a linguistic model to discern truth from deception. In this study, we construct a Chinese corpus comprised of both deceptive and truthful reviews, and aim to shed light on the different linguistic features of these two sub-corpora. The lexical distribution of the two groups of reviews is checked statistically. Then we try to identify the verbal cues which are associated with deception.

2   Related Research

Although research on verbal cues to deception is not as well developed as that on non-verbal cues, some still take textual based deception detection as their research objectives. Recently, more and more researchers begin to analyze linguistic features of deception by computerized measures. The proposed linguistic cues to deception in existing literatures mainly include [Bond & Lee 2005][Newman et al. 2003][Zhou et al. 2004][Hancock et al. 2007]:

1. Word count

Compared with truthful verbal statement, fewer words are being used in deception discourse. This is mainly due to the fact that liars are relatively unfamiliar with the content what they are talking about, thus lying usually takes more mental effort than telling the truth. Some extra cognitive operation like thinking and reasoning are needed during the procedure of fabricating lies, which causes a lie becoming relatively short in length. In addition, the presentation of lies is generally vague and ambiguous, with fewer details and less specific description [Ford 2001][DePaulo et al. 2003].

Yet a description of a real world scene or event is based mainly on memory but imagination. The retrospective memory is usually specific, detailed and vivid, thus potentially contains more perceptual description and contextual information.

However, in [Zhou et al. 2004]'s study on computer-mediated communication (e.g. e-mail), they found that, liars obviously use more words than truth-tellers. Due to the asynchronous and editable nature of such communication, liars have adequate time to adapt their discourses, thus make their speech more realistic and believable by increasing the number of words in the discourses. This is consistent with the research finding concerning the distinction between prepared and unprepared lie. When liars are required instant responses, there are significant differences between their speech and that of the truth-tellers; however, the difference is not obvious anymore if given time to rehearse their speaking. Besides, the differences in the quality of memory between experienced events and imaged events will be reduced with the lapse of time. To disperse the attention of listeners, or enhance the credibility of their claims, liars may add some extra words, providing more information than is needed.

2. The use of pronouns

Most research agrees that liars tend to use fewer self-mentions (first-person pronouns) such as *I, me, myself*. That is mainly due to the liars' lack of personal experiment of their narrated stories, or attempting to dissociate themselves from the lies [Newman et al. 2003]. The use of first-person pronouns is a proclamation of one's ownership of the statement. Through the reducing of self-mentions, liars appear to avoid personal responsibility and possible negative aftereffect for their behaviors. Accordingly, liars usually show excessive use of third-person pronouns than true-tellers [DePaulo et al. 2003].

3. Emotion words

Lying is typically associated with negative emotions such as guilt, nervousness, shame and anxiety, which leads to an increasing use of negative emotion words (e.g. hate, sad, worthless, ugly, nasty) in deceptive discourse [Newman et al. 2003][Zhou et al 2004]. However, [Burgoon et al 2003] indicate that, liars do tend to use more emotional expressions, but there is no significant difference between the use of positive and negative emotions.

4. Other lexical characteristics

Liars tend to choose ambiguous words, fuzzy words, and more general words instead of their hyponyms. Words which reflect cognitive complexity are seldom used in their speech, for example, exclusive words (e.g. but, or, except), action verbs (e.g. walk) and negations. And they also try to reduce the repeated word sequences in the discourse. Besides, by using more modal particles, liars tend to cover up their thought latency, prolong thinking time of fabricating lies, or conceal their guilty.

5. Pausing and speech rate

A pause is a short break in speaking. As a natural signal of discourse segmentation, a pause reflects what the speaker wants to emphasize or clarify. According to [Ekman 1989], pausing serves as one of the most common vocal marks of lying, which shows that the liars' speeches are not completely controlled by their thoughts. Therefore, they fill their speeches with pauses, which enable them to get more time to develop the utterances. Besides, liars may also talk without pauses when a pause is actually necessary, or use longer than normal pauses.

Speak rate can be measured in words per minute. There are several factors which affect the rate of speak, such as the speakers' emotion, thinking speed and personal differences. If one's speaking speed deviates from these constraints, he is quite likely to tell a lie [Yang 2010].

6. Other linguistic signs of unclear thinking

As mentioned above, additional cognitive load and complex mental effort build barriers for liars in organizing their speeches. Therefore, the speech behaviors that indicate unclear thought can be reliable signs of lying, which include incomplete sentences, disordered expression, repetition of thought, self-correction, halting or convoluted phrases, indirect ideas and more slip of the tongue [Walters 2001].

7. Rhetorical devices

The use of rhetorical devices enriches discourse and makes language more expressive. For most liars, they do not use rhetorical embellishment unless those devices help in enhancing the credibility of their lies, e.g., hyperbole, irony, metaphor, rhetorical question and repetition [Yang 2010].

At present, most research in this field effort on the analysis of the statement of pseudo-events or fabricated facts. In addition to those types of lies, deceptive emotion or opinion is also among the commonest forms of lies. And some studies indicate that people lie more when they are talking about their feelings and opinions. Therefore, this study focuses on the opinion oriented lies. We first construct a small scale corpus with both truthful and deceptive review texts. Then, by examining the word-distribution statistically, we aim to reveal lexical characteristic differences between the two sub-corpora.

3   Experimental Design and Corpus Collection

As it is difficult to directly collect opinion-oriented deceptive texts (for example, download from the Internet), we design a topic to collect the texts. 51 College students aged 20 to 25 are selected as participants to give a speech on the topic of "my favorite teacher".

The procedure of corpus collection is as follows:

- Each participant is given approximately 1 minute to describe one of his favorite teachers;
- The participant is then requested to think about a teacher who he dislikes, but describe the teacher with opposite attitudes (i.e., to pretend he like the teacher and thus give a false-positive comment).

Therefore, the first speech is an authentic review while the second shows deceptive opinion.

These recorded audio files are then transcribed manually in the manner of broad transcription. We retain part of the paralinguistic information of the audio files, such as pausing, lengthening, self-correction, word repetition, and incomplete sentences. The transcribed corpus comprises approximately 23,506 Chinese characters, in which 12,380 are from the sub-corpus of truthful reviews and 11,126 from the deceptive one. Below are two sentences respectively from the two sub-corpora.

(i) 我最喜欢的老师是我高中时候的数学老师，她是一个长得非常漂亮，人非常地瘦，而且非常地白，非常有女神气质的一位老师。en，除了人长得漂亮呢，我非常喜欢她的就是她课讲得非常好。她能够非常深入地解释一件数学问题。然后#，深入浅出。另外我觉得她的作#，为人也非常地好，对大家，对所有的同学都和蔼可亲。

My favorite teacher is my high school math teacher. She is very pretty, very slim and white skinned, with a goddess-like quality. uh. Another thing which makes me like her is that she is great at teaching. She can explain mathematics in-depth and # clearly to the layman. Besides, I feel that her #, she is very nice and approachable for us all the students.

(ii) 我也喜欢一个我们的研究生导师。跟他接触，他身上有很多优点，比如说对学生要求很严格，然后对待科研工作很认真，很负责任。en，他身上有我们，en，应该要学习的东西，en，所以说我很喜欢他。

I also like one of our master tutors. By contact with him, (I find that) he has many advantages. For example, he is strict with students, and very involved and responsible in research. uh. We can learn something from him. uh. So I like him very much.

4   Lexical distribution in truthful and deceptive texts

We perform statistical analysis on the lexical distributions of the two transcribed sub-corpora. The "TextMind (WenXin)" system is adopted to identify the semantic category of words. Developed by the Computational Cyber-Psychology laboratory, Institute of Psychology, Chinese academy of sciences, "TextMind" is a Chinese psychological analysis system based on LIWC (Linguistic Inquiry and Word Count) [Gao et al 2013]. LIWC divides English words into more than 80 categories according to their lexical characteristics and psychological features. The lexicon of TextMind is referred to the English lexicon of LIWC2007 and the traditional Chinese lexicon of C-LIWC. And the system also integrates the word segmentation and Part-of-speech tagging modules of both NLPIR and LTP.

Below we summarize the lexical characteristics of the two sub-corpora.

1. Word Count

Consistent with relevant studies, in our corpus of teacher review, deceptive texts (M = 160.80, SE=60.20) use fewer words than truthful ones (M=177.47, SE=52.93). However, the difference between the two is not significant (F = 0.773, p> 0.8). This may be caused by the experimental settings in which the participants are required to provide a one-minute speech. That may reduce the possibility of observing a difference.

2. Personal Pronouns

More first person pronouns (e.g. 我"I", 我们"we") are observed in truthful reviews (M=8.4, SE=3.7) than deceptive ones (M=6.9, SE=4.3), with an insignificant difference level (F = 0.743, p> 0.3). This shows that compared with people telling fact lies, people telling emotional lies are less likely to avoid referring to themselves to refrain from deception.

What is worth noted is that the second person pronoun (e.g. 你"you") plays a role as a distinguishing category in our corpus. There is a significant difference (F=7.461, p<0.01) between second person pronouns used in truthful reviews (M=0.471, SE=0.977) and deceptive reviews (M=0.098, SE=0.36). Some sentences with second person pronouns are shown below:

(iii)在她的身上你能够看得出十足十的中文人的影子
You can feel that she is a typical "Chinese language and literature" scholar.

(iv)上他的课，你从来不会感觉无聊。
You never feel boring attending his course.

(v) 和他的交谈中，你都感到他非常地真诚，恳切。
You feel that he is very sincere and earnest when communicating with him.

Here 你"you" refers to people in general. It is used to denote that the speakers' personal experiences or feelings are actually universal, thereby increasing the credibility of their speech. The second person pronouns are also used by true-tellers to enhance the effect of language expression, boost the emphasis, and help the listeners to feel connected and more into the situation.

3. Emotion words and other adjectives

In our study, emotion words turn to be insignificant in distinguishing truth and lies, as can be seen from the following table.

Table 1. Distribution of emotion words in the corpus

	Truthful reviews	Deceptive reviews	p value
Positive emotion words	M=4.39, SE=2.36	M=3.92, SE=2.34	F=1.016, p>0.3
Negative emotion words	M=0.92, SE=1.20	M=2.46, SE=2.54	F=0.225, p>0.5
All emotion words	M=5.31, SE=2.75	M=3.52, SE=4.73	F=0.340, p>0.5

The top 10 adjectives used in the two sub-corpora are listed as below. In the sub-corpus of truthful reviews, they are "好(good), 认真(serious), 漂亮(beautiful), 强(able), 幽默(humor), 亲切(kind), 耐心(patient), 枯燥(boring - typically load with negations), 清楚(clear), 风趣(funny)". In the sub-corpus of deceptive reviews, they are "好(good), 不错(not bad), 严格(strict), 认真(serious), 严厉(severe), 深刻(profound), 严谨(rigorous), 温暖(warmth), 耐心(patience), 独特(unique)".

As can be seen from the list, since the given topic is "my favorite teacher", almost all the adjectives listed are positive. However, there are still differences on the degree of positive emotion in the two lists (for example, "good" vs. "not bad").

4. Other related features

A significant difference is identified between the uses of direct speech in the two sub-corpora. More direct speech is evidenced in truthful reviews (M=0.588, SE=1.599) than deceptive reviews (M=0.078, SE=0.555, F=8.299, p<0.005).

Direct speech is quoted speech as exactly what the original speaker has said. For the fabricated opinion texts, it may bring heavy cognitive load to forge the speaker's original sayings. Therefore, liars usually do use direct speech, which lead to a far more few usage of direct speech in deceptive texts.

5   Conclusions and Future Work

According to [McCornack 1992]'s Information Manipulation Theory (IMT), in the procedure of interpersonal communication, individuals often face a dilemma of having to weigh their words. On the one hand, they need to provide their interlocutors sufficient information as is required; on the other hand they have to face with the potential risks of revealing some information. In order to reconcile these two conflicting goals, individuals have to adjust the information provided strategically, which is reflected in their external speech. Therefore, verbal cues, just like nonverbal cues, also serve as effective devices in spotting lies.

By the statistical analysis on the words used in both truthful and deceptive narratives of our self-built opinion corpus, we conclude that specific types of words can play an effective role in distinguishing the two types of texts. Admittedly, our current corpus is still inadequate. So, in the follow-up studies we plan to further expand the size of the corpus, and more effective strategies of transcription and semantic annotation are also needed.

6   Acknowledgements

The author thanks the following students from the institute of linguistics and applied linguistics, SFL, PKU for their contributions to this study. They are Yanru Xing, Yufei He and Xiaowei Li. This research is funded by National Natural Science Funds of China (No. 61305089), Beijing Higher Education Young Elite Teacher Project (No. YETP0027), and Beijing Social Science Fund (No. 14WYC041).

Reference

1. Bond G. and Lee A. Y. (2005). Language of lies in prison: Linguistic classification of prisoners' truthful and deceptive natural language. *Applied Cognitive Psychology*, 19, 313-329.

2. Burgoon J., Blair J., Qin T. and Nunamaker J. (2003). Detecting Deception through Linguistic Analysis, *Intelligence and Security Informatics*, 2665, 91-101.

3. Cohen T. R., Gunia B. C., Kim-Jun S. Y., Murnighan J. K. (2009). Do groups lie more than individuals? Honesty and deception as a function of strategic self-interest. *Journal of Experimental Social Psychology*, 45(6), 1321–1324.

4. DePaulo, B. M., Kashy, D. A., Kirkendol, S. E., Wyer, M. M., and Epstein, J. A., 1996, Lying in everyday life, *Journal of Personality and Social Psychology*, 70 (5), 979–995.

5. DePaulo B., Lindsay J. J., Molone B. E., Muhlenbruck L., Charlton K., Cooper H., 2003, Cues to deception, *Psychological Bulletin*, 129, 74-118.

6. Ekman P., 1989, *Lies: Clues to Deceit in the Marketplace, Politics and Marriage* (《如何戳穿谎言》), Shanghai Culture Publishing House. [in Chinese]

7. Ford C., 2001, *Lies!Lies!Lies!* (《说谎：你所不知道的一切》), xinhua publishing house. [in Chinese]

8. Gao R., Hao B., Li H., Gao Y., Zhu T. (2013). Developing Simplified Chinese Psychological Linguistic Analysis Dictionary for Microblog. *International Conference on Brain & Health Informatics* (BHI'13). Maebashi, Japan, 359-368

9. Hancock J., Curry L., Goorha S. and Woodworth M., 2008, On Lying and Being Lied to: A Linguistic Analysis of Deception in Computer-Mediated Communication, *Discourse Processes*, 45(1): 1-23.

10. Hancock, J. T., 2007, Digital deception: When, where and how people lie online, In K. McKenna, T. Postmes, U. Reips, & A. N. Joinson (Eds.), *Oxford handbook of Internet psychology*, Oxford, England: Oxford University Press, 287–301.

11. McCornack, S.A. (1992). Information manipulation theory, *Communication Monographs*, 59, 1-16.

12. Newman M., Pennebaker J., Berry D. and Richards J., 2003, Lying words: Predicting deception from linguistic styles, *Personality and Social Psychology Bulletin*, 29, 665–675.

13. Sun W., 2008, Overview of Research on Lies in the West (西方谎言研究理论综述), *Social Sciences Abroad*, 2, 25-31. [in Chinese]

14. Walters S., 2001, The Truth About Lying: How to Spot a Lie and Protect Yourself from Deception (《挑战谎言——识别谎言的技巧》), Nanhai Press. [in Chinese]

15. Yang F. W., 2010, *The Identification and Study on Lie* (《谎言的识别研究》), PhD dissertation, Huazhong University of Science and Technology. [in Chinese]

16. Zhang T.Y. and Zhang Y.Q., 2008, A Review on Studies of Lying and Lie-detection (说谎作为及其识别的心理学研究), *Advances in Psychological Science*, 16 (4), 651-660. [in Chinese]

17. Zhou L., Burgoon J., Numamaker J. and Twitchell D., 2004, Automating Linguistics-based Cues for Detecting Deception in Asynchronous Computer-mediated Communications, *Group Decision and Negotiation*, 13, 81-106.

An Empirical Study of Gender-related Differences in Topics selection Based on We-Media Corpus[*]

Yubo Wang

School of Chinese Language and Literature / National Institute of Chinese Language Matters and Social Development, Wuhan University, Wuhan, China
wangyubo@whu.edu.cn

Abstract. Our thesis aims to find out the gender-related differences in topics selection in Chinese We-Media through an extensive amount of classified blog corpus text. According to the Chinese blog corpus text, there is a statistically significant differences in topics selection between men and women. Based on the empirical study, we questioned the previous studies which suggest that men incline to choose politics and economic-related topics. We believe that in different communicative context, Men tend to change the topics accordingly, whereas women remain the same.

Keywords: Gender-related differences; We-Media corpus; Text classification; Topics selection; Quantitative study

1   Preface

Lately, the academia tend to shift the research emphasis from gender-related differences in language to communicative discourse patterns. Wardhaugh (1998,2010) assumed that the speech behavior and discourse patterns of both genders have various degrees of difference, which reflects on the aspects of topics selection, topics number, strategies for turn-taking and so on.

Concerning the research on the difference about men and women's discourse selection, foreign studies performed it relatively early, According to the survey regarding traditional working-class family. Klein (1971) had found out that men mainly talk about things relate to works, sports and so on when they stay together. On the contrary, women mainly talk about families, such as children, the household, conjugal relationship and etc. Krammer assumed that men always talk incessantly on aspects of business, politics, legal matter, taxes, sports. Conversely, women often centralized the topics of books, food and drink, life troubles, life-style when construct discourse. By means of investigating middle-class. Aries (1976,1982) assumed that women mainly talk about their personal situation, reveal their feelings when they are with friends (especially with the same gender), while men rarely do so, they talk a lot

---

*   Project supported by the National Social Science Fund (No. 12CYY030), the Humanity and Social Science Youth foundation of Ministry of Education of China (No. 12YJC740106).

M. Dong et al. (Eds.): CLSW 2016, LNAI 10085, pp. 708–716, 2016
DOI: 10.1007/978-3-319-49508-8_65

about sports, politics, various competition and their own perspective. Myerhoff(1980) investigated American-Jewish community, and found out that men love to talk something more abstract or conceptually, such as politics, economy, religion and so on in daily communication, Conversely , women tend to discuss something directly relate to personal life , such as children, food, health, neighbors, and family.

  The foreign scholars had an earlier discovery that there exist some differences in the topics selection among genders. For example: Klein(1971), Kramer(1974), Aries(1976,1982), Myerhoff(1980), Wardhaugh(1998) and other scholars have been researching on the middle and old aged working or middle class folks in American-Jewish community, By and large, that men usually do not involve personal emotions in the conversation between the people with their own gender. Subjects of their conversations mainly focus on politics, economic, competition, sports, commerce and so on. Conversely, women tend to choose topics that are highly related to the present situation and much more personal. Therefore, they have a tendency to talk about themselves, emotions, family, children, spousal relationship and so on .

  Our scholars start the research of gender-related differences in topics selection much later than foreign scholars. Related domestic researches such as Xu Lisheng(1997), Li Jingwei(1998), Zhao Ronghui(2003), Cui Yanying(2012), these scholars mainly explore the gender-related differences in topic selection . and researches mainly summarizes the results of foreign studies instead of perform the field research aimed at Chinese gender-related differences in topic selection.

  Xu Lisheng（1997）assumed that the topics which debated by women are usually tend to be more personal and immediate. Compared with this, men prefer topics impersonal, and they often keep a distance from the situations which occurred instantly and immediately. Jia Yuxin (1997:426) assumed that the female is characterized by emotional orientation, but the male is instrumental orientation. Zhao Ronghui (2003) charted the graph concerning tendency of the gender-related differences in topics selection. The double-sided arrow of AB stands for the continuation of different topics. Obviously, men take an interest in A topics direction (Politics and Military Affairs), whereas women keep a preference to B topics direction (Sentimental and Fashion).

  Due to the Eastern and Western Culture differences, people tend to have different topic preferences regardless of their gender identity. Therefore, foreign researches are unable to fully reflect the gender-related differences in topic selection. On the basis of extensive classified We-Media blog corpus text, our research aims to find out gender-related differences in Chinese topic selection.

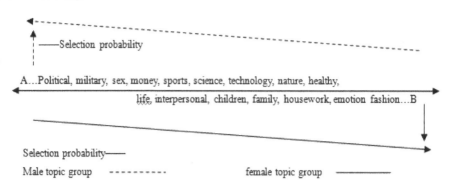

2   Classification and Preferences in topics

Firstly, we randomly picked 1008755 blog posts that possess gender characteristics of authors from the Network Media Monitoring Corpus, which was under the National Language Resource Monitoring & Research Centre. With an amount of 500889 blog posts by men and 507866 blog posts by women, these data were used to construct a We Media Corpus.

The topics of these blog posts have been sorted into 27 types according to the topic classification of Sina Blog, Blogcn, NetEase Blog and Zhao Ronghui(2003). Procedures of the text classification are listed below:

① Traditional Chinese and Simplified Chinese Conversion was applied to all blog posts;

② Text segmentation was performed on all blog posts using the text segmentation software;

③ Regular Expression and stop words list were used to filter the segmented blog posts;

④ 27 types of training corpus will be learned by the Machine Learner, forming 27 term frequency lists;

⑤ There was a manual intervention on the 27 term frequency lists. In the light of professional knowledge, Strengthen the low occurrence rate but highly distinctive proper nouns' weightage.

⑥ Naive Bayesian was used to calculate the Posterior Probability of each category. The topic which has the highest value of posterior probability was used as a classification. Table 1 shows the number of topic texts after classification.

Table 1 shows the number of topics after classification.

Table 1. The number of different topics of blog posts shows

Topics	Men	Women	Difference Value
Digressions	151511	115925	35586
Domestic life	126634	208957	-82323
Marriage	70659	79207	-8548

IT Digital	38353	17482	20871
Sports	28710	4716	23994
TV & Films	15622	10532	5090
Entertainment	8071	18017	-9946
Games	7351	699	6652
Tourism	7289	10506	-3217
Literature & Arts	6498	3072	3426
Education	5973	14094	-8121
History & Culture	5659	839	4820
Life Philosophy	4072	1631	2441
Finance& Economics	3491	633	2858
Law & Policies	3098	267	2831
Health & Medical	2746	6160	-3414
Delicacies	2562	7315	-4753
Religion Ideology	2361	273	2088
Technologies	1953	279	1674
Job Recruitment	1935	972	963
Military Affairs	1684	139	1545
Augury	1637	2035	-398
Political Regime	1334	214	1120
Property Assets	1204	457	747
Beauty & Skincare	197	2118	-1921
Trend& Consumptions	157	1337	-1180
Gender Physiology	125	10	115

2.1 Men's topic preferences

Taking all types of male topics as standard, we chart a curve graph in descending order as follow:

Table 2. Descending order graph of men's topic selection

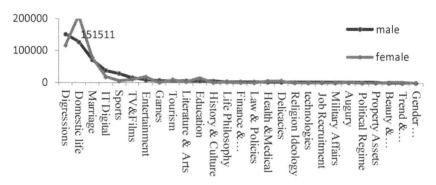

Digression is the most discussed topic in men's blog posts, as it occupied 30.25% of the total number of men's blog posts. It is a topic that could not be classified under the other 26 types of topics, as it does not have a fixed subject. Most digression come from a random comment and the texts are often short. Secondly, domestic life, marriage and IT digital account for 25.28%, 14.11% and 7.66% of men's blog posts respectively. The least discussed topic is gender physiology, which only accounts for 0.025% of the total of men's blog post.

Fig. 1. Distribution of men's Topic Preferences

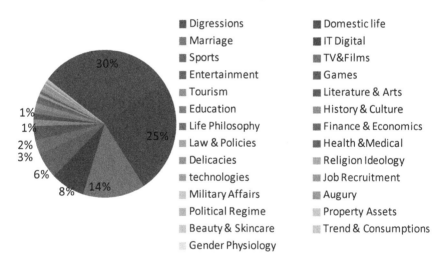

The data above suggests different perspectives from various scholars. Klein(1971), Aries(1976,1982), Myerhoff(1980), Wardhaugh(1986), Wardhaugh(1998), Zhao Ronghui(2003) and other scholars has assumed that men prefer to discuss about politics, laws, sports and economic related topics in daily chats. Zhao Ronghui(2003)used a tendency chart to conclude the gender-related differences in the choice of topics. The double-sided arrow of AB stands for continuations of different topics. Men generally have a greater interest in A side of topics (e.g. Politics and Military Affairs), but women have a greater interest in B side of topics (Sentimental and Fashion).

Politics Sex Sports Nature Life Children Chores Fashion

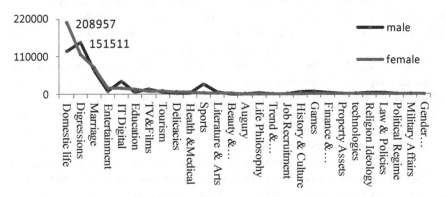

A   Military Finance Technology Health Social Family Emotions   B

Men have significantly different topic selection in the most discussable topic and daily chat in online blog. However, our research findings show that "Digression, Domestic Affairs, Marriage, IT Digital and sports" are the most discussed topics in men's blog posts. These topics account for 83% of the total number of texts, while the remaining 22 topics only account for 17% of all the blog posts. Among this 17%, Finance and Economics account for 0.7%, Political Regime accounts for 0.27% and Laws and Policies account for 0.62%. This proves that men's topic preference of We-Media differs from daily communication, and the respondent and communicative context have an effect on the choice of topics. Men have a wide variety in topics selection inclination under different occasion.

2.2   Women's topic preferences

Taking all types of female topics as standard, we chart a curve graph in descending order as follow:

Table 3. Descending order graph of female Topic selection

The most discussed topic by women is domestic affairs, which account for 41.14% of the total number while "digression, marriage, entertainment" account for 22.83%, 15.6% and 3.55% respectively. The least discussed topic is gender physiology, with only 10 posts, which account for a mere 0.002% of the total posts. Our data shows that there is no significant difference in We Media's most discussed topics and daily chats.

Fig. 2. Distribution of women's topic preferences

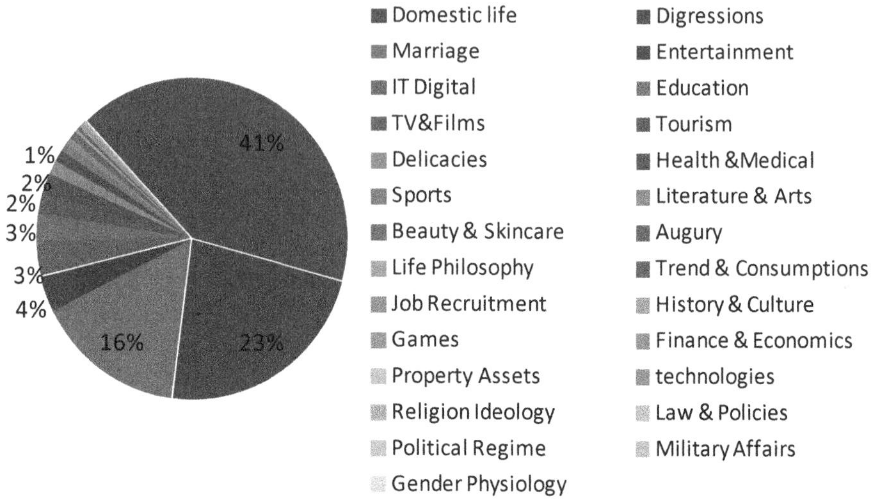

- Domestic life
- Marriage
- IT Digital
- TV&Films
- Delicacies
- Sports
- Beauty & Skincare
- Life Philosophy
- Job Recruitment
- Games
- Property Assets
- Religion Ideology
- Political Regime
- Gender Physiology
- Digressions
- Entertainment
- Education
- Tourism
- Health &Medical
- Literature & Arts
- Augury
- Trend & Consumptions
- History & Culture
- Finance & Economics
- technologies
- Law & Policies
- Military Affairs

2.3   The stability of topic preferences

The discrepancy between male and female topic selection have some differences, according to domestic and international study results in daily communicative situation.

In view of observed research results, Previous Studies assumed that men do not contact the type of topics like domestic affairs and marriage in their daily communication. However, our research results suggest that on the basis of the male blog posts, domestic affairs and marriage are the most frequently discussed topics, as it account for 39% of all blog posts. Based on the platform of We-Media corpus, we notice that there is a convergence of topic preferences between men and women. The top 3 topics like "Domestic affairs, Digressions and Marriage" are chosen by both two genders. The only difference was the sequence, for men the most discussed topic was digression, while for women the most discussed topic was domestic affairs. The results show that, male topics change in different context (We-Media and daily chats), while certain stability is observed in female choice of topics. This also suggests that under two different communicative circumstances like daily communication and online blog, men and women have some differences in topic selection.

3   Significance Level Test on Differences

Although the top 3 topic preferences of both men and women are the same, but this can not prove that there are no gender-related differences in choosing topics. With the help of statistical analysis, our thesis aims to find out whether there are statistical significance gender-related differences in topics selection.

Due to the difference in the data mode, there was also a difference in the method of testing the significant difference level. Depending on the number of sample groups in the interval data, we could use T-test or ANOVA for interval data analysis, and Chi-square tests for nominal or ordinal data. We decided to use the non parametric test to verify the significant levels of gender-related differences in the choice of topics, as these 27 topic categories are not considered as interval data, and the different value does not correspond with the normal distribution, which means it does not accord with the requirements of a parameter test.

Non-parametric test does not depend on the statistical analysis of population distribution, but is used to verify whether the data came from the same population when it does not obey the rule of normal distribution. Our research conducts the Chi-square tests for independence. With the help of data analysis software SPSS 22.0, we obtain the Chi-square tests results as below.

Table 4. Chi-Square Tests

	Value	df	Asymp. Sig. (2-sided)
Pearson Chi-Square	86702.647a	26	.000
Likelihood Ratio	92547.887	26	.000
Linear-by-Linear Association	138.716	1	.000
N of Valid Cases	1008772		
a. 0 cells (.0%) have expected count less than 5. The minimum expected count is 67.03.			

We could find out the "Pearson Chi-square" and the value of Asymp.Sig. by looking at the table above. Pearson Chi-Square value, which is the x2 value, is 86702.647; whereas the Asymp.Sig.value, in other words p-value, is .000. When the p-value is <0.05, there is a significant difference between the two. If the p-value is >0.05, there is no significant difference between the two. The degree of freedom from the test is df=(r-1)*(K-1), which means the number of rows minus 1 times the number of columns minus 1, df=(27-1)*(3-1)=52. Based on the Chi-square distribution table, the x2 threshold value that corresponds with df=52, a=0.05 is 67.50. Since the x2 value (86702.647) is greater than the threshold value, with a p-value<0.05 (0.000), we can conclude that there are statistically significant gender-related differences in choice of topics in blog platform.

4   Conclusion

Based on our research results, we are able to conclude that :(1) On the basis of blog text, there are significant gender-related differences in topics selection; (2) Men often change their topics when communicative context change, whereas women tend to remain the same. Topics such as "politics, gender, economic, sports" are common in men's daily communication but not in online blog. On the other hand, the academia assume that topics relate with family and emotions are rarely discussed by men in daily communication, nevertheless turn out to be the most discussed topics in online blogs. We suspect that reason of that change is due to the properties of We-Media platform, which characterized by personal, commutative, selective and openness. Which differentiate the context of We-Media platform from other communicative context.

There's no doubt that: gender-related differences in topic selection are not only limited to adults, this phenomenon also exist in teenagers and children, Based on the study regarding blacks and whites's daily discourse state. Brooks-Gunn(1979), Gookwin(1990) assumed that white boys mainly talk about sports , exchange various information , whereas white girls mainly discuss school affairs , expose their inner feelings. Black boys prefer publicize their own "achievement", on the contrary, black girls talk about their own appearance, make-up and interpersonal relationship.

References:
1. Wardhaugh, R. 1998.Introduction to Socialinguistics [M]. Beijing: *Foreign Language Teaching and Research Press.*
2. Goodwin, M. H. 1990.He-Said-She-Said: Talk as Social Organization among Black Children. [M].*Bloomington: Indiana University Press.*
3. Zhao Ronghui.2003. Language and gender——The study of colloquial language from the perspective of sociolinguistics [M].Shanghai: *Shanghai Foreign Language Education Press.*[In Chinese]
4. Aries, E. 1976. Interaction patterns and themes of male, female, and mixed groups. *Small Group Behaviour* .7(1), pp. 7-18.
5. Aries, E. 1982. Verbal and nonverbal behavior in single-sex and mix-sex groups. *Psychological Reports* .51, 127-34.
6. Brooks-Gunn, J. & Matthews, W. 1979. He and She: How Children Develop Their Sexrole Identity. *Englewood Cliffs, NJ: Prentice-Hall.*
7. Cui Yanying.2012.Gender differences in compliment topics in American english——Take American script"Drop Dead Diva"as example [J]. *Journal of North University of China:Social Science Edition,6.* [In Chinese]
8. Klein, J. 1971. The family in "traditional" working-class England. In M. Anderson(ed.) *Sociology of the Family,* Baltimore, Penguin.
9. Kramer, C. 1974. Wishy-washy mommy talk [J]. *Psychology Today,* 82-85.
10. Li Jingwei.1998. Language gender-related differences and its cause analysis [J]. *Shandong Foreign Language Teaching,* 12~16. [In Chinese]
11. Myerhoff, B. 1980. Number Our Day. *New York,Simon & Schuster.*
12. Wardhaugh, R. 2010.An Introduction to Sociolinguistics. 6th edition. *Oxford: Wiley Blackwell.*
13. Xu Lisheng. 1997. Studies on gender-related differences in discourse feature. *Journal of Foreign Languages,* CSRP-03-06. [In Chinese]

The interaction of semantic and orthographic processing during Chinese sinograms recognition: An ERP Study

Hao Zhang[1], Fei Chen[1], Nan Yan[1(✉)], Lan Wang[1], I-Fan Su[2] and Manwa L. Ng[2]

[1] CAS Key Laboratory of Human-Machine Intelligence-Synergy Systems, Shenzhen Institutes of Advanced Technology, Chinese Academy of Sciences, Shenzhen, China
zhanghao@siat.ac.cn, nan.yan@siat.ac.cn
[2] Division of Speech and Hearing Sciences, The University of Hong Kong, Hong Kong
ifansu@hku.hk, manwa@hku.hk

Abstract. The present study investigated the interaction of semantic and orthographic processing during compound sinogram recognition, using event related potentials (ERPs) and a picture-word matching task. The behavioral results showed that participants generally needed more time to make a response and were more prone to make mistakes, when the paired mismatch sinogram was orthographically similar or semantically related to the picture's matching name. The N400 results indicated the main effect of semantics and the significant interaction of semantics by orthography. Moreover, only under the semantically related condition (S+), the mean amplitude of N400 was more negative going in orthographically similar condition (O+) than in orthographically dissimilar one (O-), while there was no significant difference under the semantically unrelated condition (S-). Consequently, the sub-lexical orthographic information plays an important role in discriminating the sinograms sharing related semantics.

Keywords: Interaction · Semantic-Orthographic Processing · Sinogram Recognition · N400

1 Introduction

There are substantial studies confirming that the orthographic information was mandatorily co-activated during word recognition (Grainger and Jacobs, 1996; Muneaux and Ziegler, 2004; Racine and Grosjean, 2005). A number of the related studies have adopted the picture-word interference paradigm in which orthographic representations were manipulated to detect its influences on word recognition (Lupker, 1982; Underwood and Briggs, 1984), and found a facilitation effect in distractors overlapping in spelling in the tasks of visual word recognition. Several studies (Starreveld and La Heij, 1995; Roelofs et al., 1996) have manipulated the orthographic and semantic representations of the picture's name in order to observe the effects of orthographic and semantic interactions on word production. These behavioral findings indicated an interaction of linguistic codes in semantic, orthographic and phonological representation in the mental lexicon.

© Springer International Publishing AG 2016
M. Dong et al. (Eds.): CLSW 2016, LNAI 10085, pp. 717–727, 2016
DOI: 10.1007/978-3-319-49508-8_66

As a non-alphabetic hieroglyphic, Chinese is believed as an ideal candidate to test the orthographic effects on word recognition. Picture naming task has been adopted in several studies, reaching a consensus that the orthographic representation has a facilitation effect on sinogram production, and the orthographic facilitation is actually independent from phonological facilitation (Bi et al., 2009; Zhang et al., 2009; Zhang and Weekes, 2009; Zhang and Damian, 2012). Su et al. (2012) adopted the picture naming task and manipulated the semantic and orthographic relatedness to the picture's name, in order to find out the interconnectedness between semantic and orthographic processing. They put forward the proposal that the orthographic effect in Chinese word production is located at the semantic or the lemma level. However, few researches were reported on the neural activity in the interactions of semantic and orthographic processing.

With the high temporal resolution, event related potentials (ERPs) are likely to be an ideal way to explore the neural underpinnings of the interaction of semantic and orthographic processing in sinogram recognition. It is well established that the negative-going potential component N400, typically maximal over centro-parietal electrode sites, has been critically seen as an index of semantic processing, and the contextual semantic manipulations could lead to changes in N400 response (Brown and Hagoort, 1993; Lau et al., 2008). Hamm et al. (2002) manipulated the subtle semantic incongruity and the N400 effect was discovered to picture stimuli that were semantically incongruous to a prime word. Consequently, the N400 response may provide us a tractable window to explore the interactions of semantic and orthographic processing during Chinese sinograms recognition.

More than 80% of sinograms (Wang and Tsai, 2011), namely Chinese characters, are phonograms which consist of two functional components: a semantic radical and a phonetic radical, with the former one usually providing the semantic category information, and the latter one providing the articulation cues. There are substantial and growing evidences that recognizing a sinogram involves the parallel processing of its radicals (Ding et al., 2004). According to the relationship between the meaning of semantic radical and that of the host phonogram, sinograms could be divided into semantically opaque sinogram whose meaning differ significantly from the semantic radical (e.g. 骄, jiao1, meaning *pride*, the semantic radical 马, ma3, meaning *horse*) and the semantically transparent sinogram whose meaning is closely related to its semantic radical (e.g. 植, zhi2, meaning *plant*, the semantic radical 木, mu4, meaning *wood*) (Chen and Weekes, 2004). Considering the orthographic conditions of Chinese sinogram, it is feasible to manipulate the semantic radicals to produce orthographic similar and semantic related pairs (e.g. 狗-狼), orthographic similar and semantic unrelated pairs (e.g. 狗-猜), orthographic dissimilar and semantic related pairs (e.g. 狗-鼠), orthographic dissimilar and semantic unrelated pairs (e.g. 狗-眉). By adopting behavioral and electrophysiological measures, the primary aim of this study is to compare the differences in response for the aforementioned four kinds of pairs, in order to find some cues for the interaction of semantic and orthographic processing in Chinese sinogram recognition.

2 Methods

2.1 Participants and materials

Twenty (10 females) right-handed native Mandarin speakers aged 19-27 (M = 23.89 years, SD = 2.78 years) were recruited in the current study. All the participants did not record any speech or hearing problems, and had no history of neurological or psychiatric abnormalities. Each of them had normal or correct-to-normal vision, and was paid for their participation in this study. Written informed consent was obtained from each participant. Approval of the experiment was obtained from the Human Research Ethics Committee of Shenzhen Institutes of Advanced Technology.

Twenty black and white line drawings were selected from Snodgrass and Vanderwart picture database (Snodgrass and Vanderwart, 1980), all of these pictures were evaluated by naming consistency, familiarity, representation consistency and visual complexity. Each selected picture could be named by a single sinogram, and was paired with five kinds of sinograms written in modern Chinese script with a phonetic and a semantic radical. In the matching condition, the sinogram was exactly the name of the picture (e.g. 狗-狗, meaning *dog-dog*). The other four conditions were different types of mismatch: the 'O+S+' condition (orthographically similar and semantically related, e.g. 狗-狼, meaning *dog-wolf*), the 'O+S-' condition (orthographically similar and semantically unrelated, e.g. 狗-猜, meaning *dog-guess*), the 'O-S+' condition (orthographically dissimilar and semantically related, e.g. 狗-鼠, meaning *dog-mouse*), and the 'O-S-' condition (orthographically dissimilar and semantically unrelated, e.g. 狗-眉, meaning *dog-eyebrow*). On the whole, there are 20 pictures and 100 paired sinograms included in the experiment.

All the testing sinograms were matched in terms of mean character frequency[1] and mean number of strokes. Furthermore, in order to control the orthographic similarity and semantic relatedness among the four mismatch conditions, a questionnaire survey was conducted based on a 5 points Likert scale of sinogram pairs. The rating scores of orthographic similarity between O+ and O- conditions were significantly different (all $ps < 0.001$). Likewise, the rating scores of semantic relatedness between S+ and S- conditions were obviously different (all $ps < 0.001$). Properties of different kinds of paired sinograms were shown in Table. 1.

Table 1. Properties and examples of different conditions of paired sinograms for picture stimuli

Conditions	Match	Mismatch			
		O+S-	O+S+	O-S+	O-S-
Examples	狗	猜	狼	鼠	眉
	/kəu3/	/tɕʰai1/	/laŋ 2/	/ʂu3/	/mei2/

---

[1] All the stimuli were selected in a word frequency database from the Centre for Chinese Linguistics of Peking University (URL: http://ccl.pku.edu.cn:8080/ccl_corpus/CCL_CC_Sta_Xiandai.pdf, download on 6th May 2010).

	dog	guess	wolf	rat	eyebrow
Frequency	48.45 (32.35)	38.63 (30.86)	30.78 (32.7)	46.34 (28.12)	45.08 (19.96)
Strokes	9.65 (2.08)	10.15 (2.11)	10.1 (1.65)	9.55 (1.79)	9.65 (1.81)
OS Rating	N/A	2.73 (0.69)	2.74 (0.7)	1.1 (0.14)	1.06 (0.07)
SR Rating	N/A	1.2 (0.2)	3.59 (0.72)	3.61 (0.52)	1.06 (0.09)

Note. Frequency is computed as per million. "OS Rating" represents orthographic similarity rating, and "SR Rating" represents semantic relatedness rating. In these rating systems, "1" is absolutely dissimilar/unrelated, "5" is absolutely similar/related. Standard deviations are given in brackets.

2.2   Procedure

After familiarized with all the testing pictures, participants were seated in a sound-attenuating booth. Each trial began with a fixation cross (+) appeared in the center of the monitor for 500ms, then a picture (e.g. *dog*) was presented in the middle of the monitor accompanied with the paired sinogram. Participants were instructed to decide whether the paired sinogram matched with the picture's name by pressing one of two keys on a mouse. Presentation of testing trials was terminated once the participant made a response. Next trial would begin after a blank screen presented for a random duration between 800 and 1200ms (Fig. 1.). Pseudo-random stimulus sequences design was adopted to avoid the same picture appearing successively. The whole experiment consisted of 320 trials, 160 of which were matching trials, randomly interleaved with other mismatch trials: O+S+ condition (40 trials), O+S- condition (40 trials), O-S+ condition (40 trials), O-S- condition (40 trials).

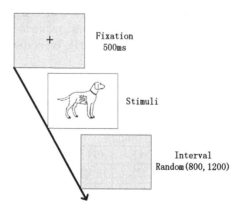

Fig. 1. Illustration of the experimental procedure

2.3   EEG recordings

The EEG data were recorded using an EGI (Electrical Geodesics, Inc.) GES410 system with 64 channel HydroCel GSN electrode nets. EEG data were recorded continuously with vertex (Cz) as the referenced electrode, and re-referenced to the average-mastoid reference in off-line analyses. In the off-line analysis, continuous data were filtered by a phase-shift free high-pass 0.5 Hz, low-pass 30 Hz filters. ERP measurement was time-locked to the visual onset of picture and paired sinogram. The EEG data were segmented from 100ms before the stimulus onset to 800ms post-stimulus onset, with the 100ms pre-stimulus used as the baseline. Trials with excessive ocular or movement artifacts were rejected, and only trials with correct responses were accepted for averaging ERP.

2.4   Data analyses

For behavioral data, mean reaction time (RT) and accuracy rate (ACC) of the four mismatch conditions were computed among each participant. To confirm the effects of semantic and orthographic processing, a repeated measures ANOVA was conducted with semantic and orthographic variations as independent variables.

For ERP data, based on previous studies the visual stimuli may trigger three components: N1, P2, and N400 (Yen et al, 2014). The chosen time windows of three components were N1 (90-130 ms), P2 (140-200 ms), and N400 (350-450 ms), which were determined by the global field power averaged across all conditions and participants (cf. Zhang et al., 2013). Statistical analyses were focused on the mean amplitude and latency of the component associated with visual word recognition: N400 (Brown et al., 2000). Greenhouse-Geisser corrections were applied when needed.

3   Results

3.1   Behavioral data

A summary of the behavioral findings was shown in Table 1. RTs from incorrect responses or deviated by more than ±3 SD were all discarded. For RTs, a repeated measures ANOVA, with semantics and orthography as two within-subject factors, showed both the main effect of semantics (F (1, 19) = 20.35, $p < 0.001$), orthography (F (1, 19) = 82.65, $p < 0.001$) and the interactions of semantics by orthography (F (1, 19) = 20.06, $p < 0.001$) were significant. Tukey's HSD post hoc comparison revealed that participants took more time to make a response in S+ conditions relative to S- conditions (S+: 755 ms; S-: 694 ms, $p < 0.001$), and in O+ conditions relative to O- conditions (O+: 733 ms; O-: 715 ms, $p < 0.001$).

For ACCs, a repeated measures ANOVA showed the main effect of semantics (F (1, 19) = 9.19, $p < 0.05$) and orthography (F (1, 19) = 36.61, $p < 0.001$), but not the interaction of semantics by orthography (F (3, 76) = 0.39, $p > 0.05$). Specifically, Tukey's HSD post hoc comparison revealed that the ACC was significantly reduced in S+ compared to S- conditions (S+: 93.6%; S-: 98.3%, $p < 0.001$), or in O+ to O-conditions (O+: 94.9%; O-: 96.9%, $p < 0.05$). This means that participants were more prone to make mistakes in semantically related or orthographic similar distractors.

Table 2. Mean reaction time (RT) and accuracy rate (ACC) of each mismatch condition (data in brackets were standard deviations)

Conditions	ACC (%)	RT (ms)
O+S-	96.9 (3.8)	713 (75)
O+S+	92.6 (4.8)	755 (86)
O-S+	94.1 (5.5)	756 (89)
O-S-	99.3 (1.2)	676 (70)

3.2   ERP data

Grand averaged waveforms of ERPs in two selected potentials are shown in Fig. 2.

3.2.1   N1-P2 analyses

Although the amplitude of P2 in orthographically dissimilar and semantically related condition (O-S+ condition) seemed to have higher values in this potential component, repeated measures ANOVA showed that neither the main effect of semantics and orthography, nor the interaction of semantics by orthography were significant in both earlier potential components (all ps > 0.05). This means that there were no basic differences among the four mismatch conditions in these two earlier neural activities.

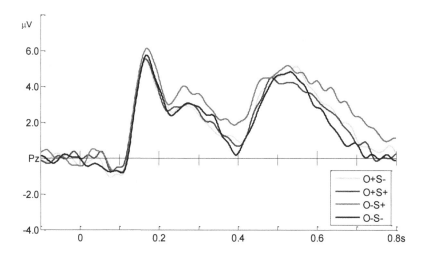

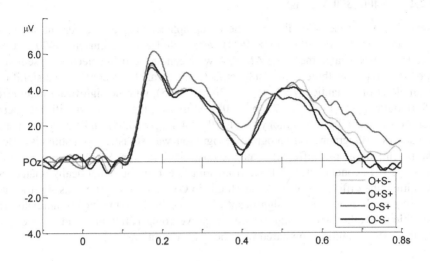

Fig. 2. Grand averaged waveforms of ERPs for Chinese sinograms recognition in electrodes of Pz and POz. The upper one represents waveforms of Pz, and the following one represents POz

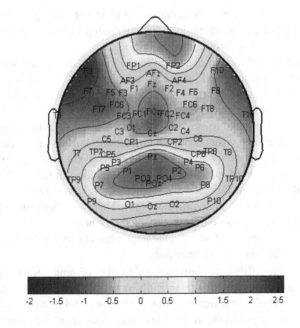

Fig. 3. Topographical map of N400 between 350 and 450 ms

3.2.2   N400 (350-450 ms) analyses

According to previous studies and the topographical map of the current study, six electrodes (P1, Pz, P2, PO3, POz, PO4) were included in the current N400 analyses (see Fig. 3.). Repeated measures ANOVA were conducted using electrodes, semantics and orthography as three within-subject factors. The analyses confirmed a significant main effect of semantics (F (1, 19) = 7.36, $p < 0.05$), with no significant main effect of orthography (F (1, 19) = 1.77, $p > 0.05$). Moreover, there was a significant interaction of semantics by orthography (F (1, 19) = 4.43, $p < 0.05$), indicating that the influence of orthography on sinogram recognition was statistically distinguishable in the magnitude across different semantic conditions (S+ vs. S-). Simple main effect analyses were conducted with Bonferroni adjustment. In the semantically related (S+) condition, the difference of N400 amplitude in O+ vs. O- condition was significant ($p < 0.05$), while there was no significant difference in the semantically unrelated (S-) condition. In other words, significantly negative going N400 amplitudes were found for the O+S+ condition compared with the O-S+ condition.

4   Discussion

The present study utilized both behavioral and electrophysiological measures with a picture-word matching task to explore the interaction between semantic and orthographic processing during sinograms recognition.

The results of the behavioral data showed the main effect of semantics and orthography in both response time (RT) and accuracy rate (ACC). That is to say, when the paired mismatch sinogram is orthographically similar or semantically related to the picture's matching name, participants generally need more time to make a response and are more prone to make mistakes. Taft and colleagues (2006) proposed a hierarchical model concerning visual word identification, and assumed that the orthography, semantics and phonology were interactively activated during word recognition. In the current picture-word matching task, the semantic information of the matching sinogram could be provided directly by the picture, and not necessarily represented by the related information of a matching sinogram. Therefore, both the orthographic and semantic information of a sinogram (i.e. a picture's name) could be co-activated automatically at the absence of visual character presentation and had an interference effect on the participants' discrimination.

The results of the ERPs data showed a main effect of semantics in the mean amplitude of N400 component, with semantically unrelated conditions being more negative-going than that of semantically related conditions. N400 contributes to the comprehension of language, and the amplitude of this component is altered by the contextual semantic surroundings (Brown and Hagoort, 1993). N400 effect of the current study was consistent with previous researches, which are focusing on the manipulation of context, showing that incongruent context generate more negative-going waveform than congruent context (Brown et al., 2000; Hamm et al., 2002).

Moreover, the results of N400 amplitude also revealed an interaction between orthography and semantics. The orthographic effect on sinogram recognition is actually regulated by different semantic conditions. Only under the semantically related circumstance (S+), the N400 difference between orthographically similar (O+) and dissimilar (O-) condition was significant while no significant difference was found under semantically unrelated condition (S-). Semantics of the overall Chinese character is the upmost deciding factor during sinogram discrimination, and orthography effect is affiliated to that of semantics.

Zhou and colleagues (1999) proposed an assumption that in the recognition of compound sinogram, the visual word input is automatically decoded into different orthographic units, and these units map to the orthographic representations in the mental lexicon simultaneously. That is to say, the processing of radicals is involved in host compound sinogram recognition. The function of a radical is taken into account, in considering the sub-lexical processing of radicals (Chen and Weekes, 2004). It has to be noted that in current study, the orthographic manipulations are concentrated on the semantic radicals. More specifically, under the orthographic similar conditions, the sinograms share the same semantic radicals. Under the semantically related condition, the sub-lexical processing of the orthography (i.e. semantic radical) may increase the overall semantic processing load of the Chinese character. The additional processing of semantic radical may account for the significant difference of N400 amplitude between the O-S+ and O+S+ condition. Consequently, the orthographic information plays an important role in understanding the overall semantics during semantic-related sinogram recognition.

5 Conclusion

In this study, both behavioral and electrophysiological measures were adopted to investigate the interaction of semantic and orthographic processing during Chinese sinogram recognition. To conclude, both the semantic and orthographic information conveyed by the sinograms affect the behavioral performance while conducting picture-word matching task. Moreover, the interaction between semantic and orthographic processing in N400 sheds light upon the hypothesis that the sub-lexical orthographic information plays an important role in distinguishing compound sonograms which overlap with each other in terms of semantics.

Acknowledgement. This study was jointly supported by a grant from National Natural Science Foundation of China (NSFC 61135003, 91420301 and 61401452), Shenzhen Speech Rehabilitation Technology Laboratory and Health and Health Services Research Fund (HHSRF).

References

1. Bi, Y., Xu, Y., Caramazza, A.: Orthographic and phonological effects in the picture–word interference paradigm: Evidence from a logographic language. Applied Psycholinguistics **30**, 637-658 (2009)
2. Brown, C., Hagoort, P.: The processing nature of the N400: Evidence from masked priming. Journal of Cognitive Neuroscience **5**, 34-44 (1993)
3. Brown, C., Hagoort, P., Chwilla, J.D. An event-related brain potential analysis of visual word priming effects. Brain and language **72**, 158-190 (2000)
4. Chen, M.J., Weekes, S.B.: Effects of semantic radicals on Chinese character categorization and character decision. Chinese Journal of psychology **46**, 181-196 (2004)
5. Ding, G., Peng, D., Taft, M. The nature of the mental representation of radicals in Chinese: a priming study. Journal of Experimental Psychology: Learning, Memory, and Cognition **30**, 530 (2004)
6. Grainger, J., Jacobs, M.A. Orthographic processing in visual word recognition: a multiple read-out model. Psychological review **3**, 518 (1996)
7. Hamm, P.J., Johnson, W.B., Kirk, J.I. Comparison of the N300 and N400 ERPs to picture stimuli in congruent and incongruent contexts. Clinical Neurophysiology **8**, 1339-1350 (2002)
8. Lau, F.E., Phillips, C., Poeppel, D. A cortical network for semantics: (de) constructing the N400. Nature Reviews Neuroscience **9**, 920-933 (2008)
9. Lupker, J.S. The role of phonetic and orthographic similarity in picture–word interference. Canadian Journal of Psychology/Revue Canadienne de Psychologie **3**, 349 (1982)
10. Mathilde, M., Johannes, Z. Locus of orthographic effects in spoken word recognition: Novel insights from the neighbor generation task. Language and cognitive processes **19**, 641-660 (2004)
11. Racine, I., Grosjean, F. The cost of deleting a schwa at the time of recognition of French words. Canadian Journal of Experimental Psychology **59**, 240–254 (2005)
12. Roelofs, A., Meyer, S.A., Levelt, J.W. Interaction between semantic and orthographic factors in conceptually driven naming: Comment on Starreveld and La Heij (1995). Journal of Experimental Psychology: Learning, Memory, and Cognition **22**, 246-251 (1996)
13. Starreveld, A.P., La, H.-W. Time-course analysis of semantic and orthographic context effects in picture naming. Journal of Experimental Psychology: Learning, Memory, and Cognition **22**, 896 (1995)
14. Su, I.-F., Yeung, S.-T., Weekes, S.B., Law, S.-P. Locus of orthographic facilitation effect in spoken word production: Evidence from Cantonese Chinese. In Chinese Spoken Language Processing (ISCSLP), 8th International Symposium on 440-444 (2012)
15. Snodgrass, G.J., Vanderwart, M. A standardized set of 260 pictures: norms for name agreement, image agreement, familiarity, and visual complexity. Journal of experimental psychology: Human learning and memory **6**, 174 (1980)
16. Taft, M. Processing of characters by native Chinese readers. In The handbook of east Asian psycholinguistics. Cambridge university press, Cambridge **1**, 237–249 (2006)
17. Underwood, G., Briggs, P. The development of word recognition processes. British Journal of Psychology **2**, 243-255 (1984)
18. Wang, W.S.-Y., Tsai, Y.C. The alphabet and the sinogram. Dyslexia across cultures. Brookes Publishing, Baltimore (2011)
19. Yum, N.Y., Law, S.-P., Su, I.-F., Lau, D.K.-Y., Mo, N.K. An ERP study of effects of regularity and consistency in delayed naming and lexicality judgment in a logographic writing system. Frontiers in Psychology **5**, 315 (2014)

20. Zhang Q., Chen, H.-C., Weekes, S.B., Yang, Y. Independent effects of orthographic and phonological facilitation on spoken word production in Mandarin. Language and speech **52**,113-126 (2009)

21. Zhang, Q., Damian, F.M. Effects of orthography on speech production in Chinese. Journal of psycholinguistic research **41**, 267-283 (2012)

22. Zhang, C., Peng, G., Wang, W. S.-Y. Achieving constancy in spoken word identification: Time course of talker normalization. Brain and language **126**,193-202 (2013)

23. Zhang Q., Weekes, S.B. Orthographic facilitation effects on spoken word production: Evidence from Chinese. Language and Cognitive Processes **24**, 1082-1096 (2009)

24. Zhou, X., Marslen-Wilson, W. Sublexical processing in reading Chinese. Reading Chinese script: A cognitive analysis, 37-63 (1999)

Study on the Effectiveness of the Regulations for Chinese Words with Variant Forms Based on a Long-Span Diachronic Corpus[*]

Gaoqi Rao[1], Meng Dai[2], Endong Xun[1†]

[1]Beijing Language and Culture University, China

[2]Beijing Normal University, China

Abstract. Chinese words with variant forms are synonymous words with same written forms. They're important objects of language planning. In this article, the diachronic use of Chinese words with variant forms involved in the *Consolidated Table of the First Batch of Chinese Words with Variant Forms* and the *Consolidated Table of the First Batch of Chinese Words with Variant Forms (Draft)* is studied using long-time span diachronic corpus and diachronic retrieval systems, and such words are categorized by their diachronic trends. Based on this method, the effectiveness of artificial regulations on Chinese words with variant forms exhibiting different trends in usage is analyzed. The analytical data show that the consolidation and standardization of Chinese words with variant forms were effectively implemented in the language situation of 2002 and 2003 and had a positive significance.

Keywords: Chinese words with variant forms; language regulation; diachronic computing; language situation

1   Introduction

Chinese words with variant forms are special vocabulary phenomena of natural language. The Chinese words as the subjects investigated in this article are written in Mandarin with variant forms. In the *Consolidated Table of the First Batch of Chinese*

---

[*] The present study is jointly funded by the Natural Science Fund of China(61300081, 61170162), the National Hi-Tech Research and Development Program (2015AA015409), 863 Program (SQ2015AA0100074), and the National Planning Office of Philosophy and Social Sciences(12&ZD173) and Social Science Fund of China "Chinese Chunk Bank Construction and Application Research".
[†] Corresponding author

© Springer International Publishing AG 2016
M. Dong et al. (Eds.): CLSW 2016, LNAI 10085, pp. 728–742, 2016
DOI: 10.1007/978-3-319-49508-8_67

Words with Variant Forms jointly released by the Ministry of Education (MOE) and the National Languages Committee(NLC) in 2002, Chinese words with variant forms are defined as synonymous words used simultaneously and written in different forms [1]. For example, the word groups "笔划-笔画" (strokes) and "身份-身分" (identity) are synonyms with various forms. Chinese words with variant forms are the results of the long-term accumulation of the Chinese language. Furthermore, the majority of modern Chinese writers inevitably use Chinese words with variant forms [2]. These words are also used quite extensively, placing unnecessary burdens and obstacles to language learning and dissemination as well as increasing the complexity of pragmatics, damaging the language dissemination and informatization.

The Consolidated Table of the First Batch of Chinese Words with Variant Forms (Trial) was compiled by four units, including the Committee for Proofreading of the Publishers Association of China, the Chinese Language Association of newspapers etc. in 2003. Li Xingjian and Yu Zhihong [3] have stated that the consolidated table was released as a recommended constructive practice as a result of research on Chinese lexicology, and as a combined product of Chinese lexical theories and practices.

The development process of the consolidated table of Chinese words with variant forms has some technicalities but it highlights the accepted fundamental principles of compliance to customs. The consolidated table of Chinese words with variant forms compiled by the MOE and the NLC significantly depended on several co-occurring corpora. In today's perspective, its scale and time span of this table are extremely limited. Language situation is time related and thus, using a corpus within a certain time span enables a more intensive sorting and investigation of Chinese words with variant forms. In this article, Chinese words with variant forms within 61 years after the founding of PR China are investigated in terms of word frequency, based on the diachronic corpus and retrieval system of a 61-year-old authoritative newspaper [4, 5]. The development regulations for Chinese words with variant forms in the diachronic pragmatics are explored, and such characters are studied and classified. By studying the changes in the word frequency in specific years, the tasks of artificial regulations in terms of the implementation are analyzed. Finally, quantitative indicators are established based on diachronic linguistics, with a view of offering advice on future language planning and quantitative references on a longer time scale.

2   On corpus resources

A diachronic retrieval system of modern Chinese vocabulary developed by the Beijing Language and Culture University collected the corpus of an authoritative newspaper from its establishment in November of 1949 till 2007, which comprise a total of 0.7 billion words. The 61-year corpus has gone through different moments of history of the PR China, with significant changes in the highly documented language and social situations. In this article, the corpus is sorted by years. The following items are left out: word segmentation punctuation marks, Latin letters, and low-frequency named entities, among others. Finally, a total of 328000 words are obtained. The size of the corpus within a different time range is shown in Table 1.

Time range	Average number of words	Average number of different words	Average number of characters	Time range	Average number of words	Average number of different words	Average number of characters
1950–59	99.1K	7.7M	12.5M	1980–89	112.6K	6.2M	10.1M
1960–69	71.6K	6.2M	10.1M	1990–99	143.1K	9.4M	15.3M
1970–79	69.1K	5.5M	9.2M	2000–07	136.3K	9.8M	16.1M

Table 1. Statistics of Changes in Corpus Size at Different Time Ranges

Belonging to an authoritative sociolect, the corpus reflects the public life of language on every time section. Notably, many of the Chinese words with variant forms included in the *Consolidated Table of the First Batch of Chinese Words with Variant Forms* and the *Consolidated Table of the First Batch of Chinese Words with Variant Forms (Draft)* were less frequently found in the public life of language. Consequently, our data could not effectively describe the use of these Chinese words during the period, thereby resulting in data sparsity issues. We believe that if a word appeared less than 10 times during the period of study, its use in the language is relatively fortuitous. In that case, resultant data are statistically ineffective. Therefore, waiting is necessary until other reliable data become available instead of using the above data as sorted investigation results. Data sparsity was observed in 70 groups of Chinese words with variant forms in first batch, accounting for 20.7% and 51 groups for the second batch, accounting for 19.3%.

3   Spontaneous regulations and basic classification

The development of language is a collective and unconscious process, and the same is true for the formation and the development of Chinese words with variant forms, even for spontaneous regulations. Whether these Chinese words have spontaneous language regulations themselves in the public life of language prior to artificial language regulations and how the effectiveness of such regulations is fundamentally significant in establishing the artificial language regulations requires determining the type of tasks of the artificial regulations. If spontaneous language regulations exist, then the tasks of artificial language regulations merely aim to describe, recognize, and consolidate the specifications. However, if spontaneous language regulations are weak or unformed, formulation of the artificial language regulations will require sorting the complex pragmatic phenomena and instituting regulations according to the ontological information and other linguistics, including the principles of sociology.

By observing Chinese words with variant forms in the long-time span corpus, using most these Chinese words is clearly biased, indicating that a variant of one Chinese word has achieved the dominant position. This conclusion could reveal some spontaneous regulations for Chinese words with variant forms in pragmatics. Based on the existence and usage of the spontaneous regulations in pragmatic practices, the Chinese words with variant forms described in Consolidated Tables I and II are classified into the advantaged and the complex type (see Fig.1, left). A variant of one Chinese word, which has dominant advantages, can be categorized into the advantaged type, whereas any other variants without the advantages or with uncertain advantages can be categorized into the complex type. Each of the two types can be subdivided by the trend characteristics (see Fig. 1, right).

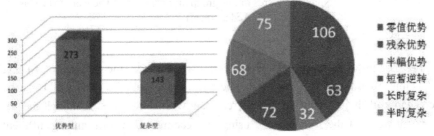

Fig. 1. (L): Quantitative Comparison of the Advantaged and Complex Types (R): Quantitative Distribution of the Two Types

3.1   Advantaged type

The advantaged type is defined as a variant of one Chinese word (i.e., the recommended one) with dominant advantages. The advantaged type can be subdivided into four types based on morphological distribution, namely, the "zero-frequency advantaged forms," "low-frequency disadvantaged forms," "disadvantaged forms with the frequency over half of the advantaged forms," and "disadvantaged forms emerging with frequency briefly exceeding the advantaged forms." Chinese words with variant forms in this category share a common trait, that is, the presence of spontaneous regulations. The important tasks of artificial regulations include the expansion and maintenance of the existing advantages of the advantaged form, thereby reducing pragmatic confusion and learning difficulties. This portion accounts for 65.6% of the total.

3.1.1 Zero-frequency disadvantaged forms: The frequency of usage of a disadvantaged form (non-recommended type) during the period studied is zero, whereas that of an advantaged form is greater than zero. This finding suggests that the advantaged form has the absolute advantage in terms of the authoritative pragmatics with spontaneous regulations. In this case, the roles of language regulations are to consolidate and determine the position of the advantaged form, thereby reducing or eliminating confusion in the language situation. The less stringent zero-frequency disadvantaged form allows the frequency of the use of the disadvantaged form for several years to be greater than zero.

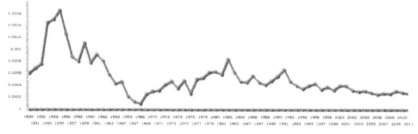

Fig. 2. "计划-计画" (Note: The words of this group mean "to plan." The word "计画" is marked in green)

Fig. 2 shows that among the word group "计划-计画," the frequency of using the recommended form "计划" went up and down in the statistics of over sixty years, whereas that of the other group, "计画" constantly remained zero. Although the development trend of the frequency of using the recommended form among different words are different, the comparative advantages of the non-recommended form underwent insignificant change. This finding clearly demonstrates that in the public life of language, the use of the recommended form has overwhelming superiority and spontaneously formed regulations. By observing the frequency of use in certain years, both the modern Chinese dictionary and the consolidated table released by the National Languages Committee showed limited effect. The spontaneous regulations formed during the public life of language prior to artificial regulations, "without worry" on the implementation of the regulations. This portion accounts for 25.5% of the total.

3.1.2 Low-frequency disadvantaged forms (hereinafter referred to as poorly advantaged)**:**
As shown in the diachronic distribution, the disadvantaged form is used sporadically, without a globally zero-advantaged form. However, even in the years with the zero-advantaged form, the frequency of the disadvantaged form is greater than or

equal to that of the advantaged form; furthermore, in the years with the frequency greater than zero, the frequency is no more than half of that of the advantaged form. This distribution shows that both the advantaged and the disadvantaged forms are slightly employed in the authoritative pragmatics. However, the advantaged form still possesses greater advantages. The tasks of artificial language regulations are to identify and convert to "zero-advantaged" form.

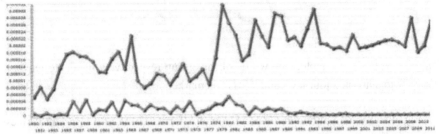

Fig. 3. 担心-耽心 (Note: The words of this group mean 'to worry about,' and '耽心' is marked in green)

Fig. 3"担心-耽心" are typical examples of having the distribution of "poorly advantaged" forms. The disadvantaged form is used sporadically. The sporadically used disadvantaged forms in the two examples emerged in the early years and in the first decade from 1990s to the 21st century; the advantaged form and the disadvantaged form are relatively identical to "zero-advantaged" form. 14 of the 39 variant Chinese words of the low-frequency disadvantaged forms in the Consolidated Table of the First Batch of Chinese Words with Variant Forms respectively show such a trend that the six decades of using the variant Chinese words experienced a transition from "poorly-advantaged" to "zero-advantaged" forms. Thus, it is with the use of 620 of variant Chinese words in the Consolidated Table of the First Batch of Chinese Words with Variant Forms (Trial). This portion accounts for 15.1% of the total.

3.1.3 Disadvantaged forms with the frequency over half of the advantaged forms(also known as the half-range advantaged form)

The frequency of using a disadvantaged form in the years over or equal to half of the 60 years is greater than zero and greater than half of the frequency of using an advantaged form in Year 0. This finding indicates that the advantages of the advantaged form in the authoritative pragmatics are unclear, having added signs of coexistence, spontaneous regulations built on the sand, and heavier burden on artificial regulations.

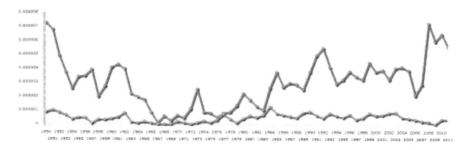

Fig. 4. 启程-起程 (Note: The words of this group respectively mean 'to leave, to set out, or to start on a journey', and "起程" is marked in green)

Fig. 4 shows that although the recommended form "启程" of the variant Chinese words "启程-起程"(sourced from the Consolidated Table of the First Batch of Chinese Words with Variant Forms (Draft)) has dominant advantages, the position of the disadvantaged form "起程" in the authoritative pragmatics cannot be ignored . In the 1970–1980s, the frequency of using the disadvantaged form eventually matched the advantaged form. In this case, the foundation for using the advantaged form is less reliable than the two cases above; thus, focusing on establishing regulations for such type is required, enabling a transition from "poorly advantaged" to "zero-advantaged" form. This portion accounts for 7.7% of the total.

3.1.4 Disadvantaged forms emerging with frequency, briefly exceeding the advantaged forms (hereinafter referred to as the transient reversal):

This type can be considered a subset of the half-advantaged form, but the frequency of using the disadvantaged form is over that of using the advantaged form in certain years. This finding indicates that although the advantaged form exists in the word, it still co-exists and shares existence with the disadvantaged form in authoritative pragmatics. Explicitly, the tasks of language planning are arduous and important.

Fig. 5. (Top): 本分-本份 (Note: The words of this group mean 'one's part or duty,' and "本份" is marked in green).

"本分-本份" (of the first batch) is shown as Fig. 5. The advantaged forms "本分" has distinct advantages, whereas the disadvantaged forms "本份" overweighs the advantaged form in the 1990s and in the middle of the first decade of the new century. The advantaged and disadvantaged forms co-occur and share, requiring artificial regulations. This portion accounts for 17.3% of the total.

3.2   Complex type

A class of complex Chinese words with variant forms is listed in the consolidated table of Chinese words with variant forms. Neither variant forms of one Chinese word of this type hold distinct advantages on a global scale (in the 60-year corpus); specifically, the frequency relationship between the two forms is complex. Based on the duration of this phenomenon, the Chinese words of this type are divided into two types, namely, the "long-time complex" and the "half-span complex" types. However, the variant forms of this type similarly have spontaneous regulations without a complete form, and sorting complex pragmatic phenomena is an important task of artificial regulations.

3.2.1 Long-time complex type: Considering the difficulty in discerning dominant advantages from disadvantages throughout the time, the language standardization should prioritize this type, e.g., "笔画-笔划" in Fig. 6. This portion accounts for 16.3% of the total.

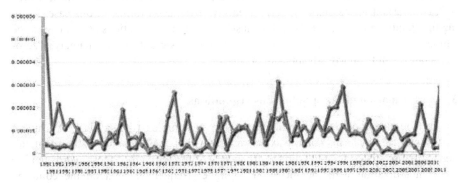

Fig. 6. 笔画-笔划 (Note: The words of this group mean 'strokes,' and "笔划" is marked in green)

3.2.2 Half-span complex type: Considering that dominant advantages can be difficult to discern in over a third of the time, the value of the standardization of this type is investigated based on the time range of its complexity. If the time range of its complexity appears in the late three decades (as in Fig. 7), it will indicate that reliable spontaneous regulations are still waiting to be formed, and sorting complex pragmatic phenomena is more difficult. This portion accounts for 18.0% of the total.

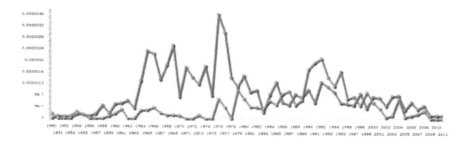

Fig. 7. 架势-架式 (Note: The words of this group mean 'stance,' and "架式" is marked in green)

3.3   Chinese words with over two variant forms

This case is similar to the classification of Chinese words with two variant forms. The effective data coverage (13 groups in the first batch and 8 groups in the second batch) can be roughly divided into two types, namely, quasi-zero-advantaged and quasi-residual-frequency type. One advantaged form exists, and two disadvantaged forms, in contrast to the advantaged form, exhibit a trend similar to that of Chinese words with two variant forms, namely, zero or poorly advantaged forms. In this case, forming the spontaneous regulations and the tasks of artificial regulations are thought to be similar to those of the Chinese words with two variant forms, namely, "zero-advantaged" and "poorly advantaged" forms.

3.4   Formation of the spontaneous regulations

Of the complex type, especially of the half-span complex type, a class of Chinese words with variant forms notably exists, among which, the formation of the spontaneous regulations is correlated with the frequency of use. Broadly, "these words tend to the standardization with the increasingly higher frequency," and on the contrary, "they are prone to be confused with lower frequency." This distribution is a subset of the distribution of the half-span complex type. This portion accounts for 89.3% of the half-span complex type.

3.4.1 'Words tending to the standardization with the increasingly higher frequency': With the higher frequency of using the words, the variant forms, which originally had no significant difference, are quickly distinguished as the advantaged and the disadvantaged forms. This distribution is a 'living fossil' of the spontaneous regulations, revealing a choice from the variant forms in sixty years.

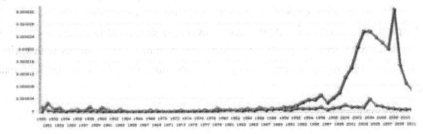

Fig. 8. 订单-定单 (Note: The words of this group mean 'order,' and '订单' is marked in green)

As seen from "订单-定单" in Fig. 8, the earlier frequency of use is extremely low. With the development of society and media, the language situation becomes more complicated, and generally speaking, the frequency of use is higher. The higher frequency of using Chinese words with variant forms causes more confusion. In such circumstances, language societies spontaneously standardize the variant forms for communication purposes. Accordingly, the advantaged variant forms being used more frequently in the early years accelerate the elimination of the disadvantaged forms for certain reasons (e.g. for "clear meaning," "clearly readable," or "simple writing," or even only for the public's acceptance), thereby resulting in a more sharply demarcated phenomenon. Why members of language societies keep pace with the higher frequency of using Chinese words with variant forms vote with "pencil and article" would require another article. This portion accounts for 65.3% of the half-span complex type.

3.4.2 'Words prone to being confused with lower frequency': This process is a reverse of the above-mentioned distribution, namely, Chinese words with variant forms having originally clearer distinctions are more difficult to distinguish because of their less frequent usage; accordingly, the variant forms tend to be confused.

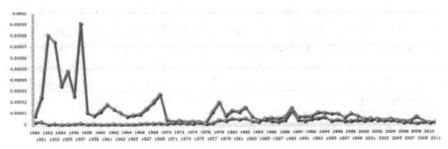

Fig. 9. 交代-交待 (Note: The words of this group respectively mean 'to tell, to leave words, or to order,' and "交待" is marked in green)

Of the word group "交代-交待" given in Fig. 9, the two variant forms coexist and share with each other because of the lower frequency of use. Difficulties in the practical communication caused by the variant forms are decreasing because of their less frequent usage. Thus, no momentum or necessity exists for language societies to continue the spontaneous regulations. Indeed, this type of Chinese words with variant forms is rare, but worth noting. This portion accounts for 24.0% of the half-span complex type.

4   Effectiveness of the consolidated table of Chinese words with variant forms

4.1   Changes in the use after the release of the regulations

The Consolidated Tables released in 2002 and 2003, respectively, gather 338 groups and 264 groups. In the 61-year diachronic corpus, the years 2002 and 2003 are taken as two key time intervals. Changes in the frequency of the use of variant Chi-

	Advantages Unchanged	Advantages Expanded	Advantages Narrowed	Unidentified
Lot 1	3 3.3%	57 **63.3%**	15 16.7%	15 16.7%
Lot 2	2 2.6%	55 **70.5%**	10 12.8%	11 14.1%

Table 2. Changes in the Use of Chinese Words with Variant Forms After Release of the Regulations

As seen from Table 2, using Chinese words with variant forms, especially those without spontaneous regulations, is normalized in the public life of language in accordance with the Consolidated Table of the First Batch of Chinese Words with Variant Forms and the Consolidated Table of the First Batch of Chinese Words with Variant Forms released in 2002 and 2003. The recommended forms hold and expand the advantages of the majority of advantaged forms, reducing the confusion and learning burdens in pragmatics. Chinese words with variant forms that expand the advantages are exemplified with the word-group "启程-起程" given in Fig. 8 and the group "本分-本份" in Fig. 6.

Those with the forms narrowing the advantages are exemplified in the word-group as Fig. 10, whereas those with the forms remaining advantages are seen in Fig. 12 (bottom). The forms' remaining advantages are notably limited to the situation that the disadvantaged form and advantaged form coexist and share with each other. The advantaged forms that maintain or reduce advantages with fewer changes in the frequency of use are excluded from the "zero-advantaged " and "half-advantaged" forms.

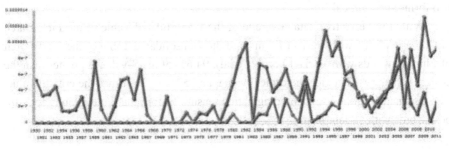

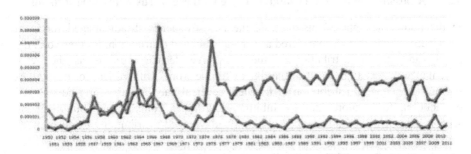

Fig. 10. (Top): 褴褛-蓝褛 (Note: The words of this group mean 'being dressed in rags,' and '褴褛' is marked in green) (Bottom): 热衷-热中 (Note: The word of this group mean 'be fond of', and '热中' is marked in green)

4.2 Quantitative analysis of the trend changes

From a statistical perspective, Chinese words with variant forms coexisting with each other are measured quantitatively. Based on the frequency ratio of the advantaged form to the disadvantaged form, it can be modified to form the following equation:

$$S = \sum_{a}^{t} \frac{1}{y_t - y_a} \cdot \frac{f_a + 1}{f_b + 1}$$
,

where f_a and f_b represent the frequencies of the advantaged and disadvantaged forms in the years. Given that the "zero-advantaged" and "poorly advantaged" forms exist, the Laplace smoothing [6] is adopted to avoid the denominator from zero. 'y_t' and 'y_n' represent the start and end years of the investigation, respectively. Obviously, the earlier the year, the greater the weighted value; furthermore, the S-value is positively correlated with the frequency of the advantaged form, and can be used for describing the importance of the advantaged form. Assuming that 'f_a' is equal to 'f_b,' the S-value 4.68 is a critical value to estimate the situation that frequencies of use of the two forms are identical.

Within the effective data coverage of the Consolidated Table of the First Batch of Chinese Words with Variant Forms and the Consolidated Table of the First Batch of Chinese Words with Variant Forms (Trial), 94.6% of the S-value is greater than the critical value, 79% is twice the critical value, and 57% is five times the critical value. The parameter can be used as a pragmatic measure to formulate regulations for Chinese words with variant forms.

4.3   A possible evolutionary model of The Chinese words with variant forms

In the poorly advantaged distribution, the zero-frequency disadvantaged forms in consecutive years can be considered as zero-advantaged distribution. Furthermore, the poorly advantaged distribution in the last three decades appears as the zero-advantaged distribution. Most of the time, Chinese words with variant forms exhibiting half-advantaged distribution of transient reversal had similar poorly advantaged distribution; furthermore, those exhibiting a half-span complex distribution in the second half has a half-advantaged or poorly advantaged distribution. These findings show the process through which language societies spontaneously formulate regulations when a word is more frequently used in the language situation.

The idealized development process of the Chinese words with variant forms is proposed to undergo several distributions as follows: complex distribution, distribution of transient reversal, half-advantaged distribution, poorly advantaged distribution, and zero-advantaged distribution. This process shows a gradual transition from highly mixed distribution to the distribution of a variant form holding the absolute advantages. Obviously, when Chinese words with variant forms are developed into a zero-advantaged distribution, language societies spontaneously formulate regulations, and such spontaneous regulations have stable effects. Being excluded from the Chinese words with variant forms will take some time. The above-mentioned distributions of the Chinese words with variant forms characterize different stages in which the words appear. However, not all words appear (full-span complex), develop (half-span complex and then transient reversal), or decline (poorly-advantaged and zero-advantaged) in the time section of this article corpus.

The artificial language regulations aim to accelerate the development of Chinese words with variant forms, allowing a quick shift from Chinese words with variant forms in complex pragmatic use to the zero-advantaged distribution. However, when language regulations appear, Chinese words with variant forms are in different stages of development. Such stages involve different tasks for the formulation of language regulations, such as to determine variant forms (at the stage of complex distribution), to expand the advantages of the advantaged forms (at the stages of transient reversal and half-advantaged distributions), and to consolidate the advantages of the advantaged forms (at the stages of poorly advantaged and zero-advantaged distributions). Ideally, Chinese words with variant forms formed for historical reasons will finally change over to the zero-advantaged distribution after being affected by the spontaneous or artificial regulations, thereby losing its variant forms.

5   Basic conclusions

First, Chinese words with variant forms are sanctioned by usage. Other principles of the words include "clear meaning," "clearly readable," "simple writing," "highly stratified," and "due consideration" [7]. Among these considerations, the first, fourth, and fifth items involve semantics, whereas the second and third items address ontological information. Investigation on the corpus mainly aimed at the principle of "conforming to conventions."

By observing the long-time span corpus, Chinese words with variant forms have can be observed to have spontaneous regulations extensively applied in pragmatics. However, the effectiveness of spontaneous regulations has varying reliability, with significant differences. Accordingly, the tasks of artificial regulations are also different. Chinese words with variant forms that exhibiting exhibited radically different trends are classified, and thus, the different tasks of the artificial regulations could be differently determined differently to consolidate the absolute advantages, to expand the minor advantages, and to sort complex pragmatics.

From the aspect of expanding the minor advantages and sorting the complex pragmatics, a conclusion can be made after the release of the *Consolidated Table of the First Batch of Chinese Words with Variant Forms*, and the *Consolidated Table of the First Batch of Chinese Words with Variant Forms (Trial)* has relatively good effects on the words of significant importance of regulations and their revisions; thus, they are effectively implemented in the public life of language. Furthermore, the consolidated tables play active roles in "improving the application performance of Chinese," "reducing the burdens on learning Chinese," and "adapting to the needs of information processing"[8].

References

1. MOE, PR China: Consolidated Table of the First Batch of Chinese Words with Variant Forms and the Consolidated Table of the First Batch of Chinese Words with Variant Forms (Draft), 2002
2. Zhou Youguang: Consolidation of Chinese Words with Variant Forms and Ambiguity of Chinese Lexicon [J], Education Paper of China, April 1st, 2002.
3. Li Xingjian, Yu Hongzhi: Studies on Words with Variant Forms in Modern Chinese[M]: Shanghai Lexicographical Publishing House, 2005:222-233.
4. Xun Endong, Rao Gaoqi, Xie Jiali, Huang Zhi-e: Diachronic Retrieval for Modern Chinese Word: System Construction and its Application[J]: 2015, 29(3):169-176.
5. Xun Endong, Rao Gaoqi, Xiao Xiaoyue, Zang Jiaojiao: The Construction of BCC Corpus in the age of Big Data. Corpus Linguistics, 2016(1): 93-118.
6. Zong Chengqing: Statistical Natural Language Processing[M]. Tsinghua University Press, 2008, 143
7. Yang Jianqiao: Problems on Multisyllable Words with Variant Forms [J], Journal on Fudan University, 2006 No.6:110-116.
8. Zhou Youguang: Preface of Regulated Dictionary of Words with Variant Forms in Modern Chinese , Shanghai Lexicographical Publishing House, 2002

Motion Constructions in Singapore Mandarin Chinese: A Typological Perspective

Yong Kang Khoo and Jingxia Lin[1]

[1] Nanyang Technological University, Singapore
ykhoo002@e.ntu.edu.sg
jingxialin@ntu.edu.sg

Abstract. Research on Singapore Mandarin Chinese has shown that it is influenced, to a certain degree, by dialects such as Min (e.g. Hokkien) and Cantonese. This has resulted in many differences between Mainland China Mandarin Chinese and Singapore Mandarin Chinese. This paper examines one such difference: the expression of self-agentive motion constructions. This study finds that Singapore Mandarin Chinese lies somewhere in between dialects and modern Mandarin Chinese with respect to lexicalization of motion events. The findings suggest that rather than the categorical patterns that have been proposed in many previous studies, the lexicalization patterns in different languages may form a continuum.

Keywords: self-agentive motion event · Singapore Mandarin Chinese · word order

1   Introduction

Motion events are those that involve the movement or maintenance of position of an object, known as the Figure, with respect to another object, known as the Ground; this movement or maintenance is known as the Path [1]. The expression of such events can be done in several ways, and can be classified typologically into two main types: the verb-framed and the satellite-framed. Modern Mandarin Chinese can be considered the latter in terms of the expression of motion events [2]. The satellites are Path complements, which includes non-deictic complements (C_{nd}) such as 上 *shang* 'up' and 下 *xia* 'down' and deictic complements (C_d) such as 来 *lai* 'come' and 去 *qu* 'go' and they indicate the Path of the Figure. Such is the case for the various Chinese dialects as well; however, the position of these complements with respect to the Ground, especially the deictic complements, differ from dialect to dialect.

In Mainland China Mandarin Chinese (MC), these Path complements can be used in three main ways. The deictic and non-deictic complements can be used either individually as simple Path complements or in conjunction as complex Path complements. They can then be used together with different manner verbs (V) and objects (O), and grammaticality of the constructions are given by factors such as the agentivity of the

© Springer International Publishing AG 2016
M. Dong et al. (Eds.): CLSW 2016, LNAI 10085, pp. 743–750, 2016
DOI: 10.1007/978-3-319-49508-8_68

manner verb and the type of object (e.g. location, patient or agent) [3, 4]. Examples of these constructions can be found in (1).

(1)   Examples of how Path complements can be used
  a.   V + C_{nd} + O
       送回学校

       song   hui   xuexiao
       send   back   school
       'send (it) back to the school'
  b.   V + O + C_d
       飞房间里来

       fei   fangjian li   lai
       fly   room   in   come
       'flew into the room'
  c.   V + C_{nd} + O + C_d
       走进房间去

       zou   jin   fangjian qu
       walk   in   room   go
       'walk into the room'

However, as far as locative nouns are concerned, these constructions seem to be only few types that are allowed in MC and there seems to be no exceptions [3].

As for the Chinese dialects, a wider range of constructions are permitted [5]. In Yiu's study, she examined the motion event constructions in five different Chinese dialects, namely Wu (吴), Cantonese (广东), and three different Min (闽) dialects, namely Hui'an (惠安), Chao'an (潮安) and Fuqing (福清). Her results showed that constructions where the deictic complement comes before the locative object are permitted in some dialects. Interestingly, there are some internal differences amongst the three Min dialects where Fuqing and Hui'an are more similar to MC in their typologies. She attributed this to language contact, given that Fuqing and Hui'an are spoken in regions nearer to where MC is the dominant dialect. This demonstrates that the typologies of languages and dialects are not as neatly defined as previously defined.

This then raises a question with regards to motion constructions in Singapore Mandarin Chinese (SC). Research on SC has shown that it has been influenced to a certain degree by Chinese dialects such as Min (e.g. Hokkien) and Cantonese [6]. This has caused variations in the language such that it can differ quite significantly from other varieties of Mandarin Chinese (like those spoken in Mainland China or Taiwan), making it typologically interesting to investigate the lexicalization patterns in SC and discuss its position with respect to MC and other Chinese dialects. This paper examines motion constructions that involve self-agentive manner verbs, with a focus on those in which the Figure moves with respect to a location noun. An analysis of these constructions provides a typological overview of SC, suggesting that SC rests in the middle of the typological continuum.

2   Approach and Data

This paper will focus on constructions expressing self-agentive directed motion events in SC, with particular focus on the distribution of the deictic complements, 来 *lai* 'come' and 去 *qu* 'go' in these constructions. The data of this study comes from a corpus of 26 episodes of five different Singaporean Chinese variety shows. These variety shows are selected as they are either talk shows or game shows and are therefore unscripted, allowing for the observation of natural speech. A total of around 360,000 characters (around 20,000 sentences) were transcribed from these shows. The sentences containing the words 来 *lai* 'come' and 去 *qu* 'go' are first identified, before narrowing the scope down to only sentences that expresses self-agentive directed motion events.

3   Major Findings

A total of 2882 sentences containing 来 *lai* 'come' and 去 *qu* 'go' were identified from the data, and out of these sentences, 70 of them are expressions of self-agentive directed motion events. A detailed breakdown can be found in Table 1.

Table 1. Word orders exhibited in SC

Construction Type	Frequency	Example
C_d: 来 *lai* 'come'		
C_{nd} + Loc + *lai*	1	进门来 jin men lai enter door come 'enter (through) the door'
2. C_{nd} + *lai* + Loc	4	回来工厂 hui lai gongchang return come factory 'return to the factory'
3. V_m + C_{nd} + *lai* + Loc	4	走进来我们家 zou jin lai women jia walk enter come our house 'walk into our house'
4. V_m + *lai* + Loc	4	跑来carpark pao lai carpark run come carpark 'run to the carpark'
5. V_m + *dao* (to) + Loc + *lai*	3	跑到家里来 pao dao jiali lai run to house come 'run to (and arrive in) the house'

C_d: 去 qu 'go'		
6. C_{nd} + Loc + qu	2	往哪里去 wang nali qu towards where go 'where (do we) go'
7. C_{nd} + qu + Loc	14	回 去 厨房 hui qu chufang return go kitchen 'go back to the kitchen'
8. V_m + C_{nd} + qu + Loc	9	跑 进 去 里面 pao jin qu limian run enter go inside 'run inside'
9. V_m + qu + Loc	16	走去哪个小贩中心 zou qu nage xiaofanzhongxin walk go which food centre 'whichever food centre (do I) go to'
10. V_m + dao (to) + Loc + qu	13	吊到那上面去 diao dao na shangmian qu hang to that above go 'hang (something) onto that'

A symmetrical distribution has been observed in the two deictic complements – all structures permitted for 来 *lai* 'come' are also permitted for 去 *qu* 'go' and this gives rise to five unique types of constructions. Out of these five different types, the following two are also permitted in MC:

(2) C_{nd} + Loc + C_d
(3) V_m + dao (to) + Loc + C_d

However, it seems that these are not preferred constructions in SC, as seen from the relatively higher usage of each of the other three types of constructions, namely "V_m + C_d + Loc", "V_m + C_{nd} + C_d + Loc" and "Cnd + Cd + Loc". This suggests that SC is rather accepting of constructions. This acceptance and flexibility is even more apparent when compared to other Chinese dialects, as given by Table 2.

It is also observed that there is a significant usage of the construction 去到 *qu dao* 'go to and arrive at', a construction that is quite uncommon in MC [7], but used so frequently in SC that it has extended beyond spatial directional constructions, such as 去到什么样的程度 *qu dao shenme yang de chengdu* 'to what extent'. It has been pointed out that the use of 到 *dao* 'to' to introduce the locative object is more common than the use of non-deictic directional complements [8] and faces less restrictions [5]. Though this observation is not part paper's focus, it might suggest that there might be a difference in the lexical items, 来 *lai* 'come' and 去 *qu* 'go', and this may also be one of the reasons behind the differences in the types of permitted word orders.

Table 2. Comparison of Word Orders across dialects and varieties. The comparison is made by putting SC and MC against the ones as summarised by Yiu [5].

	Wu	MC	SC	Fuqing	Hui'an	Chao'an	Cantonese
Simple directional complements: Self-agentive motion events							
$V_m + C_d + Loc$	*	*	✓	✓	✓	✓	✓
$V_m + to + Loc + C_d$	✓	✓	✓	✓	✓	*	*
Compound directional complements: Self-agentive motion events							
$V_m + C_{nd} + Loc + C_d$	?	✓	✓	*	*	*	*
$V_m + C_{nd} + C_d + Loc$	*	*	✓	✓	✓	✓	✓
$C_{nd} + C_d + Loc$	-	*	✓	-	-	-	-
$C_{nd} + Loc + C_d$	-	✓	✓	-	-	-	-

Note: A '-' indicates that this construction is not identified in Yiu's paper [5].

4   Discussion

From the above comparisons, there are two significant observations. First, the word orders exhibited in SC is shown to be the most accommodating out of the seven dialects and varieties of Chinese compared, having permitted all of the word orders being compared. The most significant difference between SC and MC is that the deictic complement in SC can be followed by the locative object, similar to those of Cantonese and the Min dialects while this construction is not permitted in MC. Examples of this construction in the various dialects and varieties can be found in (4). Though it is unclear from the comparison if dialects also allow for the construction of "$C_{nd} + C_d + Loc$", it should be noted that this is a construction rarely found in MC.

(4)   Construction: $V + C_{nd} + C_d + Loc$
  a.   Cantonese [5]
      佢爬咗上去山頂。
      Keoi5   paa4   zo2   soeng5   heoi3   saan1   deng2.
      s/he   climb   ASP   ascend   go   mountain top
      'S/he climbed up to the top of the mountain.'
  b.   Min (Chao'an) [5]
      伊爬起去山頂。
      I33   pe?5   khi35   khɯ53   suã33   teŋ53.
      s/he   climb   rise   go   mountain top
      'S/he climbs up to the top of the mountain.'
  c.   SC
      他们要跑出去外面。
      tamen   yao   pao   chu   qu   waimian.
      they   want   run   out   go   outside
      'They want to run out (of this place).'

Second, it is observed that the manner verb can form a complete and grammatical construction with the deictic complement and locative object in SC, while this is also not permitted in MC. Again, this is similar to those in Cantonese and Min dialects, such as those seen in (5).

(5)   Construction: V + C$_d$ + Loc
a. Cantonese [5]
行嚟学校
haang4   lai4   hok6haau6
walk   come   school
'to walk to school'
b. Min (Chao'an) [5]
走来学校
tsau35   lai213   hak2hau35
run   come   school
'to run to school'
c. SC
跑来carpark
pao   lai   carpark
run   come   carpark
'run to the carpark'

This makes the classification of the typology of SC rather challenging. On the one hand, it is a variety of modern Mandarin Chinese, and shares many typological features with other varieties such as Mainland China Mandarin Chinese. On the other hand, due to the influence by Chinese dialects, SC has displayed properties of these dialects, and has even been shown to exhibit preference to these properties over those of modern Mandarin Chinese. While Yiu classified the dialects into strong and weak VO dialects depending on whether or not the locative object can come after the deictic complement, the present study thinks that SC cannot be considered as either (at least in terms of the expression of self-agentive motion events). This means that there should be a more narrowly defined method of representing the various dialects and varieties of Chinese. Hence, we suggest the continuum in (6) as a means to better reflect the differences between the various dialects and varieties when considering the word orders in self-agentive motion events.

(6)   MC→ SC, Wu → Fuqing, Hui'an → Chao'an, Cantonese

The arrangement of Chinese dialects appears to be consistent with Yiu's discussions when speaking of the relation between the geographical locations of these dialects in Mainland China and the number of northern features the dialects exhibits [5]. Wu, being the closest to the geographical location of MC in the North, is typologically closer to MC in terms of the expression of agentive motion events, while Chao'an and Cantonese are the furthest away, being situated in the southern parts of China, would be a lot less similar in this respect. In the establishment of this continuum, Fuqing and Hui'an has been classified separately from Chao'an as the former two dialects differs slightly from Cantonese – Fuqing and Hui'an do not permit the construction "V_m + to + Loc + C_d", unlike Cantonese and Chao'an.

In the case of SC, it exists in between the MC and most of the other southern dialects (less Wu, which is grouped together with SC), given that it exhibits features from both sides of the continuum. The reason why Wu has been grouped together with SC is that Wu has exhibited properties more similar to MC than to other dialects, such as the ungrammaticality of the construction "V_m + C_d + Loc". However, Wu still maintains some differences, such as in the construction "V_m + C_{nd} + Loc + C_d", where the grammaticality is still circumstantial despite the heavy influence of MC on Wu.

5   Conclusion

In conclusion, in terms of self-agentive motion constructions, SC lies between MC and most of the southern dialects (Min and Yue), and exhibits properties from both extremes. Language contact has been observed to play a part in the formation of SC and dialects, such as Min and Yue, has influenced SC in its syntactical rules. A more specific classification, as compared to Yiu [5], has been suggested by the present paper, to account for the slight degree of variations between each dialect and variety of Chinese – such a classification would better reflect the relations of the different dialects and their differences.

We suggest that further studies in expressions of agentive motion events in these dialects and varieties of Chinese should be undertaken to address current gaps and gain a clearer picture of the exact strength of SC in relation to MC and other Chinese dialects. The usage of 到 dao 'to' should also be explored, as there seems to be varying usage of this preposition in motion event constructions [5], [8]. Such a study may help refine current notions about the positions of dialects and varieties of Chinese in the typology continuum on a larger scale and aid in the understanding of the Chinese languages as a whole.

Acknowledgment

We wish to acknowledge the funding support for this project from Nanyang Technological University under the Undergraduate Research Experience on CAmpus (URECA) programme.

References

1. Talmy, L.: Lexicalization patterns: Semantic Structure in lexical forms. In: Timothy Shopen (ed.), Language typology and syntactic description, vol. 3: Grammatical categories and the lexicon, pp. 57-149. Cambridge: Cambridge University Press. (1985)
2. Talmy, L.: A Typology of Event Integration. Toward a Cognitive Semantics: Typology and Process in Concept Structuring, vol. 2, chapter 3, pp. 214-288. MIT Press, Cambridge, MA. (2000)

3. Lu, J.M.: Concerning the verbal complement of direction and the position of object (in Chinese). In: Chinese Teaching in the World, vol. 1, pp. 5-17. (2002)
4. Cai, T.: On the position of the Compound Verbs of Direction with Location Nouns. In: Journal of College of Chinese Language and Culture of Jinan University, vol. 4, pp. 66-71. (2006)
5. Yiu, C.Y.M.: Typology of Word Order in Chinese Dialects: Revisiting the Classification of Min. In: Language and Linguistics, vol. 15, pp. 539-573. (2014)
6. Chew, C.H.: An Overview of Variations in Singapore Chinese (in Chinese). In Cheng Hai Chew (ed). 2002. The Grammar of Singapore Chinese (in Chinese), pp. 9-24. (2002)
7. Li, H.: The symmetry and asymmetry phenomenon of "lai" and "qu". M.A. Thesis, Guangxi Normal University. (2008)
8. Tang, Z. and Lamarre, C.: A Contrastive Study of the Linguistic Encoding of Motion Events in Standard Chinese and in the Guanzhong dialect of Mandarin (Shaanxi). In: Bulletin of Chinese Linguistics, vol. 2, pp. 137-170. (2007)

The Source of Implicit Negation in Mandarin Chinese Yes-No Questions

Daniel Kwang Guan CHAN [✉]

Centre for Language Studies, National University of Singapore, Singapore
daniel.chan@nus.edu.sg

Abstract. How is it possible that negation can be expressed without the explicit use of negation markers? This paper answers this question by looking at the cases of implicit negation in different types of yes-no questions in Mandarin Chinese. After arguing that Mandarin Chinese has at least three distinct classes of yes-no questions, and that the three distinct classes form a continuum of semantic features, we consider the sentence-final particle *ma* (吗), based on its etymology, as a source of the negative meaning in affirmative yes-no questions, or inversion polarity in negative yes-no questions. Finally, we propose that negative yes-no questions can be analysed like English tag questions.

Keywords. Implicit negation · Yes-no questions · Mandarin Chinese · Sentence-final particle *ma* (吗) · Rhetorical questions

1 Introduction

An interesting and somewhat puzzling property of negation is that it can be expressed without the use of actual negation markers. This is the case of certain kinds of questions, as illustrated in examples (1) and (2), a yes-no question and an open-ended question respectively.

(1) 不想去就别去。有人强迫你吗?!
   Bù xiǎng qù jiù bié qù. Yǒu rén qiángpò nǐ ma?!
   "Don't go if you don't want to go. Is anyone forcing you to go?!"

(2) 不想去就别去。谁强迫你啦?!
   Bù xiǎng qù jiù bié qù. Shéi qiángpò nǐ la?!
   "Don't go if you don't want to go. Who is forcing you to go?!"

The main research question of this paper concerns the source of negation in questions that express negation implicitly. In this paper, our scope shall be limited to the expression of implicit negation in questions of the first type (i.e. yes-no questions) in Mandarin Chinese.

Generally speaking, yes-no questions are close-ended questions that can typically be answered with either yes or no. They involve the consideration of two possible answers: an affirmative proposition <P> and a negative proposition <¬P> (i.e. the "complement" of the affirmative proposition in the mathematical sense of the word).

© Springer International Publishing AG 2016
M. Dong et al. (Eds.): CLSW 2016, LNAI 10085, pp. 751–762, 2016
DOI: 10.1007/978-3-319-49508-8_69

In Section 2, we will first present two classes of yes-no questions that are have been discussed in the literature, namely those that take the form <P / ¬P?> and <P *ma?*> (see examples (3) and (4) below). We present the work of Li and Thompson (1981) concerning the difference between these two classes of yes-no questions, and then point out a certain number of problems that such a bipartite classification poses. We claim that a third distinct class of yes-no questions, namely <¬P *ma?*>, should be considered, and show that this third class of yes-no questions present properties that are distinct from those of the first two classes. We use syntactic tests to distinguish the three classes of yes-no questions and show that all three forms of yes-no questions form a continuum on a scale of "neutrality". Section 3 will focus on the semantic contribution of the sentence-final particle *ma*, the effect it has on the inversion of the polarity of propositions, as well as its interaction with explicit negation in forming biased yes-no questions with unambiguously rhetorical meaning. We argue that would help us understand why the questions of the form <P *ma?*> and <¬P *ma?*> have precisely the properties demonstrated.

2   Types of yes-no questions

Previous works in the literature (e.g. Li & Thompson, 1979, among others) have admitted that two main types of yes-no questions exist in Mandarin Chinese. On one hand, there is the "disjunctive question" of the form <P / ¬P?>, which consists in juxtaposing the affirmative form of a verb with a negative form of the same verb, for example : *chī* "eat" and *bù chī* "not eat".

(3) 你吃不吃苹果?

Nǐ chī-bù-chī píngguǒ?

"Do you eat apples or not?"

The speaker asking the yes-no question then requires the listener to say which of the two alternative propositions considered, P or ¬P, is the correct one. On the other hand, there is the yes-no question that is identified as a question solely by virtue of the sentence-final particle *ma* (pronounced in a neutral and unstressed tone) placed right after a certain proposition P:

(4) 你吃苹果吗?

Nǐ chī píngguǒ ma?

"Do you eat apples?"

For sake of simplicity, let us refer to these two classes of yes-no questions as Type I and Type II questions.

2.1   Contexts for Types I and II questions

Li and Thompson (1979, 1981) showed that these two types of questions are not used in the same contexts. Type I questions are asked in "neutral" contexts, whereas Type II questions can be asked in "non-neutral" contexts. The terms "neutral" and "non-neutral" are defined as follows by Li and Thompson

(1979: 202): *A neutral context is one in which the questioner has no assumptions concerning the proposition that is being questioned and wishes to know whether it is true. Whenever the question brings to the speech situation an assumption about either the truth or the falsity of the proposition s/he is asking about, then that context is non-neutral with respect to that question.* In the case of the question in example (4), the question can be asked of an interlocutor who is known to not eat apples. In this case, the Type I question in (3) is not acceptable. In asking the question in (4), the speaker indicates that he has made the following negative implication (5) and orientates the expected answer from the interlocutor towards the negative response.

(5) 我以为你不吃苹果。

   Wǒ yǐwéi nǐ bù chī píngguǒ.

   "I thought you do not eat apples."

However, in the case of Type I questions, the context must be neutral, and both possible answers to the question ("yes" and "no") are considered to be equally likely. No negative implication is communicated to the interlocutor in this case.

We can summarise the findings of Li and Thompson (1979) as follows:

- Yes-no questions can be either neutral or non-neutral. (Note: We will use the terms "non-neutral" and "biased" interchangeably in the rest of this paper).
- Type I questions, i.e. disjunctive questions of the form <P or ¬P?> are always neutral.
- Type II questions, i.e. questions that are posed with the sentence-final particle *ma* can be non-neutral.
- When Type II questions are non-neutral, the sentence-final particle *ma* orientates the yes-no question towards a negative response <¬P>.

2.2   A third class of yes-no questions <¬P *ma*>

In this section, we argue for the need to identify a third class of yes-no questions, as the bipartite classification of yes-no questions presented in the earlier section is insufficient for the two following reasons. Firstly, the sentence-final particle *ma* does not always make a question a biased one. For instance, when the sentence-final particle *ma* co-occurs with an adverb like *dàodǐ* ("after all"), only a non-biased interpretation is obtained.

(6) 你到底吃苹果吗?

   Nǐ dàodǐ chī píngguǒ ma?

   "Do you eat apples?"

Secondly, the sentence-final particle *ma,* even when it is interpreted as a biased question, may not always involve a negative implication nor be oriented towards a negative response. This is the case when both syntactic negation (through the use of negation markers *bù* or *méi*) and the sentence-final particle *ma* co-occur in the same proposition, as shown in examples (7), (8) and (9):

(7) 你不吃苹果吗?
     Nǐ bù chī píngguǒ ma?
     "Don't you eat apples?"
     (Implication: You do eat apples.)

(8) 你没吃苹果吗?
     Nǐ méi chī píngguǒ ma?
     "Didn't you eat apples?"
     (Implication: You did eat apples.)

(9) 他不叫小明吗?
     Tā bú jiào Xiǎomíng ma?
     "Isn't his name Xiaoming?"
     (Implication: His name is indeed Xiaoming.)

These two problems indicate that there is a need to distinguish between yes-no questions of the form <P *ma*?>, which are ambiguous between biased and non-biased readings, and yes-no questions of the form <¬P *ma*?>, which are unambiguously biased. Moreover, the above examples show that the polarity of the implication induced by the sentence-final particle *ma* depends on the polarity of the proposition contained in the question itself, and that if the proposition contained is already in the negative, then the question will be biased towards a positive response. This leads us to consider the existence of three distinct classes of yes-no questions, which form a continuum with respect to neutrality according to their interpretations, as shown in Figure 1 below.

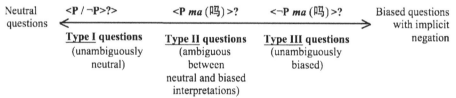

Figure 1. Continuum of yes-no questions with respect to their neutrality

Types I, II and III of yes-no questions are illustrated in (10), (11) and (12) respectively.

(10) **Type I**
     中医减肥有没有效?
     Zhōng-yī jiǎnféi yǒu-méi-yǒu xiào?
     "Is the weight-loss method through the use of Chinese medicine effective or not?"

(11) **Type II**

中医减肥有效吗？

Zhōng-yī jiǎnféi yǒu xiào ma?

"Is the weight-loss method through the use of Chinese medicine effective?"

(1st reading): Pure information-seeking question

(2nd reading): Biased question with a negative implication.

(12) **Type III**

中医减肥没有效吗？

Zhōng-yī jiǎnféi méi-yǒu xiào ma?

"Isn't the weight-loss method through the use of Chinese medicine effective?"

(Only possible reading): Biased question

The continuum shown in Figure 1 raises two interesting questions. Firstly, there seems to be an asymmetry between Type II questions (of the form <P *ma?*>) and Type III questions (of the form <¬P *ma?*>), in that only Type II questions are ambiguous and not Type III questions. This is despite the fact that both types of questions involve the same sentence-final particle *ma*. Secondly, when Type II questions are non-neutral, the biasedness is towards a negative implication or response. What contributes to this negative meaning? If it is the sentence-final particle *ma* that contributes to it, then why are Type III questions not biased in the same way?

Before discussing the answers to these questions in Section 3, we will demonstrate using syntactic tests to show that the 3 types of yes-no questions have distinct properties.

2.3 Distinguishing between the 3 types of yes-no questions

It can be shown that each of the three types of Yes-No questions has its unique set of properties, using the following syntactic tests: Firstly, as mentioned in the previous section, only neutral questions (Types I and II) are compatible with the adverb *dàodǐ*.

(13) **Type I**

中医减肥到底有没有效？

Zhōng-yī jiǎnféi dàodǐ yǒu-méi-yǒu xiào?

"Is the weight-loss method through the use of Chinese medicine effective or not?"

(14) **Type II**

中医减肥到底有效吗？

Zhōng-yī jiǎnféi dàodǐ yǒu xiào ma?

"Is the weight-loss method through the use of Chinese medicine effective?"

(15) **Type III**
*中医减肥到底没有效吗?
*Zhōng-yī jiǎnféi dàodǐ *méi-yǒu xiào ma?*
Secondly, the use of a subordinating interrogative phrase *shéi zhīdào* "who knows?" at the start of the question seems to give the same effect as the adverb *dàodǐ*.

(16) **Type I**
谁知道: 中医减肥有没有效?
Shéi zhīdào: zhōng-yī jiǎnféi yǒu-méi-yǒu xiào?
"Who knows if the weight-loss method through the use of Chinese medicine is effective or not?"

(17) **Type II**
谁知道: 中医减肥有效吗?
Shéi zhīdào: zhōng-yī jiǎnféi yǒu xiào ma?
"Who knows if the weight-loss method through the use of Chinese medicine is effective?"

(18) **Type III**
*谁知道: 中医减肥没有效吗?
Shéizhīdào: zhōng-yī jiǎnféi méi-yǒu xiào ma?
Thirdly, the adverb *nándào* seems to have the opposite effect: only biased questions are compatible with the adverb *nándào*.

(19) **Type I**
*中医减肥难道有没有效?
Zhōng-yī jiǎnféi nándào yǒu-méi-yǒu xiào?

(20) **Type II**
中医减肥难道有效吗?
Zhōng-yī jiǎnféi nándào yǒu xiào ma?
"Don't tell me the weight-loss method through the use of Chinese medicine IS effective!"
(Implication: "The weight-loss method through the use of Chinese medicine is not effective!")

(21) **Type III**
中医减肥难道没有效吗?
Zhōng-yī jiǎnféi nándào méi-yǒu xiào ma?
"Don't tell me the weight-loss method through the use of Chinese medicine is NOT effective!"
(Implication: "The weight-loss method through the use of Chinese medicine is effective!")
Fourthly, the adverb *zhēnde* seems to behave like the adverb *nándào*.

(22) **Type I**
*中医减肥真的有没有效?
Zhōng-yī jiǎnféi zhēnde yǒu-méi-yǒu xiào?

(23) **Type II**
中医减肥真的有效吗？
Zhōng-yī jiǎnféi zhēnde yǒu xiào ma?
"Is the weight-loss method through the use of Chinese medicine REALLY effective?!"
(Implication: "The weight-loss method through the use of Chinese medicine is not effective!")

(24) **Type III**
中医减肥真的没有效吗？
Zhōng-yī jiǎnféi zhēnde méi-yǒu xiào ma?
"Is the weight-loss method through the use of Chinese medicine REALLY not effective!"
(Implication: "The weight-loss method through the use of Chinese medicine is effective!")

3   Source of implicit negation of *ma*

Section 2 showed that implicit negation is available when the question carries the sentence-final particle *ma*. In this section, we suggest that this is due to the semantic trace of negation that is remnant from the etymology of this sentence-final particle. We then discuss why the polarity of the implication of biased yes-no questions is the opposite of that of the proposition contained in it.

3.1   Etymology of sentence-final *ma*

In order to understand the workings of the sentence-final particle *ma*, we will first recall a study by Pan (2007: 90–94), who demonstrated that the sentence-final particle *ma* (吗) has evolved from the former negation marker *wú* (无), which was then substituted by *me₁* (麽), *mo* (摩) ou *mo* (磨) before being replaced by *ma* (吗) towards the end of the Tang dynasty.

(25) Diachronic evolution of the interrogative *ma* (J. Pan, 2007: 94):
wu (无) → *mo* (麽 / 摩 / 磨) → '吗' (*ma*)

If Pan (2007) (among others) is right that the sentence-final particle *ma* has evolved from a negation marker, it would help us understand the two following facts. Firstly, it would explain why the sentence-final particle *ma* (吗) and the negation marker are interchangeable at the end of a sentence, like in the following pair of examples:

(26) 你吃过没？
Nǐ chī-guò méi?
"Have you eaten [this] before?"

(27) 你吃过吗？

  Nǐ chī-guò ma?

  "Have you eaten [this] before?"

Secondly, it would explain why the sentence-final particle *ma* (吗) and the negation marker cannot occur together:

(28) *你吃过吗没？

  **Nǐ chī-guò ma méi?*

(29) *你吃过没吗？

  **Nǐ chī-guò méi ma?*

We believe that these two facts are good arguments to support the etymological origin of the sentence-final particle ma: since it was evolved from a negation marker, the semantic origin must have left a trace in its current use, and this would be why it can commute with a negation marker. Nonetheless, as it is only just a semantic trace of negation observable in the sentence-final particle ma, it is not a true negation marker. Syntactically, the sentence-final particle ma and the negation marker *méi* do not share the same status: the former bears on the entire proposition, while the latter bears only on a predicate, as shown in the minimal pair of examples below:

(30) 你吃过没吃过？

  Nǐ chī-guò méi chī-guò?

  "Have you eaten [this] before or not?"

(31) *你吃过吗吃过？

  **Nǐ chī-guò ma chī-guò?*

In summary, we claim that the sentence-final particle is a true interrogative marker for yes-no questions. It was developed from a true negation marker, but became grammaticalised as an interrogative marker. This point of view allow us to discuss the source of implicit negation or the inversion of polarity in the implication of certain rhetorical yes-no questions, which we turn to next.

3.2   The sentence-final particle *ma* and the inversion of polarity

We return to the question of why the sentence-final particle *ma* seems to invert the polarity of the proposition contained in the yes-no question. Two clues point us to the answer of this question. The first was already mentioned above, namely that the sentence-final particle *ma* has exactly the same function as a negation marker at the end of an affirmative proposition, to transform it into a yes-no question. The proposition contained in the questions (26) and (27) is "You have eaten this before", and the speech act corresponding to the question invites the interlocutor to adopt a position in relation to this assertion, by answering yes or no in order to validate either the assertion P, or the negation of the assertion P, i.e. ¬P.

Although questions (26) and (27) are interchangeable in a neutral context, they are not interchangeable in a non-neutral one. The following question (32) is posed in a non-neutral context due to the assertion that precedes the yes-no question and the presence of the adverb *nándào*, but the question in (33) is not natural.

(32) 河豚鱼那么稀少，你（难道）吃过吗？

   Hétúnyú name xīshǎo, nǐ (nándào) chī-guò ma?

   "Puffer fish is so rare, have you eaten it before?"

   (Implication: You must not have eaten it before.)

(33) 河豚鱼那么稀少，你（难道）吃过没？

   *Hétúnyú name xīshǎo, nǐ (nándào) chī-guò méi?

The second clue is that, although the yes-no question that does not contain any negation marker can be interpreted as a non-neutral question, the yes-no question that does contain a negation marker can also be interpreted as a non-neutral question.

(34) 金枪鱼那么普遍，你没吃过吗？

   Jīnqiāngyú name pǔbiàn, nǐ méi chī-guò ma?

   "Tuna is so common, have you not eaten it before?"

   (Implication: You must have eaten it before.)

These two clues, taken together, suggest a triple parallelism between yes-no questions ending with the sentence-final particle *ma* in Mandarin and "tag questions" in English. For the sake of comparison, English tag questions are interrogative forms that are added after the anchor proposition to strengthen its meaning. They are generally of an inverse polarity with regard to the anchor propositions preceding them, as shown below:

(35) You haven't eaten this fish, have you?

(36) You have eaten this fish, haven't you?

(37) ??You have eaten this fish, have you?

(38) *You haven't eaten this fish, haven't you?

Schematically, the anchor propositions that are followed by tag questions take one of the following forms: <¬Q, $\underline{Q?}$> or <Q, $\underline{¬Q?}$>, where Q represents the propositional content and where the underlined part corresponds to the tag question.

Now, let us present three similarities between tag questions in English and questions bearing the sentence-final particle *ma* in Mandarin Chinese. The similarities concern (i) their pragmatic/ informational structure, (ii) the polarity of propositions making up the interrogative context, and (iii) their ambiguity. Firstly, in a non-neutral question that is asked with a sentence-final particle *ma*, the assertion that underlies the question, namely P, is presented as a doubtful - or even false - piece of information. In other words, the speaker introduces a disagreement or a deviation with the information given by P, and favours instead the contrary assertion, ¬P. In the same way, tag questions are used in the same contexts. Consider the following examples, taken from Reese and Asher (2008a: 454), in which we have underlined the tag question parts:

(39) A: Julie wouldn't do it that way.

B: Well, Julie isn't here [pause] is she?

(40) A: Can Julie do it for us?

B: Julie isn't here [pause] is she?

In (39), the utterance of B is to tell A that the fact introduced by the anchor phrase ¬Q (= Julie is not here), and consequently the manner in which Julie accomplishes the task is of no relevance in the current situation. Here, the tag question Q?, namely *is she here?*, contains the proposition Q *Julie is here*, which is presented as a false assertion: it is not true that Julie is here. In (40), the reply of B serves to reply to A's question by communicating the belief that Julie is not present, even if the speaker is open to the possibility that the belief could be false. The tag question here, therefore serves to invite A to confirm the validity of his belief, expressed by the anchor proposition, ¬Q. Here, the tag question Q?, namely *is she here?*, contains the proposition Q *Julie is here* , which is presented as a doubt or uncertainty with respect to that belief.

Secondly, just as the tag question is always of the opposite polarity with regard to the anchor proposition, the question of the form <P *ma*?> is also of the opposite polarity with regard to the implicit proposition ¬P, corresponding to the speaker's beliefs. The implicit proposition can be made explicit in Mandarin Chinese with an alternative sentence-final particle *ba*:

(41) 河豚鱼那么稀少，你没吃过吧？

Hétúnyú name xīshǎo, nǐ méi chī-guò ba?

"Puffer fish is so rare, you must not have eaten it before?"

(42) 金枪鱼那么普遍，你吃过吧？

Jīnqiāngyú name pǔbiàn, nǐ chī-guò ba?

"Tuna is so common, you must have eaten it before?"

It is important to note here that the identification of the implicit proposition in Mandarin Chinese is not arbitrary: (41) and (42) can be uttered in place of (32) and (34) respectively in exactly the same contexts. As we can see, the relation between a tag question ¬Q? (or Q?) and its corresponding anchor proposition Q (or ¬Q) is therefore comparable with the relation between the question <P *ma*?> (or <¬P *ma*?>) and the implicit proposition ¬P (or P) which reflects the belief of the speaker with respect to the question. In both cases, we have an inversion of polarity between the two component propositions.

(43) Mandarin:

Implicit proposition + Question with *ma*:   <P, ¬P?> or <¬P, P?>

(44) English

Anchor proposition + Tag question: <Q, ¬Q?> or <¬Q, Q?>

Thirdly, according to Reese and Asher (2008a: 454), even if tag questions are generally biased questions like in the following, they can be neutral questions.

(45) A: We need someone who has consulted for us before.

  B: Julie isn't here is she? (without pause)

Specifically, Reese and Asher (2008b: 8) specify that neutral tag questions "only appear to be possible when the anchor contains a negation and when there is little or no rhythmic break between the anchor and the tag". In the same way, questions asked with the sentence-final particle *ma* may be non-neutral but not always either. We have seen how they can behave like neutral question in the earlier sections, without favouring the positive or the negative reply.

The triple parallelism between tag questions in English and questions of the form <P *ma*?> that we have just presented suggests that the latter may be analysed as tag questions, where anchor propositions are not explicit.

3.3   Why negative questions with *ma* are biased questions

We have seen in this paper that the reason why a yes-no question <P *ma*?> is sometimes interpreted as a negative proposition, is that it behaves just like a tag question, associated with an invisible and implicit anchor proposition of the opposite polarity, ¬P. Now, we are left with one last question, i.e. why <¬P *ma*?> cannot be ambiguous in the same way as the question <P *ma*?> is. The answer to the question follows naturally from the above discussion and analysis that we have proposed for yes-no questions bearing the sentence-final particle *ma*. Firstly, the yes-no question <¬P *ma*?> can never ever be neutral because it is a genuine tag question, and tag questions of the negative polarity are never neutral. Indeed, if we are on the right track about the parallelism between English tag questions and Mandarin questions of the form <P *ma*?>, i.e. to treat the latter as Mandarin versions of tag questions, then we can note that tag questions can only be ambiguous when they are of the positive polarity; when they are of the negative polarity, only the biased question interpretation is possible. Hence, the reply of B in (45) could not have been replaced by (46), which cannot possibly be interpreted as a neutral question.

  (46) #Julie is here isn't she? (*without pause*)

Secondly, the yes-no question <¬P *ma*?> can never ever be neutral because in a neutral yes-no question, the sentence final particle *ma* still retains a negative semantic feature. The negation in the yes-no question of the form <¬P *ma*?> would then be in conflict with the negative semantic feature that is present in the sentence-final particle *ma*.

In summary, the yes-no question of the form <¬P *ma*?> cannot be a neutral question for two reasons: (i) it behaves like a tag question, and in order to be a neutral tag question, it must be of the positive polarity, while <¬P *ma*?> is of the negative polarity; and (ii) in order to be a neutral yes-no question, the sentence-final particle *ma* must exhibit a semantic trace of negation. This trace is in conflict with the negation (¬) that bears on P in the question of the form <¬P *ma?*>.

4   Conclusion

In this paper, we have refined the classification of yes-no questions in Mandarin Chinese, showing that they form a continuum, with unambiguously neutral questions on one end of the spectrum to unambiguously biased questions on the other end. These three classes are represented by the forms <P / ¬P?>, <P *ma?*> and <¬P *ma?*> respectively. Such a classification led us to discuss the source of implicit negation in the latter two forms of yes-no question. We have shown that the sentence-final particle is responsible for the implicit negation and that this particle turns a proposition into an equivalent of an English tag question. English tag questions are tied to anchor questions, just as Mandarin yes-no questions with *ma* are tied to the implicit proposition containing the implicit negation. (cf. Chan, 2011)

Further work remains to be done in the area of rhetorical questions in Mandarin Chinese, in particular how adverbs such as *dàodǐ* (到底), *nándào* (难道) and *zhēnde* (真的) may either induce or reject the rhetorical question interpretation. The scope should also be extended to open-ended questions such as the one in (2).

References

1. Chan, K. G. D.: La négation et la polarité en chinois contemporain. Unpublished PhD dissertation, Université Paris-7, France (2011)
2. Li, C. N., Thompson, S. A.: The pragmatics of two types of yes/no questions in Mandarin and its universal implications. Papers from the 15th Regional Meetings of the Chicago Linguistics Society (1979)
3. Li, C. N., Thompson, S. A.: Mandarin Chinese: A Functional Reference Grammar. University of California Press, Berkeley (1981)
4. Pan, J. V.: Interrogation et quantification: le rôle et la fonction des particules et des syntagmes interrogatifs en chinois mandarin. Unpublished PhD dissertation, Université de Nantes, France (2007)
5. Reese, B., Asher, N.: Prosody and the Interpretation of Tag questions. In: Puig-Waldmüller, E. (ed.) Proceedings of Sinn und Bedeutung **11**, 448–462. Universitat Pompeu Fabra, Barcelona (2008a)
6. Reese, B., Asher, N.: Intonation and Discourse: Biased Questions. In: Ishihra, S., Jannedy S., Schwarz, A. (eds.), Working Papers of the SFB632, Interdisciplinary Studies on Information Structure **8**, 1–38 (2008b)
7. Sadock, J. M.: Queclaratives. Chicago Linguistic Society **7**, 223–231 (1971)
8. Sadock, J. M.: Towards a Linguistic Theory of Speech Acts. Academic Press, New York (1974)

Study in Words and Characters Use and Contents of the Opening Addresses by Chinese University Presidents

Xinyuan Zhang, Pengyuan Liu

Language Monitoring and Social Computing Laboratory, National Language Resource Monitoring and Research Center, Faculty of Information Science, Beijing Language and Culture University, Beijing, China,100083

zhangxinyuansky@163.com, liupengyuan@pku.edu.cn

Abstract: This paper selects 213 opening addresses by Chinese university presidents between 2003 and 2015, synchronically and diachronically, this paper has devoted itself to the study of the usage of words and characters in those addresses, the contents as a whole. The location and the time those speeches were delivered have also been taken into consideration. By comparing the words and characters used in those addresses to Lexicon of Common Words in Contemporary Chinese, this paper shows that vocabulary used in addresses doesn't change dramatically with time going diachronically, and the themes and focuses of the speeches tend to vary from time to time. This paper classifies the speeches into certain types according to the frequently and individually used words, analyzes the features of their contents. The conclusion is that universities have put more emphasis on cultivating spirits, quality, ability and virtue.

Keywords: word and character usage, content analysis, the opening address, synchronic and diachronic

1   preface

In recent years' back-to-school seasons, the speeches addressed by Chinese university presidents are often widely spread. Compared with ever before, there has been a lot of changes in speech style. Through the opening speech, we can also know the face of universities and what happened in those days. Therefore, studying the opening speeches by presidents has a strong practical and historical values. At present, there have been some linguistic researches on speech. Wu Ying [1] took premier Zhu Rongji's speeches as the research object, and put forward the

© Springer International Publishing AG 2016
M. Dong et al. (Eds.): CLSW 2016, LNAI 10085, pp. 763–770, 2016
DOI: 10.1007/978-3-319-49508-8_70

corresponding policy of addressing; Hou Jinjing[2] selected 21 speeches by Xi Jinping, studied it's rhetorical style. There were researchers who took the aspects of discourse or translation (Jin Lu[3], Li Hongshuo[4], Gao Jianye[5]). On the aspect of research object, only a few targeted at the commencements, whereas few on the opening addresses. This paper intends to take the addresses by Chinese university presidents in the opening ceremony for undergraduates.

2   research object and the overall data

The data comes from universities' official websites, Baidu database and CNKI, including 213 addresses from 2003 to 2015, which covers universities of comprehensive, arts, language and so on.

Table1 research object and the overall data

Ad–dress	Character		word		Average character token	Average word token	The longest length	The shortest length
	token	type	token	type				
213	525809	3377	310943	17870	2469	1795	9014	514

3   3Investigation in word use and contents

3.1 overall synchronic study

3.1.1 Word use

Coverage rate is an important indicator of the distribution of Chinese characters' use. With the help of the National Corpus frequency statistical tools, we studied the words use in these addresses, and compare them with that in The Green Paper on Language Situation in China (GPLSC) [6].

Generally, about 600 characters could reach up to a coverage rate of 80%. However, in these addresses, only 375 characters made it. And 644 characters covered 90%

of the corpus. This shows that the opening speech tends to repeatedly use some high-frequency words, and the range is relatively narrow and more concentrated. The reason, we think, lies in that the address always has unified theme, fewer contents, high level of quotation and less rarely used words. The new characters introduced is limited even by quoting ancient classical Chinese references or epigrams with strong color in written language.

3.1.2 Comparison between corpus and Lexicon of Common Words in Contemporary Chinese

Comparing the first 2500 characters in corpus with that in Lexicon of Common Words in Contemporary Chinese, we got 2011 shared words. 489 characters in our corpus didn't show in the word list. We cut the 2500 characters into 3 parts, i.e. the first 500, No501 to No1500, and the last 1000 characters. The result indicates that these 489 characters are more concerned with name entity, the ancient Chinese words, the annual events and so on. For example, characters 韩[han2]/圳 [zhen4]/伊[yi1]/澳[ao4]/珞[luo4]/珈[jia1]etc. were mainly used in place names; characters 俞[yu2]/彰[zhang1]/邓[deng4]/钊[zhao1]/冯[feng2]/敖[ao2]etc. were related with the names of people; and 曰[yue1]/吾[wu3]/尔[er3] etc. were frequently used in ancient Chinese. Among these, the name 邓小平[Deng Xiaoping]/ 彭士禄[Peng Shilu]/ 竺可桢[Zhu Kezhen]/比尔·盖茨[Bill Gates] played an important role in those characters above rating ahead, and characters 汶[wen4]/霾 [mai2] had much to do with big events, say WenChuan Earthquake and Wu Mai in Beijing. These all reflect some characteristics of the opening addresses. Presidents of Chinese university tend to introduce the university, quote some classical Chinese archaism to encourage students, or motivate them by some anecdotes of celebrities. We can also read about their spirit, i.e. advance with the times and cultivate patriotism.

3.2 durations of different periods

3.2.1 Basic information about character and word use

As the number of addresses before 2007 and between the years of 2008 to 2010 was only a few, we divided all the data into 7 parts as below. Only 2682 characters cover all the corpus.

Table 2. Character and word use in durations of different periods

Period		03-07	08-10	2011	2012	2013	2014	2015
Number of address		19	24	26	25	35	34	50
character	type	1705	1990	2077	2135	2308	2344	2682
	token	42641	54759	64793	68800	82488	82625	129806
	average	2244	2282	2492	2752	2357	2430	2596
word	type	4017	5348	5875	6281	7036	7308	9951
	token	30710	39626	46612	49815	59901	60166	95401
	average	1616	1651	1793	1992	1711	1770	1908
High frequency	WordType	1787	2376	2487	2661	2813	3012	3651
	percent	44.49	44.43	42.33	42.37	39.98	41.22	36.69
Shared	WordType	1682						
	percent	41.87	31.45	28.63	26.78	23.91	23.02	16.90
SingleUsed	WordType	443	738	843	1075	1242	1246	2494
	percent	11.03	13.40	14.35	17.12	17.65	17.05	25.06

High-frequency words are words with a coverage of 90%. From the table above we can get, that there are differences in the number of Word Type in different periods, but very nearly the same when over the number of all word types. This indicates that the use of high-frequency words are stable. The number of shared words of all periods was 1682, and showed a tendency of decline with the passage of time. Words used only in period one were 443, then added to 2494 in 2015. Diachronically speaking, the words used in addresses gradually grew richer and the words added were usually low in frequency.

3.2.2 Diachronic study of contents based on the high-frequency words

High-frequency words can reflect the features of corpus' contents to a certain extent. By investigating high frequency words of different periods, we'd gain the features and the evolution rule. We selected the top 100 words of different periods in frequency, compared the shared words and the vocabulary rate of every period over the former period. Based on 2003-2007, the vocabulary rate of every period over the former one had a tendency of declining, i.e. words used in addresses tend to be stable.

We divided these top100 words into 5 parts based on the contents they embodied.

(1) School Entity: it means names of people or things in school, including "university, schoolmate, president, teacher, freshman, student, Tsinghua, etc."

(2) Sprit and Ability: it refers to words about students' sprits or abilities in address, including "sprit, innovation, diligence, critical thinking, responsibility, etc."

(3) Introduction of University: it means words used to describe universities, involving the size, history, hardware, development plan, and talent cultivation plan.

(4) Native Land Emotion: it means statements about big social events or life planning, or wishes of students being patriotic and ready to serve the community.

(5) The others: this part contains some words that showed no obvious link with contents, see "this year, a batch of, etc."

Based on the 5 categories, we got the vocabulary of every period and category. As we can infer, with the passage of time, 1) Addresses about sprits and abilities constantly increased, especially in recent 3 years, it has become the most important subject.2) In general, contents about introductions and school entities showed a significantly reduced trend.3) There were some fluctuations in category of native land emotion and others, but relatively stable by and large.

All the changes above reflects the increasing emphasis on the cultivation of students' spiritual quality, ability and moral character in Chinese universities. Introduction of universities getting weaker, quality, ability and moral character being emphasized, are measures to pursuit the essence of education. It's also consistent with China's continuous strengthening of constructing spiritual civilization. Meanwhile, category of native land emotion still being a consistent theme of the opening address means universities always pay great attention to develop students' sense of ownership and social responsibility.

3.3   Investigation of different types of sub-corpus

3.3.1 Character and word use in different types of sub-corpus

We divided all the data into 3 categories of Generalist University, Engineering University and Specialist University. The specialist class was then divided into 7 parts, including classes of language, finance and economic, agriculture and forestry, arts, and ethnic, normal universities.

The results showed that the average number of character/ word used in university of arts was significantly higher than that of others. This indicates that the addresses of Arts University has a relatively longer length. Character and word use in other type of universities tends to be much balance. Shared words were only 680, making up a relatively low share (the maximum was less than 30%).

Corresponding to that, words used only in one type of sub-corpus showed that words used varied with their types of university. Words used only in addresses of engineering universities reached 200, making up a proportion of 7.63%. This indicates its' uniqueness in word use. We then located and compared these 200 words in corpus, and found that words of names or originated from idioms or ancient Chinese phrases accounted for a substantial proportion.

Table 3 category of words used only in Engineering University

We then divided words in "the others" into the following categories according to their style and emotion embodied.48 of those were with

Category	number	percentage	Example
Words of name	57	28.5%	葡萄牙、匈奴、隋代、玄奘
Words from idiom	30	15%	喋喋不休、睚眦必报
Words from phrase	20	10%	厥有国语
The others	93	46.5%	

strong color in written language, 29 with strong color in oral language, and 16 were strong in derogatory sense.

3.3.2 Comparison of Top30 high frequency words within sub-corpus

We selected the top 30 words with high frequency from each sub-corpus and made a comparison. We got 8 shared words altogether. There were 大学[da4xue2], 同学[tong2xue2],学习[xue2xi2],社会[she4hui4],国家[guo2jia1],中国[zhong1 guo2],学生[xue2sheng1],学校[xue2xiao4]. Obviously, they were mainly about things or objects, and had a strong link with university, society and the country. Words used only in each sub-corpus were listed below.

Words used only in one sub-corpus can to some extent reflect some characteristics of that sub-corpus. Words in addresses of Generalist University were relatively more comprehensive. Comparing bold words and not-bold words in Table 8, we found, that the not-bold words directly indicated which category of university the address belongs to, while the bold words reflected the characteristics of their contents. For example, Engineering University emphasis on learning to question and practice ("质疑""实践" in Chinese respectively), setting up goals. Finance and Economic University pays more attentions to self-development. Agriculture and Forestry University believes in diligence("勤奋" in Chinese), and university of Politics and Laws , Arts and Ethnic takes the overall situation as the fundamental, shouldering the nation's mission and social development responsibility.

Therefore we can infer, presidents of different types of university tend to make an address centered on their characteristics and with some basic information still there. Additionally, one of the reasons of the word "同学[tong2xue2]" being high-frequently used may lie in it being the speech recipient, as this way of talking increases its frequency of use.

4   Conclusion

This paper studied the characters and words use in 213 speeches by presidents of Chinese universities from 2003 to 2015. By comparing the character and word use to Lexicon of Common Words in Contemporary Chinese, we have known how they are used and what they reflect. Speeches delivered at different times have different focuses. Speeches delivered in recent years have put more stress on students' spirits and abilities. The addresses are, to some extent, a mirror of college education, basic information, and social development in contemporary China.

Meanwhile, we only studied the character and word use and the contents of addresses. There is still much for further study. We will also enrich and balance the corpus, reduce the subjectivity of classification, and/or refer to the commencement speeches for further inquiry.

Acknowledgments

Supported by National Natural Science Foundation of China (No.61272215). Supported by Major Project of the National Language Committee of the 12th Five-Year Research Plan in 2015(No.ZDI125-55).

Reference

1. Wu Ying: Study on Linguistic Strategy of Leader's Speech from Speeches by Zhu Rongji. Lu-Dong University, 2012[in Chinese]
2. Hou Jinjing: Study on Rhetorical Style of Speeches by Xi Jinping. Sichuan Normal University,2015
3. Jin Lu: Study on Meta-functions Equivalence of Chinese and Foreign University's address in Text Translation ,Nanjing Industrial University,2012
4. Li Hongshuo: An Analysis of the Evaluation Category of Russian President's New Year's Speech, Xinjiang University,2013
5. Gao Jianye: Report on Interpretation Practice of Wen Jiabao's Speech. Hebei University,2013
6. Ministry of Education Language Information Management Division: The Green Paper on Language Situation in China, Beijing, The Commercial Press, 2008

Author Index

Printed in the United States
By Bookmasters